D0940040

# WileyPLUS is a research-based online environment for effective teaching and learning.

*WileyPLUS* builds students' confidence because it takes the guesswork out of studying by providing students with a clear roadmap:

- what to do
- how to do it
- if they did it right

It offers interactive resources along with a complete digital textbook that help students learn more. With *WileyPLUS*, students take more initiative so you'll have greater impact on their achievement in the classroom and beyond.

# For more information, visit www.wileyplus.com

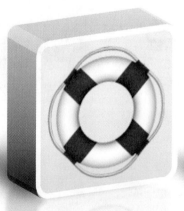

# BIG JAVA

# Late Objects

# CAY HORSTMANN

San Jose State University

**WILEY**

John Wiley & Sons, Inc.

| | |
|---|---|
| VICE PRESIDENT AND EXECUTIVE PUBLISHER | Don Fowley |
| EXECUTIVE EDITOR | Beth Lang Golub |
| CONTENT MANAGER | Kevin Holm |
| SENIOR PRODUCTION EDITOR | John Curley |
| EXECUTIVE MARKETING MANAGER | Christopher Ruel |
| CREATIVE DIRECTOR | Harry Nolan |
| SENIOR DESIGNER | Madelyn Lesure |
| SENIOR PHOTO EDITOR | Lisa Gee |
| PRODUCT DESIGNER | Thomas Kulesa |
| CONTENT EDITOR | Wendy Ashenberg |
| EDITORIAL PROGRAM ASSISTANT | Elizabeth Mills |
| MEDIA SPECIALIST | Lisa Sabatini |
| PRODUCTION SERVICES | Cindy Johnson |
| COVER PHOTOS | © Robbie Taylor/Alamy; |
| | © FLPA/John Holmes/Age Fotostock; |
| | © frans lemmens/Alamy |

This book was set in Stempel Garamond by Publishing Services, and printed and bound by R.R. Donnelley & Sons Company. The cover was printed by R.R. Donnelley & Sons, Jefferson City.

This book is printed on acid-free paper. ∞

*Library of Congress Cataloging-in-Publication Data:*
Horstmann, Cay S., 1959-
 Big Java : late objects / Cay Horstmann.
   p. cm.
  Includes index.
  ISBN 978-1-118-08788-6 (pbk. : acid-free paper)
 1. Java (Computer program language) I. Title.
 QA76.73.J38H67 2012
 005.2'762--dc23
                         2011043315

ISBN 978-1-118-08788-6 (Main Book)
ISBN 978-1-118-12942-5 (Binder-Ready Version)

Printed in the United States of America

10 9 8 7 6 5 4 3 2 1

# PREFACE

This book is an introduction to Java and computer programming that focuses on the essentials—and on effective learning. The book is designed to serve a wide range of student interests and abilities and is suitable for a first course in programming for computer scientists, engineers, and students in other disciplines. No prior programming experience is required, and only a modest amount of high school algebra is needed. Here are the key features of this book:

### Present fundamentals first.

The book takes a traditional route, first stressing control structures, methods, procedural decomposition, and arrays. Objects are used when appropriate in the early chapters. Students start designing and implementing their own classes in Chapter 8.

### Guidance and worked examples help students succeed.

Beginning programmers often ask "How do I start? Now what do I do?" Of course, an activity as complex as programming cannot be reduced to cookbook-style instructions. However, step-by-step guidance is immensely helpful for building confidence and providing an outline for the task at hand. "Problem Solving" sections stress the importance of design and planning. "How To" guides help students with common programming tasks. Additional Worked Examples are available online.

### Practice makes perfect.

Of course, programming students need to be able to implement nontrivial programs, but they first need to have the confidence that they can succeed. This book contains a substantial number of self-check questions at the end of each section. "Practice It" pointers suggest exercises to try after each section. And additional practice opportunities, including code completion questions, guided lab exercises, and skill-oriented multiple-choice questions are available online.

### A visual approach motivates the reader and eases navigation.

Photographs present visual analogies that explain the nature and behavior of computer concepts. Step-by-step figures illustrate complex program operations. Syntax boxes and example tables present a variety of typical and special cases in a compact format. It is easy to get the "lay of the land" by browsing the visuals, before focusing on the textual material.

*Visual features help the reader with navigation.*

### Focus on the essentials while being technically accurate.

An encyclopedic coverage is not helpful for a beginning programmer, but neither is the opposite—reducing the material to a list of simplistic bullet points. In this book, the essentials are presented in digestible chunks, with separate notes that go deeper into good practices or language features when the reader is ready for the additional information. You will not find artificial over-simplifications that give an illusion of knowledge.

# A Tour of the Book

This book is intended for a two-semester introduction to programming that may also include algorithms, data structures, and/or applications.

The first seven chapters follow a traditional approach to basic programming concepts. Students learn about control structures, stepwise refinement, and arrays. Objects are used only for input/output and string processing. Input/output is covered in Chapter 7, but Sections 7.1 and 7.2 can be covered with Chapter 4; in that way, students can practice writing loops that process text files. Chapter 4 also provides an

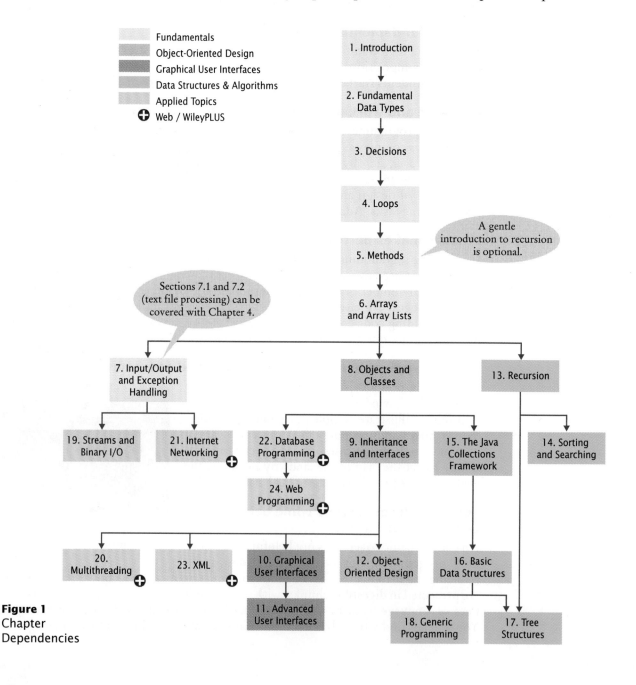

**Figure 1**
Chapter
Dependencies

optional introduction to programming drawings that consist of lines, rectangles, and ovals, with an emphasis on reinforcing loops.

After students have gained a solid foundation, they are ready to tackle the implementation of classes in Chapter 8. Chapter 9 covers inheritance and interfaces. A simple methodology for object-oriented design is presented in Chapter 12. Object-oriented design may also be covered immediately after Chapter 9 by omitting the GUI versions of the sample programs. By the end of these chapters, students will be able to implement programs with multiple interacting classes.

Graphical user interfaces are presented in Chapters 10 and 11. The first of these chapters enables students to write programs with buttons, text components, and simple drawings. If you want to go deeper, you will find layout management and additional user-interface components in the second chapter.

Chapters 13–18 cover algorithms and data structures at a level suitable for beginning students. Recursion, in Chapter 13, starts with simple examples and progresses to meaningful applications that would be difficult to implement iteratively. Chapter 14 covers quadratic sorting algorithms as well as merge sort, with an informal introduction to big-Oh notation. In Chapter 15, the Java Collections Framework is presented from the perspective of a library user, without revealing the implementations of lists and maps. You can cover this chapter anytime after Chapter 8. In Chapters 16 and 17, students learn how to implement linear and tree-based data structures, and how to analyze the efficiency of operations on these data structures. Finally, Chapter 18 covers programming with Java generics.

Chapters 19–24 feature applied topics: binary input/output, concurrent programming, networking, database programming, XML processing, and the development of web applications. Chapters 20–24 are available in electronic form on the Web and in WileyPLUS.

Any subset of these chapters can be incorporated into a custom print version of this text; ask your Wiley sales representative for details.

## Problem Solving Strategies

This book provides practical, step-by-step illustrations of techniques that can help students devise and evaluate solutions to programming problems. Introduced where they are most relevant, these strategies address barriers to success for many students. Strategies included are:

- Algorithm Design (with pseudocode)
- First Do It By Hand (doing sample calculations by hand)
- Flowcharts
- Test Cases
- Hand-Tracing
- Storyboards
- Reusable Methods
- Stepwise Refinement
- Adapting Algorithms
- Discovering Algorithms by Manipulating Physical Objects
- Tracing Objects (identifying state and behavior)
- Patterns for Object Data
- Thinking Recursively
- Estimating the Running Time of an Algorithm

## Optional Science and Business Exercises

End-of-chapter exercises include problems from scientific and business domains. Designed to engage students, the exercises illustrate the value of programming in applied fields.

## Appendices

Many instructors find it highly beneficial to require a consistent style for all assignments. If the style guide in Appendix L conflicts with instructor sentiment or local customs, however, it is available in electronic form so that it can be modified.

A. The Basic Latin and Latin-1 Subsets of Unicode
B. Java Operator Summary
C. Java Reserved Word Summary
D. The Java Library
E. Java Syntax Summary
F. HTML Summary
G. Tool Summary
H. Javadoc Summary
I. Number Systems
J. Bit and Shift Operations
K. UML Summary
L. Java Language Coding Guidelines

## Web Resources

This book is complemented by a complete suite of online resources and a robust WileyPLUS course. Go to www.wiley.com/college/horstmann to visit the online companion sites, which include

- Source code for all example programs in the book and in online examples.
- Worked Examples that apply the problem-solving steps in the book to other realistic examples.
- Video Examples in which the author explains the steps he is taking and shows his work as he solves a programming problem.
- Lab exercises that apply chapter concepts (with solutions for instructors only).
- Lecture presentation slides (in PowerPoint format).
- Solutions to all review and programming exercises (for instructors only).
- A test bank that focuses on skills, not just terminology (for instructors only).

## WileyPLUS

WileyPLUS is an online teaching and learning environment that integrates the digital textbook with instructor and student resources. See pages xiii–xiv for details.

Pointers in the book describe what students will find on the Web.

VIDEO EXAMPLE 4.2    **Drawing a Spiral**

In this Video Example, you will see how to develop a program that draws a spiral.

ONLINE EXAMPLE
A program using common loop algorithms.

# A Walkthrough of the Learning Aids

The pedagogical elements in this book work together to focus on and reinforce key concepts and fundamental principles of programming, with additional tips and detail organized to support and deepen these fundamentals. In addition to traditional features, such as chapter objectives and a wealth of exercises, each chapter contains elements geared to today's visual learner.

Throughout each chapter, **margin notes** show where new concepts are introduced and provide an outline of key ideas.

Additional **online example code** provides complete programs for students to run and modify.

Annotated **syntax boxes** provide a quick, visual overview of new language constructs.

**Annotations** explain required components and point to more information on common errors or best practices associated with the syntax.

**Analogies** to everyday objects are used to explain the nature and behavior of concepts such as variables, data types, loops, and more.

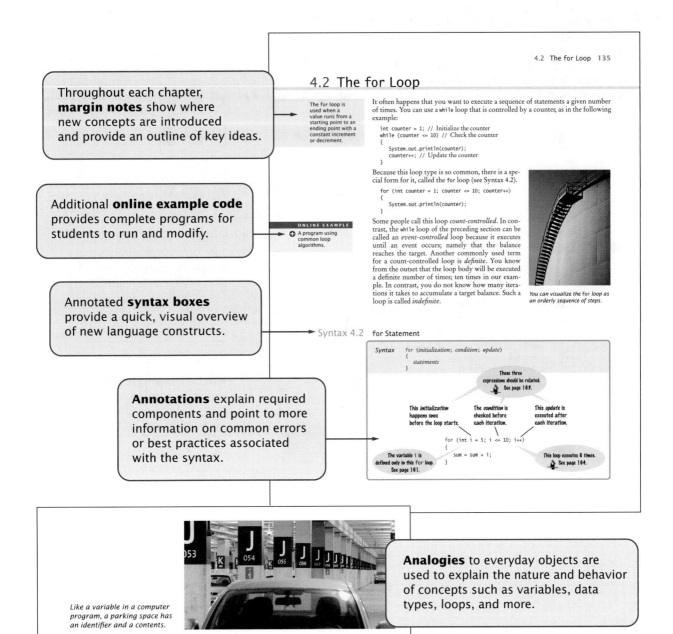

**Memorable photos** reinforce analogies and help students remember the concepts.

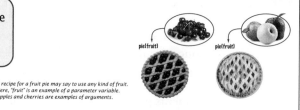

*A recipe for a fruit pie may say to use any kind of fruit. Here, "fruit" is an example of a parameter variable. Apples and cherries are examples of arguments.*

**Problem Solving sections** teach techniques for generating ideas and evaluating proposed solutions, often using pencil and paper or other artifacts. These sections emphasize that most of the planning and problem solving that makes students successful happens away from the computer.

6.5 Problem Solving: Discovering Algorithms by Manipulating Physical Objects **277**

Now how does that help us with our problem, switching the first and the second half of the array?

Let's put the first coin into place, by swapping it with the fifth coin. However, as Java programmers, we will say that we swap the coins in positions 0 and 4:

Next, we swap the coins in positions 1 and 5:

**HOW TO 1.1**  **Describing an Algorithm with Pseudocode**

This is the first of many "How To" sections in this book that give you step-by-step procedures for carrying out important tasks in developing computer programs.

Before you are ready to write a program in Java, you need to develop an algorithm—a method for arriving at a solution for a particular problem. Describe the algorithm in pseudocode: a sequence of precise steps formulated in English.

For example, consider this problem: You have the choice of buying two cars. One is more fuel efficient than the other, but also more expensive. You know the price and fuel efficiency (in miles per gallon, mpg) of both cars. You plan to keep the car for ten years. Assume a price of $4 per gallon of gas and usage of 15,000 miles per year. You will pay cash for the car and not worry about financing costs. Which car is the better deal?

**Step 1**  Determine the inputs and outputs.

In our sample problem, we have these inputs:
- **purchase price1** and **fuel efficiency1**, the price and fuel efficiency (in mpg) of the first car
- **purchase price2** and **fuel efficiency2**, the price and fuel efficiency of the second car

We simply want to know which car is the better buy. That is the desired output.

**How To guides** give step-by-step guidance for common programming tasks, emphasizing planning and testing. They answer the beginner's question, "Now what do I do?" and integrate key concepts into a problem-solving sequence.

**Worked Examples** and **Video Examples** apply the steps in the How To to a different example, showing how they can be used to plan, implement, and test a solution to another programming problem.

**WORKED EXAMPLE 1.1**  **Writing an Algorithm for Tiling a Floor**

 This Worked Example shows how to develop an algorithm for laying tile in an alternating pattern of colors.

Table 1  Variable Declarations in Java

| Variable Name | Comment |
|---|---|
| int cans = 6; | Declares an integer variable and initializes it with 6. |
| int total = cans + bottles; | The initial value need not be a constant. (Of course, cans and bottles must have been previously declared.) |
| 🚫 bottles = 1; | **Error:** The type is missing. This statement is not a declaration but an assignment of a new value to an existing variable—see Section 2.1.4. |
| 🚫 int bottles = "10"; | **Error:** You cannot initialize a number with a string. |
| int bottles; | Declares an integer variable without initializing it. This can be a cause for errors—see Common Error 2.1 on page 37. |
| int cans, bottles; | Declares two integer variables in a single statement. In this book, we will declare each variable in a separate statement. |

**Example tables** support beginners with multiple, concrete examples. These tables point out common errors and present another quick reference to the section's topic.

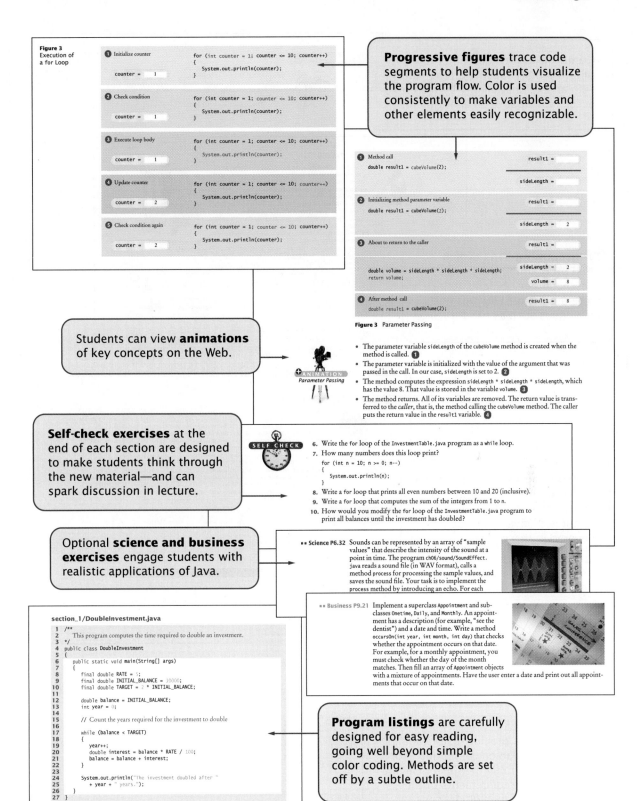

**Figure 3**
Execution of
a for Loop

❶ Initialize counter

```
for (int counter = 1; counter <= 10; counter++)
{
    System.out.println(counter);
}
```

counter =  1

❷ Check condition

```
for (int counter = 1; counter <= 10; counter++)
{
    System.out.println(counter);
}
```

counter =  1

❸ Execute loop body

```
for (int counter = 1; counter <= 10; counter++)
{
    System.out.println(counter);
}
```

counter =  1

❹ Update counter

```
for (int counter = 1; counter <= 10; counter++)
{
    System.out.println(counter);
}
```

counter =  2

❺ Check condition again

```
for (int counter = 1; counter <= 10; counter++)
{
    System.out.println(counter);
}
```

counter =  2

**Progressive figures** trace code segments to help students visualize the program flow. Color is used consistently to make variables and other elements easily recognizable.

❶ Method call
```
double result1 = cubeVolume(2);
```
result1 =
sideLength =

❷ Initializing method parameter variable
```
double result1 = cubeVolume(2);
```
result1 =
sideLength =   2

❸ About to return to the caller
```
double volume = sideLength * sideLength * sideLength;
return volume;
```
result1 =
sideLength =   2
volume =   8

❹ After method call
```
double result1 = cubeVolume(2);
```
result1 =   8

**Figure 3**   Parameter Passing

Students can view **animations** of key concepts on the Web.

ANIMATION
*Parameter Passing*

- The parameter variable sideLength of the cubeVolume method is created when the method is called. ❶
- The parameter variable is initialized with the value of the argument that was passed in the call. In our case, sideLength is set to 2. ❷
- The method computes the expression sideLength * sideLength * sideLength, which has the value 8. That value is stored in the variable volume. ❸
- The method returns. All of its variables are removed. The return value is transferred to the *caller*, that is, the method calling the cubeVolume method. The caller puts the return value in the result1 variable. ❹

**Self-check exercises** at the end of each section are designed to make students think through the new material—and can spark discussion in lecture.

SELF CHECK

6. Write the for loop of the InvestmentTable.java program as a while loop.
7. How many numbers does this loop print?
   ```
   for (int n = 10; n >= 0; n--)
   {
       System.out.println(n);
   }
   ```
8. Write a for loop that prints all even numbers between 10 and 20 (inclusive).
9. Write a for loop that computes the sum of the integers from 1 to n.
10. How would you modify the for loop of the InvestmentTable.java program to print all balances until the investment has doubled?

Optional **science and business exercises** engage students with realistic applications of Java.

•• Science P6.32  Sounds can be represented by an array of "sample values" that describe the intensity of the sound at a point in time. The program ch06/sound/SoundEffect.java reads a sound file (in WAV format), calls a method process for processing the sample values, and saves the sound file. Your task is to implement the process method by introducing an echo. For each

•• Business P9.21  Implement a superclass Appointment and subclasses Onetime, Daily, and Monthly. An appointment has a description (for example, "see the dentist") and a date and time. Write a method occursOn(int year, int month, int day) that checks whether the appointment occurs on that date. For example, for a monthly appointment, you must check whether the day of the month matches. Then fill an array of Appointment objects with a mixture of appointments. Have the user enter a date and print out all appointments that occur on that date.

**section_1/DoubleInvestment.java**
```
1  /**
2     This program computes the time required to double an investment.
3  */
4  public class DoubleInvestment
5  {
6     public static void main(String[] args)
7     {
8        final double RATE = 5;
9        final double INITIAL_BALANCE = 10000;
10       final double TARGET = 2 * INITIAL_BALANCE;
11
12       double balance = INITIAL_BALANCE;
13       int year = 0;
14
15       // Count the years required for the investment to double
16
17       while (balance < TARGET)
18       {
19          year++;
20          double interest = balance * RATE / 100;
21          balance = balance + interest;
22       }
23
24       System.out.println("The investment doubled after "
25          + year + " years.");
26    }
27 }
```

**Program listings** are carefully designed for easy reading, going well beyond simple color coding. Methods are set off by a subtle outline.

**Common Errors** describe the kinds of errors that students often make, with an explanation of why the errors occur, and what to do about them.

Common Error 6.4

### Length and Size

Unfortunately, the Java syntax for determining the number of elements in an array, an array list, and a string is not at all consistent. It is a common error to confuse these. You just have to remember the correct syntax for every data type.

| Data Type | Number of Elements |
|---|---|
| Array | a.length |
| Array list | a.size() |
| String | a.length() |

Programming Tip 3.5

### Hand-Tracing

A very useful technique for understanding whether a program works correctly is called *hand-tracing*. You simulate the program's activity on a sheet of paper. You can use this method with pseudocode or Java code.

Get an index card, a cocktail napkin, or whatever sheet of paper is within reach. Make a column for each variable. Have the program code ready. Use a marker, such as a paper clip, to mark the current statement. In your mind, execute statements one at a time. Every time the value of a variable changes, cross out the old value and write the new value below the old one.

For example, let's trace the tax program with the data from the program run on page 102. In lines 15 and 16, tax1 and tax2 are initialized to 0.

*Hand-tracing helps you understand whether a program works correctly.*

```
 8  public static void main(String[] args)
 9  {
10     final double RATE1 = 0.10;
11     final double RATE2 = 0.25;
12     final double RATE1_SINGLE_LIMIT = 32000;
13     final double RATE1_MARRIED_LIMIT = 64000;
14
15     double tax1 = 0;
16     double tax2 = 0;
17
```

| tax1 | tax2 | income | marital status |
|---|---|---|---|
| 0 | 0 | | |

**Programming Tips** explain good programming practices, and encourage students to be more productive with tips and techniques such as hand-tracing.

In lines 22 and 25, income and maritalStatus are initialized by input statements.

```
20     Scanner in = new Scanner(System.in);
21     System.out.print("Please enter your income: ");
22     double income = in.nextDouble();
23
24     System.out.print("Please enter s for single, m for married: ");
25     String maritalStatus = in.next();
```

| tax1 | tax2 | income | marital status |
|---|---|---|---|
| 0 | 0 | 80000 | m |

Special Topic 7.2

### File Dialog Boxes

In a program with a graphical user interface, you will want to use a file dialog box (such as the one shown in the figure below) whenever the users of your program need to pick a file. The JFileChooser class implements a file dialog box for the Swing user-interface toolkit.

The JFileChooser class has many options to fine-tune the display of the dialog box, but in its most basic form it is quite simple: Construct a file chooser object; then call the showOpenDialog or showSaveDialog method. Both methods show the same dialog box, but the button for selecting a file is labeled "Open" or "Save", depending on which method you call.

For better placement of the dialog box on the screen, you can specify the user-interface component over which to pop up the dialog box. If you don't care where the dialog box pops up, you can simply pass null. The showOpenDialog and showSaveDialog methods return either JFileChooser.APPROVE_OPTION, if the user has chosen a file, or JFileChooser.CANCEL_OPTION, if the user canceled the selection. If a file was chosen, then you call the getSelectedFile method to obtain a File object that describes the file. Here is a complete example:

**ONLINE EXAMPLE**
A program that demonstrates how to use a file chooser.

```
JFileChooser chooser = new JFileChooser();
Scanner in = null;
if (chooser.showOpenDialog(null) == JFileChooser.APPROVE_OPTION)
{
    File selectedFile = chooser.getSelectedFile();
    in = new Scanner(selectedFile);
    . . .
}
```

**Special Topics** present optional topics and provide additional explanation of others. New features of Java 7 are also covered in these notes.

Call with showOpenDialog method

### *Random Fact 4.1* The First Bug

According to legend, the first bug was found in the Mark II, a huge electromechanical computer at Harvard University. It really was caused by a bug—a moth was trapped in a relay switch.

Actually, from the note that the operator left in the log book next to the moth (see the figure), it appears as if the term "bug" had already been in active use at the time.

The pioneering computer scientist Maurice Wilkes wrote, "Somehow, at the Moore School and afterwards, one had always assumed there would be no particular difficulty in getting programs right. I can remember the exact instant in time at which it dawned on me that a great part of my future life would be spent finding mistakes in my own programs."

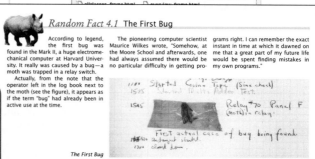

*The First Bug*

**Random Facts** provide historical and social information on computing—for interest and to fulfill the "historical and social context" requirements of the ACM/IEEE curriculum guidelines.

# WileyPLUS

WileyPLUS is an online environment that supports students and instructors. This book's WileyPLUS course can complement the printed text or replace it altogether.

## For Students

Different learning styles, different levels of proficiency, different levels of preparation—each student is unique. WileyPLUS empowers all students to take advantage of their individual strengths.

Integrated, multi-media resources—including audio and visual exhibits and demonstration problems—encourage active learning and provide multiple study paths to fit each student's learning preferences.

- Worked Examples apply the problem-solving steps in the book to another realistic example.
- Video Examples present the author explaining the steps he is taking and showing his work as he solves a programming problem.
- Animations of key concepts allow students to replay dynamic explanations that instructors usually provide on a whiteboard.

Self-assessments are linked to relevant portions of the text. Students can take control of their own learning and practice until they master the material.

- Practice quizzes can reveal areas where students need to focus.
- "Learn by doing" lab exercises can be assigned for self-study or for use in the lab.
- "Code completion" questions enable students to practice programming skills by filling in small code snippets and getting immediate feedback.

## For Instructors

WileyPLUS includes all of the instructor resources found on the companion site, and more.

WileyPLUS gives you tools for identifying those students who are falling behind, allowing you to intervene accordingly, without having to wait for them to come to office hours.

- Practice quizzes for pre-reading assessment, self-quizzing, or additional practice can be used as-is or modified for your course needs.
- Multi-step laboratory exercises can be used in lab or assigned for extra student practice.

WileyPLUS simplifies and automates student performance assessment, making assignments, and scoring student work.

- An extensive set of multiple-choice questions for quizzing and testing have been developed to focus on skills, not just terminology.
- "Code completion" questions can also be added to online quizzes.
- Solutions to all review and programming exercises are provided.

To order *Big Java, Late Objects,* with its WileyPLUS course for your students, use ISBN 978-1-118-28906-8.

## With WileyPLUS ...

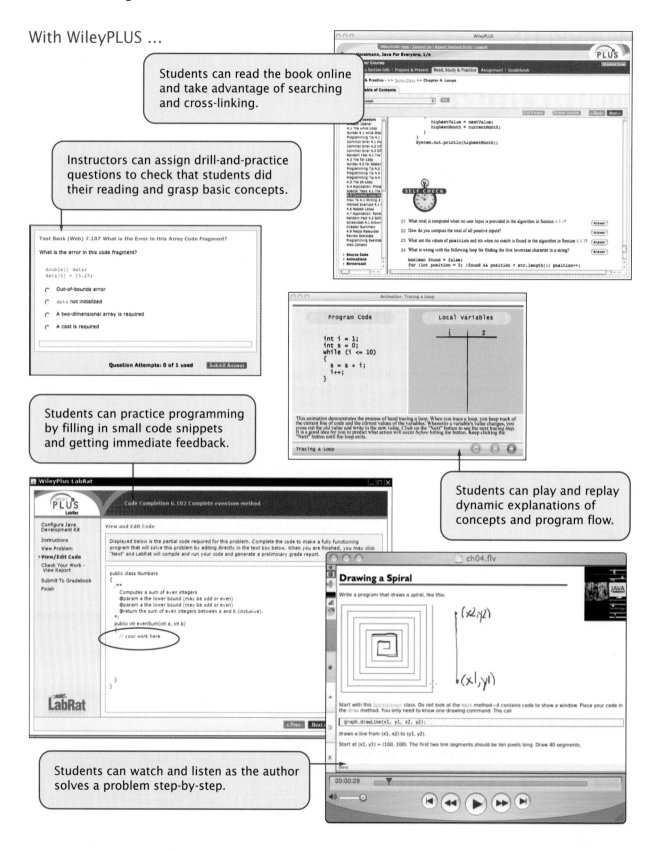

Students can read the book online and take advantage of searching and cross-linking.

Instructors can assign drill-and-practice questions to check that students did their reading and grasp basic concepts.

Students can practice programming by filling in small code snippets and getting immediate feedback.

Students can play and replay dynamic explanations of concepts and program flow.

Students can watch and listen as the author solves a problem step-by-step.

# Acknowledgments

Many thanks to Beth Lang Golub, Don Fowley, Elizabeth Mills, Thomas Kulesa, Wendy Ashenberg, Lisa Gee, Andre Legaspi, Kevin Holm, and John Curley at John Wiley & Sons, and Vickie Piercey at Publishing Services for their help with this project. An especially deep acknowledgment and thanks goes to Cindy Johnson for her hard work, sound judgment, and amazing attention to detail.

I am grateful to Jose Cordova, *University of Louisiana, Monroe*, Rick Giles, *Acadia University*, Amitava Karmaker, *University of Wisconsin, Stout*, Khaled Mansour, *Washtenaw Community College*, Patricia McDermott-Wells, *Florida International University*, Brent Seales, *University of Kentucky*, Donald Smith, *Columbia College*, and David Woolbright, *Columbus State University*, for their excellent work on the supplemental material. Thank you also to Jose-Arturo Mora-Soto, Jesica Rivero-Espinosa, and Julio-Angel Cano-Romero of the University of Madrid for their contribution of business exercises.

Many thanks to the individuals who provided feedback, reviewed the manuscript, made valuable suggestions, and brought errors and omissions to my attention. They include:

Lynn Aaron, *SUNY Rockland Community College*

Karen Arlien, *Bismarck State College*

Jay Asundi, *University of Texas, Dallas*

Eugene Backlin, *DePaul University*

William C. Barge, *Trine University*

Bruce J. Barton, *Suffolk County Community College*

Sanjiv K. Bhatia, *University of Missouri, St. Louis*

Anna Bieszczad, *California State University, Channel Islands*

Jackie Bird, *Northwestern University*

Eric Bishop, *Northland Pioneer College*

Paul Bladek, *Edmonds Community College*

Paul Logasa Bogen II, *Texas A&M University*

Irene Bruno, *George Mason University*

Paolo Bucci, *Ohio State University*

Joe Burgin, *College of Southern Maryland*

Robert P. Burton, *Brigham Young University*

Leonello Calabresi, *University of Maryland University College*

Martine Ceberio, *University of Texas, El Paso*

Uday Chakraborty, *University of Missouri, St. Louis*

Suchindran Chatterjee, *Arizona State University*

Xuemin Chen, *Texas Southern University*

Haiyan Cheng, *Willamette University*

Chakib Chraibi, *Barry University*

Ta-Tao Chuang, *Gonzaga University*

Vincent Cicirello, *Richard Stockton College*

Mark Clement, *Brigham Young University*

Gerald Cohen, *St. Joseph's College*

Ralph Conrad, *San Antonio College*

Dave Cook, *Stephen F. Austin State University*

Rebecca Crellin, *Community College of Allegheny County*

Leslie Damon, *Vermont Technical College*

Geoffrey D. Decker, *Northern Illinois University*

Khaled Deeb, *Barry University, School of Adult and Continuing Education*

Akshaye Dhawan, *Ursinus College*

Julius Dichter, *University of Bridgeport*

Mike Domaratzki, *University of Manitoba*

Philip Dorin, *Loyola Marymount University*

Anthony J. Dos Reis, *SUNY New Paltz*

Elizabeth Drake, *Santa Fe College*

Tom Duffy, *Norwalk Community College*

Michael Eckmann, *Skidmore College*

Sander Eller, *California State Polytechnic University, Pomona*

Amita Engineer, *Valencia Community College*

Dave Evans, *Pasadena Community College*

James Factor, *Alverno College*

Chris Fietkiewicz, *Case Western Reserve University*

Terrell Foty, *Portland Community College*

Valerie Frear, *Daytona State College*

Ryan Garlick, *University of North Texas*

Aaron Garrett, *Jacksonville State University*

Stephen Gilbert, *Orange Coast College*

Peter van der Goes, *Rose State College*

Billie Goldstein, *Temple University*

Michael Gourley, *University of Central Oklahoma*

Grigoriy Grinberg, *Montgomery College*

Linwu Gu, *Indiana University*

Sylvain Guinepain, *University of Oklahoma, Norman*

Bruce Haft, *Glendale Community College*

Nancy Harris, *James Madison University*

Allan M. Hart, *Minnesota State University, Mankato*

Ric Heishman, *George Mason University*

Guy Helmer, *Iowa State University*

Katherin Herbert, *Montclair State University*

Rodney Hoffman, *Occidental College*

May Hou, *Norfolk State University*

John Houlihan, *Loyola University*

Andree Jacobson, *University of New Mexico*

Eric Jiang, *University of San Diego*

Christopher M. Johnson, *Guilford College*

Jonathan Kapleau, *New Jersey Institute of Technology*

Amitava Karmaker, *University of Wisconsin, Stout*

Rajkumar Kempaiah, *College of Mount Saint Vincent*

Mugdha Khaladkar, *New Jersey Institute of Technology*

Richard Kick, *Newbury Park High School*

Julie King, *Sullivan University, Lexington*

Samuel Kohn, *Touro College*

April Kontostathis, *Ursinus College*

Ron Krawitz, *DeVry University*

Nat Kumaresan, *Georgia Perimeter College*

Debbie Lamprecht, *Texas Tech University*

Jian Lin, *Eastern Connecticut State University*

Hunter Lloyd, *Montana State University*

Cheng Luo, *Coppin State University*

Kelvin Lwin, *University of California, Merced*

Frank Malinowski, *Dalton College*

John S. Mallozzi, *Iona College*

Khaled Mansour, *Washtenaw Community College*

Kenneth Martin, *University of North Florida*

Deborah Mathews, *J. Sargeant Reynolds Community College*

Louis Mazzucco, *State University of New York at Cobleskill and Excelsior College*

Drew McDermott, *Yale University*

Hugh McGuire, *Grand Valley State University*

Michael L. Mick, *Purdue University, Calumet*

Jeanne Milostan, *University of California, Merced*
Sandeep Mitra, *SUNY Brockport*
Michel Mitri, *James Madison University*
Kenrick Mock, *University of Alaska Anchorage*
Namdar Mogharreban, *Southern Illinois University*
Shamsi Moussavi, *Massbay Community College*
Nannette Napier, *Georgia Gwinnett College*
Tony Tuan Nguyen, *De Anza College*
Michael Ondrasek, *Wright State University*
K. Palaniappan, *University of Missouri*
James Papademas, *Oakton Community College*
Gary Parker, *Connecticut College*
Jody Paul, *Metropolitan State College of Denver*
Mark Pendergast, *Florida Gulf Coast University*
James T. Pepe, *Bentley University*
Jeff Pittges, *Radford University*
Tom Plunkett, *Virginia Tech*
Linda L. Preece, *Southern Illinois University*
Vijay Ramachandran, *Colgate University*
Craig Reinhart, *California Lutheran University*
Jonathan Robinson, *Touro College*
Chaman Lal Sabharwal, *Missouri University of Science & Technology*
Katherine Salch, *Illinois Central College*
Namita Sarawagi, *Rhode Island College*
Ben Schafer, *University of Northern Iowa*
Walter Schilling, *Milwaukee School of Engineering*
Jeffrey Paul Scott, *Blackhawk Technical College*
Amon Seagull, *NOVA Southeastern University*
Linda Seiter, *John Carroll University*
Kevin Seppi, *Brigham Young University*
Ricky J. Sethi, *UCLA, USC ISI, and DeVry University*
Ali Shaykhian, *Florida Institute of Technology*
Lal Shimpi, *Saint Augustine's College*
Victor Shtern, *Boston University*
Rahul Simha, *George Washington University*
Jeff Six, *University of Delaware*
Donald W. Smith, *Columbia College*
Derek Snow, *University of Southern Alabama*
Peter Spoerri, *Fairfield University*
David R. Stampf, *Suffolk County Community College*
Peter Stanchev, *Kettering University*
Ryan Stansifer, *Florida Institute of Technology*
Stu Steiner, *Eastern Washington University*
Robert Strader, *Stephen F. Austin State University*
David Stucki, *Otterbein University*
Ashok Subramanian, *University of Missouri, St Louis*
Jeremy Suing, *University of Nebraska, Lincoln*
Dave Sullivan, *Boston University*
Vaidy Sunderam, *Emory University*
Hong Sung, *University of Central Oklahoma*
Monica Sweat, *Georgia Tech University*
Joseph Szurek, *University of Pittsburgh, Greensburg*
Jack Tan, *University of Wisconsin*
Cynthia Tanner, *West Virginia University*
Russell Tessier, *University of Massachusetts, Amherst*
Krishnaprasad Thirunarayan, *Wright State University*
Megan Thomas, *California State University, Stanislaus*
Timothy Urness, *Drake University*
Eliana Valenzuela-Andrade, *University of Puerto Rico at Arecibo*

Tammy VanDeGrift, *University of Portland*
Philip Ventura, *Broward College*
David R. Vineyard, *Kettering University*
Qi Wang, *Northwest Vista College*
Jonathan Weissman, *Finger Lakes Community College*
Reginald White, *Black Hawk Community College*
Ying Xie, *Kennesaw State University*
Arthur Yanushka, *Christian Brothers University*

Chen Ye, *University of Illinois, Chicago*
Wook-Sung Yoo, *Fairfield University*
Steve Zale, *Middlesex County College*
Bahram Zartoshty, *California State University, Northridge*
Frank Zeng, *Indiana Wesleyan University*
Hairong Zhao, *Purdue University Calumet*
Stephen Zilora, *Rochester Institute of Technology*

And a special thank you to our class testers:

Eugene Backlin and the students of DePaul University, Loop
Debra M. Duke and the students of J. Sargeant Reynolds Community College
Gerald Gordon and the students of DePaul University, Loop
Mike Gourley and the students of the University of Central Oklahoma
Mohammad Morovati and the students of the College of DuPage
Mutsumi Nakamura and the students of Arizona State University
George Novacky and the students of the University of Pittsburgh
Darrin Rothe and the students of the Milwaukee School of Engineering
Paige Rutner and the students of Georgia Southern University
Narasimha Shashidhar and the students of Sam Houston State University
Mark Sherriff and the students of the University of Virginia
Frank Zeng and the students of Indiana Wesleyan University

# CONTENTS

➕  Available online in WileyPLUS and at www.wiley.com/college/horstmann.

⊕ Available online in WileyPLUS and at www.wiley.com/college/horstmann.

## ALPHABETICAL LIST OF SYNTAX BOXES

| CHAPTER | Common Errors | How Tos and Worked Examples |
|---|---|---|

⊕  Available online in WileyPLUS and at www.wiley.com/college/horstmann.

|  Programming Tips |  Special Topics |  Random Facts |
|---|---|---|

➕ Available online in WileyPLUS and at www.wiley.com/college/horstmann.

⊕  Available online in WileyPLUS and at www.wiley.com/college/horstmann.

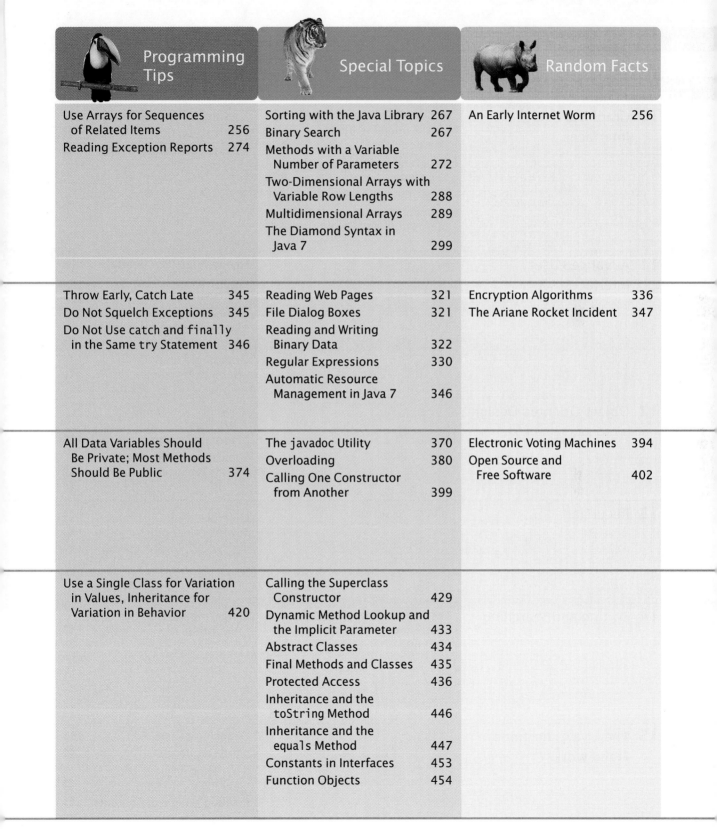

➕ Available online in WileyPLUS and at www.wiley.com/college/horstmann.

⊕ Available online in WileyPLUS and at www.wiley.com/college/horstmann.

➕ Available online in WileyPLUS and at www.wiley.com/college/horstmann.

⊕  Available online in WileyPLUS and at www.wiley.com/college/horstmann.

|  Programming Tips |  Special Topics | |  Random Facts |
|---|---|---|---|
| | Static Classes | 728 | |
| | Open Addressing | 747 | |
| | | | |
| | Wildcard Types | 828 | |
| | Reflection | 832 | |
| | | | |
| Use the Runnable Interface ⊕ <br> Check for Thread Interruptions in the run Method of a Thread ⊕ | Thread Pools ⊕ <br> Object Locks and Synchronized Methods ⊕ <br> The Java Memory Model ⊕ | | Embedded Systems ⊕ |
| Use High-Level Libraries ⊕ | | | |
| Stick with the Standard ⊕ <br> Avoid Unnecessary Data Replication ⊕ <br> Don't Replicate Columns in a Table ⊕ <br> Don't Hardwire Database Connection Parameters into Your Program ⊕ <br> Let the Database Do the Work ⊕ | Primary Keys and Indexes ⊕ <br> Transactions ⊕ <br> Object-Relational Mapping ⊕ | | Databases and Privacy ⊕ |
| Prefer XML Elements over Attributes ⊕ <br> Avoid Children with Mixed Elements and Text ⊕ | Schema Languages ⊕ <br> Other XML Technologies ⊕ | | Word Processing and Typesetting Systems ⊕ <br> Grammars, Parsers, and Compilers ⊕ |
| | Session State and Cookies ⊕ <br> AJAX ⊕ | | |

⊕  Available online in WileyPLUS and at www.wiley.com/college/horstmann.

CHAPTER **1**

# INTRODUCTION

Just as you gather tools, study a project, and make a plan for tackling it, in this chapter you will gather up the basics you need to start learning to program. After a brief introduction to computer hardware, software, and programming in general, you will learn how to write and run your first Java program. You will also learn how to diagnose and fix programming errors, and how to use pseudocode to describe an algorithm—a step-by-step description of how to solve a problem—as you plan your computer programs.

# 1.1  Computer Programs

**Computers execute very basic instructions in rapid succession.**

You have probably used a computer for work or fun. Many people use computers for everyday tasks such as electronic banking or writing a term paper. Computers are good for such tasks. They can handle repetitive chores, such as totaling up numbers or placing words on a page, without getting bored or exhausted.

The flexibility of a computer is quite an amazing phenomenon. The same machine can balance your checkbook, lay out your term paper, and play a game. In contrast, other machines carry out a much narrower range of tasks; a car drives and a toaster toasts. Computers can carry out a wide range of tasks because they execute different programs, each of which directs the computer to work on a specific task.

**A computer program is a sequence of instructions and decisions.**

The computer itself is a machine that stores data (numbers, words, pictures), interacts with devices (the monitor, the sound system, the printer), and executes programs. A **computer program** tells a computer, in minute detail, the sequence of steps that are needed to fulfill a task. The physical computer and peripheral devices are collectively called the **hardware**. The programs the computer executes are called the **software**.

Today's computer programs are so sophisticated that it is hard to believe that they are composed of extremely primitive instructions. A typical instruction may be one of the following:

- Put a red dot at a given screen position.
- Add up two numbers.
- If this value is negative, continue the program at a certain instruction.

The computer user has the illusion of smooth interaction because a program contains a huge number of such instructions, and because the computer can execute them at great speed.

**Programming is the act of designing and implementing computer programs.**

The act of designing and implementing computer programs is called **programming**. In this book, you will learn how to program a computer—that is, how to direct the computer to execute tasks.

To write a computer game with motion and sound effects or a word processor that supports fancy fonts and pictures is a complex task that requires a team of many highly-skilled programmers. Your first programming efforts will be more mundane. The concepts and skills you learn in this book form an important foundation, and you should not be disappointed if your first programs do not rival the sophisticated software that is familiar to you. Actually, you will find that there is an immense thrill even in simple programming tasks. It is an amazing experience to see the computer precisely and quickly carry out a task that would take you hours of drudgery, to make small changes in a program that lead to immediate improvements, and to see the computer become an extension of your mental powers.

**SELF CHECK**

1. What is required to play music on a computer?
2. Why is a CD player less flexible than a computer?
3. What does a computer user need to know about programming in order to play a video game?

## 1.2  The Anatomy of a Computer

To understand the programming process, you need to have a rudimentary understanding of the building blocks that make up a computer. We will look at a personal computer. Larger computers have faster, larger, or more powerful components, but they have fundamentally the same design.

At the heart of the computer lies the **central processing unit (CPU)** (see Figure 1). The inside wiring of the CPU is enormously complicated. For example, the Intel Core processor (a popular CPU for personal computers at the time of this writing) is composed of several hundred million structural elements, called *transistors*.

> The central processing unit (CPU) performs program control and data processing.

The CPU performs program control and data processing. That is, the CPU locates and executes the program instructions; it carries out arithmetic operations such as addition, subtraction, multiplication, and division; it fetches data from external memory or devices and places processed data into storage.

> Storage devices include memory and secondary storage.

There are two kinds of storage. **Primary storage** is made from memory chips: electronic circuits that can store data, provided they are supplied with electric power. **Secondary storage**, usually a **hard disk** (see Figure 2), provides slower and less expensive storage that persists without electricity. A hard disk consists of rotating platters, which are coated with a magnetic material, and read/write heads, which can detect and change the magnetic flux on the platters.

The computer stores both data and programs. They are located in secondary storage and loaded into memory when the program starts. The program then updates the data in memory and writes the modified data back to secondary storage.

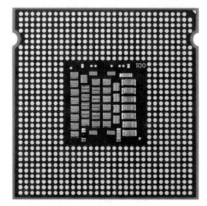

**Figure 1**   Central Processing Unit

**Figure 2**   A Hard Disk

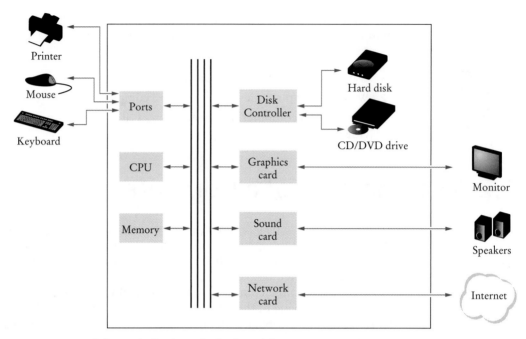

**Figure 3** Schematic Design of a Personal Computer

To interact with a human user, a computer requires peripheral devices. The computer transmits information (called *output*) to the user through a display screen, speakers, and printers. The user can enter information (called *input*) for the computer by using a keyboard or a pointing device such as a mouse.

Some computers are self-contained units, whereas others are interconnected through **networks**. Through the network cabling, the computer can read data and programs from central storage locations or send data to other computers. To the user of a networked computer, it may not even be obvious which data reside on the computer itself and which are transmitted through the network.

Figure 3 gives a schematic overview of the architecture of a personal computer. Program instructions and data (such as text, numbers, audio, or video) are stored on the hard disk, on a compact disk (or DVD), or elsewhere on the network. When a program is started, it is brought into memory, where the CPU can read it. The CPU reads the program one instruction at a time. As directed by these instructions, the CPU reads data, modifies it, and writes it back to memory or the hard disk. Some program instructions will cause the CPU to place dots on the display screen or printer or to vibrate the speaker. As these actions happen many times over and at great speed, the human user will perceive images and sound. Some program instructions read user input from the keyboard or mouse. The program analyzes the nature of these inputs and then executes the next appropriate instruction.

**SELF CHECK**

4. Where is a program stored when it is not currently running?
5. Which part of the computer carries out arithmetic operations, such as addition and multiplication?

**Practice It**    Now you can try these exercises at the end of the chapter: R1.2, R1.3.

## Random Fact 1.1  The ENIAC and the Dawn of Computing

The ENIAC (electronic numerical integrator and computer) was the first usable electronic computer. It was designed by J. Presper Eckert and John Mauchly at the University of Pennsylvania and was completed in 1946—two years before transistors were invented. The computer was housed in a large room and consisted of many cabinets containing about 18,000 vacuum tubes (see Figure 4). Vacuum tubes burned out at the rate of several tubes per day. An attendant with a shopping cart full of tubes constantly made the rounds and replaced defective ones. The computer was programmed by connecting wires on panels. Each wiring configuration would set up the computer for a particular problem. To have the computer work on a different problem, the wires had to be replugged.

Work on the ENIAC was supported by the U.S. Navy, which was interested in computations of ballistic tables that would give the trajectory of a projectile, depending on the wind resistance, initial velocity, and atmospheric conditions. To compute the trajectories, one must find the numerical solutions of certain differential equations; hence the name "numerical integrator". Before machines like the ENIAC were developed, humans did this kind of work, and until the 1950s the word "computer" referred to these people. The ENIAC was later used for peaceful purposes, such as the tabulation of U.S. Census data.

**Figure 4**   The ENIAC

# 1.3 The Java Programming Language

In order to write a computer program, you need to provide a sequence of instructions that the CPU can execute. A computer program consists of a large number of simple CPU instructions, and it is tedious and error-prone to specify them one by one. For that reason, **high-level programming languages** have been created. In a high-level language, you specify the actions that your program should carry out. A **compiler** translates the high-level instructions into the more detailed instructions required by the CPU. Many different programming languages have been designed for different purposes.

In 1991, a group led by James Gosling and Patrick Naughton at Sun Microsystems designed a programming language, code-named "Green", for use in

*James Gosling*

consumer devices, such as intelligent television "set-top" boxes. The language was designed to be simple, secure, and usable for many different processor types. No customer was ever found for this technology.

Gosling recounts that in 1994 the team realized, "We could write a really cool browser. It was one of the few things in the client/server mainstream that needed some of the weird things we'd done: architecture neutral, real-time, reliable, secure." Java was introduced to an enthusiastic crowd at the SunWorld exhibition in 1995, together with a browser that ran **applets**—Java code that can be located anywhere on the Internet. Figure 5 shows a typical example of an applet.

Since then, Java has grown at a phenomenal rate. Programmers have embraced the language because it is easier to use than its closest rival, C++. In addition, Java has a rich **library** that makes it possible to write portable programs that can bypass proprietary operating systems—a feature that was eagerly sought by those who wanted to be independent of those proprietary systems and was bitterly fought by their vendors. A "micro edition" and an "enterprise edition" of the Java library allow Java programmers to target hardware ranging from smart cards and cell phones to the largest Internet servers.

Because Java was designed for the Internet, it has two attributes that make it very suitable for beginners: safety and portability.

The safety features of the Java language make it possible to run Java programs in a browser without fear that they might attack your computer. As an added benefit, these features also help you to learn the language faster. When you make an error that results in unsafe behavior, you receive an accurate error report.

The other benefit of Java is portability. The same Java program will run, without change, on Windows, UNIX, Linux, or Macintosh. In order to achieve portability, the Java compiler does not translate Java programs directly into CPU instructions. Instead, compiled Java programs contain instructions for the Java **virtual machine**,

Java was originally designed for programming consumer devices, but it was first successfully used to write Internet applets.

Java was designed to be safe and portable, benefiting both Internet users and students.

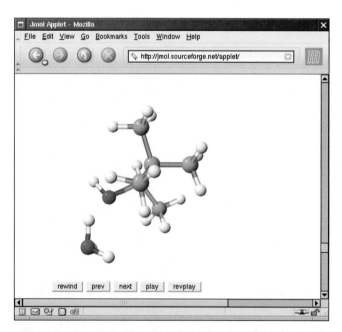

**Figure 5** An Applet for Visualizing Molecules Running in a Browser Window (http://jmol.sourceforge.net/)

Java programs are distributed as instructions for a virtual machine, making them platform-independent.

a program that simulates a real CPU. Portability is another benefit for the beginning student. You do not have to learn how to write programs for different platforms.

At this time, Java is firmly established as one of the most important languages for general-purpose programming as well as for computer science instruction. However, although Java is a good language for beginners, it is not perfect, for three reasons.

Because Java was not specifically designed for students, no thought was given to making it really simple to write basic programs. A certain amount of technical machinery is necessary in Java to write even the simplest programs. This is not a problem for professional programmers, but it can be a nuisance for beginning students. As you learn how to program in Java, there will be times when you will be asked to be satisfied with a preliminary explanation and wait for more complete detail in a later chapter.

Java has been extended many times during its life—see Table 1. In this book, we assume that you have Java version 5 or later.

Java has a very large library. Focus on learning those parts of the library that you need for your programming projects.

Finally, you cannot hope to learn all of Java in one course. The Java language itself is relatively simple, but Java contains a vast set of *library packages* that are required to write useful programs. There are packages for graphics, user-interface design, cryptography, networking, sound, database storage, and many other purposes. Even expert Java programmers cannot hope to know the contents of all of the packages—they just use those that they need for particular projects.

Using this book, you should expect to learn a good deal about the Java language and about the most important packages. Keep in mind that the central goal of this book is not to make you memorize Java minutiae, but to teach you how to think about programming.

| Table 1  Java Versions | | |
|:---:|:---:|:---:|
| Version | Year | Important New Features |
| 1.0 | 1996 | |
| 1.1 | 1997 | Inner classes |
| 1.2 | 1998 | Swing, Collections framework |
| 1.3 | 2000 | Performance enhancements |
| 1.4 | 2002 | Assertions, XML support |
| 5 | 2004 | Generic classes, enhanced for loop, auto-boxing, enumerations, annotations |
| 6 | 2006 | Library improvements |
| 7 | 2011 | Small language changes and library improvements |

**SELF CHECK**

**6.** What are the two most important benefits of the Java language?

**7.** How long does it take to learn the entire Java library?

**Practice It**    Now you can try this exercise at the end of the chapter: R1.5.

# 1.4 Becoming Familiar with Your Programming Environment

> Set aside some time to become familiar with the programming environment that you will use for your class work.

Many students find that the tools they need as programmers are very different from the software with which they are familiar. You should spend some time making yourself familiar with your programming environment. Because computer systems vary widely, this book can only give an outline of the steps you need to follow. It is a good idea to participate in a hands-on lab, or to ask a knowledgeable friend to give you a tour.

Step 1    Start the Java development environment.

Computer systems differ greatly in this regard. On many computers there is an **integrated development environment** in which you can write and test your programs. On other computers you first launch an **editor,** a program that functions like a word processor, in which you can enter your Java instructions; you then open a *console window* and type commands to execute your program. You need to find out how to get started with your environment.

> An editor is a program for entering and modifying text, such as a Java program.

Step 2    Write a simple program.

The traditional choice for the very first program in a new programming language is a program that displays a simple greeting: "Hello, World!". Let us follow that tradition. Here is the "Hello, World!" program in Java:

```java
public class HelloPrinter
{
   public static void main(String[] args)
   {
      System.out.println("Hello, World!");
   }
}
```

We will examine this program in the next section.

No matter which programming environment you use, you begin your activity by typing the program statements into an editor window.

Create a new file and call it HelloPrinter.java, using the steps that are appropriate for your environment. (If your environment requires that you supply a project name in addition to the file name, use the name hello for the project.) Enter the program instructions *exactly* as they are given above. Alternatively, locate the electronic copy in this book's companion code and paste it into your editor.

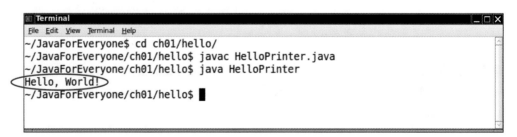

**Figure 6**   Running the HelloPrinter Program in a Console Window

**Figure 7**
Running the
`HelloPrinter`
Program in an
Integrated
Development
Environment

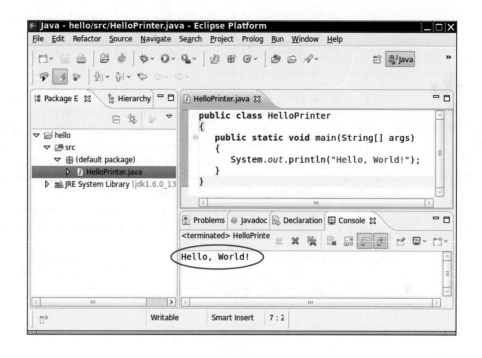

Java is case sensitive.
You must be careful
about distinguishing
between upper- and
lowercase letters.

As you write this program, pay careful attention to the various symbols, and keep in mind that Java is **case sensitive**. You must enter upper- and lowercase letters exactly as they appear in the program listing. You cannot type `MAIN` or `PrintLn`. If you are not careful, you will run into problems—see Common Error 1.2 on page 16.

Step 3    Run the program.

The process for running a program depends greatly on your programming environment. You may have to click a button or enter some commands. When you run the test program, the message

```
Hello, World!
```

will appear somewhere on the screen (see Figures 6 and 7).

The Java compiler
translates source
code into class files
that contain
instructions for the
Java virtual machine.

In order to run your program, the Java compiler translates your **source code** (that is, the statements that you wrote) into *class files*. (A class file contains instructions for the Java virtual machine.) After the compiler has translated your program into virtual machine instructions, the virtual machine executes them. Figure 8 summarizes the process of creating and running a Java program. In some programming environments,

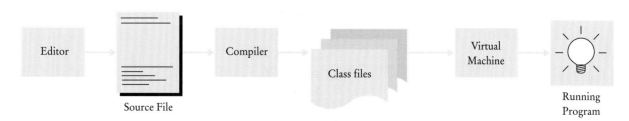

**Figure 8**    From Source Code to Running Program

the compiler and virtual machine are essentially invisible to the programmer—they are automatically executed whenever you ask to run a Java program. In other environments, you need to launch the compiler and virtual machine explicitly.

ANIMATION
*Compilation Process*

Step 4    Organize your work.

As a programmer, you write programs, try them out, and improve them. You store your programs in **files**. Files are stored in **folders** or **directories**. A folder can contain files as well as other folders, which themselves can contain more files and folders (see Figure 9). This hierarchy can be quite large, and you need not be concerned with all of its branches. However, you should create folders for organizing your work. It is a good idea to make a separate folder for your programming class. Inside that folder, make a separate folder for each program.

Some programming environments place your programs into a default location if you don't specify a folder yourself. In that case, you need to find out where those files are located.

Be sure that you understand where your files are located in the folder hierarchy. This information is essential when you submit files for grading, and for making backup copies (see Programming Tip 1.1).

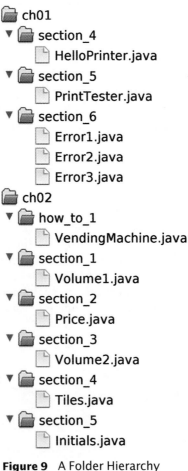

**Figure 9**   A Folder Hierarchy

8. Where is the `HelloPrinter.java` file stored on your computer?

9. What do you do to protect yourself from data loss when you work on programming projects?

**Practice It** Now you can try this exercise at the end of the chapter: R1.6.

---

**Programming Tip 1.1**

### Backup Copies

You will spend many hours creating and improving Java programs. It is easy to delete a file by accident, and occasionally files are lost because of a computer malfunction. Retyping the contents of lost files is frustrating and time-consuming. It is therefore crucially important that you learn how to safeguard files and get in the habit of doing so *before* disaster strikes. Backing up files on a memory stick is an easy and convenient storage method for many people. Another increasingly popular form of backup is Internet file storage. Here are a few pointers to keep in mind:

- *Back up often.* Backing up a file takes only a few seconds, and you will hate yourself if you have to spend many hours recreating work that you could have saved easily. I recommend that you back up your work once every thirty minutes.

- *Rotate backups.* Use more than one directory for backups, and rotate them. That is, first back up onto the first directory. Then back up onto the second directory. Then use the third, and then go back to the first. That way you always have three recent backups. If your recent changes made matters worse, you can then go back to the older version.

> Develop a strategy for keeping backup copies of your work before disaster strikes.

- *Pay attention to the backup direction.* Backing up involves copying files from one place to another. It is important that you do this right—that is, copy from your work location to the backup location. If you do it the wrong way, you will overwrite a newer file with an older version.

- *Check your backups once in a while.* Double-check that your backups are where you think they are. There is nothing more frustrating than to find out that the backups are not there when you need them.

- *Relax, then restore.* When you lose a file and need to restore it from a backup, you are likely to be in an unhappy, nervous state. Take a deep breath and think through the recovery process before you start. It is not uncommon for an agitated computer user to wipe out the last backup when trying to restore a damaged file.

---

**VIDEO EXAMPLE 1.1**

### Compiling and Running a Program

This Video Example shows how to compile and run a simple Java program.

# 1.5 Analyzing Your First Program

In this section, we will analyze the first Java program in detail. Here again is the source code:

**section_5/HelloPrinter.java**

```
1   public class HelloPrinter
2   {
3      public static void main(String[] args)
4      {
5         System.out.println("Hello, World!");
6      }
7   }
```

The line

```
public class HelloPrinter
```

indicates the declaration of a **class** called HelloPrinter.

> Classes are the fundamental building blocks of Java programs.

Every Java program consists of one or more classes. Classes are the fundamental building blocks of Java programs. You will have to wait until Chapter 8 for a full explanation of classes.

The word public denotes that the class is usable by the "public". You will later encounter private features.

In Java, every source file can contain at most one public class, and the name of the public class must match the name of the file containing the class. For example, the class HelloPrinter must be contained in a file named HelloPrinter.java.

The construction

```
public static void main(String[] args)
{
   . . .
}
```

> Every Java application contains a class with a main method. When the application starts, the instructions in the main method are executed.

declares a **method** called main. A method contains a collection of programming instructions that describe how to carry out a particular task. Every Java application must have a main method. Most Java programs contain other methods besides main, and you will see in Chapter 5 how to write other methods.

The term static is explained in more detail in Chapter 8, and the meaning of String[] args is covered in Chapter 7. At this time, simply consider

> Each class contains declarations of methods. Each method contains a sequence of instructions.

```
public class ClassName
{
   public static void main(String[] args)
   {
      . . .
   }
}
```

as a part of the "plumbing" that is required to create a Java program. Our first program has all instructions inside the main method of the class.

The main method contains one or more instructions called **statements**. Each statement ends in a semicolon (;). When a program runs, the statements in the main method are executed one by one.

## Syntax 1.1  Java Program

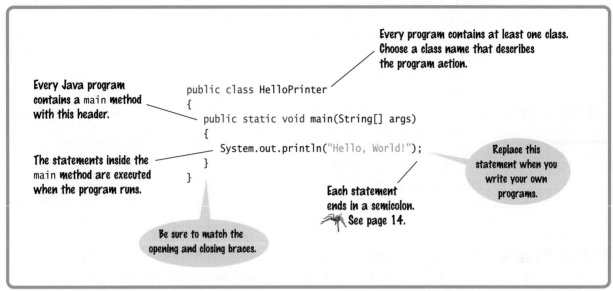

Every program contains at least one class.
Choose a class name that describes
the program action.

Every Java program
contains a main **method**
with this header.

The statements inside the
main **method** are executed
when the program runs.

```java
public class HelloPrinter
{
   public static void main(String[] args)
   {
      System.out.println("Hello, World!");
   }
}
```

Replace this
statement when you
write your own
programs.

Each statement
ends in a semicolon.
See page 14.

Be sure to match the
opening and closing braces.

In our example program, the main method has a single statement:

```java
System.out.println("Hello, World!");
```

This statement prints a line of text, namely "Hello, World!". In this statement, we *call* a method which, for reasons that we will not explain here, is specified by the rather long name System.out.println.

We do not have to implement this method—the programmers who wrote the Java library already did that for us. We simply want the method to perform its intended task, namely to print a value.

Whenever you call a method in Java, you need to specify

**A method is called by specifying the method and its arguments.**

1. The method you want to use (in this case, System.out.println).

2. Any values the method needs to carry out its task (in this case, "Hello, World!"). The technical term for such a value is an **argument**. Arguments are enclosed in parentheses. Multiple arguments are separated by commas.

A sequence of characters enclosed in quotation marks

```java
"Hello, World!"
```

**A string is a sequence of characters enclosed in quotation marks.**

is called a **string**. You must enclose the contents of the string inside quotation marks so that the compiler knows you literally mean "Hello, World!". There is a reason for this requirement. Suppose you need to print the word *main*. By enclosing it in quotation marks, "main", the compiler knows you mean the sequence of characters m a i n, not the method named main. The rule is simply that you must enclose all text strings in quotation marks, so that the compiler considers them plain text and does not try to interpret them as program instructions.

You can also print numerical values. For example, the statement

```java
System.out.println(3 + 4);
```

evaluates the expression 3 + 4 and displays the number 7.

The `System.out.println` method prints a string or a number and then starts a new line. For example, the sequence of statements

```
System.out.println("Hello");
System.out.println("World!");
```

prints two lines of text:

```
Hello
World!
```

**ONLINE EXAMPLE**

A program to demonstrate print commands.

There is a second method, `System.out.print`, that you can use to print an item without starting a new line. For example, the output of the two statements

```
System.out.print("00");
System.out.println(3 + 4);
```

is the single line

```
007
```

**SELF CHECK**

10. How do you modify the `HelloPrinter` program to greet you instead?
11. How would you modify the `HelloPrinter` program to print the word "Hello" vertically?
12. Would the program continue to work if you replaced line 5 with this statement?
    ```
    System.out.println(Hello);
    ```
13. What does the following set of statements print?
    ```
    System.out.print("My lucky number is");
    System.out.println(3 + 4 + 5);
    ```
14. What do the following statements print?
    ```
    System.out.println("Hello");
    System.out.println("");
    System.out.println("World");
    ```

**Practice It**  Now you can try these exercises at the end of the chapter: R1.7, R1.8, P1.5, P1.7.

Common Error 1.1

### Omitting Semicolons

In Java every statement must end in a semicolon. Forgetting to type a semicolon is a common error. It confuses the compiler, because the compiler uses the semicolon to find where one statement ends and the next one starts. The compiler does not use line breaks or closing braces to recognize the end of statements. For example, the compiler considers

```
System.out.println("Hello")
System.out.println("World!");
```

a single statement, as if you had written

```
System.out.println("Hello") System.out.println("World!");
```

Then it doesn't understand that statement, because it does not expect the word `System` following the closing parenthesis after `"Hello"`.

The remedy is simple. Scan every statement for a terminating semicolon, just as you would check that every English sentence ends in a period.

# 1.6 Errors

Experiment a little with the `HelloPrinter` program. What happens if you make a typing error such as

```
System.ou.println("Hello, World!");
System.out.println("Hello, Word!");
```

> A compile-time error is a violation of the programming language rules that is detected by the compiler.

In the first case, the compiler will complain. It will say that it has no clue what you mean by `ou`. The exact wording of the error message is dependent on your development environment, but it might be something like "Cannot find symbol ou". This is a **compile-time error**. Something is wrong according to the rules of the language and the compiler finds it. For this reason, compile-time errors are often called *syntax errors*. When the compiler

*Programmers spend a fair amount of time fixing compile-time and run-time errors.*

finds one or more errors, it refuses to translate the program into Java virtual machine instructions, and as a consequence you have no program that you can run. You must fix the error and compile again. In fact, the compiler is quite picky, and it is common to go through several rounds of fixing compile-time errors before compilation succeeds for the first time.

If the compiler finds an error, it will not simply stop and give up. It will try to report as many errors as it can find, so you can fix them all at once.

Sometimes, an error throws the compiler off track. Suppose, for example, you forget the quotation marks around a string: `System.out.println(Hello, World!)`. The compiler will not complain about the missing quotation marks. Instead, it will report "Cannot find symbol Hello". Unfortunately, the compiler is not very smart and it does not realize that you meant to use a string. It is up to you to realize that you need to enclose strings in quotation marks.

The error in the second line above is of a different kind. The program will compile and run, but its output will be wrong. It will print

```
Hello, Word!
```

> A run-time error causes a program to take an action that the programmer did not intend.

This is a **run-time error**. The program is syntactically correct and does something, but it doesn't do what it is supposed to do. Because run-time errors are caused by logical flaws in the program, they are often called *logic errors*.

This particular run-time error did not include an error message. It simply produced the wrong output. Some kinds of run-time errors are so severe that they generate an **exception**: an error message from the Java virtual machine. For example, if your program includes the statement

```
System.out.println(1 / 0);
```

you will get a run-time error message "Division by zero".

> **ONLINE EXAMPLE**
> ⊕ Three programs to illustrate errors.

During program development, errors are unavoidable. Once a program is longer than a few lines, it would require superhuman concentration to enter it correctly without slipping up once. You will find yourself omitting semicolons or quotation marks more often than you would like, but the compiler will track down these problems for you.

Run-time errors are more troublesome. The compiler will not find them—in fact, the compiler will cheerfully translate any program as long as its syntax is correct—

but the resulting program will do something wrong. It is the responsibility of the program author to test the program and find any run-time errors.

**SELF CHECK**

15. Suppose you omit the "" characters around Hello, World! from the HelloPrinter.java program. Is this a compile-time error or a run-time error?

16. Suppose you change println to printline in the HelloPrinter.java program. Is this a compile-time error or a run-time error?

17. Suppose you change main to hello in the HelloPrinter.java program. Is this a compile-time error or a run-time error?

18. When you used your computer, you may have experienced a program that "crashed" (quit spontaneously) or "hung" (failed to respond to your input). Is that behavior a compile-time error or a run-time error?

19. Why can't you test a program for run-time errors when it has compiler errors?

**Practice It** Now you can try these exercises at the end of the chapter: R1.9, R1.10, R1.11.

---

**Common Error 1.2**

### Misspelling Words

If you accidentally misspell a word, then strange things may happen, and it may not always be completely obvious from the error messages what went wrong. Here is a good example of how simple spelling errors can cause trouble:

```java
public class HelloPrinter
{
    public static void Main(String[] args)
    {
        System.out.println("Hello, World!");
    }
}
```

This class declares a method called Main. The compiler will not consider this to be the same as the main method, because Main starts with an uppercase letter and the Java language is case sensitive. Upper- and lowercase letters are considered to be completely different from each other, and to the compiler Main is no better match for main than rain. The compiler will cheerfully compile your Main method, but when the Java virtual machine reads the compiled file, it will complain about the missing main method and refuse to run the program. Of course, the message "missing main method" should give you a clue where to look for the error.

If you get an error message that seems to indicate that the compiler or virtual machine is on the wrong track, it is a good idea to check for spelling and capitalization. If you misspell the name of a symbol (for example, ou instead of out), the compiler will produce a message such as "cannot find symbol ou". That error message is usually a good clue that you made a spelling error.

---

# 1.7 Problem Solving: Algorithm Design

You will soon learn how to program calculations and decision making in Java. But before we look at the mechanics of implementing computations in the next chapter, let's consider how you can describe the steps that are necessary for finding the solution for a problem.

You may have run across advertisements that encourage you to pay for a computerized service that matches you up with a love partner. Think how this might work. You fill out a form and send it in. Others do the same. The data are processed by a computer program. Is it reasonable to assume that the computer can perform the task of finding the best match for you? Suppose your younger brother, not the computer, had all the forms on his desk. What instructions could you give him? You can't say, "Find the best-looking person who likes inline skating and browsing the Internet". There is no objective standard for good looks, and your brother's opinion (or that of a computer program analyzing the digitized photo) will likely be different from yours. If you can't give written instructions for someone to solve the problem, there is no way the computer can magically find the right solution. The computer can only do what you tell it to do. It just does it faster, without getting bored or exhausted.

*Finding the perfect partner is not a problem that a computer can solve.*

For that reason, a computerized match-making service cannot guarantee to find the optimal match for you. Instead, you may be presented with a set of potential partners who share common interests with you. That is a task that a computer program can solve.

Now consider the following investment problem:

> You put $10,000 into a bank account that earns 5 percent interest per year. How many years does it take for the account balance to be double the original?

Could you solve this problem by hand? Sure, you could. You figure out the balance as follows:

| year | interest | balance |
|------|----------|---------|
| 0 | | 10000 |
| 1 | 10000.00 x 0.05 = 500.00 | 10000.00 + 500.00 = 10500.00 |
| 2 | 10500.00 x 0.05 = 525.00 | 10500.00 + 525.00 = 11025.00 |
| 3 | 11025.00 x 0.05 = 551.25 | 11025.00 + 551.25 = 11576.25 |
| 4 | 11576.25 x 0.05 = 578.81 | 11576.25 + 578.81 = 12155.06 |

You keep going until the balance is at least $20,000. Then the last number in the year column is the answer.

Of course, carrying out this computation is intensely boring to you or your younger brother. But computers are very good at carrying out repetitive calculations quickly and flawlessly. What is important to the computer is a description of the steps for finding the solution. Each step must be clear and unambiguous, requiring no guesswork. Here is such a description:

Start with a year value of 0, a column for the interest, and a balance of $10,000.

| year | interest | balance |
|------|----------|---------|
| 0 | | 10000 |

> Repeat the following steps while the balance is less than $20,000
>     Add 1 to the year value.
>     Compute the interest as balance x 0.05 (i.e., 5 percent interest).
>     Add the interest to the balance.

| year | interest | balance |
|------|----------|---------|
| 0 |  | 10000 |
| 1 | 500.00 | 10500.00 |
| 14 | 942.82 | 19799.32 |
| (15) | 989.96 | 20789.28 |

> Report the final year value as the answer.

Of course, these steps are not yet in a language that a computer can understand, but you will soon learn how to formulate them in Java. This informal description is called **pseudocode**.

> Pseudocode is an informal description of a sequence of steps for solving a problem.

There are no strict requirements for pseudocode because it is read by human readers, not a computer program. Here are the kinds of pseudocode statements that we will use in this book:

- Use statements such as the following to describe how a value is set or changed:

  > total cost = purchase price + operating cost
  > Multiply the balance value by 1.05.
  > Remove the first and last character from the word.

- You can describe decisions and repetitions as follows:

  > If total cost 1 < total cost 2
  > While the balance is less than $20,000
  > For each picture in the sequence

  Use indentation to indicate which statements should be selected or repeated:

  > For each car
  >     operating cost = 10 x annual fuel cost
  >     total cost = purchase price + operating cost

  Here, the indentation indicates that both statements should be executed for each car.

- Indicate results with statements such as:

  > Choose car 1.
  > Report the final year value as the answer.

The exact wording is not important. What is important is that pseudocode describes a sequence of steps that is

- Unambiguous
- Executable
- Terminating

An algorithm for solving a problem is a sequence of steps that is unambiguous, executable, and terminating.

The step sequence is *unambiguous* when there are precise instructions for what to do at each step and where to go next. There is no room for guesswork or personal opinion. A step is *executable* when it can be carried out in practice. Had we said to use the actual interest rate that will be charged in years to come, and not a fixed rate of 5 percent per year, that step would not have been executable, because there is no way for anyone to know what that interest rate will be. A sequence of steps is *terminating* if it will eventually come to an end. In our example, it requires a bit of thought to see that the sequence will not go on forever: With every step, the balance goes up by at least $500, so eventually it must reach $20,000.

*An algorithm is a recipe for finding a solution.*

Understand the problem

Develop and describe an algorithm

Test the algorithm with simple inputs

Translate the algorithm into Java

Compile and test your program

A sequence of steps that is unambiguous, executable, and terminating is called an **algorithm**. We have found an algorithm to solve our investment problem, and thus we can find the solution by programming a computer. The existence of an algorithm is an essential prerequisite for programming a task. You need to first discover and describe an algorithm for the task that you want to solve before you start programming (see Figure 10).

**Figure 10**   The Software Development Process

**SELF CHECK**

20. Suppose the interest rate was 20 percent. How long would it take for the investment to double?

21. Suppose your cell phone carrier charges you $29.95 for up to 300 minutes of calls, and $0.45 for each additional minute, plus 12.5 percent taxes and fees. Give an algorithm to compute the monthly charge from a given number of minutes.

22. Consider the following pseudocode for finding the most attractive photo from a sequence of photos:

Pick the first photo and call it "the best so far".
For each photo in the sequence
    If it is more attractive than the "best so far"
        Discard "the best so far".
        Call this photo "the best so far".
The photo called "the best so far" is the most attractive photo in the sequence.

Is this an algorithm that will find the most attractive photo?

**23.** Suppose each photo in Self Check 22 had a price tag. Give an algorithm for finding the most expensive photo.

**24.** Suppose you have a random sequence of black and white marbles and want to rearrange it so that the black and white marbles are grouped together. Consider this algorithm:

> **Repeat until sorted**
> Locate the first black marble that is preceded by a white marble, and switch them.

What does the algorithm do with the sequence ○●○●●? Spell out the steps until the algorithm stops.

**25.** Suppose you have a random sequence of colored marbles. Consider this pseudo-code:

> **Repeat until sorted**
> Locate the first marble that is preceded by a marble of a different color, and switch them.

Why is this not an algorithm?

**Practice It** Now you can try these exercises at the end of the chapter: R1.15, R1.17, P1.4.

---

**HOW TO 1.1** **Describing an Algorithm with Pseudocode**

This is the first of many "How To" sections in this book that give you step-by-step procedures for carrying out important tasks in developing computer programs.

Before you are ready to write a program in Java, you need to develop an algorithm—a method for arriving at a solution for a particular problem. Describe the algorithm in pseudo-code: a sequence of precise steps formulated in English.

For example, consider this problem: You have the choice of buying two cars. One is more fuel efficient than the other, but also more expensive. You know the price and fuel efficiency (in miles per gallon, mpg) of both cars. You plan to keep the car for ten years. Assume a price of $4 per gallon of gas and usage of 15,000 miles per year. You will pay cash for the car and not worry about financing costs. Which car is the better deal?

**Step 1** Determine the inputs and outputs.

In our sample problem, we have these inputs:

- **purchase price1** and **fuel efficiency1**, the price and fuel efficiency (in mpg) of the first car
- **purchase price2** and **fuel efficiency2**, the price and fuel efficiency of the second car

We simply want to know which car is the better buy. That is the desired output.

**Step 2** Break down the problem into smaller tasks.

For each car, we need to know the total cost of driving it. Let's do this computation separately for each car. Once we have the total cost for each car, we can decide which car is the better deal.

> The total cost for each car is **purchase price + operating cost**.

We assume a constant usage and gas price for ten years, so the operating cost depends on the cost of driving the car for one year.

> The operating cost is **10 x annual fuel cost**.
> The annual fuel cost is **price per gallon x annual fuel consumed**.

The annual fuel consumed is **annual miles driven / fuel efficiency**. For example, if you drive the car for 15,000 miles and the fuel efficiency is 15 miles/gallon, the car consumes 1,000 gallons.

**Step 3**    Describe each subtask in pseudocode.

In your description, arrange the steps so that any intermediate values are computed before they are needed in other computations. For example, list the step

> **total cost = purchase price + operating cost**

after you have computed **operating cost**.
Here is the algorithm for deciding which car to buy:

> **For each car, compute the total cost as follows:**
>     **annual fuel consumed = annual miles driven / fuel efficiency**
>     **annual fuel cost = price per gallon x annual fuel consumed**
>     **operating cost = 10 x annual fuel cost**
>     **total cost = purchase price + operating cost**
> **If total cost1 < total cost2**
>     **Choose car1.**
> **Else**
>     **Choose car2.**

**Step 4**    Test your pseudocode by working a problem.

We will use these sample values:

> Car 1: $25,000, 50 miles/gallon
> Car 2: $20,000, 30 miles/gallon

Here is the calculation for the cost of the first car:

> **annual fuel consumed = annual miles driven / fuel efficiency = 15000 / 50 = 300**
> **annual fuel cost = price per gallon x annual fuel consumed = 4 x 300 = 1200**
> **operating cost = 10 x annual fuel cost = 10 x 1200 = 12000**
> **total cost = purchase price + operating cost = 25000 + 12000 = 37000**

Similarly, the total cost for the second car is $40,000. Therefore, the output of the algorithm is to choose car 1.

---

**WORKED EXAMPLE 1.1**     **Writing an Algorithm for Tiling a Floor**

 This Worked Example shows how to develop an algorithm for laying tile in an alternating pattern of colors.

**VIDEO EXAMPLE 1.2**    **Dividing Household Expenses**

This Video Example shows how to develop an algorithm for dividing household expenses among roommates.

# CHAPTER SUMMARY

### Define "computer program" and programming.

- Computers execute very basic instructions in rapid succession.
- A computer program is a sequence of instructions and decisions.
- Programming is the act of designing and implementing computer programs.

### Describe the components of a computer.

- The central processing unit (CPU) performs program control and data processing.
- Storage devices include memory and secondary storage.

### Describe the process of translating high-level languages to machine code.

- Java was originally designed for programming consumer devices, but it was first successfully used to write Internet applets.
- Java was designed to be safe and portable, benefiting both Internet users and students.
- Java programs are distributed as instructions for a virtual machine, making them platform-independent.
- Java has a very large library. Focus on learning those parts of the library that you need for your programming projects.

### Become familiar with your Java programming environment.

- Set aside some time to become familiar with the programming environment that you will use for your class work.
- An editor is a program for entering and modifying text, such as a Java program.
- Java is case sensitive. You must be careful about distinguishing between upper- and lowercase letters.
- The Java compiler translates source code into class files that contain instructions for the Java virtual machine.
- Develop a strategy for keeping backup copies of your work before disaster strikes.

### Describe the building blocks of a simple program.

- Classes are the fundamental building blocks of Java programs.
- Every Java application contains a class with a main method. When the application starts, the instructions in the main method are executed.
- Each class contains declarations of methods. Each method contains a sequence of instructions.
- A method is called by specifying the method and its arguments.
- A string is a sequence of characters enclosed in quotation marks.

**Classify program errors as compile-time and run-time errors.**

- A compile-time error is a violation of the programming language rules that is detected by the compiler.
- A run-time error causes a program to take an action that the programmer did not intend.

**Write pseudocode for simple algorithms.**

- Pseudocode is an informal description of a sequence of steps for solving a problem.
- An algorithm for solving a problem is a sequence of steps that is unambiguous, executable, and terminating.

## STANDARD LIBRARY ITEMS INTRODUCED IN THIS CHAPTER

```
java.io.PrintStream                    java.lang.System
    print                                  out
    println
```

## REVIEW EXERCISES

- **R1.1** Explain the difference between using a computer program and programming a computer.

- **R1.2** Which parts of a computer can store program code? Which can store user data?

- **R1.3** Which parts of a computer serve to give information to the user? Which parts take user input?

- **R1.4** A toaster is a single-function device, but a computer can be programmed to carry out different tasks. Is your cell phone a single-function device, or is it a programmable computer? (Your answer will depend on your cell phone model.)

- **R1.5** Explain two benefits of using Java over machine code.

- **R1.6** On your own computer or on a lab computer, find the exact location (folder or directory name) of
  - **a.** The sample file `HelloPrinter.java`, which you wrote with the editor
  - **b.** The Java program launcher `java.exe` or `java`
  - **c.** The library file `rt.jar` that contains the run-time library

- **R1.7** What does this program print?
```java
public class Test
{
    public static void main(String[] args)
    {
        System.out.println("39 + 3");
        System.out.println(39 + 3);
    }
}
```

▪▪ **R1.8** What does this program print? Pay close attention to spaces.

```java
public class Test
{
    public static void main(String[] args)
    {
        System.out.print("Hello");
        System.out.println("World");
    }
}
```

▪▪ **R1.9** What is the compile-time error in this program?

```java
public class Test
{
    public static void main(String[] args)
    {
        System.out.println("Hello", "World!");
    }
}
```

▪▪ **R1.10** Write three versions of the HelloPrinter.java program that have different compile-time errors. Write a version that has a run-time error.

▪ **R1.11** How do you discover syntax errors? How do you discover logic errors?

▪▪ **R1.12** Write an algorithm to settle the following question: A bank account starts out with $10,000. Interest is compounded monthly at 6 percent per year (0.5 percent per month). Every month, $500 is withdrawn to meet college expenses. After how many years is the account depleted?

▪▪▪ **R1.13** Consider the question in Exercise R1.12. Suppose the numbers ($10,000, 6 percent, $500) were user selectable. Are there values for which the algorithm you developed would not terminate? If so, change the algorithm to make sure it always terminates.

▪▪▪ **R1.14** In order to estimate the cost of painting a house, a painter needs to know the surface area of the exterior. Develop an algorithm for computing that value. Your inputs are the width, length, and height of the house, the number of windows and doors, and their dimensions. (Assume the windows and doors have a uniform size.)

▪▪ **R1.15** You want to decide whether you should drive your car to work or take the train. You know the one-way distance from your home to your place of work, and the fuel efficiency of your car (in miles per gallon). You also know the one-way price of a train ticket. You assume the cost of gas at $4 per gallon, and car maintenance at 5 cents per mile. Write an algorithm to decide which commute is cheaper.

▪▪ **R1.16** You want to find out which fraction of your car's use is for commuting to work, and which is for personal use. You know the one-way distance from your home to work. For a particular period, you recorded the beginning and ending mileage on the odometer and the number of work days. Write an algorithm to settle this question.

▪ **R1.17** In How To 1.1, you made assumptions about the price of gas and annual usage to compare cars. Ideally, you would like to know which car is the better deal without making these assumptions. Why can't a computer program solve that problem?

▪▪▪ **R1.18** The value of $\pi$ can be computed according to the following formula:

$$\frac{\pi}{4} = 1 - \frac{1}{3} + \frac{1}{5} - \frac{1}{7} + \frac{1}{9} - \cdots$$

Write an algorithm to compute $\pi$. Because the formula is an infinite series and an algorithm must stop after a finite number of steps, you should stop when you have the result determined to six significant digits.

■■ **R1.19** Suppose you put your younger brother in charge of backing up your work. Write a set of detailed instructions for carrying out his task. Explain how often he should do it, and what files he needs to copy from which folder to which location. Explain how he should verify that the backup was carried out correctly.

■ **Business R1.20** Imagine that you and a number of friends go to a luxury restaurant, and when you ask for the bill you want to split the amount and the tip (15 percent) between all. Write pseudocode for calculating the amount of money that everyone has to pay. Your program should print the amount of the bill, the tip, the total cost, and the amount each person has to pay. It should also print how much of what each person pays is for the bill and for the tip.

## PROGRAMMING EXERCISES

■ **P1.1** Write a program that prints a greeting of your choice, perhaps in a language other than English.

■■ **P1.2** Write a program that prints the sum of the first ten positive integers, $1 + 2 + ... + 10$.

■■ **P1.3** Write a program that prints the product of the first ten positive integers, $1 \times 2 \times ... \times 10$. (Use * to indicate multiplication in Java.)

■■ **P1.4** Write a program that prints the balance of an account after the first, second, and third year. The account has an initial balance of $1,000 and earns 5 percent interest per year.

■ **P1.5** Write a program that displays your name inside a box on the screen, like this:

```
Dave
```

Do your best to approximate lines with characters such as | - +.

■■■ **P1.6** Write a program that prints your name in large letters, such as

```
*   *   **    ****    ****   *   *
*   *  *  *   *   *   *   *   *   *
*****  *    *  ****    ****    * *
*   * ******  *   *   *   *     *
*   *  *    * *   *   *   *     *
```

■■ **P1.7** Write a program that prints a face similar to (but different from) the following:

```
   /////
  +"""""+
 (| o o |)
  |  ^  |
  | '_' |
  +-----+
```

■■ **P1.8** Write a program that prints an imitation of a Piet Mondrian painting. (Search the Internet if you are not familiar with his paintings.) Use character sequences such as @@@ or ::: to indicate different colors, and use - and | to form lines.

■■ **P1.9** Write a program that prints a house that looks exactly like the following:

```
     +
    + +
   +   +
  +-----+
  | .-. |
  | | | |
  +-+-+-+
```

■■■ **P1.10** Write a program that prints an animal speaking a greeting, similar to (but different from) the following:

```
/\_/\      -----
( ' ' )  / Hello \'
(  -  ) <  Junior |
 | | |   \ Coder!/
(_|_)      -----
```

■ **P1.11** Write a program that prints three items, such as the names of your three best friends or favorite movies, on three separate lines.

■ **P1.12** Write a program that prints a poem of your choice. If you don't have a favorite poem, search the Internet for "Emily Dickinson" or "e e cummings".

■■ **P1.13** Write a program that prints the United States flag, using * and = characters.

■■ **P1.14** Type in and run the following program:

```java
import javax.swing.JOptionPane;

public class DialogViewer
{
   public static void main(String[] args)
   {
      JOptionPane.showMessageDialog(null, "Hello, World!");
   }
}
```

Then modify the program to show the message "Hello, *your name*!".

■■ **P1.15** Type in and run the following program:

```java
import javax.swing.JOptionPane;

public class DialogViewer
{
   public static void main(String[] args)
   {
      String name = JOptionPane.showInputDialog("What is your name?");
      System.out.println(name);
   }
}
```

Then modify the program to print "Hello, *name*!", displaying the name that the user typed in.

■■■ **P1.16** Modify the program from Exercise P1.15 so that the dialog continues with the message "My name is Hal! What would you like me to do?" Discard the user's input and display a message such as

```
I'm sorry, Dave. I'm afraid I can't do that.
```

Replace Dave with the name that was provided by the user.

**•• P1.17** Type in and run the following program:

```java
import java.net.URL;
import javax.swing.ImageIcon;
import javax.swing.JOptionPane;

public class Test
{
    public static void main(String[] args) throws Exception
    {
        URL imageLocation = new URL(
            "http://horstmann.com/java4everyone/duke.gif");
        JOptionPane.showMessageDialog(null, "Hello", "Title",
            JOptionPane.PLAIN_MESSAGE, new ImageIcon(imageLocation));
    }
}
```

Then modify it to show a different greeting and image.

**• Business P1.18** Write a program that prints a two-column list of your friends' birthdays. In the first column, print the names of your best friends; in the second column, print their birthdays.

**• Business P1.19** In the United States there is no federal sales tax, so every state may impose its own sales taxes. Look on the Internet for the sales tax charged in five U.S. states, then write a program that prints the tax rate for five states of your choice.

```
Sales Tax Rates
---------------
Alaska:    0%
Hawaii:    4%
. . .
```

**• Business P1.20** To speak more than one language is a valuable skill in the labor market today. One of the basic skills is learning to greet people. Write a program that prints a two-column list with the greeting phrases shown in the following table; in the first column, print the phrase in English, in the second column, print the phrase in a language of your choice. If you don't speak any language other than English, use an online translator or ask a friend.

| List of Phrases to Translate |
| --- |
| Good morning. |
| It is a pleasure to meet you. |
| Please call me tomorrow. |
| Have a nice day! |

## ANSWERS TO SELF-CHECK QUESTIONS

1. A program that reads the data on the CD and sends output to the speakers and the screen.
2. A CD player can do one thing—play music CDs. It cannot execute programs.
3. Nothing.
4. In secondary storage, typically a hard disk.
5. The central processing unit.

**6.** Safety and portability.

**7.** No one person can learn the entire library—it is too large.

**8.** The answer varies among systems. A typical answer might be `/home/dave/cs1/hello/Hello-Printer.java` or `c:\Users\Dave\Workspace\hello\HelloPrinter.java`

**9.** You back up your files and folders.

**10.** Change `World` to your name (here, `Dave`):

```
System.out.println("Hello, Dave!");
```

**11.**
```
System.out.println("H");
System.out.println("e");
System.out.println("l");
System.out.println("l");
System.out.println("o");
```

**12.** No. The compiler would look for an item whose name is `Hello`. You need to enclose `Hello` in quotation marks:

```
System.out.println("Hello");
```

**13.** The printout is `My lucky number is12`. It would be a good idea to add a space after the `is`.

**14.** `Hello`
a blank line
`World`

**15.** This is a compile-time error. The compiler will complain that it does not know the meanings of the words `Hello` and `World`.

**16.** This is a compile-time error. The compiler will complain that `System.out` does not have a method called `printline`.

**17.** This is a run-time error. It is perfectly legal to give the name `hello` to a method, so the compiler won't complain. But when the program is run, the virtual machine will look for a `main` method and won't find one.

**18.** It is a run-time error. After all, the program had been compiled in order for you to run it.

**19.** When a program has compiler errors, no class file is produced, and there is nothing to run.

**20.** 4 years:

0 10,000

1 12,000

2 14,400

3 17,280

4 20,736

**21.** Is the number of minutes at most 300?

**a.** If so, the answer is $29.95 \times 1.125 = $33.70$.

**b.** If not,

**1.** Compute the difference: (number of minutes) − 300.

**2.** Multiply that difference by 0.45.

**3.** Add $29.95.

**4.** Multiply the total by 1.125. That is the answer.

**22.** No. The step **If it is more attractive than the "best so far"** is not executable because there is no objective way of deciding which of two photos is more attractive.

**23.** **Pick the first photo and call it "the most expensive so far".**
**For each photo in the sequence**
　**If it is more expensive than "the most expensive so far"**
　　**Discard "the most expensive so far".**
　　**Call this photo "the most expensive so far".**
**The photo called "the most expensive so far" is the most expensive photo in the sequence.**

**24.** The first black marble that is preceded by a white one is marked in blue:

Switching the two yields

●○○●●

The next black marble to be switched is

●○○●●

yielding

●○●○●

The next steps are

●●○○●

●●○●○

●●●○○

Now the sequence is sorted.

**25.** The sequence doesn't terminate. Consider the input ○●○●○. The first two marbles keep getting switched.

## CHAPTER 2

# FUNDAMENTAL DATA TYPES

## CHAPTER GOALS

To declare and initialize variables and constants

To understand the properties and limitations of integers and floating-point numbers

To appreciate the importance of comments and good code layout

To write arithmetic expressions and assignment statements

To create programs that read and process inputs, and display the results

To learn how to use the Java String type

## CHAPTER CONTENTS

Numbers and character strings (such as the ones on this display board) are important data types in any Java program. In this chapter, you will learn how to work with numbers and text, and how to write simple programs that perform useful tasks with them.

# 2.1 Variables

When your program carries out computations, you will want to store values so that you can use them later. In a Java program, you use **variables** to store values. In this section, you will learn how to declare and use variables.

To illustrate the use of variables, we will develop a program that solves the following problem. Soft drinks are sold in cans and bottles. A store offers a six-pack of 12-ounce cans for the same price as a two-liter bottle. Which should you buy? (Twelve fluid ounces equal approximately 0.355 liters.)

In our program, we will declare variables for the number of cans per pack and for the volume of each can. Then we will compute the volume of a six-pack in liters and print out the answer.

*What contains more soda? A six-pack of 12-ounce cans or a two-liter bottle?*

## 2.1.1 Variable Declarations

The following statement declares a variable named cansPerPack:

```
int cansPerPack = 6;
```

A **variable** is a storage location in a computer program. Each variable has a name and holds a value.

> A variable is a storage location with a name.

A variable is similar to a parking space in a parking garage. The parking space has an identifier (such as "J 053"), and it can hold a vehicle. A variable has a name (such as cansPerPack), and it can hold a value (such as 6).

*Like a variable in a computer program, a parking space has an identifier and a contents.*

Syntax 2.1    Variable Declaration

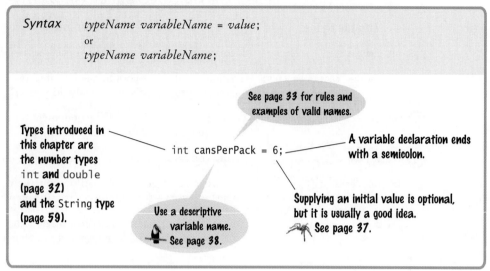

*Syntax*    *typeName variableName = value;*
or
*typeName variableName;*

See page **33** for rules and
examples of valid names.

Types introduced in
this chapter are
the number types
int **and** double
(page **32**)
and the String **type**
(page **59**).

int cansPerPack = 6;

A variable declaration ends
with a semicolon.

Use a descriptive
variable name.
See page **38**.

Supplying an initial value is optional,
but it is usually a good idea.
See page **37**.

---

When declaring a
variable, you
usually specify an
initial value.

When declaring a variable, you usually want to **initialize** it. That is, you specify the value that should be stored in the variable. Consider again this variable declaration:

```
int cansPerPack = 6;
```

The variable cansPerPack is initialized with the value 6.

When declaring a
variable, you also
specify the type of
its values.

Like a parking space that is restricted to a certain type of vehicle (such as a compact car, motorcycle, or electric vehicle), a variable in Java stores data of a specific **type**. Java supports quite a few data types: numbers, text strings, files, dates, and many others. You must specify the type whenever you declare a variable (see Syntax 2.1).

The cansPerPack variable is an **integer**, a whole number without a fractional part. In Java, this type is called int. (See the next section for more information about number types in Java.)

Note that the type comes before the variable name:

```
int cansPerPack = 6;
```

After you have declared and initialized a variable, you can use it. For example,

```
int cansPerPack = 6;
System.out.println(cansPerPack);
int cansPerCrate = 4 * cansPerPack;
```

Table 1 shows several examples of variable declarations.

*Each parking space is suitable for a particular type of vehicle,
just as each variable holds a value of a particular type.*

### Table 1  Variable Declarations in Java

| Variable Name | Comment |
|---|---|
| `int cans = 6;` | Declares an integer variable and initializes it with 6. |
| `int total = cans + bottles;` | The initial value need not be a fixed value. (Of course, cans and `bottles` must have been previously declared.) |
| 🚫 `bottles = 1;` | **Error:** The type is missing. This statement is not a declaration but an assignment of a new value to an existing variable—see Section 2.1.4. |
| 🚫 `int volume = "2";` | **Error:** You cannot initialize a number with a string. |
| `int cansPerPack;` | Declares an integer variable without initializing it. This can be a cause for errors—see Common Error 2.1 on page 37. |
| `int dollars, cents;` | Declares two integer variables in a single statement. In this book, we will declare each variable in a separate statement. |

## 2.1.2  Number Types

Use the int type for numbers that cannot have a fractional part.

In Java, there are several different types of numbers. You use the `int` type to denote a whole number without a fractional part. For example, there must be an integer number of cans in any pack of cans—you cannot have a fraction of a can.

When a fractional part is required (such as in the number 0.335), we use **floating-point numbers**. The most commonly used type for floating-point numbers in Java is called `double`. (If you want to know the reason, read Special Topic 2.1 on page 39 .) Here is the declaration of a floating-point variable:

```
double canVolume = 0.335;
```

### Table 2  Number Literals in Java

| Number | Type | Comment |
|---|---|---|
| 6 | int | An integer has no fractional part. |
| -6 | int | Integers can be negative. |
| 0 | int | Zero is an integer. |
| 0.5 | double | A number with a fractional part has type `double`. |
| 1.0 | double | An integer with a fractional part .0 has type `double`. |
| 1E6 | double | A number in exponential notation: $1 \times 10^6$ or 1000000. Numbers in exponential notation always have type `double`. |
| 2.96E-2 | double | Negative exponent: $2.96 \times 10^{-2} = 2.96 / 100 = 0.0296$ |
| 🚫 100,000 | | **Error:** Do not use a comma as a decimal separator. |
| 🚫 3 1/2 | | **Error:** Do not use fractions; use decimal notation: 3.5 |

Use the double type for floating-point numbers.

When a value such as 6 or 0.335 occurs in a Java program, it is called a **number literal**. If a number literal has a decimal point, it is a floating-point number; otherwise, it is an integer. Table 2 shows how to write integer and floating-point literals in Java.

### 2.1.3 Variable Names

When you declare a variable, you should pick a name that explains its purpose. For example, it is better to use a descriptive name, such as canVolume, than a terse name, such as cv.

In Java, there are a few simple rules for variable names:

1. Variable names must start with a letter or the underscore (_) character, and the remaining characters must be letters, numbers, or underscores. (Technically, the $ symbol is allowed as well, but you should not use it—it is intended for names that are automatically generated by tools.)

2. You cannot use other symbols such as ? or %. Spaces are not permitted inside names either. You can use uppercase letters to denote word boundaries, as in cansPerPack. This naming convention is called *camel case* because the uppercase letters in the middle of the name look like the humps of a camel.)

3. Variable names are **case sensitive**, that is, canVolume and canvolume are different names.

4. You cannot use **reserved words** such as double or class as names; these words are reserved exclusively for their special Java meanings. (See Appendix C for a listing of all reserved words in Java.)

By convention, variable names should start with a lowercase letter.

It is a convention among Java programmers that variable names should start with a lowercase letter (such as canVolume) and class names should start with an uppercase letter (such as HelloPrinter). That way, it is easy to tell them apart.

Table 3 shows examples of legal and illegal variable names in Java.

#### Table 3 Variable Names in Java

| Variable Name | Comment |
|---|---|
| canVolume1 | Variable names consist of letters, numbers, and the underscore character. |
| x | In mathematics, you use short variable names such as *x* or *y*. This is legal in Java, but not very common, because it can make programs harder to understand (see Programming Tip 2.1 on page 38). |
| ⚠ CanVolume | **Caution:** Variable names are case sensitive. This variable name is different from canVolume, and it violates the convention that variable names should start with a lowercase letter. |
| 🚫 6pack | **Error:** Variable names cannot start with a number. |
| 🚫 can volume | **Error:** Variable names cannot contain spaces. |
| 🚫 double | **Error:** You cannot use a reserved word as a variable name. |
| 🚫 ltr/fl.oz | **Error:** You cannot use symbols such as / or . |

### 2.1.4 The Assignment Statement

An assignment statement stores a new value in a variable, replacing the previously stored value.

You use the **assignment statement** to place a new value into a variable. Here is an example:

```
cansPerPack = 8;
```

The left-hand side of an assignment statement consists of a variable. The right-hand side is an expression that has a value. That value is stored in the variable, overwriting its previous contents.

There is an important difference between a variable declaration and an assignment statement:

```
int cansPerPack = 6;        Variable declaration
...
cansPerPack = 8;            Assignment statement
```

The first statement is the declaration of `cansPerPack`. It is an instruction to create a new variable of type `int`, to give it the name `cansPerPack`, and to initialize it with 6. The second statement is an *assignment statement:* an instruction to replace the contents of the *existing* variable `cansPerPack` with another value.

The assignment operator = does *not* denote mathematical equality.

The = sign doesn't mean that the left-hand side is *equal* to the right-hand side. The expression on the right is evaluated, and its value is placed into the variable on the left.

Do not confuse this *assignment operation* with the = used in algebra to denote *equality*. The assignment operator is an instruction to do something—namely, place a value into a variable. The mathematical equality states that two values are equal.

For example, in Java, it is perfectly legal to write

```
totalVolume = totalVolume + 2;
```

It means to look up the value stored in the variable `totalVolume`, add 2 to it, and place the result back into `totalVolume`. (See Figure 1.) The net effect of executing this statement is to increment `totalVolume` by 2. For example, if `totalVolume` was 2.13 before execution of the statement, it is set to 4.13 afterwards. Of course, in mathematics it would make no sense to write that $x = x + 2$. No value can equal itself plus 2.

**ANIMATION**
*Variable Initialization and Assignment*

## Syntax 2.2 Assignment

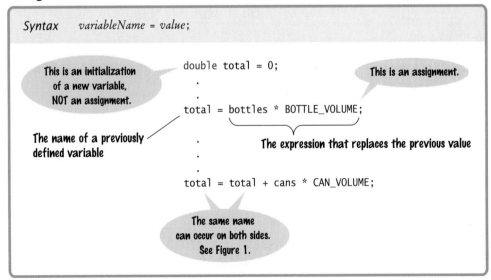

*Syntax*    *variableName = value;*

This is an initialization of a new variable, NOT an assignment.

```
double total = 0;
```

This is an assignment.

The name of a previously defined variable

```
total = bottles * BOTTLE_VOLUME;
```

The expression that replaces the previous value

```
total = total + cans * CAN_VOLUME;
```

The same name can occur on both sides. See Figure 1.

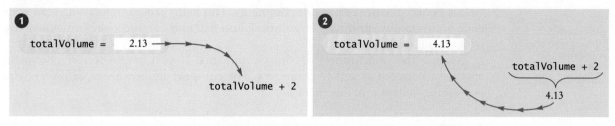

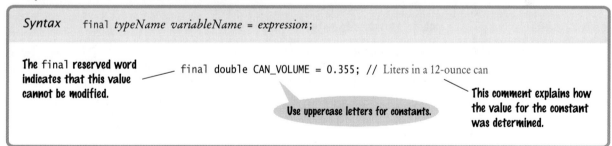

**Figure 1** Executing the Assignment totalVolume = totalVolume + 2

### 2.1.5 Constants

> You cannot change the value of a variable that is defined as final.

When a variable is defined with the reserved word final, its value can never change. Constants are commonly written using capital letters to distinguish them visually from regular variables:

```
final double BOTTLE_VOLUME = 2;
```

It is good programming style to use named constants in your program to explain the meanings of numeric values. For example, compare the statements

```
double totalVolume = bottles * 2;
```

and

```
double totalVolume = bottles * BOTTLE_VOLUME;
```

A programmer reading the first statement may not understand the significance of the number 2. The second statement, with a named constant, makes the computation much clearer.

## Syntax 2.3 Constant Declaration

*Syntax*  final *typeName* *variableName* = *expression*;

The final **reserved word indicates that this value cannot be modified.**

```
final double CAN_VOLUME = 0.355; // Liters in a 12-ounce can
```

Use uppercase letters for constants.

This comment explains how the value for the constant was determined.

### 2.1.6 Comments

As your programs get more complex, you should add **comments**, explanations for human readers of your code. For example, here is a comment that explains the value used in a variable initialization:

```
final double CAN_VOLUME = 0.355; // Liters in a 12-ounce can
```

This comment explains the significance of the value 0.355 to a human reader. The compiler does not process comments at all. It ignores everything from a // delimiter to the end of the line.

It is a good practice to provide comments. This helps programmers who read your code understand your intent. In addition, you will find comments helpful when you review your own programs.

You use the `//` delimiter for short comments. If you have a longer comment, enclose it between `/*` and `*/` delimiters. The compiler ignores these delimiters and everything in between. For example,

```
/*
    There are approximately 0.335 liters in a 12-ounce can because one ounce
    equals 0.02957353 liter; see The International Systems of Units (SI) - Conversion
    Factors for General Use (NIST Special Publication 1038).
*/
```

Finally, start a comment that explains the purpose of a program with the `/**` delimiter instead of `/*`. Tools that analyze source files rely on that convention. For example,

```
/**
    This program computes the volume (in liters) of a six-pack of soda cans.
*/
```

The following program shows the use of variables, constants, and the assignment statement. The program displays the volume of a six-pack of cans and the total volume of the six-pack and a two-liter bottle. We use constants for the can and bottle volumes. The `totalVolume` variable is initialized with the volume of the cans. Using an assignment statement, we add the bottle volume. As you can see from the program output, the six-pack of cans contains over two liters of soda.

**section_1/Volume1.java**

```java
1   /**
2       This program computes the volume (in liters) of a six-pack of soda
3       cans and the total volume of a six-pack and a two-liter bottle.
4   */
5   public class Volume1
6   {
7       public static void main(String[] args)
8       {
9           int cansPerPack = 6;
10          final double CAN_VOLUME = 0.355; // Liters in a 12-ounce can
11          double totalVolume = cansPerPack * CAN_VOLUME;
12
13          System.out.print("A six-pack of 12-ounce cans contains ");
14          System.out.print(totalVolume);
15          System.out.println(" liters.");
16
17          final double BOTTLE_VOLUME = 2; // Two-liter bottle
18
19          totalVolume = totalVolume + BOTTLE_VOLUME;
20
21          System.out.print("A six-pack and a two-liter bottle contain ");
22          System.out.print(totalVolume);
23          System.out.println(" liters.");
24      }
25  }
```

**Program Run**

```
A six-pack of 12-ounce cans contains 2.13 liters.
A six-pack and a two-liter bottle contain 4.13 liters.
```

*Just as a television commentator explains the news,*
*you use comments in your program to explain its behavior.*

**SELF CHECK**

1. Declare a variable suitable for holding the number of bottles in a case.
2. What is wrong with the following variable declaration?

   ```
   int ounces per liter = 28.35
   ```
3. Declare and initialize two variables, `unitPrice` and `quantity`, to contain the unit price of a single bottle and the number of bottles purchased. Use reasonable initial values.
4. Use the variables declared in Self Check 3 to display the total purchase price.
5. Some drinks are sold in four-packs instead of six-packs. How would you change the `Volume1.java` program to compute the total volume?
6. What is wrong with this comment?

   ```
   double canVolume = 0.355; /* Liters in a 12-ounce can //
   ```
7. Suppose the type of the `cansPerPack` variable in `Volume1.java` was changed from `int` to `double`. What would be the effect on the program?
8. Why can't the variable `totalVolume` in the `Volume1.java` program be declared as `final`?
9. How would you explain assignment using the parking space analogy?

**Practice It**     Now you can try these exercises at the end of the chapter: R2.1, R2.2, P2.1.

---

Common Error 2.1

### Using Undeclared or Uninitialized Variables

You must declare a variable before you use it for the first time. For example, the following sequence of statements would not be legal:

```
double canVolume = 12 * literPerOunce; // ERROR: literPerOunce is not yet declared
double literPerOunce = 0.0296;
```

In your program, the statements are compiled in order. When the compiler reaches the first statement, it does not know that `literPerOunce` will be declared in the next line, and it reports an error. The remedy is to reorder the declarations so that each variable is declared before it is used.

A related error is to leave a variable uninitialized:

```java
int bottles;
int bottleVolume = bottles * 2; // ERROR: bottles is not yet initialized
```

The Java compiler will complain that you are using a variable that has not yet been given a value. The remedy is to assign a value to the variable before it is used.

**Programming Tip 2.1**

### Choose Descriptive Variable Names

We could have saved ourselves a lot of typing by using shorter variable names, as in

```java
double cv = 0.355;
```

Compare this declaration with the one that we actually used, though. Which one is easier to read? There is no comparison. Just reading canVolume is a lot less trouble than reading cv and then *figuring out* it must mean "can volume".

In practical programming, this is particularly important when programs are written by more than one person. It may be obvious to *you* that cv stands for can volume and not current velocity, but will it be obvious to the person who needs to update your code years later? For that matter, will you remember yourself what cv means when you look at the code three months from now?

**Common Error 2.2**

### Overflow

Because numbers are represented in the computer with a limited number of digits, they cannot represent arbitrary numbers.

The int type has a *limited range:* It can represent numbers up to a little more than two billion. For many applications, this is not a problem, but you cannot use an int to represent the world population.

If a computation yields a value that is outside the int range, the result *overflows*. No error is displayed. Instead, the result is truncated, yielding a useless value. For example,

```java
int fiftyMillion = 50000000;
System.out.println(100 * fiftyMillion); // Expected: 5000000000
```

displays 705032704.

In situations such as this, you can switch to double values. However, read Common Error 2.3 for more information about a related issue: roundoff errors.

**Common Error 2.3**

### Roundoff Errors

Roundoff errors are a fact of life when calculating with floating-point numbers. You probably have encountered that phenomenon yourself with manual calculations. If you calculate 1/3 to two decimal places, you get 0.33. Multiplying again by 3, you obtain 0.99, not 1.00.

In the processor hardware, numbers are represented in the binary number system, using only digits 0 and 1. As with decimal numbers, you can get roundoff errors when binary digits are lost. They just may crop up at different places than you might expect.

Here is an example:

```java
double price = 4.35;
double quantity = 100;
double total = price * quantity; // Should be 100 * 4.35 = 435
System.out.println(total); // Prints 434.99999999999999
```

In the binary system, there is no exact representation for 4.35, just as there is no exact representation for 1/3 in the decimal system. The representation used by the computer is just a little less than 4.35, so 100 times that value is just a little less than 435.

You can deal with roundoff errors by rounding to the nearest integer (see Section 2.2.5) or by displaying a fixed number of digits after the decimal separator (see Section 2.3.2).

---

**Programming Tip 2.2**

### Do Not Use Magic Numbers

A **magic number** is a numeric constant that appears in your code without explanation. For example,

```java
totalVolume = bottles * 2;
```

Why 2? Are bottles twice as voluminous as cans? No, the reason is that every bottle contains 2 liters. Use a named constant to make the code self-documenting:

```java
final double BOTTLE_VOLUME = 2;
totalVolume = bottles * BOTTLE_VOLUME;
```

There is another reason for using named constants. Suppose circumstances change, and the bottle volume is now 1.5 liters. If you used a named constant, you make a single change, and you are done. Otherwise, you have to look at every value of 2 in your program and ponder whether it meant a bottle volume, or something else. In a program that is more than a few pages long, that is incredibly tedious and error-prone.

Even the most reasonable cosmic constant is going to change one day. You think there are seven days per week? Your customers on Mars are going to be pretty unhappy about your silly prejudice. Make a constant

```java
final int DAYS_PER_WEEK = 7;
```

*We prefer programs that are easy to understand over those that appear to work by magic.*

---

**Special Topic 2.1**

### Numeric Types in Java

In addition to the int and double types, Java has several other numeric types.

Java has two floating-point types. The float type uses half the storage of the double type that we use in this book, but it can only store about 7 decimal digits. (In the computer, numbers are represented in the binary number system, using digits 0 and 1.) Many years ago, when computers had far less memory than they have today, float was the standard type for floating-point computations, and programmers would indulge in the luxury of "double precision" only when they needed the additional digits. Today, the float type is rarely used.

By the way, these numbers are called "floating-point" because of their internal representation in the computer. Consider numbers 29600, 2.96, and 0.0296. They can be represented in a very similar way: namely, as a sequence of the significant digits—296—and an indication of the position of the decimal point. When the values are multiplied or divided by 10, only the position of the decimal point changes; it "floats". Computers use base 2, not base 10, but the principle is the same.

In addition to the int type, Java has integer types byte, short, and long. Their ranges are shown in Table 4. (Their strange-looking limits are related to powers of 2, another consequence of the fact that computers use binary numbers.)

| Table 4 Java Number Types | | |
|---|---|---|
| Type | Description | Size |
| int | The integer type, with range −2,147,483,648 (Integer.MIN_VALUE) ... 2,147,483,647 (Integer.MAX_VALUE, about 2.14 billion) | 4 bytes |
| byte | The type describing a single byte consisting of 8 bits, with range −128 ... 127 | 1 byte |
| short | The short integer type, with range −32,768 ... 32,767 | 2 bytes |
| long | The long integer type, with about 19 decimal digits | 8 bytes |
| double | The double-precision floating-point type, with about 15 decimal digits and a range of about $\pm 10^{308}$ | 8 bytes |
| float | The single-precision floating-point type, with about 7 decimal digits and a range of about $\pm 10^{38}$ | 4 bytes |
| char | The character type, representing code units in the Unicode encoding scheme (see Random Fact 2.2) | 2 bytes |

**Special Topic 2.2**

## Big Numbers

If you want to compute with really large numbers, you can use big number objects. Big number objects are objects of the BigInteger and BigDecimal classes in the java.math package. Unlike the number types such as int or double, big number objects have essentially no limits on their size and precision. However, computations with big number objects are much slower than those that involve number types. Perhaps more importantly, you can't use the familiar arithmetic operators such as (+ - *) with them. Instead, you have to use methods called add, subtract, and multiply. Here is an example of how to create a BigInteger object and how to call the multiply method:

```
BigInteger oneHundred = new BigInteger("100");
BigInteger fiftyMillion = new BigInteger("50000000");
System.out.println(oneHundred.multiply(fiftyMillion)); // Prints 5000000000
```

The BigDecimal type carries out floating-point computations without roundoff errors. For example,

```
BigDecimal price = new BigDecimal("4.35");
BigDecimal quantity = new BigDecimal("100");
BigDecimal total = price.multiply(quantity);
System.out.println(total); // Prints 435.00
```

# 2.2 Arithmetic

In the following sections, you will learn how to carry out arithmetic calculations in Java.

## 2.2.1 Arithmetic Operators

Java supports the same four basic arithmetic operations as a calculator—addition, subtraction, multiplication, and division—but it uses different symbols for multiplication and division.

You must write a * b to denote multiplication. Unlike in mathematics, you cannot write a b, a · b, or a × b. Similarly, division is always indicated with a /, never a ÷ or a fraction bar.

For example, $\dfrac{a + b}{2}$ becomes (a + b) / 2.

The combination of variables, literals, operators, and/or method calls is called an **expression**. For example, (a + b) / 2 is an expression.

Parentheses are used just as in algebra: to indicate in which order the parts of the expression should be computed. For example, in the expression (a + b) / 2, the sum a + b is computed first, and then the sum is divided by 2. In contrast, in the expression

    a + b / 2

only b is divided by 2, and then the sum of a and b / 2 is formed. As in regular algebraic notation, multiplication and division have a *higher precedence* than addition and subtraction. For example, in the expression a + b / 2, the / is carried out first, even though the + operation occurs further to the left.

If you mix integer and floating-point values in an arithmetic expression, the result is a floating-point value. For example, 7 + 4.0 is the floating-point value 11.0.

> Mixing integers and floating-point values in an arithmetic expression yields a floating-point value.

## 2.2.2 Increment and Decrement

> The ++ operator adds 1 to a variable; the -- operator subtracts 1.

Changing a variable by adding or subtracting 1 is so common that there is a special shorthand for it. The ++ operator increments a variable—see Figure 2:

    counter++; // Adds 1 to the variable counter

Similarly, the -- operator decrements a variable:

    counter--; // Subtracts 1 from counter

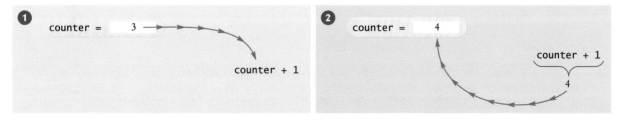

**Figure 2** Incrementing a Variable

### 2.2.3 Integer Division and Remainder

If both arguments of / are integers, the remainder is discarded.

Division works as you would expect, as long as at least one of the numbers involved is a floating-point number. That is,

```
7.0 / 4.0
7 / 4.0
7.0 / 4
```

all yield 1.75. However, if *both* numbers are integers, then the result of the division is always an integer, with the remainder discarded. That is,

```
7 / 4
```

evaluates to 1 because 7 divided by 4 is 1 with a remainder of 3 (which is discarded). This can be a source of subtle programming errors—see Common Error 2.4.

If you are interested in the remainder only, use the % operator:

```
7 % 4
```

*Integer division and the % operator yield the dollar and cent values of a piggybank full of pennies.*

The % operator computes the remainder of an integer division.

is 3, the remainder of the integer division of 7 by 4. The % symbol has no analog in algebra. It was chosen because it looks similar to /, and the remainder operation is related to division. The operator is called **modulus**. (Some people call it *modulo* or *mod*.) It has no relationship with the percent operation that you find on some calculators.

Here is a typical use for the integer / and % operations. Suppose you have an amount of pennies in a piggybank:

```
int pennies = 1729;
```

You want to determine the value in dollars and cents. You obtain the dollars through an integer division by 100:

```
int dollars = pennies / 100;   // Sets dollars to 17
```

The integer division discards the remainder. To obtain the remainder, use the % operator:

```
int cents = pennies % 100;   // Sets cents to 29
```

See Table 5 for additional examples.

| Table 5 **Integer Division and Remainder** | | |
|---|---|---|
| Expression (where n = 1729) | Value | Comment |
| n % 10 | 9 | n % 10 is always the last digit of n. |
| n / 10 | 172 | This is always n without the last digit. |
| n % 100 | 29 | The last two digits of n. |
| n / 10.0 | 172.9 | Because 10.0 is a floating-point number, the fractional part is not discarded. |
| -n % 10 | -9 | Because the first argument is negative, the remainder is also negative. |
| n % 2 | 1 | n % 2 is 0 if n is even, 1 or –1 if n is odd. |

## 2.2.4 Powers and Roots

The Java library declares many mathematical functions, such as Math.sqrt (square root) and Math.pow (raising to a power).

In Java, there are no symbols for powers and roots. To compute them, you must call methods. To take the square root of a number, you use the Math.sqrt method. For example, $\sqrt{x}$ is written as Math.sqrt(x). To compute $x^n$, you write Math.pow(x, n).

In algebra, you use fractions, exponents, and roots to arrange expressions in a compact two-dimensional form. In Java, you have to write all expressions in a linear arrangement. For example, the mathematical expression

$$b \times \left(1 + \frac{r}{100}\right)^n$$

becomes

```
b * Math.pow(1 + r / 100, n)
```

Figure 3 shows how to analyze such an expression. Table 6 shows additional mathematical methods.

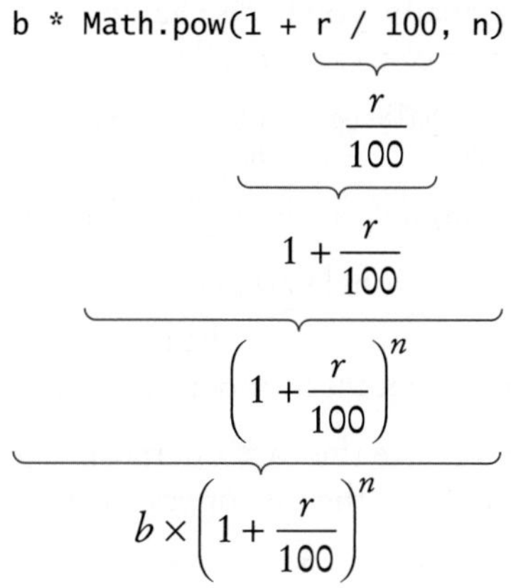

**Figure 3**
Analyzing an Expression

| Table 6  Mathematical Methods | |
|---|---|
| Method | Returns |
| Math.sqrt(x) | Square root of $x$ ($\geq 0$) |
| Math.pow(x, y) | $x^y$ ($x > 0$, or $x = 0$ and $y > 0$, or $x < 0$ and $y$ is an integer) |
| Math.sin(x) | Sine of $x$ ($x$ in radians) |
| Math.cos(x) | Cosine of $x$ |
| Math.tan(x) | Tangent of $x$ |
| Math.toRadians(x) | Convert $x$ degrees to radians (i.e., returns $x \cdot \pi/180$) |
| Math.toDegrees(x) | Convert $x$ radians to degrees (i.e., returns $x \cdot 180/\pi$) |
| Math.exp(x) | $e^x$ |
| Math.log(x) | Natural log ($\ln(x)$, $x > 0$) |

| Table 6 Mathematical Methods | |
|---|---|
| Method | Returns |
| `Math.log10(x)` | Decimal log ($\log_{10}(x)$, $x > 0$) |
| `Math.round(x)` | Closest integer to $x$ (as a `long`) |
| `Math.abs(x)` | Absolute value $\lvert x \rvert$ |
| `Math.max(x, y)` | The larger of $x$ and $y$ |
| `Math.min(x, y)` | The smaller of $x$ and $y$ |

## 2.2.5 Converting Floating-Point Numbers to Integers

Occasionally, you have a value of type `double` that you need to convert to the type `int`. It is an error to assign a floating-point value to an integer:

```
double balance = total + tax;
int dollars = balance; // Error: Cannot assign double to int
```

The compiler disallows this assignment because it is potentially dangerous:

- The fractional part is lost.
- The magnitude may be too large. (The largest integer is about 2 billion, but a floating-point number can be much larger.)

You use a cast (*typeName*) to convert a value to a different type.

You must use the **cast** operator `(int)` to convert a convert floating-point value to an integer. Write the cast operator before the expression that you want to convert:

```
double balance = total + tax;
int dollars = (int) balance;
```

The cast `(int)` converts the floating-point value `balance` to an integer by discarding the fractional part. For example, if `balance` is 13.75, then `dollars` is set to 13.

When applying the cast operator to an arithmetic expression, you need to place the expression inside parentheses:

```
int dollars = (int) (total + tax);
```

Syntax 2.4  Cast

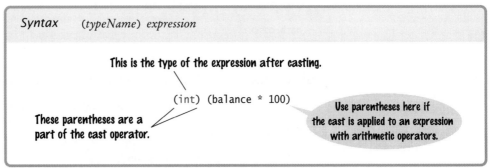

**ONLINE EXAMPLE**

A program demonstrating casts, rounding, and the % operator.

Discarding the fractional part is not always appropriate. If you want to round a floating-point number to the nearest whole number, use the `Math.round` method. This method returns a `long` integer, because large floating-point numbers cannot be stored in an `int`.

```
long rounded = Math.round(balance);
```

If `balance` is 13.75, then `rounded` is set to 14.

If you know that the result can be stored in an `int` and does not require a `long`, you can use a cast:

```
int rounded = (int) Math.round(balance);
```

## Table 7  Arithmetic Expressions

| Mathematical Expression | Java Expression | Comments |
|---|---|---|
| $\dfrac{x + y}{2}$ | `(x + y) / 2` | The parentheses are required; `x + y / 2` computes $x + \dfrac{y}{2}$. |
| $\dfrac{xy}{2}$ | `x * y / 2` | Parentheses are not required; operators with the same precedence are evaluated left to right. |
| $\left(1 + \dfrac{r}{100}\right)^n$ | `Math.pow(1 + r / 100, n)` | Use `Math.pow(x, n)` to compute $x^n$. |
| $\sqrt{a^2 + b^2}$ | `Math.sqrt(a * a + b * b)` | `a * a` is simpler than `Math.pow(a, 2)`. |
| $\dfrac{i + j + k}{3}$ | `(i + j + k) / 3.0` | If $i, j$, and $k$ are integers, using a denominator of 3.0 forces floating-point division. |
| $\pi$ | `Math.PI` | `Math.PI` is a constant declared in the `Math` class. |

**SELF CHECK**

**10.** A bank account earns interest once per year. In Java, how do you compute the interest earned in the first year? Assume variables `percent` and `balance` of type `double` have already been declared.

**11.** In Java, how do you compute the side length of a square whose area is stored in the variable `area`?

**12.** The volume of a sphere is given by

$$V = \frac{4}{3}\pi r^3$$

If the radius is given by a variable `radius` of type `double`, write a Java expression for the volume.

**13.** What is the value of `1729 / 10` and `1729 % 10`?

**14.** If `n` is a positive number, what is `(n / 10) % 10`?

**Practice It**  Now you can try these exercises at the end of the chapter: R2.3, R2.5, P2.4, P2.25.

### Unintended Integer Division

It is unfortunate that Java uses the same symbol, namely /, for both integer and floating-point division. These are really quite different operations. It is a common error to use integer division by accident. Consider this segment that computes the average of three integers.

```
int score1 = 10;
int score2 = 4;
int score3 = 9;

double average = (score1 + score2 + score3) / 3; // Error
System.out.println("Average score: " + average); // Prints 7.0, not 7.666666666666667
```

What could be wrong with that? Of course, the average of score1, score2, and score3 is

$$\frac{score1 + score2 + score3}{3}$$

Here, however, the / does not mean division in the mathematical sense. It denotes integer division because both score1 + score2 + score3 and 3 are integers. Because the scores add up to 23, the average is computed to be 7, the result of the integer division of 23 by 3. That integer 7 is then moved into the floating-point variable average. The remedy is to make the numerator or denominator into a floating-point number:

```
double total = score1 + score2 + score3;
double average = total / 3;
```

or

```
double average = (score1 + score2 + score3) / 3.0;
```

### Unbalanced Parentheses

Consider the expression

```
((a + b) * t / 2 * (1 - t)
```

What is wrong with it? Count the parentheses. There are three ( and two ). The parentheses are *unbalanced*. This kind of typing error is very common with complicated expressions. Now consider this expression.

```
(a + b) * t) / (2 * (1 - t)
```

This expression has three ( and three ), but it still is not correct. In the middle of the expression,

```
(a + b) * t) / (2 * (1 - t)
          ↑
```

there is only one ( but two ), which is an error. In the middle of an expression, the count of ( must be greater than or equal to the count of ), and at the end of the expression the two counts must be the same.

Here is a simple trick to make the counting easier without using pencil and paper. It is difficult for the brain to keep two counts simultaneously. Keep only one count when scanning the expression. Start with 1 at the first opening parenthesis, add 1 whenever you see an opening parenthesis, and subtract one whenever you see a closing parenthesis. Say the numbers aloud as you scan the

expression. If the count ever drops below zero, or is not zero at the end, the parentheses are unbalanced. For example, when scanning the previous expression, you would mutter

```
(a + b) * t) / (2 * (1 - t)
1      0 -1
```

and you would find the error.

### Programming Tip 2.3

### Spaces in Expressions

It is easier to read

```
x1 = (-b + Math.sqrt(b * b - 4 * a * c)) / (2 * a);
```

than

```
x1=(-b+Math.sqrt(b*b-4*a*c))/(2*a);
```

Simply put spaces around all operators + - * / % =. However, don't put a space after a *unary* minus: a – used to negate a single quantity, such as -b. That way, it can be easily distinguished from a *binary* minus, as in a - b.

It is customary not to put a space after a method name. That is, write Math.sqrt(x) and not Math.sqrt (x).

### Special Topic 2.3

### Combining Assignment and Arithmetic

In Java, you can combine arithmetic and assignment. For example, the instruction

```
total += cans;
```

is a shortcut for

```
total = total + cans;
```

Similarly,

```
total *= 2;
```

is another way of writing

```
total = total * 2;
```

Many programmers find this a convenient shortcut. If you like it, go ahead and use it in your own code. For simplicity, we won't use it in this book, though.

### VIDEO EXAMPLE 2.1

### Using Integer Division

A punch recipe calls for a given amount of orange soda. In this Video Example, you will see how to compute the required number of 12-ounce cans, using integer division.

*Random Fact 2.1* The Pentium Floating-Point Bug

In 1994, Intel Corporation released what was then its most powerful processor, the Pentium. Unlike previous generations of its processors, it had a very fast floating-point unit. Intel's goal was to compete aggressively with the makers of higher-end processors for engineering workstations. The Pentium was a huge success immediately.

In the summer of 1994, Dr. Thomas Nicely of Lynchburg College in Virginia ran an extensive set of computations to analyze the sums of reciprocals of certain sequences of prime numbers. The results were not always what his theory predicted, even after he took into account the inevitable roundoff errors. Then Dr. Nicely noted that the same program did produce the correct results when running on the slower 486 processor that preceded the Pentium in Intel's lineup. This should not have happened. The optimal roundoff behavior of floating-point calculations has been standardized by the Institute for Electrical and Electronic Engineers (IEEE) and Intel claimed to adhere to the IEEE standard in both the 486 and the Pentium processors. Upon further checking, Dr. Nicely discovered that indeed there was a very small set of numbers for which the product of two numbers was computed differently on the two processors. For example,

$$4{,}195{,}835 - \big((4{,}195{,}835/3{,}145{,}727) \times 3{,}145{,}727\big)$$

is mathematically equal to 0, and it did compute as 0 on a 486 processor. On his Pentium processor the result was 256.

As it turned out, Intel had independently discovered the bug in its testing and had started to produce chips that fixed it. The bug was caused by an error in a table that was used to speed up the floating-point multiplication algorithm of the processor. Intel determined that the problem was exceedingly rare. They claimed that under normal use, a typical consumer would only notice the problem once every 27,000 years. Unfortunately for Intel, Dr. Nicely had not been a normal user.

Now Intel had a real problem on its hands. It figured that the cost of replacing all Pentium processors that it had sold so far would cost a great deal of money. Intel already had more orders for the chip than it could produce, and it would be particularly galling to have to give out the scarce chips as free replacements instead of selling them. Intel's management decided to punt on the issue and initially offered to replace the processors only for those customers who could prove that their work required absolute precision in mathematical calculations. Naturally, that did not go over well with the hundreds of thousands of customers who had paid retail prices of $700 and more for a Pentium chip and did not want to live with the nagging feeling that perhaps, one day, their income tax program would produce a faulty return.

Ultimately, Intel caved in to public demand and replaced all defective chips, at a cost of about 475 million dollars.

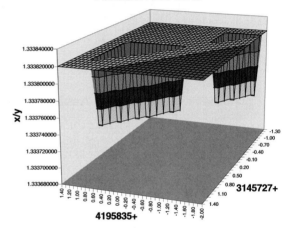

This graph shows a set of numbers for which the original Pentium processor obtained the wrong quotient.

# 2.3  Input and Output

In the following sections, you will see how to read user input and how to control the appearance of the output that your programs produce.

## 2.3.1  Reading Input

You can make your programs more flexible if you ask the program user for inputs rather than using fixed values. Consider, for example, a program that processes prices

*A supermarket scanner reads bar codes. The Java* Scanner *reads numbers and text.*

and quantities of soda containers. Prices and quantities are likely to fluctuate. The program user should provide them as inputs.

When a program asks for user input, it should first print a message that tells the user which input is expected. Such a message is called a **prompt**.

```
System.out.print("Please enter the number of bottles: "); // Display prompt
```

Use the print method, not println, to display the prompt. You want the input to appear after the colon, not on the following line. Also remember to leave a space after the colon.

Because output is sent to System.out, you might think that you use System.in for input. Unfortunately, it isn't quite that simple. When Java was first designed, not much attention was given to reading keyboard input. It was assumed that all programmers would produce graphical user interfaces with text fields and menus. System.in was given a minimal set of features and must be combined with other classes to be useful.

To read keyboard input, you use a class called Scanner. You obtain a Scanner *object* by using the following statement:

```
Scanner in = new Scanner(System.in);
```

You will learn more about objects and classes in Chapter 8. For now, simply include this statement whenever you want to read keyboard input.

Java classes are grouped into packages. Use the import statement to use classes from packages.

When using the Scanner class, you need to carry out another step: import the class from its **package**. A package is a collection of classes with a related purpose. All classes in the Java library are contained in packages. The System class belongs to the package java.lang. The Scanner class belongs to the package java.util.

Only the classes in the java.lang package are automatically available in your programs. To use the Scanner class from the java.util package, place the following declaration at the top of your program file:

```
import java.util.Scanner;
```

Once you have a scanner, you use its nextInt method to read an integer value:

```
System.out.print("Please enter the number of bottles: ");
int bottles = in.nextInt();
```

## Syntax 2.5    Input Statement

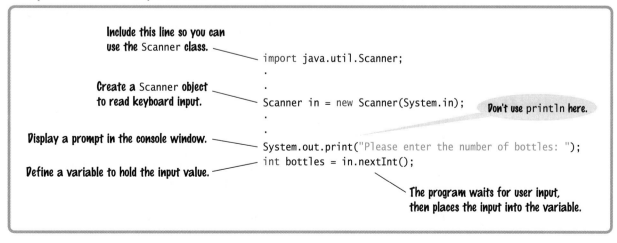

Include this line so you can use the Scanner class.

```
import java.util.Scanner;
```

Create a Scanner object to read keyboard input.

```
Scanner in = new Scanner(System.in);
```

Don't use println here.

Display a prompt in the console window.

```
System.out.print("Please enter the number of bottles: ");
```

Define a variable to hold the input value.

```
int bottles = in.nextInt();
```

The program waits for user input, then places the input into the variable.

Use the Scanner class to read keyboard input in a console window.

When the `nextInt` method is called, the program waits until the user types a number and presses the Enter key. After the user supplies the input, the number is placed into the `bottles` variable, and the program continues.

To read a floating-point number, use the `nextDouble` method instead:

```
System.out.print("Enter price: ");
double price = in.nextDouble();
```

## 2.3.2 Formatted Output

When you print the result of a computation, you often want to control its appearance. For example, when you print an amount in dollars and cents, you usually want it to be rounded to two significant digits. That is, you want the output to look like

```
Price per liter: 1.22
```

instead of

```
Price per liter: 1.215962441314554
```

Use the `printf` method to specify how values should be formatted.

The following command displays the price with two digits after the decimal point:

```
System.out.printf("%.2f", price);
```

You can also specify a *field width*:

```
System.out.printf("%10.2f", price);
```

The price is printed using ten characters: six spaces followed by the four characters 1.22.

|  |  |  |  |  |  |  | 1 | . | 2 | 2 |

The construct `%10.2f` is called a *format specifier:* it describes how a value should be formatted. The letter `f` at the end of the format specifier indicates that we are displaying a floating-point number. Use `d` for an integer and `s` for a string; see Table 8 for examples.

### Table 8 Format Specifier Examples

| Format String | Sample Output | Comments |
|---|---|---|
| "%d" | 24 | Use d with an integer. |
| "%5d" | 24 | Spaces are added so that the field width is 5. |
| "Quantity:%5d" | Quantity:    24 | Characters inside a format string but outside a format specifier appear in the output. |
| "%f" | 1.21997 | Use f with a floating-point number. |
| "%.2f" | 1.22 | Prints two digits after the decimal point. |
| "%7.2f" | 1.22 | Spaces are added so that the field width is 7. |
| "%s" | Hello | Use s with a string. |
| "%d %.2f" | 24 1.22 | You can format multiple values at once. |

*You use the* printf *method to line up your output in neat columns.*

A format string contains format specifiers and literal characters. Any characters that are not format specifiers are printed verbatim. For example, the command

```
System.out.printf("Price per liter:%10.2f", price);
```

prints

```
Price per liter:      1.22
```

You can print multiple values with a single call to the printf method. Here is a typical example:

```
System.out.printf("Quantity: %d Total: %10.2f", quantity, total);
```

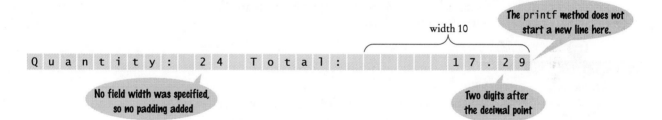

width 10

The printf method does not start a new line here.

Quantity:  24  Total:        17.29

No field width was specified, so no padding added

Two digits after the decimal point

The printf method, like the print method, does not start a new line after the output. If you want the next output to be on a separate line, you can call System.out.println(). Alternatively, Section 2.5.4 shows you how to add a newline character to the format string.

Our next example program will prompt for the price of a six-pack and the volume of each can, then print out the price per ounce. The program puts to work what you just learned about reading input and formatting output.

### section_3/Volume2.java

```
 1  import java.util.Scanner;
 2
 3  /**
 4      This program prints the price per ounce for a six-pack of cans.
 5  */
 6  public class Volume2
 7  {
 8     public static void main(String[] args)
 9     {
```

```
10      // Read price per pack
11
12      Scanner in = new Scanner(System.in);
13
14      System.out.print("Please enter the price for a six-pack: ");
15      double packPrice = in.nextDouble();
16
17      // Read can volume
18
19      System.out.print("Please enter the volume for each can (in ounces): ");
20      double canVolume = in.nextDouble();
21
22      // Compute pack volume
23
24      final double CANS_PER_PACK = 6;
25      double packVolume = canVolume * CANS_PER_PACK;
26
27      // Compute and print price per ounce
28
29      double pricePerOunce = packPrice / packVolume;
30
31      System.out.printf("Price per ounce: %8.2f", pricePerOunce);
32      System.out.println();
33   }
34 }
```

**Program Run**

```
Please enter the price for a six-pack: 2.95
Please enter the volume for each can (in ounces): 12
Price per ounce:     0.04
```

**SELF CHECK**

15. Write statements to prompt for and read the user's age using a Scanner variable named in.

16. What is wrong with the following statement sequence?
```
System.out.print("Please enter the unit price: ");
double unitPrice = in.nextDouble();
int quantity = in.nextInt();
```

17. What is problematic about the following statement sequence?
```
System.out.print("Please enter the unit price: ");
double unitPrice = in.nextInt();
```

18. What is problematic about the following statement sequence?
```
System.out.print("Please enter the number of cans");
int cans = in.nextInt();
```

19. What is the output of the following statement sequence?
```
int volume = 10;
System.out.printf("The volume is %5d", volume);
```

20. Using the printf method, print the values of the integer variables bottles and cans so that the output looks like this:
```
Bottles:        8
Cans:          24
```
The numbers to the right should line up. (You may assume that the numbers have at most 8 digits.)

**Practice It**     Now you can try these exercises at the end of the chapter: R2.10, P2.6, P2.7.

**Programming Tip 2.4**

### Use the API Documentation

The classes and methods of the Java library are listed in the **API documentation**. The API is the "**application programming interface**". A programmer who uses the Java classes to put together a computer program (or *application*) is an *application programmer*. That's you. In contrast, the programmers who designed and implemented the library classes (such as Scanner) are *system programmers*.

> The API (Application Programming Interface) documentation lists the classes and methods of the Java library.

You can find the API documentation at http://download.oracle.com/javase/7/docs/api. The API documentation describes all classes in the Java library—there are thousands of them. Fortunately, only a few are of interest to the beginning programmer. To learn more about a class, click on its name in the left hand column. You can then find out the package to which the class belongs, and which methods it supports (see Figure 4). Click on the link of a method to get a detailed description.

Appendix D contains an abbreviated version of the API documentation.

**Figure 4**   The API Documentation of the Standard Java Library

HOW TO 2.1          **Carrying out Computations**

Many programming problems require arithmetic computations. This How To shows you how to turn a problem statement into pseudocode and, ultimately, a Java program.

For example, suppose you are asked to write a program that simulates a vending machine. A customer selects an item for purchase and inserts a bill into the vending machine. The vending machine dispenses the purchased item and gives change. We will assume that all item prices are multiples of 25 cents, and the machine gives all change in dollar coins and quarters.

Your task is to compute how many coins of each type to return.

**Step 1**   Understand the problem: What are the inputs? What are the desired outputs?

In this problem, there are two inputs:
- The denomination of the bill that the customer inserts
- The price of the purchased item

There are two desired outputs:
- The number of dollar coins that the machine returns
- The number of quarters that the machine returns

**Step 2**   Work out examples by hand.

This is a very important step. If you can't compute a couple of solutions by hand, it's unlikely that you'll be able to write a program that automates the computation.

Let's assume that a customer purchased an item that cost $2.25 and inserted a $5 bill. The customer is due $2.75, or two dollar coins and three quarters, in change.

That is easy for you to see, but how can a Java program come to the same conclusion? The key is to work in pennies, not dollars. The change due the customer is 275 pennies. Dividing by 100 yields 2, the number of dollars. Dividing the remainder (75) by 25 yields 3, the number of quarters.

**Step 3**   Write pseudocode for computing the answers.

In the previous step, you worked out a specific instance of the problem. You now need to come up with a method that works in general.

Given an arbitrary item price and payment, how can you compute the coins due? First, compute the change due in pennies:

> change due = 100 x bill value - item price in pennies

To get the dollars, divide by 100 and discard the remainder:

> dollar coins = change due / 100 (without remainder)

The remaining change due can be computed in two ways. If you are familiar with the modulus operator, you can simply compute

> change due = change due % 100

Alternatively, subtract the penny value of the dollar coins from the change due:

> change due = change due - 100 x dollar coins

To get the quarters due, divide by 25:

> quarters = change due / 25

**Step 4**  Declare the variables and constants that you need, and specify their types.

Here, we have five variables:

- `billValue`
- `itemPrice`
- `changeDue`
- `dollarCoins`
- `quarters`

Should we introduce constants to explain 100 and 25 as PENNIES_PER_DOLLAR and PENNIES_PER_QUARTER? Doing so will make it easier to convert the program to international markets, so we will take this step.

It is very important that `changeDue` and PENNIES_PER_DOLLAR are of type int because the computation of `dollarCoins` uses integer division. Similarly, the other variables are integers.

**Step 5**  Turn the pseudocode into Java statements.

If you did a thorough job with the pseudocode, this step should be easy. Of course, you have to know how to express mathematical operations (such as powers or integer division) in Java.

```
changeDue = PENNIES_PER_DOLLAR * billValue - itemPrice;
dollarCoins = changeDue / PENNIES_PER_DOLLAR;
changeDue = changeDue % PENNIES_PER_DOLLAR;
quarters = changeDue / PENNIES_PER_QUARTER;
```

**Step 6**  Provide input and output.

Before starting the computation, we prompt the user for the bill value and item price:

```
System.out.print("Enter bill value (1 = $1 bill, 5 = $5 bill, etc.): ");
billValue = in.nextInt();
System.out.print("Enter item price in pennies: ");
itemPrice = in.nextInt();
```

When the computation is finished, we display the result. For extra credit, we use the `printf` method to make sure that the output lines up neatly.

```
System.out.printf("Dollar coins: %6d", dollarCoins);
System.out.printf("Quarters:     %6d", quarters);
```

**Step 7**  Provide a class with a `main` method.

Your computation needs to be placed into a class. Find an appropriate name for the class that describes the purpose of the computation. In our example, we will choose the name VendingMachine.

Inside the class, supply a `main` method.

*A vending machine takes bills
and gives change in coins.*

In the main method, you need to declare constants and variables (Step 4), carry out computations (Step 5), and provide input and output (Step 6). Clearly, you will want to first get the input, then do the computations, and finally show the output. Declare the constants at the beginning of the method, and declare each variable just before it is needed.

Here is the complete program, how_to_1/VendingMachine.java:

```java
import java.util.Scanner;

/**
   This program simulates a vending machine that gives change.
*/
public class VendingMachine
{
   public static void main(String[] args)
   {
      Scanner in = new Scanner(System.in);

      final int PENNIES_PER_DOLLAR = 100;
      final int PENNIES_PER_QUARTER = 25;

      System.out.print("Enter bill value (1 = $1 bill, 5 = $5 bill, etc.): ");
      int billValue = in.nextInt();
      System.out.print("Enter item price in pennies: ");
      int itemPrice = in.nextInt();

      // Compute change due

      int changeDue = PENNIES_PER_DOLLAR * billValue - itemPrice;
      int dollarCoins = changeDue / PENNIES_PER_DOLLAR;
      changeDue = changeDue % PENNIES_PER_DOLLAR;
      int quarters = changeDue / PENNIES_PER_QUARTER;

      // Print change due

      System.out.printf("Dollar coins: %6d", dollarCoins);
      System.out.println();
      System.out.printf("Quarters:     %6d", quarters);
      System.out.println();
   }
}
```

**Program Run**

```
Enter bill value (1 = $1 bill, 5 = $5 bill, etc.): 5
Enter item price in pennies: 225
Dollar coins:      2
Quarters:          3
```

WORKED EXAMPLE 2.1    **Computing the Cost of Stamps**

This Worked Example uses arithmetic functions to simulate a stamp vending machine.

➕ Available online in WileyPLUS and at www.wiley.com/college/horstmann.

# 2.4 Problem Solving: First Do It By Hand

A very important step for developing an algorithm is to first carry out the computations *by hand*. If you can't compute a solution yourself, it's unlikely that you'll be able to write a program that automates the computation.

To illustrate the use of hand calculations, consider the following problem.

A row of black and white tiles needs to be placed along a wall. For aesthetic reasons, the architect has specified that the first and last tile shall be black.

Your task is to compute the number of tiles needed and the gap at each end, given the space available and the width of each tile.

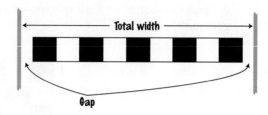

**Pick concrete values for a typical situation to use in a hand calculation.**

To make the problem more concrete, let's assume the following dimensions:

- Total width: 100 inches
- Tile width: 5 inches

The obvious solution would be to fill the space with 20 tiles, but that would not work—the last tile would be white.

Instead, look at the problem this way: The first tile must always be black, and then we add some number of white/black pairs:

The first tile takes up 5 inches, leaving 95 inches to be covered by pairs. Each pair is 10 inches wide. Therefore the number of pairs is 95 / 10 = 9.5. However, we need to discard the fractional part since we can't have fractions of tile pairs.

Therefore, we will use 9 tile pairs or 18 tiles, plus the initial black tile. Altogether, we require 19 tiles.

The tiles span 19 × 5 = 95 inches, leaving a total gap of 100 − 19 × 5 = 5 inches.

The gap should be evenly distributed at both ends. At each end, the gap is (100 − 19 × 5) / 2 = 2.5 inches.

This computation gives us enough information to devise an algorithm with arbitrary values for the total width and tile width.

**ONLINE EXAMPLE**

A program that implements this algorithm.

> number of pairs = integer part of (total width - tile width) / (2 x tile width)
> number of tiles = 1 + 2 x number of pairs
> gap at each end = (total width - number of tiles x tile width) / 2

As you can see, doing a hand calculation gives enough insight into the problem that it becomes easy to develop an algorithm.

21. Translate the pseudocode for computing the number of tiles and the gap width into Java.

22. Suppose the architect specifies a pattern with black, gray, and white tiles, like this:

Again, the first and last tile should be black. How do you need to modify the algorithm?

23. A robot needs to tile a floor with alternating black and white tiles. Develop an algorithm that yields the color (0 for black, 1 for white), given the row and column number. Start with specific values for the row and column, and then generalize.

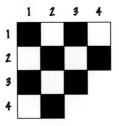

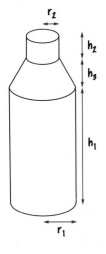

24. For a particular car, repair and maintenance costs in year 1 are estimated at $100; in year 10, at $1,500. Assuming that the repair cost increases by the same amount every year, develop pseudocode to compute the repair cost in year 3 and then generalize to year **n**.

25. The shape of a bottle is approximated by two cylinders of radius $r_1$ and $r_2$ and heights $h_1$ and $h_2$, joined by a cone section of height $h_3$.

Using the formulas for the volume of a cylinder, $V = \pi r^2 h$, and a cone section,

$$V = \pi \frac{\left(r_1^2 + r_1 r_2 + r_2^2\right)h}{3},$$

develop pseudocode to compute the volume of the bottle. Using an actual bottle with known volume as a sample, make a hand calculation of your pseudocode.

**Practice It**    Now you can try these exercises at the end of the chapter: R2.15, R2.17, R2.18.

---

WORKED EXAMPLE 2.2    **Computing Travel Time**

In this Worked Example, we develop a hand calculation to compute the time that a robot requires to retrieve an item from rocky terrain.

➕ Available online in WileyPLUS and at www.wiley.com/college/horstmann.

# 2.5 Strings

Strings are sequences of characters.

Many programs process text, not numbers. Text consists of **characters**: letters, numbers, punctuation, spaces, and so on. A **string** is a sequence of characters. For example, the string "Harry" is a sequence of five characters.

## 2.5.1 The String Type

You can declare variables that hold strings.

```
String name = "Harry";
```

We distinguish between string variables (such as the variable name declared above) and string **literals** (character sequences enclosed in quotes, such as "Harry"). A string variable is simply a variable that can hold a string, just as an integer variable can hold an integer. A string literal denotes a particular string, just as a number literal (such as 2) denotes a particular number.

The length method yields the number of characters in a string.

The number of characters in a string is called the *length* of the string. For example, the length of "Harry" is 5. You can compute the length of a string with the length method.

```
int n = name.length();
```

A string of length 0 is called the *empty string*. It contains no characters and is written as " ".

## 2.5.2 Concatenation

Use the + operator to *concatenate* strings; that is, to put them together to yield a longer string.

Given two strings, such as "Harry" and "Morgan", you can **concatenate** them to one long string. The result consists of all characters in the first string, followed by all characters in the second string. In Java, you use the + operator to concatenate two strings.

For example,

```
String fName = "Harry";
String lName = "Morgan";
String name = fName + lName;
```

results in the string

```
"HarryMorgan"
```

What if you'd like the first and last name separated by a space? No problem:

```
String name = fName + " " + lName;
```

This statement concatenates three strings: fName, the string literal " ", and lName. The result is

```
"Harry Morgan"
```

When the expression to the left or the right of a + operator is a string, the other one is automatically forced to become a string as well, and both strings are concatenated.

For example, consider this code:

```
String jobTitle = "Agent";
int employeeId = 7;
String bond = jobTitle + employeeId;
```

Whenever one of the arguments of the + operator is a string, the other argument is converted to a string.

Because jobTitle is a string, employeeId is converted from the integer 7 to the string "7". Then the two strings "Agent" and "7" are concatenated to form the string "Agent7".

This concatenation is very useful for reducing the number of System.out.print instructions. For example, you can combine

```
System.out.print("The total is ");
System.out.println(total);
```

to the single call

```
System.out.println("The total is " + total);
```

The concatenation "The total is " + total computes a single string that consists of the string "The total is ", followed by the string equivalent of the number total.

## 2.5.3 String Input

Use the next method of the Scanner class to read a string containing a single word.

You can read a string from the console:

```
System.out.print("Please enter your name: ");
String name = in.next();
```

When a string is read with the next method, only one word is read. For example, suppose the user types

```
Harry Morgan
```

as the response to the prompt. This input consists of two words. The call in.next() yields the string "Harry". You can use another call to in.next() to read the second word.

## 2.5.4 Escape Sequences

To include a quotation mark in a literal string, precede it with a backslash (\), like this:

```
"He said \"Hello\""
```

The backslash is not included in the string. It indicates that the quotation mark that follows should be a part of the string and not mark the end of the string. The sequence \" is called an **escape sequence**.

To include a backslash in a string, use the escape sequence \\, like this:

```
"C:\\Temp\\Secret.txt"
```

Another common escape sequence is \n, which denotes a **newline** character. Printing a newline character causes the start of a new line on the display. For example, the statement

```
System.out.print("*\n**\n***\n");
```

prints the characters

```
*
**
***
```

on three separate lines.

You often want to add a newline character to the end of the format string when you use System.out.printf:

```
System.out.printf("Price: %10.2f\n", price);
```

### 2.5.5 Strings and Characters

Strings are sequences of Unicode characters (see Random Fact 2.2). In Java, a **character** is a value of the type char. Characters have numeric values. You can find the values of the characters that are used in Western European languages in Appendix A. For example, if you look up the value for the character 'H', you can see that is actually encoded as the number 72.

*A string is a sequence of characters.*

Character literals are delimited by single quotes, and you should not confuse them with strings.

- 'H' is a character, a value of type char.
- "H" is a string containing a single character, a value of type String.

**String positions are counted starting with 0.**

The charAt method returns a char value from a string. The first string position is labeled 0, the second one 1, and so on.

```
H  a  r  r  y
0  1  2  3  4
```

The position number of the last character (4 for the string "Harry") is always one less than the length of the string.

For example, the statement

```
String name = "Harry";
char start = name.charAt(0);
char last = name.charAt(4);
```

sets start to the value 'H' and last to the value 'y'.

### 2.5.6 Substrings

**Use the substring method to extract a part of a string.**

Once you have a string, you can extract substrings by using the substring method. The method call

```
str.substring(start, pastEnd)
```

returns a string that is made up of the characters in the string str, starting at position start, and containing all characters up to, but not including, the position pastEnd. Here is an example:

```
String greeting = "Hello, World!";
String sub = greeting.substring(0, 5); // sub is "Hello"
```

The substring operation makes a string that consists of the first five characters taken from the string greeting.

```
H  e  l  l  o  ,     W  o  r  l  d  !
0  1  2  3  4  5  6  7  8  9  10 11 12
```

Let's figure out how to extract the substring "World". Count characters starting at 0, not 1. You find that W has position number 7. The first character that you don't want, !, is the character at position 12. Therefore, the appropriate substring command is

```
String sub2 = greeting.substring(7, 12);
```

It is curious that you must specify the position of the first character that you do want and then the first character that you don't want. There is one advantage to this setup. You can easily compute the length of the substring: It is pastEnd - start. For example, the string "World" has length 12 − 7 = 5.

If you omit the end position when calling the substring method, then all characters from the starting position to the end of the string are copied. For example,

```
String tail = greeting.substring(7); // Copies all characters from position 7 on
```

sets tail to the string "World!".

Following is a simple program that puts these concepts to work. The program asks for your name and that of your significant other. It then prints out your initials.

The operation first.substring(0, 1) makes a string consisting of one character, taken from the start of first. The program does the same for the second. Then it concatenates the resulting one-character strings with the string literal "&" to get a string of length 3, the initials string. (See Figure 5.)

*Initials are formed from the first letter of each name.*

**Figure 5** Building the initials String

### section_5/Initials.java

```
1    import java.util.Scanner;
2
3    /**
4       This program prints a pair of initials.
5    */
6    public class Initials
7    {
8       public static void main(String[] args)
9       {
10          Scanner in = new Scanner(System.in);
11
```

```
12        // Get the names of the couple
13
14        System.out.print("Enter your first name: ");
15        String first = in.next();
16        System.out.print("Enter your significant other's first name: ");
17        String second = in.next();
18
19        // Compute and display the inscription
20
21        String initials = first.substring(0, 1)
22            + "&" + second.substring(0, 1);
23        System.out.println(initials);
24     }
25 }
```

**Program Run**

```
Enter your first name: Rodolfo
Enter your significant other's first name: Sally
R&S
```

## Table 9  String Operations

| Statement | Result | Comment |
|---|---|---|
| string str = "Ja";<br>str = str + "va"; | str is set to "Java" | When applied to strings,<br>+ denotes concatenation. |
| System.out.println("Please"<br>  + " enter your name: "); | Prints<br>Please enter your name: | Use concatenation to break up strings<br>that don't fit into one line. |
| team = 49 + "ers" | team is set to "49ers" | Because "ers" is a string, 49 is converted<br>to a string. |
| String first = in.next();<br>String last = in.next();<br>(User input: Harry Morgan) | first contains "Harry"<br>last contains "Morgan" | The next method places the next word<br>into the string variable. |
| String greeting = "H & S";<br>int n = greeting.length(); | n is set to 5 | Each space counts as one character. |
| String str = "Sally";<br>char ch = str.charAt(1); | ch is set to 'a' | This is a char value, not a String. Note<br>that the initial position is 0. |
| String str = "Sally";<br>String str2 = str.substring(1, 4); | str2 is set to "all" | Extracts the substring starting at<br>position 1 and ending before position 4. |
| String str = "Sally";<br>String str2 = str.substring(1); | str2 is set to "ally" | If you omit the end position, all<br>characters from the position until the<br>end of the string are included. |
| String str = "Sally";<br>String str2 = str.substring(1, 2); | str2 is set to "a" | Extracts a String of length<br>1; contrast with str.charAt(1). |
| String last = str.substring(<br>  str.length() - 1); | last is set to the string<br>containing the last<br>character in str | The last character has position<br>str.length() - 1. |

**26.** What is the length of the string `"Java Program"`?

**27.** Consider this string variable.

```
String str = "Java Program";
```

Give a call to the substring method that returns the substring `"gram"`.

**28.** Use string concatenation to turn the string variable str from Self Check 27 into `"Java Programming"`.

**29.** What does the following statement sequence print?

```
String str = "Harry";
int n = str.length();
String mystery = str.substring(0, 1) + str.substring(n - 1, n);
System.out.println(mystery);
```

**30.** Give an input statement to read a name of the form "John Q. Public".

**Practice It** Now you can try these exercises at the end of the chapter: R2.7, R2.11, P2.15, P2.23.

---

### Instance Methods and Static Methods

In this chapter, you have learned how to read, process, and print numbers and strings. Many of these tasks involve various method calls. You may have noticed syntactical differences in these method calls. For example, to compute the square root of a number num, you call `Math.sqrt(num)`, but to compute the length of a string str, you call `str.length()`. This section explains the reasons behind these differences.

The Java language distinguishes between values of **primitive types** and **objects**. Numbers and characters, as well as the values false and true that you will see in Chapter 3, are primitive. All other values are objects. Examples of objects are

- a string such as `"Hello"`.
- a Scanner object obtained by calling `in = new Scanner(System.in)`.
- `System.in` and `System.out`.

In Java, each object belongs to a **class**. For example,

- All strings are objects of the String class.
- A scanner object belongs to the Scanner class.
- `System.out` is an object of the PrintStream class. (It is useful to know this so that you can look up the valid methods in the API documentation; see Programming Tip 2.4 on page 53.)

A class declares the methods that you can use with its objects. Here are examples of methods that are invoked on objects:

```
"Hello".substring(0, 1)
in.nextDouble()
System.out.println("Hello")
```

A method is invoked with the **dot notation**: the object is followed by the name of the method, and the method is followed by parameters enclosed in parentheses.

The method is invoked on this object.　　This is the name of the method.　　These parameters are inputs to the method.

```
System.out.println("Hello")
```

You cannot invoke methods on numbers. For example, the call `2.sqrt()` would be an error.

In Java, classes can declare methods that are *not* invoked on objects. Such methods are called **static methods**. (The term "static" is a historical holdover from the C and C++ programming languages. It has nothing to do with the usual meaning of the word.) For example, the Math class declares a static method sqrt. You call it by giving the name of the class and method, then the name of the numeric input: Math.sqrt(2).

The name of the class — The name of the static method

Math.sqrt(2)

In contrast, a method that is invoked on an object is called an **instance method**. As a rule of thumb, you use static methods when you manipulate numbers. You use instance methods when you process strings or perform input/output. You will learn more about the distinction between static and instance methods in Chapter 8.

---

**Special Topic 2.5**

## Using Dialog Boxes for Input and Output

Most program users find the console window rather old-fashioned. The easiest alternative is to create a separate pop-up window for each input.

| Input | ✕ |
| --- | --- |
| **? Enter price:** | |
| [          ] | |
| OK  Cancel | |

*An Input Dialog Box*

Call the static showInputDialog method of the JOptionPane class, and supply the string that prompts the input from the user. For example,

```
String input = JOptionPane.showInputDialog("Enter price:");
```

**ONLINE EXAMPLE**

⊕ A complete program that uses option panes for input and output.

That method returns a String object. Of course, often you need the input as a number. Use the Integer.parseInt and Double.parseDouble methods to convert the string to a number:

```
double price = Double.parseDouble(input);
```

You can also display output in a dialog box:

```
JOptionPane.showMessageDialog(null, "Price: " + price);
```

---

**VIDEO EXAMPLE 2.2**

## Computing Distances on Earth

In this Video Example, you will see how to write a program that computes the distance between any two points on Earth.

---

⊕ Available online in WileyPLUS and at www.wiley.com/college/horstmann.

## *Random Fact 2.2* International Alphabets and Unicode

The English alphabet is pretty simple: upper- and lowercase *a* to *z*. Other European languages have accent marks and special characters. For example, German has three so-called *umlaut* characters, ä, ö, ü, and a *double-s* character ß. These are not optional frills; you couldn't write a page of German text without using these characters a few times. German keyboards have keys for these characters.

*The German Keyboard Layout*

Many countries don't use the Roman script at all. Russian, Greek, Hebrew, Arabic, and Thai letters, to name just a few, have completely different shapes. To complicate matters, Hebrew and Arabic are typed from right to left. Each of these alphabets has about as many characters as the English alphabet.

*Hebrew, Arabic, and English*

The Chinese languages as well as Japanese and Korean use Chinese characters. Each character represents an idea or thing. Words are made up of one or more of these ideographic characters. Over 70,000 ideographs are known.

Starting in 1988, a consortium of hardware and software manufacturers developed a uniform encoding scheme called **Unicode** that is capable of encoding text in essentially all written languages of the world. An early version of Unicode used 16 bits for each character. The Java char type corresponds to that encoding.

Today Unicode has grown to a 21-bit code, with definitions for over 100,000 characters. There are even plans to add codes for extinct languages, such as Egyptian hieroglyphics. Unfortunately, that means that a Java char value does not always correspond to a Unicode character. Some characters in languages such as Chinese or ancient Egyptian occupy two char values.

*The Chinese Script*

---

## CHAPTER SUMMARY

### Declare variables with appropriate names and types.

- A variable is a storage location with a name.
- When declaring a variable, you usually specify an initial value.
- When declaring a variable, you also specify the type of its values.
- Use the int type for numbers that cannot have a fractional part.
- Use the double type for floating-point numbers.
- By convention, variable names should start with a lowercase letter.
- An assignment statement stores a new value in a variable, replacing the previously stored value.
- The assignment operator = does *not* denote mathematical equality.

- You cannot change the value of a variable that is defined as `final`.
- Use comments to add explanations for humans who read your code. The compiler ignores comments.

## Write arithmetic expressions in Java.

- Mixing integers and floating-point values in an arithmetic expression yields a floating-point value.
- The `++` operator adds 1 to a variable; the `--` operator subtracts 1.
- If both arguments of `/` are integers, the remainder is discarded.
- The `%` operator computes the remainder of an integer division.
- The Java library declares many mathematical functions, such as `Math.sqrt` (square root) and `Math.pow` (raising to a power).
- You use a cast (*typeName*) to convert a value to a different type.

## Write programs that read user input and print formatted output.

- Java classes are grouped into packages. Use the `import` statement to use classes from packages.
- Use the `Scanner` class to read keyboard input in a console window.
- Use the `printf` method to specify how values should be formatted.
- The API (Application Programming Interface) documentation lists the classes and methods of the Java library.

## Carry out hand calculations when developing an algorithm.

- Pick concrete values for a typical situation to use in a hand calculation.

## Write programs that process strings.

- Strings are sequences of characters.
- The `length` method yields the number of characters in a string.
- Use the `+` operator to *concatenate* strings; that is, to put them together to yield a longer string.
- Whenever one of the arguments of the `+` operator is a string, the other argument is converted to a string.
- Use the `next` method of the `Scanner` class to read a string containing a single word.
- String positions are counted starting with 0.
- Use the `substring` method to extract a part of a string.

## STANDARD LIBRARY ITEMS INTRODUCED IN THIS CHAPTER

| | | |
|---|---|---|
| java.io.PrintStream | max | java.math.BigDecimal |
|   printf | min |   add |
| java.lang.Double | pow |   multiply |
|   parseDouble | round |   subtract |
| java.lang.Integer | sin | java.math.BigInteger |
|   MAX_VALUE | sqrt |   add |
|   MIN_VALUE | tan |   multiply |
|   parseInt | toDegrees |   subtract |
| java.lang.Math | toRadians | java.util.Scanner |
|   PI | java.lang.String |   next |
|   abs |   charAt |   nextDouble |
|   cos |   length |   nextInt |
|   exp |   substring | javax.swing.JOptionPane |
|   log | java.lang.System |   showInputDialog |
|   log10 |   in |   showMessageDialog |

## REVIEW EXERCISES

**R2.1** What is the value of mystery after this sequence of statements?

```
int mystery = 1;
mystery = 1 - 2 * mystery;
mystery = mystery + 1;
```

**R2.2** What is wrong with the following sequence of statements?

```
int mystery = 1;
mystery = mystery + 1;
int mystery = 1 - 2 * mystery;
```

**R2.3** Write the following mathematical expressions in Java.

$$s = s_0 + v_0 t + \frac{1}{2} g t^2$$

$$G = 4\pi^2 \frac{a^3}{p^2(m_1 + m_2)}$$

$$FV = PV \cdot \left(1 + \frac{INT}{100}\right)^{YRS}$$

$$c = \sqrt{a^2 + b^2 - 2ab \cos\gamma}$$

**R2.4** Write the following Java expressions in mathematical notation.

   **a.** dm = m * (Math.sqrt(1 + v / c) / Math.sqrt(1 - v / c) - 1);
   **b.** volume = Math.PI * r * r * h;
   **c.** volume = 4 * Math.PI * Math.pow(r, 3) / 3;
   **d.** z = Math.sqrt(x * x + y * y);

**R2.5** What are the values of the following expressions? In each line, assume that

```
double x = 2.5;
double y = -1.5;
```

```
int m = 18;
int n = 4;
```

**a.** x + n * y - (x + n) * y
**b.** m / n + m % n
**c.** 5 * x - n / 5
**d.** 1 - (1 - (1 - (1 - (1 - n))))
**e.** Math.sqrt(Math.sqrt(n))

■ **R2.6**  What are the values of the following expressions, assuming that n is 17 and m is 18?

**a.** n / 10 + n % 10
**b.** n % 2 + m % 2
**c.** (m + n) / 2
**d.** (m + n) / 2.0
**e.** (int) (0.5 * (m + n))
**f.** (int) Math.round(0.5 * (m + n))

■■ **R2.7**  What are the values of the following expressions? In each line, assume that

```
String s = "Hello";
String t = "World";
```

**a.** s.length() + t.length()
**b.** s.substring(1, 2)
**c.** s.substring(s.length() / 2, s.length())
**d.** s + t
**e.** t + s

■ **R2.8**  Find at least five *compile-time* errors in the following program.

```
public class HasErrors
{
   public static void main();
   {
      System.out.print(Please enter two numbers:)
      x = in.readDouble;
      y = in.readDouble;
      System.out.printline("The sum is " + x + y);
   }
}
```

■■ **R2.9**  Find three *run-time* errors in the following program.

```
public class HasErrors
{
   public static void main(String[] args)
   {
      int x = 0;
      int y = 0;
      Scanner in = new Scanner("System.in");
      System.out.print("Please enter an integer:");
      x = in.readInt();
      System.out.print("Please enter another integer: ");
      x = in.readInt();
      System.out.println("The sum is " + x + y);
   }
}
```

■ **R2.10** Consider the following code segment.

```
double purchase = 19.93;
double payment = 20.00;
double change = payment - purchase;
System.out.println(change);
```

The code segment prints the change as 0.07000000000000028. Explain why. Give a recommendation to improve the code so that users will not be confused.

■ **R2.11** Explain the differences between 2, 2.0, '2', "2", and "2.0".

■ **R2.12** Explain what each of the following program segments computes.

**a.** x = 2;
     y = x + x;
**b.** s = "2";
     t = s + s;

■■ **R2.13** Write pseudocode for a program that reads a word and then prints the first character, the last character, and the characters in the middle. For example, if the input is Harry, the program prints H y arr.

■■ **R2.14** Write pseudocode for a program that reads a name (such as Harold James Morgan) and then prints a monogram consisting of the initial letters of the first, middle, and last name (such as HJM).

■■■ **R2.15** Write pseudocode for a program that computes the first and last digit of a number. For example, if the input is 23456, the program should print 2 and 6. *Hint:* %, Math.log10.

■ **R2.16** Modify the pseudocode for the program in How To 2.1 so that the program gives change in quarters, dimes, and nickels. You can assume that the price is a multiple of 5 cents. To develop your pseudocode, first work with a couple of specific values.

■■ **R2.17** A cocktail shaker is composed of three cone sections.

Using realistic values for the radii and heights, compute the total volume, using the formula given in Self Check 25 for a cone section. Then develop an algorithm that works for arbitrary dimensions.

■■■ **R2.18** You are cutting off a piece of pie like this, where $c$ is the length of the straight part (called the chord length) and $h$ is the height of the piece.

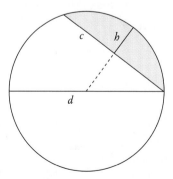

There is an approximate formula for the area: $A \approx \frac{2}{3}ch + \frac{h^3}{2c}$

However, *h* is not so easy to measure, whereas the diameter *d* of a pie is usually well-known. Calculate the area where the diameter of the pie is 12 inches and the chord length of the segment is 10 inches. Generalize to an algorithm that yields the area for any diameter and chord length.

•• **R2.19** The following pseudocode describes how to obtain the name of a day, given the day number (0 = Sunday, 1 = Monday, and so on.)

> Declare a string called names containing "SunMonTueWedThuFriSat".
> Compute the starting position as 3 x the day number.
> Extract the substring of names at the starting position with length 3.

Check this pseudocode, using the day number 4. Draw a diagram of the string that is being computed, similar to Figure 5.

••• **R2.20** The following pseudocode describes how to swap two letters in a word.

> We are given a string str and two positions i and j. (i comes before j)
> Set first to the substring from the start of the string to the last position before i.
> Set middle to the substring from positions i + 1 to j - 1.
> Set last to the substring from position j + 1 to the end of the string.
> Concatenate the following five strings: first, the string containing just the character at position j,
>     middle, the string containing just the character at position i, and last.

Check this pseudocode, using the string "Gateway" and positions 2 and 4. Draw a diagram of the string that is being computed, similar to Figure 5.

•• **R2.21** How do you get the first character of a string? The last character? How do you remove the first character? The last character?

••• **R2.22** Write a program that prints the values

```
3 * 1000 * 1000 * 1000
3.0 * 1000 * 1000 * 1000
```

Explain the results.

• **R2.23** This chapter contains a number of recommendations regarding variables and constants that make programs easier to read and maintain. Briefly summarize these recommendations.

## PROGRAMMING EXERCISES

• **P2.1** Write a program that displays the dimensions of a letter-size (8.5 × 11 inches) sheet of paper in millimeters. There are 25.4 millimeters per inch. Use constants and comments in your program.

• **P2.2** Write a program that computes and displays the perimeter of a letter-size (8.5 × 11 inches) sheet of paper and the length of its diagonal.

• **P2.3** Write a program that reads a number and displays the square, cube, and fourth power. Use the Math.pow method only for the fourth power.

•• **P2.4** Write a program that prompts the user for two integers and then prints
- The sum
- The difference

- The product
- The average
- The distance (absolute value of the difference)
- The maximum (the larger of the two)
- The minimum (the smaller of the two)

*Hint:* The max and min functions are declared in the Math class.

**•• P2.5** Enhance the output of Exercise P2.4 so that the numbers are properly aligned:

```
Sum:           45
Difference:    -5
Product:       500
Average:       22.50
Distance:       5
Maximum:       25
Minimum:       20
```

**•• P2.6** Write a program that prompts the user for a measurement in meters and then converts it to miles, feet, and inches.

**• P2.7** Write a program that prompts the user for a radius and then prints
- The area and circumference of a circle with that radius
- The volume and surface area of a sphere with that radius

**•• P2.8** Write a program that asks the user for the lengths of the sides of a rectangle. Then print
- The area and perimeter of the rectangle
- The length of the diagonal (use the Pythagorean theorem)

**• P2.9** Improve the program discussed in How To 2.1 to allow input of quarters in addition to bills.

**••• P2.10** Write a program that helps a person decide whether to buy a hybrid car. Your program's inputs should be:

- The cost of a new car
- The estimated miles driven per year
- The estimated gas price
- The efficiency in miles per gallon
- The estimated resale value after 5 years

Compute the total cost of owning the car for five years. (For simplicity, we will not take the cost of financing into account.) Obtain realistic prices for a new and used hybrid and a comparable car from the Web. Run your program twice, using today's gas price and 15,000 miles per year. Include pseudocode and the program runs with your assignment.

**•• P2.11** Write a program that asks the user to input
- The number of gallons of gas in the tank
- The fuel efficiency in miles per gallon
- The price of gas per gallon

Then print the cost per 100 miles and how far the car can go with the gas in the tank.

■ **P2.12** *File names and extensions.* Write a program that prompts the user for the drive letter (C), the path (\Windows\System), the file name (Readme), and the extension (txt). Then print the complete file name C:\Windows\System\Readme.txt. (If you use UNIX or a Macintosh, skip the drive name and use / instead of \ to separate directories.)

■■■ **P2.13** Write a program that reads a number between 1,000 and 999,999 from the user, where the user enters a comma in the input. Then print the number without a comma. Here is a sample dialog; the user input is in color:

```
Please enter an integer between 1,000 and 999,999: 23,456
23456
```

*Hint:* Read the input as a string. Measure the length of the string. Suppose it contains *n* characters. Then extract substrings consisting of the first *n* – 4 characters and the last three characters.

■■ **P2.14** Write a program that reads a number between 1,000 and 999,999 from the user and prints it with a comma separating the thousands. Here is a sample dialog; the user input is in color:

```
Please enter an integer between 1000 and 999999: 23456
23,456
```

■ **P2.15** *Printing a grid.* Write a program that prints the following grid to play tic-tac-toe.

```
+--+--+--+
|  |  |  |
+--+--+--+
|  |  |  |
+--+--+--+
|  |  |  |
+--+--+--+
```

Of course, you could simply write seven statements of the form

```
System.out.println("+--+--+--+");
```

You should do it the smart way, though. Declare string variables to hold two kinds of patterns: a comb-shaped pattern and the bottom line. Print the comb three times and the bottom line once.

■■ **P2.16** Write a program that reads in an integer and breaks it into a sequence of individual digits. For example, the input 16384 is displayed as

```
1 6 3 8 4
```

You may assume that the input has no more than five digits and is not negative.

■■ **P2.17** Write a program that reads two times in military format (0900, 1730) and prints the number of hours and minutes between the two times. Here is a sample run. User input is in color.

```
Please enter the first time: 0900
Please enter the second time: 1730
8 hours 30 minutes
```

Extra credit if you can deal with the case where the first time is later than the second:

```
Please enter the first time: 1730
Please enter the second time: 0900
15 hours 30 minutes
```

■■■ **P2.18** *Writing large letters.* A large letter H can be produced like this:

```
*   *
*   *
*****
*   *
*   *
```

It can be declared as a string literal like this:

```
final string LETTER_H = "*   *\n*   *\n*****\n*   *\n*   *\n";
```

(The \n escape sequence denotes a "newline" character that causes subsequent characters to be printed on a new line.) Do the same for the letters E, L, and O. Then write the message

```
H
E
L
L
O
```

in large letters.

■■ **P2.19** Write a program that transforms numbers 1, 2, 3, ..., 12 into the corresponding month names January, February, March, ..., December. *Hint:* Make a very long string "January February March ...", in which you add spaces such that each month name has *the same length*. Then use substring to extract the month you want.

■■ **P2.20** Write a program that prints a Christmas tree:

```
     /\'
    /  \'
   /    \'
  /      \'
  --------
    "  "
    "  "
    "  "
```

Remember to use escape sequences.

■■ **P2.21** Easter Sunday is the first Sunday after the first full moon of spring. To compute the date, you can use this algorithm, invented by the mathematician Carl Friedrich Gauss in 1800:

1. Let y be the year (such as 1800 or 2001).
2. Divide y by 19 and call the remainder a. Ignore the quotient.
3. Divide y by 100 to get a quotient b and a remainder c.
4. Divide b by 4 to get a quotient d and a remainder e.
5. Divide 8 * b + 13 by 25 to get a quotient g. Ignore the remainder.
6. Divide 19 * a + b - d - g + 15 by 30 to get a remainder h. Ignore the quotient.
7. Divide c by 4 to get a quotient j and a remainder k.
8. Divide a + 11 * h by 319 to get a quotient m. Ignore the remainder.
9. Divide 2 * e + 2 * j - k - h + m + 32 by 7 to get a remainder r. Ignore the quotient.

**10.** Divide h - m + r + 90 by 25 to get a quotient n. Ignore the remainder.

**11.** Divide h - m + r + n + 19 by 32 to get a remainder p. Ignore the quotient.

Then Easter falls on day p of month n. For example, if y is 2001:

```
a = 6                 h = 18              n = 4
b = 20, c = 1         j = 0, k = 1        p = 15
d = 5, e = 0          m = 0
g = 6                 r = 6
```

Therefore, in 2001, Easter Sunday fell on April 15. Write a program that prompts the user for a year and prints out the month and day of Easter Sunday.

■■ **Business P2.22** The following pseudocode describes how a bookstore computes the price of an order from the total price and the number of the books that were ordered.

> Read the total book price and the number of books.
> Compute the tax (7.5 percent of the total book price).
> Compute the shipping charge ($2 per book).
> The price of the order is the sum of the total book price, the tax, and the shipping charge.
> Print the price of the order.

Translate this pseudocode into a Java program.

■■ **Business P2.23** The following pseudocode describes how to turn a string containing a ten-digit phone number (such as "4155551212") into a more readable string with parentheses and dashes, like this: "(415) 555-1212".

> Take the substring consisting of the first three characters and surround it with "(" and ") ". This is the area code.
> Concatenate the area code, the substring consisting of the next three characters, a hyphen, and the substring consisting of the last four characters. This is the formatted number.

Translate this pseudocode into a Java program that reads a telephone number into a string variable, computes the formatted number, and prints it.

■■ **Business P2.24** The following pseudocode describes how to extract the dollars and cents from a price given as a floating-point value. For example, a price 2.95 yields values 2 and 95 for the dollars and cents.

> Assign the price to an integer variable dollars.
> Multiply the difference price - dollars by 100 and add 0.5.
> Assign the result to an integer variable cents.

Translate this pseudocode into a Java program. Read a price and print the dollars and cents. Test your program with inputs 2.95 and 4.35.

■■ **Business P2.25** *Giving change.* Implement a program that directs a cashier how to give change. The program has two inputs: the amount due and the amount received from the customer. Display the dollars, quarters, dimes, nickels, and pennies that the customer should receive in return. In order to avoid roundoff errors, the program user should supply both amounts in pennies, for example 274 instead of 2.74.

■ **Business P2.26** An online bank wants you to create a program that shows prospective customers how their deposits will grow. Your program should read the initial balance and the annual interest rate. Interest is compounded monthly. Print out the balances after the first three months. Here is a sample run:

```
Initial balance: 1000
Annual interest rate in percent: 6.0
After first month:     1005.00
After second month:    1010.03
After third month:     1015.08
```

▪ **Business P2.27** A video club wants to reward its best members with a discount based on the member's number of movie rentals and the number of new members referred by the member. The discount is in percent and is equal to the sum of the rentals and the referrals, but it cannot exceed 75 percent. (*Hint:* Math.min.) Write a program Discount-Calculator to calculate the value of the discount.

Here is a sample run:

```
Enter the number of movie rentals: 56
Enter the number of members referred to the video club: 3
The discount is equal to:     59.00 percent.
```

▪ **Science P2.28** Consider the following circuit.

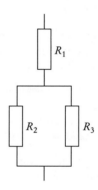

Write a program that reads the resistances of the three resistors and computes the total resistance, using Ohm's law.

▪▪ **Science P2.29** The dew point temperature $T_d$ can be calculated (approximately) from the relative humidity $RH$ and the actual temperature $T$ by

$$T_d = \frac{b \cdot f(T, RH)}{a - f(T, RH)}$$

$$f(T, RH) = \frac{a \cdot T}{b + T} + \ln(RH)$$

where $a = 17.27$ and $b = 237.7°$ C.

Write a program that reads the relative humidity (between 0 and 1) and the temperature (in degrees C) and prints the dew point value. Use the Java function log to compute the natural logarithm.

▪▪▪ **Science P2.30** The pipe clip temperature sensors shown here are robust sensors that can be clipped directly onto copper pipes to measure the temperature of the liquids in the pipes.

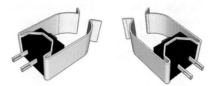

Each sensor contains a device called a *thermistor*. Thermistors are semiconductor devices that exhibit a temperature-dependent resistance described by:

$$R = R_0 \, e^{\beta\left(\frac{1}{T} - \frac{1}{T_0}\right)}$$

where $R$ is the resistance (in $\Omega$) at the temperature $T$ (in °K), and $R_0$ is the resistance (in $\Omega$) at the temperature $T_0$ (in °K). $\beta$ is a constant that depends on the material used to make the thermistor. Thermistors are specified by providing values for $R_0$, $T_0$, and $\beta$.

The thermistors used to make the pipe clip temperature sensors have $R_0 = 1075 \, \Omega$ at $T_0 = 85$ °C, and $\beta = 3969$ °K. (Notice that $\beta$ has units of °K. Recall that the temperature in °K is obtained by adding 273 to the temperature in °C.) The liquid temperature, in °C, is determined from the resistance $R$, in $\Omega$, using

$$T = \frac{\beta T_0}{T_0 \ln\left(\dfrac{R}{R_0}\right) + \beta} - 273$$

Write a Java program that prompts the user for the thermistor resistance $R$ and prints a message giving the liquid temperature in °C.

**■■■ Science P2.31**   The circuit shown below illustrates some important aspects of the connection between a power company and one of its customers. The customer is represented by three parameters, $V_t$, $P$, and $pf$. $V_t$ is the voltage accessed by plugging into a wall outlet. Customers depend on having a dependable value of $V_t$ in order for their appliances to work properly. Accordingly, the power company regulates the value of $V_t$ carefully. $P$ describes the amount of power used by the customer and is the primary factor in determining the customer's electric bill. The power factor, $pf$, is less familiar. (The power factor is calculated as the cosine of an angle so that its value will always be between zero and one.) In this problem you will be asked to write a Java program to investigate the significance of the power factor.

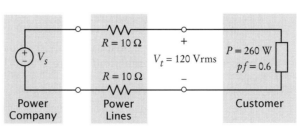

In the figure, the power lines are represented, somewhat simplistically, as resistances in Ohms. The power company is represented as an AC voltage source. The source voltage, $V_s$, required to provide the customer with power $P$ at voltage $V_t$ can be determined using the formula

$$V_s = \sqrt{\left(V_t + \frac{2RP}{V_t}\right)^2 + \left(\frac{2RP}{pfV_t}\right)^2\left(1 - pf^2\right)}$$

($V_s$ has units of Vrms.) This formula indicates that the value of $V_s$ depends on the value of $pf$. Write a Java program that prompts the user for a power factor value and then prints a message giving the corresponding value of $V_s$, using the values for $P$, $R$, and $V_t$ shown in the figure above.

■■■ **Science P2.32** Consider the following tuning circuit connected to an antenna, where $C$ is a variable capacitor whose capacitance ranges from $C_{min}$ to $C_{max}$.

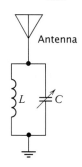

Antenna

$L$  $C$

The tuning circuit selects the frequency $f = \dfrac{2\pi}{\sqrt{LC}}$. To design this circuit for a given frequency, take $C = \sqrt{C_{min}C_{max}}$ and calculate the required inductance $L$ from $f$ and $C$. Now the circuit can be tuned to any frequency in the range $f_{min} = \dfrac{2\pi}{\sqrt{LC_{max}}}$ to $f_{max} = \dfrac{2\pi}{\sqrt{LC_{min}}}$.

Write a Java program to design a tuning circuit for a given frequency, using a variable capacitor with given values for $C_{min}$ and $C_{max}$. (A typical input is $f = 16.7$ MHz, $C_{min} = 14$ pF, and $C_{max} = 365$ pF.) The program should read in $f$ (in Hz), $C_{min}$ and $C_{max}$ (in F), and print the required inductance value and the range of frequencies to which the circuit can be tuned by varying the capacitance.

■ **Science P2.33** According to the Coulomb force law, the electric force between two charged particles of charge $Q_1$ and $Q_2$ Coulombs, that are a distance $r$ meters apart, is

$$F = \frac{Q_1 Q_2}{4\pi\varepsilon r^2}$$ Newtons, where $\varepsilon = 8.854 \times 10^{-12}$ Farads/meter. Write a program that calculates the force on a pair of charged particles, based on the user input of $Q_1$ Coulombs, $Q_2$ Coulombs, and $r$ meters, and then computes and displays the electric force.

## ANSWERS TO SELF-CHECK QUESTIONS

1. One possible answer is

   ```
   int bottlesPerCase = 8;
   ```

   You may choose a different variable name or a different initialization value, but your variable should have type `int`.

2. There are three errors:
   - You cannot have spaces in variable names.
   - The variable type should be `double` because it holds a fractional value.
   - There is a semicolon missing at the end of the statement.

3. ```
   double unitPrice = 1.95;
   int quantity = 2;
   ```

4. ```
   System.out.print("Total price: ");
   System.out.println(unitPrice * quantity);
   ```

5. Change the declaration of `cansPerPack` to

   ```
   int cansPerPack = 4;
   ```

6. You need to use a `*/` delimiter to close a comment that begins with a `/*`:

   ```
   double canVolume = 0.355;
      /* Liters in a 12-ounce can */
   ```

7. The program would compile, and it would display the same result. However, a person reading the program might find it confusing that fractional cans are being considered.

8. Its value is modified by the assignment statement.

9. Assignment would occur when one car is replaced by another in the parking space.

10. ```
    double interest = balance * percent / 100;
    ```

11. ```
    double sideLength = Math.sqrt(area);
    ```

12. ```
    4 * PI * Math.pow(radius, 3) / 3
    ```
    or `(4.0 / 3) * PI * Math.pow(radius, 3)`, but not `(4 / 3) * PI * Math.pow(radius, 3)`

13. 172 and 9

14. It is the second-to-last digit of n. For example, if n is 1729, then n / 10 is 172, and (n / 10) % 10 is 2.

15. ```
    System.out.print("How old are you? ");
    int age = in.nextInt();
    ```

16. There is no prompt that alerts the program user to enter the quantity.

17. The second statement calls `nextInt`, not `nextDouble`. If the user were to enter a price such as 1.95, the program would be terminated with an "input mismatch exception".

18. There is no colon and space at the end of the prompt. A dialog would look like this:

    ```
    Please enter the number of cans6
    ```

19. ```
    The total volume is     10
    ```

    There are four spaces between is and 10. One space originates from the format string (the space between s and %), and three spaces are added before 10 to achieve a field width of 5.

20. Here is a simple solution:

    ```
    System.out.printf("Bottles: %8d\n", bottles);
    System.out.printf("Cans:    %8d\n", cans);
    ```

    Note the spaces after Cans:. Alternatively, you can use format specifiers for the strings. You can even combine all output into a single statement:

    ```
    System.out.printf("%-9s%8d\n%-9s%8d\n",
    "Bottles: ", bottles, "Cans:", cans);
    ```

21. ```
    int pairs = (totalWidth - tileWidth)
       / (2 * tileWidth);
    int tiles = 1 + 2 * pairs;
    double gap = (totalWidth -
       tiles * tileWidth) / 2.0;
    ```

    Be sure that `pairs` is declared as an `int`.

22. Now there are groups of four tiles (gray/white/gray/black) following the initial black tile. Therefore, the algorithm is now

    **number of groups = integer part of (total width - tile width) / (4 x tile width)**
    **number of tiles = 1 + 4 x number of groups**

    The formula for the gap is not changed.

23. Clearly, the answer depends only on whether the row and column numbers are even or odd, so let's first take the remainder after dividing by 2. Then we can enumerate all expected answers:

    | Row % 2 | Column % 2 | Color |
    |---------|------------|-------|
    | 0 | 0 | 0 |
    | 0 | 1 | 1 |
    | 1 | 0 | 1 |
    | 1 | 1 | 0 |

In the first three entries of the table, the color is simply the sum of the remainders. In the fourth entry, the sum would be 2, but we want a zero. We can achieve that by taking another remainder operation:

`color = ((row % 2) + (column % 2)) % 2`

24. In nine years, the repair costs increased by $1,400. Therefore, the increase per year is $1,400 / 9 ≈ $156. The repair cost in year 3 would be $100 + 2 × $156 = $412. The repair cost in year $n$ is $100 + $n$ × $156. To avoid accumulation of roundoff errors, it is actually a good idea to use the original expression that yielded $156, that is,

`Repair cost in year n = 100 + n x 1400 / 9`

25. The pseudocode follows easily from the equations:

`bottom volume = π x r₁² x h₁`
`top volume = π x r₂² x h₂`
`middle volume = π x (r₁² + r₁ x r₂ + r₂²) x h₃ / 3`
`total volume = bottom volume + top volume + middle volume`

Measuring a typical wine bottle yields $r_1 = 3.6$, $r_2 = 1.2$, $h_1 = 15$, $h_2 = 7$, $h_3 = 6$ (all in centimeters). Therefore,

bottom volume = 610.73

top volume = 31.67

middle volume = 135.72

total volume = 778.12

The actual volume is 750 ml, which is close enough to our computation to give confidence that it is correct.

26. The length is 12. The space counts as a character.

27. `str.substring(8, 12)` or `str.substring(8)`

28. `str = str + "ming";`

29. `Hy`

30. 
```
String first = in.next();
String middle = in.next();
String last = in.next();
```

## CHAPTER 3

# DECISIONS

To implement decisions using if
  statements

To compare integers, floating-point numbers, and strings

To write statements using the Boolean data type

To develop strategies for testing your programs

To validate user input

One of the essential features of computer programs is their ability to make decisions. Like a train that changes tracks depending on how the switches are set, a program can take different actions depending on inputs and other circumstances.

In this chapter, you will learn how to program simple and complex decisions. You will apply what you learn to the task of checking user input.

# 3.1 The if Statement

The if statement allows a program to carry out different actions depending on the nature of the data to be processed.

The if statement is used to implement a decision (see Syntax 3.1). When a condition is fulfilled, one set of statements is executed. Otherwise, another set of statements is executed.

Here is an example using the if statement: In many countries, the number 13 is considered unlucky. Rather than offending superstitious tenants, building owners sometimes skip the thirteenth floor; floor 12 is immediately followed by floor 14. Of course, floor 13 is not usually left empty or, as some conspiracy theorists believe, filled with secret offices and research labs. It is simply called floor 14. The computer that controls the building elevators needs to compensate for this foible and adjust all floor numbers above 13.

Let's simulate this process in Java. We will ask the user to type in the desired floor number and then compute the actual floor. When the input is above 13, then we need to decrement the input to obtain the actual floor. For example, if the user provides an input of 20, the program determines the actual floor as 19. Otherwise, we simply use the supplied floor number.

*This elevator panel "skips" the thirteenth floor. The floor is not actually missing—the computer that controls the elevator adjusts the floor numbers above 13.*

```java
int actualFloor;

if (floor > 13)
{
   actualFloor = floor - 1;
}
else
{
   actualFloor = floor;
}
```

The flowchart in Figure 1 shows the branching behavior.

In our example, each branch of the if statement contains a single statement. You can include as many statements in each branch as you like. Sometimes, it happens that

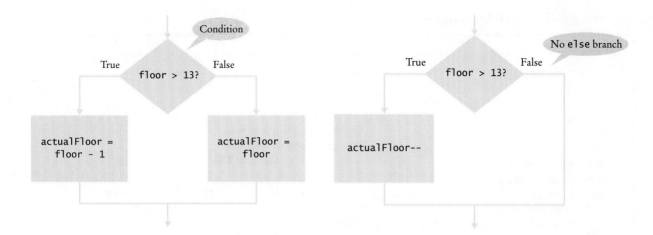

**Figure 1**
Flowchart for if Statement

**Figure 2**
Flowchart for if Statement with No else Branch

there is nothing to do in the else branch of the statement. In that case, you can omit it entirely, such as in this example:

```
int actualFloor = floor;

if (floor > 13)
{
    actualFloor--;
} // No else needed
```

See Figure 2 for the flowchart.

*An if statement is like a fork in the road. Depending upon a decision, different parts of the program are executed.*

## Syntax 3.1 if Statement

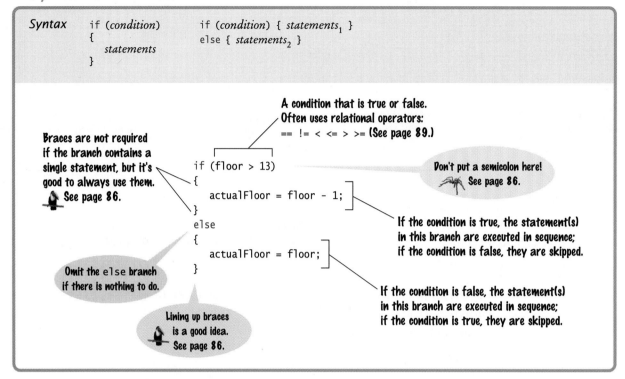

*Syntax*
```
if (condition)              if (condition) { statements₁ }
{                           else { statements₂ }
    statements
}
```

A condition that is true or false.
Often uses relational operators:
== != < <= > >= (See page 89.)

Braces are not required if the branch contains a single statement, but it's good to always use them.
🐦 See page 86.

```
if (floor > 13)
{
    actualFloor = floor - 1;
}
else
{
    actualFloor = floor;
}
```

Don't put a semicolon here!
🕷 See page 86.

If the condition is true, the statement(s) in this branch are executed in sequence; if the condition is false, they are skipped.

Omit the else branch if there is nothing to do.

Lining up braces is a good idea. See page 86.

If the condition is false, the statement(s) in this branch are executed in sequence; if the condition is true, they are skipped.

The following program puts the if statement to work. This program asks for the desired floor and then prints out the actual floor.

### section_1/ElevatorSimulation.java

```java
1   import java.util.Scanner;
2
3   /**
4      This program simulates an elevator panel that skips the 13th floor.
5   */
6   public class ElevatorSimulation
7   {
8      public static void main(String[] args)
9      {
10        Scanner in = new Scanner(System.in);
11        System.out.print("Floor: ");
12        int floor = in.nextInt();
13
14        // Adjust floor if necessary
15
16        int actualFloor;
17        if (floor > 13)
18        {
19           actualFloor = floor - 1;
20        }
21        else
22        {
```

```
23            actualFloor = floor;
24         }
25
26         System.out.println("The elevator will travel to the actual floor "
27            + actualFloor);
28      }
29 }
```

**Program Run**

```
Floor: 20
The elevator will travel to the actual floor 19
```

**SELF CHECK**

1. In some Asian countries, the number 14 is considered unlucky. Some building owners play it safe and skip *both* the thirteenth and the fourteenth floor. How would you modify the sample program to handle such a building?

2. Consider the following if statement to compute a discounted price:
   ```
   if (originalPrice > 100)
   {
      discountedPrice = originalPrice - 20;
   }
   else
   {
      discountedPrice = originalPrice - 10;
   }
   ```
   What is the discounted price if the original price is 95? 100? 105?

3. Compare this if statement with the one in Self Check 2:
   ```
   if (originalPrice < 100)
   {
      discountedPrice = originalPrice - 10;
   }
   else
   {
      discountedPrice = originalPrice - 20;
   }
   ```
   Do the two statements always compute the same value? If not, when do the values differ?

4. Consider the following statements to compute a discounted price:
   ```
   discountedPrice = originalPrice;
   if (originalPrice > 100)
   {
      discountedPrice = originalPrice - 10;
   }
   ```
   What is the discounted price if the original price is 95? 100? 105?

5. The variables fuelAmount and fuelCapacity hold the actual amount of fuel and the size of the fuel tank of a vehicle. If less than 10 percent is remaining in the tank, a status light should show a red color; otherwise it shows a green color. Simulate this process by printing out either "red" or "green".

**Practice It**   Now you can try these exercises at the end of the chapter: R3.5, R3.6, P3.31.

### Brace Layout

The compiler doesn't care where you place braces. In this book, we follow the simple rule of making { and } line up.

```
if (floor > 13)
{
    floor--;
}
```

This style makes it easy to spot matching braces. Some programmers put the opening brace on the same line as the if:

```
if (floor > 13) {
    floor--;
}
```

*Properly lining up your code makes your programs easier to read.*

This style makes it harder to match the braces, but it saves a line of code, allowing you to view more code on the screen without scrolling. There are passionate advocates of both styles.

It is important that you pick a layout style and stick with it consistently within a given programming project. Which style you choose may depend on your personal preference or a coding style guide that you need to follow.

### Always Use Braces

When the body of an if statement consists of a single statement, you need not use braces. For example, the following is legal:

```
if (floor > 13)
    floor--;
```

However, it is a good idea to always include the braces:

```
if (floor > 13)
{
    floor--;
}
```

The braces make your code easier to read. They also make it easier for you to maintain the code because you won't have to worry about adding braces when you add statements inside an if statement.

### A Semicolon After the if Condition

The following code fragment has an unfortunate error:

```
if (floor > 13) ; // ERROR
{
    floor--;
}
```

There should be no semicolon after the if condition. The compiler interprets this statement as follows: If floor is greater than 13, execute the statement that is denoted by a single semicolon, that is, the do-nothing statement. The statement enclosed in braces is no longer a part of the if statement. It is always executed. In other words, even if the value of floor is not above 13, it is decremented.

**Programming Tip 3.3**

### Tabs

Block-structured code has the property that nested statements are indented by one or more levels:

```
public class ElevatorSimulation
{
   public static void main(String[] args)
   {
      int floor;
      . . .
      if (floor > 13)
      {
         floor--;
      }
      . . .
   }

0  1  2  3    Indentation level
```

*You use the Tab key to move the cursor to the next indentation level.*

How do you move the cursor from the leftmost column to the appropriate indentation level? A perfectly reasonable strategy is to hit the space bar a sufficient number of times. With most editors, you can use the Tab key instead. A tab moves the cursor to the next indentation level. Some editors even have an option to fill in the tabs automatically.

While the Tab *key* is nice, some editors use *tab characters* for alignment, which is not so nice. Tab characters can lead to problems when you send your file to another person or a printer. There is no universal agreement on the width of a tab character, and some software will ignore tab characters altogether. It is therefore best to save your files with spaces instead of tabs. Most editors have a setting to automatically convert all tabs to spaces. Look at the documentation of your development environment to find out how to activate this useful setting.

**Special Topic 3.1**

### The Conditional Operator

Java has a *conditional operator* of the form

> *condition* ? *value₁* : *value₂*

The value of that expression is either *value₁* if the test passes or *value₂* if it fails. For example, we can compute the actual floor number as

```
actualFloor = floor > 13 ? floor - 1 : floor;
```

which is equivalent to

```
if (floor > 13) { actualFloor = floor - 1; } else { actualFloor = floor; }
```

You can use the conditional operator anywhere that a value is expected, for example:

```
System.out.println("Actual floor: " + (floor > 13 ? floor - 1 : floor));
```

We don't use the conditional operator in this book, but it is a convenient construct that you will find in many Java programs.

### Avoid Duplication in Branches

Look to see whether you *duplicate code* in each branch. If so, move it out of the if statement. Here is an example of such duplication:

```java
if (floor > 13)
{
   actualFloor = floor - 1;
   System.out.println("Actual floor: " + actualFloor);
}
else
{
   actualFloor = floor;
   System.out.println("Actual floor: " + actualFloor);
}
```

The output statement is exactly the same in both branches. This is not an error—the program will run correctly. However, you can simplify the program by moving the duplicated statement, like this:

```java
if (floor > 13)
{
   actualFloor = floor - 1;
}
else
{
   actualFloor = floor;
}
System.out.println("Actual floor: " + actualFloor);
```

Removing duplication is particularly important when programs are maintained for a long time. When there are two sets of statements with the same effect, it can easily happen that a programmer modifies one set but not the other.

# 3.2 Comparing Numbers and Strings

Use relational operators
(< <= > >= == !=)
to compare numbers.

Every if statement contains a condition. In many cases, the condition involves comparing two values. For example, in the previous examples we tested floor > 13. The comparison > is called a **relational operator**. Java has six relational operators (see Table 1).

As you can see, only two Java relational operators (> and <) look as you would expect from the mathematical notation. Computer keyboards do not have keys for ≥, ≤, or ≠, but the >=, <=, and != operators are easy to remember because they look similar. The == operator is initially confusing to most newcomers to Java.

*In Java, you use a relational operator to check whether one value is greater than another.*

| Table 1 Relational Operators | | |
|---|---|---|
| Java | Math Notation | Description |
| > | > | Greater than |
| >= | ≥ | Greater than or equal |
| < | < | Less than |
| <= | ≤ | Less than or equal |
| == | = | Equal |
| != | ≠ | Not equal |

In Java, = already has a meaning, namely assignment. The == operator denotes equality testing:

```
floor = 13; // Assign 13 to floor
```

```
if (floor == 13)   // Test whether floor equals 13
```

You must remember to use == inside tests and to use = outside tests.

## Syntax 3.2    Comparisons

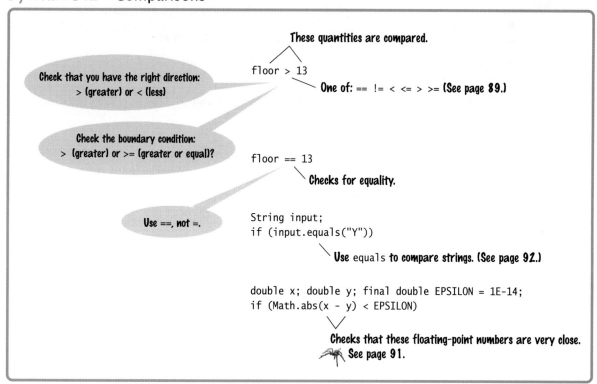

The relational operators in Table 1 have a lower precedence than the arithmetic operators. That means, you can write arithmetic expressions on either side of the relational operator without using parentheses. For example, in the expression

```
floor - 1 < 13
```

both sides (floor - 1 and 13) of the < operator are evaluated, and the results are compared. Appendix B shows a table of the Java operators and their precedence.

To test whether two strings are equal to each other, you must use the method called equals:

```
if (string1.equals(string2)) . . .
```

Do not use the == operator to compare strings. The comparison

```
if (string1 == string2) // Not useful
```

Do not use the == operator to compare strings. Use the equals method instead.

has an unrelated meaning. It tests whether the two strings are stored in the same location. You can have strings with identical contents stored in different locations, so this test never makes sense in actual programming; see Common Error 3.3 on page 92.

Table 2 summarizes how to compare values in Java.

## Table 2 Relational Operator Examples

| Expression | Value | Comment |
|---|---|---|
| 3 <= 4 | true | 3 is less than 4; <= tests for "less than or equal". |
| 🚫 3 =< 4 | **Error** | The "less than or equal" operator is <=, not =<. The "less than" symbol comes first. |
| 3 > 4 | false | > is the opposite of <=. |
| 4 < 4 | false | The left-hand side must be strictly smaller than the right-hand side. |
| 4 <= 4 | true | Both sides are equal; <= tests for "less than or equal". |
| 3 == 5 - 2 | true | == tests for equality. |
| 3 != 5 - 1 | true | != tests for inequality. It is true that 3 is not 5 – 1. |
| 🚫 3 = 6 / 2 | **Error** | Use == to test for equality. |
| 1.0 / 3.0 == 0.333333333 | false | Although the values are very close to one another, they are not exactly equal. See Common Error 3.2 on page 91. |
| 🚫 "10" > 5 | **Error** | You cannot compare a string to a number. |
| "Tomato".substring(0, 3).equals("Tom") | true | Always use the equals method to check whether two strings have the same contents. |
| "Tomato".substring(0, 3) == ("Tom") | false | Never use == to compare strings; it only checks whether the strings are stored in the same location. See Common Error 3.3 on page 92. |

**6.** Which of the following conditions are true, provided a is 3 and b is 4?

   **a.** a + 1 <= b

   **b.** a + 1 >= b

   **c.** a + 1 != b

**7.** Give the opposite of the condition

```
floor > 13
```

**8.** What is the error in this statement?

```
if (scoreA = scoreB)
{
    System.out.println("Tie");
}
```

**9.** Supply a condition in this if statement to test whether the user entered a Y:

```
System.out.println("Enter Y to quit.");
String input = in.next();
if (. . .)
{
    System.out.println("Goodbye.");
}
```

**10.** How do you test that a string str is the empty string?

**Practice It**   Now you can try these exercises at the end of the chapter: R3.4, R3.7, P3.18.

---

**Common Error 3.2**

### Exact Comparison of Floating-Point Numbers

Floating-point numbers have only a limited precision, and calculations can introduce roundoff errors. You must take these inevitable roundoffs into account when comparing floating-point numbers. For example, the following code multiplies the square root of 2 by itself. Ideally, we expect to get the answer 2:

```
double r = Math.sqrt(2.0);
if (r * r == 2.0)
{
    System.out.println("Math.sqrt(2.0) squared is 2.0");
}
else
{
    System.out.println("Math.sqrt(2.0) squared is not 2.0 but "
        + r * r);
}
```

*Take limited precision into account when comparing floating-point numbers.*

This program displays

```
Math.sqrt(2.0) squared is not 2.0 but 2.00000000000000044
```

It does not make sense in most circumstances to compare floating-point numbers exactly. Instead, we should test whether they are *close enough*. That is, the magnitude of their difference should be less than some threshold. Mathematically, we would write that $x$ and $y$ are close enough if

$$|x - y| < \varepsilon$$

for a very small number, $\varepsilon$. $\varepsilon$ is the Greek letter epsilon, a letter used to denote a very small quantity. It is common to set $\varepsilon$ to $10^{-14}$ when comparing `double` numbers:

```java
final double EPSILON = 1E-14;
double r = Math.sqrt(2.0);
if (Math.abs(r * r - 2.0) < EPSILON)
{
    System.out.println("Math.sqrt(2.0) squared is approximately 2.0");
}
```

Common Error 3.3

### Using == to Compare Strings

If you write

```java
if (nickname == "Rob")
```

then the test succeeds only if the variable `nickname` refers to the exact same location as the string literal "Rob". The test will pass if a string variable was initialized with the same string literal:

```java
String nickname = "Rob";
. . .
if (nickname == "Rob") // Test is true
```

However, if the string with the letters R o b has been assembled in some other way, then the test will fail:

```java
String name = "Robert";
String nickname = name.substring(0, 3);
. . .
if (nickname == "Rob") // Test is false
```

In this case, the `substring` method produces a string in a different memory location. Even though both strings have the same contents, the comparison fails.

You must remember never to use `==` to compare strings. Always use `equals` to check whether two strings have the same contents.

Special Topic 3.2

### Lexicographic Ordering of Strings

If two strings are not identical to each other, you still may want to know the relationship between them. The `compareTo` method compares strings in "lexicographic" order. This ordering is very similar to the way in which words are sorted in a dictionary. If

```java
string1.compareTo(string2) < 0
```

then the string `string1` comes before the string `string2` in the dictionary. For example, this is the case if `string1` is "Harry", and `string2` is "Hello". If

```java
string1.compareTo(string2) > 0
```

then `string1` comes after `string2` in dictionary order.

Finally, if

```java
string1.compareTo(string2) == 0
```

then `string1` and `string2` are equal.

*To see which of two terms comes first in the dictionary, consider the first letter in which they differ.*

There are a few technical differences between the ordering in a dictionary and the lexicographic ordering in Java. In Java:

> The compareTo method compares strings in lexicographic order.

- All uppercase letters come before the lowercase letters. For example, "Z" comes before "a".
- The space character comes before all printable characters.
- Numbers come before letters.
- For the ordering of punctuation marks, see Appendix A.

When comparing two strings, you compare the first letters of each word, then the second letters, and so on, until one of the strings ends or you find the first letter pair that doesn't match.

If one of the strings ends, the longer string is considered the "larger" one. For example, compare "car" with "cart". The first three letters match, and we reach the end of the first string. Therefore "car" comes before "cart" in lexicographic ordering.

When you reach a mismatch, the string containing the "larger" character is considered "larger". For example, let's compare "cat" with "cart". The first two letters match. Because t comes after r, the string "cat" comes after "cart" in the lexicographic ordering.

| c | a | r |

| c | a | r | t |

| c | a | t |

Letters   r comes
match    before t

*Lexicographic Ordering*

---

**HOW TO 3.1**

## Implementing an if Statement

This How To walks you through the process of implementing an if statement. We will illustrate the steps with the following example problem:

The university bookstore has a Kilobyte Day sale every October 24, giving an 8 percent discount on all computer accessory purchases if the price is less than $128, and a 16 percent discount if the price is at least $128. Write a program that asks the cashier for the original price and then prints the discounted price.

**Step 1**  Decide upon the branching condition.

In our sample problem, the obvious choice for the condition is:

**original price < 128?**

That is just fine, and we will use that condition in our solution.

But you could equally well come up with a correct solution if you choose the opposite condition: Is the original price at least $128? You might choose this condition if you put yourself into the position of a shopper who wants to know when the bigger discount applies.

*Sales discounts are often higher for expensive products. Use the if statement to implement such a decision.*

**Step 2**  Give pseudocode for the work that needs to be done when the condition is true.

In this step, you list the action or actions that are taken in the "positive" branch. The details depend on your problem. You may want to print a message, compute values, or even exit the program.

In our example, we need to apply an 8 percent discount:

**discounted price = 0.92 x original price**

**Step 3**   Give pseudocode for the work (if any) that needs to be done when the condition is *not* true.

What do you want to do in the case that the condition of Step 1 is not satisfied? Sometimes, you want to do nothing at all. In that case, use an if statement without an else branch.

In our example, the condition tested whether the price was less than $128. If that condition is *not* true, the price is at least $128, so the higher discount of 16 percent applies to the sale:

**discounted price = 0.84 x original price**

**Step 4**   Double-check relational operators.

First, be sure that the test goes in the right *direction*. It is a common error to confuse > and <. Next, consider whether you should use the < operator or its close cousin, the <= operator.

What should happen if the original price is exactly $128? Reading the problem carefully, we find that the lower discount applies if the original price is *less than* $128, and the higher discount applies when it is *at least* $128. A price of $128 should therefore *not* fulfill our condition, and we must use <, not <=.

**Step 5**   Remove duplication.

Check which actions are common to both branches, and move them outside. (See Programming Tip 3.4 on page 88.)

In our example, we have two statements of the form

**discounted price = ___ x original price**

They only differ in the discount rate. It is best to just set the rate in the branches, and to do the computation afterwards:

**If original price < 128**
    **discount rate = 0.92**
**Else**
    **discount rate = 0.84**
**discounted price = discount rate x original price**

**Step 6**   Test both branches.

Formulate two test cases, one that fulfills the condition of the if statement, and one that does not. Ask yourself what should happen in each case. Then follow the pseudocode and act each of them out.

In our example, let us consider two scenarios for the original price: $100 and $200. We expect that the first price is discounted by $8, the second by $32.

When the original price is 100, then the condition 100 < 128 is true, and we get

**discount rate = 0.92**
**discounted price = 0.92 x 100 = 92**

When the original price is 200, then the condition 200 < 128 is false, and

**discount rate = 0.84**
**discounted price = 0.84 x 200 = 168**

In both cases, we get the expected answer.

**Step 7**   Assemble the if statement in Java.

Type the skeleton

```
if ()
{
```

```
   }
   else
   {
   }
```

and fill it in, as shown in Syntax 3.1 on page 84. Omit the `else` branch if it is not needed. In our example, the completed statement is

```
if (originalPrice < 128)
{
   discountRate = 0.92;
}
else
{
   discountRate = 0.84;
}
discountedPrice = discountRate * originalPrice;
```

**ONLINE EXAMPLE**

The complete program for calculating a discounted price.

---

**WORKED EXAMPLE 3.1**  **Extracting the Middle**

This Worked Example shows how to extract the middle character from a string, or the two middle characters if the length of the string is even.

| c | r | a | t | e |
|---|---|---|---|---|
| 0 | 1 | 2 | 3 | 4 |

---

*Random Fact 3.1*  The Denver Airport Luggage Handling System

Making decisions is an essential part of any computer program. Nowhere is this more obvious than in a computer system that helps sort luggage at an airport. After scanning the luggage identification codes, the system sorts the items and routes them to different conveyor belts. Human operators then place the items onto trucks. When the city of Denver built a huge airport to replace an outdated and congested facility, the luggage system contractor went a step further. The new system was designed to replace the human operators with robotic carts. Unfortunately, the system plainly did not work. It was plagued by mechanical problems, such as luggage falling onto the tracks and jamming carts. Equally frustrating were the software glitches. Carts would uselessly accumulate at some locations when they were needed elsewhere.

The airport had been scheduled to open in 1993, but without a functioning luggage system, the opening was delayed for over a year while the contractor tried to fix the problems. The contractor never succeeded, and ultimately a manual system was installed. The delay cost the city and airlines close to a billion dollars, and the contractor, once the leading luggage systems vendor in the United States, went bankrupt.

Clearly, it is very risky to build a large system based on a technology that has never been tried on a smaller scale. As robots and the software that controls them get better over time, they will take on a larger share of luggage handling in the future. But it is likely that this will happen in an incremental fashion.

*The Denver airport originally had a fully automatic system for moving luggage, replacing human operators with robotic carts. Unfortunately, the system never worked and was dismantled before the airport was opened.*

---

Available online in WileyPLUS and at www.wiley.com/college/horstmann.

# 3.3 Multiple Alternatives

Multiple if statements can be combined to evaluate complex decisions.

In Section 3.1, you saw how to program a two-way branch with an `if` statement. In many situations, there are more than two cases. In this section, you will see how to implement a decision with multiple alternatives.

For example, consider a program that displays the effect of an earthquake, as measured by the Richter scale (see Table 3).

The 1989 Loma Prieta earthquake that damaged the Bay Bridge in San Francisco and destroyed many buildings measured 7.1 on the Richter scale.

| Table 3 Richter Scale | |
|---|---|
| Value | Effect |
| 8 | Most structures fall |
| 7 | Many buildings destroyed |
| 6 | Many buildings considerably damaged, some collapse |
| 4.5 | Damage to poorly constructed buildings |

The Richter scale is a measurement of the strength of an earthquake. Every step in the scale, for example from 6.0 to 7.0, signifies a tenfold increase in the strength of the quake.

In this case, there are five branches: one each for the four descriptions of damage, and one for no destruction. Figure 3 shows the flowchart for this multiple-branch statement.

**ANIMATION**
*Multiple Alternatives*

You use multiple `if` statements to implement multiple alternatives, like this:

```java
if (richter >= 8.0)
{
    System.out.println("Most structures fall");
}
else if (richter >= 7.0)
{
    System.out.println("Many buildings destroyed");
}
else if (richter >= 6.0)
{
    System.out.println("Many buildings considerably damaged, some collapse");
}
else if (richter >= 4.5)
{
    System.out.println("Damage to poorly constructed buildings");
}
else
{
    System.out.println("No destruction of buildings");
}
```

As soon as one of the four tests succeeds, the effect is displayed, and no further tests are attempted. If none of the four cases applies, the final `else` clause applies, and a default message is printed.

**Figure 3**
Multiple Alternatives

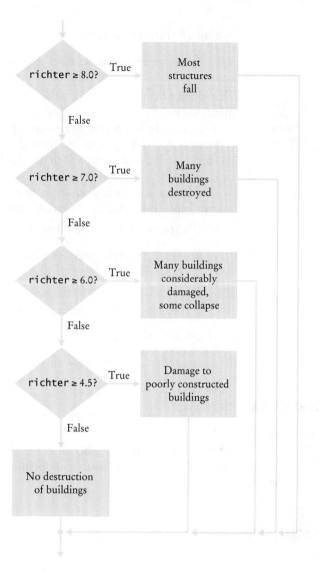

Here you must sort the conditions and test against the largest cutoff first.
Suppose we reverse the order of tests:

```
if (richter >= 4.5) // Tests in wrong order
{
    System.out.println("Damage to poorly constructed buildings");
}
else if (richter >= 6.0)
{
    System.out.println("Many buildings considerably damaged, some collapse");
}
else if (richter >= 7.0)
{
    System.out.println("Many buildings destroyed");
```

```
   }
   else if (richter >= 8.0)
   {
      System.out.println("Most structures fall");
   }
```

This does not work. Suppose the value of richter is 7.1. That value is at least 4.5, matching the first case. The other tests will never be attempted.

The remedy is to test the more specific conditions first. Here, the condition richter >= 8.0 is more specific than the condition richter >= 7.0, and the condition richter >= 4.5 is more general (that is, fulfilled by more values) than either of the first two.

In this example, it is also important that we use an if/else if/else sequence, not just multiple independent if statements. Consider this sequence of independent tests.

```
   if (richter >= 8.0) // Didn't use else
   {
      System.out.println("Most structures fall");
   }
   if (richter >= 7.0)
   {
      System.out.println("Many buildings destroyed");
   }
   if (richter >= 6.0)
   {
      System.out.println("Many buildings considerably damaged, some collapse");
   }
   if (richter >= 4.5)
   {
      System.out.println("Damage to poorly constructed buildings");
   }
```

Now the alternatives are no longer exclusive. If richter is 7.1, then the last *three* tests all match, and three messages are printed.

**When using multiple if statements, test general conditions after more specific conditions.**

**ONLINE EXAMPLE**

The complete program for printing earthquake descriptions.

**SELF CHECK**

11. In a game program, the scores of players A and B are stored in variables scoreA and scoreB. Assuming that the player with the larger score wins, write an if/else if/else sequence that prints out "A won", "B won", or "Game tied".

12. Write a conditional statement with three branches that sets s to 1 if x is positive, to –1 if x is negative, and to 0 if x is zero.

13. How could you achieve the task of Self Check 12 with only two branches?

14. Beginners sometimes write statements such as the following:

```
   if (price > 100)
   {
      discountedPrice = price - 20;
   }
   else if (price <= 100)
   {
      discountedPrice = price - 10;
   }
```

Explain how this code can be improved.

15. Suppose the user enters -1 into the earthquake program. What is printed?

**16.** Suppose we want to have the earthquake program check whether the user entered a negative number. What branch would you add to the `if` statement, and where?

**Practice It**   Now you can try these exercises at the end of the chapter: R3.22, P3.9, P3.34.

### The `switch` Statement

An `if/else if/else` sequence that compares a *value* against several alternatives can be implemented as a `switch` statement. For example,

```java
int digit = . . .;
switch (digit)
{
   case 1: digitName = "one"; break;
   case 2: digitName = "two"; break;
   case 3: digitName = "three"; break;
   case 4: digitName = "four"; break;
   case 5: digitName = "five"; break;
   case 6: digitName = "six"; break;
   case 7: digitName = "seven"; break;
   case 8: digitName = "eight"; break;
   case 9: digitName = "nine"; break;
   default: digitName = ""; break;
}
```

*The* `switch` *statement lets you choose from a fixed set of alternatives.*

This is a shortcut for

```java
int digit = . . .;
if (digit == 1) { digitName = "one"; }
else if (digit == 2) { digitName = "two"; }
else if (digit == 3) { digitName = "three"; }
else if (digit == 4) { digitName = "four"; }
else if (digit == 5) { digitName = "five"; }
else if (digit == 6) { digitName = "six"; }
else if (digit == 7) { digitName = "seven"; }
else if (digit == 8) { digitName = "eight"; }
else if (digit == 9) { digitName = "nine"; }
else { digitName = ""; }
```

It isn't much of a shortcut, but it has one advantage—it is obvious that all branches test the *same* value, namely `digit`.

The `switch` statement can be applied only in narrow circumstances. The values in the case clauses must be constants. They can be integers or characters. As of Java 7, strings are permitted as well. You cannot use a `switch` statement to branch on floating-point values.

Every branch of the switch should be terminated by a `break` instruction. If the break is missing, execution *falls through* to the next branch, and so on, until a break or the end of the `switch` is reached. In practice, this fall-through behavior is rarely useful, but it is a common cause of errors. If you accidentally forget a `break` statement, your program compiles but executes unwanted code. Many programmers consider the `switch` statement somewhat dangerous and prefer the `if` statement.

We leave it to you to use the `switch` statement for your own code or not. At any rate, you need to have a reading knowledge of `switch` in case you find it in other programmers' code.

# 3.4 Nested Branches

When a decision statement is contained inside the branch of another decision statement, the statements are *nested*.

It is often necessary to include an `if` statement inside another. Such an arrangement is called a *nested* set of statements.

Here is a typical example: In the United States, different tax rates are used depending on the taxpayer's marital status. There are different tax schedules for single and for married taxpayers. Married taxpayers add their income together and pay taxes on the total. Table 4 gives the tax rate computations, using a simplification of the schedules in effect for the 2008 tax year. A different tax rate applies to each "bracket". In this schedule, the income in the first bracket is taxed at 10 percent, and the income in the second bracket is taxed at 25 percent. The income limits for each bracket depend on the marital status.

| Table 4 Federal Tax Rate Schedule | | |
|---|---|---|
| If your status is Single and if the taxable income is | the tax is | of the amount over |
| at most $32,000 | 10% | $0 |
| over $32,000 | $3,200 + 25% | $32,000 |
| If your status is Married and if the taxable income is | the tax is | of the amount over |
| at most $64,000 | 10% | $0 |
| over $64,000 | $6,400 + 25% | $64,000 |

Nested decisions are required for problems that have two levels of decision making.

Now compute the taxes due, given a marital status and an income figure. The key point is that there are two *levels* of decision making. First, you must branch on the marital status. Then, for each marital status, you must have another branch on income level.

The two-level decision process is reflected in two levels of `if` statements in the program at the end of this section. (See Figure 4 for a flowchart.) In theory, nesting can go deeper than two levels. A three-level decision process (first by state, then by marital status, then by income level) requires three nesting levels.

**ANIMATION**
*Nested Branches*

*Computing income taxes requires multiple levels of decisions.*

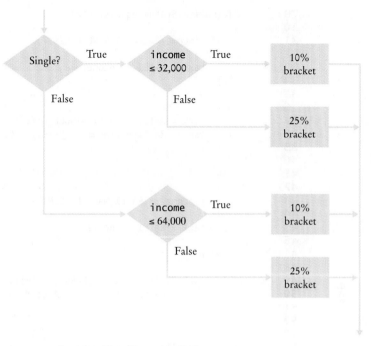

**Figure 4**  Income Tax Computation

### section_4/TaxCalculator.java

```
1   import java.util.Scanner;
2
3   /**
4      This program computes income taxes, using a simplified tax schedule.
5   */
6   public class TaxCalculator
7   {
8      public static void main(String[] args)
9      {
10        final double RATE1 = 0.10;
11        final double RATE2 = 0.25;
12        final double RATE1_SINGLE_LIMIT = 32000;
13        final double RATE1_MARRIED_LIMIT = 64000;
14
15        double tax1 = 0;
16        double tax2 = 0;
17
18        // Read income and marital status
19
20        Scanner in = new Scanner(System.in);
21        System.out.print("Please enter your income: ");
22        double income = in.nextDouble();
23
24        System.out.print("Please enter s for single, m for married: ");
25        String maritalStatus = in.next();
26
27        // Compute taxes due
28
```

```
29          if (maritalStatus.equals("s"))
30          {
31             if (income <= RATE1_SINGLE_LIMIT)
32             {
33                tax1 = RATE1 * income;
34             }
35             else
36             {
37                tax1 = RATE1 * RATE1_SINGLE_LIMIT;
38                tax2 = RATE2 * (income - RATE1_SINGLE_LIMIT);
39             }
40          }
41          else
42          {
43             if (income <= RATE1_MARRIED_LIMIT)
44             {
45                tax1 = RATE1 * income;
46             }
47             else
48             {
49                tax1 = RATE1 * RATE1_MARRIED_LIMIT;
50                tax2 = RATE2 * (income - RATE1_MARRIED_LIMIT);
51             }
52          }
53
54          double totalTax = tax1 + tax2;
55
56          System.out.println("The tax is $" + totalTax);
57       }
58    }
```

**Program Run**

```
Please enter your income: 80000
Please enter s for single, m for married: m
The tax is $10400
```

**SELF CHECK**

**17.** What is the amount of tax that a single taxpayer pays on an income of $32,000?

**18.** Would that amount change if the first nested if statement changed from

```
if (income <= RATE1_SINGLE_LIMIT)
```

to

```
if (income < RATE1_SINGLE_LIMIT)
```

**19.** Suppose Harry and Sally each make $40,000 per year. Would they save taxes if they married?

**20.** How would you modify the TaxCalculator.java program in order to check that the user entered a correct value for the marital status (i.e., s or m)?

**21.** Some people object to higher tax rates for higher incomes, claiming that you might end up with less money after taxes when you get a raise for working hard. What is the flaw in this argument?

**Practice It**    Now you can try these exercises at the end of the chapter: R3.9, R3.21, P3.18, P3.21.

Programming Tip 3.5

## Hand-Tracing

A very useful technique for understanding whether a program works correctly is called *hand-tracing*. You simulate the program's activity on a sheet of paper. You can use this method with pseudocode or Java code.

Get an index card, a cocktail napkin, or whatever sheet of paper is within reach. Make a column for each variable. Have the program code ready. Use a marker, such as a paper clip, to mark the current statement. In your mind, execute statements one at a time. Every time the value of a variable changes, cross out the old value and write the new value below the old one.

For example, let's trace the tax program with the data from the program run on page 102. In lines 15 and 16, tax1 and tax2 are initialized to 0.

*Hand-tracing helps you understand whether a program works correctly.*

```
 8  public static void main(String[] args)
 9  {
10     final double RATE1 = 0.10;
11     final double RATE2 = 0.25;
12     final double RATE1_SINGLE_LIMIT = 32000;
13     final double RATE1_MARRIED_LIMIT = 64000;
14
15     double tax1 = 0;
16     double tax2 = 0;
17
```

| tax1 | tax2 | income | marital status |
|------|------|--------|----------------|
| 0    | 0    |        |                |
|      |      |        |                |

In lines 22 and 25, income and maritalStatus are initialized by input statements.

```
20     Scanner in = new Scanner(System.in);
21     System.out.print("Please enter your income: ");
22     double income = in.nextDouble();
23
24     System.out.print("Please enter s for single, m for married: ");
25     String maritalStatus = in.next();
```

| tax1 | tax2 | income | marital status |
|------|------|--------|----------------|
| 0    | 0    | 80000  | m              |
|      |      |        |                |

Because maritalStatus is not "s", we move to the else branch of the outer if statement (line 41).

```
29     if (maritalStatus.equals("s"))
30     {
31        if (income <= RATE1_SINGLE_LIMIT)
32        {
33           tax1 = RATE1 * income;
34        }
35        else
36        {
37           tax1 = RATE1 * RATE1_SINGLE_LIMIT;
38           tax2 = RATE2 * (income - RATE1_SINGLE_LIMIT);
39        }
40     }
41     else
42     {
```

Because income is not <= 64000, we move to the else branch of the inner if statement (line 47).

```
43        if (income <= RATE1_MARRIED_LIMIT)
44        {
45           tax1 = RATE1 * income;
46        }
47        else
48        {
49           tax1 = RATE1 * RATE1_MARRIED_LIMIT;
50           tax2 = RATE2 * (income - RATE1_MARRIED_LIMIT);
51        }
```

The values of tax1 and tax2 are updated.

```
48      {
49          tax1 = RATE1 * RATE1_MARRIED_LIMIT;
50          tax2 = RATE2 * (income - RATE1_MARRIED_LIMIT);
51      }
52  }
53
```

| tax1 | tax2 | income | marital status |
|------|------|--------|----------------|
| ~~0~~ | ~~0~~ | 80000 | m |
| 6400 | 4000 | | |

Their sum totalTax is computed and printed.
Then the program ends.

```
54      double totalTax = tax1 + tax2;
55
56      System.out.println("The tax is $" + totalTax);
57  }
```

| tax1 | tax2 | income | marital status | total tax |
|------|------|--------|----------------|-----------|
| ~~0~~ | ~~0~~ | 80000 | m | |
| 6400 | 4000 | | | 10400 |

Because the program trace shows the expected output ($10,400), it successfully demonstrated that this test case works correctly.

---

Common Error 3.4

## The Dangling else Problem

When an if statement is nested inside another if statement, the following error may occur.

```
double shippingCharge = 5.00; // $5 inside continental U.S.
if (country.equals("USA"))
   if (state.equals("HI"))
      shippingCharge = 10.00; // Hawaii is more expensive
else // Pitfall!
   shippingCharge = 20.00; // As are foreign shipments
```

The indentation level seems to suggest that the else is grouped with the test country.equals("USA"). Unfortunately, that is not the case. The compiler ignores all indentation and matches the else with the preceding if. That is, the code is actually

```
double shippingCharge = 5.00; // $5 inside continental U.S.
if (country.equals("USA"))
   if (state.equals("HI"))
      shippingCharge = 10.00; // Hawaii is more expensive
   else // Pitfall!
      shippingCharge = 20.00; // As are foreign shipments
```

That isn't what you want. You want to group the else with the first if.

The ambiguous else is called a *dangling else*. You can avoid this pitfall if you always use braces, as recommended in Programming Tip 3.2 on page 86:

```
double shippingCharge = 5.00; // $5 inside continental U.S.
if (country.equals("USA"))
{
   if (state.equals("HI"))
   {
      shippingCharge = 10.00; // Hawaii is more expensive
   }
}
else
{
   shippingCharge = 20.00; // As are foreign shipments
}
```

### Enumeration Types

In many programs, you use variables that can hold one of a finite number of values. For example, in the tax return class, the marital Status variable holds one of the values "s" or "m". If, due to some programming error, the maritalStatus variable is set to another value (such as "d" or "w"), then the programming logic may produce invalid results.

In a simple program, this is not really a problem. But as programs grow over time, and more cases are added (such as the "married filing separately" status), errors can slip in. Java version 5.0 introduces a remedy: **enumeration types**. An enumeration type has a finite set of values, for example

```
public enum FilingStatus { SINGLE, MARRIED, MARRIED_FILING_SEPARATELY }
```

You can have any number of values, but you must include them all in the enum declaration.
You can declare variables of the enumeration type:

```
FilingStatus status = FilingStatus.SINGLE;
```

If you try to assign a value that isn't a FilingStatus, such as 2 or "S", then the compiler reports an error.

Use the == operator to compare enumeration values, for example:

```
if (status == FilingStatus.SINGLE) . . .
```

Place the enum declaration inside the class that implements your program, such as

```
public class TaxReturn
{
    public enum FilingStatus { SINGLE, MARRIED, MARRIED_FILING_SEPARATELY }

    public static void main(String[] args)
    {
        . . .
    }
}
```

### Computing the Plural of an English Word

The plural of apple is apples, but the plural of cherry is cherries. In this Video Example, we develop an algorithm for computing the plural of an English word.

# 3.5 Problem Solving: Flowcharts

Flow charts are made up of elements for tasks, input/output, and decisions.

You have seen examples of flowcharts earlier in this chapter. A flowchart shows the structure of decisions and tasks that are required to solve a problem. When you have to solve a complex problem, it is a good idea to draw a flowchart to visualize the flow of control.

The basic flowchart elements are shown in Figure 5.

➕ Available online in WileyPLUS and at www.wiley.com/college/horstmann.

The basic idea is simple enough. Link tasks and input/output boxes in the sequence in which they should be executed. Whenever you need to make a decision, draw a diamond with two outcomes (see Figure 6).

Each branch can contain a sequence of tasks and even additional decisions. If there are multiple choices for a value, lay them out as in Figure 7.

There is one issue that you need to be aware of when drawing flowcharts. Unconstrained branching and merging can lead to "spaghetti code", a messy network of possible pathways through a program.

There is a simple rule for avoiding spaghetti code: Never point an arrow *inside another branch*.

To understand the rule, consider this example: Shipping costs are $5 inside the United States, except that to Hawaii and Alaska they are $10. International shipping costs are also $10.

> Each branch of a decision can contain tasks and further decisions.

> Never point an arrow inside another branch.

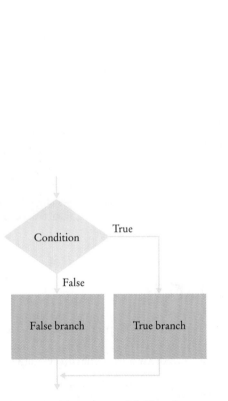

**Figure 6** Flowchart with Two Outcomes

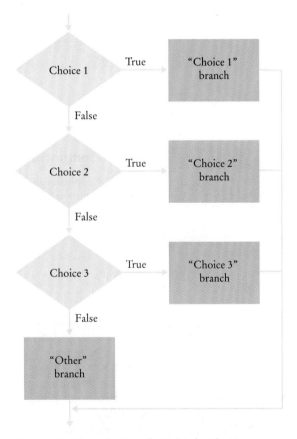

**Figure 7** Flowchart with Multiple Choices

You might start out with a flowchart like the following:

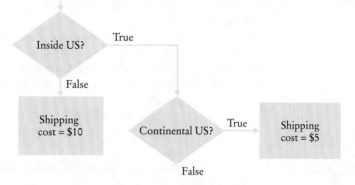

Now you may be tempted to reuse the "shipping cost = $10" task:

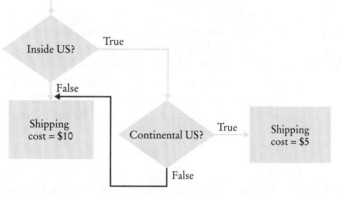

Don't do that! The red arrow points inside a different branch. Instead, add another task that sets the shipping cost to $10, like this:

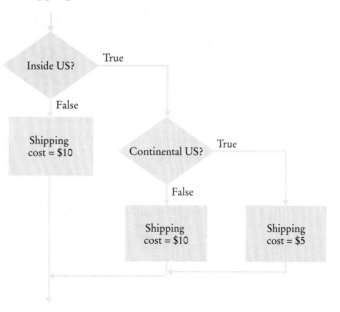

Not only do you avoid spaghetti code, but it is also a better design. In the future it may well happen that the cost for international shipments is different from that to Alaska and Hawaii.

Flowcharts can be very useful for getting an intuitive understanding of the flow of an algorithm. However, they get large rather quickly when you add more details. At that point, it makes sense to switch from flowcharts to pseudocode.

*Spaghetti code has so many pathways that it becomes impossible to understand.*

**SELF CHECK**

22. Draw a flowchart for a program that reads a value temp and prints "Frozen" if it is less than zero.

23. What is wrong with the flowchart at right?

24. How do you fix the flowchart of Self Check 23?

25. Draw a flowchart for a program that reads a value x. If it is less than zero, print "Error". Otherwise, print its square root.

26. Draw a flowchart for a program that reads a value temp. If it is less than zero, print "Ice". If it is greater than 100, print "Steam". Otherwise, print "Liquid".

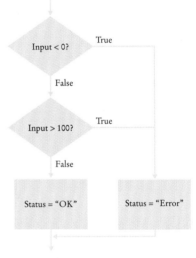

**Practice It** Now you can try these exercises at the end of the chapter: R3.12, R3.13, R3.14.

# 3.6 Problem Solving: Test Cases

Consider how to test the tax computation program from Section 3.4. Of course, you cannot try out all possible inputs of marital status and income level. Even if you could, there would be no point in trying them all. If the program correctly computes one or two tax amounts in a given bracket, then we have a good reason to believe that all amounts will be correct.

You want to aim for complete *coverage* of all decision points. Here is a plan for obtaining a comprehensive set of test cases:

*Each branch of your program should be covered by a test case.*

- There are two possibilities for the marital status and two tax brackets for each status, yielding four test cases.

- Test a handful of *boundary* conditions, such as an income that is at the boundary between two brackets, and a zero income.

- If you are responsible for error checking (which is discussed in Section 3.8), also test an invalid input, such as a negative income.

Make a list of the test cases and the expected outputs:

| Test Case | Expected Output | Comment |
|---|---|---|
| 30,000 s | 3,000 | 10% bracket |
| 72,000 s | 13,200 | 3,200 + 25% of 40,000 |
| 50,000 m | 5,000 | 10% bracket |
| 104,000 m | 16,400 | 6,400 + 25% of 40,000 |
| 32,000 s | 3,200 | boundary case |
| 0 | 0 | boundary case |

When you develop a set of test cases, it is helpful to have a flowchart of your program (see Section 3.5). Check off each branch that has a test case. Include test cases for the boundary cases of each decision. For example, if a decision checks whether an input is less than 100, test with an input of 100.

It is a good idea to design test cases before implementing a program.

   It is always a good idea to design test cases *before* starting to code. Working through the test cases gives you a better understanding of the algorithm that you are about to implement.

**SELF CHECK**

**27.** Using Figure 1 on page 83 as a guide, follow the process described in Section 3.6 to design a set of test cases for the ElevatorSimulation.java program in Section 3.1.

**28.** What is a boundary test case for the algorithm in How To 3.1 on page 93? What is the expected output?

**29.** Using Figure 3 on page 97 as a guide, follow the process described in Section 3.6 to design a set of test cases for the EarthquakeStrength.java program in Section 3.3.

**30.** Suppose you are designing a part of a program for a medical robot that has a sensor returning an *x*- and *y*-location (measured in cm). You need to check whether the sensor location is inside the circle, outside the circle, or on the boundary (specifically, having a distance of less than 1 mm from the boundary). Assume the circle has center (0, 0) and a radius of 2 cm. Give a set of test cases.

**Practice It**   Now you can try these exercises at the end of the chapter: R3.15, R3.16.

---

**Programming Tip 3.6**

## Make a Schedule and Make Time for Unexpected Problems

Commercial software is notorious for being delivered later than promised. For example, Microsoft originally promised that its Windows Vista operating system would be available late in 2003, then in 2005, then in March 2006; it finally was released in January 2007. Some of the early promises might not have been realistic. It was in Microsoft's interest to let prospective customers expect the imminent availability of the product. Had customers known the actual delivery date, they might have switched to a different product in the meantime. Undeniably, though, Microsoft had not anticipated the full complexity of the tasks it had set itself to solve.

   Microsoft can delay the delivery of its product, but it is likely that you cannot. As a student or a programmer, you are expected to manage your time wisely and to finish your assignments on time. You can probably do simple programming exercises the night before the due date, but an assignment that looks twice as hard may well take four times as long, because more things can go wrong. You should therefore make a schedule whenever you start a programming project.

First, estimate realistically how much time it will take you to:

- Design the program logic.
- Develop test cases.
- Type the program in and fix syntax errors.
- Test and debug the program.

For example, for the income tax program I might estimate an hour for the design; 30 minutes for developing test cases; an hour for data entry and fixing syntax errors; and an hour for testing and debugging. That is a total of 3.5 hours. If I work two hours a day on this project, it will take me almost two days.

*Make a schedule for your programming work and build in time for problems.*

Then think of things that can go wrong. Your computer might break down. You might be stumped by a problem with the computer system. (That is a particularly important concern for beginners. It is *very* common to lose a day over a trivial problem just because it takes time to track down a person who knows the magic command to overcome it.) As a rule of thumb, *double* the time of your estimate. That is, you should start four days, not two days, before the due date. If nothing went wrong, great; you have the program done two days early. When the inevitable problem occurs, you have a cushion of time that protects you from embarrassment and failure.

## Special Topic 3.5

### Logging

Sometimes you run a program and you are not sure where it spends its time. To get a printout of the program flow, you can insert trace messages into the program, such as this one:

```java
if (status == SINGLE)
{
    System.out.println("status is SINGLE");
    . . .
}
```

However, there is a problem with using System.out.println for trace messages. When you are done testing the program, you need to remove all print statements that produce trace messages. If you find another error, however, you need to stick the print statements back in.

To overcome this problem, you should use the Logger class, which allows you to turn off the trace messages without removing them from the program.

Instead of printing directly to System.out, use the global logger object that is returned by the call Logger.getGlobal(). (Prior to Java 7, you obtained the global logger as Logger.getLogger("global").) Then call the info method:

```java
Logger.getGlobal().info("status is SINGLE");
```

By default, the message is printed. But if you call

> Logging messages can be deactivated when testing is complete.

```java
Logger.getGlobal().setLevel(Level.OFF);
```

at the beginning of the main method of your program, all log message printing is suppressed. Set the level to Level.INFO to turn logging of info messages on again. Thus, you can turn off the log messages when your program works fine, and you can turn them back on if you find another error. In other words, using Logger.getGlobal().info is just like System.out.println, except that you can easily activate and deactivate the logging.

The Logger class has many other options for industrial-strength logging. Check out the API documentation if you want to have more control over logging.

# 3.7 Boolean Variables and Operators

The Boolean type boolean has two values, false and true.

*A Boolean variable is also called a flag because it can be either up (true) or down (false).*

Java has two Boolean operators that combine conditions: && (*and*) and || (*or*).

Sometimes, you need to evaluate a logical condition in one part of a program and use it elsewhere. To store a condition that can be true or false, you use a *Boolean variable*. Boolean variables are named after the mathematician George Boole (1815–1864), a pioneer in the study of logic.

In Java, the boolean data type has exactly two values, denoted false and true. These values are not strings or integers; they are special values, just for Boolean variables. Here is a declaration of a Boolean variable:

```java
boolean failed = true;
```

You can use the value later in your program to make a decision:

```java
if (failed) // Only executed if failed has been set to true
{
    . . .
}
```

When you make complex decisions, you often need to combine Boolean values. An operator that combines Boolean conditions is called a **Boolean operator**. In Java, the && operator (called *and*) yields true only when both conditions are true. The || operator (called *or*) yields the result true if at least one of the conditions is true.

Suppose you write a program that processes temperature values, and you want to test whether a given temperature corresponds to liquid water. (At sea level, water freezes at 0 degrees Celsius and boils at 100 degrees.) Water is liquid if the temperature is greater than zero *and* less than 100:

```java
if (temp > 0 && temp < 100) { System.out.println("Liquid"); }
```

The condition of the test has two parts, joined by the && operator. Each part is a Boolean value that can be true or false. The combined expression is true if both individual expressions are true. If either one of the expressions is false, then the result is also false (see Figure 8).

The Boolean operators && and || have a lower precedence than the relational operators. For that reason, you can write relational expressions on either side of the Boolean operators without using parentheses. For example, in the expression

```java
temp > 0 && temp < 100
```

the expressions temp > 0 and temp < 100 are evaluated first. Then the && operator combines the results. Appendix B shows a table of the Java operators and their precedence.

| A | B | A && B | A | B | A \|\| B | A | !A |
|---|---|--------|---|---|------|---|-----|
| true | true | true | true | true | true | true | false |
| true | false | false | true | false | true | false | true |
| false | true | false | false | true | true | | |
| false | false | false | false | false | false | | |

**Figure 8** Boolean Truth Tables

*At this geyser in Iceland, you can see ice, liquid water, and steam.*

To invert a condition, use the ! (*not*) operator.

Conversely, let's test whether water is *not* liquid at a given temperature. That is the case when the temperature is at most 0 *or* at least 100. Use the || (*or*) operator to combine the expressions:

```
if (temp <= 0 || temp >= 100) { System.out.println("Not liquid"); }
```

Figure 9 shows flowcharts for these examples.

Sometimes you need to *invert* a condition with the *not* Boolean operator. The ! operator takes a single condition and evaluates to true if that condition is false and to false if the condition is true. In this example, output occurs if the value of the Boolean variable frozen is false:

```
if (!frozen) { System.out.println("Not frozen"); }
```

Table 5 illustrates additional examples of evaluating Boolean operators.

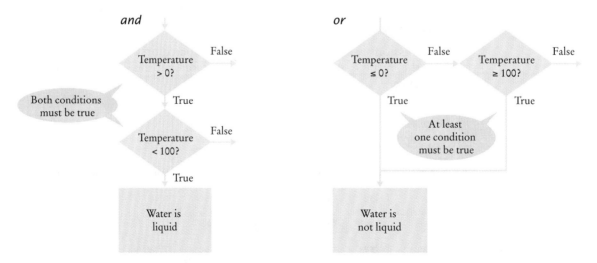

**Figure 9** Flowcharts for *and* and *or* Combinations

## Table 5  Boolean Operator Examples

| Expression | Value | Comment |
|---|---|---|
| `0 < 200 && 200 < 100` | `false` | Only the first condition is true. |
| `0 < 200 \|\| 200 < 100` | `true` | The first condition is true. |
| `0 < 200 \|\| 100 < 200` | `true` | The \|\| is not a test for "either-or". If both conditions are true, the result is true. |
| `0 < x && x < 100 \|\| x == -1` | `(0 < x && x < 100)`<br>`\|\| x == -1` | The && operator has a higher precedence than the \|\| operator (see Appendix B). |
|  `0 < x < 100` | **Error** | **Error:** This expression does not test whether x is between 0 and 100. The expression 0 < x is a Boolean value. You cannot compare a Boolean value with the integer 100. |
| `x && y > 0` | **Error** | **Error:** This expression does not test whether x and y are positive. The left-hand side of && is an integer, x, and the right-hand side, y > 0, is a Boolean value. You cannot use && with an integer argument. |
| `!(0 < 200)` | `false` | 0 < 200 is true, therefore its negation is false. |
| `frozen == true` | `frozen` | There is no need to compare a Boolean variable with true. |
| `frozen == false` | `!frozen` | It is clearer to use ! than to compare with false. |

**SELF CHECK**

**31.** Suppose x and y are two integers. How do you test whether both of them are zero?

**32.** How do you test whether at least one of them is zero?

**33.** How do you test whether *exactly one of them* is zero?

**34.** What is the value of `!!frozen`?

**35.** What is the advantage of using the type `boolean` rather than strings `"false"`/`"true"` or integers 0/1?

**Practice It**   Now you can try these exercises at the end of the chapter: R3.29, P3.25, P3.27.

### Combining Multiple Relational Operators

Consider the expression

```
if (0 <= temp <= 100) // Error
```

This looks just like the mathematical test $0 \leq temp \leq 100$. But in Java, it is a compile-time error.

Let us dissect the condition. The first half, `0 <= temp`, is a test with an outcome true or false. The outcome of that test (true or false) is then compared against 100. This seems to make no sense. Is true larger than 100 or not? Can one compare truth values and numbers? In Java, you cannot. The Java compiler rejects this statement.

Instead, use && to combine two separate tests:

```
if (0 <= temp && temp <= 100) . . .
```

Another common error, along the same lines, is to write

```
if (input == 1 || 2) . . . // Error
```

to test whether input is 1 or 2. Again, the Java compiler flags this construct as an error. You cannot apply the || operator to numbers. You need to write two Boolean expressions and join them with the || operator:

```
if (input == 1 || input == 2) . . .
```

Common Error 3.6

### Confusing && and || Conditions

It is a surprisingly common error to confuse *and* and *or* conditions. A value lies between 0 and 100 if it is at least 0 *and* at most 100. It lies outside that range if it is less than 0 *or* greater than 100. There is no golden rule; you just have to think carefully.

Often the *and* or *or* is clearly stated, and then it isn't too hard to implement it. But sometimes the wording isn't as explicit. It is quite common that the individual conditions are nicely set apart in a bulleted list, but with little indication of how they should be combined. Consider these instructions for filing a tax return. You can claim single filing status if any one of the following is true:

- You were never married.
- You were legally separated or divorced on the last day of the tax year.
- You were widowed, and did not remarry.

Since the test passes if *any one* of the conditions is true, you must combine the conditions with *or*. Elsewhere, the same instructions state that you may use the more advantageous status of married filing jointly if all five of the following conditions are true:

- Your spouse died less than two years ago and you did not remarry.
- You have a child whom you can claim as dependent.
- That child lived in your home for all of the tax year.
- You paid over half the cost of keeping up your home for this child.
- You filed a joint return with your spouse the year he or she died.

Because *all* of the conditions must be true for the test to pass, you must combine them with an *and*.

### Special Topic 3.6

### Short-Circuit Evaluation of Boolean Operators

The && and || operators are computed using short-circuit evaluation. In other words, logical expressions are evaluated from left to right, and evaluation stops as soon as the truth value is determined. When an && is evaluated and the first condition is false, the second condition is not evaluated, because it does not matter what the outcome of the second test is.

For example, consider the expression

```
quantity > 0 && price / quantity < 10
```

> The && and || operators are computed using *short-circuit evaluation:* As soon as the truth value is determined, no further conditions are evaluated.

Suppose the value of quantity is zero. Then the test quantity > 0 fails, and the second test is not attempted. That is just as well, because it is illegal to divide by zero.

Similarly, when the first condition of an || expression is true, then the remainder is not evaluated because the result must be true.

This process is called *short-circuit evaluation*.

*In a short circuit, electricity travels along the path of least resistance. Similarly, short-circuit evaluation takes the fastest path for computing the result of a Boolean expression.*

**Special Topic 3.7**

### De Morgan's Law

Humans generally have a hard time comprehending logical conditions with *not* operators applied to *and/or* expressions. De Morgan's Law, named after the logician Augustus De Morgan (1806–1871), can be used to simplify these Boolean expressions.

Suppose we want to charge a higher shipping rate if we don't ship within the continental United States.

```
if (!(country.equals("USA") && !state.equals("AK") && !state.equals("HI")))
{
    shippingCharge = 20.00;
}
```

This test is a little bit complicated, and you have to think carefully through the logic. When it is *not* true that the country is USA *and* the state is not Alaska *and* the state is not Hawaii, then charge $20.00. Huh? It is not true that some people won't be confused by this code.

The computer doesn't care, but it takes human programmers to write and maintain the code. Therefore, it is useful to know how to simplify such a condition.

De Morgan's Law has two forms: one for the negation of an *and* expression and one for the negation of an *or* expression:

> De Morgan's law tells you how to negate && and || conditions.

    !(A && B)    is the same as    !A || !B
    !(A || B)    is the same as    !A && !B

Pay particular attention to the fact that the *and* and *or* operators are *reversed* by moving the *not* inward. For example, the negation of "the state is Alaska *or* it is Hawaii",

```
!(state.equals("AK") || state.equals("HI"))
```

is "the state is not Alaska *and* it is not Hawaii":

```
!state.equals("AK") && !state.equals("HI")
```

Now apply the law to our shipping charge computation:

```
!(country.equals("USA")
    && !state.equals("AK")
    && !state.equals("HI"))
```

is equivalent to

```
!country.equals("USA")
    || !!state.equals("AK")
    || !!state.equals("HI")
```

Because two ! cancel each other out, the result is the simpler test

```
!country.equals("USA")
   || state.equals("AK")
   || state.equals("HI")
```

In other words, higher shipping charges apply when the destination is outside the United States or to Alaska or Hawaii.

To simplify conditions with negations of *and* or *or* expressions, it is usually a good idea to apply De Morgan's Law to move the negations to the innermost level.

# 3.8 Application: Input Validation

*Like a quality control worker, you want to make sure that user input is correct before processing it.*

An important application for the `if` statement is *input validation*. Whenever your program accepts user input, you need to make sure that the user-supplied values are valid before you use them in your computations.

Consider our elevator simulation program. Assume that the elevator panel has buttons labeled 1 through 20 (but not 13). The following are illegal inputs:

- The number 13
- Zero or a negative number
- A number larger than 20
- An input that is not a sequence of digits, such as `five`

In each of these cases, we will want to give an error message and exit the program.

It is simple to guard against an input of 13:

```
if (floor == 13)
{
    System.out.println("Error: There is no thirteenth floor.");
}
```

Here is how you ensure that the user doesn't enter a number outside the valid range:

```
if (floor <= 0 || floor > 20)
{
    System.out.println("Error: The floor must be between 1 and 20.");
}
```

However, dealing with an input that is not a valid integer is a more serious problem. When the statement

```
floor = in.nextInt();
```

**Call the hasNextInt or hasNextDouble method to ensure that the next input is a number.**

is executed, and the user types in an input that is not an integer (such as `five`), then the integer variable `floor` is not set. Instead, a run-time exception occurs and the program is terminated. To avoid this problem, you should first call the `hasNextInt` method which checks whether the next input is an integer. If that method returns `true`, you can safely call `nextInt`. Otherwise, print an error message and exit the program.

```
if (in.hasNextInt())
{
    int floor = in.nextInt();
    Process the input value
}
```

```
else
{
    System.out.println("Error: Not an integer.");
}
```

Here is the complete elevator simulation program with input validation:

**section_8/ElevatorSimulation2.java**

```
 1  import java.util.Scanner;
 2
 3  /**
 4     This program simulates an elevator panel that skips the 13th floor, checking for
 5     input errors.
 6  */
 7  public class ElevatorSimulation2
 8  {
 9     public static void main(String[] args)
10     {
11        Scanner in = new Scanner(System.in);
12        System.out.print("Floor: ");
13        if (in.hasNextInt())
14        {
15           // Now we know that the user entered an integer
16
17           int floor = in.nextInt();
18
19           if (floor == 13)
20           {
21              System.out.println("Error: There is no thirteenth floor.");
22           }
23           else if (floor <= 0 || floor > 20)
24           {
25              System.out.println("Error: The floor must be between 1 and 20.");
26           }
27           else
28           {
29              // Now we know that the input is valid
30
31              int actualFloor = floor;
32              if (floor > 13)
33              {
34                 actualFloor = floor - 1;
35              }
36
37              System.out.println("The elevator will travel to the actual floor "
38                 + actualFloor);
39           }
40        }
41        else
42        {
43           System.out.println("Error: Not an integer.");
44        }
45     }
46  }
```

**Program Run**

```
Floor: 13
Error: There is no thirteenth floor.
```

**SELF CHECK**

**36.** In the `ElevatorSimulation2` program, what is the output when the input is
  **a.** 100?
  **b.** −1?
  **c.** 20?
  **d.** thirteen?

**37.** Your task is to rewrite lines 19–26 of the `ElevatorSimulation2` program so that there is a single `if` statement with a complex condition. What is the condition?

```
if (. . .)
{
    System.out.println("Error: Invalid floor number");
}
```

**38.** In the Sherlock Holmes story "The Adventure of the Sussex Vampire", the inimitable detective uttered these words: "Matilda Briggs was not the name of a young woman, Watson, … It was a ship which is associated with the giant rat of Sumatra, a story for which the world is not yet prepared." Over a hundred years later, researchers found giant rats in Western New Guinea, another part of Indonesia.

Suppose you are charged with writing a program that processes rat weights. It contains the statements

```
System.out.print("Enter weight in kg: ");
double weight = in.nextDouble();
```

What input checks should you supply?

*When processing inputs, you want to reject values that are too large. But how large is too large? These giant rats, found in Western New Guinea, are about five times the size of a city rat.*

**39.** Run the following test program and supply inputs 2 and three at the prompts. What happens? Why?

```
import java.util.Scanner

public class Test
{
    public static void main(String[] args)
    {
        Scanner in = new Scanner(System.in);
        System.out.print("Enter an integer: ");
        int m = in.nextInt();
        System.out.print("Enter another integer: ");
        int n = in.nextInt();
        System.out.println(m + " " + n);
    }
}
```

**Practice It**    Now you can try these exercises at the end of the chapter: R3.3, R3.32, P3.11.

---

**VIDEO EXAMPLE 3.2**        **The Genetic Code**

Watch this Video Example to see how to build a "decoder ring" for the genetic code.

---

## *Random Fact 3.2* Artificial Intelligence

When one uses a sophisticated computer program such as a tax preparation package, one is bound to attribute some intelligence to the computer. The computer asks sensible questions and makes computations that we find a mental challenge. After all, if doing one's taxes were easy, we wouldn't need a computer to do it for us.

As programmers, however, we know that all this apparent intelligence is an illusion. Human programmers have carefully "coached" the software in all possible scenarios, and it simply replays the actions and decisions that were programmed into it.

Would it be possible to write computer programs that are genuinely intelligent in some sense? From the earliest days of computing, there was a sense that the human brain might be nothing but an immense computer, and that it might well be feasible to program computers to imitate some processes of human thought. Serious research into *artificial intelligence* began in the mid-1950s, and the first twenty years brought some impressive successes. Programs that play chess—surely an activity that appears to require remarkable intellectual powers—have become so good that they now routinely beat all but the best human players. As far back as 1975, an *expert-system* program called Mycin gained fame for being better in diagnosing meningitis in patients than the average physician.

However, there were serious setbacks as well. From 1982 to 1992, the Japanese government embarked on a massive research project, funded at over 40 billion Japanese yen. It was known as the *Fifth-Generation Project.* Its goal was to develop new hardware and software to greatly improve the performance of expert system software. At its outset, the project created fear in other countries that the Japanese computer industry was about to become the undisputed leader in the field. However, the end results were disappointing and did little to bring

artificial intelligence applications to market.

From the very outset, one of the stated goals of the AI community was to produce software that could translate text from one language to another, for example from English to Russian. That undertaking proved to be enormously complicated. Human language appears to be much more subtle and interwoven with the human experience than had originally been thought. Even the grammar-checking tools that come with word-processing programs today are more of a gimmick than a useful tool, and analyzing grammar is just the first step in translating sentences.

The CYC (from en*cyc*lopedia) project, started by Douglas Lenat in 1984, tries to codify the implicit assumptions that underlie human speech and writing. The team members started out analyzing news articles and asked themselves what unmentioned facts are necessary to actually understand the sentences. For example, consider the sentence, "Last fall she enrolled in Michigan State". The reader automatically realizes that "fall" is not related to falling down in this context, but refers to the season. While there is a state of Michigan, here Michigan State denotes the university. A priori, a computer program has none of this

knowledge. The goal of the CYC project is to extract and store the requisite facts—that is, (1) people enroll in universities; (2) Michigan is a state; (3) many states have universities named X State University, often abbreviated as X State; (4) most people enroll in a university in the fall. By 1995, the project had codified about 100,000 common-sense concepts and about a million facts of knowledge relating them. Even this massive amount of data has not proven sufficient for useful applications.

In recent years, artificial intelligence technology has seen substantial advances. One of the most astounding examples is the outcome of a series of "grand challenges" for autonomous vehicles posed by the Defense Advanced Research Projects Agency (DARPA). Competitors were invited to submit a computer-controlled vehicle that had to complete an obstacle course without a human driver or remote control. The first event, in 2004, was a disappointment, with none of the entrants finishing the route. In 2005, five vehicles completed a grueling 212 km course in the Mojave desert. Stanford's Stanley came in first, with an average speed of 30 km/h. In 2007, DARPA moved the competition to an "urban" environment, an abandoned air force base. Vehicles had to be able to interact with each other, following California traffic laws. As Stanford's Sebastian Thrun explained: "In the last Grand Challenge, it didn't really matter whether an obstacle was a rock or a bush, because either way you'd just drive around it. The current challenge is to move from just sensing the environment to understanding it."

*Winner of the 2007 DARPA Urban Challenge*

## CHAPTER SUMMARY

### Use the `if` statement to implement a decision.

- The `if` statement allows a program to carry out different actions depending on the nature of the data to be processed.

### Implement comparisons of numbers and objects.

- Use relational operators (`<` `<=` `>` `>=` `==` `!=`) to compare numbers.
- Do not use the `==` operator to compare strings. Use the `equals` method instead.
- The `compareTo` method compares strings in lexicographic order.

### Implement complex decisions that require multiple `if` statements.

- Multiple `if` statements can be combined to evaluate complex decisions.
- When using multiple `if` statements, test general conditions after more specific conditions.

### Implement decisions whose branches require further decisions.

- When a decision statement is contained inside the branch of another decision statement, the statements are *nested*.
- Nested decisions are required for problems that have two levels of decision making.

### Draw flowcharts for visualizing the control flow of a program.

- Flow charts are made up of elements for tasks, input/output, and decisions.
- Each branch of a decision can contain tasks and further decisions.
- Never point an arrow inside another branch.

### Design test cases for your programs.

- Each branch of your program should be covered by a test case.
- It is a good idea to design test cases before implementing a program.
- Logging messages can be deactivated when testing is complete.

**Use the Boolean data type to store and combine conditions that can be true or false.**

- The Boolean type `boolean` has two values, `false` and `true`.
- Java has two Boolean operators that combine conditions: `&&` (*and*) and `||` (*or*).
- To invert a condition, use the `!` (*not*) operator.
- The `&&` and `||` operators are computed using *short-circuit evaluation:* As soon as the truth value is determined, no further conditions are evaluated.
- De Morgan's law tells you how to negate `&&` and `||` conditions.

**Apply `if` statements to detect whether user input is valid.**

- Call the `hasNextInt` or `hasNextDouble` method to ensure that the next input is a number.

## STANDARD LIBRARY ITEMS INTRODUCED IN THIS CHAPTER

```
java.lang.String
    equals
    compareTo
java.util.Scanner
    hasNextDouble
    hasNextInt
```

```
java.util.logging.Level
    INFO
    OFF
java.util.logging.Logger
    getGlobal
    info
    setLevel
```

## REVIEW EXERCISES

**• R3.1** What is the value of each variable after the `if` statement?

**a.** `int n = 1; int k = 2; int r = n;`
`if (k < n) { r = k; }`

**b.** `int n = 1; int k = 2; int r;`
`if (n < k) { r = k; }`
`else { r = k + n; }`

**c.** `int n = 1; int k = 2; int r = k;`
`if (r < k) { n = r; }`
`else { k = n; }`

**d.** `int n = 1; int k = 2; int r = 3;`
`if (r < n + k) { r = 2 * n; }`
`else { k = 2 * r; }`

**• • R3.2** Explain the difference between

```
s = 0;
if (x > 0) { s++; }
if (y > 0) { s++; }
```

and

```
s = 0;
if (x > 0) { s++; }
else if (y > 0) { s++; }
```

■■ **R3.3** Find the errors in the following if statements.

**a.** `if x > 0 then System.out.print(x);`

**b.** `if (1 + x > Math.pow(x, Math.sqrt(2)) { y = y + x; }`

**c.** `if (x = 1) { y++; }`

**d.**
```
x = in.nextInt();
if (in.hasNextInt())
{
    sum = sum + x;
}
else
{
    System.out.println("Bad input for x");
}
```

**e.**
```
String letterGrade = "F";
if (grade >= 90) { letterGrade = "A"; }
if (grade >= 80) { letterGrade = "B"; }
if (grade >= 70) { letterGrade = "C"; }
if (grade >= 60) { letterGrade = "D"; }
```

■ **R3.4** What do these code fragments print?

**a.**
```
int n = 1;
int m = -1;
if (n < -m) { System.out.print(n); }
else { System.out.print(m); }
```

**b.**
```
int n = 1;
int m = -1;
if (-n >= m) { System.out.print(n); }
else { System.out.print(m); }
```

**c.**
```
double x = 0;
double y = 1;
if (Math.abs(x - y) < 1) { System.out.print(x); }
else { System.out.print(y); }
```

**d.**
```
double x = Math.sqrt(2);
double y = 2;
if (x * x == y) { System.out.print(x); }
else { System.out.print(y); }
```

■■ **R3.5** Suppose x and y are variables of type `double`. Write a code fragment that sets y to x if x is positive and to 0 otherwise.

■■ **R3.6** Suppose x and y are variables of type `double`. Write a code fragment that sets y to the absolute value of x without calling the `Math.abs` function. Use an `if` statement.

■■ **R3.7** Explain why it is more difficult to compare floating-point numbers than integers. Write Java code to test whether an integer n equals 10 and whether a floating-point number x is approximately equal to 10.

■ **R3.8** It is easy to confuse the = and == operators. Write a test program containing the statement

```
if (floor = 13)
```

What error message do you get? Write another test program containing the statement

```
count == 0;
```

What does your compiler do when you compile the program?

**R3.9** Each square on a chess board can be described by a letter and number, such as g5 in this example:

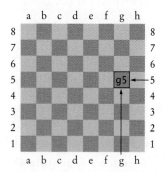

The following pseudocode describes an algorithm that determines whether a square with a given letter and number is dark (black) or light (white).

```
If the letter is an a, c, e, or g
    If the number is odd
        color = "black"
    Else
        color = "white"
Else
    If the number is even
        color = "black"
    Else
        color = "white"
```

Using the procedure in Programming Tip 3.5, trace this pseudocode with input g5.

**R3.10** Give a set of four test cases for the algorithm of Exercise R3.9 that covers all branches.

**R3.11** In a scheduling program, we want to check whether two appointments overlap. For simplicity, appointments start at a full hour, and we use military time (with hours 0–24). The following pseudocode describes an algorithm that determines whether the appointment with start time **start1** and end time **end1** overlaps with the appointment with start time **start2** and end time **end2**.

```
If start1 > start2
    s = start1
Else
    s = start2
If end1 < end2
    e = end1
Else
    e = end2
If s < e
    The appointments overlap.
Else
    The appointments don't overlap.
```

Trace this algorithm with an appointment from 10–12 and one from 11–13, then with an appointment from 10–11 and one from 12–13.

- **R3.12** Draw a flow chart for the algorithm in Exercise R3.11.

- **R3.13** Draw a flow chart for the algorithm in Exercise P3.17.

- **R3.14** Draw a flow chart for the algorithm in Exercise P3.18.

-- **R3.15** Develop a set of test cases for the algorithm in Exercise R3.11.

-- **R3.16** Develop a set of test cases for the algorithm in Exercise P3.18.

-- **R3.17** Write pseudocode for a program that prompts the user for a month and day and prints out whether it is one of the following four holidays:
  - New Year's Day (January 1)
  - Independence Day (July 4)
  - Veterans Day (November 11)
  - Christmas Day (December 25)

-- **R3.18** Write pseudocode for a program that assigns letter grades for a quiz, according to the following table:

| Score | Grade |
|-------|-------|
| 90–100 | A |
| 80–89 | B |
| 70–79 | C |
| 60–69 | D |
| < 60 | F |

-- **R3.19** Explain how the lexicographic ordering of strings in Java differs from the ordering of words in a dictionary or telephone book. *Hint:* Consider strings such as `IBM`, `wiley.com`, `Century 21`, and `While-U-Wait`.

-- **R3.20** Of the following pairs of strings, which comes first in lexicographic order?
  - **a.** `"Tom"`, `"Jerry"`
  - **b.** `"Tom"`, `"Tomato"`
  - **c.** `"church"`, `"Churchill"`
  - **d.** `"car manufacturer"`, `"carburetor"`
  - **e.** `"Harry"`, `"hairy"`
  - **f.** `"Java"`, `" Car"`
  - **g.** `"Tom"`, `"Tom"`
  - **h.** `"Car"`, `"Carl"`
  - **i.** `"car"`, `"bar"`

- **R3.21** Explain the difference between an `if/else if/else` sequence and nested `if` statements. Give an example of each.

-- **R3.22** Give an example of an `if/else if/else` sequence where the order of the tests does not matter. Give an example where the order of the tests matters.

- **R3.23** Rewrite the condition in Section 3.3 to use `<` operators instead of `>=` operators. What is the impact on the order of the comparisons?

-- **R3.24** Give a set of test cases for the tax program in Exercise P3.22. Manually compute the expected results.

■ **R3.25** Make up a Java code example that shows the dangling else problem using the following statement: A student with a GPA of at least 1.5, but less than 2, is on probation. With less than 1.5, the student is failing.

■■■ **R3.26** Complete the following truth table by finding the truth values of the Boolean expressions for all combinations of the Boolean inputs p, q, and r.

| p | q | r | (p && q) \|\| !r | !(p && (q \|\| !r)) |
|---|---|---|---|---|
| false | false | false | | |
| false | false | true | | |
| false | true | false | | |
| . . . | | | | |
| 5 more combinations | | | | |
| . . . | | | | |

■■■ **R3.27** True or false? *A* && *B* is the same as *B* && *A* for any Boolean conditions *A* and *B*.

■ **R3.28** The "advanced search" feature of many search engines allows you to use Boolean operators for complex queries, such as "(cats OR dogs) AND NOT pets". Contrast these search operators with the Boolean operators in Java.

■■ **R3.29** Suppose the value of b is false and the value of x is 0. What is the value of each of the following expressions?

**a.** b && x == 0
**b.** b \|\| x == 0
**c.** !b && x == 0
**d.** !b \|\| x == 0
**e.** b && x != 0
**f.** b \|\| x != 0
**g.** !b && x != 0
**h.** !b \|\| x != 0

■■ **R3.30** Simplify the following expressions. Here, b is a variable of type boolean.

**a.** b == true
**b.** b == false
**c.** b != true
**d.** b != false

■■■ **R3.31** Simplify the following statements. Here, b is a variable of type boolean and n is a variable of type int.

**a.** if (n == 0) { b = true; } else { b = false; }
   *(Hint:* What is the value of n == 0?)
**b.** if (n == 0) { b = false; } else { b = true; }
**c.** b = false; if (n > 1) { if (n < 2) { b = true; } }
**d.** if (n < 1) { b = true; } else { b = n > 2; }

**R3.32** What is wrong with the following program?

```java
System.out.print("Enter the number of quarters: ");
int quarters = in.nextInt();
if (in.hasNextInt())
{
   total = total + quarters * 0.25;
   System.out.println("Total: " + total);
}
else
{
   System.out.println("Input error.");
}
```

## PROGRAMMING EXERCISES

**P3.1** Write a program that reads an integer and prints whether it is negative, zero, or positive.

**P3.2** Write a program that reads a floating-point number and prints "zero" if the number is zero. Otherwise, print "positive" or "negative". Add "small" if the absolute value of the number is less than 1, or "large" if it exceeds 1,000,000.

**P3.3** Write a program that reads an integer and prints how many digits the number has, by checking whether the number is ≥ 10, ≥ 100, and so on. (Assume that all integers are less than ten billion.) If the number is negative, first multiply it with –1.

**P3.4** Write a program that reads three numbers and prints "all the same" if they are all the same, "all different" if they are all different, and "neither" otherwise.

**P3.5** Write a program that reads three numbers and prints "increasing" if they are in increasing order, "decreasing" if they are in decreasing order, and "neither" otherwise. Here, "increasing" means "strictly increasing", with each value larger than its predecessor. The sequence 3 4 4 would not be considered increasing.

**P3.6** Repeat Exercise P3.5, but before reading the numbers, ask the user whether increasing/decreasing should be "strict" or "lenient". In lenient mode, the sequence 3 4 4 is increasing and the sequence 4 4 4 is both increasing and decreasing.

**P3.7** Write a program that reads in three integers and prints "in order" if they are sorted in ascending *or* descending order, or "not in order" otherwise. For example,

```
1 2 5    in order
1 5 2    not in order
5 2 1    in order
1 2 2    in order
```

**P3.8** Write a program that reads four integers and prints "two pairs" if the input consists of two matching pairs (in some order) and "not two pairs" otherwise. For example,

```
1 2 2 1    two pairs
1 2 2 3    not two pairs
2 2 2 2    two pairs
```

■ **P3.9** Write a program that reads a temperature value and the letter C for Celsius or F for Fahrenheit. Print whether water is liquid, solid, or gaseous at the given temperature at sea level.

■ **P3.10** The boiling point of water drops by about one degree centigrade for every 300 meters (or 1,000 feet) of altitude. Improve the program of Exercise P3.9 to allow the user to supply the altitude in meters or feet.

■ **P3.11** Add error handling to Exercise P3.10. If the user does not enter a number when expected, or provides an invalid unit for the altitude, print an error message and end the program.

■■ **P3.12** Write a program that translates a letter grade into a number grade. Letter grades are A, B, C, D, and F, possibly followed by + or –. Their numeric values are 4, 3, 2, 1, and 0. There is no F+ or F–. A + increases the numeric value by 0.3, a – decreases it by 0.3. However, an A+ has value 4.0.

```
Enter a letter grade: B-
The numeric value is 2.7.
```

■■ **P3.13** Write a program that translates a number between 0 and 4 into the closest letter grade. For example, the number 2.8 (which might have been the average of several grades) would be converted to B–. Break ties in favor of the better grade; for example 2.85 should be a B.

■■ **P3.14** Write a program that takes user input describing a playing card in the following shorthand notation:

| | |
|---|---|
| A | Ace |
| 2 ... 10 | Card values |
| J | Jack |
| Q | Queen |
| K | King |
| D | Diamonds |
| H | Hearts |
| S | Spades |
| C | Clubs |

Your program should print the full description of the card. For example,

```
Enter the card notation: QS
Queen of Spades
```

■■ **P3.15** Write a program that reads in three floating-point numbers and prints the largest of the three inputs. For example:

```
Please enter three numbers: 4 9 2.5
The largest number is 9.
```

■■ **P3.16** Write a program that reads in three strings and sorts them lexicographically.

```
Enter three strings: Charlie Able Baker
Able
Baker
Charlie
```

•• **P3.17** When two points in time are compared, each given as hours (in military time, ranging from 0 and 23) and minutes, the following pseudocode determines which comes first.

> If hour1 < hour2
>     time1 comes first.
> Else if hour1 and hour2 are the same
>     If minute1 < minute2
>         time1 comes first.
>     Else if minute1 and minute2 are the same
>         time1 and time2 are the same.
>     Else
>         time2 comes first.
> Else
>     time2 comes first.

Write a program that prompts the user for two points in time and prints the time that comes first, then the other time.

•• **P3.18** The following algorithm yields the season (Spring, Summer, Fall, or Winter) for a given month and day.

> If month is 1, 2, or 3, season = "Winter"
> Else if month is 4, 5, or 6, season = "Spring"
> Else if month is 7, 8, or 9, season = "Summer"
> Else if month is 10, 11, or 12, season = "Fall"
> If month is divisible by 3 and day >= 21
>     If season is "Winter", season = "Spring"
>     Else if season is "Spring", season = "Summer"
>     Else if season is "Summer", season = "Fall"
>     Else season = "Winter"

Write a program that prompts the user for a month and day and then prints the season, as determined by this algorithm.

•• **P3.19** Write a program that reads in two floating-point numbers and tests whether they are the same up to two decimal places. Here are two sample runs.

```
Enter two floating-point numbers: 2.0 1.99998
They are the same up to two decimal places.
Enter two floating-point numbers: 2.0 1.98999
They are different.
```

••• **P3.20** Write a program that prompts for the day and month of the user's birthday and then prints a horoscope. Make up fortunes for programmers, like this:

```
Please enter your birthday (month and day): 6 16
Gemini are experts at figuring out the behavior of complicated programs.
You feel where bugs are coming from and then stay one step ahead. Tonight,
your style wins approval from a tough critic.
```

Each fortune should contain the name of the astrological sign. (You will find the names and date ranges of the signs at a distressingly large number of sites on the Internet.)

■■ **P3.21** The original U.S. income tax of 1913 was quite simple. The tax was

- 1 percent on the first $50,000.
- 2 percent on the amount over $50,000 up to $75,000.
- 3 percent on the amount over $75,000 up to $100,000.
- 4 percent on the amount over $100,000 up to $250,000.
- 5 percent on the amount over $250,000 up to $500,000.
- 6 percent on the amount over $500,000.

There was no separate schedule for single or married taxpayers. Write a program that computes the income tax according to this schedule.

■■■ **P3.22** Write a program that computes taxes for the following schedule.

| If your status is Single and if the taxable income is over | but not over | the tax is | of the amount over |
|---|---|---|---|
| $0 | $8,000 | 10% | $0 |
| $8,000 | $32,000 | $800 + 15% | $8,000 |
| $32,000 | | $4,400 + 25% | $32,000 |
| If your status is Married and if the taxable income is over | but not over | the tax is | of the amount over |
| $0 | $16,000 | 10% | $0 |
| $16,000 | $64,000 | $1,600 + 15% | $16,000 |
| $64,000 | | $8,800 + 25% | $64,000 |

■■■ **P3.23** The `TaxCalculator.java` program uses a simplified version of the 2008 U.S. income tax schedule. Look up the tax brackets and rates for the current year, for both single and married filers, and implement a program that computes the actual income tax.

■■■ **P3.24** *Unit conversion.* Write a unit conversion program that asks the users from which unit they want to convert (fl. oz, gal, oz, lb, in, ft, mi) and to which unit they want to convert (ml, l, g, kg, mm, cm, m, km). Reject incompatible conversions (such as gal → km). Ask for the value to be converted, then display the result:

```
Convert from? gal
Convert to? ml
Value? 2.5
2.5 gal = 9462.5 ml
```

■ **P3.25** Write a program that prompts the user to provide a single character from the alphabet. Print Vowel or Consonant, depending on the user input. If the user input is not a letter (between a and z or A and Z), or is a string of length > 1, print an error message.

■■■ **P3.26** *Roman numbers*. Write a program that converts a positive integer into the Roman number system. The Roman number system has digits

| | |
|---|---|
| I | 1 |
| V | 5 |
| X | 10 |
| L | 50 |
| C | 100 |
| D | 500 |
| M | 1,000 |

Numbers are formed according to the following rules:

**a.** Only numbers up to 3,999 are represented.

**b.** As in the decimal system, the thousands, hundreds, tens, and ones are expressed separately.

**c.** The numbers 1 to 9 are expressed as

| | |
|---|---|
| I | 1 |
| II | 2 |
| III | 3 |
| IV | 4 |
| V | 5 |
| VI | 6 |
| VII | 7 |
| VIII | 8 |
| IX | 9 |

As you can see, an I preceding a V or X is subtracted from the value, and you can never have more than three I's in a row.

**d.** Tens and hundreds are done the same way, except that the letters X, L, C and C, D, M are used instead of I, V, X, respectively.

Your program should take an input, such as 1978, and convert it to Roman numerals, MCMLXXVIII.

■■ **P3.27** Write a program that asks the user to enter a month (1 for January, 2 for February, and so on) and then prints the number of days in the month. For February, print "28 or 29 days".

```
Enter a month: 5
30 days
```

Do not use a separate if/else branch for each month. Use Boolean operators.

■■■ **P3.28** A year with 366 days is called a leap year. Leap years are necessary to keep the calendar synchronized with the sun because the earth revolves around the sun once every 365.25 days. Actually, that figure is not entirely precise, and for all dates after 1582 the *Gregorian correction* applies. Usually years that are divisible by 4 are leap years, for example 1996. However, years that are divisible by 100 (for example, 1900) are not leap years, but years that are divisible by 400 are leap years (for example,

2000). Write a program that asks the user for a year and computes whether that year is a leap year. Use a single if statement and Boolean operators.

**■■■ P3.29** French country names are feminine when they end with the letter e, masculine otherwise, except for the following which are masculine even though they end with e:

- le Belize
- le Cambodge
- le Mexique
- le Mozambique
- le Zaïre
- le Zimbabwe

Write a program that reads the French name of a country and adds the article: le for masculine or la for feminine, such as le Canada or la Belgique.

However, if the country name starts with a vowel, use l'; for example, l'Afghanistan.

For the following plural country names, use les:

- les Etats-Unis
- les Pays-Bas

**■■■ Business P3.30** Write a program to simulate a bank transaction. There are two bank accounts: checking and savings. First, ask for the initial balances of the bank accounts; reject negative balances. Then ask for the transactions; options are deposit, withdrawal, and transfer. Then ask for the account; options are checking and savings. Then ask for the amount; reject transactions that overdraw an account. At the end, print the balances of both accounts.

**■■ Business P3.31** Write a program that reads in the name and salary of an employee. Here the salary will denote an *hourly* wage, such as $9.25. Then ask how many hours the employee worked in the past week. Be sure to accept fractional hours. Compute the pay. Any overtime work (over 40 hours per week) is paid at 150 percent of the regular wage. Print a paycheck for the employee.

**■■ Business P3.32** When you use an automated teller machine (ATM) with your bank card, you need to use a personal identification number (PIN) to access your account. If a user fails more than three times when entering the PIN, the machine will block the card. Assume that the user's PIN is "1234" and write a program that asks the user for the PIN no more than three times, and does the following:

- If the user enters the right number, print a message saying, "Your PIN is correct", and end the program.
- If the user enters a wrong number, print a message saying, "Your PIN is incorrect" and, if you have asked for the PIN less than three times, ask for it again.
- If the user enters a wrong number three times, print a message saying "Your bank card is blocked" and end the program.

**■ Business P3.33** Calculating the tip when you go to a restaurant is not difficult, but your restaurant wants to suggest a tip according to the service diners receive. Write a program that calculates a tip according to the diner's satisfaction as follows:

- Ask for the diners' satisfaction level using these ratings: 1 = Totally satisfied, 2 = Satisfied, 3 = Dissatisfied.

- If the diner is totally satisfied, calculate a 20 percent tip.
- If the diner is satisfied, calculate a 15 percent tip.
- If the diner is dissatisfied, calculate a 10 percent tip.
- Report the satisfaction level and tip in dollars and cents.

**■ Business P3.34** A supermarket awards coupons depending on how much a customer spends on groceries. For example, if you spend $50, you will get a coupon worth eight percent of that amount. The following table shows the percent used to calculate the coupon awarded for different amounts spent. Write a program that calculates and prints the value of the coupon a person can receive based on groceries purchased.

Here is a sample run:

```
Please enter the cost of your groceries: 14
You win a discount coupon of $ 1.12. (8% of your purchase)
```

| Money Spent | Coupon Percentage |
|---|---|
| Less than $10 | No coupon |
| From $10 to $60 | 8% |
| More than $60 to $150 | 10% |
| More than $150 to $210 | 12% |
| More than $210 | 14% |

**■ Science P3.35** Write a program that prompts the user for a wavelength value and prints a description of the corresponding part of the electromagnetic spectrum, as given in the following table.

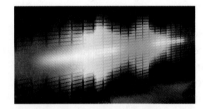

| Electromagnetic Spectrum | | |
|---|---|---|
| Type | Wavelength (m) | Frequency (Hz) |
| Radio Waves | $> 10^{-1}$ | $< 3 \times 10^9$ |
| Microwaves | $10^{-3}$ to $10^{-1}$ | $3 \times 10^9$ to $3 \times 10^{11}$ |
| Infrared | $7 \times 10^{-7}$ to $10^{-3}$ | $3 \times 10^{11}$ to $4 \times 10^{14}$ |
| Visible light | $4 \times 10^{-7}$ to $7 \times 10^{-7}$ | $4 \times 10^{14}$ to $7.5 \times 10^{14}$ |
| Ultraviolet | $10^{-8}$ to $4 \times 10^{-7}$ | $7.5 \times 10^{14}$ to $3 \times 10^{16}$ |
| X-rays | $10^{-11}$ to $10^{-8}$ | $3 \times 10^{16}$ to $3 \times 10^{19}$ |
| Gamma rays | $< 10^{-11}$ | $> 3 \times 10^{19}$ |

**■ Science P3.36** Repeat Exercise P3.35, modifying the program so that it prompts for the frequency instead.

**■■ Science P3.37** Repeat Exercise P3.35, modifying the program so that it first asks the user whether the input will be a wavelength or a frequency.

**■■■ Science P3.38** A minivan has two sliding doors. Each door can be opened by either a dashboard switch, its inside handle, or its outside handle. However, the inside handles do not work if a child lock switch is activated. In order for the sliding doors to open, the gear shift must be in park, *and* the master unlock switch must be activated. (This book's author is the long-suffering owner of just such a vehicle.)

Your task is to simulate a portion of the control software for the vehicle. The input is a sequence of values for the switches and the gear shift, in the following order:

- Dashboard switches for left and right sliding door, child lock, and master unlock (0 for off or 1 for activated)

- Inside and outside handles on the left and right sliding doors (0 or 1)

- The gear shift setting (one of P N D 1 2 3 R).

A typical input would be 0 0 0 1 0 1 0 0 0 P.

Print "left door opens" and/or "right door opens" as appropriate. If neither door opens, print "both doors stay closed".

**■ Science P3.39** Sound level $L$ in units of decibel (dB) is determined by

$$L = 20 \log_{10}(p/p_0)$$

where $p$ is the sound pressure of the sound (in Pascals, abbreviated Pa), and $p_0$ is a reference sound pressure equal to $20 \times 10^{-6}$ Pa (where $L$ is 0 dB). The following table gives descriptions for certain sound levels.

| | |
|---|---|
| Threshold of pain | 130 dB |
| Possible hearing damage | 120 dB |
| Jack hammer at 1 m | 100 dB |
| Traffic on a busy roadway at 10 m | 90 dB |
| Normal conversation | 60 dB |
| Calm library | 30 dB |
| Light leaf rustling | 0 dB |

Write a program that reads a value and a unit, either dB or Pa, and then prints the closest description from the list above.

**■■ Science P3.40** The electric circuit shown below is designed to measure the temperature of the gas in a chamber.

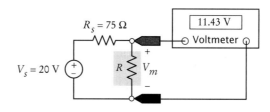

The resistor $R$ represents a temperature sensor enclosed in the chamber. The resistance $R$, in $\Omega$, is related to the temperature $T$, in °C, by the equation

$$R = R_0 + kT$$

In this device, assume $R_0 = 100\ \Omega$ and $k = 0.5$. The voltmeter displays the value of the voltage, $V_m$, across the sensor. This voltage $V_m$ indicates the temperature, $T$, of the gas according to the equation

$$T = \frac{R}{k} - \frac{R_0}{k} = \frac{R_s}{k}\frac{V_m}{V_s - V_m} - \frac{R_0}{k}$$

Suppose the voltmeter voltage is constrained to the range $V_{min} = 12$ volts $\leq V_m \leq V_{max} = 18$ volts. Write a program that accepts a value of $V_m$ and checks that it's between 12 and 18. The program should return the gas temperature in degrees Celsius when $V_m$ is between 12 and 18 and an error message when it isn't.

■■■ **Science P3.41**  Crop damage due to frost is one of the many risks confronting farmers. The figure below shows a simple alarm circuit designed to warn of frost. The alarm circuit uses a device called a thermistor to sound a buzzer when the temperature drops below freezing. Thermistors are semiconductor devices that exhibit a temperature dependent resistance described by the equation

$$R = R_0 e^{\beta\left(\frac{1}{T} - \frac{1}{T_0}\right)}$$

where $R$ is the resistance, in $\Omega$, at the temperature $T$, in °K, and $R_0$ is the resistance, in $\Omega$, at the temperature $T_0$, in °K. $\beta$ is a constant that depends on the material used to make the thermistor.

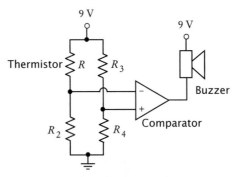

The circuit is designed so that the alarm will sound when

$$\frac{R_2}{R + R_2} < \frac{R_4}{R_3 + R_4}$$

The thermistor used in the alarm circuit has $R_0 = 33{,}192\ \Omega$ at $T_0 = 40$ °C, and $\beta = 3{,}310$ °K. (Notice that $\beta$ has units of °K. The temperature in °K is obtained by adding 273° to the temperature in °C.) The resistors $R_2$, $R_3$, and $R_4$ have a resistance of 156.3 k$\Omega$ = 156,300 $\Omega$.

Write a Java program that prompts the user for a temperature in °F and prints a message indicating whether or not the alarm will sound at that temperature.

**■ Science P3.42** A mass $m = 2$ kilograms is attached to the end of a rope of length $r = 3$ meters. The mass is whirled around at high speed. The rope can withstand a maximum tension of $T = 60$ Newtons. Write a program that accepts a rotation speed $v$ and determines whether such a speed will cause the rope to break. *Hint:* $T = mv^2/r$.

**■ Science P3.43** A mass $m$ is attached to the end of a rope of length $r = 3$ meters. The rope can only be whirled around at speeds of 1, 10, 20, or 40 meters per second. The rope can withstand a maximum tension of $T = 60$ Newtons. Write a program where the user enters the value of the mass $m$, and the program determines the greatest speed at which it can be whirled without breaking the rope. *Hint:* $T = mv^2/r$.

**■■ Science P3.44** The average person can jump off the ground with a velocity of 7 mph without fear of leaving the planet. However, if an astronaut jumps with this velocity while standing on Halley's Comet, will the astronaut ever come back down? Create a program that allows the user to input a launch velocity (in mph) from the surface of Halley's Comet and determine whether a jumper will return to the surface. If not, the program should calculate how much more massive the comet must be in order to return the jumper to the surface.

*Hint:* Escape velocity is $v_{\text{escape}} = \sqrt{2\dfrac{GM}{R}}$, where $G = 6.67 \times 10^{-11} N\,m^2/kg^2$ is the gravitational constant, $M = 1.3 \times 10^{22}$ kg is the mass of Halley's comet, and $R = 1.153 \times 10^6$ m is its radius.

## ANSWERS TO SELF-CHECK QUESTIONS

1. Change the if statement to
```
if (floor > 14)
{
    actualFloor = floor - 2;
}
```

2. 85. 90. 85.

3. The only difference is if originalPrice is 100. The statement in Self Check 2 sets discounted-Price to 90; this one sets it to 80.

4. 95. 100. 95.

5.
```
if (fuelAmount < 0.10 * fuelCapacity)
{
    System.out.println("red");
}
else
{
    System.out.println("green");
}
```

6. (a) and (b) are both true, (c) is false.

7. floor <= 13

8. The values should be compared with ==, not =.

9. input.equals("Y")

10. str.equals("") or str.length() == 0

11.
```
if (scoreA > scoreB)
{
    System.out.println("A won");
}
else if (scoreA < scoreB)
{
    System.out.println("B won");
}
else
{
    System.out.println("Game tied");
}
```

12.
```
if (x > 0) { s = 1; }
else if (x < 0) { s = -1; }
else { s = 0; }
```

**13.** You could first set s to one of the three values:
```
s = 0;
if (x > 0) { s = 1; }
else if (x < 0) { s = -1; }
```

**14.** The `if (price <= 100)` can be omitted (leaving just `else`), making it clear that the `else` branch is the sole alternative.

**15.** No destruction of buildings.

**16.** Add a branch before the final `else`:
```
else if (richter < 0)
{
    System.out.println("Error: Negative input");
}
```

**17.** 3200.

**18.** No. Then the computation is 0.10 × 32000 + 0.25 × (32000 – 32000).

**19.** No. Their individual tax is $5,200 each, and if they married, they would pay $10,400. Actually, taxpayers in higher tax brackets (which our program does not model) may pay higher taxes when they marry, a phenomenon known as the *marriage penalty*.

**20.** Change `else` in line 41 to
```
else if (maritalStatus.equals("m"))
```
and add another branch after line 52:
```
else
{
    System.out.println(
    "Error: marital status should be s or m.");
}
```

**21.** The higher tax rate is only applied on the income in the higher bracket. Suppose you are single and make $31,900. Should you try to get a $200 raise? Absolutely: you get to keep 90 percent of the first $100 and 75 percent of the next $100.

**22.**

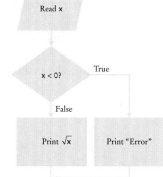

**23.** The "True" arrow from the first decision points into the "True" branch of the second decision, creating spaghetti code.

**24.** Here is one solution. In Section 3.7, you will see how you can combine the conditions for a more elegant solution.

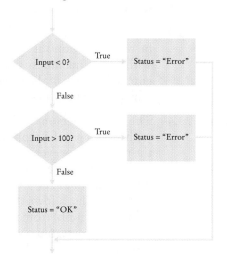

**25.**

**26.**

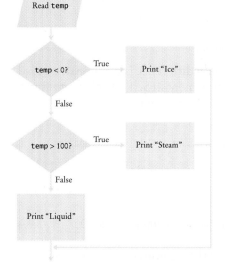

**27.**

| Test Case | Expected Output | Comment |
|---|---|---|
| 12 | 12 | Below 13th floor |
| 14 | 13 | Above 13th floor |
| 13 | ? | The specification is not clear— See Section 3.8 for a version of this program with error handling |

**29.** A boundary test case is a price of $128. A 16 percent discount should apply because the problem statement states that the larger discount applies if the price is *at least* $128. Thus, the expected output is $107.52.

**30.**

| Test Case | Expected Output | Comment |
|---|---|---|
| 9 | Most structures fall | |
| 7.5 | Many buildings destroyed | |
| 6.5 | Many buildings ... | |
| 5 | Damage to poorly... | |
| 3 | No destruction... | |
| 8.0 | Most structures fall | Boundary case. In this program, boundary cases are not as significant because the behavior of an earthquake changes gradually. |
| -1 | | The specification is not clear—see Self Check 16 for a version of this program with error handling. |

**31.**

| Test Case | Expected Output | Comment |
|---|---|---|
| (0.5, 0.5) | inside | |
| (4, 2) | outside | |
| (0, 2) | on the boundary | Exactly on the boundary |
| (1.414, 1.414) | on the boundary | Close to the boundary |
| (0, 1.9) | inside | Not less than 1 mm from the boundary |
| (0, 2.1) | outside | Not less than 1 mm from the boundary |

**32.** x == 0 && y == 0

**33.** x == 0 || y == 0

**34.** (x == 0 && y != 0) || (y == 0 && x != 0)

**35.** The same as the value of frozen.

**36.** You are guaranteed that there are no other values. With strings or integers, you would need to check that no values such as "maybe" or –1 enter your calculations.

**37.** (a) Error: The floor must be between 1 and 20.
(b) Error: The floor must be between 1 and 20.
(c) 19  (d) Error: Not an integer.

**38.** floor == 13 || floor <= 0 || floor > 20

**39.** Check for in.hasNextDouble(), to make sure a researcher didn't supply an input such as oh my. Check for weight <= 0, because any rat must surely have a positive weight. We don't know how giant a rat could be, but the New Guinea rats weighed no more than 2 kg. A regular house rat (*rattus rattus*) weighs up to 0.2 kg, so we'll say that any weight > 10 kg was surely an input error, perhaps confusing grams and kilograms. Thus, the checks are

```
if (in.hasNextDouble())
{
   double weight = in.nextDouble();
   if (weight < 0)
   {
      System.out.println(
         "Error: Weight cannot be negative.");
   }
   else if (weight > 10)
   {
      System.out.println(
         "Error: Weight > 10 kg.");
   }
   else
   {
      Process valid weight.
   }
}
else
{
   System.out.print("Error: Not a number");
}
```

**40.** The second input fails, and the program terminates without printing anything.

## CHAPTER 4

# LOOPS

To implement while, for, and do loops

To hand-trace the execution of a program

To become familiar with common
loop algorithms

To understand nested loops

To implement programs that read and process data sets

To use a computer for simulations

In a loop, a part of a program is repeated over and over, until a specific goal is reached. Loops are important for calculations that require repeated steps and for processing input consisting of many data items. In this chapter, you will learn about loop statements in Java, as well as techniques for writing programs that process input and simulate activities in the real world.

# 4.1  The while Loop

In this section, you will learn about *loop statements* that repeatedly execute instructions until a goal has been reached.

Recall the investment problem from Chapter 1. You put $10,000 into a bank account that earns 5 percent interest per year. How many years does it take for the account balance to be double the original investment?

*Because the interest earned also earns interest, a bank balance grows exponentially.*

In Chapter 1 we developed the following algorithm for this problem:

Start with a year value of 0, a column for the interest, and a balance of $10,000.

| year | interest | balance |
|------|----------|---------|
| 0    |          | $10,000 |

Repeat the following steps while the balance is less than $20,000.
    Add 1 to the year value.
    Compute the interest as balance x 0.05 (i.e., 5 percent interest).
    Add the interest to the balance.
Report the final year value as the answer.

You now know how to declare and update the variables in Java. What you don't yet know is how to carry out "Repeat steps while the balance is less than $20,000".

*In a particle accelerator, subatomic particles traverse a loop-shaped tunnel multiple times, gaining the speed required for physical experiments. Similarly, in computer science, statements in a loop are executed while a condition is true.*

**Figure 1** Flowchart of a while Loop

In Java, the while statement implements such a repetition (see Syntax 4.1). It has the form

```
while (condition)
{
    statements
}
```

> A loop executes instructions repeatedly while a condition is true.

As long as the condition remains true, the statements inside the while statement are executed. These statements are called the **body** of the while statement.

In our case, we want to increment the year counter and add interest while the balance is less than the target balance of $20,000:

```
while (balance < TARGET)
{
    year++;
    double interest = balance * RATE / 100;
    balance = balance + interest;
}
```

A while statement is an example of a **loop**. If you draw a flowchart, the flow of execution loops again to the point where the condition is tested (see Figure 1).

## Syntax 4.1 while Statement

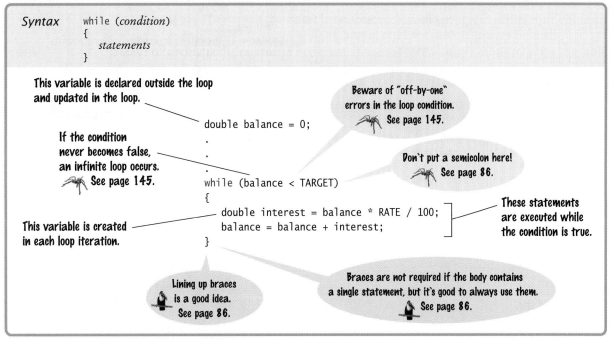

*Syntax*
```
while (condition)
{
    statements
}
```

This variable is declared outside the loop and updated in the loop.

Beware of "off-by-one" errors in the loop condition. See page 145.

If the condition never becomes false, an infinite loop occurs. See page 145.

```
double balance = 0;
.
.
.
while (balance < TARGET)
{
    double interest = balance * RATE / 100;
    balance = balance + interest;
}
```

Don't put a semicolon here! See page 86.

These statements are executed while the condition is true.

This variable is created in each loop iteration.

Lining up braces is a good idea. See page 86.

Braces are not required if the body contains a single statement, but it's good to always use them. See page 86.

When you declare a variable *inside* the loop body, the variable is created for each iteration of the loop and removed after the end of each iteration. For example, consider the interest variable in this loop:

```
while (balance < TARGET)
{
   year++;
   double interest = balance * RATE / 100;
   balance = balance + interest;
} // interest no longer declared here
```

> A new interest variable is created in each iteration.

In contrast, the balance and years variables were declared outside the loop body. That way, the same variable is used for all iterations of the loop.

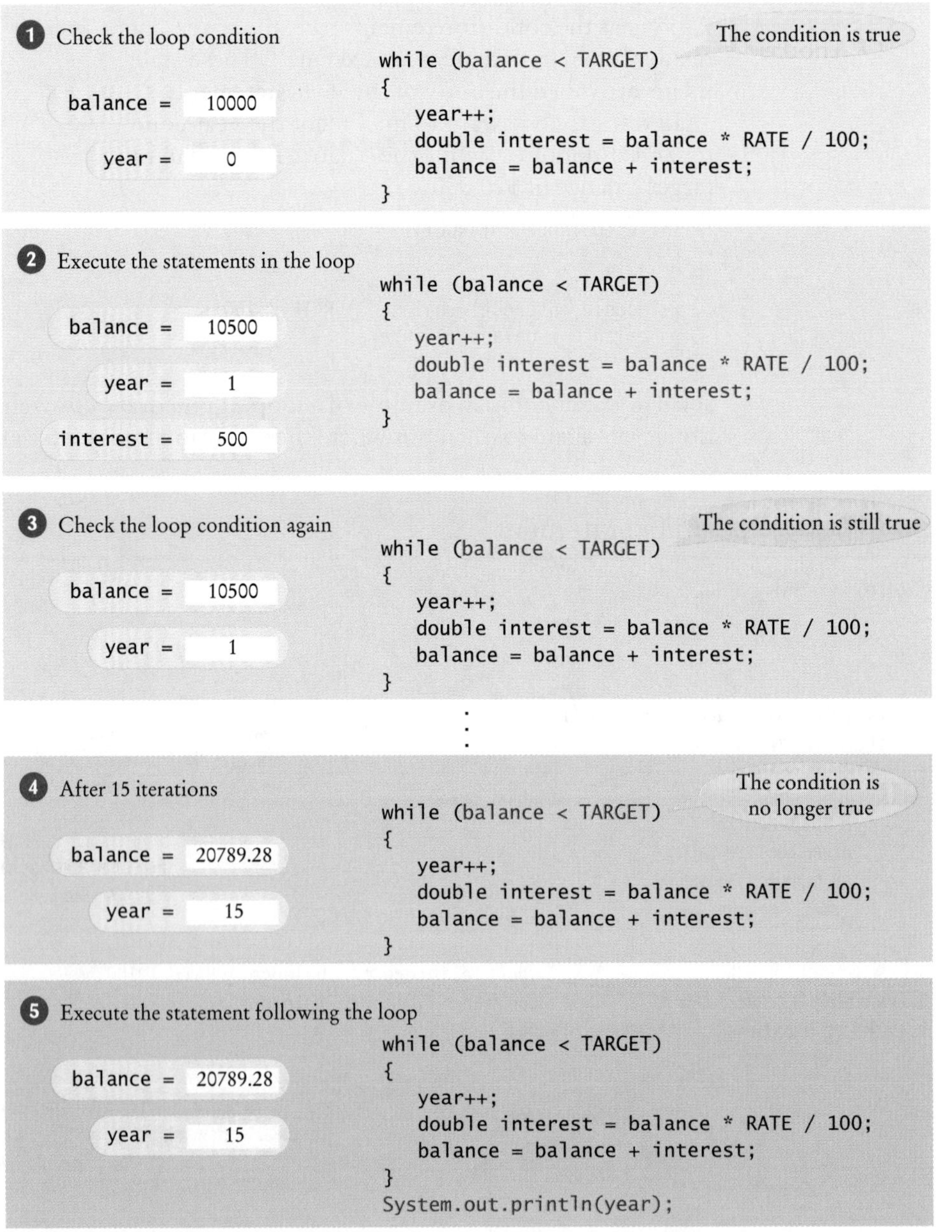

① Check the loop condition

balance = 10000

year = 0

```
while (balance < TARGET)
{
   year++;
   double interest = balance * RATE / 100;
   balance = balance + interest;
}
```

The condition is true

② Execute the statements in the loop

balance = 10500

year = 1

interest = 500

```
while (balance < TARGET)
{
   year++;
   double interest = balance * RATE / 100;
   balance = balance + interest;
}
```

③ Check the loop condition again

balance = 10500

year = 1

```
while (balance < TARGET)
{
   year++;
   double interest = balance * RATE / 100;
   balance = balance + interest;
}
```

The condition is still true

⋮

④ After 15 iterations

balance = 20789.28

year = 15

```
while (balance < TARGET)
{
   year++;
   double interest = balance * RATE / 100;
   balance = balance + interest;
}
```

The condition is no longer true

⑤ Execute the statement following the loop

balance = 20789.28

year = 15

```
while (balance < TARGET)
{
   year++;
   double interest = balance * RATE / 100;
   balance = balance + interest;
}
System.out.println(year);
```

**Figure 2**
Execution of the
DoubleInvestment
Loop

Here is the program that solves the investment problem. Figure 2 illustrates the program's execution.

### section_1/DoubleInvestment.java

```
1   /**
2       This program computes the time required to double an investment.
3   */
4   public class DoubleInvestment
5   {
6      public static void main(String[] args)
7      {
8         final double RATE = 5;
9         final double INITIAL_BALANCE = 10000;
10        final double TARGET = 2 * INITIAL_BALANCE;
11
12        double balance = INITIAL_BALANCE;
13        int year = 0;
14
15        // Count the years required for the investment to double
16
17        while (balance < TARGET)
18        {
19           year++;
20           double interest = balance * RATE / 100;
21           balance = balance + interest;
22        }
23
24        System.out.println("The investment doubled after "
25           + year + " years.");
26     }
27  }
```

### Program Run

```
The investment doubled after 15 years.
```

**SELF CHECK**

1. How many years does it take for the investment to triple? Modify the program and run it.
2. If the interest rate is 10 percent per year, how many years does it take for the investment to double? Modify the program and run it.
3. Modify the program so that the balance after each year is printed. How did you do that?
4. Suppose we change the program so that the condition of the while loop is
   ```
   while (balance <= TARGET)
   ```
   What is the effect on the program? Why?
5. What does the following loop print?
   ```
   int n = 1;
   while (n < 100)
   {
      n = 2 * n;
      System.out.print(n + " ");
   }
   ```

**Practice It** Now you can try these exercises at the end of the chapter: R4.1, R4.5, P4.14.

## Table 1 while Loop Examples

| Loop | Output | Explanation |
|---|---|---|
| ```<br>i = 0; sum = 0;<br>while (sum < 10)<br>{<br>   i++; sum = sum + i;<br>   Print i and sum;<br>}<br>``` | 1 1<br>2 3<br>3 6<br>4 10 | When sum is 10, the loop condition is false, and the loop ends. |
| ```<br>i = 0; sum = 0;<br>while (sum < 10)<br>{<br>   i++; sum = sum - i;<br>   Print i and sum;<br>}<br>``` | 1 -1<br>2 -3<br>3 -6<br>4 -10<br>. . . | Because sum never reaches 10, this is an "infinite loop" (see Common Error 4.2 on page 145). |
| ```<br>i = 0; sum = 0;<br>while (sum < 0)<br>{<br>   i++; sum = sum - i;<br>   Print i and sum;<br>}<br>``` | (No output) | The statement sum < 0 is false when the condition is first checked, and the loop is never executed. |
| ```<br>i = 0; sum = 0;<br>while (sum >= 10)<br>{<br>   i++; sum = sum + i;<br>   Print i and sum;<br>}<br>``` | (No output) | The programmer probably thought, "Stop when the sum is at least 10." However, the loop condition controls when the loop is executed, not when it ends (see Common Error 4.1 on page 144). |
| ```<br>i = 0; sum = 0;<br>while (sum < 10) ;<br>{<br>   i++; sum = sum + i;<br>   Print i and sum;<br>}<br>``` | (No output, program does not terminate) | Note the semicolon before the {. This loop has an empty body. It runs forever, checking whether sum < 0 and doing nothing in the body. |

**Common Error 4.1**

### Don't Think "Are We There Yet?"

When doing something repetitive, most of us want to know when we are done. For example, you may think, "I want to get at least $20,000," and set the loop condition to

```
balance >= TARGET
```

But the while loop thinks the opposite: How long am I allowed to keep going? The correct loop condition is

```
while (balance < TARGET)
```

In other words: "Keep at it while the balance is less than the target."

*When writing a loop condition, don't ask, "Are we there yet?" The condition determines how long the loop will keep going.*

## Infinite Loops

A very annoying loop error is an *infinite loop:* a loop that runs forever and can be stopped only by killing the program or restarting the computer. If there are output statements in the program, then reams and reams of output flash by on the screen. Otherwise, the program just sits there and *hangs*, seeming to do nothing. On some systems, you can kill a hanging program by hitting Ctrl + C. On others, you can close the window in which the program runs.

A common reason for infinite loops is forgetting to update the variable that controls the loop:

```java
int year = 1;
while (year <= 20)
{
    double interest = balance * RATE / 100;
    balance = balance + interest;
}
```

*Like this hamster who can't stop running in the treadmill, an infinite loop never ends.*

Here the programmer forgot to add a year++ command in the loop. As a result, the year always stays at 1, and the loop never comes to an end.

Another common reason for an infinite loop is accidentally incrementing a counter that should be decremented (or vice versa). Consider this example:

```java
int year = 20;
while (year > 0)
{
    double interest = balance * RATE / 100;
    balance = balance + interest;
    year++;
}
```

The year variable really should have been decremented, not incremented. This is a common error because incrementing counters is so much more common than decrementing that your fingers may type the ++ on autopilot. As a consequence, year is always larger than 0, and the loop never ends. (Actually, year may eventually exceed the largest representable positive integer and *wrap around* to a negative number. Then the loop ends—of course, with a completely wrong result.)

## Off-by-One Errors

Consider our computation of the number of years that are required to double an investment:

```java
int year = 0;
while (balance < TARGET)
{
    year++;
    balance = balance * (1 + RATE / 100);
}
System.out.println("The investment doubled after "
    + year + " years.");
```

Should year start at 0 or at 1? Should you test for balance < TARGET or for balance <= TARGET? It is easy to be *off by one* in these expressions.

Some people try to solve **off-by-one errors** by randomly inserting +1 or -1 until the program seems to work—a terrible strategy. It can take a long time to compile and test all the various possibilities. Expending a small amount of mental effort is a real time saver.

Fortunately, off-by-one errors are easy to avoid, simply by thinking through a couple of test cases and using the information from the test cases to come up with a rationale for your decisions.

Should year start at 0 or at 1? Look at a scenario with simple values: an initial balance of \$100 and an interest rate of 50 percent. After year 1, the balance is \$150, and after year 2 it is \$225, or over \$200. So the investment doubled after 2 years. The loop executed two times, incrementing year each time. Hence year must start at 0, not at 1.

> An off-by-one error is a common error when programming loops. Think through simple test cases to avoid this type of error.

| year | balance |
|------|---------|
| 0 | \$100 |
| 1 | \$150 |
| 2 | \$225 |

In other words, the `balance` variable denotes the balance after the end of the year. At the outset, the `balance` variable contains the balance after year 0 and not after year 1.

Next, should you use a < or <= comparison in the test? This is harder to figure out, because it is rare for the balance to be exactly twice the initial balance. There is one case when this happens, namely when the interest is 100 percent. The loop executes once. Now year is 1, and balance is exactly equal to 2 * `INITIAL_BALANCE`. Has the investment doubled after one year? It has. Therefore, the loop should not execute again. If the test condition is `balance < TARGET`, the loop stops, as it should. If the test condition had been `balance <= TARGET`, the loop would have executed once more.

In other words, you keep adding interest while the balance *has not yet doubled*.

## *Random Fact 4.1* The First Bug

According to legend, the first bug was found in the Mark II, a huge electromechanical computer at Harvard University. It really was caused by a bug—a moth was trapped in a relay switch.

Actually, from the note that the operator left in the log book next to the moth (see the photo), it appears as if the term "bug" had already been in active use at the time.

The pioneering computer scientist Maurice Wilkes wrote, "Somehow, at the Moore School and afterwards, one had always assumed there would be no particular difficulty in getting programs right. I can remember the exact instant in time at which it dawned on me that a great part of my future life would be spent finding mistakes in my own programs."

The First Bug

# 4.2  Problem Solving: Hand-Tracing

> Hand-tracing is a simulation of code execution in which you step through instructions and track the values of the variables.

In Programming Tip 3.5, you learned about the method of hand-tracing. When you hand-trace code or pseudocode, you write the names of the variables on a sheet of paper, mentally execute each step of the code and update the variables.

It is best to have the code written or printed on a sheet of paper. Use a marker, such as a paper clip, to mark the current line. Whenever a variable changes, cross out the old value and write the new value below. When a program produces output, also write down the output in another column.

Consider this example. What value is displayed?

```java
int n = 1729;
int sum = 0;
while (n > 0)
{
   int digit = n % 10;
   sum = sum + digit;
   n = n / 10;
}
System.out.println(sum);
```

There are three variables: n, sum, and digit.

| n | sum | digit |
|---|-----|-------|
|   |     |       |
|   |     |       |

The first two variables are initialized with 1729 and 0 before the loop is entered.

```java
      int n = 1729;
⊂⊃    int sum = 0;
      while (n > 0)
      {
         int digit = n % 10;
         sum = sum + digit;
         n = n / 10;
      }
      System.out.println(sum);
```

| n | sum | digit |
|------|-----|-------|
| 1729 | 0 |   |
|   |   |   |
|   |   |   |
|   |   |   |
|   |   |   |

Because n is greater than zero, enter the loop. The variable digit is set to 9 (the remainder of dividing 1729 by 10). The variable sum is set to 0 + 9 = 9.

```java
      int n = 1729;
      int sum = 0;
      while (n > 0)
      {
         int digit = n % 10;
⊂⊃       sum = sum + digit;
         n = n / 10;
      }
      System.out.println(sum);
```

| n | sum | digit |
|------|-----|-------|
| 1729 | ~~0~~ |   |
|   | 9 | 9 |
|   |   |   |
|   |   |   |
|   |   |   |

Finally, n becomes 172. (Recall that the remainder in the division 1729 / 10 is discarded because both arguments are integers.)

Cross out the old values and write the new ones under the old ones.

```
int n = 1729;
int sum = 0;
while (n > 0)
{
    int digit = n % 10;
    sum = sum + digit;
    n = n / 10;
}
System.out.println(sum);
```

| n | sum | digit |
|---|---|---|
| ~~1729~~ | ~~0~~ | |
| 172 | 9 | 9 |
| | | |
| | | |
| | | |

Now check the loop condition again.

```
int n = 1729;
int sum = 0;
while (n > 0)
{
    int digit = n % 10;
    sum = sum + digit;
    n = n / 10;
}
System.out.println(sum);
```

Because n is still greater than zero, repeat the loop. Now digit becomes 2, sum is set to $9 + 2 = 11$, and n is set to 17.

| n | sum | digit |
|---|---|---|
| ~~1729~~ | ~~0~~ | |
| ~~172~~ | ~~9~~ | ~~9~~ |
| 17 | 11 | 2 |
| | | |
| | | |

Repeat the loop once again, setting digit to 7, sum to $11 + 7 = 18$, and n to 1.

| n | sum | digit |
|---|---|---|
| ~~1729~~ | ~~0~~ | |
| ~~172~~ | ~~9~~ | ~~9~~ |
| ~~17~~ | ~~11~~ | ~~2~~ |
| 1 | 18 | 7 |
| | | |

Enter the loop for one last time. Now digit is set to 1, sum to 19, and n becomes zero.

| n | sum | digit |
|---|---|---|
| ~~1729~~ | ~~0~~ | |
| ~~172~~ | ~~9~~ | ~~9~~ |
| ~~17~~ | ~~11~~ | ~~2~~ |
| ~~1~~ | ~~18~~ | ~~7~~ |
| 0 | 19 | 1 |

```
        int n = 1729;
        int sum = 0;
  ⊂⊐    while (n > 0)
        {
            int digit = n % 10;
            sum = sum + digit;
            n = n / 10;
        }
        System.out.println(sum);
```

*Because n equals zero, this condition is not true.*

The condition n > 0 is now false. Continue with the statement after the loop.

```
        int n = 1729;
        int sum = 0;
        while (n > 0)
        {
            int digit = n % 10;
            sum = sum + digit;
            n = n / 10;
        }
  ⊂⊐    System.out.println(sum);
```

| n | sum | digit | output |
|---|-----|-------|--------|
| ~~1729~~ | ~~0~~ | | |
| ~~172~~ | ~~9~~ | ~~9~~ | |
| ~~17~~ | ~~11~~ | ~~2~~ | |
| ~~1~~ | ~~18~~ | ~~7~~ | |
| 0 | 19 | 1 | 19 |

**ANIMATION**
*Tracing a Loop*

This statement is an output statement. The value that is output is the value of sum, which is 19.

Of course, you can get the same answer by just running the code. However, hand-tracing can give you an *insight* that you would not get if you simply ran the code. Consider again what happens in each iteration:

- We extract the last digit of n.
- We add that digit to sum.
- We strip the digit off n.

**Hand-tracing can help you understand how an unfamiliar algorithm works.**

In other words, the loop forms the sum of the digits in n. You now know what the loop does for any value of n, not just the one in the example. (Why would anyone want to form the sum of the digits? Operations of this kind are useful for checking the validity of credit card numbers and other forms of ID numbers—see Exercise P4.32.)

**Hand-tracing can show errors in code or pseudocode.**

Hand-tracing does not just help you understand code that works correctly. It is a powerful technique for finding errors in your code. When a program behaves in a way that you don't expect, get out a sheet of paper and track the values of the variables as you mentally step through the code.

You don't need a working program to do hand-tracing. You can hand-trace pseudocode. In fact, it is an excellent idea to hand-trace your pseudocode before you go to the trouble of translating it into actual code, to confirm that it works correctly.

**SELF CHECK**

**6.** Hand-trace the following code, showing the value of n and the output.

```
int n = 5;
while (n >= 0)
{
    n--;
    System.out.print(n);
}
```

7. Hand-trace the following code, showing the value of n and the output. What potential error do you notice?

```java
int n = 1;
while (n <= 3)
{
    System.out.print(n + ", ");
    n++;
}
```

8. Hand-trace the following code, assuming that a is 2 and n is 4. Then explain what the code does for arbitrary values of a and n.

```java
int r = 1;
int i = 1;
while (i <= n)
{
    r = r * a;
    i++;
}
```

9. Trace the following code. What error do you observe?

```java
int n = 1;
while (n != 50)
{
    System.out.println(n);
    n = n + 10;
}
```

10. The following pseudocode is intended to count the number of digits in the number **n**:

    **count = 1**
    **temp = n**
    **while (temp > 10)**
        **Increment count.**
        **Divide temp by 10.0.**

    Trace the pseudocode for **n** = 123 and **n** = 100. What error do you find?

**Practice It**  Now you can try these exercises at the end of the chapter: R4.3, R4.6.

# 4.3 The for Loop

The for loop is used when a value runs from a starting point to an ending point with a constant increment or decrement.

It often happens that you want to execute a sequence of statements a given number of times. You can use a while loop that is controlled by a counter, as in the following example:

```java
int counter = 1; // Initialize the counter
while (counter <= 10) // Check the counter
{
    System.out.println(counter);
    counter++; // Update the counter
}
```

Because this loop type is so common, there is a special form for it, called the for loop (see Syntax 4.2).

```
for (int counter = 1; counter <= 10; counter++)
{
    System.out.println(counter);
}
```

Some people call this loop *count-controlled*. In contrast, the `while` loop of the preceding section can be called an *event-controlled* loop because it executes until an event occurs; namely that the balance reaches the target. Another commonly used term for a count-controlled loop is *definite*. You know from the outset that the loop body will be executed a definite number of times; ten times in our example. In contrast, you do not know how many iterations it takes to accumulate a target balance. Such a loop is called *indefinite*.

The `for` loop neatly groups the initialization, condition, and update expressions together. However, it is important to realize that these expressions are not executed together (see Figure 3).

*You can visualize the* for *loop as an orderly sequence of steps.*

ANIMATION
*The* for *Loop*

- The initialization is executed once, before the loop is entered. **1**
- The condition is checked before each iteration. **2 5**
- The update is executed after each iteration. **4**

---

**1** Initialize counter

counter = 1

```
for (int counter = 1; counter <= 10; counter++)
{
    System.out.println(counter);
}
```

**2** Check condition

counter = 1

```
for (int counter = 1; counter <= 10; counter++)
{
    System.out.println(counter);
}
```

**3** Execute loop body

counter = 1

```
for (int counter = 1; counter <= 10; counter++)
{
    System.out.println(counter);
}
```

**4** Update counter

counter = 2

```
for (int counter = 1; counter <= 10; counter++)
{
    System.out.println(counter);
}
```

**5** Check condition again

counter = 2

```
for (int counter = 1; counter <= 10; counter++)
{
    System.out.println(counter);
}
```

**Figure 3**
Execution of a
for Loop

## Syntax 4.2 for Statement

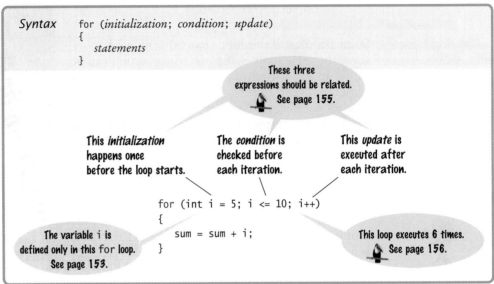

A for loop can count down instead of up:

```
for (int counter = 10; counter >= 0; counter--) . . .
```

The increment or decrement need not be in steps of 1:

```
for (int counter = 0; counter <= 10; counter = counter + 2) . . .
```

See Table 2 for additional variations.

So far, we have always declared the counter variable in the loop initialization:

```
for (int counter = 1; counter <= 10; counter++)
{
    . . .
}
// counter no longer declared here
```

### Table 2  for Loop Examples

| Loop | Values of i | Comment |
|------|-------------|---------|
| for (i = 0; i <= 5; i++) | 0 1 2 3 4 5 | Note that the loop is executed 6 times. (See Programming Tip 4.3 on page 156.) |
| for (i = 5; i >= 0; i--) | 5 4 3 2 1 0 | Use i-- for decreasing values. |
| for (i = 0; i < 9; i = i + 2) | 0 2 4 6 8 | Use i = i + 2 for a step size of 2. |
| for (i = 0; i != 9; i = i + 2) | 0 2 4 6 8 10 12 14 ... (infinite loop) | You can use < or <= instead of != to avoid this problem. |
| for (i = 1; i <= 20; i = i * 2) | 1 2 4 8 16 | You can specify any rule for modifying i, such as doubling it in every step. |
| for (i = 0; i < str.length(); i++) | 0 1 2 ... until the last valid index of the string str | In the loop body, use the expression str.charAt(i) to get the ith character. |

Such a variable is declared for all iterations of the loop, but you cannot use it after the loop. If you declare the counter variable before the loop, you can continue to use it after the loop:

```
int counter;
for (counter = 1; counter <= 10; counter++)
{
   . . .
}
// counter still declared here
```

Here is a typical use of the for loop. We want to print the balance of our savings account over a period of years, as shown in this table:

| Year | Balance |
|------|---------|
| 1 | 10500.00 |
| 2 | 11025.00 |
| 3 | 11576.25 |
| 4 | 12155.06 |
| 5 | 12762.82 |

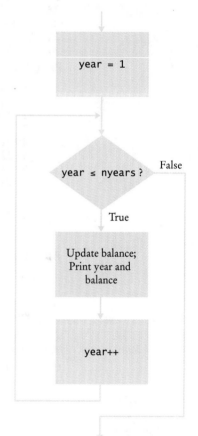

The for loop pattern applies because the variable year starts at 1 and then moves in constant increments until it reaches the target:

```
for (int year = 1; year <= nyears; year++)
{
    Update balance.
    Print year and balance.
}
```

Following is the complete program. Figure 4 shows the corresponding flowchart.

**Figure 4**   Flowchart of a for Loop

**section_3/InvestmentTable.java**

```
1   import java.util.Scanner;
2
3   /**
4      This program prints a table showing the growth of an investment.
5   */
6   public class InvestmentTable
7   {
8      public static void main(String[] args)
9      {
10        final double RATE = 5;
11        final double INITIAL_BALANCE = 10000;
```

```
12          double balance = INITIAL_BALANCE;
13
14          System.out.print("Enter number of years: ");
15          Scanner in = new Scanner(System.in);
16          int nyears = in.nextInt();
17
18          // Print the table of balances for each year
19
20          for (int year = 1; year <= nyears; year++)
21          {
22             double interest = balance * RATE / 100;
23             balance = balance + interest;
24             System.out.printf("%4d %10.2f\n", year, balance);
25          }
26       }
27    }
```

**Program Run**

```
Enter number of years: 10
   1   10500.00
   2   11025.00
   3   11576.25
   4   12155.06
   5   12762.82
   6   13400.96
   7   14071.00
   8   14774.55
   9   15513.28
  10   16288.95
```

Another common use of the for loop is to traverse all characters of a string:

```
for (int i = 0; i < str.length(); i++)
{
   char ch = str.charAt(i);
   Process ch
}
```

Note that the counter variable i starts at 0, and the loop is terminated when i reaches the length of the string. For example, if str has length 5, i takes on the values 0, 1, 2, 3, and 4. These are the valid positions in the string.

SELF CHECK

**11.** Write the for loop of the InvestmentTable.java program as a while loop.

**12.** How many numbers does this loop print?

```
for (int n = 10; n >= 0; n--)
{
   System.out.println(n);
}
```

**13.** Write a for loop that prints all even numbers between 10 and 20 (inclusive).

**14.** Write a for loop that computes the sum of the integers from 1 to n.

**15.** How would you modify the for loop of the InvestmentTable.java program to print all balances until the investment has doubled?

**Practice It**    Now you can try these exercises at the end of the chapter: R4.4, R4.10, P4.8, P4.13.

Programming Tip 4.1

### Use for Loops for Their Intended Purpose Only

A for loop is an *idiom* for a loop of a particular form. A value runs from the start to the end, with a constant increment or decrement.

The compiler won't check whether the initialization, condition, and update expressions are related. For example, the following loop is legal:

```java
// Confusing—unrelated expressions
for (System.out.print("Inputs: "); in.hasNextDouble(); sum = sum + x)
{
    x = in.nextDouble();
}
```

However, programmers reading such a for loop will be confused because it does not match their expectations. Use a while loop for iterations that do not follow the for idiom.

You should also be careful not to update the loop counter in the body of a for loop. Consider the following example:

```java
for (int counter = 1; counter <= 100; counter++)
{
    if (counter % 10 == 0) // Skip values that are divisible by 10
    {
        counter++; // Bad style—you should not update the counter in a for loop
    }
    System.out.println(counter);
}
```

Updating the counter inside a for loop is confusing because the counter is updated *again* at the end of the loop iteration. In some loop iterations, counter is incremented once, in others twice. This goes against the intuition of a programmer who sees a for loop.

If you find yourself in this situation, you can either change from a for loop to a while loop, or implement the "skipping" behavior in another way. For example:

```java
for (int counter = 1; counter <= 100; counter++)
{
    if (counter % 10 != 0) // Skip values that are divisible by 10
    {
        System.out.println(counter);
    }
}
```

Programming Tip 4.2

### Choose Loop Bounds That Match Your Task

Suppose you want to print line numbers that go from 1 to 10. Of course, you will use a loop:

```java
for (int i = 1; i <= 10; i++)
```

The values for i are bounded by the relation $1 \leq i \leq 10$. Because there are $\leq$ on both bounds, the bounds are called **symmetric**.

When traversing the characters in a string, it is more natural to use the bounds

```java
for (int i = 0; i < str.length(); i++)
```

In this loop, i traverses all valid positions in the string. You can access the ith character as str.charAt(i). The values for i are bounded by $0 \leq i < str.length()$, with a $\leq$ to the left and a $<$ to the right. That is appropriate, because str.length() is not a valid position. Such bounds are called **asymmetric**.

In this case, it is not a good idea to use symmetric bounds:

```java
for (int i = 0; i <= str.length() - 1; i++) // Use < instead
```

The asymmetric form is easier to understand.

### Count Iterations

Finding the correct lower and upper bounds for an iteration can be confusing. Should you start at 0 or at 1? Should you use <= b or < b as a termination condition?

Counting the number of iterations is a very useful device for better understanding a loop. Counting is easier for loops with asymmetric bounds. The loop

```
for (int i = a; i < b; i++)
```

is executed b - a times. For example, the loop traversing the characters in a string,

```
for (int i = 0; i < str.length(); i++)
```

runs str.length() times. That makes perfect sense, because there are str.length() characters in a string.

The loop with symmetric bounds,

```
for (int i = a; i <= b; i++)
```

is executed b - a + 1 times. That "+1" is the source of many programming errors.

For example,

```
for (int i = 0; i <= 10; i++)
```

runs 11 times. Maybe that is what you want; if not, start at 1 or use < 10.

One way to visualize this "+1" error is by looking at a fence. Each section has one fence post to the left, and there is a final post on the right of the last section. Forgetting to count the last value is often called a "fence post error".

*How many posts do you need for a fence with four sections? It is easy to be "off by one" with problems such as this one.*

# 4.4 The do Loop

Sometimes you want to execute the body of a loop at least once and perform the loop test after the body is executed. The do loop serves that purpose:

```
do
{
    statements
}
while (condition);
```

The body of the do loop is executed first, then the condition is tested.

Some people call such a loop a *post-test loop* because the condition is tested after completing the loop body. In contrast, while and for loops are *pre-test loops*. In those loop types, the condition is tested before entering the loop body.

A typical example for a do loop is input validation. Suppose you ask a user to enter a value < 100. If the user doesn't pay attention and enters a larger value, you ask again, until the value is correct. Of course, you cannot test the value until the user has entered it. This is a perfect fit for the do loop (see Figure 5):

**Figure 5**   Flowchart of a do Loop

```java
int value;
do
{
   System.out.print("Enter an integer < 100: ");
   value = in.nextInt();
}
while (value >= 100);
```

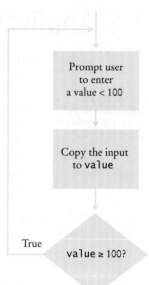

**16.** Suppose that we want to check for inputs that are at least 0 and at most 100. Modify the do loop for this check.

**17.** Rewrite the input check do loop using a while loop. What is the disadvantage of your solution?

**18.** Suppose Java didn't have a do loop. Could you rewrite any do loop as a while loop?

**19.** Write a do loop that reads integers and computes their sum. Stop when reading the value 0.

**20.** Write a do loop that reads integers and computes their sum. Stop when reading a zero or the same value twice in a row. For example, if the input is 1 2 3 4 4, then the sum is 14 and the loop stops.

**Practice It**   Now you can try these exercises at the end of the chapter: R4.9, R4.16, R4.17.

---

### Flowcharts for Loops

In Section 3.5, you learned how to use flowcharts to visualize the flow of control in a program. There are two types of loops that you can include in a flowchart; they correspond to a while loop and a do loop in Java. They differ in the placement of the condition—either before or after the loop body.

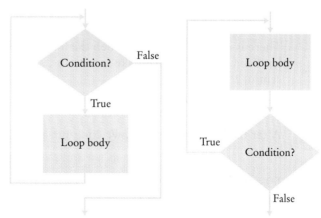

As described in Section 3.5, you want to avoid "spaghetti code" in your flowcharts. For loops, that means that you never want to have an arrow that points inside a loop body.

# 4.5 Application: Processing Sentinel Values

A sentinel value denotes the end of a data set, but it is not part of the data.

In this section, you will learn how to write loops that read and process a sequence of input values.

Whenever you read a sequence of inputs, you need to have some method of indicating the end of the sequence. Sometimes you are lucky and no input value can be zero. Then you can prompt the user to keep entering numbers, or 0 to finish the sequence. If zero is allowed but negative numbers are not, you can use –1 to indicate termination.

Such a value, which is not an actual input, but serves as a signal for termination, is called a **sentinel**.

Let's put this technique to work in a program that computes the average of a set of salary values. In our sample program, we will use –1 as a sentinel. An employee would surely not work for a negative salary, but there may be volunteers who work for free.

Inside the loop, we read an input. If the input is not –1, we process it. In order to compute the average, we need the total sum of all salaries, and the number of inputs.

*In the military, a sentinel guards a border or passage. In computer science, a sentinel value denotes the end of an input sequence or the border between input sequences.*

```java
salary = in.nextDouble();
if (salary != -1)
{
    sum = sum + salary;
    count++;
}
```

We stay in the loop while the sentinel value is not detected.

```java
while (salary != -1)
{
    . . .
}
```

There is just one problem: When the loop is entered for the first time, no data value has been read. We must make sure to initialize salary with some value other than the sentinel:

```java
double salary = 0;
// Any value other than -1 will do
```

After the loop has finished, we compute and print the average. Here is the complete program:

### section_5/SentinelDemo.java

```java
1   import java.util.Scanner;
2
3   /**
4      This program prints the average of salary values that are terminated with a sentinel.
5   */
```

```
 6  public class SentinelDemo
 7  {
 8     public static void main(String[] args)
 9     {
10        double sum = 0;
11        int count = 0;
12        double salary = 0;
13        System.out.print("Enter salaries, -1 to finish: ");
14        Scanner in = new Scanner(System.in);
15
16        // Process data until the sentinel is entered
17
18        while (salary != -1)
19        {
20           salary = in.nextDouble();
21           if (salary != -1)
22           {
23              sum = sum + salary;
24              count++;
25           }
26        }
27
28        // Compute and print the average
29
30        if (count > 0)
31        {
32           double average = sum / count;
33           System.out.println("Average salary: " + average);
34        }
35        else
36        {
37           System.out.println("No data");
38        }
39     }
40  }
```

**Program Run**

```
Enter salaries, -1 to finish: 10 10 40 -1
Average salary: 20
```

You can use a Boolean variable to control a loop. Set the variable before entering the loop, then set it to the opposite to leave the loop.

Some programmers don't like the "trick" of initializing the input variable with a value other than the sentinel. Another approach is to use a Boolean variable:

```
System.out.print("Enter salaries, -1 to finish: ");
boolean done = false;
while (!done)
{
   value = in.nextDouble();
   if (value == -1)
   {
      done = true;
   }
   else
   {
      Process value.
   }
}
```

Special Topic 4.1 on page 160 shows an alternative mechanism for leaving such a loop.

Now consider the case in which any number (positive, negative, or zero) can be an acceptable input. In such a situation, you must use a sentinel that is not a number (such as the letter Q). As you have seen in Section 3.8, the condition

```
in.hasNextDouble()
```

is `false` if the next input is not a floating-point number. Therefore, you can read and process a set of inputs with the following loop:

```
System.out.print("Enter values, Q to quit: ");
while (in.hasNextDouble())
{
    value = in.nextDouble();
    Process value.
}
```

**SELF CHECK**

**21.** What does the `SentinelDemo.java` program print when the user immediately types −1 when prompted for a value?

**22.** Why does the `SentinelDemo.java` program have *two* checks of the form

```
salary != -1
```

**23.** What would happen if the declaration of the `salary` variable in `SentinelDemo.java` was changed to

```
double salary = -1;
```

**24.** In the last example of this section, we prompt the user "Enter values, Q to quit." What happens when the user enters a different letter?

**25.** What is wrong with the following loop for reading a sequence of values?

```
System.out.print("Enter values, Q to quit: ");
do
{
    double value = in.nextDouble();
    sum = sum + value;
    count++;
}
while (in.hasNextDouble());
```

**Practice It**    Now you can try these exercises at the end of the chapter: R4.13, P4.27, P4.28.

---

Special Topic 4.1

### The Loop-and-a-Half Problem and the break Statement

Consider again this loop for processing inputs until a sentinel value has been reached:

```
boolean done = false;
while (!done)
{
    double value = in.nextDouble();
    if (value == -1)
    {
        done = true;
    }
    else
    {
        Process value.
    }
}
```

The actual test for loop termination is in the middle of the loop, not at the top. This is called a **loop and a half** because one must go halfway into the loop before knowing whether one needs to terminate.

As an alternative, you can use the break reserved word.

```
while (true)
{
   double value = in.nextDouble();
   if (value == -1) { break; }
   Process value.
}
```

The break statement breaks out of the enclosing loop, independent of the loop condition. When the break statement is encountered, the loop is terminated, and the statement following the loop is executed.

In the loop-and-a-half case, break statements can be beneficial. But it is difficult to lay down clear rules as to when they are safe and when they should be avoided. We do not use the break statement in this book.

---

Special Topic 4.2

### Redirection of Input and Output

Consider the SentinelDemo program that computes the average value of an input sequence. If you use such a program, then it is quite likely that you already have the values in a file, and it seems a shame that you have to type them all in again. The command line interface of your operating system provides a way to link a file to the input of a program, as if all the characters in the file had actually been typed by a user. If you type

> Use input redirection to read input from a file. Use output redirection to capture program output in a file.

```
java SentinelDemo < numbers.txt
```

the program is executed, but it no longer expects input from the keyboard. All input commands get their input from the file numbers.txt. This process is called *input redirection*.

Input redirection is an excellent tool for testing programs. When you develop a program and fix its bugs, it is boring to keep entering the same input every time you run the program. Spend a few minutes putting the inputs into a file, and use redirection.

You can also redirect output. In this program, that is not terribly useful. If you run

```
java SentinelDemo < numbers.txt > output.txt
```

the file output.txt contains the input prompts and the output, such as

```
Enter salaries, -1 to finish: Enter salaries, -1 to finish:
Enter salaries, -1 to finish: Enter salaries, -1 to finish:
Average salary: 15
```

However, redirecting output is obviously useful for programs that produce lots of output. You can format or print the file containing the output.

---

VIDEO EXAMPLE 4.1

### Evaluating a Cell Phone Plan

In this Video Example, you will learn how to design a program that computes the cost of a cell phone plan from actual usage data.

 Available online in WileyPLUS and at www.wiley.com/college/horstmann.

# 4.6 Problem Solving: Storyboards

When you design a program that interacts with a user, you need to make a plan for that interaction. What information does the user provide, and in which order? What information will your program display, and in which format? What should happen when there is an error? When does the program quit?

> A storyboard consists of annotated sketches for each step in an action sequence.

This planning is similar to the development of a movie or a computer game, where *storyboards* are used to plan action sequences. A storyboard is made up of panels that show a sketch of each step. Annotations explain what is happening and note any special situations. Storyboards are also used to develop software—see Figure 6.

Making a storyboard is very helpful when you begin designing a program. You need to ask yourself which information you need in order to compute the answers that the program user wants. You need to decide how to present those answers. These are important considerations that you want to settle before you design an algorithm for computing the answers.

> Developing a storyboard helps you understand the inputs and outputs that are required for a program.

Let's look at a simple example. We want to write a program that helps users with questions such as "How many tablespoons are in a pint?" or "How many inches are 30 centimeters?"

What information does the user provide?

- The quantity and unit to convert from
- The unit to convert to

What if there is more than one quantity? A user may have a whole table of centimeter values that should be converted into inches.

What if the user enters units that our program doesn't know how to handle, such as ångström?

What if the user asks for impossible conversions, such as inches to gallons?

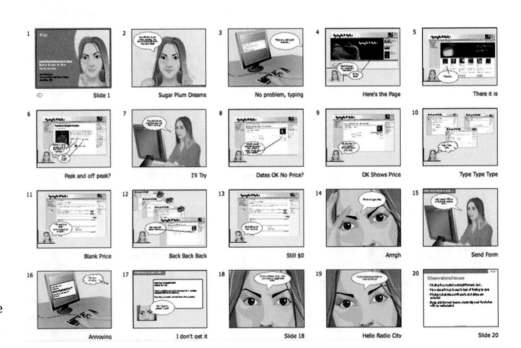

**Figure 6**
Storyboard for the Design of a Web Application

Let's get started with a storyboard panel. It is a good idea to write the user inputs in a different color. (Underline them if you don't have a color pen handy.)

---

**Converting a Sequence of Values**

What unit do you want to convert from? cm
What unit do you want to convert to? in
Enter values, terminated by zero ———————— Allows conversion of multiple values
30
30 cm = 11.81 in ————
100                    └—— Format makes clear what got converted
100 cm = 39.37 in
0
What unit do you want to convert from?

---

The storyboard shows how we deal with a potential confusion. A user who wants to know how many inches are 30 centimeters may not read the first prompt carefully and specify inches. But then the output is "30 in = 76.2 cm", alerting the user to the problem.

The storyboard also raises an issue. How is the user supposed to know that "cm" and "in" are valid units? Would "centimeter" and "inches" also work? What happens when the user enters a wrong unit? Let's make another storyboard to demonstrate error handling.

---

**Handling Unknown Units (needs improvement)**

What unit do you want to convert from? cm
What unit do you want to convert to? inches
Sorry, unknown unit.
What unit do you want to convert to? inch
Sorry, unknown unit.
What unit do you want to convert to? grrr

---

To eliminate frustration, it is better to list the units that the user can supply.

---

From unit (in, ft, mi, mm, cm, m, km, oz, lb, g, kg, tsp, tbsp, pint, gall): cm
To unit: in ————
           └—— No need to list the units again

---

We switched to a shorter prompt to make room for all the unit names. Exercise R4.21 explores a different alternative.

There is another issue that we haven't addressed yet. How does the user quit the program? The first storyboard suggests that the program will go on forever.

We can ask the user after seeing the sentinel that terminates an input sequence.

> **Exiting the Program**
>
> From unit (in, ft, mi, mm, cm, m, km, oz, lb, g, kg, tsp, tbsp, pint, gal): cm
> To unit: in
> Enter values, terminated by zero
> 30
> 30 cm = 11.81 in
> 0 ———————————— Sentinel triggers the prompt to exit
> More conversions (y, n)? n
> (Program exits)

As you can see from this case study, a storyboard is essential for developing a working program. You need to know the flow of the user interaction in order to structure your program.

**SELF CHECK**

**26.** Provide a storyboard panel for a program that reads a number of test scores and prints the average score. The program only needs to process one set of scores. Don't worry about error handling.

**27.** Google has a simple interface for converting units. You just type the question, and you get the answer.

Make storyboards for an equivalent interface in a Java program. Show a scenario in which all goes well, and show the handling of two kinds of errors.

**28.** Consider a modification of the program in Self Check 26. Suppose we want to drop the lowest score before computing the average. Provide a storyboard for the situation in which a user only provides one score.

**29.** What is the problem with implementing the following storyboard in Java?

> **Computing Multiple Averages**
>
> Enter scores: 90 80 90 100 80
> The average is 88
> Enter scores: 100 70 70 100 80
> The average is 88
> Enter scores: -1 ———————— -1 is used as a sentinel to exit the program
> (Program exits)

**30.** Produce a storyboard for a program that compares the growth of a $10,000 investment for a given number of years under two interest rates.

**Practice It** Now you can try these exercises at the end of the chapter: R4.21, R4.22, R4.23.

# 4.7  Common Loop Algorithms

In the following sections, we discuss some of the most common algorithms that are implemented as loops. You can use them as starting points for your loop designs.

## 4.7.1  Sum and Average Value

To compute an average, keep a total and a count of all values.

Computing the sum of a number of inputs is a very common task. Keep a *running total*, a variable to which you add each input value. Of course, the total should be initialized with 0.

```
double total = 0;
while (in.hasNextDouble())
{
    double input = in.nextDouble();
    total = total + input;
}
```

Note that the total variable is declared outside the loop. We want the loop to update a single variable. The input variable is declared inside the loop. A separate variable is created for each input and removed at the end of each loop iteration.

To compute an average, count how many values you have, and divide by the count. Be sure to check that the count is not zero.

```
double total = 0;
int count = 0;
while (in.hasNextDouble())
{
    double input = in.nextDouble();
    total = total + input;
    count++;
}
double average = 0;
if (count > 0)
{
    average = total / count;
}
```

## 4.7.2  Counting Matches

To count values that fulfill a condition, check all values and increment a counter for each match.

You often want to know how many values fulfill a particular condition. For example, you may want to count how many spaces are in a string. Keep a *counter*, a variable that is initialized with 0 and incremented whenever there is a match.

```
int spaces = 0;
for (int i = 0; i < str.length(); i++)
{
    char ch = str.charAt(i);
    if (ch == ' ')
    {
        spaces++;
    }
}
```

For example, if str is "My Fair Lady", spaces is incremented twice (when i is 2 and 7).

Note that the spaces variable is declared outside the loop. We want the loop to update a single variable. The ch variable is declared inside the loop. A separate variable is created for each iteration and removed at the end of each loop iteration.

This loop can also be used for scanning inputs. The following loop reads text, a word at a time, and counts the number of words with at most three letters:

```java
int shortWords = 0;
while (in.hasNext())
{
    String input = in.next();
    if (input.length() <= 3)
    {
        shortWords++;
    }
}
```

*In a loop that counts matches, a counter is incremented whenever a match is found.*

### 4.7.3 Finding the First Match

**If your goal is to find a match, exit the loop when the match is found.**

When you count the values that fulfill a condition, you need to look at all values. However, if your task is to find a match, then you can stop as soon as the condition is fulfilled.

Here is a loop that finds the first space in a string. Because we do not visit all elements in the string, a while loop is a better choice than a for loop:

```java
boolean found = false;
char ch = '?';
int position = 0;
while (!found && position < str.length())
{
    ch = str.charAt(position);
    if (ch == ' ') { found = true; }
    else { position++; }
}
```

If a match was found, then found is true, ch is the first matching character, and position is the index of the first match. If the loop did not find a match, then found remains false after the end of the loop.

Note that the variable ch is declared *outside* the while loop because you may want to use the input after the loop has finished. If it had been declared inside the loop body, you would not be able to use it outside the loop.

*When searching, you look at items until a match is found.*

### 4.7.4 Prompting Until a Match is Found

In the preceding example, we searched a string for a character that matches a condition. You can apply the same process to user input. Suppose you are asking a user to enter a positive value < 100. Keep asking until the user provides a correct input:

```java
boolean valid = false;
double input = 0;
while (!valid)
{
   System.out.print("Please enter a positive value < 100: ");
   input = in.nextDouble();
   if (0 < input && input < 100) { valid = true; }
   else { System.out.println("Invalid input."); }
}
```

Note that the variable input is declared *outside* the while loop because you will want to use the input after the loop has finished.

### 4.7.5 Maximum and Minimum

To find the largest value, update the largest value seen so far whenever you see a larger one.

To compute the largest value in a sequence, keep a variable that stores the largest element that you have encountered, and update it when you find a larger one.

```java
double largest = in.nextDouble();
while (in.hasNextDouble())
{
   double input = in.nextDouble();
   if (input > largest)
   {
      largest = input;
   }
}
```

This algorithm requires that there is at least one input.

To compute the smallest value, simply reverse the comparison:

```java
double smallest = in.nextDouble();
while (in.hasNextDouble())
{
   double input = in.nextDouble();
   if (input < smallest)
   {
      smallest = input;
   }
}
```

*To find the height of the tallest bus rider, remember the largest value so far, and update it whenever you see a taller one.*

### 4.7.6 Comparing Adjacent Values

To compare adjacent inputs, store the preceding input in a variable.

When processing a sequence of values in a loop, you sometimes need to compare a value with the value that just preceded it. For example, suppose you want to check whether a sequence of inputs contains adjacent duplicates such as 1 7 2 9 9 4 9.

Now you face a challenge. Consider the typical loop for reading a value:

```
double input;
while (in.hasNextDouble())
{
    input = in.nextDouble();
    . . .
}
```

How can you compare the current input with the preceding one? At any time, `input` contains the current input, overwriting the previous one.

The answer is to store the previous input, like this:

```
double input = 0;
while (in.hasNextDouble())
{
    double previous = input;
    input = in.nextDouble();
    if (input == previous)
    {
        System.out.println("Duplicate input");
    }
}
```

*When comparing adjacent values, store the previous value in a variable.*

One problem remains. When the loop is entered for the first time, `input` has not yet been read. You can solve this problem with an initial input operation outside the loop:

```
double input = in.nextDouble();
while (in.hasNextDouble())
{
    double previous = input;
    input = in.nextDouble();
    if (input == previous)
    {
        System.out.println("Duplicate input");
    }
}
```

**ONLINE EXAMPLE**

A program using common loop algorithms.

**SELF CHECK**

31. What total is computed when no user input is provided in the algorithm in Section 4.7.1?

32. How do you compute the total of all positive inputs?

33. What are the values of `position` and `ch` when no match is found in the algorithm in Section 4.7.3?

34. What is wrong with the following loop for finding the position of the first space in a string?

```
boolean found = false;
for (int position = 0; !found && position < str.length(); position++)
{
```

```
        char ch = str.charAt(position);
        if (ch == ' ') { found = true; }
    }
```

**35.** How do you find the position of the *last* space in a string?

**36.** What happens with the algorithm in Section 4.7.5 when no input is provided at all? How can you overcome that problem?

**Practice It**   Now you can try these exercises at the end of the chapter: P4.5, P4.9, P4.10.

---

**HOW TO 4.1**

### Writing a Loop

This How To walks you through the process of implementing a loop statement. We will illustrate the steps with the following example problem:

Read twelve temperature values (one for each month), and display the number of the month with the highest temperature. For example, according to http://worldclimate.com, the average maximum temperatures for Death Valley are (in order by month, in degrees Celsius):

18.2  22.6  26.4  31.1  36.6  42.2  45.7  44.5  40.2  33.1  24.2  17.6

In this case, the month with the highest temperature (45.7 degrees Celsius) is July, and the program should display 7.

**Step 1**   Decide what work must be done *inside* the loop.

Every loop needs to do some kind of repetitive work, such as

- Reading another item.
- Updating a value (such as a bank balance or total).
- Incrementing a counter.

If you can't figure out what needs to go inside the loop, start by writing down the steps that you would take if you solved the problem by hand. For example, with the temperature reading problem, you might write

**Read first value.**
**Read second value.**
**If second value is higher than the first, set highest temperature to that value, highest month to 2.**
**Read next value.**
**If value is higher than the first and second, set highest temperature to that value, highest month to 3.**
**Read next value.**
**If value is higher than the highest temperature seen so far, set highest temperature to that value,**
**highest month to 4.**
. . .

Now look at these steps and reduce them to a set of *uniform* actions that can be placed into the loop body. The first action is easy:

**Read next value.**

The next action is trickier. In our description, we used tests "higher than the first", "higher than the first and second", "higher than the highest temperature seen so far". We need to settle on one test that works for all iterations. The last formulation is the most general.

Similarly, we must find a general way of setting the highest month. We need a variable that stores the current month, running from 1 to 12. Then we can formulate the second loop action:

**If value is higher than the highest temperature, set highest temperature to that value, highest month to current month.**

Altogether our loop is

**Repeat**
**Read next value.**
**If value is higher than the highest temperature,**
**set highest temperature to that value,**
**set highest month to current month.**
**Increment current month.**

**Step 2**  Specify the loop condition.

What goal do you want to reach in your loop? Typical examples are

- Has a counter reached its final value?

- Have you read the last input value?

- Has a value reached a given threshold?

In our example, we simply want the current month to reach 12.

**Step 3**  Determine the loop type.

We distinguish between two major loop types. A *count-controlled* loop is executed a definite number of times. In an *event-controlled* loop, the number of iterations is not known in advance—the loop is executed until some event happens.

Count-controlled loops can be implemented as for statements. For other loops, consider the loop condition. Do you need to complete one iteration of the loop body before you can tell when to terminate the loop? In that case, choose a do loop. Otherwise, use a while loop.

Sometimes, the condition for terminating a loop changes in the middle of the loop body. In that case, you can use a Boolean variable that specifies when you are ready to leave the loop. Follow this pattern:

```
boolean done = false;
while (!done)
{
    Do some work.
    If all work has been completed
    {
        done = true;
    }
    else
    {
        Do more work.
    }
}
```

Such a variable is called a **flag**.

In summary,

- If you know in advance how many times a loop is repeated, use a for loop.

- If the loop body must be executed at least once, use a do loop.

- Otherwise, use a while loop.

In our example, we read 12 temperature values. Therefore, we choose a for loop.

**Step 4**  Set up variables for entering the loop for the first time.

List all variables that are used and updated in the loop, and determine how to initialize them. Commonly, counters are initialized with 0 or 1, totals with 0.

In our example, the variables are

```
current month
highest value
highest month
```

We need to be careful how we set up the highest temperature value. We can't simply set it to 0. After all, our program needs to work with temperature values from Antarctica, all of which may be negative.

A good option is to set the highest temperature value to the first input value. Of course, then we need to remember to read in only 11 more values, with the current month starting at 2.

We also need to initialize the highest month with 1. After all, in an Australian city, we may never find a month that is warmer than January.

**Step 5** Process the result after the loop has finished.

In many cases, the desired result is simply a variable that was updated in the loop body. For example, in our temperature program, the result is the highest month. Sometimes, the loop computes values that contribute to the final result. For example, suppose you are asked to average the temperatures. Then the loop should compute the sum, not the average. After the loop has completed, you are ready to compute the average: divide the sum by the number of inputs.

Here is our complete loop.

```
Read first value; store as highest value.
highest month = 1
For current month from 2 to 12
    Read next value.
    If value is higher than the highest value
        Set highest value to that value.
        Set highest month to current month.
```

**Step 6** Trace the loop with typical examples.

Hand trace your loop code, as described in Section 4.2. Choose example values that are not too complex—executing the loop 3–5 times is enough to check for the most common errors. Pay special attention when entering the loop for the first and last time.

Sometimes, you want to make a slight modification to make tracing feasible. For example, when hand-tracing the investment doubling problem, use an interest rate of 20 percent rather than 5 percent. When hand-tracing the temperature loop, use 4 data values, not 12.

Let's say the data are 22.6  36.6  44.5  24.2. Here is the walkthrough:

| current month | current value | highest month | highest value |
|---------------|---------------|---------------|---------------|
|               |               | ~~1~~         | ~~22.6~~      |
| ~~2~~         | ~~36.6~~      | ~~2~~         | ~~36.6~~      |
| ~~3~~         | ~~44.5~~      | 3             | 44.5          |
| 4             | 24.2          |               |               |

The trace demonstrates that **highest month** and **highest value** are properly set.

**Step 7** Implement the loop in Java.

Here's the loop for our example. Exercise P4.4 asks you to complete the program.

```java
double highestValue;
highestValue = in.nextDouble();
int highestMonth = 1;
```

```
for (int currentMonth = 2; currentMonth <= 12; currentMonth++)
{
   double nextValue = in.nextDouble();
   if (nextValue > highestValue)
   {
      highestValue = nextValue;
      highestMonth = currentMonth;
   }
}
System.out.println(highestMonth);
```

WORKED EXAMPLE 4.1    **Credit Card Processing**

This Worked Example uses a loop to remove spaces from a credit card number.

# 4.8 Nested Loops

> When the body of a loop contains another loop, the loops are nested. A typical use of nested loops is printing a table with rows and columns.

In Section 3.4, you saw how to nest two if statements. Similarly, complex iterations sometimes require a **nested loop**: a loop inside another loop statement. When processing tables, nested loops occur naturally. An outer loop iterates over all rows of the table. An inner loop deals with the columns in the current row.

In this section you will see how to print a table. For simplicity, we will simply print the powers of $x$, $x^n$, as in the table at right.

Here is the pseudocode for printing the table:

**Print table header.**
**For x from 1 to 10**
    **Print table row.**
    **Print new line.**

| $x^1$ | $x^2$ | $x^3$ | $x^4$ |
|---|---|---|---|
| 1 | 1 | 1 | 1 |
| 2 | 4 | 8 | 16 |
| 3 | 9 | 27 | 81 |
| ... | ... | ... | ... |
| 10 | 100 | 1000 | 10000 |

How do you print a table row? You need to print a value for each exponent. This requires a second loop.

**For n from 1 to 4**
    **Print $x^n$.**

This loop must be placed inside the preceding loop. We say that the inner loop is *nested* inside the outer loop.

*The hour and minute displays in a digital clock are an example of nested loops. The hours loop 12 times, and for each hour, the minutes loop 60 times.*

➕ Available online in WileyPLUS and at *www.wiley.com/college/horstmann*.

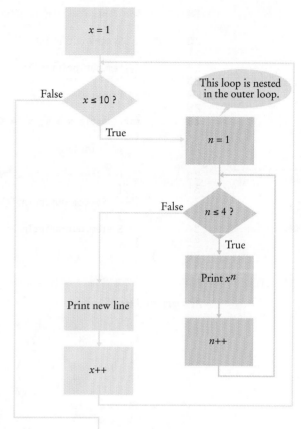

**Figure 7**
Flowchart of a Nested Loop

There are 10 rows in the outer loop. For each *x*, the program prints four columns in the inner loop (see Figure 7). Thus, a total of 10 × 4 = 40 values are printed.

Following is the complete program. Note that we also use loops to print the table header. However, those loops are not nested.

**section_8/PowerTable.java**

```
1   /**
2       This program prints a table of powers of x.
3   */
4   public class PowerTable
5   {
6       public static void main(String[] args)
7       {
8           final int NMAX = 4;
9           final double XMAX = 10;
10
11          // Print table header
12
13          for (int n = 1; n <= NMAX; n++)
14          {
15              System.out.printf("%10d", n);
16          }
17          System.out.println();
```

```
18       for (int n = 1; n <= NMAX; n++)
19       {
20          System.out.printf("%10s", "x ");
21       }
22       System.out.println();
23
24       // Print table body
25
26       for (double x = 1; x <= XMAX; x++)
27       {
28          // Print table row
29
30          for (int n = 1; n <= NMAX; n++)
31          {
32             System.out.printf("%10.0f", Math.pow(x, n));
33          }
34          System.out.println();
35       }
36    }
37 }
```

**Program Run**

|   1 |    2 |    3 |     4 |
|-----|------|------|-------|
|   x |    x |    x |     x |
|     |      |      |       |
|   1 |    1 |    1 |     1 |
|   2 |    4 |    8 |    16 |
|   3 |    9 |   27 |    81 |
|   4 |   16 |   64 |   256 |
|   5 |   25 |  125 |   625 |
|   6 |   36 |  216 |  1296 |
|   7 |   49 |  343 |  2401 |
|   8 |   64 |  512 |  4096 |
|   9 |   81 |  729 |  6561 |
|  10 |  100 | 1000 | 10000 |

**SELF CHECK**

**37.** Why is there a statement `System.out.println();` in the outer loop but not in the inner loop?

**38.** How would you change the program to display all powers from $x^0$ to $x^5$?

**39.** If you make the change in Self Check 38, how many values are displayed?

**40.** What do the following nested loops display?

```
for (int i = 0; i < 3; i++)
{
   for (int j = 0; j < 4; j++)
   {
      System.out.print(i + j);
   }
   System.out.println();
}
```

**41.** Write nested loops that make the following pattern of brackets:

```
[][][][]
[][][][]
[][][][]
```

**Practice It**    Now you can try these exercises at the end of the chapter: R4.27, P4.19, P4.21.

| Table 3   Nested Loop Examples | | |
|---|---|---|
| Nested Loops | Output | Explanation |
| ```for (i = 1; i <= 3; i++)<br>{<br>   for (j = 1; j <= 4; j++)  { Print "*" }<br>   System.out.println();<br>}``` | ```****<br>****<br>****``` | Prints 3 rows of 4 asterisks each. |
| ```for (i = 1; i <= 4; i++)<br>{<br>   for (j = 1; j <= 3; j++) { Print "*" }<br>   System.out.println();<br>}``` | ```***<br>***<br>***<br>***``` | Prints 4 rows of 3 asterisks each. |
| ```for (i = 1; i <= 4; i++)<br>{<br>   for (j = 1; j <= i; j++) { Print "*" }<br>   System.out.println();<br>}``` | ```*<br>**<br>***<br>****``` | Prints 4 rows of lengths 1, 2, 3, and 4. |
| ```for (i = 1; i <= 3; i++)<br>{<br>   for (j = 1; j <= 5; j++)<br>   {<br>      if (j % 2 == 0) { Print "*" }<br>      else { Print "-" }<br>   }<br>   System.out.println();<br>}``` | ```-*-*-<br>-*-*-<br>-*-*-``` | Prints asterisks in even columns, dashes in odd columns. |
| ```for (i = 1; i <= 3; i++)<br>{<br>   for (j = 1; j <= 5; j++)<br>   {<br>      if (i % 2 == j % 2) { Print "*" }<br>      else { Print " " }<br>   }<br>   System.out.println();<br>}``` | ```* * *<br> * *<br>* * *``` | Prints a checkerboard pattern. |

**WORKED EXAMPLE 4.2**    **Manipulating the Pixels in an Image**

This Worked Example shows how to use nested loops for manipulating the pixels in an image. The outer loop traverses the rows of the image, and the inner loop accesses each pixel of a row.

# 4.9 Application: Random Numbers and Simulations

*In a simulation, you use the computer to simulate an activity.*

A *simulation program* uses the computer to simulate an activity in the real world (or an imaginary one). Simulations are commonly used for predicting climate change, analyzing traffic, picking stocks, and many other applications in science and business. In many simulations, one or more loops are used to modify the state of a system and observe the changes. You will see examples in the following sections.

## 4.9.1 Generating Random Numbers

Many events in the real world are difficult to predict with absolute precision, yet we can sometimes know the average behavior quite well. For example, a store may know from experience that a customer arrives every five minutes. Of course, that is an average—customers don't arrive in five minute intervals. To accurately model customer traffic, you want to take that random fluctuation into account. Now, how can you run such a simulation in the computer?

*You can introduce randomness by calling the random number generator.*

The Java library has a *random number generator*, which produces numbers that appear to be completely random. Calling Math.random() yields a random floating-point number that is ≥ 0 and < 1. Call Math.random() again, and you get a different number.

The following program calls Math.random() ten times.

### section_9_1/RandomDemo.java

```
1   /**
2      This program prints ten random numbers between 0 and 1.
3   */
4   public class RandomDemo
5   {
6      public static void main(String[] args)
7      {
8         for (int i = 1; i <= 10; i++)
9         {
10           double r = Math.random();
11           System.out.println(r);
12        }
13     }
14  }
```

### Program Run

```
0.6513550469421886
0.920193662882893
0.6904776061289993
0.8862828776788884
0.7730177555323139
0.3020238718668635
0.0028504531690907164
0.9099983981705169
0.1151636530517488
0.1592258808929058
```

Actually, the numbers are not completely random. They are drawn from sequences of numbers that don't repeat for a long time. These sequences are actually computed from fairly simple formulas; they just behave like random numbers (see Exercise P4.25). For that reason, they are often called **pseudorandom** numbers.

## 4.9.2 Simulating Die Tosses

In actual applications, you need to transform the output from the random number generator into different ranges. For example, to simulate the throw of a die, you need random integers between 1 and 6.

Here is the general recipe for computing random integers between two bounds a and b. As you know from Programming Tip 4.3 on page 156, there are b - a + 1 values between a and b, including the bounds themselves. First compute

```
(int) (Math.random() * (b - a + 1))
```

to obtain a random integer between 0 and b - a, then add a, yielding a random value between a and b:

```
int r = (int) (Math.random() * (b - a + 1)) + a;
```

Here is a program that simulates the throw of a pair of dice:

**section_9_2/Dice.java**

```
1  /**
2      This program simulates tosses of a pair of dice.
3  */
4  public class Dice
5  {
6     public static void main(String[] args)
7     {
8        for (int i = 1; i <= 10; i++)
9        {
10          // Generate two random numbers between 1 and 6
11
12          int d1 = (int) (Math.random() * 6) + 1;
13          int d2 = (int) (Math.random() * 6) + 1;
14          System.out.println(d1 + " " + d2);
15       }
16       System.out.println();
17    }
18 }
```

**Program Run**

```
5 1
2 1
1 2
5 1
1 2
6 4
4 4
6 1
6 3
5 2
```

### 4.9.3 The Monte Carlo Method

The Monte Carlo method is an ingenious method for finding approximate solutions to problems that cannot be precisely solved. (The method is named after the famous casino in Monte Carlo.) Here is a typical example. It is difficult to compute the number $\pi$, but you can approximate it quite well with the following simulation.

Simulate shooting a dart into a square surrounding a circle of radius 1. That is easy: generate random $x$ and $y$ coordinates between –1 and 1.

If the generated point lies inside the circle, we count it as a *hit*. That is the case when $x^2 + y^2 \le 1$. Because our shots are entirely random, we expect that the ratio of *hits / tries* is approximately equal to the ratio of the areas of the circle and the square, that is, $\pi / 4$. Therefore, our estimate for $\pi$ is 4 × *hits / tries*. This method yields an estimate for $\pi$, using nothing but simple arithmetic.

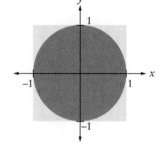

To generate a random floating-point value between –1 and 1, you compute:

```
double r = Math.random(); // 0 ≤ r < 1
double x = -1 + 2 * r; //−1 ≤ x < 1
```

As r ranges from 0 (inclusive) to 1 (exclusive), x ranges from $-1 + 2 \times 0 = -1$ (inclusive) to $-1 + 2 \times 1 = 1$ (exclusive). In our application, it does not matter that x never reaches 1. The points that fulfill the equation $x = 1$ lie on a line with area 0.

Here is the program that carries out the simulation:

**section_9_3/MonteCarlo.java**

```
1   /**
2       This program computes an estimate of pi by simulating dart throws onto a square.
3   */
4   public class MonteCarlo
5   {
6      public static void main(String[] args)
7      {
8         final int TRIES = 10000;
9
10        int hits = 0;
11        for (int i = 1; i <= TRIES; i++)
12        {
13           // Generate two random numbers between -1 and 1
14
15           double r = Math.random();
16           double x = -1 + 2 * r; // Between -1 and 1
17           r = Math.random();
18           double y = -1 + 2 * r;
19
```

```
20          // Check whether the point lies in the unit circle
21
22          if (x * x + y * y <= 1) { hits++; }
23       }
24
25       /*
26          The ratio hits / tries is approximately the same as the ratio
27          circle area / square area = pi / 4
28       */
29
30       double piEstimate = 4.0 * hits / TRIES;
31       System.out.println("Estimate for pi: " + piEstimate);
32    }
33 }
```

**Program Run**

```
Estimate for pi: 3.1504
```

**SELF CHECK**

42. How do you simulate a coin toss with the `Math.random()` method?

43. How do you simulate the picking of a random playing card?

44. Why does the loop body in `Dice.java` call `Math.random()` twice?

45. In many games, you throw a pair of dice to get a value between 2 and 12. What is wrong with this simulated throw of a pair of dice?

    ```
    int sum = (int) (Math.random() * 11) + 2;
    ```

46. How do you generate a random floating-point number ≥ 0 and < 100?

**Practice It**    Now you can try these exercises at the end of the chapter: R4.28, P4.7, P4.24.

---

Special Topic 4.3

### Drawing Graphical Shapes

In Java, it is easy to produce simple drawings such as the one in Figure 8. By writing programs that draw such patterns, you can practice programming loops. For now, we give you a program outline into which you place your drawing code. The program outline also contains the necessary code for displaying a window containing your drawing. You need not look at that code now. It will be discussed in detail in Chapter 10.

Your drawing instructions go inside the draw method:

```
public class TwoRowsOfSquares
{
    public static void draw(Graphics g)
    {
        Drawing instructions
    }
    . . .
}
```

**Figure 8** Two Rows of Squares

When the window is shown, the draw method is called, and your drawing instructions will be executed.

The draw method receives an object of type Graphics. The Graphics object has methods for drawing shapes. It also remembers the color that is used for drawing operations. You can think of the Graphics object as the equivalent of System.out for drawing shapes instead of printing values.

Table 4 shows useful methods of the Graphics class.

### Table 4 Graphics Methods

| Method | Result | Notes |
|---|---|---|
| g.drawRect(x, y, width, height) | | (x, y) is the top left corner. |
| g.drawOval(x, y, width, height) | | (x, y) is the top left corner of the box that bounds the ellipse. To draw a circle, use the same value for width and height. |
| g.fillRect(x, y, width, height) | | The rectangle is filled in. |
| g.fillOval(x, y, width, height) | | The oval is filled in. |
| g.drawLine(x1, y1, x2, y2) | | (x1, y1) and (x2, y2) are the endpoints. |
| g.drawString("Message", x, y) | Message<br>Basepoint    Baseline | (x, y) is the basepoint. |
| g.setColor(color) | From now on, draw or fill methods will use this color. | Use Color.RED, Color.GREEN, Color.BLUE, and so on. (See Table 10.1 for a complete list of predefined colors.) |

The program below draws the squares shown in Figure 8. When you want to produce your own drawings, make a copy of this program and modify it. Replace the drawing tasks in the draw method. Rename the class (for example, Spiral instead of TwoRowsOfSquares).

### special_topic_3/TwoRowsOfSquares.java

```
 1  import java.awt.Color;
 2  import java.awt.Graphics;
 3  import javax.swing.JFrame;
 4  import javax.swing.JComponent;
 5
 6  /**
 7     This program draws two rows of squares.
 8  */
 9  public class TwoRowsOfSquares
10  {
```

```
11   public static void draw(Graphics g)
12   {
13      final int width = 20;
14      g.setColor(Color.BLUE);
15
16      // Top row. Note that the top left corner of the drawing has coordinates (0, 0)
17      int x = 0;
18      int y = 0;
19      for (int i = 0; i < 10; i++)
20      {
21         g.fillRect(x, y, width, width);
22         x = x + 2 * width;
23      }
24      // Second row, offset from the first one
25      x = width;
26      y = width;
27      for (int i = 0; i < 10; i++)
28      {
29         g.fillRect(x, y, width, width);
30         x = x + 2 * width;
31      }
32   }
33
34   public static void main(String[] args)
35   {
36      // Do not look at the code in the main method
37      // Your code will go into the draw method above
38
39      JFrame frame = new JFrame();
40
41      final int FRAME_WIDTH = 400;
42      final int FRAME_HEIGHT = 400;
43
44      frame.setSize(FRAME_WIDTH, FRAME_HEIGHT);
45      frame.setDefaultCloseOperation(JFrame.EXIT_ON_CLOSE);
46
47      JComponent component = new JComponent()
48      {
49         public void paintComponent(Graphics graph)
50         {
51            draw(graph);
52         }
53      };
54
55      frame.add(component);
56      frame.setVisible(true);
57   }
58 }
```

VIDEO EXAMPLE 4.2    **Drawing a Spiral**

In this Video Example, you will see how to develop a program that draws a spiral.

➕ Available online in WileyPLUS and at www.wiley.com/college/horstmann.

## *Random Fact 4.2*  Software Piracy

As you read this, you will have written a few computer programs and experienced firsthand how much effort it takes to write even the humblest of programs. Writing a real software product, such as a financial application or a computer game, takes a lot of time and money. Few people, and fewer companies, are going to spend that kind of time and money if they don't have a reasonable chance to make more money from their effort. (Actually, some companies give away their software in the hope that users will upgrade to more elaborate paid versions. Other companies give away the software that enables users to read and use files but sell the software needed to create those files. Finally, there are individuals who donate their time, out of enthusiasm, and produce programs that you can copy freely.)

When selling software, a company must rely on the honesty of its customers. It is an easy matter for an unscrupulous person to make copies of computer programs without paying for them. In most countries that is illegal. Most governments provide legal protection, such as copyright laws and patents, to encourage the development of new products. Countries that tolerate widespread piracy have found

that they have an ample cheap supply of foreign software, but no local manufacturers willing to design good software for their own citizens, such as word processors in the local script or financial programs adapted to the local tax laws.

When a mass market for software first appeared, vendors were enraged by the money they lost through piracy. They tried to fight back by various schemes to ensure that only the legitimate owner could use the software, such as *dongles*—devices that must be attached to a printer port before the software will run. Legitimate users hated these measures. They paid for the software, but they had to suffer through inconveniences, such as having multiple dongles stick out from their computer. In the United States, market pressures forced most vendors to give up on these copy protection schemes, but they are still commonplace in other parts of the world.

Because it is so easy and inexpensive to pirate software, and the chance of being found out is minimal, you have to make a moral choice for yourself. If a package that you would really like to have is too expensive for your budget, do you steal it, or do you stay

honest and get by with a more affordable product?

Of course, piracy is not limited to software. The same issues arise for other digital products as well. You may have had the opportunity to obtain copies of songs or movies

without payment. Or you may have been frustrated by a copy protection device on your music player that made it difficult for you to listen to songs that you paid for. Admittedly, it can be difficult to have a lot of sympathy for a musical ensemble whose publisher charges a lot of money for what seems to have been very little effort on their part, at least when compared to the effort that goes into designing and implementing a software package. Nevertheless, it seems only fair that artists and authors receive some compensation for their efforts. How to pay artists, authors, and programmers fairly, without burdening honest customers, is an unsolved problem at the time of this writing, and many computer scientists are engaged in research in this area.

## CHAPTER SUMMARY

### Explain the flow of execution in a loop.

- A loop executes instructions repeatedly while a condition is true.
- An off-by-one error is a common error when programming loops. Think through simple test cases to avoid this type of error.

### Use the technique of hand-tracing to analyze the behavior of a program.

- Hand-tracing is a simulation of code execution in which you step through instructions and track the values of the variables.
- Hand-tracing can help you understand how an unfamiliar algorithm works.
- Hand-tracing can show errors in code or pseudocode.

**Use for loops for implementing count-controlled loops.**

- The for loop is used when a value runs from a starting point to an ending point with a constant increment or decrement.

**Choose between the while loop and the do loop.**

- The do loop is appropriate when the loop body must be executed at least once.

**Implement loops that read sequences of input data.**

- A sentinel value denotes the end of a data set, but it is not part of the data.
- You can use a Boolean variable to control a loop. Set the variable to true before entering the loop, then set it to false to leave the loop.
- Use input redirection to read input from a file. Use output redirection to capture program output in a file.

**Use the technique of storyboarding for planning user interactions.**

- A storyboard consists of annotated sketches for each step in an action sequence.
- Developing a storyboard helps you understand the inputs and outputs that are required for a program.

**Know the most common loop algorithms.**

- To compute an average, keep a total and a count of all values.
- To count values that fulfill a condition, check all values and increment a counter for each match.
- If your goal is to find a match, exit the loop when the match is found.
- To find the largest value, update the largest value seen so far whenever you see a larger one.
- To compare adjacent inputs, store the preceding input in a variable.

**Use nested loops to implement multiple levels of iteration.**

- When the body of a loop contains another loop, the loops are nested. A typical use of nested loops is printing a table with rows and columns.

**Apply loops to the implementation of simulations.**

- In a simulation, you use the computer to simulate an activity.
- You can introduce randomness by calling the random number generator.

## REVIEW EXERCISES

**▪ R4.1** Write a `while` loop that prints

    **a.** All squares less than n. For example, if n is 100, print 0 1 4 9 16 25 36 49 64 81.

    **b.** All positive numbers that are divisible by 10 and less than n. For example, if n is 100, print 10 20 30 40 50 60 70 80 90

    **c.** All powers of two less than n. For example, if n is 100, print 1 2 4 8 16 32 64.

**▪▪ R4.2** Write a loop that computes

    **a.** The sum of all even numbers between 2 and 100 (inclusive).

    **b.** The sum of all squares between 1 and 100 (inclusive).

    **c.** The sum of all odd numbers between a and b (inclusive).

    **d.** The sum of all odd digits of n. (For example, if n is 32677, the sum would be $3 + 7 + 7 = 17$.)

**▪ R4.3** Provide trace tables for these loops.

    **a.**
```
int i = 0; int j = 10; int n = 0;
while (i < j) { i++; j--; n++; }
```
    **b.**
```
int i = 0; int j = 0; int n = 0;
while (i < 10) { i++; n = n + i + j; j++; }
```
    **c.**
```
int i = 10; int j = 0; int n = 0;
while (i > 0) { i--; j++; n = n + i - j; }
```
    **d.**
```
int i = 0; int j = 10; int n = 0;
while (i != j) { i = i + 2; j = j - 2; n++; }
```

**▪ R4.4** What do these loops print?

    **a.** `for (int i = 1; i < 10; i++) { System.out.print(i + " "); }`

    **b.** `for (int i = 1; i < 10; i += 2) { System.out.print(i + " "); }`

    **c.** `for (int i = 10; i > 1; i--) { System.out.print(i + " "); }`

    **d.** `for (int i = 0; i < 10; i++) { System.out.print(i + " "); }`

    **e.** `for (int i = 1; i < 10; i = i * 2) { System.out.print(i + " "); }`

    **f.** `for (int i = 1; i < 10; i++) { if (i % 2 == 0) { System.out.print(i + " "); } }`

**▪ R4.5** What is an infinite loop? On your computer, how can you terminate a program that executes an infinite loop?

**▪ R4.6** Write a program trace for the pseudocode in Exercise P4.6, assuming the input values are 4 7 –2 –5 0.

**R4.7** What is an "off-by-one" error? Give an example from your own programming experience.

**R4.8** What is a sentinel value? Give a simple rule when it is appropriate to use a numeric sentinel value.

**R4.9** Which loop statements does Java support? Give simple rules for when to use each loop type.

**R4.10** How many iterations do the following loops carry out? Assume that i is not changed in the loop body.

```
a. for (int i = 1; i <= 10; i++) . . .
b. for (int i = 0; i < 10; i++) . . .
c. for (int i = 10; i > 0; i--) . . .
d. for (int i = -10; i <= 10; i++) . . .
e. for (int i = 10; i >= 0; i++) . . .
f. for (int i = -10; i <= 10; i = i + 2) . . .
g. for (int i = -10; i <= 10; i = i + 3) . . .
```

**R4.11** Write pseudocode for a program that prints a calendar such as the following:

```
Su  M  T  W Th  F Sa
             1  2  3  4
 5  6  7  8  9 10 11
12 13 14 15 16 17 18
19 20 21 22 23 24 25
26 27 28 29 30 31
```

**R4.12** Write pseudocode for a program that prints a Celsius/Fahrenheit conversion table such as the following:

```
Celsius | Fahrenheit
--------+-----------
      0 |         32
     10 |         50
     20 |         68
    . . .        . . .
    100 |        212
```

**R4.13** Write pseudocode for a program that reads a student record, consisting of the student's first and last name, followed by a sequence of test scores and a sentinel of –1. The program should print the student's average score. Then provide a trace table for this sample input:

```
Harry Morgan 94 71 86 95 -1
```

**R4.14** Write pseudocode for a program that reads a sequence of student records and prints the total score for each student. Each record has the student's first and last name, followed by a sequence of test scores and a sentinel of –1. The sequence is terminated by the word END. Here is a sample sequence:

```
Harry Morgan 94 71 86 95 -1
Sally Lin 99 98 100 95 90 -1
END
```

Provide a trace table for this sample input.

■ **R4.15** Rewrite the following for loop into a while loop.

```
int s = 0;
for (int i = 1; i <= 10; i++)
{
   s = s + i;
}
```

■ **R4.16** Rewrite the following do loop into a while loop.

```
int n = in.nextInt();
double x = 0;
double s;
do
{
   s = 1.0 / (1 + n * n);
   n++;
   x = x + s;
}
while (s > 0.01);
```

■ **R4.17** Provide trace tables of the following loops.

**a.** 
```
int s = 1;
int n = 1;
while (s < 10) { s = s + n; }
n++;
```

**b.** 
```
int s = 1;
for (int n = 1; n < 5; n++) { s = s + n; }
```

**c.** 
```
int s = 1;
int n = 1;
do
{
   s = s + n;
   n++;
}
while (s < 10 * n);
```

■ **R4.18** What do the following loops print? Work out the answer by tracing the code, not by using the computer.

**a.** 
```
int s = 1;
for (int n = 1; n <= 5; n++)
{
   s = s + n;
   System.out.print(s + " ");
}
```

**b.** 
```
int s = 1;
for (int n = 1; s <= 10; System.out.print(s + " "))
{
   n = n + 2;
   s = s + n;
}
```

**c.** 
```
int s = 1;
int n;
for (n = 1; n <= 5; n++)
{
   s = s + n;
   n++;
}
System.out.print(s + " " + n);
```

- **R4.19** What do the following program segments print? Find the answers by tracing the code, not by using the computer.

  **a.** 
  ```java
  int n = 1;
  for (int i = 2; i < 5; i++) { n = n + i; }
  System.out.print(n);
  ```

  **b.** 
  ```java
  int i;
  double n = 1 / 2;
  for (i = 2; i <= 5; i++) { n = n + 1.0 / i; }
  System.out.print(i);
  ```

  **c.** 
  ```java
  double x = 1;
  double y = 1;
  int i = 0;
  do
  {
      y = y / 2;
      x = x + y;
      i++;
  }
  while (x < 1.8);
  System.out.print(i);
  ```

  **d.** 
  ```java
  double x = 1;
  double y = 1;
  int i = 0;
  while (y >= 1.5)
  {
      x = x / 2;
      y = x + y;
      i++;
  }
  System.out.print(i);
  ```

- **R4.20** Give an example of a `for` loop where symmetric bounds are more natural. Give an example of a `for` loop where asymmetric bounds are more natural.

- **R4.21** Add a storyboard panel for the conversion program in Section 4.6 on page 162 that shows a scenario where a user enters incompatible units.

- **R4.22** In Section 4.6, we decided to show users a list of all valid units in the prompt. If the program supports many more units, this approach is unworkable. Give a storyboard panel that illustrates an alternate approach: If the user enters an unknown unit, a list of all known units is shown.

- **R4.23** Change the storyboards in Section 4.6 to support a menu that asks users whether they want to convert units, see program help, or quit the program. The menu should be displayed at the beginning of the program, when a sequence of values has been converted, and when an error is displayed.

- **R4.24** Draw a flow chart for a program that carries out unit conversions as described in Section 4.6.

- **R4.25** In Section 4.7.5, the code for finding the largest and smallest input initializes the `largest` and `smallest` variables with an input value. Why can't you initialize them with zero?

- **R4.26** What are nested loops? Give an example where a nested loop is typically used.

**R4.27** The nested loops

```java
for (int i = 1; i <= height; i++)
{
    for (int j = 1; j <= width; j++) { System.out.print("*"); }
    System.out.println();
}
```

display a rectangle of a given width and height, such as

```
****
****
****
```

Write a *single* for loop that displays the same rectangle.

**R4.28** Suppose you design an educational game to teach children how to read a clock. How do you generate random values for the hours and minutes?

**R4.29** In a travel simulation, Harry will visit one of his friends that are located in three states. He has ten friends in California, three in Nevada, and two in Utah. How do you produce a random number between 1 and 3, denoting the destination state, with a probability that is proportional to the number of friends in each state?

## PROGRAMMING EXERCISES

**P4.1** Write programs with loops that compute

   **a.** The sum of all even numbers between 2 and 100 (inclusive).

   **b.** The sum of all squares between 1 and 100 (inclusive).

   **c.** All powers of 2 from $2^0$ up to $2^{20}$.

   **d.** The sum of all odd numbers between a and b (inclusive), where a and b are inputs.

   **e.** The sum of all odd digits of an input. (For example, if the input is 32677, the sum would be $3 + 7 + 7 = 17$.)

**P4.2** Write programs that read a sequence of integer inputs and print

   **a.** The smallest and largest of the inputs.

   **b.** The number of even and odd inputs.

   **c.** Cumulative totals. For example, if the input is 1 7 2 9, the program should print 1 8 10 19.

   **d.** All adjacent duplicates. For example, if the input is 1 3 3 4 5 5 6 6 6 2, the program should print 3 5 6.

**P4.3** Write programs that read a line of input as a string and print

   **a.** Only the uppercase letters in the string.

   **b.** Every second letter of the string.

   **c.** The string, with all vowels replaced by an underscore.

   **d.** The number of vowels in the string.

   **e.** The positions of all vowels in the string.

**P4.4** Complete the program in How To 4.1 on page 169. Your program should read twelve temperature values and print the month with the highest temperature.

**•• P4.5**   Write a program that reads a set of floating-point values. Ask the user to enter the values, then print

- the average of the values.
- the smallest of the values.
- the largest of the values.
- the range, that is the difference between the smallest and largest.

Of course, you may only prompt for the values once.

**• P4.6**   Translate the following pseudocode for finding the minimum value from a set of inputs into a Java program.

> Set a Boolean variable "first" to true.
> While another value has been read successfully
>     If first is true
>         Set the minimum to the value.
>         Set first to false.
>     Else if the value is less than the minimum
>         Set the minimum to the value.
> Print the minimum.

**••• P4.7**   Translate the following pseudocode for randomly permuting the characters in a string into a Java program.

> Read a word.
> Repeat word.length() times
>     Pick a random position i in the word, but not the last position.
>     Pick a random position j > i in the word.
>     Swap the letters at positions j and i.
> Print the word.

To swap the letters, construct substrings as follows:

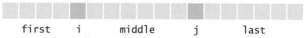

first       i       middle       j       last

Then replace the string with

```
first + word.charAt(j) + middle + word.charAt(i) + last
```

**• P4.8**   Write a program that reads a word and prints each character of the word on a separate line. For example, if the user provides the input "Harry", the program prints

```
H
a
r
r
y
```

**•• P4.9**   Write a program that reads a word and prints the word in reverse. For example, if the user provides the input "Harry", the program prints

```
yrraH
```

**• P4.10**   Write a program that reads a word and prints the number of vowels in the word. For this exercise, assume that a e i o u y are vowels. For example, if the user provides the input "Harry", the program prints 2 vowels.

■■■ **P4.11** Write a program that reads a word and prints the number of syllables in the word. For this exercise, assume that syllables are determined as follows: Each sequence of adjacent vowels a e i o u y, except for the last e in a word, is a syllable. However, if that algorithm yields a count of 0, change it to 1. For example,

| Word | Syllables |
|------|-----------|
| Harry | 2 |
| hairy | 2 |
| hare | 1 |
| the | 1 |

■■■ **P4.12** Write a program that reads a word and prints all substrings, sorted by length. For example, if the user provides the input "rum", the program prints

```
r
u
m
ru
um
rum
```

■ **P4.13** Write a program that prints all powers of 2 from $2^0$ up to $2^{20}$.

■■ **P4.14** Write a program that reads a number and prints all of its *binary digits:* Print the remainder number % 2, then replace the number with number / 2. Keep going until the number is 0. For example, if the user provides the input 13, the output should be

```
1
0
1
1
```

■■ **P4.15** *Mean and standard deviation.* Write a program that reads a set of floating-point data values. Choose an appropriate mechanism for prompting for the end of the data set.

When all values have been read, print out the count of the values, the average, and the standard deviation. The average of a data set $\{x_1, \ldots, x_n\}$ is $\bar{x} = \sum x_i / n$, where $\sum x_i = x_1 + \ldots + x_n$ is the sum of the input values. The standard deviation is

$$s = \sqrt{\frac{\sum (x_i - \bar{x})^2}{n - 1}}$$

However, this formula is not suitable for the task. By the time the program has computed $\bar{x}$, the individual $x_i$ are long gone. Until you know how to save these values, use the numerically less stable formula

$$s = \sqrt{\frac{\sum x_i^2 - \frac{1}{n}\left(\sum x_i\right)^2}{n - 1}}$$

You can compute this quantity by keeping track of the count, the sum, and the sum of squares as you process the input values.

**•• P4.16** The *Fibonacci numbers* are defined by the sequence

$$f_1 = 1$$
$$f_2 = 1$$
$$f_n = f_{n-1} + f_{n-2}$$

Reformulate that as

*Fibonacci numbers describe the growth of a rabbit population.*

```
fold1 = 1;
fold2 = 1;
fnew = fold1 + fold2;
```

After that, discard `fold2`, which is no longer needed, and set `fold2` to `fold1` and `fold1` to `fnew`. Repeat an appropriate number of times.

Implement a program that prompts the user for an integer $n$ and prints the $n$th Fibonacci number, using the above algorithm.

**••• P4.17** *Factoring of integers.* Write a program that asks the user for an integer and then prints out all its factors. For example, when the user enters 150, the program should print

```
2
3
5
5
```

**••• P4.18** *Prime numbers.* Write a program that prompts the user for an integer and then prints out all prime numbers up to that integer. For example, when the user enters 20, the program should print

```
2
3
5
7
11
13
17
19
```

Recall that a number is a prime number if it is not divisible by any number except 1 and itself.

**• P4.19** Write a program that prints a multiplication table, like this:

```
 1   2   3   4   5   6   7   8   9  10
 2   4   6   8  10  12  14  16  18  20
 3   6   9  12  15  18  21  24  27  30
     .  .  .
10  20  30  40  50  60  70  80  90 100
```

**•• P4.20** Write a program that reads an integer and displays, using asterisks, a filled and hollow square, placed next to each other. For example if the side length is 5, the program should display

```
***** *****
***** *   *
***** *   *
***** *   *
***** *****
```

**■■ P4.21** Write a program that reads an integer and displays, using asterisks, a filled diamond of the given side length. For example, if the side length is 4, the program should display

```
   *
  ***
 *****
*******
 *****
  ***
   *
```

**■■■ P4.22** *The game of Nim.* This is a well-known game with a number of variants. The following variant has an interesting winning strategy. Two players alternately take marbles from a pile. In each move, a player chooses how many marbles to take. The player must take at least one but at most half of the marbles. Then the other player takes a turn. The player who takes the last marble loses.

Write a program in which the computer plays against a human opponent. Generate a random integer between 10 and 100 to denote the initial size of the pile. Generate a random integer between 0 and 1 to decide whether the computer or the human takes the first turn. Generate a random integer between 0 and 1 to decide whether the computer plays *smart* or *stupid*. In stupid mode the computer simply takes a random legal value (between 1 and $n/2$) from the pile whenever it has a turn. In smart mode the computer takes off enough marbles to make the size of the pile a power of two minus 1—that is, 3, 7, 15, 31, or 63. That is always a legal move, except when the size of the pile is currently one less than a power of two. In that case, the computer makes a random legal move.

You will note that the computer cannot be beaten in smart mode when it has the first move, unless the pile size happens to be 15, 31, or 63. Of course, a human player who has the first turn and knows the winning strategy can win against the computer.

**■■ P4.23** *The Drunkard's Walk.* A drunkard in a grid of streets randomly picks one of four directions and stumbles to the next intersection, then again randomly picks one of four directions, and so on. You might think that on average the drunkard doesn't move very far because the choices cancel each other out, but that is actually not the case.

Represent locations as integer pairs $(x, y)$. Implement the drunkard's walk over 100 intersections, starting at (0, 0), and print the ending location.

**■■ P4.24** *The Monty Hall Paradox.* Marilyn vos Savant described the following problem (loosely based on a game show hosted by Monty Hall) in a popular magazine: "Suppose you're on a game show, and you're given the choice of three doors: Behind one door is a car; behind the others, goats. You pick a door, say No. 1, and the host, who knows what's behind the doors, opens another door, say No. 3, which has a goat. He then says to you, "Do you want to pick door No. 2?" Is it to your advantage to switch your choice?"

Ms. vos Savant proved that it is to your advantage, but many of her readers, including some mathematics professors, disagreed, arguing that the probability would not change because another door was opened.

Your task is to simulate this game show. In each iteration, randomly pick a door number between 1 and 3 for placing the car. Randomly have the player pick a door. Randomly have the game show host pick a door having a goat (but not the door that the player picked). Increment a counter for strategy 1 if the player wins by switching to the host's choice, and increment a counter for strategy 2 if the player wins by sticking with the original choice. Run 1,000 iterations and print both counters.

■ **P4.25** A simple random generator is obtained by the formula

$$r_{new} = (a \cdot r_{old} + b)\%m$$

and then setting $r_{old}$ to $r_{new}$. If $m$ is chosen as $2^{32}$, then you can compute

$$r_{new} = a \cdot r_{old} + b$$

because the truncation of an overflowing result to the int type is equivalent to computing the remainder.

Write a program that asks the user to enter a seed value for $r_{old}$. (Such a value is often called a *seed*). Then print the first 100 random integers generated by this formula, using $a = 32310901$ and $b = 1729$.

■■ **P4.26** *The Buffon Needle Experiment.* The following experiment was devised by Comte Georges-Louis Leclerc de Buffon (1707–1788), a French naturalist. A needle of length 1 inch is dropped onto paper that is ruled with lines 2 inches apart. If the needle drops onto a line, we count it as a *hit*. (See Figure 9.) Buffon discovered that the quotient *tries/hits* approximates $\pi$.

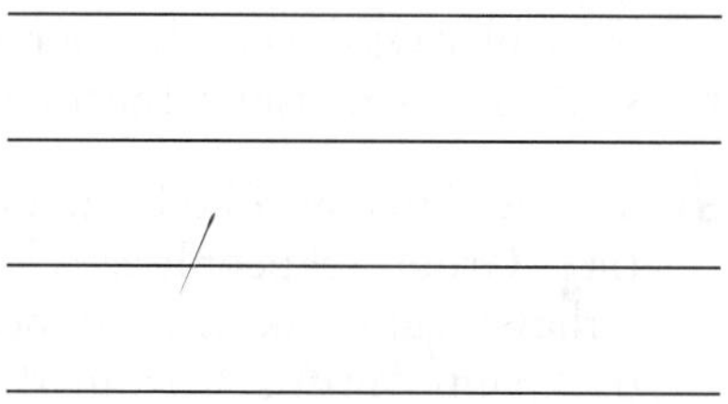

**Figure 9**
The Buffon Needle Experiment

For the Buffon needle experiment, you must generate two random numbers: one to describe the starting position and one to describe the angle of the needle with the *x*-axis. Then you need to test whether the needle touches a grid line.

Generate the *lower* point of the needle. Its *x*-coordinate is irrelevant, and you may assume its *y*-coordinate $y_{low}$ to be any random number between 0 and 2. The angle $\alpha$ between the needle and the *x*-axis can be any value between 0 degrees and 180 degrees ($\pi$ radians). The upper end of the needle has *y*-coordinate

$$y_{high} = y_{low} + \sin\alpha$$

The needle is a hit if $y_{high}$ is at least 2, as shown in Figure 10. Stop after 10,000 tries and print the quotient *tries/hits*. (This program is not suitable for computing the value of $\pi$. You need $\pi$ in the computation of the angle.)

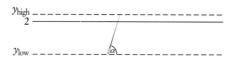

**Figure 10**
A Hit in the Buffon Needle Experiment

**■■ Business P4.27** *Currency conversion.* Write a program that first asks the user to type today's price for one dollar in Japanese yen, then reads U.S. dollar values and converts each to yen. Use 0 as a sentinel.

| | | | |
|---|---|---|---|
| CANADA | CAD | 0.9512 | 0.8883 |
| CHINA | CNY | 13.469 | 6.0910 |
| EURO | EUR | 0.6644 | 0.6100 |
| JAPAN | JPY | 109.00 | 102.00 |
| SINGAPORE | SGD | 13.712 | 12.630 |
| HONG KONG | HKD | 10.043 | 84.072 |

**■■ Business P4.28** Write a program that first asks the user to type in today's price of one dollar in Japanese yen, then reads U.S. dollar values and converts each to Japanese yen. Use 0 as the sentinel value to denote the end of dollar inputs. Then the program reads a sequence of yen amounts and converts them to dollars. The second sequence is terminated by another zero value.

**■■ Business P4.29** Your company has shares of stock it would like to sell when their value exceeds a certain target price. Write a program that reads the target price and then reads the current stock price until it is at least the target price. Your program should use a Scanner to read a sequence of double values from standard input. Once the minimum is reached, the program should report that the stock price exceeds the target price.

**■■ Business P4.30** Write an application to pre-sell a limited number of cinema tickets. Each buyer can buy as many as 4 tickets. No more than 100 tickets can be sold. Implement a program called TicketSeller that prompts the user for the desired number of tickets and then displays the number of remaining tickets. Repeat until all tickets have been sold, and then display the total number of buyers.

**■■ Business P4.31** You need to control the number of people who can be in an oyster bar at the same time. Groups of people can always leave the bar, but a group cannot enter the bar if they would make the number of people in the bar exceed the maximum of 100 occupants. Write a program that reads the sizes of the groups that arrive or depart. Use negative numbers for departures. After each input, display the current number of occupants. As soon as the bar holds the maximum number of people, report that the bar is full and exit the program.

**■■■ Business P4.32** *Credit Card Number Check.* The last digit of a credit card number is the *check digit*, which protects against transcription errors such as an error in a single digit or switching two digits. The following method is used to verify actual credit card numbers but, for simplicity, we will describe it for numbers with 8 digits instead of 16:

- Starting from the rightmost digit, form the sum of every other digit. For example, if the credit card number is 4358 9795, then you form the sum $5 + 7 + 8 + 3 = 23$.
- Double each of the digits that were not included in the preceding step. Add all digits of the resulting numbers. For example, with the number given above, doubling the digits, starting with the next-to-last one, yields 18 18 10 8. Adding all digits in these values yields $1 + 8 + 1 + 8 + 1 + 0 + 8 = 27$.
- Add the sums of the two preceding steps. If the last digit of the result is 0, the number is valid. In our case, $23 + 27 = 50$, so the number is valid.

Write a program that implements this algorithm. The user should supply an 8-digit number, and you should print out whether the number is valid or not. If it is not valid, you should print the value of the check digit that would make it valid.

**•• Science P4.33** In a predator-prey simulation, you compute the populations of predators and prey, using the following equations:

$$prey_{n+1} = prey_n \times \left(1 + A - B \times pred_n\right)$$
$$pred_{n+1} = pred_n \times \left(1 - C + D \times prey_n\right)$$

Here, $A$ is the rate at which prey birth exceeds natural death, $B$ is the rate of predation, $C$ is the rate at which predator deaths exceed births without food, and $D$ represents predator increase in the presence of food.

Write a program that prompts users for these rates, the initial population sizes, and the number of periods. Then print the populations for the given number of periods. As inputs, try $A = 0.1$, $B = C = 0.01$, and $D = 0.00002$ with initial prey and predator populations of 1,000 and 20.

**•• Science P4.34** *Projectile flight.* Suppose a cannonball is propelled straight into the air with a starting velocity $v_0$. Any calculus book will state that the position of the ball after $t$ seconds is $s(t) = -\frac{1}{2}gt^2 + v_0 t$, where $g = 9.81$ m/s$^2$ is the gravitational force of the earth. No calculus textbook ever mentions why someone would want to carry out such an obviously dangerous experiment, so we will do it in the safety of the computer.

In fact, we will confirm the theorem from calculus by a simulation. In our simulation, we will consider how the ball moves in very short time intervals $\Delta t$. In a short time interval the velocity $v$ is nearly constant, and we can compute the distance the ball moves as $\Delta s = v\Delta t$. In our program, we will simply set

```
const double DELTA_T = 0.01;
```

and update the position by

```
s = s + v * DELTA_T;
```

The velocity changes constantly—in fact, it is reduced by the gravitational force of the earth. In a short time interval, $\Delta v = -g\Delta t$, we must keep the velocity updated as

```
v = v - g * DELTA_T;
```

In the next iteration the new velocity is used to update the distance.

Now run the simulation until the cannonball falls back to the earth. Get the initial velocity as an input (100 m/s is a good value). Update the position and velocity 100 times per second, but print out the position only every full second. Also printout the values from the exact formula $s(t) = -\frac{1}{2}gt^2 + v_0 t$ for comparison.

*Note:* You may wonder whether there is a benefit to this simulation when an exact formula is available. Well, the formula from the calculus book is *not* exact. Actually, the gravitational force diminishes the farther the cannonball is away from the surface of the earth. This complicates the algebra sufficiently that it is not possible to give an exact formula for the actual motion, but the computer simulation can simply be extended to apply a variable gravitational force. For cannonballs, the calculus-book formula is actually good enough, but computers are necessary to compute accurate trajectories for higher-flying objects such as ballistic missiles.

■■■ **Science P4.35** A simple model for the hull of a ship is given by

$$|y| = \frac{B}{2}\left[1 - \left(\frac{2x}{L}\right)^2\right]\left[1 - \left(\frac{z}{T}\right)^2\right]$$

where $B$ is the beam, $L$ is the length, and $T$ is the draft. (*Note:* There are two values of $y$ for each $x$ and $z$ because the hull is symmetric from starboard to port.)

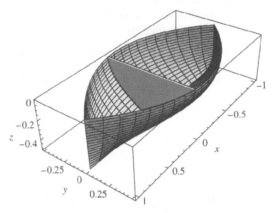

The cross-sectional area at a point $x$ is called the "section" in nautical parlance. To compute it, let $z$ go from 0 to $-T$ in $n$ increments, each of size $T/n$. For each value of $z$, compute the value for $y$. Then sum the areas of trapezoidal strips. At right are the strips where $n = 4$.

Write a program that reads in values for $B$, $L$, $T$, $x$, and $n$ and then prints out the cross-sectional area at $x$.

■ **Science P4.36** Radioactive decay of radioactive materials can be modeled by the equation $A = A_0 e^{-t(\log 2/h)}$, where $A$ is the amount of the material at time $t$, $A_0$ is the amount at time 0, and $h$ is the half-life.

Technetium-99 is a radioisotope that is used in imaging of the brain. It has a half-life of 6 hours. Your program should display the relative amount $A / A_0$ in a patient body every hour for 24 hours after receiving a dose.

■■■ **Science P4.37** The photo at left shows an electric device called a "transformer". Transformers are often constructed by wrapping coils of wire around a ferrite core. The figure below illustrates a situation that occurs in various audio devices such as cell phones and music players. In this circuit, a transformer is used to connect a speaker to the output of an audio amplifier.

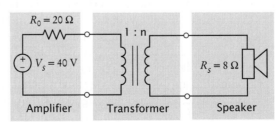

The symbol used to represent the transformer is intended to suggest two coils of wire. The parameter $n$ of the transformer is called the "turns ratio" of the transformer. (The number of times that a wire is wrapped around the core to form a coil is called the number of turns in the coil. The turns ratio is literally the ratio of the number of turns in the two coils of wire.)

When designing the circuit, we are concerned primarily with the value of the power delivered to the speakers—that power causes the speakers to produce the sounds we want to hear. Suppose we were to connect the speakers directly to the amplifier without using the transformer. Some fraction of the power available from the amplifier would get to the speakers. The rest of the available power would be lost in the amplifier itself. The transformer is added to the circuit to increase the fraction of the amplifier power that is delivered to the speakers.

The power, $P_s$, delivered to the speakers is calculated using the formula

$$P_s = R_s \left( \frac{n V_s}{n^2 R_0 + R_s} \right)^2$$

Write a program that models the circuit shown and varies the turns ratio from 0.01 to 2 in 0.01 increments, then determines the value of the turns ratio that maximizes the power delivered to the speakers.

■ **Graphics P4.38**  Write a program to plot the following face.

■ **Graphics P4.39**  Write a graphical application that displays a checkerboard with 64 squares, alternating white and black.

■■■ **Graphics P4.40**  Write a graphical application that draws a spiral, such as the following:

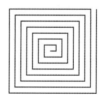

■■ **Graphics P4.41**  It is easy and fun to draw graphs of curves with the Java graphics library. Simply draw 100 line segments joining the points $(x, f(x))$ and $(x + d, f(x + d))$, where $x$ ranges from $x_{min}$ to $x_{max}$ and $d = (x_{max} - x_{min})/100$.
Draw the curve $f(x) = 0.00005x^3 - 0.03x^2 + 4x + 200$, where $x$ ranges from 0 to 400 in this fashion.

■■■ **Graphics P4.42**  Draw a picture of the "four-leaved rose" whose equation in polar coordinates is $r = \cos(2\theta)$. Let $\theta$ go from 0 to $2\pi$ in 100 steps. Each time, compute $r$ and then compute the $(x, y)$ coordinates from the polar coordinates by using the formula

$$x = r \cdot \cos(\theta), \quad y = r \cdot \sin(\theta)$$

## ANSWERS TO SELF-CHECK QUESTIONS

1. 23 years.
2. 7 years.
3. Add a statement

   ```
   System.out.println(balance);
   ```

   as the last statement in the `while` loop.
4. The program prints the same output. This is because the balance after 14 years is slightly below $20,000, and after 15 years, it is slightly above $20,000.
5. 2 4 8 16 32 64 128

   Note that the value 128 is printed even though it is larger than 100.
6.

   | n | output |
   |---|--------|
   | ~~5~~ | |
   | ~~4~~ | 4 |
   | ~~3~~ | 3 |
   | ~~2~~ | 2 |
   | ~~1~~ | 1 |
   | ~~0~~ | 0 |
   | -1 | -1 |

7.

   | n | output |
   |---|--------|
   | ~~1~~ | 1, |
   | ~~2~~ | 1, 2, |
   | ~~3~~ | 1, 2, 3, |
   | 4 | |

   There is a comma after the last value. Usually, commas are between values only.
8.

   | a | n | r | i |
   |---|---|---|---|
   | 2 | 4 | ~~1~~ | ~~1~~ |
   | | | ~~2~~ | ~~2~~ |
   | | | 4 | 3 |
   | | | ~~8~~ | 4 |
   | | | 16 | 5 |

   The code computes $a^n$.
9.

   | n | output |
   |---|--------|
   | ~~1~~ | 1 |
   | ~~11~~ | 11 |
   | ~~21~~ | 21 |
   | ~~31~~ | 31 |
   | ~~41~~ | 41 |
   | ~~51~~ | 51 |
   | ~~61~~ | 61 |
   | ... | |

   This is an infinite loop. n is never equal to 50.
10.

   | count | temp |
   |-------|------|
   | 1 | 123 |
   | 2 | 12.3 |
   | 3 | 1.23 |

This yields the correct answer. The number 123 has 3 digits.

| count | temp |
|-------|------|
| 1 | 100 |
| 2 | 10.0 |

This yields the wrong answer. The number 100 also has 3 digits. The loop condition should have been

```
while (temp >= 10)
```

11.
```
int year = 1;
while (year <= nyears)
{
    double interest = balance * RATE / 100;
    balance = balance + interest;
    System.out.printf("%4d %10.2f\n",
        year, balance);
    year++;
}
```

12. 11 numbers: 10 9 8 7 6 5 4 3 2 1 0

13.
```
for (int i = 10; i <= 20; i = i + 2)
{
    System.out.println(i);
}
```

14.
```
int sum = 0;
for (int i = 1; i <= n; i++)
{
    sum = sum + i;
}
```

15.
```
for (int year = 1;
    balance <= 2 * INITIAL_BALANCE; year++)
```

However, it is best not to use a for loop in this case because the loop condition does not relate to the year variable. A `while` loop would be a better choice.

16.
```
do
{
    System.out.print(
        "Enter a value between 0 and 100: ");
    value = in.nextInt();
}
while (value < 0 || value > 100);
```

17.
```
int value = 100;
while (value >= 100)
{
    System.out.print("Enter a value < 100: ");
    value = in.nextInt();
}
```

Here, the variable `value` had to be initialized with an artificial value to ensure that the loop is entered at least once.

**18.** Yes. The do loop

```
do { body } while (condition);
```

is equivalent to this `while` loop:

```
boolean first = true;
while (first || condition)
{
    body;
    first = false;
}
```

**19.**
```
int x;
int sum = 0;
do
{
    x = in.nextInt();
    sum = sum + x;
}
while (x != 0);
```

**20.**
```
int x = 0;
int previous;
do
{
    previous = x;
    x = in.nextInt();
    sum = sum + x;
}
while (x != 0 && previous != x);
```

**21.** `No data`

**22.** The first check ends the loop after the sentinel has been read. The second check ensures that the sentinel is not processed as an input value.

**23.** The `while` loop would never be entered. The user would never be prompted for input. Because `count` stays 0, the program would then print `"No data"`.

**24.** The `nextDouble` method also returns `false`. A more accurate prompt would have been: "Enter values, a key other than a digit to quit." But that might be more confusing to the program user who would need now ponder which key to choose.

**25.** If the user doesn't provide any numeric input, the first call to `in.nextDouble()` will fail.

**26.** *Computing the average*

```
Enter scores, Q to quit: 90 80 90 100 80 Q
The average is 88
(Program exits)
```

**27.** *Simple conversion*

```
                                    ─── Only one value can be converted
Your conversion question: How many in are 30 cm
30 cm = 11.81 in
(Program exits) ─────── Run program again for another question
```

*Unknown unit*

```
Your conversion question: How many inches are 30 cm?
Unknown unit: inches
Known units are in, ft, mi, mm, cm, m, km, oz, lb, g, kg, tsp, tbsp, pint, gal
(Program exits)
```

*Program doesn't understand question syntax*

```
Your conversion question: What is an ångström?
Please formulate your question as "How many (unit) are (value) (unit)?"
(Program exits)
```

**28.** *One score is not enough*

```
Enter scores, Q to quit: 90 Q
Error: At least two scores are required.
(Program exits)
```

**29.** It would not be possible to implement this interface using the Java features we have covered up to this point. There is no way for the program to know when the first set of inputs ends. (When you read numbers with `value = in.nextDouble()`, it is your choice whether to put them on a single line or multiple lines.)

**30.** *Comparing two interest rates*

```
First interest rate in percent: 5
Second interest rate in percent: 10
Years: 5
Year    5%        10%

0    10000.00    10000.00 ──── This row clarifies that 1 means
1    10500.00    11000.00       the end of the first year
2    11025.00    12100.00
3    11576.25    13310.00
4    12155.06    14641.00
5    12762.82    16105.10
```

**31.** The total is zero.

**32.**
```
double total = 0;
while (in.hasNextDouble())
{
    double input = in.nextDouble();
    if (input > 0) { total = total + input; }
}
```

**33.** `position` is `str.length()` and `ch` is unchanged from its initial value, `'?'`. Note that `ch` must be initialized with some value—otherwise the compiler will complain about a possibly uninitialized variable.

**34.** The loop will stop when a match is found, but you cannot access the match because neither `position` nor `ch` are defined outside the loop.

**35.** Start the loop at the end of string:

```
boolean found = false;
int i = str.length() - 1;
while (!found && i >= 0)
{
    char ch = str.charAt(i);
    if (ch == ' ') { found = true; }
    else { i--; }
}
```

**36.** The initial call to `in.nextDouble()` fails, terminating the program. One solution is to do all input in the loop and introduce a Boolean variable that checks whether the loop is entered for the first time.

```
double input = 0;
boolean first = true;
while (in.hasNextDouble())
{
    double previous = input;
    input = in.nextDouble();
    if (first) { first = false; }
    else if (input == previous)
    {
        System.out.println("Duplicate input");
    }
}
```

**37.** All values in the inner loop should be displayed on the same line.

**38.** Change lines 13, 18, and 30 to `for (int n = 0; n <= NMAX; n++)`. Change `NMAX` to 5.

**39.** 60: The outer loop is executed 10 times, and the inner loop 6 times.

**40.** 0123
1234
2345

**41.**
```
for (int i = 1; i <= 3; i++)
{
    for (int j = 1; j <= 4; j++)
    {
        System.out.print("[]");
    }
    System.out.println();
}
```

**42.** Compute `(int) (Math.random() * 2)`, and use 0 for heads, 1 for tails, or the other way around.

**43.** Compute `(int) (Math.random() * 4)` and associate the numbers 0 . . . 3 with the four suits. Then compute `(int) (Math.random() * 13)` and associate the numbers 0 . . . 12 with Jack, Ace, 2 . . . 10, Queen, and King.

**44.** We need to call it once for each die. If we printed the same value twice, the die tosses would not be independent.

**45.** The call will produce a value between 2 and 12, but all values have the same probability. When throwing a pair of dice, the number 7 is six times as likely as the number 2. The correct formula is

```
int sum = (int) (Math.random() * 6) + (int)
(Math.random() * 6) + 2;
```

**46.** `Math.random() * 100.0`

# METHODS

A method packages a computation consisting of multiple steps into a form that can be easily understood and reused. (The person in the image to the left is in the middle of executing the method "make espresso".)

In this chapter, you will learn how to design and implement your own methods. Using the process of stepwise refinement, you will be able to break up complex tasks into sets of cooperating methods.

# 5.1 Methods as Black Boxes

A method is a
named sequence
of instructions.

A **method** is a sequence of instructions with a name. You have already encountered several methods. For example, the Math.pow method, which was introduced in Chapter 2, contains instructions to compute a power $x^y$. Moreover, every Java program has a method called main.

You *call* a method in order to execute its instructions. For example, consider the following program fragment:

```
public static void main(String[] args)
{
    double result = Math.pow(2, 3);
    . . .
}
```

By using the expression Math.pow(2, 3), main *calls* the Math.pow method, asking it to compute $2^3$. The instructions of the Math.pow method execute and compute the result. The Math.pow method *returns* its result back to main, and the main method resumes execution (see Figure 1).

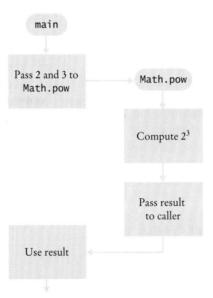

**Figure 1**  Execution Flow During a Method Call

**Figure 2**
The Math.pow Method
as a Black Box

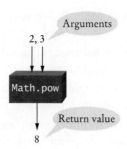

Arguments

2, 3

Math.pow

Return value

8

Arguments are
supplied when a
method is called.

When another method calls the Math.pow method, it provides "inputs", such as the values 2 and 3 in the call Math.pow(2, 3). These values are called the **arguments** of the method call. Note that they are not necessarily inputs provided by a human user. They are simply the values for which we want the method to compute a result. The "output" that the Math.pow method computes is called the **return value**.

The return value is
the result that the
method computes.

Methods can receive multiple arguments, but they return only one value. It is also possible to have methods with no arguments. An example is the Math.random method that requires no argument to produce a random number.

The return value of a method is returned to the calling method, where it is processed according to the statement containing the method call. For example, suppose your program contains a statement

```
double result = Math.pow(2, 3);
```

When the Math.pow method returns its result, the return value is stored in the variable result.

Do not confuse returning a value with producing program output. If you want the return value to be printed, you need to add a statement such as System.out.print(result).

At this point, you may wonder how the Math.pow method performs its job. For example, how does Math.pow compute that $2^3$ is 8? By multiplying $2 \times 2 \times 2$? With logarithms? Fortunately, as a user of the method, you *don't need to know* how the method is implemented. You just need to know the *specification* of the method: If you provide arguments $x$ and $y$, the method returns $x^y$. Engineers use the term *black box* for a device with a given specification but unknown implementation. You can think of Math.pow as a black box, as shown in Figure 2.

When you design your own methods, you will want to make them appear as black boxes to other programmers. Those programmers want to use your methods without knowing what goes on inside. Even if you are the only person working on a program, making each method into a black box pays off: there are fewer details that you need to keep in mind.

*Although a thermostat is usually white, you can think of it as a "black box". The input is the desired temperature, and the output is a signal to the heater or air conditioner.*

**SELF CHECK**

1. Consider the method call `Math.pow(3, 2)`. What are the arguments and return values?

2. What is the return value of the method call `Math.pow(Math.pow(2, 2), 2)`?

3. The `Math.ceil` method in the Java standard library is described as follows: The method receives a single argument *a* of type `double` and returns the smallest `double` value $\geq a$ that is an integer. What is the return value of `Math.ceil(2.3)`?

4. It is possible to determine the answer to Self Check 3 without knowing how the `Math.ceil` method is implemented. Use an engineering term to describe this aspect of the `Math.ceil` method.

**Practice It**    Now you can try these exercises at the end of the chapter: R5.3, R5.6.

# 5.2 Implementing Methods

In this section, you will learn how to implement a method from a given specification. We will use a very simple example: a method to compute the volume of a cube with a given side length.

*The `cubeVolume` method uses a given side length to compute the volume of a cube.*

When writing this method, you need to

> When declaring a method, you provide a name for the method, a variable for each argument, and a type for the result.

- Pick a name for the method (`cubeVolume`).
- Declare a variable for each argument (`double sideLength`). These variables are called the **parameter variables**.
- Specify the type of the return value (`double`).
- Add the `public static` modifiers. We will discuss the meanings of these modifiers in Chapter 8. For now, you should simply add them to your methods.

Put all this information together to form the first line of the method's declaration:

```java
public static double cubeVolume(double sideLength)
```

This line is called the **header** of the method. Next, specify the *body* of the method. The body contains the variable declarations and statements that are executed when the method is called.

The volume of a cube of side length *s* is *s* × *s* × *s*. However, for greater clarity, our parameter variable has been called `sideLength`, not *s*, so we need to compute `sideLength * sideLength * sideLength`.

We will store this value in a variable called `volume`:

```java
double volume = sideLength * sideLength * sideLength;
```

In order to return the result of the method, use the `return` statement:

```java
return volume;
```

*The* return *statement gives the method's result to the caller.*

The body of a method is enclosed in braces. Here is the complete method:

```java
public static double cubeVolume(double sideLength)
{
    double volume = sideLength * sideLength * sideLength;
    return volume;
}
```

Let's put this method to use. We'll supply a main method that calls the cubeVolume method twice.

```java
public static void main(String[] args)
{
    double result1 = cubeVolume(2);
    double result2 = cubeVolume(10);
    System.out.println("A cube with side length 2 has volume " + result1);
    System.out.println("A cube with side length 10 has volume " + result2);
}
```

When the method is called with different arguments, the method returns different results. Consider the call cubeVolume(2). The argument 2 corresponds to the sideLength parameter variable. Therefore, in this call, sideLength is 2. The method computes

## Syntax 5.1 Static Method Declaration

**Syntax**
```
public static returnType methodName(parameterType parameterName, . . . )
{
    method body
}
```

Type of return value     Type of parameter variable

Name of method     Name of parameter variable

```
public static double cubeVolume(double sideLength)
{
    double volume = sideLength * sideLength * sideLength;
    return volume;
}
```

Method body, executed when method is called.

return **statement** exits method and returns result.

sideLength * sideLength * sideLength, or 2 * 2 * 2. When the method is called with a different argument, say 10, then the method computes 10 * 10 * 10.

Now we combine both methods into a test program. Note that both methods are contained in the same class. Also note the comment that describes the behavior of the cubeVolume method. (Programming Tip 5.1 describes the format of the comment.)

### section_2/Cubes.java

```
1   /**
2       This program computes the volumes of two cubes.
3   */
4   public class Cubes
5   {
6      public static void main(String[] args)
7      {
8         double result1 = cubeVolume(2);
9         double result2 = cubeVolume(10);
10        System.out.println("A cube with side length 2 has volume " + result1);
11        System.out.println("A cube with side length 10 has volume " + result2);
12     }
13
14     /**
15         Computes the volume of a cube.
16         @param sideLength the side length of the cube
17         @return the volume
18     */
19     public static double cubeVolume(double sideLength)
20     {
21        double volume = sideLength * sideLength * sideLength;
22        return volume;
23     }
24  }
```

### Program Run

```
A cube with side length 2 has volume 8
A cube with side length 10 has volume 1000
```

**SELF CHECK**

5. What is the value of cubeVolume(3)?

6. What is the value of cubeVolume(cubeVolume(2))?

7. Provide an alternate implementation of the body of the cubeVolume method by calling the Math.pow method.

8. Declare a method squareArea that computes the area of a square of a given side length.

9. Consider this method:

```
public static int mystery(int x, int y)
{
   double result = (x + y) / (y - x);
   return result;
}
```

What is the result of the call mystery(2, 3)?

**Practice It**    Now you can try these exercises at the end of the chapter: R5.1, R5.2, P5.5, P5.22.

## Method Comments

Whenever you write a method, you should *comment* its behavior. Comments are for human readers, not compilers. The Java language provides a standard layout for method comments, called the **javadoc** convention, as shown here:

```
/**
    Computes the volume of a cube.
    @param sideLength the side length of the cube
    @return the volume
*/
public static double cubeVolume(double sideLength)
{
    double volume = sideLength * sideLength * sideLength;
    return volume;
}
```

> Method comments explain the purpose of the method, the meaning of the parameter variables and return value, as well as any special requirements.

Comments are enclosed in /** and */ delimiters. The first line of the comment describes the purpose of the method. Each @param clause describes a parameter variable and the @return clause describes the return value.

Note that the method comment does not document the implementation (*how* the method carries out its work) but rather the design (*what* the method does). The comment allows other programmers to use the method as a "black box".

# 5.3 Parameter Passing

> Parameter variables hold the arguments supplied in the method call.

In this section, we examine the mechanism of parameter passing more closely. When a method is called, variables are created for receiving the method's arguments. These variables are called **parameter variables**. (Another commonly used term is **formal parameters**.) The values that are supplied to the method when it is called are the **arguments** of the call. (These values are also commonly called the **actual parameters**.) Each parameter variable is initialized with the corresponding argument.

Consider the method call illustrated in Figure 3:

```
double result1 = cubeVolume(2);
```

*A recipe for a fruit pie may say to use any kind of fruit. Here, "fruit" is an example of a parameter variable. Apples and cherries are examples of arguments.*

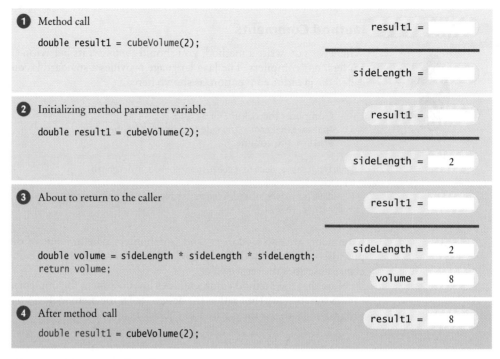

**1** Method call

```
double result1 = cubeVolume(2);
```

result1 =

sideLength =

**2** Initializing method parameter variable

```
double result1 = cubeVolume(2);
```

result1 =

sideLength = 2

**3** About to return to the caller

```
double volume = sideLength * sideLength * sideLength;
return volume;
```

result1 =

sideLength = 2

volume = 8

**4** After method call

```
double result1 = cubeVolume(2);
```

result1 = 8

**Figure 3** Parameter Passing

**ANIMATION**
*Parameter Passing*

- The parameter variable `sideLength` of the `cubeVolume` method is created when the method is called. **1**
- The parameter variable is initialized with the value of the argument that was passed in the call. In our case, `sideLength` is set to 2. **2**
- The method computes the expression `sideLength * sideLength * sideLength`, which has the value 8. That value is stored in the variable `volume`. **3**
- The method returns. All of its variables are removed. The return value is transferred to the *caller*, that is, the method calling the `cubeVolume` method. The caller puts the return value in the `result1` variable. **4**

Now consider what happens in a subsequent call, `cubeVolume(10)`. A new parameter variable is created. (Recall that the previous parameter variable was removed when the first call to `cubeVolume` returned.) It is initialized with 10, and the process repeats. After the second method call is complete, its variables are again removed.

**SELF CHECK**

10. What does this program print? Use a diagram like Figure 3 to find the answer.
```
public static double mystery(int x, int y)
{
   double z = x + y;
   z = z / 2.0;
   return z;
}
public static void main(String[] args)
{
   int a = 5;
   int b = 7;
```

```
        System.out.println(mystery(a, b));
    }
```

11. What does this program print? Use a diagram like Figure 3 to find the answer.

```
public static int mystery(int x)
{
    int y = x * x;
    return y;
}
public static void main(String[] args)
{
    int a = 4;
    System.out.println(mystery(a + 1));
}
```

12. What does this program print? Use a diagram like Figure 3 to find the answer.

```
public static int mystery(int n)
{
    n++;
    n++;
    return n;
}
public static void main(String[] args)
{
    int a = 5;
    System.out.println(mystery(a));
}
```

**Practice It**    Now you can try these exercises at the end of the chapter: R5.5, R5.14, P5.8.

---

**Programming Tip 5.2**

## Do Not Modify Parameter Variables

In Java, a parameter variable is just like any other variable. You can modify the values of the parameter variables in the body of a method. For example,

```
public static int totalCents(int dollars, int cents)
{
    cents = dollars * 100 + cents; // Modifies parameter variable
    return cents;
}
```

However, many programmers find this practice confusing (see Common Error 5.1). To avoid the confusion, simply introduce a separate variable:

```
public static int totalCents(int dollars, int cents)
{
    int result = dollars * 100 + cents;
    return result;
}
```

---

**Common Error 5.1**

## Trying to Modify Arguments

The following method contains a common error: trying to modify an argument.

```
public static int addTax(double price, double rate)
{
    double tax = price * rate / 100;
    price = price + tax; // Has no effect outside the method
```

```
        return tax;
    }
```

Now consider this call:

```
double total = 10;
addTax(total, 7.5); // Does not modify total
```

When the addTax method is called, price is set to 10. Then price is changed to 10.75. When the method returns, all of its parameter variables are removed. Any values that have been assigned to them are simply forgotten. Note that total is *not* changed. In Java, a method can never change the contents of a variable that was passed as an argument.

# 5.4 Return Values

The return statement terminates a method call and yields the method result.

You use the return statement to specify the result of a method. In the preceding examples, each return statement returned a variable. However, the return statement can return the value of any expression. Instead of saving the return value in a variable and returning the variable, it is often possible to eliminate the variable and return a more complex expression:

```
public static double cubeVolume(double sideLength)
{
    return sideLength * sideLength * sideLength;
}
```

When the return statement is processed, the method exits *immediately*. Some programmers find this behavior convenient for handling exceptional cases at the beginning of the method:

```
public static double cubeVolume(double sideLength)
{
    if (sideLength < 0) { return 0; }
    // Handle the regular case
    . . .
}
```

If the method is called with a negative value for sideLength, then the method returns 0 and the remainder of the method is not executed. (See Figure 4.)

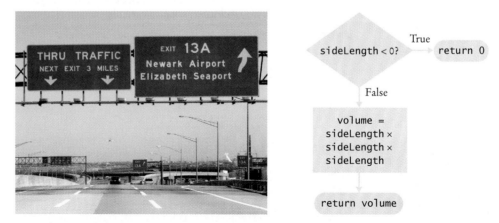

**Figure 4**  A return Statement Exits a Method Immediately

Every branch of a method needs to return a value. Consider the following incorrect method:

```java
public static double cubeVolume(double sideLength)
{
   if (sideLength >= 0)
   {
      return sideLength * sideLength * sideLength;
   } // Error—no return value if sideLength < 0
}
```

The compiler reports this as an error. A correct implementation is:

```java
public static double cubeVolume(double sideLength)
{
   if (sideLength >= 0)
   {
      return sideLength * sideLength * sideLength;
   }
   else
   {
      return 0;
   }
}
```

Many programmers dislike the use of multiple return statements in a method. You can avoid multiple returns by storing the method result in a variable that you return in the last statement of the method. For example:

```java
public static double cubeVolume(double sideLength)
{
   double volume;
   if (sideLength >= 0)
   {
      volume = sideLength * sideLength * sideLength;
   }
   else
   {
      volume = 0;
   }
   return volume;
}
```

**ONLINE EXAMPLE**

A program showing a method with multiple return statements.

**SELF CHECK**

13. Suppose we change the body of the `cubeVolume` method to

```java
if (sideLength <= 0) { return 0; }
return sideLength * sideLength * sideLength;
```

How does this method differ from the one described in this section?

14. What does this method do?

```java
public static boolean mystery (int n)
{
   if (n % 2 == 0) { return true };
   else { return false; }
}
```

15. Implement the `mystery` method of Self Check 14 with a single `return` statement.

**Practice It**   Now you can try these exercises at the end of the chapter: R5.13, P5.20.

Common Error 5.2

### Missing Return Value

It is a compile-time error if some branches of a method return a value and others do not. Consider this example:

```
public static int sign(double number)
{
    if (number < 0) { return -1; }
    if (number > 0) { return 1; }
    // Error: missing return value if number equals 0
}
```

This method computes the sign of a number: –1 for negative numbers and +1 for positive numbers. If the argument is zero, however, no value is returned. The remedy is to add a statement `return 0;` to the end of the method.

HOW TO 5.1

### Implementing a Method

A method is a computation that can be used multiple times with different arguments, either in the same program or in different programs. Whenever a computation is needed more than once, turn it into a method.

To illustrate this process, suppose that you are helping archaeologists who research Egyptian pyramids. You have taken on the task of writing a method that determines the volume of a pyramid, given its height and base length.

**Step 1** Describe what the method should do.

Provide a simple English description, such as "Compute the volume of a pyramid whose base is a square."

**Step 2** Determine the method's "inputs".

Make a list of *all* the parameters that can vary. It is common for beginners to implement methods that are overly specific. For example, you may know that the great pyramid of Giza, the largest of the Egyptian pyramids, has a height of 146 meters and a base length of 230 meters. You should *not* use these numbers in your calculation, even if the original problem only asked about the great pyramid. It is just as easy—and far more useful—to write a method that computes the volume of *any* pyramid.

> Turn computations that can be reused into methods.

In our case, the parameters are the pyramid's height and base length. At this point, we have enough information to document the method:

```
/**
    Computes the volume of a pyramid whose base is a square.
    @param height  the height of the pyramid
    @param baseLength  the length of one side of the pyramid's base
    @return  the volume of the pyramid
*/
```

**Step 3** Determine the types of the parameter variables and the return value.

The height and base length can both be floating-point numbers. Therefore, we will choose the type `double` for both parameter variables. The computed volume is also a floating-point number, yielding a return type of `double`. Therefore, the method will be declared as

```
public static double pyramidVolume(double height, double baseLength)
```

**Step 4** Write pseudocode for obtaining the desired result.

In most cases, a method needs to carry out several steps to find the desired answer. You may need to use mathematical formulas, branches, or loops. Express your method in pseudocode.
An Internet search yields the fact that the volume of a pyramid is computed as

**volume = 1/3 x height x base area**

Because the base is a square, we have

**base area = base length x base length**

Using these two equations, we can compute the volume from the arguments.

**Step 5** Implement the method body.

In our example, the method body is quite simple. Note the use of the `return` statement to return the result.

```
public static double pyramidVolume(double height, double baseLength)
{
    double baseArea = baseLength * baseLength;
    return height * baseArea / 3;
}
```

**Step 6** Test your method.

After implementing a method, you should test it in isolation. Such a test is called a **unit test**. Work out test cases by hand, and make sure that the method produces the correct results. For example, for a pyramid with height 9 and base length 10, we expect the area to be 1/3 × 9 × 100 = 300. If the height is 0, we expect an area of 0.

```
public static void main(String[] args)
{
    System.out.println("Volume: " + pyramidVolume(9, 10));
    System.out.println("Expected: 300");
    System.out.println("Volume: " + pyramidVolume(0, 10));
    System.out.println("Expected: 0");
}
```

**ONLINE EXAMPLE**

➕ The program for calculating a pyramid's volume.

The output confirms that the method worked as expected:

```
Volume: 300
Expected: 300
Volume: 0
Expected: 0
```

---

## WORKED EXAMPLE 5.1    Generating Random Passwords

This Worked Example creates a method that generates passwords of a given length with at least one digit and one special character.

Enter your current password: [            ]
Enter your new password: [            ]
Retype your new password: [            ]

➕ Available online in WileyPLUS and at www.wiley.com/college/horstmann.

# 5.5 Methods Without Return Values

Use a return type of void to indicate that a method does not return a value.

Sometimes, you need to carry out a sequence of instructions that does not yield a value. If that instruction sequence occurs multiple times, you will want to package it into a method. In Java, you use the return type void to indicate the absence of a return value.

Here is a typical example: Your task is to print a string in a box, like this:

```
-------
!Hello!
-------
```

*A* void *method returns no value, but it can produce output.*

However, different strings can be substituted for Hello. A method for this task can be declared as follows:

```
public static void boxString(String contents)
```

Now you develop the body of the method in the usual way, by formulating a general method for solving the task.

**Print a line that contains the - character n + 2 times, where n is the length of the string.**
**Print a line containing the contents, surrounded with a ! to the left and right.**
**Print another line containing the - character n + 2 times.**

Here is the method implementation:

```
/**
    Prints a string in a box.
    @param contents the string to enclose in a box
*/
public static void boxString(String contents)
{
    int n = contents.length();
    for (int i = 0; i < n + 2; i++) { System.out.print("-"); }
    System.out.println();
    System.out.println("!" + contents + "!");
    for (int i = 0; i < n + 2; i++) { System.out.print("-"); }
    System.out.println();
}
```

**ONLINE EXAMPLE**

 A complete program demonstrating the boxString method.

Note that this method doesn't compute any value. It performs some actions and then returns to the caller.

Because there is no return value, you cannot use boxString in an expression. You can call

```
boxString("Hello");
```

but not

```
result = boxString("Hello"); // Error: boxString doesn't return a result.
```

If you want to return from a void method before reaching the end, you use a return statement without a value. For example,

```
public static void boxString(String contents)
{
```

```
    int n = contents.length();
    if (n == 0)
    {
        return; // Return immediately
    }
    . . .
}
```

**16.** How do you generate the following printout, using the boxString method?

```
-------
!Hello!
-------

-------
!World!
-------
```

**17.** What is wrong with the following statement?

```
System.out.print(boxString("Hello"));
```

**18.** Implement a method shout that prints a line consisting of a string followed by three exclamation marks. For example, shout("Hello") should print Hello!!!. The method should not return a value.

**19.** How would you modify the boxString method to leave a space around the string that is being boxed, like this:

```
---------
! Hello !
---------
```

**20.** The boxString method contains the code for printing a line of - characters twice. Place that code into a separate method printLine, and use that method to simplify boxString. What is the code of both methods?

**Practice It** Now you can try these exercises at the end of the chapter: R5.4, P5.25.

# 5.6 Problem Solving: Reusable Methods

Eliminate replicated code or pseudocode by defining a method.

You have used many methods from the standard Java library. These methods have been provided as a part of the Java platform so that programmers need not recreate them. Of course, the Java library doesn't cover every conceivable need. You will often be able to save yourself time by designing your own methods that can be used for multiple problems.

When you write nearly identical code or pseudocode multiple times, either in the same program or in separate programs, consider introducing a method. Here is a typical example of code replication:

```
int hours;
do
{
    System.out.print("Enter a value between 0 and 23: ");
    hours = in.nextInt();
}
while (hours < 0 || hours > 23);
```

```
int minutes;
do
{
    System.out.print("Enter a value between 0 and 59: ");
    minutes = in.nextInt();
}
while (minutes < 0 || minutes > 59);
```

This program segment reads two variables, making sure that each of them is within a certain range. It is easy to extract the common behavior into a method:

```
/**
    Prompts a user to enter a value up to a given maximum until the user
    provides a valid input.
    @param high the largest allowable input
    @return the value provided by the user (between 0 and high, inclusive)
*/
public static int readIntUpTo(int high)
{
    int input;
    Scanner in = new Scanner(System.in);
    do
    {
        System.out.print("Enter a value between 0 and " + high + ": ");
        input = in.nextInt();
    }
    while (input < 0 || input > high);
    return input;
}
```

Then use this method twice:

```
int hours = readIntUpTo(23);
int minutes = readIntUpTo(59);
```

We have now removed the replication of the loop—it only occurs once, inside the method.

Note that the method can be reused in other programs that need to read integer values. However, we should consider the possibility that the smallest value need not always be zero.

Here is a better alternative:

Design your methods to be reusable. Supply parameter variables for the values that can vary when the method is reused.

```
/**
    Prompts a user to enter a value within a given range until the user
    provides a valid input.
    @param low the smallest allowable input
    @param high the largest allowable input
    @return the value provided by the user (between low and high, inclusive)
*/
public static int readIntBetween(int low, int high)
{
    int input;
    Scanner in = new Scanner(System.in);
    do
    {
        System.out.print("Enter a value between " + low + " and " + high + ": ");
        input = in.nextInt();
    }
    while (input < low || input > high);
    return input;
}
```

*When carrying out the same task multiple times, use a method.*

In our program, we call

```
int hours = readIntBetween(0, 23);
```

Another program can call

```
int month = readIntBetween(1, 12);
```

In general, you will want to provide parameter variables for the values that vary when a method is reused.

**SELF CHECK**

**21.** Consider the following statements:
```
int totalPennies = (int) Math.round(100 * total) % 100;
int taxPennies = (int) Math.round(100 * (total * taxRate)) % 100;
```
Introduce a method to reduce code duplication.

**22.** Consider this method that prints a page number on the left or right side of a page:
```
if (page % 2 == 0) { System.out.println(page); }
else { System.out.println("                                " + page); }
```
Introduce a method with return type `boolean` to make the condition in the `if` statement easier to understand.

**23.** Consider the following method that computes compound interest for an account with an initial balance of $10,000 and an interest rate of 5 percent:
```
public static double balance(int years) { return 10000 * Math.pow(1.05, years); }
```
How can you make this method more reusable?

**24.** The comment explains what the following loop does. Use a method instead.
```
// Counts the number of spaces
int spaces = 0;
for (int i = 0; i < input.length(); i++)
{
    if (input.charAt(i) == ' ') { spaces++; }
}
```

**25.** In Self Check 24, you were asked to implement a method that counts spaces. How can you generalize it so that it can count any character? Why would you want to do this?

**Practice It** Now you can try these exercises at the end of the chapter: R5.7, P5.21.

# 5.7 Problem Solving: Stepwise Refinement

Use the process of stepwise refinement to decompose complex tasks into simpler ones.

One of the most powerful strategies for problem solving is the process of **stepwise refinement**. To solve a difficult task, break it down into simpler tasks. Then keep breaking down the simpler tasks into even simpler ones, until you are left with tasks that you know how to solve.

Now apply this process to a problem of everyday life. You get up in the morning and simply must **get coffee**. How do you get coffee? You see whether you can get someone else, such as your mother or mate, to bring you some. If that fails, you must **make coffee**.

*A production process is broken down into sequences of assembly steps.*

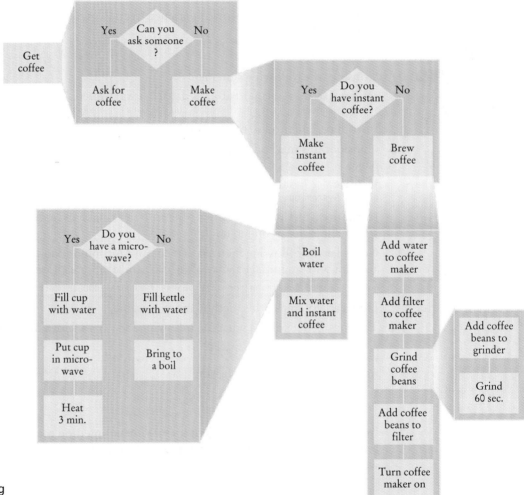

**Figure 5**
Flowchart of Coffee-Making Solution

How do you make coffee? If there is instant coffee available, you can **make instant coffee**. How do you make instant coffee? Simply **boil water** and mix the boiling water with the instant coffee. How do you boil water? If there is a microwave, then you fill a cup with water, place it in the microwave and heat it for three minutes. Otherwise, you fill a kettle with water and heat it on the stove until the water comes to a boil. On the other hand, if you don't have instant coffee, you must **brew coffee**. How do you brew coffee? You add water to the coffee maker, put in a filter, **grind coffee**, put the coffee in the filter, and turn the coffee maker on. How do you grind coffee? You add coffee beans to the coffee grinder and push the button for 60 seconds.

Figure 5 shows a flowchart view of the coffee-making solution. Refinements are shown as expanding boxes. In Java, you implement a refinement as a method. For example, a method `brewCoffee` would call `grindCoffee`, and `brewCoffee` would be called from a method `makeCoffee`.

Let us apply the process of stepwise refinement to a programming problem. When printing a check, it is customary to write the check amount both as a number ("$274.15") and as a text string ("two hundred seventy four dollars and 15 cents"). Doing so reduces the recipient's temptation to add a few digits in front of the amount.

For a human, this isn't particularly difficult, but how can a computer do this? There is no built-in method that turns 274 into "two hundred seventy four". We need to program this method. Here is the description of the method we want to write:

```
/**
    Turns a number into its English name.
    @param number a positive integer < 1,000
    @return the name of number (e.g., "two hundred seventy four")
*/
public static String intName(int number)
```

How can this method do its job? Consider a simple case first. If the number is between 1 and 9, we need to compute "one" ... "nine". In fact, we need the same computation *again* for the hundreds (two hundred). Any time you need something more than once, it is a good idea to turn that into a method. Rather than writing the entire method, write only the comment:

```
/**
    Turns a digit into its English name.
    @param digit an integer between 1 and 9
    @return the name of digit ("one" ... "nine")
*/
public static String digitName(int digit)
```

Numbers between 10 and 19 are special cases. Let's have a separate method `teenName` that converts them into strings "eleven", "twelve", "thirteen", and so on:

```
/**
    Turns a number between 10 and 19 into its English name.
    @param number an integer between 10 and 19
    @return the name of the number ("ten" ... "nineteen")
*/
public static String teenName(int number)
```

When you discover that you need a method, write a description of the parameter variables and return values.

A method may require simpler methods to carry out its work.

Next, suppose that the number is between 20 and 99. The name of such a number has two parts, such as "seventy four". We need a way of producing the first part, "twenty", "thirty", and so on. Again, we will put that computation into a separate method:

```
/**
    Gives the name of the tens part of a number between 20 and 99.
    @param number an integer between 20 and 99
    @return the name of the tens part of the number ("twenty" ... "ninety")
*/
public static String tensName(int number)
```

Now let us write the pseudocode for the `intName` method. If the number is between 100 and 999, then we show a digit and the word "hundred" (such as "two hundred"). We then remove the hundreds, for example reducing 274 to 74. Next, suppose the remaining part is at least 20 and at most 99. If the number is evenly divisible by 10, we use `tensName`, and we are done. Otherwise, we print the tens with `tensName` (such as "seventy") and remove the tens, reducing 74 to 4. In a separate branch, we deal with numbers that are at between 10 and 19. Finally, we print any remaining single digit (such as "four").

> part = number (The part that still needs to be converted)
> name = "" (The name of the number)
>
> If part >= 100
>     name = name of hundreds in part + " hundred"
>     Remove hundreds from part.
>
> If part >= 20
>     Append tensName(part) to name.
>     Remove tens from part.
> Else if part >= 10
>     Append teenName(part) to name.
>     part = 0
>
> If (part > 0)
>     Append digitName(part) to name.

Translating the pseudocode into Java is straightforward. The result is shown in the source listing at the end of this section.

Note how we rely on helper methods to do much of the detail work. Using the process of stepwise refinement, we now need to consider these helper methods.

Let's start with the `digitName` method. This method is so simple to implement that pseudocode is not really required. Simply use an `if` statement with nine branches:

```
public static String digitName(int digit)
{
    if (digit == 1) { return "one" };
    if (digit == 2) { return "two" };
    . . .
}
```

The `teenName` and `tensName` methods are similar.

ANIMATION
*Tracing a Method*

This concludes the process of stepwise refinement. Here is the complete program:

**section_7/IntegerName.java**

```java
import java.util.Scanner;

/**
   This program turns an integer into its English name.
*/
public class IntegerName
{
   public static void main(String[] args)
   {
      Scanner in = new Scanner(System.in);
      System.out.print("Please enter a positive integer < 1000: ");
      int input = in.nextInt();
      System.out.println(intName(input));
   }

   /**
      Turns a number into its English name.
      @param number a positive integer < 1,000
      @return the name of the number (e.g. "two hundred seventy four")
   */
   public static String intName(int number)
   {
      int part = number; // The part that still needs to be converted
      String name = ""; // The name of the number

      if (part >= 100)
      {
         name = digitName(part / 100) + " hundred";
         part = part % 100;
      }

      if (part >= 20)
      {
         name = name + " " + tensName(part);
         part = part % 10;
      }
      else if (part >= 10)
      {
         name = name + " " + teenName(part);
         part = 0;
      }

      if (part > 0)
      {
         name = name + " " + digitName(part);
      }

      return name;
   }

   /**
      Turns a digit into its English name.
      @param digit an integer between 1 and 9
      @return the name of digit ("one" ... "nine")
   */
```

```
56    public static String digitName(int digit)
57    {
58       if (digit == 1) { return "one"; }
59       if (digit == 2) { return "two"; }
60       if (digit == 3) { return "three"; }
61       if (digit == 4) { return "four"; }
62       if (digit == 5) { return "five"; }
63       if (digit == 6) { return "six"; }
64       if (digit == 7) { return "seven"; }
65       if (digit == 8) { return "eight"; }
66       if (digit == 9) { return "nine"; }
67       return "";
68    }
69
70    /**
71       Turns a number between 10 and 19 into its English name.
72       @param number  an integer between 10 and 19
73       @return  the name of the given number ("ten" . . . "nineteen")
74    */
75    public static String teenName(int number)
76    {
77       if (number == 10) { return "ten"; }
78       if (number == 11) { return "eleven"; }
79       if (number == 12) { return "twelve"; }
80       if (number == 13) { return "thirteen"; }
81       if (number == 14) { return "fourteen"; }
82       if (number == 15) { return "fifteen"; }
83       if (number == 16) { return "sixteen"; }
84       if (number == 17) { return "seventeen"; }
85       if (number == 18) { return "eighteen"; }
86       if (number == 19) { return "nineteen"; }
87       return "";
88    }
89
90    /**
91       Gives the name of the tens part of a number between 20 and 99.
92       @param number  an integer between 20 and 99
93       @return  the name of the tens part of the number ("twenty" . . . "ninety")
94    */
95    public static String tensName(int number)
96    {
97       if (number >= 90) { return "ninety"; }
98       if (number >= 80) { return "eighty"; }
99       if (number >= 70) { return "seventy"; }
100      if (number >= 60) { return "sixty"; }
101      if (number >= 50) { return "fifty"; }
102      if (number >= 40) { return "forty"; }
103      if (number >= 30) { return "thirty"; }
104      if (number >= 20) { return "twenty"; }
105      return "";
106   }
107 }
```

**Program Run**

```
Please enter a positive integer < 1000: 729
seven hundred twenty nine
```

26. Explain how you can improve the intName method so that it can handle arguments up to 9999.

27. Why does line 40 set part = 0?

28. What happens when you call intName(0)? How can you change the intName method to handle this case correctly?

29. Trace the method call intName(72), as described in Programming Tip 5.4.

30. Use the process of stepwise refinement to break down the task of printing the following table into simpler tasks.

```
+-----+-----------+
|  i  | i * i * i |
+-----+-----------+
|   1 |         1 |
|   2 |         8 |
   . . .        . . .
|  20 |      8000 |
+-----+-----------+
```

**Practice It** Now you can try these exercises at the end of the chapter: R5.12, P5.11, P5.24.

**Programming Tip 5.3**

### Keep Methods Short

There is a certain cost for writing a method. You need to design, code, and test the method. The method needs to be documented. You need to spend some effort to make the method reusable rather than tied to a specific context. To avoid this cost, it is always tempting just to stuff more and more code in one place rather than going through the trouble of breaking up the code into separate methods. It is quite common to see inexperienced programmers produce methods that are several hundred lines long.

As a rule of thumb, a method that is so long that its code will not fit on a single screen in your development environment should probably be broken up.

**Programming Tip 5.4**

### Tracing Methods

When you design a complex method, it is a good idea to carry out a manual walkthrough before entrusting your program to the computer.

Take an index card, or some other piece of paper, and write down the method call that you want to study. Write the name of the method and the names and values of the parameter variables, like this:

| intName(number = 416) |
| --- |
|  |
|  |

Then write the names and initial values of the method variables. Write them in a table, because you will update them as you walk through the code.

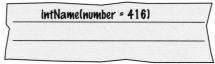

| intName(number = 416) | |
| --- | --- |
| **part** | **name** |
| 416 | "" |
|  |  |

We enter the test part >= 100. part / 100 is 4 and part % 100 is 16. digitName(4) is easily seen to be "four". (Had digitName been complicated, you would have started another sheet of paper to figure out that method call. It is quite common to accumulate several sheets in this way.)

Now name has changed to name + " " + digitName(part / 100) + " hundred", that is "four hundred", and part has changed to part % 100, or 16.

| intName(number = 416) | |
|---|---|
| **part** | **name** |
| ~~416~~ | ~~""~~ |
| 16 | "four hundred" |
| | |

Now you enter the branch part >= 10. teenName(16) is sixteen, so the variables now have the values

| intName(number = 416) | |
|---|---|
| **part** | **name** |
| ~~416~~ | ~~""~~ |
| ~~16~~ | ~~"four hundred"~~ |
| 0 | "four hundred sixteen" |
| | |

Now it becomes clear why you need to set part to 0 in line 40. Otherwise, you would enter the next branch and the result would be "four hundred sixteen six". Tracing the code is an effective way to understand the subtle aspects of a method.

## Programming Tip 5.5

### Stubs

When writing a larger program, it is not always feasible to implement and test all methods at once. You often need to test a method that calls another, but the other method hasn't yet been implemented. Then you can temporarily replace the missing method with a **stub**. A stub is a method that returns a simple value that is sufficient for testing another method. Here are examples of stub methods:

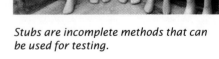

*Stubs are incomplete methods that can be used for testing.*

```
/**
    Turns a digit into its English name.
    @param digit an integer between 1 and 9
    @return the name of digit ("one" . . . "nine")
*/
public static String digitName(int digit)
{
    return "mumble";
}

/**
    Gives the name of the tens part of a number between 20 and 99.
    @param number an integer between 20 and 99
    @return the tens name of the number ("twenty" . . . "ninety")
```

```
*/
public static String tensName(int number)
{
    return "mumblety";
}
```

If you combine these stubs with the intName method and test it with an argument of 274, you will get a result of "mumble hundred mumblety mumble", which indicates that the basic logic of the intName method is working correctly.

---

**WORKED EXAMPLE 5.2**    **Calculating a Course Grade**

This Worked Example uses stepwise refinement to solve the problem of converting a set of letter grades into an average grade for a course.

---

# 5.8 Variable Scope

As your programs get larger and contain more variables, you may encounter problems where you cannot access a variable that is defined in a different part of your program, or where two variable definitions conflict with each other. In order to resolve these problems, you need to be familiar with the concept of *variable scope*.

> The scope of a variable is the part of the program in which it is visible.

The **scope** of a variable is the part of the program in which you can access it. For example, the scope of a method's parameter variable is the entire method. In the following code segment, the scope of the parameter variable sideLength is the entire cubeVolume method but not the main method.

```
public static void main(String[] args)
{
    System.out.println(cubeVolume(10));
}

public static double cubeVolume(double sideLength)
{
    return sideLength * sideLength * sideLength;
}
```

A variable that is defined within a method is called a **local variable**. When a local variable is declared in a block, its scope ranges from its declaration until the end of the block. For example, in the code segment below, the scope of the square variable is highlighted.

```
public static void main(String[] args)
{
    int sum = 0;
    for (int i = 1; i <= 10; i++)
    {
        int square = i * i;
        sum = sum + square;
    }
    System.out.println(sum);
}
```

➕ Available online in WileyPLUS and at www.wiley.com/college/horstmann.

The scope of a variable that is declared in a for statement extends to the end of the statement:

```java
public static void main(String[] args)
{
    int sum = 0;
    for (int i = 1; i <= 10; i++)
    {
        sum = sum + i * i;
    }
    System.out.println(sum);
}
```

Here is an example of a scope problem. The following code will not compile:

```java
public static void main(String[] args)
{
    double sideLength = 10;
    int result = cubeVolume();
    System.out.println(result);
}

public static double cubeVolume()
{
    return sideLength * sideLength * sideLength; // ERROR
}
```

Note the scope of the variable sideLength. The cubeVolume method attempts to read the variable, but it cannot—the scope of sideLength does not extend outside the main method. The remedy is to pass it as an argument, as we did in Section 5.2.

It is possible to use the same variable name more than once in a program. Consider the result variables in the following example:

```java
public static void main(String[] args)
{
    int result = square(3) + square(4);
    System.out.println(result);
}

public static int square(int n)
{
    int result = n * n;
    return result;
}
```

*In the same way that there can be a street named "Main Street" in different cities, a Java program can have multiple variables with the same name.*

Two local or parameter variables can have the same name, provided that their scopes do not overlap.

Each result variable is declared in a separate method, and their scopes do not overlap.

You can even have two variables with the same name in the same method, provided that their scopes do not overlap:

```java
public static void main(String[] args)
{
    int sum = 0;
    for (int i = 1; i <= 10; i++)
    {
        sum = sum + i;
    }

    for (int i = 1; i <= 10; i++)
    {
        sum = sum + i * i;
    }
    System.out.println(sum);
}
```

It is not legal to declare two variables with the same name in the same method in such a way that their scopes overlap. For example, the following is not legal:

```java
public static int sumOfSquares(int n)
{
    int sum = 0;
    for (int i = 1; i <= n; i++)
    {
        int n = i * i; // ERROR
        sum = sum + n;
    }
    return sum;
}
```

The scope of the local variable n is contained within the scope of the parameter variable n. In this case, you need to rename one of the variables.

**SELF CHECK**

Consider this sample program:

```java
1   public class Sample
2   {
3      public static void main(String[] args)
4      {
5         int x = 4;
6         x = mystery(x + 1);
7         System.out.println(s);
8      }
9
10     public static int mystery(int x)
11     {
12        int s = 0;
13        for (int i = 0; i < x; x++)
14        {
15           int x = i + 1;
16           s = s + x;
```

```
17        }
18     return s;
19   }
20 }
```

**31.** Which lines are in the scope of the variable i declared in line 13?

**32.** Which lines are in the scope of the parameter variable x declared in line 10?

**33.** The program declares two local variables with the same name whose scopes don't overlap. What are they?

**34.** There is a scope error in the mystery method. How do you fix it?

**35.** There is a scope error in the main method. What is it, and how do you fix it?

**Practice It**    Now you can try these exercises at the end of the chapter: R5.9, R5.10.

---

VIDEO EXAMPLE 5.1    **Debugging**

In this Video Example, you will learn how to use a debugger to find errors in a program.

---

# 5.9 Recursive Methods (Optional)

A recursive method is a method that calls itself. This is not as unusual as it sounds at first. Suppose you face the arduous task of cleaning up an entire house. You may well say to yourself, "I'll pick a room and clean it, and then I'll clean the other rooms." In other words, the cleanup task calls itself, but with a simpler input. Eventually, all the rooms will be cleaned.

*Cleaning up a house can be solved recursively:*
*Clean one room, then clean up the rest.*

➕  Available online in WileyPLUS and at www.wiley.com/college/horstmann.

In Java, a recursive method uses the same principle. Here is a typical example. We want to print triangle patterns like this:

```
[]
[][]
[][][]
[][][][]
```

Specifically, our task is to provide a method

```
public static void printTriangle(int sideLength)
```

The triangle given above is printed by calling `printTriangle(4)`. To see how recursion helps, consider how a triangle with side length 4 can be obtained from a triangle with side length 3.

```
[]
[][]
[][][]
[][][][]
```

**Print the triangle with side length 3.**
**Print a line with four [].**

A recursive computation solves a problem by using the solution of the same problem with simpler inputs.

More generally, here are the Java instructions for an arbitrary side length:

```java
public static void printTriangle(int sideLength)
{
    printTriangle(sideLength - 1);
    for (int i = 0; i < sideLength; i++)
    {
        System.out.print("[]");
    }
    System.out.println();
}
```

For a recursion to terminate, there must be special cases for the simplest inputs.

There is just one problem with this idea. When the side length is 1, we don't want to call `printTriangle(0)`, `printTriangle(-1)`, and so on. The solution is simply to treat this as a special case, and not to print anything when `sideLength` is less than 1.

```java
public static void printTriangle(int sideLength)
{
    if (sideLength < 1) { return; }
    printTriangle(sideLength - 1);
    for (int i = 0; i < sideLength; i++)
    {
        System.out.print("[]");
    }
    System.out.println();
}
```

Look at the `printTriangle` method one more time and notice how utterly reasonable it is. If the side length is 0, nothing needs to be printed. The next part is just as reasonable. Print the smaller triangle *and don't think about why that works*. Then print a row of []. Clearly, the result is a triangle of the desired size.

There are two key requirements to make sure that the recursion is successful:

- Every recursive call must simplify the task in some way.
- There must be special cases to handle the simplest tasks directly.

The `printTriangle` method calls itself again with smaller and smaller side lengths. Eventually the side length must reach 0, and the method stops calling itself.

*This set of Russian dolls looks similar to the call pattern of a recursive method.*

Here is what happens when we print a triangle with side length 4:

- The call `printTriangle(4)` calls `printTriangle(3)`.
  - The call `printTriangle(3)` calls `printTriangle(2)`.
    - The call `printTriangle(2)` calls `printTriangle(1)`.
      - The call `printTriangle(1)` calls `printTriangle(0)`.
        - The call `printTriangle(0)` returns, doing nothing.
      - The call `printTriangle(1)` prints [].
    - The call `printTriangle(2)` prints [][].
  - The call `printTriangle(3)` prints [][][].
- The call `printTriangle(4)` prints [][][][].

**ANIMATION**
*Tracing a Recursion*

The call pattern of a recursive method looks complicated, and the key to the successful design of a recursive method is *not to think about it*.

Recursion is not really necessary to print triangle shapes. You can use nested loops, like this:

```java
public static void printTriangle(int sideLength)
{
    for (int i = 0; i < sideLength; i++)
    {
        for (int j = 0; j < i; j++)
        {
            System.out.print("[]");
        }
        System.out.println();
    }
}
```

**ONLINE EXAMPLE**

The complete
TrianglePrinter
program.

However, this pair of loops is a bit tricky. Many people find the recursive solution simpler to understand.

**SELF CHECK**

**36.** Consider this slight modification of the `printTriangle` method:

```java
public static void printTriangle(int sideLength)
{
    if (sideLength < 1) { return; }
    for (int i = 0; i < sideLength; i++)
    {
        System.out.print("[]");
```

```
    }
    System.out.println();
    printTriangle(sideLength - 1);
}
```

What is the result of `printTriangle(4)`?

**37.** Consider this recursive method:

```
public static int mystery(int n)
{
    if (n <= 0) { return 0; }
    return n + mystery(n - 1);
}
```

What is `mystery(4)`?

**38.** Consider this recursive method:

```
public static int mystery(int n)
{
    if (n <= 0) { return 0; }
    return mystery(n / 2) + 1;
}
```

What is `mystery(20)`?

**39.** Write a recursive method for printing n box shapes [] in a row.

**40.** The `intName` method in Section 5.7 accepted arguments < 1,000. Using a recursive call, extend its range to 999,999. For example an input of 12,345 should return `"twelve thousand three hundred forty five"`.

**Practice It**    Now you can try these exercises at the end of the chapter: R5.16, P5.16, P5.18.

---

**HOW TO 5.2**

### Thinking Recursively

To solve a problem recursively requires a different mindset than to solve it by programming loops. In fact, it helps if you are, or pretend to be, a bit lazy and let others do most of the work for you. If you need to solve a complex problem, pretend that "someone else" will do most of the heavy lifting and solve the problem for all simpler inputs. Then you only need to figure out how you can turn the solutions with simpler inputs into a solution for the whole problem.

To illustrate the recursive thinking process, consider the problem of Section 4.2, computing the sum of the digits of a number. We want to design a method `digitSum` that computes the sum of the digits of an integer n.

For example, `digitSum(1729)` = 1 + 7 + 2 + 9 = 19

**Step 1**    Break the input into parts that can themselves be inputs to the problem.

In your mind, focus on a particular input or set of inputs for the task that you want to solve, and think how you can simplify the inputs. Look for simplifications that can be solved by the same task, and whose solutions are related to the original task.

> The key to finding a recursive solution is reducing the input to a simpler input for the same problem.

In the digit sum problem, consider how we can simplify an input such as n = 1729. Would it help to subtract 1? After all, `digitSum(1729)` = `digitSum(1728)` + 1. But consider n = 1000. There seems to be no obvious relationship between `digitSum(1000)` and `digitSum(999)`.

A much more promising idea is to remove the last digit, that is, to compute n / 10 = 172. The digit sum of 172 is directly related to the digit sum of 1729.

**Step 2**    Combine solutions with simpler inputs into a solution of the original problem.

In your mind, consider the solutions for the simpler inputs that you have discovered in Step 1. Don't worry *how* those solutions are obtained. Simply have faith that the solutions are readily available. Just say to yourself: These are simpler inputs, so someone else will solve the problem for me.

In the case of the digit sum task, ask yourself how you can obtain digitSum(1729) if you know digitSum(172). You simply add the last digit (9) and you are done. How do you get the last digit? As the remainder n % 10. The value digitSum(n) can therefore be obtained as

> When designing a recursive solution, do not worry about multiple nested calls. Simply focus on reducing a problem to a slightly simpler one.

    digitSum(n / 10) + n % 10

Don't worry how digitSum(n / 10) is computed. The input is smaller, and therefore it works.

**Step 3**    Find solutions to the simplest inputs.

A recursive computation keeps simplifying its inputs. To make sure that the recursion comes to a stop, you must deal with the simplest inputs separately. Come up with special solutions for them. That is usually very easy.

Look at the simplest inputs for the digitSum problem:

- A number with a single digit
- 0

---

## *Random Fact 5.1*  The Explosive Growth of Personal Computers

In 1971, Marcian E. "Ted" Hoff, an engineer at Intel Corporation, was working on a chip for a manufacturer of electronic calculators. He realized that it would be a better idea to develop a *general-purpose* chip that could be *programmed* to interface with the keys and display of a calculator, rather than to do yet another custom design. Thus, the *microprocessor* was born. At the time, its primary application was as a controller for calculators, washing machines, and the like. It took years for the computer industry to notice that a genuine central processing unit was now available as a single chip.

Hobbyists were the first to catch on. In 1974 the first computer *kit*, the Altair 8800, was available from MITS Electronics for about $350. The kit consisted of the microprocessor, a circuit board, a very small amount of memory, toggle switches, and a row of display lights. Purchasers had to solder and assemble it, then program it in machine language through the toggle switches. It was not a big hit.

The first big hit was the Apple II. It was a real computer with a keyboard, a monitor, and a floppy disk drive. When it was first released, users had a $3,000 machine that could play Space Invaders, run a primitive bookkeeping program, or let users program it in BASIC. The original Apple II did not even support lowercase letters, making it worthless for word processing. The breakthrough came in 1979 with a new spreadsheet program, VisiCalc. In a spreadsheet, you enter financial data and their relationships into a grid of rows and columns (see the figure at right). Then you modify some of the data and watch in real time how the others change. For example, you can see how changing the mix of widgets in a manufacturing plant might affect estimated costs and profits. Middle managers in companies, who understood computers and were fed up with having to wait for hours or days to get their data runs back from the computing center, snapped up VisiCalc and the computer that was needed to run it. For them, the computer was a spreadsheet machine.

The next big hit was the IBM Personal Computer, ever after known as the PC. It was the first widely available personal computer that used Intel's 16-bit processor, the 8086, whose successors are still being used in personal computers today. The success of the PC was based not on any engineering breakthroughs but on the fact that it was easy to *clone*. IBM published the computer's specifications in order to encourage third parties to develop plug-in cards. Perhaps IBM did not foresee that functionally equivalent versions of their computer could be recreated by others, but a variety of PC clone vendors emerged, and ultimately IBM stopped selling personal computers.

IBM never produced an *operating system* for its PCs—that is, the software that organizes the interaction between the user and the computer, starts application programs, and manages disk storage and other resources. Instead, IBM offered customers the option of three separate operating systems. Most customers couldn't care less about the operating system.

A number with a single digit is its own digit sum, so you can stop the recursion when n < 10, and return n in that case. Or, you can be even lazier. If n has a single digit, then digitSum(n / 10) + n % 10 equals digitSum(0) + n. You can simply terminate the recursion when n is zero.

**Step 4**   Implement the solution by combining the simple cases and the reduction step.

Now you are ready to implement the solution. Make separate cases for the simple inputs that you considered in Step 3. If the input isn't one of the simplest cases, then implement the logic you discovered in Step 2.

Here is the complete digitSum method:

```java
public static int digitSum(int n)
{
    if (n == 0) { return 0; } // Special case for terminating the recursion
    return digitSum(n / 10) + n % 10; // General case
}
```

**ONLINE EXAMPLE**

⊕ A program illustrating the digitSum method.

---

**VIDEO EXAMPLE 5.2**   **Fully Justified Text**

In printed books (such as this one), all but the last line of a paragraph have the same length. In this Video Example, you will see how to achieve this effect.

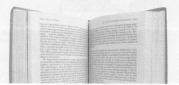

---

They chose the system that was able to launch most of the few applications that existed at the time. It happened to be DOS (Disk Operating System) by Microsoft. Microsoft licensed the same operating system to other hardware vendors and encouraged software companies to write DOS applications.

A huge number of useful application programs for PC-compatible machines was the result.

PC applications were certainly useful, but they were not easy to learn. Every vendor developed a different *user interface:* the collection of keystrokes, menu options, and settings that a user needed to master to use a software package effectively. Data exchange between applications was difficult, because each program used a different data format. The Apple Macintosh changed all that in 1984. The designers of the Macintosh had the vision to supply an intuitive user interface with the computer and to force software developers to adhere to it. It took Microsoft and PC-compatible manufacturers years to catch up.

Most personal computers are used for accessing information from online sources, entertainment, word processing, and home finance. Some analysts predict that the personal computer will merge with the television set and cable network into an entertainment and information appliance.

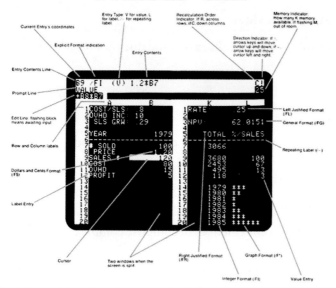

*The Visicalc Spreadsheet Running on an Apple II*

---

⊕ Available online in WileyPLUS and at www.wiley.com/college/horstmann.

**Understand the concepts of methods, arguments, and return values.**

- A method is a named sequence of instructions.
- Arguments are supplied when a method is called.
- The return value is the result that the method computes.

**Be able to implement methods.**

- When declaring a method, you provide a name for the method, a variable for each argument, and a type for the result.
- Method comments explain the purpose of the method, the meaning of the parameter variables and return value, as well as any special requirements.

**Describe the process of parameter passing.**

- Parameter variables hold the arguments supplied in the method call.

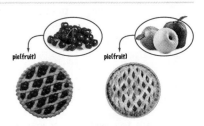

**Describe the process of returning a value from a method.**

- The return statement terminates a method call and yields the method result.
- Turn computations that can be reused into methods.

**Design and implement methods without return values.**

- Use a return type of void to indicate that a method does not return a value.

**Develop methods that can be reused for multiple problems.**

- Eliminate replicated code or pseudocode by defining a method.
- Design your methods to be reusable. Supply parameter variables for the values that can vary when the method is reused.

**Apply the design principle of stepwise refinement.**

- Use the process of stepwise refinement to decompose complex tasks into simpler ones.
- When you discover that you need a method, write a description of the parameter variables and return values.
- A method may require simpler methods to carry out its work.

**Determine the scope of variables in a program.**

- The scope of a variable is the part of the program in which it is visible.
- Two local or parameter variables can have the same name, provided that their scopes do not overlap.

**Understand recursive method calls and implement simple recursive methods.**

- A recursive computation solves a problem by using the solution of the same problem with simpler inputs.
- For a recursion to terminate, there must be special cases for the simplest inputs.
- The key to finding a recursive solution is reducing the input to a simpler input for the same problem.
- When designing a recursive solution, do not worry about multiple nested calls. Simply focus on reducing a problem to a slightly simpler one.

## REVIEW EXERCISES

- **R5.1** In which sequence are the lines of the Cubes.java program in Section 5.2 executed, starting with the first line of main?

- **R5.2** Write method headers for methods with the following descriptions.
    - **a.** Computing the larger of two integers
    - **b.** Computing the smallest of three floating-point numbers
    - **c.** Checking whether an integer is a prime number, returning true if it is and false otherwise
    - **d.** Checking whether a string is contained inside another string
    - **e.** Computing the balance of an account with a given initial balance, an annual interest rate, and a number of years of earning interest
    - **f.** Printing the balance of an account with a given initial balance and an annual interest rate over a given number of years
    - **g.** Printing the calendar for a given month and year
    - **h.** Computing the weekday for a given day, month, and year (as a string such as "Monday")
    - **i.** Generating a random integer between 1 and $n$

- **R5.3** Give examples of the following methods from the Java library.
    - **a.** A method with a double argument and a double return value
    - **b.** A method with two double arguments and a double return value
    - **c.** A method with a String argument and a double return value
    - **d.** A method with no arguments and a double return value

- **R5.4** True or false?
    - **a.** A method has exactly one return statement.
    - **b.** A method has at least one return statement.

    **c.** A method has at most one return value.

    **d.** A method with return value `void` never has a `return` statement.

    **e.** When executing a `return` statement, the method exits immediately.

    **f.** A method with return value `void` must print a result.

    **g.** A method without parameter variables always returns the same value.

■■ **R5.5** Consider these methods:

```
public static double f(double x) { return g(x) + Math.sqrt(h(x)); }
public static double g(double x) { return 4 * h(x); }
public static double h(double x) { return x * x + k(x) - 1; }
public static double k(double x) { return 2 * (x + 1); }
```

Without actually compiling and running a program, determine the results of the following method calls.

    **a.** `double x1 = f(2);`

    **b.** `double x2 = g(h(2));`

    **c.** `double x3 = k(g(2) + h(2));`

    **d.** `double x4 = f(0) + f(1) + f(2);`

    **e.** `double x5 = f(-1) + g(-1) + h(-1) + k(-1);`

■ **R5.6** What is the difference between an argument and a return value? How many arguments can a method call have? How many return values?

■■ **R5.7** Design a method that prints a floating-point number as a currency value (with a $ sign and two decimal digits).

    **a.** Indicate how the programs `ch02/section_3/Volume2.java` and `ch04/section_3/InvestmentTable.java` should change to use your method.

    **b.** What change is required if the programs should show a different currency, such as euro?

■■ **Business R5.8** Write pseudocode for a method that translates a telephone number with letters in it (such as 1-800-FLOWERS) into the actual phone number. Use the standard letters on a phone pad.

■■ **R5.9** Describe the scope error in the following program and explain how to fix it.

```
public class Conversation
{
   public static void main(String[] args)
   {
      Scanner in = new Scanner(System.in);
```

```
                System.out.print("What is your first name? ");
                String input = in.next();
                System.out.println("Hello, " + input);
                System.out.print("How old are you? ");
                int input = in.nextInt();
                input++;
                System.out.println("Next year, you will be " + input);
            }
        }
```

**■■ R5.10** For each of the variables in the following program, indicate the scope. Then determine what the program prints, without actually running the program.

```
 1   public class Sample
 2   {
 3      public static void main(String[] args)
 4      {
 5         int i = 10;
 6         int b = g(i);
 7         System.out.println(b + i);
 8      }
 9
10      public static int f(int i)
11      {
12         int n = 0;
13         while (n * n <= i) { n++; }
14         return n - 1;
15      }
16
17      public static int g(int a)
18      {
19         int b = 0;
20         for (int n = 0; n < a; n++)
21         {
22            int i = f(n);
23            b = b + i;
24         }
25         return b;
26      }
27   }
```

**■■ R5.11** Use the process of stepwise refinement to describe the process of making scrambled eggs. Discuss what you do if you do not find eggs in the refrigerator.

**■ R5.12** Perform a walkthrough of the `intName` method with the following arguments:

   **a.** 5

   **b.** 12

   **c.** 21

   **d.** 301

   **e.** 324

   **f.** 0

   **g.** -2

**■■ R5.13** Consider the following method:

```
public static int f(int a)
{
   if (a < 0) { return -1; }
   int n = a;
```

```
        while (n > 0)
        {
            if (n % 2 == 0) // n is even
            {
                n = n / 2;
            }
            else if (n == 1) { return 1; }
            else { n = 3 * n + 1; }
        }
        return 0;
    }
```

Perform traces of the computations f(-1), f(0), f(1), f(2), f(10), and f(100).

**■■■ R5.14** Consider the following method that is intended to swap the values of two integers:

```
public static void falseSwap(int a, int b)
{
    int temp = a;
    a = b;
    b = temp;
}

public static void main(String[] args)
{
    int x = 3;
    int y = 4;
    falseSwap(x, y);
    System.out.println(x + " " + y);
}
```

Why doesn't the falseSwap method swap the contents of x and y?

**■■■ R5.15** Give pseudocode for a recursive method for printing all substrings of a given string. For example, the substrings of the string "rum" are "rum" itself, "ru", "um", "r", "u", "m", and the empty string. You may assume that all letters of the string are different.

**■■■ R5.16** Give pseudocode for a recursive method that sorts all letters in a string. For example, the string "goodbye" would be sorted into "bdegooy".

## PROGRAMMING EXERCISES

**■ P5.1** Write the following methods and provide a program to test them.

**a.** double smallest(double x, double y, double z), returning the smallest of the arguments

**b.** double average(double x, double y, double z), returning the average of the arguments

**■■ P5.2** Write the following methods and provide a program to test them.

**a.** boolean allTheSame(double x, double y, double z), returning true if the arguments are all the same

**b.** boolean allDifferent(double x, double y, double z), returning true if the arguments are all different

**c.** boolean sorted(double x, double y, double z), returning true if the arguments are sorted, with the smallest one coming first

■■ **P5.3** Write the following methods.

    **a.** `int firstDigit(int n)`, returning the first digit of the argument

    **b.** `int lastDigit(int n)`, returning the last digit of the argument

    **c.** `int digits(int n)`, returning the number of digits of the argument

For example, `firstDigit(1729)` is 1, `lastDigit(1729)` is 9, and `digits(1729)` is 4. Provide a program that tests your methods.

■ **P5.4** Write a method

```
public static String middle(String str)
```

that returns a string containing the middle character in `str` if the length of `str` is odd, or the two middle characters if the length is even. For example, `middle("middle")` returns `"dd"`.

■ **P5.5** Write a method

```
public static String repeat(String str, int n)
```

that returns the string `str` repeated `n` times. For example, `repeat("ho", 3)` returns `"hohoho"`.

■■ **P5.6** Write a method

```
public static int countVowels(String str)
```

that returns a count of all vowels in the string `str`. Vowels are the letters a, e, i, o, and u, and their uppercase variants.

■■ **P5.7** Write a method

```
public static int countWords(String str)
```

that returns a count of all words in the string `str`. Words are separated by spaces. For example, `countWords("Mary had a little lamb")` should return 5.

■■ **P5.8** It is a well-known phenomenon that most people are easily able to read a text whose words have two characters flipped, provided the first and last letter of each word are not changed. For example,

> I dn'ot gvie a dman for a man taht can olny sepll a wrod one way. (Mrak Taiwn)

Write a method `String scramble(String word)` that constructs a scrambled version of a given word, randomly flipping two characters other than the first and last one. Then write a program that reads words and prints the scrambled words.

■ **P5.9** Write methods

```
public static double sphereVolume(double r)

public static double sphereSurface(double r)

public static double cylinderVolume(double r, double h)

public static double cylinderSurface(double r, double h)

public static double coneVolume(double r, double h)

public static double coneSurface(double r, double h)
```

that compute the volume and surface area of a sphere with radius r, a cylinder with a circular base with radius r and height h, and a cone with a circular base with radius r and height h. Then write a program that prompts the user for the values of r and h, calls the six methods, and prints the results.

■■ **P5.10** Write a method

```
public static double readDouble(String prompt)
```

that displays the prompt string, followed by a space, reads a floating-point number in, and returns it. Here is a typical usage:

```
salary = readDouble("Please enter your salary:");
percentageRaise = readDouble("What percentage raise would you like?");
```

■■ **P5.11** Enhance the `intName` method so that it works correctly for values < 1,000,000,000.

■■ **P5.12** Enhance the `intName` method so that it works correctly for negative values and zero. *Caution:* Make sure the improved method doesn't print 20 as "twenty zero".

■■■ **P5.13** For some values (for example, 20), the `intName` method returns a string with a leading space (" twenty"). Repair that blemish and ensure that spaces are inserted only when necessary. *Hint:* There are two ways of accomplishing this. Either ensure that leading spaces are never inserted, or remove leading spaces from the result before returning it.

■■■ **P5.14** Write a method `String getTimeName(int hours, int minutes)` that returns the English name for a point in time, such as "ten minutes past two", "half past three", "a quarter to four", or "five o'clock". Assume that `hours` is between 1 and 12.

■■ **P5.15** Write a recursive method

```
public static String reverse(String str)
```

that computes the reverse of a string. For example, `reverse("flow")` should return "wolf". *Hint:* Reverse the substring starting at the second character, then add the first character at the end. For example, to reverse "flow", first reverse "low" to "wol", then add the "f" at the end.

■■ **P5.16** Write a recursive method

```
public static boolean isPalindrome(String str)
```

that returns `true` if `str` is a palindrome, that is, a word that is the same when reversed. Examples of palindrome are "deed", "rotor", or "aibohphobia". *Hint:* A word is a palindrome if the first and last letters match and the remainder is also a palindrome.

■■ **P5.17** Use recursion to implement a method `public static boolean find(String str, String match)` that tests whether `match` is contained in `str`:

```
boolean b = find("Mississippi", "sip"); // Sets b to true
```

*Hint:* If `str` starts with `match`, then you are done. If not, consider the string that you obtain by removing the first character.

■ **P5.18** Use recursion to determine the number of digits in an integer `n`. *Hint:* If `n` is < 10, it has one digit. Otherwise, it has one more digit than `n / 10`.

■ **P5.19** Use recursion to compute $a^n$, where $n$ is a positive integer. *Hint:* If $n$ is 1, then $a^n = a$. If $n$ is even, then $a^n = (a^{n/2})^2$. Otherwise, $a^n = a \times a^{n-1}$.

■■ **P5.20** *Leap years.* Write a method

```
public static boolean isLeapYear(int year)
```

that tests whether a year is a leap year: that is, a year with 366 days. Exercise P3.28 describes how to test whether a year is a leap year. In this exercise, use multiple `if` statements and `return` statements to return the result as soon as you know it.

•• **P5.21** In Exercise P3.26 you were asked to write a program to convert a number to its representation in Roman numerals. At the time, you did not know how to eliminate duplicate code, and as a consequence the resulting program was rather long. Rewrite that program by implementing and using the following method:

```
public static String romanDigit(int n, String one, String five, String ten)
```

That method translates one digit, using the strings specified for the one, five, and ten values. You would call the method as follows:

```
romanOnes = romanDigit(n % 10, "I", "V", "X");
n = n / 10;
romanTens = romanDigit(n % 10, "X", "L", "C");
. . .
```

•• **Business P5.22** Write a method that computes the balance of a bank account with a given initial balance and interest rate, after a given number of years. Assume interest is compounded yearly.

•• **Business P5.23** Write a program that prints instructions to get coffee, asking the user for input whenever a decision needs to be made. Decompose each task into a method, for example:

```
public static void brewCoffee()
{
    System.out.println("Add water to the coffee maker.");
    System.out.println("Put a filter in the coffee maker.");
    grindCoffee();
    System.out.println("Put the coffee in the filter.");
    . . .
}
```

•• **Business P5.24** Write a program that prints a paycheck. Ask the program user for the name of the employee, the hourly rate, and the number of hours worked. If the number of hours exceeds 40, the employee is paid "time and a half", that is, 150 percent of the hourly rate on the hours exceeding 40. Your check should look similar to that in the figure below. Use fictitious names for the payer and the bank. Be sure to use stepwise refinement and break your solution into several methods. Use the `intName` method to print the dollar amount of the check.

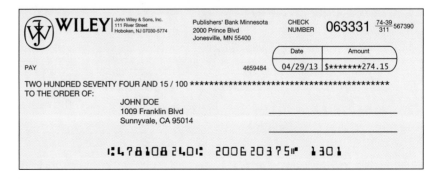

•• **Business P5.25** *Postal bar codes.* For faster sorting of letters, the United States Postal Service encourages companies that send large volumes of mail to use a bar code denoting the zip code (see Figure 6).

**\*\*\*\*\*\*\*\*\*\*\*\*\*\*\***    ECRLOT    **\*\***    CO57

CODE  C671RTS2
JOHN DOE                                                CO57
1009 FRANKLIN BLVD
SUNNYVALE        CA  95014 – 5143

‖‖‖·‖·‖·‖‖‖····‖‖·‖·‖·‖‖····‖‖·‖··‖‖·‖·‖·‖

**Figure 6**   A Postal Bar Code

The encoding scheme for a five-digit zip code is shown in Figure 7. There are full-height frame bars on each side. The five encoded digits are followed by a check digit, which is computed as follows: Add up all digits, and choose the check digit to make the sum a multiple of 10. For example, the zip code 95014 has a sum of 19, so the check digit is 1 to make the sum equal to 20.

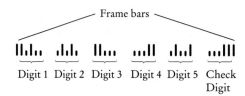

Digit 1   Digit 2   Digit 3   Digit 4   Digit 5   Check
                                                   Digit

**Figure 7**   Encoding for Five-Digit Bar Codes

Each digit of the zip code, and the check digit, is encoded according to the table below, where 1 denotes a full bar and 0 a half bar:

| Digit | Bar 1 (weight 7) | Bar 2 (weight 4) | Bar 3 (weight 2) | Bar 4 (weight 1) | Bar 5 (weight 0) |
|-------|------------------|------------------|------------------|------------------|------------------|
| 1 | 0 | 0 | 0 | 1 | 1 |
| 2 | 0 | 0 | 1 | 0 | 1 |
| 3 | 0 | 0 | 1 | 1 | 0 |
| 4 | 0 | 1 | 0 | 0 | 1 |
| 5 | 0 | 1 | 0 | 1 | 0 |
| 6 | 0 | 1 | 1 | 0 | 0 |
| 7 | 1 | 0 | 0 | 0 | 1 |
| 8 | 1 | 0 | 0 | 1 | 0 |
| 9 | 1 | 0 | 1 | 0 | 0 |
| 0 | 1 | 1 | 0 | 0 | 0 |

The digit can be easily computed from the bar code using the column weights 7, 4, 2, 1, 0. For example, 01100 is $0 \times 7 + 1 \times 4 + 1 \times 2 + 0 \times 1 + 0 \times 0 = 6$. The only exception is 0, which would yield 11 according to the weight formula.

Write a program that asks the user for a zip code and prints the bar code. Use : for half bars, | for full bars. For example, 95014 becomes

||:|:::|:|:|||::::::||:|::|:::|||

Provide these methods:

```
public static void printDigit(int d)
public static void printBarCode(int zipCode)
```

**■■■ Business P5.26** Write a program that reads in a bar code (with : denoting half bars and | denoting full bars) and prints out the zip code it represents. Print an error message if the bar code is not correct.

**■■ Business P5.27** Write a program that converts a Roman number such as MCMLXXVIII to its decimal number representation. *Hint:* First write a method that yields the numeric value of each of the letters. Then use the following algorithm:

> total = 0
> While the roman number string is not empty
>     If value(first character) is at least value(second character), or the string has length 1
>         Add value(first character) to total.
>         Remove the character.
>     Else
>         Add the difference value(second character) – value(first character) to total.
>         Remove both characters.

**■■ Business P5.28** A non-governmental organization needs a program to calculate the amount of financial assistance for needy families. The formula is as follows:

- If the annual household income is between $30,000 and $40,000 and the household has at least three children, the amount is $1,000 per child.
- If the annual household income is between $20,000 and $30,000 and the household has at least two children, the amount is $1,500 per child.
- If the annual household income is less than $20,000, the amount is $2,000 per child.

Implement a method for this computation. Write a program that asks for the household income and number of children for each applicant, printing the amount returned by your method. Use –1 as a sentinel value for the input.

**■■■ Business P5.29** In a social networking service, a user has friends, the friends have other friends, and so on. We are interested in knowing how many people can be reached from a person by following a given number of friendship relations. This number is called the "degree of separation": one for friends, two for friends of friends, and so on. Because we do not have the data from an actual social network, we will simply use an average of the number of friends per user.

Write a recursive method

```
public static double reachablePeople(int degree, double averageFriendsPerUser)
```

Use that method in a program that prompts the user for the desired degree and average, and then prints the number of reachable people. This number should include the original user.

**■■ Business P5.30** Having a secure password is a very important practice, when much of our information is stored online. Write a program that validates a new password, following these rules:

- The password must be at least 8 characters long.
- The password must have at least one uppercase and one lowercase letter
- The password must have at least one digit.

Write a program that asks for a password, then asks again to confirm it. If the passwords don't match or the rules are not fulfilled, prompt again. Your program should include a method that checks whether a password is valid.

**■■■ Science P5.31** You are designing an element for a control panel that displays a temperature value between 0 and 100. The element's color should vary continuously from blue (when the temperature is 0) to red (when the temperature is 100). Write a method `public static int colorForValue(double temperature)` that returns a color value for the given temperature. Colors are encoded as red/green/blue values, each between 0 and 255. The three colors are combined into a single integer, using the formula

```
color = 65536 × red + 256 × green + blue
```

Each of the intermediate colors should be fully saturated; that is, it should be on the outside of the color cube, along the path that goes from blue through cyan, green, and yellow to red.

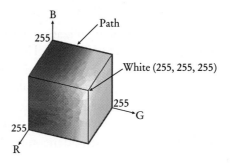

You need to know how to *interpolate* between values. In general, if an output $y$ should vary from $c$ to $d$ as an input $x$ varies from $a$ to $b$, then $y$ is computed as follows:

$$z = (x - a) / (b - a)$$

$$y = d z + c (1 - z)$$

If the temperature is between 0 and 25 degrees, interpolate between blue and cyan, whose (red, green, blue) components are (0, 0, 255) and (0, 255, 255). For temperature values between 25 and 50, interpolate between (0, 255, 255) and (0, 255, 0), which represents the color green. Do the same for the remaining two path segments.

You need to interpolate each color component separately and then combine the interpolated colors to a single integer.

Be sure to use appropriate helper methods to solve your task.

**■■ Science P5.32** In a movie theater, the angle $\theta$ at which a viewer sees the picture on the screen depends on the distance $x$ of the viewer from the screen. For a movie theater with the dimensions shown in the picture below, write a method that computes the angle for a given distance.

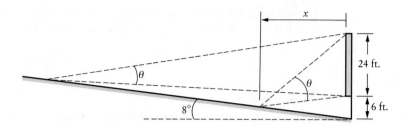

Next, provide a more general method that works for theaters with arbitrary dimensions.

■■ **Science P5.33** The effective focal length $f$ of a lens of thickness $d$ that has surfaces with radii of curvature $R_1$ and $R_2$ is given by

$$\frac{1}{f} = (n - 1)\left[\frac{1}{R_1} - \frac{1}{R_2} + \frac{(n-1)d}{nR_1R_2}\right]$$

where $n$ is the refractive index of the lens medium. Write a method that computes $f$ in terms of the other parameters.

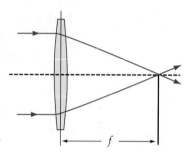

■■ **Science P5.34** A laboratory container is shaped like the frustum of a cone:

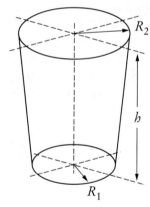

Write methods to compute the volume and surface area, using these equations:

$$V = \tfrac{1}{3}\pi h\left(R_1^2 + R_2^2 + R_1R_2\right)$$

$$S = \pi\left(R_1 + R_2\right)\sqrt{\left(R_2 - R_1\right)^2 + h^2} + \pi R_1^2$$

■■ **Science P5.35** Electric wire, like that in the photo, is a cylindrical conductor covered by an insulating material. The resistance of a piece of wire is given by the formula

$$R = \frac{\rho L}{A} = \frac{4\rho L}{\pi d^2}$$

where $\rho$ is the resistivity of the conductor, and $L$, $A$, and $d$ are the length, cross-sectional area, and diameter of the wire. The resistivity of copper is $1.678 \times 10^{-8}\ \Omega\ \text{m}$.

The wire diameter, $d$, is commonly specified by the American wire gauge (AWG), which is an integer, $n$. The diameter of an AWG $n$ wire is given by the formula

$$d = 0.127 \times 92^{\frac{36-n}{39}} \text{ mm}$$

Write a method

```
public static double diameter(int wireGauge)
```

that accepts the wire gauge and returns the corresponding wire diameter. Write another method

```
public static double copperWireResistance(double length, int wireGauge)
```

that accepts the length and gauge of a piece of copper wire and returns the resistance of that wire. The resistivity of aluminum is $2.82 \times 10^{-8}$ Ω m. Write a third method

```
public static double aluminumWireResistance(double length, int wireGauge)
```

that accepts the length and gauge of a piece of aluminum wire and returns the resistance of that wire.

Write a program to test these methods.

**■■ Science P5.36** The drag force on a car is given by

$$F_D = \frac{1}{2}\rho v^2 A C_D$$

where $\rho$ is the density of air (1.23 kg/m³), $v$ is the velocity in units of m/s, $A$ is the projected area of the car (2.5 m²), and $C_D$ is the drag coefficient (0.2).

The amount of power in watts required to overcome such drag force is $P = F_D v$, and the equivalent horsepower required is Hp $= P/746$. Write a program that accepts a car's velocity and computes the power in watts and in horsepower needed to overcome the resulting drag force. *Note:* 1 mph $= 0.447$ m/s.

## ANSWERS TO SELF-CHECK QUESTIONS

**1.** The arguments are 3 and 2. The return value is 9.

**2.** The inner call to Math.pow returns $2^2 = 4$. Therefore, the outer call returns $4^2 = 16$.

**3.** 3.0

**4.** Users of the method can treat it as a *black box*.

**5.** 27

**6.** $8 \times 8 \times 8 = 512$

**7.** 
```
double volume = Math.pow(sideLength, 3);
return volume;
```

**8.** 
```
public static double squareArea(
    double sideLength)
{
    double area = sideLength * sideLength;
    return area;
}
```

**9.** (2 + 3) / (3 - 2) = 5

**10.** When the mystery method is called, x is set to 5, y is set to 7, and z becomes 12.0. Then z is changed to 6.0, and that value is returned and printed.

**11.** When the method is called, x is set to 5. Then y is set to 25, and that value is returned and printed.

**12.** When the method is called, n is set to 5. Then n is incremented twice, setting it to 7. That value is returned and printed.

**13.** It acts the same way: If sideLength is 0, it returns 0 directly instead of computing 0 × 0 × 0.

**14.** It returns true if n is even; false if n is odd.

15.
```java
public static boolean mystery(int n)
{
    return n % 2 == 0;
}
```

16.
```java
boxString("Hello");
boxString("World");
```

17. The `boxString` method does not return a value. Therefore, you cannot use it in a call to the print method.

18.
```java
public static void shout(String message)
{
    System.out.println(message ++ "!!!");
}
```

19.
```java
public static void boxString(String contents)
{
    int n = contents.length();
    for (int i = 0; i < n + 4; i++)
    {
        System.out.print("-");
    }
    System.out.println();
    System.out.println("! " + contents + " !");
    for (int i = 0; i < n + 4; i++)
    {
        System.out.print("-");
    }
    System.out.println()
}
```

20.
```java
public static void printLine(int count)
{
    for (int i = 0; i < count; i++)
    {
        System.out.print("-");
    }
    System.out.println();
}
public static void boxString(String contents)
{
    int n = contents.length();
    printLine(n + 2);
    System.out.println("!" + contents + "!");
    printLine(n + 2);
}
```

21.
```java
int totalPennies = getPennies(total);
int taxPennies = getPennies(total * taxRate);
```
where the method is defined as
```java
/**
    @param amount an amount in dollars and cents
    @return the number of pennies in the amount
*/
public static int getPennies(double amount)
{
    return (int) Math.round(100 * amount) % 100;
}
```

22.
```java
if (isEven(page)) . . .
```
where the method is defined as follows:
```java
public static boolean isEven(int n)
{
    return n % 2 == 0;
}
```

23. Add parameter variables so you can pass the initial balance and interest rate to the method:
```java
public static double balance(
    double initialBalance, double rate,
    int years)
{
    return initialBalance * pow(
        1 + rate / 100, years);
}
```

24.
```java
int spaces = countSpaces(input);
```
where the method is defined as follows:
```java
/**
    @param str any string
    @return the number of spaces in str
*/
public static int countSpaces(String str)
{
    int count = 0;
    for (int i = 0; i < str.length(); i++)
    {
        if (str.charAt(i) == ' ')
        {
            count++;
        }
    }
    return count;
}
```

25. It is very easy to replace the space with any character.
```java
/**
    @param str any string
    @param ch a character whose occurrences
        should be counted
    @return the number of times that ch occurs
        in str
*/
public static int count(String str, char ch)
{
    int count = 0;
    for (int i = 0; i < str.length(); i++)
    {
        if (str.charAt(i) == ch) { count++; }
    }
    return count;
}
```
This is useful if you want to count other characters. For example, `count(input, ",")` counts the commas in the input.

**26.** Change line 28 to

```
name = name + digitName(part / 100)
  + " hundred";
```

In line 25, add the statement

```
if (part >= 1000)
{
    name = digitName(part / 1000) + "thousand ";
    part = part % 1000;
}
```

In line 18, change 1000 to 10000 in the comment.

**27.** In the case of "teens", we already have the last digit as part of the name.

**28.** Nothing is printed. One way of dealing with this case is to add the following statement before line 23.

```
if (number == 0) { return "zero"; }
```

**29.** Here is the approximate trace:

| intName(number = 72) | |
|---|---|
| part | name |
| ~~72~~ | ~~"seventy"~~ |
| 2 | " seventy two" |
| | |

Note that the string starts with a blank space. Exercise P5.13 asks you to eliminate it.

**30.** Here is one possible solution. Break up the task **print table** into **print header** and **print body**. The **print header** task calls **print separator**, prints the header cells, and calls **print separator** again. The **print body** task repeatedly calls **print row** and then calls **print separator**.

**31.** Lines 14–17.

**32.** Lines 11–19.

**33.** The variables x defined in lines 5 and 15.

**34.** Rename the local variable x that is declared in line 15, or rename the parameter variable x that is declared in line 10.

**35.** The main method accesses the local variable s of the mystery method. Assuming that the main method intended to print the last value of s before the method returned, it should simply print the return value that is stored in its local variable x.

**36.**
```
[][][][]
[][][]
[][]
[]
```

**37.** $4 + 3 + 2 + 1 + 0 = 10$

**38.** mystery(10) + 1 = mystery(5) + 2 = mystery(2) + 3 = mystery(1) + 4 = mystery(0) + 5 = 5

**39.** The idea is to print one [], then print n - 1 of them.

```
public static void printBoxes(int n)
{
    if (n == 0) { return; }
    System.out.print("[]");
    printBoxes(n - 1);
}
```

**40.** Simply add the following to the beginning of the method:

```
if (part >= 1000)
{
    return intName(part / 1000) + " thousand "
        + intName(part % 1000);
}
```

# ARRAYS AND
# ARRAY LISTS

## CHAPTER CONTENTS

In many programs, you need to collect large numbers of values. In Java, you use the array and array list constructs for this purpose. Arrays have a more concise syntax, whereas array lists can automatically grow to any desired size. In this chapter, you will learn about arrays, array lists, and common algorithms for processing them.

# 6.1 Arrays

We start this chapter by introducing the array data type. Arrays are the fundamental mechanism in Java for collecting multiple values. In the following sections, you will learn how to declare arrays and how to access array elements.

## 6.1.1 Declaring and Using Arrays

Suppose you write a program that reads a sequence of values and prints out the sequence, marking the largest value, like this:

```
32
54
67.5
29
35
80
115 <= largest value
44.5
100
65
```

You do not know which value to mark as the largest one until you have seen them all. After all, the last value might be the largest one. Therefore, the program must first store all values before it can print them.

Could you simply store each value in a separate variable? If you know that there are ten values, then you could store the values in ten variables value1, value2, value3, …, value10. However, such a sequence of variables is not very practical to use. You would have to write quite a bit of code ten times, once for each of the variables. In Java, an **array** is a much better choice for storing a sequence of values of the same type.

Here we create an array that can hold ten values of type double:

```
new double[10]
```

The number of elements (here, 10) is called the *length* of the array.

The new operator constructs the array. You will want to store the array in a variable so that you can access it later.

The type of an array variable is the type of the element to be stored, followed by []. In this example, the type is double[], because the element type is double.

Here is the declaration of an array variable of type double[] (see Figure 1):

```
double[] values; ❶
```

When you declare an array variable, it is not yet initialized. You need to initialize the variable with the array:

```
double[] values = new double[10]; ❷
```

> An array collects a sequence of values of the same type.

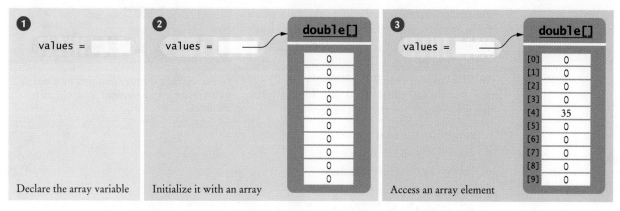

**Figure 1** An Array of Size 10

Now values is initialized with an array of 10 numbers. By default, each number in the array is 0.

When you declare an array, you can specify the initial values. For example,

```
double[] moreValues = { 32, 54, 67.5, 29, 35, 80, 115, 44.5, 100, 65 };
```

When you supply initial values, you don't use the new operator. The compiler determines the length of the array by counting the initial values.

To access a value in an array, you specify which "slot" you want to use. That is done with the [] operator:

```
values[4] = 35; ❸
```

Now the number 4 slot of values is filled with 35 (see Figure 1). This "slot number" is called an *index*. Each slot in an array contains an *element*.

Because values is an array of double values, each element values[i] can be used like any variable of type double. For example, you can display the element with index 4 with the following command:

```
System.out.println(values[4]);
```

Individual elements in an array are accessed by an integer index i, using the notation *array*[i].

An array element can be used like any variable.

## Syntax 6.1 Arrays

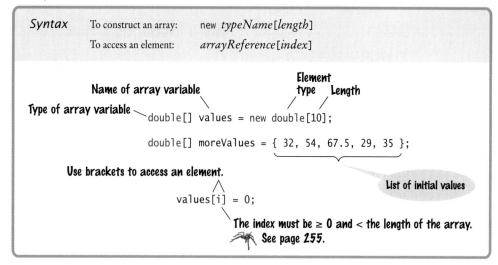

*Syntax*    To construct an array:    new *typeName*[*length*]
            To access an element:    *arrayReference*[*index*]

Name of array variable

Element type    Length

Type of array variable
```
double[] values = new double[10];
```

```
double[] moreValues = { 32, 54, 67.5, 29, 35 };
```

List of initial values

Use brackets to access an element.
```
values[i] = 0;
```

The index must be ≥ 0 and < the length of the array.
See page *255*.

Before continuing, we must take care of an important detail of Java arrays. If you look carefully at Figure 1, you will find that the *fifth* element was filled when we changed `values[4]`. In Java, the elements of arrays are numbered *starting at 0*. That is, the legal elements for the `values` array are

*Like a mailbox that is identified by a box number, an array element is identified by an index.*

> `values[0]`, the first element
>
> `values[1]`, the second element
>
> `values[2]`, the third element
>
> `values[3]`, the fourth element
>
> `values[4]`, the fifth element
>
> . . .
>
> `values[9]`, the tenth element

In other words, the declaration

> `double[] values = new double[10];`

creates an array with ten elements. In this array, an index can be any integer ranging from 0 to 9.

You have to be careful that the index stays within the valid range. Trying to access an element that does not exist in the array is a serious error. For example, if `values` has ten elements, you are not allowed to access `values[20]`. Attempting to access an element whose index is not within the valid index range is called a **bounds error**. The compiler does not catch this type of error. When a bounds error occurs at run time, it causes a run-time exception.

Here is a very common bounds error:

> `double[] values = new double[10];`
> `values[10] = value;`

There is no `values[10]` in an array with ten elements—the index can range from 0 to 9.

To avoid bounds errors, you will want to know how many elements are in an array. The expression `values.length` yields the length of the `values` array. Note that there are no parentheses following `length`.

An array index must be at least zero and less than the size of the array.

A bounds error, which occurs if you supply an invalid array index, can cause your program to terminate.

## Table 1 Declaring Arrays

| | |
|---|---|
| `int[] numbers = new int[10];` | An array of ten integers. All elements are initialized with zero. |
| `final int LENGTH = 10;`<br>`int[] numbers = new int[LENGTH];` | It is a good idea to use a named constant instead of a "magic number". |
| `int length = in.nextInt();`<br>`double[] data = new double[length];` | The length need not be a constant. |
| `int[] squares = { 0, 1, 4, 9, 16 };` | An array of five integers, with initial values. |
| `String[] friends = { "Emily", "Bob", "Cindy" };` | An array of three strings. |
| 🚫 `double[] data = new int[10];` | **Error:** You cannot initialize a `double[]` variable with an array of type `int[]`. |

Use the expression
*array*.length to find
the number of
elements in an array.

The following code ensures that you only access the array when the index variable i is within the legal bounds:

```
if (0 <= i && i < values.length) { values[i] = value; }
```

Arrays suffer from a significant limitation: *their length is fixed*. If you start out with an array of 10 elements and later decide that you need to add additional elements, then you need to make a new array and copy all elements of the existing array into the new array. We will discuss this process in detail in Section 6.3.9.

To visit all elements of an array, use a variable for the index. Suppose values has ten elements and the integer variable i is set to 0, 1, 2, and so on, up to 9. Then the expression values[i] yields each element in turn. For example, this loop displays all elements in the values array.

```
for (int i = 0; i < 10; i++)
{
    System.out.println(values[i]);
}
```

Note that in the loop condition the index is *less than* 10 because there is no element corresponding to values[10].

## 6.1.2 Array References

If you look closely at Figure 1, you will note that the variable values does not store any numbers. Instead, the array is stored elsewhere and the values variable holds a **reference** to the array. (The reference denotes the location of the array in memory.) When you access the elements in an array, you need not be concerned about the fact that Java uses array references. This only becomes important when copying array references.

When you copy an array variable into another, both variables refer to the same array (see Figure 2).

An array reference
specifies the location
of an array. Copying
the reference yields a
second reference to
the same array.

```
int[] scores = { 10, 9, 7, 4, 5 };
int[] values = scores; // Copying array reference
```

You can modify the array through either of the variables:

```
scores[3] = 10;
System.out.println(values[3]); // Prints 10
```

Section 6.3.9 shows how you can make a copy of the *contents* of the array.

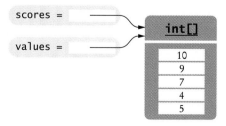

**Figure 2**
Two Array Variables Referencing the Same Array

### 6.1.3 Partially Filled Arrays

*With a partially filled array, you need to remember how many elements are filled.*

An array cannot change size at run time. This is a problem when you don't know in advance how many elements you need. In that situation, you must come up with a good guess on the maximum number of elements that you need to store. For example, we may decide that we sometimes want to store more than ten elements, but never more than 100:

```java
final int LENGTH = 100;
double[] values = new double[LENGTH];
```

In a typical program run, only a part of the array will be occupied by actual elements. We call such an array a **partially filled array**. You must keep a *companion variable* that counts how many elements are actually used. In Figure 3 we call the companion variable currentSize.

The following loop collects inputs and fills up the values array:

```java
int currentSize = 0;
Scanner in = new Scanner(System.in);
while (in.hasNextDouble())
{
   if (currentSize < values.length)
   {
      values[currentSize] = in.nextDouble();
      currentSize++;
   }
}
```

**With a partially filled array, keep a companion variable for the current size.**

At the end of this loop, currentSize contains the actual number of elements in the array. Note that you have to stop accepting inputs if the currentSize companion variable reaches the array length.

To process the gathered array elements, you again use the companion variable, not the array length. This loop prints the partially filled array:

**ONLINE EXAMPLE**

A program demonstrating array operations.

```java
for (int i = 0; i < currentSize; i++)
{
   System.out.println(values[i]);
}
```

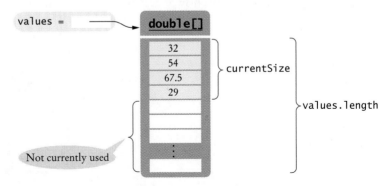

**Figure 3** A Partially Filled Array

1. Declare an array of integers containing the first five prime numbers.

2. Assume the array `primes` has been initialized as described in Self Check 1. What does it contain after executing the following loop?

```
for (int i = 0; i < 2; i++)
{
    primes[4 - i] = primes[i];
}
```

3. Assume the array `primes` has been initialized as described in Self Check 1. What does it contain after executing the following loop?

```
for (int i = 0; i < 5; i++)
{
    primes[i]++;
}
```

4. Given the declaration

```
int[] values = new int[10];
```

write statements to put the integer 10 into the elements of the array `values` with the lowest and the highest valid index.

5. Declare an array called `words` that can hold ten elements of type `String`.

6. Declare an array containing two strings, `"Yes"`, and `"No"`.

7. Can you produce the output on page 250 without storing the inputs in an array, by using an algorithm similar to the algorithm for finding the maximum in Section 4.7.5?

**Practice It** Now you can try these exercises at the end of the chapter: R6.1, R6.2, R6.6, P6.1.

---

### Bounds Errors

Perhaps the most common error in using arrays is accessing a nonexistent element.

```
double[] values = new double[10];
values[10] = 5.4;
    // Error—values has 10 elements, and the index can range from 0 to 9
```

If your program accesses an array through an out-of-bounds index, there is no compiler error message. Instead, the program will generate an exception at run time.

---

### Uninitialized Arrays

A common error is to allocate an array variable, but not an actual array.

```
double[] values;
values[0] = 29.95; // Error—values not initialized
```

The Java compiler will catch this error. The remedy is to initialize the variable with an array:

```
double[] values = new double[10];
```

**Programming Tip 6.1**

## Use Arrays for Sequences of Related Items

Arrays are intended for storing sequences of values with the same meaning. For example, an array of test scores makes perfect sense:

```
int[] scores = new int[NUMBER_OF_SCORES];
```

But an array

```
int[] personalData = new int[3];
```

that holds a person's age, bank balance, and shoe size in positions 0, 1, and 2 is bad design. It would be tedious for the programmer to remember which of these data values is stored in which array location. In this situation, it is far better to use three separate variables.

## *Random Fact 6.1*  An Early Internet Worm

In November 1988, Robert Morris, a student at Cornell University, launched a so-called virus program that infected about 6,000 computers connected to the Internet across the United States. Tens of thousands of computer users were unable to read their e-mail or otherwise use their computers. All major universities and many high-tech companies were affected. (The Internet was much smaller then than it is now.)

The particular kind of virus used in this attack is called a *worm*. The worm program crawled from one computer on the Internet to the next. The worm would attempt to connect to finger, a program in the UNIX operating system for finding information on a user who has an account on a particular computer on the network. Like many programs in UNIX, finger was written in the C language. In order to store the user name, the finger program allocated an array of 512 characters, under the assumption that nobody would ever provide such a long input. Unfortunately, C does not check that an array index is less than the length of the array. If you write into an array using an index that is too large, you simply overwrite memory locations that belong to some other objects. In some versions of the finger program, the programmer had been lazy and had not checked whether the array holding the input characters was large enough

to hold the input. So the worm program purposely filled the 512-character array with 536 bytes. The excess 24 bytes would overwrite a return address, which the attacker knew was stored just after the array. When that method was finished, it didn't return to its caller but to code supplied by the worm (see the figure, A "Buffer Overrun" Attack). That code ran under the same super-user privileges as finger, allowing the worm to gain entry into the remote system. Had the programmer who wrote finger been more conscientious, this particular attack would not be possible.

In Java, as in C, all programmers must be very careful not to overrun array boundaries. However, in Java, this error causes a run-time exception, and it never corrupts memory outside the array. This is one of the safety features of Java.

One may well speculate what would possess the virus author to spend many weeks to plan the antisocial act of breaking into thousands of computers and disabling them. It appears that the break-in was fully intended by the author, but the disabling of the computers was a bug, caused by continuous reinfection. Morris was sentenced to 3 years probation, 400 hours of community service, and a $10,000 fine.

In recent years, computer attacks have intensified and the motives have become more sinister. Instead

of disabling computers, viruses often steal financial data or use the attacked computers for sending spam e-mail. Sadly, many of these attacks continue to be possible because of poorly written programs that are susceptible to buffer overrun errors.

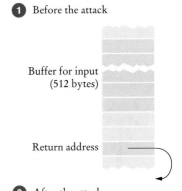

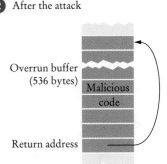

*A "Buffer Overrun" Attack*

# 6.2 The Enhanced for Loop

You can use the enhanced for loop to visit all elements of an array.

Often, you need to visit all elements of an array. The *enhanced for loop* makes this process particularly easy to program.

Here is how you use the enhanced for loop to total up all elements in an array named values:

```java
double[] values = . . .;
double total = 0;
for (double element : values)
{
    total = total + element;
}
```

The loop body is executed for each element in the array values. At the beginning of each loop iteration, the next element is assigned to the variable element. Then the loop body is executed. You should read this loop as "for each element in values".

This loop is equivalent to the following for loop and an explicit index variable:

```java
for (int i = 0; i < values.length; i++)
{
    double element = values[i];
    total = total + element;
}
```

Note an important difference between the enhanced for loop and the basic for loop. In the enhanced for loop, the *element variable* is assigned values[0], values[1], and so on. In the basic for loop, the *index variable* i is assigned 0, 1, and so on.

Use the enhanced for loop if you do not need the index values in the loop body.

Keep in mind that the enhanced for loop has a very specific purpose: getting the elements of a collection, from the beginning to the end. It is not suitable for all array algorithms. In particular, the enhanced for loop does not allow you to modify the contents of an array. The following loop does not fill an array with zeroes:

```java
for (double element : values)
{
    element = 0; // ERROR: this assignment does not modify array elements
}
```

When the loop is executed, the variable element is set to values[0]. Then element is set to 0, then to values[1], then to 0, and so on. The values array is not modified. The remedy is simple: Use a basic for loop:

**ONLINE EXAMPLE**

⊕ An program that demonstrates the enhanced for loop.

```java
for (int i = 0; i < values.length; i++)
{
    values[i] = 0; // OK
}
```

*The enhanced for loop is a convenient mechanism for traversing all elements in a collection.*

## Syntax 6.2    The Enhanced for Loop

*Syntax*    for (*typeName variable* : *collection*)
{
    *statements*
}

This variable is set in each loop iteration.
It is only defined inside the loop.

An array

for (double element : values)
{
    sum = sum + element;
}

These statements
are executed for each
element.

The variable
contains an element,
not an index.

**SELF CHECK**

**8.** What does this enhanced for loop do?

```
int counter = 0;
for (double element : values)
{
    if (element == 0) { counter++; }
}
```

**9.** Write an enhanced for loop that prints all elements in the array values.

**10.** Write an enhanced for loop that multiplies all elements in a double[] array named factors, accumulating the result in a variable named product.

**11.** Why is the enhanced for loop not an appropriate shortcut for the following basic for loop?

```
for (int i = 0; i < values.length; i++) { values[i] = i * i; }
```

**Practice It**    Now you can try these exercises at the end of the chapter: R6.7, R6.8, R6.9.

# 6.3  Common Array Algorithms

In the following sections, we discuss some of the most common algorithms for working with arrays. If you use a partially filled array, remember to replace values.length with the companion variable that represents the current size of the array.

## 6.3.1  Filling

This loop fills an array with squares (0, 1, 4, 9, 16, ...). Note that the element with index 0 contains $0^2$, the element with index 1 contains $1^2$, and so on.

```
for (int i = 0; i < values.length; i++)
{
    values[i] = i * i;
}
```

### 6.3.2 Sum and Average Value

You have already encountered this algorithm in Section 4.7.1. When the values are located in an array, the code looks much simpler:

```java
double total = 0;
for (double element : values)
{
    total = total + element;
}
double average = 0;
if (values.length > 0) { average = total / values.length; }
```

### 6.3.3 Maximum and Minimum

Use the algorithm from Section 4.7.5 that keeps a variable for the largest element already encountered. Here is the implementation of that algorithm for an array:

```java
double largest = values[0];
for (int i = 1; i < values.length; i++)
{
    if (values[i] > largest)
    {
        largest = values[i];
    }
}
```

Note that the loop starts at 1 because we initialize largest with values[0].

To compute the smallest element, reverse the comparison.

These algorithms require that the array contain at least one element.

### 6.3.4 Element Separators

When separating elements, don't place a separator before the first element.

When you display the elements of an array, you usually want to separate them, often with commas or vertical lines, like this:

```
32 | 54 | 67.5 | 29 | 35
```

Note that there is one fewer separator than there are numbers. Print the separator before each element in the sequence *except the initial one* (with index 0) like this:

```java
for (int i = 0; i < values.length; i++)
{
    if (i > 0)
    {
        System.out.print(" | ");
    }
    System.out.print(values[i]);
}
```

If you want comma separators, you can use the Arrays.toString method. The expression

```java
Arrays.toString(values)
```

returns a string describing the contents of the array values in the form

```
[32, 54, 67.5, 29, 35]
```

*To print five elements, you need four separators.*

The elements are surrounded by a pair of brackets and separated by commas. This method can be convenient for debugging:

```java
System.out.println("values=" + Arrays.toString(values));
```

## 6.3.5 Linear Search

*To search for a specific element, visit the elements and stop when you encounter the match.*

You often need to search for the position of a specific element in an array so that you can replace or remove it. Visit all elements until you have found a match or you have come to the end of the array. Here we search for the position of the first element in an array that is equal to 100:

```java
int searchedValue = 100;
int pos = 0;
boolean found = false;
while (pos < values.length && !found)
{
    if (values[pos] == searchedValue)
    {
        found = true;
    }
    else
    {
        pos++;
    }
}
if (found) { System.out.println("Found at position: " + pos); }
else { System.out.println("Not found"); }
```

A linear search inspects elements in sequence until a match is found.

This algorithm is called **linear search** or *sequential search* because you inspect the elements in sequence. If the array is sorted, you can use the more efficient **binary search** algorithm—see Special Topic 6.2 on page 267.

## 6.3.6 Removing an Element

Suppose you want to remove the element with index pos from the array values. As explained in Section 6.1.3, you need a companion variable for tracking the number of elements in the array. In this example, we use a companion variable called currentSize.

If the elements in the array are not in any particular order, simply overwrite the element to be removed with the *last* element of the array, then decrement the current-Size variable. (See Figure 4.)

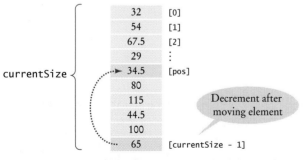

**Figure 4**
Removing an Element in an Unordered Array

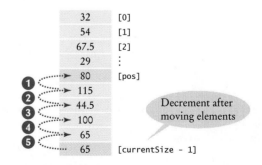

**Figure 5**
Removing an Element in an Ordered Array

```
values[pos] = values[currentSize - 1];
currentSize--;
```

**ANIMATION**
*Removing from an Array*

The situation is more complex if the order of the elements matters. Then you must move all elements following the element to be removed to a lower index, and then decrement the variable holding the size of the array. (See Figure 5.)

```
for (int i = pos + 1; i < currentSize; i++)
{
    values[i - 1] = values[i];
}
currentSize--;
```

## 6.3.7 Inserting an Element

**ANIMATION**
*Inserting into an Array*

In this section, you will see how to insert an element into an array. Note that you need a companion variable for tracking the array size, as explained in Section 6.1.3.

If the order of the elements does not matter, you can simply insert new elements at the end, incrementing the variable tracking the size.

```
if (currentSize < values.length)
{
    currentSize++;
    values[currentSize - 1] = newElement;
}
```

It is more work to insert an element at a particular position in the middle of an array. First, move all elements after the insertion location to a higher index. Then insert the new element (see Figure 7).

Note the order of the movement: When you remove an element, you first move the next element to a lower index, then the one after that, until you finally get to the end of the array. When you insert an element, you start at the end of the array, move that element to a higher index, then move the one before that, and so on until you finally get to the insertion location.

> Before inserting an element, move elements to the end of the array *starting with the last one.*

```
if (currentSize < values.length)
{
    currentSize++;
    for (int i = currentSize - 1; i > pos; i--)
    {
        values[i] = values[i - 1];
    }
    values[pos] = newElement;
}
```

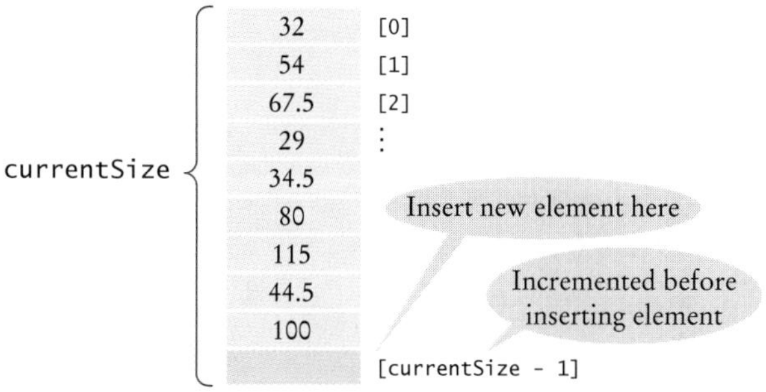

**Figure 6**
Inserting an Element in an Unordered Array

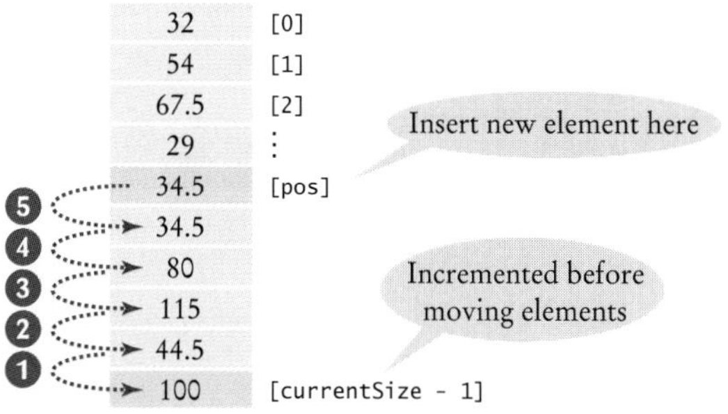

**Figure 7**
Inserting an Element in an Ordered Array

### 6.3.8 Swapping Elements

You often need to swap elements of an array. For example, you can sort an array by repeatedly swapping elements that are not in order.

Consider the task of swapping the elements at positions i and j of an array values. We'd like to set values[i] to values[j]. But that overwrites the value that is currently stored in values[i], so we want to save that first:

```
double temp = values[i];
values[i] = values[j];
```

Now we can set values[j] to the saved value.

```
values[j] = temp;
```

Figure 8 shows the process.

> Use a temporary variable when swapping two elements.

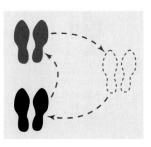

*To swap two elements, you need a temporary variable.*

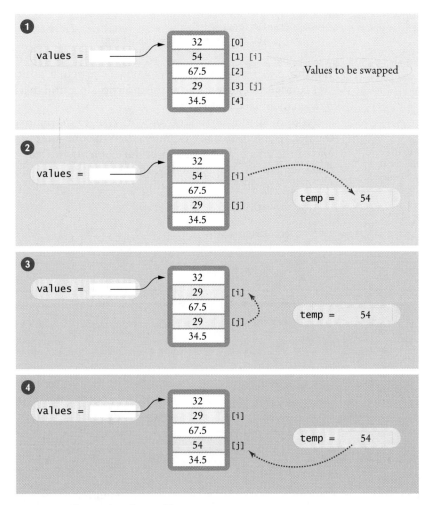

**Figure 8** Swapping Array Elements

### 6.3.9  Copying Arrays

Array variables do not themselves hold array elements. They hold a reference to the actual array. If you copy the reference, you get another reference to the same array (see Figure 9):

```
double[] values = new double[6];
. . .  // Fill array
double[] prices = values;  ❶
```

If you want to make a true copy of an array, call the `Arrays.copyOf` method (as shown in Figure 9).

```
double[] prices = Arrays.copyOf(values, values.length);  ❷
```

The call `Arrays.copyOf(values, n)` allocates an array of length n, copies the first n elements of values (or the entire values array if n > values.length) into it, and returns the new array.

> Use the Arrays.
> copyOf method to
> copy the elements of
> an array into a
> new array.

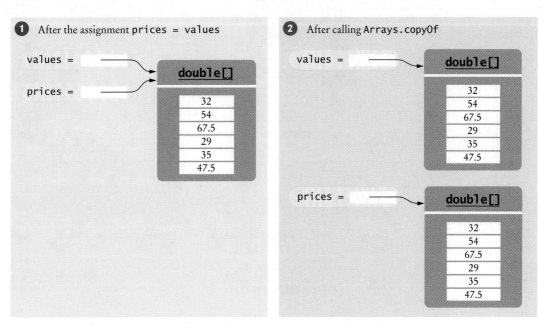

**Figure 9**   Copying an Array Reference versus Copying an Array

In order to use the `Arrays` class, you need to add the following statement to the top of your program:

```
import java.util.Arrays;
```

Another use for `Arrays.copyOf` is to grow an array that has run out of space. The following statements have the effect of doubling the length of an array (see Figure 10):

```
double[] newValues = Arrays.copyOf(values, 2 * values.length);  ❶
values = newValues;  ❷
```

The `copyOf` method was added in Java 6. If you use Java 5, replace

```
double[] newValues = Arrays.copyOf(values, n)
```

with

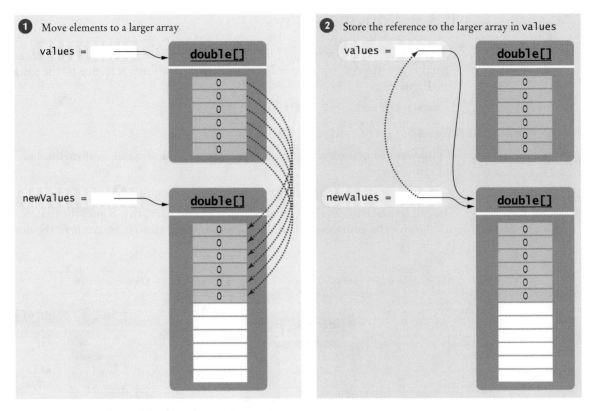

**Figure 10**    Growing an Array

```
double[] newValues = new double[n];
for (int i = 0; i < n && i < values.length; i++)
{
    newValues[i] = values[i];
}
```

## 6.3.10 Reading Input

If you know how many inputs the user will supply, it is simple to place them into an array:

```
double[] inputs = new double[NUMBER_OF_INPUTS];
for (i = 0; i < inputs.length; i++)
{
    inputs[i] = in.nextDouble();
}
```

However, this technique does not work if you need to read a sequence of arbitrary length. In that case, add the inputs to an array until the end of the input has been reached.

```
int currentSize = 0;
while (in.hasNextDouble() && currentSize < inputs.length)
{
    inputs[currentSize] = in.nextDouble();
    currentSize++;
}
```

Now inputs is a partially filled array, and the companion variable currentSize is set to the number of inputs.

However, this loop silently throws away inputs that don't fit into the array. A better approach is to grow the array to hold all inputs.

```java
double[] inputs = new double[INITIAL_SIZE];
int currentSize = 0;
while (in.hasNextDouble())
{
    // Grow the array if it has been completely filled
    if (currentSize >= inputs.length)
    {
        inputs = Arrays.copyOf(inputs, 2 * inputs.length); // Grow the inputs array
    }

    inputs[currentSize] = in.nextDouble();
    currentSize++;
}
```

When you are done, you can discard any excess (unfilled) elements:

```java
inputs = Arrays.copyOf(inputs, currentSize);
```

The following program puts these algorithms to work, solving the task that we set ourselves at the beginning of this chapter: to mark the largest value in an input sequence.

### section_3/LargestInArray.java

```java
1   import java.util.Scanner;
2
3   /**
4      This program reads a sequence of values and prints them, marking the largest value.
5   */
6   public class LargestInArray
7   {
8      public static void main(String[] args)
9      {
10         final int LENGTH = 100;
11         double[] values = new double[LENGTH];
12         int currentSize = 0;
13
14         // Read inputs
15
16         System.out.println("Please enter values, Q to quit:");
17         Scanner in = new Scanner(System.in);
18         while (in.hasNextDouble() && currentSize < values.length)
19         {
20            values[currentSize] = in.nextDouble();
21            currentSize++;
22         }
23
24         // Find the largest value
25
26         double largest = values[0];
27         for (int i = 1; i < currentSize; i++)
28         {
29            if (values[i] > largest)
30            {
31               largest = values[i];
32            }
33         }
```

```
34
35          // Print all values, marking the largest
36
37          for (int i = 0; i < currentSize; i++)
38          {
39             System.out.print(values[i]);
40             if (values[i] == largest)
41             {
42                System.out.print(" <== largest value");
43             }
44             System.out.println();
45          }
46       }
47  }
```

**Program Run**

```
Please enter values, Q to quit:
34.5 80 115 44.5 Q
34.5
80
115 <== largest value
44.5
```

**12.** Given these inputs, what is the output of the LargestInArray program?

```
20 10 20 Q
```

**13.** Write a loop that counts how many elements in an array are equal to zero.

**14.** Consider the algorithm to find the largest element in an array. Why don't we initialize largest and i with zero, like this?

```
double largest = 0;
for (int i = 0; i < values.length; i++)
{
   if (values[i] > largest)
   {
      largest = values[i];
   }
}
```

**15.** When printing separators, we skipped the separator before the initial element. Rewrite the loop so that the separator is printed *after* each element, except for the last element.

**16.** What is wrong with these statements for printing an array with separators?

```
System.out.print(values[0]);
for (int i = 1; i < values.length; i++)
{
   System.out.print(", " + values[i]);
}
```

**17.** When finding the position of a match, we used a while loop, not a for loop. What is wrong with using this loop instead?

```
for (pos = 0; pos < values.length && !found; pos++)
{
   if (values[pos] > 100)
   {
      found = true;
   }
```

```
    }
```

**18.** When inserting an element into an array, we moved the elements with larger index values, starting at the end of the array. Why is it wrong to start at the insertion location, like this?

```
for (int i = pos; i < currentSize - 1; i++)
{
    values[i + 1] = values[i];
}
```

**Practice It**  Now you can try these exercises at the end of the chapter: R6.17, R6.20, P6.15.

---

**Common Error 6.3**

### Underestimating the Size of a Data Set

Programmers commonly underestimate the amount of input data that a user will pour into an unsuspecting program. Suppose you write a program to search for text in a file. You store each line in a string, and keep an array of strings. How big do you make the array? Surely nobody is going to challenge your program with an input that is more than 100 lines. Really? It is very easy to feed in the entire text of *Alice in Wonderland* or *War and Peace* (which are available on the Internet). All of a sudden, your program has to deal with tens or hundreds of thousands of lines. You either need to allow for large inputs or politely reject the excess input.

---

**Special Topic 6.1**

### Sorting with the Java Library

Sorting an array efficiently is not an easy task. You will learn in Chapter 14 how to implement efficient sorting algorithms. Fortunately, the Java library provides an efficient sort method.

To sort an array values, call

```
Arrays.sort(values);
```

If the array is partially filled, call

```
Arrays.sort(values, 0, currentSize);
```

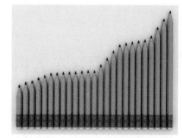

---

**Special Topic 6.2**

### Binary Search

When an array is sorted, there is a much faster search algorithm than the linear search of Section 6.3.5.

Consider the following sorted array values.

| [0] | [1] | [2] | [3] | [4] | [5] | [6] | [7] |
|-----|-----|-----|-----|-----|-----|-----|-----|
| 1 | 5 | 8 | 9 | 12 | 17 | 20 | 32 |

We would like to see whether the number 15 is in the array. Let's narrow our search by finding whether the number is in the first or second half of the array. The last point in the first half of the values array, values[3], is 9, which is smaller than the number we are looking for. Hence, we should look in the second half of the array for a match, that is, in the sequence:

| [0] | [1] | [2] | [3] | [4] | [5] | [6] | [7] |
|-----|-----|-----|-----|-----|-----|-----|-----|
| 1 | 5 | 8 | 9 | 12 | 17 | 20 | 32 |

Now the last element of the first half of this sequence is 17; hence, the number must be located in the sequence:

```
[0] [1] [2] [3] [4] [5] [6] [7]
 1   5   8   9  12  17  20  32
```

The last element of the first half of this very short sequence is 12, which is smaller than the number that we are searching, so we must look in the second half:

```
[0] [1] [2] [3] [4] [5] [6] [7]
 1   5   8   9  12  17  20  32
```

We still don't have a match because $15 \neq 17$, and we cannot divide the subsequence further. If we wanted to insert 15 into the sequence, we would need to insert it just before values[5].

This search process is called a **binary search**, because we cut the size of the search in half in each step. That cutting in half works only because we know that the array is sorted. Here is an implementation in Java:

```java
boolean found = false;
int low = 0;
int high = values.length - 1;
int pos = 0;
while (low <= high && !found)
{
    pos = (low + high) / 2; // Midpoint of the subsequence
    if (values[pos] == searchedNumber) { found = true; }
    else if (values[pos] < searchedNumber) { low = pos + 1; } // Look in second half
    else { high = pos - 1; } // Look in first half
}
if (found) { System.out.println("Found at position " + pos); }
else { System.out.println("Not found. Insert before position " + pos); }
```

# 6.4 Using Arrays with Methods

In this section, we will explore how to write methods that process arrays.

Arrays can occur as method arguments and return values.

When you define a method with an array argument, you provide a parameter variable for the array. For example, the following method computes the sum of an array of floating-point numbers:

```java
public static double sum(double[] values)
{
    double total = 0;
    for (double element : values)
    {
        total = total + element;
    }
    return total;
}
```

This method visits the array elements, but it does not modify them. It is also possible to modify the elements of an array. The following method multiplies all elements of an array by a given factor:

```java
public static void multiply(double[] values, double factor)
{
    for (int i = 0; i < values.length; i++)
    {
```

```
            values[i] = values[i] * factor;
        }
    }
```

Figure 11 traces the method call

```
    multiply(scores, 10);
```

Note these steps:

- The parameter variables `values` and `factor` are created. **①**
- The parameter variables are initialized with the arguments that are passed in the call. In our case, `values` is set to `scores` and `factor` is set to 10. Note that `values` and `scores` are references to the *same* array. **②**
- The method multiplies all array elements by 10. **③**
- The method returns. Its parameter variables are removed. However, `scores` still refers to the array with the modified elements. **④**

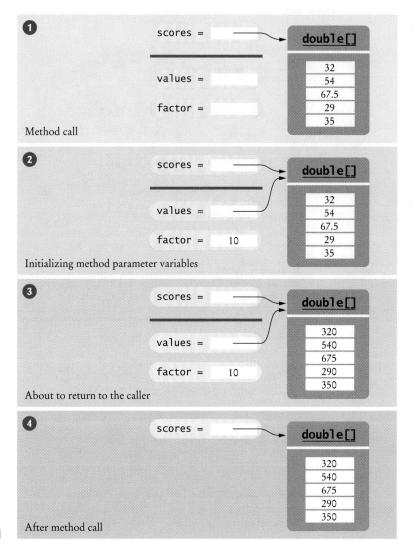

**Figure 11**
Trace of Call to
the `multiply` Method

A method can return an array. Simply build up the result in the method and return it. In this example, the squares method returns an array of squares from $0^2$ up to $(n-1)^2$:

```java
public static int[] squares(int n)
{
   int[] result = new int[n];
   for (int i = 0; i < n; i++)
   {
      result[i] = i * i;
   }
   return result;
}
```

The following example program reads values from standard input, multiplies them by 10, and prints the result in reverse order. The program uses three methods:

- The readInputs method returns an array, using the algorithm of Section 6.3.10.
- The multiply method has an array argument. It modifies the array elements.
- The printReversed method also has an array argument, but it does not modify the array elements.

### section_4/Reverse.java

```java
 1   import java.util.Scanner;
 2
 3   /**
 4      This program reads, scales, and reverses a sequence of numbers.
 5   */
 6   public class Reverse
 7   {
 8      public static void main(String[] args)
 9      {
10         double[] numbers = readInputs(5);
11         multiply(numbers, 10);
12         printReversed(numbers);
13      }
14
15      /**
16         Reads a sequence of floating-point numbers.
17         @param numberOfInputs the number of inputs to read
18         @return an array containing the input values
19      */
20      public static double[] readInputs(int numberOfInputs)
21      {
22         System.out.println("Enter " + numberOfInputs + " numbers: ");
23         Scanner in = new Scanner(System.in);
24         double[] inputs = new double[numberOfInputs];
25         for (int i = 0; i < inputs.length; i++)
26         {
27            inputs[i] = in.nextDouble();
28         }
29         return inputs;
30      }
31
32      /**
33         Multiplies all elements of an array by a factor.
34         @param values an array
35         @param factor the value with which element is multiplied
36      */
```

```
37    public static void multiply(double[] values, double factor)
38    {
39       for (int i = 0; i < values.length; i++)
40       {
41          values[i] = values[i] * factor;
42       }
43    }
44
45    /**
46       Prints an array in reverse order.
47       @param values an array of numbers
48       @return an array that contains the elements of values in reverse order
49    */
50    public static void printReversed(double[] values)
51    {
52       // Traverse the array in reverse order, starting with the last element
53       for (int i = values.length - 1; i >= 0; i--)
54       {
55          System.out.print(values[i] + " ");
56       }
57       System.out.println();
58    }
59 }
```

**Program Run**

```
Enter 5 numbers:
12 25 20 0 10
100.0 0.0 200.0 250.0 120.0
```

**SELF CHECK**

19. How do you call the squares method to compute the first five squares and store the result in an array `numbers`?

20. Write a method `fill` that fills all elements of an array of integers with a given value. For example, the call `fill(scores, 10)` should fill all elements of the array `scores` with the value 10.

21. Describe the purpose of the following method:

```java
public static int[] mystery(int length, int n)
{
   int[] result = new int[length];
   for (int i = 0; i < result.length; i++)
   {
      result[i] = (int) (n * Math.random());
   }
   return result;
}
```

22. Consider the following method that reverses an array:

```java
public static int[] reverse(int[] values)
{
   int[] result = new int[values.length];
   for (int i = 0; i < values.length; i++)
   {
      result[i] = values[values.length - 1 - i];
   }
   return result;
}
```

Suppose the reverse method is called with an array scores that contains the numbers 1, 4, and 9. What is the contents of scores after the method call?

**23.** Provide a trace diagram of the reverse method when called with an array that contains the values 1, 4, and 9.

**Practice It**    Now you can try these exercises at the end of the chapter: R6.25, P6.6, P6.7.

---

### Methods with a Variable Number of Parameters

Starting with Java version 5.0, it is possible to declare methods that receive a variable number of parameters. For example, we can write a sum method that can compute the sum of any number of arguments:

```
int a = sum(1, 3); // Sets a to 4
int b = sum(1, 7, 2, 9); // Sets b to 19
```

The modified sum method must be declared as

```
public static void sum(int... values)
```

The ... symbol indicates that the method can receive any number of int arguments. The values parameter variable is actually an int[] array that contains all arguments that were passed to the method. The method implementation traverses the values array and processes the elements:

```
public void sum(int... values)
{
    int total = 0;
    for (int i = 0; i < values.length; i++) // values is an int[]
    {
        total = total + values[i];
    }
    return total;
}
```

---

# 6.5 Problem Solving: Adapting Algorithms

By combining fundamental algorithms, you can solve complex programming tasks.

In Section 6.3, you were introduced to a number of fundamental array algorithms. These algorithms form the building blocks for many programs that process arrays. In general, it is a good problem-solving strategy to have a repertoire of fundamental algorithms that you can combine and adapt.

Consider this example problem: You are given the quiz scores of a student. You are to compute the final quiz score, which is the sum of all scores after dropping the lowest one. For example, if the scores are

```
8  7  8.5  9.5  7  4  10
```

then the final score is 50.

We do not have a ready-made algorithm for this situation. Instead, consider which algorithms may be related. These include:

- Calculating the sum (Section 6.3.2)
- Finding the minimum value (Section 6.3.3)
- Removing an element (Section 6.3.6)

We can formulate a plan of attack that combines these algorithms:

**Find the minimum.**
**Remove it from the array.**
**Calculate the sum.**

Let's try it out with our example. The minimum of

```
    [0] [1] [2] [3] [4] [5] [6]
     8   7  8.5 9.5  7   4  10
```

is 4. How do we remove it?

Now we have a problem. The removal algorithm in Section 6.3.6 locates the element to be removed by using the *position* of the element, not the value.

But we have another algorithm for that:

- Linear search (Section 6.3.5)

We need to fix our plan of attack:

**Find the minimum value.**
**Find its position.**
**Remove that position from the array.**
**Calculate the sum.**

Will it work? Let's continue with our example.

We found a minimum value of 4. Linear search tells us that the value 4 occurs at position 5.

```
    [0] [1] [2] [3] [4] [5] [6]
     8   7  8.5 9.5  7   4  10
```

We remove it:

```
    [0] [1] [2] [3] [4] [5]
     8   7  8.5 9.5  7  10
```

Finally, we compute the sum: $8 + 7 + 8.5 + 9.5 + 7 + 10 = 50$.

This walkthrough demonstrates that our strategy works.

Can we do better? It seems a bit inefficient to find the minimum and then make another pass through the array to obtain its position.

We can adapt the algorithm for finding the minimum to yield the position of the minimum. Here is the original algorithm:

```java
double smallest = values[0];
for (int i = 1; i < values.length; i++)
{
   if (values[i] < smallest)
   {
      smallest = values[i];
   }
}
```

> You should be familiar with the implementation of fundamental algorithms so that you can adapt them.

When we find the smallest value, we also want to update the position:

```java
if (values[i] < smallest)
{
   smallest = values[i];
   smallestPosition = i;
}
```

In fact, then there is no reason to keep track of the smallest value any longer. It is simply `values[smallestPosition]`. With this insight, we can adapt the algorithm as follows:

```java
int smallestPosition = 0;
for (int i = 1; i < values.length; i++)
{
   if (values[i] < values[smallestPosition])
   {
      smallestPosition = i;
   }
}
```

**ONLINE EXAMPLE**

A program that computes the final score using the adapted algorithm for finding the minimum.

With this adaptation, our problem is solved with the following strategy:

**Find the position of the minimum.**
**Remove it from the array.**
**Calculate the sum.**

The next section shows you a technique for discovering a new algorithm when none of the fundamental algorithms can be adapted to a task.

**SELF CHECK**

24. Section 6.3.6 has two algorithms for removing an element. Which of the two should be used to solve the task described in this section?

25. It isn't actually necessary to *remove* the minimum in order to compute the total score. Describe an alternative.

26. How can you print the number of positive and negative values in a given array, using one or more of the algorithms in Section 4.7?

27. How can you print all positive values in an array, separated by commas?

28. Consider the following algorithm for collecting all matches in an array:

```java
int matchesSize = 0;
for (int i = 0; i < values.length; i++)
{
   if (values[i] fulfills the condition)
   {
      matches[matchesSize] = values[i];
      matchesSize++;
   }
}
```

How can this algorithm help you with Self Check 27?

**Practice It**    Now you can try these exercises at the end of the chapter: R6.26, R6.27.

---

**Programming Tip 6.2**

### Reading Exception Reports

You will sometimes have programs that terminate, reporting an "exception", such as

```
Exception in thread "main" java.lang.ArrayIndexOutOfBoundsException: 10
    at Homework1.processValues(Homework1.java:14)
    at Homework1.main(Homework1.java:36)
```

Quite a few students give up at that point, saying "it didn't work", or "my program died", without reading the error message. Admittedly, the format of the exception report is not very friendly. But, with some practice, it is easy to decipher it.

There are two pieces of useful information:

1. The name of the exception, such as `ArrayIndexOutOfBoundsException`
2. The stack trace, that is, the method calls that led to the exception, such as `Homework1.java:14` and `Homework1.java:36` in our example.

The name of the exception is always in the first line of the report, and it ends in `Exception`. If you get an `ArrayIndexOutOfBoundsException`, then there was a problem with an invalid array index. That is useful information.

To determine the line number of the offending code, look at the file names and line numbers. The first line of the stack trace is the method that actually generated the exception. The last line of the stack trace is a line in `main`. In our example, the exception was caused by line 14 of `Homework1.java`. Open up the file, go to that line, and look at it! Also look at the name of the exception. In most cases, these two pieces of information will make it completely obvious what went wrong, and you can easily fix your error.

Sometimes, the exception was thrown by a method that is in the standard library. Here is a typical example:

```
Exception in thread "main" java.lang.StringIndexOutOfBoundsException: String index
    out of range: -4
   at java.lang.String.substring(String.java:1444)
   at Homework2.main(Homework2.java:29)
```

The exception happened in the `substring` method of the `String` class, but the real culprit is the first method in a file that you wrote. In this example, that is `Homework2.main`, and you should look at line 29 of `Homework2.java`.

---

## HOW TO 6.1    Working with Arrays

In many data processing situations, you need to process a sequence of values. This How To walks you through the steps for storing input values in an array and carrying out computations with the array elements.

Consider again the problem from Section 6.5: A final quiz score is computed by adding all the scores, except for the lowest one. For example, if the scores are

8  7  8.5  9.5  7  5  10

then the final score is 50.

**Step 1**   Decompose your task into steps.

You will usually want to break down your task into multiple steps, such as

- Reading the data into an array.
- Processing the data in one or more steps.
- Displaying the results.

When deciding how to process the data, you should be familiar with the array algorithms in Section 6.3. Most processing tasks can be solved by using one or more of these algorithms.

In our sample problem, we will want to read the data. Then we will remove the minimum and compute the total. For example, if the input is 8 7 8.5 9.5 7 5 10, we will remove the minimum of 5, yielding 8 7 8.5 9.5 7 10. The sum of those values is the final score of 50.

Thus, we have identified three steps:

**Read inputs.**
**Remove the minimum.**
**Calculate the sum.**

**Step 2**    Determine which algorithm(s) you need.

Sometimes, a step corresponds to exactly one of the basic array algorithms in Section 6.3. That is the case with calculating the sum (Section 6.3.2) and reading the inputs (Section 6.3.10). At other times, you need to combine several algorithms. To remove the minimum value, you can find the minimum value (Section 6.3.3), find its position (Section 6.3.5), and remove the element at that position (Section 6.3.6).

We have now refined our plan as follows:

**Read inputs.**
**Find the minimum.**
**Find its position.**
**Remove the minimum.**
**Calculate the sum.**

This plan will work—see Section 6.5. But here is an alternate approach. It is easy to compute the sum and subtract the minimum. Then we don't have to find its position. The revised plan is

**Read inputs.**
**Find the minimum.**
**Calculate the sum.**
**Subtract the minimum.**

**Step 3**    Use methods to structure the program.

Even though it may be possible to put all steps into the main method, this is rarely a good idea. It is better to make each processing step into a separate method. In our example, we will implement three methods:

- readInputs
- sum
- minimum

The main method simply calls these methods:

```
double[] scores = readInputs();
double total = sum(scores) - minimum(scores);
System.out.println("Final score: " + total);
```

**Step 4**    Assemble and test the program.

Place your methods into a class. Review your code and check that you handle both normal and exceptional situations. What happens with an empty array? One that contains a single element? When no match is found? When there are multiple matches? Consider these boundary conditions and make sure that your program works correctly.

In our example, it is impossible to compute the minimum if the array is empty. In that case, we should terminate the program with an error message *before* attempting to call the minimum method.

What if the minimum value occurs more than once? That means that a student had more than one test with the same low score. We subtract only one of the occurrences of that low score, and that is the desired behavior.

The following table shows test cases and their expected output:

| Test Case | Expected Output | Comment |
|---|---|---|
| 8 7 8.5 9.5 7 5 10 | 50 | See Step 1. |
| 8 7 7 9 | 24 | Only one instance of the low score should be removed. |
| 8 | 0 | After removing the low score, no score remains. |
| (no inputs) | **Error** | That is not a legal input. |

Here's the complete program (how_to_1/Scores.java):

```java
import java.util.Arrays;
import java.util.Scanner;

/**
   This program computes a final score for a series of quiz scores: the sum after dropping
   the lowest score. The program uses arrays.
*/
public class Scores
{
   public static void main(String[] args)
   {
      double[] scores = readInputs();
      if (scores.length == 0)
      {
         System.out.println("At least one score is required.");
      }
      else
      {
         double total = sum(scores) - minimum(scores);
         System.out.println("Final score: " + total);
      }
   }

   /**
      Reads a sequence of floating-point numbers.
      @return an array containing the numbers
   */
   public static double[] readInputs()
   {
      // Read the input values into an array

      final int INITIAL_SIZE = 10;
      double[] inputs = new double[INITIAL_SIZE];
      System.out.println("Please enter values, Q to quit:");
      Scanner in = new Scanner(System.in);
      int currentSize = 0;
      while (in.hasNextDouble())
      {
         // Grow the array if it has been completely filled
```

```
            if (currentSize >= inputs.length)
            {
                inputs = Arrays.copyOf(inputs, 2 * inputs.length);
            }
            inputs[currentSize] = in.nextDouble();
            currentSize++;
        }

        return Arrays.copyOf(inputs, currentSize);
    }

    /**
        Computes the sum of the values in an array.
        @param values an array
        @return the sum of the values in values
    */
    public static double sum(double[] values)
    {
        double total = 0;
        for (double element : values)
        {
            total = total + element;
        }
        return total;
    }

    /**
        Gets the minimum value from an array.
        @param values an array of size >= 1
        @return the smallest element of values
    */
    public static double minimum(double[] values)
    {
        double smallest = values[0];
        for (int i = 1; i < values.length; i++)
        {
            if (values[i] < smallest)
            {
                smallest = values[i];
            }
        }
        return smallest;
    }
}
```

## WORKED EXAMPLE 6.1    Rolling the Dice

This Worked Example shows how to analyze a set of die tosses to see whether the die is "fair".

# 6.6 Problem Solving: Discovering Algorithms by Manipulating Physical Objects

*Manipulating physical objects can give you ideas for discovering algorithms.*

In Section 6.5, you saw how to solve a problem by combining and adapting known algorithms. But what do you do when none of the standard algorithms is sufficient for your task? In this section, you will learn a technique for discovering algorithms by manipulating physical objects.

Consider the following task: You are given an array whose size is an even number, and you are to switch the first and the second half. For example, if the array contains the eight numbers

9   13  21  4   11  7   1   3

then you should change it to

11  7   1   3   9   13  21  4

Many students find it quite challenging to come up with an algorithm. They may know that a loop is required, and they may realize that elements should be inserted (Section 6.3.7) or swapped (Section 6.3.8), but they do not have sufficient intuition to draw diagrams, describe an algorithm, or write down pseudocode.

One useful technique for discovering an algorithm is to manipulate physical objects. Start by lining up some objects to denote an array. Coins, playing cards, or small toys are good choices.

Here we arrange eight coins:

**Use a sequence of coins, playing cards, or toys to visualize an array of values.**

Now let's step back and see what we can do to change the order of the coins. We can remove a coin (Section 6.3.6):

*Visualizing the removal of an array element*

We can insert a coin (Section 6.3.7):

*Visualizing the insertion of an array element*

Or we can swap two coins (Section 6.3.8).

*Visualizing the swapping of two coins*

Go ahead—line up some coins and try out these three operations right now so that you get a feel for them.

Now how does that help us with our problem, switching the first and the second half of the array?

Let's put the first coin into place, by swapping it with the fifth coin. However, as Java programmers, we will say that we swap the coins in positions 0 and 4:

Next, we swap the coins in positions 1 and 5:

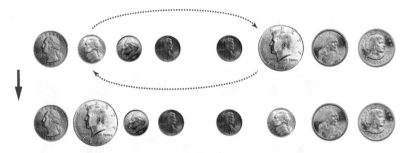

Two more swaps, and we are done:

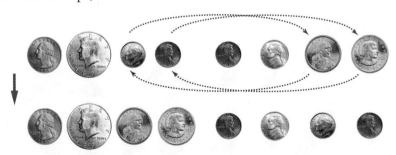

Now an algorithm is becoming apparent:

```
i = 0
j = ... (we'll think about that in a minute)
While (don't know yet)
    Swap elements at positions i and j
    i++
    j++
```

Where does the variable j start? When we have eight coins, the coin at position zero is moved to position 4. In general, it is moved to the middle of the array, or to position **size / 2**.

And how many iterations do we make? We need to swap all coins in the first half. That is, we need to swap **size / 2** coins. The pseudocode is

**ONLINE EXAMPLE**

A program that implements the algorithm that switches the first and second halves of an array.

```
i = 0
j = size / 2
While (i < size / 2)
    Swap elements at positions i and j
    i++
    j++
```

It is a good idea to make a walkthrough of the pseudocode (see Section 4.2). You can use paper clips to denote the positions of the variables i and j. If the walkthrough is successful, then we know that there was no "off-by-one" error in the pseudocode. Self Check 29 asks you to carry out the walkthrough, and Exercise P6.8 asks you to translate the pseudocode to Java. Exercise R6.28 suggests a different algorithm for switching the two halves of an array, by repeatedly removing and inserting coins.

You can use paper clips as position markers or counters.

Many people find that the manipulation of physical objects is less intimidating than drawing diagrams or mentally envisioning algorithms. Give it a try when you need to design a new algorithm!

**SELF CHECK**

29. Walk through the algorithm that we developed in this section, using two paper clips to indicate the positions for i and j. Explain why there are no bounds errors in the pseudocode.

30. Take out some coins and simulate the following pseudocode, using two paper clips to indicate the positions for i and j.

```
i = 0
j = size - 1
While (i < j)
    Swap elements at positions i and j
    i++
    j--
```

What does the algorithm do?

31. Consider the task of rearranging all elements in an array so that the even numbers come first. Otherwise, the order doesn't matter. For example, the array

1 4 14 2 1 3 5 6 23

could be rearranged to

4 2 14 6 1 5 3 23 1

Using coins and paperclips, discover an algorithm that solves this task by swapping elements, then describe it in pseudocode.

32. Discover an algorithm for the task of Self Check 31 that uses removal and insertion of elements instead of swapping.

33. Consider the algorithm in Section 4.7.4 that finds the largest element in a sequence of inputs—*not* the largest element in an array. Why is this algorithm better visualized by picking playing cards from a deck rather than arranging toy soldiers in a sequence?

**Practice It**    Now you can try these exercises at the end of the chapter: R6.28, R6.29, P6.8.

---

**VIDEO EXAMPLE 6.1**    **Removing Duplicates from an Array**

In this Video Example, we will discover an algorithm for removing duplicates from an array.

# 6.7 Two-Dimensional Arrays

It often happens that you want to store collections of values that have a two-dimensional layout. Such data sets commonly occur in financial and scientific applications. An arrangement consisting of rows and columns of values is called a *two-dimensional array*, or a *matrix*.

Let's explore how to store the example data shown in Figure 12: the medal counts of the figure skating competitions at the 2010 Winter Olympics.

|               | Gold | Silver | Bronze |
|---------------|------|--------|--------|
| Canada        | 1    | 0      | 1      |
| China         | 1    | 1      | 0      |
| Germany       | 0    | 0      | 1      |
| Korea         | 1    | 0      | 0      |
| Japan         | 0    | 1      | 1      |
| Russia        | 0    | 1      | 1      |
| United States | 1    | 1      | 0      |

**Figure 12**   Figure Skating Medal Counts

➕ Available online in WileyPLUS and at www.wiley.com/college/horstmann.

### 6.7.1 Declaring Two-Dimensional Arrays

*Use a two-dimensional array to store tabular data.*

In Java, you obtain a two-dimensional array by supplying the number of rows and columns. For example, `new int[7][3]` is an array with seven rows and three columns. You store a reference to such an array in a variable of type `int[][]`. Here is a complete declaration of a two-dimensional array, suitable for holding our medal count data:

```java
final int COUNTRIES = 7;
final int MEDALS = 3;
int[][] counts = new int[COUNTRIES][MEDALS];
```

Alternatively, you can declare and initialize the array by grouping each row:

```java
int[][] counts =
   {
      { 1, 0, 1 },
      { 1, 1, 0 },
      { 0, 0, 1 },
      { 1, 0, 0 },
      { 0, 1, 1 },
      { 0, 1, 1 },
      { 1, 1, 0 }
   };
```

As with one-dimensional arrays, you cannot change the size of a two-dimensional array once it has been declared.

### Syntax 6.3  Two-Dimensional Array Declaration

```
                                          Number of rows
              Name      Element type      Number of columns
                \           \            /  /
   double[][] tableEntries = new double[7][3];
                                              All values are initialized with 0.

        Name
          \
   int[][] data = {
                                    List of initial values
                    { 16, 3, 2, 13 },
                    { 5, 10, 11, 8 },
                    { 9, 6, 7, 12 },
                    { 4, 15, 14, 1 },
                 };
```

### 6.7.2 Accessing Elements

*Individual elements in a two-dimensional array are accessed by using two index values, array[i][j].*

To access a particular element in the two-dimensional array, you need to specify two index values in separate brackets to select the row and column, respectively (see Figure 13):

```java
int medalCount = counts[3][1];
```

To access all elements in a two-dimensional array, you use two nested loops. For example, the following loop prints all elements of counts:

```java
for (int i = 0; i < COUNTRIES; i++)
{
    // Process the ith row
    for (int j = 0; j < MEDALS; j++)
    {
        // Process the jth column in the ith row
        System.out.printf("%8d", counts[i][j]);
    }
    System.out.println(); // Start a new line at the end of the row
}
```

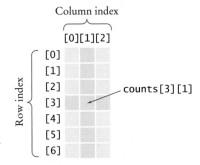

**Figure 13**
Accessing an Element in a
Two-Dimensional Array

### 6.7.3 Locating Neighboring Elements

Some programs that work with two-dimensional arrays need to locate the elements that are adjacent to an element. This task is particularly common in games. Figure 14 shows how to compute the index values of the neighbors of an element.

For example, the neighbors of counts[3][1] to the left and right are counts[3][0] and counts[3][2]. The neighbors to the top and bottom are counts[2][1] and counts[4][1].

You need to be careful about computing neighbors at the boundary of the array. For example, counts[0][1] has no neighbor to the top. Consider the task of computing the sum of the neighbors to the top and bottom of the element count[i][j]. You need to check whether the element is located at the top or bottom of the array:

```java
int total = 0;
if (i > 0) { total = total + counts[i - 1][j]; }
if (i < ROWS - 1) { total = total + counts[i + 1][j]; }
```

|  |  |  |
|---|---|---|
| [i - 1][j - 1] | [i - 1][j] | [i - 1][j + 1] |
| [i][j - 1] | [i][j] | [i][j + 1] |
| [i + 1][j - 1] | [i + 1][j] | [i + 1][j + 1] |

**Figure 14**
Neighboring Locations in a
Two-Dimensional Array

### 6.7.4  Computing Row and Column Totals

A common task is to compute row or column totals. In our example, the row totals give us the total number of medals won by a particular country.

Finding the right index values is a bit tricky, and it is a good idea to make a quick sketch. To compute the total of row i, we need to visit the following elements:

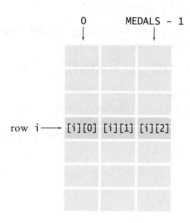

As you can see, we need to compute the sum of counts[i][j], where j ranges from 0 to MEDALS - 1. The following loop computes the total:

```
int total = 0;
for (int j = 0; j < MEDALS; j++)
{
    total = total + counts[i][j];
}
```

Computing column totals is similar. Form the sum of counts[i][j], where i ranges from 0 to COUNTRIES - 1.

```
int total = 0;
for (int i = 0; i < COUNTRIES; i++)
{
    total = total + counts[i][j];
}
```

**ANIMATION**
*Tracing a Nested
Loop in a 2D Array*

## 6.7.5 Two-Dimensional Array Parameters

When you pass a two-dimensional array to a method, you will want to recover the dimensions of the array. If values is a two-dimensional array, then

- values.length is the number of rows.
- values[0].length is the number of columns. (See Special Topic 6.4 for an explanation of this expression.)

For example, the following method computes the sum of all elements in a two-dimensional array:

```java
public static int sum(int[][] values)
{
   int total = 0;
   for (int i = 0; i < values.length; i++)
   {
      for (int j = 0; j < values[0].length; j++)
      {
         total = total + values[i][j];
      }
   }
   return total;
}
```

Working with two-dimensional arrays is illustrated in the following program. The program prints out the medal counts and the row totals.

### section_7/Medals.java

```java
1   /**
2       This program prints a table of medal winner counts with row totals.
3   */
4   public class Medals
5   {
6      public static void main(String[] args)
7      {
8         final int COUNTRIES = 7;
9         final int MEDALS = 3;
10
11        String[] countries =
12           {
13              "Canada",
14              "China",
15              "Germany",
16              "Korea",
17              "Japan",
18              "Russia",
19              "United States"
20           };
21
22        int[][] counts =
23           {
24              { 1, 0, 1 },
25              { 1, 1, 0 },
26              { 0, 0, 1 },
27              { 1, 0, 0 },
28              { 0, 1, 1 },
29              { 0, 1, 1 },
30              { 1, 1, 0 }
```

```
31          };
32
33          System.out.println("          Country    Gold  Silver  Bronze    Total");
34
35          // Print countries, counts, and row totals
36          for (int i = 0; i < COUNTRIES; i++)
37          {
38              // Process the ith row
39              System.out.printf("%15s", countries[i]);
40
41              int total = 0;
42
43              // Print each row element and update the row total
44              for (int j = 0; j < MEDALS; j++)
45              {
46                  System.out.printf("%8d", counts[i][j]);
47                  total = total + counts[i][j];
48              }
49
50              // Display the row total and print a new line
51              System.out.printf("%8d\n", total);
52          }
53      }
54  }
```

**Program Run**

| Country | Gold | Silver | Bronze | Total |
|---|---|---|---|---|
| Canada | 1 | 0 | 1 | 2 |
| China | 1 | 1 | 0 | 2 |
| Germany | 0 | 0 | 1 | 1 |
| Korea | 1 | 0 | 0 | 1 |
| Japan | 0 | 1 | 1 | 2 |
| Russia | 0 | 1 | 1 | 2 |
| United States | 1 | 1 | 0 | 2 |

**SELF CHECK**

**34.** What results do you get if you total the columns in our sample data?

**35.** Consider an 8 × 8 array for a board game:

```
int[][] board = new int[8][8];
```

Using two nested loops, initialize the board so that zeroes and ones alternate, as on a checkerboard:

```
0 1 0 1 0 1 0 1
1 0 1 0 1 0 1 0
0 1 0 1 0 1 0 1
. . .
1 0 1 0 1 0 1 0
```

*Hint:* Check whether i + j is even.

**36.** Declare a two-dimensional array for representing a tic-tac-toe board. The board has three rows and columns and contains strings "x", "o", and " ".

**37.** Write an assignment statement to place an "x" in the upper-right corner of the tic-tac-toe board in Self Check 36.

**38.** Which elements are on the diagonal joining the upper-left and the lower-right corners of the tic-tac-toe board in Self Check 36?

**Practice It** Now you can try these exercises at the end of the chapter: R6.30, P6.18, P6.19.

WORKED EXAMPLE 6.2 **A World Population Table**

This Worked Example shows how to print world population data in a table with row and column headers, and with totals for each of the data columns.

Special Topic 6.4

## Two-Dimensional Arrays with Variable Row Lengths

When you declare a two-dimensional array with the command

```
int[][] a = new int[3][3];
```

then you get a 3 × 3 matrix that can store 9 elements:

```
a[0][0] a[0][1] a[0][2]
a[1][0] a[1][1] a[1][2]
a[2][0] a[2][1] a[2][2]
```

In this matrix, all rows have the same length.

In Java it is possible to declare arrays in which the row length varies. For example, you can store an array that has a triangular shape, such as:

```
b[0][0]
b[1][0] b[1][1]
b[2][0] b[2][1] b[2][2]
```

To allocate such an array, you must work harder. First, you allocate space to hold three rows. Indicate that you will manually set each row by leaving the second array index empty:

```
double[][] b = new double[3][];
```

Then allocate each row separately (see Figure 15):

```
for (int i = 0; i < b.length; i++)
{
    b[i] = new double[i + 1];
}
```

You can access each array element as b[i][j]. The expression b[i] selects the ith row, and the [j] operator selects the jth element in that row.

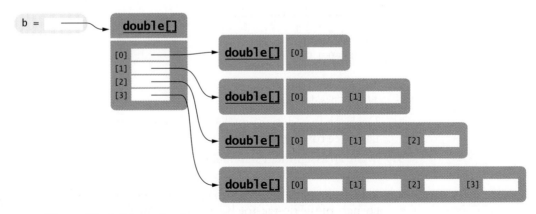

**Figure 15** A Triangular Array

+ Available online in WileyPLUS and at www.wiley.com/college/horstmann.

Note that the number of rows is b.length, and the length of the ith row is b[i].length. For example, the following pair of loops prints a ragged array:

```java
for (int i = 0; i < b.length; i++)
{
   for (int j = 0; j < b[i].length; j++)
   {
      System.out.print(b[i][j]);
   }
   System.out.println();
}
```

Alternatively, you can use two enhanced for loops:

```java
for (double[] row : b)
{
   for (double element : row)
   {
      System.out.print(element);
   }
   System.out.println();
}
```

Naturally, such "ragged" arrays are not very common.

Java implements plain two-dimensional arrays in exactly the same way as ragged arrays: as arrays of one-dimensional arrays. The expression new int[3][3] automatically allocates an array of three rows, and three arrays for the rows' contents.

---

**Special Topic 6.5**

### Multidimensional Arrays

You can declare arrays with more than two dimensions. For example, here is a three-dimensional array:

```java
int[][][] rubiksCube = new int[3][3][3];
```

Each array element is specified by three index values:

```java
rubiksCube[i][j][k]
```

---

# 6.8  Array Lists

An array list stores a sequence of values whose size can change.

When you write a program that collects inputs, you don't always know how many inputs you will have. In such a situation, an **array list** offers two significant advantages:

- Array lists can grow and shrink as needed.
- The ArrayList class supplies methods for common tasks, such as inserting and removing elements.

In the following sections, you will learn how to work with array lists.

*An array list expands to hold as many elements as needed.*

## Syntax 6.4  Array Lists

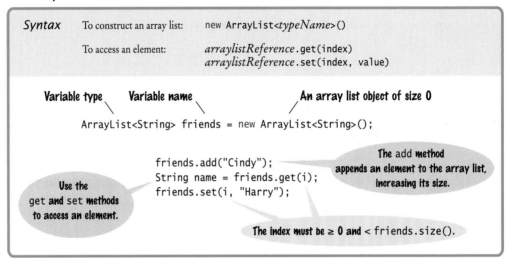

*Syntax*   To construct an array list:   `new ArrayList<`*typeName*`>()`

To access an element:   *arraylistReference*`.get(index)`
*arraylistReference*`.set(index, value)`

**Variable type**   **Variable name**   **An array list object of size 0**

`ArrayList<String> friends = new ArrayList<String>();`

`friends.add("Cindy");`
`String name = friends.get(i);`
`friends.set(i, "Harry");`

**Use the**
**get and set methods**
**to access an element.**

**The add method**
**appends an element to the array list,**
**increasing its size.**

**The index must be ≥ 0 and < friends.size().**

## 6.8.1 Declaring and Using Array Lists

The following statement declares an array list of strings:

```
ArrayList<String> names = new ArrayList<String>();
```

The ArrayList class
is a generic class:
ArrayList<*Type*>
collects elements of
the specified type.

The ArrayList class is contained in the java.util package. In order to use array lists in your program, you need to use the statement import java.util.ArrayList.

The type ArrayList<String> denotes an array list of String elements. The angle brackets around the String type tell you that String is a **type parameter**. You can replace String with any other class and get a different array list type. For that reason, ArrayList is called a **generic class**. However, you cannot use primitive types as type parameters—there is no ArrayList<int> or ArrayList<double>. Section 6.8.5 shows how you can collect numbers in an array list.

It is a common error to forget the initialization:

```
ArrayList<String> names;
names.add("Harry"); // Error—names not initialized
```

Here is the proper initialization:

```
ArrayList<String> names = new ArrayList<String>();
```

Note the () after new ArrayList<String> on the right-hand side of the initialization. It indicates that the **constructor** of the ArrayList<String> class is being called. We will discuss constructors in Chapter 8.

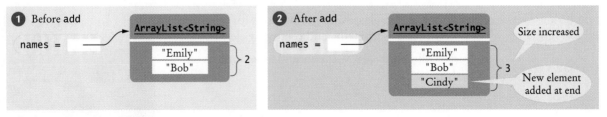

**Figure 16**  Adding an Element with add

When the `ArrayList<String>` is first constructed, it has size 0. You use the `add` method to add an element to the end of the array list.

```
names.add("Emily"); // Now names has size 1 and element "Emily"
names.add("Bob"); // Now names has size 2 and elements "Emily", "Bob"
names.add("Cindy"); // names has size 3 and elements "Emily", "Bob", and "Cindy"
```

> Use the size method to obtain the current size of an array list.

The size increases after each call to `add` (see Figure 16). The `size` method yields the current size of the array list.

To obtain an array list element, use the `get` method, not the `[]` operator. As with arrays, index values start at 0. For example, `names.get(2)` retrieves the name with index 2, the third element in the array list:

```
String name = names.get(2);
```

> Use the get and set methods to access an array list element at a given index.

As with arrays, it is an error to access a nonexistent element. A very common bounds error is to use the following:

```
int i = names.size();
name = names.get(i);  // Error
```

The last valid index is `names.size() - 1`.

To set an array list element to a new value, use the `set` method.

```
names.set(2, "Carolyn");
```

This call sets position 2 of the `names` array list to `"Carolyn"`, overwriting whatever value was there before.

The set method overwrites existing values. It is different from the `add` method, which adds a new element to the array list.

You can insert an element in the middle of an array list. For example, the call `names.add(1, "Ann")` adds a new element at position 1 and moves all elements with index 1 or larger by one position. After each call to the `add` method, the size of the array list increases by 1 (see Figure 17).

> *An array list has methods for adding and removing elements in the middle.*

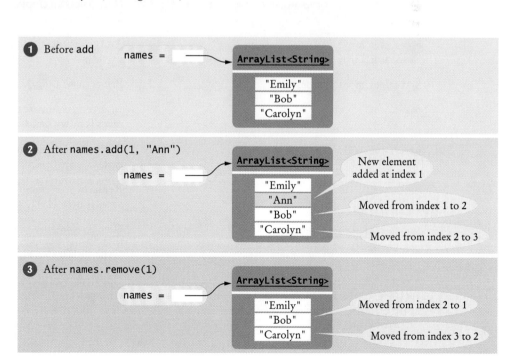

**1** Before `add`

names =  →  **ArrayList<String>**
"Emily"
"Bob"
"Carolyn"

**2** After `names.add(1, "Ann")`

names =  →  **ArrayList<String>**
"Emily"
"Ann"  — New element added at index 1
"Bob"  — Moved from index 1 to 2
"Carolyn"  — Moved from index 2 to 3

**3** After `names.remove(1)`

names =  →  **ArrayList<String>**
"Emily"
"Bob"  — Moved from index 2 to 1
"Carolyn"  — Moved from index 3 to 2

**Figure 17**
Adding and Removing Elements in the Middle of an Array List

> Use the add and remove methods to add and remove array list elements.

Conversely, the remove method removes the element at a given position, moves all elements after the removed element down by one position, and reduces the size of the array list by 1. Part 3 of Figure 17 illustrates the result of names.remove(1).

With an array list, it is very easy to get a quick printout. Simply pass the array list to the println method:

```
System.out.println(names); // Prints [Emily, Bob, Carolyn]
```

## 6.8.2 Using the Enhanced for Loop with Array Lists

You can use the enhanced for loop to visit all elements of an array list. For example, the following loop prints all names:

```
ArrayList<String> names = . . . ;
for (String name : names)
{
    System.out.println(name);
}
```

This loop is equivalent to the following basic for loop:

```
for (int i = 0; i < names.size(); i++)
{
    String name = names.get(i);
    System.out.println(name);
}
```

| Table 2  Working with Array Lists | |
|---|---|
| `ArrayList<String> names = new ArrayList<String>();` | Constructs an empty array list that can hold strings. |
| `names.add("Ann");`<br>`names.add("Cindy");` | Adds elements to the end. |
| `System.out.println(names);` | Prints [Ann, Cindy]. |
| `names.add(1, "Bob");` | Inserts an element at index 1.<br>names is now [Ann, Bob, Cindy]. |
| `names.remove(0);` | Removes the element at index 0.<br>names is now [Bob, Cindy]. |
| `names.set(0, "Bill");` | Replaces an element with a different value.<br>names is now [Bill, Cindy]. |
| `String name = names.get(i);` | Gets an element. |
| `String last = names.get(names.size() - 1);` | Gets the last element. |
| `ArrayList<Integer> squares = new ArrayList<Integer>();`<br>`for (int i = 0; i < 10; i++)`<br>`{`<br>`   squares.add(i * i);`<br>`}` | Constructs an array list holding the first ten squares. |

### 6.8.3 Copying Array Lists

As with arrays, you need to remember that array list variables hold references. Copying the reference yields two references to the same array list (see Figure 18).

```
ArrayList<String> friends = names;
friends.add("Harry");
```

Now both `names` and `friends` reference the same array list to which the string `"Harry"` was added.

If you want to make a copy of an array list, construct the copy and pass the original list into the constructor:

```
ArrayList<String> newNames = new ArrayList<String>(names);
```

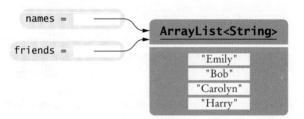

**Figure 18** Copying an Array List Reference

### 6.8.4 Array Lists and Methods

Like arrays, array lists can be method arguments and return values. Here is an example: a method that receives a list of strings and returns the reversed list.

```
public static ArrayList<String> reverse(ArrayList<String> names)
{
    // Allocate a list to hold the method result
    ArrayList<String> result = new ArrayList<String>();

    // Traverse the names list in reverse order, starting with the last element
    for (int i = names.size() - 1; i >= 0; i--)
    {
        // Add each name to the result
        result.add(names.get(i));
    }
    return result;
}
```

If this method is called with an array list containing the names Emily, Bob, Cindy, it returns a new array list with the names Cindy, Bob, Emily.

### 6.8.5 Wrappers and Auto-boxing

**To collect numbers in array lists, you must use wrapper classes.**

In Java, you cannot directly insert primitive type values—numbers, characters, or `boolean` values—into array lists. For example, you cannot form an `ArrayList<double>`. Instead, you must use one of the **wrapper classes** shown in the following table.

| Primitive Type | Wrapper Class |
|:---:|:---:|
| byte | Byte |
| boolean | Boolean |
| char | Character |
| double | Double |
| float | Float |
| int | Integer |
| long | Long |
| short | Short |

For example, to collect `double` values in an array list, you use an `ArrayList<Double>`. Note that the wrapper class names start with uppercase letters, and that two of them differ from the names of the corresponding primitive type: `Integer` and `Character`.

Conversion between primitive types and the corresponding wrapper classes is automatic. This process is called **auto-boxing** (even though *auto-wrapping* would have been more consistent).

For example, if you assign a `double` value to a `Double` variable, the number is automatically "put into a box" (see Figure 19).

```
Double wrapper = 29.95;
```

Conversely, wrapper values are automatically "unboxed" to primitive types.

```
double x = wrapper;
```

Because boxing and unboxing is automatic, you don't need to think about it. Simply remember to use the wrapper type when you declare array lists of numbers. From then on, use the primitive type and rely on auto-boxing.

```
ArrayList<Double> values = new ArrayList<Double>();
values.add(29.95);
double x = values.get(0);
```

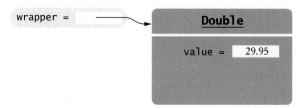

**Figure 19** A Wrapper Class Variable

*Like truffles that must be in a wrapper to be sold,
a number must be placed in a wrapper to be stored in an array list.*

### 6.8.6   Using Array Algorithms with Array Lists

The array algorithms in Section 6.3 can be converted to array lists simply by using the array list methods instead of the array syntax (see Table 3 on page 297). For example, this code snippet finds the largest element in an array:

```
double largest = values[0];
for (int i = 1; i < values.length; i++)
{
   if (values[i] > largest)
   {
      largest = values[i];
   }
}
```

Here is the same algorithm, now using an array list:

```
double largest = values.get(0);
for (int i = 1; i < values.size(); i++)
{
   if (values.get(i) > largest)
   {
      largest = values.get(i);
   }
}
```

### 6.8.7   Storing Input Values in an Array List

When you collect an unknown number of inputs, array lists are *much* easier to use than arrays. Simply read inputs and add them to an array list:

```
ArrayList<Double> inputs = new ArrayList<Double>();
while (in.hasNextDouble())
{
   inputs.add(in.nextDouble());
}
```

### 6.8.8  Removing Matches

It is easy to remove elements from an array list, by calling the remove method. A common processing task is to remove all elements that match a particular condition. Suppose, for example, that we want to remove all strings of length < 4 from an array list.

Of course, you traverse the array list and look for matching elements:

```
ArrayList<String> words = ...;
for (int i = 0; i < words.size(); i++)
{
   String word = words.get(i);
   if (word.length() < 4)
   {
      Remove the element at index i.
   }
}
```

But there is a subtle problem. After you remove the element, the for loop increments i, skipping past the *next* element.

Consider this concrete example, where words contains the strings "Welcome", "to", "the", "island!". When i is 1, we remove the word "to" at index 1. Then i is incremented to 2, and the word "the", which is now at position 1, is never examined.

| i | words |
|---|---|
| ~~0~~ | ~~"Welcome", "to", "the", "island"~~ |
| ~~1~~ | "Welcome", "the", "island" |
| 2 | |

We should not increment the index when removing a word. The appropriate pseudo-code is

**If the element at index i matches the condition**
    **Remove the element.**
**Else**
    **Increment i.**

Because we don't always increment the index, a for loop is not appropriate for this algorithm. Instead, use a while loop:

```
int i = 0;
while (i < words.size())
{
    String word = words.get(i);
    if (word.length() < 4)
    {
        words.remove(i);
    }
    else
    {
        i++;
    }
}
```

## 6.8.9 Choosing Between Array Lists and Arrays

For most programming tasks, array lists are easier to use than arrays. Array lists can grow and shrink. On the other hand, arrays have a nicer syntax for element access and initialization.

Which of the two should you choose? Here are some recommendations.

- If the size of a collection never changes, use an array.
- If you collect a long sequence of primitive type values and you are concerned about efficiency, use an array.
- Otherwise, use an array list.

**ONLINE EXAMPLE**

A version of the Scores program using an array list.

The following program shows how to mark the largest value in a sequence of values. This program uses an array list. Note how the program is an improvement over the array version on page 265. This program can process input sequences of arbitrary length.

## Table 3   Comparing Array and Array List Operations

| Operation | Arrays | Array Lists |
|---|---|---|
| Get an element. | `x = values[4];` | `x = values.get(4)` |
| Replace an element. | `values[4] = 35;` | `values.set(4, 35);` |
| Number of elements. | `values.length` | `values.size()` |
| Number of filled elements. | `currentSize` (companion variable, see Section 6.1.3) | `values.size()` |
| Remove an element. | See Section 6.3.6 | `values.remove(4);` |
| Add an element, growing the collection. | See Section 6.3.7 | `values.add(35);` |
| Initializing a collection. | `int[] values = { 1, 4, 9 };` | No initializer list syntax; call add three times. |

### section_8/LargestInArrayList.java

```java
import java.util.ArrayList;
import java.util.Scanner;

/**
   This program reads a sequence of values and prints them, marking the largest value.
*/
public class LargestInArrayList
{
   public static void main(String[] args)
   {
      ArrayList<Double> values = new ArrayList<Double>();

      // Read inputs

      System.out.println("Please enter values, Q to quit:");
      Scanner in = new Scanner(System.in);
      while (in.hasNextDouble())
      {
         values.add(in.nextDouble());
      }

      // Find the largest value

      double largest = values.get(0);
      for (int i = 1; i < values.size(); i++)
      {
         if (values.get(i) > largest)
         {
            largest = values.get(i);
         }
      }

      // Print all values, marking the largest
```

```
35        for (double element : values)
36        {
37           System.out.print(element);
38           if (element == largest)
39           {
40              System.out.print(" <== largest value");
41           }
42           System.out.println();
43        }
44     }
45  }
```

**Program Run**

```
Please enter values, Q to quit:
35 80 115 44.5 Q
35
80
115 <== largest value
44.5
```

**SELF CHECK**

**39.** Declare an array list primes of integers that contains the first five prime numbers (2, 3, 5, 7, and 11).

**40.** Given the array list primes declared in Self Check 39, write a loop to print its elements in reverse order, starting with the last element.

**41.** What does the array list names contain after the following statements?

```
ArrayList<String> names = new ArrayList<String>;
names.add("Bob");
names.add(0, "Ann");
names.remove(1);
names.add("Cal");
```

**42.** What is wrong with this code snippet?

```
ArrayList<String> names;
names.add(Bob);
```

**43.** Consider this method that appends the elements of one array list to another.

```
public static void append(ArrayList<String> target, ArrayList<String> source)
{
   for (int i = 0; i < source.size(); i++)
   {
      target.add(source.get(i));
   }
}
```

What are the contents of names1 and names2 after these statements?

```
ArrayList<String> names1 = new ArrayList<String>();
names1.add("Emily");
names1.add("Bob");
names1.add("Cindy");
ArrayList<String> names2 = new ArrayList<String>();
names2.add("Dave");
append(names1, names2);
```

**44.** Suppose you want to store the names of the weekdays. Should you use an array list or an array of seven strings?

45. The section_8 directory of your source code contains an alternate implementation of the problem solution in How To 6.1 on page 275. Compare the array and array list implementations. What is the primary advantage of the latter?

**Practice It**  Now you can try these exercises at the end of the chapter: R6.10, R6.34, P6.21, P6.23.

**Common Error 6.4**

### Length and Size

Unfortunately, the Java syntax for determining the number of elements in an array, an array list, and a string is not at all consistent.

| Data Type | Number of Elements |
|-----------|--------------------|
| Array | `a.length` |
| Array list | `a.size()` |
| String | `a.length()` |

It is a common error to confuse these. You just have to remember the correct syntax for every data type.

**Special Topic 6.6**

### The Diamond Syntax in Java 7

Java 7 introduces a convenient syntax enhancement for declaring array lists and other generic classes. In a statement that declares and constructs an array list, you need not repeat the type parameter in the constructor. That is, you can write

```
ArrayList<String> names = new ArrayList<>();
```

instead of

```
ArrayList<String> names = new ArrayList<String>();
```

This shortcut is called the "diamond syntax" because the empty brackets <> look like a diamond shape.

**VIDEO EXAMPLE 6.2**  **Game of Life**

Conway's *Game of Life* simulates the growth of a population, using only two simple rules. This Video Example shows you how to implement this famous "game".

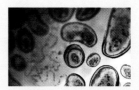

➕ Available online in WileyPLUS and at www.wiley.com/college/horstmann.

## CHAPTER SUMMARY

**Use arrays for collecting values.**

- An array collects a sequence of values of the same type.
- Individual elements in an array are accessed by an integer index i, using the notation *array*[i].
- An array element can be used like any variable.
- An array index must be at least zero and less than the size of the array.
- A bounds error, which occurs if you supply an invalid array index, can cause your program to terminate.
- Use the expression *array*.length to find the number of elements in an array.
- An array reference specifies the location of an array. Copying the reference yields a second reference to the same array.
- With a partially filled array, keep a companion variable for the current size.

**Know when to use the enhanced for loop.**

- You can use the enhanced for loop to visit all elements of an array.
- Use the enhanced for loop if you do not need the index values in the loop body.

**Know and use common array algorithms.**

- When separating elements, don't place a separator before the first element.
- A linear search inspects elements in sequence until a match is found.
- Before inserting an element, move elements to the end of the array *starting with the last one*.
- Use a temporary variable when swapping two elements.
- Use the Arrays.copyOf method to copy the elements of an array into a new array.

**Implement methods that process arrays.**

- Arrays can occur as method arguments and return values.

**Combine and adapt algorithms for solving a programming problem.**

- By combining fundamental algorithms, you can solve complex programming tasks.
- You should be familiar with the implementation of fundamental algorithms so that you can adapt them.

**Discover algorithms by manipulating physical objects.**

- Use a sequence of coins, playing cards, or toys to visualize an array of values.
- You can use paper clips as position markers or counters.

**Use two-dimensional arrays for data that is arranged in rows and columns.**

- Use a two-dimensional array to store tabular data.
- Individual elements in a two-dimensional array are accessed by using two index values, *array*[i][j].

**Use array lists for managing collections whose size can change.**

- An array list stores a sequence of values whose size can change.
- The ArrayList class is a generic class: ArrayList<*Type*> collects elements of the specified type.
- Use the size method to obtain the current size of an array list.
- Use the get and set methods to access an array list element at a given index.
- Use the add and remove methods to add and remove array list elements.
- To collect numbers in array lists, you must use wrapper classes.

## STANDARD LIBRARY ITEMS INTRODUCED IN THIS CHAPTER

```
java.lang.Boolean               java.util.ArrayList<E>
java.lang.Double                   add
java.lang.Integer                  get
java.util.Arrays                   remove
   copyOf                          set
   toString                        size
```

## REVIEW EXERCISES

**■■ R6.1** Write code that fills an array values with each set of numbers below.

|     |   |   |   |    |    |    |    |    |    |     |    |
|-----|---|---|---|----|----|----|----|----|----|-----|----|
| **a.** 1 | 2 | 3 | 4 | 5 | 6 | 7 | 8 | 9 | 10 | | |
| **b.** 0 | 2 | 4 | 6 | 8 | 10 | 12 | 14 | 16 | 18 | 20 | |
| **c.** 1 | 4 | 9 | 16 | 25 | 36 | 49 | 64 | 81 | 100 | | |
| **d.** 0 | 0 | 0 | 0 | 0 | 0 | 0 | 0 | 0 | 0 | | |
| **e.** 1 | 4 | 9 | 16 | 9 | 7 | 4 | 9 | 11 | | | |
| **f.** 0 | 1 | 0 | 1 | 0 | 1 | 0 | 1 | 0 | 1 | | |
| **g.** 0 | 1 | 2 | 3 | 4 | 0 | 1 | 2 | 3 | 4 | | |

▪▪ **R6.2** Consider the following array:

```
int[] a = { 1, 2, 3, 4, 5, 4, 3, 2, 1, 0 };
```

What is the value of total after the following loops complete?

**a.** 
```
int total = 0;
for (int i = 0; i < 10; i++) { total = total + a[i]; }
```
**b.** 
```
int total = 0;
for (int i = 0; i < 10; i = i + 2) { total = total + a[i]; }
```
**c.** 
```
int total = 0;
for (int i = 1; i < 10; i = i + 2) { total = total + a[i]; }
```
**d.** 
```
int total = 0;
for (int i = 2; i <= 10; i++) { total = total + a[i]; }
```
**e.** 
```
int total = 0;
for (int i = 1; i < 10; i = 2 * i) { total = total + a[i]; }
```
**f.** 
```
int total = 0;
for (int i = 9; i >= 0; i--) { total = total + a[i]; }
```
**g.** 
```
int total = 0;
for (int i = 9; i >= 0; i = i - 2) { total = total + a[i]; }
```
**h.** 
```
int total = 0;
for (int i = 0; i < 10; i++) { total = a[i] - total; }
```

▪▪ **R6.3** Consider the following array:

```
int[] a = { 1, 2, 3, 4, 5, 4, 3, 2, 1, 0 };
```

What are the contents of the array a after the following loops complete?

**a.** `for (int i = 1; i < 10; i++) { a[i] = a[i - 1]; }`
**b.** `for (int i = 9; i > 0; i--) { a[i] = a[i - 1]; }`
**c.** `for (int i = 0; i < 9; i++) { a[i] = a[i + 1]; }`
**d.** `for (int i = 8; i >= 0; i--) { a[i] = a[i + 1]; }`
**e.** `for (int i = 1; i < 10; i++) { a[i] = a[i] + a[i - 1]; }`
**f.** `for (int i = 1; i < 10; i = i + 2) { a[i] = 0; }`
**g.** `for (int i = 0; i < 5; i++) { a[i + 5] = a[i]; }`
**h.** `for (int i = 1; i < 5; i++) { a[i] = a[9 - i]; }`

▪▪▪ **R6.4** Write a loop that fills an array values with ten random numbers between 1 and 100. Write code for two nested loops that fill values with ten *different* random numbers between 1 and 100.

▪▪ **R6.5** Write Java code for a loop that simultaneously computes both the maximum and minimum of an array.

▪ **R6.6** What is wrong with each of the following code segments?

**a.** 
```
int[] values = new int[10];
for (int i = 1; i <= 10; i++)
{
   values[i] = i * i;
}
```
**b.** 
```
int[] values;
for (int i = 0; i < values.length; i++)
{
   values[i] = i * i;
}
```

**■■ R6.7**  Write enhanced for loops for the following tasks.

    **a.** Printing all elements of an array in a single row, separated by spaces.

    **b.** Computing the product of all elements in an array.

    **c.** Counting how many elements in an array are negative.

**■■ R6.8**  Rewrite the following loops without using the enhanced for loop construct. Here, values is an array of floating-point numbers.

    **a.** `for (double x : values) { total = total + x; }`

    **b.** `for (double x : values) { if (x == target) { return true; } }`

    **c.** `int i = 0;`
       `for (double x : values) { values[i] = 2 * x; i++; }`

**■■ R6.9**  Rewrite the following loops, using the enhanced for loop construct. Here, values is an array of floating-point numbers.

    **a.** `for (int i = 0; i < values.length; i++) { total = total + values[i]; }`

    **b.** `for (int i = 1; i < values.length; i++) { total = total + values[i]; }`

    **c.** `for (int i = 0; i < values.length; i++)`
       `{`
          `if (values[i] == target) { return i; }`
       `}`

**■ R6.10**  What is wrong with each of the following code segments?

    **a.** `ArrayList<int> values = new ArrayList<int>();`

    **b.** `ArrayList<Integer> values = new ArrayList();`

    **c.** `ArrayList<Integer> values = new ArrayList<Integer>;`

    **d.** `ArrayList<Integer> values = new ArrayList<Integer>();`
       `for (int i = 1; i <= 10; i++)`
       `{`
          `values.set(i - 1, i * i);`
       `}`

    **e.** `ArrayList<Integer> values;`
       `for (int i = 1; i <= 10; i++)`
       `{`
          `values.add(i * i);`
       `}`

**■ R6.11**  What is an index of an array? What are the legal index values? What is a bounds error?

**■ R6.12**  Write a program that contains a bounds error. Run the program. What happens on your computer?

**■ R6.13**  Write a loop that reads ten numbers and a second loop that displays them in the opposite order from which they were entered.

**■ R6.14**  Trace the flow of the linear search loop in Section 6.3.5, where values contains the elements 80 90 100 120 110. Show two columns, for pos and found. Repeat the trace when values contains 80 90 100 70.

**■ R6.15**  Trace both mechanisms for removing an element described in Section 6.3.6. Use an array values with elements 110 90 100 120 80, and remove the element at index 2.

**■■ R6.16** For the operations on partially filled arrays below, provide the header of a method. Do not implement the methods.

    **a.** Sort the elements in decreasing order.

    **b.** Print all elements, separated by a given string.

    **c.** Count how many elements are less than a given value.

    **d.** Remove all elements that are less than a given value.

    **e.** Place all elements that are less than a given value in another array.

**■ R6.17** Trace the flow of the loop in Section 6.3.4 with the given example. Show two columns, one with the value of i and one with the output.

**■ R6.18** Consider the following loop for collecting all elements that match a condition; in this case, that the element is larger than 100.

```
ArrayList<Double> matches = new ArrayList<Double>();
for (double element : values)
{
    if (element > 100)
    {
        matches.add(element);
    }
}
```

Trace the flow of the loop, where values contains the elements 110 90 100 120 80. Show two columns, for element and matches.

**■ R6.19** Trace the flow of the loop in Section 6.3.5, where values contains the elements 80 90 100 120 110. Show two columns, for pos and found. Repeat the trace when values contains the elements 80 90 120 70.

**■■ R6.20** Trace the algorithm for removing an element described in Section 6.3.6. Use an array values with elements 110 90 100 120 80, and remove the element at index 2.

**■■ R6.21** Give pseudocode for an algorithm that rotates the elements of an array by one position, moving the initial element to the end of the array, like this:

**■■ R6.22** Give pseudocode for an algorithm that removes all negative values from an array, preserving the order of the remaining elements.

**■■ R6.23** Suppose values is a *sorted* array of integers. Give pseudocode that describes how a new value can be inserted in its proper position so that the resulting array stays sorted.

**■■■ R6.24** A *run* is a sequence of adjacent repeated values. Give pseudocode for computing the length of the longest run in an array. For example, the longest run in the array with elements

    1 2 5 5 3 1 2 4 3 2 2 2 2 3 6 5 5 6 3 1

has length 4.

**••• R6.25** What is wrong with the following method that aims to fill an array with random numbers?

```java
public static void fillWithRandomNumbers(double[] values)
{
    double[] numbers = new double[values.length];
    for (int i = 0; i < numbers.length; i++)
    {
        numbers[i] = Math.random();
    }
    values = numbers;
}
```

**•• R6.26** You are given two arrays denoting *x*- and *y*-coordinates of a set of points in the plane. For plotting the point set, we need to know the *x*- and *y*-coordinates of the smallest rectangle containing the points.

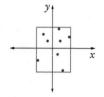

How can you obtain these values from the fundamental algorithms in Section 6.3?

**• R6.27** Solve the problem described in Section 6.5 by sorting the array first. How do you need to modify the algorithm for computing the total?

**•• R6.28** Solve the task described in Section 6.6 using an algorithm that removes and inserts elements instead of switching them. Write the pseudocode for the algorithm, assuming that methods for removal and insertion exist. Act out the algorithm with a sequence of coins and explain why it is less efficient than the swapping algorithm developed in Section 6.6.

**•• R6.29** Develop an algorithm for finding the most frequently occurring value in an array of numbers. Use a sequence of coins. Place paper clips below each coin that count how many other coins of the same value are in the sequence. Give the pseudocode for an algorithm that yields the correct answer, and describe how using the coins and paper clips helped you find the algorithm.

**•• R6.30** Write Java statements for performing the following tasks with an array declared as

```java
int[][] values = new int[ROWS][COLUMNS];
```

- Fill all entries with 0.
- Fill elements alternately with 0s and 1s in a checkerboard pattern.
- Fill only the elements at the top and bottom row with zeroes.
- Compute the sum of all elements.
- Print the array in tabular form.

**•• R6.31** Write pseudocode for an algorithm that fills the first and last column as well as the first and last row of a two-dimensional array of integers with −1.

**• R6.32** Section 6.8.8 shows that you must be careful about updating the index value when you remove elements from an array list. Show how you can avoid this problem by traversing the array list backwards.

■■ **R6.33** True or false?

    **a.** All elements of an array are of the same type.

    **b.** Arrays cannot contain strings as elements.

    **c.** Two-dimensional arrays always have the same number of rows and columns.

    **d.** Elements of different columns in a two-dimensional array can have different types.

    **e.** A method cannot return a two-dimensional array.

    **f.** A method cannot change the length of an array argument.

    **g.** A method cannot change the number of columns of an argument that is a two-dimensional array.

■■ **R6.34** How do you perform the following tasks with array lists in Java?

    **a.** Test that two array lists contain the same elements in the same order.

    **b.** Copy one array list to another.

    **c.** Fill an array list with zeroes, overwriting all elements in it.

    **d.** Remove all elements from an array list.

■ **R6.35** True or false?

    **a.** All elements of an array list are of the same type.

    **b.** Array list index values must be integers.

    **c.** Array lists cannot contain strings as elements.

    **d.** Array lists can change their size, getting larger or smaller.

    **e.** A method cannot return an array list.

    **f.** A method cannot change the size of an array list argument.

## PROGRAMMING EXERCISES

■■ **P6.1** Write a program that initializes an array with ten random integers and then prints four lines of output, containing

    • Every element at an even index.

    • Every even element.

    • All elements in reverse order.

    • Only the first and last element.

■■ **P6.2** Write array methods that carry out the following tasks for an array of integers. For each method, provide a test program.

    **a.** Swap the first and last elements in the array.

    **b.** Shift all elements by one to the right and move the last element into the first position. For example, 1 4 9 16 25 would be transformed into 25 1 4 9 16.

    **c.** Replace all even elements with 0.

    **d.** Replace each element except the first and last by the larger of its two neighbors.

**e.** Remove the middle element if the array length is odd, or the middle two elements if the length is even.

**f.** Move all even elements to the front, otherwise preserving the order of the elements.

**g.** Return the second-largest element in the array.

**h.** Return true if the array is currently sorted in increasing order.

**i.** Return true if the array contains two adjacent duplicate elements.

**j.** Return true if the array contains duplicate elements (which need not be adjacent).

**■ P6.3** Modify the `LargestInArray.java` program in Section 6.3 to mark both the smallest and the largest elements.

**■■ P6.4** Write a method `sumWithoutSmallest` that computes the sum of an array of values, except for the smallest one, in a single loop. In the loop, update the sum and the smallest value. After the loop, return the difference.

**■ P6.5** Write a method `public static void removeMin` that removes the minimum value from a partially filled array without calling other methods.

**■■ P6.6** Compute the *alternating sum* of all elements in an array. For example, if your program reads the input

$$1 \quad 4 \quad 9 \quad 16 \quad 9 \quad 7 \quad 4 \quad 9 \quad 11$$

then it computes

$$1 - 4 + 9 - 16 + 9 - 7 + 4 - 9 + 11 = -2$$

**■ P6.7** Write a method that reverses the sequence of elements in an array. For example, if you call the method with the array

$$1 \quad 4 \quad 9 \quad 16 \quad 9 \quad 7 \quad 4 \quad 9 \quad 11$$

then the array is changed to

$$11 \quad 9 \quad 4 \quad 7 \quad 9 \quad 16 \quad 9 \quad 4 \quad 1$$

**■ P6.8** Write a method that implements the algorithm developed in Section 6.6.

**■■ P6.9** Write a method

```
public static boolean equals(int[] a, int[] b)
```

that checks whether two arrays have the same elements in the same order.

**■■ P6.10** Write a method

```
public static boolean sameSet(int[] a, int[] b)
```

that checks whether two arrays have the same elements in some order, ignoring duplicates. For example, the two arrays

$$1 \quad 4 \quad 9 \quad 16 \quad 9 \quad 7 \quad 4 \quad 9 \quad 11$$

and

$$11 \quad 11 \quad 7 \quad 9 \quad 16 \quad 4 \quad 1$$

would be considered identical. You will probably need one or more helper methods.

■■■ **P6.11** Write a method

```
public static boolean sameElements(int[] a, int[] b)
```

that checks whether two arrays have the same elements in some order, with the same multiplicities. For example,

$$1 \quad 4 \quad 9 \quad 16 \quad 9 \quad 7 \quad 4 \quad 9 \quad 11$$

and

$$11 \quad 1 \quad 4 \quad 9 \quad 16 \quad 9 \quad 7 \quad 4 \quad 9$$

would be considered identical, but

$$1 \quad 4 \quad 9 \quad 16 \quad 9 \quad 7 \quad 4 \quad 9 \quad 11$$

and

$$11 \quad 11 \quad 7 \quad 9 \quad 16 \quad 4 \quad 1 \quad 4 \quad 9$$

would not. You will probably need one or more helper methods.

■■ **P6.12** A *run* is a sequence of adjacent repeated values. Write a program that generates a sequence of 20 random die tosses in an array and that prints the die values, marking the runs by including them in parentheses, like this:

```
1 2 (5 5) 3 1 2 4 3 (2 2 2 2) 3 6 (5 5) 6 3 1
```

Use the following pseudocode:

```
Set a boolean variable inRun to false.
For each valid index i in the array
    If inRun
        If values[i] is different from the preceding value
            Print ).
            inRun = false.
    If not inRun
        If values[i] is the same as the following value
            Print (.
            inRun = true.
    Print values[i].
If inRun, print ).
```

■■ **P6.13** Write a program that generates a sequence of 20 random die tosses in an array and that prints the die values, marking only the longest run, like this:

```
1 2 5 5 3 1 2 4 3 (2 2 2 2) 3 6 5 5 6 3 1
```

If there is more than one run of maximum length, mark the first one.

■■ **P6.14** Write a program that generates a sequence of 20 random values between 0 and 99 in an array, prints the sequence, sorts it, and prints the sorted sequence. Use the sort method from the standard Java library.

■■■ **P6.15** Write a program that produces ten random permutations of the numbers 1 to 10. To generate a random permutation, you need to fill an array with the numbers 1 to 10 so that no two entries of the array have the same contents. You could do it by brute force, by generating random values until you have a value that is not yet in the array. But that is inefficient. Instead, follow this algorithm.

Make a second array and fill it with the numbers 1 to 10.
Repeat 10 times
    Pick a random element from the second array.
    Remove it and append it to the permutation array.

■■ **P6.16** It is a well-researched fact that men in a restroom generally prefer to maximize their distance from already occupied stalls, by occupying the middle of the longest sequence of unoccupied places.

For example, consider the situation where ten stalls are empty.

_ _ _ _ _ _ _ _ _ _

The first visitor will occupy a middle position:

_ _ _ _ _ X _ _ _ _

The next visitor will be in the middle of the empty area at the left.

_ _ X _ _ X _ _ _ _

Write a program that reads the number of stalls and then prints out diagrams in the format given above when the stalls become filled, one at a time. *Hint:* Use an array of boolean values to indicate whether a stall is occupied.

■■■ **P6.17** In this assignment, you will model the game of *Bulgarian Solitaire*. The game starts with 45 cards. (They need not be playing cards. Unmarked index cards work just as well.) Randomly divide them into some number of piles of random size. For example, you might start with piles of size 20, 5, 1, 9, and 10. In each round, you take one card from each pile, forming a new pile with these cards. For example, the sample starting configuration would be transformed into piles of size 19, 4, 8, 9, and 5. The solitaire is over when the piles have size 1, 2, 3, 4, 5, 6, 7, 8, and 9, in some order. (It can be shown that you always end up with such a configuration.)

In your program, produce a random starting configuration and print it. Then keep applying the solitaire step and print the result. Stop when the solitaire final configuration is reached.

■■■ **P6.18** *Magic squares.* An $n \times n$ matrix that is filled with the numbers $1, 2, 3, \ldots, n^2$ is a magic square if the sum of the elements in each row, in each column, and in the two diagonals is the same value.

| 16 | 3 | 2 | 13 |
| 5 | 10 | 11 | 8 |
| 9 | 6 | 7 | 12 |
| 4 | 15 | 14 | 1 |

Write a program that reads in 16 values from the keyboard and tests whether they form a magic square when put into a 4 × 4 array. You need to test two features:

**1.** Does each of the numbers 1, 2, ..., 16 occur in the user input?

**2.** When the numbers are put into a square, are the sums of the rows, columns, and diagonals equal to each other?

■■■ **P6.19** Implement the following algorithm to construct magic $n \times n$ squares; it works only if $n$ is odd.

> Set row = n - 1, column = n / 2.
> For k = 1 ... n * n
>     Place k at [row][column].
>     Increment row and column.
>     If the row or column is n, replace it with 0.
>     If the element at [row][column] has already been filled
>         Set row and column to their previous values.
>     Decrement row.

Here is the $5 \times 5$ square that you get if you follow this method:

| 11 | 18 | 25 | 2 | 9 |
|----|----|----|----|----|
| 10 | 12 | 19 | 21 | 3 |
| 4 | 6 | 13 | 20 | 22 |
| 23 | 5 | 7 | 14 | 16 |
| 17 | 24 | 1 | 8 | 15 |

Write a program whose input is the number $n$ and whose output is the magic square of order $n$ if $n$ is odd.

■■ **P6.20** Write a method that computes the average of the neighbors of a two-dimensional array element in the eight directions shown in Figure 14.

```
public static double neighborAverage(int[][] values, int row, int column)
```

However, if the element is located at the boundary of the array, only include the neighbors that are in the array. For example, if row and column are both 0, there are only three neighbors.

■■ **P6.21** Write a program that reads a sequence of input values and displays a bar chart of the values, using asterisks, like this:

```
**********************
*****************************************
****************************
***************************
*************
```

You may assume that all values are positive. First figure out the maximum value. That value's bar should be drawn with 40 asterisks. Shorter bars should use proportionally fewer asterisks.

■■■ **P6.22** Improve the program of Exercise P6.21 to work correctly when the data set contains negative values.

■■ **P6.23** Improve the program of Exercise P6.21 by adding captions for each bar. Prompt the user for the captions and data values. The output should look like this:

```
      Egypt ***********************
     France *****************************************
      Japan ****************************
    Uruguay ***************************
Switzerland *************
```

**■■ P6.24** A theater seating chart is implemented as a two-dimensional array of ticket prices, like this:

```
10 10 10 10 10 10 10 10 10 10
10 10 10 10 10 10 10 10 10 10
10 10 10 10 10 10 10 10 10 10
10 10 20 20 20 20 20 20 10 10
10 10 20 20 20 20 20 20 10 10
10 10 20 20 20 20 20 20 10 10
20 20 30 30 40 40 30 30 20 20
20 30 30 40 50 50 40 30 30 20
30 40 50 50 50 50 50 50 40 30
```

Write a program that prompts users to pick either a seat or a price. Mark sold seats by changing the price to 0. When a user specifies a seat, make sure it is available. When a user specifies a price, find any seat with that price.

**■■■ P6.25** Write a program that plays tic-tac-toe. The tic-tac-toe game is played on a 3 × 3 grid as in the photo at right. The game is played by two players, who take turns. The first player marks moves with a circle, the second with a cross. The player who has formed a horizontal, vertical, or diagonal sequence of three marks wins. Your program should draw the game board, ask the user for the coordinates of the next mark, change the players after every successful move, and pronounce the winner.

**■ P6.26** Write a method

```
public static ArrayList<Integer> append(ArrayList<Integer> a, ArrayList<Integer> b)
```

that appends one array list after another. For example, if a is

$$1 \quad 4 \quad 9 \quad 16$$

and b is

$$9 \quad 7 \quad 4 \quad 9 \quad 11$$

then append returns the array list

$$1 \quad 4 \quad 9 \quad 16 \quad 9 \quad 7 \quad 4 \quad 9 \quad 11$$

**■■ P6.27** Write a method

```
public static ArrayList<Integer> merge(ArrayList<Integer> a, ArrayList<Integer> b)
```

that merges two array lists, alternating elements from both array lists. If one array list is shorter than the other, then alternate as long as you can and then append the remaining elements from the longer array list. For example, if a is

$$1 \quad 4 \quad 9 \quad 16$$

and b is

$$9 \quad 7 \quad 4 \quad 9 \quad 11$$

then merge returns the array list

$$1 \quad 9 \quad 4 \quad 7 \quad 9 \quad 4 \quad 16 \quad 9 \quad 11$$

**•• P6.28** Write a method

```
public static ArrayList<Integer> mergeSorted(ArrayList<Integer> a,
    ArrayList<Integer> b)
```

that merges two *sorted* array lists, producing a new sorted array list. Keep an index into each array list, indicating how much of it has been processed already. Each time, append the smallest unprocessed element from either array list, then advance the index. For example, if a is

$$1 \quad 4 \quad 9 \quad 16$$

and b is

$$4 \quad 7 \quad 9 \quad 11$$

then mergeSorted returns the array list

$$1 \quad 4 \quad 4 \quad 7 \quad 9 \quad 9 \quad 9 \quad 11 \quad 16$$

**•• Business P6.29** A pet shop wants to give a discount to its clients if they buy one or more pets and at least five other items. The discount is equal to 20 percent of the cost of the other items, but not the pets.

Implement a method

```
public static void discount(double[] prices, boolean[] isPet, int nItems)
```

The method receives information about a particular sale. For the ith item, prices[i] is the price before any discount, and isPet[i] is true if the item is a pet.

Write a program that prompts a cashier to enter each price and then a Y for a pet or N for another item. Use a price of –1 as a sentinel. Save the inputs in an array. Call the method that you implemented, and display the discount.

**•• Business P6.30** A supermarket wants to reward its best customer of each day, showing the customer's name on a screen in the supermarket. For that purpose, the customer's purchase amount is stored in an ArrayList<Double> and the customer's name is stored in a corresponding ArrayList<String>.

Implement a method

```
public static String nameOfBestCustomer(ArrayList<Double> sales,
    ArrayList<String> customers)
```

that returns the name of the customer with the largest sale.

Write a program that prompts the cashier to enter all prices and names, adds them to two array lists, calls the method that you implemented, and displays the result. Use a price of 0 as a sentinel.

**••• Business P6.31** Improve the program of Exercise P6.30 so that it displays the top customers, that is, the topN customers with the largest sales, where topN is a value that the user of the program supplies.

Implement a method

```
public static ArrayList<String> nameOfBestCustomers(ArrayList<Double> sales,
    ArrayList<String> customers, int topN)
```

If there were fewer than topN customers, include all of them.

**•• Science P6.32** Sounds can be represented by an array of "sample values" that describe the intensity of the sound at a point in time. The program ch06/sound/SoundEffect.java reads a sound file (in WAV format), calls a method process for processing the sample values, and saves the sound file. Your task is to implement the process method by introducing an echo. For each sound value, add the value from 0.2 seconds ago. Scale the result so that no value is larger than 32767.

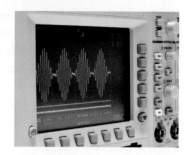

**••• Science P6.33** You are given a two-dimensional array of values that give the height of a terrain at different points in a square. Write a method

```
public static void floodMap(double[][] heights, double waterLevel)
```

that prints out a flood map, showing which of the points in the terrain would be flooded if the water level was the given value. In the flood map, print a * for each flooded point and a space for each point that is not flooded.

Here is a sample map:

Then write a program that reads one hundred terrain height values and shows how the terrain gets flooded when the water level increases in ten steps from the lowest point in the terrain to the highest.

**•• Science P6.34** Sample values from an experiment often need to be smoothed out. One simple approach is to replace each value in an array with the average of the value and its two neighboring values (or one neighboring value if it is at either end of the array). Implement a method

```
public static void smooth(double[] values, int size)
```

that carries out this operation. You should not create another array in your solution.

**•• Science P6.35** Modify the ch06/animation/BlockAnimation.java program to show an animated sine wave. In the *i*th frame, shift the sine wave by *i* degrees.

**••• Science P6.36** Write a program that models the movement of an object with mass *m* that is attached to an oscillating spring. When a spring is displaced from its equilibrium position by an amount $x$, Hooke's law states that the restoring force is

$$F = -kx$$

where $k$ is a constant that depends on the spring. (Use 10 N/m for this simulation.)

Start with a given displacement $x$ (say, 0.5 meter). Set the initial velocity $v$ to 0. Compute the acceleration $a$

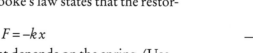
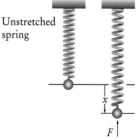

Unstretched spring

from Newton's law ($F = ma$) and Hooke's law, using a mass of 1 kg. Use a small time interval $\Delta t = 0.01$ second. Update the velocity—it changes by $a\Delta t$. Update the displacement—it changes by $v\Delta t$.

Every ten iterations, plot the spring displacement as a bar, where 1 pixel represents 1 cm. Use the technique in Special Topic 4.3 for creating an image.

**■■ Graphics P6.37** Using the technique of Special Topic 4.3, generate the image of a checkerboard.

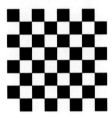

**■ Graphics P6.38** Using the technique of Special Topic 4.3, generate the image of a sine wave. Draw a line of pixels for every five degrees.

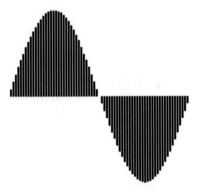

## ANSWERS TO SELF-CHECK QUESTIONS

1. `int[] primes = { 2, 3, 5, 7, 11 };`
2. `2, 3, 5, 3, 2`
3. `3, 4, 6, 8, 12`
4. `values[0] = 10;`
   `values[9] = 10;`

   or better: `values[values.length - 1] = 10;`
5. `String[] words = new String[10];`
6. `String[] words = { "Yes", "No" };`
7. No. Because you don't store the values, you need to print them when you read them. But

you don't know where to add the <= until you have seen all values.

8. It counts how many elements of `values` are zero.
9. `for (double x : values)`
   `{`
   `    System.out.println(x);`
   `}`
10. `double product = 1;`
    `for (double f : factors)`
    `{`
    `    product = product * f;`

```
}
```

**11.** The loop writes a value into `values[i]`. The enhanced `for` loop does not have the index variable `i`.

**12.** `20 <== largest value`
`10`
`20 <== largest value`

**13.**
```
int count = 0;
for (double x : values)
{
    if (x == 0) { count++; }
}
```

**14.** If all elements of `values` are negative, then the result is incorrectly computed as 0.

**15.**
```
for (int i = 0; i < values.length; i++)
{
    System.out.print(values[i]);
    if (i < values.length - 1)
    {
        System.out.print(" | ");
    }
}
```

Now you know why we set up the loop the other way.

**16.** If the array has no elements, then the program terminates with an exception.

**17.** If there is a match, then pos is incremented before the loop exits.

**18.** This loop sets all elements to `values[pos]`.

**19.** `int[] numbers = squares(5);`

**20.**
```
public static void fill(int[] values, int value)
{
    for (int i = 0; i < values.length; i++)
    {
        values[i] = value; }
}
```

**21.** The method returns an array whose length is given in the first argument. The array is filled with random integers between 0 and n - 1.

**22.** The contents of scores is unchanged. The reverse method returns a new array with the reversed numbers.

**23.**

| values | result | i |
|--------|--------|---|
| [1, 4, 9] | [0, 0, 0] | 0 |
| | [9, 0, 0] | 1 |
| | [9, 4, 0] | 2 |
| | [9, 4, 1] | |

**24.** Use the first algorithm. The order of elements does not matter when computing the sum.

**25.** Find the minimum value.
Calculate the sum.
Subtract the minimum value.

**26.** Use the algorithm for counting matches (Section 4.7.2) twice, once for counting the positive values and once for counting the negative values.

**27.** You need to modify the algorithm in Section 6.3.4.
```
boolean first = true;
for (int i = 0; i < values.length; i++)
{
    if (values[i] > 0))
    {
        if (first) { first = false; }
        else { System.out.print(", "); }
    }
    System.out.print(values[i]);
}
```
Note that you can no longer use i > 0 as the criterion for printing a separator.

**28.** Use the algorithm to collect all positive elements in an array, then use the algorithm in Section 6.3.4 to print the array of matches.

**29.** The paperclip for i assumes positions 0, 1, 2, 3. When i is incremented to 4, the condition i < size / 2 becomes false, and the loop ends. Similarly, the paperclip for j assumes positions 4, 5, 6, 7, which are the valid positions for the second half of the array.

**30.** It reverses the elements in the array.

**31.** Here is one solution. The basic idea is to move all odd elements to the end. Put one paper clip at the beginning of the array and one at the end. If the element at the first paper clip is odd, swap it with the one at the other paper clip and move that paper clip to the left. Otherwise, move the first paper clip to the right. Stop when the two paper clips meet. Here is the pseudocode:

i = 0
j = size - 1

**While (i < j)**
    **If (a[i] is odd)**
        **Swap elements at positions i and j.**
        **j--**
    **Else**
        **i++**

**32.** Here is one solution. The idea is to remove all odd elements and move them to the end. The trick is to know when to stop. Nothing is gained by moving odd elements into the area that already contains moved elements, so we want to mark that area with another paper clip.

**i = 0**
**moved = size**
**While (i < moved)**
    **If (a[i] is odd)**
        **Remove the element at position i and add it**
            **at the end.**
        **moved--**

**33.** When you read inputs, you get to see values one at a time, and you can't peek ahead. Picking cards one at a time from a deck of cards simulates this process better than looking at a sequence of items, all of which are revealed.

**34.** You get the total number of gold, silver, and bronze medals in the competition. In our example, there are four of each.

**35.**
```
for (int i = 0; i < 8; i++)
{
    for (int j = 0; j < 8; j++)
    {
        board[i][j] = (i + j) % 2;
    }
}
```

**36.** `String[][] board = new String[3][3];`

**37.** `board[0][2] = "x";`

**38.** `board[0][0], board[1][1], board[2][2]`

**39.**
```
ArrayList<Integer> primes =
    new ArrayList<Integer>();
primes.add(2);
primes.add(3);
primes.add(5);
primes.add(7);
primes.add(11);
```

**40.**
```
for (int i = primes.size() - 1; i >= 0; i--)
{
    System.out.println(primes.get(i));
}
```

**41.** `"Ann"`, `"Cal"`

**42.** The `names` variable has not been initialized.

**43.** `names1` contains "Emily", "Bob", "Cindy", "Dave"; `names2` contains "Dave"

**44.** Because the number of weekdays doesn't change, there is no disadvantage to using an array, and it is easier to initialize:

```
String[] weekdayNames = { "Monday", "Tuesday",
    "Wednesday", "Thursday", "Friday",
    "Saturday", "Sunday" };
```

**45.** Reading inputs into an array list is much easier.

## CHAPTER 7

# INPUT/OUTPUT AND EXCEPTION HANDLING

## CHAPTER GOALS

To read and write text files

To process command line arguments

To throw and catch exceptions

To implement programs that propagate checked exceptions

## CHAPTER CONTENTS

In this chapter, you will learn how to read and write files—a very useful skill for processing real world data. As an application, you will learn how to encrypt data. (The Enigma machine shown at left is an encryption device used by Germany in World War II. Pioneering British computer scientists broke the code and were able to intercept encoded messages, which was a significant help in winning the war.) The remainder of this chapter tells you how your programs can report and recover from problems, such as missing files or malformed content, using the exception-handling mechanism of the Java language.

# 7.1 Reading and Writing Text Files

We begin this chapter by discussing the common task of reading and writing files that contain text. Examples of text files include not only files that are created with a simple text editor, such as Windows Notepad, but also Java source code and HTML files.

**Use the Scanner class for reading text files.**

In Java, the most convenient mechanism for reading text is to use the Scanner class. You already know how to use a Scanner for reading console input. To read input from a disk file, the Scanner class relies on another class, File, which describes disk files and directories. (The File class has many methods that we do not discuss in this book; for example, methods that delete or rename a file.)

To begin, construct a File object with the name of the input file:

```
File inputFile = new File("input.txt");
```

Then use the File object to construct a Scanner object:

```
Scanner in = new Scanner(inputFile);
```

This Scanner object reads text from the file input.txt. You can use the Scanner methods (such as nextInt, nextDouble, and next) to read data from the input file.

For example, you can use the following loop to process numbers in the input file:

```
while (in.hasNextDouble())
{
   double value = in.nextDouble();
   Process value.
}
```

**When writing text files, use the PrintWriter class and the print/println/printf methods.**

To write output to a file, you construct a PrintWriter object with the desired file name, for example

```
PrintWriter out = new PrintWriter("output.txt");
```

If the output file already exists, it is emptied before the new data are written into it. If the file doesn't exist, an empty file is created.

The PrintWriter class is an enhancement of the PrintStream class that you already know—System.out is a PrintStream object. You can use the familiar print, println, and printf methods with any PrintWriter object:

```
out.println("Hello, World!");
out.printf("Total: %8.2f\n", total);
```

Close all files when
you are done
processing them.

When you are done processing a file, be sure to *close* the Scanner or PrintWriter:

```
in.close();
out.close();
```

If your program exits without closing the PrintWriter, some of the output may not be written to the disk file.

The following program puts these concepts to work. It reads a file containing numbers, and writes the numbers to another file, lined up in a column and followed by their total.

For example, if the input file has the contents

```
32 54 67.5 29 35 80
115 44.5 100 65
```

then the output file is

```
        32.00
        54.00
        67.50
        29.00
        35.00
        80.00
       115.00
        44.50
       100.00
        65.00
Total:  622.00
```

There is one additional issue that we need to tackle. If the input or output file for a Scanner doesn't exist, a FileNotFoundException occurs when the Scanner object is constructed. The compiler insists that we specify what the program should do when that happens. Similarly, the PrintWriter constructor generates this exception if it cannot open the file for writing. (This can happen if the name is illegal or the user does not have the authority to create a file in the given location.) In our sample program, we want to terminate the main method if the exception occurs. To achieve this, we label the main method with a throws declaration:

```
public static void main(String[] args) throws FileNotFoundException
```

You will see in Section 7.4 how to deal with exceptions in a more professional way.

The File, PrintWriter, and FileNotFoundException classes are contained in the java.io package.

### section_1/Total.java

```
 1   import java.io.File;
 2   import java.io.FileNotFoundException;
 3   import java.io.PrintWriter;
 4   import java.util.Scanner;
 5
 6   /**
 7       This program reads a file with numbers, and writes the numbers to another
 8       file, lined up in a column and followed by their total.
 9   */
10   public class Total
11   {
12      public static void main(String[] args) throws FileNotFoundException
13      {
```

```
14      // Prompt for the input and output file names
15
16      Scanner console = new Scanner(System.in);
17      System.out.print("Input file: ");
18      String inputFileName = console.next();
19      System.out.print("Output file: ");
20      String outputFileName = console.next();
21
22      // Construct the Scanner and PrintWriter objects for reading and writing
23
24      File inputFile = new File(inputFileName);
25      Scanner in = new Scanner(inputFile);
26      PrintWriter out = new PrintWriter(outputFileName);
27
28      // Read the input and write the output
29
30      double total = 0;
31
32      while (in.hasNextDouble())
33      {
34         double value = in.nextDouble();
35         out.printf("%15.2f\n", value);
36         total = total + value;
37      }
38
39      out.printf("Total: %8.2f\n", total);
40
41      in.close();
42      out.close();
43   }
44 }
```

**SELF CHECK**

1. What happens when you supply the same name for the input and output files to the Total program? Try it out if you are not sure.

2. What happens when you supply the name of a nonexistent input file to the Total program? Try it out if you are not sure.

3. Suppose you wanted to add the total to an existing file instead of writing a new file. Self Check 1 indicates that you cannot simply do this by specifying the same file for input and output. How can you achieve this task? Provide the pseudo-code for the solution.

4. How do you modify the program so that it shows the average, not the total, of the inputs?

5. How can you modify the Total program so that it writes the values in two columns, like this:

```
    32.00    54.00
    67.50    29.00
    35.00    80.00
   115.00    44.50
   100.00    65.00
Total:      622.00
```

**Practice It**    Now you can try these exercises at the end of the chapter: R7.1, R7.2, P7.1.

### Backslashes in File Names

When you specify a file name as a string literal, and the name contains backslash characters (as in a Windows file name), you must supply each backslash twice:

```
File inputFile = new File("c:\\homework\\input.dat");
```

A single backslash inside a quoted string is an **escape character** that is combined with the following character to form a special meaning, such as \n for a newline character. The \\ combination denotes a single backslash.

When a user supplies a file name to a program, however, the user should not type the backslash twice.

### Constructing a Scanner with a String

When you construct a PrintWriter with a string, it writes to a file:

```
PrintWriter out = new PrintWriter("output.txt");
```

However, this does *not* work for a Scanner. The statement

```
Scanner in = new Scanner("input.txt"); // Error?
```

does *not* open a file. Instead, it simply reads through the string: in.next() returns the string "input.txt". (This is occasionally useful—see Section 7.2.4.)

You must simply remember to use File objects in the Scanner constructor:

```
Scanner in = new Scanner(new File("input.txt")); // OK
```

### Reading Web Pages

You can read the contents of a web page with this sequence of commands:

```
String address = "http://horstmann.com/index.html";
URL pageLocation = new URL(address);
Scanner in = new Scanner(pageLocation.openStream());
```

Now simply read the contents of the web page with the Scanner in the usual way. The URL constructor and the openStream method can throw an IOException, so you need to tag the main method with throws IOException. (See Section 7.4.3 for more information on the throws clause.)

The URL class is contained in the java.net package.

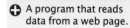

**ONLINE EXAMPLE**

➕ A program that reads data from a web page.

### File Dialog Boxes

In a program with a graphical user interface, you will want to use a file dialog box (such as the one shown in the figure below) whenever the users of your program need to pick a file. The JFileChooser class implements a file dialog box for the Swing user-interface toolkit.

The JFileChooser class has many options to fine-tune the display of the dialog box, but in its most basic form it is quite simple: Construct a file chooser object; then call the showOpenDialog or showSaveDialog method. Both methods show the same dialog box, but the button for selecting a file is labeled "Open" or "Save", depending on which method you call.

For better placement of the dialog box on the screen, you can specify the user-interface component over which to pop up the dialog box. If you don't care where the dialog box pops up, you can simply pass `null`. The `showOpenDialog` and `showSaveDialog` methods return either `JFileChooser.APPROVE_OPTION`, if the user has chosen a file, or `JFileChooser.CANCEL_OPTION`, if the user canceled the selection. If a file was chosen, then you call the `getSelectedFile` method to obtain a `File` object that describes the file. Here is a complete example:

**ONLINE EXAMPLE**

✚ A program that demonstrates how to use a file chooser.

```java
JFileChooser chooser = new JFileChooser();
Scanner in = null;
if (chooser.showOpenDialog(null) == JFileChooser.APPROVE_OPTION)
{
    File selectedFile = chooser.getSelectedFile();
    in = new Scanner(selectedFile);
    . . .
}
```

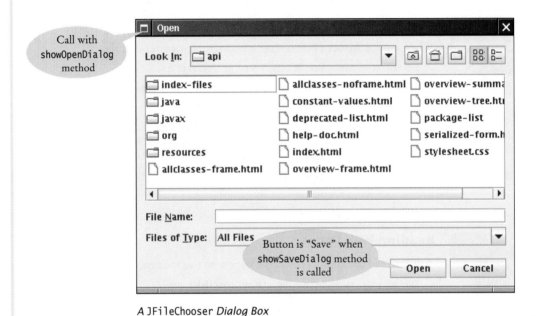

Call with `showOpenDialog` method

Button is "Save" when `showSaveDialog` method is called

*A* JFileChooser *Dialog Box*

## Special Topic 7.3

## Reading and Writing Binary Data

You use the `Scanner` and `PrintWriter` classes to read and write text files. Text files contain sequences of characters. Other files, such as images, are not made up of characters but of bytes. A **byte** is a fundamental storage unit in a computer—a number consisting of eight binary digits. (A byte can represent unsigned integers between 0 and 255 or signed integers between –128 and 127.) The Java library has a different set of classes, called streams, for working with binary files. While modifying binary files is quite challenging and beyond the scope of this book, we give you a simple example of copying binary data from a web site to a file.

You use an `InputStream` to read binary data. For example,

```java
URL imageLocation = new URL("http://horstmann.com/java4everyone/duke.gif");
InputStream in = imageLocation.openStream();
```

To write binary data to a file, use a `FileOutputStream`:

```java
FileOutputStream out = new FileOutputStream("duke.gif");
```

The read method of an input stream reads a single byte and returns –1 when no further input is available. The write method of an output stream writes a single byte.

The following loop copies all bytes from an input stream to an output stream:

```
boolean done = false;
while (!done)
{
    int input = in.read(); // -1 or a byte between 0 and 255
    if (input == -1) { done = true; }
    else { out.write(input); }
}
```

# 7.2  Text Input and Output

In the following sections, you will learn how to process text with complex contents, and you will learn how to cope with challenges that often occur with real data.

## 7.2.1  Reading Words

The next method reads a string that is delimited by white space.

The next method of the Scanner class reads the next string. Consider the loop

```
while (in.hasNext())
{
    String input = in.next();
    System.out.println(input);
}
```

If the user provides the input:

```
Mary had a little lamb
```

this loop prints each word on a separate line:

```
Mary
had
a
little
lamb
```

However, the words can contain punctuation marks and other symbols. The next method returns any sequence of characters that is not white space. *White space* includes spaces, tab characters, and the newline characters that separate lines. For example, the following strings are considered "words" by the next method:

```
snow.
1729
C++
```

(Note the period after snow—it is considered a part of the word because it is not white space.)

Here is precisely what happens when the next method is executed. Input characters that are white space are *consumed*—that is, removed from the input. However, they do not become part of the word. The first character that is not white space becomes the first character of the word. More characters are added until either another white space character occurs, or the end of the input file has been reached. However, if the end of the input file is reached before any character was added to the word, a "no such element exception" occurs.

Sometimes, you want to read just the words and discard anything that isn't a letter. You achieve this task by calling the useDelimiter method on your Scanner object:

```
Scanner in = new Scanner(. . .);
in.useDelimiter("[^A-Za-z]+");
```

Here, we set the character pattern that separates words to "any sequence of characters other than letters". (See Special Topic 7.4.) With this setting, punctuation and numbers are not included in the words returned by the next method.

## 7.2.2 Reading Characters

Sometimes, you want to read a file one character at a time. You will see an example in Section 7.3 where we encrypt the characters of a file. You achieve this task by calling the useDelimiter method on your Scanner object with an empty string:

```
Scanner in = new Scanner(. . .);
in.useDelimiter("");
```

Now each call to next returns a string consisting of a single character. Here is how you can process the characters:

```
while (in.hasNext())
{
    char ch = in.next().charAt(0);
    Process ch.
}
```

## 7.2.3 Classifying Characters

The Character class has methods for classifying characters.

When you read a character, or when you analyze the characters in a word or line, you often want to know what kind of character it is. The Character class declares several useful methods for this purpose. Each of them has an argument of type char and returns a boolean value (see Table 1 ).

For example, the call

```
Character.isDigit(ch)
```

returns true if ch is a digit ('0' ... '9' or a digit in another writing system—see Random Fact 2.2), false otherwise.

### Table 1 Character Testing Methods

| Method | Examples of Accepted Characters |
|---|---|
| isDigit | 0, 1, 2 |
| isLetter | A, B, C, a, b, c |
| isUpperCase | A, B, C |
| isLowerCase | a, b, c |
| isWhiteSpace | space, newline, tab |

## 7.2.4 Reading Lines

When each line of a file is a data record, it is often best to read entire lines with the nextLine method:

```
String line = in.nextLine();
```

The next input line (without the newline character) is placed into the string line. You can then take the line apart for further processing.

The hasNextLine method returns true if there is at least one more line in the input, false when all lines have been read. To ensure that there is another line to process, call the hasNextLine method before calling nextLine.

Here is a typical example of processing lines in a file. A file with population data from the CIA Fact Book site (https://www.cia.gov/library/publications/the-world-factbook/index.html) contains lines such as the following:

```
China   1330044605
India   1147995898
United States 303824646
. . .
```

Because some country names have more than one word, it would be tedious to read this file using the next method. For example, after reading United, how would your program know that it needs to read another word before reading the population count?

Instead, read each input line into a string:

```
while (in.hasNextLine())
{
    String line = nextLine();
    Process line.
}
```

Use the isDigit and isWhiteSpace methods introduced to find out where the name ends and the number starts.

Locate the first digit:

```
int i = 0;
while (!Character.isDigit(line.charAt(i))) { i++; }
```

Then extract the country name and population:

```
String countryName = line.substring(0, i);
String population = line.substring(i);
```

However, the country name contains one or more spaces at the end. Use the trim method to remove them:

```
countryName = countryName.trim();
```

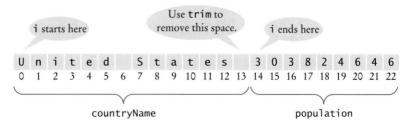

The trim method returns the string with all white space at the beginning and end removed.

There is one additional problem. The population is stored in a string, not a number. In Section 7.2.6, you will see how to convert the string to a number.

## 7.2.5 Scanning a String

In the preceding section, you saw how to break a string into parts by looking at individual characters. Another approach is occasionally easier. You can use a Scanner object to read the characters from a string:

```
Scanner lineScanner = new Scanner(line);
```

Then you can use lineScanner like any other Scanner object, reading words and numbers:

```
String countryName = lineScanner.next(); // Read first word
// Add more words to countryName until number encountered
while (!lineScanner.hasNextInt())
{
    countryName = countryName + " " + lineScanner.next();
}
int populationValue = lineScanner.nextInt();
```

## 7.2.6 Converting Strings to Numbers

Sometimes you have a string that contains a number, such as the population string in Section 7.2.4. For example, suppose that the string is the character sequence "303824646". To get the integer value 303824646, you use the Integer.parseInt method:

```
int populationValue = Integer.parseInt(population);
    // populationValue is the integer 303824646
```

If a string contains the digits of a number, you use the Integer.parseInt or Double.parseDouble method to obtain the number value.

To convert a string containing floating-point digits to its floating-point value, use the Double.parseDouble method. For example, suppose input is the string "3.95".

```
double price = Double.parseDouble(input);
    // price is the floating-point number 3.95
```

You need to be careful when calling the Integer.parseInt and Double.parseDouble methods. The argument must be a string containing the digits of an integer, without any additional characters. Not even spaces are allowed! In our situation, we happen to know that there won't be any spaces at the beginning of the string, but there might be some at the end. Therefore, we use the trim method:

```
int populationValue = Integer.parseInt(population.trim());
```

How To 7.1 on page 333 continues this example.

## 7.2.7 Avoiding Errors When Reading Numbers

You have used the nextInt and nextDouble methods of the Scanner class many times, but here we will have a look at what happens in "abnormal" situations. Suppose you call

```
int value = in.nextInt();
```

The nextInt method recognizes numbers such as 3 or -21. However, if the input is not a properly formatted number, an "input mismatch exception" occurs. For example, consider an input containing the characters

```
2 1 s t   c e n t u r y
```

White space is consumed and the word 21st is read. However, this word is not a properly formatted number, causing an input mismatch exception in the nextInt method.

If there is no input at all when you call nextInt or nextDouble, a "no such element exception" occurs. To avoid exceptions, use the hasNextInt method to screen the input when reading an integer. For example,

```
if (in.hasNextInt())
{
   int value = in.nextInt();
   . . .
}
```

Similarly, you should call the hasNextDouble method before calling nextDouble.

## 7.2.8 Mixing Number, Word, and Line Input

The nextInt, nextDouble, and next methods *do not* consume the white space that follows the number or word. This can be a problem if you alternate between calling nextInt/nextDouble/next and nextLine. Suppose a file contains country names and population values in this format:

```
China
1330044605
India
1147995898
United States
303824646
```

Now suppose you read the file with these instructions:

```
while (in.hasNextLine())
{
   String countryName = in.nextLine();
   int population = in.nextInt();
   Process the country name and population.
}
```

Initially, the input contains

```
C h i n a \n 1 3 3 0 0 4 4 6 0 5 \n I n d i a \n
```

After the first call to the nextLine method, the input contains

```
1 3 3 0 0 4 4 6 0 5 \n I n d i a \n
```

After the call to nextInt, the input contains

```
\n I n d i a \n
```

Note that the nextInt call did *not* consume the newline character. Therefore, the second call to nextLine reads an empty string!

The remedy is to add a call to nextLine after reading the population value:

```
String countryName = in.nextLine();
int population = in.nextInt();
in.nextLine(); // Consume the newline
```

The call to nextLine consumes any remaining white space *and* the newline character.

## 7.2.9 Formatting Output

When you write numbers or strings, you often want to control how they appear. For example, dollar amounts are usually formatted with two significant digits, such as

```
Cookies:     3.20
```

You know from Section 2.3.2 how to achieve this output with the `printf` method. In this section, we discuss additional options of the `printf` method.

Suppose you need to print a table of items and prices, each stored in an array, such as this one:

```
Cookies:     3.20
Linguine:    2.95
Clams:      17.29
```

Note that the item strings line up to the left, whereas the numbers line up to the right. By default, the `printf` method lines up values to the right. To specify left alignment, you add a hyphen (-) before the field width:

```
System.out.printf("%-10s%10.2f", items[i] + ":", prices[i]);
```

Here, we have two format specifiers.

- `%-10s` formats a left-justified string. The string `items[i] + ":"` is padded with spaces so it becomes ten characters wide. The - indicates that the string is placed on the left, followed by sufficient spaces to reach a width of 10.

- `%10.2f` formats a floating-point number, also in a field that is ten characters wide. However, the spaces appear to the left and the value to the right.

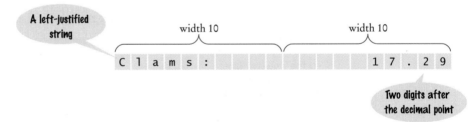

A construct such as `%-10s` or `%10.2f` is called a *format specifier:* it describes how a value should be formatted.

| | Table 2 Format Flags | |
|---|---|---|
| Flag | Meaning | Example |
| - | Left alignment | 1.23 followed by spaces |
| 0 | Show leading zeroes | 001.23 |
| + | Show a plus sign for positive numbers | +1.23 |
| ( | Enclose negative numbers in parentheses | (1.23) |
| , | Show decimal separators | 12,300 |
| ^ | Convert letters to uppercase | 1.23E+1 |

| Code | Type | Example |
|:---:|:---:|:---:|
| d | Decimal integer | 123 |
| f | Fixed floating-point | 12.30 |
| e | Exponential floating-point | 1.23e+1 |
| g | General floating-point (exponential notation is used for very large or very small values) | 12.3 |
| s | String | Tax: |

Table 3 **Format Types**

A format specifier has the following structure:

- The first character is a %
- Next, there are optional "flags" that modify the format, such as - to indicate left alignment. See Table 2 for the most common format flags.
- Next is the field width, the total number of characters in the field (including the spaces used for padding), followed by an optional precision for floating-point numbers.
- The format specifier ends with the format type, such as f for floating-point values or s for strings. There are quite a few format types—Table 3 shows the most important ones.

**SELF CHECK**

6. Suppose the input contains the characters `Hello, World!`. What are the values of word and input after this code fragment?

```
String word = in.next();
String input = in.nextLine();
```

7. Suppose the input contains the characters `995.0 Fred`. What are the values of number and input after this code fragment?

```
int number = 0;
if (in.hasNextInt()) { number = in.nextInt(); }
String input = in.next();
```

8. Suppose the input contains the characters `6E6 6,995.00`. What are the values of x1 and x2 after this code fragment?

```
double x1 = in.nextDouble();
double x2 = in.nextDouble();
```

9. Your input file contains a sequence of numbers, but sometimes a value is not available and is marked as `N/A`. How can you read the numbers and skip over the markers?

10. How can you remove spaces from the country name in Section 7.2.4 without using the trim method?

**Practice It**    Now you can try these exercises at the end of the chapter: P7.2, P7.4, P7.5.

Special Topic 7.4

### Regular Expressions

Regular expressions describe character patterns. For example, numbers have a simple form. They contain one or more digits. The regular expression describing numbers is [0-9]+. The set [0-9] denotes any digit between 0 and 9, and the + means "one or more".

The search commands of professional programming editors understand regular expressions. Moreover, several utility programs use regular expressions to locate matching text. A commonly used program that uses regular expressions is *grep* (which stands for "global regular expression print"). You can run grep from a command line or from inside some compilation environments. Grep is part of the UNIX operating system, and versions are available for Windows. It needs a regular expression and one or more files to search. When grep runs, it displays a set of lines that match the regular expression.

Suppose you want to find all magic numbers (see Programming Tip 2.2) in a file.

```
grep [0-9]+ Homework.java
```

lists all lines in the file Homework.java that contain sequences of digits. That isn't terribly useful; lines with variable names x1 will be listed. OK, you want sequences of digits that do *not* immediately follow letters:

```
grep [^A-Za-z][0-9]+ Homework.java
```

The set [^A-Za-z] denotes any characters that are *not* in the ranges A to Z and a to z. This works much better, and it shows only lines that contain actual numbers.

The useDelimiter method of the Scanner class accepts a regular expression to describe delimiters—the blocks of text that separate words. As already mentioned, if you set the delimiter pattern to [^A-Za-z]+, a delimiter is a sequence of one or more characters that are not letters.

For more information on regular expressions, consult one of the many tutorials on the Internet by pointing your search engine to "regular expression tutorial".

VIDEO EXAMPLE 7.1

### Computing a Document's Readability

In this Video Example, we develop a program that computes the Flesch Readability Index for a document.

# 7.3 Command Line Arguments

Depending on the operating system and Java development environment used, there are different methods of starting a program—for example, by selecting "Run" in the compilation environment, by clicking on an icon, or by typing the name of the program at the prompt in a command shell window. The latter method is called "invoking the program from the command line". When you use this method, you must of course type the name of the program, but you can also type in additional information that the program can use. These additional strings are called **command line arguments**. For example, if you start a program with the command line

```
java ProgramClass -v input.dat
```

then the program receives two command line arguments: the strings "-v" and "input.dat". It is entirely up to the program what to do with these strings. It is customary to interpret strings starting with a hyphen (-) as program options.

⊕ Available online in WileyPLUS and at www.wiley.com/college/horstmann.

Should you support command line arguments for your programs, or should you prompt users, perhaps with a graphical user interface? For a casual and infrequent user, an interactive user interface is much better. The user interface guides the user along and makes it possible to navigate the application without much knowledge. But for a frequent user, a command line interface has a major advantage: it is easy to automate. If you need to process hundreds of files every day, you could spend all your time typing file names into file chooser dialog boxes. However, by using batch files or shell scripts (a feature of your computer's operating system), you can automatically call a program many times with different command line arguments.

Your program receives its command line arguments in the args parameter of the main method:

```java
public static void main(String[] args)
```

In our example, args is an array of length 2, containing the strings

```
args[0]:    "-v"
args[1]:    "input.dat"
```

> **Programs that start from the command line receive the command line arguments in the main method.**

Let us write a program that *encrypts* a file—that is, scrambles it so that it is unreadable except to those who know the decryption method. Ignoring 2,000 years of progress in the field of encryption, we will use a method familiar to Julius Caesar, replacing A with a D, B with an E, and so on (see Figure 1).

The program takes the following command line arguments:

- An optional -d flag to indicate decryption instead of encryption
- The input file name
- The output file name

For example,

```
java CaesarCipher input.txt encrypt.txt
```

encrypts the file input.txt and places the result into encrypt.txt.

```
java CaesarCipher -d encrypt.txt output.txt
```

decrypts the file encrypt.txt and places the result into output.txt.

*The emperor Julius Caesar used a simple scheme to encrypt messages.*

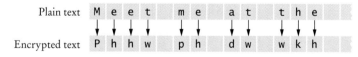

**Figure 1** Caesar Cipher

### section_3/CaesarCipher.java

```java
1   import java.io.File;
2   import java.io.FileNotFoundException;
3   import java.io.PrintWriter;
4   import java.util.Scanner;
```

```
 5
 6   /**
 7       This program encrypts a file using the Caesar cipher.
 8   */
 9   public class CaesarCipher
10   {
11      public static void main(String[] args) throws FileNotFoundException
12      {
13         final int DEFAULT_KEY = 3;
14         int key = DEFAULT_KEY;
15         String inFile = "";
16         String outFile = "";
17         int files = 0; // Number of command line arguments that are files
18
19         for (int i = 0; i < args.length; i++)
20         {
21            String arg = args[i];
22            if (arg.charAt(0) == '-')
23            {
24               // It is a command line option
25
26               char option = arg.charAt(1);
27               if (option == 'd') { key = -key; }
28               else { usage(); return; }
29            }
30            else
31            {
32               // It is a file name
33
34               files++;
35               if (files == 1) { inFile = arg; }
36               else if (files == 2) { outFile = arg; }
37            }
38         }
39         if (files != 2) { usage(); return; }
40
41         Scanner in = new Scanner(new File(inFile));
42         in.useDelimiter(""); // Process individual characters
43         PrintWriter out = new PrintWriter(outFile);
44
45         while (in.hasNext())
46         {
47            char from = in.next().charAt(0);
48            char to = encrypt(from, key);
49            out.print(to);
50         }
51         in.close();
52         out.close();
53      }
54
55      /**
56          Encrypts upper- and lowercase characters by shifting them
57          according to a key.
58          @param ch the letter to be encrypted
59          @param key the encryption key
60          @return the encrypted letter
61      */
62      public static char encrypt(char ch, int key)
63      {
64         int base = 0;
```

```
65        if ('A' <= ch && ch <= 'Z') { base = 'A'; }
66        else if ('a' <= ch && ch <= 'z') { base = 'a'; }
67        else { return ch; } // Not a letter
68        int offset = ch - base + key;
69        final int LETTERS = 26; // Number of letters in the Roman alphabet
70        if (offset > LETTERS) { offset = offset - LETTERS; }
71        else if (offset < 0) { offset = offset + LETTERS; }
72        return (char) (base + offset);
73     }
74
75     /**
76        Prints a message describing proper usage.
77     */
78     public static void usage()
79     {
80        System.out.println("Usage: java CaesarCipher [-d] infile outfile");
81     }
82  }
```

**SELF CHECK**

**11.** If the program is invoked with java CaesarCipher -d file1.txt, what are the elements of args?

**12.** Trace the program when it is invoked as in Self Check 11.

**13.** Will the program run correctly if the program is invoked with java CaesarCipher file1.txt file2.txt -d? If so, why? If not, why not?

**14.** Encrypt CAESAR using the Caesar cipher.

**15.** How can you modify the program so that the user can specify an encryption key other than 3 with a -k option, for example

```
java CaesarCipher -k15 input.txt output.txt
```

**Practice It**    Now you can try these exercises at the end of the chapter: R7.4, P7.8, P7.9.

---

HOW TO 7.1              **Processing Text Files**

Processing text files that contain real data can be surprisingly challenging. This How To gives you step-by-step guidance.

As an example, we will consider this task: Read two country data files, worldpop.txt and worldarea.txt (supplied with the book's companion code). Both files contain the same countries in the same order. Write a file world_pop_density.txt that contains country names and population densities (people per square km), with the country names aligned left and the numbers aligned right:

```
Afghanistan              50.56
Akrotiri                127.64
Albania                 125.91
Algeria                  14.18
American Samoa          288.92
. . .
```

*Singapore is one of the most densely populated countries in the world.*

**Step 1** Understand the processing task.

As always, you need to have a clear understanding of the task before designing a solution. Can you carry out the task by hand (perhaps with smaller input files)? If not, get more information about the problem.

One important aspect that you need to consider is whether you can process the data as it becomes available, or whether you need to store it first. For example, if you are asked to write out sorted data, you first need to collect all input, perhaps by placing it in an array list. However, it is often possible to process the data "on the go", without storing it.

In our example, we can read each file a line at a time and compute the density for each line because our input files store the population and area data in the same order.

The following pseudocode describes our processing task.

> While there are more lines to be read
>     Read a line from each file.
>     Extract the country name.
>     population = number following the country name in the line from the first file
>     area = number following the country name in the line from the second file
>     If area != 0
>         density = population / area
>     Print country name and density.

**Step 2** Determine which files you need to read and write.

This should be clear from the problem. In our example, there are two input files, the population data and the area data, and one output file.

**Step 3** Choose a mechanism for obtaining the file names.

There are three options:
- Hard-coding the file names (such as "worldpop.txt").
- Asking the user:
  ```
  Scanner in = new Scanner(System.in);
  System.out.print("Enter filename: ");
  String inFile = in.nextLine();
  ```
- Using command-line arguments for the file names.

In our example, we use hard-coded file names for simplicity.

**Step 4** Choose between line, word, and character-based input.

As a rule of thumb, read lines if the input data is grouped by lines. That is the case with tabular data, such as in our example, or when you need to report line numbers.

When gathering data that can be distributed over several lines, then it makes more sense to read words. Keep in mind that you lose all white space when you read words.

Reading characters is mostly useful for tasks that require access to individual characters. Examples include analyzing character frequencies, changing tabs to spaces, or encryption.

**Step 5** With line-oriented input, extract the required data.

It is simple to read a line of input with the nextLine method. Then you need to get the data out of that line. You can extract substrings, as described in Section 7.2.4.

Typically, you will use methods such as Character.isWhitespace and Character.isDigit to find the boundaries of substrings.

If you need any of the substrings as numbers, you must convert them, using Integer.parseInt or Double.parseDouble.

**Step 6**   Use methods to factor out common tasks.

Processing input files usually has repetitive tasks, such as skipping over white space or extracting numbers from strings. It really pays off to develop a set of methods to handle these tedious operations.

In our example, we have two common tasks that call for helper methods: extracting the country name and the value that follows. We will implement methods

```java
public static String extractCountry(String line)
public static double extractValue(String line)
```

These methods are implemented as described in Section 7.2.4.

Here is the complete source code (how_to_1/PopulationDensity.java).

```java
import java.io.File;
import java.io.FileNotFoundException;
import java.io.PrintWriter;
import java.util.Scanner;

/**
    This program reads data files of country populations and areas and prints the
    population density for each country.
*/
public class PopulationDensity
{
    public static void main(String[] args) throws FileNotFoundException
    {
        // Construct Scanner objects for input files

        Scanner in1 = new Scanner(new File("worldpop.txt"));
        Scanner in2 = new Scanner(new File("worldarea.txt"));

        // Construct PrintWriter for the output file

        PrintWriter out = new PrintWriter("world_pop_density.txt");

        // Read lines from each file

        while (in1.hasNextLine() && in2.hasNextLine())
        {
            String line1 = in1.nextLine();
            String line2 = in2.nextLine();

            // Extract country and associated value
            String country = extractCountry(line1);
            double population = extractValue(line1);
            double area = extractValue(line2);

            // Compute and print the population density
            double density = 0;
            if (area != 0) // Protect against division by zero
            {
                density = population / area;
            }
            out.printf("%-40s%15.2f\n", country, density);
        }

        in1.close();
        in2.close();
        out.close();
    }
```

```java
/**
   Extracts the country from an input line.
   @param line a line containing a country name, followed by a number
   @return the country name
*/
public static String extractCountry(String line)
{
   int i = 0; // Locate the start of the first digit
   while (!Character.isDigit(line.charAt(i))) { i++; }
   return line.substring(0, i).trim(); // Extract the country name
}

/**
   Extracts the value from an input line.
   @param line a line containing a country name, followed by a value
   @return the value associated with the country
*/
public static double extractValue(String line)
{
   int i = 0; // Locate the start of the first digit
   while (!Character.isDigit(line.charAt(i))) { i++; }
   // Extract and convert the value
   return Double.parseDouble(line.substring(i).trim());
}
}
```

## Random Fact 7.1 Encryption Algorithms

The exercises at the end of this chapter give a few algorithms for encrypting text. Don't actually use any of those methods to send secret messages to your lover. Any skilled cryptographer can *break* these schemes in a very short time—that is, reconstruct the original text without knowing the secret keyword.

In 1978, Ron Rivest, Adi Shamir, and Leonard Adleman introduced an encryption method that is much more powerful. The method is called *RSA encryption*, after the last names of its inventors. The exact scheme is too complicated to present here, but it is not actually difficult to follow. You can find the details in http://theory.lcs.mit.edu/~rivest/rsapaper.pdf.

RSA is a remarkable encryption method. There are two keys: a public key and a private key. (See the figure.) You can print the public key on your business card (or in your e-mail signature block) and give it to any-

one. Then anyone can send you messages that only you can decrypt. Even though everyone else knows the public key, and even if they intercept all the messages coming to you, they cannot break the scheme and actually read the messages. In 1994, hundreds of researchers, collaborating over the Internet, cracked an RSA message encrypted with a 129-digit key. Messages encrypted with a key of 230 digits or more are expected to be secure.

The inventors of the algorithm obtained a *patent* for it. A patent is a deal that society makes with an inventor. For a period of 20 years, the inventor has an exclusive right for its commercialization, may collect royalties from others wishing to manufacture the invention, and may even stop competitors from using it altogether. In return, the inventor must publish the invention, so that others may learn from it, and must relinquish all claim to it after the monopoly period ends. The presumption is that in the absence

of patent law, inventors would be reluctant to go through the trouble of inventing, or they would try to cloak their techniques to prevent others from copying their devices.

There has been some controversy about the RSA patent. Had there not been patent protection, would the inventors have published the method anyway, thereby giving the benefit to society without the cost of the 20-year monopoly? In this case, the answer is probably yes. The inventors were academic researchers, who live on salaries rather than sales receipts and are usually rewarded for their discoveries by a boost in their reputation and careers. Would their followers have been as active in discovering (and patenting) improvements? There is no way of knowing, of course. Is an algorithm even patentable, or is it a mathematical fact that belongs to nobody? The patent office did take the latter attitude for a long time. The RSA inventors and many others described their

**Analyzing Baby Names**

In this Worked Example, you will use data from the Social Security Administration to analyze the most popular baby names.

# 7.4 Exception Handling

There are two aspects to dealing with program errors: *detection* and *handling*. For example, the Scanner constructor can detect an attempt to read from a non-existent file. However, it cannot handle that error. A satisfactory way of handling the error might be to terminate the program, or to ask the user for another file name. The Scanner class cannot choose between these alternatives. It needs to report the error to another part of the program.

In Java, *exception handling* provides a flexible mechanism for passing control from the point of error detection to a handler that can deal with the error. In the following sections, we will look into the details of this mechanism.

inventions in terms of imaginary electronic devices, rather than algorithms, to circumvent that restriction. Nowadays, the patent office will award software patents.

There is another interesting aspect to the RSA story. A programmer, Phil Zimmermann, developed a program called PGP (for *Pretty Good Privacy*) that is based on RSA. Anyone can use the program to encrypt messages, and decryption is not feasible even with the most powerful computers. You can get a copy of a free PGP implementation from the GNU project (http://www.gnupg.org). The existence of strong encryption methods bothers the United States government to no end. Criminals and foreign agents can send communications that the police and intelligence agencies cannot decipher. The government considered charging Zimmermann with breaching a law that forbids the unauthorized export of munitions, arguing that he should have known that his program would appear on the Internet. There have been serious proposals to make it illegal for private citizens to use these encryption methods, or to keep the keys secret from law enforcement.

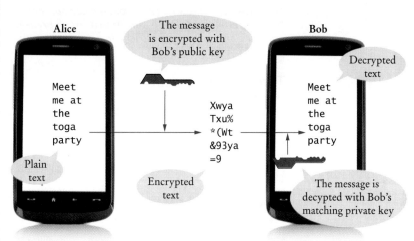

*Public-Key Encryption*

## 7.4.1 Throwing Exceptions

> To signal an exceptional condition, use the throw statement to throw an exception object.

When you detect an error condition, your job is really easy. You just *throw* an appropriate exception object, and you are done. For example, suppose someone tries to withdraw too much money from a bank account.

```
if (amount > balance)
{
    // Now what?
}
```

First look for an appropriate exception class. The Java library provides many classes to signal all sorts of exceptional conditions. Figure 2 shows the most useful ones. (The classes are arranged as a tree-shaped hierarchy, with more specialized classes at the bottom of the tree. We will discuss such hierarchies in more detail in Chapter 9.)

Look around for an exception type that might describe your situation. How about the `ArithmeticException`? Is it an arithmetic error to have a negative balance? No—Java can deal with negative numbers. Is the amount to be withdrawn illegal? Indeed it is. It is just too large. Therefore, let's throw an `IllegalArgumentException`.

```
if (amount > balance)
{
    throw new IllegalArgumentException("Amount exceeds balance");
}
```

> When you throw an exception, processing continues in an exception handler.

When you throw an exception, execution does not continue with the next statement but with an **exception handler**. That is the topic of the next section.

*When you throw an exception, the normal control flow is terminated. This is similar to a circuit breaker that cuts off the flow of electricity in a dangerous situation.*

Syntax 7.1     Throwing an Exception

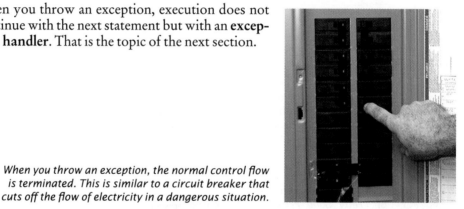

*Syntax*     throw *exceptionObject*;

Most exception objects can be constructed with an error message.

A new exception object is constructed, then thrown.

```
if (amount > balance)
{
    throw new IllegalArgumentException("Amount exceeds balance");
}
balance = balance - amount;
```

This line is not executed when the exception is thrown.

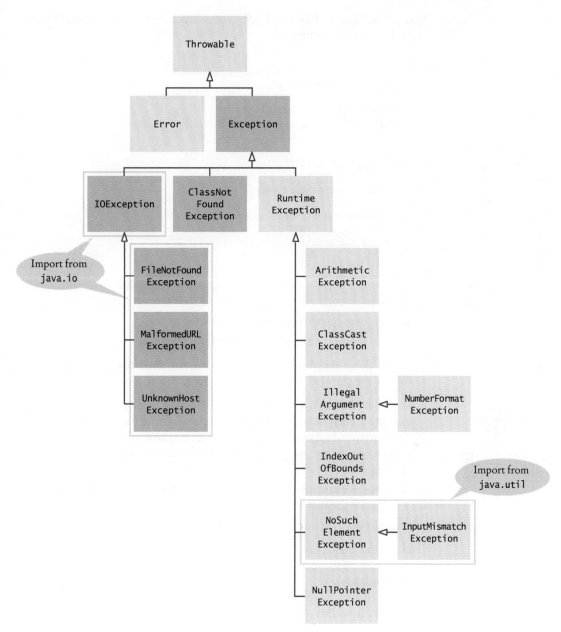

**Figure 2** A Part of the Hierarchy of Exception Classes

## 7.4.2 Catching Exceptions

Place the statements
that can cause an
exception inside a
try block, and the
handler inside a
catch clause.

Every exception should be handled somewhere in your program. If an exception has
no handler, an error message is printed, and your program terminates. Of course,
such an unhandled exception is confusing to program users.

You handle exceptions with the try/catch statement. Place the statement into a
location of your program that knows how to handle a particular exception. The try
block contains one or more statements that may cause an exception of the kind that

you are willing to handle. Each catch clause contains the handler for an exception type. Here is an example:

```
try
{
   String filename = . . .;
   Scanner in = new Scanner(new File(filename));
   String input = in.next();
   int value = Integer.parseInt(input);
   . . .
}
catch (IOException exception)
{
   exception.printStackTrace();
}
catch (NumberFormatException exception)
{
   System.out.println(exception.getMessage());
}
```

Three exceptions may be thrown in this try block:

- The Scanner constructor can throw a FileNotFoundException.
- Scanner.next can throw a NoSuchElementException.
- Integer.parseInt can throw a NumberFormatException.

If any of these exceptions is actually thrown, then the rest of the instructions in the try block are skipped. Here is what happens for the various exception types:

- If a FileNotFoundException is thrown, then the catch clause for the IOException is executed. (If you look at Figure 2, you will note that FileNotFoundException is a descendant of IOException.) If you want to show the user a different message for a FileNotFoundException, you must place the catch clause *before* the clause for an IOException.
- If a NumberFormatException occurs, then the second catch clause is executed.
- A NoSuchElementException is *not caught* by any of the catch clauses. The exception remains thrown until it is caught by another try block.

Each catch clause contains a handler. When the catch (IOException exception) block is executed, then some method in the try block has failed with an IOException (or one of its descendants).

In this handler, we produce a printout of the chain of method calls that led to the exception, by calling

```
exception.printStackTrace()
```

*You should only catch those exceptions that you can handle.*

## Syntax 7.2    Catching Exceptions

*Syntax*
```
try
{
    statement
    statement
    . . .
}
catch (ExceptionClass exceptionObject)
{
    statement
    statement
    . . .
}
```

This constructor can throw a
`FileNotFoundException`.

```
try
{
    Scanner in = new Scanner(new File("input.txt"));
    String input = in.next();
    process(input);
}
catch (IOException exception)
{
    System.out.println("Could not open input file");
}
catch (Exception except)
{
    System.out.println(except.getMessage);
}
```

This is the exception that was thrown.

When an `IOException` is thrown,
execution resumes here.

A `FileNotFoundException`
is a special case of an `IOException`.

Additional catch clauses
can appear here. Place
more specific exceptions
before more general ones.

In the second exception handler, we call `exception.getMessage()` to retrieve the message associated with the exception. When the `parseInt` method throws a `NumberFormatException`, the message contains the string that it was unable to format. When you throw an exception, you can provide your own message string. For example, when you call

```
throw new IllegalArgumentException("Amount exceeds balance");
```

the message of the exception is the string provided in the constructor.

In these sample `catch` clauses, we merely inform the user of the source of the problem. Often, it is better to give the user another chance to provide a correct input—see Section 7.5 for a solution.

## 7.4.3 Checked Exceptions

In Java, the exceptions that you can throw and catch fall into three categories.

- Internal errors are reported by descendants of the type `Error`. One example is the `OutOfMemoryError`, which is thrown when all available computer memory has been used up. These are fatal errors that happen rarely, and we will not consider them in this book.

- Descendants of `RuntimeException`, such as as `IndexOutOfBoundsException` or `IllegalArgumentException` indicate errors in your code. They are called **unchecked exceptions**.

Checked exceptions are due to external circumstances that the programmer cannot prevent. The compiler checks that your program handles these exceptions.

- All other exceptions are **checked exceptions**. These exceptions indicate that something has gone wrong for some external reason beyond your control. In Figure 2, the checked exceptions are shaded in a darker color.

Why have two kinds of exceptions? A checked exception describes a problem that can occur, no matter how careful you are. For example, an IOException can be caused by forces beyond your control, such as a disk error or a broken network connection. The compiler takes checked exceptions very seriously and ensures that they are handled. Your program will not compile if you don't indicate how to deal with a checked exception.

The unchecked exceptions, on the other hand, are your fault. The compiler does not check whether you handle an unchecked exception, such as an IndexOutOfBounds-Exception. After all, you should check your index values rather than install a handler for that exception.

If you have a handler for a checked exception in the same method that may throw it, then the compiler is satisfied. For example,

```
try
{
    File inFile = new File(filename);
    Scanner in = new Scanner(inFile); // Throws FileNotFoundException
    . . .
}
catch (FileNotFoundException exception) // Exception caught here
{
    . . .
}
```

Add a throws clause to a method that can throw a checked exception.

However, it commonly happens that the current method *cannot handle* the exception. In that case, you need to tell the compiler that you are aware of this exception and that you want your method to be terminated when it occurs. You supply a method with a throws clause.

```
public static String readData(String filename) throws FileNotFoundException
{
    File inFile = new File(filename);
    Scanner in = new Scanner(inFile);
    . . .
}
```

The throws clause signals the caller of your method that it may encounter a FileNotFoundException. Then the caller needs to make the same decision—handle the exception, or declare that the exception may be thrown.

It sounds somehow irresponsible not to handle an exception when you know that it happened. Actually, the opposite is true. Java provides an exception handling facility so that an exception can be sent to the *appropriate* handler. Some methods detect errors, some methods handle them, and some methods just pass them along. The throws clause simply ensures that no exceptions get lost along the way.

*Just as trucks with large or hazardous loads carry warning signs, the* throws *clause warns the caller that an exception may occur.*

## Syntax 7.3    The throws Clause

*Syntax*      *modifiers returnType methodName(parameterType parameterName, . . .)*
                 throws *ExceptionClass, ExceptionClass, . . .*

```
public static String readData(String filename)
    throws FileNotFoundException, NumberFormatException
```

**You must specify all checked exceptions that this method may throw.**

**You may also list unchecked exceptions.**

## 7.4.4 The finally Clause

> Once a try block is entered, the statements in a finally clause are guaranteed to be executed, whether or not an exception is thrown.

Occasionally, you need to take some action whether or not an exception is thrown. The finally construct is used to handle this situation. Here is a typical situation.

It is important to close a PrintWriter to ensure that all output is written to the file. In the following code segment, we open a stream, call one or more methods, and then close the stream:

```
PrintWriter out = new PrintWriter(filename);
writeData(out);
out.close(); // May never get here
```

Now suppose that one of the methods before the last line throws an exception. Then the call to close is never executed! You solve this problem by placing the call to close inside a finally clause:

```
PrintWriter out = new PrintWriter(filename);
try
{
    writeData(out);
}
finally
{
    out.close();
}
```

In a normal case, there will be no problem. When the try block is completed, the finally clause is executed, and the writer is closed. However, if an exception occurs, the finally clause is also executed before the exception is passed to its handler.

**ONLINE EXAMPLE**

A program that demonstrates throwing and catching exceptions.

Use the finally clause whenever you need to do some clean up, such as closing a file, to ensure that the clean up happens no matter how the method exits.

*All visitors to a foreign country have to go through passport control, no matter what happened on their trip. Similarly, the code in a* finally *clause is always executed, even when an exception has occurred.*

## Syntax 7.4 The finally Clause

```
Syntax    try
          {
              statement
              statement
              . . .
          }
          finally
          {
              statement
              statement
              . . .
          }
```

*This variable must be declared outside the try block so that the finally clause can access it.*

```
PrintWriter out = new PrintWriter(filename);
try
{
    writeData(out);
}
finally
{
    out.close();
}
```

*This code may throw exceptions.*

*This code is always executed, even if an exception occurs.*

---

**SELF CHECK**

**16.** Suppose balance is 100 and amount is 200. What is the value of balance after these statements?

```
if (amount > balance)
{
    throw new IllegalArgumentException("Amount exceeds balance");
}
balance = balance - amount;
```

**17.** When depositing an amount into a bank account, we don't have to worry about overdrafts—except when the amount is negative. Write a statement that throws an appropriate exception in that case.

**18.** Consider the method

```
public static void main(String[] args)
{
    try
    {
        Scanner in = new Scanner(new File("input.txt"));
        int value = in.nextInt();
        System.out.println(value);
    }
    catch (IOException exception)
    {
        System.out.println("Error opening file.");
    }
}
```

Suppose the file with the given file name exists and has no contents. Trace the flow of execution.

**19.** Why is an `ArrayIndexOutOfBoundsException` not a checked exception?

**20.** Is there a difference between catching checked and unchecked exceptions?

**21.** What is wrong with the following code, and how can you fix it?

```
public static void writeAll(String[] lines, String filename)
{
    PrintWriter out = new PrintWriter(filename);
    for (String line : lines)
    {
        out.println(line.toUpperCase());
    }
    out.close();
}
```

**Practice It**  Now you can try these exercises at the end of the chapter: R7.7, R7.8, R7.9.

---

**Programming Tip 7.1**

### Throw Early, Catch Late

When a method detects a problem that it cannot solve, it is better to throw an exception rather than try to come up with an imperfect fix. For example, suppose a method expects to read a number from a file, and the file doesn't contain a number. Simply using a zero value would be a poor choice because it hides the actual problem and perhaps causes a different problem elsewhere.

> Throw an exception as soon as a problem is detected. Catch it only when the problem can be handled.

Conversely, a method should only catch an exception if it can really remedy the situation. Otherwise, the best remedy is simply to have the exception propagate to its caller, allowing it to be caught by a competent handler.

These principles can be summarized with the slogan "throw early, catch late".

---

**Programming Tip 7.2**

### Do Not Squelch Exceptions

When you call a method that throws a checked exception and you haven't specified a handler, the compiler complains. In your eagerness to continue your work, it is an understandable impulse to shut the compiler up by squelching the exception:

```
try
{
    Scanner in = new Scanner(new File(filename));
    // Compiler complained about FileNotFoundException
    . . .
}
catch (FileNotFoundException e) {} // So there!
```

The do-nothing exception handler fools the compiler into thinking that the exception has been handled. In the long run, this is clearly a bad idea. Exceptions were designed to transmit problem reports to a competent handler. Installing an incompetent handler simply hides an error condition that could be serious.

Programming Tip 7.3

### Do Not Use catch and finally in the Same try Statement

It is possible to have a finally clause following one or more catch clauses. Then the code in the finally clause is executed whenever the try block is exited in any of three ways:

1. After completing the last statement of the try block
2. After completing the last statement of a catch clause, if this try block caught an exception
3. When an exception was thrown in the try block and not caught

It is tempting to combine catch and finally clauses, but the resulting code can be hard to understand, and it is often incorrect. Instead, use two statements:

- a try/finally statement to close resources
- a separate try/catch statement to handle errors

For example,

```
try
{
    PrintWriter out = new PrintWriter(filename);
    try
    {
        Write output.
    }
    finally
    {
        out.close();
    }
}
catch (IOException exception)
{
    Handle exception.
}
```

Note that the nested statements work correctly if the PrintWriter constructor throws an exception, too.

Special Topic 7.5

### Automatic Resource Management in Java 7

In Java 7, you can use a new form of the try block that automatically closes a PrintWriter or Scanner object. Here is the syntax:

```
try (PrintWriter out = new PrintWriter(filename))
{
    Write output to out.
}
```

The close method is automatically invoked on the out object when the try block ends, whether or not an exception has occurred. A finally statement is not required.

## Random Fact 7.2  The Ariane Rocket Incident

The European Space Agency (ESA), Europe's counterpart to NASA, had developed a rocket model called Ariane that it had successfully used several times to launch satellites and scientific experiments into space. However, when a new version, the Ariane 5, was launched on June 4, 1996, from ESA's launch site in Kourou, French Guiana, the rocket veered off course about 40 seconds after liftoff. Flying at an angle of more than 20 degrees, rather than straight up, exerted such an aerodynamic force that the boosters separated, which triggered the automatic self-destruction mechanism. The rocket blew itself up.

The ultimate cause of this accident was an unhandled exception! The rocket contained two identical devices (called inertial reference systems) that processed flight data from measuring devices and turned the data into information about the rocket position.

The onboard computer used the position information for controlling the boosters. The same inertial reference systems and computer software had worked fine on the Ariane 4.

However, due to design changes to the rocket, one of the sensors measured a larger acceleration force than had been encountered in the Ariane 4. That value, expressed as a floating-point value, was stored in a 16-bit integer (like a short variable in Java). Unlike Java, the Ada language, used for the device software, generates an exception if a floating-point number is too large to be converted to an integer. Unfortunately, the programmers of the device had decided that this situation would never happen and didn't provide an exception handler.

When the overflow did happen, the exception was triggered and, because there was no handler, the device shut itself off. The onboard computer sensed the failure and switched over to the backup device. However, that device had shut itself off for exactly the same reason, something that the designers of the rocket had not expected. They figured that the devices might fail for mechanical reasons, and the chance of two devices having the same mechanical failure was considered remote. At that point, the rocket was without reliable position information and went off course.

Perhaps it would have been better if the software hadn't been so thorough? If it had ignored the overflow, the device wouldn't have been shut off. It would have computed bad data. But then the device would have reported wrong position data, which could have been just as fatal. Instead, a correct implementation should have caught overflow exceptions and come up with some strategy to recompute the flight data. Clearly, giving up was not a reasonable option in this context.

The advantage of the exception-handling mechanism is that it makes these issues explicit to programmers—something to think about when you curse the Java compiler for complaining about uncaught exceptions.

*The Explosion of the Ariane Rocket*

# 7.5  Application: Handling Input Errors

This section walks through an example program that includes exception handling. The program, DataAnalyzer.java, asks the user for the name of a file. The file is expected to contain data values. The first line of the file should contain the total number of values, and the remaining lines contain the data. A typical input file looks like this:

```
3
1.45
-2.1
0.05
```

When designing a program, ask yourself what kinds of exceptions can occur.

What can go wrong? There are two principal risks.

- The file might not exist.
- The file might have data in the wrong format.

Who can detect these faults? The Scanner constructor will throw an exception when the file does not exist. The methods that process the input values need to throw an exception when they find an error in the data format.

What exceptions can be thrown? The Scanner constructor throws a FileNot-FoundException when the file does not exist, which is appropriate in our situation. When there are fewer data items than expected, or when the file doesn't start with the count of values, the program will throw an NoSuchElementException. Finally, when there are more inputs than expected, an IOException should be thrown.

For each exception, you need to decide which part of your program can competently handle it.

Who can remedy the faults that the exceptions report? Only the main method of the DataAnalyzer program interacts with the user, so it catches the exceptions, prints appropriate error messages, and gives the user another chance to enter a correct file:

```java
// Keep trying until there are no more exceptions
boolean done = false;
while (!done)
{
    try
    {
        Prompt user for file name.

        double[] data = readFile(filename);

        Process data.

        done = true;
    }
    catch (FileNotFoundException exception)
    {
        System.out.println("File not found.");
    }
    catch (NoSuchElementException exception)
    {
        System.out.println("File contents invalid.");
    }
    catch (IOException exception)
    {
        exception.printStackTrace();
    }
}
```

The first two catch clauses in the main method give a human-readable error report if bad data was encountered or the file was not found. However, if another IOException occurs, then it prints a stack trace so that a programmer can diagnose the problem.

The following readFile method constructs the Scanner object and calls the readData method. It does not handle any exceptions. If there is a problem with the input file, it simply passes the exception to its caller.

```java
public static double[] readFile(String filename) throws IOException
{
    File inFile = new File(filename);
    Scanner in = new Scanner(inFile);
    try
    {
```

```
      return readData(in);
   }
   finally
   {
      in.close();
   }
}
```

Note how the `finally` clause ensures that the file is closed even when an exception occurs.

Also note that the `throws` clause of the `readFile` method need not include the `FileNotFoundException` class because it is a special case of an `IOException`.

The `readData` method reads the number of values, constructs an array, and fills it with the data values.

```
public static double[] readData(Scanner in) throws IOException
{
   int numberOfValues = in.nextInt(); // May throw NoSuchElementException
   double[] data = new double[numberOfValues];

   for (int i = 0; i < numberOfValues; i++)
   {
      data[i] = in.nextDouble(); // May throw NoSuchElementException
   }

   if (in.hasNext())
   {
      throw new IOException("End of file expected");
   }
   return data;
}
```

As discussed in Section 7.2.7, the calls to the `nextInt` and `nextDouble` methods can throw a `NoSuchElementException` when there is no input at all or an `InputMismatchException` if the input is not a number. As you can see from Figure 2 on page 340, an `InputMismatchException` is a special case of a `NoSuchElementException`.

You need not declare the `NoSuchElementException` in the `throws` clause because it is not a checked exception, but you can include it for greater clarity.

There are three potential errors:

- The file might not start with an integer.
- There might not be a sufficient number of data values.
- There might be additional input after reading all data values.

In the first two cases, the `Scanner` throws a `NoSuchElementException`. Note again that this is *not* a checked exception—we could have avoided it by calling `hasNextInt`/`hasNextDouble` first. However, this method does not know what to do in this case, so it allows the exception to be sent to a handler elsewhere.

When we find that there is additional unexpected input, we throw an `IOException`. To see the exception handling at work, look at a specific error scenario.

1. `main` calls `readFile`.
2. `readFile` calls `readData`.
3. `readData` calls `Scanner.nextInt`.
4. There is no integer in the input, and `Scanner.nextInt` throws a `NoSuchElementException`.

5. `readData` has no catch clause. It terminates immediately.

6. `readFile` has no catch clause. It terminates immediately after executing the `finally` clause and closing the file.

7. The first catch clause in `main` is for a `FileNotFoundException`. The exception that is currently being thrown is a `NoSuchElementException`, and this handler doesn't apply.

8. The next catch clause is for a `NoSuchElementException`, and execution resumes here. That handler prints a message to the user. Afterward, the user is given another chance to enter a file name. Note that the statements for processing the data have been skipped.

This example shows the separation between error detection (in the `readData` method) and error handling (in the `main` method). In between the two is the `readFile` method, which simply passes the exceptions along.

### section_5/DataAnalyzer.java

```
1   import java.io.File;
2   import java.io.FileNotFoundException;
3   import java.io.IOException;
4   import java.util.Scanner;
5   import java.util.NoSuchElementException;
6
7   /**
8       This program processes a file containing a count followed by data values.
9       If the file doesn't exist or the format is incorrect, you can specify another file.
10  */
11  public class DataAnalyzer
12  {
13      public static void main(String[] args)
14      {
15          Scanner in = new Scanner(System.in);
16
17          // Keep trying until there are no more exceptions
18
19          boolean done = false;
20          while (!done)
21          {
22              try
23              {
24                  System.out.print("Please enter the file name: ");
25                  String filename = in.next();
26
27                  double[] data = readFile(filename);
28
29                  // As an example for processing the data, we compute the sum
30
31                  double sum = 0;
32                  for (double d : data) { sum = sum + d; }
33                  System.out.println("The sum is " + sum);
34
35                  done = true;
36              }
37              catch (FileNotFoundException exception)
38              {
39                  System.out.println("File not found.");
```

```
40              }
41              catch (NoSuchElementException exception)
42              {
43                  System.out.println("File contents invalid.");
44              }
45              catch (IOException exception)
46              {
47                  exception.printStackTrace();
48              }
49          }
50      }
51
52      /**
53          Opens a file and reads a data set.
54          @param filename the name of the file holding the data
55          @return the data in the file
56      */
57      public static double[] readFile(String filename) throws IOException
58      {
59          File inFile = new File(filename);
60          Scanner in = new Scanner(inFile);
61          try
62          {
63              return readData(in);
64          }
65          finally
66          {
67              in.close();
68          }
69      }
70
71      /**
72          Reads a data set.
73          @param in the scanner that scans the data
74          @return the data set
75      */
76      public static double[] readData(Scanner in) throws IOException
77      {
78          int numberOfValues = in.nextInt(); // May throw NoSuchElementException
79          double[] data = new double[numberOfValues];
80
81          for (int i = 0; i < numberOfValues; i++)
82          {
83              data[i] = in.nextDouble(); // May throw NoSuchElementException
84          }
85
86          if (in.hasNext())
87          {
88              throw new IOException("End of file expected");
89          }
90          return data;
91      }
92 }
```

**22.** Why doesn't the readFile method catch any exceptions?

**23.** Consider the try/finally statement in the readFile method. Why was the in variable declared outside the try block?

**24.** Suppose the user specifies a file that exists and is empty. Trace the flow of execution in the `DataAnalyzer` program.

**25.** Why didn't the `readData` method call `hasNextInt`/`hasNextDouble` to ensure that the `NoSuchElementException` is not thrown?

**Practice It**    Now you can try these exercises at the end of the chapter: R7.15, R7.16, P7.13.

---

**VIDEO EXAMPLE 7.2**    **Detecting Accounting Fraud**

In this Video Example, you will see how to detect accounting fraud by analyzing digit distributions. You will learn how to read data from the Internet and handle exceptional situations.

---

## CHAPTER SUMMARY

### Develop programs that read and write files.

- Use the `Scanner` class for reading text files.
- When writing text files, use the `PrintWriter` class and the `print`/`println`/`printf` methods.
- Close all files when you are done processing them.

### Be able to process text in files.

- The `next` method reads a string that is delimited by white space.
- The `Character` class has methods for classifying characters.
- The `nextLine` method reads an entire line.
- If a string contains the digits of a number, you use the `Integer.parseInt` or `Double.parseDouble` method to obtain the number value.

### Process the command line arguments of a program.

- Programs that start from the command line receive the command line arguments in the `main` method.

### Use exception handling to transfer control from an error location to an error handler.

- To signal an exceptional condition, use the `throw` statement to throw an exception object.
- When you throw an exception, processing continues in an exception handler.
- Place the statements that can cause an exception inside a `try` block, and the handler inside a `catch` clause.

---

➕ Available online in WileyPLUS and at www.wiley.com/college/horstmann.

- Checked exceptions are due to external circumstances that the programmer cannot prevent. The compiler checks that your program handles these exceptions.
- Add a throws clause to a method that can throw a checked exception.
- Once a try block is entered, the statements in a finally clause are guaranteed to be executed, whether or not an exception is thrown.
- Throw an exception as soon as a problem is detected. Catch it only when the problem can be handled.

**Use exception handling in a program that processes input.**

- When designing a program, ask yourself what kinds of exceptions can occur.
- For each exception, you need to decide which part of your program can competently handle it.

## STANDARD LIBRARY ITEMS INTRODUCED IN THIS CHAPTER

```
java.io.File                      java.lang.NumberFormatException
java.io.FileNotFoundException     java.lang.RuntimeException
java.io.IOException               java.lang.Throwable
java.io.PrintWriter                  getMessage
   close                             printStackTrace
java.lang.Character               java.net.URL
   isDigit                           openStream
   isLetter                       java.util.InputMismatchException
   isLowerCase                    java.util.NoSuchElementException
   isUpperCase                    java.util.Scanner
   isWhiteSpace                      close
java.lang.Double                     hasNextLine
   parseDouble                       nextLine
java.lang.Error                      useDelimiter
java.lang.Integer                 javax.swing.JFileChooser
   parseInt                          getSelectedFile
java.lang.IllegalArgumentException   showOpenDialog
java.lang.NullPointerException       showSaveDialog
```

## REVIEW EXERCISES

■■ **R7.1** What happens if you try to open a file for reading that doesn't exist? What happens if you try to open a file for writing that doesn't exist?

■■ **R7.2** What happens if you try to open a file for writing, but the file or device is write-protected (sometimes called read-only)? Try it out with a short test program.

■ **R7.3** How do you open a file whose name contains a backslash, like c:temp\output.dat?

■ **R7.4** If a program Woozle is started with the command

```
java Woozle -Dname=piglet -I\eeyore -v heff.txt a.txt lump.txt
```

what are the values of args[0], args[1], and so on?

■ **R7.5** What is the difference between throwing an exception and catching an exception?

■ **R7.6** What is a checked exception? What is an unchecked exception? Give an example for each. Which exceptions do you need to declare with the `throws` reserved word?

■■ **R7.7** Why don't you need to declare that your method might throw an `IndexOutOfBounds-Exception`?

■■ **R7.8** When your program executes a `throw` statement, which statement is executed next?

■■ **R7.9** What happens if an exception does not have a matching `catch` clause?

■■ **R7.10** What can your program do with the exception object that a `catch` clause receives?

■■ **R7.11** Is the type of the exception object always the same as the type declared in the `catch` clause that catches it? If not, why not?

■ **R7.12** What is the purpose of the `finally` clause? Give an example of how it can be used.

■■ **R7.13** What happens when an exception is thrown, the code of a `finally` clause executes, and that code throws an exception of a different kind than the original one? Which one is caught by a surrounding `catch` clause? Write a sample program to try it out.

■■ **R7.14** Which exceptions can the `next` and `nextInt` methods of the `Scanner` class throw? Are they checked exceptions or unchecked exceptions?

■■ **R7.15** Suppose the program in Section 7.5 reads a file containing the following values:

```
1
2
3
4
```

What is the outcome? How could the program be improved to give a more accurate error report?

■■ **R7.16** Can the `readFile` method in Section 7.5 throw a `NullPointerException`? If so, how?

## PROGRAMMING EXERCISES

■ **P7.1** Write a program that carries out the following tasks:

> Open a file with the name hello.txt.
> Store the message "Hello, World!" in the file.
> Close the file.
> Open the same file again.
> Read the message into a string variable and print it.

■ **P7.2** Write a program that reads a file containing text. Read each line and send it to the output file, preceded by *line numbers*. If the input file is

```
Mary had a little lamb
Whose fleece was white as snow.
And everywhere that Mary went,
The lamb was sure to go!
```

then the program produces the output file

```
/* 1 */ Mary had a little lamb
/* 2 */ Whose fleece was white as snow.
/* 3 */ And everywhere that Mary went,
/* 4 */ The lamb was sure to go!
```

The line numbers are enclosed in /* */ delimiters so that the program can be used for numbering Java source files.

Prompt the user for the input and output file names.

- **P7.3** Repeat Exercise P7.2, but allow the user to specify the file name on the command-line. If the user doesn't specify any file name, then prompt the user for the name.

- **P7.4** Write a program that reads a file containing two columns of floating-point numbers. Prompt the user for the file name. Print the average of each column.

- **P7.5** Write a program that asks the user for a file name and prints the number of characters, words, and lines in that file.

- **P7.6** Write a program Find that searches all files specified on the command line and prints out all lines containing a specified word. For example, if you call

  ```
  java Find ring report.txt address.txt Homework.java
  ```

  then the program might print

  ```
  report.txt: has broken up an international ring of DVD bootleggers that
  address.txt: Kris Kringle, North Pole
  address.txt: Homer Simpson, Springfield
  Homework.java: String filename;
  ```

  The specified word is always the first command line argument.

- **P7.7** Write a program that checks the spelling of all words in a file. It should read each word of a file and check whether it is contained in a word list. A word list is available on most Linux systems in the file /usr/share/dict/words. (If you don't have access to a Linux system, your instructor should be able to get you a copy.) The program should print out all words that it cannot find in the word list.

- **P7.8** Write a program that replaces each line of a file with its reverse. For example, if you run

  ```
  java Reverse HelloPrinter.java
  ```

  then the contents of HelloPrinter.java are changed to

  ```
  retnirPolleH ssalc cilbup
  {
  )sgra ][gnirtS(niam diov citats cilbup
  {
  wodniw elosnoc eht ni gniteerg a yalpsiD //

  ;)"!dlroW ,olleH"(nltnirp.tuo.metsyS
  }
  }
  ```

  Of course, if you run Reverse twice on the same file, you get back the original file.

- **P7.9** Write a program that reads each line in a file, reverses its lines, and writes them to another file. For example, if the file input.txt contains the lines

  ```
  Mary had a little lamb
  Its fleece was white as snow
  And everywhere that Mary went
  The lamb was sure to go.
  ```

  and you run

  ```
  reverse input.txt output.txt
  ```

  then output.txt contains

```
The lamb was sure to go.
And everywhere that Mary went
Its fleece was white as snow
Mary had a little lamb
```

**■■ P7.10** Get the data for names in prior decades from the Social Security Administration. Paste the table data in files named babynames80s.txt, etc. Modify the worked_example_1/BabyNames.java program so that it prompts the user for a file name. The numbers in the files have comma separators, so modify the program to handle them. Can you spot a trend in the frequencies?

**■■ P7.11** Write a program that reads in worked_example_1/babynames.txt and produces two files, boynames.txt and girlnames.txt, separating the data for the boys and girls.

**■■■ P7.12** Write a program that reads a file in the same format as worked_example_1/babynames.txt and prints all names that are both boy and girl names (such as Alexis or Morgan).

**■■ P7.13** Write a program that asks the user to input a set of floating-point values. When the user enters a value that is not a number, give the user a second chance to enter the value. After two chances, quit reading input. Add all correctly specified values and print the sum when the user is done entering data. Use exception handling to detect improper inputs.

**■■ P7.14** Using the mechanism described in Special Topic 7.1, write a program that reads all data from a web page and writes them to a file. Prompt the user for the web page URL and the file.

**■■ P7.15** Using the mechanism described in Special Topic 7.1, write a program that reads all data from a web page and prints all hyperlinks of the form

```
<a href="link">link text</a>
```

Extra credit if your program can follow the links that it finds and find links in those web pages as well. (This is the method that search engines such as Google use to find web sites.)

**■■ Business P7.16** A hotel salesperson enters sales in a text file. Each line contains the following, separated by semicolons: The name of the client, the service sold (such as Dinner, Conference, Lodging, and so on), the amount of the sale, and the date of that event. Write a program that reads such a file and displays the total amount for each service category. Display an error if the file does not exist or the format is incorrect.

**■■ Business P7.17** Write a program that reads a text file as described in Exercise P7.16, and that writes a separate file for each service category, containing the entries for that category. Name the output files Dinner.txt, Conference.txt, and so on.

**■■ Business P7.18** A store owner keeps a record of daily cash transactions in a text file. Each line contains three items: The invoice number, the cash amount, and the letter P if the amount was paid or R if it was received. Items are separated by spaces. Write a program that prompts the store owner for the amount of cash at the beginning and end of the day, and the name of the file. Your program should check whether the actual amount of cash at the end of the day equals the expected value.

**■■■ Science P7.19** After the switch in the figure below closes, the voltage (in volts) across the capacitor is represented by the equation

$$v(t) = B\left(1 - e^{-t/(RC)}\right)$$

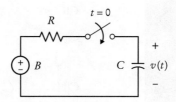

Suppose the parameters of the electric circuit are $B = 12$ volts, $R = 500\ \Omega$, and $C = 0.25\ \mu F$. Consequently

$$v(t) = 12\left(1 - e^{-0.008t}\right)$$

where $t$ has units of μs. Read a file params.txt containing the values for $B$, $R$, $C$, and the starting and ending values for $t$. Write a file rc.txt of values for the time $t$ and the corresponding capacitor voltage $v(t)$, where $t$ goes from the given starting value to the given ending value in 100 steps. In our example, if $t$ goes from 0 to 1,000 μs, the twelfth entry in the output file would be:

    110   7.02261

**■■■ Science P7.20** The figure below shows a plot of the capacitor voltage from the circuit shown in Exercise P7.19. The capacitor voltage increases from 0 volts to $B$ volts. The "rise time" is defined as the time required for the capacitor voltage to change from $v_1 = 0.05 \times B$ to $v_2 = 0.95 \times B$.

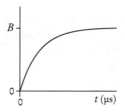

The file rc.txt contains a list of values of time $t$ and the corresponding capacitor voltage $v(t)$. A time in μs and the corresponding voltage in volts are printed on the same line. For example, the line

    110   7.02261

indicates that the capacitor voltage is 7.02261 volts when the time is 110 μs. The time is increasing in the data file.

Write a program that reads the file rc.txt and uses the data to calculate the rise time. Approximate $B$ by the voltage in the last line of the file, and find the data points that are closest to $0.05 \times B$ and $0.95 \times B$.

■■ **Science P7.21** Suppose a file contains bond energies and bond lengths for covalent bonds in the following format:

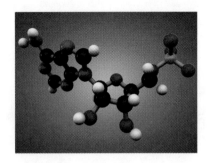

| Single, double, or triple bond | Bond energy (kJ/mol) | Bond length (nm) |
| --- | --- | --- |
| C\|C | 370 | 0.154 |
| C\|\|C | 680 | 0.13 |
| C\|\|\|C | 890 | 0.12 |
| C\|H | 435 | 0.11 |
| C\|N | 305 | 0.15 |
| C\|O | 360 | 0.14 |
| C\|F | 450 | 0.14 |
| C\|Cl | 340 | 0.18 |
| O\|H | 500 | 0.10 |
| O\|O | 220 | 0.15 |
| O\|Si | 375 | 0.16 |
| N\|H | 430 | 0.10 |
| N\|O | 250 | 0.12 |
| F\|F | 160 | 0.14 |
| H\|H | 435 | 0.074 |

Write a program that accepts data from one column and returns the corresponding data from the other columns in the stored file. If input data matches different rows, then return all matching row data. For example, a bond length input of 0.12 should return triple bond C|||C and bond energy 890 kJ/mol *and* single bond N|O and bond energy 250 kJ/mol.

## ANSWERS TO SELF-CHECK QUESTIONS

1. When the `PrintWriter` object is created, the output file is emptied. Sadly, that is the same file as the input file. The input file is now empty and the `while` loop exits immediately.

2. The program throws a `FileNotFoundException` and terminates.

3. Open a scanner for the file.
   For each number in the scanner
       Add the number to an array.
   Close the scanner.
   Set total to 0.
   Open a print writer for the file.
   For each number in the array
       Write the number to the print writer.
       Add the number to total.
   Write total to the print writer.
   Close the print writer.

4. Add a variable count that is incremented whenever a number is read. In the end, print the average, not the total, as
   ```
   out.printf("Average: %8.2f\n", total / count);
   ```
   Because the string "Average" is three characters longer than "Total", change the other output to `out.printf("%18.2f\n", value)`.

5. Add a variable count that is incremented whenever a number is read. Only write a new line when it is even.
   ```
   count++;
   out.printf("%8.2f", value);
   if (count % 2 == 0) { out.println(); }
   ```
   At the end of the loop, write a new line if count is odd, then write the total:
   ```
   if (count % 2 == 1) { out.println(); }
   out.printf("Total: %10.2f\n", total);
   ```

6. `word` is `"Hello,"` and `input` is `"World!"`

7. Because `995.0` is not an integer, the call `in.hasNextInt()` returns false, and the call `in.nextInt()` is skipped. The value of `number` stays 0, and `input` is set to the string `"995.0"`.

8. `x1` is set to 6000000. Because a comma is not considered a part of a floating-point number in Java, the second call to `nextDouble` causes an input mismatch exception and `x2` is not set.

9. Read them as strings, and convert those strings to numbers that are not equal to `N/A`:
   ```
   String input = in.next();
   if (!input.equals("N/A"))
   {
       double value = Double.parseDouble(input);
       Process value.
   }
   ```

10. Locate the last character of the country name:
    ```
    int j = i - 1;
    while (!Character.isWhiteSpace(line.charAt(j)))
    {
        j--;
    }
    ```
    Then extract the country name:
    ```
    String countryName = line.substring(0, j + 1);
    ```

11. `args[0]` is `"-d"` and `args[1]` is `"file1.txt"`

12. 

| key | inFile | outFile | i | arg |
|-----|--------|---------|---|-----|
| ~~3~~ | ~~null~~ | null | ~~0~~ | ~~-d~~ |
| -3 | file1.txt | | ~~1~~ | file1.txt |
| | | | 2 | |

Then the program prints a message
```
Usage: java CaesarCipher [-d] infile outfile
```

13. The program will run correctly. The loop that parses the options does not depend on the positions in which the options appear.

14. FDHVDU

15. Add the lines
    ```
    else if (option == 'k')
    {
        key = Integer.parseInt(
            args[i].substring(2));
    }
    ```
    after line 27 and update the usage information.

16. It is still 100. The last statement was not executed because the exception was thrown.

17. ```
    if (amount < 0)
    {
        throw new IllegalArgumentException(
            "Negative amount");
    }
    ```
    ```

18. The Scanner constructor succeeds because the file exists. The nextInt method throws a NoSuchElementException. This is *not* an IOException. Therefore, the error is not caught. Because there is no other handler, an error message is printed and the program terminates.

19. Because programmers should simply check that their array index values are valid instead of trying to handle an ArrayIndexOutOfBounds-Exception.

20. No. You can catch both exception types in the same way, as you can see in the code example on page 339.

21. There are two mistakes. The PrintWriter constructor can throw a FileNotFoundException. You should supply a throws clause. And if one of the array elements is null, a NullPointerException is thrown. In that case, the out.close() statement is never executed. You should use a try/finally statement.

22. The exceptions are better handled in the main method.

23. If it had been declared inside the try block, its scope would only have extended until the end of the try block, and it would not have been accessible in the finally clause.

24. main calls readFile, which calls readData. The call in.nextInt() throws a NoSuchElementException. The readFile method doesn't catch it, so it propagates back to main, where it is caught. An error message is printed, and the user can specify another file.

25. We *want* to throw that exception, so that someone else can handle the problem of a bad data file.

# OBJECTS AND CLASSES

To understand the concepts of classes, objects, and encapsulation

To implement instance variables, methods, and constructors

To be able to design, implement, and test your own classes

To understand the behavior of object references, static variables, and static methods

## CHAPTER CONTENTS

This chapter introduces you to object-oriented programming, an important technique for writing complex programs. In an object-oriented program, you don't simply manipulate numbers and strings, but you work with objects that are meaningful for your application. Objects with the same behavior (such as the windmills to the left) are grouped into classes. A programmer provides the desired behavior by specifying and implementing methods for these classes. In this chapter, you will learn how to discover, specify, and implement your own classes, and how to use them in your programs.

# 8.1 Object-Oriented Programming

You have learned how to structure your programs by decomposing tasks into methods. This is an excellent practice, but experience shows that it does not go far enough. It is difficult to understand and update a program that consists of a large collection of methods.

To overcome this problem, computer scientists invented **object-oriented programming**, a programming style in which tasks are solved by collaborating objects. Each object has its own set of data, together with a set of methods that act upon the data.

You have already experienced this programming style when you used strings, the System.out object, or a Scanner object. Each of these objects has a set of methods. For example, you can use the length and substring methods to work with String objects.

When you develop an object-oriented program, you create your own objects that describe what is important in your application. For example, in a student database you might work with Student and Course objects. Of course, then you must supply methods for these objects.

A class describes a set of objects with the same behavior.

In Java, a programmer doesn't implement a single object. Instead, the programmer provides a **class**. A class describes a set of objects with the same behavior. For example, the String class describes the behavior of all strings. The class specifies how

*A Car class describes passenger vehicles that can carry 4–5 people and a small amount of luggage.*

a string stores its characters, which methods can be used with strings, and how the methods are implemented.

In contrast, the PrintStream class describes the behavior of objects that can be used to produce output. One such object is System.out, and you have seen in Chapter 7 how to create PrintStream objects that send output to a file.

Each class defines a specific set of methods that you can use with its objects. For example, when you have a String object, you can invoke the length method:

```
"Hello, World".length()
```

We say that the length method is a method of the String class. The PrintStream class has a different set of methods. For example, the call

```
System.out.length()
```

would be illegal—the PrintStream class has no length method. However, PrintStream has a println method, and the call

```
out.println("Hello, World!")
```

is legal.

The set of all methods provided by a class, together with a description of their behavior, is called the **public interface** of the class.

> Every class has a public interface: a collection of methods through which the objects of the class can be manipulated.

When you work with an object of a class, you do not know how the object stores its data, or how the methods are implemented. You need not know how a String organizes a character sequence, or how a PrintWriter object sends data to a file. All you need to know is the public interface—which methods you can apply, and what these methods do. The process of providing a public interface, while hiding the implementation details, is called **encapsulation**.

> Encapsulation is the act of providing a public interface and hiding the implementation details.

When you design your own classes, you will use encapsulation. That is, you will specify a set of public methods and hide the implementation details. Other programmers on your team can then use your classes without having to know their implementations, just as you are able to make use of the String and PrintStream classes.

> Encapsulation enables changes in the implementation without affecting users of a class.

If you work on a program that is being developed over a long period of time, it is common for implementation details to change, usually to make objects more efficient or more capable. When the implementation is hidden, the improvements do not affect the programmers that use the objects.

*You can drive a car by operating the steering wheel and pedals, without knowing how the engine works. Similarly, you use an object through its methods. The implementation is hidden.*

*A driver of an electric car doesn't have to learn new controls even though the car engine is very different. Neither does the programmer who uses an object with an improved implementation—as long as the same methods are used.*

**SELF CHECK**

1. Is the method call "Hello, World".println() legal? Why or why not?
2. When using a String object, you do not know how it stores its characters. How can you access them?
3. Describe a way in which a String object might store its characters.
4. Suppose the providers of your Java compiler decide to change the way that a String object stores its characters, and they update the String method implementations accordingly. Which parts of your code do you need to change when you get the new compiler?

**Practice It**    Now you can try these exercises at the end of the chapter: R8.1, R8.4.

# 8.2 Implementing a Simple Class

In this section, we look at the implementation of a very simple class. You will see how objects store their data, and how methods access the data of an object. Knowing how a very simple class operates will help you design and implement more complex classes later in this chapter.

Our first example is a class that models a *tally counter*, a mechanical device that is used to count people—for example, to find out how many people attend a concert or board a bus (see Figure 1).

Whenever the operator pushes a button, the counter value advances by one. We model this operation with a count method. A physical counter has a display to show the current value. In our simulation, we use a getValue method instead.

**Figure 1**    A Tally Counter

Here is an example of using the Counter class. First, we construct an object of the class:

```
Counter tally = new Counter();
```

In Java, you use the new operator to construct objects. We will discuss object construction in more detail in Section 8.6.

Next, we invoke methods on our object. First, we invoke the count method twice, simulating two button pushes. Then we invoke the getValue method to check how many times the button was pushed.

```
tally.count();
tally.count();
int result = tally.getValue(); // Sets result to 2
```

We can invoke the methods again, and the result will be different.

```
tally.count();
tally.count();
result = tally.getValue(); // Sets result to 4
```

As you can see, the tally object remembers the effect of prior method calls.

When implementing the Counter class, we need to specify how each counter object stores its data. In this simple example, that is very straightforward. Each counter needs a variable that keeps track of how many times the counter has been advanced.

An object stores its data in **instance variables**. An *instance* of a class is an object of the class. Thus, an instance variable is a storage location that is present in each object of the class.

You specify instance variables in the class declaration:

```
public class Counter
{
    private int value;
    . . .
}
```

An instance variable declaration consists of the following parts:

- An **modifier** (private)
- The **type** of the instance variable (such as int)
- The name of the instance variable (such as value)

**An object's instance variables store the data required for executing its methods.**

## Syntax 8.1    Instance Variable Declaration

```
Syntax    public class ClassName
          {
              private typeName variableName;
              . . .
          }
```

```
                              public class Counter          Each object of this class
                              {                             has a separate copy of
                                  private int value;        this instance variable.
    Instance variables should      . . .
      always be private.         }
                                                 Type of the variable
```

Each object of a class has its own set of instance variables. For example, if concert-Counter and boardingCounter are two objects of the Counter class, then each object has its own value variable (see Figure 2).

> Each object of a class has its own set of instance variables.

As you will see in Section 8.6, the instance variable value is set to 0 when a Counter object is constructed.

Next, let us have a quick look at the implementation of the methods of the Counter class. The count method advances the counter value by 1.

```java
public void count()
{
    value = value + 1;
}
```

We will cover the syntax of the method header in Section 8.3. For now, focus on the body of the method inside the braces.

Note how the count method increments the instance variable value. *Which* instance variable? The one belonging to the object on which the method is invoked. For example, consider the call

> An instance method can access the instance variables of the object on which it acts.

```java
concertCounter.count();
```

This call advances the value variable of the concertCounter object.

The methods that you invoke on an object are called **instance methods** to distinguish them from the static methods of Chapter 5.

Finally, look at the other instance method of the Counter class. The getValue method returns the current value:

```java
public int getValue()
{
    return value;
}
```

This method is required so that users of the Counter class can find out how often a particular counter has been clicked. A user cannot simply access the value instance variable. That variable has been declared with the access specifier private.

> A private instance variable can only be accessed by the methods of its own class.

The private specifier restricts access to the methods of the *same class*. For example, the value variable can be accessed by the count and getValue methods of the Counter class but not a method of another class. Those other methods need to use the getValue method if they want to find out the counter's value, or the count method if they want to change it.

**ONLINE EXAMPLE**

⊕ The complete Counter class and a CounterTester program.

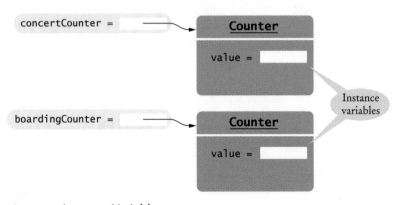

**Figure 2** Instance Variables

*These clocks have common behavior, but each of them has a different state. Similarly, objects of a class can have their instance variables set to different values.*

Private instance variables are an essential part of encapsulation. They allow a programmer to hide the implementation of a class from a class user.

**SELF CHECK**

5. Supply the body of a method `public void reset()` that resets the counter back to zero.

6. Consider a change to the implementation of the counter. Instead of using an integer counter, we use a string of | characters to keep track of the clicks, just like a human might do.

```
public class Counter
{
    private String strokes = "";
    public void count()
    {
        strokes = strokes + "|";
    }
    . . .
}
```

How do you implement the `getValue` method with this data representation?

7. Suppose another programmer has used the original `Counter` class. What changes does that programmer have to make in order to use the modified class?

8. Suppose you use a class `Clock` with private instance variables `hours` and `minutes`. How can you access these variables in your program?

**Practice It**   Now you can try these exercises at the end of the chapter: P8.1, P8.2.

# 8.3  Specifying the Public Interface of a Class

When designing a class, you start by specifying its **public interface**. The public interface of a class consists of all methods that a user of the class may want to apply to its objects.

Let's consider a simple example. We want to use objects that simulate cash registers. A cashier who rings up a sale presses a key to start the sale, then rings up each item. A display shows the amount owed as well as the total number of items purchased.

In our simulation, we want to call the following methods on a cash register object:

- Add the price of an item.
- Get the total amount owed, and the count of items purchased.
- Clear the cash register to start a new sale.

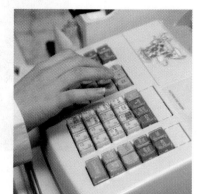

Here is an outline of the CashRegister class. We supply comments for all of the methods to document their purpose.

```java
/**
    A simulated cash register that tracks the item
    count and the total amount due.
*/
public class CashRegister
{
    private data—see Section 8.4

    /**
        Adds an item to this cash register.
        @param price the price of this item
    */
    public void addItem(double price)
    {
        implementation—see Section 8.5
    }

    /**
        Gets the price of all items in the current sale.
        @return the total price
    */
    public double getTotal()
    {
        implementation—see Section 8.5
    }

    /**
        Gets the number of items in the current sale.
        @return the item count
    */
    public int getCount()
    {
        implementation—see Section 8.5
    }

    /**
        Clears the item count and the total.
    */
    public void clear()
    {
        implementation—see Section 8.5
    }
}
```

The method declarations and comments make up the *public interface* of the class. The data and the method bodies make up the *private implementation* of the class.

Note that the methods of the CashRegister class are instance methods. They are *not* declared as static. You invoke them on objects (or instances) of the CashRegister class.

**Figure 3**
An Object Reference
and an Object

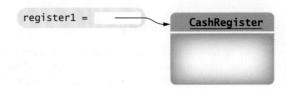

To see an instance method in action, we first need to construct an object:

```
CashRegister register1 = new CashRegister();
    // Constructs a CashRegister object
```

This statement initializes the register1 variable with a reference to a new CashRegister object—see Figure 3. (We discuss the process of object construction in Section 8.6 and object references in Section 8.10.)

Once the object has been constructed, we are ready to invoke a method:

```
register1.addItem(1.95); // Invokes a method
```

> A mutator method changes the object on which it operates.

When you look at the public interface of a class, it is useful to classify its methods as *mutators* and *accessors*. A **mutator** method modifies the object on which it operates. The CashRegister class has two mutators: addItem and clear. After you call either of these methods, the object has changed. You can observe that change by calling the getTotal or getCount method.

> An accessor method does not change the object on which it operates.

An **accessor** method queries the object for some information without changing it. The CashRegister class has two accessors: getTotal and getCount. Applying either of these methods to a CashRegister object simply returns a value and does not modify the object. For example, the following statement prints the current total and count:

```
System.out.println(register1.getTotal()) + " " + register1.getCount());
```

Now we know *what* a CashRegister object can do, but not *how* it does it. Of course, to use CashRegister objects in our programs, we don't need to know.

In the next sections, you will see how the CashRegister class is implemented.

**SELF CHECK**

9. What does the following code segment print?

```
CashRegister reg = new CashRegister();
reg.clear();
reg.addItem(0.95);
reg.addItem(0.95);
System.out.println(reg.getCount() + " " + reg.getTotal());
```

10. What is wrong with the following code segment?

```
CashRegister reg = new CashRegister();
reg.clear();
reg.addItem(0.95);
System.out.println(reg.getAmountDue());
```

11. Declare a method getDollars of the CashRegister class that yields the amount of the total sale as a dollar value without the cents.

12. Name two accessor methods of the String class.

13. Is the nextInt method of the Scanner class an accessor or a mutator?

14. Provide documentation comments for the Counter class of Section 8.2.

**Practice It** Now you can try these exercises at the end of the chapter: R8.2, R8.8.

## The javadoc Utility

The javadoc utility formats documentation comments into a neat set of documents that you can view in a web browser. It makes good use of the seemingly repetitive phrases. The first sentence of each method comment is used for a *summary table* of all methods of your class (see Figure 4). The @param and @return comments are neatly formatted in the detail description of each method (see Figure 5). If you omit any of the comments, then javadoc generates documents that look strangely empty.

This documentation format may look familiar. It is the same format that is used in the official Java documentation. The programmers who implement the Java library use javadoc themselves. They too document every class, every method, every parameter, and every return value, and then use javadoc to extract the documentation.

Many integrated programming environments can execute javadoc for you. Alternatively, you can invoke the javadoc utility from a shell window, by issuing the command

```
javadoc MyClass.java
```

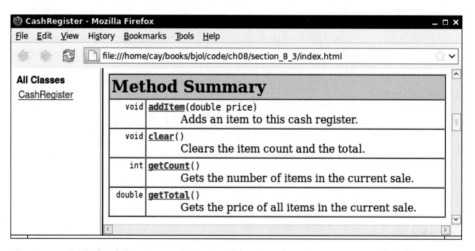

**Figure 4**   A Method Summary Generated by javadoc

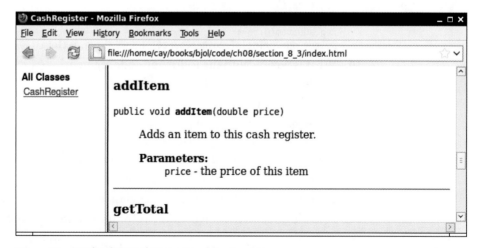

**Figure 5**   Method Detail Generated by javadoc

The javadoc utility produces files such as MyClass.html in HTML format, which you can inspect in a browser. You can use hyperlinks to navigate to other classes and methods.

You can run javadoc before implementing any methods. Just leave all the method bodies empty. Don't run the compiler—it would complain about missing return values. Simply run javadoc on your file to generate the documentation for the public interface that you are about to implement.

The javadoc tool is wonderful because it does one thing right: It allows you to put the documentation *together with your code*. That way, when you update your programs, you can see right away which documentation needs to be updated. Hopefully, you will update it right then and there. Afterward, run javadoc again and get updated information that is timely and nicely formatted.

# 8.4 Designing the Data Representation

An object stores its data in **instance variables**. These are variables that are declared inside the class (see Syntax 8.1).

When implementing a class, you have to determine which data each object needs to store. The object needs to have all the information necessary to carry out any method call.

Go through all methods and consider their data requirements. It is a good idea to start with the accessor methods. For example, a CashRegister object must be able to return the correct value for the getTotal method. That means, it must either store all entered prices and compute the total in the method call, or it must store the total.

Now apply the same reasoning to the getCount method. If the cash register stores all entered prices, it can count them in the getCount method. Otherwise, you need to have a variable for the count.

> For each accessor method, an object must either store or compute the result.

The addItem method receives a price as an argument, and it must record the price. If the CashRegister object stores an array of entered prices, then the addItem method appends the price. On the other hand, if we decide to store just the item total and count, then the addItem method updates these two variables.

Finally, the clear method must prepare the cash register for the next sale, either by emptying the array of prices or by setting the total and count to zero.

We have now discovered two different ways of representing the data that the object needs. Either of them will work, and we have to make a choice. We will choose the simpler one: variables for the total price and the item count. (Other options are explored in Exercises P8.16 and P8.17.)

> Commonly, there is more than one way of representing the data of an object, and you must make a choice.

*Like a wilderness explorer who needs to carry all items that may be needed, an object needs to store the data required for any method calls.*

```
int itemCount;
double totalPrice;
```

The instance variables are declared in the class, but outside any methods, with the private modifier:

```
public class CashRegister
{
    private int itemCount;
    private double totalPrice;
    . . .
}
```

Be sure that your data representation supports method calls in any order.

Note that method calls can come in *any order*. For example, consider the CashRegister class. After calling

```
register1.getTotal()
```

a program can make another call to

```
register1.addItem(1.95)
```

You should not assume that you can clear the sum in a call to getTotal. Your data representation should allow for method calls that come in arbitrary order, in the same way that occupants of a car can push the various buttons and levers in any order they choose.

**ONLINE EXAMPLE**

The CashRegister class with instance variables.

**SELF CHECK**

**15.** What is wrong with this code segment?

```
CashRegister register2 = new CashRegister();
register2.clear();
register2.addItem(0.95);
System.out.println(register2.totalPrice);
```

**16.** Consider a class Time that represents a point in time, such as 9 A.M. or 3:30 P.M. Give two sets of instance variables that can be used for implementing the Time class. (*Hint for the second set:* Military time.)

**17.** Suppose the implementor of the Time class changes from one implementation strategy to another, keeping the public interface unchanged. What do the programmers who use the Time class need to do?

**18.** Consider a class Grade that represents a letter grade, such as A+ or B. Give two different sets of instance variables that can be used for implementing the Grade class.

**Practice It**   Now you can try these exercises at the end of the chapter: R8.6, R8.16.

# 8.5 Implementing Instance Methods

When implementing a class, you need to provide the bodies for all methods. Implementing an instance method is very similar to implementing a static method, with one essential difference: You can access the instance variables of the class in the method body.

For example, here is the implementation of the addItem method of the CashRegister class. (You can find the remaining methods at the end of the next section.)

```
public void addItem(double price)
{
    itemCount++;
    totalPrice = totalPrice + price;
}
```

## Syntax 8.2    Instance Methods

*Syntax*    *modifiers returnType methodName(parameterType parameterName, . . . )*
           {
              *method body*
           }

```
public class CashRegister
{
   . . .
   public void addItem(double price)         Explicit parameter
   {
      itemCount++;
      totalPrice = totalPrice + price;
   }
   . . .
}
```

*Instance variables of the implicit parameter*

---

**The object on which a method is applied is the implicit parameter.**

Whenever you use an instance variable, such as `itemCount` or `totalPrice`, in a method, it denotes that instance variable *of the object on which the method was invoked.* For example, consider the call

```
register1.addItem(1.95);
```

The first statement in the `addItem` method is

```
itemCount++;
```

Which `itemCount` is incremented? In this call, it is the `itemCount` of the `register1` object. (See Figure 6.)

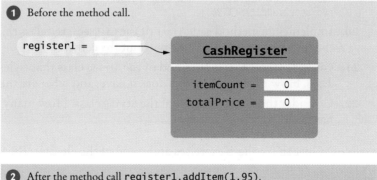

❶ Before the method call.

register1 =

**CashRegister**

itemCount = 0
totalPrice = 0

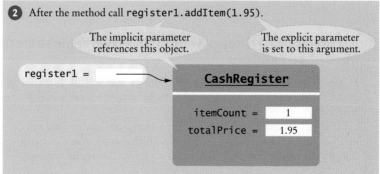

❷ After the method call `register1.addItem(1.95)`.

The implicit parameter references this object.

The explicit parameter is set to this argument.

register1 =

**CashRegister**

itemCount = 1
totalPrice = 1.95

**Figure 6**
Implicit and Explicit Parameters

*When an item is added, it affects the instance variables of the cash register object on which the method is invoked.*

Explicit parameters of a method are listed in the method declaration.

The object on which a method is invoked is called the **implicit parameter** of the method. In Java, you do not actually write the implicit parameter in the method declaration. For that reason, the parameter is called "implicit".

In contrast, parameters that are explicitly mentioned in the method declaration, such as the totalPrice parameter variable, are called **explicit parameters**. Every method has exactly one implicit parameter and zero or more explicit parameters.

**SELF CHECK**

**19.** What are the values of register1.itemCount, register1.totalPrice, register2.itemCount, and register2.totalPrice after these statements?

```
CashRegister register1 = new CashRegister();
register1.addItem(0.90);
register1.addItem(0.95);
CashRegister register2 = new CashRegister();
register2.addItem(1.90);
```

**20.** Implement a method getDollars of the CashRegister class that yields the amount of the total sale as a dollar value without the cents.

**21.** Consider the substring method of the String class that is described in Section 2.5.6. How many parameters does it have, and what are their types?

**22.** Consider the length method of the String class. How many parameters does it have, and what are their types?

**Practice It** Now you can try these exercises at the end of the chapter: R8.10, P8.16, P8.17, P8.18.

---

Programming Tip 8.1

### All Instance Variables Should Be Private; Most Methods Should Be Public

It is possible to declare instance variables as public, but you should not do that in your own code. Always use encapsulation, with private instance variables that are manipulated with methods.

Typically, methods are public. However, sometimes you have a method that is used only as a helper method by other methods. In that case, you can make the helper method private. Simply use the private reserved word when declaring the method.

# 8.6 Constructors

A constructor
initializes the
instance variables
of an object.

A **constructor** initializes the instance variables of an object. The constructor is automatically called whenever an object is created with the new operator.

You have seen the new operator in Chapter 2. It is used whenever a new object is required. For example, the expression new Scanner(System.in) in the statement

```
Scanner in = new Scanner(System.in);
```

A constructor is
invoked when an
object is created with
the new operator.

constructs a new object of the Scanner class. Specifically, a constructor of the Scanner class is called with the argument System.in. That constructor initializes the Scanner object.

The name of a
constructor is
the same as the
class name.

The name of a constructor is identical to the name of its class. For example:

```
public class CashRegister
{
    . . .

    /**
        Constructs a cash register with cleared item count and total.
    */
    public CashRegister() // A constructor
    {
        itemCount = 0;
        totalPrice = 0;
    }
}
```

Constructors never return values, but you do not use the void reserved word when declaring them.

A class can have
multiple
constructors.

Many classes have more than one constructor. This allows you to declare objects in different ways. Consider for example a BankAccount class that has two constructors:

```
public class BankAccount
{
    . . .

    /**
        Constructs a bank account with a zero balance.
    */
    public BankAccount() { . . . }

    /**
        Constructs a bank account with a given balance.
        @param initialBalance the initial balance
    */
    public BankAccount(double initialBalance) { . . . }
}
```

Both constructors have the same name as the class, BankAccount. The first constructor has no parameter variables, whereas the second constructor has a parameter variable of type double.

The compiler picks
the constructor
that matches the
construction
arguments.

When you construct an object, the compiler chooses the constructor that matches the arguments that you supply. For example,

```
BankAccount joesAccount = new BankAccount();
    // Uses BankAccount() constructor
BankAccount lisasAccount = new BankAccount(499.95);
    // Uses BankAccount(double) constructor
```

## Syntax 8.3 Constructors

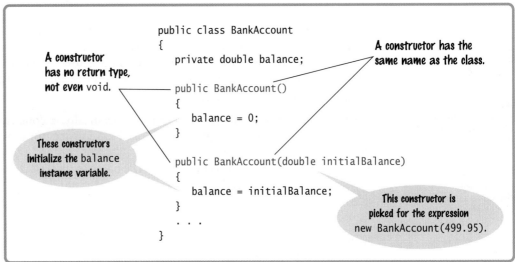

```
                          public class BankAccount
                          {
                              private double balance;

                              public BankAccount()
                              {
                                  balance = 0;
                              }

                              public BankAccount(double initialBalance)
                              {
                                  balance = initialBalance;
                              }
                              . . .
                          }
```

A constructor
has no return type,
**not even** void.

A constructor has the
same name as the class.

These constructors
initialize the balance
instance variable.

This constructor is
picked for the expression
new BankAccount(499.95).

---

**By default, numbers are initialized as 0, Booleans as false, and object references as null.**

If you do not initialize an instance variable in a constructor, it is automatically set to a default value:

- Numbers are set to zero.
- Boolean variables are initialized as false.
- Object and array references are set to the special value null that indicates that no object is associated with the variable (see Section 8.10). This is usually not desirable, and you should initialize object references in your constructors (see Common Error 8.1 on page 378).

In this regard, instance variables differ from local variables declared inside methods. The computer reports an error if you use a local variable that has not been explicitly initialized.

**If you do not provide a constructor, a constructor with no arguments is generated.**

If you do not supply any constructor for a class, the compiler automatically generates a constructor. That constructor has no arguments, and it initializes all instance variables with their default values. Therefore, every class has at least one constructor.

You have now encountered all concepts that are necessary to implement the CashRegister class.

*A constructor is like a set of assembly instructions for an object.*

The complete code for the class is given here. In the next section, you will see how to test the class.

**section_6/CashRegister.java**

```java
1   /**
2       A simulated cash register that tracks the item count and
3       the total amount due.
4   */
5   public class CashRegister
6   {
7       private int itemCount;
8       private double totalPrice;
9
10      /**
11          Constructs a cash register with cleared item count and total.
12      */
13      public CashRegister()
14      {
15          itemCount = 0;
16          totalPrice = 0;
17      }
18
19      /**
20          Adds an item to this cash register.
21          @param price the price of this item
22      */
23      public void addItem(double price)
24      {
25          itemCount++;
26          totalPrice = totalPrice + price;
27      }
28
29      /**
30          Gets the price of all items in the current sale.
31          @return the total amount
32      */
33      public double getTotal()
34      {
35          return totalPrice;
36      }
37
38      /**
39          Gets the number of items in the current sale.
40          @return the item count
41      */
42      public int getCount()
43      {
44          return itemCount;
45      }
46
47      /**
48          Clears the item count and the total.
49      */
50      public void clear()
51      {
52          itemCount = 0;
53          totalPrice = 0;
54      }
55  }
```

**23.** Consider this class:

```java
public class Person
{
    private String name;

    public Person(String firstName, String lastName)
    {
        name = lastName + ", " + firstName;
    }
    . . .
}
```

If an object is constructed as

```java
Person harry = new Person("Harry", "Morgan");
```

what is its `name` instance variable?

**24.** Provide an implementation for a `Person` constructor so that after the call

```java
Person p = new Person();
```

the `name` instance variable of `p` is `"unknown"`.

**25.** What happens if you supply no constructor for the `CashRegister` class?

**26.** Consider the following class:

```java
public class Item
{
    private String description;
    private double price;

    public Item() { . . . }
    // Additional methods omitted
}
```

Provide an implementation for the constructor. Be sure that no instance variable is set to `null`.

**27.** Which constructors should be supplied in the `Item` class so that each of the following declarations compiles?

   **a.** `Item item2 = new Item("Corn flakes");`

   **b.** `Item item3 = new Item(3.95);`

   **c.** `Item item4 = new Item("Corn flakes", 3.95);`

   **d.** `Item item1 = new Item();`

   **e.** `Item item5;`

**Practice It**    Now you can try these exercises at the end of the chapter: R8.12, P8.4, P8.5.

---

Common Error 8.1

### Forgetting to Initialize Object References in a Constructor

Just as it is a common error to forget to initialize a local variable, it is easy to forget about instance variables. Every constructor needs to ensure that all instance variables are set to appropriate values.

If you do not initialize an instance variable, the Java compiler will initialize it for you. Numbers are initialized with 0, but object references—such as string variables—are set to the `null` reference.

Of course, 0 is often a convenient default for numbers. However, null is hardly ever a convenient default for objects. Consider this "lazy" constructor for a modified version of the BankAccount class:

```
public class BankAccount
{
   private double balance;
   private String owner;
   . . .
   public BankAccount(double initialBalance)
   {
      balance = initialBalance;
   }
}
```

In this case, balance is initialized, but the owner variable is set to a null reference. This can be a problem—it is illegal to call methods on the null reference.

To avoid this problem, it is a good idea to initialize every instance variable:

```
public BankAccount(double initialBalance)
{
   balance = initialBalance;
   owner = "None";
}
```

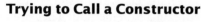

## Common Error 8.2

### Trying to Call a Constructor

A constructor is not a method. You must use it in combination with the new reserved word:

```
CashRegister register1 = new CashRegister();
```

After an object has been constructed, you cannot invoke the constructor on that object again. For example, you cannot call the constructor to clear an object:

```
. . .
register1.CashRegister(); // Error
```

It is true that the constructor can set a *new* CashRegister object to the cleared state, but you cannot invoke a constructor on an *existing* object. However, you can replace the object with a new one:

```
register1 = new CashRegister(); // OK
```

## Common Error 8.3

### Declaring a Constructor as void

Do not use the void reserved word when you declare a constructor:

```
public void BankAccount() // Error—don't use void!
```

This would declare a method with return type void and *not* a constructor. Unfortunately, the Java compiler does not consider this a syntax error.

Special Topic 8.2

### Overloading

When the same method name is used for more than one method, then the name is **overloaded**. In Java you can overload method names provided that the parameter types are different. For example, you can declare two methods, both called print:

```
public void print(CashRegister register)
public void print(BankAccount account)
```

When the print method is called,

```
print(x);
```

the compiler looks at the type of x. If x is a CashRegister object, the first method is called. If x is an BankAccount object, the second method is called. If x is neither, the compiler generates an error.

We have not used the overloading feature in this book. Instead, we gave each method a unique name, such as printRegister or printAccount. However, we have no choice with constructors. Java demands that the name of a constructor equal the name of the class. If a class has more than one constructor, then that name must be overloaded.

# 8.7 Testing a Class

In the preceding section, we completed the implementation of the CashRegister class. What can you do with it? Of course, you can compile the file CashRegister.java. However, you can't *execute* the CashRegister class. It doesn't contain a main method. That is normal—most classes don't contain a main method. They are meant to be combined with a class that has a main method.

> A unit test verifies that a class works correctly in isolation, outside a complete program.

In the long run, your class may become a part of a larger program that interacts with users, stores data in files, and so on. However, before integrating a class into a program, it is always a good idea to test it in isolation. Testing in isolation, outside a complete program, is called **unit testing**.

To test your class, you have two choices. Some interactive development environments, such as BlueJ (http://bluej.org) and Dr. Java (http://drjava.org), have commands for constructing objects and invoking methods. Then you can test a class simply by constructing an object, calling methods, and verifying that you get the expected return values. Figure 7 shows the result of calling the getTotal method on a CashRegister object in BlueJ.

*An engineer tests a part in isolation. This is an example of unit testing.*

> To test a class, use an environment for interactive testing, or write a tester class to execute test instructions.

Alternatively, you can write a *tester class*. A tester class is a class with a main method that contains statements to run methods of another class. A tester class typically carries out the following steps:

1. Construct one or more objects of the class that is being tested.
2. Invoke one or more methods.
3. Print out one or more results.
4. Print the expected results.

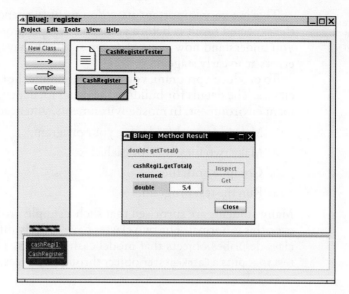

**Figure 7**   The Return Value of the getTotal Method in BlueJ

Here is a class to run methods of the CashRegister class. The main method constructs an object of type CashRegister, invokes the addItem method three times, and then displays the result of the getCount and getTotal methods.

**section_7/CashRegisterTester.java**

```java
1   /**
2      This program tests the CashRegister class.
3   */
4   public class CashRegisterTester
5   {
6      public static void main(String[] args)
7      {
8         CashRegister register1 = new CashRegister();
9         register1.addItem(1.95);
10        register1.addItem(0.95);
11        register1.addItem(2.50);
12        System.out.println(register1.getCount());
13        System.out.println("Expected: 3");
14        System.out.printf("%.2f\n", register1.getTotal());
15        System.out.println("Expected: 5.40");
16     }
17  }
```

**Program Run**

```
3
Expected: 3
5.40
Expected: 5.40
```

In our sample program, we add three items totaling $5.40. When displaying the method results, we also display messages that describe the values we expect to see.

> Determining the expected result in advance is an important part of testing.

This is a very important step. You want to spend some time thinking about what the expected result is before you run a test program. This thought process will help you understand how your program should behave, and it can help you track down errors at an early stage.

To produce a program, you need to combine the CashRegister and CashRegisterTester classes. The details for building the program depend on your compiler and development environment. In most environments, you need to carry out these steps:

1. Make a new subfolder for your program.
2. Make two files, one for each class.
3. Compile both files.
4. Run the test program.

Many students are surprised that such a simple program contains two classes. However, this is normal. The two classes have entirely different purposes. The CashRegister class describes objects that model cash registers. The CashRegisterTester class runs a test that puts a CashRegister object through its paces.

**SELF CHECK**

**28.** How would you enhance the tester class to test the clear method?

**29.** When you run the CashRegisterTester program, how many objects of class CashRegister are constructed? How many objects of type CashRegisterTester?

**30.** Why is the CashRegisterTester class unnecessary in development environments that allow interactive testing, such as BlueJ?

**Practice It**    Now you can try these exercises at the end of the chapter: P8.10, P8.11, P8.21.

---

## HOW TO 8.1    Implementing a Class

A very common task is to implement a class whose objects can carry out a set of specified actions. This How To walks you through the necessary steps.

As an example, consider a class Menu. An object of this class can display a menu such as

```
1) Open new account
2) Log into existing account
3) Help
4) Quit
```

Then the menu waits for the user to supply a value. If the user does not supply a valid value, the menu is redisplayed, and the user can try again.

**Step 1**    Get an informal list of the responsibilities of your objects.

Be careful that you restrict yourself to features that are actually required in the problem. With real-world items, such as cash registers or bank accounts, there are potentially dozens of features that might be worth implementing. But your job is not to faithfully model the real world. You need to determine only those responsibilities that you need for solving your specific problem.

In the case of the menu, you need to

Display the menu.
Get user input.

Now look for hidden responsibilities that aren't part of the problem description. How do objects get created? Which mundane activities need to happen, such as clearing the cash register at the beginning of each sale?

In the menu example, consider how a menu is produced. The programmer creates an empty menu object and then adds options "Open new account", "Help", and so on. That is another responsibility:

**Add an option.**

**Step 2**   Specify the public interface.

Turn the list in Step 1 into a set of methods, with specific types for the parameter variables and the return values. Many programmers find this step simpler if they write out method calls that are applied to a sample object, like this:

```
Menu mainMenu = new Menu();
mainMenu.addOption("Open new account");
// Add more options
int input = mainMenu.getInput();
```

Now we have a specific list of methods.

- `void addOption(String option)`

- `int getInput()`

What about displaying the menu? There is no sense in displaying the menu without also asking the user for input. However, `getInput` may need to display the menu more than once if the user provides a bad input. Thus, `display` is a good candidate for a private method.

To complete the public interface, you need to specify the constructors. Ask yourself what information you need in order to construct an object of your class. Sometimes you will want two constructors: one that sets all instance variables to a default and one that sets them to user-supplied values.

In the case of the menu example, we can get by with a single constructor that creates an empty menu.

Here is the public interface:

```
public class Menu
{
    public Menu() { . . . }
    public void addOption(String option) { . . . }
    public int getInput() { . . . }
}
```

**Step 3**   Document the public interface.

Supply a documentation comment for the class, then comment each method.

```
/**
    A menu that is displayed on a console.
*/
public class Menu
{
    /**
        Constructs a menu with no options.
    */
    public Menu() { . . . }

    /**
        Adds an option to the end of this menu.
        @param option the option to add
    */
    public void addOption(String option) { . . . }
```

```
/**
    Displays the menu, with options numbered starting with 1,
    and prompts the user for input. Repeats until a valid input
    is supplied.
    @return the number that the user supplied
*/
public int getInput() { . . . }
}
```

**Step 4**    Determine instance variables.

Ask yourself what information an object needs to store to do its job. The object needs to be able to process every method using just its instance variables and the method arguments.

Go through each method, perhaps starting with a simple one or an interesting one, and ask yourself what the object needs to carry out the method's task. Which data items are required in addition to the method arguments? Make instance variables for those data items.

In our example, let's start with the addOption method. We clearly need to store the added menu option so that the menu can be displayed later. How should we store the options? As an array list of strings? As one long string? Both approaches can be made to work. We will use an array list here. Exercise P8.3 asks you to implement the other approach.

```
public class Menu
{
    private ArrayList<String> options;
    . . .
}
```

Now consider the getInput method. It shows the stored options and reads an integer. When checking that the input is valid, we need to know the number of menu items. Because we store them in an array list, the number of menu items is simply obtained as the size of the array list. If you stored the menu items in one long string, you might want to keep another instance variable that stores the item count.

We will also need a scanner to read the user input, which we will add as another instance variable:

```
private Scanner in;
```

**Step 5**    Implement constructors and methods.

Implement the constructors and methods in your class, one at a time, starting with the easiest ones. For example, here is the implementation of the addOption method:

```
public void addOption(String option)
{
    options.add(option);
}
```

Here is the getInput method. This method is a bit more sophisticated. It loops until a valid input has been obtained, displaying the menu options before reading the input.

```
public int getInput()
{
    int input;
    do
    {
        for (int i = 0; i < options.size(); i++)
        {
            int choice = i + 1;
            System.out.println(choice + ") " + options.get(i));
        }
        input = in.nextInt();
    }
    while (input < 1 || input > options.size());
```

```
        return input;
    }
```

Finally, we need to supply a constructor to initialize the instance variables:

```
public Menu()
{
    options = new ArrayList<String>();
    in = new Scanner(System.in);
}
```

If you find that you have trouble with the implementation of some of your methods, you may need to rethink your choice of instance variables. It is common for a beginner to start out with a set of instance variables that cannot accurately describe the state of an object. Don't hesitate to go back and rethink your implementation strategy.

Once you have completed the implementation, compile your class and fix any compiler errors.

**Step 6**    Test your class.

Write a short tester program and execute it. The tester program should carry out the method calls that you found in Step 2.

```
public class MenuTester
{
    public static void main(String[] args)
    {
        Menu mainMenu = new Menu();
        mainMenu.addOption("Open new account");
        mainMenu.addOption("Log into existing account");
        mainMenu.addOption("Help");
        mainMenu.addOption("Quit");
        int input = mainMenu.getInput();
        System.out.println("Input: " + input);
    }
}
```

**Program Run**

```
1) Open new account
2) Log into existing account
3) Help
4) Quit
5
1) Open new account
2) Log into existing account
3) Help
4) Quit
3
Input: 3
```

**ONLINE EXAMPLE**

⊕ The complete Menu and MenuTester classes.

---

**WORKED EXAMPLE 8.1**    **Implementing a Bank Account Class**

⊕ This Worked Example shows how to develop a class that simulates a bank account.

---

⊕ Available online in WileyPLUS and at www.wiley.com/college/horstmann.

**Paying Off a Loan**

When you take out a loan, the bank tells you how much you need to pay and for how long. Where do these numbers come from? This Video Example uses a Loan object to demonstrate how a loan is paid off.

# 8.8  Problem Solving: Tracing Objects

You have seen how the technique of hand-tracing is useful for understanding how a program works. When your program contains objects, it is useful to adapt the technique so that you gain a better understanding about object data and encapsulation.

> Write the methods on the front of a card, and the instance variables on the back.

Use an index card or a sticky note for each object. On the front, write the methods that the object can execute. On the back, make a table for the values of the instance variables.

Here is a card for a CashRegister object:

| CashRegister reg1 | | itemCount | totalPrice |
|---|---|---|---|
| clear | | | |
| addItem(price) | | | |
| getTotal | | | |
| getCount | | | |

*front*                    *back*

In a small way, this gives you a feel for encapsulation. An object is manipulated through its public interface (on the front of the card), and the instance variables are hidden in the back.

When an object is constructed, fill in the initial values of the instance variables:

| itemCount | totalPrice |
|---|---|
| 0 | 0 |

> Update the values of the instance variables when a mutator method is called.

Whenever a mutator method is executed, cross out the old values and write the new ones below. Here is what happens after a call to the addItem method:

| itemCount | totalPrice |
|---|---|
| ~~0~~ | ~~0~~ |
| 1 | 19.95 |

➕ Available online in WileyPLUS and at www.wiley.com/college/horstmann.

If you have more than one object in your program, you will have multiple cards, one for each object:

| itemCount | totalPrice |
|-----------|------------|
| ~~0~~ | ~~0~~ |
| 1 | 19.95 |

| itemCount | totalPrice |
|-----------|------------|
| ~~0~~ | ~~0~~ |
| 1 | 19.95 |
| 2 | 34.95 |

These diagrams are also useful when you design a class. Suppose you are asked to enhance the CashRegister class to compute the sales tax. Add a method getSalesTax to the front of the card. Now turn the card over, look over the instance variables, and ask yourself whether the object has sufficient information to compute the answer. Remember that each object is an autonomous unit. Any data value that can be used in a computation must be

- An instance variable.
- A method argument.
- A static variable (uncommon; see Section 8.11).

To compute the sales tax, we need to know the tax rate and the total of the taxable items. (Food items are usually not subject to sales tax.) We don't have that information available. Let us introduce additional instance variables for the tax rate and the taxable total. The tax rate can be set in the constructor (assuming it stays fixed for the lifetime of the object). When adding an item, we need to be told whether the item is taxable. If so, we add its price to the taxable total.

For example, consider the following statements.

```
CashRegister reg2(7.5); // 7.5 percent sales tax
reg2.addItem(3.95, false); // Not taxable
reg2.addItem(19.95, true); // Taxable
```

**ONLINE EXAMPLE**

An enhanced CashRegister class that computes the sales tax.

When you record the effect on a card, it looks like this:

| itemCount | totalPrice | taxableTotal | taxRate |
|-----------|------------|--------------|---------|
| ~~0~~ | ~~0~~ | ~~0~~ | 7.5 |
| ~~1~~ | ~~3.95~~ | | |
| 2 | 23.90 | 19.95 | |

With this information, it becomes easy to compute the tax. It is **taxableTotal x taxRate / 100**. Tracing the object helped us understand the need for additional instance variables.

**SELF CHECK**

**31.** Consider a Car class that simulates fuel consumption in a car. We will assume a fixed efficiency (in miles per gallon) that is supplied in the constructor. There are methods for adding gas, driving a given distance, and checking the amount of gas left in the tank. Make a card for a Car object, choosing suitable instance variables and showing their values after the object was constructed.

**32.** Trace the following method calls:

```
Car myCar(25);
myCar.addGas(20);
myCar.drive(100);
myCar.drive(200);
myCar.addGas(5);
```

**33.** Suppose you are asked to simulate the odometer of the car, by adding a method getMilesDriven. Add an instance variable to the object's card that is suitable for computing this method.

**34.** Trace the methods of Self Check 32, updating the instance variable that you added in Self Check 33.

**Practice It** Now you can try these exercises at the end of the chapter: R8.13, R8.14, R8.15.

# 8.9 Problem Solving: Patterns for Object Data

When you design a class, you first consider the needs of the programmers who use the class. You provide the methods that the users of your class will call when they manipulate objects. When you implement the class, you need to come up with the instance variables for the class. It is not always obvious how to do this. Fortunately, there is a small set of recurring patterns that you can adapt when you design your own classes. We introduce these patterns in the following sections.

## 8.9.1 Keeping a Total

An instance variable for the total is updated in methods that increase or decrease the total amount.

Many classes need to keep track of a quantity that can go up or down as certain methods are called. Examples:

- A bank account has a balance that is increased by a deposit, decreased by a withdrawal.
- A cash register has a total that is increased when an item is added to the sale, cleared after the end of the sale.
- A car has gas in the tank, which is increased when fuel is added and decreased when the car drives.

In all of these cases, the implementation strategy is similar. Keep an instance variable that represents the current total. For example, for the cash register:

```
private double totalPrice;
```

Locate the methods that affect the total. There is usually a method to increase it by a given amount.

```
public void addItem(double price)
{
    totalPrice = totalPrice + price;
}
```

Depending on the nature of the class, there may be a method that reduces or clears the total. In the case of the cash register, there is a `clear` method:

```java
public void clear()
{
    total = 0;
}
```

There is usually a method that yields the current total. It is easy to implement:

```java
public double getTotal()
{
    return totalPrice;
}
```

All classes that manage a total follow the same basic pattern. Find the methods that affect the total and provide the appropriate code for increasing or decreasing it. Find the methods that report or use the total, and have those methods read the current total.

## 8.9.2  Counting Events

A counter that counts events is incremented in methods that correspond to the events.

You often need to count how often certain events occur in the life of an object. For example:

- In a cash register, you want to know how many items have been added in a sale.
- A bank account charges a fee for each transaction; you need to count them.

Keep a counter, such as

```java
private int itemCount;
```

Increment the counter in those methods that correspond to the events that you want to count.

```java
public void addItem(double price)
{
    totalPrice = totalPrice + price;
    itemCount++;
}
```

You may need to clear the counter, for example at the end of a sale or a statement period.

```java
public void clear()
{
    total = 0;
    itemCount = 0;
}
```

There may or may not be a method that reports the count to the class user. The count may only be used to compute a fee or an average. Find out which methods in your class make use of the count, and read the current value in those methods.

## 8.9.3  Collecting Values

Some objects collect numbers, strings, or other objects. For example, each multiple-choice question has a number of choices. A cash register may need to store all prices of the current sale.

Use an array list or an array to store the values. (An array list is usually simpler because you won't need to track the number of values.) For example,

```java
public class Question
{
    private ArrayList<String> choices;
    . . .
}
```

In the constructor, initialize the instance variable to an empty collection:

```java
public Question()
{
    choices = new ArrayList<String>();
}
```

*A shopping cart object needs to manage a collection of items.*

You need to supply some mechanism for adding values. It is common to provide a method for appending a value to the collection:

```java
public void add(String question)
{
    choices.add(question);
}
```

The user of a `Question` object can call this method multiple times to add the various choices.

### 8.9.4 Managing Properties of an Object

A property is a value of an object that an object user can set and retrieve. For example, a `Student` object may have a name and an ID.

Provide an instance variable to store the property's value and methods to get and set it.

```java
public class Student
{
    private String name;
    . . .
    public String getName() { return name; }
    public void setName(String newName) { name = newName; }
    . . .
}
```

It is common to add error checking to the setter method. For example, we may want to reject a blank name:

```java
public void setName(String newName)
{
    if (newName.length() > 0) { name = newName; }
}
```

Some properties should not change after they have been set in the constructor. For example, a student's ID may be fixed (unlike the student's name, which may change). In that case, don't supply a setter method.

```java
public class Student
{
```

```
    private int id;
    . . .
    public Student(int anId) { id = anId; }
    public String getId() { return id; }
    // No setId method
    . . .
}
```

## 8.9.5 Modeling Objects with Distinct States

Some objects have behavior that varies depending on what has happened in the past. For example, a Fish object may look for food when it is hungry and ignore food after it has eaten. Such an object would need to remember whether it has recently eaten.

Supply an instance variable that models the state, together with some constants for the state values:

```
public class Fish
{
    private int hungry;

    public static final int NOT_HUNGRY = 0;
    public static final int SOMEWHAT_HUNGRY = 1;
    public static final int VERY_HUNGRY = 2;
    . . .
}
```

(Alternatively, you can use an enumeration—see Special Topic 3.4.)

Determine which methods change the state. In this example, a fish that has just eaten food, won't be hungry. But as the fish moves, it will get hungrier.

```
public void eat()
{
    hungry = NOT_HUNGRY;
    . . .
}

public void move()
{
    . . .
    if (hungry < VERY_HUNGRY) { hungry++; }
}
```

*If a fish is in a hungry state, its behavior changes.*

Finally, determine where the state affects behavior. A fish that is very hungry will want to look for food first.

```
public void move()
{
   if (hungry == VERY_HUNGRY)
   {
      Look for food.
   }
   . . .
}
```

## 8.9.6 Describing the Position of an Object

Some objects move around during their lifetime, and they remember their current position. For example,

To model a moving object, you need to store and update its position.

- A train drives along a track and keeps track of the distance from the terminus.
- A simulated bug living on a grid crawls from one grid location to the next, or makes 90 degree turns to the left or right.
- A cannonball is shot into the air, then descends as it is pulled by the gravitational force.

Such objects need to store their position. Depending on the nature of their movement, they may also need to store their orientation or velocity.

If the object moves along a line, you can represent the position as a distance from a fixed point.

```
private double distanceFromTerminus;
```

If the object moves in a grid, remember its current location and direction in the grid:

```
private int row;
private int column;
private int direction; // 0 = North, 1 = East, 2 = South, 3 = West
```

When you model a physical object such as a cannonball, you need to track both the position and the velocity, possibly in two or three dimensions. Here we model a cannonball that is shot upward into the air:

```
private double zPosition;
private double zVelocity;
```

There will be methods that update the position. In the simplest case, you may be told by how much the object moves:

```
public void move(double distanceMoved)
{
   distanceFromTerminus = distanceFromTerminus + distanceMoved;
}
```

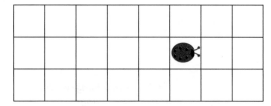

*A bug in a grid needs to store its row, column, and direction.*

If the movement happens in a grid, you need to update the row or column, depending on the current orientation.

```java
public void moveOneUnit()
{
    if (direction == NORTH) { row--; }
    else if (direction == EAST) { column++; }
    . . .
}
```

Exercise P8.25 shows you how to update the position of a physical object with known velocity.

Whenever you have a moving object, keep in mind that your program will *simulate* the actual movement in some way. Find out the rules of that simulation, such as movement along a line or in a grid with integer coordinates. Those rules determine how to represent the current position. Then locate the methods that move the object, and update the positions according to the rules of the simulation.

**SELF CHECK**

**35.** Suppose we want to count the number of transactions in a bank account in a statement period, and we add a counter to the BankAccount class:

```java
public class BankAccount
{
    private int transactionCount;
    . . .
}
```

In which methods does this counter need to be updated?

**36.** In the example in Section 8.9.3, why is the add method required? That is, why can't the user of a Question object just call the add method of the ArrayList<String> class?

**37.** Suppose we want to enhance the CashRegister class in Section 8.6 to track the prices of all purchased items for printing a receipt. Which instance variable should you provide? Which methods should you modify?

**38.** Consider an Employee class with properties for tax ID number and salary. Which of these properties should have only a getter method, and which should have getter and setter methods?

**39.** Look at the direction instance variable in the bug example in Section 8.9.6. This is an example of which pattern?

**Practice It**    Now you can try these exercises at the end of the chapter: P8.6, P8.7, P8.12.

**VIDEO EXAMPLE 8.2**    **Modeling a Robot Escaping from a Maze**

In this Video Example, we will program classes that model a robot escaping from a maze.

⊕  Available online in WileyPLUS and at *www.wiley.com/college/horstmann*.

## *Random Fact 8.1* Electronic Voting Machines

In the 2000 presidential elections in the United States, votes were tallied by a variety of machines. Some machines processed cardboard ballots into which voters punched holes to indicate their choices (see below). When voters were not careful, remains of paper—the now infamous "chads"—were partially stuck in the punch cards, causing votes to be miscounted. A manual recount was necessary, but it was not carried out everywhere due to time constraints and procedural wrangling. The election was very close, and there remain doubts in the minds of many people whether the election outcome would have been different if the voting machines had accurately counted the intent of the voters.

*Punch Card Ballot*

Subsequently, voting machine manufacturers have argued that electronic voting machines would avoid the problems caused by punch cards or optically scanned forms. In an electronic voting machine, voters indicate their preferences by pressing buttons or touching icons on a computer screen. Typically, each voter is presented with a summary screen for review before casting the ballot. The process is very similar to using a bank's automated teller machine.

It seems plausible that these machines make it more likely that a vote is counted in the same way that the voter intends. However, there has been significant controversy surrounding some types of electronic voting machines. If a machine simply records the votes and prints out the totals after the election has been completed, then how do you know that the machine worked correctly? Inside the machine is a computer that executes a program, and, as you may know from your own experience, programs can have bugs.

In fact, some electronic voting machines do have bugs. There have been isolated cases where machines reported tallies that were impossible. When a machine reports far more or far fewer votes than voters, then it is clear that it malfunctioned. Unfortunately, it is then impossible to find out the actual votes. Over time, one would expect these bugs to be fixed in the software. More insidiously, if the results are plausible, nobody may ever investigate.

Many computer scientists have spoken out on this issue and confirmed that it is impossible, with today's technology, to tell that software is error free and has not been tampered with. Many of them recommend that electronic voting machines should employ a *voter verifiable audit trail*. (A good source of information is http://verifiedvoting.org.) Typically, a voter-verifiable machine prints out a ballot. Each voter has a chance to review the printout, and then deposits it in an old-fashioned ballot box. If there is a problem with the electronic equipment, the printouts can be scanned or counted by hand.

As this book is written, this concept is strongly resisted both by manufacturers of electronic voting machines and by their customers, the cities and counties that run elections. Manufacturers are reluctant to increase the cost of the machines because they may not be able to pass the cost increase on to their customers, who tend to have tight budgets. Election officials fear problems with malfunctioning printers, and some of them have publicly stated that they actually prefer equipment that eliminates bothersome recounts.

What do you think? You probably use an automated bank teller machine to get cash from your bank account. Do you review the paper record that the machine issues? Do you check your bank statement? Even if you don't, do you put your faith in other people who double-check their balances, so that the bank won't get away with widespread cheating?

Is the integrity of banking equipment more important or less important than that of voting machines? Won't every voting process have some room for error and fraud anyway? Is the added cost for equipment, paper, and staff time reasonable to combat a potentially slight risk of malfunction and fraud? Computer scientists cannot answer these questions—an informed society must make these tradeoffs. But, like all professionals, they have an obligation to speak out and give accurate testimony about the capabilities and limitations of computing equipment.

*Touch Screen Voting Machine*

# 8.10  Object References

In Java, a variable whose type is a class does not actually hold an object. It merely holds the *memory location* of an object. The object itself is stored elsewhere—see Figure 8.

We use the technical term **object reference** to denote the memory location of an object. When a variable contains the memory location of an object, we say that it *refers* to an object. For example, after the statement

```
CashRegister reg1 = new CashRegister();
```

the variable reg1 refers to the CashRegister object that the new operator constructed. Technically speaking, the new operator returned a reference to the new object, and that reference is stored in the reg1 variable.

> An object reference specifies the location of an object.

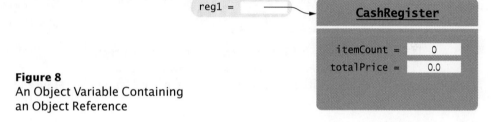

**Figure 8**
An Object Variable Containing
an Object Reference

## 8.10.1  Shared References

> Multiple object variables can contain references to the same object.

You can have two (or more) object variables that store references to the same object, for example by assigning one to the other.

```
CashRegister reg2 = reg1;
```

Now you can access the same CashRegister object both as reg1 and as reg2, as shown in Figure 9.

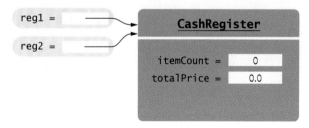

**Figure 9**
Two Object Variables
Referring to the Same Object

> Primitive type variables store values. Object variables store references.

In this regard, object variables differ from variables for primitive types (numbers, characters, and boolean values). When you declare

```
int num1 = 0;
```

then the num1 variable holds the number 0, not a reference to the number (see Figure 10).

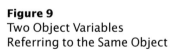

**Figure 10**   A Variable of Type int Stores a Number

You can see the difference between primitive type variables and object variables when you make a copy of a variable. When you copy a number, the original and the copy of the number are independent values. But when you copy an object reference, both the original and the copy are references to the same object.

Consider the following code, which copies a number and then changes the copy (see Figure 11):

```
int num1 = 0; ①
int num2 = num1; ②
num2++; ③
```

Now the variable num1 contains the value 0, and num2 contains 1.

> When copying an object reference, you have two references to the same object.

Now consider the seemingly analogous code with CashRegister objects (see Figure 12):

```
CashRegister reg1 = new CashRegister(); ①
CashRegister reg2 = reg1; ②
reg2.addItem(2.95); ③
```

Because reg1 and reg2 refer to the same cash register after step ②, both variables now refer to a cash register with item count 1 and total price 2.95.

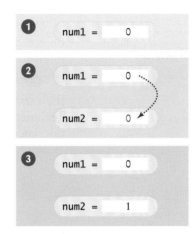

**Figure 11**  Copying Numbers

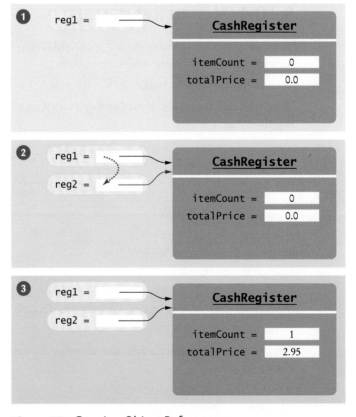

**Figure 12**  Copying Object References

There is a reason for the difference between numbers and objects. In the computer, each number requires a small amount of memory. But objects can be very large. It is far more efficient to manipulate only the memory location.

## 8.10.2  The `null` Reference

The null reference refers to no object.

An object reference can have the special value `null` if it refers to no object at all. It is common to use the `null` value to indicate that a value has never been set. For example,

```
String middleInitial = null; // No middle initial
```

You use the `==` operator (and not `equals`) to test whether an object reference is a `null` reference:

```
if (middleInitial == null)
{
    System.out.println(firstName + " " + lastName);
}
else
{
    System.out.println(firstName + " " + middleInitial + ". " + lastName);
}
```

Note that the `null` reference is not the same as the empty string `""`. The empty string is a valid string of length 0, whereas a `null` indicates that a `String` variable refers to no string at all.

It is an error to invoke a method on a `null` reference. For example,

```
CashRegister reg = null;
System.out.println(reg.getTotal()); // Error—cannot invoke a method on null
```

This code causes a "null pointer exception" at run time.

The `null` reference is the default value for an object reference that is contained inside another object or an array of objects. In order to avoid run-time errors, you need to replace these `null` references with references to actual objects.

For example, suppose you construct an array of bank accounts:

```
BankAccount[] accounts = new BankAccount[NACCOUNTS];
```

You now have an array filled with `null` references. If you want an array of actual bank accounts, you need to construct them:

```
for (int i = 0; i < accounts.length; i++)
{
    accounts[i] = new BankAccount();
}
```

## 8.10.3  The `this` Reference

In a method, the this reference refers to the implicit parameter.

Every instance method receives the implicit parameter in a variable called `this`.

For example, consider the method call

```
reg1.addItem(2.95);
```

When the method is called, the parameter variable `this` refers to the same object as `reg1` (see Figure 13).

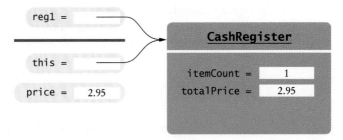

**Figure 13** The Implicit Parameter of a Method Call

You don't usually need to use the this reference, but you can. For example, you can write the addItem method like this:

```
void addItem(double price)
{
   this.itemCount++;
   this.totalPrice = this.totalPrice + price;
}
```

Some programmers like to use the this reference to make it clear that itemCount and totalPrice are instance variables and not local variables. You may want to try it out and see if you like that style.

There is another situation where the this reference can make your programs easier to read. Consider a constructor or instance method that calls another instance method *on the same object*. For example, the CashRegister constructor can call the clear method instead of duplicating its code:

```
public CashRegister()
{
   clear();
}
```

This call is easier to understand when you use the this reference:

```
public CashRegister()
{
   this.clear();
}
```

It is now more obvious that the method is invoked on the object that is being constructed.

Finally, some people like to use the this reference in constructors. Here is a typical example:

```
public class Student
{
   private int id;
   private String name;

   public Student(int id, String name)
   {
      this.id = id;
      this.name = name;
   }
}
```

The expression id refers to the parameter variable, and this.id to the instance variable. In general, if both a local variable and an instance variable have the same name, you can access the local variable by its name, and the instance variable with the this reference.

You can implement the constructor without using the this reference. Simply choose other names for the parameter variables:

```
public Student(int anId, String aName)
{
    id = anId;
    name = aName;
}
```

**40.** Suppose we have a variable

```
String greeting = "Hello";
```

What is the effect of this statement?

```
String greeting2 = greeting;
```

**41.** After calling String greeting3 = greeting2.toUpperCase(), what are the contents of greeting and greeting2?

**42.** What is the value of s.length() if s is

**a.** the empty string ""?

**b.** null?

**43.** What is the type of this in the call greeting.substring(1, 4)?

**44.** Supply a method addItems(int quantity, double price) in the CashRegister class to add multiple instances of the same item. Your implementation should repeatedly call the addItem method. Use the this reference.

**Practice It** Now you can try these exercises at the end of the chapter: R8.19, R8.20.

Special Topic 8.3

## Calling One Constructor from Another

Consider the BankAccount class outlined in Section 8.6. It has two constructors: a constructor without arguments to initialize the balance with zero, and another constructor to supply an initial balance. Rather than explicitly setting the balance to zero, one constructor can call another constructor of the same class instead. There is a shorthand notation to achieve this result:

```
public class BankAccount
{
    public BankAccount (double initialBalance)
    {
        balance = initialBalance;
    }

    public BankAccount()
    {
        this(0);
    }
    . . .
}
```

The command this(0); means "Call another constructor of this class and supply the value 0". Such a call to another constructor can occur only as the *first line in a constructor*.

> This syntax is a minor convenience. We will not use it in this book. Actually, the use of the reserved word this is a little confusing. Normally, this denotes a reference to the implicit parameter, but if this is followed by parentheses, it denotes a call to another constructor of this class.

# 8.11 Static Variables and Methods

A static variable belongs to the class, not to any object of the class.

Sometimes, a value properly belongs to a class, not to any object of the class. You use a **static variable** for this purpose. Here is a typical example: We want to assign bank account numbers sequentially. That is, we want the bank account constructor to construct the first account with number 1001, the next with number 1002, and so on. To solve this problem, we need to have a single value of lastAssignedNumber that is a property of the *class*, not any object of the class. Such a variable is called a static variable, because you declare it using the static reserved word.

*The reserved word* static *is a holdover from the C++ language. Its use in Java has no relationship to the normal use of the term.*

```java
public class BankAccount
{
    private double balance;
    private int accountNumber;
    private static int lastAssignedNumber = 1000;

    public BankAccount()
    {
        lastAssignedNumber++;
        accountNumber = lastAssignedNumber;
    }
    . . .
}
```

Every BankAccount object has its own balance and accountNumber instance variables, but there is only a single copy of the lastAssignedNumber variable (see Figure 14). That variable is stored in a separate location, outside any BankAccount objects.

Like instance variables, static variables should always be declared as private to ensure that methods of other classes do not change their values. However, static *constants* may be either private or public. For example, the BankAccount class can define a public constant value, such as

```java
public class BankAccount
{
    public static final double OVERDRAFT_FEE = 29.95;
    . . .
}
```

Methods from any class can refer to such a constant as BankAccount.OVERDRAFT_FEE.

A static method is not invoked on an object.

Sometimes a class defines methods that are not invoked on an object. Such a method is called a **static method**. A typical example of a static method is the sqrt method in the Math class. Because numbers aren't objects, you can't invoke methods on them. For example, if x is a number, then the call x.sqrt() is not legal in Java.

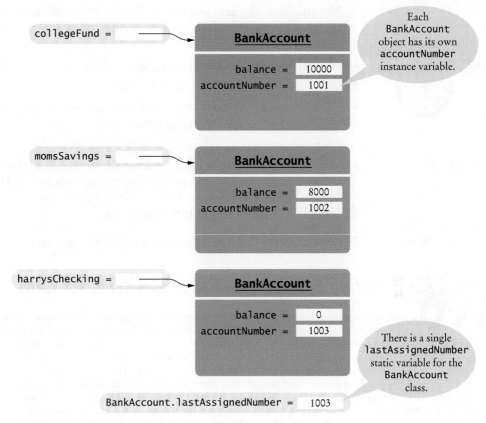

**Figure 14** A Static Variable and Instance Variables

Therefore, the Math class provides a static method that is invoked as Math.sqrt(x). No object of the Math class is constructed. The Math qualifier simply tells the compiler where to find the sqrt method.

You can define your own static methods for use in other classes. Here is an example:

```java
public class Financial
{
   /**
      Computes a percentage of an amount.
      @param percentage the percentage to apply
      @param amount the amount to which the percentage is applied
      @return the requested percentage of the amount
   */
   public static double percentOf(double percentage, double amount)
   {
      return (percentage / 100) * amount;
   }
}
```

When calling this method, supply the name of the class containing it:

```java
double tax = Financial.percentOf(taxRate, total);
```

**ONLINE EXAMPLE**

A program with static methods and variables.

You had to use static methods in Chapter 5 before you knew how to implement your own objects. However, in object-oriented programming, static methods are not very common.

Nevertheless, the `main` method is always static. When the program starts, there aren't any objects. Therefore, the first method of a program must be a static method.

**SELF CHECK**

45. Name two static variables of the `System` class.
46. Name a static constant of the `Math` class.
47. The following method computes the average of an array of numbers:

    ```
    public static double average(double[] values)
    ```

    Why should it not be defined as an instance method?
48. Harry tells you that he has found a great way to avoid those pesky objects: Put all code into a single class and declare all methods and variables `static`. Then `main` can call the other static methods, and all of them can access the static variables. Will Harry's plan work? Is it a good idea?

**Practice It** Now you can try these exercises at the end of the chapter: P8.14, P8.15.

## *Random Fact 8.2* Open Source and Free Software

Most companies that produce software regard the source code as a trade secret. After all, if customers or competitors had access to the source code, they could study it and create similar programs without paying the original vendor. For the same reason, customers dislike secret source code. If a company goes out of business or decides to discontinue support for a computer program, its users are left stranded. They are unable to fix bugs or adapt the program to a new operating system. Nowadays, some software packages are distributed with "open source" or "free software" licenses. Here, the term "free" doesn't refer to price, but to the freedom to inspect and modify the source code. Richard Stallman, a famous computer scientist and winner of a MacArthur "genius" grant, pioneered the concept of free software. He is the inventor of the Emacs text editor and the originator of the GNU project that aims to create an entirely free version of a UNIX compatible operating system. All programs of the GNU project are licensed under the General Public License or GPL. The GPL allows you to make as many copies as you wish, make any modifications to the source, and redistribute the original and modified programs, charging nothing at all or whatever the market will bear. In return, you must agree that your modifications also fall under the GPL. You must give out the source code to any changes that you distribute, and anyone else can distribute them under the same conditions. The GPL, and similar open source licenses, form a social contract. Users of the software enjoy the freedom to use and modify the software, and in return they are obligated to share any improvements that they make. Many programs, such as the Linux operating system and the GNU C++ compiler, are distributed under the GPL.

Some commercial software vendors have attacked the GPL as "viral" and "undermining the commercial software sector". Other companies have a more nuanced strategy, producing proprietary software while also contributing to open source projects.

Frankly, open source is not a panacea and there is plenty of room for the commercial software sector. Open source software often lacks the polish of commercial software because many of the programmers are volunteers who are interested in solving their own problems, not in making a product that is easy to use by others. Some product categories are not available at all as open source software because the development work is unattractive when there is little promise of commercial gain. Open source software has been most successful in areas that are of interest to programmers, such as the Linux operating system, Web servers, and programming tools.

On the positive side, the open software community can be very competitive and creative. It is quite common to see several competing projects that take ideas from each other, all rapidly becoming more capable. Having many programmers involved, all reading the source code, often means that bugs tend to get squashed quickly. Eric Raymond describes open source development in his famous article "The Cathedral and the Bazaar" (http://catb.org/~esr/writings/cathedral-bazaar/cathedral-bazaar/index.html). He writes "Given enough eyeballs, all bugs are shallow".

*Richard Stallman, a pioneer of the free source movement.*

## CHAPTER SUMMARY

### Understand the concepts of classes, objects, and encapsulation.

- A class describes a set of objects with the same behavior.
- Every class has a public interface: a collection of methods through which the objects of the class can be manipulated.
- Encapsulation is the act of providing a public interface and hiding the implementation details.
- Encapsulation enables changes in the implementation without affecting users of a class.

### Understand instance variables and method implementations of a simple class.

- An object's instance variables store the data required for executing its methods.
- Each object of a class has its own set of instance variables.
- An instance method can access the instance variables of the object on which it acts.
- A private instance variable can only be accessed by the methods of its own class.

### Write method headers that describe the public interface of a class.

- You can use method headers and method comments to specify the public interface of a class.
- A mutator method changes the object on which it operates.
- An accessor method does not change the object on which it operates.

### Choose an appropriate data representation for a class.

- For each accessor method, an object must either store or compute the result.
- Commonly, there is more than one way of representing the data of an object, and you must make a choice.
- Be sure that your data representation supports method calls in any order.

### Provide the implementation of instance methods for a class.

- The object on which a method is applied is the implicit parameter.
- Explicit parameters of a method are listed in the method declaration.

### Design and implement constructors.

- A constructor initializes the instance variables of an object.
- A constructor is invoked when an object is created with the new operator.
- The name of a constructor is the same as the class name.
- A class can have multiple constructors.
- The compiler picks the constructor that matches the construction arguments.

- By default, numbers are initialized as 0, Booleans as `false`, and object references as `null`.
- If you do not provide a constructor, a constructor with no arguments is generated.

**Write tests that verify that a class works correctly.**

- A unit test verifies that a class works correctly in isolation, outside a complete program.
- To test a class, use an environment for interactive testing, or write a tester class to execute test instructions.
- Determining the expected result in advance is an important part of testing.

**Use the technique of object tracing for visualizing object behavior.**

- Write the methods on the front of a card, and the instance variables on the back.
- Update the values of the instance variables when a mutator method is called.

**Use patterns to design the data representation of a class.**

- An instance variable for the total is updated in methods that increase or decrease the total amount.
- A counter that counts events is incremented in methods that correspond to the events.
- An object can collect other objects in an array or array list.
- An object property can be accessed with a getter method and changed with a setter method.
- If your object can have one of several states that affect the behavior, supply an instance variable for the current state.
- To model a moving object, you need to store and update its position.

**Describe the behavior of object references.**

- An object reference specifies the location of an object.
- Multiple object variables can contain references to the same object.
- Primitive type variables store values. Object variables store references.
- When copying an object reference, you have two references to the same object.
- The `null` reference refers to no object.
- In a method, the `this` reference refers to the implicit parameter.

**Understand the behavior of static variables and methods.**

- A static variable belongs to the class, not to any object of the class.
- A static method is not invoked on an object.

## REVIEW EXERCISES

- **R8.1** What is encapsulation? Why is it useful?

- **R8.2** What values are returned by the calls reg1.getCount(), reg1.getTotal(), reg2.getCount(), and reg2.getTotal() after these statements?

      CashRegister reg1 = new CashRegister();
      reg1.addItem(3.25);
      reg1.addItem(1.95);
      CashRegister reg2 = new CashRegister();
      reg2.addItem(3.25);
      reg2.clear();

- **R8.3** Consider the Menu class in How To 8.1 on page 382. What is displayed when the following calls are executed?

      Menu simpleMenu = new Menu();
      simpleMenu.addOption("Ok");
      simpleMenu.addOption("Cancel");
      int response = simpleMenu.getInput();

- **R8.4** What is the *public interface* of a class? How does it differ from the *implementation* of a class?

- ■■ **R8.5** Consider the data representation of a cash register that keeps track of sales tax in Section 8.8. Instead of tracking the taxable total, track the total sales tax. Redo the walkthrough with this change.

- ■■■ **R8.6** Suppose the CashRegister needs to support a method void undo() that undoes the addition of the preceding item. This enables a cashier to quickly undo a mistake. What instance variables should you add to the CashRegister class to support this modification?

- **R8.7** What is an instance method, and how does it differ from a static method?

- **R8.8** What is a mutator method? What is an accessor method?

- **R8.9** What is an implicit parameter? How does it differ from an explicit parameter?

- **R8.10** How many implicit parameters can an instance method have? How many implicit parameters can a static method have? How many explicit parameters can an instance method have?

- **R8.11** What is a constructor?

- **R8.12** How many constructors can a class have? Can you have a class with no constructors? If a class has more than one constructor, which of them gets called?

- **R8.13** Using the object tracing technique described in Section 8.8, trace the program at the end of Section 8.7.

- ■■ **R8.14** Using the object tracing technique described in Section 8.8, trace the program in Worked Example 8.1.

- ■■■ **R8.15** Design a modification of the BankAccount class in Worked Example 8.1 in which the first five transactions per month are free and a $1 fee is charged for every additional transaction. Provide a method that deducts the fee at the end of a month. What additional instance variables do you need? Using the object tracing technique described in Section 8.8, trace a scenario that shows how the fees are computed over two months.

■■■ **R8.16** Instance variables are "hidden" by declaring them as private, but they aren't hidden very well at all. Anyone can read the class declaration. Explain to what extent the private reserved word hides the private implementation of a class.

■■■ **R8.17** You can read the itemCount instance variable of the CashRegister class with the getCount accessor method. Should there be a setCount mutator method to change it? Explain why or why not.

■■■ **R8.18** In a static method, it is easy to differentiate between calls to instance methods and calls to static methods. How do you tell them apart? Why is it not as easy for methods that are called from an instance method?

■■ **R8.19** What is the this reference? Why would you use it?

■■ **R8.20** What is the difference between the number zero, the null reference, the value false, and the empty string?

## PROGRAMMING EXERCISES

■ **P8.1** We want to add a button to the tally counter in Section 8.2 that allows an operator to undo an accidental button click. Provide a method

```
public void undo()
```

that simulates such a button. As an added precaution, make sure that the operator cannot click the undo button more often than the count button.

■ **P8.2** Simulate a tally counter that can be used to admit a limited number of people. First, the limit is set with a call

```
public void setLimit(int maximum)
```

If the count button was clicked more often than the limit, simulate an alarm by printing out a message "Limit exceeded".

■■■ **P8.3** Reimplement the Menu class so that it stores all menu items in one long string. *Hint:* Keep a separate counter for the number of options. When a new option is added, append the option count, the option, and a newline character.

■■ **P8.4** Implement a class Address. An address has a house number, a street, an optional apartment number, a city, a state, and a postal code. Supply two constructors: one with an apartment number and one without. Supply a print method that prints the address with the street on one line and the city, state, and zip code on the next line. Supply a method public boolean comesBefore(Address other) that tests whether this address comes before another when the addresses are compared by postal code.

■ **P8.5** Implement a class SodaCan with methods getSurfaceArea() and get-Volume(). In the constructor, supply the height and radius of the can.

■■ **P8.6** Implement a class Car with the following properties. A car has a certain fuel efficiency (measured in miles/gallon) and a certain amount of fuel in the gas tank. The efficiency is specified in the constructor, and the initial fuel level is 0. Supply a method drive that simulates driving the car for a certain distance, reducing the fuel level in the gas tank, and methods getGas-Level, to return the current fuel level, and addGas, to tank up. Sample usage:

```
Car myHybrid = new Car(50); // 50 miles per gallon
myHybrid.addGas(20); // Tank 20 gallons
myHybrid.drive(100); // Drive 100 miles
System.out.println(myHybrid.getGasLevel()); // Print fuel remaining
```

**■■ P8.7** Implement a class Student. For the purpose of this exercise, a student has a name and a total quiz score. Supply an appropriate constructor and methods getName(), addQuiz(int score), getTotalScore(), and getAverageScore(). To compute the latter, you also need to store the *number of quizzes* that the student took.

**■■ P8.8** Modify the Student class of Exercise P8.7 to compute grade point averages. Methods are needed to add a grade and get the current GPA. Specify grades as elements of a class Grade. Supply a constructor that constructs a grade from a string, such as "B+". You will also need a method that translates grades into their numeric values (for example, "B+" becomes 3.3).

**■■■ P8.9** Declare a class ComboLock that works like the combination lock in a gym locker, as shown here. The lock is constructed with a combination—three numbers between 0 and 39. The reset method resets the dial so that it points to 0. The turnLeft and turnRight methods turn the dial by a given number of ticks to the left or right. The open method attempts to open the lock. The lock opens if the user first turned it right to the first number in the combination, then left to the second, and then right to the third.

```
public class ComboLock
{
    . . .
    public ComboLock(int secret1, int secret2, int secret3) { . . . }
    public void reset() { . . . }
    public void turnLeft(int ticks) { . . . }
    public void turnRight(int ticks) { . . . }
    public boolean open() { . . . }
}
```

**■■ P8.10** Implement a VotingMachine class that can be used for a simple election. Have methods to clear the machine state, to vote for a Democrat, to vote for a Republican, and to get the tallies for both parties.

**■■ P8.11** Provide a class for authoring a simple letter. In the constructor, supply the names of the sender and the recipient:

```
public Letter(String from, String to)
```

Supply a method

```
public void addLine(String line)
```

to add a line of text to the body of the letter. Supply a method

```
public String getText()
```

that returns the entire text of the letter. The text has the form:

> Dear *recipient name*:
> *blank line*
> *first line of the body*
> *second line of the body*
> . . .

*last line of the body*
*blank line*
Sincerely,
*blank line*
*sender name*

Also supply a main method that prints this letter.

```
Dear John:

I am sorry we must part.
I wish you all the best.

Sincerely,

Mary
```

Construct an object of the Letter class and call addLine twice.

■■ **P8.12** Write a class Bug that models a bug moving along a horizontal line. The bug moves either to the right or left. Initially, the bug moves to the right, but it can turn to change its direction. In each move, its position changes by one unit in the current direction. Provide a constructor

```
public Bug(int initialPosition)
```

and methods

- public void turn()
- public void move()
- public int getPosition()

Sample usage:

```
Bug bugsy = new Bug(10);
bugsy.move(); // Now the position is 11
bugsy.turn();
bugsy.move(); // Now the position is 10
```

Your main method should construct a bug, make it move and turn a few times, and print the actual and expected positions.

■■ **P8.13** Implement a class Moth that models a moth flying in a straight line. The moth has a position, the distance from a fixed origin. When the moth moves toward a point of light, its new position is halfway between its old position and the position of the light source. Supply a constructor

```
public Moth(double initialPosition)
```

and methods

- public void moveToLight(double lightPosition)
- public void getPosition()

Your main method should construct a moth, move it toward a couple of light sources, and check that the moth's position is as expected.

■■■ **P8.14** Write static methods

- public static double sphereVolume(double r)
- public static double sphereSurface(double r)
- public static double cylinderVolume(double r, double h)
- public static double cylinderSurface(double r, double h)

- `public static double coneVolume(double r, double h)`
- `public static double coneSurface(double r, double h)`

that compute the volume and surface area of a sphere with a radius r, a cylinder with a circular base with radius r and height h, and a cone with a circular base with radius r and height h. Place them into a class Geometry. Then write a program that prompts the user for the values of r and h, calls the six methods, and prints the results.

**■■ P8.15** Solve Exercise P8.14 by implementing classes Sphere, Cylinder, and Cone. Which approach is more object-oriented?

**■■ Business P8.16** Reimplement the CashRegister class so that it keeps track of the price of each added item in an ArrayList<Double>. Remove the itemCount and totalPrice instance variables. Reimplement the clear, addItem, getTotal, and getCount methods. Add a method displayAll that displays the prices of all items in the current sale.

**■■ Business P8.17** Reimplement the CashRegister class so that it keeps track of the total price as an integer: the total cents of the price. For example, instead of storing 17.29, store the integer 1729. Such an implementation is commonly used because it avoids the accumulation of roundoff errors. Do not change the public interface of the class.

**■■ Business P8.18** After closing time, the store manager would like to know how much business was transacted during the day. Modify the CashRegister class to enable this functionality. Supply methods getSalesTotal and getSalesCount to get the total amount of all sales and the number of sales. Supply a method resetSales that resets any counters and totals so that the next day's sales start from zero.

**■■ Business P8.19** Implement a class Portfolio. This class has two objects, checking and savings, of the type BankAccount that was developed in Worked Example 8.1 (ch08/worked_example_1/BankAccount.java in your code files). Implement four methods:

- `public void deposit(double amount, String account)`
- `public void withdraw(double amount, String account)`
- `public void transfer(double amount, String account)`
- `public double getBalance(String account)`

Here the account string is "S" or "C". For the deposit or withdrawal, it indicates which account is affected. For a transfer, it indicates the account from which the money is taken; the money is automatically transferred to the other account.

**■■ Business P8.20** Design and implement a class Country that stores the name of the country, its population, and its area. Then write a program that reads in a set of countries and prints

- The country with the largest area.
- The country with the largest population.
- The country with the largest population density (people per square kilometer (or mile)).

**■■ Business P8.21** Design a class Message that models an e-mail message. A message has a recipient, a sender, and a message text. Support the following methods:

- A constructor that takes the sender and recipient
- A method append that appends a line of text to the message body
- A method toString that makes the message into one long string like this: "From: Harry Morgan\nTo: Rudolf Reindeer\n . . ."

Write a program that uses this class to make a message and print it.

■■ **Business P8.22** Design a class `Mailbox` that stores e-mail messages, using the `Message` class of Exercise P8.21. Implement the following methods:

- `public void addMessage(Message m)`
- `public Message getMessage(int i)`
- `public void removeMessage(int i)`

■■ **Business P8.23** Design a `Customer` class to handle a customer loyalty marketing campaign. After accumulating $100 in purchases, the customer receives a $10 discount on the next purchase. Provide methods

- `void makePurchase(double amount)`
- `boolean discountReached()`

Provide a test program and test a scenario in which a customer has earned a discount and then made over $90, but less than $100 in purchases. This should not result in a second discount. Then add another purchase that results in the second discount.

■■■ **Business P8.24** The Downtown Marketing Association wants to promote downtown shopping with a loyalty program similar to the one in Exercise P8.23. Shops are identified by a number between 1 and 20. Add a new parameter variable to the `makePurchase` method that indicates the shop. The discount is awarded if a customer makes purchases in at least three different shops, spending a total of $100 or more.

■■■ **Science P8.25** Design a class `Cannonball` to model a cannonball that is fired into the air. A ball has

- An $x$- and a $y$-position.
- An $x$- and a $y$-velocity.

Supply the following methods:

- A constructor with an $x$-position (the $y$-position is initially 0)
- A method `move(double sec)` that moves the ball to the next position (First compute the distance traveled in sec seconds, using the current velocities, then update the $x$- and $y$-positions; then update the $y$-velocity by taking into account the gravitational acceleration of $-9.81$ m/s$^2$; the $x$-velocity is unchanged.)
- Methods `getX` and `getY` that get the current location of the cannonball
- A method `shoot` whose arguments are the angle $\alpha$ and initial velocity $v$ (Compute the $x$-velocity as $v \cos \alpha$ and the $y$-velocity as $v \sin \alpha$; then keep calling `move` with a time interval of 0.1 seconds until the $y$-position is 0; call `getX` and `getY` after every move and display the position.)

Use this class in a program that prompts the user for the starting angle and the initial velocity. Then call `shoot`.

■■ **Science P8.26** The colored bands on the top-most resistor shown in the photo below indicate a resistance of 6.2 k$\Omega$ ±5 percent. The resistor tolerance of ±5 percent indicates the acceptable variation in the resistance. A 6.2 k$\Omega$ ±5 percent resistor could have a resistance as small as 5.89 k$\Omega$ or as large as 6.51 k$\Omega$. We say that 6.2 k$\Omega$ is the *nominal value* of the resistance and that the actual value of the resistance can be any value between 5.89 k$\Omega$ and 6.51 k$\Omega$.

Write a program that represents a resistor as a class. Provide a single constructor that accepts values for the nominal resistance and tolerance and then determines the actual value randomly. The class should provide public methods to get the nominal resistance, tolerance, and the actual resistance.

Write a `main` method for the program that demonstrates that the class works properly by displaying actual resistances for ten 330 Ω ±10 percent resistors.

■■ **Science P8.27**   In the `Resistor` class from Exercise P8.26, supply a method that returns a description of the "color bands" for the resistance and tolerance. A resistor has four color bands:

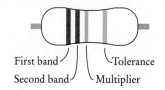

First band / Second band / Tolerance / Multiplier

- The first band is the first significant digit of the resistance value.
- The second band is the second significant digit of the resistance value.
- The third band is the decimal multiplier.
- The fourth band indicates the tolerance.

| Color | Digit | Multiplier | Tolerance |
|---|---|---|---|
| Black | 0 | $\times 10^0$ | — |
| Brown | 1 | $\times 10^1$ | ±1% |
| Red | 2 | $\times 10^2$ | ±2% |
| Orange | 3 | $\times 10^3$ | — |
| Yellow | 4 | $\times 10^4$ | — |
| Green | 5 | $\times 10^5$ | ±0.5% |
| Blue | 6 | $\times 10^6$ | ±0.25% |
| Violet | 7 | $\times 10^7$ | ±0.1% |
| Gray | 8 | $\times 10^8$ | ±0.05% |
| White | 9 | $\times 10^9$ | — |
| Gold | — | $\times 10^{-1}$ | ±5% |
| Silver | — | $\times 10^{-2}$ | ±10% |
| None | — | — | ±20% |

For example (using the values from the table as a key), a resistor with red, violet, green, and gold bands (left to right) will have 2 as the first digit, 7 as the second digit, a multiplier of $10^5$, and a tolerance of ±5 percent, for a resistance of 2,700 kΩ, plus or minus 5 percent.

■■■ **Science P8.28** The figure below shows a frequently used electric circuit called a "voltage divider". The input to the circuit is the voltage $v_i$. The output is the voltage $v_o$. The output of a voltage divider is proportional to the input, and the constant of proportionality is called the "gain" of the circuit. The voltage divider is represented by the equation

$$G = \frac{v_o}{v_i} = \frac{R_2}{R_1 + R_2}$$

where $G$ is the gain and $R_1$ and $R_2$ are the resistances of the two resistors that comprise the voltage divider.

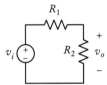

Manufacturing variations cause the actual resistance values to deviate from the nominal values, as described in Exercise P8.26. In turn, variations in the resistance values cause variations in the values of the gain of the voltage divider. We calculate the *nominal value of the gain* using the nominal resistance values and the *actual value of the gain* using actual resistance values.

Write a program that contains two classes, VoltageDivider and Resistor. The Resistor class is described in Exercise P8.26. The VoltageDivider class should have two instance variables that are objects of the Resistor class. Provide a single constructor that accepts two Resistor objects, nominal values for their resistances, and the resistor tolerance. The class should provide public methods to get the nominal and actual values of the voltage divider's gain.

Write a main method for the program that demonstrates that the class works properly by displaying nominal and actual gain for ten voltage dividers each consisting of 5% resistors having nominal values $R_1 = 250\ \Omega$ and $R_2 = 750\ \Omega$.

## ANSWERS TO SELF-CHECK QUESTIONS

1. No—the object "Hello, World" belongs to the String class, and the String class has no println method.

2. Through the substring and charAt methods.

3. As an ArrayList<Character>. As a char array.

4. None. The methods will have the same effect, and your code could not have manipulated String objects in any other way.

5. ```
public void reset()
{
    value = 0;
}
```

6. ```
public int getValue()
{
```

```
    return strokes.length();
}
```

7. None—the public interface has not changed.

8. You cannot access the instance variables directly. You must use the methods provided by the Clock class.

9. 2 1.90

10. There is no method named getAmountDue.

11. `public int getDollars();`

12. length, substring. In fact, all methods of the String class are accessors.

13. A mutator. Getting the next number removes it from the input, thereby modifying it. Not

convinced? Consider what happens if you call the `nextInt` method twice. You will usually get two different numbers. But if you call an accessor twice on an object (without a mutation between the two calls), you are sure to get the same result.

14. 
```java
/**
    This class models a tally counter.
*/
public class Counter
{
    private int value;

    /**
        Gets the current value of this counter.
        @return the current value
    */
    public int getValue()
    {
        return value;
    }

    /**
        Advances the value of this counter by 1.
    */
    public void count()
    {
        value = value + 1;
    }
```

15. The code tries to access a private instance variable.

16. (1) `int hours; // Between 1 and 12`
`int minutes; // Between 0 and 59`
`boolean pm; // True for P.M., false for A.M.`

    (2) `int hours; // Military time, between 0 and 23`
`int minutes; // Between 0 and 59`

    (3) `int totalMinutes // Between 0 and 60 * 24 - 1`

17. They need not change their programs at all because the public interface has not changed. They need to recompile with the new version of the `Time` class.

18. (1) `String letterGrade; // "A+", "B"`

    (2) `double numberGrade; // 4.3, 3.0`

19. `2 1.85 1 1.90`

20. 
```java
public int getDollars()
{
    int dollars = (int) totalPrice;
        // Truncates cents
    return dollars;
}
```

21. Three parameters: two explicit parameters of type `int`, and one implicit parameter of type `String`.

22. One parameter: the implicit parameter of type `String`. The method has no explicit parameters.

23. `"Morgan, Harry"`

24. `public Person() { name = "unknown"; }`

25. A constructor is generated that has the same effect as the constructor provided in this section. It sets both instance variables to zero.

26. 
```java
public Item()
{
    price = 0;
    description = "";
}
```

    The `price` instance variable need not be initialized because it is set to zero by default, but it is clearer to initialize it explicitly.

27. (a) `Item(String)` (b) `Item(double)`
(c) `Item(String, double)` (d) `Item()`
(e) No constructor has been called.

28. Add these lines:
```java
register1.clear();
System.out.println(register1.getCount());
System.out.println("Expected: 0");
System.out.printf("%.2f\n",
    register1.getTotal());
System.out.println("Expected: 0.00");
```

29. `1, 0`

30. These environments allow you to call methods on an object without creating a `main` method.

31.

```
Car myCar

Car(mpg)
addGas(amount)
drive(distance)
getGasLeft
```

*front*

| gasLeft | milesPerGallon |
|---------|----------------|
| 0       | 25             |

*back*

**32.**

| gasLeft | milesPerGallon |
|---------|----------------|
| ~~0~~ | 25 |
| ~~20~~ | |
| ~~16~~ | |
| ~~8~~ | |
| 13 | |

**33.**

| gasLeft | milesPerGallon | totalMiles |
|---------|----------------|------------|
| 0 | 25 | 0 |

**34.**

| gasLeft | milesPerGallon | totalMiles |
|---------|----------------|------------|
| ~~0~~ | 25 | 0 |
| ~~20~~ | | |
| ~~16~~ | | 100 |
| ~~8~~ | | 300 |
| 13 | | |

**35.** It needs to be incremented in the deposit and withdraw methods. There also needs to be some method to reset it after the end of a statement period.

**36.** The ArrayList<String> instance variable is private, and the class users cannot acccess it.

**37.** Add an ArrayList<Double> prices. In the addItem method, add the current price. In the reset method, replace the array list with an empty one. Also supply a method printReceipt that prints the prices.

**38.** The tax ID of an employee does not change, and no setter method should be supplied. The salary of an employee can change, and both getter and setter methods should be supplied.

**39.** It is an example of the "state pattern" described in Section 8.9.5. The direction is a state that changes when the bug turns, and it affects how the bug moves.

**40.** Both greeting and greeting2 refer to the same string "Hello".

**41.** They both still refer to the string "Hello". The toUpperCase method computes the string "HELLO", but it is not a mutator—the original string is unchanged.

**42.** (a) 0

(b) A null pointer exception is thrown.

**43.** It is a reference of type String.

**44.**
```
public void addItems(int quantity, double price)
{
    for (int i = 1; i <= quantity; i++)
    {
        this.addItem(price);
    }
}
```

**45.** System.in and System.out

**46.** Math.PI

**47.** The method needs no data of any object. The only required input is the values argument.

**48.** Yes, it works. Static methods can call each other and access static variables—any method can. But it is a terrible idea. A program that consists of a single class with many methods is hard to understand.

# CHAPTER 9

# INHERITANCE AND INTERFACES

## CHAPTER GOALS

To learn about inheritance

To implement subclasses that inherit and override superclass methods

To understand the concept of polymorphism

To be familiar with the common superclass Object and its methods

To work with interface types

## CHAPTER CONTENTS

Objects from related classes usually share common behavior. For example, shovels, rakes, and clippers all perform gardening tasks. In this chapter, you will learn how the notion of inheritance expresses the relationship between specialized and general classes. By using inheritance, you will be able to share code between classes and provide services that can be used by multiple classes.

# 9.1 Inheritance Hierarchies

**A subclass inherits data and behavior from a superclass.**

In object-oriented design, **inheritance** is a relationship between a more general class (called the **superclass**) and a more specialized class (called the **subclass**). The subclass inherits data and behavior from the superclass. For example, consider the relationships between different kinds of vehicles depicted in Figure 1.

Every car *is a* vehicle. Cars share the common traits of all vehicles, such as the ability to transport people from one place to another. We say that the class Car inherits from the class Vehicle. In this relationship, the Vehicle class is the superclass and the Car class is the subclass. In Figure 2, the superclass and subclass are joined with an arrow that points to the superclass.

**You can always use a subclass object in place of a superclass object.**

Suppose we have an algorithm that manipulates a Vehicle object. Because a car is a special kind of vehicle, we can use a Car object in such an algorithm, and it will work correctly. The **substitution principle** states that you can always use a subclass object when a superclass object is expected. For example, consider a method that takes an argument of type Vehicle:

```
void processVehicle(Vehicle v)
```

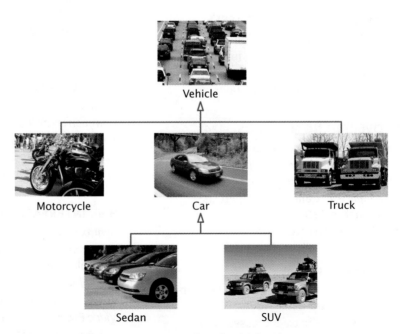

**Figure 1** An Inheritance Hierarchy of Vehicle Classes

**Figure 2**
An Inheritance Diagram

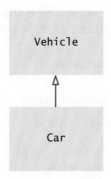

Because Car is a subclass of Vehicle, you can call that method with a Car object:

```
Car myCar = new Car(. . .);
processVehicle(myCar);
```

Why provide a method that processes Vehicle objects instead of Car objects? That method is more useful because it can handle *any* kind of vehicle (including Truck and Motorcycle objects). In general, when we group classes into an inheritance hierarchy, we can share common code among the classes.

In this chapter, we will consider a simple hierarchy of classes. Most likely, you have taken computer-graded quizzes. A quiz consists of questions, and there are different kinds of questions:

- Fill-in-the-blank
- Choice (single or multiple)
- Numeric (where an approximate answer is ok; e.g., 1.33 when the actual answer is 4/3)
- Free response

*We will develop a simple but flexible quiz-taking program to illustrate inheritance.*

Figure 3 shows an inheritance hierarchy for these question types.

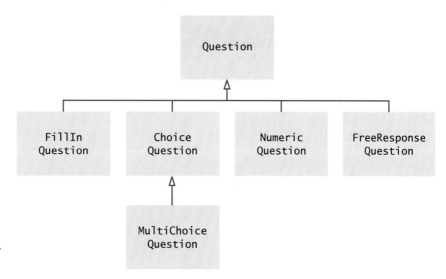

**Figure 3**
Inheritance Hierarchy
of Question Types

At the root of this hierarchy is the `Question` type. A question can display its text, and it can check whether a given response is a correct answer.

**section_1/Question.java**

```java
 1  /**
 2     A question with a text and an answer.
 3  */
 4  public class Question
 5  {
 6     private String text;
 7     private String answer;
 8
 9     /**
10        Constructs a question with empty question and answer.
11     */
12     public Question()
13     {
14        text = "";
15        answer = "";
16     }
17
18     /**
19        Sets the question text.
20        @param questionText the text of this question
21     */
22     public void setText(String questionText)
23     {
24        text = questionText;
25     }
26
27     /**
28        Sets the answer for this question.
29        @param correctResponse the answer
30     */
31     public void setAnswer(String correctResponse)
32     {
33        answer = correctResponse;
34     }
35
36     /**
37        Checks a given response for correctness.
38        @param response the response to check
39        @return true if the response was correct, false otherwise
40     */
41     public boolean checkAnswer(String response)
42     {
43        return response.equals(answer);
44     }
45
46     /**
47        Displays this question.
48     */
49     public void display()
50     {
51        System.out.println(text);
52     }
53  }
```

This question class is very basic. It does not handle multiple-choice questions, numeric questions, and so on. In the following sections, you will see how to form subclasses of the Question class.

Here is a simple test program for the Question class:

### section_1/QuestionDemo1.java

```java
1   import java.util.ArrayList;
2   import java.util.Scanner;
3
4   /**
5      This program shows a simple quiz with one question.
6   */
7   public class QuestionDemo1
8   {
9      public static void main(String[] args)
10     {
11        Scanner in = new Scanner(System.in);
12
13        Question q = new Question();
14        q.setText("Who was the inventor of Java?");
15        q.setAnswer("James Gosling");
16
17        q.display();
18        System.out.print("Your answer: ");
19        String response = in.nextLine();
20        System.out.println(q.checkAnswer(response));
21     }
22  }
```

### Program Run

```
Who was the inventor of Java?
Your answer: James Gosling
true
```

**SELF CHECK**

1. Consider classes Manager and Employee. Which should be the superclass and which should be the subclass?

2. What are the inheritance relationships between classes BankAccount, Checking-Account, and SavingsAccount?

3. Figure 7.2 shows an inheritance diagram of exception classes in Java. List all superclasses of the class RuntimeException.

4. Consider the method doSomething(Car c). List all vehicle classes from Figure 1 whose objects *cannot* be passed to this method.

5. Should a class Quiz inherit from the class Question? Why or why not?

**Practice It**   Now you can try these exercises at the end of the chapter: R9.1, R9.7, R9.9.

### Use a Single Class for Variation in Values, Inheritance for Variation in Behavior

The purpose of inheritance is to model objects with different *behavior*. When students first learn about inheritance, they have a tendency to overuse it, by creating multiple classes even though the variation could be expressed with a simple instance variable.

Consider a program that tracks the fuel efficiency of a fleet of cars by logging the distance traveled and the refueling amounts. Some cars in the fleet are hybrids. Should you create a subclass HybridCar? Not in this application. Hybrids don't behave any differently than other cars when it comes to driving and refueling. They just have a better fuel efficiency. A single Car class with an instance variable

```
double milesPerGallon;
```

is entirely sufficient.

However, if you write a program that shows how to repair different kinds of vehicles, then it makes sense to have a separate class HybridCar. When it comes to repairs, hybrid cars behave differently from other cars.

# 9.2 Implementing Subclasses

In this section, you will see how to form a subclass and how a subclass automatically inherits functionality from its superclass.

Suppose you want to write a program that handles questions such as the following:

```
In which country was the inventor of Java born?
1. Australia
2. Canada
3. Denmark
4. United States
```

You could write a ChoiceQuestion class from scratch, with methods to set up the question, display it, and check the answer. But you don't have to. Instead, use inheritance and implement ChoiceQuestion as a subclass of the Question class (see Figure 4).

In Java, you form a subclass by specifying what makes the subclass different from its superclass.

> A subclass inherits all methods that it does not override.

Subclass objects automatically have the instance variables that are declared in the superclass. You only declare instance variables that are not part of the superclass objects.

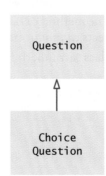

**Figure 4**
The ChoiceQuestion Class is a Subclass of the Question Class

*Like the manufacturer of a stretch limo, who starts with a regular car and modifies it, a programmer makes a subclass by modifying another class.*

A subclass can override a superclass method by providing a new implementation.

The subclass inherits all public methods from the superclass. You declare any methods that are *new* to the subclass, and *change* the implementation of inherited methods if the inherited behavior is not appropriate. When you supply a new implementation for an inherited method, you **override** the method.

A ChoiceQuestion object differs from a Question object in three ways:

- Its objects store the various choices for the answer.
- There is a method for adding answer choices.
- The display method of the ChoiceQuestion class shows these choices so that the respondent can choose one of them.

When the ChoiceQuestion class inherits from the Question class, it needs to spell out these three differences:

```
public class ChoiceQuestion extends Question
{
    // This instance variable is added to the subclass
    private ArrayList<String> choices;

    // This method is added to the subclass
    public void addChoice(String choice, boolean correct) { . . . }

    // This method overrides a method from the superclass
    public void display() { . . . }
}
```

The extends reserved word indicates that a class inherits from a superclass.

The reserved word extends denotes inheritance.

Figure 5 shows the layout of a ChoiceQuestion object. It has the text and answer instance variables that are declared in the Question superclass, and it adds an additional instance variable, choices.

The addChoice method is specific to the ChoiceQuestion class. You can only apply it to ChoiceQuestion objects, not general Question objects.

In contrast, the display method is a method that already exists in the superclass. The subclass overrides this method, so that the choices can be properly displayed.

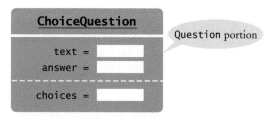

**Figure 5** Data Layout of Subclass Object

## Syntax 9.1 Subclass Declaration

*Syntax*
```
public class SubclassName extends SuperclassName
{
    instance variables
    methods
}
```

The reserved word extends denotes inheritance.

**Declare instance variables that are added to the subclass.**

**Declare methods that are added to the subclass.**

**Declare methods that the subclass overrides.**

*Subclass* / *Superclass*

```
public class ChoiceQuestion extends Question
{
    private ArrayList<String> choices

    public void addChoice(String choice, boolean correct) { . . . }

    public void display() { . . . }
}
```

All other methods of the Question class are automatically inherited by the Choice-Question class.

You can call the inherited methods on a subclass object:

```
choiceQuestion.setAnswer("2");
```

However, the private instance variables of the superclass are inaccessible. Because these variables are private data of the superclass, only the superclass has access to them. The subclass has no more access rights than any other class.

In particular, the ChoiceQuestion methods cannot directly access the instance variable answer. These methods must use the public interface of the Question class to access its private data, just like every other method.

To illustrate this point, let's implement the addChoice method. The method has two arguments: the choice to be added (which is appended to the list of choices), and a Boolean value to indicate whether this choice is correct. For example,

```
question.addChoice("Canada", true);
```

The first argument is added to the choices variable. If the second argument is true, then the answer instance variable becomes the number of the current choice. For example, if choices.size() is 2, then answer is set to the string "2".

```
public void addChoice(String choice, boolean correct)
{
    choices.add(choice);
    if (correct)
    {
        // Convert choices.size() to string
        String choiceString = "" + choices.size();
        setAnswer(choiceString);
    }
}
```

You can't just access the answer variable in the superclass. Fortunately, the Question class has a setAnswer method. You can call that method. On which object? The question that you are currently modifying—that is, the implicit parameter of the ChoiceQuestion.addChoice method. As you saw in Chapter 8, if you invoke a method on the implicit parameter, you don't have to specify the implicit parameter and can write just the method name:

```
setAnswer(choiceString);
```

If you prefer, you can make it clear that the method is executed on the implicit parameter:

```
this.setAnswer(choiceString);
```

**SELF CHECK**

**6.** Suppose q is an object of the class Question and cq an object of the class ChoiceQuestion. Which of the following calls are legal?

   **a.** q.setAnswer(response)

   **b.** cq.setAnswer(response)

   **c.** q.addChoice(choice, true)

   **d.** cq.addChoice(choice, true)

**7.** Suppose the class Employee is declared as follows:

```
public class Employee
{
    private String name;
    private double baseSalary;

    public void setName(String newName) { . . . }
    public void setBaseSalary(double newSalary) { . . . }
    public String getName() { . . . }
    public double getSalary() { . . . }
}
```

Declare a class Manager that inherits from the class Employee and adds an instance variable bonus for storing a salary bonus. Omit constructors and methods.

**8.** Which instance variables does the Manager class from Self Check 7 have?

**9.** In the Manager class, provide the method header (but not the implementation) for a method that overrides the getSalary method from the class Employee.

**10.** Which methods does the Manager class from Self Check 9 inherit?

**Practice It**   Now you can try these exercises at the end of the chapter: R9.3, P9.6, P9.10.

**Common Error 9.1**

### Replicating Instance Variables from the Superclass

A subclass has no access to the private instance variables of the superclass.

```
public ChoiceQuestion(String questionText)
{
    text = questionText; // Error—tries to access private superclass variable
}
```

When faced with a compiler error, beginners commonly "solve" this issue by adding *another* instance variable with the same name to the subclass:

```
public class ChoiceQuestion extends Question
{
```

```
            private ArrayList<String> choices;
            private String text; // Don't!
            . . .
      }
```

Sure, now the constructor compiles, but it doesn't set the correct text! Such a ChoiceQuestion object has two instance variables, both named text. The constructor sets one of them, and the display method displays the other.

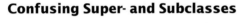

**ChoiceQuestion**

text =
answer =

choices =
text =

Question portion

### Confusing Super- and Subclasses

If you compare an object of type ChoiceQuestion with an object of type Question, you find that

- The reserved word extends suggests that the ChoiceQuestion object is an extended version of a Question.
- The ChoiceQuestion object is larger; it has an added instance variable, choices.
- The ChoiceQuestion object is more capable; it has an addChoice method.

It seems a superior object in every way. So why is ChoiceQuestion called the *subclass* and Question the *superclass*?

The *super/sub* terminology comes from set theory. Look at the set of all questions. Not all of them are ChoiceQuestion objects; some of them are other kinds of questions. Therefore, the set of ChoiceQuestion objects is a *subset* of the set of all Question objects, and the set of Question objects is a *superset* of the set of ChoiceQuestion objects. The more specialized objects in the subset have a richer state and more capabilities.

# 9.3 Overriding Methods

An overriding method can extend or replace the functionality of the superclass method.

The subclass inherits the methods from the superclass. If you are not satisfied with the behavior of an inherited method, you *override* it by specifying a new implementation in the subclass.

Consider the display method of the ChoiceQuestion class. It overrides the superclass display method in order to show the choices for the answer. This method *extends* the functionality of the superclass version. This means that the subclass method carries out the action of the superclass method (in our case, displaying the question text), and it also does some additional work (in our case, displaying the choices). In other cases, a subclass method *replaces* the functionality of a superclass method, implementing an entirely different behavior.

Let us turn to the implementation of the display method of the ChoiceQuestion class. The method needs to

- Display the question text.
- Display the answer choices.

The second part is easy because the answer choices are an instance variable of the subclass.

```java
public class ChoiceQuestion
{
   . . .
   public void display()
   {
      // Display the question text
      . . .
      // Display the answer choices
      for (int i = 0; i < choices.size(); i++)
      {
         int choiceNumber = i + 1;
         System.out.println(choiceNumber + ": " + choices.get(i));
      }
   }
}
```

But how do you get the question text? You can't access the text variable of the super-class directly because it is private.

Instead, you can call the `display` method of the superclass, by using the reserved word super:

Use the reserved word super to call a superclass method.

```java
public void display()
{
   // Display the question text
   super.display(); // OK
   // Display the answer choices
   . . .
}
```

If you omit the reserved word super, then the method will not work as intended.

ANIMATION
*Inheritance*

```java
public void display()
{
   // Display the question text
   display(); // Error—invokes this.display()
   . . .
}
```

Because the implicit parameter this is of type ChoiceQuestion, and there is a method named display in the ChoiceQuestion class, that method will be called—but that is just the method you are currently writing! The method would call itself over and over.

Here is the complete program that lets you take a quiz consisting of two Choice-Question objects. We construct both objects and pass them to a method presentQuestion. That method displays the question to the user and checks whether the user response is correct.

### section_3/QuestionDemo2.java

```java
1  import java.util.Scanner;
2
3  /**
4     This program shows a simple quiz with two choice questions.
5  */
6  public class QuestionDemo2
7  {
8     public static void main(String[] args)
9     {
```

```
10        ChoiceQuestion first = new ChoiceQuestion();
11        first.setText("What was the original name of the Java language?");
12        first.addChoice("*7", false);
13        first.addChoice("Duke", false);
14        first.addChoice("Oak", true);
15        first.addChoice("Gosling", false);
16
17        ChoiceQuestion second = new ChoiceQuestion();
18        second.setText("In which country was the inventor of Java born?");
19        second.addChoice("Australia", false);
20        second.addChoice("Canada", true);
21        second.addChoice("Denmark", false);
22        second.addChoice("United States", false);
23
24        presentQuestion(first);
25        presentQuestion(second);
26    }
27
28    /**
29        Presents a question to the user and checks the response.
30        @param q the question
31    */
32    public static void presentQuestion(ChoiceQuestion q)
33    {
34        q.display();
35        System.out.print("Your answer: ");
36        Scanner in = new Scanner(System.in);
37        String response = in.nextLine();
38        System.out.println(q.checkAnswer(response));
39    }
40 }
```

## section_3/ChoiceQuestion.java

```
1  import java.util.ArrayList;
2
3  /**
4      A question with multiple choices.
5  */
6  public class ChoiceQuestion extends Question
7  {
8      private ArrayList<String> choices;
9
10     /**
11         Constructs a choice question with no choices.
12     */
13     public ChoiceQuestion()
14     {
15         choices = new ArrayList<String>();
16     }
17
18     /**
19         Adds an answer choice to this question.
20         @param choice the choice to add
21         @param correct true if this is the correct choice, false otherwise
22     */
23     public void addChoice(String choice, boolean correct)
24     {
```

```
25          choices.add(choice);
26          if (correct)
27          {
28             // Convert choices.size() to string
29             String choiceString = "" + choices.size();
30             setAnswer(choiceString);
31          }
32       }
33
34       public void display()
35       {
36          // Display the question text
37          super.display();
38          // Display the answer choices
39          for (int i = 0; i < choices.size(); i++)
40          {
41             int choiceNumber = i + 1;
42             System.out.println(choiceNumber + ": " + choices.get(i));
43          }
44       }
45    }
```

**Program Run**

```
What was the original name of the Java language?
1: *7
2: Duke
3: Oak
4: Gosling
Your answer: *7
false
In which country was the inventor of Java born?
1: Australia
2: Canada
3: Denmark
4: United States
Your answer: 2
true
```

**SELF CHECK**

**11.** What is wrong with the following implementation of the display method?

```
public class ChoiceQuestion
{
   . . .
   public void display()
   {
      System.out.println(text);
      for (int i = 0; i < choices.size(); i++)
      {
         int choiceNumber = i + 1;
         System.out.println(choiceNumber + ": " + choices.get(i));
      }
   }
}
```

**12.** What is wrong with the following implementation of the display method?

```
public class ChoiceQuestion
{
```

```
 . . .
public void display()
{
   this.display();
   for (int i = 0; i < choices.size(); i++)
   {
      int choiceNumber = i + 1;
      System.out.println(choiceNumber + ": " + choices.get(i));
   }
}
}
```

13. Look again at the implementation of the addChoice method that calls the setAnswer method of the superclass. Why don't you need to call super.setAnswer?

14. In the Manager class of Self Check 7, override the getName method so that managers have a * before their name (such as *Lin, Sally).

15. In the Manager class of Self Check 9, override the getSalary method so that it returns the sum of the salary and the bonus.

**Practice It**    Now you can try these exercises at the end of the chapter: P9.1, P9.2, P9.11.

---

Common Error 9.3

### Accidental Overloading

In Java, two methods can have the same name, provided they differ in their parameter types. For example, the PrintStream class has methods called println with headers

```
void println(int x)
```

and

```
void println(String x)
```

These are different methods, each with its own implementation. The Java compiler considers them to be completely unrelated. We say that the println name is **overloaded**. This is different from overriding, where a subclass method provides an implementation of a method whose parameter variables have the *same* types.

If you mean to override a method but use a parameter variable with a different type, then you accidentally introduce an overloaded method. For example,

```
public class ChoiceQuestion extends Question
{
   . . .
   public void display(PrintStream out)
   // Does not override void display()
   {
      . . .
   }
}
```

The compiler will not complain. It thinks that you want to provide a method just for Print-Stream arguments, while inheriting another method void display().

When overriding a method, be sure to check that the types of the parameter variables match exactly.

## Forgetting to Use super When Invoking a Superclass Method

A common error in extending the functionality of a superclass method is to forget the reserved word super. For example, to compute the salary of a manager, get the salary of the underlying Employee object and add a bonus:

```
public class Manager
{
    . . .
    public double getSalary()
    {
        double baseSalary = getSalary();
            // Error: should be super.getSalary()
        return baseSalary + bonus;
    }
}
```

Here getSalary() refers to the getSalary method applied to the implicit parameter of the method. The implicit parameter is of type Manager, and there is a getSalary method in the Manager class. Calling that method is a recursive call, which will never stop. Instead, you must tell the compiler to invoke the superclass method.

Whenever you call a superclass method from a subclass method with the same name, be sure to use the reserved word super.

## Calling the Superclass Constructor

Consider the process of constructing a subclass object. A subclass constructor can only initialize the instance variables of the subclass. But the superclass instance variables also need to be initialized. Unless you specify otherwise, the superclass instance variables are initialized with the constructor of the superclass that has no arguments.

> Unless specified otherwise, the subclass constructor calls the superclass constructor with no arguments.

In order to specify another constructor, you use the super reserved word, together with the arguments of the superclass constructor, as the *first statement* of the subclass constructor.

For example, suppose the Question superclass had a constructor for setting the question text. Here is how a subclass constructor could call that superclass constructor:

> To call a superclass constructor, use the super reserved word in the first statement of the subclass constructor.

```
public ChoiceQuestion(String questionText)
{
    super(questionText);
    choices = new ArrayList<String>();
}
```

In our example program, we used the superclass constructor with no arguments. However, if all superclass constructors have arguments, you must use the super syntax and provide the arguments for a superclass constructor.

> The constructor of a subclass can pass arguments to a superclass constructor, using the reserved word super.

When the reserved word super is followed by a parenthesis, it indicates a call to the superclass constructor. When used in this way, the constructor call must be *the first statement of the subclass constructor*. If super is followed by a period and a method name, on the other hand, it indicates a call to a superclass method, as you saw in the preceding section. Such a call can be made anywhere in any subclass method.

Syntax 9.2    Constructor with Superclass Initializer

> *Syntax*    public *ClassName*(*parameterType parameterName*, . . .)
> {
>     super(*arguments*);
>     . . .
> }

**The superclass constructor is called first.**

```
public ChoiceQuestion(String questionText)
{
    super(questionText);
    choices = new ArrayList<String>;
}
```

*If you omit the superclass constructor call, the superclass constructor with no arguments is invoked.*

**The constructor body can contain additional statements.**

# 9.4 Polymorphism

In this section, you will learn how to use inheritance for processing objects of different types in the same program.

Consider our first sample program. It presented two Question objects to the user. The second sample program presented two ChoiceQuestion objects. Can we write a program that shows a mixture of both question types?

With inheritance, this goal is very easy to realize. In order to present a question to the user, we need not know the exact type of the question. We just display the question and check whether the user supplied the correct answer. The Question superclass has methods for this purpose. Therefore, we can simply declare the parameter variable of the presentQuestion method to have the type Question:

```
public static void presentQuestion(Question q)
{
    q.display();
    System.out.print("Your answer: ");
    Scanner in = new Scanner(System.in);
    String response = in.nextLine();
    System.out.println(q.checkAnswer(response));
}
```

As discussed in Section 9.1, we can substitute a subclass object whenever a superclass object is expected:

```
ChoiceQuestion second = new ChoiceQuestion();
. . .
presentQuestion(second); // OK to pass a ChoiceQuestion
```

> A subclass reference can be used when a superclass reference is expected.

When the presentQuestion method executes, the object references stored in second and q refer to the same object of type ChoiceQuestion (see Figure 6).

However, the *variable* q knows less than the full story about the object to which it refers (see Figure 7).

Because q is a variable of type Question, you can call the display and checkAnswer methods. You cannot call the addChoice method, though—it is not a method of the Question superclass.

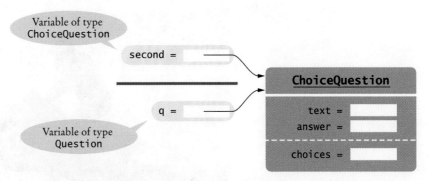

**Figure 6** Variables of Different Types Referring to the Same Object

ANIMATION
*Polymorphism*

This is as it should be. After all, it happens that in this method call, q refers to a ChoiceQuestion. In another method call, q might refer to a plain Question or an entirely different subclass of Question.

Now let's have a closer look inside the presentQuestion method. It starts with the call

```
q.display(); // Does it call Question.display or ChoiceQuestion.display?
```

Which display method is called? If you look at the program output on page 433, you will see that the method called depends on the contents of the parameter variable q. In the first case, q refers to a Question object, so the Question.display method is called. But in the second case, q refers to a ChoiceQuestion, so the ChoiceQuestion.display method is called, showing the list of choices.

In Java, method calls *are always determined by the type of the actual object*, not the type of the variable containing the object reference. This is called **dynamic method lookup**.

Polymorphism ("having multiple shapes") allows us to manipulate objects that share a set of tasks, even though the tasks are executed in different ways.

Dynamic method lookup allows us to treat objects of different classes in a uniform way. This feature is called **polymorphism**. We ask multiple objects to carry out a task, and each object does so in its own way.

Polymorphism makes programs *easily extensible*. Suppose we want to have a new kind of question for calculations, where we are willing to accept an approximate answer. All we need to do is to declare a new class NumericQuestion that extends Question, with its own checkAnswer method. Then we can call the presentQuestion method with a mixture of plain questions, choice questions, and numeric questions. The presentQuestion method need not be changed at all! Thanks to dynamic method lookup, method calls to the display and checkAnswer methods automatically select the correct method of the newly declared classes.

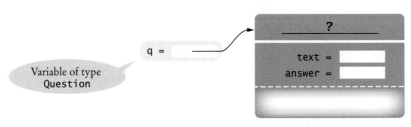

**Figure 7** A Question Reference Can Refer to an Object of Any Subclass of Question

*In the same way that vehicles can differ in their method of locomotion, polymorphic objects carry out tasks in different ways.*

### section_4/QuestionDemo3.java

```java
1  import java.util.Scanner;
2
3  /**
4     This program shows a simple quiz with two question types.
5  */
6  public class QuestionDemo3
7  {
8     public static void main(String[] args)
9     {
10        Question first = new Question();
11        first.setText("Who was the inventor of Java?");
12        first.setAnswer("James Gosling");
13
14        ChoiceQuestion second = new ChoiceQuestion();
15        second.setText("In which country was the inventor of Java born?");
16        second.addChoice("Australia", false);
17        second.addChoice("Canada", true);
18        second.addChoice("Denmark", false);
19        second.addChoice("United States", false);
20
21        presentQuestion(first);
22        presentQuestion(second);
23     }
24
25     /**
26        Presents a question to the user and checks the response.
27        @param q the question
28     */
29     public static void presentQuestion(Question q)
30     {
31        q.display();
32        System.out.print("Your answer: ");
33        Scanner in = new Scanner(System.in);
34        String response = in.nextLine();
35        System.out.println(q.checkAnswer(response));
36     }
37  }
```

**Program Run**

```
Who was the inventor of Java?
Your answer: Bjarne Stroustrup
false
In which country was the inventor of Java born?
1: Australia
2: Canada
3: Denmark
4: United States
Your answer: 2
true
```

**SELF CHECK**

16. Assuming SavingsAccount is a subclass of BankAccount, which of the following code fragments are valid in Java?

    **a.** BankAccount account = new SavingsAccount();

    **b.** SavingsAccount account2 = new BankAccount();

    **c.** BankAccount account = null;

    **d.** SavingsAccount account2 = account;

17. If account is a variable of type BankAccount that holds a non-null reference, what do you know about the object to which account refers?

18. Declare an array quiz that can hold a mixture of Question and ChoiceQuestion objects.

19. Consider the code fragment

    ```
    ChoiceQuestion cq = . . .; // A non-null value
    cq.display();
    ```

    Which actual method is being called?

20. Is the method call Math.sqrt(2) resolved through dynamic method lookup?

**Practice It**    Now you can try these exercises at the end of the chapter: R9.6, P9.4, P9.20.

---

**Special Topic 9.2**

### Dynamic Method Lookup and the Implicit Parameter

Suppose we add the presentQuestion method to the Question class itself:

```
void presentQuestion()
{
    display();
    System.out.print("Your answer: ");
    Scanner in = new Scanner(System.in);
    String response = in.nextLine();
    System.out.println(checkAnswer(response));
}
```

Now consider the call

```
ChoiceQuestion cq = new ChoiceQuestion();
cq.setText("In which country was the inventor of Java born?");
. . .
cq.presentQuestion();
```

Which `display` and `checkAnswer` method will the `presentQuestion` method call? If you look inside the code of the `presentQuestion` method, you can see that these methods are executed on the implicit parameter.

```java
public class Question
{
    public void presentQuestion()
    {
        this.display();
        System.out.print("Your answer: ");
        Scanner in = new Scanner(System.in);
        String response = in.nextLine();
        System.out.println(this.checkAnswer(response));
    }
}
```

The implicit parameter `this` in our call is a reference to an object of type `ChoiceQuestion`. Because of dynamic method lookup, the `ChoiceQuestion` versions of the `display` and `checkAnswer` methods are called automatically. This happens even though the `presentQuestion` method is declared in the `Question` class, which has *no knowledge* of the `ChoiceQuestion` class.

As you can see, polymorphism is a very powerful mechanism. The `Question` class supplies a `presentQuestion` method that specifies the common nature of presenting a question, namely to display it and check the response. How the displaying and checking are carried out is left to the subclasses.

## Special Topic 9.3

## Abstract Classes

When you extend an existing class, you have the choice whether or not to override the methods of the superclass. Sometimes, it is desirable to *force* programmers to override a method. That happens when there is no good default for the superclass, and only the subclass programmer can know how to implement the method properly.

Here is an example: Suppose the First National Bank of Java decides that every account type must have some monthly fees. Therefore, a `deductFees` method should be added to the `Account` class:

```java
public class Account
{
    public void deductFees() { . . . }
    . . .
}
```

But what should this method do? Of course, we could have the method do nothing. But then a programmer implementing a new subclass might simply forget to implement the `deductFees` method, and the new account would inherit the do-nothing method of the superclass. There is a better way—declare the `deductFees` method as an **abstract method**:

```java
public abstract void deductFees();
```

An abstract method has no implementation. This forces the implementors of subclasses to specify concrete implementations of this method. (Of course, some subclasses might decide to implement a do-nothing method, but then that is their choice—not a silently inherited default.)

> An abstract method is a method whose implementation is not specified.

You cannot construct objects of classes with abstract methods. For example, once the `Account` class has an abstract method, the compiler will flag an attempt to create a `new Account()` as an error.

> An abstract class is a class that cannot be instantiated.

A class for which you cannot create objects is called an **abstract class**. A class for which you can create objects is sometimes called a **concrete class**. In Java, you must declare all abstract classes with the reserved word abstract:

```
public abstract class Account
{
    public abstract void deductFees();
    . . .
}

public class SavingsAccount extends Account // Not abstract
{
    . . .
    public void deductFees() // Provides an implementation
    {
        . . .
    }
}
```

Note that you cannot construct an *object* of an abstract class, but you can still have an *object reference* whose type is an abstract class. Of course, the actual object to which it refers must be an instance of a concrete subclass:

```
Account anAccount; // OK
anAccount = new Account(); // Error—Account is abstract
anAccount = new SavingsAccount(); // OK
anAccount = null; // OK
```

The reason for using abstract classes is to force programmers to create subclasses. By specifying certain methods as abstract, you avoid the trouble of coming up with useless default methods that others might inherit by accident.

Special Topic 9.4

## Final Methods and Classes

In Special Topic 9.3 you saw how you can force other programmers to create subclasses of abstract classes and override abstract methods. Occasionally, you may want to do the opposite and *prevent* other programmers from creating subclasses or from overriding certain methods. In these situations, you use the final reserved word. For example, the String class in the standard Java library has been declared as

```
public final class String { . . . }
```

That means that nobody can extend the String class. When you have a reference of type String, it must contain a String object, never an object of a subclass.

You can also declare individual methods as final:

```
public class SecureAccount extends BankAccount
{
    . . .
    public final boolean checkPassword(String password)
    {
        . . .
    }
}
```

This way, nobody can override the checkPassword method with another method that simply returns true.

### Protected Access

We ran into a hurdle when trying to implement the display method of the ChoiceQuestion class. That method wanted to access the instance variable text of the superclass. Our remedy was to use the appropriate method of the superclass to display the text.

Java offers another solution to this problem. The superclass can declare an instance variable as *protected:*

```
public class Question
{
    protected String text;
    . . .
}
```

Protected data in an object can be accessed by the methods of the object's class and all its subclasses. For example, ChoiceQuestion inherits from Question, so its methods can access the protected instance variables of the Question superclass.

Some programmers like the protected access feature because it seems to strike a balance between absolute protection (making instance variables private) and no protection at all (making instance variables public). However, experience has shown that protected instance variables are subject to the same kinds of problems as public instance variables. The designer of the superclass has no control over the authors of subclasses. Any of the subclass methods can corrupt the superclass data. Furthermore, classes with protected variables are hard to modify. Even if the author of the superclass would like to change the data implementation, the protected variables cannot be changed, because someone somewhere out there might have written a subclass whose code depends on them.

In Java, protected variables have another drawback—they are accessible not just by subclasses, but also by other classes in the same package (see Section 12.4 for information about packages).

It is best to leave all data private. If you want to grant access to the data to subclass methods only, consider making the *accessor* method protected.

### Developing an Inheritance Hierarchy

When you work with a set of classes, some of which are more general and others more specialized, you want to organize them into an inheritance hierarchy. This enables you to process objects of different classes in a uniform way.

As an example, we will consider a bank that offers customers the following account types:

- A savings account that earns interest. The interest compounds monthly and is computed on the minimum monthly balance.
- A checking account that has no interest, gives you three free withdrawals per month, and charges a $1 transaction fee for each additional withdrawal.

The program will manage a set of accounts of both types, and it should be structured so that other account types can be added without affecting the main processing loop. Supply a menu

```
D)eposit W)ithdraw M)onth end Q)uit
```

For deposits and withdrawals, query the account number and amount. Print the balance of the account after each transaction.

In the "Month end" command, accumulate interest or clear the transaction counter, depending on the type of the bank account. Then print the balance of all accounts.

**Step 1**    List the classes that are part of the hierarchy.

In our case, the problem description yields two classes: SavingsAccount and CheckingAccount. Of course, you could implement each of them separately. But that would not be a good idea because the classes would have to repeat common functionality, such as updating an account balance. We need another class that can be responsible for that common functionality. The problem statement does not explicitly mention such a class. Therefore, we need to discover it. Of course, in this case, the solution is simple. Savings accounts and checking accounts are special cases of a bank account. Therefore, we will introduce a common superclass BankAccount.

**Step 2**    Organize the classes into an inheritance hierarchy.

Draw an inheritance diagram that shows super- and subclasses. Here is one for our example:

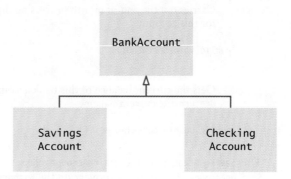

**Step 3**    Determine the common responsibilities.

In Step 2, you will have identified a class at the base of the hierarchy. That class needs to have sufficient responsibilities to carry out the tasks at hand. To find out what those tasks are, write pseudocode for processing the objects.

```
For each user command
    If it is a deposit or withdrawal
        Deposit or withdraw the amount from the specified account.
        Print the balance.
    If it is month end processing
        For each account
            Call month end processing.
            Print the balance.
```

From the pseudocode, we obtain the following list of common responsibilities that every bank account must carry out:

```
Deposit money.
Withdraw money.
Get the balance.
Carry out month end processing.
```

**Step 4**    Decide which methods are overridden in subclasses.

For each subclass and each of the common responsibilities, decide whether the behavior can be inherited or whether it needs to be overridden. Be sure to declare any methods that are inherited or overridden in the root of the hierarchy.

```
public class BankAccount
{
    . . .
```

```
    /**
        Makes a deposit into this account.
        @param amount the amount of the deposit
    */
    public void deposit(double amount) { . . . }

    /**
        Makes a withdrawal from this account, or charges a penalty if
        sufficient funds are not available.
        @param amount the amount of the withdrawal
    */
    public void withdraw(double amount) { . . . }

    /**
        Carries out the end of month processing that is appropriate
        for this account.
    */
    public void monthEnd() { . . . }

    /**
        Gets the current balance of this bank account.
        @return the current balance
    */
    public double getBalance() { . . . }
}
```

The SavingsAccount and CheckingAccount classes both override the monthEnd method. The SavingsAccount class must also override the withdraw method to track the minimum balance. The CheckingAccount class must update a transaction count in the withdraw method.

**Step 5** Declare the public interface of each subclass.

Typically, subclasses have responsibilities other than those of the superclass. List those, as well as the methods that need to be overridden. You also need to specify how the objects of the subclasses should be constructed.

In this example, we need a way of setting the interest rate for the savings account. In addition, we need to specify constructors and overridden methods.

```
public class SavingsAccount extends BankAccount
{
    . . .
    /**
        Constructs a savings account with a zero balance.
    */
    public SavingsAccount() { . . . }

    /**
        Sets the interest rate for this account.
        @param rate the monthly interest rate in percent
    */
    public void setInterestRate(double rate) { . . . }

    // These methods override superclass methods
    public void withdraw(double amount) { . . . }
    public void monthEnd() { . . . }
}

public class CheckingAccount extends BankAccount
{
    . . .
    /**
```

Constructs a checking account with a zero balance.
```
*/
public CheckingAccount() { . . . }

// These methods override superclass methods
public void withdraw(double amount) { . . . }
public void monthEnd() { . . . }
}
```

**Step 6**  Identify instance variables.

List the instance variables for each class. If you find an instance variable that is common to all classes, be sure to place it in the base of the hierarchy.

All accounts have a balance. We store that value in the BankAccount superclass:

```
public class BankAccount
{
   private double balance;
   . . .
}
```

The SavingsAccount class needs to store the interest rate. It also needs to store the minimum monthly balance, which must be updated by all withdrawals.

```
public class SavingsAccount extends BankAccount
{
   private double interestRate;
   private double minBalance;
   . . .
}
```

The CheckingAccount class needs to count the withdrawals, so that the charge can be applied after the free withdrawal limit is reached.

```
public class CheckingAccount extends BankAccount
{
   private int withdrawals;
   . . .
}
```

**Step 7**  Implement constructors and methods.

The methods of the BankAccount class update or return the balance.

```
public void deposit(double amount)
{
   balance = balance + amount;
}

public void withdraw(double amount)
{
   balance = balance - amount;
}

public double getBalance()
{
   return balance;
}
```

At the level of the BankAccount superclass, we can say nothing about end of month processing. We choose to make that method do nothing:

```
public void monthEnd()
{
}
```

In the `withdraw` method of the `SavingsAccount` class, the minimum balance is updated. Note the call to the superclass method:

```java
public void withdraw(double amount)
{
    super.withdraw(amount);
    double balance = getBalance();
    if (balance < minBalance)
    {
        minBalance = balance;
    }
}
```

In the `monthEnd` method of the `SavingsAccount` class, the interest is deposited into the account. We must call the `deposit` method because we have no direct access to the `balance` instance variable. The minimum balance is reset for the next month.

```java
public void monthEnd()
{
    double interest = minBalance * interestRate / 100;
    deposit(interest);
    minBalance = getBalance();
}
```

The `withdraw` method of the `CheckingAccount` class needs to check the withdrawal count. If there have been too many withdrawals, a charge is applied. Again, note how the method invokes the superclass method:

```java
public void withdraw(double amount)
{
    final int FREE_WITHDRAWALS = 3;
    final int WITHDRAWAL_FEE = 1;

    super.withdraw(amount);
    withdrawals++;
    if (withdrawals > FREE_WITHDRAWALS)
    {
        super.withdraw(WITHDRAWAL_FEE);
    }
}
```

End of month processing for a checking account simply resets the withdrawal count.

```java
public void monthEnd()
{
    withdrawals = 0;
}
```

**Step 8** Construct objects of different subclasses and process them.

In our sample program, we allocate 5 checking accounts and 5 savings accounts and store their addresses in an array of bank accounts. Then we accept user commands and execute deposits, withdrawals, and monthly processing.

```java
BankAccount[] accounts = . . .;
. . .
Scanner in = new Scanner(System.in);
boolean done = false;
while (!done)
{
    System.out.print("D)eposit  W)ithdraw  M)onth end  Q)uit: ");
    String input = in.next();
    if (input.equals("D") || input.equals("W")) // Deposit or withdrawal
    {
```

```
                    System.out.print("Enter account number and amount: ");
                    int num = in.nextInt();
                    double amount = in.nextDouble();

                    if (input.equals("D")) { accounts[num].deposit(amount); }
                    else { accounts[num].withdraw(amount); }

                    System.out.println("Balance: " + accounts[num].getBalance());
                }
                else if (input.equals("M")) // Month end processing
                {
                    for (int n = 0; n < accounts.length; n++)
                    {
                        accounts[n].monthEnd();
                        System.out.println(n + " " + accounts[n].getBalance());
                    }
                }
                else if (input == "Q")
                {
                    done = true;
                }
        }
```

## WORKED EXAMPLE 9.1

### Implementing an Employee Hierarchy for Payroll Processing

This Worked Example shows how to implement payroll processing that works for different kinds of employees.

## VIDEO EXAMPLE 9.1

### Building a Discussion Board

In this Video Example, we will build a discussion board for students and instructors.

# 9.5 Object: The Cosmic Superclass

In Java, every class that is declared without an explicit extends clause automatically extends the class Object. That is, the class Object is the direct or indirect superclass of *every* class in Java (see Figure 8). The Object class defines several very general methods, including

- toString, which yields a string describing the object (Section 9.5.1).
- equals, which compares objects with each other (Section 9.5.2).
- hashCode, which yields a numerical code for storing the object in a set (see Special Topic 15.1).

➕ Available online in WileyPLUS and at www.wiley.com/college/horstmann.

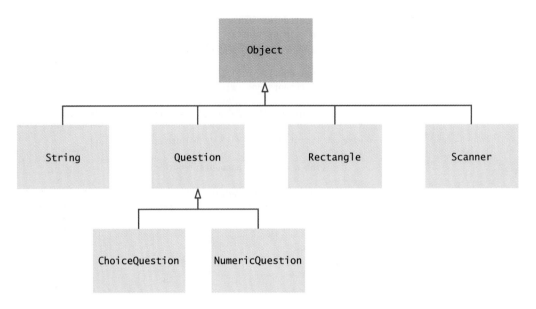

**Figure 8**  The Object Class Is the Superclass of Every Java Class

## 9.5.1 Overriding the toString Method

The toString method returns a string representation for each object. It is often used for debugging. For example, consider the Rectangle class in the standard Java library. Its toString method shows the state of a rectangle:

```
Rectangle box = new Rectangle(5, 10, 20, 30);
String s = box.toString();
    // Sets s to "java.awt.Rectangle[x=5,y=10,width=20,height=30]"
```

The toString method is called automatically whenever you concatenate a string with an object. Here is an example:

```
"box=" + box;
```

On one side of the + concatenation operator is a string, but on the other side is an object reference. The Java compiler automatically invokes the toString method to turn the object into a string. Then both strings are concatenated. In this case, the result is the string

```
"box=java.awt.Rectangle[x=5,y=10,width=20,height=30]"
```

The compiler can invoke the toString method, because it knows that *every* object has a toString method: Every class extends the Object class, and that class declares toString.

As you know, numbers are also converted to strings when they are concatenated with other strings. For example,

```
int age = 18;
String s = "Harry's age is " + age;
    // Sets s to "Harry's age is 18"
```

In this case, the toString method is *not* involved. Numbers are not objects, and there is no toString method for them. Fortunately, there is only a small set of primitive types, and the compiler knows how to convert them to strings.

Let's try the toString method for the BankAccount class:

```
BankAccount momsSavings = new BankAccount(5000);
String s = momsSavings.toString(); // Sets s to something like "BankAccount@d24606bf"
```

That's disappointing—all that's printed is the name of the class, followed by the **hash code**, a seemingly random code. The hash code can be used to tell objects apart—different objects are likely to have different hash codes. (See Special Topic 15.1 for the details.)

We don't care about the hash code. We want to know what is *inside* the object. But, of course, the toString method of the Object class does not know what is inside the BankAccount class. Therefore, we have to override the method and supply our own version in the BankAccount class. We'll follow the same format that the toString method of the Rectangle class uses: first print the name of the class, and then the values of the instance variables inside brackets.

```
public class BankAccount
{
    . . .
    public String toString()
    {
        return "BankAccount[balance=" + balance + "]";
    }
}
```

This works better:

```
BankAccount momsSavings = new BankAccount(5000);
String s = momsSavings.toString(); // Sets s to "BankAccount[balance=5000]"
```

## 9.5.2  The equals Method

In addition to the toString method, the Object class also provides an equals method, whose purpose is to check whether two objects have the same contents:

```
if (stamp1.equals(stamp2)) . . .        // Contents are the same—see Figure 9
```

This is different from the test with the == operator, which tests whether two references are identical, referring to the *same object:*

```
if (stamp1 == stamp2) . . .       // Objects are the same—see Figure 10
```

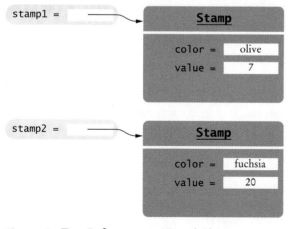

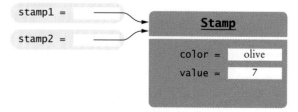

**Figure 9**  Two References to Equal Objects            **Figure 10**  Two References to the Same Object

Let's implement the `equals` method for a `Stamp` class. You need to override the `equals` method of the `Object` class:

```
public class Stamp
{
    private String color;
    private int value;
    . . .
    public boolean equals(Object otherObject)
    {
        . . .
    }
    . . .
}
```

*The* equals *method checks whether two objects have the same contents.*

Now you have a slight problem. The `Object` class knows nothing about stamps, so it declares the `otherObject` parameter variable of the `equals` method to have the type `Object`. When overriding the method, you are not allowed to change the type of the parameter variable. Cast the parameter variable to the class `Stamp`:

```
Stamp other = (Stamp) otherObject;
```

Then you can compare the two stamps:

```
public boolean equals(Object otherObject)
{
    Stamp other = (Stamp) otherObject;
    return color.equals(other.color)
        && value == other.value;
}
```

Note that this `equals` method can access the instance variables of *any* `Stamp` object: the access `other.color` is perfectly legal.

### 9.5.3 The instanceof Operator

As you have seen, it is legal to store a subclass reference in a superclass variable:

```
ChoiceQuestion cq = new ChoiceQuestion();
Question q = cq; // OK
Object obj = cq; // OK
```

Very occasionally, you need to carry out the opposite conversion, from a superclass reference to a subclass reference.

For example, you may have a variable of type `Object`, and you happen to know that it actually holds a `Question` reference. In that case, you can use a cast to convert the type:

> If you know that an object belongs to a given class, use a cast to convert the type.

```
Question q = (Question) obj;
```

However, this cast is somewhat dangerous. If you are wrong, and `obj` actually refers to an object of an unrelated type, then a "class cast" exception is thrown.

To protect against bad casts, you can use the `instanceof` operator. It tests whether an object belongs to a particular type. For example,

> The `instanceof` operator tests whether an object belongs to a particular type.

```
obj instanceof Question
```

returns `true` if the type of `obj` is convertible to `Question`. This happens if `obj` refers to an actual `Question` or to a subclass such as `ChoiceQuestion`.

## Syntax 9.3   The instanceof Operator

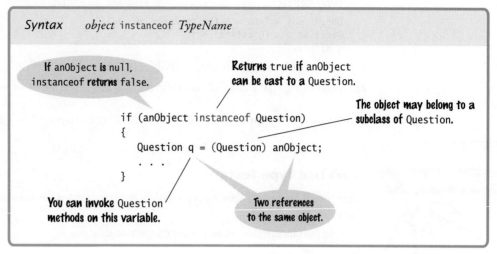

**Syntax**   *object* instanceof *TypeName*

If anObject is null, instanceof returns false.

Returns true if anObject can be cast to a Question.

The object may belong to a subclass of Question.

```
if (anObject instanceof Question)
{
    Question q = (Question) anObject;
    . . .
}
```

You can invoke Question methods on this variable.

Two references to the same object.

Using the instanceof operator, a safe cast can be programmed as follows:

```
if (obj instanceof Question)
{
    Question q = (Question) obj;
}
```

Note that instanceof is *not* a method. It is an operator, just like + or <. However, it does not operate on numbers. To the left is an object, and to the right a type name.

Do *not* use the instanceof operator to bypass polymorphism:

```
if (q instanceof ChoiceQuestion) // Don't do this—see Common Error 9.5 on page 446
{
    // Do the task the ChoiceQuestion way
}
else if (q instanceof Question)
{
    // Do the task the Question way
}
```

**ONLINE EXAMPLE**

A program that demonstrates the toString method and the instanceof operator.

In this case, you should implement a method doTheTask in the Question class, override it in ChoiceQuestion, and call

```
q.doTheTask();
```

**SELF CHECK**

21. Why does the call
    ```
    System.out.println(System.out);
    ```
    produce a result such as java.io.PrintStream@7a84e4?

22. Will the following code fragment compile? Will it run? If not, what error is reported?
    ```
    Object obj = "Hello";
    System.out.println(obj.length());
    ```

**23.** Will the following code fragment compile? Will it run? If not, what error is reported?

```java
Object obj = "Who was the inventor of Java?";
Question q = (Question) obj;
q.display();
```

**24.** Why don't we simply store all objects in variables of type `Object`?

**25.** Assuming that x is an object reference, what is the value of x `instanceof Object`?

**Practice It**      Now you can try these exercises at the end of the chapter: P9.7, P9.8, P9.12.

---

Common Error 9.5

### Don't Use Type Tests

Some programmers use specific type tests in order to implement behavior that varies with each class:

```java
if (q instanceof ChoiceQuestion) // Don't do this
{
    // Do the task the ChoiceQuestion way
}
else if (q instanceof Question)
{
    // Do the task the Question way
}
```

This is a poor strategy. If a new class such as `NumericQuestion` is added, then you need to revise all parts of your program that make a type test, adding another case:

```java
else if (q instanceof NumericQuestion)
{
    // Do the task the NumericQuestion way
}
```

In contrast, consider the addition of a class `NumericQuestion` to our quiz program. *Nothing* needs to change in that program because it uses polymorphism, not type tests.

    Whenever you find yourself trying to use type tests in a hierarchy of classes, reconsider and use polymorphism instead. Declare a method `doTheTask` in the superclass, override it in the subclasses, and call

```java
q.doTheTask();
```

---

Special Topic 9.6

### Inheritance and the `toString` Method

You just saw how to write a `toString` method: Form a string consisting of the class name and the names and values of the instance variables. However, if you want your `toString` method to be usable by subclasses of your class, you need to work a bit harder. Instead of hardcoding the class name, call the `getClass` method (which every class inherits from the `Object` class) to obtain an object that describes a class and its properties. Then invoke the `getName` method to get the name of the class:

```java
public String toString()
{
    return getClass().getName() + "[balance=" + balance + "]";
}
```

Then the `toString` method prints the correct class name when you apply it to a subclass, say a `SavingsAccount`.

```
SavingsAccount momsSavings = . . . ;
System.out.println(momsSavings);
// Prints "SavingsAccount[balance=10000]"
```

Of course, in the subclass, you should override toString and add the values of the subclass instance variables. Note that you must call super.toString to get the instance variables of the superclass—the subclass can't access them directly.

```java
public class SavingsAccount extends BankAccount
{
   . . .
   public String toString()
   {
      return super.toString() + "[interestRate=" + interestRate + "]";
   }
}
```

Now a savings account is converted to a string such as SavingsAccount[balance= 10000][interest-Rate=5]. The brackets show which variables belong to the superclass.

---

### Inheritance and the equals Method

You just saw how to write an equals method: Cast the otherObject parameter variable to the type of your class, and then compare the instance variables of the implicit parameter and the explicit parameter.

But what if someone called stamp1.equals(x) where x wasn't a Stamp object? Then the bad cast would generate an exception. It is a good idea to test whether otherObject really is an instance of the Stamp class. The easiest test would be with the instanceof operator. However, that test is not specific enough. It would be possible for otherObject to belong to some subclass of Stamp. To rule out that possibility, you should test whether the two objects belong to the same class. If not, return false.

```java
if (getClass() != otherObject.getClass()) { return false; }
```

Moreover, the Java language specification demands that the equals method return false when otherObject is null.

Here is an improved version of the equals method that takes these two points into account:

```java
public boolean equals(Object otherObject)
{
   if (otherObject == null) { return false; }
   if (getClass() != otherObject.getClass()) { return false; }
   Stamp other = (Stamp) otherObject;
   return color.equals(other.color) && value == other.value;
}
```

When you implement equals in a subclass, you should first call equals in the superclass to check whether the superclass instance variables match. Here is an example:

```java
public CollectibleStamp extends Stamp
{
   private int year;
   . . .
   public boolean equals(Object otherObject)
   {
      if (!super.equals(otherObject)) { return false; }
      CollectibleStamp other = (CollectibleStamp) otherObject;
      return year == other.year;
   }
}
```

# 9.6 Interface Types

It is often possible to design a general and reusable mechanism for processing objects by focusing on the essential operations that an algorithm needs. You use *interface types* to express these operations.

## 9.6.1 Defining an Interface

Consider the following method that computes the average balance in an array of BankAccount objects:

```
public static double average(BankAccount[] objects)
{
   if (objects.length == 0) { return 0; }
   double sum = 0;
   for (BankAccount obj : objects)
   {
      sum = sum + obj.getBalance();
   }
   return sum / objects.length;
}
```

Now suppose you have an array of Country objects and want to determine the average of the areas:

```
public static double average(Country[] objects)
{
   if (objects.length == 0) { return 0; }
   double sum = 0;
   for (Country obj : objects)
   {
      sum = sum + obj.getArea();
   }
   return sum / objects.length;
}
```

Clearly, the algorithm for computing the result is the same in both cases, but the details of measurement differ. How can we write a *single* method that computes the averages of both bank accounts and countries?

*This standmixer provides the "rotation" service to any attachment that conforms to a common interface. Similarly, the average method at the end of this section works with any class that implements a common interface.*

## Syntax 9.4   Interface Types

| | | |
|---|---|---|
| *Syntax* | *Declaring:* | `public interface` *InterfaceName*<br>`{`<br>    *method declarations*<br>`}` |
| | *Implementing:* | `public class` *ClassName* `implements` *InterfaceName*, *InterfaceName*, . . .<br>`{`<br>    *instance variables*<br>    *methods*<br>`}` |

```
                          public interface Measurable
Interface methods         {                              ──── Interface methods
are always public. ────       double getMeasure();           have no implementation.
                          }
```

```
                          public class BankAccount implements Measurable
                          {
                              . . .                           A class can implement one
                                                              or more interface types.
     Other
  BankAccount  ────           public double getMeasure()
   methods.                   {
                                  return balance;           ──── Implementation for the method that
                              }                                  was declared in the interface type.
                          }
```

Suppose that the classes agree on a single method `getMeasure` that obtains the measure to be used in the data analysis. For bank accounts, `getMeasure` returns the balance. For countries, `getMeasure` returns the area. Other classes can participate too, provided that their `getMeasure` method returns an appropriate value.

Then we can implement a single method that computes

```
sum = sum + obj.getMeasure();
```

What is the type of the variable `obj`? Any class that has a `getMeasure` method.

> A Java interface type contains the return types, names, and parameter variables of a set of methods.

In Java, an **interface type** is used to specify required operations. We will declare an interface type that we call `Measurable`:

```
public interface Measurable
{
    double getMeasure();
}
```

The interface declaration lists all methods that the interface type requires. The `Measurable` interface type requires a single method, but in general, an interface type can require multiple methods. (Note that the `Measurable` type is not a type in the standard library—it is a type that was created specifically for this book.)

> Unlike a class, an interface type provides no implementation.

An interface type is similar to a class, but there are several important differences:

- All methods in an interface type are *abstract;* that is, they have a name, parameter variables, and a return type, but they don't have an implementation.
- All methods in an interface type are automatically public.
- An interface type cannot have instance variables.
- An interface type cannot have static methods.

By using an interface type for a parameter variable, a method can accept objects from many classes.

We can use the interface type `Measurable` to implement a "universal" method for computing averages:

```java
public static double average(Measurable[] objects)
{
    if (objects.length == 0) { return 0; }
    double sum = 0;
    for (Measurable obj : objects)
    {
        sum = sum + obj.getMeasure();
    }
    return sum / objects.length;
}
```

## 9.6.2 Implementing an Interface

The `implements` reserved word indicates which interfaces a class implements.

The average method is usable for objects of any class that **implements** the `Measurable` interface. A class implements an interface type if it declares the interface in an `implements` clause, and if it implements the method or methods that the interface requires. Let's modify the `BankAccount` class to implement the `Measurable` interface.

```java
public class BankAccount implements Measurable
{
    public double getMeasure()
    {
        return balance;
    }
    . . .
}
```

Note that the class must declare the method as `public`, whereas the interface type need not—all methods in an interface type are public.

Similarly, it is an easy matter to implement a `Country` class that implements the `Measurable` interface.

```java
public class Country implements Measurable
{
    public double getMeasure()
    {
        return area;
    }
    . . .
}
```

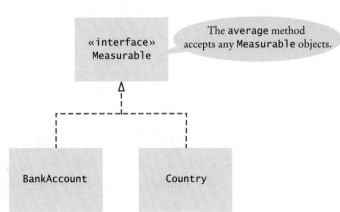

The average method accepts any **Measurable** objects.

**Figure 11**
Classes that Implement the `Measurable` Interface

A reference to a BankAccount or Country can be converted to a Measurable reference. The sample program at the end of this section shows how the same average method can compute the average of a collection of bank accounts or countries.

In summary, the Measurable interface expresses what all measurable objects have in common. This commonality makes it possible to write methods such as average that are usable for many classes.

Figure 11 shows a diagram of the classes and interfaces in this program. A dotted arrow with a triangular tip denotes the "implements" relationship.

### section_6/MeasurableDemo.java

```
1   /**
2         This program demonstrates the measurable BankAccount and Country classes.
3   */
4   public class MeasurableDemo
5   {
6      public static void main(String[] args)
7      {
8         Measurable[] accounts = new Measurable[3];
9         accounts[0] = new BankAccount(0);
10        accounts[1] = new BankAccount(10000);
11        accounts[2] = new BankAccount(2000);
12
13        System.out.println("Average balance: "
14           + average(accounts));
15
16        Measurable[] countries = new Measurable[3];
17        countries[0] = new Country("Uruguay", 176220);
18        countries[1] = new Country("Thailand", 514000);
19        countries[2] = new Country("Belgium", 30510);
20
21        System.out.println("Average area: "
22           + average(countries));
23     }
24
25     /**
26         Computes the average of the measures of the given objects.
27         @param objects an array of Measurable objects
28         @return the average of the measures
29     */
30     public static double average(Measurable[] objects)
31     {
32        if (objects.length == 0) { return 0; }
33        double sum = 0;
34        for (Measurable obj : objects)
35        {
36           sum = sum + obj.getMeasure();
37        }
38        return sum / objects.length;
39     }
40  }
```

### Program Run

```
Average balance: 4000.0
Average area: 240243.33333333334
```

### 9.6.3 The Comparable Interface

Implement the Comparable interface so that objects of your class can be compared, for example, in a sort method.

In the preceding sections, we defined the Measurable interface and provided an average method that works with any classes implementing that interface. In this section, you will learn about the Comparable interface of the standard Java library.

The Measurable interface is used for measuring a single object. The Comparable interface is more complex because comparisons involve two objects. The interface declares a compareTo method. The call

```
a.compareTo(b)
```

must return a negative number if a should come before b, zero if a and b are the same, and a positive number otherwise.

The Comparable interface has a single method:

```java
public interface Comparable
{
    int compareTo(Object otherObject);
}
```

For example, the BankAccount class can implement Comparable like this:

```java
public class BankAccount implements Comparable
{
    . . .
    public int compareTo(Object otherObject)
    {
        BankAccount other = (BankAccount) otherObject;
        if (balance < other.balance) { return -1; }
        if (balance > other.balance) { return 1; }
        return 0;
    }
    . . .
}
```

This compareTo method compares bank accounts by their balance. Note that the compareTo method has a parameter variable of type Object. To turn it into a BankAccount reference, we use a cast:

```java
BankAccount other = (BankAccount) otherObject;
```

Once the BankAccount class implements the Comparable interface, you can sort an array of bank accounts with the Arrays.sort method:

```java
BankAccount[] accounts = new BankAccount[3];
accounts[0] = new BankAccount(10000);
accounts[1] = new BankAccount(0);
accounts[2] = new BankAccount(2000);
Arrays.sort(accounts);
```

*The* compareTo *method checks whether another object is larger or smaller.*

The accounts array is now sorted by increasing balance.

**SELF CHECK**

26. Suppose you want to use the average method to find the average salary of Employee objects. What condition must the Employee class fulfill?
27. Why can't the average method have a parameter variable of type Object[]?
28. Why can't you use the average method to find the average length of String objects?
29. What is wrong with this code?
    ```
    Measurable meas = new Measurable();
    System.out.println(meas.getMeasure());
    ```
30. How can you sort an array of Country objects by increasing area?
31. Can you use the Arrays.sort method to sort an array of String objects? Check the API documentation for the String class.

**Practice It**   Now you can try these exercises at the end of the chapter: R9.14, P9.15, P9.16.

---

Common Error 9.6

### Forgetting to Declare Implementing Methods as Public

The methods in an interface are not declared as public, because they are public by default. However, the methods in a class are *not* public by default. It is a common error to forget the public reserved word when declaring a method from an interface:

```java
public class BankAccount implements Measurable
{
    double getMeasure() // Oops—should be public
    {
        return balance;
    }
    . . .
}
```

Then the compiler complains that the method has a weaker access level, namely package access instead of public access (see Section 12.4). The remedy is to declare the method as public.

---

Special Topic 9.8

### Constants in Interfaces

Interfaces cannot have instance variables, but it is legal to specify **constants**.

When declaring a constant in an interface, you can (and should) omit the reserved words public static final, because all variables in an interface are automatically public static final. For example,

```java
public interface Measurable
{
    double OUNCES_PER_LITER = 33.814;
    . . .
}
```

To use this constant in your programs, add the interface name:

```java
Measurable.OUNCES_PER_LITER
```

## Function Objects

In the preceding section, you saw how the `Measurable` interface type makes it possible to provide services that work for many classes—provided they are willing to implement the interface type. But what can you do if a class does not do so? For example, we might want to compute the average length of a collection of strings, but `String` does not implement `Measurable`.

Let's rethink our approach. The average method needs to measure each object. When the objects are required to be of type `Measurable`, the responsibility for measuring lies with the objects themselves, which is the cause of the limitation that we noted. It would be better if another object could carry out the measurement. Let's move the measurement method into a different interface:

```
public interface Measurer
{
    double measure(Object anObject);
}
```

The `measure` method measures an object and returns its measurement. We use a parameter variable of type `Object`, the "lowest common denominator" of all classes in Java, because we do not want to restrict which classes can be measured.

We add a parameter variable of type `Measurer` to the average method:

```
public static double average(Object[] objects, Measurer meas)
{
    if (objects.length == 0) { return 0; }
    double sum = 0;
    for (Object obj : objects)
    {
        sum = sum + meas.measure(obj);
    }
    return sum / objects.length;
}
```

When calling the method, you need to supply a `Measurer` object. That is, you need to implement a class with a `measure` method, and then create an object of that class. Let's do that for measuring strings:

```
public class StringMeasurer implements Measurer
{
    public double measure(Object obj)
    {
        String str = (String) obj; // Cast obj to String type
        return str.length();
    }
}
```

Note that the `measure` method must accept an argument of type `Object`, even though this particular measurer just wants to measure strings. The parameter variable must have the same type as in the `Measurer` interface. Therefore, the `Object` parameter variable is cast to the `String` type.

Finally, we are ready to compute the average length of an array of strings:

```
String[] words = { "Mary", "had", "a", "little", "lamb" };
Measurer lengthMeasurer = new StringMeasurer();
double result = average(words, lengthMeasurer); // result is set to 3.6
```

An object such as `lengthMeasurer` is called a *function object*. The sole purpose of the object is to execute a single method, in our case `measure`. (In mathematics, as well as many other programming languages, the term "function" is used where Java uses "method".)

The `Comparator` interface, discussed in Special Topic 14.5, is another example of an interface for function objects.

VIDEO EXAMPLE 9.2    **Drawing Geometric Shapes**

In this Video Example, you will see how to use inheritance to describe and draw different geometric shapes.

## CHAPTER SUMMARY

### Explain the notions of inheritance, superclass, and subclass.

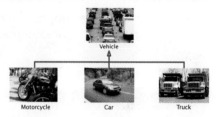

- A subclass inherits data and behavior from a superclass.
- You can always use a subclass object in place of a superclass object.

### Implement subclasses in Java.

- A subclass inherits all methods that it does not override.
- A subclass can override a superclass method by providing a new implementation.
- The extends reserved word indicates that a class inherits from a superclass.

### Implement methods that override methods from a superclass.

- An overriding method can extend or replace the functionality of the superclass method.
- Use the reserved word super to call a superclass method.
- Unless specified otherwise, the subclass constructor calls the superclass constructor with no arguments.
- To call a superclass constructor, use the super reserved word in the first statement of the subclass constructor.
- The constructor of a subclass can pass arguments to a superclass constructor, using the reserved word super.

### Use polymorphism for processing objects of related types.

- A subclass reference can be used when a superclass reference is expected.
- Polymorphism ("having multiple shapes") allows us to manipulate objects that share a set of tasks, even though the tasks are executed in different ways.
- An abstract method is a method whose implementation is not specified.
- An abstract class is a class that cannot be instantiated.

### Use the toString method and instanceof operator with objects.

- Override the toString method to yield a string that describes the object's state.
- The equals method checks whether two objects have the same contents.

➕ Available online in WileyPLUS and at www.wiley.com/college/horstmann.

- If you know that an object belongs to a given class, use a cast to convert the type.
- The instanceof operator tests whether an object belongs to a particular type.

**Use interface types for algorithms that process objects of different classes.**

- A Java interface type contains the return types, names, and parameter variables of a set of methods.
- Unlike a class, an interface type provides no implementation.
- By using an interface type for a parameter variable, a method can accept objects from many classes.
- The implements reserved word indicates which interfaces a class implements.
- Implement the Comparable interface so that objects of your class can be compared, for example, in a sort method.

## REVIEW EXERCISES

**■ R9.1** Identify the superclass and subclass in each of the following pairs of classes.

    **a.** Employee, Manager

    **b.** GraduateStudent, Student

    **c.** Person, Student

    **d.** Employee, Professor

    **e.** BankAccount, CheckingAccount

    **f.** Vehicle, Car

    **g.** Vehicle, Minivan

    **h.** Car, Minivan

    **i.** Truck, Vehicle

**■ R9.2** Consider a program for managing inventory in a small appliance store. Why isn't it useful to have a superclass SmallAppliance and subclasses Toaster, CarVacuum, TravelIron, and so on?

**■ R9.3** Which methods does the ChoiceQuestion class inherit from its superclass? Which methods does it override? Which methods does it add?

**■ R9.4** Which methods does the SavingsAccount class in How To 9.1 inherit from its superclass? Which methods does it override? Which methods does it add?

**■ R9.5** List the instance variables of a CheckingAccount object from How To 9.1.

**■■ R9.6** Suppose the class Sub extends the class Sandwich. Which of the following assignments are legal?

```
Sandwich x = new Sandwich();
Sub y = new Sub();
```

    **a.** x = y;

    **b.** y = x;

    **c.** y = new Sandwich();

    **d.** x = new Sub();

- **R9.7** Draw an inheritance diagram that shows the inheritance relationships between these classes.
  - Person
  - Employee
  - Student
  - Instructor
  - Classroom
  - Object

- **R9.8** In an object-oriented traffic simulation system, we have the classes listed below. Draw an inheritance diagram that shows the relationships between these classes.

  - Vehicle
  - Car
  - Truck
  - Sedan
  - Coupe
  - PickupTruck
  - SportUtilityVehicle
  - Minivan
  - Bicycle
  - Motorcycle

- **R9.9** What inheritance relationships would you establish among the following classes?

  - Student
  - Professor
  - TeachingAssistant
  - Employee
  - Secretary
  - DepartmentChair
  - Janitor
  - SeminarSpeaker
  - Person
  - Course
  - Seminar
  - Lecture
  - ComputerLab

- ■■ **R9.10** How does a cast such as (BankAccount) x differ from a cast of number values such as (int) x?

- ■■■ **R9.11** Which of these conditions returns true? Check the Java documentation for the inheritance patterns. Recall that System.out is an object of the PrintStream class.

  **a.** System.out instanceof PrintStream
  **b.** System.out instanceof OutputStream
  **c.** System.out instanceof LogStream
  **d.** System.out instanceof Object
  **e.** System.out instanceof Closeable
  **f.** System.out instanceof Writer

- ■■ **R9.12** Suppose C is a class that implements the interfaces I and J. Which of the following assignments require a cast?

  ```
  C c = . . .;
  I i = . . .;
  J j = . . .;
  ```

  **a.** c = i;
  **b.** j = c;
  **c.** i = j;

- ■■ **R9.13** Suppose C is a class that implements the interfaces I and J, and i is declared as

  ```
  I i = new C();
  ```

Which of the following statements will throw an exception?

**a.** C c = (C) i;

**b.** J j = (J) i;

**c.** i = (I) null;

**■■ R9.14** Suppose the class Sandwich implements the Edible interface, and you are given the variable declarations

```
Sandwich sub = new Sandwich();
Rectangle cerealBox = new Rectangle(5, 10, 20, 30);
Edible e = null;
```

Which of the following assignment statements are legal?

**a.** e = sub;

**b.** sub = e;

**c.** sub = (Sandwich) e;

**d.** sub = (Sandwich) cerealBox;

**e.** e = cerealBox;

**f.** e = (Edible) cerealBox;

**g.** e = (Rectangle) cerealBox;

**h.** e = (Rectangle) null;

## PROGRAMMING EXERCISES

**■■ P9.1** Add a class NumericQuestion to the question hierarchy of Section 9.1. If the response and the expected answer differ by no more than 0.01, then accept the response as correct.

**■■ P9.2** Add a class FillInQuestion to the question hierarchy of Section 9.1. Such a question is constructed with a string that contains the answer, surrounded by _ _, for example, "The inventor of Java was _James Gosling_". The question should be displayed as

```
The inventor of Java was _____
```

**■ P9.3** Modify the checkAnswer method of the Question class so that it does not take into account different spaces or upper/lowercase characters. For example, the response "JAMES gosling" should match an answer of "James Gosling".

**■■ P9.4** Add a class AnyCorrectChoiceQuestion to the question hierarchy of Section 9.1 that allows multiple correct choices. The respondent should provide any one of the correct choices. The answer string should contain all of the correct choices, separated by spaces. Provide instructions in the question text.

**■■ P9.5** Add a class MultiChoiceQuestion to the question hierarchy of Section 9.1 that allows multiple correct choices. The respondent should provide all correct choices, separated by spaces. Provide instructions in the question text.

**■■ P9.6** Add a method addText to the Question superclass and provide a different implementation of ChoiceQuestion that calls addText rather than storing an array list of choices.

**■ P9.7** Provide toString methods for the Question and ChoiceQuestion classes.

**■■ P9.8** Implement a superclass `Person`. Make two classes, `Student` and `Instructor`, that inherit from `Person`. A person has a name and a year of birth. A student has a major, and an instructor has a salary. Write the class declarations, the constructors, and the methods `toString` for all classes. Supply a test program that tests these classes and methods.

**■■ P9.9** Make a class `Employee` with a name and salary. Make a class `Manager` inherit from `Employee`. Add an instance variable, named `department`, of type `String`. Supply a method `toString` that prints the manager's name, department, and salary. Make a class `Executive` inherit from `Manager`. Supply appropriate `toString` methods for all classes. Supply a test program that tests these classes and methods.

**■■ P9.10** The `Rectangle` class of the standard Java library does not supply a method to compute the area or the perimeter of a rectangle. Provide a subclass `BetterRectangle` of the `Rectangle` class that has `getPerimeter` and `getArea` methods. *Do not add any instance variables*. In the constructor, call the `setLocation` and `setSize` methods of the `Rectangle` class. Provide a program that tests the methods that you supplied.

**■■■ P9.11** Repeat Exercise P9.10, but in the `BetterRectangle` constructor, invoke the superclass constructor.

**■■ P9.12** A labeled point has *x*- and *y*-coordinates and a string label. Provide a class `LabeledPoint` with a constructor `LabeledPoint(int x, int y, String label)` and a `toString` method that displays x, y, and the label.

**■■ P9.13** Reimplement the `LabeledPoint` class of Exercise P9.12 by storing the location in a `java.awt.Point` object. Your `toString` method should invoke the `toString` method of the `Point` class.

**■■ P9.14** Modify the `SodaCan` class of Exercise P8.5 to implement the `Measurable` interface. The measure of a soda can should be its surface area. Write a program that computes the average surface area of an array of soda cans.

**■■ P9.15** A person has a name and a height in centimeters. Use the `average` method in Section 9.6 to process a collection of `Person` objects.

**■■■ P9.16** Write a method

```
public static Measurable maximum(Measurable[] objects)
```

that returns the object with the largest measure. Use that method to determine the country with the largest area from an array of countries.

**■■■ P9.17** Declare an interface `Filter` as follows:

```
public interface Filter
{
    boolean accept(Object x);
}
```

Write a method

```
public static ArrayList<Object> collectAll(ArrayList<Object> objects, Filter f)
```

that returns all objects in the `objects` array that are accepted by the given filter.

Provide a class `ShortWordFilter` whose `filter` method accepts all strings of length < 5.

Then write a program that reads all words from `System.in`, puts them into an `Array-List<Object>`, calls `collectAll`, and prints a list of the short words.

■■■ **P9.18** The System.out.printf method has predefined formats for printing integers, floating-point numbers, and other data types. But it is also extensible. If you use the S format, you can print any class that implements the Formattable interface. That interface has a single method:

```
void formatTo(Formatter formatter, int flags, int width, int precision)
```

In this exercise, you should make the BankAccount class implement the Formattable interface. Ignore the flags and precision and simply format the bank balance, using the given width. In order to achieve this task, you need to get an Appendable reference like this:

```
Appendable a = formatter.out();
```

Appendable is another interface with a method

```
void append(CharSequence sequence)
```

CharSequence is yet another interface that is implemented by (among others) the String class. Construct a string by first converting the bank balance into a string and then padding it with spaces so that it has the desired width. Pass that string to the append method.

■■■ **P9.19** Enhance the formatTo method of Exercise P9.18 by taking into account the precision.

■■ **Business P9.20** Change the CheckingAccount class in How To 9.1 so that a $1 fee is levied for deposits or withdrawals in excess of three free monthly transactions. Place the code for computing the fee into a separate method that you call from the deposit and withdraw methods.

■■ **Business P9.21** Implement a superclass Appointment and subclasses Onetime, Daily, and Monthly. An appointment has a description (for example, "see the dentist") and a date. Write a method occursOn(int year, int month, int day) that checks whether the appointment occurs on that date. For example, for a monthly appointment, you must check whether the day of the month matches. Then fill an array of Appointment objects with a mixture of appointments. Have the user enter a date and print out all appointments that occur on that date.

■■ **Business P9.22** Improve the appointment book program of Exercise P9.21. Give the user the option to add new appointments. The user must specify the type of the appointment, the description, and the date.

■■■ **Business P9.23** Improve the appointment book program of Exercises P9.21 and P9.22 by letting the user save the appointment data to a file and reload the data from a file. The saving part is straightforward: Make a method save. Save the type, description, and date to a file. The loading part is not so easy. First determine the type of the appointment to be loaded, create an object of that type, and then call a load method to load the data.

■■■ **Science P9.24** In this problem, you will model a circuit consisting of an arbitrary configuration of resistors. Provide a superclass Circuit with a instance method getResistance. Provide a subclass Resistor representing a single resistor. Provide subclasses Serial and Parallel, each of which contains an ArrayList<Circuit>. A Serial circuit models a series of circuits, each of which can be a single resistor or another circuit. Similarly, a

`Parallel` circuit models a set of circuits in parallel. For example, the following circuit is a `Parallel` circuit containing a single resistor and one `Serial` circuit:

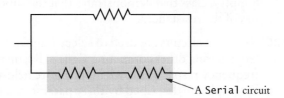

~A `Serial` circuit

Use Ohm's law to compute the combined resistance.

**■■ Science P9.25** Part (a) of the figure below shows a symbolic representation of an electric circuit called an *amplifier*. The input to the amplifier is the voltage $v_i$ and the output is the voltage $v_o$. The output of an amplifier is proportional to the input. The constant of proportionality is called the "gain" of the amplifier.

Parts (b), (c), and (d) show schematics of three specific types of amplifier: the *inverting amplifier*, *noninverting amplifier*, and *voltage divider amplifier*. Each of these three amplifiers consists of two resistors and an op amp. The value of the gain of each amplifier depends on the values of its resistances. In particular, the gain, $g$, of the inverting amplifier is given by $g = -\dfrac{R_2}{R_1}$. Similarly the gains of the noninverting amplifier and voltage divider amplifier are given by $g = 1 + \dfrac{R_2}{R_1}$ and $g = \dfrac{R_2}{R_1 + R_2}$, respectively.

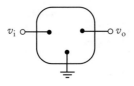

$v_i$       $v_o$

(a) Amplifier

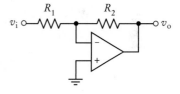

(b) Inverting amplifier

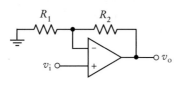

(c) Noninverting amplifier

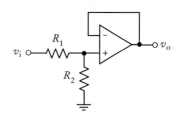

(d) Voltage divider amplifier

Write a Java program that represents the amplifier as a superclass and represents the inverting, noninverting, and voltage divider amplifiers as subclasses. Give the subclass two methods, `getGain` and a `getDescription` method that returns a string identifying the amplifier. Each subclass should have a constructor with two arguments, the resistances of the amplifier.

The subclasses need to override the getGain and getDescription methods of the superclass.

Supply a class that demonstrates that the subclasses all work properly for sample values of the resistances.

•• **Science P9.26** Resonant circuits are used to select a signal (e.g., a radio station or TV channel) from among other competing signals. Resonant circuits are characterized by the frequency response shown in the figure below. The resonant frequency response is completely described by three parameters: the resonant frequency, $\omega_o$, the bandwidth, $B$, and the gain at the resonant frequency, $k$.

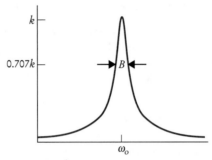

Frequency (rad/s, log scale)

Two simple resonant circuits are shown in the figure below. The circuit in (a) is called a *parallel resonant circuit*. The circuit in (b) is called a *series resonant circuit*. Both resonant circuits consist of a resistor having resistance $R$, a capacitor having capacitance $C$, and an inductor having inductance $L$.

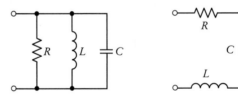

(a) Parallel resonant circuit    (b) Series resonant circuit

These circuits are designed by determining values of $R$, $C$, and $L$ that cause the resonant frequency response to be described by specified values of $\omega_o$, $B$, and $k$. The design equations for the parallel resonant circuit are:

$$R = k, \quad C = \frac{1}{BR}, \text{ and } \quad L = \frac{1}{\omega_o^2 C}$$

Similarly, the design equations for the series resonant circuit are:

$$R = \frac{1}{k}, \quad L = \frac{R}{B}, \text{ and } \quad C = \frac{1}{\omega_o^2 L}$$

Write a Java program that represents ResonantCircuit as a superclass and represents the SeriesResonantCircuit and ParallelResonantCircuit as subclasses. Give the superclass three private instance variables representing the parameters $\omega_o$, $B$, and $k$ of the resonant frequency response. The superclass should provide public instance methods to get and set each of these variables. The superclass should also provide a `display` method that prints a description of the resonant frequency response.

Each subclass should provide a method that designs the corresponding resonant circuit. The subclasses should also override the `display` method of the superclass to print descriptions of both the frequency response (the values of $\omega_o$, $B$, and $k$) and the circuit (the values of $R$, $C$, and $L$).

All classes should provide appropriate constructors.

Supply a class that demonstrates that the subclasses all work properly.

## ANSWERS TO SELF-CHECK QUESTIONS

1. Because every manager is an employee but not the other way around, the `Manager` class is more specialized. It is the subclass, and `Employee` is the superclass.

2. `CheckingAccount` and `SavingsAccount` both inherit from the more general class `BankAccount`.

3. `Exception`, `Throwable`

4. Vehicle, truck, motorcycle

5. It shouldn't. A quiz isn't a question; it *has* questions.

6. a, b, d

7. 
```
public class Manager extends Employee
{
    private double bonus;
    // Constructors and methods omitted
}
```

8. `name`, `baseSalary`, and `bonus`

9. 
```
public class Manager extends Employee
{
    . . .
    public double getSalary() { . . . }
}
```

10. `getName`, `setName`, `setBaseSalary`

11. The method is not allowed to access the instance variable `text` from the superclass.

12. The type of the `this` reference is `ChoiceQuestion`. Therefore, the `display` method of `ChoiceQuestion` is selected, and the method calls itself.

13. Because there is no ambiguity. The subclass doesn't have a `setAnswer` method.

14. 
```
public String getName()
{
    return "*" + super.getName();
}
```

15. 
```
public double getSalary()
{
    return super.getSalary() + bonus;
}
```

16. a only.

17. It belongs to the class `BankAccount` or one of its subclasses.

18. `Question[] quiz = new Question[SIZE];`

19. You cannot tell from the fragment — `cq` may be initialized with an object of a subclass of `ChoiceQuestion`. The `display` method of whatever object `cq` references is invoked.

20. No. This is a static method of the `Math` class. There is no implicit parameter object that could be used to dynamically look up a method.

21. Because the implementor of the `PrintStream` class did not supply a `toString` method.

22. The second line will not compile. The class `Object` does not have a method `length`.

23. The code will compile, but the second line will throw a class cast exception because `Question` is not a subclass of `String`.

24. There are only a few methods that can be invoked on variables of type `Object`.

25. The value is `false` if x is `null` and `true` otherwise.

26. It must implement the `Measurable` interface and provide a `getMeasure` method returning the salary.

27. The `Object` class doesn't have a `getMeasure` method.

28. You cannot modify the `String` class to implement `Measurable` — it is a library class. See Special Topic 9.9 for a solution.

**29.** Measurable is not a class. You cannot construct objects of type Measurable.

**30.** Have the Country class implement the Comparable interface, as shown below, and call Arrays.sort.

```
public class Country implements Comparable
{
    . . .
    public int compareTo(Object otherObject)
    {
        Country other = (Country) otherObject;
        if (area < other.area) return -1;
        if (area > other.area) return 1;
        return 0;
    }
}
```

**31.** Yes, you can, because String implements the Comparable interface type.

CHAPTER **10**

# GRAPHICAL
# USER
# INTERFACES

In this chapter, you will learn how to write graphical user-interface applications that contain buttons, text components, and graphical components such as charts. You will be able to process the events that are generated by button clicks, process the user input, and update the textual and graphical output.

# 10.1 Frame Windows

A graphical application shows information inside a **frame**: a window with a title bar, as shown in Figure 1. In the following sections, you will learn how to display a frame and how to place user-interface components inside it.

*A graphical user interface is displayed inside a frame.*

## 10.1.1 Displaying a Frame

> To show a frame, construct a JFrame object, set its size, and make it visible.

To show a frame, carry out the following steps:

1. Construct an object of the JFrame class:

   ```
   JFrame frame = new JFrame();
   ```

2. Set the size of the frame:

   ```
   final int FRAME_WIDTH = 300;
   final int FRAME_HEIGHT = 400;
   frame.setSize(FRAME_WIDTH, FRAME_HEIGHT);
   ```

   This frame will be 300 pixels wide and 400 pixels tall. If you omit this step the frame will be 0 by 0 pixels, and you won't be able to see it. (Pixels are the tiny dots from which digital images are composed.)

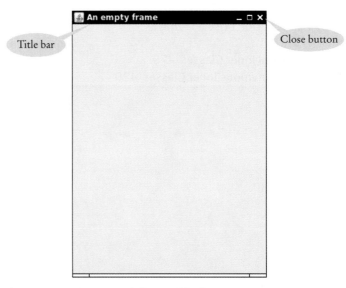

**Figure 1** A Frame Window

466

3. If you'd like, set the title of the frame:

```
frame.setTitle("An empty frame");
```

If you omit this step, the title bar is simply left blank.

4. Set the "default close operation":

```
frame.setDefaultCloseOperation(JFrame.EXIT_ON_CLOSE);
```

When the user closes the frame, the program automatically exits. Don't omit this step. If you do, the program keeps running even after the frame is closed.

5. Make the frame visible:

```
frame.setVisible(true);
```

The simple program below shows all of these steps. It produces the empty frame shown in Figure 1.

The JFrame class is a part of the javax.swing package. Swing is the nickname for the graphical user-interface library in Java. The "x" in javax denotes the fact that Swing started out as a Java *extension* before it was added to the standard library.

**section_1_1/EmptyFrameViewer.java**

```java
1   import javax.swing.JFrame;
2
3   /**
4      This program displays an empty frame.
5   */
6   public class EmptyFrameViewer
7   {
8      public static void main(String[] args)
9      {
10        JFrame frame = new JFrame();
11
12        final int FRAME_WIDTH = 300;
13        final int FRAME_HEIGHT = 400;
14        frame.setSize(FRAME_WIDTH, FRAME_HEIGHT);
15        frame.setTitle("An empty frame");
16        frame.setDefaultCloseOperation(JFrame.EXIT_ON_CLOSE);
17
18        frame.setVisible(true);
19     }
20  }
```

## 10.1.2 Adding User-Interface Components to a Frame

An empty frame is not very interesting. You will want to add some user-interface components, such as buttons and text labels. However, if you add components directly to the frame, they get placed on top of each other.

*When building a graphical user interface, you add components to a frame.*

Use a JPanel to group multiple user-interface components together.

If you have more than one component, put them into a **panel** (a container for other user-interface components), and then add the panel to the frame:

```
JPanel panel = new JPanel();
panel.add(button);
panel.add(label);
frame.add(panel);
```

You first construct the components, providing the text that should appear on them:

```
JButton button = new JButton("Click me!");
JLabel label = new JLabel("Hello, World!");
```

Then you add the components to the frame, as shown above. Figure 2 shows the result. When you run the program, you can click the button, but nothing will happen. You will see in Section 10.2 how to attach an action to a button.

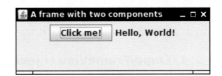

**Figure 2**   A Frame with a Button and a Label

### section_1_2/FIlledFrameViewer.java

```java
1   import javax.swing.JButton;
2   import javax.swing.JFrame;
3   import javax.swing.JLabel;
4   import javax.swing.JPanel;
5
6   /**
7      This program shows a frame that is filled with two components.
8   */
9   public class FilledFrameViewer
10  {
11     public static void main(String[] args)
12     {
13        JFrame frame = new JFrame();
14
15        JButton button = new JButton("Click me!");
16        JLabel label = new JLabel("Hello, World!");
17
18        JPanel panel = new JPanel();
19        panel.add(button);
20        panel.add(label);
21        frame.add(panel);
22
23        final int FRAME_WIDTH = 300;
24        final int FRAME_HEIGHT = 100;
25        frame.setSize(FRAME_WIDTH, FRAME_HEIGHT);
26        frame.setTitle("A frame with two components");
27        frame.setDefaultCloseOperation(JFrame.EXIT_ON_CLOSE);
28
29        frame.setVisible(true);
30     }
31  }
```

### 10.1.3 Using Inheritance to Customize Frames

Declare a JFrame subclass for a complex frame.

As you add more user-interface components to a frame, the frame can get quite complex. Your programs will become easier to understand when you use inheritance for complex frames.

To do so, design a subclass of JFrame. Store the components as instance variables. Initialize them in the constructor of your subclass. This approach makes it easy to add helper methods for organizing your code.

It is also a good idea to set the frame size in the frame constructor. The frame usually has a better idea of the preferred size than the program displaying it.

For example,

```java
public class FilledFrame extends JFrame
{
    // Use instance variables for components
    private JButton button;
    private JLabel label;

    private static final int FRAME_WIDTH = 300;
    private static final int FRAME_HEIGHT = 100;

    public FilledFrame()
    {
        // Now we can use a helper method
        createComponents();

        // It is a good idea to set the size in the frame constructor
        setSize(FRAME_WIDTH, FRAME_HEIGHT);
    }

    private void createComponents()
    {
        button = new JButton("Click me!");
        label = new JLabel("Hello, World!");
        JPanel panel = new JPanel();
        panel.add(button);
        panel.add(label);
        add(panel);
    }
}
```

*In Java, you can use inheritance to customize a frame.*

Of course, we still need a class with a main method:

```java
public class FilledFrameViewer2
{
    public static void main(String[] args)
    {
        JFrame frame = new FilledFrame();
        frame.setTitle("A frame with two components");
        frame.setDefaultCloseOperation(JFrame.EXIT_ON_CLOSE);
        frame.setVisible(true);
    }
}
```

**ONLINE EXAMPLE**

The complete FilledFrame program.

1. How do you display a square frame with a title bar that reads "Hello, World!"?
2. How can a program display two frames at once?
3. How can a program show a frame with two buttons labeled Yes and No?
4. Why does the `FilledFrameViewer2` class declare the frame variable to have class `JFrame`, not `FilledFrame`?
5. How many Java source files are required by the application in Section 10.1.3 when we use inheritance to declare the frame class?
6. Why does the `createComponents` method of `FilledFrame` call `add(panel)`, whereas the `main` method of `FilledFrameViewer` calls `frame.add(panel)`?

**Practice It**    Now you can try these exercises at the end of the chapter: R10.1, R10.4, P10.1.

---

Special Topic 10.1

### Adding the `main` Method to the Frame Class

Have another look at the `FilledFrame` and `FilledFrameViewer2` classes. Some programmers prefer to combine these two classes, by adding the `main` method to the frame class:

```java
public class FilledFrame extends JFrame
{
    . . .
    public static void main(String[] args)
    {
        JFrame frame = new FilledFrame();
        frame.setTitle("A frame with two components");
        frame.setDefaultCloseOperation(JFrame.EXIT_ON_CLOSE);
        frame.setVisible(true);
    }

    public FilledFrame()
    {
        createComponents();
        setSize(FRAME_WIDTH, FRAME_HEIGHT);
    }
    . . .
}
```

This is a convenient shortcut that you will find in many programs, but it does not separate the responsibilities between the frame class and the program.

---

# 10.2 Events and Event Handling

In an application that interacts with the user through a console window, user input is under control of the program. The program asks the user for input in a specific order. For example, a program might ask the user to supply first a name, then a dollar amount. But the programs that you use every day on your computer don't work like that. In a program with a modern **graphical user interface**, the *user* is in control. The user can use both the mouse and the keyboard and can manipulate many parts of the user interface in any desired order. For example, the user can enter information into text fields, pull down menus, click buttons, and drag scroll bars in any order. The program must react to the user commands in whatever order they arrive. Having to deal with many possible inputs in random order is quite a bit harder than simply forcing the user to supply input in a fixed order.

In the following sections, you will learn how to write Java programs that can react to user-interface events.

## 10.2.1  Listening to Events

Whenever the user of a graphical program types characters or uses the mouse anywhere inside one of the windows of the program, the program receives a notification that an **event** has occurred. For example, whenever the mouse moves a tiny interval over a window, a "mouse move" event is generated. Clicking a button or selecting a menu item generates an "action" event.

Most programs don't want to be flooded by irrelevant events. For example, when a button is clicked with the mouse, the mouse moves over the button, then the mouse button is pressed, and finally the button is released. Rather than receiving all these mouse events, a program can indicate that it only cares about button clicks, not about the underlying mouse events. On the other hand, if the mouse input is used

*In an event-driven user interface, the program receives an event whenever the user manipulates an input component.*

for drawing shapes on a virtual canvas, a program needs to closely track mouse events.

Every program must indicate which events it needs to receive. It does that by installing **event listener** objects. These objects are instances of classes that you must provide. The methods of your event listener classes contain the instructions that you want to have executed when the events occur.

To install a listener, you need to know the **event source**. The event source is the user-interface component, such as a button, that generates a particular event. You add an event listener object to the appropriate event sources. Whenever the event occurs, the event source calls the appropriate methods of all attached event listeners.

This sounds somewhat abstract, so let's run through an extremely simple program that prints a message whenever a button is clicked. Button listeners must belong to a class that implements the ActionListener interface:

```
public interface ActionListener
{
    void actionPerformed(ActionEvent event);
}
```

This particular interface has a single method, actionPerformed. It is your job to supply a class whose actionPerformed method contains the instructions that you want executed whenever the button is clicked. Here is a very simple example of such a listener class:

### section_2_1/ClickListener.java

```
1   import java.awt.event.ActionEvent;
2   import java.awt.event.ActionListener;
3
```

```
4   /**
5      An action listener that prints a message.
6   */
7   public class ClickListener implements ActionListener
8   {
9      public void actionPerformed(ActionEvent event)
10     {
11        System.out.println("I was clicked.");
12     }
13  }
```

We ignore the `event` parameter variable of the `actionPerformed` method—it contains additional details about the event, such as the time at which it occurred. Note that the event handling classes are defined in the `java.awt.event` package. (AWT is the Abstract Window Toolkit, the Java library for dealing with windows and events.)

Once the listener class has been declared, we need to construct an object of the class and add it to the button:

Attach an ActionListener to each button so that your program can react to button clicks.

```
ActionListener listener = new ClickListener();
button.addActionListener(listener);
```

Whenever the button is clicked, the Java event handling library calls

```
listener.actionPerformed(event);
```

As a result, the message is printed.

You can test this program out by opening a console window, starting the `ButtonViewer1` program from that console window, clicking the button, and watching the messages in the console window (see Figure 3).

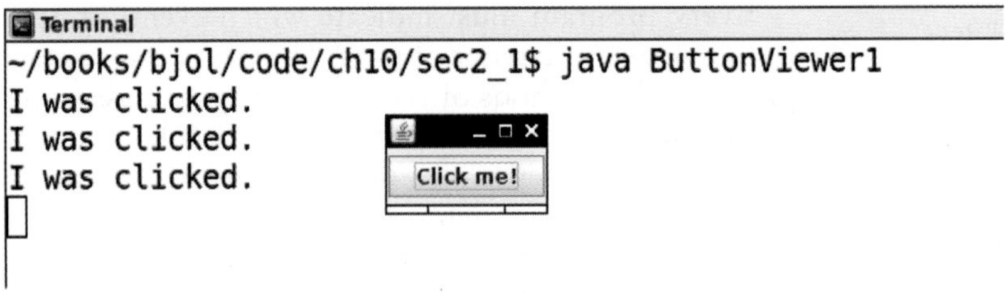

**Figure 3**  Implementing an Action Listener

### section_2_1/ButtonFrame1.java

```
1   import java.awt.event.ActionListener;
2   import javax.swing.JButton;
3   import javax.swing.JFrame;
4   import javax.swing.JPanel;
5
6   /**
7      This frame demonstrates how to install an action listener.
8   */
9   public class ButtonFrame1 extends JFrame
10  {
11     private static final int FRAME_WIDTH = 100;
12     private static final int FRAME_HEIGHT = 60;
13
```

```
14   public ButtonFrame1()
15   {
16      createComponents();
17      setSize(FRAME_WIDTH, FRAME_HEIGHT);
18   }
19
20   private void createComponents()
21   {
22      JButton button = new JButton("Click me!");
23      JPanel panel = new JPanel();
24      panel.add(button);
25      add(panel);
26
27      ActionListener listener = new ClickListener();
28      button.addActionListener(listener);
29   }
30 }
```

### section_2_1/ButtonViewer1.java

```
1   import javax.swing.JFrame;
2
3   /**
4      This program demonstrates how to install an action listener.
5   */
6   public class ButtonViewer1
7   {
8      public static void main(String[] args)
9      {
10        JFrame frame = new ButtonFrame1();
11        frame.setDefaultCloseOperation(JFrame.EXIT_ON_CLOSE);
12        frame.setVisible(true);
13     }
14  }
```

## 10.2.2 Using Inner Classes for Listeners

*An inner class is a class that is declared inside another class.*

In the preceding section, you saw how to specify button actions. The code for the button action is placed into a listener class. It is common to implement listener classes as **inner classes** like this:

```
public class ButtonFrame2 extends JFrame
{
   . . .
   // This inner class is declared inside the frame class
   class ClickListener implements ActionListener
   {
      . . .
   }

   private void createComponents()
   {
      button = new JButton("Click me!");
      ActionListener listener = new ClickListener();
      button.addActionListener(listener);
      . . .
   }
}
```

An inner class is simply a class that is declared inside another class.

There are two advantages to making a listener class into an inner class. First, listener classes tend to be very short. You can put the inner class close to where it is needed, without cluttering up the remainder of the project. Moreover, inner classes have a very attractive feature: Their methods can access instance variables and methods of the surrounding class.

Methods of an inner class can access variables from the surrounding class.

This feature is particularly useful when implementing event handlers. It allows the inner class to access variables without having to receive them as constructor or method arguments.

Let's look at an example. Instead of printing the message "I was clicked", we want to show it in a label. If we make the action listener into an inner class of the frame class, its actionPerformed method can access the label instance variable and call the setText method, which changes the label text.

```java
public class ButtonFrame2 extends JFrame
{
   private JButton button;
   private JLabel label;
   . . .
   class ClickListener implements ActionListener
   {
      public void actionPerformed(ActionEvent event)
      {
         // Accesses label variable from surrounding class
         label.setText("I was clicked");
      }
   }
   . . .
}
```

Having the listener as a regular class is unattractive—the listener would need to be constructed with a reference to the label field (see Exercise P10.5).

### section_2_2/ButtonFrame2.java

```java
 1  import java.awt.event.ActionEvent;
 2  import java.awt.event.ActionListener;
 3  import javax.swing.JButton;
 4  import javax.swing.JFrame;
 5  import javax.swing.JLabel;
 6  import javax.swing.JPanel;
 7
 8  public class ButtonFrame2 extends JFrame
 9  {
10     private JButton button;
11     private JLabel label;
12
13     private static final int FRAME_WIDTH = 300;
14     private static final int FRAME_HEIGHT = 100;
15
16     public ButtonFrame2()
17     {
18        createComponents();
19        setSize(FRAME_WIDTH, FRAME_HEIGHT);
20     }
21
```

```
22      /**
23          An action listener that changes the label text.
24      */
25      class ClickListener implements ActionListener
26      {
27          public void actionPerformed(ActionEvent event)
28          {
29              label.setText("I was clicked.");
30          }
31      }
32
33      private void createComponents()
34      {
35          button = new JButton("Click me!");
36          ActionListener listener = new ClickListener();
37          button.addActionListener(listener);
38
39          label = new JLabel("Hello, World!");
40
41          JPanel panel = new JPanel();
42          panel.add(button);
43          panel.add(label);
44          add(panel);
45      }
46  }
```

## 10.2.3 Application: Showing Growth of an Investment

In this section, we will build a practical application with a graphical user interface. A frame displays the amount of money in a bank account. Whenever the user clicks a button, 5 percent interest is added, and the new balance is displayed (see Figure 4).

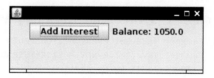

**Figure 4**
Clicking the Button
Grows the Investment

We need a button and a label for the user interface. We also need to store the current balance:

```
public class InvestmentFrame extends JFrame
{
    private JButton button;
    private JLabel resultLabel;
    private double balance;

    private static final double INTEREST_RATE = 5;
    private static final double INITIAL_BALANCE = 1000;
    . . .
}
```

We initialize the balance when the frame is constructed. Then we add the button and label to a panel, and the panel to the frame:

```
public InvestmentFrame()
{
```

```
      balance = INITIAL_BALANCE;

      createComponents();
      setSize(FRAME_WIDTH, FRAME_HEIGHT);
   }
```

Now we are ready for the hard part—the event listener that handles button clicks. As in the preceding section, it is necessary to declare a class that implements the Action-Listener interface, and to place the button action into the actionPerformed method. Our listener class adds interest and displays the new balance:

```
class AddInterestListener implements ActionListener
{
   public void actionPerformed(ActionEvent event)
   {
      double interest = balance * INTEREST_RATE / 100;
      balance = balance + interest;
      resultLabel.setText("Balance: " + balance);
   }
}
```

We make this class an inner class so that it can access the balance and resultLabel instance variables.

Finally, we need to add an instance of the listener class to the button:

```
private void createComponents()
{
   button = new JButton("Add Interest");
   ActionListener listener = new AddInterestListener();
   button.addActionListener(listener);
   . . .
}
```

Here is the complete program. It demonstrates how to add multiple components to a frame, by using a panel, and how to implement listeners as inner classes.

### section_2_3/InvestmentFrame.java

```
 1   import java.awt.event.ActionEvent;
 2   import java.awt.event.ActionListener;
 3   import javax.swing.JButton;
 4   import javax.swing.JFrame;
 5   import javax.swing.JLabel;
 6   import javax.swing.JPanel;
 7
 8   public class InvestmentFrame extends JFrame
 9   {
10      private JButton button;
11      private JLabel resultLabel;
12      private double balance;
13
14      private static final int FRAME_WIDTH = 300;
15      private static final int FRAME_HEIGHT = 100;
16
17      private static final double INTEREST_RATE = 5;
18      private static final double INITIAL_BALANCE = 1000;
19
20      public InvestmentFrame()
21      {
22         balance = INITIAL_BALANCE;
```

```
23
24          createComponents();
25          setSize(FRAME_WIDTH, FRAME_HEIGHT);
26       }
27
28       /**
29          Adds interest to the balance and updates the display.
30       */
31       class AddInterestListener implements ActionListener
32       {
33          public void actionPerformed(ActionEvent event)
34          {
35             double interest = balance * INTEREST_RATE / 100;
36             balance = balance + interest;
37             resultLabel.setText("Balance: " + balance);
38          }
39       }
40
41       private void createComponents()
42       {
43          button = new JButton("Add Interest");
44          ActionListener listener = new AddInterestListener();
45          button.addActionListener(listener);
46
47          resultLabel = new JLabel("Balance: " + balance);
48
49          JPanel panel = new JPanel();
50          panel.add(button);
51          panel.add(resultLabel);
52          add(panel);
53       }
54    }
```

### section_2_3/InvestmentViewer.java

```
1     import javax.swing.JFrame;
2
3     /**
4        This program shows the growth of an investment.
5     */
6     public class InvestmentViewer
7     {
8        public static void main(String[] args)
9        {
10          JFrame frame = new InvestmentFrame();
11          frame.setDefaultCloseOperation(JFrame.EXIT_ON_CLOSE);
12          frame.setVisible(true);
13       }
14    }
```

**SELF CHECK**

7.  Which objects are the event source and the event listener in the ButtonViewer program?

8.  Why is it legal to assign a ClickListener object to a variable of type ActionListener?

9.  When do you call the actionPerformed method?

10. Why would an inner class method want to access a variable from a surrounding scope?

**11.** How do you place the "Balance: . . ." message to the left of the "Add Interest" button?

**Practice It** Now you can try these exercises at the end of the chapter: R10.7, P10.2, P10.5.

### Common Error 10.1

### Modifying Parameter Types in the Implementing Method

When you implement an interface, you must declare each method *exactly* as it is specified in the interface. Accidentally making small changes to the parameter variable types is a common error. Here is the classic example,

```
class MyListener implements ActionListener
{
    public void actionPerformed()
    // Oops . . . forgot ActionEvent parameter variable
    {
        . . .
    }
}
```

As far as the compiler is concerned, this class fails to provide the method

```
public void actionPerformed(ActionEvent event)
```

You have to read the error message carefully and pay attention to the parameter variable and return types to find your error.

### Common Error 10.2

### Forgetting to Attach a Listener

If you run your program and find that your buttons seem to be dead, double-check that you attached the button listener. The same holds for other user-interface components. It is a surprisingly common error to program the listener class and the event handler action without actually attaching the listener to the event source.

### Programming Tip 10.1

### Don't Use a Frame as a Listener

In this book, we use inner classes for event listeners. That approach works for many different event types. Once you master the technique, you don't have to think about it anymore. Many development environments automatically generate code with inner classes, so it is a good idea to be familiar with them.

However, some programmers bypass the event listener classes and turn a frame into a listener, like this:

```
public class InvestmentFrame extends JFrame
        implements ActionListener   // This approach is not recommended
{
    . . .
    public InvestmentFrame()
    {
        button = new JButton("Add Interest");
        button.addActionListener(this);
        . . .
```

```
      }

   public void actionPerformed(ActionEvent event)
   {
   }
   . . .
}
```

Now the `actionPerformed` method is a part of the `InvestmentFrame` class rather than part of a separate listener class. The listener is installed as `this`.

We don't recommend this technique. If the viewer class contains two buttons that each generate action events, then the `actionPerformed` method must investigate the event source, which leads to code that is tedious and error-prone.

Special Topic 10.2

## Local Inner Classes

An inner class can be declared completely inside a method. For example,

```
public static void main(String[] args)
{
   . . .
   class ClickListener implements ActionListener
   {
      public void actionPerformed(ActionEvent event)
      {
         . . .
      }
   }

   JButton button = new JButton("Click me");
   button.addActionListener(new ClickListener());
   . . .
}
```

This places the inner class exactly where you need it, next to the button.

The methods of a class that is defined inside a method can access the variables of the enclosing method, provided they are declared as `final`. For example,

```
public static void main(String[] args)
{
   final JLabel label = new JLabel("Hello, World!");
   . . .
   class ClickListener implements ActionListener
   {
      public void actionPerformed(ActionEvent event)
      {
         label.setText("I was clicked");
         // Accesses label variable from enclosing method
      }
   }
   . . .
   button.addActionListener(new ClickListener());
}
```

That sounds quite restrictive, but it is usually not an issue if the variable is an object reference. Keep in mind that an object variable is `final` when the variable always refers to the same object. The state of the object can change, but the variable can't refer to a different object. For example, in our program, we never intended to have the `label` variable refer to multiple labels, so there was no harm in declaring it as `final`.

However, you can't change a numeric or Boolean local variable from an inner class. For example, the following would not work:

```java
public static void main(String[] args)
{
   final double balance = INITIAL_BALANCE;
   . . .
   class AddInterestListener implements ActionListener
   {
      public void actionPerformed(ActionEvent event)
      {
         double interest = balance * (1 + INTEREST_RATE);
         balance = balance + interest;
            // Error: Can't modify a final numeric variable
      }
   }
   . . .
}
```

The remedy is to use an object instead:

```java
public static void main(String[] args)
{
   final BankAccount account = new BankAccount();
   account.deposit(INITIAL_BALANCE);
   . . .
   class AddInterestListener implements ActionListener
   {
      public void actionPerformed(ActionEvent event)
      {
         double interest = balance * (1 + INTEREST_RATE);
         account.deposit(interest);
            // Ok—we don't change the reference, just the object's state
      }
   }
   . . .
}
```

## Anonymous Inner Classes

An entity is anonymous if it does not have a name. In a program, something that is only used once doesn't usually need a name. For example, you can replace

```java
String buttonLabel = "Add Interest";
JButton button = new JButton(buttonLabel);
```

with

```java
JButton button = new JButton("Add Interest");
```

The string `"Add Interest"` is an anonymous object. Programmers like anonymous objects, because they don't have to go through the trouble of coming up with a name. If you have struggled with the decision whether to call a label `l`, `label`, or `buttonLabel`, you'll understand this sentiment.

Event listeners often give rise to a similar situation. You construct a single object of an event listener class. Afterward, the class is never used again. In Java, it is possible to declare an anonymous class if all you ever need is a single object of the class.

Here is an example:

```
button = new JButton("Add Interest");
button.addActionListener(new ActionListener()
   {
       public void actionPerformed(ActionEvent event)
       {
          double interest = balance * (1 + INTEREST_RATE);
          account.deposit(interest);
       }
   });
```

This means: Define a class that implements the ActionListener interface with the given action-Performed method. Construct an object of that class and pass it to the addActionListener method.

Many programmers like this style because it is so compact. Moreover, GUI builders in integrated development environments often generate code of this form.

# 10.3  Processing Text Input

We continue our discussion with graphical user interfaces that accept text input. Of course, a graphical application can receive text input by calling the showInputDialog method of the JOptionPane class, but popping up a separate dialog box for each input is not a natural user interface. Most graphical programs collect text input through **text components** (see Figures 5 and 7). In the following two sections, you will learn how to add text components to a graphical application, and how to read what the user types into them.

## 10.3.1  Text Fields

Use a JTextField
component for
reading a single line
of input. Place a
JLabel next to each
text field.

The JTextField class provides a text field for reading a single line of text. When you construct a text field, you need to supply the width—the approximate number of characters that you expect the user to type.

```
final int FIELD_WIDTH = 10;
rateField = new JTextField(FIELD_WIDTH);
```

Users can type additional characters, but then a part of the contents of the field becomes invisible.

You will want to label each text field so that the user knows what to type into it. Construct a JLabel object for each label:

```
JLabel rateLabel = new JLabel("Interest Rate: ");
```

You want to give the user an opportunity to enter all information into the text fields before processing it. Therefore, you should supply a button that the user can press to indicate that the input is ready for processing.

**Figure 5**
An Application
with a Text Field

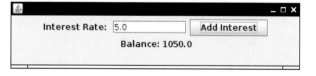

When that button is clicked, its `actionPerformed` method should read the user input from each text field, using the `getText` method of the `JTextField` class. The `getText` method returns a `String` object. In our sample program, we turn the string into a number, using the `Double.parseDouble` method. After updating the account, we show the balance in another label.

```java
class AddInterestListener implements ActionListener
{
    public void actionPerformed(ActionEvent event)
    {
        double rate = Double.parseDouble(rateField.getText());
        double interest = balance * rate / 100;
        balance = balance + interest;
        resultLabel.setText("Balance: " + balance);
    }
}
```

The following application is a useful prototype for a graphical user-interface front end for arbitrary calculations. You can easily modify it for your own needs. Place input components into the frame. In the `actionPerformed` method, carry out the needed calculations. Display the result in a label.

**section_3_1/InvestmentFrame2.java**

```java
 1   import java.awt.event.ActionEvent;
 2   import java.awt.event.ActionListener;
 3   import javax.swing.JButton;
 4   import javax.swing.JFrame;
 5   import javax.swing.JLabel;
 6   import javax.swing.JPanel;
 7   import javax.swing.JTextField;
 8
 9   /**
10       A frame that shows the growth of an investment with variable interest.
11   */
12   public class InvestmentFrame2 extends JFrame
13   {
14       private static final int FRAME_WIDTH = 450;
15       private static final int FRAME_HEIGHT = 100;
16
17       private static final double DEFAULT_RATE = 5;
18       private static final double INITIAL_BALANCE = 1000;
19
20       private JLabel rateLabel;
21       private JTextField rateField;
22       private JButton button;
23       private JLabel resultLabel;
24       private double balance;
25
26       public InvestmentFrame2()
27       {
28           balance = INITIAL_BALANCE;
29
30           resultLabel = new JLabel("Balance: " + balance);
31
32           createTextField();
33           createButton();
34           createPanel();
35
```

```
36        setSize(FRAME_WIDTH, FRAME_HEIGHT);
37     }
38
39     private void createTextField()
40     {
41        rateLabel = new JLabel("Interest Rate: ");
42
43        final int FIELD_WIDTH = 10;
44        rateField = new JTextField(FIELD_WIDTH);
45        rateField.setText("" + DEFAULT_RATE);
46     }
47
48     /**
49        Adds interest to the balance and updates the display.
50     */
51     class AddInterestListener implements ActionListener
52     {
53        public void actionPerformed(ActionEvent event)
54        {
55           double rate = Double.parseDouble(rateField.getText());
56           double interest = balance * rate / 100;
57           balance = balance + interest;
58           resultLabel.setText("Balance: " + balance);
59        }
60     }
61
62     private void createButton()
63     {
64        button = new JButton("Add Interest");
65
66        ActionListener listener = new AddInterestListener();
67        button.addActionListener(listener);
68     }
69
70     private void createPanel()
71     {
72        panel = new JPanel();
73        panel.add(rateLabel);
74        panel.add(rateField);
75        panel.add(button);
76        panel.add(resultLabel);
77        add(panel);
78     }
79  }
```

## 10.3.2 Text Areas

Use a JTextArea to show multiple lines of text.

In the preceding section, you saw how to construct text fields. A text field holds a single line of text. To display multiple lines of text, use the JTextArea class.

*You can use a text area for reading or displaying multi-line text.*

When constructing a text area, you can specify the number of rows and columns:

```
final int ROWS = 10; // Lines of text
final int COLUMNS = 30; // Characters in each row
JTextArea textArea = new JTextArea(ROWS, COLUMNS);
```

Use the setText method to set the text of a text field or text area. The append method adds text to the end of a text area. Use newline characters to separate lines, like this:

```
textArea.append(balance + "\n");
```

If you want to use a text field or text area for display purposes only, call the set-Editable method like this

```
textArea.setEditable(false);
```

Now the user can no longer edit the contents of the field, but your program can still call setText and append to change it.

As shown in Figure 6, the JTextField and JTextArea classes are subclasses of the class JTextComponent. The methods setText and setEditable are declared in the JText-Component class and inherited by JTextField and JTextArea. However, the append method is declared in the JTextArea class.

To add scroll bars to a text area, use a JScrollPane, like this:

You can add scroll bars to any component with a JScrollPane.

```
JTextArea textArea = new JTextArea(ROWS, COLUMNS);
JScrollPane scrollPane = new JScrollPane(textArea);
```

Then add the scroll pane to the panel. Figure 7 shows the result.

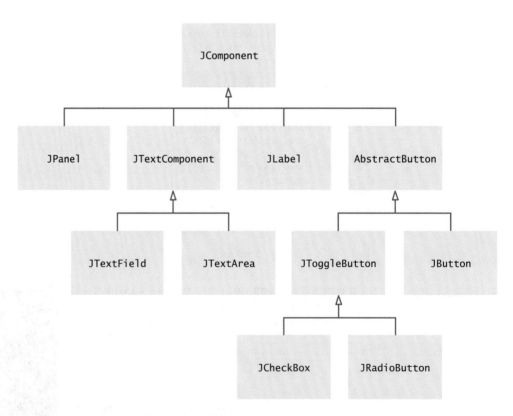

**Figure 6**  A Part of the Hierarchy of Swing User-Interface Components

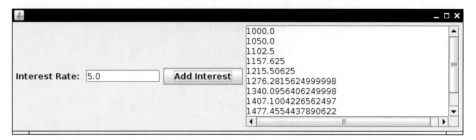

**Figure 7**   The Investment Application with a Text Area Inside Scroll Bars

The following sample program puts these concepts together. A user can enter numbers into the interest rate text field and then click on the "Add Interest" button. The interest rate is applied, and the updated balance is appended to the text area. The text area has scroll bars and is not editable.

This program is similar to the previous investment viewer program, but it keeps track of all the bank balances, not just the last one.

### section_3_2/InvestmentFrame3.java

```java
1   import java.awt.event.ActionEvent;
2   import java.awt.event.ActionListener;
3   import javax.swing.JButton;
4   import javax.swing.JFrame;
5   import javax.swing.JLabel;
6   import javax.swing.JPanel;
7   import javax.swing.JScrollPane;
8   import javax.swing.JTextArea;
9   import javax.swing.JTextField;
10
11  /**
12     A frame that shows the growth of an investment with variable interest,
13     using a text area.
14  */
15  public class InvestmentFrame3 extends JFrame
16  {
17     private static final int FRAME_WIDTH = 400;
18     private static final int FRAME_HEIGHT = 250;
19
20     private static final int AREA_ROWS = 10;
21     private static final int AREA_COLUMNS = 30;
22
23     private static final double DEFAULT_RATE = 5;
24     private static final double INITIAL_BALANCE = 1000;
25
26     private JLabel rateLabel;
27     private JTextField rateField;
28     private JButton button;
29     private JTextArea resultArea;
30     private double balance;
31
32     public InvestmentFrame3()
33     {
34        balance = INITIAL_BALANCE;
35        resultArea = new JTextArea(AREA_ROWS, AREA_COLUMNS);
```

```
36            resultArea.setText(balance + "\n");
37            resultArea.setEditable(false);
38
39            createTextField();
40            createButton();
41            createPanel();
42
43            setSize(FRAME_WIDTH, FRAME_HEIGHT);
44        }
45
46        private void createTextField()
47        {
48            rateLabel = new JLabel("Interest Rate: ");
49
50            final int FIELD_WIDTH = 10;
51            rateField = new JTextField(FIELD_WIDTH);
52            rateField.setText("" + DEFAULT_RATE);
53        }
54
55        class AddInterestListener implements ActionListener
56        {
57            public void actionPerformed(ActionEvent event)
58            {
59                double rate = Double.parseDouble(rateField.getText());
60                double interest = balance * rate / 100;
61                balance = balance + interest;
62                resultArea.append(balance + "\n");
63            }
64        }
65
66        private void createButton()
67        {
68            button = new JButton("Add Interest");
69
70            ActionListener listener = new AddInterestListener();
71            button.addActionListener(listener);
72        }
73
74        private void createPanel()
75        {
76            JPanel = new JPanel();
77            panel.add(rateLabel);
78            panel.add(rateField);
79            panel.add(button);
80            JScrollPane scrollPane = new JScrollPane(resultArea);
81            panel.add(scrollPane);
82            add(panel);
83        }
84    }
```

**SELF CHECK**

12. What happens if you omit the first JLabel object in the program of Section 10.3.1?

13. If a text field holds an integer, what expression do you use to read its contents?

14. What is the difference between a text field and a text area?

15. Why did the InvestmentFrame3 program call resultArea.setEditable(false)?

**16.** How would you modify the InvestmentFrame3 program if you didn't want to use scroll bars?

**Practice It** Now you can try these exercises at the end of the chapter: R10.13, P10.9, P10.10.

# 10.4 Creating Drawings

You often want to include simple drawings such as graphs or charts in your programs. The Java library does not have any standard components for this purpose, but it is fairly easy to make your own drawings. The following sections show how.

## 10.4.1 Drawing on a Component

We start out with a simple bar chart (see Figure 8) that is composed of three rectangles.

*You can make simple drawings out of lines, rectangles, and circles.*

You cannot draw directly onto a frame. Instead, you add a component to the frame and draw on the component. To do so, extend the JComponent class and override its paintComponent method.

> In order to display a drawing, provide a class that extends the JComponent class.

```
public class ChartComponent extends JComponent
{
    public void paintComponent(Graphics g)
    {
        Drawing instructions
    }
}
```

> Place drawing instructions inside the paintComponent method. That method is called whenever the component needs to be repainted.

When the component is shown for the first time, its paintComponent method is called automatically. The method is also called when the window is resized, or when it is shown again after it was hidden.

The paintComponent method receives an object of type Graphics. The Graphics object stores the graphics state—the current color, font, and so on, that are used for drawing operations. The Graphics class has methods for drawing geometric shapes. The call

```
g.fillRect(x, y, width, height)
```

draws a solid rectangle with upper-left corner (*x*, *y*) and the given width and height.

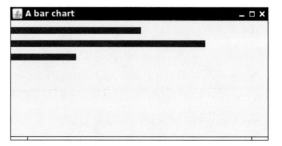

**Figure 8** Drawing a Bar Chart

The Graphics class has methods to draw rectangles and other shapes.

Here we draw three rectangles. They line up on the left because they all have $x = 0$. They also all have the same height.

```
public class ChartComponent extends JComponent
{
    public void paintComponent(Graphics g)
    {
        g.fillRect(0, 10, 200, 10);
        g.fillRect(0, 30, 300, 10);
        g.fillRect(0, 50, 100, 10);
    }
}
```

Note that the coordinate system is different from the one used in mathematics. The origin (0, 0) is at the upper-left corner of the component, and the $y$-coordinate grows downward.

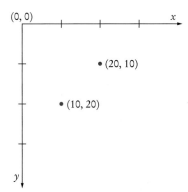

Here is the source code for the `ChartComponent` class. As you can see from the `import` statements, the Graphics class is part of the java.awt package.

**section_4_1/ChartComponent.java**

```
 1  import java.awt.Graphics;
 2  import javax.swing.JComponent;
 3
 4  /**
 5     A component that draws a bar chart.
 6  */
 7  public class ChartComponent extends JComponent
 8  {
 9      public void paintComponent(Graphics g)
10      {
11          g.fillRect(0, 10, 200, 10);
12          g.fillRect(0, 30, 300, 10);
13          g.fillRect(0, 50, 100, 10);
14      }
15  }
```

Now we need to add the component to a frame, and show the frame. Because the frame is so simple, we don't make a frame subclass. Here is the viewer class:

**section_4_1/ChartViewer.java**

```
 1  import javax.swing.JComponent;
 2  import javax.swing.JFrame;
```

```
 3
 4   public class ChartViewer
 5   {
 6      public static void main(String[] args)
 7      {
 8         JFrame frame = new JFrame();
 9
10         frame.setSize(400, 200);
11         frame.setTitle("A bar chart");
12         frame.setDefaultCloseOperation(JFrame.EXIT_ON_CLOSE);
13
14         JComponent component = new ChartComponent();
15         frame.add(component);
16
17         frame.setVisible(true);
18      }
19   }
```

## 10.4.2 Ovals, Lines, Text, and Color

In the preceding section, you learned how to write a program that draws rectangles. Now we turn to additional graphical elements that allow you to draw quite a few interesting pictures.

To draw an oval, you specify its *bounding box* (see Figure 9) in the same way that you would specify a rectangle, namely by the $x$- and $y$-coordinates of the top-left corner and the width and height of the box. Then the call

```
g.drawOval(x, y, width, height);
```

draws the outline of an oval. To draw a circle, simply set the width and height to the same values:

```
g.drawOval(x, y, diameter, diameter);
```

Notice that $(x, y)$ is the top-left corner of the bounding box, not the center of the circle.

> Use drawRect, drawOval, and drawLine to draw geometric shapes.

If you want to fill the inside of an oval, use the fillOval method instead. Conversely, if you want only the outline of a rectangle, with no filling, use the drawRect method.

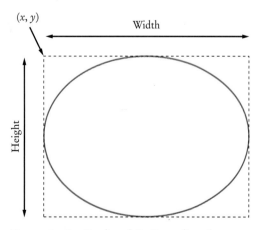

**Figure 9** An Oval and Its Bounding Box

**Figure 10**
Basepoint and Baseline

To draw a line, call the drawLine method with the *x*- and *y*-coordinates of both end points:

```
g.drawLine(x1, y1, x2, y2);
```

You often want to put text inside a drawing, for example, to label some of the parts. Use the drawString method of the Graphics class to draw a string anywhere in a window. You must specify the string and the *x*- and *y*-coordinates of the basepoint of the first character in the string (see Figure 10). For example,

The drawString method draws a string, starting at its basepoint.

```
g.drawString("Message", 50, 100);
```

When you first start drawing, all shapes and strings are drawn with a black pen. To change the color, you need to supply an object of type Color. Java uses the RGB color model. That is, you specify a color by the amounts of the primary colors—red, green, and blue—that make up the color. The amounts are given as integers between 0 (primary color not present) and 255 (maximum amount present). For example,

```
Color magenta = new Color(255, 0, 255);
```

constructs a Color object with maximum red, no green, and maximum blue, yielding a bright purple color called magenta.

| Table 1 Predefined Colors | | |
|---|---|---|
| Color | | RGB Values |
| Color.BLACK | | 0, 0, 0 |
| Color.BLUE | | 0, 0, 255 |
| Color.CYAN | | 0, 255, 255 |
| Color.GRAY | | 128, 128, 128 |
| Color.DARKGRAY | | 64, 64, 64 |
| Color.LIGHTGRAY | | 192, 192, 192 |
| Color.GREEN | | 0, 255, 0 |
| Color.MAGENTA | | 255, 0, 255 |
| Color.ORANGE | | 255, 200, 0 |
| Color.PINK | | 255, 175, 175 |
| Color.RED | | 255, 0, 0 |
| Color.WHITE | | 255, 255, 255 |
| Color.YELLOW | | 255, 255, 0 |

For your convenience, a variety of colors have been predefined in the Color class. Table 1 shows those predefined colors and their RGB values. For example, Color.PINK has been predefined to be the same color as new Color(255, 175, 175).

To draw a shape in a different color, first set the color of the Graphics object, then call the drawing method:

> When you set a new color in the graphics context, it is used for subsequent drawing operations.

```
g.setColor(Color.YELLOW);
g.fillOval(350, 25, 35, 20); // Fills the oval in yellow
```

The following program puts all these shapes to work, creating a simple chart (see Figure 11.

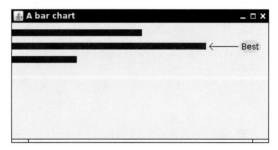

**Figure 11**  A Bar Chart with a Label

### section_4_2/ChartComponent2.java

```java
1   import java.awt.Color;
2   import java.awt.Graphics;
3   import javax.swing.JComponent;
4
5   /**
6      A component that draws a demo chart.
7   */
8   public class ChartComponent2 extends JComponent
9   {
10     public void paintComponent(Graphics g)
11     {
12        // Draw the bars
13        g.fillRect(0, 10, 200, 10);
14        g.fillRect(0, 30, 300, 10);
15        g.fillRect(0, 50, 100, 10);
16
17        // Draw the arrow
18        g.drawLine(350, 35, 305, 35);
19        g.drawLine(305, 35, 310, 30);
20        g.drawLine(305, 35, 310, 40);
21
22        // Draw the highlight and the text
23        g.setColor(Color.YELLOW);
24        g.fillOval(350, 25, 35, 20);
25        g.setColor(Color.BLACK);
26        g.drawString("Best", 355, 40);
27     }
28  }
```

**section_4_2/ChartViewer2.java**

```
1   import javax.swing.JComponent;
2   import javax.swing.JFrame;
3
4   public class ChartViewer2
5   {
6      public static void main(String[] args)
7      {
8         JFrame frame = new JFrame();
9
10        frame.setSize(400, 200);
11        frame.setTitle("A bar chart");
12        frame.setDefaultCloseOperation(JFrame.EXIT_ON_CLOSE);
13
14        JComponent component = new ChartComponent2();
15        frame.add(component);
16
17        frame.setVisible(true);
18     }
19  }
```

## 10.4.3 Application: Visualizing the Growth of an Investment

In this section, we will add a bar chart to the investment program of Section 10.3. Whenever the user clicks on the "Add Interest" button, another bar is added to the bar chart (see Figure 12).

The chart class of the preceding section produced a fixed bar chart. We will develop an improved version that can draw a chart with any values. The chart keeps an array list of the values:

```
public class ChartComponent extends JComponent
{
   private ArrayList<Double> values;
   private double maxValue;
   . . .
}
```

When drawing the bars, we need to scale the values to fit into the chart. For example, if the investment program adds a value such as 10050 to the chart, we don't want to draw a bar that is 10,050 pixels long. In order to scale the values, we need to know the largest value that should still fit inside the chart. We will ask the user of the chart component to provide that maximum in the constructor:

```
public ChartComponent(double max)
{
   values = new ArrayList<Double>();
   maxValue = max;
}
```

We compute the width of a bar as

```
int barWidth = (int) (getWidth() * value / maxValue);
```

The getWidth method returns the width of the component in pixels. If the value to be drawn equals maxValue, the bar stretches across the entire component width.

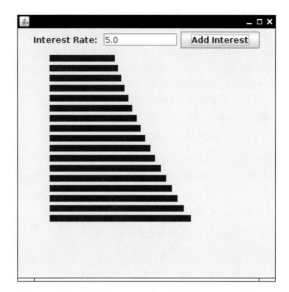

**Figure 12** Clicking on the "Add Interest" Button
Adds a Bar to the Chart

Here is the complete paintComponent method. We stack the bars horizontally and leave small gaps between them:

```java
public void paintComponent(Graphics g)
{
   final int GAP = 5;
   final int BAR_HEIGHT = 10;

   int y = GAP;
   for (double value : values)
   {
      int barWidth = (int) (getWidth() * value / maxValue);
      g.fillRect(0, y, barWidth, BAR_HEIGHT);
      y = y + BAR_HEIGHT + GAP;
   }
}
```

Whenever the user clicks the "Add Interest" button, a value is added to the array list. Afterward, it is essential to call the repaint method:

```java
public void append(double value)
{
   values.add(value);
   repaint();
}
```

The call to repaint forces a call to the paintComponent method. The paintComponent method redraws the component. Then the graph is drawn again, now showing the appended value.

Why not call paintComponent directly? The simple answer is that you can't—you don't have a Graphics object that you can pass as an argument. Instead, you need to ask the Swing library to make the call to paintComponent at its earliest convenience. That is what the repaint method does.

Call the repaint method whenever the state of a painted component changes.

When placing a painted component into a panel, you need to specify its preferred size.

We need to address another issue with painted components. If you place a painted component into a panel, you need to specify its preferred size. Otherwise, the panel will assume that the preferred size is 0 by 0 pixels, and you won't be able to see the component. Specifying the preferred size of a painted component is conceptually similar to specifying the number of rows and columns in a text area.

Call the setPreferredSize method with a Dimension object as argument. A Dimension argument wraps a width and a height into a single object. The call has the form

```java
chart.setPreferredSize(new Dimension(CHART_WIDTH, CHART_HEIGHT));
```

That's all that is required to add a diagram to an application. Here is the code for the chart and frame classes; the viewer class is with the book's companion code.

### section_4_3/ChartComponent.java

```java
1   import java.awt.Color;
2   import java.awt.Graphics;
3   import java.util.ArrayList;
4   import javax.swing.JComponent;
5
6   /**
7       A component that draws a chart.
8   */
9   public class ChartComponent extends JComponent
10  {
11     private ArrayList<Double> values;
12     private double maxValue;
13
14     public ChartComponent(double max)
15     {
16        values = new ArrayList<Double>();
17        maxValue = max;
18     }
19
20     public void append(double value)
21     {
22        values.add(value);
23        repaint();
24     }
25
26     public void paintComponent(Graphics g)
27     {
28        final int GAP = 5;
29        final int BAR_HEIGHT = 10;
30
31        int y = GAP;
32        for (double value : values)
33        {
34           int barWidth = (int) (getWidth() * value / maxValue);
35           g.fillRect(0, y, barWidth, BAR_HEIGHT);
36           y = y + BAR_HEIGHT + GAP;
37        }
38     }
39  }
```

### section_4_3/InvestmentFrame4.java

```java
1   import java.awt.Dimension;
2   import java.awt.event.ActionEvent;
```

```
3   import java.awt.event.ActionListener;
4   import javax.swing.JButton;
5   import javax.swing.JFrame;
6   import javax.swing.JLabel;
7   import javax.swing.JPanel;
8   import javax.swing.JTextField;
9
10  /**
11     A frame that shows the growth of an investment with variable interest,
12     using a bar chart.
13  */
14  public class InvestmentFrame4 extends JFrame
15  {
16     private static final int FRAME_WIDTH = 400;
17     private static final int FRAME_HEIGHT = 400;
18
19     private static final int CHART_WIDTH = 300;
20     private static final int CHART_HEIGHT = 300;
21
22     private static final double DEFAULT_RATE = 5;
23     private static final double INITIAL_BALANCE = 1000;
24
25     private JLabel rateLabel;
26     private JTextField rateField;
27     private JButton button;
28     private ChartComponent chart;
29     private double balance;
30
31     public InvestmentFrame4()
32     {
33        balance = INITIAL_BALANCE;
34        chart = new ChartComponent(3 * INITIAL_BALANCE);
35        chart.setPreferredSize(new Dimension(CHART_WIDTH, CHART_HEIGHT));
36        chart.append(INITIAL_BALANCE);
37
38        createTextField();
39        createButton();
40        createPanel();
41
42        setSize(FRAME_WIDTH, FRAME_HEIGHT);
43     }
44
45     private void createTextField()
46     {
47        rateLabel = new JLabel("Interest Rate: ");
48
49        final int FIELD_WIDTH = 10;
50        rateField = new JTextField(FIELD_WIDTH);
51        rateField.setText("" + DEFAULT_RATE);
52     }
53
54     class AddInterestListener implements ActionListener
55     {
56        public void actionPerformed(ActionEvent event)
57        {
58           double rate = Double.parseDouble(rateField.getText());
59           double interest = balance * rate / 100;
60           balance = balance + interest;
61           chart.append(balance);
62        }
```

```
63        }
64
65        private void createButton()
66        {
67            button = new JButton("Add Interest");
68
69            ActionListener listener = new AddInterestListener();
70            button.addActionListener(listener);
71        }
72
73        private void createPanel()
74        {
75            JPanel panel = new JPanel();
76            panel.add(rateLabel);
77            panel.add(rateField);
78            panel.add(button);
79            panel.add(chart);
80            add(panel);
81        }
82    }
```

**SELF CHECK**

**17.** How do you modify the program in Section 10.4.1 to draw two squares?

**18.** What happens if you call `fillOval` instead `fillRect` in the program of Section 10.4.1?

**19.** Give instructions to draw a circle with center (100, 100) and radius 25.

**20.** Give instructions to draw a letter "V" by drawing two line segments.

**21.** Give instructions to draw a string consisting of the letter "V".

**22.** What are the RGB color values of `Color.BLUE`?

**23.** How do you draw a yellow square on a red background?

**24.** What would happen in the investment viewer program if we simply painted each bar as

```
g.fillRect(0, y, value, BAR_HEIGHT);
```

in the `paintComponent` method of the `ChartComponent` class?

**25.** What would happen if you omitted the call to `repaint` in the `append` method of the `ChartComponent` class?

**26.** What would happen if you omitted the call to `chart.setPreferredSize` in the `InvestmentFrame4` constructor?

**Practice It**  Now you can do: R10.18, P10.17, P10.18.

---

Common Error 10.3

### Forgetting to Repaint

When you change the data in a painted component, the component is not automatically painted with the new data. You must call the `repaint` method of the component. Your component's `paintComponent` method will then be invoked. Note that you should not call the `paint-Component` method directly.

The best place to call `repaint` is in the method of your component that modifies the data values:

```
void changeData(. . .)
{
    Update data values
    repaint();
}
```

This is a concern only for your own painted components. When you make a change to a standard Swing component such as a `JLabel`, the component is automatically repainted.

## Common Error 10.4

### By Default, Components Have Zero Width and Height

You must be careful when you add a painted component, such as a component displaying a chart, to a panel. The default size for a `JComponent` is 0 by 0 pixels, and the component will not be visible. The remedy is to call the `setPreferredSize` method:

```
chart.setPreferredSize(new Dimension(CHART_WIDTH, CHART_HEIGHT));
```

This is an issue only for painted components. Buttons, labels, and so on, know how to compute their preferred size.

## HOW TO 10.1

### Drawing Graphical Shapes

Suppose you want to write a program that displays graphical shapes such as cars, aliens, charts, or any other images that can be obtained from rectangles, lines, and ellipses. These instructions give you a step-by-step procedure for decomposing a drawing into parts and implementing a program that produces the drawing.

In this How To we will create a program to draw a national flag.

**Step 1**  Determine the shapes that you need for the drawing.

You can use the following shapes:

- Squares and rectangles
- Circles and ellipses
- Lines

The outlines of these shapes can be drawn in any color, and you can fill the insides of these shapes with any color. You can also use text to label parts of your drawing.

Some national flag designs consist of three equally wide sections of different colors, side by side, as in the Italian flag shown below.

You could draw such a flag using three rectangles. But if the middle rectangle is white, as it is, for example, in the flag of Italy (green, white, red), it is easier and looks better to draw a line on the top and bottom of the middle portion:

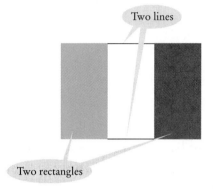

Two lines

Two rectangles

**Step 2**   Find the coordinates for the shapes.

You now need to find the exact positions for the geometric shapes.

- For rectangles, you need the $x$- and $y$-position of the top-left corner, the width, and the height.
- For ellipses, you need the top-left corner, width, and height of the bounding rectangle.
- For lines, you need the $x$- and $y$-positions of the starting point and the end point.
- For text, you need the $x$- and $y$-position of the basepoint.

A commonly-used size for a window is 300 by 300 pixels. You may not want the flag crammed all the way to the top, so perhaps the upper-left corner of the flag should be at point (100, 100).

Many flags, such as the flag of Italy, have a width : height ratio of 3 : 2. (You can often find exact proportions for a particular flag by doing a bit of Internet research on one of several Flags of the World sites.) For example, if you make the flag 90 pixels wide, then it should be 60 pixels tall. (Why not make it 100 pixels wide? Then the height would be $100 \cdot 2 / 3 \approx 67$, which seems more awkward.)

Now you can compute the coordinates of all the important points of the shape:

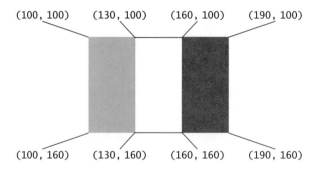

**Step 3**   Write Java statements to draw the shapes.

In our example, there are two rectangles and two lines:

```
g.setColor(Color.GREEN);
g.fillRect(100, 100, 30, 60);

g.setColor(Color.RED);
g.fillRect(160, 100, 30, 60);
```

```
g.setColor(Color.BLACK);
g.drawLine(130, 100, 160, 100);
g.drawLine(130, 160, 160, 160);
```

If you are more ambitious, then you can express the coordinates in terms of a few variables. In the case of the flag, we have arbitrarily chosen the top-left corner and the width. All other coordinates follow from those choices. If you decide to follow the ambitious approach, then the rectangles and lines are determined as follows:

```
g.fillRect(xLeft, yTop, width / 3, width * 2 / 3);
. . .
g.fillRect(xLeft + 2 * width / 3, yTop, width / 3, width * 2 / 3);
. . .
g.drawLine(xLeft + width / 3, yTop, xLeft + width * 2 / 3, yTop);
g.drawLine(xLeft + width / 3, yTop + width * 2 / 3,
   xLeft + width * 2 / 3, yTop + width * 2 / 3);
```

**Step 4**   Consider using methods or classes for repetitive steps.

Do you need to draw more than one flag? Perhaps with different sizes? Then it is a good idea to design a method or class, so you won't have to repeat the same drawing instructions.
For example, you can write a method

```
void drawItalianFlag(Graphics g, int xLeft, int yTop, int width)
{
   Draw a flag at the given location and size
}
```

Place the instructions from the preceding step into this method. Then you can call

```
drawItalianFlag(g, 10, 10, 100);
drawItalianFlag(g, 10, 125, 150);
```

in the paintComponent method to draw two flags.

**Step 5**   Place the drawing instructions in the paintComponent method.

```
public class ItalianFlagComponent extends JComponent
{
   public void paintComponent(Graphics g)
   {
      Drawing instructions
   }
}
```

If your drawing is simple, simply place all drawing statements here. Otherwise, call the methods you created in Step 4.

**Step 6**   Write the viewer class.

Provide a viewer class, with a main method in which you construct a frame, add your component, and make your frame visible. The viewer class is completely routine; you only need to change a single line to show a different component.

```
public class ItalianFlagViewer
{
   public static void main(String[] args)
   {
      JFrame frame = new JFrame();

      frame.setSize(300, 400);
      frame.setDefaultCloseOperation(JFrame.EXIT_ON_CLOSE);

      JComponent component = new ItalianFlagComponent();
      frame.add(component);
```

```
        frame.setVisible(true);
    }
}
```

---

## WORKED EXAMPLE 10.1 · Coding a Bar Chart Creator

In this Worked Example, we will develop a simple program for creating bar charts. The user enters labels and values for the bars, and the program displays the chart.

## VIDEO EXAMPLE 10.1 · Solving Crossword Puzzles

**WILEY PLUS**

In this Video Example, we develop a program that finds words for solving a crossword puzzle.

---

## CHAPTER SUMMARY

**Display frames and add components inside frames.**

- To show a frame, construct a JFrame object, set its size, and make it visible.
- Use a JPanel to group multiple user-interface components together.
- Declare a JFrame subclass for a complex frame.

**Explain the event concept and handle button events.**

- User-interface events include key presses, mouse moves, button clicks, menu selections, and so on.
- An event listener belongs to a class created by the application programmer. Its methods describe the actions to be taken when an event occurs.
- Event sources report on events. When an event occurs, the event source notifies all event listeners.
- Attach an ActionListener to each button so that your program can react to button clicks.
- Methods of an inner class can access variables from the surrounding class.

**Use text components for reading text input.**

- Use a JTextField component for reading a single line of input. Place a JLabel next to each text field.
- Use a JTextArea to show multiple lines of text.
- You can add scroll bars to any component with a JScrollPane.

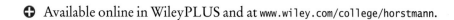 Available online in WileyPLUS and at www.wiley.com/college/horstmann.

**Create simple drawings with rectangles, ovals, lines, and text.**

- In order to display a drawing, provide a class that extends the JComponent class.
- Place drawing instructions inside the paintComponent method. That method is called whenever the component needs to be repainted.
- The Graphics class has methods to draw rectangles and other shapes.
- Use drawRect, drawOval, and drawLine to draw geometric shapes.
- The drawString method draws a string, starting at its basepoint.
- When you set a new color in the graphics context, it is used for subsequent drawing operations.
- Call the repaint method whenever the state of a painted component changes.
- When placing a painted component into a panel, you need to specify its preferred size.

## STANDARD LIBRARY ITEMS INTRODUCED IN THIS CHAPTER

java.awt.Color
java.awt.Component
  addMouseListener
  getHeight
  getWidth
  repaint
  setPreferredSize
  setSize
  setVisible
java.awt.Container
  add
java.awt.Dimension
java.awt.Frame
  setTitle

java.awt.Graphics
  setColor
  drawLine
  drawOval
  drawRect
  drawString
  fillOval
  fillRect
java.awt.event.ActionEvent
*java.awt.event.ActionListener*
  actionPerformed
javax.swing.AbstractButton
  addActionListener
javax.swing.JComponent
  paintComponent

javax.swing.JFrame
  setDefaultCloseOperation
javax.swing.JButton
javax.swing.JLabel
javax.swing.JPanel
javax.swing.JScrollPane
javax.swing.JTextArea
  append
javax.swing.JTextField
javax.swing.text.JTextComponent
  getText
  isEditable
  setEditable
  setText

## REVIEW EXERCISES

- **R10.1** What is the difference between a frame and a panel?

- **R10.2** From a programmer's perspective, what is the most important difference between the user interface of a console application and a graphical application?

- **R10.3** Why are separate viewer and frame classes used for graphical programs?

- **R10.4** What happens if you add a button and a label directly to a JFrame without using a JPanel? What happens if you add the label first? Try it out, by modifying the program in Section 10.1.2, and report your observations.

- **R10.5** What is an event object? An event source? An event listener?

- **R10.6** Who calls the actionPerformed method of an event listener? When does the call to the actionPerformed method occur?

■■ **R10.7** You can exit a graphical program by calling System.exit(0). Describe how to provide an Exit button that functions in the same way as closing the window. Should you still call setDefaultCloseOperation on the frame?

■ **R10.8** How would you add a counter to the program in Section 10.2.1 that prints how often the button has been clicked? Where is the counter updated?

■■ **R10.9** How would you add a counter to the program in Section 10.2.2 that shows how often the button has been clicked? Where is the counter updated? Where is it displayed?

■■■ **R10.10** How would you reorganize the InvestmentViewer program in Section 10.2.3 if you needed to make AddInterestListener into a top-level class (that is, not an inner class)?

■■■ **R10.11** Why are we using inner classes for event listeners? If Java did not have inner classes, could we still implement event listeners? How?

■■■ **R10.12** Is it a requirement to use inheritance for frames, as described in Section 10.1.3? (*Hint:* Consider Special Topic 10.1.)

■ **R10.13** What is the difference between a label, a text field, and a text area?

■■ **R10.14** Name a method that is declared in JTextArea, a method that JTextArea inherits from JTextComponent, and a method that JTextArea inherits from JComponent.

■■ **R10.15** Why did the program in Section 10.3.2 use a text area and not a label to show how the interest accumulates? How could you have achieved a similar effect with an array of labels?

■■ **R10.16** Who calls the paintComponent method of a component? When does the call to the paintComponent method occur?

■ **R10.17** In the program of Section 10.4.2, why was the oval drawn before the string?

■■ **R10.18** How would you modify the chart component in Section 10.4.3 to draw a vertical bar chart? (*Careful:* The *y*-values grow downward.)

■■ **R10.19** How do you specify a text color?

■■ **R10.20** What is the difference between the paintComponent and repaint methods?

■■ **R10.21** Explain why the call to the getWidth method in the ChartComponent class has no explicit parameter.

■ **R10.22** How would you modify the drawItalianFlag method in How To 10.1 to draw any flag with a white vertical stripe in the middle and two arbitrary colors to the left and right?

## PROGRAMMING EXERCISES

■ **P10.1** Write a program that shows a square frame filled with 100 buttons labeled 1 to 100. Nothing needs to happen when you press any of the buttons.

■ **P10.2** Enhance the ButtonViewer1 program in Section 10.2.1 so that it prints a message "I was clicked *n* times!" whenever the button is clicked. The value *n* should be incremented with each click.

■■ **P10.3** Enhance the `ButtonViewer1` program in Section 10.2.1 so that it has two buttons, each of which prints a message "I was clicked *n* times!" whenever the button is clicked. Each button should have a separate click count.

■■ **P10.4** Enhance the `ButtonViewer1` program in Section 10.2.1 so that it has two buttons labeled A and B, each of which prints a message "Button *x* was clicked!", where *x* is A or B.

■■ **P10.5** Implement a `ButtonViewer1` program as in Exercise P10.3 using only a single listener class. *Hint:* Pass the button label to the constructor of the listener.

■ **P10.6** Enhance the `ButtonViewer1` program so that it prints the date and time at which the button was clicked. *Hint:* `System.out.println(new java.util.Date())` prints the current date and time.

■■■ **P10.7** Implement the `ClickListener` in the `ButtonViewer2` program of Section 10.2.2 as a regular class (that is, not an inner class). *Hint:* Store a reference to the label. Add a constructor to the listener class that sets the reference.

■■ **P10.8** Add error handling to the program in Section 10.3.2. If the interest rate is not a floating-point number, or if it less than 0, display an error message, using a `JOption-Pane` (see Special Topic 2.5).

■ **P10.9** Write a graphical application simulating a bank account. Supply text fields and buttons for depositing and withdrawing money, and for displaying the current balance in a label.

■ **P10.10** Write a graphical application describing an earthquake, as in Section 3.3. Supply a text field and button for entering the strength of the earthquake. Display the earthquake description in a label.

■ **P10.11** Write a graphical application for computing statistics of a data set. Supply a text field and button for adding floating-point values, and display the current minimum, maximum, and average in a label.

■ **P10.12** Write an application with three labeled text fields, one each for the initial amount of a savings account, the annual interest rate, and the number of years. Add a button "Calculate" and a read-only text area to display the balance of the savings account after the end of each year.

■■ **P10.13** In the application from Exercise P10.12, replace the text area with a bar chart that shows the balance after the end of each year.

■ **P10.14** Write a graphics program that draws your name in red, contained inside a blue rectangle. Provide a class `NameViewer` and a class `NameComponent`.

■■ **P10.15** Write a graphics program that draws 12 strings, one each for the 12 standard colors, besides `Color.WHITE`, each in its own color. Provide a class `ColorNameViewer` and a class `ColorNameComponent`.

■■ **P10.16** Write a program that draws two solid squares: one in pink and one in purple. Use a standard color for one of them and a custom color for the other. Provide a class `TwoSquareViewer` and a class `TwoSquareComponent`.

■■ **P10.17** Write a program to plot the following face. Provide a class FaceViewer and a class Face-Component.

■■ **P10.18** Draw a "bull's eye"—a set of concentric rings in alternating black and white colors. *Hint:* Fill a black circle, then fill a smaller white circle on top, and so on. Your program should be composed of classes BullsEyeComponent and BullsEyeViewer.

■■ **P10.19** Write a program that draws a picture of a house. It could be as simple as the accompanying figure, or if you like, make it more elaborate (3-D, skyscraper, marble columns in the entryway, whatever).

■■ **P10.20** Extend Exercise P10.19 by supplying a drawHouse method in which you can specify the position and size. Then populate your frame with a few houses of different sizes.

■■ **P10.21** Extend Exercise P10.20 so that you can make the houses appear in different colors. The color should be passed as an argument to the drawHouse method. Populate your frame with houses of different colors.

■■ **P10.22** Improve the output quality of the investment application in Section 10.3.2. Format the numbers with two decimal digits, using the String.format method. Set the font of the text area to a fixed width font, using the call

```
textArea.setFont(new Font(Font.MONOSPACED, Font.PLAIN, 12));
```

■■ **P10.23** Write a program that draws a 3D view of a cylinder.

■■ **P10.24** Write a program to plot the string "HELLO", using only lines and circles. Do not call drawString, and do not use System.out. Make classes LetterH, LetterE, LetterL, and LetterO.

■■ **P10.25** Modify the drawItalianFlag method in How To 10.1 to draw any flag with three horizontal colored stripes. Write a program that displays the German and Hungarian flags.

**•• P10.26** Write a program that displays the Olympic rings. Color the rings in the Olympic colors. Provide a method `drawRing` that draws a ring of a given position and color.

**••• P10.27** Write a program that prompts the user to enter an integer in a text field. When a Draw button is clicked, draw as many rectangles at random positions in a component as the user requested.

**•• P10.28** Write a program that asks the user to enter an integer *n* into a text field. When a Draw button is clicked, draw an *n*-by-*n* grid in a component.

**•• P10.29** Write a program that has a Draw button and a component in which a random mixture of rectangles, ellipses, and lines, with random positions, is displayed each time the Draw button is clicked.

**•• P10.30** Make a bar chart to plot the following data set. Label each bar. Provide a class `BarChartViewer` and a class `BarChartComponent`.

| Bridge Name | Longest Span (ft) |
|---|---|
| Golden Gate | 4,200 |
| Brooklyn | 1,595 |
| Delaware Memorial | 2,150 |
| Mackinac | 3,800 |

**••• P10.31** Write a program that draws a clock face with a time that the user enters in two text fields (one for the hours, one for the minutes).

*Hint:* You need to determine the angles of the hour hand and the minute hand. The angle of the minute hand is easy; the minute hand travels 360 degrees in 60 minutes. The angle of the hour hand is harder; it travels 360 degrees in 12 × 60 minutes.

**••• P10.32** Write a program that fills the window with a large ellipse, with a black outline and filled with your favorite color. The ellipse should touch the window boundaries, even if the window is resized.

**•• Business P10.33** Implement a graphical application that simulates a cash register. Provide a text field for the item price and two buttons for adding the item to the sale, one for taxable items and one for nontaxable items. In a text area, display the register tape that lists all items (labeling the taxable items with a *), followed by the amount due. Provide another button for starting a new sale.

**•• Business P10.34** Write a graphical application to implement a currency converter between euros and U.S. dollars, and vice versa. Provide two text fields for the euro and dollar amounts. Between them, place two buttons labeled > and < for updating the field on the right or left. For this exercise, use a conversion rate of 1 euro = 1.42 U.S. dollars.

■■ **Business P10.35** Write a graphical application that produces a restaurant bill. Provide buttons for ten popular dishes or drink items. (You decide on the items and their prices.) Provide text fields for entering less popular items and prices. In a text area, show the bill, including tax and a suggested tip.

## ANSWERS TO SELF-CHECK QUESTIONS

1. Modify the `EmptyFrameViewer` program as follows:

   ```
   final int FRAME_WIDTH = 300;
   final int FRAME_HEIGHT = 300;
   . . .
   frame.setTitle("Hello, World!");
   ```

2. Construct two `JFrame` objects, set each of their sizes, and call `setVisible(true)` on each of them.

3. Add the following panel to the frame:

   ```
   JButton button1 = new JButton("Yes");
   JButton button2 = new JButton("No");
   JPanel panel = new JPanel();
   panel.add(button1);
   panel.add(button2);
   ```

4. There was no need to invoke any methods that are specific to `FilledFrame`. It is always a good idea to use the most general type when declaring a variable.

5. Two: `FilledFrameViewer2`, `FilledFrame`.

6. It's an instance method of `FilledFrame`, so the frame is the implicit parameter.

7. The `button` object is the event source. The `listener` object is the event listener.

8. The `ClickListener` class implements the `ActionListener` interface.

9. You don't. The Swing library calls the method when the button is clicked.

10. Direct access is simpler than the alternative— passing the variable as an argument to a constructor or method.

11. First add `label` to the `panel`, then add `button`.

12. Then the text field is not labeled, and the user will not know its purpose.

13. `Integer.parseInt(textField.getText())`

14. A text field holds a single line of text; a text area holds multiple lines.

15. The text area is intended to display the program output. It does not collect user input.

16. Don't construct a `JScrollPane` but add the `resultArea` object directly to the panel.

17. Here is one possible solution:

    ```
    g.fillRect(0, 0, 50, 50);
    g.fillRect(0, 100, 50, 50);
    ```

18. The program shows three very elongated ellipses instead of the rectangles.

19. `g.drawOval(75, 75, 50, 50);`

20. ```
    g.drawLine(0, 0, 10, 30);
    g.drawLine(10, 30, 20, 0);
    ```

21. `g.drawString("V", 0, 30);`

22. `0, 0, 255`

23. First fill a big red square, then fill a small yellow square inside:

    ```
    g.setColor(Color.RED);
    g.fillRect(0, 0, 200, 200);
    g.setColor(Color.YELLOW);
    g.fillRect(50, 50, 100, 100);
    ```

24. All the bars would stretch all the way to the right of the component since they would be much longer than the component's width.

25. The chart would not be repainted when the user hits the "Add Interest" button.

26. The chart would be shown at size 0 by 0; that is, it would be invisible.
    ```

# ADVANCED USER INTERFACES

The graphical applications with which you are familiar have many visual gadgets for information entry: buttons, scroll bars, menus, and so on. In this chapter, you will learn how to use the most common user-interface components in the Java Swing toolkit, and how to search the Java documentation for information about other components. You will also learn more about event handling, so you can use timer events in animations and process mouse events in interactive graphical programs.

# 11.1 Layout Management

**User-interface components are arranged by placing them inside containers. Containers can be placed inside larger containers.**

**Each container has a layout manager that directs the arrangement of its components.**

**Three useful layout managers are the border layout, flow layout, and grid layout.**

**When adding a component to a container with the border layout, specify the NORTH, SOUTH, WEST, EAST, or CENTER position.**

Up to now, you have had limited control over the layout of user-interface components. You learned how to add components to a panel, and the panel arranged the components from left to right. However, in many applications, you need more sophisticated arrangements.

In Java, you build up user interfaces by adding components into containers such as panels. Each container has its own **layout manager**, which determines how components are laid out.

By default, a JPanel uses a **flow layout**.

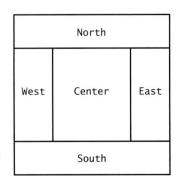

*A layout manager arranges user-interface components.*

A flow layout simply arranges its components from left to right and starts a new row when there is no more room in the current row.

Another commonly used layout manager is the **border layout**. The border layout groups components into five areas: center, north, south, west, and east (see Figure 1). Each area can hold a single component, or it can be empty.

The border layout is the default layout manager for a frame (or, more technically, the frame's content pane). But you can also use the border layout in a panel:

```
panel.setLayout(new BorderLayout());
```

Now the panel is controlled by a border layout, not the flow layout. When adding a component, you specify the position, like this:

```
panel.add(component, BorderLayout.NORTH);
```

|  | North |  |
|---|---|---|
| West | Center | East |
|  | South |  |

**Figure 1**
Components Expand to Fill
Space in the Border Layout

| 7 | 8 | 9 |
|---|---|---|
| 4 | 5 | 6 |
| 1 | 2 | 3 |
| 0 | . | CE |

**Figure 2**  The Grid Layout

The content pane of a frame has a border layout by default. A panel has a flow layout by default.

The **grid layout** manager arranges components in a grid with a fixed number of rows and columns. All components are resized so that they all have the same width and height. Like the border layout, it also expands each component to fill the entire allotted area. (If that is not desirable, you need to place each component inside a panel.) Figure 2 shows a number pad panel that uses a grid layout. To create a grid layout, you supply the number of rows and columns in the constructor, then add the components, row by row, left to right:

```
JPanel buttonPanel = new JPanel();
buttonPanel.setLayout(new GridLayout(4, 3));
buttonPanel.add(button7);
buttonPanel.add(button8);
buttonPanel.add(button9);
buttonPanel.add(button4);
  . . .
```

Sometimes you want to have a tabular arrangement of the components where columns have different sizes or one component spans multiple columns. A more complex layout manager called the *grid bag layout* can handle these situations. The grid bag layout is quite complex to use, however, and we do not cover it in this book; see, for example, Cay S. Horstmann and Gary Cornell, *Core Java 2 Volume 1: Fundamentals*, 8th edition (Prentice Hall, 2008), for more information. Java 6 introduced a *group layout* that is designed for use by interactive tools—see Programming Tip 11.1 on page 520.

Fortunately, you can create acceptable-looking layouts in nearly all situations by nesting panels. You give each panel an appropriate layout manager. Panels don't have visible borders, so you can use as many panels as you need to organize your components. Figure 3 shows an example. The keypad buttons are contained in a panel with grid layout. That panel is itself contained in a larger panel with border layout. The text field is in the northern position of the larger panel.

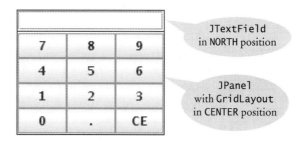

**Figure 3**  Nesting Panels

The following code produces the arrangement in Figure 3:

```
JPanel keypadPanel = new JPanel();
keypadPanel.setLayout(new BorderLayout());
buttonPanel = new JPanel();
buttonPanel.setLayout(new GridLayout(4, 3));
buttonPanel.add(button7);
buttonPanel.add(button8);
// . . .
keypadPanel.add(buttonPanel, BorderLayout.CENTER);
JTextField display = new JTextField();
keypadPanel.add(display, BorderLayout.NORTH);
```

**SELF CHECK**

1. What happens if you place two buttons in the northern position of a border layout? Try it out with a small program.

2. How do you add two buttons to the northern position of a frame so that they are shown next to each other?

3. How can you stack three buttons one above the other?

4. What happens when you place one button in the northern position of a border layout and another in the center position? Try it out with a small program if you aren't sure.

5. Some calculators have a double-wide 0 button, as shown below. How can you achieve that?

**Practice It** Now you can try these exercises at the end of the chapter: R11.1, R11.3, P11.1.

# 11.2 Choices

In the following sections, you will see how to present a finite set of choices to the user. Which Swing component you use depends on whether the choices are mutually exclusive or not, and on the amount of space you have for displaying the choices.

## 11.2.1 Radio Buttons

For a small set of mutually exclusive choices, use a group of radio buttons or a combo box.

If the choices are mutually exclusive, use a set of **radio buttons**. In a radio button set, only one button can be selected at a time. When the user selects another button in the same set, the previously selected button is automatically turned off. (These buttons are called radio buttons because they work like the station selector buttons on a car radio: If you select a new station,

*In an old fashioned radio, pushing down one station button released the others.*

the old station is automatically deselected.) For example, in Figure 4, the font sizes are mutually exclusive. You can select small, medium, or large, but not a combination of them.

Add radio buttons to a ButtonGroup so that only one button in the group is selected at any time.

To create a set of radio buttons, first create each button individually, and then add all buttons in the set to a `ButtonGroup` object:

```
JRadioButton smallButton = new JRadioButton("Small");
JRadioButton mediumButton = new JRadioButton("Medium");
JRadioButton largeButton = new JRadioButton("Large");

ButtonGroup group = new ButtonGroup();
group.add(smallButton);
group.add(mediumButton);
group.add(largeButton);
```

Note that the button group does *not* place the buttons close to each other in the container. The purpose of the button group is simply to find out which buttons to turn off when one of them is turned on. It is still your job to arrange the buttons on the screen.

The `isSelected` method is called to find out whether a button is currently selected or not. For example,

```
if (largeButton.isSelected()) { size = LARGE_SIZE; }
```

Unfortunately, there is no convenient way of finding out which button in a group is currently selected. You have to call `isSelected` on each button. Because users will expect one radio button in a radio button group to be selected, call `setSelected(true)` on the default radio button before making the enclosing frame visible.

You can place a border around a panel to group its contents visually.

If you have multiple button groups, it is a good idea to group them together visually. It is a good idea to use a panel for each set of radio buttons, but the panels themselves are invisible. You can add a *border* to a panel to make it visible. In Figure 4, for example, the panels containing the Size radio buttons and Style check boxes have borders.

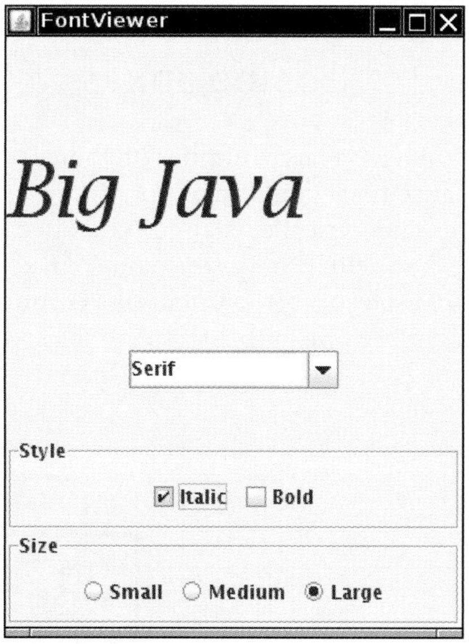


**Figure 4** A Combo Box, Check Boxes, and Radio Buttons

There are a large number of border types. We will show only a couple of variations and leave it to the border enthusiasts to look up the others in the Swing documentation. The `EtchedBorder` class yields a border with a three-dimensional, etched effect. You can add a border to any component, but most commonly you apply it to a panel:

```
JPanel panel = new JPanel();
panel.setBorder(new EtchedBorder());
```

If you want to add a title to the border (as in Figure 4), you need to construct a `Titled-Border`. You make a titled border by supplying a basic border and then the title you want. Here is a typical example:

```
panel.setBorder(new TitledBorder(new EtchedBorder(), "Size"));
```

## 11.2.2  Check Boxes

For a binary choice, use a check box.

A **check box** is a user-interface component with two states: checked and unchecked. You use a group of check boxes when one selection does not exclude another. For example, the choices for "Bold" and "Italic" in Figure 4 are not exclusive. You can choose either, both, or neither. Therefore, they are implemented as a set of separate check boxes. Radio buttons and check boxes have different visual appearances. Radio buttons are round and have a black dot when selected. Check boxes are square and have a check mark when selected.

You construct a check box by providing the name in the constructor:

```
JCheckBox italicCheckBox = new JCheckBox("Italic");
```

Because check box settings do not exclude each other, you do not place a set of check boxes inside a button group.

As with radio buttons, you use the `isSelected` method to find out whether a check box is currently checked or not.

## 11.2.3  Combo Boxes

For a large set of choices, use a combo box.

If you have a large number of choices, you don't want to make a set of radio buttons, because that would take up a lot of space. Instead, you can use a **combo box**. This component is called a combo box because it is a combination of a list and a text field. The text field displays the name of the current selection. When you click on the arrow to the right of the text field of a combo box, a list of selections drops down, and you can choose one of the items in the list (see Figure 5).

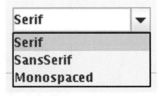

**Figure 5**  An Open Combo Box

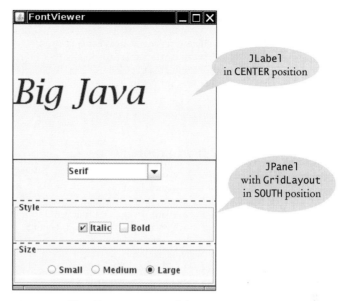

**Figure 6**   The Components of the `FontFrame`

If the combo box is *editable*, you can also type in your own selection. To make a combo box editable, call the `setEditable` method.

You add strings to a combo box with the `addItem` method.

```
JComboBox facenameCombo = new JComboBox();
facenameCombo.addItem("Serif");
facenameCombo.addItem("SansSerif");
. . .
```

You get the item that the user has selected by calling the `getSelectedItem` method. However, because combo boxes can store other objects in addition to strings, the `getSelectedItem` method has return type `Object`. Hence, in our example, you must cast the returned value back to `String`:

```
String selectedString = (String) facenameCombo.getSelectedItem();
```

You can select an item for the user with the `setSelectedItem` method.

Radio buttons, check boxes, and combo boxes generate an `ActionEvent` whenever the user selects an item. In the following program, we don't care which component was clicked—all components notify the same listener object. Whenever the user clicks on any one of them, we simply ask each component for its current content, using the `isSelected` and `getSelectedItem` methods. We then redraw the label with the new font.

Figure 6 shows how the components are arranged in the frame.

> Radio buttons, check boxes, and combo boxes generate action events, just as buttons do.

### section_2/FontViewer.java

```
1   import javax.swing.JFrame;
2
3   /**
4       This program allows the user to view font effects.
5   */
6   public class FontViewer
7   {
```

```
 8      public static void main(String[] args)
 9      {
10         JFrame frame = new FontFrame();
11         frame.setDefaultCloseOperation(JFrame.EXIT_ON_CLOSE);
12         frame.setTitle("FontViewer");
13         frame.setVisible(true);
14      }
15   }
```

### section_2/FontFrame.java

```
 1   import java.awt.BorderLayout;
 2   import java.awt.Font;
 3   import java.awt.GridLayout;
 4   import java.awt.event.ActionEvent;
 5   import java.awt.event.ActionListener;
 6   import javax.swing.ButtonGroup;
 7   import javax.swing.JButton;
 8   import javax.swing.JCheckBox;
 9   import javax.swing.JComboBox;
10   import javax.swing.JFrame;
11   import javax.swing.JLabel;
12   import javax.swing.JPanel;
13   import javax.swing.JRadioButton;
14   import javax.swing.border.EtchedBorder;
15   import javax.swing.border.TitledBorder;
16
17   /**
18      This frame contains a text sample and a control panel
19      to change the font of the text.
20   */
21   public class FontFrame extends JFrame
22   {
23      private static final int FRAME_WIDTH = 300;
24      private static final int FRAME_HEIGHT = 400;
25
26      private JLabel label;
27      private JCheckBox italicCheckBox;
28      private JCheckBox boldCheckBox;
29      private JRadioButton smallButton;
30      private JRadioButton mediumButton;
31      private JRadioButton largeButton;
32      private JComboBox facenameCombo;
33      private ActionListener listener;
34
35      /**
36         Constructs the frame.
37      */
38      public FontFrame()
39      {
40         // Construct text sample
41         label = new JLabel("Big Java");
42         add(label, BorderLayout.CENTER);
43
44         // This listener is shared among all components
45         listener = new ChoiceListener();
46
47         createControlPanel();
48         setLabelFont();
```

```
49        setSize(FRAME_WIDTH, FRAME_HEIGHT);
50    }
51
52    class ChoiceListener implements ActionListener
53    {
54        public void actionPerformed(ActionEvent event)
55        {
56            setLabelFont();
57        }
58    }
59
60    /**
61        Creates the control panel to change the font.
62    */
63    public void createControlPanel()
64    {
65        JPanel facenamePanel = createComboBox();
66        JPanel sizeGroupPanel = createCheckBoxes();
67        JPanel styleGroupPanel = createRadioButtons();
68
69        // Line up component panels
70
71        JPanel controlPanel = new JPanel();
72        controlPanel.setLayout(new GridLayout(3, 1));
73        controlPanel.add(facenamePanel);
74        controlPanel.add(sizeGroupPanel);
75        controlPanel.add(styleGroupPanel);
76
77        // Add panels to content pane
78
79        add(controlPanel, BorderLayout.SOUTH);
80    }
81
82    /**
83        Creates the combo box with the font style choices.
84        @return the panel containing the combo box
85    */
86    public JPanel createComboBox()
87    {
88        facenameCombo = new JComboBox();
89        facenameCombo.addItem("Serif");
90        facenameCombo.addItem("SansSerif");
91        facenameCombo.addItem("Monospaced");
92        facenameCombo.setEditable(true);
93        facenameCombo.addActionListener(listener);
94
95        JPanel panel = new JPanel();
96        panel.add(facenameCombo);
97        return panel;
98    }
99
100    /**
101        Creates the check boxes for selecting bold and italic styles.
102        @return the panel containing the check boxes
103    */
104    public JPanel createCheckBoxes()
105    {
106        italicCheckBox = new JCheckBox("Italic");
107        italicCheckBox.addActionListener(listener);
108
```

```
109        boldCheckBox = new JCheckBox("Bold");
110        boldCheckBox.addActionListener(listener);
111
112        JPanel panel = new JPanel();
113        panel.add(italicCheckBox);
114        panel.add(boldCheckBox);
115        panel.setBorder(new TitledBorder(new EtchedBorder(), "Style"));
116
117        return panel;
118     }
119
120     /**
121        Creates the radio buttons to select the font size.
122        @return the panel containing the radio buttons
123     */
124     public JPanel createRadioButtons()
125     {
126        smallButton = new JRadioButton("Small");
127        smallButton.addActionListener(listener);
128
129        mediumButton = new JRadioButton("Medium");
130        mediumButton.addActionListener(listener);
131
132        largeButton = new JRadioButton("Large");
133        largeButton.addActionListener(listener);
134        largeButton.setSelected(true);
135
136        // Add radio buttons to button group
137
138        ButtonGroup group = new ButtonGroup();
139        group.add(smallButton);
140        group.add(mediumButton);
141        group.add(largeButton);
142
143        JPanel panel = new JPanel();
144        panel.add(smallButton);
145        panel.add(mediumButton);
146        panel.add(largeButton);
147        panel.setBorder(new TitledBorder(new EtchedBorder(), "Size"));
148
149        return panel;
150     }
151
152     /**
153        Gets user choice for font name, style, and size
154        and sets the font of the text sample.
155     */
156     public void setLabelFont()
157     {
158        // Get font name
159        String facename = (String) facenameCombo.getSelectedItem();
160
161        // Get font style
162
163        int style = 0;
164        if (italicCheckBox.isSelected())
165        {
166           style = style + Font.ITALIC;
167        }
```

```
168          if (boldCheckBox.isSelected())
169          {
170             style = style + Font.BOLD;
171          }
172
173          // Get font size
174
175          int size = 0;
176
177          final int SMALL_SIZE = 24;
178          final int MEDIUM_SIZE = 36;
179          final int LARGE_SIZE = 48;
180
181          if (smallButton.isSelected()) { size = SMALL_SIZE; }
182          else if (mediumButton.isSelected()) { size = MEDIUM_SIZE; }
183          else if (largeButton.isSelected()) { size = LARGE_SIZE; }
184
185          // Set font of text field
186
187          label.setFont(new Font(facename, style, size));
188          label.repaint();
189       }
190 }
```

**SELF CHECK**

6. What is the advantage of a JComboBox over a set of radio buttons? What is the disadvantage?

7. What happens when you put two check boxes into a button group? Try it out if you are not sure.

8. How can you nest two etched borders, like this?

9. Why do all user-interface components in the FontFrame class share the same listener?

10. Why was the combo box placed inside a panel? What would have happened if it had been added directly to the control panel?

11. How could the following user interface be improved?

Bold ● Yes ○ No

**Practice It**   Now you can try these exercises at the end of the chapter: R11.11, P11.3, P11.4.

HOW TO 11.1    **Laying Out a User Interface**

A graphical user interface is made up of components such as buttons and text fields. The Swing library uses containers and layout managers to arrange these components. This How To explains how to group components into containers and how to pick the right layout managers.

**Step 1**   Make a sketch of your desired component layout.

Draw all the buttons, labels, text fields, and borders on a sheet of paper. Graph paper works best.

Here is an example—a user interface for ordering pizza. The user interface contains

- Three radio buttons
- Two check boxes
- A label: "Your Price:"
- A text field
- A border

**Step 2**   Find groupings of adjacent components with the same layout.

Usually, the component arrangement is complex enough that you need to use several panels, each with its own layout manager. Start by looking at adjacent components that are arranged top to bottom or left to right. If several components are surrounded by a border, they should be grouped together.

Here are the groupings from the pizza user interface:

**Step 3**   Identify layouts for each group.

When components are arranged horizontally, choose a flow layout. When components are arranged vertically, use a grid layout with one column.

In the pizza user interface example, you would choose

- A (3, 1) grid layout for the radio buttons
- A (2, 1) grid layout for the check boxes
- A flow layout for the label and text field

**Step 4**   Group the groups together.

Look at each group as one blob, and group the blobs together into larger groups, just as you grouped the components in the preceding step. If you note one large blob surrounded by smaller blobs, you can group them together in a border layout.

You may have to repeat the grouping again if you have a very complex user interface. You are done if you have arranged all groups in a single container.

For example, the three component groups of the pizza user interface can be arranged as:

- A group containing the first two component groups, placed in the center of a container with a border layout.

- The third component group, in the southern area of that container.

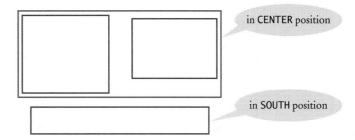

In this step, you may run into a couple of complications. The group "blobs" tend to vary in size more than the individual components. If you place them inside a grid layout, the grid layout forces them all to be the same size. Also, you occasionally would like a component from one group to line up with a component from another group, but there is no way for you to communicate that intent to the layout managers.

These problems can be overcome by using more sophisticated layout managers or implementing a custom layout manager. However, those techniques are beyond the scope of this book. Sometimes, you may want to start over with Step 1, using a component layout that is easier to manage. Or you can decide to live with minor imperfections of the layout. Don't worry about achieving the perfect layout—after all, you are learning programming, not user-interface design.

**Step 5**  Write the code to generate the layout.

This step is straightforward but potentially tedious, especially if you have a large number of components.

Start by constructing the components. Then construct a panel for each component group and set its layout manager if it is not a flow layout (the default for panels). Add a border to the panel if required. Finally, add the components to their panels. Continue in this fashion until you reach the outermost containers, which you add to the frame.

Here is an outline of the code required for the pizza user interface:

```
JPanel radioButtonPanel = new JPanel();
radioButtonPanel.setLayout(new GridLayout(3, 1));
radioButtonPanel.setBorder(new TitledBorder(new EtchedBorder(), "Size"));
radioButtonPanel.add(smallButton);
radioButtonPanel.add(mediumButton);
radioButtonPanel.add(largeButton);

JPanel checkBoxPanel = new JPanel();
checkBoxPanel.setLayout(new GridLayout(2, 1));
checkBoxPanel.add(pepperoniButton());
checkBoxPanel.add(anchoviesButton());

JPanel pricePanel = new JPanel(); // Uses FlowLayout by default
pricePanel.add(new JLabel("Your Price: "));
pricePanel.add(priceTextField);
```

```
JPanel centerPanel = new JPanel(); // Uses FlowLayout
centerPanel.add(radioButtonPanel);
centerPanel.add(checkBoxPanel);

// Frame uses BorderLayout by default
add(centerPanel, BorderLayout.CENTER);
add(pricePanel, BorderLayout.SOUTH);
```

Programming Tip 11.1

## Use a GUI Builder

As you have seen, implementing even a simple graphical user interface in Java is quite tedious. You have to write a lot of code for constructing components, using layout managers, and providing event handlers. Most of the code is repetitive.

A GUI builder takes away much of the tedium. Most GUI builders help you in three ways:

- You drag and drop components onto a panel. The GUI builder writes the layout management code for you.

- You customize components with a dialog box, setting properties such as fonts, colors, text, and so on. The GUI builder writes the customization code for you.

- You provide event handlers by picking the event to process and providing just the code snippet for the listener method. The GUI builder writes the boilerplate code for attaching a listener object.

Java 6 introduced GroupLayout, a powerful layout manager that was specifically designed to be used by GUI builders. The free NetBeans development environment, available from http://netbeans.org, makes use of this layout manager—see Figure 7.

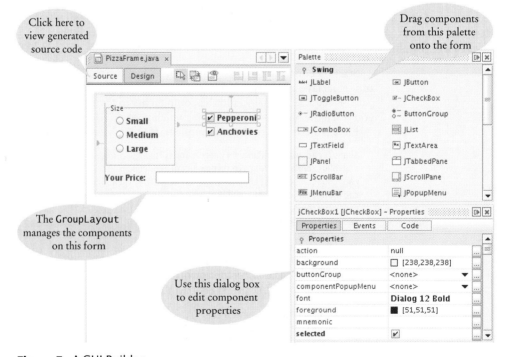

**Figure 7** A GUI Builder

If you need to build a complex user interface, you will find that learning to use a GUI builder is a very worthwhile investment. You will spend less time writing boring code, and you will have more fun designing your user interface and focusing on the functionality of your program.

WORKED EXAMPLE 11.1 **Programming a Working Calculator**

In this Worked Example, we implement arithmetic and scientific operations for a calculator. The sample program in Section 11.1 showed how to lay out the buttons for a simple calculator, and we use that program as a starting point.

# 11.3 Menus

A frame contains a menu bar. The menu bar contains menus. A menu contains submenus and menu items.

Anyone who has ever used a graphical user interface is familiar with pull-down menus (see Figure 8). At the top of the frame is a *menu bar* that contains the top-level menus. Each menu is a collection of *menu items* and *submenus*.

The sample program for this section builds up a small but typical menu and traps the action events from the menu items. The program allows the user to specify the font for a label by selecting a face name, font size, and font style. In Java it is easy to create these menus.

You add the menu bar to the frame:

```
public class MyFrame extends JFrame
{
   public MyFrame()
   {
      JMenuBar menuBar = new JMenuBar();
      setJMenuBar(menuBar);
      . . .
   }
   . . .
}
```

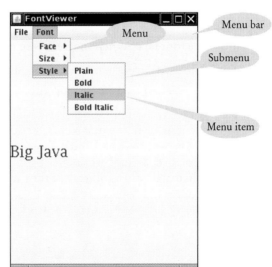

**Figure 8**
Pull-Down Menus

➕ Available online in WileyPLUS and at www.wiley.com/college/horstmann.

*A menu provides a list of available choices.*

Menus are then added to the menu bar:

```
JMenu fileMenu = new JMenu("File");
JMenu fontMenu = new JMenu("Font");
menuBar.add(fileMenu);
menuBar.add(fontMenu);
```

You add menu items and submenus with the add method:

```
JMenuItem exitItem = new JMenuItem("Exit");
fileMenu.add(exitItem);

JMenu styleMenu = new JMenu("Style");
fontMenu.add(styleMenu); // A submenu
```

**Menu items generate action events.**

A menu item has no further submenus. When the user selects a menu item, the menu item sends an action event. Therefore, you want to add a listener to each menu item:

```
ActionListener listener = new ExitItemListener();
exitItem.addActionListener(listener);
```

You add action listeners only to menu items, not to menus or the menu bar. When the user clicks on a menu name and a submenu opens, no action event is sent.

To keep the program readable, it is a good idea to use a separate method for each menu or set of related menus. For example,

```
public JMenu createFaceMenu()
{
    JMenu menu = new JMenu("Face");
    menu.add(createFaceItem("Serif"));
    menu.add(createFaceItem("SansSerif"));
    menu.add(createFaceItem("Monospaced"));
    return menu;
}
```

Now consider the createFaceItem method. It has a string parameter variable for the name of the font face. When the item is selected, its action listener needs to

1. Set the current face name to the menu item text.
2. Make a new font from the current face, size, and style, and apply it to the label.

We have three menu items, one for each supported face name. Each of them needs to set a different name in the first step. Of course, we can make three listener classes SerifListener, SansSerifListener, and MonospacedListener, but that is not very elegant. After all, the actions only vary by a single string. We can store that string inside the listener class and then make three objects of the same listener class:

```
class FaceItemListener implements ActionListener
{
    private String name;

    public FaceItemListener(String newName) { name = newName; }
```

```
   public void actionPerformed(ActionEvent event)
   {
      faceName = name; // Sets an instance variable of the frame class
      setLabelFont();
   }
}
```

Now we can install a listener object with the appropriate name:

```
public JMenuItem createFaceItem(String name)
{
   JMenuItem item = new JMenuItem(name);
   ActionListener listener = new FaceItemListener(name);
   item.addActionListener(listener);
   return item;
}
```

This approach is still a bit tedious. We can do better by using a local inner class (see Special Topic 10.2). When we move the declaration of the inner class inside the createFaceItem method, the actionPerformed method can access the name parameter variable directly. However, we need to observe a technical rule. Because name is a local variable, it must be declared as final to be accessible from an inner class method.

```
public JMenuItem createFaceItem(final String name)
// Final variables can be accessed from an inner class method
{
   class FaceItemListener implements ActionListener // A local inner class
   {
      public void actionPerformed(ActionEvent event)
      {
         facename = name; // Accesses the local variable name
         setLabelFont();
      }
   }

   JMenuItem item = new JMenuItem(name);
   ActionListener listener = new FaceItemListener();
   item.addActionListener(listener);
   return item;
}
```

The same strategy is used for the createSizeItem and createStyleItem methods.

### section_3/FontViewer2.java

```
1   import javax.swing.JFrame;
2
3   /**
4      This program uses a menu to display font effects.
5   */
6   public class FontViewer2
7   {
8      public static void main(String[] args)
9      {
10        JFrame frame = new FontFrame2();
11        frame.setDefaultCloseOperation(JFrame.EXIT_ON_CLOSE);
12        frame.setTitle("FontViewer");
13        frame.setVisible(true);
14     }
15  }
```

**section_3/FontFrame2.java**

```java
1   import java.awt.BorderLayout;
2   import java.awt.Font;
3   import java.awt.event.ActionEvent;
4   import java.awt.event.ActionListener;
5   import javax.swing.JFrame;
6   import javax.swing.JLabel;
7   import javax.swing.JMenu;
8   import javax.swing.JMenuBar;
9   import javax.swing.JMenuItem;
10
11  /**
12     This frame has a menu with commands to change the font
13     of a text sample.
14  */
15  public class FontFrame2 extends JFrame
16  {
17     private static final int FRAME_WIDTH = 300;
18     private static final int FRAME_HEIGHT = 400;
19
20     private JLabel label;
21     private String facename;
22     private int fontstyle;
23     private int fontsize;
24
25     /**
26        Constructs the frame.
27     */
28     public FontFrame2()
29     {
30        // Construct text sample
31        label = new JLabel("Big Java");
32        add(label, BorderLayout.CENTER);
33
34        // Construct menu
35        JMenuBar menuBar = new JMenuBar();
36        setJMenuBar(menuBar);
37        menuBar.add(createFileMenu());
38        menuBar.add(createFontMenu());
39
40        facename = "Serif";
41        fontsize = 24;
42        fontstyle = Font.PLAIN;
43
44        setLabelFont();
45        setSize(FRAME_WIDTH, FRAME_HEIGHT);
46     }
47
48     class ExitItemListener implements ActionListener
49     {
50        public void actionPerformed(ActionEvent event)
51        {
52           System.exit(0);
53        }
54     }
55
56     /**
57        Creates the File menu.
```

```
58          @return the menu
59       */
60       public JMenu createFileMenu()
61       {
62          JMenu menu = new JMenu("File");
63          JMenuItem exitItem = new JMenuItem("Exit");
64          ActionListener listener = new ExitItemListener();
65          exitItem.addActionListener(listener);
66          menu.add(exitItem);
67          return menu;
68       }
69
70       /**
71          Creates the Font submenu.
72          @return the menu
73       */
74       public JMenu createFontMenu()
75       {
76          JMenu menu = new JMenu("Font");
77          menu.add(createFaceMenu());
78          menu.add(createSizeMenu());
79          menu.add(createStyleMenu());
80          return menu;
81       }
82
83       /**
84          Creates the Face submenu.
85          @return the menu
86       */
87       public JMenu createFaceMenu()
88       {
89          JMenu menu = new JMenu("Face");
90          menu.add(createFaceItem("Serif"));
91          menu.add(createFaceItem("SansSerif"));
92          menu.add(createFaceItem("Monospaced"));
93          return menu;
94       }
95
96       /**
97          Creates the Size submenu.
98          @return the menu
99       */
100      public JMenu createSizeMenu()
101      {
102         JMenu menu = new JMenu("Size");
103         menu.add(createSizeItem("Smaller", -1));
104         menu.add(createSizeItem("Larger", 1));
105         return menu;
106      }
107
108      /**
109         Creates the Style submenu.
110         @return the menu
111      */
112      public JMenu createStyleMenu()
113      {
114         JMenu menu = new JMenu("Style");
115         menu.add(createStyleItem("Plain", Font.PLAIN));
116         menu.add(createStyleItem("Bold", Font.BOLD));
```

```
117          menu.add(createStyleItem("Italic", Font.ITALIC));
118          menu.add(createStyleItem("Bold Italic", Font.BOLD
119                + Font.ITALIC));
120          return menu;
121       }
122
123       /**
124          Creates a menu item to change the font face and set its action listener.
125          @param name the name of the font face
126          @return the menu item
127       */
128       public JMenuItem createFaceItem(final String name)
129       {
130          class FaceItemListener implements ActionListener
131          {
132             public void actionPerformed(ActionEvent event)
133             {
134                facename = name;
135                setLabelFont();
136             }
137          }
138
139          JMenuItem item = new JMenuItem(name);
140          ActionListener listener = new FaceItemListener();
141          item.addActionListener(listener);
142          return item;
143       }
144
145       /**
146          Creates a menu item to change the font size
147          and set its action listener.
148          @param name the name of the menu item
149          @param increment the amount by which to change the size
150          @return the menu item
151       */
152       public JMenuItem createSizeItem(String name, final int increment)
153       {
154          class SizeItemListener implements ActionListener
155          {
156             public void actionPerformed(ActionEvent event)
157             {
158                fontsize = fontsize + increment;
159                setLabelFont();
160             }
161          }
162
163          JMenuItem item = new JMenuItem(name);
164          ActionListener listener = new SizeItemListener();
165          item.addActionListener(listener);
166          return item;
167       }
168
169       /**
170          Creates a menu item to change the font style
171          and set its action listener.
172          @param name the name of the menu item
173          @param style the new font style
174          @return the menu item
175       */
```

```
176    public JMenuItem createStyleItem(String name, final int style)
177    {
178       class StyleItemListener implements ActionListener
179       {
180          public void actionPerformed(ActionEvent event)
181          {
182             fontstyle = style;
183             setLabelFont();
184          }
185       }
186
187       JMenuItem item = new JMenuItem(name);
188       ActionListener listener = new StyleItemListener();
189       item.addActionListener(listener);
190       return item;
191    }
192
193    /**
194       Sets the font of the text sample.
195    */
196    public void setLabelFont()
197    {
198       Font f = new Font(facename, fontstyle, fontsize);
199       label.setFont(f);
200    }
201 }
```

**SELF CHECK**

12. Why do JMenu objects not generate action events?

13. Can you add a menu item directly to the menu bar? Try it out. What happens?

14. Why is the increment parameter variable in the createSizeItem method declared as final?

15. Why can't the createFaceItem method simply set the faceName instance variable, like this:

```
class FaceItemListener implements ActionListener
{
   public void actionPerformed(ActionEvent event)
   {
      setLabelFont();
   }
}

public JMenuItem createFaceItem(String name)
{
   JMenuItem item = new JMenuItem(name);
   faceName = name;
   ActionListener listener = new FaceItemListener();
   item.addActionListener(listener);
   return item;
}
```

16. In this program, the font specification (name, size, and style) is stored in instance variables. Why was this not necessary in the program of the previous section?

**Practice It** Now you can try these exercises at the end of the chapter: R11.12, P11.6, P11.7.

# 11.4 Exploring the Swing Documentation

You should learn to navigate the API documentation to find out more about user-interface components.

In the preceding sections, you saw the basic properties of the most common user-interface components. We purposefully omitted many options and variations to simplify the discussion. You can go a long way by using only the simplest properties of these components. If you want to implement a more sophisticated effect, you can look inside the Swing documentation. You may find the documentation intimidating at first glance, though. The purpose of this section is to show you how you can use the documentation to your advantage without being overwhelmed.

*In order to use the Swing library effectively, you need to study the API documentation.*

As an example, consider a program for mixing colors by specifying the red, green, and blue values. How can you specify the colors? Of course, you could supply three text fields, but sliders would be more convenient for users of your program (see Figure 9).

The Swing user-interface toolkit has a large set of user-interface components. How do you know if there is a slider? You can buy a book that illustrates all Swing components. Or you can run the sample application included in the Java Development Kit that shows off all Swing components (see Figure 10). Or you can look at the names of all of the classes that start with J and decide that JSlider may be a good candidate.

Next, you need to ask yourself a few questions:

* How do I construct a JSlider?
* How can I get notified when the user has moved it?
* How can I tell to which value the user has set it?

**Figure 9**   A Color Viewer with Sliders

**Figure 10**
The SwingSet Demo

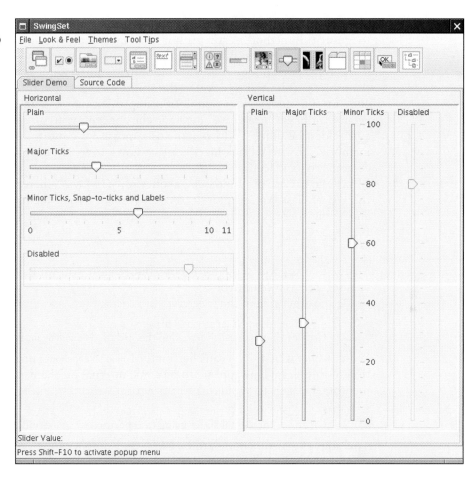

When you look at the documentation of the JSlider class, you will probably not be happy. There are over 50 methods in the JSlider class and over 250 inherited methods, and some of the method descriptions look downright scary, such as the one in Figure 11. Apparently some folks out there are concerned about the valueIsAdjusting property, whatever that may be, and the designers of this class felt it necessary to

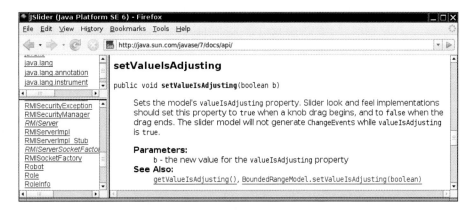

**Figure 11**   A Mysterious Method Description from the API Documentation

supply a method to tweak that property. Until you too feel that need, your best bet is to ignore this method. As the author of an introductory book, it pains me to tell you to ignore certain facts. But the truth of the matter is that the Java library is so large and complex that nobody understands it in its entirety, not even the designers of Java themselves. You need to develop the ability to separate fundamental concepts from ephemeral minutiae. For example, it is important that you understand the concept of event handling. Once you understand the concept, you can ask the question, "What event does the slider send when the user moves it?" But it is not important that you memorize how to set tick marks or that you know how to implement a slider with a custom look and feel.

Let's go back to our fundamental questions. In Java 6, there are six constructors for the `JSlider` class. You want to learn about one or two of them. You must strike a balance somewhere between the trivial and the bizarre. Consider

> `public JSlider()`
>> Creates a horizontal slider with the range 0 to 100 and an initial value of 50.

Maybe that is good enough for now, but what if you want another range or initial value? It seems too limited.

On the other side of the spectrum, there is

> `public JSlider(BoundedRangeModel brm)`
>> Creates a horizontal slider using the specified `BoundedRangeModel`.

Whoa! What is that? You can click on the `BoundedRangeModel` link to get a long explanation of this class. This appears to be some internal mechanism for the Swing implementors. Let's try to avoid this constructor if we can. Looking further, we find

> `public JSlider(int min, int max, int value)`
>> Creates a horizontal slider using the specified `min`, `max`, and `value`.

This sounds general enough to be useful and simple enough to be usable. You might want to stash away the fact that you can have vertical sliders as well.

Next, you want to know what events a slider generates. There is no `addAction-Listener` method. That makes sense. Adjusting a slider seems different from clicking a button, and Swing uses a different event type for these events. There is a method

> `public void addChangeListener(ChangeListener l)`

Click on the `ChangeListener` link to find out more about this interface. It has a single method

> `void stateChanged(ChangeEvent e)`

Apparently, that method is called whenever the user moves the slider. What is a `Change-Event`? Once again, click on the link, to find out that this event class has *no* methods of its own, but it inherits the `getSource` method from its superclass `EventObject`. The get-Source method tells us which component generated this event, but we don't need that information—we know that the event came from the slider.

Now let's make a plan: Add a change event listener to each slider. When the slider is changed, the `stateChanged` method is called. Find out the new value of the slider. Recompute the color value and repaint the color panel. That way, the color panel is continually repainted as the user moves one of the sliders.

To compute the color value, you will still need to get the current value of the slider. Look at all the methods that start with `get`. Sure enough, you find

> `public int getValue()`
>> Returns the slider's value.

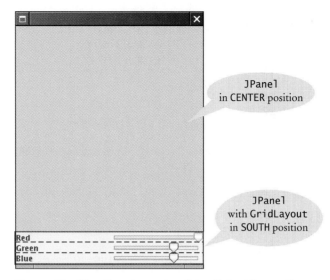

**JPanel** in CENTER position

**JPanel** with GridLayout in SOUTH position

Red
Green
Blue

**Figure 12**   The Components of the Color Viewer Frame

Now you know everything you need to write the program. The program uses one new Swing component and one event listener of a new type. After having mastered the basics, you may want to explore the capabilities of the component further, for example by adding tick marks—see Exercise P11.9.

Figure 12 shows how the components are arranged in the frame.

**section_4/ColorViewer.java**

```
 1  import javax.swing.JFrame;
 2
 3  public class ColorViewer
 4  {
 5     public static void main(String[] args)
 6     {
 7        JFrame frame = new ColorFrame();
 8        frame.setDefaultCloseOperation(JFrame.EXIT_ON_CLOSE);
 9        frame.setVisible(true);
10     }
11  }
```

**section_4/ColorFrame.java**

```
 1  import java.awt.BorderLayout;
 2  import java.awt.Color;
 3  import java.awt.GridLayout;
 4  import javax.swing.JFrame;
 5  import javax.swing.JLabel;
 6  import javax.swing.JPanel;
 7  import javax.swing.JSlider;
 8  import javax.swing.event.ChangeListener;
 9  import javax.swing.event.ChangeEvent;
10
11  public class ColorFrame extends JFrame
12  {
13     private static final int FRAME_WIDTH = 300;
14     private static final int FRAME_HEIGHT = 400;
```

```
15
16      private JPanel colorPanel;
17      private JSlider redSlider;
18      private JSlider greenSlider;
19      private JSlider blueSlider;
20
21      public ColorFrame()
22      {
23         colorPanel = new JPanel();
24
25         add(colorPanel, BorderLayout.CENTER);
26         createControlPanel();
27         setSampleColor();
28         setSize(FRAME_WIDTH, FRAME_HEIGHT);
29      }
30
31      class ColorListener implements ChangeListener
32      {
33         public void stateChanged(ChangeEvent event)
34         {
35            setSampleColor();
36         }
37      }
38
39      public void createControlPanel()
40      {
41         ChangeListener listener = new ColorListener();
42
43         redSlider = new JSlider(0, 255, 255);
44         redSlider.addChangeListener(listener);
45
46         greenSlider = new JSlider(0, 255, 175);
47         greenSlider.addChangeListener(listener);
48
49         blueSlider = new JSlider(0, 255, 175);
50         blueSlider.addChangeListener(listener);
51
52         JPanel controlPanel = new JPanel();
53         controlPanel.setLayout(new GridLayout(3, 2));
54
55         controlPanel.add(new JLabel("Red"));
56         controlPanel.add(redSlider);
57
58         controlPanel.add(new JLabel("Green"));
59         controlPanel.add(greenSlider);
60
61         controlPanel.add(new JLabel("Blue"));
62         controlPanel.add(blueSlider);
63
64         add(controlPanel, BorderLayout.SOUTH);
65      }
66
67      /**
68         Reads the slider values and sets the panel to
69         the selected color.
70      */
71      public void setSampleColor()
72      {
73         // Read slider values
74
```

```
75        int red = redSlider.getValue();
76        int green = greenSlider.getValue();
77        int blue = blueSlider.getValue();
78
79        // Set panel background to selected color
80
81        colorPanel.setBackground(new Color(red, green, blue));
82        colorPanel.repaint();
83    }
84 }
```

**SELF CHECK**

17. Suppose you want to allow users to pick a color from a color dialog box. Which class would you use? Look in the API documentation.

18. Why does a slider emit change events and not action events?

**Practice It**    Now you can try these exercises at the end of the chapter: R11.14, P11.2, P11.9.

# 11.5  Using Timer Events for Animations

In this section we introduce timer events and show how you can use them to implement simple animations.

The Timer class in the javax.swing package generates a sequence of action events, spaced at even time intervals. (You can think of a timer as an invisible button that is automatically clicked.) This is useful whenever you want to send continuous updates to a component. For example, in an animation, you may want to update a scene ten times per second and redisplay the image to give the illusion of movement.

> A timer generates action events at fixed intervals.

When you use a timer, you specify the frequency of the events and an object of a class that implements the ActionListener interface. Place whatever action you want to occur inside the actionPerformed method. Finally, start the timer.

```
class MyListener implements ActionListener
{
    public void actionPerformed(ActionEvent event)
    {
        Action that is executed at each timer event
    }
}

MyListener listener = new MyListener();
Timer t = new Timer(interval, listener);
t.start();
```

Then the timer calls the actionPerformed method of the listener object every interval milliseconds.

*A Swing timer notifies a listener with each "tick".*

Our sample program will display a moving rectangle. We first supply a Rectangle-Component class with a moveRectangleBy method that moves the rectangle by a given amount.

### section_5/RectangleComponent.java

```java
1   import java.awt.Graphics;
2   import javax.swing.JComponent;
3
4   /**
5      This component displays a rectangle that can be moved.
6   */
7   public class RectangleComponent extends JComponent
8   {
9      private static final int RECTANGLE_WIDTH = 20;
10     private static final int RECTANGLE_HEIGHT = 30;
11
12     private int xLeft;
13     private int yTop;
14
15     public RectangleComponent()
16     {
17        xLeft = 0;
18        yTop = 0;
19     }
20
21     public void paintComponent(Graphics g)
22     {
23        g.fillRect(xLeft, yTop, RECTANGLE_WIDTH, RECTANGLE_HEIGHT);
24     }
25
26     /**
27        Moves the rectangle by a given amount.
28        @param dx the amount to move in the x-direction
29        @param dy the amount to move in the y-direction
30     */
31     public void moveRectangleBy(int dx, int dy)
32     {
33        xLeft = xLeft + dx;
34        yTop = yTop + dy;
35        repaint();
36     }
37  }
```

To make an animation, the timer listener should update and repaint a component several times per second.

Note the call to repaint in the moveRectangleBy method. This call is necessary to ensure that the component is repainted after the position of the rectangle has been changed. The call to repaint forces a call to the paintComponent method. The paintComponent method redraws the component, causing the rectangle to appear at the updated location.

The actionPerformed method of the timer listener moves the rectangle one pixel down and to the right:

```java
scene.moveRectangleBy(1, 1);
```

Because the actionPerformed method is called many times per second, the rectangle appears to move smoothly across the frame.

**section_5/RectangleFrame.java**

```java
1   import java.awt.event.ActionEvent;
2   import java.awt.event.ActionListener;
3   import javax.swing.JFrame;
4   import javax.swing.Timer;
5
6   /**
7      This frame contains a moving rectangle.
8   */
9   public class RectangleFrame extends JFrame
10  {
11     private static final int FRAME_WIDTH = 300;
12     private static final int FRAME_HEIGHT = 400;
13
14     private RectangleComponent scene;
15
16     class TimerListener implements ActionListener
17     {
18        public void actionPerformed(ActionEvent event)
19        {
20           scene.moveRectangleBy(1, 1);
21        }
22     }
23
24     public RectangleFrame()
25     {
26        scene = new RectangleComponent();
27        add(scene);
28
29        setSize(FRAME_WIDTH, FRAME_HEIGHT);
30
31        ActionListener listener = new TimerListener();
32
33        final int DELAY = 100; // Milliseconds between timer ticks
34        Timer t = new Timer(DELAY, listener);
35        t.start();
36     }
37  }
```

**SELF CHECK**

19. Why does a timer require a listener object?

20. How can you make the rectangle move backwards?

21. Describe two ways of modifying the program so that the rectangle moves twice as fast.

22. How can you make a car move instead of a rectangle?

23. How can you make two rectangles move in parallel in the scene?

24. What would happen if you omitted the call to repaint in the moveRectangleBy method?

**Practice It**   Now you can try these exercises at the end of the chapter: P11.12, P11.13, P11.14.

# 11.6 Mouse Events

You use a mouse
listener to capture
mouse events.

If you write programs that show drawings, and you want users to manipulate the drawings with a mouse, then you need to listen to mouse events. Mouse listeners are more complex than action listeners, the listeners that process button clicks and timer ticks.

A mouse listener must implement the Mouse-Listener interface, which contains the following five methods:

*In Swing, a mouse event isn't a gathering of rodents; it's notification of a mouse click by the program user.*

```
public interface MouseListener
{
    void mousePressed(MouseEvent event);
        // Called when a mouse button has been pressed on a component
    void mouseReleased(MouseEvent event);
        // Called when a mouse button has been released on a component
    void mouseClicked(MouseEvent event);
        // Called when the mouse has been clicked on a component
    void mouseEntered(MouseEvent event);
        // Called when the mouse enters a component
    void mouseExited(MouseEvent event);
        // Called when the mouse exits a component
}
```

The mousePressed and mouseReleased methods are called whenever a mouse button is pressed or released. If a button is pressed and released in quick succession, and the mouse has not moved, then the mouseClicked method is called as well. The mouseEntered and mouseExited methods can be used to highlight a user-interface component whenever the mouse is pointing inside it.

The most commonly used method is mousePressed. Users generally expect that their actions are processed as soon as the mouse button is pressed.

You add a mouse listener to a component by calling the addMouseListener method:

```
public class MyMouseListener implements MouseListener
{
    public void mousePressed(MouseEvent event)
    {
        int x = event.getX();
        int y = event.getY();
        Process mouse event at (x, y)
    }

    // Do-nothing methods
    public void mouseReleased(MouseEvent event) {}
    public void mouseClicked(MouseEvent event) {}
    public void mouseEntered(MouseEvent event) {}
    public void mouseExited(MouseEvent event) {}
}

MouseListener listener = new MyMouseListener();
component.addMouseListener(listener);
```

In our sample program, a user clicks on a component containing a rectangle. Whenever the mouse button is pressed, the rectangle is moved to the mouse location. We first enhance the RectangleComponent class and add a moveRectangleTo method to move the rectangle to a new position.

### section_6/RectangleComponent2.java

```
1   import java.awt.Graphics;
2   import java.awt.Rectangle;
3   import javax.swing.JComponent;
4
5   /**
6      This component displays a rectangle that can be moved.
7   */
8   public class RectangleComponent2 extends JComponent
9   {
10     private static final int RECTANGLE_WIDTH = 20;
11     private static final int RECTANGLE_HEIGHT = 30;
12
13     private int xLeft;
14     private int yTop;
15
16     public RectangleComponent2()
17     {
18        xLeft = 0;
19        yTop = 0;
20     }
21
22     public void paintComponent(Graphics g)
23     {
24        g.fillRect(xLeft, yTop, RECTANGLE_WIDTH, RECTANGLE_HEIGHT);
25     }
26
27     /**
28        Moves the rectangle to the given location.
29        @param x the x-position of the new location
30        @param y the y-position of the new location
31     */
32     public void moveRectangleTo(int x, int y)
33     {
34        xLeft = x;
35        yTop = y;
36        repaint();
37     }
38   }
```

Note the call to repaint in the moveRectangleTo method. As you saw before, this call causes the component to repaint itself and show the rectangle in the new position.

Now, add a mouse listener to the component. Whenever the mouse is pressed, the listener moves the rectangle to the mouse location.

```
class MousePressListener implements MouseListener
{
   public void mousePressed(MouseEvent event)
   {
      int x = event.getX();
      int y = event.getY();
      scene.moveRectangleTo(x, y);
   }
   . . .
}
```

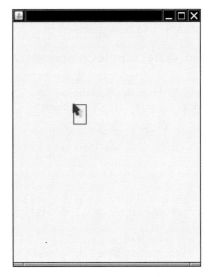

**Figure 13**   Clicking the Mouse Moves the Rectangle

It often happens that a particular listener specifies actions only for one or two of the listener methods. Nevertheless, all five methods of the interface must be implemented. The unused methods are simply implemented as do-nothing methods.

Go ahead and run the `RectangleViewer2` program. Whenever you click the mouse inside the frame, the top-left corner of the rectangle moves to the mouse pointer (see Figure 13).

### section_6/RectangleViewer2.java

```java
1   import javax.swing.JFrame;
2
3   /**
4      This program displays a rectangle that can be moved with the mouse.
5   */
6   public class RectangleViewer2
7   {
8      public static void main(String[] args)
9      {
10        JFrame frame = new RectangleFrame2();
11        frame.setDefaultCloseOperation(JFrame.EXIT_ON_CLOSE);
12        frame.setVisible(true);
13     }
14  }
```

### section_6/RectangleFrame2.java

```java
1   import java.awt.event.MouseListener;
2   import java.awt.event.MouseEvent;
3   import javax.swing.JFrame;
4
5   /**
6      This frame contains a moving rectangle.
7   */
8   public class RectangleFrame2 extends JFrame
9   {
```

```
10        private static final int FRAME_WIDTH = 300;
11        private static final int FRAME_HEIGHT = 400;
12
13        private RectangleComponent2 scene;
14
15        class MousePressListener implements MouseListener
16        {
17           public void mousePressed(MouseEvent event)
18           {
19              int x = event.getX();
20              int y = event.getY();
21              scene.moveRectangleTo(x, y);
22           }
23
24           // Do-nothing methods
25           public void mouseReleased(MouseEvent event) {}
26           public void mouseClicked(MouseEvent event) {}
27           public void mouseEntered(MouseEvent event) {}
28           public void mouseExited(MouseEvent event) {}
29        }
30
31        public RectangleFrame2()
32        {
33           scene = new RectangleComponent2();
34           add(scene);
35
36           MouseListener listener = new MousePressListener();
37           scene.addMouseListener(listener);
38
39           setSize(FRAME_WIDTH, FRAME_HEIGHT);
40        }
41  }
```

**SELF CHECK**

**25.** Why was the moveRectangleBy method in RectangleComponent2 replaced with a moveRectangleTo method?

**26.** Why must the MousePressListener class supply five methods?

**27.** How could you change the behavior of the program so that a new rectangle is added whenever the mouse is clicked?

**Practice It**   Now you can try these exercises at the end of the chapter: R11.21, P11.22, P11.23.

Special Topic 11.1

### Keyboard Events

If you program a game, you may want to process keystrokes, such as the arrow keys. Add a key listener to the component on which you draw the game scene. The KeyListener interface has three methods. As with a mouse listener, you are most interested in key press events, and you can leave the other two methods empty. Your key listener class should look like this:

```
class MyKeyListener implements KeyListener
{
   public void keyPressed(KeyEvent event)
   {
      String key = KeyStroke.getKeyStrokeForEvent(event).toString();
      key = key.replace("pressed ", "");
      Process key.
```

```
   }

   // Do-nothing methods
   public void keyReleased(KeyEvent event) {}
   public void keyTyped(KeyEvent event) {}
}
```

The call `KeyStroke.getKeyStrokeForEvent(event).toString()` turns the event object into a text description of the key, such as "pressed LEFT". In the next line, we eliminate the "pressed " prefix. The remainder is a string such as "LEFT" or "A" that describes the key that was pressed. You can find a list of all key names in the API documentation of the KeyStroke class.

*Whenever the program user presses a key, a key event is generated.*

As always, remember to attach the listener to the event source:

```
KeyListener listener = new MyKeyListener();
scene.addKeyListener(listener);
```

In order to receive key events, your component must call

```
scene.setFocusable(true);
```

**ONLINE EXAMPLE**

A complete program that uses the arrow keys to move a rectangle.

---

**Special Topic 11.2**

## Event Adapters

In the preceding section you saw how to install a mouse listener in a mouse event source and how the listener methods are called when an event occurs. Usually, a program is not interested in all listener notifications. For example, a program may only be interested in mouse clicks and may not care that these mouse clicks are composed of "mouse pressed" and "mouse released" events. Of course, the program could supply a listener that declares all those methods in which it has no interest as "do-nothing" methods, for example:

```
class MouseClickListener implements MouseListener
{
   public void mouseClicked(MouseEvent event)
   {
      Mouse click action
   }

   // Four do-nothing methods
   public void mouseEntered(MouseEvent event) {}
   public void mouseExited(MouseEvent event) {}
   public void mousePressed(MouseEvent event) {}
   public void mouseReleased(MouseEvent event) {}
}
```

To avoid this labor, some friendly soul has created a MouseAdapter class that implements the MouseListener interface such that all methods do nothing. You can *extend* that class, inheriting the do-nothing methods and overriding the methods that you care about, like this:

```
class MouseClickListener extends MouseAdapter
{
   public void mouseClicked(MouseEvent event)
   {
      Mouse click action
   }
}
```

There is also a KeyAdapter that implements the KeyListener interface (see Special Topic 11.1), providing three do-nothing methods.

## WORKED EXAMPLE 11.2 — **Adding Mouse and Keyboard Support to the Bar Chart Creator**

In this Worked Example, we will enhance the bar chart creator of Worked Example 10.1 and add support for mouse and keyboard operations.

## VIDEO EXAMPLE 11.1 — **Designing a Baby Naming Program**

In this Video Example, you will see how to design a user interface for a program that suggests baby names.

## CHAPTER SUMMARY

**Learn how to arrange multiple components in a container.**

- User-interface components are arranged by placing them inside containers. Containers can be placed inside larger containers.
- Each container has a layout manager that directs the arrangement of its components.
- Three useful layout managers are the border layout, flow layout, and grid layout.
- When adding a component to a container with the border layout, specify the NORTH, SOUTH, WEST, EAST, or CENTER position.
- The content pane of a frame has a border layout by default. A panel has a flow layout by default.

**Select among the Swing components for presenting choices to the user.**

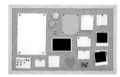

- For a small set of mutually exclusive choices, use a group of radio buttons or a combo box.
- Add radio buttons to a ButtonGroup so that only one button in the group is selected at any time.
- You can place a border around a panel to group its contents visually.
- For a binary choice, use a check box.
- For a large set of choices, use a combo box.
- Radio buttons, check boxes, and combo boxes generate action events, just as buttons do.

**Implement menus in a Swing program.**

- A frame contains a menu bar. The menu bar contains menus. A menu contains submenus and menu items.
- Menu items generate action events.

Available online in WileyPLUS and at www.wiley.com/college/horstmann.

## Use the Swing documentation.

- You should learn to navigate the API documentation to find out more about user-interface components.

## Use timer events to implement animations.

- A timer generates action events at fixed intervals.
- To make an animation, the timer listener should update and repaint a component several times per second.

## Write programs that process mouse events.

- You use a mouse listener to capture mouse events.

---

## STANDARD LIBRARY ITEMS INTRODUCED IN THIS CHAPTER

java.awt.BorderLayout
   CENTER
   EAST
   NORTH
   SOUTH
   WEST
java.awt.Component
   addKeyListener
   addMouseListener
   setFocusable
java.awt.Container
   setLayout
java.awt.FlowLayout
java.awt.Font
   BOLD
   ITALIC
java.awt.GridLayout
java.awt.event.KeyEvent
*java.awt.event.KeyListener*
   keyPressed
   keyReleased
   keyTyped
java.awt.event.MouseEvent
   getX
   getY
*java.awt.event.MouseListener*
   mouseClicked
   mouseEntered
   mouseExited
   mousePressed
   mouseReleased
javax.swing.AbstractButton
   isSelected
   setSelected

javax.swing.ButtonGroup
   add
javax.swing.JCheckBox
javax.swing.JComboBox
   addItem
   getSelectedItem
   isEditable
   setEditable
   setSelectedItem
javax.swing.JComponent
   setBorder
   setFocusable
   setFont
javax.swing.JFrame
   setJMenuBar
javax.swing.JMenu
   add
javax.swing.JMenuBar
   add
javax.swing.JMenuItem
javax.swing.JRadioButton
javax.swing.JSlider
   addChangeListener
   getValue
javax.swing.KeyStroke
   getKeyStrokeForEvent
javax.swing.Timer
   start
   stop
javax.swing.border.EtchedBorder
javax.swing.border.TitledBorder
javax.swing.event.ChangeEvent
*javax.swing.event.ChangeListener*
   stateChanged

## REVIEW EXERCISES

- **R11.1** Can you use a flow layout for the components in a frame? If yes, how?

- **R11.2** What is the advantage of a layout manager over telling the container "place this component at position $(x, y)$"?

- **R11.3** What happens when you place a single button into the CENTER area of a container that uses a border layout? Try it out by writing a small sample program if you aren't sure of the answer.

- **R11.4** What happens if you place multiple buttons directly into the SOUTH area, without using a panel? Try it out by writing a small sample program if you aren't sure of the answer.

- **R11.5** What happens when you add a button to a container that uses a border layout and omit the position? Try it out and explain.

- **R11.6** What happens when you try to add a button to another button? Try it out and explain.

- **R11.7** The control panel in Section 11.4 uses a grid layout manager. Explain a drawback of the grid that is apparent in Figure 12. What could you do to overcome this drawback?

- **R11.8** What is the difference between the grid layout and the grid bag layout?

- **R11.9** Can you add icons to check boxes, radio buttons, and combo boxes? Browse the Java documentation to find out. Then write a small test program to verify your findings.

- **R11.10** What is the difference between radio buttons and check boxes?

- **R11.11** Why do you need a button group for radio buttons but not for check boxes?

- **R11.12** What is the difference between a menu bar, a menu, and a menu item?

- **R11.13** When browsing through the Java documentation for more information about sliders, we ignored the JSlider constructor with no arguments. Why? Would it have worked in our sample program?

- **R11.14** How do you construct a vertical slider? Consult the Swing documentation for an answer.

- **R11.15** Why doesn't a JComboBox send out change events?

- **R11.16** What component would you use to show a set of choices, as in a combo box, but so that several items are visible at the same time? Run the Swing demo application or look at a book with Swing example programs to find the answer.

- **R11.17** How many Swing user-interface components are there? Look at the Java documentation to get an approximate answer.

- **R11.18** How many methods does the JProgressBar component have? Be sure to count inherited methods. Look at the Java documentation.

- **R11.19** What is the difference between an ActionEvent and a MouseEvent?

- **R11.20** What information does an action event object carry? What additional information does a mouse event object carry? *Hint:* Check the API documentation.

■■ **R11.21** Why does the ActionListener interface have only one method, whereas the Mouse-Listener has five methods?

## PROGRAMMING EXERCISES

■ **P11.1** Write an application with three buttons labeled "Red", "Green", and "Blue" that changes the background color of a panel in the center of the frame to red, green, or blue.

■■ **P11.2** Add icons to the buttons of Exercise P11.1. Use a JButton constructor with an Icon argument and supply an ImageIcon.

■ **P11.3** Write an application with three radio buttons labeled "Red", "Green", and "Blue" that changes the background color of a panel in the center of the frame to red, green, or blue.

■ **P11.4** Write an application with three check boxes labeled "Red", "Green", and "Blue" that adds a red, green, or blue component to the background color of a panel in the center of the frame. This application can display a total of eight color combinations.

■ **P11.5** Write an application with a combo box containing three items labeled "Red", "Green", and "Blue" that change the background color of a panel in the center of the frame to red, green, or blue.

■ **P11.6** Write an application with a Color menu and menu items labeled "Red", "Green", and "Blue" that change the background color of a panel in the center of the frame to red, green, or blue.

■ **P11.7** Write a program that displays a number of rectangles at random positions. Supply menu items "Fewer" and "More" that generate fewer or more random rectangles. Each time the user selects "Fewer", the count should be halved. Each time the user clicks on "More", the count should be doubled.

■■ **P11.8** Modify the program of Exercise P11.7 to replace the buttons with a slider to generate more or fewer random rectangles.

■■ **P11.9** Modify the slider program in Section 11.4 to add a set of tick marks to each slider that show the exact slider position.

■■■ **P11.10** Enhance the font viewer program to allow the user to select different font faces. Research the API documentation to find out how to find the available fonts on the user's system.

■■■ **P11.11** Write a program that lets users design charts such as the following:

```
┌──────────────────────────────────────────────┐
│ Golden Gate                                    │
├──────────────────────┐
│ Brooklyn             │
├──────────────────────────────┐
│ Delaware Memorial            │
├────────────────────────────────────┐
│ Mackinac                           │
└────────────────────────────────────┘
```

Use appropriate components to ask for the length, label, and color, then apply them when the user clicks an "Add Item" button.

■ **P11.12** Write a program that uses a timer to print the current time once a second. *Hint:* The following code prints the current time:

```
Date now = new Date();
System.out.println(now);
```

The Date class is in the java.util package.

■■■ **P11.13** Change the RectangleComponent for the animation in Section 11.5 so that the rectangle bounces off the edges of the component rather than simply moving outside.

■■ **P11.14** Change the rectangle animation in Section 11.5 so that it shows two rectangles moving in opposite directions.

■■ **P11.15** Write a program that animates a car so that it moves across a frame.

■■■ **P11.16** Write a program that animates two cars moving across a frame in opposite directions (but at different heights so that they don't collide.)

■■■ **P11.17** Write a program that displays a scrolling message in a panel. Use a timer for the scrolling effect. In the timer's action listener, move the starting position of the message and repaint. When the message has left the window, reset the starting position to the other corner. Provide a user interface to customize the message text, font, foreground and background colors, and the scrolling speed and direction.

■ **P11.18** Change the RectangleComponent for the mouse listener program in Section 11.6 so that a new rectangle is added to the component whenever the mouse is clicked. *Hint:* Store all points on which the user clicked, and draw all rectangles in the paintComponent method.

■ **P11.19** Write a program that prompts the user to enter the *x*- and *y*-positions of a center point and a radius, using text fields. When the user clicks a "Draw" button, draw a circle with that center and radius in a component.

■■ **P11.20** Write a program that allows the user to specify a circle by typing the radius in a text field and then clicking on the center. Note that you don't need a "Draw" button.

■ **P11.21** Write a program that allows the user to specify a circle with two mouse presses, the first one on the center and the second on a point on the periphery. *Hint:* In the mouse press handler, you must keep track of whether you already received the center point in a previous mouse press.

■■■ **P11.22** Write a program that allows the user to specify a triangle with three mouse presses. After the first mouse press, draw a small dot. After the second mouse press, draw a line joining the first two points. After the third mouse press, draw the entire triangle. The fourth mouse press erases the old triangle and starts a new one.

■■■ **P11.23** Implement a program that allows two players to play tic-tac-toe. Draw the game grid and an indication of whose turn it is (X or O). Upon the next click, check that the mouse click falls into an empty location, fill the location with the mark of the current player, and give the other player a turn. If the game is won, indicate the winner. Also supply a button for starting over.

■■■ **P11.24** Write a program that lets users design bar charts with a mouse. When the user clicks inside a bar, the next mouse click extends the length of the bar to the *x*-coordinate of the mouse click. (If it is at or near 0, the bar is removed.) When the user clicks below the last bar, a new bar is added whose length is the *x*-coordinate of the mouse click.

■■ **Business P11.25** Write a program with a graphical interface that allows the user to convert an amount of money between U.S. dollars (USD), euros (EUR), and British pounds (GBP). The user interface should have the following elements: a text box to enter the amount to be converted, two combo boxes to allow the user to select the currencies, a button to make the conversion, and a label to show the result. Display a warning if the user does not choose different currencies. Use the following conversion rates:

> 1 EUR is equal to 1.42 USD.
>
> 1 GBP is equal to 1.64 USD.
>
> 1 GBP is equal to 1.13 EUR.

■■ **Business P11.26** Write a program with a graphical interface that implements a login window with text fields for the user name and password. When the login is successful, hide the login window and open a new window with a welcome message. Follow these rules for validating the password:

**1.** The user name is not case sensitive.

**2.** The password is case sensitive.

**3.** The user has three opportunities to enter valid credentials.

Otherwise, display an error message and terminate the program. When the program starts, read the file users.txt. Each line in that file contains a username and password, separated by a space. You should make a users.txt file for testing your program.

■■ **Business P11.27** In Exercise P11.26, the password is shown as it is typed. Browse the Swing documentation to find an appropriate component for entering a password. Improve the solution of Exercise P11.26 by using this component instead of a text field. Each time the user types a letter, show a ■ character.

## ANSWERS TO SELF-CHECK QUESTIONS

**1.** Only the second one is displayed.

**2.** First add them to a panel, then add the panel to the north end of a frame.

**3.** Place them inside a panel with a GridLayout that has three rows and one column.

**4.** The button in the north stretches horizontally to fill the width of the frame. The height of the northern area is the normal height.

**5.** To get the double-wide button, put it in the south of a panel with border layout whose center has a 3 × 2 grid layout with the keys 7, 8, 4, 5, 1, 2. Put that panel in the west of another border layout panel whose eastern area has a 4 × 1 grid layout with the remaining keys.

**6.** If you have many options, a set of radio buttons takes up a large area. A combo box can show many options without using up much space. But the user cannot see the options as easily.

**7.** If one of them is checked, the other one is unchecked. You should use radio buttons if that is the behavior you want.

**8.** You can't nest borders, but you can nest panels with borders:

```
JPanel p1 = new JPanel();
p1.setBorder(new EtchedBorder());
JPanel p2 = new JPanel();
p2.setBorder(new EtchedBorder());
p1.add(p2);
```

**9.** When any of the component settings is changed, the program simply queries all of them and updates the label.

**10.** To keep it from growing too large. It would have grown to the same width and height as the two panels below it.

**11.** Instead of using radio buttons with two choices, use a checkbox.

**12.** When you open a menu, you have not yet made a selection. Only `JMenuItem` objects correspond to selections.

**13.** Yes, you can—`JMenuItem` is a subclass of `JMenu`. The item shows up on the menu bar. When you click on it, its listener is called. But the behavior feels unnatural for a menu bar and is likely to confuse users.

**14.** The parameter variable is accessed in a method of an inner class.

**15.** Then the `faceName` variable is set when the menu item is added to the menu, not when the user selects the menu.

**16.** In the previous program, the user-interface components effectively served as storage for the font specification. Their current settings were used to construct the font. But a menu doesn't save settings; it just generates an action.

**17.** `JColorChooser`.

**18.** Action events describe one-time changes, such as button clicks. Change events describe continuous changes.

**19.** The timer needs to call some method whenever the time interval expires. It calls the `action-Performed` method of the listener object.

**20.** Call `scene.moveRectangleBy(-1, -1)` in the `action-Performed` method.

**21.** You can cut the timer delay in half (to 50 milliseconds between ticks), or you can double the distance by which the rectangle moves, by calling `scene.moveRectangleBy(2, 2)`.

**22.** The component class would need to draw a car at positon $(x, y)$ instead of a rectangle.

**23.** There are two entirely different ways:

   **a.** Add a second `RectangleComponent` to the frame, using a grid layout. Change the `actionPerformed` method of the `TimerListener` to call `moveRectangleBy` on both components.

   **b.** Draw a second rectangle in the `paint-Component` method of `RectangleComponent`.

**24.** The moved rectangles won't be painted, and the rectangle will appear to be stationary until the frame is repainted for an external reason.

**25.** Because you know the current mouse position, not the amount by which the mouse has moved.

**26.** It implements the `MouseListener` interface, which has five methods.

**27.** The `RectangleComponent2` class needs to keep track of the locations of multiple rectangles. It can do that with an array list of `Point` or `Rect-angle` objects. The `paintComponent` method needs to draw them all. Replace the `moveRectangleTo` method with an `addRectangleAt` method that adds a rectangle at a given $(x, y)$ position.

# OBJECT-ORIENTED DESIGN

Successfully implementing a software system—as simple as your next homework project or as complex as the next air traffic monitoring system—requires a great deal of planning and design. In fact, for larger projects, the amount of time spent on planning and design is much greater than the amount of time spent on programming and testing.

Do you find that most of your homework time is spent in front of the computer, keying in code and fixing bugs? If so, you can probably save time by focusing on a better design before you start coding. This chapter tells you how to approach the design of an object-oriented program in a systematic manner.

# 12.1 Classes and Their Responsibilities

When you design a program, you work from a *requirements specification*, a description of what your program should do. The designer's task is to discover structures that make it possible to implement the requirements in a computer program. In the following sections, we will examine the steps of the design process.

## 12.1.1 Discovering Classes

> To discover classes, look for nouns in the problem description.

When you solve a problem using objects and classes, you need to determine the classes required for the implementation. You may be able to reuse existing classes, or you may need to implement new ones.

One simple approach for discovering classes and methods is to look for the nouns and verbs in the requirements specification. Often, *nouns* correspond to classes, and *verbs* correspond to methods.

For example, suppose your job is to print an invoice such as the one in Figure 1. Obvious classes that come to mind are Invoice, LineItem, and Customer. It is a good idea to keep a list of *candidate classes* on a whiteboard or a sheet of paper. As you brainstorm, simply put all ideas for classes onto the list. You can always cross out the ones that weren't useful after all.

> Concepts from the problem domain are good candidates for classes.

In general, concepts from the problem domain, be it science, business, or a game, often make good classes. Examples are

- Cannonball
- CashRegister
- Monster

The name for such a class should be a noun that describes the concept.

Not all classes can be discovered from the program requirements. Most complex programs need classes for tactical purposes, such as file or database access, user interfaces, control mechanisms, and so on.

Some of the classes that you need may already exist, either in the standard library or in a program that you developed previously. You also may be able to use inheritance to extend existing classes into classes that match your needs.

# INVOICE

Sam's Small Appliances
100 Main Street
Anytown, CA 98765

| Item | Qty | Price | Total |
|------|-----|-------|-------|
| Toaster | 3 | $29.95 | $89.85 |
| Hair Dryer | 1 | $24.95 | $24.95 |
| Car Vacuum | 2 | $19.99 | $39.98 |

**AMOUNT DUE:  $154.78**

**Figure 1**  An Invoice

What might not be a good class? If you can't tell from the class name what an object of the class is supposed to do, then you are probably not on the right track. For example, your homework assignment might be to write a program that prints paychecks. Suppose you start by trying to design a class PaycheckProgram. What would an object of this class do? An object of this class would have to do everything that the homework needs to do. That doesn't simplify anything. A better class would be Paycheck. Then your program can manipulate one or more Paycheck objects.

Another common mistake, often made by students who are used to writing programs that consist of static methods, is to turn an action into a class. For example, if your homework assignment is to compute a paycheck, you may consider writing a class ComputePaycheck. But can you visualize a "ComputePaycheck" object? The fact that "ComputePaycheck" isn't a noun tips you off that you are on the wrong track. On the other hand, a Paycheck class makes intuitive sense. The word "paycheck" is a noun. You can visualize a paycheck object. You can then think about useful methods of the Paycheck class, such as computeTaxes, that help you solve the assignment.

*In a class scheduling system, potential classes from the problem domain include Class, LectureHall, Instructor, and Student.*

Finally, a common error is to overdo the class discovery process. For example, should an address be an object of an `Address` class, or should it simply be a string? There is no perfect answer—it depends on the task that you want to solve. If your software needs to analyze addresses (for example, to determine shipping costs), then an `Address` class is an appropriate design. However, if your software will never need such a capability, you should not waste time on an overly complex design. It is your job to find a balanced design; one that is neither too limiting nor excessively general.

## 12.1.2 The CRC Card Method

Once you have identified a set of classes, you define the behavior for each class. Find out what methods you need to provide for each class in order to solve the programming problem. A simple rule for finding these methods is to look for *verbs* in the task description, then match the verbs to the appropriate objects. For example, in the invoice program, a class needs to compute the amount due. Now you need to figure out *which class* is responsible for this method. Do customers compute what they owe? Do invoices total up the amount due? Do the items total themselves up? The best choice is to make "compute amount due" the responsibility of the `Invoice` class.

An excellent way to carry out this task is the "**CRC card** method." *CRC* stands for "*c*lasses", "*r*esponsibilities", "*c*ollaborators", and in its simplest form, the method works as follows: Use an index card for each *class* (see Figure 2). As you think about verbs in the task description that indicate methods, you pick the card of the class that you think should be responsible, and write that *responsibility* on the card.

For each responsibility, you record which other classes are needed to fulfill it. Those classes are the **collaborators**.

For example, suppose you decide that an invoice should compute the amount due. Then you write "compute amount due" on the left-hand side of an index card with the title `Invoice`.

If a class can carry out that responsibility by itself, do nothing further. But if the class needs the help of other classes, write the names of these collaborators on the right-hand side of the card.

To compute the total, the invoice needs to ask each line item about its total price. Therefore, the `LineItem` class is a collaborator.

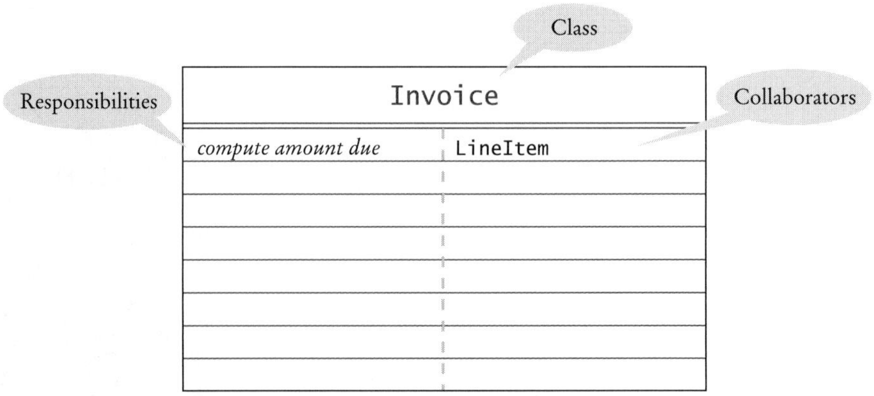

> A CRC card describes a class, its responsibilities, and its collaborating classes.

**Figure 2** A CRC Card

This is a good time to look up the index card for the `LineItem` class. Does it have a "get total price" method? If not, add one.

How do you know that you are on the right track? For each responsibility, ask yourself how it can actually be done, using the responsibilities written on the various cards. Many people find it helpful to group the cards on a table so that the collaborators are close to each other, and to simulate tasks by moving a token (such as a coin) from one card to the next to indicate which object is currently active.

Keep in mind that the responsibilities that you list on the CRC card are on a *high level*. Sometimes a single responsibility may need two or more Java methods for carrying it out. Some researchers say that a CRC card should have no more than three distinct responsibilities.

The CRC card method is informal on purpose, so that you can be creative and discover classes and their properties. Once you find that you have settled on a good set of classes, you will want to know how they are related to each other. Can you find classes with common properties, so that some responsibilities can be taken care of by a common superclass? Can you organize classes into clusters that are independent of each other? Finding class relationships and documenting them with diagrams is the topic of Section 12.2.

## 12.1.3 Cohesion

The public interface of a class is cohesive if all of its features are related to the concept that the class represents.

A class should represent a single concept. The public methods and constants that the public interface exposes should be *cohesive*. That is, all interface features should be closely related to the single concept that the class represents.

If you find that the public interface of a class refers to multiple concepts, then that is a good sign that it may be time to use separate classes instead. Consider, for example, the public interface of a `CashRegister` class:

```java
public class CashRegister
{
    public static final double NICKEL_VALUE = 0.05;
    public static final double DIME_VALUE = 0.1;
    public static final double QUARTER_VALUE = 0.25;
    . . .
    public void enterPayment(int dollars, int quarters,
        int dimes, int nickels, int pennies) { . . . }
    . . .
}
```

There are really two concepts here: a cash register that holds coins and computes their total, and the values of individual coins. (For simplicity, we assume that the cash register only holds coins, not bills. Exercise P12.2 discusses a more general solution.)

It makes sense to have a separate `Coin` class and have coins responsible for knowing their values.

```java
public class Coin
{
    . . .
    public Coin(double aValue, String aName) { . . . }
    public double getValue() { . . . }
    . . .
}
```

Then the CashRegister class can be simplified:

```
public class CashRegister
{
    . . .
    public void enterPayment(int coinCount, Coin coinType) { . . . }
    . . .
}
```

Now the CashRegister class no longer needs to know anything about coin values. The same class can equally well handle euros or zorkmids!

This is clearly a better solution, because it separates the responsibilities of the cash register and the coins.

**SELF CHECK**

1. What is the rule of thumb for finding classes?
2. Your job is to write a program that plays chess. Might ChessBoard be an appropriate class? How about MovePiece?
3. Suppose the invoice is to be saved to a file. Name a likely collaborator.
4. Looking at the invoice in Figure 1, what is a likely responsibility of the Customer class?
5. What do you do if a CRC card has ten responsibilities?

**Practice It**    Now you can try these exercises at the end of the chapter: R12.4, R12.5, R12.12.

# 12.2  Relationships Between Classes

When designing a program, it is useful to document the relationships between classes. This helps you in a number of ways. For example, if you find classes with common behavior, you can save effort by placing the common behavior into a superclass. If you know that some classes are *not* related to each other, you can assign different programmers to implement each of them, without worrying that one of them has to wait for the other.

In the following sections, we will describe the most common types of relationships.

## 12.2.1 Dependency

A class depends on another class if it uses objects of that class.

Many classes need other classes in order to do their jobs. For example, in Section 12.1.3, we described a design of a CashRegister class that depends on the Coin class to determine the value of the payment.

The dependency relationship is sometimes nicknamed the "knows about" relationship. The cash register in Section 12.1.3 knows that there are coin objects. In contrast, the Coin class does *not* depend on the CashRegister class. Coins have no idea that they are being collected in cash registers, and they can carry out their work without ever calling any method in the CashRegister class.

To visualize relationships, such as dependency between classes, programmers draw class diagrams. In this book, we use the UML ("Unified Modeling Language") notation for objects and classes. UML is a notation for object-oriented analysis and

**Figure 3**
Dependency Relationship
Between the CashRegister
and Coin Classes

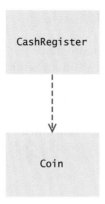

design invented by Grady Booch, Ivar Jacobson, and James Rumbaugh, three leading researchers in object-oriented software development. The UML notation distinguishes between *object diagrams* and *class diagrams*. An object diagram shows individual objects, their attributes, and the relationships between them. Chapter 8 has several object diagrams. A class diagram shows classes and the relationships between them. In Chapter 9, you saw class diagrams that show inheritance relationships. In the UML notation, we underline the names of classes in object diagrams but not in class diagrams.

In a class diagram, you denote dependency by a dashed line with a ⤞-shaped open arrow tip. The arrow tip points to the class on which the other class depends. Figure 3 shows a class diagram indicating that the CashRegister class depends on the Coin class.

If many classes of a program depend on each other, then we say that the **coupling** between classes is high. Conversely, if there are few dependencies between classes, then we say that the coupling is low (see Figure 4).

Why does coupling matter? If the Coin class changes in the next release of the program, all the classes that depend on it may be affected. If the change is drastic, the coupled classes must all be updated. Furthermore, if we would like to use a class in another program, we have to take with it all the classes on which it depends. Thus, we want to remove unnecessary coupling between classes.

It is a good practice to minimize the coupling (i.e., dependency) between classes.

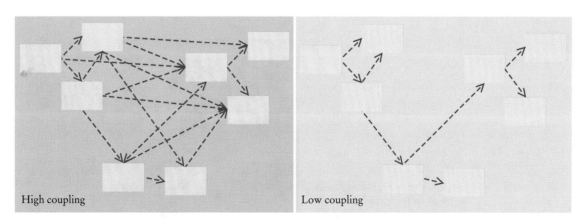

High coupling                                      Low coupling

**Figure 4**   High and Low Coupling Between Classes

## 12.2.2 Aggregation

Another fundamental relationship between classes is the "aggregation" relationship (which is informally known as the "has-a" relationship).

The **aggregation** relationship states that objects of one class contain objects of another class. Consider a quiz that is made up of questions. Because each quiz has one or more questions, we say that the class Quiz *aggregates* the class Question. In the UML notation, aggregation is denoted by a line with a diamond-shaped symbol attached to the aggregating class (see Figure 5).

**Figure 5**
Class Diagram
Showing Aggregation

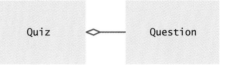

Finding out about aggregation is very helpful for deciding how to implement classes. For example, when you implement the Quiz class, you will want to store the questions of a quiz as an instance variable.

Because a quiz can have any number of questions, an array or array list is a good choice for collecting them:

```
public class Quiz
{
    private ArrayList<Question> questions;
    . . .
}
```

Aggregation is a stronger form of dependency. If a class has objects of another class, it certainly knows about the other class. However, the converse is not true. For example, a class may use the Scanner class without ever declaring an instance variable of class Scanner. The class may simply construct a local variable of type Scanner, or its methods may receive Scanner objects as arguments. This use is not aggregation because the objects of the class don't contain Scanner objects—they just create or receive them for the duration of a single method.

Generally, you need aggregation when an object needs to remember another object *between method calls*.

*A car has a motor and tires. In object-oriented design, this "has-a" relationship is called aggregation.*

## 12.2.3 Inheritance

Inheritance is a relationship between a more general class (the superclass) and a more specialized class (the subclass). This relationship is often described as the "is-a" relationship. Every truck *is a* vehicle. Every savings account *is a* bank account.

Inheritance is sometimes abused. For example, consider a `Tire` class that describes a car tire. Should the class `Tire` be a subclass of a class `Circle`? It sounds convenient. There are quite a few useful methods in the `Circle` class—for example, the `Tire` class may inherit methods that compute the radius, perimeter, and center point, which should come in handy when drawing tire shapes. Though it may be convenient for the programmer, this arrangement makes no sense conceptually. It isn't true that every tire is a circle. Tires are car parts, whereas circles are geometric objects. There is a relationship between tires and circles, though. A tire *has a* circle as its boundary. Use aggregation:

> Inheritance (the *is-a* relationship) is sometimes inappropriately used when the *has-a* relationship would be more appropriate.

```
public class Tire
{
   private String rating;
   private Circle boundary;
   . . .
}
```

Here is another example: Every car *is a* vehicle. Every car *has a* tire (in fact, it typically has four or, if you count the spare, five). Thus, you would use inheritance from `Vehicle` and use aggregation of `Tire` objects:

> Aggregation (the *has-a* relationship) denotes that objects of one class contain references to objects of another class.

```
public class Car extends Vehicle
{
   private Tire[] tires;
   . . .
}
```

See Figure 6 for the UML diagram.

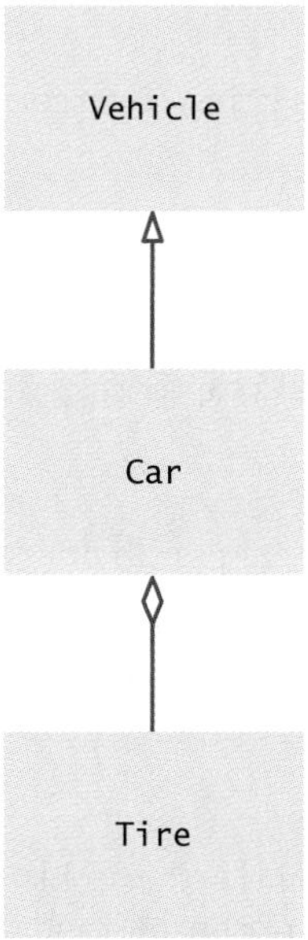

**Figure 6**
UML Notation for
Inheritance and Aggregation

You need to be able to distinguish the UML notation for inheritance, interface implementation, aggregation, and dependency.

The arrows in the UML notation can get confusing. Table 1 shows a summary of the four UML relationship symbols that we use in this book.

| Table 1 | UML Relationship Symbols | | |
|---|---|---|---|
| Relationship | Symbol | Line Style | Arrow Tip |
| Inheritance | ——————▷ | Solid | Triangle |
| Interface Implementation | - - - - - - ▷ | Dotted | Triangle |
| Aggregation | ◇——————— | Solid | Diamond |
| Dependency | - - - - - - ▷ | Dotted | Open |

**SELF CHECK**

6. Consider the `CashRegisterTester` class of Chapter 8. On which classes does it depend?

7. Consider the `Question` and `ChoiceQuestion` objects of Chapter 9. How are they related?

8. Consider the `Quiz` class described in Section 12.2.2. Suppose a quiz contains a mixture of `Question` and `ChoiceQuestion` objects. Which classes does the `Quiz` class depend on?

9. Why should coupling be minimized between classes?

10. In an e-mail system, messages are stored in a mailbox. Draw a UML diagram that shows the appropriate aggregation relationship.

11. You are implementing a system to manage a library, keeping track of which books are checked out by whom. Should the `Book` class aggregate `Patron` or the other way around?

12. In a library management system, what would be the relationship between classes `Patron` and `Author`?

**Practice It**    Now you can try these exercises at the end of the chapter: R12.8, R12.9, R12.13.

---

**HOW TO 12.1**    **Using CRC Cards and UML Diagrams in Program Design**

Before writing code for a complex problem, you need to design a solution. The methodology introduced in this chapter suggests that you follow a design process that is composed of the following tasks:

• Discover classes.
• Determine the responsibilities of each class.
• Describe the relationships between the classes.

CRC cards and UML diagrams help you discover and record this information.

**Step 1**    Discover classes.

Highlight the nouns in the problem description. Make a list of the nouns. Cross out those that don't seem to be reasonable candidates for classes.

**Step 2**    Discover responsibilities.

Make a list of the major tasks that your system needs to fulfill. From those tasks, pick one that is not trivial and that is intuitive to you. Find a class that is responsible for carrying out that task. Make an index card and write the name and the task on it. Now ask yourself how an object of the class can carry out the task. It probably needs help from other objects. Then make CRC cards for the classes to which those objects belong and write the responsibilities on them.

Don't be afraid to cross out, move, split, or merge responsibilities. Rip up cards if they become too messy. This is an informal process.

You are done when you have walked through all major tasks and are satisfied that they can all be solved with the classes and responsibilities that you discovered.

**Step 3**    Describe relationships.

Make a class diagram that shows the relationships between all the classes that you discovered.

Start with inheritance—the *is-a* relationship between classes. Is any class a specialization of another? If so, draw inheritance arrows. Keep in mind that many designs, especially for simple programs, don't use inheritance extensively.

The "collaborators" column of the CRC card tells you which classes are used by that class. Draw dependency arrows for the collaborators on the CRC cards.

Some dependency relationships give rise to aggregations. For each of the dependency relationships, ask yourself: How does the object locate its collaborator? Does it navigate to it directly because it stores a reference? In that case, draw an aggregation arrow. Or is the collaborator a method parameter variable or return value? Then simply draw a dependency arrow.

---

**Special Topic 12.1**

## Attributes and Methods in UML Diagrams

Sometimes it is useful to indicate class *attributes* and *methods* in a class diagram. An **attribute** is an externally observable property that objects of a class have. For example, name and price would be attributes of the Product class. Usually, attributes correspond to instance variables. But they don't have to—a class may have a different way of organizing its data. For example, a GregorianCalendar object from the Java library has attributes day, month, and year, and it would be appropriate to draw a UML diagram that shows these attributes. However, the class doesn't actually have instance variables that store these quantities. Instead, it internally represents all dates by counting the milliseconds from January 1, 1970—an implementation detail that a class user certainly doesn't need to know about.

You can indicate attributes and methods in a class diagram by dividing a class rectangle into three compartments, with the class name in the top, attributes in the middle, and methods in the bottom (see the figure below). You need not list *all* attributes and methods in a particular diagram. Just list the ones that are helpful for understanding whatever point you are making with a particular diagram.

Also, don't list as an attribute what you also draw as an aggregation. If you denote by aggregation the fact that a Car has Tire objects, don't add an attribute tires.

*Attributes and Methods in a Class Diagram*

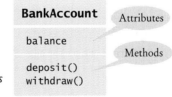

Special Topic 12.2

## Multiplicities

Some designers like to write *multiplicities* at the end(s) of an aggregation relationship to denote how many objects are aggregated. The notations for the most common multiplicities are:

- any number (zero or more): *
- one or more: 1..*
- zero or one: 0..1
- exactly one: 1

The figure below shows that a customer has one or more bank accounts.

*An Aggregation Relationship with Multiplicities*

Special Topic 12.3

## Aggregation, Association, and Composition

Some designers find the aggregation or *has-a* terminology unsatisfactory. For example, consider customers of a bank. Does the bank "have" customers? Do the customers "have" bank accounts, or does the bank "have" them? Which of these "has" relationships should be modeled by aggregation? This line of thinking can lead us to premature implementation decisions.

Early in the design phase, it makes sense to use a more general relationship between classes called **association**. A class is associated with another if you can *navigate* from objects of one class to objects of the other class. For example, given a Bank object, you can navigate to Customer objects, perhaps by accessing an instance variable, or by making a database lookup.

The UML notation for an association relationship is a solid line, with optional arrows that show in which directions you can navigate the relationship. You can also add words to the line ends to further explain the nature of the relationship. The figure below shows that you can navigate from Bank objects to Customer objects, but you cannot navigate the other way around. That is, in this particular design, the Customer class has no mechanism to determine in which banks it keeps its money.

*An Association Relationship*

The UML standard also recognizes a stronger form of the aggregation relationship called **composition**, where the aggregated objects do not have an existence independent of the containing object. For example, composition models the relationship between a bank and its accounts. If a bank closes, the account objects cease to exist as well. In the UML notation, composition looks like aggregation with a filled-in diamond.

*A Composition Relationship*

Frankly, the differences between aggregation, association, and composition can be confusing, even to experienced designers. If you find the distinction helpful, by all means use the relationship that you find most appropriate. But don't spend time pondering subtle differences between these concepts. From the practical point of view of a Java programmer, it is useful to know when objects of one class have references to objects of another class. The aggregation or *has-a* relationship accurately describes this phenomenon.

## Make Parallel Arrays into Arrays of Objects

Sometimes, you find yourself using arrays or array lists of the same length, each of which stores a part of what conceptually should be an object. In that situation, it is a good idea to reorganize your program and use a single array or array list whose elements are objects.

For example, suppose an invoice contains a series of item descriptions and prices. One solution is to keep two arrays:

```
String[] descriptions;
double[] prices;
```

Each of the arrays will have the same length, and the ith *slice*, consisting of descriptions[i] and prices[i], contains data that need to be processed together. These arrays are called **parallel arrays** (see Figure 7).

Parallel arrays become a headache in larger programs. The programmer must ensure that the arrays always have the same length and that each slice is filled with values that actually belong together. Moreover, any method that operates on a slice must get all values of the slice as arguments, which is tedious to program.

The remedy is simple. Look at the slice and find the *concept* that it represents. Then make the concept into a class. In this example, each slice contains the description and price of an item; turn this into a class:

> Avoid parallel arrays by changing them into arrays of objects.

```
public class Item
{
    private String description;
    private double price;
    . . .
}
```

**Figure 7**
Parallel Arrays

You can now eliminate the parallel arrays and replace them with a single array:

```
Item[] items;
```

Each slot in the resulting array corresponds to a slice in the set of parallel arrays (see Figure 8).

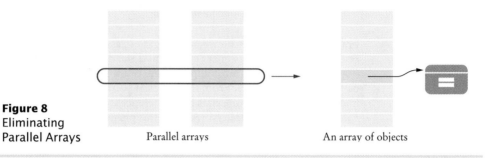

**Figure 8**
Eliminating
Parallel Arrays

Parallel arrays                    An array of objects

### Consistency

In this chapter you learned of two criteria for improving the quality of the public interface of a class. You should maximize cohesion and remove unnecessary coupling. There is another criterion that we would like you to pay attention to—*consistency*. When you have a set of methods, follow a consistent scheme for their names and parameter variables. This is simply a sign of good craftsmanship.

Sadly, you can find any number of inconsistencies in the standard Java library. Here is an example. To show an input dialog box, you call

```
JOptionPane.showInputDialog(promptString)
```

To show a message dialog box, you call

```
JOptionPane.showMessageDialog(null, messageString)
```

What's the `null` argument? It turns out that the `showMessageDialog` method needs an argument to specify the parent window, or `null` if no parent window is required. But the `showInputDialog` method requires no parent window. Why the inconsistency? There is no reason. It would have been an easy matter to supply a `showMessageDialog` method that exactly mirrors the `showInputDialog` method.

Inconsistencies such as these are not fatal flaws, but they are an annoyance, particularly because they can be so easily avoided.

# 12.3 Application: Printing an Invoice

In this book, we discuss a five-part program development process that is particularly well suited for beginning programmers:

1. Gather requirements.
2. Use CRC cards to find classes, responsibilities, and collaborators.
3. Use UML diagrams to record class relationships.
4. Use javadoc to document method behavior.
5. Implement your program.

There isn't a lot of notation to learn. The class diagrams are simple to draw. The deliverables of the design phase are obviously useful for the implementation phase—you simply take the source files and start adding the method code. Of course, as your projects get more complex, you will want to learn more about formal design methods. There are many techniques to describe object scenarios, call sequencing, the large-scale structure of programs, and so on, that are very beneficial even for relatively simple projects. *The Unified Modeling Language User Guide* gives a good overview of these techniques.

In this section, we will walk through the object-oriented design technique with a very simple example. In this case, the methodology may feel overblown, but it is a good introduction to the mechanics of each step. You will then be better prepared for the more complex programs that you will encounter in the future.

## 12.3.1 Requirements

**Start the development process by gathering and documenting program requirements.**

Before you begin designing a solution, you should gather all requirements for your program in plain English. Write down what your program should do. It is helpful to include typical scenarios in addition to a general description.

The task of our sample program is to print out an invoice. An invoice describes the charges for a set of products in certain quantities. (We omit complexities such as dates, taxes, and invoice and customer numbers.) The program simply prints the billing address, all line items, and the amount due. Each line item contains the description and unit price of a product, the quantity ordered, and the total price.

*An invoice lists the charges for each item and the amount due.*

```
              I N V O I C E

   Sam's Small Appliances
   100 Main Street
   Anytown, CA 98765

   Description              Price  Qty  Total
   Toaster                  29.95   3   89.85
   Hair dryer               24.95   1   24.95
   Car vacuum               19.99   2   39.98

   AMOUNT DUE: $154.78
```

Also, in the interest of simplicity, we do not provide a user interface. We just supply a test program that adds line items to the invoice and then prints it.

## 12.3.2 CRC Cards

**Use CRC cards to find classes, responsibilities, and collaborators.**

When designing an object-oriented program, you need to discover classes. Classes correspond to nouns in the requirements specification. In this problem, it is pretty obvious what the nouns are:

```
   Invoice        Address        LineItem
   Product        Description    Price
   Quantity       Total          Amount due
```

(Of course, Toaster doesn't count—it is the description of a LineItem object and therefore a data value, not the name of a class.)

Description and price are attributes of the Product class. What about the quantity? The quantity is not an attribute of a Product. Just as in the printed invoice, let's have a class LineItem that records the product and the quantity (such as "3 toasters").

The total and amount due are computed—not stored anywhere. Thus, they don't lead to classes.

After this process of elimination, we are left with four candidates for classes:

```
Invoice
Address
LineItem
Product
```

Each of them represents a useful concept, so let's make them all into classes.

The purpose of the program is to print an invoice. However, the Invoice class won't necessarily know whether to display the output in System.out, in a text area, or in a file. Therefore, let's relax the task slightly and make the invoice responsible for *formatting* the invoice. The result is a string (containing multiple lines) that can be printed out or displayed. Record that responsibility on a CRC card:

| Invoice |
| --- |
| *format the invoice* |
| |
| |
| |
| |
| |
| |

How does an invoice format itself? It must format the billing address, format all line items, and then add the amount due. How can the invoice format an address? It can't—that really is the responsibility of the Address class. This leads to a second CRC card:

| Address |
| --- |
| *format the address* |
| |
| |
| |
| |
| |
| |

Similarly, formatting of a line item is the responsibility of the LineItem class.

The `format` method of the `Invoice` class calls the `format` methods of the `Address` and `LineItem` classes. Whenever a method uses another class, you list that other class as a collaborator. In other words, `Address` and `LineItem` are collaborators of `Invoice`:

| Invoice | |
|---|---|
| *format the invoice* | Address |
| | LineItem |
| | |
| | |
| | |
| | |
| | |

When formatting the invoice, the invoice also needs to compute the total amount due. To obtain that amount, it must ask each line item about the total price of the item.

How does a line item obtain that total? It must ask the product for the unit price, and then multiply it by the quantity. That is, the `Product` class must reveal the unit price, and it is a collaborator of the `LineItem` class.

| Product | |
|---|---|
| *get description* | |
| *get unit price* | |
| | |
| | |
| | |
| | |
| | |
| | |

| LineItem | |
|---|---|
| *format the item* | Product |
| *get total price* | |
| | |
| | |
| | |
| | |
| | |

Finally, the invoice must be populated with products and quantities, so that it makes sense to format the result. That too is a responsibility of the `Invoice` class.

| Invoice | |
|---|---|
| *format the invoice* | Address |
| *add a product and quantity* | LineItem |
| | Product |
| | |
| | |
| | |
| | |

We now have a set of CRC cards that completes the CRC card process.

## 12.3.3 UML Diagrams

**Use UML diagrams to record class relationships.**

After you have discovered classes and their relationships with CRC cards, you should record your findings in a UML diagram. The dependency relationships come from the collaboration column on the CRC cards. Each class depends on the classes with which it collaborates. In our example, the Invoice class collaborates with the Address, LineItem, and Product classes. The LineItem class collaborates with the Product class.

Now ask yourself which of these dependencies are actually aggregations. How does an invoice know about the address, line item, and product objects with which it collaborates? An invoice object must hold references to the address and the line items when it formats the invoice. But an invoice object need not hold a reference to a product object when adding a product. The product is turned into a line item, and then it is the item's responsibility to hold a reference to it.

Therefore, the Invoice class aggregates the Address and LineItem classes. The LineItem class aggregates the Product class. However, there is no *has-a* relationship between an invoice and a product. An invoice doesn't store products directly—they are stored in the LineItem objects.

There is no inheritance in this example.

Figure 9 shows the class relationships that we discovered.

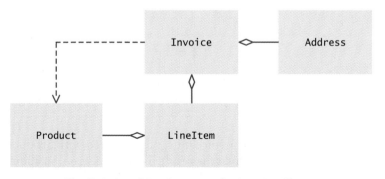

**Figure 9** The Relationships Between the Invoice Classes

## 12.3.4 Method Documentation

Use javadoc comments (with the method bodies left blank) to record the behavior of classes.

The final step of the design phase is to write the documentation of the discovered classes and methods. Simply write a Java source file for each class, write the method comments for those methods that you have discovered, and leave the bodies of the methods blank.

```java
/**
    Describes an invoice for a set of purchased products.
*/
public class Invoice
{
    /**
        Adds a charge for a product to this invoice.
        @param aProduct the product that the customer ordered
        @param quantity the quantity of the product
    */
    public void add(Product aProduct, int quantity)
    {
    }

    /**
        Formats the invoice.
        @return the formatted invoice
    */
    public String format()
    {
    }
}


/**
    Describes a quantity of an article to purchase.
*/
public class LineItem
{
    /**
        Computes the total cost of this line item.
        @return the total price
    */
    public double getTotalPrice()
    {
    }

    /**
        Formats this item.
        @return a formatted string of this item
    */
    public String format()
    {
    }
}


/**
    Describes a product with a description and a price.
*/
public class Product
{
```

```
    /**
        Gets the product description.
        @return the description
    */
    public String getDescription()
    {
    }

    /**
        Gets the product price.
        @return the unit price
    */
    public double getPrice()
    {
    }
}


/**
    Describes a mailing address.
*/
public class Address
{
    /**
        Formats the address.
        @return the address as a string with three lines
    */
    public String format()
    {
    }
}
```

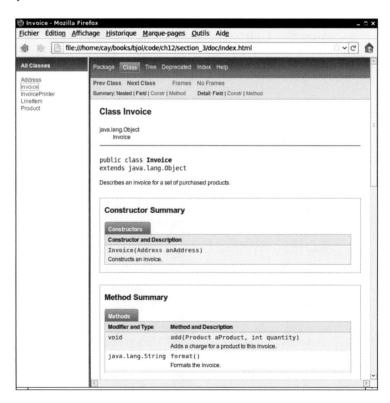

**Figure 10**
Class Documentation
in HTML Format

Then run the `javadoc` program to obtain a neatly formatted version of your documentation in HTML format (see Figure 10).

This approach for documenting your classes has a number of advantages. You can share the HTML documentation with others if you work in a team. You use a format that is immediately useful—Java source files that you can carry into the implementation phase. And, most importantly, you supply the comments for the key methods—a task that less prepared programmers leave for later, and often neglect for lack of time.

## 12.3.5 Implementation

**After completing the design, implement your classes.**

After you have completed the object-oriented design, you are ready to implement the classes.

You already have the method parameter variables and comments from the previous step. Now look at the UML diagram to add instance variables. Aggregated classes yield instance variables. Start with the `Invoice` class. An invoice aggregates `Address` and `LineItem`. Every invoice has one billing address, but it can have many line items. To store multiple `LineItem` objects, you can use an array list. Now you have the instance variables of the `Invoice` class:

```java
public class Invoice
{
    private Address billingAddress;
    private ArrayList<LineItem> items;
    . . .
}
```

A line item needs to store a `Product` object and the product quantity. That leads to the following instance variables:

```java
public class LineItem
{
    private int quantity;
    private Product theProduct;
    . . .
}
```

The methods themselves are now easy to implement. Here is a typical example. You already know what the `getTotalPrice` method of the `LineItem` class needs to do—get the unit price of the product and multiply it with the quantity.

```java
/**
    Computes the total cost of this line item.
    @return the total price
*/
public double getTotalPrice()
{
    return theProduct.getPrice() * quantity;
}
```

We will not discuss the other methods in detail—they are equally straightforward.

Finally, you need to supply constructors, another routine task.

The entire program is shown below. It is a good practice to go through it in detail and match up the classes and methods against the CRC cards and UML diagram.

In this chapter, you learned a systematic approach for building a relatively complex program. However, object-oriented design is definitely not a spectator sport. To really learn how to design and implement programs, you have to gain experience by repeating this process with your own projects. It is quite possible that you don't immediately home in on a good solution and that you need to go back and reorganize your classes and responsibilities. That is normal and only to be expected. The purpose of the object-oriented design process is to spot these problems in the design phase, when they are still easy to rectify, instead of in the implementation phase, when massive reorganization is more difficult and time consuming.

### section_3/InvoicePrinter.java

```java
 1  /**
 2      This program demonstrates the invoice classes by
 3      printing a sample invoice.
 4  */
 5  public class InvoicePrinter
 6  {
 7     public static void main(String[] args)
 8     {
 9        Address samsAddress
10           = new Address("Sam's Small Appliances",
11           "100 Main Street", "Anytown", "CA", "98765");
12
13        Invoice samsInvoice = new Invoice(samsAddress);
14        samsInvoice.add(new Product("Toaster", 29.95), 3);
15        samsInvoice.add(new Product("Hair dryer", 24.95), 1);
16        samsInvoice.add(new Product("Car vacuum", 19.99), 2);
17
18        System.out.println(samsInvoice.format());
19     }
20  }
```

### section_3/Invoice.java

```java
 1  import java.util.ArrayList;
 2
 3  /**
 4      Describes an invoice for a set of purchased products.
 5  */
 6  public class Invoice
 7  {
 8     private Address billingAddress;
 9     private ArrayList<LineItem> items;
10
11     /**
12         Constructs an invoice.
13         @param anAddress the billing address
14     */
15     public Invoice(Address anAddress)
16     {
17        items = new ArrayList<LineItem>();
18        billingAddress = anAddress;
19     }
20
21     /**
22         Adds a charge for a product to this invoice.
23         @param aProduct the product that the customer ordered
24         @param quantity the quantity of the product
25     */
26     public void add(Product aProduct, int quantity)
27     {
28        LineItem anItem = new LineItem(aProduct, quantity);
```

```
29          items.add(anItem);
30      }
31
32      /**
33          Formats the invoice.
34          @return the formatted invoice
35      */
36      public String format()
37      {
38          String r = "                          I N V O I C E\n\n"
39              + billingAddress.format()
40              + String.format("\n\n%-30s%8s%5s%8s\n",
41              "Description", "Price", "Qty", "Total");
42
43          for (LineItem item : items)
44          {
45              r = r + item.format() + "\n";
46          }
47
48          r = r + String.format("\nAMOUNT DUE: $%8.2f", getAmountDue());
49
50          return r;
51      }
52
53      /**
54          Computes the total amount due.
55          @return the amount due
56      */
57      private double getAmountDue()
58      {
59          double amountDue = 0;
60          for (LineItem item : items)
61          {
62              amountDue = amountDue + item.getTotalPrice();
63          }
64          return amountDue;
65      }
66 }
```

## section_3/LineItem.java

```
1  /**
2      Describes a quantity of an article to purchase.
3  */
4  public class LineItem
5  {
6      private int quantity;
7      private Product theProduct;
8
9      /**
10          Constructs an item from the product and quantity.
11          @param aProduct the product
12          @param aQuantity the item quantity
13      */
14      public LineItem(Product aProduct, int aQuantity)
15      {
16          theProduct = aProduct;
17          quantity = aQuantity;
18      }
19
```

```
20      /**
21          Computes the total cost of this line item.
22          @return the total price
23      */
24      public double getTotalPrice()
25      {
26          return theProduct.getPrice() * quantity;
27      }
28
29      /**
30          Formats this item.
31          @return a formatted string of this line item
32      */
33      public String format()
34      {
35          return String.format("%-30s%8.2f%5d%8.2f",
36              theProduct.getDescription(), theProduct.getPrice(),
37              quantity, getTotalPrice());
38      }
39  }
```

**section_3/Product.java**

```
1   /**
2       Describes a product with a description and a price.
3   */
4   public class Product
5   {
6       private String description;
7       private double price;
8
9       /**
10          Constructs a product from a description and a price.
11          @param aDescription the product description
12          @param aPrice the product price
13      */
14      public Product(String aDescription, double aPrice)
15      {
16          description = aDescription;
17          price = aPrice;
18      }
19
20      /**
21          Gets the product description.
22          @return the description
23      */
24      public String getDescription()
25      {
26          return description;
27      }
28
29      /**
30          Gets the product price.
31          @return the unit price
32      */
33      public double getPrice()
34      {
35          return price;
36      }
37  }
```

**section_3/Address.java**

```java
1   /**
2       Describes a mailing address.
3   */
4   public class Address
5   {
6       private String name;
7       private String street;
8       private String city;
9       private String state;
10      private String zip;
11
12      /**
13          Constructs a mailing address.
14          @param aName the recipient name
15          @param aStreet the street
16          @param aCity the city
17          @param aState the two-letter state code
18          @param aZip the ZIP postal code
19      */
20      public Address(String aName, String aStreet,
21              String aCity, String aState, String aZip)
22      {
23          name = aName;
24          street = aStreet;
25          city = aCity;
26          state = aState;
27          zip = aZip;
28      }
29
30      /**
31          Formats the address.
32          @return the address as a string with three lines
33      */
34      public String format()
35      {
36          return name + "\n" + street + "\n"
37              + city + ", " + state + " " + zip;
38      }
39  }
```

**SELF CHECK**

13. Which class is responsible for computing the amount due? What are its collaborators for this task?

14. Why do the format methods return String objects instead of directly printing to System.out?

**Practice It** Now you can try these exercises at the end of the chapter: R12.18, P12.6, P12.7.

---

**WORKED EXAMPLE 12.1** **Simulating an Automatic Teller Machine**

This Worked Example applies the object-oriented design methodology to the simulation of an automatic teller machine that works with both a console-based and graphical user interface.

➕ Available online in WileyPLUS and at www.wiley.com/college/horstmann.

# 12.4 Packages

A Java program consists of a collection of classes. So far, most of your programs have consisted of a small number of classes. As programs get larger, however, simply distributing the classes over multiple files isn't enough. An additional structuring mechanism is needed.

In Java, packages provide this structuring mechanism. A Java **package** is a set of related classes. For example, the Java library consists of dozens of packages, some of which are listed in Table 2. The following sections show how you can make use of packages in your programs.

A package is a set of related classes.

| Table 2 Important Packages in the Java Library | | |
| --- | --- | --- |
| Package | Purpose | Sample Class |
| java.lang | Language support | Math |
| java.util | Utilities | Scanner |
| java.io | Input and output | PrintStream |
| java.awt | Abstract Windowing Toolkit | Color |
| java.net | Networking | Socket |
| java.sql | Database access through Structured Query Language | ResultSet |
| javax.swing | Swing user interface | JButton |
| org.w3c.dom | Document Object Model for XML documents | Document |

## 12.4.1 Organizing Related Classes into Packages

To put a class in a package, you must place

```
package packageName;
```

as the first statement in its source file. A package name consists of one or more identifiers separated by periods. (See Section 12.4.3 for tips on constructing package names.)

For example, let's put a BankAccount class into a package named com.horstmann. The BankAccount.java file must start as follows:

```
package com.horstmann;

public class BankAccount
{
    . . .
}
```

In addition to the named packages (such as java.util or com.horstmann), there is a special package, called the *default package*, which has no name. If you did not include any package statement at the top of your source file, the class is placed in the default package.

*In Java, related classes are grouped into packages.*

## 12.4.2 Importing Packages

If you want to use a class from a package, you can refer to it by its full name (package name plus class name). For example, java.util.Scanner refers to the Scanner class in the java.util package:

```
java.util.Scanner in = new java.util.Scanner(System.in);
```

Naturally, that is somewhat inconvenient. You can instead *import* a name with an import statement:

```
import java.util.Scanner;
```

The import directive lets you refer to a class from a package by its class name, without the package prefix.

Then you can refer to the class as Scanner without the package prefix.

You can import *all classes* of a package with an import statement that ends in .*. For example, you can use the statement

```
import java.util.*;
```

to import all classes from the java.util package. That statement lets you refer to classes like Scanner or ArrayList without a java.util prefix.

However, you never need to import the classes in the java.lang package explicitly. That is the package containing the most basic Java classes, such as Math and Object. These classes are always available to you. In effect, an automatic import java.lang.*; statement has been placed into every source file.

Finally, you don't need to import other classes in the same package. For example, in the source code of the class problem1.Tester, you don't need to import the class problem1.BankAccount. The compiler will find the BankAccount class without an import statement because it is located in the same package, problem1.

## 12.4.3 Package Names

Placing related classes into a package is clearly a convenient way to organize classes. However, there is a more important reason for packages: to avoid **name clashes**. In a large project, it is inevitable that two people will come up with the same name for the same concept. This even happens in the standard Java class library (which has now grown to thousands of classes). There is a class Timer in the java.util package and another class called Timer in the javax.swing package. You can still tell the Java compiler exactly which Timer class you need by referring to them as java.util.Timer and javax.swing.Timer.

Of course, for the package-naming convention to work, there must be some way to ensure that package names are unique. It wouldn't be good if the car maker BMW placed all its Java code into the package `bmw`, and some other programmer (perhaps Britney M. Walters) had the same bright idea. To avoid this problem, the inventors of Java recommend that you use a package-naming scheme that takes advantage of the uniqueness of Internet domain names.

For example, I have a domain name `horstmann.com`, and there is nobody else on the planet with the same domain name. (I was lucky that the domain name `horstmann.com` had not been taken by anyone else when I applied. If your name is Walters, you will sadly find that someone else beat you to `walters.com`.) To get a package name, turn the domain name around to produce a package name prefix, such as `com.horstmann`.

> Use a domain name in reverse to construct an unambiguous package name.

If you don't have your own domain name, you can still create a package name that has a high probability of being unique by writing your e-mail address backwards. For example, if Britney Walters has an e-mail address `walters@cs.sjsu.edu`, then she can use a package name `edu.sjsu.cs.walters` for her own classes.

Some instructors will want you to place each of your assignments into a separate package, such as `problem1`, `problem2`, and so on. The reason is again to avoid name collision. You can have two classes, `problem1.BankAccount` and `problem2.BankAccount`, with slightly different properties.

## 12.4.4 How Classes Are Located

> The path of a class file must match its package name.

A package is located in a subdirectory that matches the package name. For example, a package `homework1` is located in a directory `homework1`. If the package name has multiple parts, such as `com.horstmann.javabook`, then you use a subdirectory for each part: `com/horstmann/javabook`.

For example, if you do your homework assignment in a *base directory* `/home/britney/assignments`, then you can place the class files for the `problem1` package into the directory `/home/britney/assignments/problem1`, as shown in Figure 11. (Here, we are using UNIX-style file names. Under Windows, you would use a directory such as `c:\Users\Britney\assignments\problem1`.)

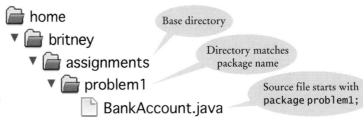

**Figure 11**
Base Directories
and Subdirectories
for Packages

**SELF CHECK**

**15.** Which of the following are packages?

   **a.** `java`

   **b.** `java.lang`

   **c.** `java.util`

   **d.** `java.lang.Math`

**16.** Is a Java program without `import` statements limited to using the default and `java.lang` packages?

17. Suppose your homework assignments are located in the directory `/home/me/cs101` (`c:\Users\me\cs101` on Windows). Your instructor tells you to place your homework into packages. In which directory do you place the class `hw1.problem1.TicTacToeTester`?

**Practice It**    Now you can try these exercises at the end of the chapter: R12.19, P12.15, P12.16.

## CHAPTER SUMMARY

### Recognize how to discover classes and their responsibilities.

- To discover classes, look for nouns in the problem description.
- Concepts from the problem domain are good candidates for classes.
- A CRC card describes a class, its responsibilities, and its collaborating classes.
- The public interface of a class is cohesive if all of its features are related to the concept that the class represents.

### Categorize class relationships and produce UML diagrams that describe them.

- A class depends on another class if it uses objects of that class.
- It is a good practice to minimize the coupling (i.e., dependency) between classes.
- A class aggregates another if its objects contain objects of the other class.
- Inheritance (the *is-a* relationship) is sometimes inappropriately used when the *has-a* relationship would be more appropriate.
- Aggregation (the *has-a* relationship) denotes that objects of one class contain references to objects of another class.
- You need to be able to distinguish the UML notation for inheritance, interface implementation, aggregation, and dependency.
- Avoid parallel arrays by changing them into arrays of objects.

### Apply an object-oriented development process to designing a program.

- Start the development process by gathering and documenting program requirements.
- Use CRC cards to find classes, responsibilities, and collaborators.
- Use UML diagrams to record class relationships.
- Use `javadoc` comments (with the method bodies left blank) to record the behavior of classes.
- After completing the design, implement your classes.

### Use packages to structure the classes in your program.

- A package is a set of related classes.
- The `import` directive lets you refer to a class from a package by its class name, without the package prefix.
- Use a domain name in reverse to construct an unambiguous package name.
- The path of a class file must match its package name.

## REVIEW EXERCISES

■■ **R12.1** List the steps in the process of object-oriented design that this chapter recommends for student use.

■ **R12.2** Give a rule of thumb for how to find classes when designing a program.

■ **R12.3** Give a rule of thumb for how to find methods when designing a program.

■■ **R12.4** After discovering a method, why is it important to identify the object that is *responsible* for carrying out the action?

■■ **R12.5** Look at the public interface of the java.lang.System class and discuss whether or not it is cohesive.

■■ **R12.6** On which classes does the class Integer in the Java standard library depend?

■■ **R12.7** On which classes does the class java.awt.Rectangle in the standard library depend?

■ **R12.8** What relationship is appropriate between the following classes: aggregation, inheritance, or neither?

    **a.** University–Student
    **b.** Student–TeachingAssistant
    **c.** Student–Freshman
    **d.** Student–Professor
    **e.** Car–Door
    **f.** Truck–Vehicle
    **g.** Traffic–TrafficSign
    **h.** TrafficSign–Color

■■ **R12.9** Every BMW is a vehicle. Should a class BMW inherit from the class Vehicle? BMW is a vehicle manufacturer. Does that mean that the class BMW should inherit from the class VehicleManufacturer?

■■ **R12.10** Some books on object-oriented programming recommend using inheritance so that the class Circle extends the class java.awt.Point. Then the Circle class inherits the setLocation method from the Point superclass. Explain why the setLocation method need not be overridden in the subclass. Why is it nevertheless not a good idea to have Circle inherit from Point? Conversely, would inheriting Point from Circle fulfill the *is-a* rule? Would it be a good idea?

■ **R12.11** Write CRC cards for the Coin and CashRegister classes described in Section 12.1.3.

■ **R12.12** Write CRC cards for the Quiz and Question classes in Section 12.2.2.

■■ **R12.13** Draw a UML diagram for the Quiz, Question, and ChoiceQuestion classes. The Quiz class is described in Section 12.2.2.

■■■ **R12.14** A file contains a set of records describing countries. Each record consists of the name of the country, its population, and its area. Suppose your task is to write a program that reads in such a file and prints

    • The country with the largest area
    • The country with the largest population
    • The country with the largest population density (people per square kilometer)

Think through the problems that you need to solve. What classes and methods will you need? Produce a set of CRC cards, a UML diagram, and a set of javadoc comments.

■■■ **R12.15** Discover classes and methods for generating a student report card that lists all classes, grades, and the grade point average for a semester. Produce a set of CRC cards, a UML diagram, and a set of javadoc comments.

■■ **R12.16** Consider the following problem description:

> Users place coins in a vending machine and select a product by pushing a button. If the inserted coins are sufficient to cover the purchase price of the product, the product is dispensed and change is given. Otherwise, the inserted coins are returned to the user.

What classes should you use to implement a solution?

■■ **R12.17** Consider the following problem description:

> Employees receive their biweekly paychecks. They are paid their hourly rates for each hour worked; however, if they worked more than 40 hours per week, they are paid overtime at 150 percent of their regular wage.

What classes should you use to implement a solution?

■■ **R12.18** Consider the following problem description:

> Customers order products from a store. Invoices are generated to list the items and quantities ordered, payments received, and amounts still due. Products are shipped to the shipping address of the customer, and invoices are sent to the billing address.

Draw a UML diagram showing the aggregation relationships between the classes `Invoice`, `Address`, `Customer`, and `Product`.

■■ **R12.19** Every Java program can be rewritten to avoid `import` statements. Explain how, and rewrite `BabyNames.java` from Worked Example 7.1 to avoid `import` statements.

■ **R12.20** What is the default package? Have you used it before this chapter in your programming?

## PROGRAMMING EXERCISES

■■ **P12.1** Modify the `giveChange` method of the `CashRegister` class in the sample code for Section 12.1 so that it returns the number of coins of a particular type to return:

```
int giveChange(Coin coinType)
```

The caller needs to invoke this method for each coin type, in decreasing value.

■ **P12.2** Real cash registers can handle both bills and coins. Design a single class that expresses the commonality of these concepts. Redesign the `CashRegister` class and provide a method for entering payments that are described by your class. Your primary challenge is to come up with a good name for this class.

■ **P12.3** Enhance the invoice-printing program by providing for two kinds of line items: One kind describes products that are purchased in certain numerical quantities (such as "3 toasters"), another describes a fixed charge (such as "shipping: $5.00"). *Hint:* Use inheritance. Produce a UML diagram of your modified implementation.

•• **P12.4** The invoice-printing program is somewhat unrealistic because the formatting of the LineItem objects won't lead to good visual results when the prices and quantities have varying numbers of digits. Enhance the format method in two ways: Accept an int[] array of column widths as an argument. Use the NumberFormat class to format the currency values.

•• **P12.5** The invoice-printing program has an unfortunate flaw—it mixes "application logic" (the computation of total charges) and "presentation" (the visual appearance of the invoice). To appreciate this flaw, imagine the changes that would be necessary to draw the invoice in HTML for presentation on the Web. Reimplement the program, using a separate InvoiceFormatter class to format the invoice. That is, the Invoice and LineItem methods are no longer responsible for formatting. However, they will acquire other responsibilities, because the InvoiceFormatter class needs to query them for the values that it requires.

••• **P12.6** Write a program that teaches arithmetic to a young child. The program tests addition and subtraction. In level 1, it tests only addition of numbers less than 10 whose sum is less than 10. In level 2, it tests addition of arbitrary one-digit numbers. In level 3, it tests subtraction of one-digit numbers with a nonnegative difference.

Generate random problems and get the player's input. The player gets up to two tries per problem. Advance from one level to the next when the player has achieved a score of five points.

••• **P12.7** Implement a simple e-mail messaging system. A message has a recipient, a sender, and a message text. A mailbox can store messages. Supply a number of mailboxes for different users and a user interface for users to log in, send messages to other users, read their own messages, and log out. Follow the design process that was described in this chapter.

•• **P12.8** Write a program that simulates a vending machine. Products can be purchased by inserting coins with a value at least equal to the cost of the product. A user selects a product from a list of available products, adds coins, and either gets the product or gets the coins returned. The coins are returned if insufficient money was supplied or if the product is sold out. The machine does not give change if too much money was added. Products can be restocked and money removed by an operator. Follow the design process that was described in this chapter. Your solution should include a class VendingMachine that is not coupled with the Scanner or PrintStream classes.

••• **P12.9** Write a program to design an appointment calendar. An appointment includes the date, starting time, ending time, and a description; for example,

```
Dentist 2012/10/1 17:30 18:30
CS1 class 2012/10/2 08:30 10:00
```

Supply a user interface to add appointments, remove canceled appointments, and print out a list of appointments for a particular day. Follow the design process that was described in this chapter. Your solution should include a class Appointment-Calendar that is not coupled with the Scanner or PrintStream classes.

•• **P12.10** Modify the implementation of the classes in the ATM simulation in Worked Example 12.1 so that the bank manages a collection of bank accounts and a separate collection of customers. Allow joint accounts in which some accounts can have more than one customer.

••• **P12.11**  Write a program that administers and grades quizzes. A quiz consists of questions. There are four types of questions: text questions, number questions, choice questions with a single answer, and choice questions with multiple answers. When grading a text question, ignore leading or trailing spaces and letter case. When grading a numeric question, accept a response that is approximately the same as the answer.

A quiz is specified in a text file. Each question starts with a letter indicating the question type (T, N, S, M), followed by a line containing the question text. The next line of a non-choice question contains the answer. Choice questions have a list of choices that is terminated by a blank line. Each choice starts with + (correct) or - (incorrect). Here is a sample file:

```
T
Which Java reserved word is used to declare a subclass?
extends
S
What is the original name of the Java language?
- *7
- C--
+ Oak
- Gosling

M
Which of the following types are supertypes of Rectangle?
- PrintStream
+ Shape
+ RectangularShape
+ Object
- String

N
What is the square root of 2?
1.41421356
```

Your program should read in a quiz file, prompt the user for responses to all questions, and grade the responses. Follow the design process that was described in this chapter.

•• **P12.12**  Produce a requirements document for a program that allows a company to send out personalized mailings, either by e-mail or through the postal service. Template files contain the message text, together with variable fields (such as Dear [Title] [Last Name] . . .). A database (stored as a text file) contains the field values for each recipient. Use HTML as the output file format. Then design and implement the program.

••• **P12.13**  Write a tic-tac-toe game that allows a human player to play against the computer. Your program will play many turns against a human opponent, and it will learn. When it is the computer's turn, the computer randomly selects an empty field, except that it won't ever choose a losing combination. For that purpose, your program must keep an array of losing combinations. Whenever the human wins, the immediately preceding combination is stored as losing. For example, suppose that X = computer and O = human. Suppose the current combination is

Now it is the human's turn, who will of course choose

```
O | X | X
--+---+--
  | O |
--+---+--
  |   | O
```

The computer should then remember the preceding combination

```
O | X | X
--+---+--
  | O |
--+---+--
  |   |
```

as a losing combination. As a result, the computer will never again choose that combination from

```
O | X |
--+---+--
  | O |
--+---+--
  |   |
```

or

```
O |   | X
--+---+--
  | O |
--+---+--
  |   |
```

Discover classes and supply a UML diagram before you begin to program.

- **P12.14** Place the CashRegister and Coin classes of the sample program in Section 12.1 into the package com.horstmann. Keep the CashRegisterTester class in the default package.

- **P12.15** Place all classes of the sample program in Section 12.3 into the package com.horstmann. How do you start the program in your programming environment?

- **P12.16** Place the classes from Worked Example 12.1 in a package whose name is derived from your e-mail address, as described in Section 12.4.3.

- ■■■ Business **P12.17** Implement a program that prints paychecks for a group of student assistants. Deduct federal income and Social Security taxes. (You may want to use the tax computation used in Chapter 3. Find out about Social Security taxes on the Internet.) Your program should prompt for the name, hourly wage, and hours worked for each student.

- ■■■ Business **P12.18** *Airline seating.* Write a program that assigns seats on an airplane. Assume the airplane has 20 seats in first class (5 rows of 4 seats each, separated by an aisle) and 90 seats in economy class (15 rows of 6 seats each, separated by an aisle). Your program should take three commands: add passengers, show seating, and quit. When passengers are added, ask for the class (first or economy), the number of passengers traveling together (1 or 2 in first class; 1 to 3 in economy), and the seating preference (aisle or window in first class; aisle, center, or window in economy). Then try to find a match and assign the seats. If no match exists, print a message. Your solution should include a class Airplane that is not coupled with the Scanner or PrintStream classes. Follow the design process that was described in this chapter.

■■■ **Business P12.19** In an airplane, each passenger has a touch screen for ordering a drink and a snack. Some items are free and some are not. The system prepares two reports for speeding up service:

  **1.** A list of all seats, ordered by row, showing the charges that must be collected.

  **2.** A list of how many drinks and snacks of each type must be prepared for the front and the rear of the plane.

Follow the design process that was described in this chapter to identify classes, and implement a program that simulates the system.

■■■ **Graphics P12.20** Implement a program to teach a young child to read the clock. In the game, present an analog clock, such as the one shown at left. Generate random times and display the clock. Accept guesses from the player. Reward the player for correct guesses. After two incorrect guesses, display the correct answer and make a new random time. Implement several levels of play. In level 1, only show full hours. In level 2, show quarter hours. In level 3, show five-minute multiples, and in level 4, show any number of minutes. After a player has achieved five correct guesses at one level, advance to the next level.

*An Analog Clock*

■■■ **Graphics P12.21** Write a program that can be used to design a suburban scene, with houses, streets, and cars. Users can add houses and cars of various colors to a street. Write more specific requirements that include a detailed description of the user interface. Then, discover classes and methods, provide UML diagrams, and implement your program.

■■■ **Graphics P12.22** Write a simple graphics editor that allows users to add a mixture of shapes (ellipses, rectangles, and lines in different colors) to a panel. Supply commands to load and save the picture. Discover classes, supply a UML diagram, and implement your program.

## ANSWERS TO SELF-CHECK QUESTIONS

**1.** Look for nouns in the problem description.

**2.** Yes (ChessBoard) and no (MovePiece).

**3.** PrintStream

**4.** To produce the shipping address of the customer.

**5.** Reword the responsibilities so that they are at a higher level, or come up with more classes to handle the responsibilities.

**6.** The CashRegisterTester class depends on the CashRegister and System classes.

**7.** The ChoiceQuestion class inherits from the Question class.

**8.** The Quiz class depends on the Question class but probably not ChoiceQuestion, if we assume that the methods of the Quiz class manipulate generic Question objects, as they did in Chapter 9.

**9.** If a class doesn't depend on another, it is not affected by interface changes in the other class.

**10.**

**11.** Typically, a library system wants to track which books a patron has checked out, so it makes more sense to have Patron aggregate Book. However, there is not always one true answer in design. If you feel strongly that it is important to identify the patron who checked out a particular book (perhaps to notify the patron to return it because it was requested by someone else), then you can argue that the aggregation should go the other way around.

**12.** There would be no relationship.

**13.** The `Invoice` class is responsible for computing the amount due. It collaborates with the `LineItem` class.

**14.** This design decision reduces coupling. It enables us to reuse the classes when we want to show the invoice in a dialog box or on a web page.

**15.** (a) No; (b) Yes; (c) Yes; (d) No

**16.** No—you simply use fully qualified names for all other classes, such as `java.util.Random` and `java.awt.Rectangle`.

**17.** `/home/me/cs101/hw1/problem1` or, on Windows, `c:\Users\me\cs101\hw1\problem1`.

CHAPTER **13**

# RECURSION

## CHAPTER GOALS

To learn to "think recursively"

To be able to use recursive
  helper methods

To understand the relationship between recursion and iteration

To understand when the use of recursion affects the efficiency of an algorithm

To analyze problems that are much easier to solve by recursion than by iteration

To process data with recursive structures using mutual recursion

## CHAPTER CONTENTS

The method of recursion is a powerful technique for breaking up complex computational problems into simpler, often smaller, ones. The term "recursion" refers to the fact that the same computation recurs, or occurs repeatedly, as the problem is solved. Recursion is often the most natural way of thinking about a problem, and there are some computations that are very difficult to perform without recursion. This chapter shows you both simple and complex examples of recursion and teaches you how to "think recursively".

# 13.1 Triangle Numbers Revisited

Chapter 5 contains a simple introduction to writing recursive methods—methods that call themselves with simpler inputs. In that chapter, you saw how to print triangle patterns such as this one:

```
[]
[][]
[][][]
[][][][]
```

The key observation is that you can print a triangle pattern of a given side length, provided you know how to print the smaller triangle pattern that is shown in blue.

*Using the same method as the one described in this section, you can compute the volume of a Mayan pyramid.*

In this section, we will modify the example slightly and use recursion to compute the area of a triangle shape of side length *n*, assuming that each [] square has area 1. This value is sometimes called the *n*th *triangle number*. For example, as you can tell from looking at the above triangle, the third triangle number is 6 and the fourth triangle number is 10.

We will develop an object-oriented solution that gives another perspective on recursive problem solving. Instead of calling a method with simpler values, we will construct a simpler object.

Here is the outline of the class that we will develop:

```java
public class Triangle
{
    private int width;

    public Triangle(int aWidth)
    {
        width = aWidth;
    }

    public int getArea()
    {
        . . .
    }
}
```

If the width of the triangle is 1, then the triangle consists of a single square, and its area is 1. Let's take care of this case first:

```java
public int getArea()
{
   if (width == 1) { return 1; }
   . . .
}
```

To deal with the general case, consider this picture:

```
[]
[][]
[][][]
[][][][]
```

Suppose we knew the area of the smaller, colored triangle. Then we could easily compute the area of the larger triangle as

```java
smallerArea + width
```

How can we get the smaller area? Let's make a smaller triangle and ask it!

```java
Triangle smallerTriangle = new Triangle(width - 1);
int smallerArea = smallerTriangle.getArea();
```

Now we can complete the getArea method:

```java
public int getArea()
{
   if (width == 1) { return 1; }
   else
   {
      Triangle smallerTriangle = new Triangle(width - 1);
      int smallerArea = smallerTriangle.getArea();
      return smallerArea + width;
   }
}
```

Here is an illustration of what happens when we compute the area of a triangle of width 4.

> A recursive computation solves a problem by using the solution to the same problem with simpler inputs.

- The getArea method makes a smaller triangle of width 3.
- It calls getArea on that triangle.
  - That method makes a smaller triangle of width 2.
  - It calls getArea on that triangle.
    - That method makes a smaller triangle of width 1.
    - It calls getArea on that triangle.
      - That method returns 1.
    - The method returns smallerArea + width = 1 + 2 = 3.
  - The method returns smallerArea + width = 3 + 3 = 6.
- The method returns smallerArea + width = 6 + 4 = 10.

This solution has one remarkable aspect. To solve the area problem for a triangle of a given width, we use the fact that we can solve the same problem for a lesser width. This is called a *recursive* solution.

The call pattern of a **recursive method** looks complicated, and the key to the successful design of a recursive method is *not to think about it*. Instead, look at the getArea method one more time and notice how utterly reasonable it is. If the width is 1, then, of course, the area is 1. The next part is just as reasonable. Compute the area of the smaller triangle *and don't think about why that works*. Then the area of the larger triangle is clearly the sum of the smaller area and the width.

There are two key requirements to make sure that the recursion is successful:

- Every recursive call must simplify the computation in some way.
- There must be special cases to handle the simplest computations directly.

> For a recursion to terminate, there must be special cases for the simplest values.

The getArea method calls itself again with smaller and smaller width values. Eventually the width must reach 1, and there is a special case for computing the area of a triangle with width 1. Thus, the getArea method always succeeds.

Actually, you have to be careful. What happens when you call the area of a triangle with width –1? It computes the area of a triangle with width –2, which computes the area of a triangle with width –3, and so on. To avoid this, the getArea method should return 0 if the width is ≤ 0.

Recursion is not really necessary to compute the triangle numbers. The area of a triangle equals the sum

```
1 + 2 + 3 + . . . + width
```

Of course, we can program a simple loop:

```
double area = 0;
for (int i = 1; i <= width; i++)
{
    area = area + i;
}
```

Many simple recursions can be computed as loops. However, loop equivalents for more complex recursions—such as the one in our next example—can be complex.

Actually, in this case, you don't even need a loop to compute the answer. The sum of the first *n* integers can be computed as

$$1 + 2 + \cdots + n = n \times (n + 1)/2$$

**ANIMATION**
*Tracing a Recursion*

Thus, the area equals

```
width * (width + 1) / 2
```

Therefore, neither recursion nor a loop is required to solve this problem. The recursive solution is intended as a "warm-up" to introduce you to the concept of recursion.

**section_1/Triangle.java**

```
1   /**
2       A triangular shape composed of stacked unit squares like this:
3       []
4       [][]
5       [][][]
6       . . .
7   */
8   public class Triangle
9   {
10      private int width;
11
12      /**
13          Constructs a triangular shape.
14          @param aWidth the width (and height) of the triangle
15      */
```

```
16      public Triangle(int aWidth)
17      {
18         width = aWidth;
19      }
20
21      /**
22         Computes the area of the triangle.
23         @return the area
24      */
25      public int getArea()
26      {
27         if (width <= 0) { return 0; }
28         else if (width == 1) { return 1; }
29         else
30         {
31            Triangle smallerTriangle = new Triangle(width - 1);
32            int smallerArea = smallerTriangle.getArea();
33            return smallerArea + width;
34         }
35      }
36   }
```

### section_1/TriangleTester.java

```
1   public class TriangleTester
2   {
3      public static void main(String[] args)
4      {
5         Triangle t = new Triangle(10);
6         int area = t.getArea();
7         System.out.println("Area: " + area);
8         System.out.println("Expected: 55");
9      }
10  }
```

### Program Run

```
Area: 55
Expected: 55
```

**SELF CHECK**

1. Why is the statement `else if (width == 1) { return 1; }` in the final version of the getArea method unnecessary?

2. How would you modify the program to recursively compute the area of a square?

3. In some cultures, numbers containing the digit 8 are lucky numbers. What is wrong with the following method that tries to test whether a number is lucky?

```
public static boolean isLucky(int number)
{
   int lastDigit = number % 10;
   if (lastDigit == 8) { return true; }
   else
   {
      return isLucky(number / 10); // Test the number without the last digit
   }
}
```

4. In order to compute a power of two, you can take the next-lower power and double it. For example, if you want to compute $2^{11}$ and you know that $2^{10} = 1024$, then $2^{11} = 2 \times 1024 = 2048$. Write a recursive method `public static int pow2(int n)` that is based on this observation.

5. Consider the following recursive method:

```java
public static int mystery(int n)
{
   if (n <= 0) { return 0; }
   else
   {
      int smaller = n - 1;
      return mystery(smaller) + n * n;
   }
}
```

What is `mystery(4)`?

**Practice It**    Now you can try these exercises at the end of the chapter: P13.1, P13.2, P13.10.

---

**Common Error 13.1**

### Infinite Recursion

A common programming error is an infinite recursion: a method calling itself over and over with no end in sight. The computer needs some amount of memory for bookkeeping for each call. After some number of calls, all memory that is available for this purpose is exhausted. Your program shuts down and reports a "stack overflow".

Infinite recursion happens either because the arguments don't get simpler or because a special terminating case is missing. For example, suppose the `getArea` method was allowed to compute the area of a triangle with width 0. If it weren't for the special test, the method would construct triangles with width –1, –2, –3, and so on.

---

# 13.2 Problem Solving: Thinking Recursively

How To 5.2 in Chapter 5 tells you how to solve a problem recursively by pretending that "someone else" will solve the problem for simpler inputs and by focusing on how to turn the simpler solutions into a solution for the whole problem.

In this section, we walk through these steps with a more complex problem: testing whether a sentence is a *palindrome*—a string that is equal to itself when you reverse all characters. Typical examples are

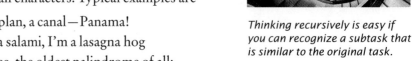

- A man, a plan, a canal—Panama!

- Go hang a salami, I'm a lasagna hog

and, of course, the oldest palindrome of all:

- Madam, I'm Adam

*Thinking recursively is easy if you can recognize a subtask that is similar to the original task.*

When testing for a palindrome, we match upper- and lowercase letters, and ignore all spaces and punctuation marks.

We want to implement the following `isPalindrome` method:

```
/**
    Tests whether a text is a palindrome.
    @param text a string that is being checked
    @return true if text is a palindrome, false otherwise
*/
public static boolean isPalindrome(String Text)
{
    . . .
}
```

**Step 1**   Consider various ways to simplify inputs.

In your mind, focus on a particular input or set of inputs for the problem that you want to solve. Think how you can simplify the inputs in such a way that the same problem can be applied to the simpler input.

When you consider simpler inputs, you may want to remove just a little bit from the original input—maybe remove one or two characters from a string, or remove a small portion of a geometric shape. But sometimes it is more useful to cut the input in half and then see what it means to solve the problem for both halves.

In the palindrome test problem, the input is the string that we need to test. How can you simplify the input? Here are several possibilities:

- Remove the first character.
- Remove the last character.
- Remove both the first and last characters.
- Remove a character from the middle.
- Cut the string into two halves.

These simpler inputs are all potential inputs for the palindrome test.

**Step 2**   Combine solutions with simpler inputs into a solution of the original problem.

In your mind, consider the solutions for the simpler inputs that you discovered in Step 1. Don't worry *how* those solutions are obtained. Simply have faith that the solutions are readily available. Just say to yourself: These are simpler inputs, so someone else will solve the problem for me.

Now think how you can turn the solution for the simpler inputs into a solution for the input that you are currently thinking about. Maybe you need to add a small quantity, perhaps related to the quantity that you lopped off to arrive at the simpler input. Maybe you cut the original input in half and have solutions for each half. Then you may need to add both solutions to arrive at a solution for the whole.

Consider the methods for simplifying the inputs for the palindrome test. Cutting the string in half doesn't seem like a good idea. If you cut

```
"Madam, I'm Adam"
```

in half, you get two strings:

```
"Madam, I"
```

and

```
"'m Adam"
```

The first string isn't a palindrome. Cutting the input in half and testing whether the halves are palindromes seems a dead end.

The most promising simplification is to remove the first *and* last characters. Removing the M at the front and the m at the back yields

```
"adam, I'm Ada"
```

Suppose you can verify that the shorter string is a palindrome. Then *of course* the original string is a palindrome—we put the same letter in the front and the back. That's extremely promising. A word is a palindrome if

- The first and last letters match (ignoring letter case).

and

- The word obtained by removing the first and last letters is a palindrome.

Again, don't worry how the test works for the shorter string. It just works.

There is one other case to consider. What if the first or last letter of the word is not a letter? For example, the string

```
"A man, a plan, a canal, Panama!"
```

ends in a ! character, which does not match the A in the front. But we should ignore non-letters when testing for palindromes. Thus, when the last character is not a letter but the first character is a letter, it doesn't make sense to remove both the first and the last characters. That's not a problem. Remove only the last character. If the shorter string is a palindrome, then it stays a palindrome when you attach a nonletter.

The same argument applies if the first character is not a letter. Now we have a complete set of cases.

- If the first and last characters are both letters, then check whether they match. If so, remove both and test the shorter string.
- Otherwise, if the last character isn't a letter, remove it and test the shorter string.
- Otherwise, the first character isn't a letter. Remove it and test the shorter string.

In all three cases, you can use the solution to the simpler problem to arrive at a solution to your problem.

**Step 3**   Find solutions to the simplest inputs.

A recursive computation keeps simplifying its inputs. Eventually it arrives at very simple inputs. To make sure that the recursion comes to a stop, you must deal with the simplest inputs separately. Come up with special solutions for them, which is usually very easy.

However, sometimes you get into philosophical questions dealing with *degenerate* inputs: empty strings, shapes with no area, and so on. Then you may want to investigate a slightly larger input that gets reduced to such a trivial input and see what value you should attach to the degenerate inputs so that the simpler value, when used according to the rules you discovered in Step 2, yields the correct answer.

Let's look at the simplest strings for the palindrome test:

- Strings with two characters
- Strings with a single character
- The empty string

We don't have to come up with a special solution for strings with two characters. Step 2 still applies to those strings—either or both of the characters are removed. But we do need to worry about strings of length 0 and 1. In those cases, Step 2 can't apply. There aren't two characters to remove.

The empty string is a palindrome—it's the same string when you read it backwards. If you find that too artificial, consider a string "mm". According to the rule discovered in Step 2, this string is a palindrome if the first and last characters of that string match and the remainder—that is, the empty string—is also a palindrome. Therefore, it makes sense to consider the empty string a palindrome.

A string with a single letter, such as "I", is a palindrome. How about the case in which the character is not a letter, such as "!"? Removing the ! yields the empty string, which is a palindrome. Thus, we conclude that all strings of length 0 or 1 are palindromes.

**Step 4**  Implement the solution by combining the simple cases and the reduction step.

Now you are ready to implement the solution. Make separate cases for the simple inputs that you considered in Step 3. If the input isn't one of the simplest cases, then implement the logic you discovered in Step 2.

Here is the isPalindrome method:

```java
public static boolean isPalindrome(String text)
{
    int length = text.length();

    // Separate case for shortest strings.
    if (length <= 1) { return true; }
    else
    {
        // Get first and last characters, converted to lowercase.
        char first = Character.toLowerCase(text.charAt(0));
        char last = Character.toLowerCase(text.charAt(length - 1));

        if (Character.isLetter(first) && Character.isLetter(last))
        {
            // Both are letters.
            if (first == last)
            {
                // Remove both first and last character.
                String shorter = text.substring(1, length - 1);
                return isPalindrome(shorter);
            }
            else
            {
                return false;
            }
        }
        else if (!Character.isLetter(last))
        {
            // Remove last character.
            String shorter = text.substring(0, length - 1);
            return isPalindrome(shorter);
        }
        else
        {
            // Remove first character.
            String shorter = text.substring(1);
            return isPalindrome(shorter);
        }
    }
}
```

6. Consider the task of removing all punctuation marks from a string. How can we break the string into smaller strings that can be processed recursively?

7. In a recursive method that removes all punctuation marks from a string, we decide to remove the last character, then recursively process the remainder. How do you combine the results?

8. How do you find solutions for the simplest inputs when removing punctuation marks from a string?

9. Provide pseudocode for a recursive method that removes punctuation marks from a string, using the answers to Self Checks 6–8.

**Practice It**   Now you can try these exercises at the end of the chapter: R13.3, P13.3, P13.6.

---

**WORKED EXAMPLE 13.1**   **Finding Files**

In this Worked Example, we find all files with a given extension in a directory tree.

```
code
  ch01
    section_4
      HelloPrinter.java
```

# 13.3 Recursive Helper Methods

> Sometimes it is easier to find a recursive solution if you make a slight change to the original problem.

Sometimes it is easier to find a recursive solution if you change the original problem slightly. Then the original problem can be solved by calling a recursive helper method.

Here is a typical example: Consider the palindrome test of Section 13.2. It is a bit inefficient to construct new string objects in every step. Now consider the following change in the problem. Rather than testing whether the entire sentence is a palindrome, let's check whether a substring is a palindrome:

*Sometimes, a task can be solved by handing it off to a recursive helper method.*

```
/**
    Tests whether a substring is a palindrome.
    @param text a string that is being checked
    @param start the index of the first character of the substring
    @param end the index of the last character of the substring
    @return true if the substring is a palindrome
*/
public static boolean isPalindrome(String text, int start, int end)
```

This method turns out to be even easier to implement than the original test. In the recursive calls, simply adjust the start and end parameter variables to skip over matching letter pairs and characters that are not letters. There is no need to construct new String objects to represent the shorter strings.

```
public static boolean isPalindrome(String text, int start, int end)
{
```

---

➕ Available online in WileyPLUS and at www.wiley.com/college/horstmann.

```
// Separate case for substrings of length 0 and 1.
if (start >= end) { return true; }
else
{
   // Get first and last characters, converted to lowercase.
   char first = Character.toLowerCase(text.charAt(start));
   char last = Character.toLowerCase(text.charAt(end));

   if (Character.isLetter(first) && Character.isLetter(last))
   {
      if (first == last)
      {
         // Test substring that doesn't contain the matching letters.
         return isPalindrome(text, start + 1, end - 1);
      }
      else
      {
         return false;
      }
   }
   else if (!Character.isLetter(last))
   {
      // Test substring that doesn't contain the last character.
      return isPalindrome(text, start, end - 1);
   }
   else
   {
      // Test substring that doesn't contain the first character.
      return isPalindrome(text, start + 1, end);
   }
}
}
```

You should still supply a method to solve the whole problem—the user of your method shouldn't have to know about the trick with the substring positions. Simply call the helper method with positions that test the entire string:

```
public static boolean isPalindrome(String text)
{
   return isPalindrome(text, 0, text.length() - 1);
}
```

**ONLINE EXAMPLE**

 The Palindromes class with a helper method.

Note that this call is *not* a recursive method call. The isPalindrome(String) method calls the helper method isPalindrome(String, int, int). In this example, we use overloading to declare two methods with the same name. The isPalindrome method with just a String parameter variable is the method that we expect the public to use. The second method, with one String and two int parameter variables, is the recursive helper method. If you prefer, you can avoid overloaded methods by choosing a different name for the helper method, such as substringIsPalindrome.

Use the technique of recursive helper methods whenever it is easier to solve a recursive problem that is equivalent to the original problem—but more amenable to a recursive solution.

**SELF CHECK**

**10.** Do we have to give the same name to both isPalindrome methods?

**11.** When does the recursive isPalindrome method stop calling itself?

**12.** To compute the sum of the values in an array, add the first value to the sum of the remaining values, computing recursively. Of course, it would be inefficient to set up an actual array of the remaining values. Which recursive helper method can solve the problem?

**13.** How can you write a recursive method `public static void sum(int[] a)` without needing a helper function?

**Practice It**   Now you can try these exercises at the end of the chapter: P13.4, P13.7, 13.11.

# 13.4 The Efficiency of Recursion

As you have seen in this chapter, recursion can be a powerful tool to implement complex algorithms. On the other hand, recursion can lead to algorithms that perform poorly. In this section, we will analyze the question of when recursion is beneficial and when it is inefficient.

*In most cases, iterative and recursive approaches have comparable efficiency.*

Consider the Fibonacci sequence: a sequence of numbers defined by the equation

$$f_1 = 1$$
$$f_2 = 1$$
$$f_n = f_{n-1} + f_{n-2}$$

That is, each value of the sequence is the sum of the two preceding values. The first ten terms of the sequence are

$$1, 1, 2, 3, 5, 8, 13, 21, 34, 55$$

It is easy to extend this sequence indefinitely. Just keep appending the sum of the last two values of the sequence. For example, the next entry is $34 + 55 = 89$.

We would like to write a method that computes $f_n$ for any value of $n$. Here we translate the definition directly into a recursive method:

**section_4/RecursiveFib.java**

```java
import java.util.Scanner;

/**
   This program computes Fibonacci numbers using a recursive method.
*/
public class RecursiveFib
{
   public static void main(String[] args)
   {
      Scanner in = new Scanner(System.in);
      System.out.print("Enter n: ");
      int n = in.nextInt();

      for (int i = 1; i <= n; i++)
      {
         long f = fib(i);
         System.out.println("fib(" + i + ") = " + f);
      }
```

```
19          }
20
21      /**
22          Computes a Fibonacci number.
23          @param n an integer
24          @return the nth Fibonacci number
25      */
26      public static long fib(int n)
27      {
28          if (n <= 2) { return 1; }
29          else { return fib(n - 1) + fib(n - 2); }
30      }
31  }
```

**Program Run**

```
Enter n: 50
fib(1) = 1
fib(2) = 1
fib(3) = 2
fib(4) = 3
fib(5) = 5
fib(6) = 8
fib(7) = 13
. . .
fib(50) = 12586269025
```

That is certainly simple, and the method will work correctly. But watch the output closely as you run the test program. The first few calls to the fib method are fast. For larger values, though, the program pauses an amazingly long time between outputs.

That makes no sense. Armed with pencil, paper, and a pocket calculator you could calculate these numbers pretty quickly, so it shouldn't take the computer anywhere near that long.

To find out the problem, let us insert **trace messages** into the method:

**section_4/RecursiveFibTracer.java**

```
1  import java.util.Scanner;
2
3  /**
4      This program prints trace messages that show how often the
5      recursive method for computing Fibonacci numbers calls itself.
6  */
7  public class RecursiveFibTracer
8  {
9      public static void main(String[] args)
10     {
11         Scanner in = new Scanner(System.in);
12         System.out.print("Enter n: ");
13         int n = in.nextInt();
14
15         long f = fib(n);
16
17         System.out.println("fib(" + n + ") = " + f);
18     }
19
20     /**
```

```
21          Computes a Fibonacci number.
22          @param n  an integer
23          @return the nth Fibonacci number
24      */
25      public static long fib(int n)
26      {
27          System.out.println("Entering fib: n = " + n);
28          long f;
29          if (n <= 2) { f = 1; }
30          else { f = fib(n - 1) + fib(n - 2); }
31          System.out.println("Exiting fib: n = " + n
32                  + " return value = " + f);
33          return f;
34      }
35  }
```

**Program Run**

```
Enter n: 6
Entering fib: n = 6
Entering fib: n = 5
Entering fib: n = 4
Entering fib: n = 3
Entering fib: n = 2
Exiting fib: n = 2 return value = 1
Entering fib: n = 1
Exiting fib: n = 1 return value = 1
Exiting fib: n = 3 return value = 2
Entering fib: n = 2
Exiting fib: n = 2 return value = 1
Exiting fib: n = 4 return value = 3
Entering fib: n = 3
Entering fib: n = 2
Exiting fib: n = 2 return value = 1
Entering fib: n = 1
Exiting fib: n = 1 return value = 1
Exiting fib: n = 3 return value = 2
Exiting fib: n = 5 return value = 5
Entering fib: n = 4
Entering fib: n = 3
Entering fib: n = 2
Exiting fib: n = 2 return value = 1
Entering fib: n = 1
Exiting fib: n = 1 return value = 1
Exiting fib: n = 3 return value = 2
Entering fib: n = 2
Exiting fib: n = 2 return value = 1
Exiting fib: n = 4 return value = 3
Exiting fib: n = 6 return value = 8
fib(6) = 8
```

Figure 1 shows the pattern of recursive calls for computing fib(6). Now it is becoming apparent why the method takes so long. It is computing the same values over and over. For example, the computation of fib(6) calls fib(4) twice and fib(3) three times. That is very different from the computation we would do with pencil and paper. There we would just write down the values as they were computed and add up the last two to get the next one until we reached the desired entry; no sequence value would ever be computed twice.

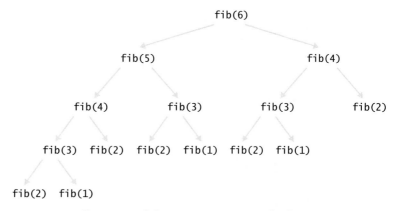

**Figure 1**  Call Pattern of the Recursive `fib` Method

If we imitate the pencil-and-paper process, then we get the following program:

**section_4/LoopFib.java**

```
1   import java.util.Scanner;
2
3   /**
4      This program computes Fibonacci numbers using an iterative method.
5   */
6   public class LoopFib
7   {
8      public static void main(String[] args)
9      {
10        Scanner in = new Scanner(System.in);
11        System.out.print("Enter n: ");
12        int n = in.nextInt();
13
14        for (int i = 1; i <= n; i++)
15        {
16           long f = fib(i);
17           System.out.println("fib(" + i + ") = " + f);
18        }
19     }
20
21     /**
22        Computes a Fibonacci number.
23        @param n an integer
24        @return the nth Fibonacci number
25     */
26     public static long fib(int n)
27     {
28        if (n <= 2) { return 1; }
29        else
30        {
31           long olderValue = 1;
32           long oldValue = 1;
33           long newValue = 1;
34           for (int i = 3; i <= n; i++)
35           {
36              newValue = oldValue + olderValue;
37              olderValue = oldValue;
38              oldValue = newValue;
```

```
39              }
40              return newValue;
41          }
42      }
43  }
```

**Program Run**

```
Enter n: 50
fib(1) = 1
fib(2) = 1
fib(3) = 2
fib(4) = 3
fib(5) = 5
fib(6) = 8
fib(7) = 13
 . . .
fib(50) = 12586269025
```

This method runs *much* faster than the recursive version.

In this example of the fib method, the recursive solution was easy to program because it exactly followed the mathematical definition, but it ran far more slowly than the iterative solution, because it computed many intermediate results multiple times.

Can you always speed up a recursive solution by changing it into a loop? Frequently, the iterative and recursive solution have essentially the same performance. For example, here is an iterative solution for the palindrome test:

Occasionally, a recursive solution runs much slower than its iterative counterpart. However, in most cases, the recursive solution is only slightly slower.

```java
public static boolean isPalindrome(String text)
{
    int start = 0;
    int end = text.length() - 1;
    while (start < end)
    {
        char first = Character.toLowerCase(text.charAt(start));
        char last = Character.toLowerCase(text.charAt(end));

        if (Character.isLetter(first) && Character.isLetter(last))
        {
            // Both are letters.
            if (first == last)
            {
                start++;
                end--;
            }
            else
            {
                return false;
            }
        }
        if (!Character.isLetter(last)) { end--; }
        if (!Character.isLetter(first)) { start++; }
    }
    return true;
}
```

**ONLINE EXAMPLE**

The LoopPalindromes class.

This solution keeps two index variables: start and end. The first index starts at the beginning of the string and is advanced whenever a letter has been matched or a nonletter has been ignored. The second index starts at the end of the string and moves toward the beginning. When the two index variables meet, the iteration stops.

Both the iteration and the recursion run at about the same speed. If a palindrome has $n$ characters, the iteration executes the loop between $n/2$ and $n$ times, depending on how many of the characters are letters, because one or both index variables are moved in each step. Similarly, the recursive solution calls itself between $n/2$ and $n$ times, because one or two characters are removed in each step.

In such a situation, the iterative solution tends to be a bit faster, because each recursive method call takes a certain amount of processor time. In principle, it is possible for a smart compiler to avoid recursive method calls if they follow simple patterns, but most Java compilers don't do that. From that point of view, an iterative solution is preferable.

However, many problems have recursive solutions that are easier to understand and implement correctly than their iterative counterparts. Sometimes there is no obvious iterative solution at all—see the example in the next section. There is a certain elegance and economy of thought to recursive solutions that makes them more appealing. As the computer scientist (and creator of the GhostScript interpreter for the PostScript graphics description language) L. Peter Deutsch put it: "To iterate is human, to recurse divine."

> In many cases, a recursive solution is easier to understand and implement correctly than an iterative solution.

**SELF CHECK**

14. Is it faster to compute the triangle numbers recursively, as shown in Section 13.1, or is it faster to use a loop that computes $1 + 2 + 3 + \ldots + \text{width}$?

15. You can compute the factorial function either with a loop, using the definition that $n! = 1 \times 2 \times \ldots \times n$, or recursively, using the definition that $0! = 1$ and $n! = (n - 1)! \times n$. Is the recursive approach inefficient in this case?

16. To compute the sum of the values in an array, you can split the array in the middle, recursively compute the sums of the halves, and add the results. Compare the performance of this algorithm with that of a loop that adds the values.

**Practice It**    Now you can try these exercises at the end of the chapter: R13.7, R13.9. P13.5, P13.25.

# 13.5 Permutations

> The permutations of a string can be obtained more naturally through recursion than with a loop.

In this section, we will study a more complex example of recursion that would be difficult to program with a simple loop. (As Exercise P13.11 shows, it is possible to avoid the recursion, but the resulting solution is quite complex, and no faster).

We will design a method that lists all permutations of a string. A permutation is simply a rearrangement of the letters in the string. For example, the string "eat" has six permutations (including the original string itself):

```
"eat"
"eta"
"aet"
"ate"
"tea"
"tae"
```

*Using recursion, you can find all arrangements of a set of objects.*

Now we need a way to generate the permutations recursively. Consider the string "eat". Let's simplify the problem. First, we'll generate all permutations that start with the letter 'e', then those that start with 'a', and finally those that start with 't'. How do we generate the permutations that start with 'e'? We need to know the permutations of the substring "at". But that's the same problem—to generate all permutations—with a simpler input, namely the shorter string "at". Thus, we can use recursion. Generate the permutations of the substring "at". They are

```
"at"
"ta"
```

For each permutation of that substring, prepend the letter 'e' to get the permutations of "eat" that start with 'e', namely

```
"eat"
"eta"
```

Now let's turn our attention to the permutations of "eat" that start with 'a'. We need to produce the permutations of the remaining letters, "et". They are:

```
"et"
"te"
```

We add the letter 'a' to the front of the strings and obtain

```
"aet"
"ate"
```

We generate the permutations that start with 't' in the same way.

That's the idea. The implementation is fairly straightforward. In the `permutations` method, we loop through all positions in the word to be permuted. For each of them, we compute the shorter word that is obtained by removing the ith letter:

```
String shorter = word.substring(0, i) + word.substring(i + 1);
```

We compute the permutations of the shorter word:

```
ArrayList<String> shorterPermutations = permutations(shorter);
```

Finally, we add the removed letter to the front of all permutations of the shorter word.

```
for (String s : shorterPermutations)
{
    result.add(word.charAt(i) + s);
}
```

As always, we have to provide a special case for the simplest strings. The simplest possible string is the empty string, which has a single permutation—itself.

Here is the complete `Permutations` class:

**section_5/Permutations.java**

```
1   import java.util.ArrayList;
2
3   /**
4      This class computes permutations of a string.
5   */
6   public class Permutations
7   {
8      public static void main(String[] args)
9      {
10         for (String s : permutations("eat"))
11         {
```

```
12                System.out.println(s);
13            }
14        }
15
16        /**
17            Gets all permutations of a given word.
18            @param word the string to permute
19            @return a list of all permutations
20        */
21        public static ArrayList<String> permutations(String word)
22        {
23            ArrayList<String> result = new ArrayList<String>();
24
25            // The empty string has a single permutation: itself
26            if (word.length() == 0)
27            {
28                result.add(word);
29                return result;
30            }
31            else
32            {
33                // Loop through all character positions
34                for (int i = 0; i < word.length(); i++)
35                {
36                    // Form a shorter word by removing the ith character
37                    String shorter = word.substring(0, i) + word.substring(i + 1);
38
39                    // Generate all permutations of the simpler word
40                    ArrayList<String> shorterPermutations = permutations(shorter)
41
42                    // Add the removed character to the front of
43                    // each permutation of the simpler word
44                    for (String s : shorterPermutations)
45                    {
46                        result.add(word.charAt(i) + s);
47                    }
48                }
49                // Return all permutations
50                return result;
51            }
52        }
53    }
```

**Program Run**

```
eat
eta
aet
ate
tea
tae
```

Compare the Permutations and Triangle classes. Both of them work on the same principle. When they work on a more complex input, they first solve the problem for a simpler input. Then they combine the result for the simpler input with additional work to deliver the results for the more complex input. There really is no particular complexity behind that process as long as you think about the solution on that level only.

However, behind the scenes, the simpler input creates even simpler input, which creates yet another simplification, and so on, until one input is so simple that the result can be obtained without further help. It is interesting to think about this process, but it can also be confusing. What's important is that you can focus on the one level that matters—putting a solution together from the slightly simpler problem, ignoring the fact that the simpler problem also uses recursion to get its results.

*Random Fact 13.1* The Limits of Computation

Have you ever wondered how your instructor or grader makes sure your programming homework is correct? In all likelihood, they look at your solution and perhaps run it with some test inputs. But usually they have a correct solution available. That suggests that there might be an easier way. Perhaps they could feed your program and their correct program into a "program comparator", a computer program that analyzes both programs and determines whether they both compute the same results. Of course, your solution and the program that is known to be correct need not be identical—what matters is that they produce the same output when given the same input.

How could such a program comparator work? Well, the Java compiler knows how to read a program and make sense of the classes, methods, and statements. So it seems plausible that someone could, with some effort, write a program that reads two Java programs, analyzes what they do, and determines whether they solve the same task. Of course, such a program would be very attractive to instructors, because it could automate the grading process. Thus, even though no such program exists today, it might be tempting to try to develop one and sell it to universities around the world.

However, before you start raising venture capital for such an effort, you should know that theoretical computer scientists have proven that it is impossible to develop such a program, *no matter how hard you try*.

There are quite a few of these unsolvable problems. The first one,

called the *halting problem*, was discovered by the British researcher Alan Turing in 1936. Because his research occurred before the first actual computer was constructed, Turing had to devise a theoretical device, the *Turing machine*, to explain how computers could work. The Turing machine consists of a long magnetic tape, a read/write head, and a program that has numbered instructions of the form: "If the current symbol under the head is *x*, then replace it with *y*, move the head one unit left or right, and continue with instruction *n*" (see figure below). Interestingly enough, with only these instructions, you can program just as much as with Java, even though it is incredibly tedious to do so. Theoretical computer scientists like Turing machines because they can be described using nothing more than the laws of mathematics.

Expressed in terms of Java, the halting problem states: "It is impossible to write a program with two inputs, namely the source code of an arbitrary Java program *P* and a string *I*, that decides whether the program *P*, when executed with the input *I*, will halt—that is, the program will not get into an infinite loop with the given input". Of course, for some kinds of programs and inputs, it is possible to decide whether the program halts with the given input. The halting problem asserts that it is impossible to come up with a single decision-making algorithm that works with all programs and inputs. Note that you can't simply run the program *P* on the input *I* to settle this question. If the program runs for 1,000 days, you don't know that the program is in an infinite loop. Maybe

you just have to wait another day for it to stop.

Such a "halt checker", if it could be written, might also be useful for grading homework. An instructor could use it to screen student submissions to see if they get into an infinite loop with a particular input, and then stop checking them. However, as Turing demonstrated, such a program cannot be written. His argument is ingenious and quite simple.

Suppose a "halt checker" program existed. Let's call it *H*. From *H*, we will develop another program, the "killer" program *K*. *K* does the following computation. Its input is a string containing the source code for a program *R*. It then applies the halt checker on the input program *R* and the input string *R*. That is, it checks whether the program *R* halts if its input is its own source code. It sounds bizarre to feed a program to itself, but it isn't impossible.

*Alan Turing*

**17.** What are all permutations of the four-letter word beat?

**18.** Our recursion for the permutation generator stops at the empty string. What simple modification would make the recursion stop at strings of length 0 or 1?

**19.** Why isn't it easy to develop an iterative solution for the permutation generator?

**Practice It**   Now you can try these exercises at the end of the chapter: P13.11, P13.12, P13.13.

---

For example, the Java compiler is written in Java, and you can use it to compile itself. Or, as a simpler example, a word counting program can count the words in its own source code.

When *K* gets the answer from *H* that *R* halts when applied to itself, it is programmed to enter an infinite loop. Otherwise *K* exits. In Java, the program might look like this:

```
public class Killer
{
   public static void main(
      String[] args)
   {
      String r = read program input;
      HaltChecker checker =
         new HaltChecker();
      if (checker.check(r, r))
      {
         while (true)
         { // Infinite loop
         }
      }
      else
      {
         return;
      }
   }
}
```

Now ask yourself: What does the halt checker answer when asked whether *K* halts when given *K* as the input? Maybe it finds out that *K* gets into an infinite loop with such an input. But wait, that can't be right. That would mean that checker.check(r, r) returns false when r is the program code of *K*. As you can plainly see, in that case, the killer method returns, so K didn't get into an infinite loop. That shows that *K* must halt when analyzing itself, so

checker.check(r, r) should return true. But then the killer method doesn't terminate—it goes into an infinite loop. That shows that it is logically impossible to implement a program that can check whether *every* program halts on a particular input.

It is sobering to know that there are *limits* to computing. There are problems that no computer program, no matter how ingenious, can answer.

Theoretical computer scientists are working on other research involving the nature of computation. One important question that remains unsettled to this day deals with problems that in practice are very time-consuming to solve. It may be that these problems are intrinsically hard, in which case it would be pointless to try to look for better algorithms. Such theoretical research can have important practical applications. For example, right now, nobody knows whether the most common encryption schemes used today could be broken by discovering a new algorithm. Knowing that no fast algorithms exist for breaking a particular code could make us feel more comfortable about the security of encryption.

Program

| Instruction number | If tape symbol is | Replace with | Then move head | Then go to instruction |
|---|---|---|---|---|
| 1 | 0 | 2 | right | 2 |
|   | 1 | 1 | left | 4 |
| 2 | 0 | 0 | right | 2 |
|   | 1 | 1 | right | 2 |
|   | 2 | 0 | left | 3 |
| 3 | 0 | 0 | left | 3 |
|   | 1 | 1 | left | 3 |
|   | 2 | 2 | right | 1 |
| 4 | 1 | 1 | right | 5 |
|   | 2 | 0 | left | 4 |

Control unit

Read/write head

Tape

*The Turing Machine*

# 13.6 Mutual Recursion

In a mutual recursion, a set of cooperating methods calls each other repeatedly.

In the preceding examples, a method called itself to solve a simpler problem. Sometimes, a set of cooperating methods calls each other in a recursive fashion. In this section, we will explore such a **mutual recursion**. This technique is significantly more advanced than the simple recursion that we discussed in the preceding sections.

We will develop a program that can compute the values of arithmetic expressions such as

```
3+4*5
(3+4)*5
1-(2-(3-(4-5)))
```

Computing such an expression is complicated by the fact that * and / bind more strongly than + and -, and that parentheses can be used to group subexpressions.

Figure 2 shows a set of **syntax diagrams** that describes the syntax of these expressions. To see how the syntax diagrams work, consider the expression 3+4*5:

- Enter the *expression* syntax diagram. The arrow points directly to *term*, giving you no alternative.
- Enter the *term* syntax diagram. The arrow points to *factor*, again giving you no choice.
- Enter the *factor* diagram. You have two choices: to follow the top branch or the bottom branch. Because the first input token is the number 3 and not a (, follow the bottom branch.
- Accept the input token because it matches the number. The unprocessed input is now +4*5.
- Follow the arrow out of *number* to the end of *factor*. As in a method call, you now back up, returning to the end of the *factor* element of the *term* diagram.

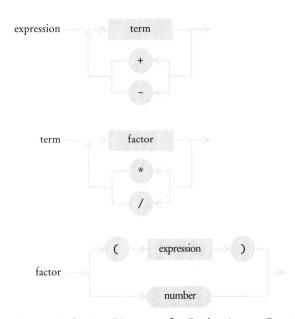

**Figure 2** Syntax Diagrams for Evaluating an Expression

- Now you have another choice—to loop back in the *term* diagram, or to exit. The next input token is a +, and it matches neither the * or the / that would be required to loop back. So you exit, returning to *expression*.

- Again, you have a choice, to loop back or to exit. Now the + matches one of the choices in the loop. Accept the + in the input and move back to the *term* element. The remaining input is 4*5.

In this fashion, an expression is broken down into a sequence of terms, separated by + or -, each term is broken down into a sequence of factors, each separated by * or /, and each factor is either a parenthesized expression or a number. You can draw this break-down as a tree. Figure 3 shows how the expressions 3+4*5 and (3+4)*5 are derived from the syntax diagram.

Why do the syntax diagrams help us compute the value of the tree? If you look at the syntax trees, you will see that they accurately represent which operations should be carried out first. In the first tree, 4 and 5 should be multiplied, and then the result should be added to 3. In the second tree, 3 and 4 should be added, and the result should be multiplied by 5.

At the end of this section, you will find the implementation of the Evaluator class, which evaluates these expressions. The Evaluator makes use of an Expression-Tokenizer class, which breaks up an input string into tokens—numbers, operators, and parentheses. (For simplicity, we only accept positive integers as numbers, and we don't allow spaces in the input.)

When you call nextToken, the next input token is returned as a string. We also supply another method, peekToken, which allows you to see the next token without consuming it. To see why the peekToken method is necessary, consider the syntax diagram of the term type. If the next token is a "*" or "/", you want to continue adding and subtracting terms. But if the next token is another character, such as a "+" or "-", you want to stop without actually consuming it, so that the token can be considered later.

To compute the value of an expression, we implement three methods: getExpressionValue, getTermValue, and getFactorValue. The getExpressionValue method first calls getTermValue to get the value of the first term of the expression. Then it

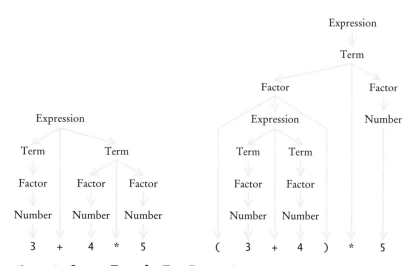

**Figure 3**  Syntax Trees for Two Expressions

checks whether the next input token is one of + or -. If so, it calls getTermValue again and adds or subtracts it.

```
public int getExpressionValue()
{
   int value = getTermValue();
   boolean done = false;
   while (!done)
   {
      String next = tokenizer.peekToken();
      if ("+".equals(next) || "-".equals(next))
      {
         tokenizer.nextToken(); // Discard "+" or "-"
         int value2 = getTermValue();
         if ("+".equals(next)) { value = value + value2; }
         else { value = value - value2; }
      }
      else
      {
         done = true;
      }
   }
   return value;
}
```

The getTermValue method calls getFactorValue in the same way, multiplying or dividing the factor values.

Finally, the getFactorValue method checks whether the next input is a number, or whether it begins with a ( token. In the first case, the value is simply the value of the number. However, in the second case, the getFactorValue method makes a recursive call to getExpressionValue. Thus, the three methods are mutually recursive.

```
public int getFactorValue()
{
   int value;
   String next = tokenizer.peekToken();
   if ("(".equals(next))
   {
      tokenizer.nextToken(); // Discard "("
      value = getExpressionValue();
      tokenizer.nextToken(); // Discard ")"
   }
   else
   {
      value = Integer.parseInt(tokenizer.nextToken());
   }
   return value;
}
```

To see the mutual recursion clearly, trace through the expression (3+4)*5:

- getExpressionValue calls getTermValue
  - getTermValue calls getFactorValue
    - getFactorValue consumes the ( input
    - getFactorValue calls getExpressionValue
      - getExpressionValue returns eventually with the value of 7, having consumed 3 + 4. This is the recursive call.
    - getFactorValue consumes the ) input

- getFactorValue returns 7
- getTermValue consumes the inputs * and 5 and returns 35
- getExpressionValue returns 35

As always with a recursive solution, you need to ensure that the recursion terminates. In this situation, that is easy to see when you consider the situation in which getExpressionValue calls itself. The second call works on a shorter subexpression than the original expression. At each recursive call, at least some of the tokens of the input string are consumed, so eventually the recursion must come to an end.

**section_6/Evaluator.java**

```
1   /**
2       A class that can compute the value of an arithmetic expression.
3   */
4   public class Evaluator
5   {
6       private ExpressionTokenizer tokenizer;
7
8       /**
9           Constructs an evaluator.
10          @param anExpression a string containing the expression
11          to be evaluated
12      */
13      public Evaluator(String anExpression)
14      {
15          tokenizer = new ExpressionTokenizer(anExpression);
16      }
17
18      /**
19          Evaluates the expression.
20          @return the value of the expression
21      */
22      public int getExpressionValue()
23      {
24          int value = getTermValue();
25          boolean done = false;
26          while (!done)
27          {
28              String next = tokenizer.peekToken();
29              if ("+".equals(next) || "-".equals(next))
30              {
31                  tokenizer.nextToken(); // Discard "+" or "-"
32                  int value2 = getTermValue();
33                  if ("+".equals(next)) { value = value + value2; }
34                  else { value = value - value2; }
35              }
36              else
37              {
38                  done = true;
39              }
40          }
41          return value;
42      }
43
44      /**
45          Evaluates the next term found in the expression.
46          @return the value of the term
47      */
```

```
48        public int getTermValue()
49        {
50           int value = getFactorValue();
51           boolean done = false;
52           while (!done)
53           {
54              String next = tokenizer.peekToken();
55              if ("*".equals(next) || "/".equals(next))
56              {
57                 tokenizer.nextToken();
58                 int value2 = getFactorValue();
59                 if ("*".equals(next)) { value = value * value2; }
60                 else { value = value / value2; }
61              }
62              else
63              {
64                 done = true;
65              }
66           }
67           return value;
68        }
69
70        /**
71           Evaluates the next factor found in the expression.
72           @return the value of the factor
73        */
74        public int getFactorValue()
75        {
76           int value;
77           String next = tokenizer.peekToken();
78           if ("(".equals(next))
79           {
80              tokenizer.nextToken(); // Discard "("
81              value = getExpressionValue();
82              tokenizer.nextToken(); // Discard ")"
83           }
84           else
85           {
86              value = Integer.parseInt(tokenizer.nextToken());
87           }
88           return value;
89        }
90     }
```

## section_6/ExpressionTokenizer.java

```
1     /**
2        This class breaks up a string describing an expression
3        into tokens: numbers, parentheses, and operators.
4     */
5     public class ExpressionTokenizer
6     {
7        private String input;
8        private int start; // The start of the current token
9        private int end; // The position after the end of the current token
10
11       /**
12          Constructs a tokenizer.
13          @param anInput the string to tokenize
14       */
```

```
15    public ExpressionTokenizer(String anInput)
16    {
17       input = anInput;
18       start = 0;
19       end = 0;
20       nextToken(); //  Find the first token
21    }
22
23    /**
24       Peeks at the next token without consuming it.
25       @return the next token or null if there are no more tokens
26    */
27    public String peekToken()
28    {
29       if (start >= input.length()) { return null; }
30       else { return input.substring(start, end); }
31    }
32
33    /**
34       Gets the next token and moves the tokenizer to the following token.
35       @return the next token or null if there are no more tokens
36    */
37    public String nextToken()
38    {
39       String r = peekToken();
40       start = end;
41       if (start >= input.length()) { return r; }
42       if (Character.isDigit(input.charAt(start)))
43       {
44          end = start + 1;
45          while (end < input.length()
46                && Character.isDigit(input.charAt(end)))
47          {
48             end++;
49          }
50       }
51       else
52       {
53          end = start + 1;
54       }
55       return r;
56    }
57 }
```

## section_6/ExpressionCalculator.java

```
1  import java.util.Scanner;
2
3  /**
4     This program calculates the value of an expression
5     consisting of numbers, arithmetic operators, and parentheses.
6  */
7  public class ExpressionCalculator
8  {
9     public static void main(String[] args)
10    {
11       Scanner in = new Scanner(System.in);
12       System.out.print("Enter an expression: ");
13       String input = in.nextLine();
14       Evaluator e = new Evaluator(input);
```

```
15          int value = e.getExpressionValue();
16          System.out.println(input + "=" + value);
17      }
18  }
```

**Program Run**

```
Enter an expression: 3+4*5
3+4*5=23
```

**SELF CHECK**

20. What is the difference between a term and a factor? Why do we need both concepts?
21. Why does the expression evaluator use mutual recursion?
22. What happens if you try to evaluate the illegal expression 3+4*)5? Specifically, which method throws an exception?

**Practice It**    Now you can try these exercises at the end of the chapter: R13.11, P13.16.

# 13.7 Backtracking

Backtracking examines partial solutions, abandoning unsuitable ones and returning to consider other candidates.

Backtracking is a problem solving technique that builds up partial solutions that get increasingly closer to the goal. If a partial solution cannot be completed, one abandons it and returns to examining the other candidates.

Backtracking can be used to solve crossword puzzles, escape from mazes, or find solutions to systems that are constrained by rules. In order to employ backtracking for a particular problem, we need two characteristic properties:

1. A procedure to examine a partial solution and determine whether to
   - Accept it as an actual solution.
   - Abandon it (either because it violates some rules or because it is clear that it can never lead to a valid solution).
   - Continue extending it.
2. A procedure to extend a partial solution, generating one or more solutions that come closer to the goal.

*In a backtracking algorithm, one explores all paths towards a solution. When one path is a dead end, one needs to backtrack and try another choice.*

**Figure 4**
A Solution to the
Eight Queens Problem

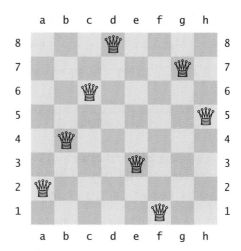

Backtracking can then be expressed with the following recursive algorithm:

Solve(partialSolution)
    Examine(partialSolution).
    If accepted
        Add partialSolution to the list of solutions.
    Else if not abandoned
        For each p in extend(partialSolution)
            Solve(p).

Of course, the processes of examining and extending a partial solution depend on the nature of the problem.

As an example, we will develop a program that finds all solutions to the eight queens problem: the task of positioning eight queens on a chess board so that none of them attacks another according to the rules of chess. In other words, there are no two queens on the same row, column, or diagonal. Figure 4 shows a solution.

In this problem, it is easy to examine a partial solution. If two queens attack another, reject it. Otherwise, if it has eight queens, accept it. Otherwise, continue.

It is also easy to extend a partial solution. Simply add another queen on an empty square.

However, in the interest of efficiency, we will be a bit more systematic about the extension process. We will place the first queen in row 1, the next queen in row 2, and so on.

We provide a class `PartialSolution` that collects the queens in a partial solution, and that has methods to examine and extend the solution:

```
public class PartialSolution
{
   private Queen[] queens;

   public int examine() { . . . }
   public PartialSolution[] extend() { . . . }
}
```

The `examine` method simply checks whether two queens attack each other:

```
public int examine()
{
```

```
         for (int i = 0; i < queens.length; i++)
         {
            for (int j = i + 1; j < queens.length; j++)
            {
               if (queens[i].attacks(queens[j])) { return ABANDON; }
            }
         }
         if (queens.length == NQUEENS) { return ACCEPT; }
         else { return CONTINUE; }
      }
```

The extend method takes a given solution and makes eight copies of it. Each copy gets a new queen in a different column.

```
   public PartialSolution[] extend()
   {
      // Generate a new solution for each column
      PartialSolution[] result = new PartialSolution[NQUEENS];
      for (int i = 0; i < result.length; i++)
      {
         int size = queens.length;

         // The new solution has one more row than this one
         result[i] = new PartialSolution(size + 1);

         // Copy this solution into the new one
         for (int j = 0; j < size; j++)
         {
            result[i].queens[j] = queens[j];
         }

         // Append the new queen into the ith column
         result[i].queens[size] = new Queen(size, i);
      }
      return result;
   }
```

You will find the Queen class at the end of the section. The only challenge is to determine when two queens attack each other diagonally. Here is an easy way of checking that. Compute the slope and check whether it is ±1. This condition can be simplified as follows:

$$(\text{row}_2 - \text{row}_1)/(\text{column}_2 - \text{column}_1) = \pm 1$$

$$\text{row}_2 - \text{row}_1 = \pm(\text{column}_2 - \text{column}_1)$$

$$|\text{row}_2 - \text{row}_1| = |\text{column}_2 - \text{column}_1|$$

Have a close look at the solve method in the EightQueens class on page 617. The method is a straightforward translation of the pseudocode for backtracking. Note how there is nothing specific about the eight queens problem in this method—it works for any partial solution with an examine and extend method (see Exercise P13.19).

Figure 5 shows the solve method in action for a four queens problem. Starting from a blank board, there are four partial solutions with a queen in row 1 **1**. When the queen is in column 1, there are four partial solutions with a queen in row 2 **2**. Two of them are immediately abandoned immediately. The other two lead to partial solutions with three queens **3** and **4**, all but one of which are abandoned. One partial solution is extended to four queens, but all of those are abandoned as well **5**.

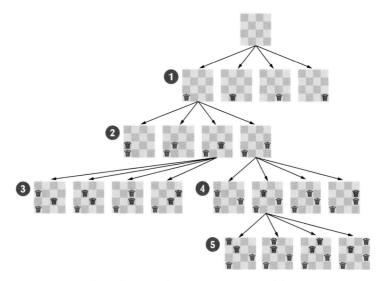

**Figure 5** Backtracking in the Four Queens Problem

Then the algorithm backtracks, giving up on a queen in position a1, instead extending the solution with the queen in position b1 (not shown).

When you run the program, it lists 92 solutions, including the one in Figure 4. Exercise P13.21 asks you to remove those that are rotations or reflections of another.

**section_7/PartialSolution.java**

```java
1  /**
2      A partial solution to the eight queens puzzle.
3  */
4  public class PartialSolution
5  {
6      private Queen[] queens;
7      private static final int NQUEENS = 8;
8
9      public static final int ACCEPT = 1;
10     public static final int ABANDON = 2;
11     public static final int CONTINUE = 3;
12
13     /**
14         Constructs a partial solution of a given size.
15         @param size the size
16     */
17     public PartialSolution(int size)
18     {
19         queens = new Queen[size];
20     }
21
22     /**
23         Examines a partial solution.
24         @return one of ACCEPT, ABANDON, CONTINUE
25     */
26     public int examine()
27     {
```

```
28        for (int i = 0; i < queens.length; i++)
29        {
30           for (int j = i + 1; j < queens.length; j++)
31           {
32              if (queens[i].attacks(queens[j])) { return ABANDON; }
33           }
34        }
35        if (queens.length == NQUEENS) { return ACCEPT; }
36        else { return CONTINUE; }
37     }
38
39     /**
40        Yields all extensions of this partial solution.
41        @return an array of partial solutions that extend this solution.
42     */
43     public PartialSolution[] extend()
44     {
45        // Generate a new solution for each column
46        PartialSolution[] result = new PartialSolution[NQUEENS];
47        for (int i = 0; i < result.length; i++)
48        {
49           int size = queens.length;
50
51           // The new solution has one more row than this one
52           result[i] = new PartialSolution(size + 1);
53
54           // Copy this solution into the new one
55           for (int j = 0; j < size; j++)
56           {
57              result[i].queens[j] = queens[j];
58           }
59
60           // Append the new queen into the ith column
61           result[i].queens[size] = new Queen(size, i);
62        }
63        return result;
64     }
65
66     public String toString() { return Arrays.toString(queens); }
67  }
```

### section_7/Queen.java

```
1   /**
2      A queen in the eight queens problem.
3   */
4   public class Queen
5   {
6      private int row;
7      private int column;
8
9      /**
10        Constructs a queen at a given position.
11        @param r the row
12        @param c the column
13     */
14     public Queen(int r, int c)
15     {
```

```java
16          row = r;
17          column = c;
18       }
19
20       /**
21          Checks whether this queen attacks another.
22          @param other the other queen
23          @return true if this and the other queen are in the same
24          row, column, or diagonal
25       */
26       public boolean attacks(Queen other)
27       {
28          return row == other.row
29             || column == other.column
30             || Math.abs(row - other.row) == Math.abs(column - other.column);
31       }
32
33       public String toString()
34       {
35          return "" + "abcdefgh".charAt(column) + (row + 1) ;
36       }
37    }
```

### section_7/EightQueens.java

```java
1    import java.util.Arrays;
2
3    /**
4       This class solves the eight queens problem using backtracking.
5    */
6    public class EightQueens
7    {
8       public static void main(String[] args)
9       {
10          solve(new PartialSolution(0));
11       }
12
13       /**
14          Prints all solutions to the problem that can be extended from
15          a given partial solution.
16          @param sol the partial solution
17       */
18       public static void solve(PartialSolution sol)
19       {
20          int exam = sol.examine();
21          if (exam == PartialSolution.ACCEPT)
22          {
23             System.out.println(sol);
24          }
25          else if (exam != PartialSolution.ABANDON)
26          {
27             for (PartialSolution p : sol.extend())
28             {
29                solve(p);
30             }
31          }
32       }
33    }
```

**Program Run**

```
[a1, e2, h3, f4, c5, g6, b7, d8]
[a1, f2, h3, c4, g5, d6, b7, e8]
[a1, g2, d3, f4, h5, b6, e7, c8]
 . . .
[f1, a2, e3, b4, h5, c6, g7, d8]
 . . .
[h1, c2, a3, f4, b5, e6, g7, d8]
[h1, d2, a3, c4, f5, b6, g7, e8]
```
(92 solutions)

**SELF CHECK**

23. Why does j begin at $i + 1$ in the examine method?
24. Continue tracing the four queens problem as shown in Figure 5. How many solutions are there with the first queen in position a2?
25. How many solutions are there altogether for the four queens problem?

**Practice It**  Now you can try these exercises at the end of the chapter: P13.19, P13.23, P13.24.

---

**WORKED EXAMPLE 13.2**  **Towers of Hanoi**

No discussion of recursion would be complete without the "Towers of Hanoi". In this Worked Example, we solve the classic puzzle with an elegant recursive solution.

---

## CHAPTER SUMMARY

**Understand the control flow in a recursive computation.**

- A recursive computation solves a problem by using the solution to the same problem with simpler inputs.
- For a recursion to terminate, there must be special cases for the simplest values.

**Design a recursive solution to a problem.**

**Identify recursive helper methods for solving a problem.**

- Sometimes it is easier to find a recursive solution if you make a slight change to the original problem.

---

➕ Available online in WileyPLUS and at www.wiley.com/college/horstmann.

**Contrast the efficiency of recursive and non-recursive algorithms.**

- Occasionally, a recursive solution runs much slower than its iterative counterpart. However, in most cases, the recursive solution is only slightly slower.
- In many cases, a recursive solution is easier to understand and implement correctly than an iterative solution.

**Review a complex recursion example that cannot be solved with a simple loop.**

- The permutations of a string can be obtained more naturally through recursion than with a loop.

**Recognize the phenomenon of mutual recursion in an expression evaluator.**

- In a mutual recursion, a set of cooperating methods calls each other repeatedly.

**Use backtracking to solve problems that require trying out multiple paths.**

- Backtracking examines partial solutions, abandoning unsuitable ones and returning to consider other candidates.

## REVIEW EXERCISES

- **R13.1** Define the terms
    - **a.** Recursion
    - **b.** Iteration
    - **c.** Infinite recursion
    - **d.** Recursive helper method

- **R13.2** Outline, but do not implement, a recursive solution for finding the smallest value in an array.

- **R13.3** Outline, but do not implement, a recursive solution for sorting an array of numbers. *Hint:* First find the smallest value in the array.

- **R13.4** Outline, but do not implement, a recursive solution for generating all subsets of the set $\{1, 2, \ldots, n\}$.

- **R13.5** Exercise P13.15 shows an iterative way of generating all permutations of the sequence $(0, 1, \ldots, n-1)$. Explain why the algorithm produces the correct result.

- **R13.6** Write a recursive definition of $x^n$, where $n \geq 0$, similar to the recursive definition of the Fibonacci numbers. *Hint:* How do you compute $x^n$ from $x^{n-1}$? How does the recursion terminate?

- **R13.7** Improve upon Exercise R13.6 by computing $x^n$ as $(x^{n/2})^2$ if $n$ is even. Why is this approach significantly faster? *Hint:* Compute $x^{1023}$ and $x^{1024}$ both ways.

- **R13.8** Write a recursive definition of $n! = 1 \times 2 \times \ldots \times n$, similar to the recursive definition of the Fibonacci numbers.

- **R13.9** Find out how often the recursive version of `fib` calls itself. Keep a static variable `fibCount` and increment it once in every call to `fib`. What is the relationship between `fib(n)` and `fibCount`?

- **R13.10** Let moves($n$) be the number of moves required to solve the Towers of Hanoi problem (see Worked Example 13.2). Find a formula that expresses moves($n$) in terms of moves($n-1$). Then show that moves($n$) = $2^n - 1$.

- **R13.11** Trace the expression evaluator program from Section 13.6 with inputs `3 - 4 + 5`, `3 - (4 + 5)`, `(3 - 4) * 5`, and `3 * 4 + 5 * 6`.

## PROGRAMMING EXERCISES

- **P13.1** Given a class `Rectangle` with instance variables `width` and `height`, provide a recursive `getArea` method. Construct a rectangle whose width is one less than the original and call its `getArea` method.

- **P13.2** Given a class `Square` with instance variable `width`, provide a recursive `getArea` method. Construct a square whose width is one less than the original and call its `getArea` method.

- **P13.3** Write a recursive method `String reverse(String text)` that reverses a string. For example, `reverse("Hello!")` returns the string `"!olleH"`. Implement a recursive solution by removing the first character, reversing the remaining text, and combining the two.

- **P13.4** Redo Exercise P13.3 with a recursive helper method that reverses a substring of the message text.

- **P13.5** Implement the `reverse` method of Exercise P13.3 as an iteration.

- **P13.6** Use recursion to implement a method

  ```
  public static boolean find(String text, String str)
  ```

  that tests whether a given text contains a string. For example, `find("Mississippi", "sip")` returns true.

  *Hint:* If the text starts with the string you want to match, then you are done. If not, consider the text that you obtain by removing the first character.

- **P13.7** Use recursion to implement a method

  ```
  public static int indexOf(String text, String str)
  ```

  that returns the starting position of the first substring of the text that matches `str`. Return –1 if `str` is not a substring of the text.

  For example, `s.indexOf("Mississippi", "sip")` returns 6.

  *Hint:* This is a bit trickier than Exercise P13.6, because you must keep track of how far the match is from the beginning of the text. Make that value a parameter variable of a helper method.

- **P13.8** Using recursion, find the largest element in an array.

  *Hint:* Find the largest element in the subset containing all but the last element. Then compare that maximum to the value of the last element.

**P13.9** Using recursion, compute the sum of all values in an array.

**P13.10** Using recursion, compute the area of a polygon. Cut off a triangle and use the fact that a triangle with corners $(x_1, y_1)$, $(x_2, y_2)$, $(x_3, y_3)$ has area

$$\frac{\left|x_1y_2 + x_2y_3 + x_3y_1 - y_1x_2 - y_2x_3 - y_3x_1\right|}{2}$$

**P13.11** The following method was known to the ancient Greeks for computing square roots. Given a value $x > 0$ and a guess $g$ for the square root, a better guess is $(x + g/x) / 2$. Write a recursive helper method `public static squareRootGuess(double x, double g)`. If $g^2$ is approximately equal to $x$, return $g$, otherwise, return `squareRootGuess` with the better guess. Then write a method `public static squareRoot(double x)` that uses the helper method.

**P13.12** Implement a `SubstringGenerator` that generates all substrings of a string. For example, the substrings of the string `"rum"` are the seven strings

```
"r", "ru", "rum", "u", "um", "m", ""
```

*Hint:* First enumerate all substrings that start with the first character. There are $n$ of them if the string has length $n$. Then enumerate the substrings of the string that you obtain by removing the first character.

**P13.13** Implement a `SubsetGenerator` that generates all subsets of the characters of a string. For example, the subsets of the characters of the string `"rum"` are the eight strings

```
"rum", "ru", "rm", "r", "um", "u", "m", ""
```

Note that the subsets don't have to be substrings—for example, `"rm"` isn't a substring of `"rum"`.

**P13.14** In this exercise, you will change the `permutations` method of Section 13.4 (which computed all permutations at once) to a `PermutationIterator` (which computes them one at a time).

```
public class PermutationIterator
{
   public PermutationIterator(String s) { . . . }
   public String nextPermutation() { . . . }
   public boolean hasMorePermutations() { . . . }
}
```

Here is how you would print out all permutations of the string `"eat"`:

```
PermutationIterator iter = new PermutationIterator("eat");
while (iter.hasMorePermutations())
{
   System.out.println(iter.nextPermutation());
}
```

Now we need a way to iterate through the permutations recursively. Consider the string `"eat"`. As before, we'll generate all permutations that start with the letter `'e'`, then those that start with `'a'`, and finally those that start with `'t'`. How do we generate the permutations that start with `'e'`? Make another `PermutationIterator` object (called `tailIterator`) that iterates through the permutations of the substring `"at"`. In the `nextPermutation` method, simply ask `tailIterator` what *its* next permutation is, and then add the `'e'` at the front. However, there is one special case. When the tail generator runs out of permutations, all permutations that start with the current letter have been enumerated. Then

- Increment the current position.
- Compute the tail string that contains all letters except for the current one.
- Make a new permutation iterator for the tail string.

You are done when the current position has reached the end of the string.

■■■ **P13.15** The following class generates all permutations of the numbers $0, 1, 2, \ldots, n-1$, without using recursion.

```java
public class NumberPermutationIterator
{
    private int[] a;

    public NumberPermutationIterator(int n)
    {
        a = new int[n];
        done = false;
        for (int i = 0; i < n; i++) { a[i] = i; }
    }

    public int[] nextPermutation()
    {
        if (a.length <= 1) { return a; }

        for (int i = a.length - 1; i > 0; i--)
        {
            if (a[i - 1] < a[i])
            {
                int j = a.length - 1;
                while (a[i - 1] > a[j]) { j--; }
                swap(i - 1, j);
                reverse(i, a.length - 1);
                return a;
            }
        }
        return a;
    }

    public boolean hasMorePermutations()
    {
        if (a.length <= 1) { return false; }
        for (int i = a.length - 1; i > 0; i--)
        {
            if (a[i - 1] < a[i]) { return true; }
        }
        return false;
    }

    public void swap(int i, int j)
    {
        int temp = a[i];
        a[i] = a[j];
        a[j] = temp;
    }

    public void reverse(int i, int j)
    {
        while (i < j) { swap(i, j); i++; j--; }
```

```
        }
    }
```

The algorithm uses the fact that the set to be permuted consists of distinct numbers. Thus, you cannot use the same algorithm to compute the permutations of the characters in a string. You can, however, use this class to get all permutations of the character positions and then compute a string whose ith character is word.charAt(a[i]). Use this approach to reimplement the PermutationIterator of Exercise P13.14 without recursion.

■■ **P13.16** Extend the expression evaluator in Section 13.6 so that it can handle the % operator as well as a "raise to a power" operator ∧. For example, 2 ∧ 3 should evaluate to 8. As in mathematics, raising to a power should bind more strongly than multiplication: 5 * 2 ∧ 3 is 40.

■■■ **P13.17** Implement an iterator that produces the moves for the Towers of Hanoi puzzle described in Worked Example 13.2. Provide methods hasMoreMoves and nextMove. The nextMove method should yield a string describing the next move. For example, the following code prints all moves needed to move five disks from peg 1 to peg 3:

```
DiskMover mover = new DiskMover(5, 1, 3);
while (mover.hasMoreMoves())
{
    System.out.println(mover.nextMove());
}
```

*Hint:* A disk mover that moves a single disk from one peg to another simply has a nextMove method that returns a string

```
Move disk from peg source to target
```

A disk mover with more than one disk to move must work harder. It needs another DiskMover to help it move the first $d - 1$ disks. The nextMove asks that disk mover for its next move until it is done. Then the nextMove method issues a command to move the $d$th disk. Finally, it constructs another disk mover that generates the remaining moves.

It helps to keep track of the state of the disk mover:

- BEFORE_LARGEST: A helper mover moves the smaller pile to the other peg.
- LARGEST: Move the largest disk from the source to the destination.
- AFTER_LARGEST: The helper mover moves the smaller pile from the other peg to the target.
- DONE: All moves are done.

■■■ **P13.18** *Escaping a Maze.* You are currently located inside a maze. The walls of the maze are indicated by asterisks (*).

```
* *******
*     * *
* ***** *
* * *   *
* * *** *
*   *   *
*** * * *
*     * *
******* *
```

Use the following recursive approach to check whether you can escape from the maze: If you are at an exit, return true. Recursively check whether you can escape from one of the empty neighboring locations without visiting the current location. This method merely tests whether there is a path out of the maze. Extra credit if you can print out a path that leads to an exit.

**■■ P13.19** The backtracking algorithm will work for any problem whose partial solutions can be examined and extended. Provide a `PartialSolution` interface type with methods `examine` and `extend`, a `solve` method that works with this interface type, and a class `EightQueensPartialSolution` that implements the interface.

**■■ P13.20** Using the `PartialSolution` interface and `solve` method from Exercise P13.19, provide a class `MazePartialSolution` for solving the maze escape problem of Exercise P13.18.

**■■■ P13.21** Refine the program for solving the eight queens problem so that rotations and reflections of previously displayed solutions are not shown. Your program should display twelve unique solutions.

**■■■ P13.22** Refine the program for solving the eight queens problem so that the solutions are written to an HTML file, using tables with black and white background for the board and the Unicode character ♕ `'\u2655'` for the white queen.

**■■ P13.23** Generalize the program for solving the eight queens problem to the *n* queens problem. Your program should prompt for the value of *n* and display the solutions.

**■■ P13.24** Using backtracking, write a program that solves summation puzzles in which each letter should be replaced by a digit, such as

> `send + more = money`

Other examples are `base + ball = games` and `kyoto + osaka = tokyo`.

**■■ P13.25** The recursive computation of Fibonacci numbers can be speeded up significantly by keeping track of the values that have already been computed. Provide an implementation of the `fib` method that uses this strategy. Whenever you return a new value, also store it in an auxiliary array. However, before embarking on a computation, consult the array to find whether the result has already been computed. Compare the running time of your improved implementation with that of the original recursive implementation and the loop implementation.

**■■■ Graphics P13.26** *The Koch Snowflake.* A snowflake-like shape is recursively defined as follows. Start with an equilateral triangle:

Next, increase the size by a factor of three and replace each straight line with four line segments:

Repeat the process:

Write a program that draws the iterations of the snowflake shape. Supply a button that, when clicked, produces the next iteration.

## ANSWERS TO SELF-CHECK QUESTIONS

1. Suppose we omit the statement. When computing the area of a triangle with width 1, we compute the area of the triangle with width 0 as 0, and then add 1, to arrive at the correct area.

2. You would compute the smaller area recursively, then return

   ```
   smallerArea + width + width - 1.
   ```

   ```
   [][][][]
   [][][][]
   [][][][]
   [][][][]
   ```

   Of course, it would be simpler to compute the area simply as width * width. The results are identical because

   $$1 + 0 + 2 + 1 + 3 + 2 + \cdots + n + n - 1 =$$
   $$\frac{n(n+1)}{2} + \frac{(n-1)n}{2} = n^2$$

3. There is no provision for stopping the recursion. When a number < 10 isn't 8, then the method should return false and stop.

4. ```
   public static int pow2(int n)
   {
       if (n <= 0) { return 1; } // 2^0 is 1
       else { return 2 * pow2(n - 1); }
   }
   ```

5. mystery(4) calls mystery(3)
   
   mystery(3) calls mystery(2)
   
   mystery(2) calls mystery(1)
   
   mystery(1) calls mystery(0)
   
   mystery(0) returns 0.
   
   mystery(1) returns 0 + 1 * 1 = 1
   
   mystery(2) returns 1 + 2 * 2 = 5
   
   mystery(3) returns 5 + 3 * 3 = 14
   
   mystery(4) returns 14 + 4 * 4 = 30

6. In this problem, *any* decomposition will work fine. We can remove the first or last character and then remove punctuation marks from the remainder. Or we can break the string in two substrings, and remove punctuation marks from each.

7. If the last character is a punctuation mark, then you simply return the shorter string with punctuation marks removed. Otherwise, you reattach the last character to that result and return it.

8. The simplest input is the empty string. It contains no punctuation marks, so you simply return it.

9. If str is empty, return str.
   last = last letter in str
   simplerResult = removePunctuation(
           str with last letter removed)
   If (last is a punctuation mark)
       Return simplerResult.
   Else
       Return simplerResult + last.

10. No—the second one could be given a different name such as substringIsPalindrome.

11. When start >= end, that is, when the investigated string is either empty or has length 1.

12. A sumHelper(int[] a, int start, int size). The method calls sumHelper(a, start + 1, size).

13. Call sum(a, size - 1) and add the *last* element, a[size - 1].

14. The loop is slightly faster. It is even faster to simply compute width * (width + 1) / 2.

15. No, the recursive solution is about as efficient as the iterative approach. Both require $n - 1$ multiplications to compute $n!$.

16. The recursive algorithm performs about as well as the loop. Unlike the recursive Fibonacci algorithm, this algorithm doesn't call itself again on the same input. For example, the sum of the array 1 4 9 16 25 36 49 64 is computed as the sum of 1 4 9 16 and 25 36 49 64, then as the sums of 1 4, 9 16, 25 36, and 49 64, which can be computed directly.

17. They are b followed by the six permutations of eat, e followed by the six permutations of
   ```

bat, a followed by the six permutations of bet, and t followed by the six permutations of bea.

**18.** Simply change if (word.length() == 0) to if (word.length() <= 1), because a word with a single letter is also its sole permutation.

**19.** An iterative solution would have a loop whose body computes the next permutation from the previous ones. But there is no obvious mechanism for getting the next permutation. For example, if you already found permutations eat, eta, and aet, it is not clear how you use that information to get the next permutation. Actually, there is an ingenious mechanism for doing just that, but it is far from obvious—see Exercise P13.15.

**20.** Factors are combined by multiplicative operators (* and /); terms are combined by additive operators (+, -). We need both so that multiplication can bind more strongly than addition.

**21.** To handle parenthesized expressions, such as 2+3*(4+5). The subexpression 4+5 is handled by a recursive call to getExpressionValue.

**22.** The Integer.parseInt call in getFactorValue throws an exception when it is given the string ")".

**23.** We want to check whether any queen[i] attacks any queen[j], but attacking is symmetric. That is, we can choose to compare only those for which i < j (or, alternatively, those for which i > j). We don't want to call the attacks method when i equals j; it would return true.

**24.** One solution:

**25.** Two solutions: The one from Self Check 24, and its mirror image.

# SORTING AND SEARCHING

To study several sorting and
searching algorithms

To appreciate that algorithms for the same
task can differ widely in performance

To understand the big-Oh notation

To estimate and compare the performance of algorithms

To write code to measure the running time of a program

One of the most common tasks in data processing is sorting. For example, an array of employees often needs to be displayed in alphabetical order or sorted by salary. In this chapter, you will learn several sorting methods as well as techniques for comparing their performance. These techniques are useful not just for sorting algorithms, but also for analyzing other algorithms.

Once an array of elements is sorted, one can rapidly locate individual elements. You will study the *binary search* algorithm that carries out this fast lookup.

# 14.1 Selection Sort

In this section, we show you the first of several sorting algorithms. A *sorting algorithm* rearranges the elements of a collection so that they are stored in sorted order. To keep the examples simple, we will discuss how to sort an array of integers before going on to sorting strings or more complex data. Consider the following array a:

[0] [1] [2] [3] [4]

| 11 | 9 | 17 | 5 | 12 |

The selection sort algorithm sorts an array by repeatedly finding the smallest element of the unsorted tail region and moving it to the front.

An obvious first step is to find the smallest element. In this case the smallest element is 5, stored in a[3]. We should move the 5 to the beginning of the array. Of course, there is already an element stored in a[0], namely 11. Therefore we cannot simply move a[3] into a[0] without moving the 11 somewhere else. We don't yet know where the 11 should end up, but we know for certain that it should not be in a[0]. We simply get it out of the way by *swapping* it with a[3]:

[0] [1] [2] [3] [4]

| 5 | 9 | 17 | 11 | 12 |

Now the first element is in the correct place. The darker color in the figure indicates the portion of the array that is already sorted.

*In selection sort, pick the smallest element and swap it with the first one. Pick the smallest element of the remaining ones and swap it with the next one, and so on.*

Next we take the minimum of the remaining entries a[1] . . . a[4]. That minimum value, 9, is already in the correct place. We don't need to do anything in this case and can simply extend the sorted area by one to the right:

Repeat the process. The minimum value of the unsorted region is 11, which needs to be swapped with the first value of the unsorted region, 17:

Now the unsorted region is only two elements long, but we keep to the same successful strategy. The minimum value is 12, and we swap it with the first value, 17:

That leaves us with an unprocessed region of length 1, but of course a region of length 1 is always sorted. We are done.

Let's program this algorithm. For this program, as well as the other programs in this chapter, we will use a utility method to generate an array with random entries. We place it into a class `ArrayUtil` so that we don't have to repeat the code in every example. To show the array, we call the static `toString` method of the `Arrays` class in the Java library and print the resulting string (see Section 6.3.4). We also add a method for swapping elements to the `ArrayUtil` class. (See Section 6.3.8 for details about swapping array elements.)

This algorithm will sort any array of integers. If speed were not an issue, or if there simply were no better sorting method available, we could stop the discussion of sorting right here. As the next section shows, however, this algorithm, while entirely correct, shows disappointing performance when run on a large data set.

Special Topic 14.2 discusses insertion sort, another simple sorting algorithm.

### section_1/SelectionSorter.java

```
 1   /**
 2       The sort method of this class sorts an array, using the selection
 3       sort algorithm.
 4   */
 5   public class SelectionSorter
 6   {
 7       /**
 8           Sorts an array, using selection sort.
 9           @param a the array to sort
10       */
11       public static void sort(int[] a)
12       {
13           for (int i = 0; i < a.length - 1; i++)
14           {
15               int minPos = minimumPosition(a, i);
16               ArrayUtil.swap(a, minPos, i);
17           }
18       }
```

```
19
20      /**
21         Finds the smallest element in a tail range of the array.
22         @param a the array to sort
23         @param from the first position in a to compare
24         @return the position of the smallest element in the
25         range a[from] . . . a[a.length - 1]
26      */
27      private static int minimumPosition(int[] a, int from)
28      {
29         int minPos = from;
30         for (int i = from + 1; i < a.length; i++)
31         {
32            if (a[i] < a[minPos]) { minPos = i; }
33         }
34         return minPos;
35      }
36   }
```

### section_1/SelectionSortDemo.java

```
1    import java.util.Arrays;
2
3    /**
4       This program demonstrates the selection sort algorithm by
5       sorting an array that is filled with random numbers.
6    */
7    public class SelectionSortDemo
8    {
9       public static void main(String[] args)
10      {
11         int[] a = ArrayUtil.randomIntArray(20, 100);
12         System.out.println(Arrays.toString(a));
13
14         SelectionSorter.sort(a);
15
16         System.out.println(Arrays.toString(a));
17      }
18   }
```

### section_1/ArrayUtil.java

```
1    import java.util.Random;
2
3    /**
4       This class contains utility methods for array manipulation.
5    */
6    public class ArrayUtil
7    {
8       private static Random generator = new Random();
9
10      /**
11         Creates an array filled with random values.
12         @param length the length of the array
13         @param n the number of possible random values
14         @return an array filled with length numbers between
15         0 and n - 1
16      */
17      public static int[] randomIntArray(int length, int n)
18      {
```

```
19        int[] a = new int[length];
20        for (int i = 0; i < a.length; i++)
21        {
22            a[i] = generator.nextInt(n);
23        }
24
25        return a;
26    }
27
28    /**
29        Swaps two entries of an array.
30        @param a the array
31        @param i the first position to swap
32        @param j the second position to swap
33    */
34    public static void swap(int[] a, int i, int j)
35    {
36        int temp = a[i];
37        a[i] = a[j];
38        a[j] = temp;
39    }
40 }
```

**Program Run**

```
[65, 46, 14, 52, 38, 2, 96, 39, 14, 33, 13, 4, 24, 99, 89, 77, 73, 87, 36, 81]
[2, 4, 13, 14, 14, 24, 33, 36, 38, 39, 46, 52, 65, 73, 77, 81, 87, 89, 96, 99]
```

**SELF CHECK**

1. Why do we need the temp variable in the swap method? What would happen if you simply assigned a[i] to a[j] and a[j] to a[i]?
2. What steps does the selection sort algorithm go through to sort the sequence 6 5 4 3 2 1?
3. How can you change the selection sort algorithm so that it sorts the elements in descending order (that is, with the largest element at the beginning of the array)?
4. Suppose we modified the selection sort algorithm to start at the end of the array, working toward the beginning. In each step, the current position is swapped with the minimum. What is the result of this modification?

**Practice It**   Now you can try these exercises at the end of the chapter: R14.2, R14.10, P14.1, P14.2.

# 14.2  Profiling the Selection Sort Algorithm

To measure the performance of a program, you could simply run it and use a stopwatch to measure how long it takes. However, most of our programs run very quickly, and it is not easy to time them accurately in this way. Furthermore, when a program takes a noticeable time to run, a certain amount of that time may simply be used for loading the program from disk into memory and displaying the result (for which we should not penalize it).

In order to measure the running time of an algorithm more accurately, we will create a StopWatch class. This class works like a real stopwatch. You can start it, stop it, and read out the elapsed time. The class uses the `System.currentTimeMillis` method, which returns the milliseconds that have elapsed since midnight at the start of January 1, 1970. Of course, you don't care about the absolute number of seconds since this historical moment, but the *difference* of two such counts gives us the number of milliseconds in a given time interval.

Here is the code for the `StopWatch` class:

**section_2/StopWatch.java**

```
1   /**
2       A stopwatch accumulates time when it is running. You can
3       repeatedly start and stop the stopwatch. You can use a
4       stopwatch to measure the running time of a program.
5   */
6   public class StopWatch
7   {
8       private long elapsedTime;
9       private long startTime;
10      private boolean isRunning;
11
12      /**
13          Constructs a stopwatch that is in the stopped state
14          and has no time accumulated.
15      */
16      public StopWatch()
17      {
18          reset();
19      }
20
21      /**
22          Starts the stopwatch. Time starts accumulating now.
23      */
24      public void start()
25      {
26          if (isRunning) { return; }
27          isRunning = true;
28          startTime = System.currentTimeMillis();
29      }
30
31      /**
32          Stops the stopwatch. Time stops accumulating and is
33          is added to the elapsed time.
34      */
35      public void stop()
36      {
37          if (!isRunning) { return; }
38          isRunning = false;
39          long endTime = System.currentTimeMillis();
40          elapsedTime = elapsedTime + endTime - startTime;
41      }
42
43      /**
44          Returns the total elapsed time.
45          @return the total elapsed time
46      */
47      public long getElapsedTime()
48      {
49          if (isRunning)
50          {
```

```
51              long endTime = System.currentTimeMillis();
52              return elapsedTime + endTime - startTime;
53          }
54          else
55          {
56              return elapsedTime;
57          }
58      }
59
60      /**
61          Stops the watch and resets the elapsed time to 0.
62      */
63      public void reset()
64      {
65          elapsedTime = 0;
66          isRunning = false;
67      }
68  }
```

Here is how to use the stopwatch to measure the sorting algorithm's performance:

### section_2/SelectionSortTimer.java

```
1  import java.util.Scanner;
2
3  /**
4      This program measures how long it takes to sort an
5      array of a user-specified size with the selection
6      sort algorithm.
7  */
8  public class SelectionSortTimer
9  {
10     public static void main(String[] args)
11     {
12         Scanner in = new Scanner(System.in);
13         System.out.print("Enter array size: ");
14         int n = in.nextInt();
15
16         // Construct random array
17
18         int[] a = ArrayUtil.randomIntArray(n, 100);
19
20         // Use stopwatch to time selection sort
21
22         StopWatch timer = new StopWatch();
23
24         timer.start();
25         SelectionSorter.sort(a);
26         timer.stop();
27
28         System.out.println("Elapsed time: "
29                 + timer.getElapsedTime() + " milliseconds");
30     }
31  }
```

### Program Run

```
Enter array size: 50000
Elapsed time: 13321 milliseconds
```

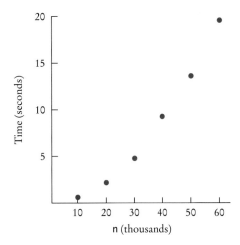

| n | Milliseconds |
|---|---|
| 10,000 | 786 |
| 20,000 | 2,148 |
| 30,000 | 4,796 |
| 40,000 | 9,192 |
| 50,000 | 13,321 |
| 60,000 | 19,299 |

**Figure 1**   Time Taken by Selection Sort

To measure the running time of a method, get the current time immediately before and after the method call.

By starting to measure the time just before sorting, and stopping the stopwatch just after, you get the time required for the sorting process, without counting the time for input and output.

The table in Figure 1 shows the results of some sample runs. These measurements were obtained with an Intel processor with a clock speed of 2 GHz, running Java 6 on the Linux operating system. On another computer the actual numbers will look different, but the relationship between the numbers will be the same.

The graph in Figure 1 shows a plot of the measurements. As you can see, when you double the size of the data set, it takes about four times as long to sort it.

**SELF CHECK**

**5.** Approximately how many seconds would it take to sort a data set of 80,000 values?
**6.** Look at the graph in Figure 1. What mathematical shape does it resemble?

**Practice It**   Now you can try these exercises at the end of the chapter: P14.3, P14.6.

# 14.3 Analyzing the Performance of the Selection Sort Algorithm

Let us count the number of operations that the program must carry out to sort an array with the selection sort algorithm. We don't actually know how many machine operations are generated for each Java instruction, or which of those instructions are more time-consuming than others, but we can make a simplification. We will simply count how often an array element is *visited*. Each visit requires about the same amount of work by other operations, such as incrementing subscripts and comparing values.

Let $n$ be the size of the array. First, we must find the smallest of $n$ numbers. To achieve that, we must visit $n$ array elements. Then we swap the elements, which takes two visits. (You may argue that there is a certain probability that we don't need to swap the values. That is true, and one can refine the computation to reflect that observation. As we will soon see, doing so would not affect the overall conclusion.) In the next step, we need to visit only $n - 1$ elements to find the minimum. In the following step, $n - 2$ elements are visited to find the minimum. The last step visits two elements to find the minimum. Each step requires two visits to swap the elements. Therefore, the total number of visits is

$$n + 2 + (n - 1) + 2 + \cdots + 2 + 2 = n + (n - 1) + \cdots + 2 + (n - 1) \cdot 2$$
$$= 2 + \cdots + (n - 1) + n + (n - 1) \cdot 2$$
$$= \frac{n(n + 1)}{2} - 1 + (n - 1) \cdot 2$$

because

$$1 + 2 + \cdots + (n - 1) + n = \frac{n(n + 1)}{2}$$

After multiplying out and collecting terms of $n$, we find that the number of visits is

$$\tfrac{1}{2}n^2 + \tfrac{5}{2}n - 3$$

We obtain a quadratic equation in $n$. That explains why the graph of Figure 1 looks approximately like a parabola.

Now simplify the analysis further. When you plug in a large value for $n$ (for example, 1,000 or 2,000), then $\frac{1}{2}n^2$ is 500,000 or 2,000,000. The lower term, $\frac{5}{2}n - 3$, doesn't contribute much at all; it is only 2,497 or 4,997, a drop in the bucket compared to the hundreds of thousands or even millions of comparisons specified by the $\frac{1}{2}n^2$ term. We will just ignore these lower-level terms. Next, we will ignore the constant factor $\frac{1}{2}$. We are not interested in the actual count of visits for a single $n$. We want to compare the ratios of counts for different values of $n$. For example, we can say that sorting an array of 2,000 numbers requires four times as many visits as sorting an array of 1,000 numbers:

$$\frac{\left(\frac{1}{2} \cdot 2000^2\right)}{\left(\frac{1}{2} \cdot 1000^2\right)} = 4$$

The factor $\frac{1}{2}$ cancels out in comparisons of this kind. We will simply say, "The number of visits is of order $n^2$". That way, we can easily see that the number of comparisons increases fourfold when the size of the array doubles: $(2n)^2 = 4n^2$.

To indicate that the number of visits is of order $n^2$, computer scientists often use **big-Oh notation**: The number of visits is $O(n^2)$. This is a convenient shorthand. (See Special Topic 14.1 for a formal definition.)

To turn a polynomial expression such as

$$\tfrac{1}{2}n^2 + \tfrac{5}{2}n - 3$$

into big-Oh notation, simply locate the fastest-growing term, $n^2$, and ignore its constant coefficient, no matter how large or small it may be.

We observed before that the actual number of machine operations, and the actual amount of time that the computer spends on them, is approximately proportional to the number of element visits. Maybe there are about 10 machine operations

Computer scientists use the big-Oh notation to describe the growth rate of a function.

(increments, comparisons, memory loads, and stores) for every element visit. The number of machine operations is then approximately $10 \times \frac{1}{2}n^2$. As before, we aren't interested in the coefficient, so we can say that the number of machine operations, and hence the time spent on the sorting, is of the order $n^2$ or $O(n^2)$.

The sad fact remains that doubling the size of the array causes a fourfold increase in the time required for sorting it with selection sort. When the size of the array increases by a factor of 100, the sorting time increases by a factor of 10,000. To sort an array of a million entries (for example, to create a telephone directory), takes 10,000 times as long as sorting 10,000 entries. If 10,000 entries can be sorted in about 3/4 of a second (as in our example), then sorting one million entries requires well over two hours. We will see in the next section how one can dramatically improve the performance of the sorting process by choosing a more sophisticated algorithm.

> Selection sort is an $O(n^2)$ algorithm. Doubling the data set means a fourfold increase in processing time.

**SELF CHECK**

7. If you increase the size of a data set tenfold, how much longer does it take to sort it with the selection sort algorithm?

8. How large does $n$ need to be so that $\frac{1}{2}n^2$ is bigger than $\frac{5}{2}n - 3$?

9. Section 6.3.6 has two algorithms for removing an element from an array of length $n$. How many array visits does each algorithm require on average?

10. Describe the number of array visits in Self Check 9 using the big-Oh notation.

11. What is the big-Oh running time of checking whether an array is already sorted?

12. Consider this algorithm for sorting an array. Set $k$ to the length of the array. Find the maximum of the first $k$ elements. Remove it, using the second algorithm of Section 6.3.6. Decrement $k$ and place the removed element into the $k$th position. Stop if $k$ is 1. What is the algorithm's running time in big-Oh notation?

**Practice It**    Now you can try these exercises at the end of the chapter: R14.4, R14.6, R14.8.

---

> Special Topic 14.1

### Oh, Omega, and Theta

We have used the big-Oh notation somewhat casually in this chapter to describe the growth behavior of a function. Here is the formal definition of the big-Oh notation: Suppose we have a function $T(n)$. Usually, it represents the processing time of an algorithm for a given input of size n. But it could be any function. Also, suppose that we have another function $f(n)$. It is usually chosen to be a simple function, such as $f(n) = n^k$ or $f(n) = \log(n)$, but it too can be any function. We write

$$T(n) = O(f(n))$$

if $T(n)$ grows at a rate that is bounded by $f(n)$. More formally, we require that for all $n$ larger than some threshold, the ratio $T(n)/f(n) \le C$ for some constant value $C$.

If $T(n)$ is a polynomial of degree $k$ in $n$, then one can show that $T(n) = O(n^k)$. Later in this chapter, we will encounter functions that are $O(\log(n))$ or $O(n\log(n))$. Some algorithms take much more time. For example, one way of sorting a sequence is to compute all of its permutations, until you find one that is in increasing order. Such an algorithm takes $O(n!)$ time, which is very bad indeed.

Table 1 shows common big-Oh expressions, sorted by increasing growth.

Strictly speaking, $T(n) = O(f(n))$ means that $T$ grows no faster than $f$. But it is permissible for $T$ to grow much more slowly. Thus, it is technically correct to state that $T(n) = n^2 + 5n - 3$ is $O(n^3)$ or even $O(n^{10})$.

| Table 1  Common Big-Oh Growth Rates ||
| Big-Oh Expression | Name |
| --- | --- |
| $O(1)$ | Constant |
| $O(\log(n))$ | Logarithmic |
| $O(n)$ | Linear |
| $O(n \log(n))$ | Log-linear |
| $O(n^2)$ | Quadratic |
| $O(n^3)$ | Cubic |
| $O(2^n)$ | Exponential |
| $O(n!)$ | Factorial |

Computer scientists have invented additional notation to describe the growth behavior of functions more accurately. The expression

$$T(n) = \Omega(f(n))$$

means that $T$ grows at least as fast as $f$, or, formally, that for all $n$ larger than some threshold, the ratio $T(n)/f(n) \geq C$ for some constant value $C$. (The $\Omega$ symbol is the capital Greek letter omega.) For example, $T(n) = n^2 + 5n - 3$ is $\Omega(n^2)$ or even $\Omega(n)$.

The expression

$$T(n) = \Theta(f(n))$$

means that $T$ and $f$ grow at the same rate — that is, both $T(n) = O(f(n))$ and $T(n) = \Omega(f(n))$ hold. (The $\Theta$ symbol is the capital Greek letter theta.)

The $\Theta$ notation gives the most precise description of growth behavior. For example, $T(n) = n^2 + 5n - 3$ is $\Theta(n^2)$ but not $\Theta(n)$ or $\Theta(n^3)$.

The notations are very important for the precise analysis of algorithms. However, in casual conversation it is common to stick with big-Oh, while still giving an estimate as good as one can make.

Special Topic 14.2

### Insertion Sort

Insertion sort is another simple sorting algorithm. In this algorithm, we assume that the initial sequence

```
a[0] a[1] . . . a[k]
```

of an array is already sorted. (When the algorithm starts, we set k to 0.) We enlarge the initial sequence by inserting the next array element, a[k + 1], at the proper location. When we reach the end of the array, the sorting process is complete.

For example, suppose we start with the array

| 11 | 9 | 16 | 5 | 7 |

Of course, the initial sequence of length 1 is already sorted. We now add a[1], which has the value 9. The element needs to be inserted before the element 11. The result is

| 9 | 11 | 16 | 5 | 7 |

Next, we add a[2], which has the value 16. This element does not have to be moved.

| 9 | 11 | 16 | 5 | 7 |

We repeat the process, inserting a[3] or 5 at the very beginning of the initial sequence.

| 5 | 9 | 11 | 16 | 7 |

Finally, a[4] or 7 is inserted in its correct position, and the sorting is completed.

The following class implements the insertion sort algorithm:

```java
public class InsertionSorter
{
   /**
      Sorts an array, using insertion sort.
      @param a the array to sort
   */
   public static void sort(int[] a)
   {
      for (int i = 1; i < a.length; i++)
      {
         int next = a[i];
         // Move all larger elements up
         int j = i;
         while (j > 0 && a[j - 1] > next)
         {
            a[j] = a[j - 1];
            j--;
         }
         // Insert the element
         a[j] = next;
      }
   }
}
```

How efficient is this algorithm? Let $n$ denote the size of the array. We carry out $n - 1$ iterations. In the $k$th iteration, we have a sequence of $k$ elements that is already sorted, and we need to insert a new element into the sequence. For each insertion, we need to visit the elements of the initial sequence until we have found the location in which the new element can be inserted. Then we need to move up the remaining elements of the sequence. Thus, $k + 1$ array elements are visited. Therefore, the total number of visits is

$$2 + 3 + \cdots + n = \frac{n(n + 1)}{2} - 1$$

**ONLINE EXAMPLE**

A program to illustrate sorting with insertion sort.

We conclude that insertion sort is an $O(n^2)$ algorithm, on the same order of efficiency as selection sort.

Insertion sort has a desirable property: Its performance is $O(n)$ if the array is already sorted—see Exercise R14.17. This is a useful property in practical applications, in which data sets are often partially sorted.

> Insertion sort is an $O(n^2)$ algorithm.

*Insertion sort is the method that many people use to sort playing cards. Pick up one card at a time and insert it so that the cards stay sorted.*

# 14.4 Merge Sort

In this section, you will learn about the merge sort algorithm, a much more efficient algorithm than selection sort. The basic idea behind merge sort is very simple.

Suppose we have an array of 10 integers. Let us engage in a bit of wishful thinking and hope that the first half of the array is already perfectly sorted, and the second half is too, like this:

| 5 | 9 | 10 | 12 | 17 | 1 | 8 | 11 | 20 | 32 |

Now it is simple to *merge* the two sorted arrays into one sorted array, by taking a new element from either the first or the second subarray, and choosing the smaller of the elements each time:

In fact, you may have performed this merging before if you and a friend had to sort a pile of papers. You and the friend split the pile in half, each of you sorted your half, and then you merged the results together.

That is all well and good, but it doesn't seem to solve the problem for the computer. It still must sort the first and second halves of the array, because it can't very well ask a few buddies to pitch in. As it turns out, though, if the computer keeps dividing the array into smaller and smaller subarrays, sorting each half and merging them back together, it carries out dramatically fewer steps than the selection sort requires.

Let's write a `MergeSorter` class that implements this idea. When the `MergeSorter` sorts an array, it makes two arrays, each half the size of the original, and sorts them recursively. Then it merges the two sorted arrays together:

*In merge sort, one sorts each half, then merges the sorted halves.*

```java
public static void sort(int[] a)
{
    if (a.length <= 1) { return; }
    int[] first = new int[a.length / 2];
    int[] second = new int[a.length - first.length];
    // Copy the first half of a into first, the second half into second
    . . .
    sort(first);
    sort(second);
    merge(first, second, a);
}
```

The merge method is tedious but quite straightforward. You will find it in the code that follows.

**section_4/MergeSorter.java**

```
1   /**
2       The sort method of this class sorts an array, using the merge
3       sort algorithm.
4   */
5   public class MergeSorter
6   {
7       /**
8           Sorts an array, using merge sort.
9           @param a the array to sort
10      */
11      public static void sort(int[] a)
12      {
13          if (a.length <= 1) { return; }
14          int[] first = new int[a.length / 2];
15          int[] second = new int[a.length - first.length];
16          // Copy the first half of a into first, the second half into second
17          for (int i = 0; i < first.length; i++)
18          {
19              first[i] = a[i];
20          }
21          for (int i = 0; i < second.length; i++)
22          {
23              second[i] = a[first.length + i];
24          }
25          sort(first);
26          sort(second);
27          merge(first, second, a);
28      }
29
30      /**
31          Merges two sorted arrays into an array.
32          @param first the first sorted array
33          @param second the second sorted array
34          @param a the array into which to merge first and second
35      */
36      private static void merge(int[] first, int[] second, int[] a)
37      {
38          int iFirst = 0;   // Next element to consider in the first array
39          int iSecond = 0;  // Next element to consider in the second array
40          int j = 0;   // Next open position in a
41
42          // As long as neither iFirst nor iSecond past the end, move
43          // the smaller element into a
44          while (iFirst < first.length && iSecond < second.length)
45          {
46              if (first[iFirst] < second[iSecond])
47              {
48                  a[j] = first[iFirst];
49                  iFirst++;
50              }
51              else
52              {
53                  a[j] = second[iSecond];
54                  iSecond++;
```

```
55            }
56            j++;
57        }
58
59        // Note that only one of the two loops below copies entries
60        // Copy any remaining entries of the first array
61        while (iFirst < first.length)
62        {
63            a[j] = first[iFirst];
64            iFirst++; j++;
65        }
66        // Copy any remaining entries of the second half
67        while (iSecond < second.length)
68        {
69            a[j] = second[iSecond];
70            iSecond++; j++;
71        }
72    }
73 }
```

### section_4/MergeSortDemo.java

```java
1  import java.util.Arrays;
2
3  /**
4     This program demonstrates the merge sort algorithm by
5     sorting an array that is filled with random numbers.
6  */
7  public class MergeSortDemo
8  {
9     public static void main(String[] args)
10    {
11        int[] a = ArrayUtil.randomIntArray(20, 100);
12        System.out.println(Arrays.toString(a));
13
14        MergeSorter.sort(a);
15
16        System.out.println(Arrays.toString(a));
17    }
18 }
```

### Program Run

```
[8, 81, 48, 53, 46, 70, 98, 42, 27, 76, 33, 24, 2, 76, 62, 89, 90, 5, 13, 21]
[2, 5, 8, 13, 21, 24, 27, 33, 42, 46, 48, 53, 62, 70, 76, 76, 81, 89, 90, 98]
```

**SELF CHECK**

13. Why does only one of the two `while` loops at the end of the `merge` method do any work?

14. Manually run the merge sort algorithm on the array 8 7 6 5 4 3 2 1.

15. The merge sort algorithm processes an array by recursively processing two halves. Describe a similar recursive algorithm for computing the sum of all elements in an array.

**Practice It**  Now you can try these exercises at the end of the chapter: R14.11, P14.4, P14.16.

# 14.5 Analyzing the Merge Sort Algorithm

The merge sort algorithm looks a lot more complicated than the selection sort algorithm, and it appears that it may well take much longer to carry out these repeated subdivisions. However, the timing results for merge sort look much better than those for selection sort.

Figure 2 shows a table and a graph comparing both sets of perfor0mance data. As you can see, merge sort is a tremendous improvement. To understand why, let us estimate the number of array element visits that are required to sort an array with the merge sort algorithm. First, let us tackle the merge process that happens after the first and second halves have been sorted.

Each step in the merge process adds one more element to a. That element may come from first or second, and in most cases the elements from the two halves must be compared to see which one to take. We'll count that as 3 visits (one for a and one each for first and second) per element, or $3n$ visits total, where $n$ denotes the length of a. Moreover, at the beginning, we had to copy from a to first and second, yielding another $2n$ visits, for a total of $5n$.

If we let $T(n)$ denote the number of visits required to sort a range of $n$ elements through the merge sort process, then we obtain

$$T(n) = T\left(\frac{n}{2}\right) + T\left(\frac{n}{2}\right) + 5n$$

because sorting each half takes $T(n/2)$ visits. Actually, if $n$ is not even, then we have one subarray of size $(n - 1)/2$ and one of size $(n + 1)/2$. Although it turns out that this detail does not affect the outcome of the computation, we will nevertheless assume for now that $n$ is a power of 2, say $n = 2^m$. That way, all subarrays can be evenly divided into two parts.

Unfortunately, the formula

$$T(n) = 2T\left(\frac{n}{2}\right) + 5n$$

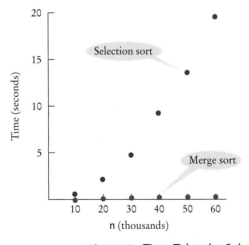

| n | Merge Sort (milliseconds) | Selection Sort (milliseconds) |
|---|---|---|
| 10,000 | 40 | 786 |
| 20,000 | 73 | 2,148 |
| 30,000 | 134 | 4,796 |
| 40,000 | 170 | 9,192 |
| 50,000 | 192 | 13,321 |
| 60,000 | 205 | 19,299 |

**Figure 2** Time Taken by Selection Sort

does not clearly tell us the relationship between $n$ and $T(n)$. To understand the relationship, let us evaluate $T(n/2)$, using the same formula:

$$T\left(\frac{n}{2}\right) = 2T\left(\frac{n}{4}\right) + 5\frac{n}{2}$$

Therefore

$$T(n) = 2 \times 2T\left(\frac{n}{4}\right) + 5n + 5n$$

Let us do that again:

$$T\left(\frac{n}{4}\right) = 2T\left(\frac{n}{8}\right) + 5\frac{n}{4}$$

hence

$$T(n) = 2 \times 2 \times 2T\left(\frac{n}{8}\right) + 5n + 5n + 5n$$

This generalizes from 2, 4, 8, to arbitrary powers of 2:

$$T(n) = 2^k T\left(\frac{n}{2^k}\right) + 5nk$$

Recall that we assume that $n = 2^m$; hence, for $k = m$,

$$T(n) = 2^m T\left(\frac{n}{2^m}\right) + 5nm$$
$$= nT(1) + 5nm$$
$$= n + 5n\log_2(n)$$

Because $n = 2^m$, we have $m = \log_2(n)$.

To establish the growth order, we drop the lower-order term $n$ and are left with $5n\log_2(n)$. We drop the constant factor 5. It is also customary to drop the base of the logarithm, because all logarithms are related by a constant factor. For example,

$$\log_2(x) = \log_{10}(x)/\log_{10}(2) \approx \log_{10}(x) \times 3.32193$$

Hence we say that merge sort is an $O(n\log(n))$ algorithm.

Is the $O(n\log(n))$ merge sort algorithm better than the $O(n^2)$ selection sort algorithm? You bet it is. Recall that it took $100^2 = 10,000$ times as long to sort a million records as it took to sort 10,000 records with the $O(n^2)$ algorithm. With the $O(n\log(n))$ algorithm, the ratio is

> Merge sort is an $O(n \log(n))$ algorithm. The $n \log(n)$ function grows much more slowly than $n^2$.

$$\frac{1,000,000\log(1,000,000)}{10,000\log(10,000)} = 100\left(\frac{6}{4}\right) = 150$$

Suppose for the moment that merge sort takes the same time as selection sort to sort an array of 10,000 integers, that is, 3/4 of a second on the test machine. (Actually, it is much faster than that.) Then it would take about 0.75 × 150 seconds, or under two minutes, to sort a million integers. Contrast that with selection sort, which would take over two hours for the same task. As you can see, even if it takes you several hours to learn about a better algorithm, that can be time well spent.

In this chapter we have barely begun to scratch the surface of this interesting topic. There are many sorting algorithms, some with even better performance than merge sort, and the analysis of these algorithms can be quite challenging. These important issues are often revisited in later computer science courses.

**SELF CHECK**

16. Given the timing data for the merge sort algorithm in the table at the beginning of this section, how long would it take to sort an array of 100,000 values?

17. If you double the size of an array, how much longer will the merge sort algorithm take to sort the new array?

**Practice It**  Now you can try these exercises at the end of the chapter: R14.7, R14.14, R14.16.

---

**Special Topic 14.3**

### The Quicksort Algorithm

Quicksort is a commonly used algorithm that has the advantage over merge sort that no temporary arrays are required to sort and merge the partial results.

The quicksort algorithm, like merge sort, is based on the strategy of divide and conquer. To sort a range a[from] . . . a[to] of the array a, first rearrange the elements in the range so that no element in the range a[from] . . . a[p] is larger than any element in the range a[p + 1] . . . a[to]. This step is called *partitioning* the range.

For example, suppose we start with a range

> 5 3 2 6 4 1 7

Here is a partitioning of the range. Note that the partitions aren't yet sorted.

> 3 3 2 1 4 | 6 5 7

You'll see later how to obtain such a partition. In the next step, sort each partition, by recursively applying the same algorithm on the two partitions. That sorts the entire range, because the largest element in the first partition is at most as large as the smallest element in the second partition.

> 1 2 3 3 4 | 5 6 7

Quicksort is implemented recursively as follows:

```java
public static void sort(int[] a, int from, int to)
{
   if (from >= to) { return; }
   int p = partition(a, from, to);
   sort(a, from, p);
   sort(a, p + 1, to);
}
```

Let us return to the problem of partitioning a range. Pick an element from the range and call it the *pivot*. There are several variations of the quicksort algorithm. In the simplest one, we'll pick the first element of the range, a[from], as the pivot.

Now form two regions a[from] . . . a[i], consisting of values at most as large as the pivot and a[j] . . . a[to], consisting of values at least as large as the pivot. The region a[i + 1] . . . a[j - 1] consists of values that haven't been analyzed yet. (See the figure below.) At the beginning, both the left and right areas are empty; that is, i = from - 1 and j = to + 1.

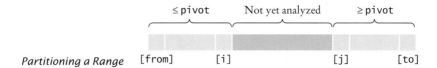

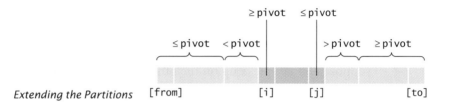

*Partitioning a Range*

Then keep incrementing i while a[i] < pivot and keep decrementing j while a[j] > pivot. The figure below shows i and j when that process stops.

*Extending the Partitions*

Now swap the values in positions i and j, increasing both areas once more. Keep going while i < j. Here is the code for the partition method:

```
private static int partition(int[] a, int from, int to)
{
   int pivot = a[from];
   int i = from - 1;
   int j = to + 1;
   while (i < j)
   {
      i++; while (a[i] < pivot) { i++; }
      j--; while (a[j] > pivot) { j--; }
      if (i < j) { ArrayUtil.swap(a, i, j); }
   }
   return j;
}
```

On average, the quicksort algorithm is an $O(n \log(n))$ algorithm. There is just one unfortunate aspect to the quicksort algorithm. Its *worst-case* run-time behavior is $O(n^2)$. Moreover, if the pivot element is chosen as the first element of the region, that worst-case behavior occurs when the input set is already sorted—a common situation in practice. By selecting the pivot element more cleverly, we can make it extremely unlikely for the worst-case behavior to occur. Such "tuned" quicksort algorithms are commonly used, because their performance is generally excellent. For example, the sort method in the Arrays class uses a quicksort algorithm.

Another improvement that is commonly made in practice is to switch to insertion sort when the array is short, because the total number of operations using insertion sort is lower for short arrays. The Java library makes that switch if the array length is less than seven.

**ONLINE EXAMPLE**

⊕ A program to demonstrate the quicksort algorithm.

*In quicksort, one partitions the elements into two groups, holding the smaller and larger elements. Then one sorts each group.*

# 14.6 Searching

Searching for an element in an array is an extremely common task. As with sorting, the right choice of algorithms can make a big difference.

## 14.6.1 Linear Search

Suppose you need to find your friend's telephone number. You look up the friend's name in the telephone book, and naturally you can find it quickly, because the telephone book is sorted alphabetically. Now suppose you have a telephone number and you must know to what party it belongs. You could of course call that number, but suppose nobody picks up on the other end. You could look through the telephone book, a number at a time, until you find the number. That would obviously be a tremendous amount of work, and you would have to be desperate to attempt it.

This thought experiment shows the difference between a search through an unsorted data set and a search through a sorted data set. The following two sections will analyze the difference formally.

> A linear search examines all values in an array until it finds a match or reaches the end.

If you want to find a number in a sequence of values that occur in arbitrary order, there is nothing you can do to speed up the search. You must simply look through all elements until you have found a match or until you reach the end. This is called a **linear** or **sequential search**.

> A linear search locates a value in an array in $O(n)$ steps.

How long does a linear search take? If we assume that the element v is present in the array a, then the average search visits $n/2$ elements, where $n$ is the length of the array. If it is not present, then all $n$ elements must be inspected to verify the absence. Either way, a linear search is an $O(n)$ algorithm.

Here is a class that performs linear searches through an array a of integers. When searching for a value, the search method returns the first index of the match, or -1 if the value does not occur in a.

**section_6_1/LinearSearcher.java**

```java
1  /**
2      A class for executing linear searches in an array.
3  */
4  public class LinearSearcher
5  {
6      /**
7          Finds a value in an array, using the linear search
8          algorithm.
9          @param a the array to search
10         @param value the value to find
11         @return the index at which the value occurs, or -1
12         if it does not occur in the array
13     */
14     public static int search(int[] a, int value)
15     {
16         for (int i = 0; i < a.length; i++)
17         {
18             if (a[i] == value) { return i; }
19         }
20         return -1;
```

```
21     }
22 }
```

**section_6_1/LinearSearchDemo.java**

```java
 1 import java.util.Arrays;
 2 import java.util.Scanner;
 3
 4 /**
 5    This program demonstrates the linear search algorithm.
 6 */
 7 public class LinearSearchDemo
 8 {
 9    public static void main(String[] args)
10    {
11       int[] a = ArrayUtil.randomIntArray(20, 100);
12       System.out.println(Arrays.toString(a));
13       Scanner in = new Scanner(System.in);
14
15       boolean done = false;
16       while (!done)
17       {
18          System.out.print("Enter number to search for, -1 to quit: ");
19          int n = in.nextInt();
20          if (n == -1)
21          {
22             done = true;
23          }
24          else
25          {
26             int pos = LinearSearcher.search(a, n);
27             System.out.println("Found in position " + pos);
28          }
29       }
30    }
31 }
```

**Program Run**

```
[46, 99, 45, 57, 64, 95, 81, 69, 11, 97, 6, 85, 61, 88, 29, 65, 83, 88, 45, 88]
Enter number to search for, -1 to quit: 12
Found in position -1
Enter number to search for, -1 to quit: -1
```

## 14.6.2 Binary Search

Now let us search for an item in a data sequence that has been previously sorted. Of course, we could still do a linear search, but it turns out we can do much better than that.

Consider the following sorted array a. The data set is:

| [0] | [1] | [2] | [3] | [4] | [5] | [6] | [7] |
|-----|-----|-----|-----|-----|-----|-----|-----|
| 1 | 5 | 8 | 9 | 12 | 17 | 20 | 32 |

We would like to see whether the value 15 is in the data set. Let's narrow our search by finding whether the value is in the first or second half of the array. The last value in the first half of the data set, a[3], is 9, which is smaller than the value we are looking for. Hence, we should look in the second half of the array for a match, that is, in the sequence:

```
     [0] [1] [2] [3] [4] [5] [6] [7]
      1   5   8   9  12  17  20  32
```

Now the last value of the first half of this sequence is 17; hence, the value must be located in the sequence:

```
     [0] [1] [2] [3] [4] [5] [6] [7]
      1   5   8   9  12  17  20  32
```

The last value of the first half of this very short sequence is 12, which is smaller than the value that we are searching, so we must look in the second half:

```
     [0] [1] [2] [3] [4] [5] [6] [7]
      1   5   8   9  12  17  20  32
```

It is trivial to see that we don't have a match, because $15 \neq 17$. If we wanted to insert 15 into the sequence, we would need to insert it just before a[5].

This search process is called a **binary search**, because we cut the size of the search in half in each step. That cutting in half works only because we know that the sequence of values is sorted.

The following class implements binary searches in a sorted array of integers. The search method returns the position of the match if the search succeeds, or -1 if the value is not found in a. Here, we show a recursive version of the binary search algorithm. See Special Topic 6.2 for an iterative version.

> A binary search locates a value in a sorted array by determining whether the value occurs in the first or second half, then repeating the search in one of the halves.

### section_6_2/BinarySearcher.java

```java
1   /**
2       A class for executing binary searches in an array.
3   */
4   public class BinarySearcher
5   {
6       /**
7           Finds a value in a range of a sorted array, using the binary
8           search algorithm.
9           @param a  the array in which to search
10          @param low  the low index of the range
11          @param high the high index of the range
12          @param value  the value to find
13          @return the index at which the value occurs, or -1
14          if it does not occur in the array
15      */
16      public int search(int[] a, int low, int high, int value)
17      {
18          if (low <= high)
19          {
20              int mid = (low + high) / 2;
21
22              if (a[mid] == value)
23              {
24                  return mid;
25              }
26              else if (a[mid] < value )
27              {
```

```
28                    return search(a, mid + 1, high, value);
29                }
30                else
31                {
32                    return search(a, low, mid - 1, value);
33                }
34            }
35            else
36            {
37                return -1;
38            }
39        }
40    }
```

Now let's determine the number of visits to array elements required to carry out a binary search. We can use the same technique as in the analysis of merge sort. Because we look at the middle element, which counts as one visit, and then search either the left or the right subarray, we have

$$T(n) = T\left(\frac{n}{2}\right) + 1$$

Using the same equation,

$$T\left(\frac{n}{2}\right) = T\left(\frac{n}{4}\right) + 1$$

By plugging this result into the original equation, we get

$$T(n) = T\left(\frac{n}{4}\right) + 2$$

That generalizes to

$$T(n) = T\left(\frac{n}{2^k}\right) + k$$

As in the analysis of merge sort, we make the simplifying assumption that $n$ is a power of 2, $n = 2^m$, where $m = \log_2(n)$. Then we obtain

$$T(n) = 1 + \log_2(n)$$

Therefore, binary search is an $O(\log(n))$ algorithm.

A binary search locates a value in a sorted array in $O(\log(n))$ steps.

That result makes intuitive sense. Suppose that $n$ is 100. Then after each search, the size of the search range is cut in half, to 50, 25, 12, 6, 3, and 1. After seven comparisons we are done. This agrees with our formula, because $\log_2(100) \approx 6.64386$, and indeed the next larger power of 2 is $2^7 = 128$.

Because a binary search is so much faster than a linear search, is it worthwhile to sort an array first and then use a binary search? It depends. If you search the array only once, then it is more efficient to pay for an $O(n)$ linear search than for an $O(n \log(n))$ sort and an $O(\log(n))$ binary search. But if you will be making many searches in the same array, then sorting it is definitely worthwhile.

**18.** Suppose you need to look through 1,000,000 records to find a telephone number. How many records do you expect to search before finding the number?

**19.** Why can't you use a "for each" loop for (int element : a) in the search method?

**20.** Suppose you need to look through a sorted array with 1,000,000 elements to find a value. Using the binary search algorithm, how many records do you expect to search before finding the value?

**Practice It** Now you can try these exercises at the end of the chapter: R14.12, P14.15, P14.18.

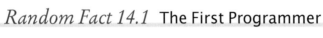

## *Random Fact 14.1* The First Programmer

Before pocket calculators and personal computers existed, navigators and engineers used mechanical adding machines, slide rules, and tables of logarithms and trigonometric functions to speed up computations. Unfortunately, the tables—for which values had to be computed by hand—were notoriously inaccurate. The mathematician Charles Babbage (1791–1871) had the insight that if a machine could be constructed that produced printed tables automatically, both calculation and typesetting errors could be avoided. Babbage set out to develop a machine for this purpose, which he called a *Difference*

*Engine* because it used successive differences to compute polynomials. For example, consider the function $f(x) = x^3$. Write down the values for $f(1)$, $f(2)$, $f(3)$, and so on. Then take the *differences* between successive values:

```
  1
       7
  8
       19
 27
       37
 64
       61
125
       91
216
```

Repeat the process, taking the difference of successive values in the second column, and then repeat once again:

```
  1
       7
  8        12
       19        6
 27        18
       37        6
 64        24
       61        6
125        30
       91
216
```

Now the differences are all the same. You can retrieve the function values by a pattern of additions—you need to know the values at the fringe of the pattern and the constant difference. You can try it out yourself: Write the highlighted numbers on a sheet of paper and fill in the others by adding the numbers that are in the north and northwest positions.

This method was very attractive, because mechanical addition machines had been known for some time. They consisted of cog wheels, with 10 cogs per wheel, to represent digits, and mechanisms to handle the carry from one digit to the next. Mechanical multiplication machines, on the other hand, were fragile and unreliable. Babbage built a successful prototype of the Difference Engine and, with his own money and government grants, proceeded to build the table-printing machine. However, because of funding problems and the difficulty of building the machine to the required precision, it was never completed.

While working on the Difference Engine, Babbage conceived of a much grander vision that he called the *Analytical Engine*. The Difference Engine was designed to carry out a limited set of computations—it was no smarter than a pocket calculator is today. But Babbage realized that such a machine could be made *programmable* by storing programs as well as data. The internal storage of the Analytical Engine was to consist of 1,000 registers of 50 decimal digits each. Programs and constants were to be stored on punched cards—a technique that was, at that time, commonly used on looms for weaving patterned fabrics.

Ada Augusta, Countess of Lovelace (1815–1852), the only child of Lord Byron, was a friend and sponsor of Charles Babbage. Ada Lovelace was one of the first people to realize the potential of such a machine, not just for computing mathematical tables but for processing data that were not numbers. She is considered by many to be the world's first programmer.

*Replica of Babbage's Difference Engine*

# 14.7 Problem Solving: Estimating the Running Time of an Algorithm

In this chapter, you have learned how to estimate the running time of sorting algorithms. As you have seen, being able to differentiate between $O(n \log(n))$ and $O(n^2)$ running times has great practical implications. Being able to estimate the running times of other algorithms is an important skill. In this section, we will practice estimating the running time of array algorithms.

## 14.7.1 Linear Time

Let us start with a simple example, an algorithm that counts how many elements have a particular value:

```
int count = 0;
for (int i = 0; i < a.length; i++)
{
    if (a[i] == value) { count++; }
}
```

What is the running time in terms of $n$, the length of the array?

Start with looking at the pattern of array element visits. Here, we visit each element once. It helps to visualize this pattern. Imagine the array as a sequence of light bulbs. As the $i$th element gets visited, imagine the $i$th bulb lighting up.

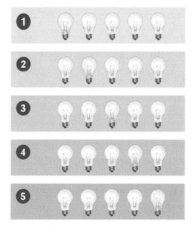

Now look at the work per visit. Does each visit involve a fixed number of actions, independent of $n$? In this case, it does. There are just a few actions—read the element, compare it, maybe increment a counter.

Therefore, the running time is $n$ times a constant, or $O(n)$.

What if we don't always run to the end of the array? For example, suppose we want to check whether the value occurs in the array, without counting it:

A loop with $n$ iterations has $O(n)$ running time if each step consists of a fixed number of actions.

```
boolean found = false;
for (int i = 0; !found && i < a.length; i++)
{
    if (a[i] == value) { found = true; }
}
```

Then the loop can stop in the middle:

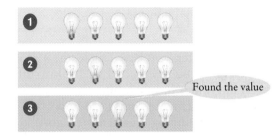

Found the value

Is this still $O(n)$? It is, because in some cases the match may be at the very end of the array. Also, if there is no match, one must traverse the entire array.

## 14.7.2 Quadratic Time

Now let's turn to a more interesting case. What if we do a lot of work with each visit? Here is an example. We want to find the most frequent element in an array.

Suppose the array is

| 8 | 7 | 5 | 7 | 7 | 5 | 4 |
|---|---|---|---|---|---|---|

It's obvious by looking at the values that 7 is the most frequent one. But now imagine an array with a few thousand values.

| 8 | 7 | 5 | 7 | 7 | 5 | 4 | 1 | 2 | 3 | 3 | 4 | 9 | 12 | 3 | 2 | 5 | ⋯ | 11 | 9 | 2 | 3 | 7 | 8 |
|---|---|---|---|---|---|---|---|---|---|---|---|---|----|---|---|---|---|----|---|---|---|---|---|

We can count how often the value 8 occurs, then move on to count how often 7 occurs, and so on. For example, in the first array, 8 occurs once, and 7 occurs three times. Where do we put the counts? Let's put them into a second array of the same length.

|   a: | 8 | 7 | 5 | 7 | 7 | 5 | 4 |
|------|---|---|---|---|---|---|---|
| counts: | 1 | 3 | 2 | 3 | 3 | 2 | 1 |

Then we take the maximum of the counts. It is 3. We look up where the 3 occurs in the counts, and find the corresponding value. Thus, the most common value is 7.

Let us first estimate how long it takes to compute the counts.

```
for (int i = 0; i < a.length; i++)
{
    counts[i] = Count how often a[i] occurs in a
}
```

**A loop with $n$ iterations has $O(n^2)$ running time if each step takes $O(n)$ time.**

We still visit each array element once, but now the work per visit is much larger. As you have seen in the previous section, each counting action is $O(n)$. When we do $O(n)$ work in each step, the total running time is $O(n^2)$.

This algorithm has three phases:

1. Compute all counts.
2. Compute the maximum.
3. Find the maximum in the counts.

We have just seen that the first phase is $O(n^2)$. Computing the maximum is $O(n)$—look at the algorithm in Section 6.3.3 and note that each steps involves a fixed amount of work. Finally, we just saw that finding a value is $O(n)$.

How can we estimate the total running time from the estimates of each phase? Of course, the total time is the sum of the individual times, but for big-Oh estimates, we take the *maximum* of the estimates. To see why, imagine that we had actual equations for each of the times:

*The big-Oh running time for doing several steps in a row is the largest of the big-Oh times for each step.*

$$T_1(n) = an^2 + bn + c$$
$$T_2(n) = dn + e$$
$$T_3(n) = fn + g$$

Then the sum is

$$T(n) = T_1(n) + T_2(n) + T_3(n) = an^2 + (b + d + f)n + c + e + g$$

But only the largest term matters, so $T(n)$ is $O(n^2)$.

Thus, we have found that our algorithm for finding the most frequent element is $O(n^2)$.

### 14.7.3  The Triangle Pattern

Let us see if we can speed up the algorithm from the preceding section. It seems wasteful to count elements again if we have already counted them.

Can we save time by eliminating repeated counting of the same element? That is, before counting a[i], should we first check that it didn't occur in a[0] ... a[i - 1]?

Let us estimate the cost of these additional checks. In the *i*th step, the amount of work is proportional to *i*. That's not quite the same as in the preceding section, where you saw that a loop with *n* iterations, each of which takes $O(n)$ time, is $O(n^2)$. Now each step just takes $O(i)$ time.

To get an intuitive feel for this situation, look at the light bulbs again. In the second iteration, we visit a[0] again. In the third iteration, we visit a[0] and a[1] again, and so on. The light bulb pattern is

*A loop with $n$ iterations has $O(n^2)$ running time if the $i$th step takes $O(i)$ time.*

If there are $n$ light bulbs, about half of the square above, or $n^2/2$ of them, light up. That's unfortunately still $O(n^2)$.

Here is another idea for time saving. When we count a[i], there is no need to do the counting in a[0] ... a[i - 1]. If a[i] never occurred before, we get an accurate count by just looking at a[i] ... a[n - 1]. And if it did, we already have an accurate count. Does that help us? Not really—it's the triangle pattern again, but this time in the other direction.

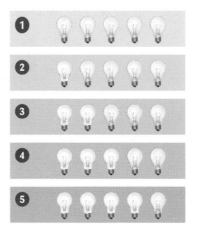

That doesn't mean that these improvements aren't worthwhile. If an $O(n^2)$ algorithm is the best one can do for a particular problem, you still want to make it as fast as possible. However, we will not pursue this plan further because it turns out that we can do much better.

## 14.7.4 Logarithmic Time

Logarithmic time estimates arise from algorithms that cut work in half in each step. You have seen this in the algorithms for binary search and merge sort, and you will see it again in Chapter 17.

In particular, when you use sorting or binary search in a phase of an algorithm, you will encounter logarithmic time in the big-Oh estimates.

> An algorithm that cuts the size of work in half in each step runs in $O(\log(n))$ time.

Consider this idea for improving our algorithm for finding the most frequent element. Suppose we first *sort* the array:

$$8 \ 7 \ 5 \ 7 \ 5 \ 4 \ \longrightarrow \ 4 \ 5 \ 5 \ 7 \ 7 \ 7 \ 8$$

That cost us $O(n \log(n))$ time. If we can complete the algorithm in $O(n)$ time, we will have found a better algorithm than the $O(n^2)$ algorithm of the preceding sections.

To see why this is possible, imagine traversing the sorted array. As long as you find a value that was equal to its predecessor, you increment a counter. When you find a different value, save the counter and start counting anew:

$$\text{a:} \quad 4 \ 5 \ 5 \ 7 \ 7 \ 7 \ 8$$
$$\text{counts:} \quad 1 \ 1 \ 2 \ 1 \ 2 \ 3 \ 1$$

Or in code,

```java
int count = 0;
for (int i = 0; i < a.length; i++)
{
```

```
        count++;
        if (i == a.length - 1 || a[i] != a[i + 1])
        {
            counts[i] = count;
            count = 0;
        }
    }
```

That's a constant amount of work per iteration, even though it visits two elements:

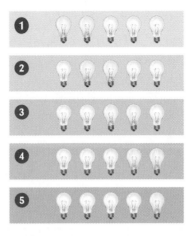

**ONLINE EXAMPLE**

⊕ A program for
comparing the speed
of algorithms that
find the most
frequent element.

$2n$ is still $O(n)$. Thus, we can compute the counts in $O(n)$ time from a sorted array. The entire algorithm is now $O(n \log(n))$.

Note that we don't actually need to keep all counts, only the highest one that we encountered so far (see Exercise P14.8). That is a worthwhile improvement, but it does not change the big-Oh estimate of the running time.

**SELF CHECK**

21. What is the "light bulb pattern" of visits in the following algorithm to check whether an array is a palindrome?

```
for (int i = 0; i < a.length / 2; i++)
{
    if (a[i] != a[a.length - 1 - i]) { return false; }
}
return true;
```

22. What is the big-Oh running time of the following algorithm to check whether the first element is duplicated in an array?

```
for (int i = 1; i < a.length; i++)
{
    if (a[0] == a[i]) { return true; }
}
return false;
```

23. What is the big-Oh running time of the following algorithm to check whether an array has a duplicate value?

```
for (int i = 0; i < a.length; i++)
{
    for (j = i + 1; j < a.length; j++)
    {
        if (a[i] == a[j]) { return true; }
```

```
      }
   }
   return false;
```

24. Describe an $O(n \log(n))$ algorithm for checking whether an array has duplicates.

25. What is the big-Oh running time of the following algorithm to find an element in an $n \times n$ array?

```
for (int i = 0; i < n; i++)
{
   for (j = 0; j < n; j++)
   {
      if (a[i][j] == value) { return true; }
   }
}
return false;
```

26. If you apply the algorithm of Section 14.7.4 to an $n \times n$ array, what is the big-Oh efficiency of finding the most frequent element in terms of $n$?

**Practice It**  Now you can try these exercises at the end of the chapter: R14.9, R14.13, R14.19, P14.8.

# 14.8 Sorting and Searching in the Java Library

When you write Java programs, you don't have to implement your own sorting algorithms. The Arrays and Collections classes provide sorting and searching methods that we will introduce in the following sections.

## 14.8.1 Sorting

> The Arrays class implements a sorting method that you should use for your Java programs.

The Arrays class contains static sort methods to sort arrays of integers and floating-point numbers. For example, you can sort an array of integers simply as

```
int[] a = . . .;
Arrays.sort(a);
```

That sort method uses the quicksort algorithm—see Special Topic 14.3 for more information about that algorithm.

> The Collections class contains a sort method that can sort array lists.

If your data are contained in an ArrayList, use the Collections.sort method instead; it uses the merge sort algorithm:

```
ArrayList<String> names = . . .;
Collections.sort(names);
```

## 14.8.2 Binary Search

The Arrays and Collections classes contain static binarySearch methods that implement the binary search algorithm, but with a useful enhancement. If a value is not found in the array, then the returned value is not −1, but −k − 1, where k is the position before which the element should be inserted. For example,

```
int[] a = { 1, 4, 9 };
int v = 7;
int pos = Arrays.binarySearch(a, v);
// Returns -3; v should be inserted before position 2
```

## 14.8.3 Comparing Objects

The sort method of the Arrays class sorts objects of classes that implement the Comparable interface.

In application programs, you often need to sort or search through collections of objects. Therefore, the Arrays and Collections classes also supply sort and binarySearch methods for objects. However, these methods cannot know how to compare arbitrary objects. Suppose, for example, that you have an array of Country objects. It is not obvious how the countries should be sorted. Should they be sorted by their names or by their areas? The sort and binarySearch methods cannot make that decision for you. Instead, they require that the objects belong to classes that implement the Comparable interface type that was introduced in Section 9.6.3. That interface has a single method:

```
public interface Comparable
{
    int compareTo(Object otherObject);
}
```

The call

```
a.compareTo(b)
```

must return a negative number if a should come before b, 0 if a and b are the same, and a positive number otherwise.

Several classes in the standard Java library, such as the String and Date classes, implement the Comparable interface.

You can implement the Comparable interface for your own classes as well. For example, to sort a collection of countries, the Country class would need to implement this interface and provide a compareTo method:

```
public class Country implements Comparable
{
    public int compareTo(Object otherObject)
    {
        Country other = (Country) otherObject;
        if (area < other.area) { return -1; }
        else if (area == other.area) { return 0; }
        else { return 1; }
    }
}
```

This method compares countries by their area. Now you can pass an array of countries to the Arrays.sort method:

```
Country[] countries = new Country[n];
// Add countries
Arrays.sort(countries); // Sorts by increasing area
```

**ONLINE EXAMPLE**

➕ A program to demonstrate the Java library methods for sorting and searching.

Whenever you need to carry out sorting or searching, use the methods in the Arrays and Collections classes and not those that you write yourself. The library algorithms have been fully debugged and optimized. Thus, the primary purpose of this chapter was not to teach you how to implement practical sorting and searching algorithms. Instead, you have learned something more important, namely that different algorithms can vary widely in performance, and that it is worthwhile to learn more about the design and analysis of algorithms.

**27.** Why can't the `Arrays.sort` method sort an array of `Rectangle` objects?

**28.** What steps would you need to take to sort an array of `BankAccount` objects by increasing balance?

**29.** Why is it useful that the `Arrays.binarySearch` method indicates the position where a missing element should be inserted?

**30.** Why does `Arrays.binarySearch` return $-k - 1$ and not $-k$ to indicate that a value is not present and should be inserted before position $k$?

**Practice It**    Now you can try these exercises at the end of the chapter: P14.14, P14.19, P14.20.

---

**Common Error 14.1**

### The `compareTo` Method Can Return Any Integer, Not Just –1, 0, and 1

The call `a.compareTo(b)` is allowed to return *any* negative integer to denote that a should come before b, not necessarily the value –1. That is, the test

```
if (a.compareTo(b) == -1) // ERROR!
```

is generally wrong. Instead, you should test

```
if (a.compareTo(b) < 0) // OK
```

Why would a `compareTo` method ever want to return a number other than –1, 0, or 1? Sometimes, it is convenient to just return the difference of two integers. For example, the `compareTo` method of the `String` class compares characters in matching positions:

```
char c1 = charAt(i);
char c2 = other.charAt(i);
```

If the characters are different, then the method simply returns their difference:

```
if (c1 != c2) { return c1 - c2; }
```

This difference is a negative number if c1 is less than c2, but it is not necessarily the number –1.

---

**Special Topic 14.4**

### The Parameterized `Comparable` Interface

As of Java version 5, the `Comparable` interface is a parameterized type, similar to the `ArrayList` type:

```
public interface Comparable<T>
{
    int compareTo(T other)
}
```

The type parameter specifies the type of the objects that this class is willing to accept for comparison. Usually, this type is the same as the class type itself. For example, the `Country` class would implement `Comparable<Country>`, like this:

```
public class Country implements Comparable<Country>
{
    . . .
    public int compareTo(Country other)
    {
        if (area < other.area) { return -1; }
        else if (area == other.area) { return 0; }
        else { return 1; }
    }
}
```

```
    . . .
}
```

The type parameter has a significant advantage: You need not use a cast to convert an `Object` parameter variable into the desired type.

Special Topic 14.5

## The `Comparator` Interface

Sometimes you want to sort an array or array list of objects, but the objects don't belong to a class that implements the `Comparable` interface. Or, perhaps, you want to sort the array in a different order. For example, you may want to sort countries by name rather than by value.

You wouldn't want to change the implementation of a class simply to call `Arrays.sort`. Fortunately, there is an alternative. One version of the `Arrays.sort` method does not require that the objects belong to classes that implement the `Comparable` interface. Instead, you can supply arbitrary objects. However, you must also provide a *comparator* object whose job is to compare objects. The comparator object must belong to a class that implements the `Comparator` interface. That interface has a single method, `compare`, which compares two objects.

As of Java version 5, the `Comparator` interface is a parameterized type. The type parameter specifies the type of the `compare` parameter variables. For example, `Comparator<Country>` looks like this:

```java
public interface Comparator<Country>
{
    int compare(Country a, Country b);
}
```

The call

```java
comp.compare(a, b)
```

must return a negative number if a should come before b, 0 if a and b are the same, and a positive number otherwise. (Here, `comp` is an object of a class that implements `Comparator<Country>`.)

For example, here is a `Comparator` class for country:

```java
public class CountryComparator implements Comparator<Country>
{
    public int compare(Country a, Country b)
    {
        if (a.area < b.area) { return -1; }
        else if (a.area == b.area) { return 0; }
        else { return 1; }
    }
}
```

To sort an array of countries by area, call

```java
Arrays.sort(countries, new CountryComparator());
```

## WORKED EXAMPLE 14.1    **Enhancing the Insertion Sort Algorithm**

In this Worked Example, we will implement an improvement of the insertion sort algorithm shown in Special Topic 14.2, which is called *Shell sort* after its inventor, Donald Shell.

➕ Available online in WileyPLUS and at www.wiley.com/college/horstmann.

## CHAPTER SUMMARY

### Describe the selection sort algorithm.

- The selection sort algorithm sorts an array by repeatedly finding the smallest element of the unsorted tail region and moving it to the front.

### Measure the running time of a method.

- To measure the running time of a method, get the current time immediately before and after the method call.

### Use the big-Oh notation to describe the running time of an algorithm.

- Computer scientists use the big-Oh notation to describe the growth rate of a function.
- Selection sort is an $O(n^2)$ algorithm. Doubling the data set means a fourfold increase in processing time.
- Insertion sort is an $O(n^2)$ algorithm.

### Describe the merge sort algorithm.

- The merge sort algorithm sorts an array by cutting the array in half, recursively sorting each half, and then merging the sorted halves.

### Contrast the running times of the merge sort and selection sort algorithms.

- Merge sort is an $O(n \log(n))$ algorithm. The $n \log(n)$ function grows much more slowly than $n^2$.

### Describe the running times of the linear search algorithm and the binary search algorithm.

- A linear search examines all values in an array until it finds a match or reaches the end.
- A linear search locates a value in an array in $O(n)$ steps.
- A binary search locates a value in a sorted array by determining whether the value occurs in the first or second half, then repeating the search in one of the halves.
- A binary search locates a value in a sorted array in $O(\log(n))$ steps.

### Practice developing big-Oh estimates of algorithms.

- A loop with $n$ iterations has $O(n)$ running time if each step consists of a fixed number of actions.
- A loop with $n$ iterations has $O(n^2)$ running time if each step takes $O(n)$ time.
- The big-Oh running time for doing several steps in a row is the largest of the big-Oh times for each step.

- A loop with $n$ iterations has $O(n^2)$ running time if the $i$th step takes $O(i)$ time.
- An algorithm that cuts the size of work in half in each step runs in $O(\log(n))$ time.

**Use the Java library methods for sorting and searching data.**

- The Arrays class implements a sorting method that you should use for your Java programs.
- The Collections class contains a sort method that can sort array lists.
- The sort method of the Arrays class sorts objects of classes that implement the Comparable interface.

## STANDARD LIBRARY ITEMS INTRODUCED IN THIS CHAPTER

java.lang.Comparable<T>
   compareTo
java.lang.System
   currentTimeMillis
java.util.Arrays
   binarySearch
   sort

java.util.Collections
   binarySearch
   sort
java.util.Comparator<T>
   compare

## REVIEW EXERCISES

- **R14.1** What is the difference between searching and sorting?

- **R14.2** *Checking against off-by-one errors.* When writing the selection sort algorithm of Section 14.1, a programmer must make the usual choices of < versus <=, a.length versus a.length - 1, and from versus from + 1. This is fertile ground for off-by-one errors. Conduct code walkthroughs of the algorithm with arrays of length 0, 1, 2, and 3 and check carefully that all index values are correct.

- **R14.3** For the following expressions, what is the order of the growth of each?

    **a.** $n^2 + 2n + 1$

    **b.** $n^{10} + 9n^9 + 20n^8 + 145n^7$

    **c.** $(n + 1)^4$

    **d.** $(n^2 + n)^2$

    **e.** $n + 0.001n^3$

    **f.** $n^3 - 1000n^2 + 10^9$

    **g.** $n + \log(n)$

    **h.** $n^2 + n\log(n)$

    **i.** $2^n + n^2$

    **j.** $\dfrac{n^3 + 2n}{n^2 + 0.75}$

- **R14.4** We determined that the actual number of visits in the selection sort algorithm is

$$T(n) = \tfrac{1}{2}n^2 + \tfrac{5}{2}n - 3$$

We characterized this method as having $O(n^2)$ growth. Compute the actual ratios

$$T(2{,}000)/T(1{,}000)$$
$$T(4{,}000)/T(1{,}000)$$
$$T(10{,}000)/T(1{,}000)$$

and compare them with

$$f(2{,}000)/f(1{,}000)$$
$$f(4{,}000)/f(1{,}000)$$
$$f(10{,}000)/f(1{,}000)$$

where $f(n) = n^2$.

- **R14.5** Suppose algorithm $A$ takes five seconds to handle a data set of 1,000 records. If the algorithm $A$ is an $O(n)$ algorithm, approximately how long will it take to handle a data set of 2,000 records? Of 10,000 records?

- ■ **R14.6** Suppose an algorithm takes five seconds to handle a data set of 1,000 records. Fill in the following table, which shows the approximate growth of the execution times depending on the complexity of the algorithm.

|        | $O(n)$ | $O(n^2)$ | $O(n^3)$ | $O(n \log(n))$ | $O(2^n)$ |
|--------|--------|----------|----------|----------------|----------|
| 1,000  | 5      | 5        | 5        | 5              | 5        |
| 2,000  |        |          |          |                |          |
| 3,000  |        | 45       |          |                |          |
| 10,000 |        |          |          |                |          |

For example, because $3{,}000^2/1{,}000^2 = 9$, the algorithm would take nine times as long, or 45 seconds, to handle a data set of 3,000 records.

- ■ **R14.7** Sort the following growth rates from slowest to fastest growth.

| | |
|---|---|
| $O(n)$ | $O(n \log(n))$ |
| $O(n^3)$ | $O(2^n)$ |
| $O(n^n)$ | $O(\sqrt{n})$ |
| $O(\log(n))$ | $O(n\sqrt{n})$ |
| $O(n^2 \log(n))$ | $O(n^{\log(n)})$ |

- **R14.8** What is the growth rate of the standard algorithm to find the minimum value of an array? Of finding both the minimum and the maximum?

**■ R14.9** What is the big-Oh time estimate of the following method in terms of $n$, the length of a? Use the "light bulb pattern" method of Section 14.7 to visualize your result.

```java
public static void swap(int[] a)
{
   int i = 0;
   int j = a.length - 1;
   while (i < j)
   {
      int temp = a[i];
      a[i] = a[j];
      a[j] = temp;
      i++;
      j--;
   }
}
```

**■ R14.10** Trace a walkthrough of selection sort with these sets:

**a.** 4   7   11   4   9   5   11   7   3   5

**b.** −7   6   8   7   5   9   0   11   10   5   8

**■ R14.11** Trace a walkthrough of merge sort with these sets:

**a.** 5   11   7   3   5   4   7   11   4   9

**b.** 9   0   11   10   5   8   −7   6   8   7   5

**■ R14.12** Trace a walkthrough of:

**a.** Linear search for 7 in     −7   1   3   3   4   7   11   13

**b.** Binary search for 8 in    −7   2   2   3   4   7   8   11   13

**c.** Binary search for 8 in    −7   1   2   3   5   7   10   13

**■■ R14.13** Your task is to remove all duplicates from an array. For example, if the array has the values

4 7 11 4 9 5 11 7 3 5

then the array should be changed to

4 7 11 9 5 3

Here is a simple algorithm. Look at a[i]. Count how many times it occurs in a. If the count is larger than 1, remove it. What is the growth rate of the time required for this algorithm?

**■■■ R14.14** Modify the merge sort algorithm to remove duplicates in the merging step to obtain an algorithm that removes duplicates from an array. Note that the resulting array does not have the same ordering as the original one. What is the efficiency of this algorithm?

**■■ R14.15** Consider the following algorithm to remove all duplicates from an array. Sort the array. For each element in the array, look at its next neighbor to decide whether it is present more than once. If so, remove it. Is this a faster algorithm than the one in Exercise R14.13?

**■■■ R14.16** Develop an $O(n \log(n))$ algorithm for removing duplicates from an array if the resulting array must have the same ordering as the original array. When a value occurs multiple times, all but its first occurrence should be removed.

■■■ **R14.17** Why does insertion sort perform significantly better than selection sort if an array is already sorted?

■■■ **R14.18** Consider the following speedup of the insertion sort algorithm of Special Topic 14.2. For each element, use the enhanced binary search algorithm that yields the insertion position for missing elements. Does this speedup have a significant impact on the efficiency of the algorithm?

■■ **R14.19** Consider the following algorithm known as *bubble sort*:

> While the array is not sorted
>     For each adjacent pair of elements
>         If the pair is not sorted
>             Swap its elements.

What is the big-Oh efficiency of this algorithm?

■■ **R14.20** The *radix sort* algorithm sorts an array of $n$ integers with $d$ digits, using ten auxiliary arrays. First place each value $v$ into the auxiliary array whose index corresponds to the last digit of $v$. Then move all values back into the original array, preserving their order. Repeat the process, now using the next-to-last (tens) digit, then the hundreds digit, and so on. What is the big-Oh time of this algorithm in terms of $n$ and $d$? When is this algorithm preferable to merge sort?

■■ **R14.21** A *stable sort* does not change the order of elements with the same value. This is a desirable feature in many applications. Consider a sequence of e-mail messages. If you sort by date and then by sender, you'd like the second sort to preserve the relative order of the first, so that you can see all messages from the same sender in date order. Is selection sort stable? Insertion sort? Why or why not?

■■ **R14.22** Give an $O(n)$ algorithm to sort an array of $n$ bytes (numbers between –128 and 127). *Hint:* Use an array of counters.

■■ **R14.23** You are given a sequence of arrays of words, representing the pages of a book. Your task is to build an index (a sorted array of words), each element of which has an array of sorted numbers representing the pages on which the word appears. Describe an algorithm for building the index and give its big-Oh running time in terms of the total number of words.

■■ **R14.24** Given two arrays of $n$ integers each, describe an $O(n \log(n))$ algorithm for determining whether they have an element in common.

■■■ **R14.25** Given an array of $n$ integers and a value $v$, describe an $O(n \log(n))$ algorithm to find whether there are two values $x$ and $y$ in the array with sum $v$.

■■ **R14.26** Given two arrays of $n$ integers each, describe an $O(n \log(n))$ algorithm for finding all elements that they have in common.

■■ **R14.27** Suppose we modify the quicksort algorithm from Special Topic 14.3, selecting the middle element instead of the first one as pivot. What is the running time on an array that is already sorted?

■■ **R14.28** Suppose we modify the quicksort algorithm from Special Topic 14.3, selecting the middle element instead of the first one as pivot. Find a sequence of values for which this algorithm has an $O(n^2)$ running time.

## PROGRAMMING EXERCISES

- **P14.1** Modify the selection sort algorithm to sort an array of integers in descending order.

- **P14.2** Modify the selection sort algorithm to sort an array of coins by their value.

- **P14.3** Write a program that automatically generates the table of sample run times for the selection sort algorithm. The program should ask for the smallest and largest value of n and the number of measurements and then make all sample runs.

- **P14.4** Modify the merge sort algorithm to sort an array of strings in lexicographic order.

- **P14.5** Write a telephone lookup program. Read a data set of 1,000 names and telephone numbers from a file that contains the numbers in random order. Handle lookups by name and also reverse lookups by phone number. Use a binary search for both lookups.

- **P14.6** Implement a program that measures the performance of the insertion sort algorithm described in Special Topic 14.2.

- **P14.7** Implement the bubble sort algorithm described in Exercise R14.19.

- **P14.8** Implement the algorithm described in Section 14.7.4, but only remember the value with the highest frequency so far:

    ```
    int mostFrequent = 0;
    int highestFrequency = -1;
    for (int i = 0; i < a.length; i++)
        Count how often a[i] occurs in a[i + 1]...a[n - 1]
        If it occurs more often than highestFrequency
            highestFrequency = that count
            mostFrequent = a[i]
    ```

- **P14.9** Implement the following modification of the quicksort algorithm, due to Bentley and McIlroy. Instead of using the first element as the pivot, use an approximation of the median. (Partitioning at the actual median would yield an $O(n \log(n))$ algorithm, but we don't know how to compute it quickly enough.)

    If $n \leq 7$, use the middle element. If $n \leq 40$, use the median of the first, middle, and last element. Otherwise compute the "pseudomedian" of the nine elements a[i * (n - 1) / 8], where i ranges from 0 to 8. The pseudomedian of nine values is $\text{med}(\text{med}(v_0, v_1, v_2), \text{med}(v_3, v_4, v_5), \text{med}(v_6, v_7, v_8))$.

    Compare the running time of this modification with that of the original algorithm on sequences that are nearly sorted or reverse sorted, and on sequences with many identical elements. What do you observe?

- **P14.10** Bentley and McIlroy suggest the following modification to the quicksort algorithm when dealing with data sets that contain many repeated elements.

    Instead of partitioning as

    | ≤ | ≥ |

    (where ≤ denotes the elements that are ≤ the pivot), it is better to partition as

However, that is tedious to achieve directly. They recommend to partition as

and then swap the two = regions into the middle. Implement this modification and check whether it improves performance on data sets with many repeated elements.

- **P14.11** Implement the radix sort algorithm described in Exercise R14.20 to sort arrays of numbers between 0 and 999.

- **P14.12** Implement the radix sort algorithm described in Exercise R14.20 to sort arrays of numbers between 0 and 999. However, use a single auxiliary array, not ten.

- **P14.13** Implement the radix sort algorithm described in Exercise R14.20 to sort arbitrary `int` values (positive or negative).

- **P14.14** Write a program that sorts an `ArrayList<Country>` in decreasing order so that the most largest country is at the beginning of the array. Use a `Comparator`.

- **P14.15** Consider the binary search algorithm in Section 14.8. If no match is found, the `search` method returns –1. Modify the method so that if a is not found, the method returns $-k - 1$, where $k$ is the position before which the element should be inserted. (This is the same behavior as `Arrays.binarySearch`.)

- **P14.16** Implement the sort method of the merge sort algorithm without recursion, where the length of the array is a power of 2. First merge adjacent regions of size 1, then adjacent regions of size 2, then adjacent regions of size 4, and so on.

- **P14.17** Implement the sort method of the merge sort algorithm without recursion, where the length of the array is an arbitrary number. Keep merging adjacent regions whose size is a power of 2, and pay special attention to the last area whose size is less.

- **P14.18** Use insertion sort and the binary search from Exercise P14.15 to sort an array as described in Exercise R14.18. Implement this algorithm and measure its performance.

- **P14.19** Supply a class `Person` that implements the `Comparable` interface. Compare persons by their names. Ask the user to input ten names and generate ten `Person` objects. Using the `compareTo` method, determine and the first and last person among them and print them.

- **P14.20** Sort an array list of strings by increasing *length*. *Hint:* Supply a `Comparator`.

- **P14.21** Sort an array list of strings by increasing length, and so that strings of the same length are sorted lexicographically. *Hint:* Supply a `Comparator`.

## ANSWERS TO SELF-CHECK QUESTIONS

1. Dropping the temp variable would not work. Then a[i] and a[j] would end up being the same value.

2. 1 | 5 4 3 2 6

   1 2 | 4 3 5 6

   1 2 3 4 5 6

3. In each step, find the *maximum* of the remaining elements and swap it with the current element (or see Self Check 4).

4. The modified algorithm sorts the array in descending order.

5. Four times as long as 40,000 values, or about 37 seconds.

6. A parabola.

7. It takes about 100 times longer.

8. If $n$ is 4, then $\frac{1}{2}n^2$ is 8 and $\frac{5}{2}n - 3$ is 7.

9. The first algorithm requires one visit, to store the new element. The second algorithm requires $T(p) = 2 \times (n - p - 1)$ visits, where $p$ is the location at which the element is removed. We don't know where that element is, but if elements are removed at random locations, on average, half of the removals will be above the middle and half below, so we can assume an average $p$ of $n / 2$ and $T(n) = 2 \times (n - n / 2 - 1) = n - 2$.

10. The first algorithm is $O(1)$, the second $O(n)$.

11. We need to check that a[0] ≤ a[1], a[1] ≤ a[2], and so on, visiting $2n - 2$ elements. Therefore, the running time is $O(n)$.

12. Let $n$ be the length of the array. In the $k$th step, we need $k$ visits to find the minimum. To remove it, we need an average of $k - 2$ visits (see Self Check 9). One additional visit is required to add it to the end. Thus, the $k$th step requires $2k - 1$ visits. Because $k$ goes from $n$ to 2, the total number of visits is

$$2n - 1 + 2(n - 1) - 1 + ... + 2 \cdot 3 - 1 + 2 \cdot 2 - 1 =$$
$$2(n + (n - 1) + ... + 3 + 2 + 1 - 1) - (n - 1) =$$
$$n(n + 1) - 2 - n + 1 = n^2 - 3$$

(because $1 + 2 + 3 + ... + (n - 1) + n = n(n + 1)/2$) Therefore, the total number of visits is $O(n^2)$.

13. When the preceding while loop ends, the loop condition must be false, that is, iFirst >= first.length or iSecond >= second.length (De Morgan's Law).

14. First sort 8 7 6 5. Recursively, first sort 8 7. Recursively, first sort 8. It's sorted. Sort 7. It's sorted. Merge them: 7 8. Do the same with 6 5 to get 5 6. Merge them to 5 6 7 8. Do the same with 4 3 2 1: Sort 4 3 by sorting 4 and 3 and merging them to 3 4. Sort 2 1 by sorting 2 and 1 and merging them to 1 2. Merge 3 4 and 1 2 to 1 2 3 4. Finally, merge 5 6 7 8 and 1 2 3 4 to 1 2 3 4 5 6 7 8.

15. If the array size is 1, return its only element as the sum. Otherwise, recursively compute the sum of the first and second subarray and return the sum of these two values.

16. Approximately $(100{,}000 \cdot \log(100{,}000)) / (50{,}000 \cdot \log(50{,}000)) = 2 \cdot 5 / 4.7 = 2.13$ times the time required for 50,000 values. That's $2.13 \cdot 192$ milliseconds or approximately 409 milliseconds.

17. $\dfrac{2n \log(2n)}{n \log(n)} = 2\dfrac{(1 + \log(2))}{\log(n)}$.

    For $n > 2$, that is a value $< 3$.

18. On average, you'd make 500,000 comparisons.

19. The search method returns the index at which the match occurs, not the data stored at that location.

20. You would search about 20. (The binary log of 1,024 is 10.)

21.

22. It is an $O(n)$ algorithm.

23. It is an $O(n^2)$ algorithm—the number of visits follows a triangle pattern.

24. Sort the array, then make a linear scan to check for adjacent duplicates.

25. It is an $O(n^2)$ algorithm—the outer and inner loop each have $n$ iterations.

26. Because an $n \times n$ array has $m = n^2$ elements, and the algorithm in Section 14.7.4, when applied to an array with $m$ elements, is $O(m \log(m))$, we have an $O(n^2\log(n))$ algorithm. Recall that $\log(n^2) = 2 \log(n)$, and the factor of 2 is irrelevant in the big-Oh notation.

27. The `Rectangle` class does not implement the `Comparable` interface.

28. The `BankAccount` class would need to implement the `Comparable` interface. Its `compareTo` method must compare the bank balances.

29. Then you know where to insert it so that the array stays sorted, and you can keep using binary search.

30. Otherwise, you would not know whether a value is present when the method returns 0.

# THE JAVA COLLECTIONS FRAMEWORK

To learn how to use the collection classes supplied in the Java library

To use iterators to traverse collections

To choose appropriate collections for solving programming problems

To study applications of stacks and queues

If you want to write a program that collects objects (such as the stamps to the left), you have a number of choices. Of course, you can use an array list, but computer scientists have invented other mechanisms that may be better suited for the task. In this chapter, we introduce the collection classes and interfaces that the Java library offers. You will learn how to use the Java collection classes, and how to choose the most appropriate collection type for a problem.

# 15.1 An Overview of the Collections Framework

A collection groups together elements and allows them to be retrieved later.

When you need to organize multiple objects in your program, you can place them into a **collection**. The ArrayList class that was introduced in Chapter 6 is one of many collection classes that the standard Java library supplies. In this chapter, you will learn about the Java *collections framework*, a hierarchy of interface types and classes for collecting objects. Each interface type is implemented by one or more classes (see Figure 1).

At the root of the hierarchy is the Collection interface. That interface has methods for adding and removing elements, and so on. Table 1 on page 672 shows all the methods. Because all collections implement this interface, its methods are available for all collection classes. For example, the size method reports the number of elements in *any* collection.

The List interface describes an important category of collections. In Java, a *list* is a collection that remembers the order of its elements (see Figure 2). The ArrayList class implements the List interface. The Java library supplies another class, LinkedList, that also implements the List interface. Unlike an array list, a linked list allows speedy insertion and removal of elements in the middle of the list. We will discuss that class in the next section.

A list is a collection that remembers the order of its elements.

You use a list whenever you want to retain the order that you established. For example, on your bookshelf, you may order books by topic. A list is an appropriate data structure for such a collection because the ordering matters to you.

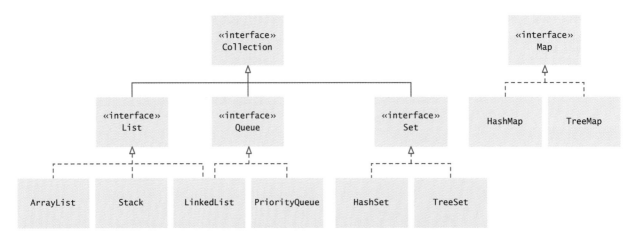

**Figure 1** Interfaces and Classes in the Java Collections Framework

**Figure 2**   A List of Books

**Figure 3**   A Set of Books

**Figure 4**   A Stack of Books

However, in many applications, you don't really care about the order of the elements in a collection. Consider a mail-order dealer of books. Without customers browsing the shelves, there is no need to order books by topic. Such a collection without an intrinsic order is called a **set**—see Figure 3.

> A set is an unordered collection of unique elements.

Because a set does not track the order of the elements, it can arrange them in a way that speeds up the operations of finding, adding, and removing elements. Computer scientists have invented mechanisms for this purpose. The Java library provides classes that are based on two such mechanisms (called *hash tables* and *binary search trees*). You will learn in this chapter how to choose between them.

Another way of gaining efficiency in a collection is to reduce the number of operations. A **stack** remembers the order of its elements, but it does not allow you to insert elements in every position. You can add and remove elements only at the top—see Figure 4.

In a **queue**, you add items to one end (the tail) and remove them from the other end (the head). For example, you could keep a queue of books, adding required reading at the tail and taking a book from the head whenever you have time to read another one. We will discuss stacks and queues in Section 15.5.

> A map keeps associations between key and value objects.

Finally, a **map** manages associations between *keys* and *values*. Every key in the map has an associated value. The map stores the keys, values, and the associations between them. For an example, consider a library that puts a bar code on each book.

The program used to check books in and out needs to look up the book associated with each bar code. A map associating bar codes with books can solve this problem—see Figure 5. We will discuss maps in Section 15.4.

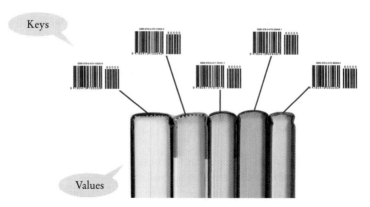

**Figure 5**   A Map from Bar Codes to Books

ONLINE EXAMPLE

A sample program that demonstrates several collection classes.

### Table 1 The Methods of the Collection Interface

| | |
|---|---|
| `Collection<String> coll =`<br>`   new ArrayList<String>();` | The `ArrayList` class implements the `Collection` interface. |
| `coll = new TreeSet<String>();` | The `TreeSet` class (Section 15.3) also implements the `Collection` interface. |
| `int n = coll.size();` | Gets the size of the collection. n is now 0. |
| `coll.add("Harry");`<br>`coll.add("Sally");` | Adds elements to the collection. |
| `String s = coll.toString();` | Returns a string with all elements in the collection. s is now `"[Harry, Sally]"` |
| `System.out.println(coll);` | Invokes the `toString` method and prints `[Harry, Sally]`. |
| `coll.remove("Harry");`<br>`boolean b = coll.remove("Tom");` | Removes an element from the collection, returning `false` if the element is not present. b is false. |
| `b = coll.contains("Sally");` | Checks whether this collection contains a given element. b is now true. |
| `for (String s : coll)`<br>`{`<br>`   System.out.println(s);`<br>`}` | You can use the "for each" loop with any collection. This loop prints the elements on separate lines. |
| `Iterator<String> iter = coll.iterator()` | You use an iterator for visiting the elements in the collection (see Section 15.2.3). |

**SELF CHECK**

1. A gradebook application stores a collection of quizzes. Should it use a list or a set?
2. A student information system stores a collection of student records for a university. Should it use a list or a set?
3. Why is a queue of books a better choice than a stack for organizing your required reading?
4. As you can see from Figure 1, the Java collections framework does not consider a map a collection. Give a reason for this decision.

**Practice It**   Now you can try these exercises at the end of the chapter: R15.1, R15.2, R15.3.

# 15.2 Linked Lists

A **linked list** is a data structure used for collecting a sequence of objects that allows efficient addition and removal of elements in the middle of the sequence. In the following sections, you will learn how a linked list manages its elements and how you can use linked lists in your programs.

## 15.2.1 The Structure of Linked Lists

To understand the inefficiency of arrays and the need for a more efficient data structure, imagine a program that maintains a sequence of employee names. If an employee leaves the company, the name must be removed. In an array, the hole in the sequence needs to be closed up by moving all objects that come after it. Conversely, suppose an employee is added in the middle of the sequence. Then all names following the new hire must be moved toward the end. Moving a large number of elements can involve a substantial amount of processing time. A linked list structure avoids this movement.

*Each node in a linked list is connected to the neighboring nodes.*

> A linked list consists of a number of nodes, each of which has a reference to the next node.

A linked list uses a sequence of *nodes*. A node is an object that stores an element and references to the neighboring nodes in the sequence (see Figure 6).

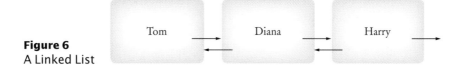

**Figure 6**
A Linked List

When you insert a new node into a linked list, only the neighboring node references need to be updated (see Figure 7).

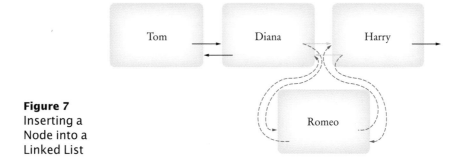

**Figure 7**
Inserting a
Node into a
Linked List

The same is true when you remove a node (see Figure 8). What's the catch? Linked lists allow speedy insertion and removal, but element access can be slow.

**Figure 8**
Removing a
Node from a
Linked List

> Adding and removing elements at a given location in a linked list is efficient.

> Visiting the elements of a linked list in sequential order is efficient, but random access is not.

For example, suppose you want to locate the fifth element. You must first traverse the first four. This is a problem if you need to access the elements in arbitrary order. The term "random access" is used in computer science to describe an access pattern in which elements are accessed in arbitrary (not necessarily random) order. In contrast, sequential access visits the elements in sequence.

Of course, if you mostly visit all elements in sequence (for example, to display or print the elements), the inefficiency of random access is not a problem. You use linked lists when you are concerned about the efficiency of inserting or removing elements and you rarely need element access in random order.

## 15.2.2 The LinkedList Class of the Java Collections Framework

The Java library provides a LinkedList class in the java.util package. It is a **generic class**, just like the ArrayList class. That is, you specify the type of the list elements in angle brackets, such as LinkedList<String> or LinkedList<Employee>.

Table 2 shows important methods of the LinkedList class. (Remember that the LinkedList class also inherits the methods of the Collection interface shown in Table 1.)

As you can see from Table 2, there are methods for accessing the beginning and the end of the list directly. However, to visit the other elements, you need a list **iterator**. We discuss iterators next.

### Table 2 Working with Linked Lists

| | |
|---|---|
| `LinkedList<String> list = new LinkedList<String>();` | An empty list. |
| `list.addLast("Harry");` | Adds an element to the end of the list. Same as add. |
| `list.addFirst("Sally");` | Adds an element to the beginning of the list. list is now [Sally, Harry]. |
| `list.getFirst();` | Gets the element stored at the beginning of the list; here "Sally". |
| `list.getLast();` | Gets the element stored at the end of the list; here "Harry". |
| `String removed = list.removeFirst();` | Removes the first element of the list and returns it. removed is "Sally" and list is [Harry]. Use removeLast to remove the last element. |
| `ListIterator<String> iter = list.listIterator()` | Provides an iterator for visiting all list elements (see Table 3 on page 676). |

## 15.2.3 List Iterators

An iterator encapsulates a position anywhere inside the linked list. Conceptually, you should think of the iterator as pointing between two elements, just as the cursor in a word processor points between two characters (see Figure 9). In the conceptual view, think of each element as being like a letter in a word processor, and think of the iterator as being like the blinking cursor between letters.

You obtain a list iterator with the `listIterator` method of the `LinkedList` class:

```
LinkedList<String> employeeNames = . . .;
ListIterator<String> iterator = employeeNames.listIterator();
```

ANIMATION
*List Iterators*

Note that the iterator class is also a generic type. A `ListIterator<String>` iterates through a list of strings; a `ListIterator<Book>` visits the elements in a `LinkedList<Book>`.

Initially, the iterator points before the first element. You can move the iterator position with the `next` method:

```
iterator.next();
```

The `next` method throws a `NoSuchElementException` if you are already past the end of the list. You should always call the iterator's `hasNext` method before calling `next`—it returns `true` if there is a next element.

```
if (iterator.hasNext())
{
    iterator.next();
}
```

The `next` method returns the element that the iterator is passing. When you use a `ListIterator<String>`, the return type of the `next` method is `String`. In general, the return type of the `next` method matches the list iterator's type parameter (which reflects the type of the elements in the list).

You traverse all elements in a linked list of strings with the following loop:

```
while (iterator.hasNext())
{
    String name = iterator.next();
    Do something with name
}
```

As a shorthand, if your loop simply visits all elements of the linked list, you can use the "for each" loop:

```
for (String name : employeeNames)
{
    Do something with name
}
```

Then you don't have to worry about iterators at all. Behind the scenes, the `for` loop uses an iterator to visit all list elements.

**Figure 9** A Conceptual View of the List Iterator

The nodes of the `LinkedList` class store two links: one to the next element and one to the previous one. Such a list is called a **doubly-linked list.** You can use the `previous` and `hasPrevious` methods of the `ListIterator` interface to move the iterator position backward.

The `add` method adds an object after the iterator, then moves the iterator position past the new element.

```
iterator.add("Juliet");
```

You can visualize insertion to be like typing text in a word processor. Each character is inserted after the cursor, then the cursor moves past the inserted character (see Figure 9). Most people never pay much attention to this—you may want to try it out and watch carefully how your word processor inserts characters.

The `remove` method removes the object that was returned by the last call to `next` or `previous`. For example, this loop removes all names that fulfill a certain condition:

```
while (iterator.hasNext())
{
    String name = iterator.next();
    if (condition is fulfilled for name)
    {
        iterator.remove();
    }
}
```

You have to be careful when calling `remove`. It can be called only *once* after calling `next` or `previous`, and you cannot call it immediately after a call to `add`. If you call the method improperly, it throws an `IllegalStateException`.

Table 3 summarizes the methods of the `ListIterator` interface. The `ListIterator` interface extends a more general `Iterator` interface that is suitable for arbitrary collections, not just lists. The table indicates which methods are specific to list iterators.

Following is a sample program that inserts strings into a list and then iterates through the list, adding and removing elements. Finally, the entire list is printed. The comments indicate the iterator position.

| Table 3 Methods of the `Iterator` and `ListIterator` Interfaces | |
| --- | --- |
| `String s = iter.next();` | Assume that `iter` points to the beginning of the list `[Sally]` before calling `next`. After the call, `s` is `"Sally"` and the iterator points to the end. |
| `iter.previous();`<br>`iter.set("Juliet");` | The `set` method updates the last element returned by `next` or `previous`. The list is now `[Juliet]`. |
| `iter.hasNext()` | Returns `false` because the iterator is at the end of the collection. |
| `if (iter.hasPrevious())`<br>`{`<br>`    s = iter.previous();`<br>`}` | `hasPrevious` returns `true` because the iterator is not at the beginning of the list. `previous` and `hasPrevious` are `ListIterator` methods. |
| `iter.add("Diana");` | Adds an element before the iterator position (`ListIterator` only). The list is now `[Diana, Juliet]`. |
| `iter.next();`<br>`iter.remove();` | `remove` removes the last element returned by `next` or `previous`. The list is now `[Diana]`. |

**section_2/ListDemo.java**

```java
 1  import java.util.LinkedList;
 2  import java.util.ListIterator;
 3
 4  /**
 5     This program demonstrates the LinkedList class.
 6  */
 7  public class ListDemo
 8  {
 9     public static void main(String[] args)
10     {
11        LinkedList<String> staff = new LinkedList<String>();
12        staff.addLast("Diana");
13        staff.addLast("Harry");
14        staff.addLast("Romeo");
15        staff.addLast("Tom");
16
17        // | in the comments indicates the iterator position
18
19        ListIterator<String> iterator = staff.listIterator(); // |DHRT
20        iterator.next(); // D|HRT
21        iterator.next(); // DH|RT
22
23        // Add more elements after second element
24
25        iterator.add("Juliet"); // DHJ|RT
26        iterator.add("Nina"); // DHJN|RT
27
28        iterator.next(); // DHJNR|T
29
30        // Remove last traversed element
31
32        iterator.remove(); // DHJN|T
33
34        // Print all elements
35
36        System.out.println(staff);
37        System.out.println("Expected: [Diana, Harry, Juliet, Nina, Tom]");
38     }
39  }
```

**Program Run**

```
[Diana, Harry, Juliet, Nina, Tom]
Expected: [Diana, Harry, Juliet, Nina, Tom]
```

**SELF CHECK**

5. Do linked lists take more storage space than arrays of the same size?

6. Why don't we need iterators with arrays?

7. Suppose the list lst contains elements "A", "B", "C", and "D". Draw the contents of the list and the iterator position for the following operations:

```java
ListIterator<String> iter = letters.iterator();
iter.next();
iter.next();
iter.remove();
iter.next();
iter.add("E");
```

```
iter.next();
iter.add("F");
```

8. Write a loop that removes all strings with length less than four from a linked list of strings called words.

9. Write a loop that prints every second element of a linked list of strings called words.

**Practice It**    Now you can try these exercises at the end of the chapter: R15.4, R15.7, P15.1.

## Random Fact 15.1 Standardization

You encounter the benefits of standardization every day. When you buy a light bulb, you can be assured that it fits the socket without having to measure the socket at home and the light bulb in the store. In fact, you may have experienced how painful the lack of standards can be if you have ever purchased a flashlight with nonstandard bulbs. Replacement bulbs for such a flashlight can be difficult and expensive to obtain.

Programmers have a similar desire for standardization. Consider the important goal of platform independence for Java programs. After you compile a Java program into class files, you can execute the class files on any computer that has a Java virtual machine. For this to work, the behavior of the virtual machine has to be strictly defined. If all virtual machines don't behave exactly the same way, then the slogan of "write once, run anywhere" turns into "write once, debug everywhere". In order for multiple implementors to create compatible virtual machines, the virtual machine needed to be standardized. That is, someone needed to create a definition of the virtual machine and its expected behavior.

Who creates standards? Some of the most successful standards have been created by volunteer groups such as the Internet Engineering Task Force (IETF) and the World Wide Web Consortium (W3C). The IETF standardizes protocols used in the Internet, such as the protocol for exchanging e-mail messages. The W3C standardizes the Hypertext Markup Language (HTML), the format for web pages. These standards have been instrumental in the creation of the World Wide Web as an open platform that is not controlled by any one company.

Many programming languages, such as C++ and Scheme, have been standardized by independent standards organizations, such as the American National Standards Institute (ANSI) and the International Organization for Standardization—called ISO for short (not an acronym; see http://www.iso.org/iso/about/discover-iso_isos-name.htm). ANSI and ISO are associations of industry professionals who develop standards for everything from car tires to credit card shapes to programming languages.

When a company invents a new technology, it has an interest in its invention becoming a standard, so that other vendors produce tools that work with the invention and thus increase its likelihood of success. On the other hand, by handing over the invention to a standards committee, especially one that insists on a fair process, the company may lose control over the standard. For that reason, Sun Microsystems, the inventor of Java, never agreed to have a third-party organization standardize the Java language. They put in place their own standard-

ization process, involving other companies but refusing to relinquish control. Another unfortunate but common tactic is to create a weak standard. For example, Netscape and Microsoft chose the European Computer Manufacturers Association (ECMA) to standardize the JavaScript language. ECMA was willing to settle for something less than truly useful, standardizing the behavior of the core language and just a few of its libraries.

Of course, many important pieces of technology aren't standardized at all. Consider the Windows operating system. Although Windows is often called a de-facto standard, it really is no standard at all. Nobody has ever attempted to define formally what the Windows operating system should do. The behavior changes at the whim of its vendor. That suits Microsoft just fine, because it makes it impossible for a third party to create its own version of Windows.

As a computer professional, there will be many times in your career when you need to make a decision whether to support a particular standard. Consider a simple example. In this chapter, you learn about the collection classes from the standard Java library. However, many computer scientists dislike these classes because of their numerous design issues. Should you use the Java collections in your own code, or should you implement a better set of collections? If you do the former, you have to deal with a design that is less than optimal. If you do the latter, other programmers may have a hard time understanding your code because they aren't familiar with your classes.

# 15.3 Sets

As you learned in Section 15.1, a **set** organizes its values in an order that is optimized for efficiency, which may not be the order in which you add elements. Inserting and removing elements is faster with a set than with a list.

In the following sections, you will learn how to choose a set implementation and how to work with sets.

## 15.3.1 Choosing a Set Implementation

> The HashSet and TreeSet classes both implement the Set interface.

The Set interface in the standard Java library has the same methods as the Collection interface, shown in Table 1. However, there is an essential difference between arbitrary collections and sets. A set does not admit duplicates. If you add an element to a set that is already present, the insertion is ignored.

The HashSet and TreeSet classes implement the Set interface. These two classes provide set implementations based on two different mechanisms, called **hash tables** and **binary search trees**. Both implementations arrange the set elements so that finding, adding, and removing elements is fast, but they use different strategies.

> Set implementations arrange the elements so that they can locate them quickly.

The basic idea of a hash table is simple. Set elements are grouped into smaller collections of elements that share the same characteristic. You can imagine a hash set of books as having a group for each color, so that books of the same color are in the same group. To find whether a book is already present, you just need to check it against the books in the same color group. Actually, hash tables don't use colors, but integer values (called hash codes) that can be computed from the elements.

In order to use a hash table, the elements must have a method to compute those integer values. This method is called hashCode. The elements must also belong to a class with a properly defined equals method (see Special Topic 9.7).

> You can form hash sets holding objects of type String, Integer, Double, Point, Rectangle, or Color.

Many classes in the standard library implement these methods, for example String, Integer, Double, Point, Rectangle, Color, and all the collection classes. Therefore, you can form a HashSet<String>, HashSet<Rectangle>, or even a HashSet<HashSet<Integer>>.

Suppose you want to form a set of elements belonging to a class that you declared, such as a HashSet<Book>. Then you need to provide hashCode and equals methods for the class Book. There is one exception to this rule. If all elements are distinct (for example, if your program never has two Book objects with the same author and title), then you can simply inherit the hashCode and equals methods of the Object class.

*On this shelf, books of the same color are grouped together. Similarly, in a hash table, objects with the same hash code are placed in the same group.*

*A tree set keeps its elements in sorted order.*

The TreeSet class uses a different strategy for arranging its elements. Elements are kept in sorted order. For example, a set of books might be arranged by height, or alphabetically by author and title. The elements are not stored in an array—that would make adding and removing elements too slow. Instead, they are stored in nodes, as in a linked list. However, the nodes are not arranged in a linear sequence but in a tree shape.

> You can form tree sets for any class that implements the Comparable interface, such as String or Integer.

In order to use a TreeSet, it must be possible to compare the elements and determine which one is "larger". You can use a TreeSet for classes such as String and Integer that implement the Comparable interface, which we discussed in Section 9.6.3. (That section also shows you how you can implement comparison methods for your own classes.)

As a rule of thumb, you should choose a TreeSet if you want to visit the set's elements in sorted order. Otherwise choose a HashSet—as long as the hash function is well chosen, it is a bit more efficient.

When you construct a HashSet or TreeSet, store the reference in a Set<String> variable, either as

```
Set<String> names = new HashSet<String>();
```
or
```
Set<String> names = new TreeSet<String>();
```

After you construct the collection object, the implementation no longer matters; only the interface is important.

## 15.3.2 Working with Sets

Adding and removing set elements are accomplished with the add and remove methods:

```
names.add("Romeo");
names.remove("Juliet");
```

> Sets don't have duplicates. Adding a duplicate of an element that is already present is ignored.

As in mathematics, a set collection in Java rejects duplicates. Adding an element has no effect if the element is already in the set. Similarly, attempting to remove an element that isn't in the set is ignored.

The contains method tests whether an element is contained in the set:

```
if (names.contains("Juliet")) . . .
```

Finally, to list all elements in the set, get an iterator. As with list iterators, you use the next and hasNext methods to step through the set.

```
Iterator<String> iter = names.iterator();
while (iter.hasNext())
{
   String name = iter.next();
   Do something with name
}
```

You can also use the "for each" loop instead of explicitly using an iterator:

```
for (String name : names)
{
    Do something with name
}
```

A set iterator visits the elements in the order in which the set implementation keeps them.

A set iterator visits the elements in the order in which the set implementation keeps them. This is not necessarily the order in which you inserted them. The order of elements in a hash set seems quite random because the hash code spreads the elements into different groups. When you visit elements of a tree set, they always appear in sorted order, even if you inserted them in a different order.

There is an important difference between the `Iterator` that you obtain from a set and the `ListIterator` that a list yields. The `ListIterator` has an `add` method to add an element at the list iterator position. The `Iterator` interface has no such method. It makes no sense to add an element at a particular position in a set, because the set can order the elements any way it likes. Thus, you always add elements directly to a set, never to an iterator of the set.

You cannot add an element to a set at an iterator position.

However, you can remove a set element at an iterator position, just as you do with list iterators.

Also, the `Iterator` interface has no `previous` method to go backward through the elements. Because the elements are not ordered, it is not meaningful to distinguish between "going forward" and "going backward".

| Table 4  Working with Sets | |
|---|---|
| `Set<String> names;` | Use the interface type for variable declarations. |
| `names = new HashSet<String>();` | Use a `TreeSet` if you need to visit the elements in sorted order. |
| `names.add("Romeo");` | Now `names.size()` is 1. |
| `names.add("Fred");` | Now `names.size()` is 2. |
| `names.add("Romeo");` | `names.size()` is still 2. You can't add duplicates. |
| `if (names.contains("Fred"))` | The contains method checks whether a value is contained in the set. In this case, the method returns true. |
| `System.out.println(names);` | Prints the set in the format [Fred, Romeo]. The elements need not be shown in the order in which they were inserted. |
| `for (String name : names)`<br>`{`<br>`    . . .`<br>`}` | Use this loop to visit all elements of a set. |
| `names.remove("Romeo");` | Now `names.size()` is 1. |
| `names.remove("Juliet");` | It is not an error to remove an element that is not present. The method call has no effect. |

The following program shows a practical application of sets. It reads in all words from a dictionary file that contains correctly spelled words and places them in a set. It then reads all words from a document—here, the book *Alice in Wonderland*—into a second set. Finally, it prints all words from that set that are not in the dictionary set. These are the potential misspellings. (As you can see from the output, we used an American dictionary, and words with British spelling, such as *clamour*, are flagged as potential errors.)

**section_3/SpellCheck.java**

```java
1   import java.util.HashSet;
2   import java.util.Scanner;
3   import java.util.Set;
4   import java.io.File;
5   import java.io.FileNotFoundException;
6
7   /**
8      This program checks which words in a file are not present in a dictionary.
9   */
10  public class SpellCheck
11  {
12     public static void main(String[] args)
13        throws FileNotFoundException
14     {
15        // Read the dictionary and the document
16
17        Set<String> dictionaryWords = readWords("words");
18        Set<String> documentWords = readWords("alice30.txt");
19
20        // Print all words that are in the document but not the dictionary
21
22        for (String word : documentWords)
23        {
24           if (!dictionaryWords.contains(word))
25           {
26              System.out.println(word);
27           }
28        }
29     }
30
31     /**
32        Reads all words from a file.
33        @param filename the name of the file
34        @return a set with all lowercased words in the file. Here, a
35        word is a sequence of upper- and lowercase letters.
36     */
37     public static Set<String> readWords(String filename)
38        throws FileNotFoundException
39     {
40        Set<String> words = new HashSet<String>();
41        Scanner in = new Scanner(new File(filename));
42        // Use any characters other than a-z or A-Z as delimiters
43        in.useDelimiter("[^a-zA-Z]+");
44        while (in.hasNext())
45        {
46           words.add(in.next().toLowerCase());
47        }
```

```
48        return words;
49    }
50 }
```

**Program Run**

```
neighbouring
croqueted
pennyworth
dutchess
comfits
xii
dinn
clamour
...
```

**10.** Arrays and lists remember the order in which you added elements; sets do not. Why would you want to use a set instead of an array or list?

**11.** Why are set iterators different from list iterators?

**12.** What is wrong with the following test to check whether the Set<String> s contains the elements "Tom", "Diana", and "Harry"?

```
if (s.toString().equals("[Tom, Diana, Harry]")) . . .
```

**13.** How can you correctly implement the test of Self Check 12?

**14.** Write a loop that prints all elements that are in both Set<String> s and Set<String> t.

**15.** Suppose you changed line 40 of the SpellCheck program to use a TreeSet instead of a HashSet. How would the output change?

**Practice It** Now you can try these exercises at the end of the chapter: P15.7, P15.8, P15.13.

---

**Programming Tip 15.1**

### Use Interface References to Manipulate Data Structures

It is considered good style to store a reference to a HashSet or TreeSet in a variable of type Set:

```
Set<String> words = new HashSet<String>();
```

This way, you have to change only one line if you decide to use a TreeSet instead.

If a method can operate on arbitrary collections, use the Collection interface type for the parameter variable:

```
public static void removeLongWords(Collection<String> words)
```

In theory, we should make the same recommendation for the List interface, namely to save ArrayList and LinkedList references in variables of type List. However, the List interface has get and set methods for random access, even though these methods are very inefficient for linked lists. You can't write efficient code if you don't know whether the methods that you are calling are efficient or not. This is plainly a serious design error in the standard library, and it makes the List interface somewhat unattractive.

# 15.4 Maps

The HashMap and TreeMap classes both implement the Map interface.

A **map** allows you to associate elements from a *key set* with elements from a *value collection*. You use a map when you want to look up objects by using a key. For example, Figure 10 shows a map from the names of people to their favorite colors.

Just as there are two kinds of set implementations, the Java library has two implementations for the Map interface: HashMap and TreeMap.

After constructing a HashMap or TreeMap, you can store the reference to the map object in a Map reference:

```
Map<String, Color> favoriteColors = new HashMap<String, Color>();
```

Use the put method to add an association:

```
favoriteColors.put("Juliet", Color.RED);
```

You can change the value of an existing association, simply by calling put again:

```
favoriteColors.put("Juliet", Color.BLUE);
```

The get method returns the value associated with a key.

```
Color julietsFavoriteColor = favoriteColors.get("Juliet");
```

If you ask for a key that isn't associated with any values, then the get method returns null.

To remove an association, call the remove method with the key:

```
favoriteColors.remove("Juliet");
```

ANIMATION
*Using a Map*

| Table 5 Working with Maps | |
|---|---|
| `Map<String, Integer> scores;` | Keys are strings, values are Integer wrappers. Use the interface type for variable declarations. |
| `scores = new TreeMap<String, Integer>();` | Use a HashMap if you don't need to visit the keys in sorted order. |
| `scores.put("Harry", 90);`<br>`scores.put("Sally", 95);` | Adds keys and values to the map. |
| `scores.put("Sally", 100);` | Modifies the value of an existing key. |
| `int n = scores.get("Sally");`<br>`Integer n2 = scores.get("Diana");` | Gets the value associated with a key, or null if the key is not present. n is 100, n2 is null. |
| `System.out.println(scores);` | Prints scores.toString(), a string of the form {Harry=90, Sally=100} |
| `for (String key : scores.keySet())`<br>`{`<br>`    Integer value = scores.get(key);`<br>`    . . .`<br>`}` | Iterates through all map keys and values. |
| `scores.remove("Sally");` | Removes the key and value. |

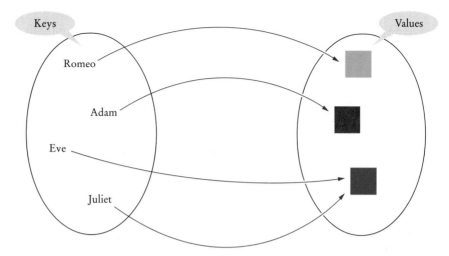

**Figure 10** A Map

To find all keys and values in a map, iterate through the key set and find the values that correspond to the keys.

Sometimes you want to enumerate all keys in a map. The keySet method yields the set of keys. You can then ask the key set for an iterator and get all keys. From each key, you can find the associated value with the get method. Thus, the following instructions print all key/value pairs in a map m:

```
Set<String> keySet = m.keySet();
for (String key : keySet)
{
   Color value = m.get(key);
   System.out.println(key + "->" + value);
}
```

This sample program shows a map in action:

### section_4/MapDemo.java

```
1   import java.awt.Color;
2   import java.util.HashMap;
3   import java.util.Map;
4   import java.util.Set;
5
6   /**
7      This program demonstrates a map that maps names to colors.
8   */
9   public class MapDemo
10  {
11     public static void main(String[] args)
12     {
13        Map<String, Color> favoriteColors = new HashMap<String, Color>();
14        favoriteColors.put("Juliet", Color.BLUE);
15        favoriteColors.put("Romeo", Color.GREEN);
16        favoriteColors.put("Adam", Color.RED);
17        favoriteColors.put("Eve", Color.BLUE);
18
19        // Print all keys and values in the map
20
21        Set<String> keySet = favoriteColors.keySet();
```

```
22          for (String key : keySet)
23          {
24              Color value = favoriteColors.get(key);
25              System.out.println(key + " : " + value);
26          }
27      }
28  }
```

**Program Run**

```
Juliet : java.awt.Color[r=0,g=0,b=255]
Adam : java.awt.Color[r=255,g=0,b=0]
Eve : java.awt.Color[r=0,g=0,b=255]
Romeo : java.awt.Color[r=0,g=255,b=0]
```

**SELF CHECK**

16. What is the difference between a set and a map?

17. Why is the collection of the keys of a map a set and not a list?

18. Why is the collection of the values of a map not a set?

19. Suppose you want to track how many times each word occurs in a document. Declare a suitable map variable.

20. What is a Map<String, HashSet<String>>? Give a possible use for such a structure.

**Practice It**   Now you can try these exercises at the end of the chapter: R15.17, P15.9, P15.14.

---

HOW TO 15.1        **Choosing a Collection**

Suppose you need to store objects in a collection. You have now seen a number of different data structures. This How To reviews how to pick an appropriate collection for your application.

**Step 1**   Determine how you access the values.

You store values in a collection so that you can later retrieve them. How do you want to access individual values? You have several choices:

- Values are accessed by an integer position. Use an ArrayList.
- Values are accessed by a key that is not a part of the object. Use a map.
- Values are accessed only at one of the ends. Use a queue (for first-in, first-out access) or a stack (for last-in, first-out access).
- You don't need to access individual values by position. Refine your choice in Steps 3 and 4.

**Step 2**   Determine the element types or key/value types.

For a list or set, determine the type of the elements that you want to store. For example, if you collect a set of books, then the element type is Book.

Similarly, for a map, determine the types of the keys and the associated values. If you want to look up books by ID, you can use a Map<Integer, Book> or Map<String, Book>, depending on your ID type.

**Step 3** Determine whether element or key order matters.

When you visit elements from a collection or keys from a map, do you care about the order in which they are visited? You have several choices:

- Elements or keys must be sorted. Use a TreeSet or TreeMap. Go to Step 6.
- Elements must be in the same order in which they were inserted. Your choice is now narrowed down to a LinkedList or an ArrayList.
- It doesn't matter. As long as you get to visit all elements, you don't care in which order. If you chose a map in Step 1, use a HashMap and go to Step 5.

**Step 4** For a collection, determine which operations must be fast.

You have several choices:

- Finding elements must be fast. Use a HashSet.
- It must be fast to add or remove elements at the beginning, or, provided that you are already inspecting an element there, another position. Use a LinkedList.
- You only insert or remove at the end, or you collect so few elements that you aren't concerned about speed. Use an ArrayList.

**Step 5** For hash sets and maps, decide whether you need to implement the hashCode and equals methods.

- If your elements or keys belong to a class that someone else implemented, check whether the class has its own hashCode and equals methods. If so, you are all set. This is the case for most classes in the standard Java library, such as String, Integer, Rectangle, and so on.
- If not, decide whether you can compare the elements by identity. This is the case if you never construct two distinct elements with the same contents. In that case, you need not do anything—the hashCode and equals methods of the Object class are appropriate.
- Otherwise, you need to implement your own equals and hashCode methods—see Special Topics 9.7 and Special Topic 15.1.

**Step 6** If you use a tree, decide whether to supply a comparator.

Look at the class of the set elements or map keys. Does that class implement the Comparable interface? If so, is the sort order given by the compareTo method the one you want? If yes, then you don't need to do anything further. This is the case for many classes in the standard library, in particular for String and Integer.

If not, then your element class must implement the Comparable interface (Section 9.6.3), or you must declare a class that implements the Comparator interface (see Special Topic 14.5).

---

**WORKED EXAMPLE 15.1** **Word Frequency**

In this Worked Example, we read a text file and print a list of all words in the file in alphabetical order, together with a count that indicates how often each word occurred in the file.

➕ Available online in WileyPLUS and at www.wiley.com/college/horstmann.

### Hash Functions

If you use a hash set or hash map with your own classes, you may need to implement a hash function. A **hash function** is a function that computes an integer value, the **hash code**, from an object in such a way that different objects are likely to yield different hash codes. Because hashing is so important, the `Object` class has a `hashCode` method. The call

```
int h = x.hashCode();
```

computes the hash code of any object x. If you want to put objects of a given class into a `HashSet` or use the objects as keys in a `HashMap`, the class should override this method. The method should be implemented so that different objects are likely to have different hash codes.

*A good hash function produces different hash values for each object so that they are scattered about in a hash table.*

For example, the `String` class declares a hash function for strings that does a good job of producing different integer values for different strings. Table 6 shows some examples of strings and their hash codes.

> A hash function computes an integer value from an object.

It is possible for two or more distinct objects to have the same hash code; this is called a *collision*. For example, the strings `"Ugh"` and `"VII"` happen to have the same hash code, but these collisions are very rare for strings (see Exercise P15.15).

> A good hash function minimizes *collisions*— identical hash codes for different objects.

The `hashCode` method of the `String` class combines the characters of a string into a numerical code. The code isn't simply the sum of the character values—that would not scramble the character values enough. Strings that are permutations of another (such as `"eat"` and `"tea"`) would all have the same hash code.

Here is the method the standard library uses to compute the hash code for a string:

```
final int HASH_MULTIPLIER = 31;
int h = 0;
for (int i = 0; i < s.length(); i++)
{
   h = HASH_MULTIPLIER * h + s.charAt(i);
}
```

For example, the hash code of `"eat"` is

```
31 * (31 * 'e' + 'a') + 't' = 100184
```

| Table 6 Sample Strings and Their Hash Codes | |
| --- | --- |
| String | Hash Code |
| `"eat"` | 100184 |
| `"tea"` | 114704 |
| `"Juliet"` | –2065036585 |
| `"Ugh"` | 84982 |
| `"VII"` | 84982 |

The hash code of "tea" is quite different, namely

```
31 * (31 * 't' + 'e') + 'a' = 114704
```

(Use the Unicode table from Appendix A to look up the character values: 'a' is 97, 'e' is 101, and 't' is 116.)

For your own classes, you should make up a hash code that combines the hash codes of the instance variables in a similar way. For example, let us declare a hashCode method for the Country class from Section 9.6.

> Override hashCode methods in your own classes by combining the hash codes for the instance variables.

There are two instance variables: the country name and the area. First, compute their hash codes. You know how to compute the hash code of a string. To compute the hash code of a floating-point number, first wrap the floating-point number into a Double object, and then compute its hash code.

```java
public class Country
{
    public int hashCode()
    {
        int h1 = name.hashCode();
        int h2 = new Double(area).hashCode();
        . . .
    }
}
```

Then combine the two hash codes:

```java
final int HASH_MULTIPLIER = 29;
int h = HASH_MULTIPLIER * h1 + h2;
return h;
```

Use a prime number as the hash multiplier—it scrambles the values well.

If you have more than two instance variables, then combine their hash codes as follows:

```java
int h = HASH_MULTIPLIER * h1 + h2;
h = HASH_MULTIPLIER * h + h3;
h = HASH_MULTIPLIER * h + h4;
. . .
return h;
```

If one of the instance variables is an integer, just use the value as its hash code.

When you supply your own hashCode method for a class, you must also provide a compatible equals method. The equals method is used to differentiate between two objects that happen to have the same hash code.

The equals and hashCode methods must be *compatible* with each other. Two objects that are equal must yield the same hash code.

> A class's hashCode method must be compatible with its equals method.

**ONLINE EXAMPLE**

A program that demonstrates a hash set with objects of the Country class.

You get into trouble if your class declares an equals method but not a hashCode method. Suppose the Country class declares an equals method (checking that the name and area are the same), but no hashCode method. Then the hashCode method is inherited from the Object superclass. That method computes a hash code from the *memory location* of the object. Then it is very likely that two objects with the same contents will have different hash codes, in which case a hash set will store them as two distinct objects.

However, if you declare *neither* equals *nor* hashCode, then there is no problem. The equals method of the Object class considers two objects equal only if their memory location is the same. That is, the Object class has compatible equals and hashCode methods. Of course, then the notion of equality is very restricted: Only identical objects are considered equal. That can be a perfectly valid notion of equality, depending on your application.

# 15.5 Stacks, Queues, and Priority Queues

In the following sections, we cover stacks, queues, and priority queues. These data structures each have a different policy for data removal. Removing an element yields the most recently added element, the least recently added, or the element with the highest priority.

## 15.5.1 Stacks

A stack is a collection of elements with "last-in, first-out" retrieval.

A **stack** lets you insert and remove elements only at one end, traditionally called the *top* of the stack. New items can be added to the top of the stack. Items are removed from the top of the stack as well. Therefore, they are removed in the order that is opposite from the order in which they have been added, called *last-in, first-out* or *LIFO* order. For example, if you add items A, B, and C and then remove them, you obtain C, B, and A. With stacks, the addition and removal operations are called push and pop.

*The last pancake that has been added to this stack will be the first one that is consumed.*

```
Stack<String> s = new Stack<String>();
s.push("A"); s.push("B"); s.push("C");
while (s.size() > 0)
{
    System.out.print(s.pop() + " "); // Prints C B A
}
```

*The Undo key pops commands off a stack, so that the last command is the first to be undone.*

There are many applications for stacks in computer science. Consider the undo feature of a word processor. It keeps the issued commands in a stack. When you select "Undo", the *last* command is undone, then the next-to-last, and so on.

Another important example is the **run-time stack** that a processor or virtual machine keeps to store the values of variables in nested methods. Whenever a new method is called, its parameter variables and local variables are pushed onto a stack. When the method exits, they are popped off again.

You will see other applications in Section 15.6.

The Java library provides a simple Stack class with methods push, pop, and peek—the latter gets the top element of the stack but does not remove it (see Table 7).

| Table 7 Working with Stacks | |
|---|---|
| `Stack<Integer> s = new Stack<Integer>();` | Constructs an empty stack. |
| `s.push(1);`<br>`s.push(2);`<br>`s.push(3);` | Adds to the top of the stack; s is now [1, 2, 3]. (Following the toString method of the Stack class, we show the top of the stack at the end.) |
| `int top = s.pop();` | Removes the top of the stack; top is set to 3 and s is now [1, 2]. |
| `head = s.peek();` | Gets the top of the stack without removing it; head is set to 2. |

## 15.5.2 Queues

A queue is a
collection of
elements with
"first-in, first-out"
retrieval.

A **queue** lets you add items to one end of the queue (the *tail*) and remove them from the other end of the queue (the *head*). Queues yield items in a *first-in, first-out* or *FIFO* fashion. Items are removed in the same order in which they were added.

A typical application is a print queue. A printer may be accessed by several applications, perhaps running on different computers. If each of the applications tried to access the printer at the same time, the printout would be garbled. Instead,

*To visualize a queue, think of people lining up.*

each application places its print data into a file and adds that file to the print queue. When the printer is done printing one file, it retrieves the next one from the queue. Therefore, print jobs are printed using the "first-in, first-out" rule, which is a fair arrangement for users of the shared printer.

The Queue interface in the standard Java library has methods add to add an element to the tail of the queue, remove to remove the head of the queue, and peek to get the head element of the queue without removing it (see Table 8).

The LinkedList class implements the Queue interface. Whenever you need a queue, simply initialize a Queue variable with a LinkedList object:

```
Queue<String> q = new LinkedList<String>();
q.add("A"); q.add("B"); q.add("C");
while (q.size() > 0) { System.out.print(q.remove() + " "); } // Prints A B C
```

The standard library provides several queue classes that we do not discuss in this book. Those classes are intended for work sharing when multiple activities (called threads) run in parallel.

### Table 8  Working with Queues

| | |
|---|---|
| `Queue<Integer> q = new LinkedList<Integer>();` | The LinkedList class implements the Queue interface. |
| `q.add(1);`<br>`q.add(2);`<br>`q.add(3);` | Adds to the tail of the queue; q is now [1, 2, 3]. |
| `int head = q.remove();` | Removes the head of the queue; head is set to 1 and q is [2, 3]. |
| `head = q.peek();` | Gets the head of the queue without removing it; head is set to 2. |

## 15.5.3 Priority Queues

When removing an
element from a
priority queue, the
element with the
most urgent priority
is retrieved.

A **priority queue** collects elements, each of which has a *priority*. A typical example of a priority queue is a collection of work requests, some of which may be more urgent than others. Unlike a regular queue, the priority queue does not maintain a first-in, first-out discipline. Instead, elements are retrieved according to their priority. In other words, new items can be inserted in any order. But whenever an item is removed, it is the item with the most urgent priority.

*When you retrieve an item from a priority queue, you always get the most urgent one.*

It is customary to give low values to urgent priorities, with priority 1 denoting the most urgent priority. Thus, each removal operation extracts the *minimum* element from the queue.

For example, consider this code in which we add objects of a class Work-Order into a priority queue. Each work order has a priority and a description.

```
PriorityQueue<WorkOrder> q = new PriorityQueue<WorkOrder>();
q.add(new WorkOrder(3, "Shampoo carpets"));
q.add(new WorkOrder(1, "Fix broken sink"));
q.add(new WorkOrder(2, "Order cleaning supplies"));
```

When calling q.remove() for the first time, the work order with priority 1 is removed. The next call to q.remove() removes the work order whose priority is highest among those remaining in the queue—in our example, the work order with priority 2. If there happen to be two elements with the same priority, the priority queue will break ties arbitrarily.

Because the priority queue needs to be able to tell which element is the smallest, the added elements should belong to a class that implements the Comparable interface. (See Section 9.6.3 for a description of that interface type.)

Table 9 shows the methods of the PriorityQueue class in the standard Java library.

**ONLINE EXAMPLE**

⊕ Programs that demonstrate stacks, queues, and priority queues.

### Table 9 Working with Priority Queues

| | |
|---|---|
| `PriorityQueue<Integer> q =`<br>`   new PriorityQueue<Integer>();` | This priority queue holds Integer objects. In practice, you would use objects that describe tasks. |
| `q.add(3); q.add(1); q.add(2);` | Adds values to the priority queue. |
| `int first = q.remove();`<br>`int second = q.remove();` | Each call to remove removes the lowest priority item: first is set to 1, second to 2. |
| `int next = q.peek();` | Gets the smallest value in the priority queue without removing it. |

**SELF CHECK**

21. Why would you want to declare a variable as

    `Queue<String> q = new LinkedList<String>()`

    instead of simply declaring it as a linked list?

22. Why wouldn't you want to use an array list for implementing a queue?

23. What does this code print?

    ```
    Queue<String> q = new LinkedList<String>();
    q.add("A");
    q.add("B");
    q.add("C");
    while (q.size() > 0) { System.out.print(q.remove() + " "); }
    ```

24. Why wouldn't you want to use a stack to manage print jobs?

25. In the sample code for a priority queue, we used a WorkOrder class. Could we have used strings instead?

    ```
    PriorityQueue<String> q = new PriorityQueue<String>();
    q.add("3 - Shampoo carpets");
    q.add("1 - Fix broken sink");
    q.add("2 - Order cleaning supplies");
    ```

**Practice It**  Now you can try these exercises at the end of the chapter: R15.12, P15.3, P15.4.

# 15.6 Stack and Queue Applications

Stacks and queues are, despite their simplicity, very versatile data structures. In the following sections, you will see some of their most useful applications.

## 15.6.1 Balancing Parentheses

A stack can be used to check whether parentheses in an expression are balanced.

In Common Error 2.5, you saw a simple trick for detecting unbalanced parentheses in an expression such as

```
-(b * b - (4 * a * c ) ) / (2 * a)
 1         2           1 0 1       0
```

Increment a counter when you see a ( and decrement it when you see a ). The counter should never be negative, and it should be zero at the end of the expression.

That works for expressions in Java, but in mathematical notation, one can have more than one kind of parentheses, such as

$$-\{\,[\,b\cdot b-(4\cdot a\cdot c)\,]\,/\,(2\cdot a)\,\}$$

To see whether such an expression is correctly formed, place the parentheses on a stack:

**When you see an opening parenthesis, push it on the stack.**
**When you see a closing parenthesis, pop the stack.**
**If the opening and closing parentheses don't match**
     **The parentheses are unbalanced. Exit.**
**If at the end the stack is empty**
     **The parentheses are balanced.**
**Else**
     **The parentheses are not balanced.**

**ONLINE EXAMPLE**
A program for checking balanced parentheses.

Here is a walkthrough of the sample expression:

| Stack | Unread expression | Comments |
|---|---|---|
| Empty | -{ [b * b - (4 * a * c ) ] / (2 * a) } | |
| { | [b * b - (4 * a * c ) ] / (2 * a) } | |
| { [ | b * b - (4 * a * c ) ] / (2 * a) } | |
| { [ ( | 4 * a * c ) ] / (2 * a) } | |
| { [ | ] / (2 * a) } | ( matches ) |
| { | / (2 * a) } | [ matches ] |
| { ( | 2 * a) } | |
| { | } | ( matches ) |
| Empty | No more input | { matches } |
| | | The parentheses are balanced |

## 15.6.2 Evaluating Reverse Polish Expressions

Consider how you write arithmetic expressions, such as (3 + 4) × 5. The parentheses are needed so that 3 and 4 are added before multiplying the result by 5.

However, you can eliminate the parentheses if you write the operators *after* the numbers, like this: 3 4 + 5 × (see Random Fact 15.2 on page 701). To evaluate this expression, apply + to 3 and 4, yielding 7, and then simplify 7 5 × to 35. It gets trickier for complex expressions. For example, 3 4 5 + × means to compute 4 5 + (that is, 9), and then evaluate 3 9 ×. If we evaluate this expression left-to-right, we need to leave the 3 somewhere while we work on 4 5 +. Where? We put it on a stack. The algorithm for evaluating reverse Polish expressions is simple:

> If you read a number
>> Push it on the stack.
> Else if you read an operand
>> Pop two values off the stack.
>> Combine the values with the operand.
>> Push the result back onto the stack.
> Else if there is no more input
>> Pop and display the result.

Here is a walkthrough of evaluating the expression 3 4 5 + ×:

| Stack | Unread expression | Comments |
|---|---|---|
| Empty | 3 4 5 + x | |
| 3 | 4 5 + x | Numbers are pushed on the stack |
| 3 4 | 5 + x | |
| 3 4 5 | + x | |
| 3 9 | x | Pop 4 and 5, push 4 5 + |
| 27 | No more input | Pop 3 and 9, push 3 9 x |
| Empty | | Pop and display the result, 27 |

The following program simulates a reverse Polish calculator:

**section_6_2/Calculator.java**

```java
1   import java.util.Scanner;
2   import java.util.Stack;
3
4   /**
5       This calculator uses the reverse Polish notation.
6   */
7   public class Calculator
8   {
9       public static void main(String[] args)
10      {
11          Scanner in = new Scanner(System.in);
12          Stack<Integer> results = new Stack<Integer>();
13          System.out.println("Enter one number or operator per line, Q to quit. ");
14          boolean done = false;
```

```
15        while (!done)
16        {
17            String input = in.nextLine();
18
19            // If the command is an operator, pop the arguments and push the result
20
21            if (input.equals("+"))
22            {
23                results.push(results.pop() + results.pop());
24            }
25            else if (input.equals("-"))
26            {
27                Integer arg2 = results.pop();
28                results.push(results.pop() - arg2);
29            }
30            else if (input.equals("*") || input.equals("x"))
31            {
32                results.push(results.pop() * results.pop());
33            }
34            else if (input.equals("/"))
35            {
36                Integer arg2 = results.pop();
37                results.push(results.pop() / arg2);
38            }
39            else if (input.equals("Q") || input.equals("q"))
40            {
41                done = true;
42            }
43            else
44            {
45                // Not an operator--push the input value
46
47                results.push(Integer.parseInt(input));
48            }
49            System.out.println(results);
50        }
51    }
52 }
```

### 15.6.3  Evaluating Algebraic Expressions

Using two stacks, you can evaluate expressions in standard algebraic notation.

In the preceding section, you saw how to evaluate expressions in reverse Polish notation, using a single stack. If you haven't found that notation attractive, you will be glad to know that one can evaluate an expression in the standard algebraic notation using two stacks—one for numbers and one for operators.

*Use two stacks to evaluate algebraic expressions.*

First, consider a simple example, the expression 3 + 4. We push the numbers on the number stack and the operators on the operator stack. Then we pop both numbers and the operator, combine the numbers with the operator, and push the result.

| | Number stack | Operator stack | Unprocessed input | Comments |
|---|---|---|---|---|
| | Empty | Empty | 3 + 4 | |
| **1** | 3 | | + 4 | |
| **2** | 3 | + | 4 | |
| **3** | 4<br>3 | + | No more input | Evaluate the top. |
| **4** | 7 | | | The result is 7. |

This operation is fundamental to the algorithm. We call it "evaluating the top".

In algebraic notation, each operator has a *precedence*. The + and - operators have the lowest precedence, * and / have a higher (and equal) precedence.

Consider the expression 3 × 4 + 5. Here are the first processing steps:

| | Number stack | Operator stack | Unprocessed input | Comments |
|---|---|---|---|---|
| | Empty | Empty | 3 × 4 + 5 | |
| **1** | 3 | | × 4 + 5 | |
| **2** | 3 | × | 4 + 5 | |
| **3** | 4<br>3 | × | + 5 | Evaluate × before +. |

Because × has a higher precedence than +, we are ready to evaluate the top:

| | Number stack | Operator stack | | Comments |
|---|---|---|---|---|
| **4** | 12 | + | 5 | |
| **5** | 5<br>12 | + | No more input | Evaluate the top. |
| **6** | 17 | | | That is the result. |

With the expression, 3 + 4 × 5, we add × to the operator stack because we must first read the next number; then we can evaluate × and then the +:

| | Number stack | Operator stack | Unprocessed input | Comments |
|---|---|---|---|---|
| | Empty | Empty | 3 + 4 × 5 | |
| **1** | 3 | | + 4 × 5 | |
| **2** | 3 | + | 4 + 5 | |

| | Number stack | Operator stack | | Comments |
|---|---|---|---|---|
| **3** | 4 <br> 3 | + | × 5 | Don't evaluate + yet. |
| **4** | 4 <br> 3 | × <br> + | 5 | |

In other words, we keep operators on the stack until they are ready to be evaluated. Here is the remainder of the computation:

| | Number stack | Operator stack | | Comments |
|---|---|---|---|---|
| **5** | 5 <br> 4 <br> 3 | × <br> + | No more input | Evaluate the top. |
| **6** | 20 <br> 3 | + | | Evaluate top again. |
| **7** | 23 | | | That is the result. |

To see how parentheses are handled, consider the expression 3 × (4 + 5). A ( is pushed on the operator stack. The + is pushed as well. When we encounter the ), we know that we are ready to evaluate the top until the matching ( reappears:

| | Number stack <br> Empty | Operator stack <br> Empty | Unprocessed input <br> 3 × (4 + 5) | Comments |
|---|---|---|---|---|
| **1** | 3 | | × (4 + 5) | |
| **2** | 3 | × | (4 + 5) | |
| **3** | 3 | ( <br> × | 4 + 5) | Don't evaluate × yet. |
| **4** | 4 <br> 3 | ( <br> × | + 5) | |
| **5** | 4 <br> 3 | + <br> ( <br> × | 5) | |
| **6** | 5 <br> 4 <br> 3 | + <br> ( <br> × | ) | Evaluate the top. |
| **7** | 9 <br> 3 | ( <br> × | No more input | Pop (. |
| **8** | 9 <br> 3 | × | | Evaluate top again. |
| **9** | 27 | | | That is the result. |

Here is the algorithm:

> **If you read a number**
>    Push it on the number stack.
> **Else if you read a (**
>    Push it on the operator stack.
> **Else if you read an operator op**
>    While the top of the stack has a higher precedence than op
>       Evaluate the top.
>    Push op on the operator stack.
> **Else if you read a )**
>    While the top of the stack is not a (
>       Evaluate the top.
>    Pop the (.
> **Else if there is no more input**
>    While the operator stack is not empty
>       Evaluate the top.

At the end, the remaining value on the number stack is the value of the expression.

The algorithm makes use of this helper method that evaluates the topmost operator with the topmost numbers:

> **Evaluate the top:**
> Pop two numbers off the number stack.
> Pop an operator off the operator stack.
> Combine the numbers with that operator.
> Push the result on the number stack.

**ONLINE EXAMPLE**

✛ The complete code for the expression calculator.

## 15.6.4 Backtracking

Use a stack to remember choices you haven't yet made so that you can backtrack to them.

Suppose you are inside a maze. You need to find the exit. What should you do when you come to an intersection? You can continue exploring one of the paths, but you will want to remember the other ones. If your chosen path didn't work, you can go back to one of the other choices and try again.

Of course, as you go along one path, you may reach further intersections, and you need to remember your choice again. Simply use a stack to remember the paths that still need to be tried. The process of returning to a

*A stack can be used to track positions in a maze.*

choice point and trying another choice is called *backtracking*. By using a stack, you return to your more recent choices before you explore the earlier ones.

Figure 11 shows an example. We start at a point in the maze, at position (3, 4). There are four possible paths. We push them all on a stack ❶. We pop off the topmost one, traveling north from (3, 4). Following this path leads to position (1, 4). We now push two choices on the stack, going west or east ❷. Both of them lead to dead ends ❸❹.

Now we pop off the path from (3,4) going east. That too is a dead end ❺. Next is the path from (3, 4) going south. At (5, 4), it comes to an intersection. Both choices are pushed on the stack ❻. They both lead to dead ends ❼❽.

Finally, the path from (3, 4) going west leads to an exit ❾.

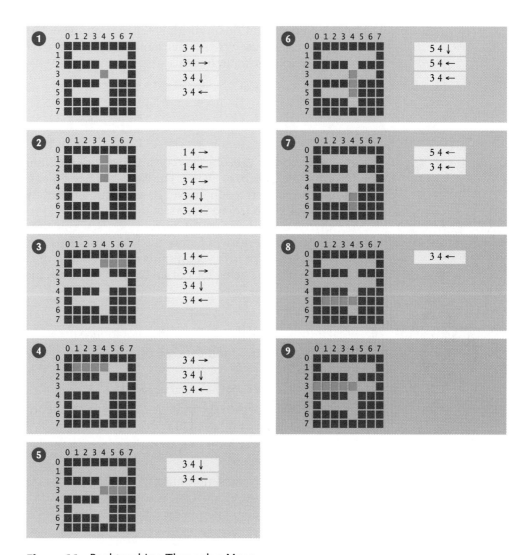

**Figure 11**   Backtracking Through a Maze

Using a stack, we have found a path out of the maze. Here is the pseudocode for our maze-finding algorithm:

> Push all paths from the point on which you are standing on a stack.
> While the stack is not empty
>   Pop a path from the stack.
>   Follow the path until you reach an exit, intersection, or dead end.
>   If you found an exit
>     Congratulations!
>   Else if you found an intersection
>     Push all paths meeting at the intersection, except the current one, onto the stack.

This algorithm will find an exit from the maze, provided that the maze has no *cycles*. If it is possible that you can make a circle and return to a previously visited intersection along a different sequence of paths, then you need to work harder—see Exercise P15.25.

How you implement this algorithm depends on the description of the maze. In the example code, we use a two-dimensional array of characters, with spaces for corridors and asterisks for walls, like this:

```
* * * * * * * *
*           *
* * * *   * * *
*               *
* * * *   * * *
*           * * *
* * * *   * * *
* * * * * * * *
```

In the example code, a `Path` object is constructed with a starting position and a direction (North, East, South, or West). The `Maze` class has a method that extends a path until it reaches an intersection or exit, or until it is blocked by a wall, and a method that computes all paths from an intersection point.

Note that you can use a queue instead of a stack in this algorithm. Then you explore the earlier alternatives before the later ones. This can work just as well for finding an answer, but it isn't very intuitive in the context of exploring a maze—you would have to imagine being teleported back to the initial intersections rather than just walking back to the last one.

**ONLINE EXAMPLE**

+ A complete program demonstrating backtracking.

**SELF CHECK**

26. What is the value of the reverse Polish notation expression 2 3 4 + 5 × ×?

27. Why does the branch for the subtraction operator in the `Calculator` program not simply execute

    `results.push(results.pop() - results.pop());`

28. In the evaluation of the expression 3 – 4 + 5 with the algorithm of Section 15.6.3, which operator gets evaluated first?

29. In the algorithm of Section 15.6.3, are the operators on the operator stack always in increasing precedence?

30. Consider the following simple maze. Assuming that we start at the marked point and push paths in the order West, South, East, North, in which order are the lettered points visited, using the algorithm of Section 15.6.4?

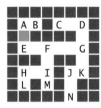

**Practice It** Now you can try these exercises at the end of the chapter: R15.21, P15.21, P15.22, P15.25, P15.26.

**WORKED EXAMPLE 15.2** **Simulating a Queue of Waiting Customers**

+ This Worked Example shows how to use a queue to simulate an actual queue of waiting customers.

+ Available online in WileyPLUS and at www.wiley.com/college/horstmann.

*Random Fact 15.2* Reverse Polish Notation

In the 1920s, the Polish mathematician Jan Łukasiewicz realized that it is possible to dispense with parentheses in arithmetic expressions, provided that you write the operators *before* their arguments, for example, + 3 4 instead of 3 + 4. Thirty years later, Australian computer scientist Charles Hamblin noted that an even better scheme would be to have the operators *follow* the operands. This was termed **reverse Polish notation** or RPN.

| Standard Notation | Reverse Polish Notation |
|---|---|
| 3 + 4 | 3 4 + |
| 3 + 4 × 5 | 3 4 5 × + |
| 3 × (4 + 5) | 3 4 5 + × |
| (3 + 4) × (5 + 6) | 3 4 + 5 6 + × |
| 3 + 4 + 5 | 3 4 + 5 + |

Reverse Polish notation might look strange to you, but that is just an accident of history. Had earlier mathematicians realized its advantages, today's schoolchildren might be using it and not worrying about precedence rules and parentheses.

In 1972, Hewlett-Packard introduced the HP 35 calculator that used reverse Polish notation. The calculator had no keys labeled with parentheses or an equals symbol. There is just a key labeled ENTER to push a number onto a stack. For that reason, Hewlett-Packard's marketing department used to refer to their product as "the calculators that have no equal".

Over time, calculator vendors have adapted to the standard algebraic notation rather than forcing its users to learn a new notation. However, those users who have made the effort to learn reverse Polish notation tend to be fanatic proponents, and to this day, some Hewlett-Packard calculator models still support it.

*The Calculator with No Equal*

---

VIDEO EXAMPLE 15.1 **Building a Table of Contents**

In this Video Example, you will see how to build a table of contents for a book.

---

## CHAPTER SUMMARY

### Understand the architecture of the Java collections framework.

- A collection groups together elements and allows them to be retrieved later.
- A list is a collection that remembers the order of its elements.
- A set is an unordered collection of unique elements.
- A map keeps associations between key and value objects.

### Understand and use linked lists.

- A linked list consists of a number of nodes, each of which has a reference to the next node.
- Adding and removing elements at a given position in a linked list is efficient.

➕ Available online in WileyPLUS and at www.wiley.com/college/horstmann.

- Visiting the elements of a linked list in sequential order is efficient, but random access is not.
- You use a list iterator to access elements inside a linked list.

## Choose a set implementation and use it to manage sets of values.

- The HashSet and TreeSet classes both implement the Set interface.
- Set implementations arrange the elements so that they can locate them quickly.
- You can form hash sets holding objects of type String, Integer, Double, Point, Rectangle, or Color.

- You can form tree sets for any class that implements the Comparable interface, such as String or Integer.
- Sets don't have duplicates. Adding a duplicate of an element that is already present is ignored.
- A set iterator visits the elements in the order in which the set implementation keeps them.
- You cannot add an element to a set at an iterator position.

## Use maps to model associations between keys and values.

- The HashMap and TreeMap classes both implement the Map interface.
- To find all keys and values in a map, iterate through the key set and find the values that correspond to the keys.
- A hash function computes an integer value from an object.
- A good hash function minimizes *collisions*—identical hash codes for different objects.

- Override hashCode methods in your own classes by combining the hash codes for the instance variables.
- A class's hashCode method must be compatible with its equals method.

## Use the Java classes for stacks, queues, and priority queues.

- A stack is a collection of elements with "last-in, first-out" retrieval.
- A queue is a collection of elements with "first-in, first-out" retrieval.

- When removing an element from a priority queue, the element with the most urgent priority is retrieved.

## Solve programming problems using stacks and queues.

- A stack can be used to check whether parentheses in an expression are balanced.
- Use a stack to evaluate expressions in reverse Polish notation.
- Using two stacks, you can evaluate expressions in standard algebraic notation.
- Use a stack to remember choices you haven't yet made so that you can backtrack to them.

## STANDARD LIBRARY ITEMS INTRODUCED IN THIS CHAPTER

*java.util.Collection<E>*
  add
  contains
  iterator
  remove
  size
java.util.HashMap<K, V>
java.util.HashSet<K, V>
*java.util.Iterator<E>*
  hasNext
  next
  remove
java.util.LinkedList<E>
  addFirst
  addLast

  getFirst
  getLast
  removeFirst
  removeLast
*java.util.List<E>*
  listIterator
*java.util.ListIterator<E>*
  add
  hasPrevious
  previous
  set
*java.util.Map<K, V>*
  get
  keySet
  put
  remove

*java.util.Queue<E>*
  peek
java.util.PriorityQueue<E>
  remove
*java.util.Set<E>*
java.util.Stack<E>
  peek
  pop
  push
java.util.TreeMap<K, V>
java.util.TreeSet<K, V>

## REVIEW EXERCISES

■■ **R15.1** An invoice contains a collection of purchased items. Should that collection be implemented as a list or set? Explain your answer.

■■ **R15.2** Consider a program that manages an appointment calendar. Should it place the appointments into a list, stack, queue, or priority queue? Explain your answer.

■■■ **R15.3** One way of implementing a calendar is as a map from date objects to event objects. However, that only works if there is a single event for a given date. How can you use another collection type to allow for multiple events on a given date?

■ **R15.4** Explain what the following code prints. Draw a picture of the linked list after each step.

```
LinkedList<String> staff = new LinkedList<String>();
staff.addFirst("Harry");
staff.addFirst("Diana");
staff.addFirst("Tom");
System.out.println(staff.removeFirst());
System.out.println(staff.removeFirst());
System.out.println(staff.removeFirst());
```

■ **R15.5** Explain what the following code prints. Draw a picture of the linked list after each step.

```
LinkedList<String> staff = new LinkedList<String>();
staff.addFirst("Harry");
staff.addFirst("Diana");
staff.addFirst("Tom");
System.out.println(staff.removeLast());
System.out.println(staff.removeFirst());
System.out.println(staff.removeLast());
```

■ **R15.6** Explain what the following code prints. Draw a picture of the linked list after each step.

```
LinkedList<String> staff = new LinkedList<String>();
staff.addFirst("Harry");
staff.addLast("Diana");
staff.addFirst("Tom");
System.out.println(staff.removeLast());
System.out.println(staff.removeFirst());
System.out.println(staff.removeLast());
```

■ **R15.7** Explain what the following code prints. Draw a picture of the linked list and the iterator position after each step.

```
LinkedList<String> staff = new LinkedList<String>();
ListIterator<String> iterator = staff.listIterator();
iterator.add("Tom");
iterator.add("Diana");
iterator.add("Harry");
iterator = staff.listIterator();
if (iterator.next().equals("Tom")) { iterator.remove(); }
while (iterator.hasNext())  { System.out.println(iterator.next()); }
```

■ **R15.8** Explain what the following code prints. Draw a picture of the linked list and the iterator position after each step.

```
LinkedList<String> staff = new LinkedList<String>();
ListIterator<String> iterator = staff.listIterator();
iterator.add("Tom");
iterator.add("Diana");
iterator.add("Harry");
iterator = staff.listIterator();
iterator.next();
iterator.next();
iterator.add("Romeo");
iterator.next();
iterator.add("Juliet");
iterator = staff.listIterator();
iterator.next();
iterator.remove();
while (iterator.hasNext()) { System.out.println(iterator.next()); }
```

■■ **R15.9** What advantages do linked lists have over arrays? What disadvantages do they have?

■■ **R15.10** Suppose you need to organize a collection of telephone numbers for a company division. There are currently about 6,000 employees, and you know that the phone switch can handle at most 10,000 phone numbers. You expect several hundred look-ups against the collection every day. Would you use an array list or a linked list to store the information?

■■ **R15.11** Suppose you need to keep a collection of appointments. Would you use a linked list or an array list of Appointment objects?

■ **R15.12** Suppose you write a program that models a card deck. Cards are taken from the top of the deck and given out to players. As cards are returned to the deck, they are placed on the bottom of the deck. Would you store the cards in a stack or a queue?

■ **R15.13** Suppose the strings "A" ... "Z" are pushed onto a stack. Then they are popped off the stack and pushed onto a second stack. Finally, they are all popped off the second stack and printed. In which order are the strings printed?

**• R15.14** What is the difference between a set and a map?

**•• R15.15** The union of two sets *A* and *B* is the set of all elements that are contained in *A*, *B*, or both. The intersection is the set of all elements that are contained in *A* and *B*. How can you compute the union and intersection of two sets, using the add and contains methods, together with an iterator?

**•• R15.16** How can you compute the union and intersection of two sets, using some of the methods that the java.util.Set interface provides, but without using an iterator? (Look up the interface in the API documentation.)

**• R15.17** Can a map have two keys with the same value? Two values with the same key?

**•• R15.18** A map can be implemented as a set of (*key, value*) pairs. Explain.

**••• R15.19** Verify the hash code of the string "Juliet" in Table 6.

**••• R15.20** Verify that the strings "VII" and "Ugh" have the same hash code.

**• R15.21** Consider the algorithm for traversing a maze from Section 15.6.4 Assume that we start at position A and push in the order West, South, East, and North. In which order will the lettered locations of the sample maze be visited?

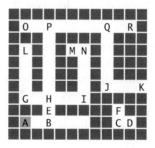

**• R15.22** Repeat Exercise R15.21, using a queue instead of a stack.

## PROGRAMMING EXERCISES

**•• P15.1** Write a method

```
public static void downsize(LinkedList<String> employeeNames, int n)
```

that removes every nth employee from a linked list.

**•• P15.2** Write a method

```
public static void reverse(LinkedList<String> strings)
```

that reverses the entries in a linked list.

**•• P15.3** Use a stack to reverse the words of a sentence. Keep reading words until you have a word that ends in a period, adding them onto a stack. When you have a word with a period, pop the words off and print them. Stop when there are no more words in the input. For example, you should turn the input

```
Mary had a little lamb. Its fleece was white as snow.
```

into

```
Lamb little a had mary. Snow as white was fleece its.
```

Pay attention to capitalization and the placement of the period.

**■ P15.4** Your task is to break a number into its individual digits, for example, to turn 1729 into 1, 7, 2, and 9. It is easy to get the last digit of a number $n$ as n % 10. But that gets the numbers in reverse order. Solve this problem with a stack. Your program should ask the user for an integer, then print its digits separated by spaces.

**■■ P15.5** A homeowner rents out parking spaces in a driveway during special events. The driveway is a "last-in, first-out" stack. Of course, when a car owner retrieves a vehicle that wasn't the last one in, the cars blocking it must temporarily move to the street so that the requested vehicle can leave. Write a program that models this behavior, using one stack for the driveway and one stack for the street. Use integers as license plate numbers. Positive numbers add a car, negative numbers remove a car, zero stops the simulation. Print out the stack after each operation is complete.

**■ P15.6** Implement a to do list. Tasks have a priority between 1 and 9, and a description. When the user enters the command add *priority description,* the program adds a new task. When the user enters next, the program removes and prints the most urgent task. The quit command quits the program. Use a priority queue in your solution.

**■ P15.7** Write a program that reads text from a file and breaks it up into individual words. Insert the words into a tree set. At the end of the input file, print all words, followed by the size of the resulting set. This program determines how many unique words a text file has.

**■■ P15.8** Implement the *sieve of Eratosthenes:* a method for computing prime numbers, known to the ancient Greeks. This method will compute all prime numbers up to $n$. Choose an $n$. First insert all numbers from 2 to $n$ into a set. Then erase all multiples of 2 (except 2); that is, 4, 6, 8, 10, 12, .... Erase all multiples of 3; that is, 6, 9, 12, 15, .... Go up to $\sqrt{n}$. Then print the set.

**■■ P15.9** Write a program that keeps a map in which both keys and values are strings—the names of students and their course grades. Prompt the user of the program to add or remove students, to modify grades, or to print all grades. The printout should be sorted by name and formatted like this:

```
Carl: B+
Joe: C
Sarah: A
```

**■■■ P15.10** Reimplement Exercise P15.9 so that the keys of the map are objects of class Student. A student should have a first name, a last name, and a unique integer ID. For grade changes and removals, lookup should be by ID. The printout should be sorted by last name. If two students have the same last name, then use the first name as a tie breaker. If the first names are also identical, then use the integer ID. *Hint:* Use two maps.

**■■■ P15.11** Write a class Polynomial that stores a polynomial such as

$$p(x) = 5x^{10} + 9x^7 - x - 10$$

as a linked list of terms. A term contains the coefficient and the power of $x$. For example, you would store $p(x)$ as

$$(5,10),(9,7),(-1,1),(-10,0)$$

Supply methods to add, multiply, and print polynomials. Supply a constructor that makes a polynomial from a single term. For example, the polynomial p can be constructed as

```
Polynomial p = new Polynomial(new Term(-10, 0));
p.add(new Polynomial(new Term(-1, 1)));
p.add(new Polynomial(new Term(9, 7)));
p.add(new Polynomial(new Term(5, 10)));
```

Then compute $p(x) \times p(x)$.

```
Polynomial q = p.multiply(p);
q.print();
```

**••• P15.12** Repeat Exercise P15.11, but use a Map<Integer, Double> for the coefficients.

**• P15.13** Insert all words from a large file (such as the novel "War and Peace", which is available on the Internet) into a hash set and a tree set. Time the results. Which data structure is faster?

**••• P15.14** Write a program that reads a Java source file and produces an index of all identifiers in the file. For each identifier, print all lines in which it occurs. For simplicity, we will consider each string consisting only of letters, numbers, and underscores an identifer. Declare a Scanner in for reading from the source file and call in.useDelimiter("[^A-Za-z0-9_]+"). Then each call to next returns an identifier.

**•• P15.15** Try to find two words with the same hash code in a large file. Keep a Map<Integer, HashSet<String>>. When you read in a word, compute its hash code $h$ and put the word in the set whose key is $h$. Then iterate through all keys and print the sets whose size is > 1.

**•• P15.16** Supply compatible hashCode and equals methods to the Student class described in Exercise P15.10. Test the hash code by adding Student objects to a hash set.

**• P15.17** Supply compatible hashCode and equals methods to the BankAccount class of Chapter 8. Test the hashCode method by printing out hash codes and by adding BankAccount objects to a hash set.

**•• P15.18** A labeled point has $x$- and $y$-coordinates and a string label. Provide a class LabeledPoint with a constructor LabeledPoint(int x, int y, String label) and hashCode and equals methods. Two labeled points are considered the same when they have the same location and label.

**•• P15.19** Reimplement the LabeledPoint class of the preceding exercise by storing the location in a java.awt.Point object. Your hashCode and equals methods should call the hashCode and equals methods of the Point class.

**•• P15.20** Modify the LabeledPoint class of Exercise P15.18 so that it implements the Comparable interface. Sort points first by their $x$-coordinates. If two points have the same $x$-coordinate, sort them by their $y$-coordinates. If two points have the same $x$- and $y$-coordinates, sort them by their label. Write a tester program that checks all cases by inserting points into a TreeSet.

**• P15.21** Write a program that checks whether a sequence of HTML tags is properly nested. For each opening tag, such as <p>, there must be a closing tag </p>. A tag such as <p> may have other tags inside, for example

```
<p> <ul> <li> </li> </ul> <a> </a> </p>
```

The inner tags must be closed before the outer ones. Your program should process a file containing tags. For simplicity, assume that the tags are separated by spaces, and that there is no text inside the tags.

- **P15.22** Add a % (remainder) operator to the expression calculator of Section 15.6.3.

- **P15.23** Add a ∧ (power) operator to the expression calculator of Section 15.6.3. For example, 2 ∧ 3 evaluates to 8. As in mathematics, your power operator should be evaluated from the right. That is, 2 ∧ 3 ∧ 2 is 2 ∧ (3 ∧ 2), not (2 ∧ 3) ∧ 2. (That's more useful because you could get the latter as 2 ∧ (3 × 2).)

- **P15.24** Modify the expression calculator of Section 15.6.3 to convert an expression into reverse Polish notation. *Hint:* Instead of evaluating the top and pushing the result, append the instructions to a string.

- **P15.25** Modify the maze solver program of Section 15.6.4 to handle mazes with cycles. Keep a set of visited intersections. When you have previously seen an intersection, treat it as a dead end and do not add paths to the stack.

- **P15.26** In a paint program, a "flood fill" fills all empty pixels of a drawing with a given color, stopping when it reaches occupied pixels. In this exercise, you will implement a simple variation of this algorithm, flood-filling a 10 × 10 array of integers that are initially 0.

  > Prompt for the starting row and column.
  > Push the (row, column) pair onto a stack.

  You will need to provide a simple Pair class.

  Repeat the following operations until the stack is empty.

  > Pop off the (row, column) pair from the top of the stack.
  > If it has not yet been filled, fill the corresponding array location with a number 1, 2, 3, and so on
  >    (to show the order in which the square is filled).
  > Push the coordinates of any unfilled neighbors in the north, east, south, or west direction on the stack.

  When you are done, print the entire array.

- **P15.27** Repeat Exercise P15.26, but use a queue instead.

- **P15.28** Use a stack to enumerate all permutations of a string. Suppose you want to find all permutations of the string meat.

  > Push the string +meat on the stack.
  > While the stack is not empty
  >   Pop off the top of the stack.
  >   If that string ends in a + (such as tame+)
  >     Remove the + and add the string to the list of permutations.
  >   Else
  >     Remove each letter in turn from the right of the +.
  >     Insert it just before the +.
  >     Push the resulting string on the stack.

  For example, after popping e+mta, you push em+ta, et+ma, and ea+mt.

- **P15.29** Repeat Exercise P15.28, but use a queue instead.

**■ ■ Business P15.30** An airport has only one runway. When it is busy, planes wishing to take off or land have to wait. Implement a simulation, using two queues, one each for the planes waiting to take off and land. Landing planes get priority. The user enters commands takeoff *flightSymbol*, land *flightSymbol*, next, and quit. The first two commands place the flight in the appropriate queue. The next command finishes the current takeoff or landing and enables the next one, printing the action (takeoff or land) and the flight symbol.

**■ ■ Business P15.31** Suppose you buy 100 shares of a stock at $12 per share, then another 100 at $10 per share, and then sell 150 shares at $15. You have to pay taxes on the gain, but exactly what is the gain? In the United States, the FIFO rule holds: You first sell all shares of the first batch for a profit of $300, then 50 of the shares from the second batch, for a profit of $250, yielding a total profit of $550. Write a program that can make these calculations for arbitrary purchases and sales of shares in a single company. The user enters commands buy *quantity price*, sell *quantity* (which causes the gain to be displayed), and quit. *Hint:* Keep a queue of objects of a class Block that contains the quantity and price of a block of shares.

**■ ■ ■ Business P15.32** Extend Exercise P15.31 to a program that can handle shares of multiple companies. The user enters commands buy *symbol quantity price* and sell *symbol quantity*. *Hint:* Keep a Map<String, Queue<Block>> that manages a separate queue for each stock symbol.

**■ ■ ■ Business P15.33** Consider the problem of finding the least expensive routes to all cities in a network from a given starting point.

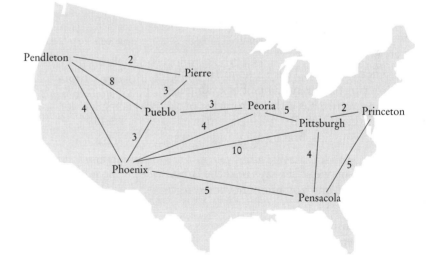

For example, in this network, the least expensive route from Pendleton to Peoria has cost 8 (going through Pierre and Pueblo).

The following helper class expresses the distance to another city:

```java
public class DistanceTo implements Comparable<DistanceTo>
{
    private String target;
    private int distance;
```

```
public DistanceTo(String city, int dist) { target = city; distance = dist; }
public String getTarget() { return target; }
public int getDistance() { return distance; }
public int compareTo(DistanceTo other) { return distance - other.distance; }
}
```

All direct connections between cities are stored in a Map<String, TreeSet<DistanceTo>>. The algorithm now proceeds as follows:

> **Let from be the starting point.**
> **Add DistanceTo(from, 0) to a priority queue.**
> **Construct a map shortestKnownDistance from city names to distances.**
> **While the priority queue is not empty**
> > **Get its smallest element.**
> > **If its target is not a key in shortestKnownDistance**
> > > **Let d be the distance to that target.**
> > > **Put (target, d) into shortestKnownDistance.**
> > > **For all cities c that have a direct connection from target**
> > > > **Add DistanceTo(c, d + distance from target to c) to the priority queue.**

When the algorithm has finished, **shortestKnownDistance** contains the shortest distance from the starting point to all reachable targets.

Your task is to write a program that implements this algorithm. Your program should read in lines of the form *city1 city2 distance*. The starting point is the first city in the first line. Print the shortest distances to all other cities.

## ANSWERS TO SELF-CHECK QUESTIONS

1. A list is a better choice because the application will want to retain the order in which the quizzes were given.

2. A set is a better choice. There is no intrinsically useful ordering for the students. For example, the registrar's office has little use for a list of all students by their GPA. By storing them in a set, adding, removing, and finding students can be fast.

3. With a stack, you would always read the latest required reading, and you might never get to the oldest readings.

4. A collection stores elements, but a map stores associations between elements.

5. Yes, for two reasons. A linked list needs to store the neighboring node references, which are not needed in an array, Moreover, there is some overhead for storing an object. In a linked list, each node is a separate object that incurs this overhead, whereas an array is a single object.

6. We can simply access each array element with an integer index.

7. |ABCD
   A|BCD
   AB|CD
   A|CD
   AC|D
   ACE|D
   ACED|
   ACEDF|

8. ```
   ListIterator<String> iter = words.iterator();
   while (iter.hasNext())
   {
       String str = iter.next();
       if (str.length() < 4) { iter.remove(); }
   }
   ```

9. ```
   ListIterator<String> iter = words.iterator();
   while (iter.hasNext())
   {
       System.out.println(iter.next());
       if (iter.hasNext())
       {
           iter.next(); // Skip the next element
       }
   }
   ```

10. Adding and removing elements as well as testing for membership is faster with sets.

11. Sets do not have an ordering, so it doesn't make sense to add an element at a particular iterator position, or to traverse a set backward.

12. You do not know in which order the set keeps the elements.

13. Here is one possibility:

```
if (s.size() == 3 && s.contains("Tom")
        && s.contains("Diana")
        && s.contains("Harry"))
    . . .
```

14.
```
for (String str : s)
{
    if (t.contains(str))
    {
        System.out.println(str);
    }
}
```

15. The words would be listed in sorted order.

16. A set stores elements. A map stores associations between keys and values.

17. The ordering does not matter, and you cannot have duplicates.

18. Because it might have duplicates.

19. `Map<String, Integer> wordFrequency;`

Note that you cannot use a `Map<String, int>` because you cannot use primitive types as type parameters in Java.

20. It associates strings with sets of strings. One application would be a thesaurus that lists synonyms for a given word. For example, the key `"improve"` might have as its value the set `["ameliorate", "better", "enhance", "enrich", "perfect", "refine"]`.

21. This way, we can ensure that only queue operations can be invoked on the q object.

22. Depending on whether you consider the 0 position the head or the tail of the queue, you would either add or remove elements at that position. Both are expensive operations.

23. A B C

24. Stacks use a "last-in, first-out" discipline. If you are the first one to submit a print job and lots of people add print jobs before the printer has a chance to deal with your job, they get their printouts first, and you have to wait until all other jobs are completed.

25. Yes—the smallest string (in lexicographic ordering) is removed first. In the example, that is the string starting with 1, then the string starting with 2, and so on. However, the scheme breaks down if a priority value exceeds 9. For example, a string `"10 - Line up braces"` comes before `"2 - Order cleaning supplies"` in lexicographic order.

26. 70.

27. It would then subtract the first argument from the second. Consider the input 5 3 –. The stack contains 5 and 3, with the 3 on the top. Then `results.pop() - results.pop()` computes $3 - 5$.

28. The – gets executed first because + doesn't have a higher precedence.

29. No, because there may be parentheses on the stack. The parentheses separate groups of operators, each of which is in increasing precedence.

30. A B E F G D C K J N

# BASIC DATA STRUCTURES

CHAPTER GOALS

To understand the implementation of
linked lists and array lists

To analyze the efficiency of fundamental operations
of lists and arrays

To implement the stack and queue data types

To implement a hash table and understand the efficiency of its operations

This chapter deals with simple data structures in which elements are arranged in a linear sequence. You will learn how linked lists, array lists, stacks, queues, and hash tables are implemented. You will study how these data structures add, remove, and locate elements, and how to use this information to analyze their efficiency. Estimating efficiency will help you choose the best implementation for a given task.

# 16.1  Implementing Linked Lists

In the last chapter you saw how to use the linked list class supplied by the Java library. Now we will look at the implementation of a simplified version of this class. This will show you how the list operations manipulate the links as the list is modified.

To keep this sample code simple, we will not implement all methods of the linked list class. We will implement only a singly-linked list, and the list class will supply direct access only to the first list element, not the last one. (A worked example and several exercises explore additional implementation options.) Our list will not use a type parameter. We will simply store raw Object values and insert casts when retrieving them. (You will see how to use type parameters in Chapter 18.) The result will be a fully functional list class that shows how the links are updated when elements are added or removed, and how the iterator traverses the list.

## 16.1.1  The Node Class

A linked list stores elements in a sequence of nodes. We need a class to represent the nodes. In a singly-linked list, a Node object stores an element and a reference to the next node.

Because the methods of both the linked list class and the iterator class have frequent access to the Node instance variables, we do not make the instance variables of the Node class private. Instead, we make Node a private **inner class** of the LinkedList class. An inner class is a class that is defined inside another class. The methods of the outer class can access the public features of the inner class. However, because the inner class is private, it cannot be accessed anywhere other than from the outer class.

```
public class LinkedList
{
   . . .
   class Node
   {
      public Object data;
      public Node next;
   }
}
```

Our LinkedList class holds a reference first to the first node (or null, if the list is completely empty):

```
public class LinkedList
{
   private Node first;
```

A linked list object holds a reference to the first node, and each node holds a reference to the next node.

```
    public LinkedList() { first = null; }

    public Object getFirst()
    {
        if (first == null) { throw new NoSuchElementException(); }
        return first.data;
    }
}
```

## 16.1.2 Adding and Removing the First Element

When adding or removing the first element, the reference to the first node must be updated.

Figure 1 shows the addFirst method in action. When a new node is added, it becomes the head of the list, and the node that was the old list head becomes its next node:

```
public class LinkedList
{
    . . .
    public void addFirst(Object element)
    {
        Node newNode = new Node(); ❶
        newNode.data = element;
        newNode.next = first; ❷
        first = newNode; ❸
    }
    . . .
}
```

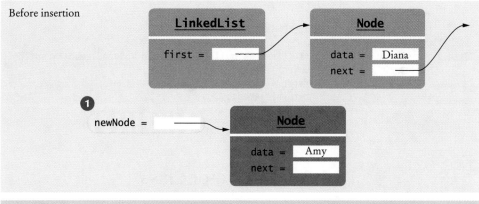

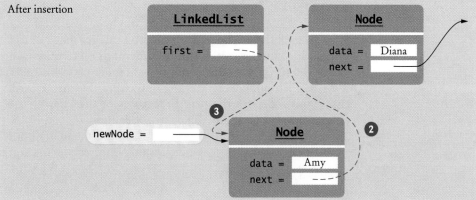

**Figure 1**
Adding a Node
to the Head of a
Linked List

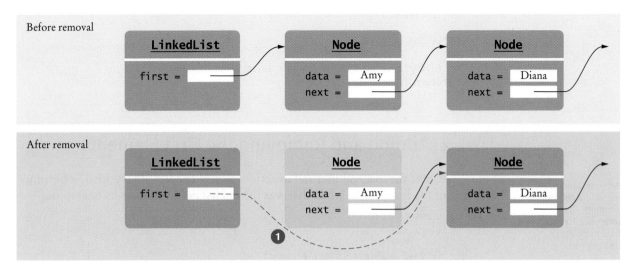

**Figure 2** Removing the First Node from a Linked List

Removing the first element of the list works as follows. The data of the first node are saved and later returned as the method result. The successor of the first node becomes the first node of the shorter list (see Figure 2). Then there are no further references to the old node, and the garbage collector will eventually recycle it.

```java
public class LinkedList
{
    . . .
    public Object removeFirst()
    {
        if (first == null) { throw new NoSuchElementException(); }
        Object element = first.data;
        first = first.next; ❶
        return element;
    }
    . . .
}
```

## 16.1.3 The Iterator Class

The ListIterator interface in the standard library declares nine methods. Our simpli-fied ListIterator interface omits four of them (the methods that move the iterator backward and the methods that report an integer index of the iterator). Our interface requires us to implement list iterator methods next, hasNext, remove, add, and set.

Our LinkedList class declares a private inner class LinkedListIterator, which imple-ments our simplified ListIterator interface. Because LinkedListIterator is an inner class, it has access to the private features of the LinkedList class—in particular, the instance variable first and the private Node class.

Note that clients of the LinkedList class don't actually know the name of the itera-tor class. They only know it is a class that implements the ListIterator interface.

```java
public class LinkedList
{
    . . .
```

```java
public ListIterator listIterator()
{
   return new LinkedListIterator();
}

class LinkedListIterator implements ListIterator
{
   private Node position;
   private Node previous;
   private boolean isAfterNext;

   public LinkedListIterator()
   {
      position = null;
      previous = null;
      isAfterNext = false;
   }
   . . .
}
}
```

A list iterator object has a reference to the last visited node.

Each iterator object has a reference, position, to the last visited node. We also store a reference to the last node before that, previous. We will need that reference to adjust the links properly in the remove method. Finally, because calls to remove and set are only valid after a call to next, we use the isAfterNext flag to track when the next method has been called.

## 16.1.4 Advancing an Iterator

To advance an iterator, update the position and remember the old position for the remove method.

When advancing an iterator with the next method, the position reference is updated to position.next, and the old position is remembered in previous. The previous position is used for just one purpose: to remove the element if the remove method is called after the next method.

There is a special case, however—if the iterator points before the first element of the list, then the old position is null, and position must be set to first:

```java
class LinkedListIterator implements ListIterator
{
   . . .
   public Object next()
   {
      if (!hasNext()) { throw new NoSuchElementException(); }
      previous = position; // Remember for remove
      isAfterNext = true;

      if (position == null)
      {
         position = first;
      }
      else
      {
         position = position.next;
      }

      return position.data;
   }
   . . .
}
```

The next method is supposed to be called only when the iterator is not yet at the end of the list, so we declare the hasNext method accordingly. The iterator is at the end if the list is empty (that is, first == null) or if there is no element after the current position (position.next == null):

```
class LinkedListIterator implements ListIterator
{
    . . .
    public boolean hasNext()
    {
        if (position == null)
        {
            return first != null;
        }
        else
        {
            return position.next != null;
        }
    }
    . . .
}
```

## 16.1.5 Removing an Element

Next, we implement the remove method of the list iterator. Recall that, in order to remove an element, one must first call next and then call remove on the iterator.

If the element to be removed is the first element, we just call removeFirst. Otherwise, an element in the middle of the list must be removed, and the node preceding it needs to have its next reference updated to skip the removed element (see Figure 3).

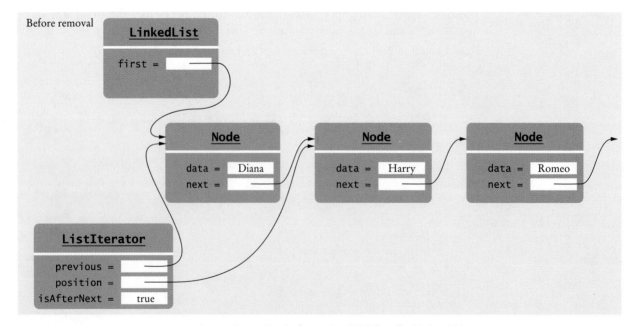

**Figure 3** Removing a Node from the Middle of a Linked List

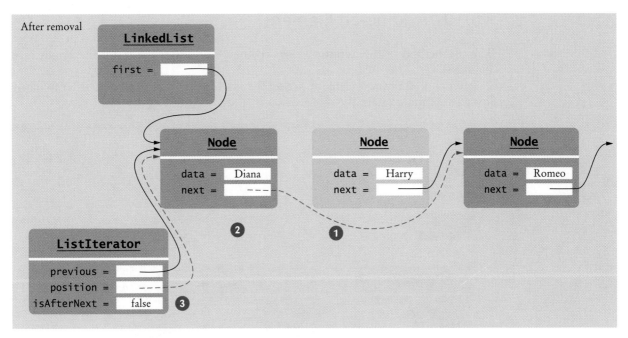

**Figure 3 (continued)**   Removing a Node from the Middle of a Linked List

We also need to update the position reference so that a subsequent call to the next method skips over the element after the removed one.

If the previous reference equals position, then this call to remove does not immediately follow a call to next, and we throw an IllegalStateException.

Note that, according to the specification of the remove method, it is illegal to call remove twice in a row. Our implementation handles this situation correctly. After completion of the remove method, previous equals position, and an exception occurs if remove is called again.

```
class LinkedListIterator implements ListIterator
{
   . . .
   public void remove()
   {
      if (!isAfterNext) { throw new IllegalStateException(); }

      if (position == first)
      {
         removeFirst();
      }
      else
      {
         previous.next = position.next;  ❶
      }
      position = previous;  ❷

      isAfterNext = false;  ❸
   }
   . . .
}
```

## 16.1.6 Adding an Element

The add method of the iterator inserts the new node after the last visited node (see Figure 4).

After adding the new element, we set the isAfterNext flag to false, in order to disallow a subsequent call to the remove or set method.

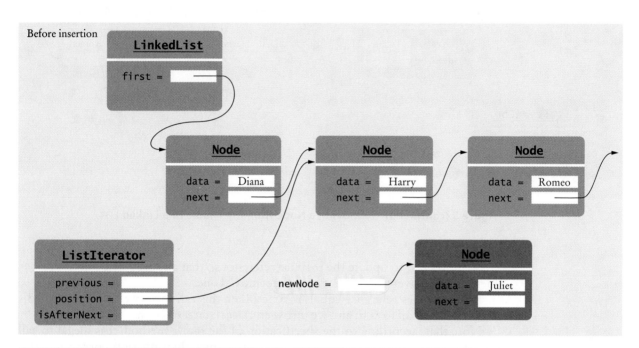

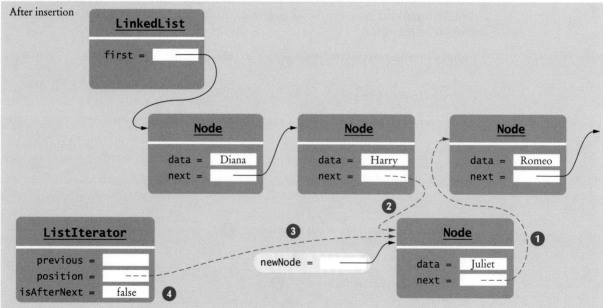

**Figure 4** Adding a Node to the Middle of a Linked List

```
class LinkedListIterator implements ListIterator
{
   . . .
   public void add(Object element)
   {
      if (position == null)
      {
         addFirst(element);
         position = first;
      }
      else
      {
         Node newNode = new Node();
         newNode.data = element;
         newNode.next = position.next;      ❶
         position.next = newNode;           ❷
         position = newNode;                ❸
      }
      isAfterNext = false;                  ❹
   }
   . . .
}
```

### 16.1.7 Setting an Element to a Different Value

The set method changes the data stored in the previously visited element:

```
public void set(Object element)
{
   if (!isAfterNext) { throw new IllegalStateException(); }
   position.data = element;
}
```

As with the remove method, a call to set is only valid if it was preceded by a call to the next method. We throw an exception if we find that there was a call to add or remove immediately before calling set.

You will find the complete implementation of our LinkedList class after the next section.

### 16.1.8 Efficiency of Linked List Operations

In a doubly-linked list, accessing an element is an $O(n)$ operation; adding and removing an element is $O(1)$.

Now that you have seen how linked list operations are implemented, we can determine their efficiency.

Consider first the cost of accessing an element. To get the $k$th element of a linked list, you start at the beginning of the list and advance the iterator $k$ times. Suppose it takes an amount of time $T$ to advance the iterator once. This quantity is independent of the iterator position—advancing an iterator does some checking and then it follows the next reference of the current node (see Section 16.1.4).

Therefore, advancing the iterator to the $k$th element consumes $kT$ time. If the linked list has $n$ elements and $k$ is chosen at random, then $k$ will average out to be $n / 2$, and $kT$ is on average $nT / 2$. Since $T / 2$ is a constant, this is an $O(n)$ expression. We have determined that accessing an element in a linked list of length $n$ is an $O(n)$ operation.

*To get to the kth node of a linked list, one must skip over the preceding nodes.*

Now consider the cost of adding an element at a given position, assuming that we already have an iterator to the position. Look at the implementation of the add method in Section 16.1.6. To add an element, one updates a couple of references in the neighboring nodes and the iterator. This operation requires a constant number of steps, independent of the size of the linked list.

Using the big-Oh notation, an operation that requires a bounded amount of time, regardless of the total number of elements in the structure, is denoted as $O(1)$. Adding an element to a linked list takes $O(1)$ time.

Similar reasoning shows that removing an element at a given position is an $O(1)$ operation.

Now consider the task of adding an element at the end of the list. We first need to get to the end, at a cost of $O(n)$. Then it takes $O(1)$ time to add the element. However, we can improve on this performance if we add a reference to the last node to the LinkedList class:

```java
public class LinkedList
{
    private Node first;
    private Node last;
    . . .
}
```

Of course, this reference must be updated when the last node changes, as elements are added or removed. In order to keep the code as simple as possible, our implementation does not have a reference to the last node. However, we will always assume that a linked list implementation can access the last element in constant time. This is the case for the LinkedList class in the standard Java library, and it is an easy enhancement to our implementation. Worked Example 16.1 shows how to add the last reference, update it as necessary, and provide an addLast method for adding an element at the end.

The code for the addLast method is very similar to the addFirst method in Section 16.1.2. It too requires constant time, independent of the length of the list. We conclude that, with an appropriate implementation, adding an element at the end of a linked list is an $O(1)$ operation.

How about removing the last element? We need a reference to the next-to-last element, so that we can set its next reference to null. (See Figure 5.)

We also need to update the last reference and set it to the next-to-last reference. But how can we get that next-to-last reference? It takes $n - 1$ iterations to obtain it,

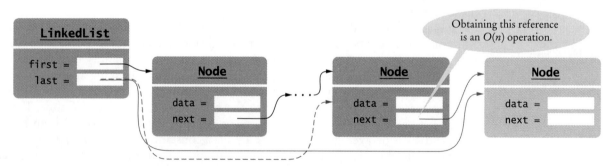

**Figure 5** Removing the Last Element of a Singly-Linked List

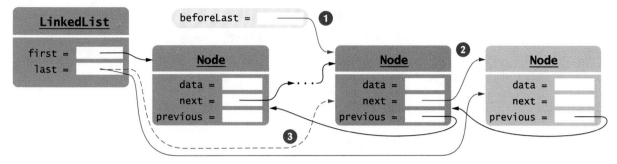

**Figure 6**   Removing the Last Element of a Doubly-Linked List

starting at the beginning of the list. Thus, removing an element from the back of a singly-linked list is an $O(n)$ operation.

We can do better in a doubly-linked list, such as the one in the standard Java library. In a doubly-linked list, each node has a reference to the previous node in addition to the next one (see Figure 6).

```java
public class LinkedList
{
   . . .
   class Node
   {
      public Object data;
      public Node next;
      public Node previous;
   }
}
```

In that case, removal of the last element takes a constant number of steps:

```java
Node beforeLast = last.previous; ❶
beforeLast.next = null; ❷
last = beforeLast; ❸
```

Therefore, removing an element from the end of a doubly-linked list is also an $O(1)$ operation. Worked Example 16.1 contains a full implementation.

Table 1 summarizes the efficiency of linked list operations.

| Table 1   **Efficiency of Linked List Operations** | | |
|---|---|---|
| Operation | Singly-Linked List | Doubly-Linked List |
| Access an element. | $O(n)$ | $O(n)$ |
| Add/remove at an iterator position. | $O(1)$ | $O(1)$ |
| Add/remove first element. | $O(1)$ | $O(1)$ |
| Add last element. | $O(1)$ | $O(1)$ |
| Remove last element. | $O(n)$ | $O(1)$ |

**section_1/LinkedList.java**

```java
import java.util.NoSuchElementException;

/**
    A linked list is a sequence of nodes with efficient
    element insertion and removal. This class
    contains a subset of the methods of the standard
    java.util.LinkedList class.
*/
public class LinkedList
{
    private Node first;

    /**
        Constructs an empty linked list.
    */
    public LinkedList()
    {
        first = null;
    }

    /**
        Returns the first element in the linked list.
        @return the first element in the linked list
    */
    public Object getFirst()
    {
        if (first == null) { throw new NoSuchElementException(); }
        return first.data;
    }

    /**
        Removes the first element in the linked list.
        @return the removed element
    */
    public Object removeFirst()
    {
        if (first == null) { throw new NoSuchElementException(); }
        Object element = first.data;
        first = first.next;
        return element;
    }

    /**
        Adds an element to the front of the linked list.
        @param element the element to add
    */
    public void addFirst(Object element)
    {
        Node newNode = new Node();
        newNode.data = element;
        newNode.next = first;
        first = newNode;
    }

    /**
        Returns an iterator for iterating through this list.
        @return an iterator for iterating through this list
    */
```

```
59      public ListIterator listIterator()
60      {
61         return new LinkedListIterator();
62      }
63
64      class Node
65      {
66         public Object data;
67         public Node next;
68      }
69
70      class LinkedListIterator implements ListIterator
71      {
72         private Node position;
73         private Node previous;
74         private boolean isAfterNext;
75
76         /**
77            Constructs an iterator that points to the front
78            of the linked list.
79         */
80         public LinkedListIterator()
81         {
82            position = null;
83            previous = null;
84            isAfterNext = false;
85         }
86
87         /**
88            Moves the iterator past the next element.
89            @return the traversed element
90         */
91         public Object next()
92         {
93            if (!hasNext()) { throw new NoSuchElementException(); )
94            previous = position; // Remember for remove
95            isAfterNext = true;
96
97            if (position == null)
98            {
99               position = first;
100           }
101           else
102           {
103              position = position.next;
104           }
105
106           return position.data;
107        }
108
109        /**
110           Tests if there is an element after the iterator position.
111           @return true if there is an element after the iterator position
112        */
113        public boolean hasNext()
114        {
115           if (position == null)
116           {
117              return first != null;
118           }
```

```
119              else
120              {
121                 return position.next != null;
122              }
123           }
124
125           /**
126              Adds an element before the iterator position
127              and moves the iterator past the inserted element.
128              @param element the element to add
129           */
130           public void add(Object element)
131           {
132              if (position == null)
133              {
134                 addFirst(element);
135                 position = first;
136              }
137              else
138              {
139                 Node newNode = new Node();
140                 newNode.data = element;
141                 newNode.next = position.next;
142                 position.next = newNode;
143                 position = newNode;
144              }
145
146              isAfterNext = false;
147           }
148
149           /**
150              Removes the last traversed element. This method may
151              only be called after a call to the next method.
152           */
153           public void remove()
154           {
155              if (!isAfterNext) { throw new IllegalStateException(); }
156
157              if (position == first)
158              {
159                 removeFirst();
160              }
161              else
162              {
163                 previous.next = position.next;
164              }
165              position = previous;
166              isAfterNext = false;
167           }
168
169           /**
170              Sets the last traversed element to a different value.
171              @param element the element to set
172           */
173           public void set(Object element)
174           {
175              if (!isAfterNext) { throw new IllegalStateException(); }
176              position.data = element;
177           }
178        }
```

**179    }**

**section_1/ListIterator.java**

```
1   /**
2       A list iterator allows access to a position in a linked list.
3       This interface contains a subset of the methods of the
4       standard java.util.ListIterator interface. The methods for
5       backward traversal are not included.
6   */
7   public interface ListIterator
8   {
9       /**
10          Moves the iterator past the next element.
11          @return the traversed element
12      */
13      Object next();
14
15      /**
16          Tests if there is an element after the iterator position.
17          @return true if there is an element after the iterator position
18      */
19      boolean hasNext();
20
21      /**
22          Adds an element before the iterator position
23          and moves the iterator past the inserted element.
24          @param element the element to add
25      */
26      void add(Object element);
27
28      /**
29          Removes the last traversed element. This method may
30          only be called after a call to the next method.
31      */
32      void remove();
33
34      /**
35          Sets the last traversed element to a different value.
36          @param element the element to set
37      */
38      void set(Object element);
39  }
```

**SELF CHECK**

1. Trace through the addFirst method when adding an element to an empty list.

2. Conceptually, an iterator is located between two elements (see Figure 9 in Chapter 15). Does the position instance variable refer to the element to the left or the element to the right?

3. Why does the add method have two separate cases?

4. Assume that a last reference is added to the LinkedList class, as described in Section 16.1.8. How does the add method of the ListIterator need to change?

5. Provide an implementation of an addLast method for the LinkedList class, assuming that there is no last reference.

6. Expressed in big-Oh notation, what is the efficiency of the addFirst method of the LinkedList class? What is the efficiency of the addLast method of Self Check 5?

**7.** How much slower is the binary search algorithm for a linked list compared to the linear search algorithm?

**Practice It** Now you can try these exercises at the end of the chapter: R16.1, P16.2, P16.4, P16.6.

Special Topic 16.1

### Static Classes

You first saw the use of inner classes for event handlers in Chapter 10. Inner classes are useful in that context, because their methods have the privilege of accessing private instance variables of outer-class objects. The same is true for the `LinkedListIterator` inner class in the sample code for this section. The iterator needs to access the `first` instance variable of its linked list.

However, there is a cost for this feature. Every object of the inner class has a reference to the object of the enclosing class that constructed it. If an inner class has no need to access the enclosing class, you can declare the class as static and eliminate the reference to the enclosing class. This is the case with the `Node` class.

You can declare it as follows:

```
public class LinkedList
{
    . . .
    static class Node
    {
        . . .
    }
}
```

However, the `LinkedListIterator` class cannot be a static class. Its methods must access the `first` element of the enclosing `LinkedList`.

WORKED EXAMPLE 16.1    **Implementing a Doubly-Linked List**

This Worked Example modifies a singly-linked list to implement a doubly-linked list.

# 16.2 Implementing Array Lists

Array lists were introduced in Chapter 6. They are conceptually similar to linked lists, allowing you to add and remove elements at any position. In the following sections, we will develop an implementation of an array list, study the efficiency of operations on array lists, and compare them with the equivalent operations on linked lists.

## 16.2.1 Getting and Setting Elements

An array list maintains a reference to an array of elements that we call the **buffer**. The buffer is large enough to hold all elements in the collection—in fact, it is usually larger to allow for adding additional elements. When the buffer gets full, it is replaced by a larger one. We discuss that process in Section 16.2.3.

➕ Available online in WileyPLUS and at www.wiley.com/college/horstmann.

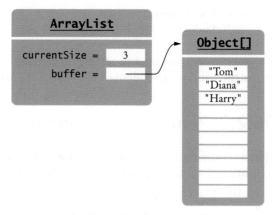

**Figure 7** An Array List Stores its Elements in an Array

In addition to the buffer, an array list has an instance field that stores the current number of elements (see Figure 7).

For simplicity, our ArrayList implementation does not work with arbitrary element types, but it simply manages elements of type Object. (Chapter 18 shows how to implement classes with type parameters.)

```java
public class ArrayList
{
   private Object[] buffer;
   private int currentSize;

   public ArrayList()
   {
      final int INITIAL_SIZE = 10;
      buffer = new Object[INITIAL_SIZE];
      currentSize = 0;
   }

   public int size() { return currentSize; }
   . . .
}
```

To access array list elements, we provide get and set methods. These methods simply check for valid positions and access the buffer at the given position:

```java
private void checkBounds(int n)
{
   if (n < 0 || n >= currentSize)
   {
      throw new IndexOutOfBoundsException();
   }
}

public Object get(int pos)
{
   checkBounds(pos);
   return buffer[pos];
}

public void set(int pos, Object element)
{
```

```
    checkBounds(pos);
    buffer[pos] = element;
}
```

Getting or setting an array list element is an $O(1)$ operation.

As you can see, getting and setting an element can be carried out with a bounded set of instructions, independent of the size of the array list. These are $O(1)$ operations.

## 16.2.2 Removing or Adding Elements

When removing an element at position $k$, the elements with higher index values need to move (see Figure 8). Here is the implementation, following Section 6.3.6:

```java
public Object remove(int pos)
{
    checkBounds(pos);

    Object removed = buffer[pos];

    for (int i = pos + 1; i < currentSize; i++)
    {
        buffer[i - 1] = buffer[i];
    }

    currentSize--;
    return removed;
}
```

How many elements are affected? If we assume that removal happens at random locations, then on average, each removal moves $n / 2$ elements, where $n$ is the size of the array list.

The same argument holds for inserting an element. On average, $n / 2$ elements need to be moved. Therefore, we say that adding and removing elements are $O(n)$ operations.

Inserting or removing an array list element is an $O(n)$ operation.

There is one situation where adding an element to an array list isn't so costly: when the insertion happens *after* the last element. If the current size is less than the length of the buffer, the size is incremented and the new element is simply stored in the buffer. This is an $O(1)$ operation.

```java
public boolean addLast(Object newElement)
{
    growBufferIfNecessary();
    currentSize++;

    buffer[currentSize - 1] = newElement;
    return true;
}
```

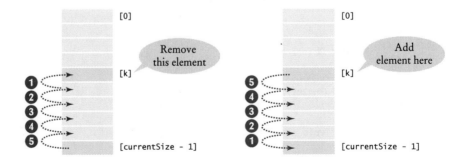

**Figure 8**
Removing and
Adding Elements

One issue remains: If there is no more room in the buffer, then we need to grow the buffer. That is the topic of the next section.

## 16.2.3  Growing the Buffer

Before inserting an element into a buffer that is completely full, we must replace the buffer with a bigger one. This new buffer is typically twice the size of the current buffer. (See Figure 9.) The existing elements are then copied into the new buffer. Reallocation is an $O(n)$ operation because all elements need to be copied to the new buffer.

*When an array list is completely full, we must move the contents to a larger buffer.*

```java
private void growBufferIfNecessary()
{
   if (currentSize == buffer.length)
   {
      Object[] newBuffer =
         new Object[2 * buffer.length]; ❶
      for (int i = 0; i < buffer.length; i++)
      {
         newBuffer[i] = buffer[i]; ❷
      }
      buffer = newBuffer; ❸
   }
}
```

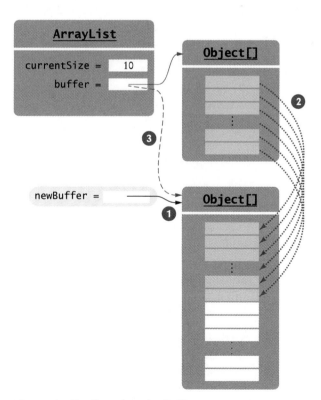

**Figure 9**   Reallocating the Buffer

If we carefully analyze the total cost of a sequence of addLast operations, it turns out that these reallocations are not as expensive as they first appear. The key observation is that buffer growth does not happen very often. Suppose we start with an array list of capacity 10 and double the size with each reallocation. We must reallocate the buffer when it reaches sizes 10, 20, 40, 80, 160, 320, 640, 1280, and so on.

Let us assume that one insertion without reallocation takes time $T_1$ and that reallocation of $k$ elements takes time $kT_2$. What is the cost of 1280 addLast operations?

Of course, we pay $1280 \cdot T_1$ for the insertions. The reallocation cost is

$$10T_2 + 20T_2 + 40T_2 + \cdots + 1280T_2 = (1 + 2 + 4 + \cdots + 128) \cdot 10 \cdot T_2$$
$$= 255 \cdot 10 \cdot T_2$$
$$< 256 \cdot 10 \cdot T_2$$
$$= 1280 \cdot 2 \cdot T_2$$

Therefore, the total cost is a bit less than

$$1280 \cdot (T_1 + 2T_2)$$

In general, the total cost of $n$ addLast operations is less than $n \cdot (T_1 + 2T_2)$. Because the second factor is a constant, we conclude that $n$ addLast operations take $O(n)$ time.

We know that it isn't quite true that an individual addLast operation takes $O(1)$ time. After all, occasionally a call to addLast is unlucky and must reallocate the buffer.

But if the cost of that reallocation is distributed over the preceding addLast operations, then the surcharge for each of them is still a constant amount. We say that addLast takes *amortized* $O(1)$ time, which is written as $O(1)+$. (Accountants say that a cost is amortized when it is distributed over multiple periods.)

In our implementation, we do not shrink the array when elements are removed. However, it turns out that you can (occasionally) shrink the array and still have $O(1)+$ performance for removing the last element (see Exercise P16.22).

> Adding or removing the last element in an array list takes amortized $O(1)$ time.

## Table 2  Efficiency of Array List and Linked List Operations

| Operation | Array List | Doubly-Linked List |
|---|---|---|
| Add/remove element at end. | $O(1)+$ | $O(1)$ |
| Add/remove element in the middle. | $O(n)$ | $O(1)$ |
| Get $k$th element. | $O(1)$ | $O(k)$ |

**ONLINE EXAMPLE**

⊕ A program to demonstrate this array list implementation.

**SELF CHECK**

8. Why is it much more expensive to get the $k$th element in a linked list than in an array list?

9. Why is it much more expensive to insert an element at the beginning of an array list than at the beginning of a linked list?

10. What is the efficiency of adding an element exactly in the middle of a linked list? An array list?

11. Suppose we insert an element at the beginning of an array list, and the buffer must be grown to hold the new element. What is the efficiency of the add operation in this situation?

**12.** Using big-Oh notation, what is the cost of adding an element to an array list as the second-to-last element?

**Practice It**   Now you can try these exercises at the end of the chapter: R16.9, R16.10, R16.11.

# 16.3  Implementing Stacks and Queues

In Section 15.5, we introduced the stack and queue data types. Stacks and queues are very simple. Elements are added and retrieved, either in *last-in, first-out* order or in *first-in, first-out* order.

In the following sections, we will study several implementations of stacks and queues and determine how efficient they are.

## 16.3.1  Stacks as Linked Lists

> A stack can be implemented as a linked list, adding and removing elements at the front.

Let us first implement a stack as a sequence of nodes. New elements are added (or "pushed") to an end of the sequence, and they are removed (or "popped") from the same end.

Which end? It is up to us to choose, and we will make the least expensive choice: to add and remove elements at the front (see Figure 10).

The push and pop operations are identical to the addFirst and removeFirst operations from Section 16.1.2. They are both $O(1)$ operations.

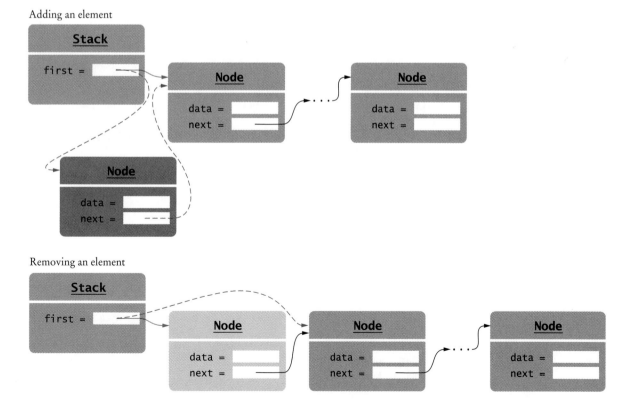

**Figure 10**   Push and Pop for a Stack Implemented as a Linked List

Here is the complete implementation:

**section_3_1/LinkedListStack.java**

```java
1   import java.util.NoSuchElementException;
2
3   /**
4       An implementation of a stack as a sequence of nodes.
5   */
6   public class LinkedListStack
7   {
8      private Node first;
9
10     /**
11         Constructs an empty stack.
12     */
13     public LinkedListStack()
14     {
15        first = null;
16     }
17
18     /**
19         Adds an element to the top of the stack.
20         @param element the element to add
21     */
22     public void push(Object element)
23     {
24        Node newNode = new Node();
25        newNode.data = element;
26        newNode.next = first;
27        first = newNode;
28     }
29
30     /**
31         Removes the element from the top of the stack.
32         @return the removed element
33     */
34     public Object pop()
35     {
36        if (first == null) { throw new NoSuchElementException(); }
37        Object element = first.data;
38        first = first.next;
39        return element;
40     }
41
42     /**
43         Checks whether this stack is empty.
44         @return true if the stack is empty
45     */
46     public boolean empty()
47     {
48        return first == null;
49     }
50
51     class Node
52     {
53        public Object data;
54        public Node next;
55     }
56  }
```

## 16.3.2 Stacks as Arrays

When implementing a stack as an array list, add and remove elements at the back.

In the preceding section, you saw how a list was implemented as a sequence of nodes. In this section, we will instead store the values in an array, thus saving the storage of the node references.

Again, it is up to us at which end of the array we place new elements. This time, it is better to add and remove elements at the back of the array (see Figure 11).

Of course, an array may eventually fill up as more elements are pushed on the stack. As with the `ArrayList` implementation of Section 16.2, the array must grow when it gets full.

The push and pop operations are identical to the `addLast` and `removeLast` operations of an array list. They are both $O(1)+$ operations.

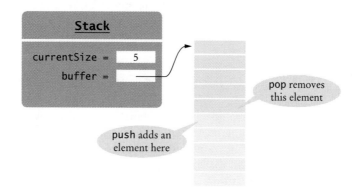

**Figure 11**   A Stack Implemented as an Array

## 16.3.3 Queues as Linked Lists

A queue can be implemented as a linked list, adding elements at the back and removing them at the front.

We now turn to the implementation of a queue. When implementing a queue as a sequence of nodes, we add nodes at one end and remove them at the other. As we discussed in Section 16.1.8, a singly-linked node sequence is not able to remove the last node in $O(1)$ time. Therefore, it is best to remove elements at the front and add them at the back (see Figure 12).

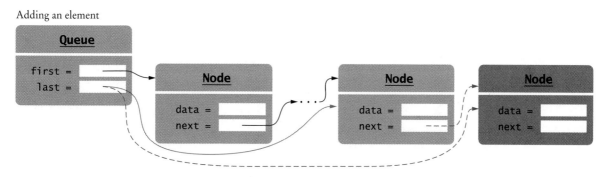

**Figure 12**   A Queue Implemented as a Linked List

Removing an element

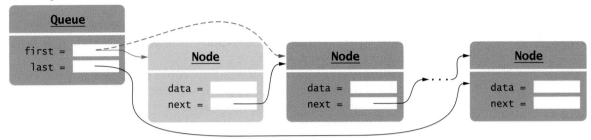

**Figure 12 (continued)** A Queue Implemented as a Linked List

The add and remove operations of a queue are $O(1)$ operations because they are the same as the addLast and removeFirst operations of a doubly-linked list. Note that we need a reference to the last node so that we can efficiently add elements.

## 16.3.4 Queues as Circular Arrays

When storing queue elements in an array, we have a problem: elements get added at one end of the array and removed at the other. But adding or removing the first element of an array is an $O(n)$ operation, so it seems that we cannot avoid this expensive operation, no matter which end we choose for adding elements and which for removing.

However, we can solve this problem with a trick. We add elements at the end, but when we remove them, we don't actually move the remaining elements. Instead, we increment the index at which the head of the queue is located (see Figure 13).

*In a circular array, we wrap around to the beginning after the last element.*

In a circular array implementation of a queue, element locations wrap from the end of the array to the beginning.

After adding sufficiently many elements, the last element of the buffer will be filled. However, if there were also a few calls to remove, then there is additional room

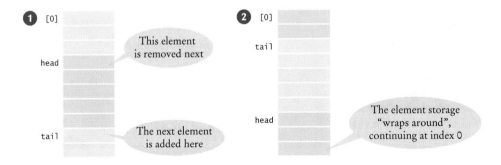

**Figure 13** Queue Elements in a Circular Array

in the front of the buffer. Then we "wrap around" and start storing elements again at index 0—see part 2 of Figure 13. For that reason, the array is called "circular".

Eventually, of course, the tail reaches the head, and a larger buffer must be allocated.

As you can see from the source code that follows, adding or removing an element requires a bounded set of operations, independent of the queue size, except for buffer reallocation. However, as discussed in Section 16.2.3, reallocation happens rarely enough that the total cost is still amortized constant time, $O(1)+$.

**section_3_4/CircularArrayQueue.java**

```java
 1  import java.util.NoSuchElementException;
 2
 3  /**
 4      An implementation of a queue as a circular array.
 5  */
 6  public class CircularArrayQueue
 7  {
 8      private Object[] buffer;
 9      private int currentSize;
10      private int head;
11      private int tail;
12
13      /**
14          Constructs an empty queue.
15      */
16      public CircularArrayQueue()
17      {
18          final int INITIAL_SIZE = 10;
19          buffer = new Object[INITIAL_SIZE];
20          currentSize = 0;
21          head = 0;
22          tail = 0;
23      }
24
25      /**
26          Checks whether this queue is empty.
27          @return true if this queue is empty
28      */
29      public boolean empty() { return currentSize == 0; }
30
31      /**
32          Adds an element to the tail of this queue.
33          @param newElement the element to add
34      */
35      public void add(Object newElement)
36      {
37          growBufferIfNecessary();
38          currentSize++;
39          buffer[tail] = newElement;
40          tail = (tail + 1) % buffer.length;
41      }
42
43      /**
44          Removes an element from the head of this queue.
45          @return the removed element
46      */
47      public Object remove()
48      {
49          if (currentSize == 0) { throw new NoSuchElementException(); }
50          Object removed = buffer[head];
51          head = (head + 1) % buffer.length;
```

```
52          currentSize--;
53          return removed;
54      }
55
56      /**
57          Grows the buffer if the current size equals the buffer's capacity.
58      */
59      private void growBufferIfNecessary()
60      {
61          if (currentSize == buffer.length)
62          {
63              Object[] newBuffer = new Object[2 * buffer.length];
64              for (int i = 0; i < buffer.length; i++)
65              {
66                  newBuffer[i] = buffer[(head + i) % buffer.length];
67              }
68              buffer = newBuffer;
69              head = 0;
70              tail = currentSize;
71          }
72      }
73  }
```

**SELF CHECK**

13. Add a method `peek` to the `Stack` implementation in Section 16.3.1 that returns the top of the stack without removing it.

14. When implementing a stack as a sequence of nodes, why isn't it a good idea to push and pop elements at the back end?

15. When implementing a stack as an array, why isn't it a good idea to push and pop elements at index 0?

16. What is wrong with this implementation of the `empty` method for the circular array queue?

    ```
    public boolean empty()
    {
        return head == 0 && tail == 0;
    }
    ```

17. What is wrong with this implementation of the `empty` method for the circular array queue?

    ```
    public boolean empty()
    {
        return head == tail;
    }
    ```

18. Have a look at the `growBufferIfNecessary` method of the `CircularArrayQueue` class. Why isn't the loop simply

    ```
    for (int i = 0; i < buffer.length; i++)
    {
        newBuffer[i] = buffer[i];
    }
    ```

**Practice It**    Now you can try these exercises at the end of the chapter: R16.20, R16.23, P16.23, P16.24.

# 16.4  Implementing a Hash Table

In Section 15.3, you were introduced to the set data structure and its two implementations in the Java collections framework, hash sets and tree sets. In these sections, you will see how hash sets are implemented and how efficient their operations are.

## 16.4.1  Hash Codes

> A good hash function minimizes *collisions*—identical hash codes for different objects.

The basic idea behind hashing is to place objects into an array, at a location that can be determined from the object itself. Each object has a **hash code**, an integer value that is computed from an object in such a way that different objects are likely to yield different hash codes.

Table 3 shows some examples of strings and their hash codes. Special Topic 15.1 shows how these values are computed.

It is possible for two or more distinct objects to have the same hash code; this is called a *collision*. For example, the strings "VII" and "Ugh" happen to have the same hash code.

| Table 3  **Sample Strings and Their Hash Codes** | | | |
|---|---|---|---|
| String | Hash Code | String | Hash Code |
| "Adam" | 2035631 | "Juliet" | –2065036585 |
| "Eve" | 70068 | "Katherine" | 2079199209 |
| "Harry" | 69496448 | "Sue" | 83491 |
| "Jim" | 74478 | "Ugh" | 84982 |
| "Joe" | 74656 | "VII" | 84982 |

## 16.4.2  Hash Tables

> A hash table uses the hash code to determine where to store each element.

A hash code is used as an array index into a **hash table**, an array that stores the set elements. In the simplest implementation of a hash table, you could make a very long array and insert each object at the location of its hash code (see Figure 14).

If there are no collisions, it is a very simple matter to find out whether an object is already present in the set or not. Compute its hash code and check whether the array position with that hash code is already occupied. This doesn't require a search through the entire array!

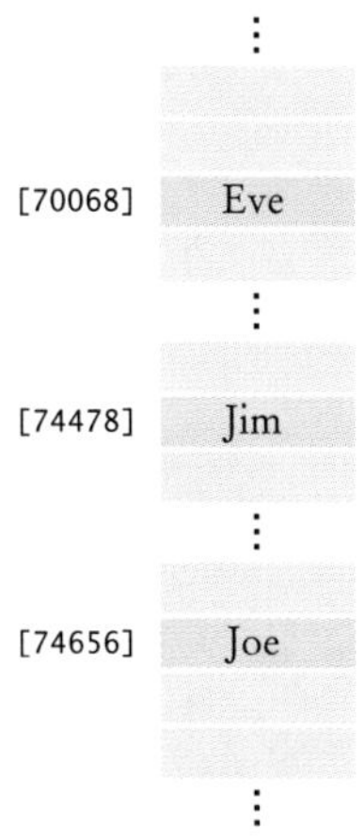

**Figure 14**
A Simplistic Implementation
of a Hash Table

*Elements with the same hash code are placed in the same bucket.*

Of course, it is not feasible to allocate an array that is large enough to hold all possible integer index positions. Therefore, we must pick an array of some reasonable size and then "compress" the hash code to become a valid array index. Compression can be easily achieved by using the remainder operation:

```
int h = x.hashCode();
if (h < 0) { h = -h; }
position = h % arrayLength;
```

See Exercise P16.30 for an alternative compression technique.

A hash table can be implemented as an array of *buckets*—sequences of nodes that hold elements with the same hash code.

After compressing the hash code, it becomes more likely that several objects will collide. There are several techniques for handling collisions. The most common one is called *separate chaining*. All colliding elements are collected in a "bucket", a linked list of elements with the same position value (see Figure 15). Special Topic 16.2 discusses *open addressing*, in which colliding elements are placed in empty locations of the hash table.

In the following, we will use the first technique. Each entry of the hash table points to a sequence of nodes containing elements with the same (compressed) hash code.

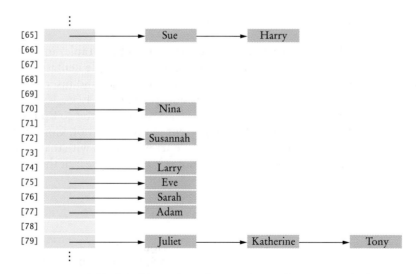

**Figure 15** A Hash Table with Buckets to Store Elements with the Same Hash Code

### 16.4.3  Finding an Element

Let's assume that our hash table has been filled with a number of elements. Now we want to find out whether a given element is already present.

Here is the algorithm for finding an object obj in a hash table:

1. Compute the hash code and compress it. This gives an index h into the hash table.

2. Iterate through the elements of the bucket at position h. For each element of the bucket, check whether it is equal to obj.

3. If a match is found among the elements of that bucket, then obj is in the set. Otherwise, it is not.

How efficient is this operation? It depends on the hash code computation. In the best case, in which there are no collisions, all buckets either are empty or have a single element.

But in practice, some collisions will occur. We need to make some assumptions that are reasonable in practice.

First, we assume that the hash code does a good job scattering the elements into different buckets. In practice, the hash functions described in Special Topic 15.1 work well.

Next, we assume that the table is large enough. This is measured by the *load factor* $F = n / L$, where $n$ is the number of elements and $L$ the table length. For example, if the table is an array of length 1,000, and it has 700 elements, then the load factor is 0.7.

If the load factor gets too large, the elements should be moved into a larger table. The hash table in the standard Java library reallocates the table when the load factor exceeds 0.75.

Under these assumptions, each bucket can be expected to have, on average, $F$ elements.

Finally, we assume that the hash code, its compression, and the equals method can be computed in bounded time, independent of the size of the set.

Now let us compute the cost of finding an element. Computing the array index takes constant time, due to our last assumption. Now we traverse a chain of buckets, which on average has a bounded length $F$. Finally, we invoke the equals method on each bucket element, which we also assume to be $O(1)$. The entire operation takes constant or $O(1)$ time.

> If there are no or only a few collisions, then adding, locating, and removing hash table elements takes constant or $O(1)$ time.

### 16.4.4  Adding and Removing Elements

Adding an element is a straightforward extension of the algorithm for finding an object. First compute the hash code to locate the bucket in which the element should be inserted:

1. Compute the compressed hash code h.

2. Iterate through the elements of the bucket at position h. For each element of the bucket, check whether it is equal to obj.

3. If a match is found among the elements of that bucket, then exit.

4. Otherwise, add a node containing obj to the beginning of the node sequence.

5. If the load factor exceeds a fixed threshold, reallocate the table.

As you saw in the preceding section, the first three steps are $O(1)$. Inserting at the beginning of a node sequence is also $O(1)$. As with array lists, we can choose the new table to be twice the size of the old table, and amortize the cost of reallocation over the preceding insertions. That is, adding an element to a hash table is $O(1)+$.

Removing an element is equally simple. First compute the hash code to locate the bucket in which the element should be inserted. Try finding the object in that bucket. If it is present, remove it. Otherwise, do nothing. Again, this is a constant time operation. If we shrink a table that becomes too sparse, the cost is $O(1)+$.

## 16.4.5 Iterating over a Hash Table

An iterator for a linked list points to the current node in a list. A hash table has multiple node chains. When we are at the end of one chain, we need to move to the start of the next one. Therefore, the iterator also needs to store the bucket number (see Figure 16).

When the iterator points into the middle of a node chain, then it is easy to advance it to the next element. However, when the iterator points to the last node in a chain, then we must skip past all empty buckets. When we find a non-empty bucket, we advance the iterator to its first node:

```
if (current != null && current.next != null)
{
    current = current.next; // Move to next element in bucket
}
else // Move to next bucket
{
    do
    {
        bucket++;
        if (bucket == buckets.length)
        {
            throw new NoSuchElementException();
        }
        current = buckets[bucket];
    }
    while (current == null);
}
```

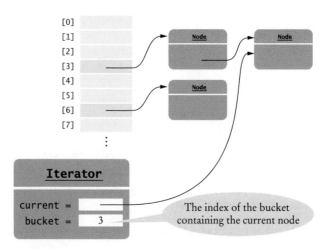

**Figure 16** An Iterator to a Hash Table

As you can see, the cost of iterating over all elements of a hash table is proportional to the table length. Note that the table length could be in excess of $O(n)$ if the table is sparsely filled. This can be avoided if we shrink the table when the load factor gets too small. In that case, iterating over the entire table is $O(n)$, and each iteration step is $O(1)$.

Table 4 summarizes the efficiency of the operations on a hash table.

| Table 4  Hash Table Efficiency | |
|---|---|
| Operation | Hash Table |
| Find an element. | $O(1)$ |
| Add/remove an element. | $O(1)+$ |
| Iterate through all elements. | $O(n)$ |

Here is an implementation of a hash set. For simplicity, we do not reallocate the table when it grows or shrinks, and we do not support the remove operation on iterators. Exercises P16.33 and P16.34 ask you to provide these enhancements.

**section_4/HashSet.java**

```java
1   import java.util.Iterator;
2   import java.util.NoSuchElementException;
3
4   /**
5      This class implements a hash set using separate chaining.
6   */
7   public class HashSet
8   {
9      private Node[] buckets;
10     private int currentSize;
11
12     /**
13        Constructs a hash table.
14        @param bucketsLength the length of the buckets array
15     */
16     public HashSet(int bucketsLength)
17     {
18        buckets = new Node[bucketsLength];
19        currentSize = 0;
20     }
21
22     /**
23        Tests for set membership.
24        @param x an object
25        @return true if x is an element of this set
26     */
27     public boolean contains(Object x)
28     {
29        int h = x.hashCode();
30        if (h < 0) { h = -h; }
31        h = h % buckets.length;
32
```

```
33        Node current = buckets[h];
34        while (current != null)
35        {
36           if (current.data.equals(x)) { return true; }
37           current = current.next;
38        }
39        return false;
40     }
41
42     /**
43        Adds an element to this set.
44        @param x an object
45        @return true if x is a new object, false if x was
46        already in the set
47     */
48     public boolean add(Object x)
49     {
50        int h = x.hashCode();
51        if (h < 0) { h = -h; }
52        h = h % buckets.length;
53
54        Node current = buckets[h];
55        while (current != null)
56        {
57           if (current.data.equals(x)) { return false; }
58              // Already in the set
59           current = current.next;
60        }
61        Node newNode = new Node();
62        newNode.data = x;
63        newNode.next = buckets[h];
64        buckets[h] = newNode;
65        currentSize++;
66        return true;
67     }
68
69     /**
70        Removes an object from this set.
71        @param x an object
72        @return true if x was removed from this set, false
73        if x was not an element of this set
74     */
75     public boolean remove(Object x)
76     {
77        int h = x.hashCode();
78        if (h < 0) { h = -h; }
79        h = h % buckets.length;
80
81        Node current = buckets[h];
82        Node previous = null;
83        while (current != null)
84        {
85           if (current.data.equals(x))
86           {
87              if (previous == null) { buckets[h] = current.next; }
88              else { previous.next = current.next; }
89              currentSize--;
90              return true;
91           }
92           previous = current;
```

```
 93              current = current.next;
 94           }
 95           return false;
 96        }
 97
 98        /**
 99           Returns an iterator that traverses the elements of this set.
100           @return a hash set iterator
101        */
102        public Iterator iterator()
103        {
104           return new HashSetIterator();
105        }
106
107        /**
108           Gets the number of elements in this set.
109           @return the number of elements
110        */
111        public int size()
112        {
113           return currentSize;
114        }
115
116        class Node
117        {
118           public Object data;
119           public Node next;
120        }
121
122        class HashSetIterator implements Iterator
123        {
124           private int bucket;
125           private Node current;
126
127           /**
128              Constructs a hash set iterator that points to the
129              first element of the hash set.
130           */
131           public HashSetIterator()
132           {
133              current = null;
134              bucket = -1;
135           }
136
137           public boolean hasNext()
138           {
139              if (current != null && current.next != null) { return true; }
140              for (int b = bucket + 1; b < buckets.length; b++)
141              {
142                 if (buckets[b] != null) { return true; }
143              }
144              return false;
145           }
146
147           public Object next()
148           {
149              if (current != null && current.next != null)
150              {
151                 current = current.next; // Move to next element in bucket
152              }
```

```
153          else // Move to next bucket
154          {
155             do
156             {
157                bucket++;
158                if (bucket == buckets.length)
159                {
160                   throw new NoSuchElementException();
161                }
162                current = buckets[bucket];
163             }
164             while (current == null);
165          }
166          return current.data;
167       }
168
169       public void remove()
170       {
171          throw new UnsupportedOperationException();
172       }
173    }
174 }
```

**section_4/HashSetDemo.java**

```
1  import java.util.Iterator;
2
3  /**
4     This program demonstrates the hash set class.
5  */
6  public class HashSetDemo
7  {
8     public static void main(String[] args)
9     {
10        HashSet names = new HashSet(101);
11
12        names.add("Harry");
13        names.add("Sue");
14        names.add("Nina");
15        names.add("Susannah");
16        names.add("Larry");
17        names.add("Eve");
18        names.add("Sarah");
19        names.add("Adam");
20        names.add("Tony");
21        names.add("Katherine");
22        names.add("Juliet");
23        names.add("Romeo");
24        names.remove("Romeo");
25        names.remove("George");
26
27        Iterator iter = names.iterator();
28        while (iter.hasNext())
29        {
30           System.out.println(iter.next());
31        }
32     }
33 }
```

**Program Run**

```
Harry
Sue
Nina
Susannah
Larry
Eve
Sarah
Adam
Juliet
Katherine
Tony
```

**SELF CHECK**

19. If a hash function returns 0 for all values, will the hash table work correctly?

20. If a hash table has size 1, will it work correctly?

21. Suppose you have two hash tables, each with $n$ elements. To find the elements that are in both tables, you iterate over the first table, and for each element, check whether it is contained in the second table. What is the big-Oh efficiency of this algorithm?

22. In which order does the iterator visit the elements of the hash table?

23. What does the hasNext method of the HashSetIterator do when it has reached the end of a bucket?

24. Why doesn't the iterator have an add method?

**Practice It** Now you can try these exercises at the end of the chapter: P16.30, P16.31, P16.33.

---

**Special Topic 16.2**

## Open Addressing

In the preceding sections, you studied a hash table implementation that uses separate chaining for collision handling, placing all elements with the same hash code in a bucket. This implementation is fast and easy to understand, but it requires storage for the links to the nodes. If one places the elements directly into the hash table, then one doesn't need to store any links. This alternative technique is called *open addressing*. It can be beneficial if one must minimize the memory usage of a hash table.

Of course, open addressing makes collision handling more complicated. If you have two elements with (compressed) hash code $h$, and the first one is placed at index $h$, then the second must be placed in another location.

There are different techniques for placing colliding elements. The simplest is *linear probing*. If possible, place the colliding element at index $h + 1$. If that slot is occupied, try $h + 2$, $h + 3$, and so on, wrapping around to 0, 1, 2, and so on, if necessary. This sequence of index values is called the *probing sequence*. (You can see other probing sequences in Exercises P16.36 and P16.37.) If the probing sequence contains no empty slots, one must reallocate to a larger table.

How do we find an element in such a hash table? We compute the hash code and traverse the probing sequence until we either find a match or an empty slot. As long as the hash table is not too full, this is still an $O(1)$ operation, but it may require more comparisons than with separate chaining. With separate chaining, we only compare objects with the same hash code.

With open addressing, there may be some objects with different hash codes that happen to lie on the probing sequence.

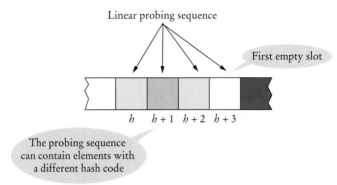

Adding an element is similar. Try finding the element first. If it is not present, add it in the first empty slot in the probing sequence.

Removing an element is trickier. You cannot simply empty the slot at which you find the element. Instead, you must traverse the probing sequence, look for the last element with the same hash code, and move that element into the slot of the removed element (Exercise P16.35).

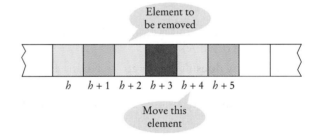

Alternatively, you can replace the removed element with a special "inactive" marker that, unlike an empty slot, does not indicate the end of a probing sequence. When adding another element, you can overwrite an inactive slot (Exercise P16.38).

## CHAPTER SUMMARY

### Describe the implementation and efficiency of linked list operations.

- A linked list object holds a reference to the first node, and each node holds a reference to the next node.
- When adding or removing the first element, the reference to the first node must be updated.
- A list iterator object has a reference to the last visited node.
- To advance an iterator, update the position and remember the old position for the remove method.
- In a doubly-linked list, accessing an element is an $O(n)$ operation; adding and removing an element is $O(1)$.

**Understand the implementation and efficiency of array list operations.**

- Getting or setting an array list element is an $O(1)$ operation.
- Inserting or removing an array list element is an $O(n)$ operation.
- Adding or removing the last element in an array list takes amortized $O(1)$ time.

**Compare different implementations of stacks and queues.**

- A stack can be implemented as a linked list, adding and removing elements at the front.
- When implementing a stack as an array list, add and remove elements at the back.
- A queue can be implemented as a linked list, adding elements at the back and removing them at the front.
- In a circular array implementation of a queue, element locations wrap from the end of the array to the beginning.

**Understand the implementation of hash tables and the efficiencies of its operations.**

- A good hash function minimizes *collisions*—identical hash codes for different objects.
- A hash table uses the hash code to determine where to store each element.
- A hash table can be implemented as an array of *buckets*—sequences of nodes that hold elements with the same hash code.
- If there are no or only a few collisions, then adding, locating, and removing hash table elements takes constant or $O(1)$ time.

## REVIEW EXERCISES

■ **R16.1** The linked list class in the Java library supports operations addLast and removeLast. To carry out these operations efficiently, the LinkedList class has an added reference last to the last node in the linked list. Draw a "before/after" diagram of the changes to the links in a linked list when the addLast method is executed.

■■ **R16.2** The linked list class in the Java library supports bidirectional iterators. To go backward efficiently, each Node has an added reference, previous, to the predecessor node in the linked list. Draw a "before/after" diagram of the changes to the links in a linked list when the addFirst and removeFirst methods execute. The diagram should show how the previous references need to be updated.

■ **R16.3** What is the big-Oh efficiency of replacing all negative values in a linked list of Integer objects with zeroes? Of removing all negative values?

■ **R16.4** What is the big-Oh efficiency of replacing all negative values in an array list of Integer objects with zeroes? Of removing all negative values?

■■ **R16.5** In the LinkedList implementation of Section 16.1, we use a flag isAfterNext to ensure that calls to the remove and set methods occur only when they are allowed.

It is not actually necessary to introduce a new instance variable for this check. Instead, one can set the previous instance variable to null at the end of every call to add or remove. With that change, how should the remove and set methods check whether they are allowed?

■ **R16.6** What is the big-Oh efficiency of the size method of Exercise P16.4?

■ **R16.7** Show that the introduction of the size method in Exercise P16.4 does not affect the big-Oh efficiency of the other list operations.

■■ **R16.8** Given the size operation of Exercise P16.4 and the get operation of Exercise P16.7, what is the big-Oh efficiency of this loop?

```
for (int i = 0; i < myList.size(); i++) { System.out.println(myList.get(i)); }
```

■■ **R16.9** Given the size operation of Exercise P16.4 and the get operation of Exercise P16.9, what is the big-Oh efficiency of this loop?

```
for (int i = 0; i < myList.size(); i++) { System.out.println(myList.get(i)); }
```

■■ **R16.10** It is not safe to remove the first element of a linked list with the removeFirst method when an iterator has just traversed the first element. Explain the problem by tracing the code and drawing a diagram.

■■ **R16.11** Continue Exercise R16.10 by providing a code example that demonstrates the problem.

■■■ **R16.12** It is not safe to simultaneously modify a linked list using two iterators. Find a situation where two iterators refer to the same linked list, and when you add an element with one iterator and remove an element with the other, the result is incorrect. Explain the problem by tracing the code and drawing a diagram.

■■■ **R16.13** Continue Exercise R16.12 by providing a code example that demonstrates the problem.

■■■ **R16.14** In the implementation of the LinkedList class of the standard Java library, the problem described in Exercises R16.10 and R16.12 results in a ConcurrentModification-Exception. Describe how the LinkedList class and the iterator classes can discover that a list was modified through multiple sources. *Hint:* Count mutating operations. Where are the counts stored? Where are they updated? Where are they checked?

■ **R16.15** Consider the efficiency of locating the $k$th element in a linked list of length $n$. If $k > n / 2$, it is more efficient to start at the end of the list and move the iterator to the previous element. Why doesn't this increase in efficiency improve the big-Oh estimate of element access in a linked list?

■ **R16.16** A linked list implementor, hoping to improve the speed of accessing elements, provides an array of Node references, pointing to every tenth node. Then the operation get(n) looks up the reference at position n / 10 and follows n % 10 links.

   **a.** With this implementation, what is the efficiency of the get operation?

   **b.** What is the disadvantage of this implementation?

■ **R16.17** Suppose an array list implementation were to add ten elements at each reallocation instead of doubling the capacity. Show that the addLast operation no longer has amortized constant time.

■ **R16.18** Consider an array list implementation with a removeLast method that shrinks the buffer to half of its size when it is at most half full. Give a sequence of addLast and removeLast calls that does not have amortized $O(1)$ efficiency.

■■■ **R16.19** Suppose the ArrayList implementation of Section 16.2 had a removeLast method that shrinks the buffer by 50 percent when it is less than 25 percent full. Show that any sequence of addLast and removeLast calls has amortized $O(1)$ efficiency.

■ **R16.20** Given a queue with $O(1)$ methods add, remove, and size, what is the big-Oh efficiency of moving the element at the head of the queue to the tail? Of moving the element at the tail of the queue to the head? (The order of the other queue elements should be unchanged.)

■ **R16.21** A deque (double-ended queue) is a data structure with operations addFirst, removeFirst, addLast, and removeLast. What is the $O(1)$ efficiency of these operations if the deque is implemented as

    **a.** a singly-linked list?

    **b.** a doubly-linked list?

    **c.** a circular array?

■■ **R16.22** In our circular array implementation of a queue, can you compute the value of the currentSize from the values of the head and tail fields? Why or why not?

■ **R16.23** Draw the contents of a circular array implementation of a queue, with an initial buffer size of 10, after each of the following loops:

    **a.** `for (int i = 1; i <= 5; i++) { q.add(i); }`

    **b.** `for (int i = 1; i <= 3; i++) { q.remove(); }`

    **c.** `for (int i = 1; i <= 10; i++) { q.add(i); }`

    **d.** `for (int i = 1; i <= 8; i++) { q.remove(); }`

■■ **R16.24** Suppose you are stranded on a desert island on which stacks are plentiful, but you need a queue. How can you implement a queue using two stacks? What is the big-Oh running time of the queue operations?

■■ **R16.25** Suppose you are stranded on a desert island on which queues are plentiful, but you need a stack. How can you implement a stack using two queues? What is the big-Oh running time of the stack operations?

■■ **R16.26** Craig Coder doesn't like the fact that he has to implement a hash function for the objects that he wants to collect in a hash table. "Why not assign a unique ID to each object?" he asks. What is wrong with his idea?

## PROGRAMMING EXERCISES

■■■ **P16.1** Add a method reverse to our implementation of the LinkedList class that reverses the links in a list. Implement this method by directly rerouting the links, not by using an iterator.

■■ **P16.2** Consider a version of the LinkedList class of Section 16.1 in which the addFirst method has been replaced with the following faulty version:

```
public void addFirst(Object element)
{
    Node newNode = new Node();
    first = newNode;
    newNode.data = element;
    newNode.next = first;
}
```

Develop a program ListTest with a test case that shows the error. That is, the program should print a failure message with this implementation but not with the correct implementation.

•• **P16.3** Consider a version of the LinkedList class of Section 16.1 in which the iterator's hasNext method has been replaced with the following faulty version:

```
public boolean hasNext()
{
    return position != null;
}
```

Develop a program ListTest with a test case that shows the error. That is, the program should print a failure message with this implementation but not with the correct implementation.

• **P16.4** Add a method size to our implementation of the LinkedList class that computes the number of elements in the list by following links and counting the elements until the end of the list is reached.

•• **P16.5** Solve Exercise P16.4 recursively by calling a recursive helper method

```
private static int size(Node start)
```

*Hint:* If start is null, then the size is 0. Otherwise, it is one larger than the size of start.next.

• **P16.6** Add an instance variable currentSize to our implementation of the LinkedList class. Modify the add, addLast, and remove methods of both the linked list and the list iterator to update the currentSize variable so that it always contains the correct size. Change the size method of Exercise P16.4 so that it simply returns the value of this instance variable.

• **P16.7** Add methods Object get(int n) and void set(int n, Object newElement) to the LinkedList class. Use a helper method

```
private static Node getNode(int n)
```

that starts at first and follows n links.

• **P16.8** Solve Exercise P16.7 by using a recursive helper method

```
private static Node getNode(Node start, int distance)
```

••• **P16.9** Improve the efficiency of the get and set methods of Exercise P16.7 by storing (or "caching") the last known (node, index) pair. If n is larger than the last known index, start from the corresponding node instead of the front of the list. Be sure to discard the last known pair when it is no longer accurate. (This can happen when another method edits the list).

•• **P16.10** Add a method boolean contains(Object obj) that checks whether our LinkedList implementation contains a given object. Implement this method by directly traversing the links, not by using an iterator.

Use the `equals` method to determine whether `obj` equals `node.data` for a given node.

**•• P16.11** Solve Exercise P16.10 recursively, by calling a recursive helper method

```
private static boolean contains(Node start, Object obj)
```

*Hint:* If `start` is `null`, then it can't contain the object. Otherwise, check `start.data` before recursively moving on to `start.next`.

**•• P16.12** A linked list class with an $O(1)$ `addLast` method needs an efficient mechanism to get to the end of the list, for example by setting an instance variable to the last element. It is then possible to remove the reference to the first node if one makes the `next` reference of the last node point to the first node, so that all nodes form a cycle. Such an implementation is called a circular linked list. Turn the linked list implementation of Section 16.1 into a circular singly-linked list.

**••• P16.13** In a circular doubly-linked list, the `previous` reference of the first node points to the last node, and the `next` reference of the last node points to the first node. Change the doubly-linked list implementation of Worked Example 16.1 into a circular list. You should remove the `last` instance variable because you can reach the last element as `first.previous`.

**•• P16.14** Modify the insertion sort algorithm of Special Topic 14.2 to sort a linked list.

**•• P16.15** The LISP language, created in 1960, implements linked lists in a very elegant way. You will explore a Java analog in this set of exercises. Conceptually, the *tail* of a list—that is, the list with its head node removed—is also a list. The tail of that list is again a list, and so on, until you reach the empty list. Here is a Java interface for such a list:

```
public interface LispList
{
    boolean empty();
    Object head();
    LispList tail();
    . . .
}
```

There are two kinds of lists, empty lists and nonempty lists:

```
public class EmptyList extends LispList { ... }
public class NonEmptyList extends LispList { ... }
```

These classes are quite trivial. The `EmptyList` class has no instance variables. Its `head` and `tail` methods simply throw an `UnsupportedOperationException`, and its `empty` method returns `true`. The `NonEmptyList` class has instance variables for the head and tail.

Here is one way of making a lisp list with three elements:

```
LispList list = new NonEmptyList("A", new NonEmptyList("B",
    new NonEmptyList("C", new EmptyList())));
```

This is a bit tedious, and it is a good idea to supply a convenience method `cons` that calls the constructor, as well as a static variable `NIL` that is an instance of an empty list. Then our list construction becomes

```
LispList list = LispList.NIL.cons("C").cons("B").cons("A");
```

Note that you need to build up the list starting from the (empty) tail.

To see the elegance of this approach, consider the implementation of a toString method that produces a string containing all list elements. The method must be implemented by both subclasses:

```java
public class EmptyList
{
    ...
    public String toString() { return ""; }
}

public class NonEmptyList
{
    ...
    public String toString() { return head() + " " + tail().toString(); }
}
```

Note that no if statement is required. A list is either empty or nonempty, and the correct toString method is invoked due to polymorphism.

In this exercise, complete the LispList interface and the EmptyList and NonEmptyList classes. Write a test program that constructs a list and prints it.

- **P16.16** Add a method length to the LispList interface of Exercise P16.15 that returns the length of the list. Implement the method in the EmptyList and NonEmptyList classes.

- **P16.17** Add a method

    ```java
    LispList merge(LispList other)
    ```

    to the LispList interface of Exercise P16.15. Implement the method in the EmptyList and NonEmptyList classes. When merging two lists, alternate between the elements, then add the remainder of the longer list. For example, merging the lists with elements 1 2 3 4 and 5 6 yields 1 5 2 6 3 4.

- **P16.18** Add a method

    ```java
    boolean contains(Object obj)
    ```

    to the LispList interface of Exercise P16.15 that returns true if the list contains an element that equals obj.

- **P16.19** Reimplement the LinkedList class of Section 16.1 so that the Node and LinkedList-Iterator classes are not inner classes.

- **P16.20** Reimplement the LinkedList class of Section 16.1 so that it implements the java.util. LinkedList interface. *Hint:* Extend the java.util.AbstractList class.

- **P16.21** Provide a listIterator method for the ArrayList implementation in Section 16.2. Your method should return an object of a class implementing java.util.ListIterator. Also have the ArrayList class implement the Iterable interface type and provide a test program that demonstrates that your array list can be used in an enhanced for loop.

- **P16.22** Provide a removeLast method for the ArrayList implementation in Section 16.2 that shrinks the buffer by 50 percent when it is less than 25 percent full.

- **P16.23** Complete the implementation of a stack in Section 16.3.2, using an array for storing the elements.

- **P16.24** Complete the implementation of a queue in Section 16.3.3, using a sequence of nodes for storing the elements.

- **P16.25** Add a method firstToLast to the implementation of a queue in Exercise P16.24. The method moves the element at the head of the queue to the tail of the queue. The element that was second in line will now be at the head.

- **P16.26** Add a method lastToFirst to the implementation of a queue in Exercise P16.24. The method moves the element at the tail of the queue to the head.

- **P16.27** Add a method firstToLast, as described in Exercise P16.25, to the circular array implementation of a queue.

- **P16.28** Add a method lastToFirst, as described in Exercise P16.26, to the circular array implementation of a queue.

- - **P16.29** A deque (double-ended queue) is a data structure with operations addFirst, removeFirst, addLast, removeLast, and size. Implement a deque as a circular array, so that these operations have amortized constant time.

- **P16.30** Implement the hash set in Section 16.4, using the "MAD (multiply-add-divide) method" for hash code compression. For that method, you choose a prime number $p$ larger than the length $L$ of the hash table and two values $a$ and $b$ between 1 and $p - 1$. Then reduce $h$ to $((a h + b) \% p) \% L$.

- **P16.31** Add methods to count collisions to the hash set in Section 16.4 and the one in Exercise P16.30. Insert all words from a dictionary (which you can find in /usr/share/dict/words on a UNIX or Linux computer) into both hash set implementations. Does the MAD method reduce collisions? (Use a table size that equals the number of words in the file. Choose $p$ to be the next prime greater than $L$, $a = 3$, and $b = 5$.)

- **P16.32** The hasNext method of the hash set implementation in Section 16.4 finds the location of the next element, but when next is called, the same search happens again. Improve the efficiency of these methods so that next (or a repeated call to hasNext) uses the position located by a preceding call to hasNext.

- - **P16.33** Reallocate the buckets of the hash set implementation in Section 16.4 when the load factor is greater than 1.0 or less than 0.5, doubling or halving its size. Note that you need to recompute the hash values of all elements.

- - - **P16.34** Implement the remove operation for iterators on the hash set in Section 16.4.

- - - **P16.35** Implement a hash table with open addressing. When removing an element that is followed by other elements with the same hash code, replace it with the last such element.

- - - **P16.36** Modify Exercise P16.35 to use *quadratic probing*. The $i$th index in the probing sequence is computed as $(h + i^2) \% L$.

- - - **P16.37** Modify Exercise P16.35 to use *double hashing*. The $i$th index in the probing sequence is computed as $(h + i h_2(k)) \% L$, where $k$ is the original hash key before compression and $h_2$ is a function mapping integers to non-zero values. A common choice is $h_2(k) = 1 + k \% q$ for a prime $q$ less than $L$.

- - - **P16.38** Modify Exercise P16.35 so that you mark removed elements with an "inactive" element. You can't use null—that is already used for empty elements. Instead, declare a static variable

    ```
    private static final Object INACTIVE = new Object();
    ```

    Use the test if (table[i] == INACTIVE) to check whether a table entry is inactive.

## ANSWERS TO SELF-CHECK QUESTIONS

1. When the list is empty, `first` is `null`. A new `Node` is allocated. Its `data` instance variable is set to the element that is being added. It's `next` instance variable is set to `null` because `first` is `null`. The `first` instance variable is set to the new node. The result is a linked list of length 1.

2. It refers to the element to the left. You can see that by tracing out the first call to `next`. It leaves `position` to refer to the first node.

3. If `position` is `null`, we must be at the head of the list, and inserting an element requires updating the `first` reference. If we are in the middle of the list, the `first` reference should not be changed.

4. If an element is added after the last one, then the last reference must be updated to point to the new element. After

   `position.next = newNode;`

   add

   `if (position == last) { last = newNode; }`

5. ```
   public void addLast(Object element)
   {
       if (first == null) { addFirst(element); }
       else
       {
           Node last = first;
           while (last.next != null)
           {
               last = last.next;
           }
           last.next = new Node();
           last.next.data = element;
       }
   }
   ```

6. $O(1)$ and $O(n)$.

7. To locate the middle element takes $n/2$ steps. To locate the middle of the subinterval to the left or right takes another $n/4$ steps. The next lookup takes $n/8$ steps. Thus, we expect almost $n$ steps to locate an element. At this point, you are better off just making a linear search that, on average, takes $n/2$ steps.

8. In a linked list, one must follow $k$ links to get to the $k$th elements. In an array list, one can reach the $k$th element directly as `buffer[k]`.

9. In a linked list, one merely updates references to the first and second node—a constant cost

that is independent of the number of elements that follow. In an array list of size $n$, inserting an element at the beginning requires us to move all $n$ elements.

10. It is $O(n)$ in both cases. In the case of the linked list, it costs $O(n)$ steps to move an iterator to the middle.

11. It is still $O(n)$. Reallocating the array is an $O(n)$ operation, and moving the array elements also requires $O(n)$ time.

12. $O(1)+$. The cost of moving one element is $O(1)$, but every so often one has to pay for a reallocation.

13. ```
    public Object peek()
    {
        if (first == null)
        {
            throw new NoSuchElementException();
        }
        return first.data;
    }
    ```

14. Removing an element from a singly-linked list is $O(n)$.

15. Adding and removing an element at index 0 is $O(n)$.

16. The queue can be empty when the head and tail are at a position other than zero. For example, after the calls `q.add(obj)` and `q.remove()`, the queue is empty, but `head` and `tail` are 1.

17. Indeed, if the queue is empty, then the head and tail are equal. But that situation also occurs when the buffer is completely full.

18. Then the circular wrapping wouldn't work. If we simply added new elements without reordering the existing ones, the new buffer layout would be

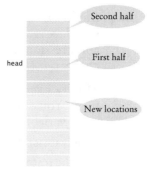

**19.** Yes, the hash set will work correctly. All elements will be inserted into a single bucket.

**20.** Yes, but there will be a single bucket containing all elements. Finding, adding, and removing elements is $O(n)$.

**21.** The iteration takes $O(n)$ steps. Each step makes an $O(1)$ containment check. Therefore, the total cost is $O(n)$.

**22.** Elements are visited by increasing (compressed) hash code. This ordering will appear random to users of the hash table.

**23.** It locates the next bucket in the bucket array and points to its first element.

**24.** In a set, it doesn't make sense to add an element at a specific position.

# TREE STRUCTURES

To study trees and binary trees

To understand how binary search trees
can implement sets

To learn how red-black trees provide performance
guarantees for set operations

To choose appropriate methods for tree traversal

To become familiar with the heap data structure

To use heaps for implementing priority queues and for sorting

In this chapter, we study data structures that organize elements hierarchically, creating arrangements that resemble trees. These data structures offer better performance for adding, removing, and finding elements than the linear structures you have seen so far. You will learn about commonly used tree-shaped structures and study their implementation and performance.

# 17.1 Basic Tree Concepts

A tree is composed of nodes, each of which can have child nodes.

In computer science, a **tree** is a hierarchical data structure composed of *nodes*. Each node has a sequence of *child nodes*, and one of the nodes is the *root node*.

Like a linked list, a tree is composed of nodes, but with a key difference. In a linked list, a node can have only one child node, so the data structure is a linear chain of nodes.

The root is the node with no parent. A leaf is a node with no children.

*A family tree shows the descendants of a common ancestor.*

In a tree, a node can have more than one child. The resulting shape resembles an actual tree with branches. However, in computer science, it is customary to draw trees upside-down, with the root on top (see Figure 1).

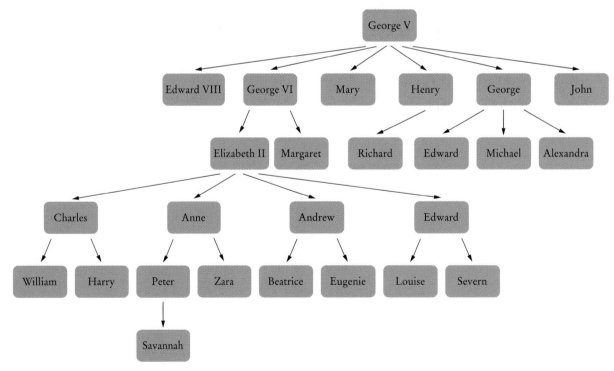

**Figure 1** A Family Tree

Trees are commonly used to represent hierarchical relationships. When we talk about nodes in a tree, it is customary to use intuitive words such as roots and leaves, but also parents, children, and siblings—see Table 1 for commonly used terms.

## Table 1  Tree Terminology

| Term | Definition | Example (using Figure 1) |
|---|---|---|
| Node | The building block of a tree: A tree is composed of linked nodes. | This tree has 26 nodes: George V, Edward VIII, ..., Savannah. |
| Child | Each node has, by definition, a sequence of links to other nodes called its child nodes. | The children of Elizabeth II are Charles, Anne, Andrew, and Edward. |
| Leaf | A node with no child nodes. | This tree has 16 leaves, including William, Harry, and Savannah. |
| Interior node | A node that is not a leaf. | George V or George VI, but not Mary. |
| Parent | If the node $c$ is a child of the node $p$, then $p$ is a parent of $c$. | Elizabeth II is the parent of Charles. |
| Sibling | If the node $p$ has children $c$ and $d$, then these nodes are siblings. | Charles and Anne are siblings. |
| Root | The node with no parent. By definition, each tree has one root node. | George V. |
| Path | A sequence of nodes $c_1, c_2, ..., c_k$ where $c_{i+1}$ is a child of $c_i$. | Elizabeth II, Anne, Peter, Savannah is a path of length 4. |
| Descendant | $d$ is a descendant of $c$ if there is a path from $c$ to $d$. | Peter is a descendant of Elizabeth II but not of Henry. |
| Ancestor | $c$ is an ancestor of $d$ if $d$ is a descendant of $c$. | Elizabeth II is an ancestor of Peter, but Henry is not. |
| Subtree | The subtree rooted at node $n$ is the tree formed by taking $n$ as the root node and including all its descendants. | The subtree with root Anne is |
| Height | The number of nodes in the longest path from the root to a leaf. (Some authors define the height to be the number of edges in the longest path, which is one less than the height used in this book.) | This tree has height 6. The longest path is George V, George VI, Elizabeth II, Anne, Peter, Savannah. |

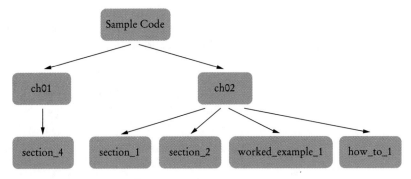

**Figure 2** A Directory Tree

Trees have many applications in computer science; see for example Figures 2 and 3.

There are multiple ways of implementing a tree. Here we present an outline of a simple implementation that is further explored in Exercises P17.1 and P17.2. A node holds a data item and a list of references to the child nodes. A tree holds a reference to the root node.

> A tree class uses a node class to represent nodes and has an instance variable for the root node.

```java
public class Tree
{
   private Node root;

   class Node
   {
      public Object data;
      public List<Node> children;
   }

   public Tree(Object rootData)
   {
      root = new Node();
      root.data = rootData;
      root.children = new ArrayList<Node>();
   }

   public void addSubtree(Tree subtree)
   {
      root.children.add(subtree.root);
   }
   . . .
}
```

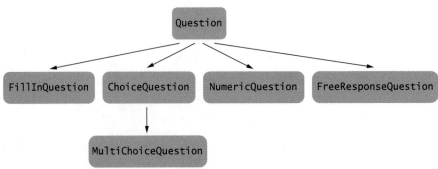

**Figure 3** An Inheritance Tree

Note that, as with linked lists, the `Node` class is nested inside the `Tree` class. It is considered an implementation detail. Users of the class only work with `Tree` objects.

When computing properties of trees, it is often convenient to use recursion. For example, consider the task of computing the tree size, that is, the number of nodes in the tree. Compute the sizes of its subtrees, add them up, and add one for the root.

For example, in Figure 1, the tree with root node Elizabeth II has four subtrees, with node counts 3, 4, 3, and 3, yielding a count of $1 + 3 + 4 + 3 + 3 = 14$ for that tree.

Formally, if $r$ is the root node of a tree, then

$$\text{size}(r) = 1 + \text{size}(c_1) + \ldots + \text{size}(c_k), \text{ where } c_1 \ldots c_k \text{ are the children of } r$$

*When computing tree properties, it is common to recursively visit smaller and smaller subtrees.*

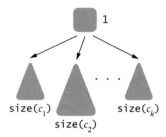

*Many tree properties are computed with recursive methods.*

To implement this size method, first provide a recursive helper:

```
class Node
{
    . . .
    public int size()
    {
        int sum = 0;
        for (Node child : children) { sum = sum + child.size(); }
        return 1 + sum;
    }
}
```

Then call this helper method from a method of the `Tree` class:

```
public class Tree
{
    . . .
    public int size() { return root.size(); }
}
```

**ONLINE EXAMPLE**

The code for the Tree class and recursive size method.

It is useful to allow an *empty tree*; a tree whose root node is `null`. This is analogous to an empty list—a list with no elements. Because we can't invoke the helper method on a `null` reference, we need to refine the `Tree` class's size method:

```
public int size()
{
    if (root == null) { return 0; }
    else { return root.size(); }
}
```

**SELF CHECK**

1. What are the paths starting with Anne in the tree shown in Figure 1?
2. What are the roots of the subtrees consisting of 3 nodes in the tree shown in Figure 1?
3. What is the height of the subtree with root Anne?
4. What are all possible shapes of trees of height 3 with two leaves?

5. Describe a recursive algorithm for counting all leaves in a tree.
6. Using the public interface of the Tree class in this section, construct a tree that is identical to the subtree with root Anne in Figure 1.
7. Is the size method of the Tree class recursive? Why or why not?

**Practice It**   Now you can try these exercises at the end of the chapter: R17.1, R17.2, P17.3.

# 17.2 Binary Trees

A binary tree consists of nodes, each of which has at most two child nodes.

In the following sections, we discuss **binary trees**, trees in which each node has at most two children. As you will see throughout this chapter, binary trees have many very important applications.

*In a binary tree, each node has a left and a right child node.*

## 17.2.1 Binary Tree Examples

*A decision tree contains questions to decide among a number of options.*

In this section, you will see several typical examples of binary trees. Figure 4 shows a *decision tree* for guessing an animal from one of several choices. Each non-leaf node contains a question. The left subtree corresponds to a "yes" answer, and the right subtree to a "no" answer.

This is a binary tree because every node has either two children (if it is a decision) or no children (if it is a conclusion). Exercises P17.6 and P17.8 show you how you can build decision trees that ask good questions for a particular data set.

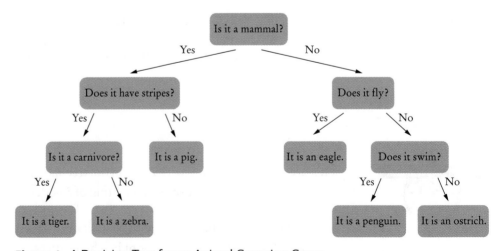

**Figure 4**   A Decision Tree for an Animal Guessing Game

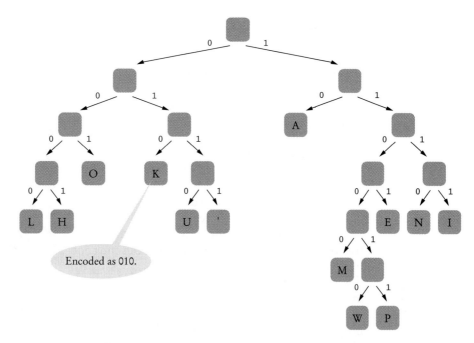

**Figure 5**   A Huffman Tree for Encoding the Thirteen Characters of Hawaiian Text

In a Huffman tree, the left and right turns on the paths to the leaves describe binary encodings.

Another example of a binary tree is a *Huffman tree*. In a Huffman tree, the leaves contain symbols that we want to encode. To encode a particular symbol, walk along the path from the root to the leaf containing the symbol, and produce a zero for every left turn and a one for every right turn. For example, in the Huffman tree of Figure 5, an H is encoded as 0001 and an A as 10. Worked Example 17.1 shows how to build a Huffman tree that gives the shortest codes for the most frequent symbols.

An expression tree shows the order of evaluation in an arithmetic expression.

Binary trees are also used to show the evaluation order in arithmetic expressions. For example, Figure 6 shows the trees for the expressions

```
(3 + 4) * 5
3 + 4 * 5
```

The leaves of the expression trees contain numbers, and the interior nodes contain the operators. Because each operator has two operands, the tree is binary.

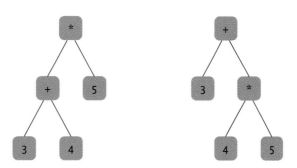

**Figure 6**   Expression Trees

## 17.2.2 Balanced Trees

In a balanced tree, all paths from the root to the leaves have approximately the same length.

When we use binary trees to store data, as we will in Section 17.3, we would like to have trees that are *balanced*. In a balanced tree, all paths from the root to one of the leaf nodes have approximately the same length. Figure 7 shows examples of a balanced and an unbalanced tree.

Recall that the height of a tree is the number of nodes in the longest path from the root to a leaf. The trees in Figure 7 have height 5. As you can see, for a given height, a balanced tree can hold more nodes than an unbalanced tree.

We care about the height of a tree because many tree operations proceed along a path from the root to a leaf, and their efficiency is better expressed by the height of the tree than the number of elements in the tree.

*In a balanced binary tree, each subtree has approximately the same number of nodes.*

A binary tree of height $h$ can have up to $n = 2^h - 1$ nodes. For example, a completely filled binary tree of height 4 has $1 + 2 + 4 + 8 = 15 = 2^4 - 1$ nodes (see Figure 8).

In other words, $h = \log_2(n + 1)$ for a completely filled binary tree. For a balanced tree, we still have $h \approx \log_2 n$. For example, the height of a balanced binary tree with 1,000 nodes is approximately 10 (because $1000 \approx 1024 = 2^{10}$). A balanced binary tree with 1,000,000 nodes has approximately height 20 (because $10^6 \approx 2^{20}$). As you will see in Section 17.3, you can find any element in such a tree in about 20 steps. That is a lot faster than traversing the 1,000,000 elements of a list.

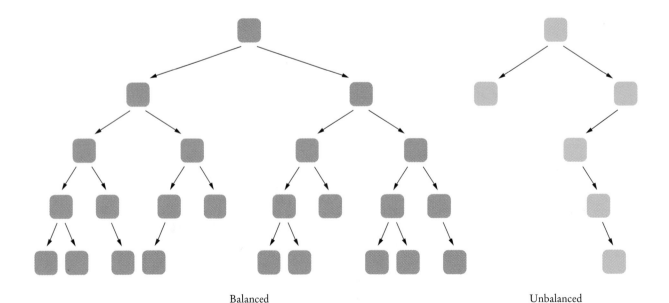

Balanced                                                    Unbalanced

**Figure 7** Balanced and Unbalanced Trees

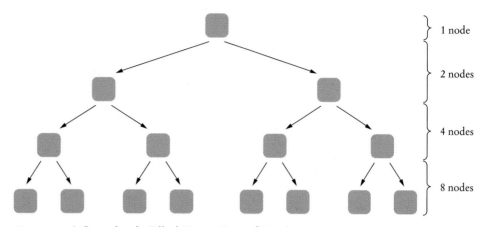

**Figure 8**   A Completely Filled Binary Tree of Height 4

## 17.2.3 A Binary Tree Implementation

Every node in a binary tree has references to two children, a left child and a right child. Either one may be null. A node in which both children are null is a leaf.

A binary tree can be implemented in Java as follows:

```java
public class BinaryTree
{
   private Node root;

   public BinaryTree() { root = null; } // An empty tree

   public BinaryTree(Object rootData, BinaryTree left, BinaryTree right)
   {
      root = new Node();
      root.data = rootData;
      root.left = left.root;
      root.right = right.root;
   }

   class Node
   {
      public Object data;
      public Node left;
      public Node right;
   }

   . . .
}
```

As with general trees, we often use recursion to define operations on binary trees. Consider computing the height of a tree; that is, the number of nodes in the longest path from the root to a leaf.

To get the height of the tree $t$, take the larger of the heights of the children and add one, to account for the root.

$$\text{height}(t) = 1 + \max(\text{height}(l), \text{height}(r))$$

where $l$ and $r$ are the left and right subtrees.

Chapter 17 Tree Structures

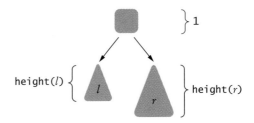

When we implement this method, we could add a `height` method to the `Node` class. However, nodes can be `null` and you can't call a method on a `null` reference. It is easier to make the recursive helper method a static method of the `Tree` class, like this:

```
public class BinaryTree
{
    . . .
    private static int height(Node n)
    {
        if (n == null) { return 0; }
        else { return 1 + Math.max(height(n.left), height(n.right)); }
    }
    . . .
}
```

To get the height of the tree, we provide this public method:

```
public class BinaryTree
{
    . . .
    public int height() { return height(root); }
}
```

 A program that implements the animal guessing game in Figure 4.

Note that there are two `height` methods: a public method with no arguments, returning the height of the tree, and a private recursive helper method, returning the height of a subtree with a given node as its root.

**SELF CHECK**

8. Encode ALOHA, using the Huffman code in Figure 5.
9. In an expression tree, where is the operator stored that gets executed *last*?
10. What is the expression tree for the expression 3 − 4 − 5?
11. How many leaves do the binary trees in Figure 4, Figure 5, and Figure 6 have? How many interior nodes?
12. Show how the recursive `height` helper method can be implemented as an instance method of the `Node` class. What is the disadvantage of that approach?

**Practice It** Now you can try these exercises at the end of the chapter: R17.4, P17.4, P17.5, P17.6.

---

**WORKED EXAMPLE 17.1** **Building a Huffman Tree**

This Worked Example shows how to build a Huffman tree for compressing the color data of an image.

⊕ Available online in WileyPLUS and at www.wiley.com/college/horstmann.

# 17.3  Binary Search Trees

A set implementation is allowed to rearrange its elements in any way it chooses so that it can find elements quickly. Suppose a set implementation *sorts* its entries. Then it can use **binary search** to locate elements quickly. Binary search takes $O(\log(n))$ steps, where $n$ is the size of the set. For example, binary search in an array of 1,000 elements is able to locate an element in at most 10 steps by cutting the size of the search interval in half in each step.

If we use an array to store the elements of a set, inserting or removing an element is an $O(n)$ operation. In the following sections, you will see how tree-shaped data structures can keep elements in sorted order with more efficient insertion and removal.

## 17.3.1  The Binary Search Property

All nodes in a binary search tree fulfill the property that the descendants to the left have smaller data values than the node data value, and the descendants to the right have larger data values.

A **binary search tree** is a binary tree in which *all nodes* fulfill the following property:

- The data values of *all* descendants to the left are less than the data value stored in the node, and *all* descendants to the right have greater data values.

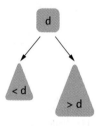

The tree in Figure 9 is a binary search tree.

We can verify the binary search property for each node in Figure 9. Consider the node "Juliet". All descendants to the left have data before "Juliet". All descendants on the right have data after "Juliet". Move on to "Eve". There is a single descendant to the left, with data "Adam" before "Eve", and a single descendant to the right, with data "Harry" after "Eve". Check the remaining nodes in the same way.

Figure 10 shows a binary tree that is not a binary search tree. Look carefully—the root node passes the test, but its two children do not.

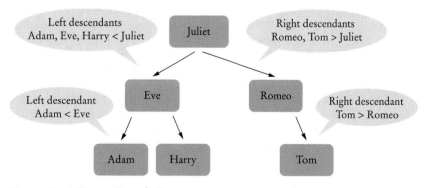

**Figure 9**  A Binary Search Tree

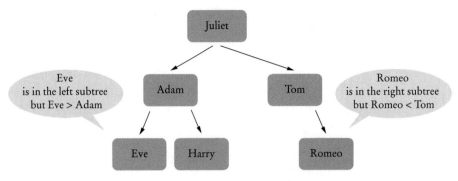

**Figure 10** A Binary Tree That Is Not a Binary Search Tree

When you implement binary search tree classes, the data variable should have type
Comparable, not Object. After all, you must be able to compare the values in a binary
search tree in order to place them into the correct position.

```
public class BinarySearchTree
{
   private Node root;

   public BinarySearchTree() { . . . }
   public void add(Comparable obj) { . . . }
   . . .
   class Node
   {
      public Comparable data;
      public Node left;
      public Node right;

      public void addNode(Node newNode) { . . . }
      . . .
   }
}
```

## 17.3.2 Insertion

To insert a value into
a binary search tree,
keep comparing the
value with the node
data and follow the
nodes to the left or
right, until reaching a
null node.

To insert data into the tree, use the following algorithm:

- If you encounter a non-null node reference, look at its data value. If the data value
  of that node is larger than the one you want to insert, continue the process with
  the left child. If the node's data value is smaller than the one you want to insert,
  continue the process with the right child.
- If you encounter a null node reference, replace it with the new node.

For example, consider the tree in Figure 11. It is the result of the following statements:

```
BinarySearchTree tree = new BinarySearchTree();
tree.add("Juliet"); ❶
tree.add("Tom"); ❷
tree.add("Diana"); ❸
tree.add("Harry"); ❹
```

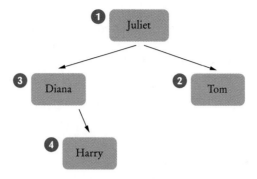

**Figure 11**   Binary Search Tree After Four Insertions

We want to insert a new element Romeo into it:

```
tree.add("Romeo");  ❺
```

Start with the root node, Juliet. Romeo comes after Juliet, so you move to the right subtree. You encounter the node Tom. Romeo comes before Tom, so you move to the left subtree. But there is no left subtree. Hence, you insert a new Romeo node as the left child of Tom (see Figure 12).

You should convince yourself that the resulting tree is still a binary search tree. When Romeo is inserted, it must end up as a right descendant of Juliet—that is what the binary search tree condition means for the root node Juliet. The root node doesn't care where in the right subtree the new node ends up. Moving along to Tom, the right child of Juliet, all it cares about is that the new node Romeo ends up somewhere on its left. There is nothing to its left, so Romeo becomes the new left child, and the resulting tree is again a binary search tree.

Here is the code for the add method of the BinarySearchTree class:

```java
public void add(Comparable obj)
{
   Node newNode = new Node();
   newNode.data = obj;
   newNode.left = null;
   newNode.right = null;
   if (root == null) { root = newNode; }
   else { root.addNode(newNode); }
}
```

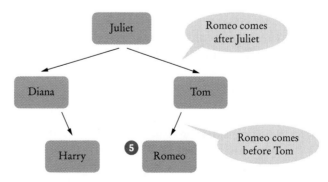

**Figure 12**   Binary Search Tree After Five Insertions

If the tree is empty, simply set its root to the new node. Otherwise, you know that the new node must be inserted somewhere within the nodes, and you can ask the root node to perform the insertion. That node object calls the `addNode` method of the `Node` class, which checks whether the new object is less than the object stored in the node. If so, the element is inserted in the left subtree; if not, it is inserted in the right subtree:

```
class Node
{
    . . .
    public void addNode(Node newNode)
    {
        int comp = newNode.data.compareTo(data);
        if (comp < 0)
        {
            if (left == null) { left = newNode; }
            else { left.addNode(newNode); }
        }
        else if (comp > 0)
        {
            if (right == null) { right = newNode; }
            else { right.addNode(newNode); }
        }
    }
    . . .
}
```

Let's trace the calls to `addNode` when inserting `Romeo` into the tree in Figure 11. The first call to `addNode` is

```
root.addNode(newNode)
```

Because `root` points to `Juliet`, you compare `Juliet` with `Romeo` and find that you must call

```
root.right.addNode(newNode)
```

The node `root.right` is `Tom`. Compare the data values again (`Tom` vs. `Romeo`) and find that you must now move to the left. Since `root.right.left` is `null`, set `root.right.left` to `newNode`, and the insertion is complete (see Figure 12).

Unlike a linked list or an array, and like a hash table, a binary tree has no *insert positions*. You cannot select the position where you would like to insert an element into a binary search tree. The data structure is *self-organizing*; that is, each element finds its own place.

## 17.3.3 Removal

We will now discuss the removal algorithm. Our task is to remove a node from the tree. Of course, we must first *find* the node to be removed. That is a simple matter, due to the characteristic property of a binary search tree. Compare the data value to be removed with the data value that is stored in the root node. If it is smaller, keep looking in the left subtree. Otherwise, keep looking in the right subtree.

Let us now assume that we have located the node that needs to be removed. First, let us consider the easiest case. If the node to be removed has no children at all, then the parent link is simply set to `null` (Figure 13).

When the node to be removed has only one child, the situation is still simple (see Figure 14).

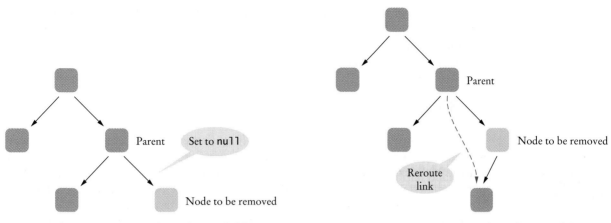

**Figure 13** Removing a Node with No Children

**Figure 14** Removing a Node with One Child

When removing a node with only one child from a binary search tree, the child replaces the node to be removed.

When removing a node with two children from a binary search tree, replace it with the smallest node of the right subtree.

To remove the node, simply modify the parent link that points to the node so that it points to the child instead.

The case in which the node to be removed has two children is more challenging. Rather than removing the node, it is easier to replace its data value with the next larger value in the tree. That replacement preserves the binary search tree property. (Alternatively, you could use the largest element of the left subtree—see Exercise P17.12).

To locate the next larger value, go to the right subtree and find its smallest data value. Keep following the left child links. Once you reach a node that has no left child, you have found the node containing the smallest data value of the subtree. Now remove that node—it is easily removed because it has at most one child to the right. Then store its data value in the original node that was slated for removal. Figure 15 shows the details.

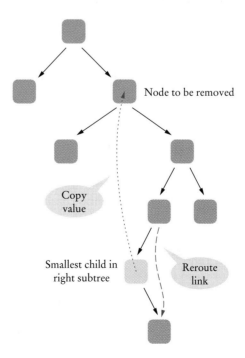

**Figure 15**
Removing a Node
with Two Children

At the end of this section, you will find the source code for the `BinarySearchTree` class. It contains the `add` and `remove` methods that we just described, as well as a `find` method that tests whether a value is present in a binary search tree, and a `print` method that we will analyze in Section 17.4.

## 17.3.4 Efficiency of the Operations

In a balanced tree, all paths from the root to the leaves have about the same length.

Now that you have seen the implementation of this data structure, you may well wonder whether it is any good. Like nodes in a list, the nodes are allocated one at a time. No existing elements need to be moved when a new element is inserted or removed; that is an advantage. How fast insertion and removal are, however, depends on the shape of the tree. These operations are fast if the tree is balanced.

Because the operations of finding, adding, and removing an element process the nodes along a path from the root to a leaf, their execution time is proportional to the height of the tree, and not to the total number of nodes in the tree.

For a balanced tree, we have $h \approx O(\log(n))$. Therefore, inserting, finding, or removing an element is an $O(\log(n))$ operation. On the other hand, if the tree happens to be *unbalanced*, then binary tree operations can be slow—in the worst case, as slow as insertion into a linked list. Table 2 summarizes these observations.

If a binary search tree is balanced, then adding, locating, or removing an element takes $O(\log(n))$ time.

If elements are added in fairly random order, the resulting tree is likely to be well balanced. However, if the incoming elements happen to be in sorted order already, then the resulting tree is completely unbalanced. Each new element is inserted at the end, and the entire tree must be traversed every time to find that end!

Binary search trees work well for random data, but if you suspect that the data in your application might be sorted or have long runs of sorted data, you should not use a binary search tree. There are more sophisticated tree structures whose methods keep trees balanced at all times. In these tree structures, one can guarantee that finding, adding, and removing elements takes $O(\log(n))$ time. The standard Java library uses *red-black trees*, a special form of balanced binary trees, to implement sets and maps. We discuss these structures in Section 17.5.

### Table 2 Efficiency of Binary Search Tree Operations

| Operation | Balanced Binary Search Tree | Unbalanced Binary Search Tree |
|---|---|---|
| Finding an element. | $O(\log(n))$ | $O(n)$ |
| Adding an element. | $O(\log(n))$ | $O(n)$ |
| Removing an element. | $O(\log(n))$ | $O(n)$ |

**section_3/BinarySearchTree.java**

```
 1   /**
 2      This class implements a binary search tree whose
 3      nodes hold objects that implement the Comparable
 4      interface.
 5   */
```

```
6   public class BinarySearchTree
7   {
8      private Node root;
9
10     /**
11        Constructs an empty tree.
12     */
13     public BinarySearchTree()
14     {
15        root = null;
16     }
17
18     /**
19        Inserts a new node into the tree.
20        @param obj the object to insert
21     */
22     public void add(Comparable obj)
23     {
24        Node newNode = new Node();
25        newNode.data = obj;
26        newNode.left = null;
27        newNode.right = null;
28        if (root == null) { root = newNode; }
29        else { root.addNode(newNode); }
30     }
31
32     /**
33        Tries to find an object in the tree.
34        @param obj the object to find
35        @return true if the object is contained in the tree
36     */
37     public boolean find(Comparable obj)
38     {
39        Node current = root;
40        while (current != null)
41        {
42           int d = current.data.compareTo(obj);
43           if (d == 0) { return true; }
44           else if (d > 0) { current = current.left; }
45           else { current = current.right; }
46        }
47        return false;
48     }
49
50     /**
51        Tries to remove an object from the tree. Does nothing
52        if the object is not contained in the tree.
53        @param obj the object to remove
54     */
55     public void remove(Comparable obj)
56     {
57        // Find node to be removed
58
59        Node toBeRemoved = root;
60        Node parent = null;
61        boolean found = false;
62        while (!found && toBeRemoved != null)
63        {
64           int d = toBeRemoved.data.compareTo(obj);
65           if (d == 0) { found = true; }
```

```
 66        else
 67        {
 68           parent = toBeRemoved;
 69           if (d > 0) { toBeRemoved = toBeRemoved.left; }
 70           else { toBeRemoved = toBeRemoved.right; }
 71        }
 72     }
 73
 74     if (!found) { return; }
 75
 76     // toBeRemoved contains obj
 77
 78     // If one of the children is empty, use the other
 79
 80     if (toBeRemoved.left == null || toBeRemoved.right == null)
 81     {
 82        Node newChild;
 83        if (toBeRemoved.left == null)
 84        {
 85           newChild = toBeRemoved.right;
 86        }
 87        else
 88        {
 89           newChild = toBeRemoved.left;
 90        }
 91
 92        if (parent == null) // Found in root
 93        {
 94           root = newChild;
 95        }
 96        else if (parent.left == toBeRemoved)
 97        {
 98           parent.left = newChild;
 99        }
100        else
101        {
102           parent.right = newChild;
103        }
104        return;
105     }
106
107     // Neither subtree is empty
108
109     // Find smallest element of the right subtree
110
111     Node smallestParent = toBeRemoved;
112     Node smallest = toBeRemoved.right;
113     while (smallest.left != null)
114     {
115        smallestParent = smallest;
116        smallest = smallest.left;
117     }
118
119     // smallest contains smallest child in right subtree
120
121     // Move contents, unlink child
122
123     toBeRemoved.data = smallest.data;
124     if (smallestParent == toBeRemoved)
125     {
```

```
126              smallestParent.right = smallest.right;
127          }
128          else
129          {
130              smallestParent.left = smallest.right;
131          }
132      }
133
134      /**
135          Prints the contents of the tree in sorted order.
136      */
137      public void print()
138      {
139          print(root);
140          System.out.println();
141      }
142
143      /**
144          Prints a node and all of its descendants in sorted order.
145          @param parent the root of the subtree to print
146      */
147      private static void print(Node parent)
148      {
149          if (parent == null) { return; }
150          print(parent.left);
151          System.out.print(parent.data + " ");
152          print(parent.right);
153      }
154
155      /**
156          A node of a tree stores a data item and references
157          to the left and right child nodes.
158      */
159      class Node
160      {
161          public Comparable data;
162          public Node left;
163          public Node right;
164
165          /**
166              Inserts a new node as a descendant of this node.
167              @param newNode the node to insert
168          */
169          public void addNode(Node newNode)
170          {
171              int comp = newNode.data.compareTo(data);
172              if (comp < 0)
173              {
174                  if (left == null) { left = newNode; }
175                  else { left.addNode(newNode); }
176              }
177              else if (comp > 0)
178              {
179                  if (right == null) { right = newNode; }
180                  else { right.addNode(newNode); }
181              }
182          }
183      }
184 }
```

**13.** What is the difference between a tree, a binary tree, and a balanced binary tree?

**14.** Are the left and right children of a binary search tree always binary search trees? Why or why not?

**15.** Draw all binary search trees containing data values A, B, and C.

**16.** Give an example of a string that, when inserted into the tree of Figure 12, becomes a right child of Romeo.

**17.** Trace the removal of the node "Tom" from the tree in Figure 12.

**18.** Trace the removal of the node "Juliet" from the tree in Figure 12.

**Practice It**  Now you can try these exercises at the end of the chapter: R17.7, R17.13, R17.15, P17.10.

# 17.4 Tree Traversal

We often want to visit all elements in a tree. There are many different orderings in which one can visit, or *traverse*, the tree elements. The following sections introduce the most common ones.

## 17.4.1 Inorder Traversal

Suppose you inserted a number of data values into a binary search tree. What can you do with them? It turns out to be surprisingly simple to print all elements in sorted order. You *know* that all data in the left subtree of any node must come before the root node and before all data in the right subtree. That is, the following algorithm will print the elements in sorted order:

> **Print the left subtree.**
> **Print the root data.**
> **Print the right subtree.**

Let's try this out with the tree in Figure 12 on page 771. The algorithm tells us to

> To visit all elements in a tree, visit the root and recursively visit the subtrees.

1. Print the left subtree of Juliet; that is, Diana and descendants.
2. Print Juliet.
3. Print the right subtree of Juliet; that is, Tom and descendants.

How do you print the subtree starting at Diana?

1. Print the left subtree of Diana. There is nothing to print.
2. Print Diana.
3. Print the right subtree of Diana, that is, Harry.

That is, the left subtree of Juliet is printed as

    Diana Harry

The right subtree of Juliet is the subtree starting at Tom. How is it printed? Again, using the same algorithm:

1. Print the left subtree of Tom, that is, Romeo.
2. Print Tom.
3. Print the right subtree of Tom. There is nothing to print.

Thus, the right subtree of Juliet is printed as

    Romeo Tom

Now put it all together: the left subtree, Juliet, and the right subtree:

    Diana Harry Juliet Romeo Tom

The tree is printed in sorted order.

It is very easy to implement this print method. We start with a recursive helper method:

```
private static void print(Node parent)
{
    if (parent == null) { return; }
    print(parent.left);
    System.out.print(parent.data + " ");
    print(parent.right);
}
```

To print the entire tree, start this recursive printing process at the root:

```
public void print()
{
    print(root);
}
```

This visitation scheme is called *inorder traversal* (visit the left subtree, the root, the right subtree). There are two related traversal schemes, called *preorder traversal* and *postorder traversal*, which we discuss in the next section.

## 17.4.2 Preorder and Postorder Traversals

We distinguish between preorder, inorder, and postorder traversal.

In Section 17.4.1, we visited a binary tree in order: first the left subtree, then the root, then the right subtree. By modifying the visitation rules, we obtain other traversals.

In preorder traversal, we visit the root *before* visiting the subtrees, and in postorder traversal, we visit the root *after* the subtrees.

*When visiting all nodes of a tree, one needs to choose a traversal order.*

| **Preorder(n)** | **Postorder(n)** |
|---|---|
| **Visit n.** | **For each child c of n** |
| **For each child c of n** | **Postorder(c).** |
| **Preorder(c).** | **Visit n.** |

These two visitation schemes will not print a binary search tree in sorted order. However, they are important in other applications. Here is an example.

In Section 17.2, you saw trees for arithmetic expressions. Their leaves store numbers, and their interior nodes store operators. The expression trees describe the order in which the operators are applied.

Let's apply postorder traversal to the expression trees in Figure 6 on page 765. The first tree yields

    3 4 + 5 *

whereas the second tree yields

    3 4 5 * +

You can interpret the traversal result as an expression in "reverse Polish notation" (see Random Fact 15.2), or equivalently, instructions for a stack-based calculator (see Section 15.6.2).

Here is another example of the importance of traversal order. Consider a directory tree such as the following:

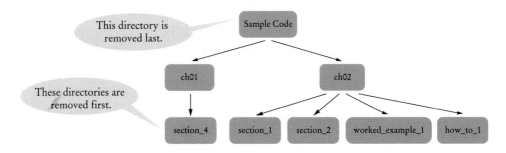

Consider the task of removing all directories from such a tree, with the restriction that you can only remove a directory when it contains no other directories. In this case, you use a postorder traversal.

Conversely, if you want to copy the directory tree, you start copying the root, because you need a target directory into which to place the children. This calls for preorder traversal.

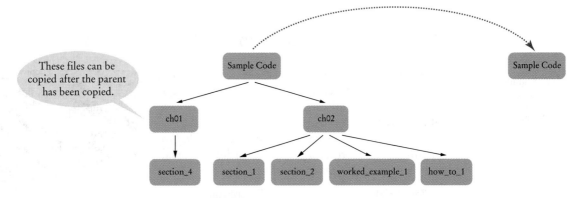

Note that pre- and postorder traversal can be defined for *any* trees, not just binary trees (see the sample code for this section). However, inorder traversal makes sense only for binary trees.

## 17.4.3 The Visitor Pattern

In the preceding sections, we simply printed each tree node that we visited. Often, we want to process the nodes in some other way. To make visitation more generic, we define an interface type

```
public interface Visitor
{
    void visit(Object data);
}
```

The preorder method receives an object of some class that implements this interface type, and calls its `visit` method:

```
private static void preorder(Node n, Visitor v)
{
   if (n == null) { return; }
   v.visit(n.data);
   for (Node c : n.children) { preorder(c, v); }
}

public void preorder(Visitor v) { preorder(root, v); }
```

Methods for postorder and, for a binary tree, inorder traversals can be implemented in the same way.

Let's say we want to count short names (with at most five letters). The following visitor will do the job. We'll make it into an inner class of the method that uses it.

```
public static void main(String[] args)
{
   BinarySearchTree bst = . . .;

   class ShortNameCounter implements Visitor
   {
      public int counter = 0;
      public void visit(Object data)
      {
         if (data.toString().length() <= 5) { counter++; }
      }
   }

   ShortNameCounter v = new ShortNameCounter();
   bst.inorder(v);
   System.out.println("Short names: " + v.counter);
}
```

Here, the visitor object accumulates the count. After the visit is complete, we can obtain the result. Because the class is an inner class, we don't worry about making the counter private.

## 17.4.4  Depth-First and Breadth-First Search

The traversals in the preceding sections are expressed using recursion. If you want to process the nodes of a tree, you supply a visitor, which is applied to all nodes. Sometimes, it is useful to use an iterative approach instead. Then you can stop processing nodes when a goal has been met.

To visit the nodes of a tree iteratively, we replace the recursive calls with a stack that keeps track of the children that need to be visited. Here is the algorithm:

*In a depth-first search, one moves as quickly as possible to the deepest nodes of the tree.*

    Push the root node on a stack.
    While the stack is not empty
        Pop the stack; let n be the popped node.
        Process n.
        Push the children of n on the stack, starting with the last one.

This algorithm is called *depth-first search* because it goes deeply into the tree and then backtracks when it reaches the leaves (see Figure 16). Note that the tree can be an arbitrary tree—it need not be binary.

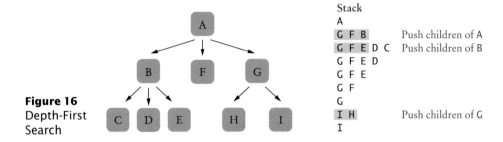

**Figure 16**
Depth-First
Search

We push the children on the stack in right-to-left order so that the visit starts with the leftmost path. If the leftmost child had been pushed first, we would still have a depth-first search, just in a less intuitive order.

If we replace the stack with a queue, the visitation order changes. Instead of going deeply into the tree, we first visit all nodes at the same level before going on to the next level. This is called *breadth-first search* (Figure 17).

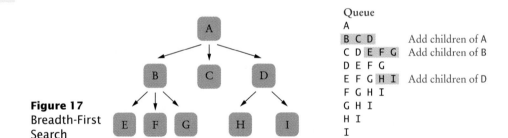

**Figure 17**
Breadth-First
Search

For this algorithm, we modify the Visitor interface of Section 17.4.3. The visit method now returns a flag indicating whether the traversal should continue. For example, if you want to visit the first ten nodes, you should provide an implementation of the Visitor interface whose visit method returns false when it has visited the tenth node.

Here is an implementation of the breadth-first algorithm:

```
public interface Visitor
{
    boolean visit(Object data);
}

public void breadthFirst(Visitor v)
{
    if (root == null) { return; }
    Queue<Node> q = new LinkedList<Node>();
    q.add(root);
    boolean more = true;
    while (more && q.size() > 0)
    {
        Node n = q.remove();
        more = v.visit(n);
```

```
        if (more)
        {
            for (Node c : n.children) { q.add(c); }
        }
    }
}
```

For depth-first search, replace the queue with a stack (Exercise P17.17).

## 17.4.5 Tree Iterators

The Java collection library uses iterators to process elements of a tree, like this:

```
TreeSet<String> t = . . .
Iterator<String> iter = t.iterator();
String first = iter.next();
String second = iter.next();
```

It is easy to implement such an iterator with depth-first or breadth-first search. Make the stack or queue into an instance variable of the iterator object. The next method executes one iteration of the loop that you saw in the last section.

```
class BreadthFirstIterator
{
    private Queue<Node> q;
    public BreadthFirstIterator(Node root)
    {
        q = new LinkedList<Node>();
        if (root != null) { q.add(root); }
    }
    public boolean hasNext() { return q.size() > 0; }
    public Object next()
    {
        Node n = q.remove();
        for (Node c : n.children) { q.add(c); }
        return n.data;
    }
}
```

Note that there is no visit method. The user of the iterator receives the node data, processes it, and decides whether to call next again.

This iterator produces the nodes in breadth-first order. For a binary search tree, one would want the nodes in sorted order instead. Exercise P17.20 shows how to implement such an iterator.

**SELF CHECK**

19. What are the inorder traversals of the two trees in Figure 6 on page 765?

20. Are the trees in Figure 6 binary search trees?

21. Why did we have to declare the variable v in the sample program in Section 17.4.4 as ShortNameCounter and not as Visitor?

22. Consider this modification of the recursive inorder traversal. We want traversal to stop as soon as the visit method returns false for a node.

```
public static void inorder(Node n, Visitor v)
{
    if (n == 0) { return; }
    inorder(n.left, v);
    if (v.visit(n.data)) { inorder(n.right, v); }
```

}

Why doesn't that work?

23. In what order are the nodes in Figure 17 visited if one pushes children on the stack from left to right instead of right to left?

24. What are the first eight visited nodes in the breadth-first traversal of the tree in Figure 1?

**Practice It** Now you can try these exercises at the end of the chapter: R17.11, R17.14, P17.16.

# 17.5 Red-Black Trees

As you saw in Section 17.3, insertion and removal in a binary search tree are $O(\log(n))$ operations *provided that the tree is balanced*. In this section, you will learn about **red-black trees**, a special kind of binary search tree that rebalances itself after each insertion or removal. With red-black trees, we can guarantee efficiency of these operations. In fact, the Java Collections framework uses red-black trees to implement tree sets and tree maps.

## 17.5.1 Basic Properties of Red-Black Trees

In a red-black tree, node coloring rules ensure that the tree is balanced.

A red-black tree is a binary search tree with the following additional properties:

- Every node is colored red or black.
- The root is black.
- A red node cannot have a red child (the "no double reds" rule).
- All paths from the root to a null have the same number of black nodes (the "equal exit cost" rule).

Of course, the nodes aren't actually colored. Each node simply has a flag to indicate whether it is considered red or black. (The choice of these colors is traditional; one could have equally well used some other attributes. Perhaps, in an alternate universe, students learn about chocolate-vanilla trees.)

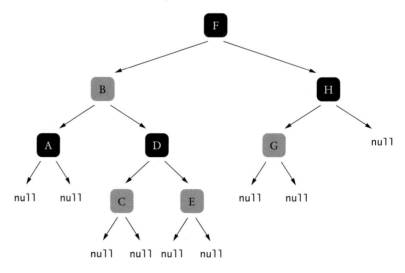

**Figure 18**
A Red-Black Tree

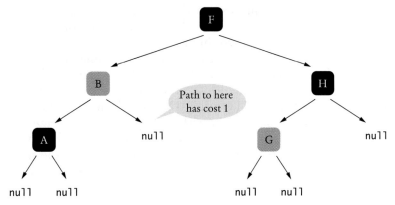

**Figure 19**   A Tree That Violates the "Equal Exit Cost" Rule

Instead of thinking of the colors, imagine each node to be a toll booth. As you travel from the root to one of the null references (an exit), you have to pay $1 at each black toll booth, but the red toll booths are free. The "equal exit cost" rule says that the cost of the trip is the same, no matter which exit you choose.

Figure 18 shows an example of a red-black tree, and Figures 19 and 20 show examples of trees that violate the "equal exit cost" and "no double reds" rules.

Note that the "equal exit cost" rule applies to paths to null references, *not* to leaves of the tree. For example, the last node of the path in Figure 19 that violates the rule is not a leaf.

*Think of each node of a red-black tree as a toll booth. The total toll to each exit is the same.*

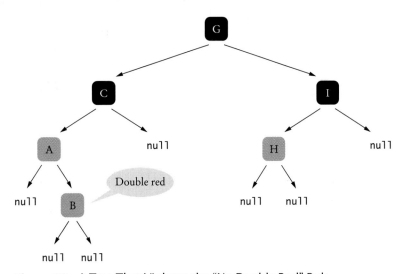

**Figure 20**   A Tree That Violates the "No Double Red" Rule

The "equal exit cost" rule eliminates highly unbalanced trees. You can't have null references high up in the tree. In other words, the nodes that aren't near the leaves need to have two children.

The "no double reds" rule gives some flexibility to add nodes without having to restructure the tree all the time. Some paths can be a bit longer than others—by alternating red and black nodes—but none can be longer than twice the black height.

The cost of traveling on a path from a given node to a null (that is, the number of black nodes on the path), is called the *black height* of the node. The cost of traveling from the root to a null is called the black height of the tree.

A tree with given black height *bh* can't be too sparse—it must have at least $2^{bh} - 1$ nodes (see Exercise R17.18). Or, if we turn this relationship around,

$$2^{bh} - 1 \le n$$
$$2^{bh} \le n + 1$$
$$bh \le \log(n + 1)$$

The "no double reds" rule says that the total height *h* of a tree is at most twice the black height:

$$h \le 2 \cdot bh \le 2 \cdot \log(n + 1)$$

Therefore the height is $O(\log(n))$.

## 17.5.2 Insertion

To insert a new node into a red-black tree, first insert it as you would into a regular binary search tree (see Section 17.3.2). Note that the new node is a leaf.

If it is the first node of the tree, it must be black. Otherwise, color it red. If its parent is black, we still have a red-black tree, and we are done.

However, if the parent is also red, we have a "double red" and need to fix it. Because the rest of the tree is a proper red-black tree, we know that the grandparent is black.

There are four possible configurations of a "double red", shown in Figure 21.

Of course, our tree is a binary search tree, and we will now take advantage of that fact. In each tree of Figure 21, we labeled the smallest, middle, and largest of the three nodes as $n_1$, $n_2$, and $n_3$. We also labeled their children in sorted order, starting with $t_1$. To fix the "double red", rearrange the three nodes as shown in Figure 22, keeping their data values, but updating their left and right references.

> To rebalance a red-black tree after inserting an element, fix all double-red violations.

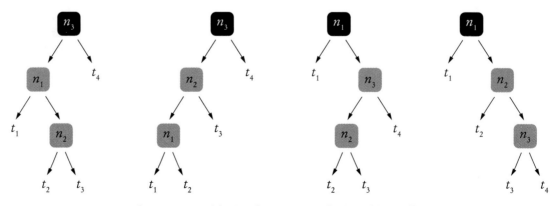

**Figure 21** The Four Possible Configurations of a "Double Red"

**Figure 22**
Fixing the "Double Red"
Violation

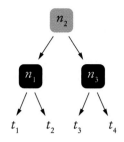

Because the fix preserves the sort order, the result is a binary search tree. The fix does not change the number of black nodes on a path. Therefore, it preserves the "equal exit cost" rule.

If the parent of $n_2$ is black, we get a red-black tree, and we are done. If that parent is red, we have another "double red", but it is one level closer to the root. In that case, fix the double-red violation of $n_2$ and its parent. You may have to continue fixing double-red violations, moving closer to the root each time. If the red parent is the root, simply turn it black. This increments all path costs, preserving the "equal exit cost" rule.

Worked Example 17.2 has an implementation of this algorithm.

We can determine the efficiency with more precision than we were able to in Section 17.5.1. To find the insertion location requires at most $h$ steps, where $h$ is the height of the tree. To fix the "double red" violations takes at most $h / 2$ steps. (Look carefully at Figures 21 and 22 to see that each fix pushes the violation up *two* nodes. If the top node of each subtree in Figure 21 has height $t$, then the nodes of the double-red violation have heights $t + 1$ and $t + 2$. In Figure 22, the top node also has height $t$. If there is a double-red violation, it is between that node and its parent at height $t - 1$.) We know from Section 17.5.1 that $h = O(\log(n))$. Therefore, insertion into a red-black tree is guaranteed to be $O(\log(n))$.

## 17.5.3 Removal

To remove a node from a red-black tree, you first use the removal algorithm for binary search trees (Section 17.3.3). Note that in that algorithm, the removed node has at most one child. We never remove a node with two children; instead, we fill it with the value of another node with at most one child and remove that node.

Two cases are easy. First, if the node to be removed is red, there is no problem with the removal—the resulting tree is still a red-black tree.

Next, assume that the node to be removed has a child. Because of the "equal exit cost" rule, the child must be red. Simply remove the parent and color the child black.

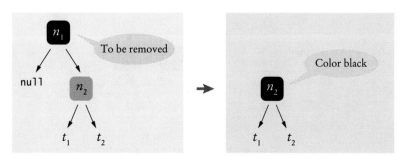

The troublesome case is the removal of a black leaf. We can't just remove it because the exit cost to the `null` replacing it would be too low. Instead, we'll first turn it into a red node.

To turn a black node into a red one, we will temporarily "bubble up" the costs, raising the cost of the parent by 1 and lowering the cost of the children by 1.

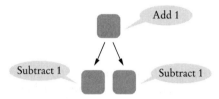

This process leaves all path costs unchanged, and it turns the black leaf into a red one which we can safely remove.

Now consider a black leaf that is to be removed. Because of the equal-exit rule, it must have a sibling. The sibling and the parent can be black or red, but they can't both be red. The leaf to be removed can be to the left or to the right. The figure at right shows all possible cases.

In the first column, bubbling up will work perfectly—it simply turns the red node into a black one and the black ones into red ones. One of the red ones is removed. The other may cause a double-red violation with one of its children, which we fix if necessary.

But in the other cases, a new problem arises. Adding 1 to a black parent yields a price of 2, which we call *double-black*. Subtracting 1 from a red child yields a *negative-red* node with a price of –1. These are not valid nodes in a red-black tree, and we need to eliminate them.

A negative-red node is always below a double-black one, and the pair can be eliminated by the transformation shown in Figure 23.

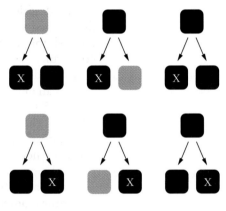

**Before removing a node in a red-black tree, turn it red and fix any double-black and double-red violations.**

**Figure 23**  Eliminating a Negative-Red Node with a Double-Black Parent

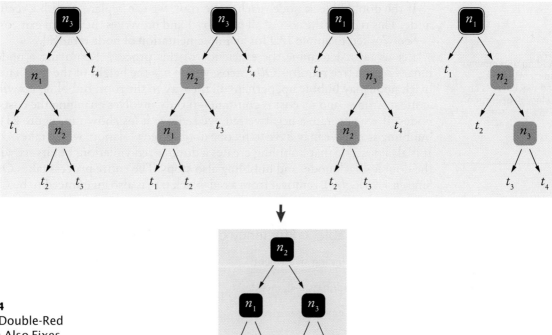

**Figure 24**
Fixing a Double-Red
Violation Also Fixes
a Double-Black
Grandparent

Sometimes, the creation of a double-black node also causes a double-red violation
below. We can fix the double-red violation as in the preceding section, but now we
color the middle node black instead of red—see Figure 24.

To see that this transformation is valid, imagine a trip through one of the node
sequences in Figure 24 from the top node to one of the trees below. The price of that
portion of the trip is 2 for each tree, both before and after the transformation.

Sometimes, neither of the two transformations applies, and then we need to "bubble up" again, which pushes the double-black node closer to the root. Figure 25 shows
the possible cases.

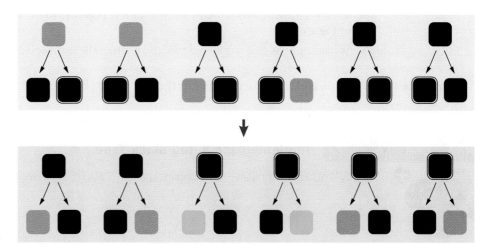

**Figure 25**
Bubbling Up a
Double-Black Node

If the double-black node reaches the root, we can replace it with a regular black node. This reduces the cost of all paths by 1 and preserves the "equal exit cost" rule. See Worked Example 17.2 for an implementation of node removal.

Adding or removing an element in a red-black tree is an $O(\log(n))$ operation.

Let us now determine the efficiency of this process. Removing a node from a binary search tree requires $O(h)$ steps, where $h$ is the height of the tree. The double-black node may bubble up, perhaps all the way to the root. Bubbling up will happen at most $h$ times, and its cost is constant—it only involves changing the costs of three nodes. If we generate a negative red, we remove it (as shown in Figure 23), and the bubbling stops. We may have to fix one double-red violation, which takes $O(h)$ steps. It is also possible that bubbling creates a double-red violation, but its fix will absorb the double-black node, and bubbling also stops. The entire process takes $O(h)$ steps. Since $h = O(\log(n))$, removal from a red-black tree is also guaranteed to be $O(\log(n))$.

| Table 3 Efficiency of Red-Black Tree Operations | |
|---|---|
| Finding an element. | $O(\log(n))$ |
| Adding an element. | $O(\log(n))$ |
| Removing an element. | $O(\log(n))$ |

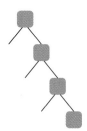

**SELF CHECK**

**25.** Consider the extreme example of a tree with only right children and at least three nodes. Why can't this be a red-black tree?

**26.** What are the shapes and colorings of all possible red-black trees that have four nodes?

**27.** Why does Figure 21 show all possible configurations of a double-red violation?

**28.** When inserting an element, can there ever be a triple-red violation in Figure 21? That is, can you have a red node with two red children? (For example, in the first tree, can $t_1$ have a red root?)

**29.** When removing an element, show that it is possible to have a triple-red violation in Figure 23.

**30.** What happens to a triple-red violation when the double-red fix is applied?

**Practice It** Now you can try these exercises at the end of the chapter: R17.18, R17.20, P17.13.

---

**WORKED EXAMPLE 17.2** **Implementing a Red-Black Tree**

In this Worked Example, we will implement a red-black tree as described in Section 17.5.

⊕ Available online in WileyPLUS and at www.wiley.com/college/horstmann.

# 17.6 Heaps

In this section, we discuss a tree structure that is particularly suited for implementing a priority queue, in which the smallest element can be removed efficiently. (Priority queues were introduced in Section 15.5.3.)

A **heap** (or, for greater clarity, *min-heap*) is a binary tree with two properties:

1. A heap is *almost completely filled:* all nodes are filled in, except the last level which may have some nodes missing toward the right (see Figure 26).

2. All nodes of the tree fulfill the *heap property:* all descendants of the node have values that are at least as large as the node value (see Figure 27 on page 792).

In particular, because the root fulfills the heap property, its value is the minimum of all values in the tree.

A heap is superficially similar to a binary search tree, but there are two important differences:

*In an almost complete tree, all layers but one are completely filled.*

> A heap is an almost completely filled binary tree in which the values of all nodes are at most as large as those of their descendants.

1. The shape of a heap is very regular. Binary search trees can have arbitrary shapes.

2. In a heap, the left and right subtrees both store elements that are larger than the root element. In contrast, in a binary search tree, smaller elements are stored in the left subtree and larger elements are stored in the right subtree.

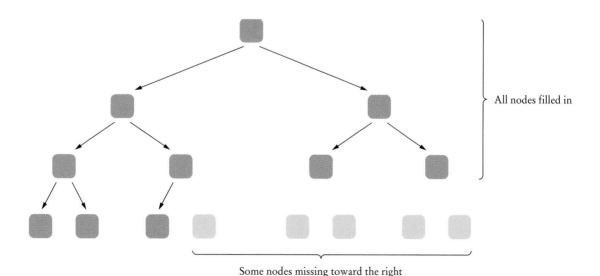

Some nodes missing toward the right

All nodes filled in

**Figure 26**   An Almost Completely Filled Tree

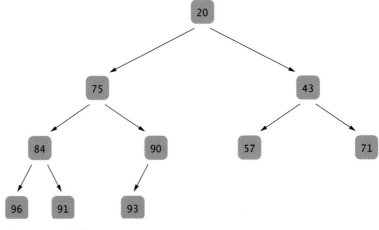

**Figure 27** A Heap

Suppose you have a heap and want to insert a new element. After insertion, the heap property should again be fulfilled. The following algorithm carries out the insertion (see Figure 28).

1. First, add a vacant slot to the end of the tree.
2. Next, demote the parent of the empty slot if it is larger than the element to be inserted. That is, move the parent value into the vacant slot, and move the vacant slot up. Repeat this demotion as long as the parent of the vacant slot is larger than the element to be inserted.
3. At this point, either the vacant slot is at the root, or the parent of the vacant slot is smaller than the element to be inserted. Insert the element into the vacant slot.

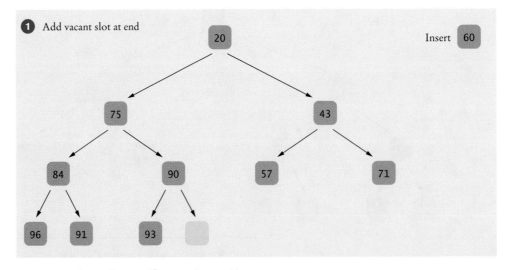

**Figure 28** Inserting an Element into a Heap

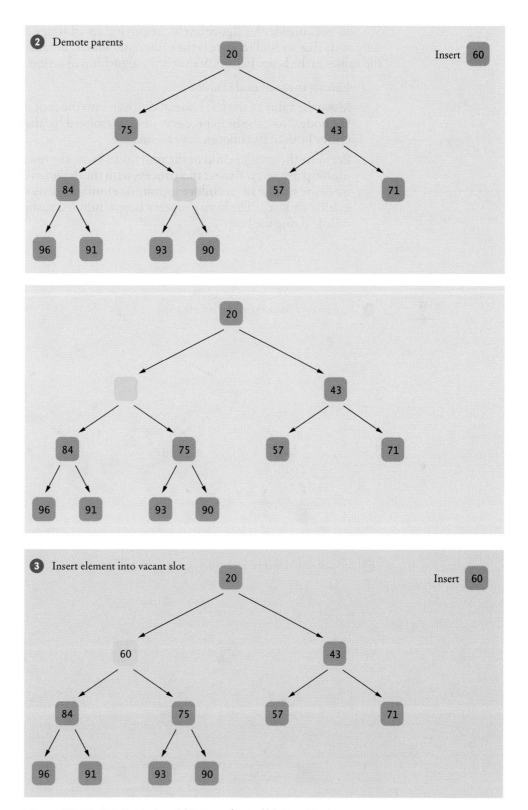

**Figure 28 (continued)** Inserting an Element into a Heap

We will not consider an algorithm for removing an arbitrary node from a heap. The only node that we will remove is the root node, which contains the minimum of all of the values in the heap. Figure 29 shows the algorithm in action.

1. Extract the root node value.
2. Move the value of the last node of the heap into the root node, and remove the last node. Now the heap property may be violated for the root node, because one or both of its children may be smaller.
3. Promote the smaller child of the root node. Now the root node again fulfills the heap property. Repeat this process with the demoted child. That is, promote the smaller of its children. Continue until the demoted child has no smaller children. The heap property is now fulfilled again. This process is called "fixing the heap".

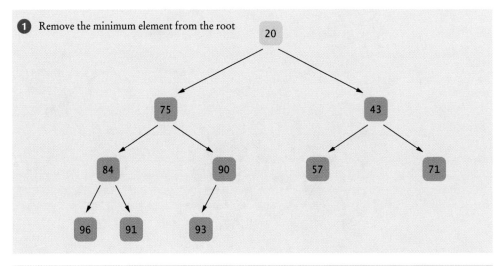

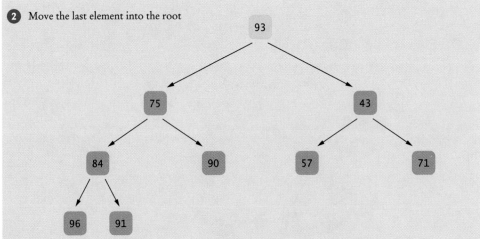

**Figure 29** Removing the Minimum Value from a Heap

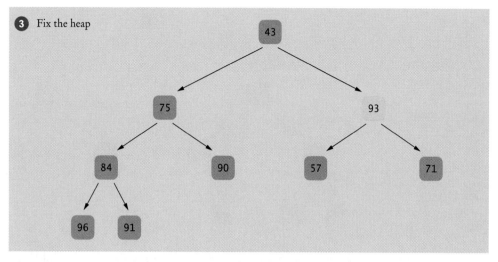

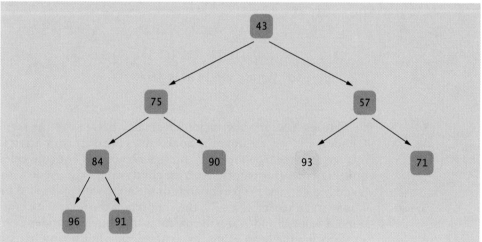

**Figure 29 (continued)** Removing the Minimum Value from a Heap

Inserting and removing heap elements is very efficient. The reason lies in the balanced shape of a heap. The insertion and removal operations visit at most $h$ nodes, where $h$ is the height of the tree. A heap of height $h$ contains at least $2^{h-1}$ elements, but less than $2^h$ elements. In other words, if $n$ is the number of elements, then

$$2^{h-1} \leq n < 2^h$$

or

$$h - 1 \leq \log_2(n) < h$$

This argument shows that the insertion and removal operations in a heap with $n$ elements take $O(\log(n))$ steps.

Contrast this finding with the situation of a binary search tree. When a binary search tree is unbalanced, it can degenerate into a linked list, so that in the worst case insertion and removal are $O(n)$ operations.

Inserting or removing a heap element is an $O(\log(n))$ operation.

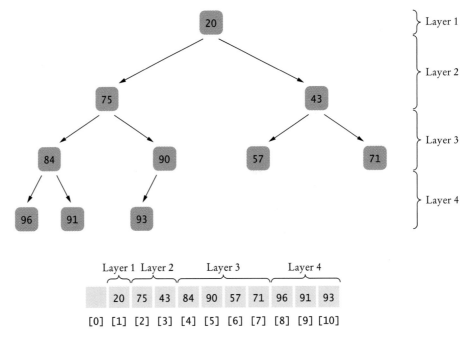

**Figure 30** Storing a Heap in an Array

The regular layout of a heap makes it possible to store heap nodes efficiently in an array.

Heaps have another major advantage. Because of the regular layout of the heap nodes, it is easy to store the node values in an array or array list. First store the first layer, then the second, and so on (see Figure 30). For convenience, we leave the 0 element of the array empty. Then the child nodes of the node with index $i$ have index $2 \cdot i$ and $2 \cdot i + 1$, and the parent node of the node with index $i$ has index $i/2$. For example, as you can see in Figure 30, the children of the node with index 4 are the nodes with index values 8 and 9, and the parent is the node with index 2.

Storing the heap values in an array may not be intuitive, but it is very efficient. There is no need to allocate individual nodes or to store the links to the child nodes. Instead, child and parent positions can be determined by very simple computations.

The program at the end of this section contains an implementation of a heap. For greater clarity, the computation of the parent and child index positions is carried out in methods getParentIndex, getLeftChildIndex, and getRightChildIndex. For greater efficiency, the method calls could be avoided by using expressions index / 2, 2 * index, and 2 * index + 1 directly.

In this section, we have organized our heaps such that the smallest element is stored in the root. It is also possible to store the largest element in the root, simply by reversing all comparisons in the heap-building algorithm. If there is a possibility of misunderstanding, it is best to refer to the data structures as min-heap or max-heap.

The test program demonstrates how to use a min-heap as a priority queue.

### section_6/MinHeap.java

```
1   import java.util.*;
2
3   /**
4      This class implements a heap.
5   */
```

```
6    public class MinHeap
7    {
8       private ArrayList<Comparable> elements;
9
10      /**
11          Constructs an empty heap.
12      */
13      public MinHeap()
14      {
15         elements = new ArrayList<Comparable>();
16         elements.add(null);
17      }
18
19      /**
20          Adds a new element to this heap.
21          @param newElement the element to add
22      */
23      public void add(Comparable newElement)
24      {
25         // Add a new leaf
26         elements.add(null);
27         int index = elements.size() - 1;
28
29         // Demote parents that are larger than the new element
30         while (index > 1
31             && getParent(index).compareTo(newElement) > 0)
32         {
33            elements.set(index, getParent(index));
34            index = getParentIndex(index);
35         }
36
37         // Store the new element in the vacant slot
38         elements.set(index, newElement);
39      }
40
41      /**
42          Gets the minimum element stored in this heap.
43          @return the minimum element
44      */
45      public Comparable peek()
46      {
47         return elements.get(1);
48      }
49
50      /**
51          Removes the minimum element from this heap.
52          @return the minimum element
53      */
54      public Comparable remove()
55      {
56         Comparable minimum = elements.get(1);
57
58         // Remove last element
59         int lastIndex = elements.size() - 1;
60         Comparable last = elements.remove(lastIndex);
61
62         if (lastIndex > 1)
63         {
64            elements.set(1, last);
65            fixHeap();
```

```
 66            }
 67
 68            return minimum;
 69        }
 70
 71        /**
 72            Turns the tree back into a heap, provided only the root
 73            node violates the heap condition.
 74        */
 75        private void fixHeap()
 76        {
 77            Comparable root = elements.get(1);
 78
 79            int lastIndex = elements.size() - 1;
 80            // Promote children of removed root while they are smaller than last
 81
 82            int index = 1;
 83            boolean more = true;
 84            while (more)
 85            {
 86                int childIndex = getLeftChildIndex(index);
 87                if (childIndex <= lastIndex)
 88                {
 89                    // Get smaller child
 90
 91                    // Get left child first
 92                    Comparable child = getLeftChild(index);
 93
 94                    // Use right child instead if it is smaller
 95                    if (getRightChildIndex(index) <= lastIndex
 96                        && getRightChild(index).compareTo(child) < 0)
 97                    {
 98                        childIndex = getRightChildIndex(index);
 99                        child = getRightChild(index);
100                    }
101
102                    // Check if larger child is smaller than root
103                    if (child.compareTo(root) < 0)
104                    {
105                        // Promote child
106                        elements.set(index, child);
107                        index = childIndex;
108                    }
109                    else
110                    {
111                        // Root is smaller than both children
112                        more = false;
113                    }
114                }
115                else
116                {
117                    // No children
118                    more = false;
119                }
120            }
121
122            // Store root element in vacant slot
123            elements.set(index, root);
124        }
125
```

```
126      /**
127           Checks whether this heap is empty.
128      */
129      public boolean empty()
130      {
131          return elements.size() == 1;
132      }
133
134      /**
135           Returns the index of the left child.
136           @param index the index of a node in this heap
137           @return the index of the left child of the given node
138      */
139      private static int getLeftChildIndex(int index)
140      {
141          return 2 * index;
142      }
143
144      /**
145           Returns the index of the right child.
146           @param index the index of a node in this heap
147           @return the index of the right child of the given node
148      */
149      private static int getRightChildIndex(int index)
150      {
151          return 2 * index + 1;
152      }
153
154      /**
155           Returns the index of the parent.
156           @param index the index of a node in this heap
157           @return the index of the parent of the given node
158      */
159      private static int getParentIndex(int index)
160      {
161          return index / 2;
162      }
163
164      /**
165           Returns the value of the left child.
166           @param index the index of a node in this heap
167           @return the value of the left child of the given node
168      */
169      private Comparable getLeftChild(int index)
170      {
171          return elements.get(2 * index);
172      }
173
174      /**
175           Returns the value of the right child.
176           @param index the index of a node in this heap
177           @return the value of the right child of the given node
178      */
179      private Comparable getRightChild(int index)
180      {
181          return elements.get(2 * index + 1);
182      }
183
184      /**
185           Returns the value of the parent.
```

```
186          @param index the index of a node in this heap
187          @return the value of the parent of the given node
188       */
189       private Comparable getParent(int index)
190       {
191          return elements.get(index / 2);
192       }
193    }
```

### section_6/WorkOrder.java

```
1     /**
2         This class encapsulates a work order with a priority.
3     */
4     public class WorkOrder implements Comparable
5     {
6        private int priority;
7        private String description;
8
9        /**
10           Constructs a work order with a given priority and description.
11           @param aPriority the priority of this work order
12           @param aDescription the description of this work order
13        */
14        public WorkOrder(int aPriority, String aDescription)
15        {
16           priority = aPriority;
17           description = aDescription;
18        }
19
20        public String toString()
21        {
22           return "priority=" + priority + ", description=" + description;
23        }
24
25        public int compareTo(Object otherObject)
26        {
27           WorkOrder other = (WorkOrder) otherObject;
28           if (priority < other.priority) { return -1; }
29           if (priority > other.priority) { return 1; }
30           return 0;
31        }
32    }
```

### section_6/HeapDemo.java

```
1     /**
2         This program demonstrates the use of a heap as a priority queue.
3     */
4     public class HeapDemo
5     {
6        public static void main(String[] args)
7        {
8           MinHeap q = new MinHeap();
9           q.add(new WorkOrder(3, "Shampoo carpets"));
10          q.add(new WorkOrder(7, "Empty trash"));
11          q.add(new WorkOrder(8, "Water plants"));
12          q.add(new WorkOrder(10, "Remove pencil sharpener shavings"));
13          q.add(new WorkOrder(6, "Replace light bulb"));
14          q.add(new WorkOrder(1, "Fix broken sink"));
```

```
15        q.add(new WorkOrder(9, "Clean coffee maker"));
16        q.add(new WorkOrder(2, "Order cleaning supplies"));
17
18        while (!q.empty())
19        {
20            System.out.println(q.remove());
21        }
22    }
23 }
```

**Program Run**

```
priority=1, description=Fix broken sink
priority=2, description=Order cleaning supplies
priority=3, description=Shampoo carpets
priority=6, description=Replace light bulb
priority=7, description=Empty trash
priority=8, description=Water plants
priority=9, description=Clean coffee maker
priority=10, description=Remove pencil sharpener shavings
```

**SELF CHECK**

**31.** The software that controls the events in a user interface keeps the events in a data structure. Whenever an event such as a mouse move or repaint request occurs, the event is added. Events are retrieved according to their importance. What abstract data type is appropriate for this application?

**32.** In an almost-complete tree with 100 nodes, how many nodes are missing in the lowest level?

**33.** If you traverse a heap in preorder, will the nodes be in sorted order?

**34.** What is the heap that results from inserting 1 into the following?

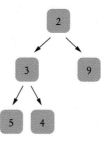

**35.** What is the result of removing the minimum from the following?

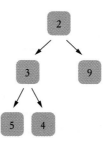

**Practice It**    Now you can try these exercises at the end of the chapter: R17.24, R17.25, P17.22.

# 17.7 The Heapsort Algorithm

The heapsort algorithm is based on inserting elements into a heap and removing them in sorted order.

Heaps are not only useful for implementing priority queues, they also give rise to an efficient sorting algorithm, heapsort. In its simplest form, the heapsort algorithm works as follows. First insert all elements to be sorted into the heap, then keep extracting the minimum.

This algorithm is an $O(n \log(n))$ algorithm: each insertion and removal is $O(\log(n))$, and these steps are repeated $n$ times, once for each element in the sequence that is to be sorted.

Heapsort is an $O(n \log(n))$ algorithm.

The algorithm can be made a bit more efficient. Rather than inserting the elements one at a time, we will start with a sequence of values in an array. Of course, that array does not represent a heap. We will use the procedure of "fixing the heap" that you encountered in the preceding section as part of the element removal algorithm. "Fixing the heap" operates on a binary tree whose child trees are heaps but whose root value may not be smaller than the descendants. The procedure turns the tree into a heap, by repeatedly promoting the smallest child value, moving the root value to its proper location.

Of course, we cannot simply apply this procedure to the initial sequence of unsorted values—the child trees of the root are not likely to be heaps. But we can first fix small subtrees into heaps, then fix larger trees. Because trees of size 1 are automatically heaps, we can begin the fixing procedure with the subtrees whose roots are located in the next-to-last level of the tree.

The sorting algorithm uses a generalized `fixHeap` method that fixes a subtree:

```
public static void fixHeap(int[] a, int rootIndex, int lastIndex)
```

The subtree is specified by the index of its root and of its last node.

The `fixHeap` method needs to be invoked on all subtrees whose roots are in the next-to-last level. Then the subtrees whose roots are in the next level above are fixed, and so on. Finally, the fixup is applied to the root node, and the tree is turned into a heap (see Figure 31).

That repetition can be programmed easily. Start with the *last* node on the next-to-lowest level and work toward the left. Then go to the next higher level. The node index values then simply run backward from the index of the last node to the index of the root.

```
int n = a.length - 1;
for (int i = (n - 1) / 2; i >= 0; i--)
{
    fixHeap(a, i, n);
}
```

It can be shown that this procedure turns an arbitrary array into a heap in $O(n)$ steps.

Note that the loop ends with index 0. When working with a given array, we don't have the luxury of skipping the 0 entry. We consider the 0 entry the root and adjust the formulas for computing the child and parent index values.

After the array has been turned into a heap, we repeatedly remove the root element. Recall from the preceding section that removing the root element is achieved by placing the last element of the tree in the root and calling the `fixHeap` method. Because we call the $O(\log(n))$ `fixHeap` method $n$ times, this process requires $O(n \log(n))$ steps.

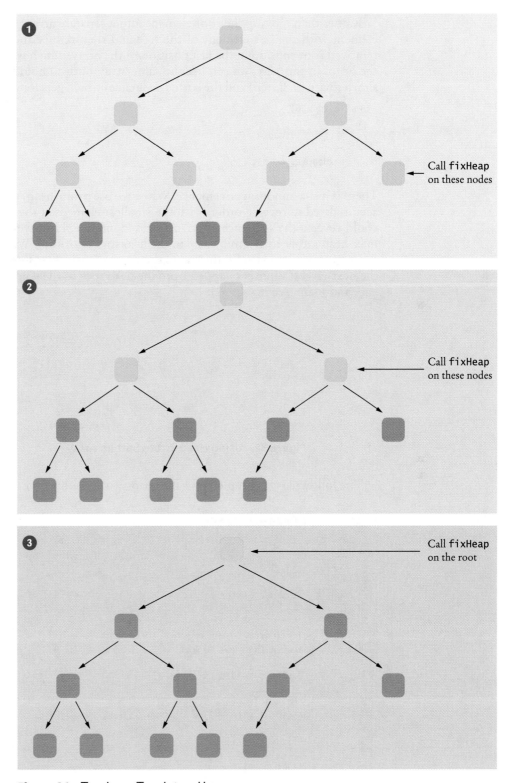

**Figure 31**   Turning a Tree into a Heap

Rather than moving the root element into a separate array, we can *swap* the root element with the last element of the tree and then reduce the tree size. Thus, the removed root ends up in the last position of the array, which is no longer needed by the heap. In this way, we can use the same array both to hold the heap (which gets shorter with each step) and the sorted sequence (which gets longer with each step).

```java
while (n > 0)
{
   ArrayUtil.swap(a, 0, n);
   n--;
   fixHeap(a, 0, n);
}
```

There is just a minor inconvenience. When we use a min-heap, the sorted sequence is accumulated in reverse order, with the smallest element at the end of the array. We could reverse the sequence after sorting is complete. However, it is easier to use a max-heap rather than a min-heap in the heapsort algorithm. With this modification, the largest value is placed at the end of the array after the first step. After the next step, the next-largest value is swapped from the heap root to the second position from the end, and so on (see Figure 32).

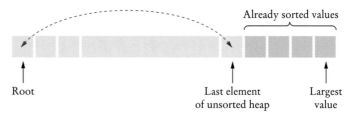

**Figure 32** Using Heapsort to Sort an Array

The following class implements the heapsort algorithm:

**section_7/HeapSorter.java**

```java
1  /**
2     The sort method of this class sorts an array, using the heap
3     sort algorithm.
4  */
5  public class HeapSorter
6  {
7     /**
8        Sorts an array, using selection sort.
9        @param a the array to sort
10    */
11    public static void sort(int[] a)
12    {
13       int n = a.length - 1;
14       for (int i = (n - 1) / 2; i >= 0; i--)
15       {
16          fixHeap(a, i, n);
17       }
18       while (n > 0)
19       {
20          ArrayUtil.swap(a, 0, n);
21          n--;
```

```
22              fixHeap(a, 0, n);
23          }
24      }
25
26      /**
27          Ensures the heap property for a subtree, provided its
28          children already fulfill the heap property.
29          @param a the array to sort
30          @param rootIndex the index of the subtree to be fixed
31          @param lastIndex the last valid index of the tree that
32          contains the subtree to be fixed
33      */
34      private static void fixHeap(int[] a, int rootIndex, int lastIndex)
35      {
36          // Remove root
37          int rootValue = a[rootIndex];
38
39          // Promote children while they are larger than the root
40
41          int index = rootIndex;
42          boolean more = true;
43          while (more)
44          {
45              int childIndex = getLeftChildIndex(index);
46              if (childIndex <= lastIndex)
47              {
48                  // Use right child instead if it is larger
49                  int rightChildIndex = getRightChildIndex(index);
50                  if (rightChildIndex <= lastIndex
51                      && a[rightChildIndex] > a[childIndex])
52                  {
53                      childIndex = rightChildIndex;
54                  }
55
56                  if (a[childIndex] > rootValue)
57                  {
58                      // Promote child
59                      a[index] = a[childIndex];
60                      index = childIndex;
61                  }
62                  else
63                  {
64                      // Root value is larger than both children
65                      more = false;
66                  }
67              }
68              else
69              {
70                  // No children
71                  more = false;
72              }
73          }
74
75          // Store root value in vacant slot
76          a[index] = rootValue;
77      }
78
79      /**
80          Returns the index of the left child.
81          @param index the index of a node in this heap
```

```
82          @return the index of the left child of the given node
83      */
84      private static int getLeftChildIndex(int index)
85      {
86          return 2 * index + 1;
87      }
88
89      /**
90          Returns the index of the right child.
91          @param index the index of a node in this heap
92          @return the index of the right child of the given node
93      */
94      private static int getRightChildIndex(int index)
95      {
96          return 2 * index + 2;
97      }
98  }
```

**SELF CHECK**

36. Which algorithm requires less storage, heapsort or merge sort?
37. Why are the computations of the left child index and the right child index in the HeapSorter different than in MinHeap?
38. What is the result of calling HeapSorter.fixHeap(a, 0, 4) where a contains 1 4 9 5 3?
39. Suppose after turning the array into a heap, it is 9 4 5 1 3. What happens in the first iteration of the while loop in the sort method?
40. Does heapsort sort an array that is already sorted in $O(n)$ time?

**Practice It**    Now you can try these exercises at the end of the chapter: R17.28, P17.24.

# CHAPTER SUMMARY

**Describe and implement general trees.**

- A tree is composed of nodes, each of which can have child nodes.
- The root is the node with no parent. A leaf is a node with no children.
- A tree class uses a node class to represent nodes and has an instance variable for the root node.
- Many tree properties are computed with recursive methods.

**Describe binary trees and their applications.**

- A binary tree consists of nodes, each of which has at most two child nodes.
- In a Huffman tree, the left and right turns on the paths to the leaves describe binary encodings.
- An expression tree shows the order of evaluation in an arithmetic expression.
- In a balanced tree, all paths from the root to the leaves have approximately the same length.

**Explain the implementation of a binary search tree and its performance characteristics.**

- All nodes in a binary search tree fulfill the property that the descendants to the left have smaller data values than the node data value, and the descendants to the right have larger data values.
- To insert a value into a binary search tree, keep comparing the value with the node data and follow the nodes to the left or right, until reaching a null node.
- When removing a node with only one child from a binary search tree, the child replaces the node to be removed.
- When removing a node with two children from a binary search tree, replace it with the smallest node of the right subtree.
- In a balanced tree, all paths from the root to the leaves have about the same length.
- If a binary search tree is balanced, then adding, locating, or removing an element takes $O(\log(n))$ time.

**Describe preorder, inorder, and postorder tree traversal.**

- To visit all elements in a tree, visit the root and recursively visit the subtrees.
- We distinguish between preorder, inorder, and postorder traversal.
- Postorder traversal of an expression tree yields the instructions for evaluating the expression on a stack-based calculator.
- Depth-first search uses a stack to track the nodes that it still needs to visit.
- Breadth-first search first visits all nodes on the same level before visiting the children.

**Describe how red-black trees provide guaranteed $O(\log(n))$ operations.**

- In a red-black tree, node coloring rules ensure that the tree is balanced.
- To rebalance a red-black tree after inserting an element, fix all double-red violations.
- Before removing a node in a red-black tree, turn it red and fix any double-black and double-red violations.
- Adding or removing an element in a red-black tree is an $O(\log(n))$ operation.

**Describe the heap data structure and the efficiency of its operations.**

- A heap is an almost completely filled tree in which the values of all nodes are at most as large as those of their descendants.
- Inserting or removing a heap element is an $O(\log(n))$ operation.
- The regular layout of a heap makes it possible to store heap nodes efficiently in an array.

**Describe the heapsort algorithm and its run-time performance.**

- The heapsort algorithm is based on inserting elements into a heap and removing them in sorted order.
- Heapsort is an $O(n \log(n))$ algorithm.

## REVIEW EXERCISES

- **R17.1** What are all possible shapes of trees of height $h$ with one leaf? Of height 2 with $k$ leaves?

- **R17.2** Describe a recursive algorithm for finding the maximum number of siblings in a tree.

- **R17.3** Describe a recursive algorithm for finding the total path length of a tree. The total path length is the sum of the lengths of all paths from the root to the leaves. (The length of a path is the number of nodes on the path.) What is the efficiency of your algorithm?

- **R17.4** Show that a binary tree with $l$ leaves has at least $l-1$ interior nodes, and exactly $l-1$ interior nodes if all of them have two children.

- **R17.5** What is the difference between a binary tree and a binary search tree? Give examples of each.

- **R17.6** What is the difference between a balanced tree and an unbalanced tree? Give examples of each.

- **R17.7** The following elements are inserted into a binary search tree. Make a drawing that shows the resulting tree after each insertion.

      Adam
      Eve
      Romeo
      Juliet
      Tom
      Diana
      Harry

- **R17.8** Insert the elements of Exercise R17.7 in opposite order. Then determine how the BinarySearchTree.print method from Section 17.4 prints out both the tree from Exercise R17.7 and this tree. Explain how the printouts are related.

- **R17.9** Consider the following tree. In which order are the nodes printed by the BinarySearchTree.print method? The numbers identify the nodes. The data stored in the nodes is not shown.

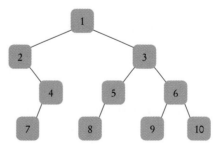

- **R17.10** Design an algorithm for finding the $k$th element (in sort order) of a binary search tree. How efficient is your algorithm?

- **R17.11** Design an $O(\log(n))$ algorithm for finding the $k$th element in a binary search tree, provided that each node has an instance variable containing the size of the subtree. Also describe how these instance variables can be maintained by the insertion and removal operations without affecting their big-Oh efficiency.

**R17.12** Design an algorithm for deciding whether two binary trees have the same shape. What is the running time of your algorithm?

**R17.13** Insert the following eleven words into a binary search tree:

Mary had a little lamb. Its fleece was white as snow.

Draw the resulting tree.

**R17.14** What is the result of printing the tree from Exercise R17.13 using preorder, inorder, and postorder traversal?

**R17.15** Locate nodes with no children, one child, and two children in the tree of Exercise R17.13. For each of them, show the tree of size 10 that is obtained after removing the node.

**R17.16** Repeat Exercise R17.13 for a red-black tree.

**R17.17** Repeat Exercise R17.15 for a red-black tree.

**R17.18** Show that a red-black tree with black height $bh$ has at least $2^{bh} - 1$ nodes. *Hint:* Look at the root. A black child has black height $bh - 1$. A red child must have two black children of black height $bh - 1$.

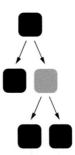

**R17.19** Let $rbts(bh)$ be the number of red-black trees with black height $bh$. Give a recursive formula for $rbts(bh)$ in terms of $rbts(bh - 1)$. How many red-black trees have heights 1, 2, and 3? *Hint:* Look at the hint for Exercise R17.18.

**R17.20** What is the maximum number of nodes in a red-black tree with black height $bh$?

**R17.21** Show that any red-black tree must have fewer interior red nodes than it has black nodes.

**R17.22** Show that the "black root" rule for red-black trees is not essential. That is, if one allows trees with a red root, insertion and deletion still occur in $O(\log(n))$ time.

**R17.23** Many textbooks use "dummy nodes"—black nodes with two `null` children—instead of regular `null` references in red-black trees. In this representation, all non-dummy nodes of a red-black tree have two children. How does this simplify the description of the removal algorithm?

**R17.24** Could a priority queue be implemented efficiently as a binary search tree? Give a detailed argument for your answer.

**R17.25** Will preorder, inorder, or postorder traversal print a heap in sorted order? Why or why not?

**R17.26** Prove that a heap of height $h$ contains at least $2^{h-1}$ elements but less than $2^h$ elements.

■■■ **R17.27** Suppose the heap nodes are stored in an array, starting with index 1. Prove that the child nodes of the heap node with index $i$ have index $2 \cdot i$ and $2 \cdot i + 1$, and the parent node of the heap node with index $i$ has index $i/2$.

■■ **R17.28** Simulate the heapsort algorithm manually to sort the array

```
11 27 8 14 45 6 24 81 29 33
```

Show all steps.

## PROGRAMMING EXERCISES

■■■ **P17.1** A general tree (in which each node can have arbitrarily many children) can be implemented as a binary tree in this way: For each node with $n$ children, use a chain of $n$ binary nodes. Each `left` reference points to a child and each `right` reference points to the next node in the chain. Using the binary tree implementation of Section 17.2, implement a tree class with the same interface as the one in Section 17.1.

■■■ **P17.2** A general tree in which all non-leaf nodes have `null` data can be implemented as a list of lists. For example, the tree

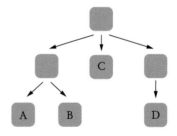

is the list [[A, B], C, [D]].

Using the list implementation from Section 16.1, implement a tree class with the same interface as the one in Section 17.1. *Hint:* Use `n instanceof List` to check whether a list element `n` is a subtree or a leaf.

■ **P17.3** Write a method that counts the number of all leaves in a tree.

■ **P17.4** Add a method `countNodesWithOneChild` to the `BinaryTree` class.

■ **P17.5** Add a method `swapChildren` that swaps all left and right children to the `BinaryTree` class.

■■ **P17.6** Implement the animal guessing game described in Section 17.2.1. Start with the tree in Figure 4, but present the leaves as "Is it a(n) X?" If it wasn't, ask the user what the animal was, and ask for a question that is true for that animal but false for X. For example,

```
Is it a mammal? Y
Does it have stripes? N
Is it a pig? N
I give up. What is it? A hamster
Please give me a question that is true for a hamster and false for a pig.
Is it small and cuddly?
```

In this way, the program learns additional facts.

■■■ **P17.7** Continue Exercise P17.6 and write the tree to a file when the program exits. Load the file when the program starts again.

■■■ **P17.8** The ID3 algorithm describes how to build a decision tree for a given a set of sample facts. The tree asks the most important questions first. We have a set of criteria (such as "Is it a mammal?") and an objective that we want to decide (such as "Can it swim?"). Each fact has a value for each criterion and the objective. Here is a set of five facts about animals. (Each row is a fact.) There are four criteria and one objective (the columns of the table). For simplicity, we assume that the values of the criteria and objective are binary (Y or N).

| Is it a mammal? | Does it have fur? | Does it have a tail? | Does it lay eggs? | Can it swim? |
|:---:|:---:|:---:|:---:|:---:|
| N | N | Y | Y | N |
| N | N | N | Y | Y |
| N | N | Y | Y | Y |
| Y | N | Y | N | Y |
| Y | Y | Y | N | N |

We now need several definitions. Given any probability value $p$ between 0 and 1, its uncertainty is

$$U(p) = -p\log_2(p) - (1-p)\log_2(1-p)$$

If $p$ is 0 or 1, the outcome is certain, and the uncertainty $U(p)$ is 0. If $p = 1/2$, then the outcome is completely uncertain and $U(p) = 1$.

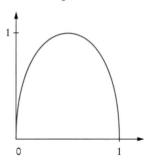

Let $n$ be the number of facts and $n(c = Y)$ be the number of facts for which the criterion $c$ has the value Y. Then the uncertainty $U(c, o)$ that $c$ contributes to the outcome $o$ is the weighted average of two uncertainties:

$$U(c,o) = \frac{n(c = Y)}{n} \cdot U\left(\frac{n(c = Y, o = Y)}{n(c = Y)}\right) + \frac{n(c = N)}{n} \cdot U\left(\frac{n(c = N, o = Y)}{n(c = N)}\right)$$

Find the criterion $c$ that minimizes the uncertainty $U(c, o)$. That question becomes the root of your tree. Recursively, repeat for the subsets of the facts for which $c$ is Y (in the left subtree) and N (in the right subtree). If it happens that the objective is constant, then you have a leaf with an answer, and the recursion stops.

In our example, we have

Two out of five are mammals.

One of those two swims.

Three out of five aren't mammals.

Two of those three swim.

Is it a mammal?    $\frac{2}{5} \cdot U\left(\frac{1}{2}\right) + \frac{3}{5} \cdot U\left(\frac{2}{3}\right) = 0.95$

Does it have fur?    $\frac{1}{5} \cdot U\left(\frac{0}{1}\right) + \frac{4}{5} \cdot U\left(\frac{3}{4}\right) = 0.65$

Does it have a tail?    $\frac{4}{5} \cdot U\left(\frac{2}{4}\right) + \frac{1}{5} \cdot U\left(\frac{1}{1}\right) = 0.8$

Does it lay eggs?    $\frac{3}{5} \cdot U\left(\frac{2}{3}\right) + \frac{2}{5} \cdot U\left(\frac{1}{2}\right) = 0.95$

Therefore, we choose "Does it have fur?" as our first criterion.

In the left subtree, look at the animals with fur. There is only one, a non-swimmer, so you can declare "It doesn't swim." For the right subtree, you now have four facts (the animals without fur) and three criteria. Repeat the process.

**•• P17.9** Reimplement the addNode method of the Node class in BinarySearchTree as a static method of the BinarySearchTree class:

```
private static Node addNode(Node parent, Node newNode)
```

If parent is null, return newNode. Otherwise, recursively add newNode to parent and return parent. Your implementation should replace the three null checks in the add and original addNode methods with just one null check.

**• P17.10** Write a method of the BinarySearchTree class

```
Comparable smallest()
```

that returns the smallest element of a tree. You will also need to add a method to the Node class.

**••• P17.11** Change the BinarySearchTree.print method to print the tree as a tree shape. You can print the tree sideways. Extra credit if you instead display the tree with the root node centered on the top.

**••• P17.12** In the BinarySearchTree class, modify the remove method so that a node with two children is replaced by the largest child of the left subtree.

**•• P17.13** Write a method for the RedBlackTree class of Worked Example 17.2 that checks that the tree fulfills the rules for a red-black tree.

**••• P17.14** Reimplement the remove method in the RedBlackTree class of Worked Example 17.2 so that the node is first removed using the binary search tree removal algorithm, and the tree is rebalanced after removal.

- **P17.15** Add methods

  ```
  void preorder(Visitor v)
  void inorder(Visitor v)
  void postorder(Visitor v)
  ```

  to the BinaryTree class of Section 17.2.

- **P17.16** Using a visitor, compute the average value of the elements in a binary tree filled with Integer objects.

- **P17.17** Add a method void depthFirst(Visitor v) to the Tree class of Section 17.4. Keep visiting until the visit method returns false.

- **P17.18** Implement an inorder method for the BinaryTree class of Section 17.2 so that it stops visiting when the visit method returns false. (*Hint:* Have inorder return false when visit returns false.)

- **P17.19** Modify the expression evaluator from Section 13.6 to produce an expression tree. (Note that the resulting tree is a binary tree but not a binary search tree.) Then use postorder traversal to evaluate the expression, using a stack for the intermediate results.

- **P17.20** Implement an iterator for the BinarySearchTree class that visits the nodes in sorted order. *Hint:* In the constructor, keep pushing left nodes on a stack until you reach null. In each call to next, deliver the top of the stack as the visited node, but first push the left nodes in its right subtree.

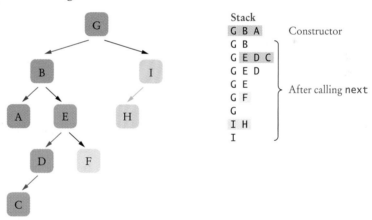

- **P17.21** Implement an iterator for the RedBlackTree class in Worked Example 17.2 that visits the nodes in sorted order. *Hint:* Take advantage of the parent links.

- **P17.22** Modify the implementation of the MinHeap class so that the parent and child index positions and elements are computed directly, without calling helper methods.

- **P17.23** Modify the implementation of the MinHeap class so that the 0 element of the array is not wasted.

- **P17.24** Time the results of heapsort and merge sort. Which algorithm behaves better in practice?

1.  There are four paths:

    Anne

    Anne, Peter

    Anne, Zara

    Anne, Peter, Savannah

2.  There are three subtrees with three nodes—they have roots Charles, Andrew, and Edward.

3.  3.

4.

5.  If n is a leaf, the leaf count is 1
    Otherwise
        Let c1 ... cn be the children of n
        The leaf count is leafCount(c1) + ...
            + leafCount(cn)

6.  ```
    Tree t1 = new Tree("Anne");
    Tree t2 = new Tree("Peter");
    t1.addSubtree(t2);
    Tree t3 = new Tree("Zara");
    t1.addSubtree(t3);
    Tree t4 = new Tree("Savannah");
    t2.addSubtree(t4);
    ```

7.  It is not. However, it calls a recursive method—the size method of the Node class.

8.  A=10, L=0000, O=001, H=0001, therefore ALOHA = 100000001000110

9.  In the root.

10.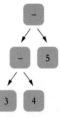

11. Figure 4: 6 leaves, 5 interior nodes.

    Figure 5: 13 leaves, 12 interior nodes.

    Figure 6: 3 leaves, 2 interior nodes

    You might guess from these data that the number of leaves always equals the number of interior nodes + 1. That is true if all interior nodes have two children, but it is false otherwise—consider this tree whose root only has one child.

12. ```
    public class Tree
    {
        . . .
        public int height()
        {
            if (root == null) { return 0; }
            else { return root.height(); }
        }

        class Node
        {
            . . .
            public int height()
            {
                int leftHeight = 0;
                if (left != null)
                {
                    leftHeight = left.height();
                }
                int rightHeight = 0;
                if (right != null)
                {
                    rightHeight = right.height();
                }
                return 1 + Math.max(
                    leftHeight, rightHeight);
            }
        }
    }
    ```

    This solution requires three null checks; the solution in Section 17.2.3 only requires one.

13. In a tree, each node can have any number of children. In a binary tree, a node has at most two children. In a balanced binary tree, all nodes have approximately as many descendants to the left as to the right.

14. Yes—because the binary search condition holds for all nodes of the tree, it holds for all nodes of the subtrees.

15.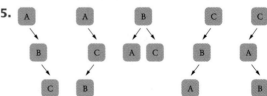

**16.** For example, Sarah. Any string between Romeo and Tom will do.

**17.** "Tom" has a single child. That child replaces "Tom" in the parent "Juliet".

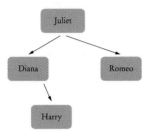

**18.** "Juliet" has two children. We look for the smallest child in the right subtree, "Romeo". The data replaces "Juliet", and the node is removed from its parent "Tom".

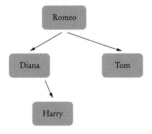

**19.** For both trees, the inorder traversal is 3 + 4 * 5.

**20.** No—for example, consider the children of +. Even without looking up the Unicode values for 3, 4, and +, it is obvious that + isn't between 3 and 4.

**21.** Because we need to call v.counter in order to retrieve the result.

**22.** When the method returns to its caller, the caller can continue traversing the tree. For example, suppose the tree is

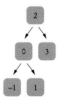

Let's assume that we want to stop visiting as soon as we encounter a zero, so visit returns false when it receives a zero. We first call inorder on the node containing 2. That calls inorder on the node containing 0, which calls inorder on the node containing –1. Then visit is called on 0, returning false. Therefore, inorder is not called on the node containing 1, and the inorder call on the node containing 0 is finished, returning to the inorder call on the root node. Now visit is called on 2, returning true, and the visitation continues, even though it shouldn't. See Exercise P17.18 for a fix.

**23.** AGIHFBEDC

**24.** That's the royal family tree, the first tree in the chapter: George V, Edward VIII, George VI, Mary, Henry, George, John, Elizabeth II

**25.** The root must be black, and the second or third node must also be black, because of the "no double reds" rule. The left null of the root has black height 1, but the null child of the next black node has black height 2.

**26.**

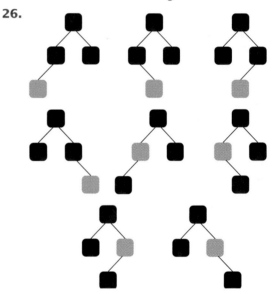

**27.** The top red node can be the left or right child of the black parent, and the bottom red node can be the left or right child of its (red) parent, yielding four configurations.

**28.** No. Look at the first tree. At the beginning, $n_2$ must have been the inserted node. Because the tree was a valid red-black tree before insertion, $t_1$ couldn't have had a red root. Now consider the step after one double-red removal. The parent of $n_2$ in Figure 22 may be red, but then $n_2$ can't have a red sibling—otherwise the tree would not have been a red-black tree.

**29.** Consider this scenario, where X is the black leaf to be removed.

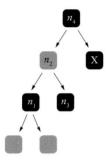

Bubble up:

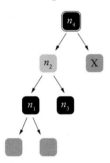

Fix the negative-red:

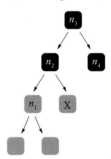

**30.** It goes away. Suppose the sibling of the red grandchild in Figure 21 is also red. That means that one of the $t_i$ has a red root. However, all of them become children of the black $n_1$ and $n_3$ in Figure 22.

**31.** A priority queue is appropriate because we want to get the important events first, even if they have been inserted later.

**32.** 27. The next power of 2 greater than 100 is 128, and a completely filled tree has 127 nodes.

**33.** Generally not. For example, the heap in Figure 30 in preorder is 20 75 84 90 96 91 93 43 57 71.

**34.**

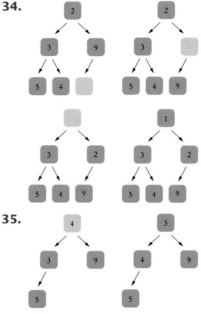

**35.**

**36.** Heapsort requires less storage because it doesn't need an auxiliary array.

**37.** The `MinHeap` wastes the 0 entry to make the formulas more intuitive. When sorting an array, we don't want to waste the 0 entry, so we adjust the formulas instead.

**38.** In tree form, that is

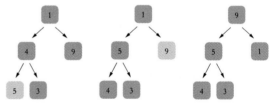

Remember, it's a max-heap!

**39.** The 9 is swapped with 3, and the heap is fixed up again, yielding

 5 4 3 1 | 9.

**40.** Unfortunately not. The largest element is removed first, and it must be moved to the root, requiring $O(\log(n))$ steps. The second-largest element is still toward the end of the array, again requiring $O(\log(n))$ steps, and so on.

# GENERIC CLASSES

## CHAPTER GOALS

To understand the objective of
generic programming

To implement generic classes and methods

To explain the execution of generic methods in the virtual machine

To describe the limitations of generic programming in Java

## CHAPTER CONTENTS

In the supermarket, a generic product can be sourced from multiple suppliers. In computer science, generic programming involves the design and implementation of data structures and algorithms that work for multiple types. You have already seen the generic ArrayList class that can be used to collect elements of arbitrary types. In this chapter, you will learn how to implement your own generic classes and methods.

# 18.1 Generic Classes and Type Parameters

**Generic programming** is the creation of programming constructs that can be used with many different types. For example, the Java library programmers who implemented the ArrayList class used the technique of generic programming. As a result, you can form array lists that collect elements of different types, such as Array-List<String>, ArrayList<BankAccount>, and so on.

The LinkedList class that we implemented in Section 16.1 is also an example of generic programming—you can store objects of any class inside a LinkedList. That LinkedList class achieves genericity by using *inheritance*. It uses references of type Object and is therefore capable of storing objects of any class. For example, you can add elements of type String because the String class extends Object. In contrast, the ArrayList and LinkedList classes from the standard Java library are *generic classes*. Each of these classes has a type parameter for specifying the type of its elements. For example, an ArrayList<String> stores String elements.

> In Java, generic programming can be achieved with inheritance or with type parameters.

When declaring a generic class, you supply a variable for each type parameter. For example, the standard library declares the class ArrayList<E>, where E is the type variable that denotes the element type. You use the same variable in the declaration of the methods, whenever you need to refer to that type. For example, the ArrayList<E> class declares methods

> A generic class has one or more type parameters.

```
public void add(E element)
public E get(int index)
```

You could use another name, such as ElementType, instead of E. However, it is customary to use short, uppercase names for type parameters.

In order to use a generic class, you need to *instantiate* the type parameter, that is, supply an actual type. You can supply any class or interface type, for example

> Type parameters can be instantiated with class or interface types.

```
ArrayList<BankAccount>
ArrayList<Measurable>
```

However, you cannot substitute any of the eight primitive types for a type parameter. It would be an error to declare an ArrayList<double>. Use the corresponding wrapper class instead, such as ArrayList<Double>.

When you instantiate a generic class, the type that you supply replaces all occurrences of the type variable in the declaration of the class. For example, the add method for ArrayList<BankAccount> has the type variable E replaced with the type BankAccount:

```
public void add(BankAccount element)
```

Contrast that with the add method of the LinkedList class in Chapter 16:

```
public void add(Object element)
```

The add method of the generic ArrayList class is safer. It is impossible to add a String object into an ArrayList<BankAccount>, but you can accidentally add a String into a LinkedList that is intended to hold bank accounts:

```
ArrayList<BankAccount> accounts1 = new ArrayList<BankAccount>();
LinkedList accounts2 = new LinkedList(); // Should hold BankAccount objects
accounts1.add("my savings"); // Compile-time error
accounts2.addFirst("my savings"); // Not detected at compile time
```

The latter will result in a class cast exception when some other part of the code retrieves the string, believing it to be a bank account:

```
BankAccount account = (BankAccount) accounts2.getFirst(); // Run-time error
```

Type parameters make generic code safer and easier to read.

Code that uses the generic ArrayList class is also easier to read. When you spot an ArrayList<BankAccount>, you know right away that it must contain bank accounts. When you see a LinkedList, you have to study the code to find out what it contains.

In Chapters 16 and 17, we used inheritance to implement generic linked lists, hash tables, and binary trees, because you were already familiar with the concept of inheritance. Using type parameters requires new syntax and additional techniques—those are the topic of this chapter.

**SELF CHECK**

1. The standard library provides a class HashMap<K, V> with key type K and value type V. Declare a hash map that maps strings to integers.

2. The binary search tree class in Chapter 17 is an example of generic programming because you can use it with any classes that implement the Comparable interface. Does it achieve genericity through inheritance or type parameters?

3. Does the following code contain an error? If so, is it a compile-time or run-time error?

   ```
   ArrayList<Integer> a = new ArrayList<Integer>();
   String s = a.get(0);
   ```

4. Does the following code contain an error? If so, is it a compile-time or run-time error?

   ```
   ArrayList<Double> a = new ArrayList<Double>();
   a.add(3);
   ```

5. Does the following code contain an error? If so, is it a compile-time or run-time error?

   ```
   LinkedList a = new LinkedList();
   a.addFirst("3.14");
   double x = (Double) a.removeFirst();
   ```

**Practice It**    Now you can try these exercises at the end of the chapter: R18.4, R18.5, R18.6.

# 18.2  Implementing Generic Types

In this section, you will learn how to implement your own generic classes. We will write a very simple generic class that stores *pairs* of objects, each of which can have an arbitrary type. For example,

```
Pair<String, Integer> result = new Pair<String, Integer>("Harry Morgan", 1729);
```

## Syntax 18.1 Declaring a Generic Class

*Syntax*   *modifier* class *GenericClassName*<*TypeVariable*$_1$, *TypeVariable*$_2$, . . .>
{
    *instance variables*
    *constructors*
    *methods*
}

Supply a variable for each type parameter.

```
public class Pair<T, S>
{
    private T first;
    private S second;
    . . .
    public T getFirst() { return first; }
    . . .
}
```

A method with a variable return type

Instance variables with a variable data type

The getFirst and getSecond methods retrieve the first and second values of the pair:

```
String name = result.getFirst();
Integer number = result.getSecond();
```

This class can be useful when you implement a method that computes two values at the same time. A method cannot simultaneously return a String and an Integer, but it can return a single object of type Pair<String, Integer>.

The generic Pair class requires two type parameters, one for the type of the first element and one for the type of the second element.

We need to choose variables for the type parameters. It is considered good form to use short uppercase names for type variables, such as those in the following table:

| Type Variable | Meaning |
|:---:|:---|
| E | Element type in a collection |
| K | Key type in a map |
| V | Value type in a map |
| T | General type |
| S, U | Additional general types |

You place the type variables for a generic class after the class name, enclosed in angle brackets (< and >):

```
public class Pair<T, S>
```

When you declare the instance variables and methods of the Pair class, use the variable T for the first element type and S for the second element type:

```
public class Pair<T, S>
{
```

Type variables of a generic class follow the class name and are enclosed in angle brackets.

```
   private T first;
   private S second;

   public Pair(T firstElement, S secondElement)
   {
      first = firstElement;
      second = secondElement;
   }
   public T getFirst() { return first; }
   public S getSecond() { return second; }
}
```

Use type parameters for the types of generic instance variables, method parameter variables, and return values.

Some people find it simpler to start out with a regular class, choosing some actual types instead of the type parameters. For example,

```
public class Pair // Here we start out with a pair of String and Integer values
{
   private String first;
   private Integer second;

   public Pair(String firstElement, Integer secondElement)
   {
      first = firstElement;
      second = secondElement;
   }

   public String getFirst() { return first; }
   public Integer getSecond() { return second; }
}
```

Now it is an easy matter to replace all String types with the type variable T and all Integer types with the type variable S.

This completes the declaration of the generic Pair class. It is ready to use whenever you need to form a pair of two objects of arbitrary types.

The following sample program shows how to make use of a Pair for returning two values from a method.

### section_2/Pair.java

```
1   /**
2       This class collects a pair of elements of different types.
3   */
4   public class Pair<T, S>
5   {
6      private T first;
7      private S second;
8
9      /**
10         Constructs a pair containing two given elements.
11         @param firstElement the first element
12         @param secondElement the second element
13      */
14      public Pair(T firstElement, S secondElement)
15      {
16         first = firstElement;
17         second = secondElement;
18      }
19
```

```
20      /**
21          Gets the first element of this pair.
22          @return the first element
23      */
24      public T getFirst() { return first; }
25
26      /**
27          Gets the second element of this pair.
28          @return the second element
29      */
30      public S getSecond() { return second; }
31
32      public String toString() { return "(" + first + ", " + second + ")"; }
33  }
```

### section_2/PairDemo.java

```
1   public class PairDemo
2   {
3      public static void main(String[] args)
4      {
5         String[] names = { "Tom", "Diana", "Harry" };
6         Pair<String, Integer> result = firstContaining(names, "a");
7         System.out.println(result.getFirst());
8         System.out.println("Expected: Diana");
9         System.out.println(result.getSecond());
10        System.out.println("Expected: 1");
11     }
12
13     /**
14        Gets the first String containing a given string, together
15        with its index.
16        @param strings an array of strings
17        @param sub a string
18        @return a pair (strings[i], i) where strings[i] is the first
19        strings[i] containing str, or a pair (null, -1) if there is no
20        match.
21     */
22     public static Pair<String, Integer> firstContaining(
23        String[] strings, String sub)
24     {
25        for (int i = 0; i < strings.length; i++)
26        {
27           if (strings[i].contains(sub))
28           {
29              return new Pair<String, Integer>(strings[i], i);
30           }
31        }
32        return new Pair<String, Integer>(null, -1);
33     }
34  }
```

### Program Run

```
Diana
Expected: Diana
1
Expected: 1
```

6. How would you use the generic Pair class to construct a pair of strings "Hello" and "World"?

7. How would you use the generic Pair class to construct a pair containing "Hello" and 1729?

8. What is the difference between an ArrayList<Pair<String, Integer>> and a Pair<ArrayList<String>, Integer>?

9. Write a method roots with a Double parameter variable x that returns both the positive and negative square root of x if x ≥ 0 or null otherwise.

10. How would you implement a class Triple that collects three values of arbitrary types?

**Practice It**  Now you can try these exercises at the end of the chapter: P18.1, P18.2, P18.9.

# 18.3  Generic Methods

A generic method
is a method with a
type parameter.

A **generic method** is a method with a type parameter. Such a method can occur in a class that in itself is not generic. You can think of it as a template for a set of methods that differ only by one or more types. For example, we may want to declare a method that can print an array of any type:

```
public class ArrayUtil
{
   /**
      Prints all elements in an array.
      @param a the array to print
   */
   public static <T> void print(T[] a)
   {
      . . .
   }
   . . .
}
```

As described in the previous section, it is often easier to see how to implement a generic method by starting with a concrete example. This method prints the elements in an array of *strings:*

```
public class ArrayUtil
{
   public static void print(String[] a)
   {
      for (String e : a)
      {
         System.out.print(e + " ");
      }
      System.out.println();
   }
   . . .
}
```

## Syntax 18.2 Declaring a Generic Method

*Syntax*     *modifiers* <*TypeVariable₁*, *TypeVariable₂*, . . .> *returnType methodName*(*parameters*)
{
    *body*
}

> Supply the type variable before the return type.

```
public static <E> String toString(ArrayList<E> a)
{
    String result = "";
    for (E e : a)
    {
        result = result + e + " ";
    }
    return result;
}
```

> Local variable with a variable data type

---

**Supply the type parameters of a generic method between the modifiers and the method return type.**

In order to make the method into a generic method, replace String with a type parameter, say E, to denote the element type of the array. Add a type parameter list, enclosed in angle brackets, between the modifiers (public static) and the return type (void):

```
public static <E> void print(E[] a)
{
    for (E e : a)
    {
        System.out.print(e + " ");
    }
    System.out.println();
}
```

**When calling a generic method, you need not instantiate the type parameters.**

When you call the generic method, you need not specify which type to use for the type parameter. (In this regard, generic methods differ from generic classes.) Simply call the method with appropriate arguments, and the compiler will match up the type parameters with the argument types. For example, consider this method call:

```
Rectangle[] rectangles = . . .;
ArrayUtil.print(rectangles);
```

**ONLINE EXAMPLE**

A sample program with a generic method for printing an array of objects and a non-generic method for printing an array of integers.

The type of the rectangles argument is Rectangle[], and the type of the parameter variable is E[]. The compiler deduces that E is Rectangle.

This particular generic method is a static method in an ordinary class. You can also declare generic methods that are not static. You can even have generic methods in generic classes.

As with generic classes, you cannot replace type parameters with primitive types. The generic print method can print arrays of any type *except* the eight primitive types. For example, you cannot use the generic print method to print an array of type int[]. That is not a major problem. Simply implement a print(int[] a) method in addition to the generic print method.

**SELF CHECK**

**11.** Exactly what does the generic print method print when you pass an array of BankAccount objects containing two bank accounts with zero balances?

**12.** Is the getFirst method of the Pair class a generic method?

**13.** Consider this `fill` method:

```
public static <T> void fill(List<T> lst, T value)
{
    for (int i = 0; i < lst.size(); i++) { lst.set(i, value); }
}
```

If you have an array list

```
ArrayList<String> a = new ArrayList<String>(10);
```

how do you fill it with ten "*"?

**14.** What happens if you pass 42 instead of "*" to the `fill` method?

**15.** Consider this `fill` method:

```
public static <T> fill(T[] arr, T value)
{
    for (int i = 0; i < arr.length; i++) { arr[i] = value; }
}
```

What happens when you execute the following statements?

```
String[] a = new String[10];
fill(a, 42);
```

**Practice It**   Now you can try these exercises at the end of the chapter: P18.3, P18.4, P18.19.

# 18.4  Constraining Type Parameters

Type parameters can be constrained with bounds.

It is often necessary to specify what types can be used in a generic class or method. Consider a generic method that finds the average of the values in an array list of objects. How can you compute averages when you know nothing about the element type? You need to have a mechanism for measuring the elements. In Section 9.6, we designed an interface for that purpose:

```
public interface Measurable
{
    double getMeasure();
}
```

*You can place restrictions on the type parameters of generic classes and methods.*

We can constrain the type of the elements, requiring that the type implement the `Measurable` type. In Java, this is achieved by adding the clause `extends Measurable` after the type parameter:

```
public static <E extends Measurable> double average(ArrayList<E> objects)
```

This means, "E or one of its superclasses extends or implements `Measurable`". In this situation, we say that E is a subtype of the `Measurable` type.

Here is the complete average method:

```
public static <E extends Measurable> double average(ArrayList<E> objects)
{
    if (objects.size() == 0) { return 0; }
    double sum = 0;
    for (E obj : objects)
    {
```

```
      sum = sum + obj.getMeasure();
   }
   return sum / objects.size();
}
```

Note the call `obj.getMeasure()`. The variable `obj` has type `E`, and `E` is a subtype of `Measurable`. Therefore, we know that it is legal to apply the `getMeasure` method to `obj`.

If the `BankAccount` class implements the `Measurable` interface, then you can call the `average` method with an array list of `BankAccount` objects. But you cannot compute the average of an array list of strings because the `String` class does not implement the `Measurable` interface.

Now consider the task of finding the minimum in an array list. We can return the element with the smallest measure (see Self Check 17). However, the `Measurable` interface was created for this book and is not widely used. Instead, we will use the `Comparable` interface type that many classes implement. The `Comparable` interface is itself a generic type. The type parameter specifies the type of the parameter variable of the `compareTo` method:

```
public interface Comparable<T>
{
   int compareTo(T other);
}
```

For example, `String` implements `Comparable<String>`. You can compare strings with other strings, but not with objects of different classes.

If the array list has elements of type `E`, then we want to require that `E` implements `Comparable<E>`. Here is the method:

```
public static <E extends Comparable<E>> E min(ArrayList<E> objects)
{
   E smallest = objects.get(0);
   for (int i = 1; i < objects.size(); i++)
   {
      E obj = objects.get(i);
      if (obj.compareTo(smallest) < 0)
      {
         smallest = obj;
      }
   }
   return smallest;
}
```

Because of the type constraint, we know that `obj` has a method

```
int compareTo(E other)
```

Therefore, the call

```
obj.compareTo(smallest)
```

is valid.

Very occasionally, you need to supply two or more type bounds. Then you separate them with the `&` character, for example

**ONLINE EXAMPLE**

A sample program that demonstrates a constraint on a type parameter.

```
<E extends Comparable<E> & Measurable>
```

The extends reserved word, when applied to type parameters, actually means "extends or implements". The bounds can be either classes or interfaces, and the type parameter can be replaced with a class or interface type.

**SELF CHECK**

16. How would you constrain the type parameter for a generic `BinarySearchTree` class?

17. Modify the `min` method to compute the minimum of an array list of elements that implements the `Measurable` interface.

18. Could we have declared the `min` method of Self Check 17 without type parameters, like this?

    ```
    public static Measurable min(ArrayList<Measurable> a)
    ```

19. Could we have declared the `min` method of Self Check 17 without type parameters for arrays, like this?

    ```
    public static Measurable min(Measurable[] a)
    ```

20. How would you implement the generic `average` method for arrays?

21. Is it necessary to use a generic `average` method for arrays of measurable objects?

**Practice It**    Now you can try these exercises at the end of the chapter: P18.5, P18.7, P18.20.

---

**Common Error 18.1**

### Genericity and Inheritance

If `SavingsAccount` is a subclass of `BankAccount`, is `ArrayList<SavingsAccount>` a subclass of `ArrayList<BankAccount>`? Perhaps surprisingly, it is not. Inheritance of type parameters does not lead to inheritance of generic classes. There is no relationship between `ArrayList<SavingsAccount>` and `ArrayList<BankAccount>`.

This restriction is necessary for type checking. Without the restriction, it would be possible to add objects of unrelated types to a collection. Suppose it was possible to assign an `ArrayList<SavingsAccount>` object to a variable of type `ArrayList<BankAccount>`:

```
ArrayList<SavingsAccount> savingsAccounts = new ArrayList<SavingsAccount>();
ArrayList<BankAccount> bankAccounts = savingsAccounts;
    // Not legal, but suppose it was
BankAccount harrysChecking = new CheckingAccount();
    // CheckingAccount is another subclass of BankAccount
bankAccounts.add(harrysChecking); // OK—can add BankAccount object
```

But `bankAccounts` and `savingsAccounts` refer to the same array list! If the assignment was legal, we would be able to add a `CheckingAccount` into an `ArrayList<SavingsAccount>`.

In many situations, this limitation can be overcome by using wildcards—see Special Topic 18.1.

---

**Common Error 18.2**

### The Array Store Exception

In Common Error 18.1, you saw that one cannot assign a subclass list to a superclass list. For example, an `ArrayList<SavingsAccount>` cannot be used where an `ArrayList<BankAccount>` is expected.

This is surprising, because you *can* perform the equivalent assignment with arrays. For example,

```
SavingsAccount[] savingsAccounts = new SavingsAccount[10];
BankAccount bankAccounts = savingsAccounts; // Legal
```

But there was a reason the assignment wasn't legal for array lists—it would have allowed storing a `CheckingAccount` into `savingsAccounts`.

Let's try that with arrays:

```
BankAccount harrysChecking = new CheckingAccount();
bankAccounts[harrysChecking]; // Throws ArrayStoreException
```

This code compiles. The object harrysChecking is a CheckingAccount and hence a BankAccount. But bankAccounts and savingsAccounts are references to the same array—an array of type Savings-Account[]. When the program runs, that array refuses to store a CheckingAccount, and throws an ArrayStoreException.

Both ArrayList and arrays avoid the type error, but they do it in different ways. The Array-List class avoids it at compile-time, and arrays avoid it at run-time. Generally, we prefer a compile-time error notification, but the cost is steep, as you can see from Special Topic 18.1. It is a lot of work to tell the compiler precisely which conversions should be permitted.

**Special Topic 18.1**

## Wildcard Types

It is often necessary to formulate subtle constraints on type parameters. Wildcard types were invented for this purpose. There are three kinds of wildcard types:

| Name | Syntax | Meaning |
|---|---|---|
| Wildcard with lower bound | ? extends B | Any subtype of B |
| Wildcard with upper bound | ? super B | Any supertype of B |
| Unbounded wildcard | ? | Any type |

A wildcard type is a type that can remain unknown. For example, we can declare the following method in the LinkedList<E> class:

```
public void addAll(LinkedList<? extends E> other)
{
   ListIterator<E> iter = other.listIterator();
   while (iter.hasNext())
   {
      add(iter.next());
   }
}
```

The method adds all elements of other to the end of the linked list.

The addAll method doesn't require a specific type for the element type of other. Instead, it allows you to use any type that is a subtype of E. For example, you can use addAll to add a LinkedList<SavingsAccount> to a LinkedList<BankAccount>.

To see a wildcard with a super bound, have another look at the min method:

```
public static <E extends Comparable<E>> E min(ArrayList<E> a)
```

However, this bound is too restrictive. Suppose the BankAccount class implements Comparable<BankAccount>. Then the subclass SavingsAccount also implements Comparable<Bank-Account> and *not* Comparable<SavingsAccount>. If you want to use the min method with a Savings-Account array list, then the type parameter of the Comparable interface should be *any supertype* of the array list's element type:

```
public static <E extends Comparable<? super E>> E min(ArrayList<E> a)
```

Here is an example of an unbounded wildcard. The Collections class declares a method

```
public static void reverse(List<?> list)
```

**ONLINE EXAMPLE**

⊕ A program that demonstrates the need for wildcards.

You can think of that declaration as a shorthand for

```
public static <T> void reverse(List<T> list)
```

Common Error 18.2 compares this limitation with the seemingly more permissive behavior of arrays in Java.

# 18.5  Type Erasure

The virtual machine erases type parameters, replacing them with their bounds or Objects.

Because generic types are a fairly recent addition to the Java language, the virtual machine that executes Java programs does not work with generic classes or methods. Instead, type parameters are "erased", that is, they are replaced with ordinary Java types. Each type parameter is replaced with its bound, or with Object if it is not bounded.

For example, the generic class Pair<T, S> turns into the following raw class:

```
public class Pair
{
   private Object first;
   private Object second;

   public Pair(Object firstElement, Object secondElement)
   {
      first = firstElement;
      second = secondElement;
   }
   public Object getFirst() { return first; }
   public Object getSecond() { return second; }
}
```

As you can see, the type parameters T and S have been replaced by Object. The result is an ordinary class.

The same process is applied to generic methods. Consider this method:

```
public static <E extends Measurable> E min(E[] objects)
{
   E smallest = objects[0];
   for (int i = 1; i < objects.length; i++)
   {
      E obj = objects[i];
      if (obj.getMeasure() < smallest.getMeasure())
      {
         smallest = obj;
      }
   }
   return smallest;
}
```

*In the Java virtual machine, generic types are erased.*

When erasing the type parameter, it is replaced with its bound, the Measurable interface:

```
public static Measurable min(Measurable[] objects)
{
   Measurable smallest = objects[0];
   for (int i = 1; i < objects.length; i++)
   {
      Measurable obj = objects[i];
      if (obj.getMeasure() < smallest.getMeasure())
      {
         smallest = obj;
      }
   }
   return smallest;
}
```

> You cannot construct objects or arrays of a generic type.

Knowing about type erasure helps you understand the limitations of Java generics. For example, you cannot construct new objects of a generic type. The following method, which tries to fill an array with copies of default objects, would be wrong:

```
public static <E> void fillWithDefaults(E[] a)
{
   for (int i = 0; i < a.length; i++)
   {
      a[i] = new E(); // ERROR
   }
}
```

To see why this is a problem, carry out the type erasure process, as if you were the compiler:

```
public static void fillWithDefaults(Object[] a)
{
   for (int i = 0; i < a.length; i++)
   {
      a[i] = new Object(); // Not useful
   }
}
```

Of course, if you start out with a Rectangle[] array, you don't want it to be filled with Object instances. But that's what the code would do after erasing types.

In situations such as this one, the compiler will report an error. You then need to come up with another mechanism for solving your problem. In this particular example, you can supply a default object:

```
public static <E> void fill(E[] a, E defaultValue)
{
   for (int i = 0; i < a.length; i++)
   {
      a[i] = defaultValue;
   }
}
```

Similarly, you cannot construct an array of a generic type:

```
public class Stack<E>
{
   private E[] elements;
   . . .
   public Stack()
   {
      elements = new E[MAX_SIZE]; // Error
```

```
      }
   }
```

Because the array construction expression `new E[]` would be erased to `new Object[]`, the compiler disallows it. A remedy is to use an array list instead:

```
public class Stack<E>
{
   private ArrayList<E> elements;
   . . .
   public Stack()
   {
      elements = new ArrayList<E>(); // Ok
   }
   . . .
}
```

Another solution is to use an array of objects and provide a cast when reading elements from the array:

```
public class Stack<E>
{
   private Object[] elements;
   private int currentSize;
   . . .
   public Stack()
   {
      elements = new Object[MAX_SIZE]; // Ok
   }
   . . .
   public E pop()
   {
      size--;
      return (E) elements[currentSize];
   }
}
```

The cast `(E)` generates a warning because it cannot be checked at run time.

These limitations are frankly awkward. It is hoped that a future version of Java will no longer erase types so that the current restrictions due to erasure can be lifted.

**SELF CHECK**

22. Suppose we want to eliminate the type bound in the `min` method of Section 18.5, by declaring the parameter variable as an array of `Comparable<E>` objects. Why doesn't this work?

23. What is the erasure of the `print` method in Section 18.3?

24. Could the `Stack` example be implemented as follows?

```
public class Stack<E>
{
   private E[] elements;
   . . .
   public Stack()
   {
      elements = (E[]) new Object[MAX_SIZE];
   }
   . . .
}
```

**25.** The `ArrayList<E>` class has a method

```
Object[] toArray()
```

Why doesn't the method return an `E[]`?

**26.** The `ArrayList<E>` class has a second method

```
E[] toArray(E[] a)
```

Why can this method return an array of type `E[]`? (*Hint:* Special Topic 18.2.)

**27.** Why can't the method

```
static <T> T[] copyOf(T[] original, int newLength)
```

be implemented without reflection?

**Practice It**   Now you can try these exercises at the end of the chapter: R18.11, R18.14, P18.22.

## Using Generic Types in a Static Context

You cannot use type parameters to declare static variables, static methods, or static inner classes. For example, the following would be illegal:

```java
public class LinkedList<E>
{
   private static E defaultValue; // ERROR
   . . .
   public static List<E> replicate(E value, int n) { . . . } // ERROR
   private static class Node { public E data; public Node next; } // ERROR
}
```

In the case of static variables, this restriction is very sensible. After the generic types are erased, there is only a single variable `LinkedList.defaultValue`, whereas the static variable declaration gives the false impression that there is a separate variable for each `LinkedList<E>`.

For static methods and inner classes, there is an easy workaround; simply add a type parameter:

```java
public class LinkedList<E>
{
   . . .
   public static <T> List<T> replicate(T value, int n) { . . . } // OK
   private static class Node<T> { public T data; public Node<T> next; } // OK
}
```

## Reflection

As you have seen, type erasure makes it impossible for a generic method to construct a generic array. There is an advanced technique called *reflection* that you can sometimes use to overcome this limitation. Reflection lets you work with classes in a running program.

In Java, the virtual machine keeps a `Class` object for each class that has been loaded. That object has information about each class, as well as methods to construct new objects of the class.

Given an object, you can get its class object by calling `getClass`:

```java
Class objsClass = obj.getClass();
```

You can then make a new instance of that class by calling the `newInstance` method:

```
Object newObj = objsClass.newInstance();
```

This method throws an exception if it cannot access a constructor with no arguments.
   Given an array, you can get the type of the elements this way:

```
Class arrayClass = array.getClass();
Class elementClass = arrayClass.getComponentType();
```

If you want to create a new array, use the `Array.newInstance` method:

```
Object[] newArray = Array.newInstance(elementClass, length);
```

Using these methods, you can implement the `fillWithDefaults` method:

```
public static <E> void fillWithDefaults(E[] a)
{
   Class arrayClass = a.getClass();
   Class elementClass = arrayClass.getComponentType();
   try
   {
      for (int i = 0; i < a.length; i++)
      {
         a[i] = elementClass.newInstance();
      }
   }
   catch (. . .) { . . . }
}
```

Note that we must ask for the element type of a. It does no good asking for `a[0].getClass`. The
array might have length 0, or `a[0]` might be `null`, or `a[0]` might be an instance of a subclass of E.
   Here is another example. The `Arrays` class implements a method

```
static <T> T[] copyOf(T[] original, int newLength)
```

That method can't simply call

```
T[] result = new T[newLength]; // Error
```

Instead, it must construct a new array with the same element type as the original:

```
Class arrayClass = original.getClass();
Class elementClass = arrayClass.getComponentType();
T[] newArray = (T[]) Array.newInstance(elementClass, newLength);
```

For this technique to work, you must have an element or array of the desired type. You
couldn't use it to build a `Stack<E>` that uses an `E[]` array because the stack starts out empty.

---

WORKED EXAMPLE 18.1    **Making a Generic Binary Search Tree Class**

In this Worked Example, we will turn the binary search tree class from Chapter 17 into a
generic `BinarySearchTree<E>` that stores elements of type E.

---

## CHAPTER SUMMARY

**Describe generic classes and type parameters.**

- In Java, generic programming can be achieved with inheritance or with type parameters.
- A generic class has one or more type parameters.
- Type parameters can be instantiated with class or interface types.
- Type parameters make generic code safer and easier to read.

**Implement generic classes and interfaces.**

- Type variables of a generic class follow the class name and are enclosed in angle brackets.
- Use type parameters for the types of generic instance variables, method parameter variables, and return values.

**Implement generic methods.**

- A generic method is a method with a type parameter.
- Supply the type parameters of a generic method between the modifiers and the method return type.
- When calling a generic method, you need not instantiate the type parameters.

**Specify constraints on type parameters.**

- Type parameters can be constrained with bounds.

**Recognize how erasure of type parameters places limitations on generic programming in Java.**

- The virtual machine erases type parameters, replacing them with their bounds or `Objects`.
- You cannot construct objects or arrays of a generic type.

## REVIEW EXERCISES

- **R18.1** What is a type parameter?
- **R18.2** What is the difference between a generic class and an ordinary class?
- **R18.3** What is the difference between a generic class and a generic method?
- **R18.4** Find an example of a non-static generic method in the standard Java library.
- **R18.5** Find four examples of a generic class with two type parameters in the standard Java library.

•• **R18.6** Find an example of a generic class in the standard library that is not a collection class.

• **R18.7** Why is a bound required for the type parameter T in the following method?

```
<T extends Comparable> int binarySearch(T[] a, T key)
```

•• **R18.8** Why is a bound not required for the type parameter E in the HashSet<E> class?

• **R18.9** What is an ArrayList<Pair<T, T>>?

•• **R18.10** Explain the type bounds of the following method of the Collections class.

```
public static <T extends Comparable<? super T>> void sort(List<T> a)
```

Why doesn't T extends Comparable or T extends Comparable<T> suffice?

• **R18.11** What happens when you pass an ArrayList<String> to a method with an ArrayList parameter variable? Try it out and explain.

••• **R18.12** What happens when you pass an ArrayList<String> to a method with an ArrayList parameter variable, and the method stores an object of type BankAccount into the array list? Try it out and explain.

•• **R18.13** What is the result of the following test?

```
ArrayList<BankAccount> accounts = new ArrayList<BankAccount>();
if (accounts instanceof ArrayList<String>) . . .
```

Try it out and explain.

•• **R18.14** The ArrayList<E> class in the standard Java library must manage an array of objects of type E, yet it is not legal to construct a generic array of type E[] in Java. Locate the implementation of the ArrayList class in the library source code that is a part of the JDK. Explain how this problem is overcome.

## PROGRAMMING EXERCISES

• **P18.1** Modify the generic Pair class so that both values have the same type.

• **P18.2** Add a method swap to the Pair class of Exercise P18.1 that swaps the first and second elements of the pair.

•• **P18.3** Implement a static generic method PairUtil.swap whose argument is a Pair object, using the generic class declared in Section 18.2. The method should return a new pair, with the first and second element swapped.

•• **P18.4** Write a static generic method PairUtil.minmax that computes the minimum and maximum elements of an array of type T and returns a pair containing the minimum and maximum value. Require that the array elements implement the Measurable interface of Chapter 9.

•• **P18.5** Repeat Exercise P18.4, but require that the array elements implement the Comparable interface.

••• **P18.6** Repeat Exercise P18.5, but refine the bound of the type parameter to extend the generic Comparable type.

•• **P18.7** Implement a generic version of the binary search algorithm.

•• **P18.8** Implement a generic version of the selection sort algorithm.

■■■ **P18.9** Implement a generic version of the merge sort algorithm. Your program should compile without warnings.

■ **P18.10** Implement a generic version of the LinkedList class of Chapter 16.

■■ **P18.11** Turn the HashSet implementation of Chapter 16 into a generic class. Use an array list instead of an array to store the buckets.

■■ **P18.12** Provide suitable hashCode and equals methods for the Pair class of Section 18.2 and implement a HashMap class, using a HashSet<Pair<K, V>>.

■■■ **P18.13** Implement a generic version of the permutation generator in Section 13.5. Generate all permutations of a List<E>.

■■ **P18.14** Write a generic static method print that prints the elements of any object that implements the Iterable<E> interface. The elements should be separated by commas. Place your method into an appropriate utility class.

■■ **P18.15** Turn the MinHeap class of Chapter 17 into a generic class. As with the TreeSet class of the standard library, allow a Comparator to compare elements. If no comparator is supplied, assume that the element type implements the Comparable interface.

■■ **P18.16** Make the Measurable interface from Chapter 9 into a generic class. Provide a static method that returns the largest element of an ArrayList<T>, provided that the elements are instances of Measurable<T>. Be sure to return a value of type T.

■■■ **P18.17** Enhance Exercise P18.16 so that the elements of the ArrayList<T> can implement Measurable<U> for appropriate types U.

■■ **P18.18** Make the Measurer interface from Chapter 9 into a generic class. Provide a static method T max(T[] values, Measurer<T> meas).

■ **P18.19** Provide a static method void append(ArrayList<T> a, ArrayList<T> b) that appends the elements of b to a.

■■ **P18.20** Modify the method of Exercise P18.19 so that the second array list can contain elements of a subclass. For example, if people is an ArrayList<Person> and students is an ArrayList<Student>, then append(people, students) should compile but append(students, people) should not.

■■ **P18.21** Modify the method of Exercise P18.19 so that it leaves the first array list unchanged and returns a new array list containing the elements of both array lists.

■■ **P18.22** Modify the method of Exercise P18.21 so that it receives and returns arrays, not array lists. *Hint:* Arrays.copyOf.

■ **P18.23** Provide a static method that reverses the elements of a generic array list.

■ **P18.24** Provide a static method that returns the reverse of a generic array list, without modifying the original list.

■■ **P18.25** Provide a static method that checks whether a generic array list is a palindrome; that is, whether the values at index i and n - 1 - i are equal to each other, where n is the size of the array list.

■■ **P18.26** Provide a static method that checks whether the elements of a generic array list are in increasing order. The elements must be comparable.

## ANSWERS TO SELF-CHECK QUESTIONS

**1.** `HashMap<String, Integer>`

**2.** It uses inheritance.

**3.** This is a compile-time error. You cannot assign the `Integer` expression `a.get(0)` to a string.

**4.** This is a compile-time error. The compiler won't convert 3 to a `Double`. *Remedy:* Call `a.add(3.0)`.

**5.** This is a run-time error. `a.removeFirst()` yields a `String` that cannot be converted into a `Double`. *Remedy:* Call `a.addFirst(3.14)`;

**6.** `new Pair<String, String>("Hello", "World")`

**7.** `new Pair<String, Integer>("Hello", 1729)`

**8.** An `ArrayList<Pair<String, Integer>>` contains multiple pairs, for example `[(Tom, 1), (Harry, 3)]`. A `Pair<ArrayList<String>, Integer>` contains a list of strings and a single integer, such as `([Tom, Harry], 1)`.

**9.**
```
public static Pair<Double, Double> roots(
      Double x)
{
   if (x >= 0)
   {
      double r = Math.sqrt(x);
      return new Pair<Double, Double>(r, -r);
   }
   else { return null; }
}
```

**10.** You have three type parameters: `Triple<T, S, U>`. Add an instance variable `U third`, a constructor argument for initializing it, and a method `U getThird()` for returning it.

**11.** The output depends on the implementation of the `toString` method in the `BankAccount` class.

**12.** No—the method has no type parameters. It is an ordinary method in a generic class.

**13.** `fill(a, "*")`

**14.** You get a compile-time error. An integer cannot be converted to a string.

**15.** You get a run-time error. Unfortunately, the call compiles, with `T = Object`. This choice is justified because a `String[]` array is convertible to an `Object[]` array, and 42 becomes `new Integer(42)`, which is convertible to an `Object`. But when the program tries to store an `Integer` in the `String[]` array, an exception is thrown.

**16.**
```
public class BinarySearchTree<E
      extends Comparable<E>>
```
or, if you read Special Topic 18.1,
```
public class BinarySearchTree<E
      extends Comparable<? superE>>
```

**17.**
```
public static <E extends Measurable> E min(
      ArrayList<E> objects)
{
   E smallest = objects.get(0);
   for (int i = 1; i < objects.size(); i++)
   {
      E obj = objects.get(i);
      if (obj.getMeasure()
         < smallest.getMeasure())
      {
         smallest = obj;
      }
   }
   return smallest;
}
```

**18.** No. As described in Common Error 18.1, you cannot convert an `ArrayList<BankAccount>` to an `ArrayList<Measurable>`, even if `BankAccount` implements `Measurable`.

**19.** Yes, but this method would not be as useful. Suppose accounts is an array of `BankAccount` objects. With this method, `min(accounts)` would return a result of type `Measurable`, whereas the generic method yields a `BankAccount`.

**20.**
```
public static <E extends Measurable>
      double average(E[] objects)
{
   if (objects.length == 0) { return 0; }
   double sum = 0;
   for (E obj : objects)
   {
      sum = sum + obj.getMeasure();
   }
   return sum / objects.length;
}
```

**21.** No. You can define
```
public static double average(
      Measurable[] objects)
{
   if (objects.length == 0) { return 0; }
   double sum = 0;
   for (Measurable obj : objects)
   {
      sum = sum + obj.getMeasure();
   }
   return sum / objects.length;
```

```
}
```

For example, if `BankAccount` implements `Measurable`, a `BankAccount[]` array is convertible to a `Measurable[]` array. Contrast with Self Check 19, where the return type was a generic type. Here, the return type is `double`, and there is no need for using generic types.

22. 
```
public static <E> Comparable<E> min(
    Comparable<E>[] objects)
```

is an error. You cannot have an array of a generic type.

23. 
```
public static void print(Object[] a)
{
    for (Object e : a)
    {
        System.out.print(e + " ");
    }
    System.out.println();
}
```

24. This code compiles (with a warning), but it is a poor technique. In the future, if type erasure no longer happens, the code will be wrong. The cast from `Object[]` to `String[]` will cause a class cast exception.

25. Internally, `ArrayList` uses an `Object[]` array. Because of type erasure, it can't make an `E[]` array. The best it can do is make a copy of its internal `Object[]` array.

26. It can use reflection to discover the element type of the parameter a, and then construct another array with that element type (or just call the `Arrays.copyOf` method).

27. The method needs to construct a new array of type T. However, that is not possible in Java without reflection.

# 19

# STREAMS AND BINARY INPUT/ OUTPUT

In this chapter you will learn more about how to write Java programs that interact with files and other sources of bytes and characters. You will learn about reading and writing text and binary data, and the differences between sequential and random access to data in a file. As an application of file processing, you will study a program that encrypts and decrypts data stored in a binary format. Finally, you will see how you can use object serialization to save and load complex objects with very little effort.

# 19.1 Readers, Writers, and Streams

There are two fundamentally different ways to store data: in *text* format or *binary* format. In text format, data items are represented in human-readable form, as a sequence of *characters*. For example, in text form, the integer 12,345 is stored as the sequence of five characters:

    '1' '2' '3' '4' '5'

In binary form, data items are represented in **bytes**. A byte is composed of 8 **bits** and can denote one of 256 values. For example, in binary format, the integer 12,345 is stored as a sequence of four bytes:

    0 0 48 57

(because $12,345 = 48 \cdot 256 + 57$).

The Java library provides two sets of classes for handling input and output. *Streams* handle binary data. *Readers* and *writers* handle data in text form. Figure 1 shows a part of the hierarchy of the Java classes for input and output.

Text input and output are more convenient for humans, because it is easier to produce input (just use a text editor) and it is easier to check that output is correct (just look at the output file in an editor). However, binary storage is more compact and more efficient.

The Reader and Writer classes were designed to process information in text form. You have already used the PrintWriter class in Chapter 7. However, for reading text,

> Streams access sequences of bytes. Readers and writers access sequences of characters.

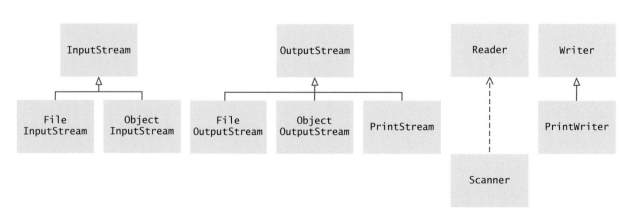

**Figure 1** Java Classes for Input and Output

the `Scanner` class is more convenient than the `Reader` class. Internally, the `Scanner` class makes use of readers to read characters.

If you store information in binary form, as a sequence of bytes, use the `InputStream` and `OutputStream` classes and their subclasses.

Why use two sets of classes? Characters are made up of bytes, but there is some variation in how each character is represented. For example, the character 'é' is encoded as a single byte with value 223 in the ISO-8859-1 encoding that has been commonly used in North America and Western Europe. However, in the UTF-8 encoding that is capable of encoding all Unicode characters, the character is represented by two bytes, 195 and 169. In the UTF-16 encoding, another encoding for Unicode, the same character is encoded as 0 223.

The `Reader` and `Writer` classes have the responsibility of converting between bytes and characters. By default, these classes use the character encoding of the computer executing the program. You can specify a different encoding in the constructor of the `Scanner` or `PrintWriter`, like this:

```
Scanner in = new Scanner(input, "UTF-8");
    // Input can be a File or InputStream
PrintWriter out = new PrintWriter(output, "UTF-8");
    // Output can be a File or OutputStream
```

Unfortunately, there is no way of automatically determining the character encoding that is used in a particular text. You need to know which character encoding was used when the text was written. If you only exchange data with users from the same country, then you can use the default encoding of your computer. Otherwise, it is a good idea to use the UTF-8 encoding.

You learned in Chapter 7 how to process text files. In the remainder of this chapter, we will focus on binary files.

1. Suppose you need to read an image file that contains color values for each pixel in the image. Will you use a `Reader` or an `InputStream`?

2. Special Topic 7.1 introduced the `openStream` method of the `URL` class, which returns an `InputStream`:

```
URL locator = new URL("http://bigjava.com/index.html");
InputStream in = locator.openStream();
```

Why doesn't the `URL` class provide a `Reader` instead?

**Practice It** Now you can try these exercises at the end of the chapter: R19.1, R19.2, R19.4.

# 19.2 Binary Input and Output

> Use `FileInputStream` and `FileOutputStream` classes to read and write binary data from and to disk files.

In this section, you will learn how to process binary data. To read binary data from a disk file, you create a `FileInputStream` object:

```
InputStream inputStream = new FileInputStream("input.bin");
```

Similarly, you use `FileOutputStream` objects to write data to a disk file in binary form:

```
OutputStream outputStream = new FileOutputStream("output.bin");
```

The `InputStream` class has a method, `read`, to read a single byte at a time. (The `FileInputStream` class overrides this method to read the bytes from a disk file.) The

The InputStream.
read method returns
an integer, either –1
to indicate end of
input, or a byte
between 0 and 255.

`InputStream.read` method returns an `int`, not a `byte`, so that it can signal either that a byte has been read or that the end of input has been reached. It returns the byte read as an integer between 0 and 255 or, when it is at the end of the input, it returns –1.

You should test the return value. Only process the input when it is not –1:

```
InputStream in = . . .;
int next = in.read();
if (next != -1)
{
    Process next   // A value between 0 and 255
}
```

The OutputStream.
write method writes
a single byte.

The `OutputStream` class has a `write` method to write a single byte. The parameter variable of the `write` method has type `int`, but only the lowest eight bits of the argument are written to the stream:

```
OutputStream out = . . .;
int value = . . .; // Should be between 0 and 255
out.write(value);
```

When you are done writing to the file, you should close it:

```
out.close();
```

These basic methods are the only input and output methods that the input and output stream classes provide. The Java stream package is built on the principle that each class should have a very focused responsibility. The job of an input stream is to get bytes, not to analyze them. If you want to read numbers, strings, or other objects, you have to combine the class with other classes whose responsibility is to group individual bytes or characters together into numbers, strings, and objects. You will see an example of those classes in Section 19.4.

As an application of a task that involves reading and writing individual bytes, we will implement an encryption program. The program scrambles the bytes in a file so that the file is unreadable except to those who know the decryption method and the secret keyword. We will use the Caesar cipher that you saw in Section 7.3, but now we will encode all bytes. The person performing any encryption chooses an *encryption key*; here the key is a number between 1 and 255 that indicates the shift to be used in encrypting each byte. (Julius Caesar used a key of 3, replacing A with D, B with E, and so on—see Figure 2).

To decrypt, simply use the negative of the encryption key. For example, to decrypt a message encoded with a key of 3, use a key of –3.

In this program we read each value separately, encrypt it, and write the encrypted value:

```
int next = in.read();
if (next == -1)
{
    done = true;
}
else
{
    int encrypted = encrypt(next);
    out.write(encrypted);
}
```

In a more complex encryption program, you would read a block of bytes, encrypt the block, and write it out.

**Figure 2**
The Caesar Cipher

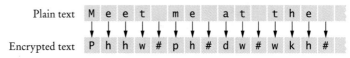

Try out the program on a file of your choice. You will find that the encrypted file is unreadable. In fact, because the newline characters are transformed, you may not be able to read the encrypted file in a text editor. To decrypt, simply run the program again and supply the negative of the encryption key.

**section_2/CaesarCipher.java**

```java
 1  import java.io.InputStream;
 2  import java.io.OutputStream;
 3  import java.io.IOException;
 4
 5  /**
 6     This class encrypts files using the Caesar cipher.
 7     For decryption, use an encryptor whose key is the
 8     negative of the encryption key.
 9  */
10  public class CaesarCipher
11  {
12     private int key;
13
14     /**
15        Constructs a cipher object with a given key.
16        @param aKey the encryption key
17     */
18     public CaesarCipher(int aKey)
19     {
20        key = aKey;
21     }
22
23     /**
24        Encrypts the contents of a stream.
25        @param in the input stream
26        @param out the output stream
27     */
28     public void encryptStream(InputStream in, OutputStream out)
29           throws IOException
30     {
31        boolean done = false;
32        while (!done)
33        {
34           int next = in.read();
35           if (next == -1)
36           {
37              done = true;
38           }
39           else
40           {
41              int encrypted = encrypt(next);
42              out.write(encrypted);
43           }
44        }
45     }
46
```

```
47   /**
48       Encrypts a value.
49       @param b the value to encrypt (between 0 and 255)
50       @return the encrypted value
51   */
52   public int encrypt(int b)
53   {
54       return (b + key) % 256;
55   }
56 }
```

### section_2/CaesarEncryptor.java

```
1    import java.io.File;
2    import java.io.FileInputStream;
3    import java.io.FileOutputStream;
4    import java.io.InputStream;
5    import java.io.IOException;
6    import java.io.OutputStream;
7    import java.util.Scanner;
8
9    /**
10       This program encrypts a file, using the Caesar cipher.
11   */
12   public class CaesarEncryptor
13   {
14      public static void main(String[] args)
15      {
16         Scanner in = new Scanner(System.in);
17         try
18         {
19            System.out.print("Input file: ");
20            String inFile = in.next();
21            System.out.print("Output file: ");
22            String outFile = in.next();
23            System.out.print("Encryption key: ");
24            int key = in.nextInt();
25
26            InputStream inStream = new FileInputStream(inFile);
27            OutputStream outStream = new FileOutputStream(outFile);
28
29            CaesarCipher cipher = new CaesarCipher(key);
30            cipher.encryptStream(inStream, outStream);
31
32            inStream.close();
33            outStream.close();
34         }
35         catch (IOException exception)
36         {
37            System.out.println("Error processing file: " + exception);
38         }
39      }
40   }
```

**3.** Why does the read method of the InputStream class return an int and not a byte?

**4.** Decrypt the following message: Khoor/#Zruog$.

**5.** Can you use the sample program from this section to encrypt a binary file, for example, an image file?

**Practice It**  Now you can try these exercises at the end of the chapter: R19.6, P19.1, P19.5.

### Negative byte Values

The read method of the InputStream class returns –1 or the byte that was read, a value between 0 and 255. It is tempting to place this value into a variable of type byte, but that turns out not to be a good idea.

```
int next = in.read();
if (next != -1)
{
   byte input = (byte) next; // Not recommended
   ...
}
```

In Java, the byte type is a *signed* type. There are 256 values of the byte type, from –128 to 127. When converting an int value between 128 and 255 to a byte, the result is a negative value. This can be inconvenient. For example, consider this test:

```
int next = in.read();
byte input = (byte) next;
if (input == 'é') . . .
```

The condition is never true, even if next is equal to the Unicode value for the 'é' character. That Unicode value happens to be 233, but a single byte is always a value between –128 and 127.

The remedy is to work with int values. Don't use the byte type.

# 19.3  Random Access

Reading a file sequentially from beginning to end can be inefficient. In this section, you will learn how to directly access arbitrary locations in a file. Consider a file that contains a set of bank accounts. We want to change the balances of some of the accounts. We could read all account data into an array list, update the information that has changed, and save the data out again. But if the data set in the file is very large, we may end up doing a lot of reading and writing just to update a handful of records. It would be better if we could locate the changed information in the file and simply replace it.

This is quite different from the file access you programmed in Chapter 7, where you read from a file, starting at the beginning and reading the entire contents until you reached the end. That access pattern is called **sequential access**. Now we would like to access specific locations in a file and change only those locations. This access pattern is called **random access** (see Figure 3). There is nothing "random" about random access—the term simply means that you can read and modify any byte stored at any location in the file.

> In sequential file access, a file is processed one byte at a time.

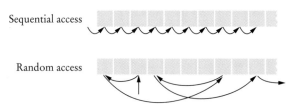

**Figure 3** Sequential and Random Access

Only disk files support random access; the System.in and System.out streams, which are attached to the keyboard and the terminal window, do not. Each disk file has a special **file pointer** position. Normally, the file pointer is at the end of the file, and any output is appended to the end. However, if you move the file pointer to the middle of the file and write to the file, the output overwrites what is already there. The next read command starts reading input at the file pointer location. You can move the file pointer just beyond the last byte currently in the file but no further.

> Random access allows access at arbitrary locations in the file, without first reading the bytes preceding the access location.

In Java, you use a RandomAccessFile object to access a file and move a file pointer. To open a random access file, you supply a file name and a string to specify the *open mode*. You can open a file either for reading only ("r") or for reading and writing ("rw"). For example, the following command opens the file bank.dat for both reading and writing:

```
RandomAccessFile f = new RandomAccessFile("bank.dat", "rw");
```

The method call

```
f.seek(position);
```

moves the file pointer to the given position, counted from the beginning of the file. The first byte of a file has position 0. To find out the current position of the file pointer (counted from the beginning of the file), use

```
long position = f.getFilePointer();
```

> A file pointer is a position in a random access file. Because files can be very large, the file pointer is of type long.

Because files can be very large, the file pointer values are long integers. To determine the number of bytes in a file, use the length method:

```
long fileLength = f.length();
```

In the example program at the end of this section, we use a random access file to store a set of bank accounts, each of which has an account number and a current balance. The test program lets you pick an account and deposit money into it.

If you want to manipulate a data set in a file, you have to pay special attention to the formatting of the data. Suppose you just store the data as text. Say account 1001 has a balance of $900, and account 1015 has a balance of 0.

1 0 0 1   9 0 0   1 0 1 5   0

We want to deposit $100 into account 1001. Suppose we move the file pointer to the first character of the old value:

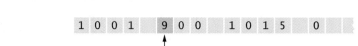

If we now simply write out the new value, the result is

$$1 \quad 0 \quad 0 \quad 1 \qquad 1 \quad 0 \quad 0 \quad 0 \quad 1 \quad 0 \quad 1 \quad 5 \qquad 0$$

That is not working too well. The update is overwriting the space that separates the values.

In order to be able to update values in a file, you must give each value a *fixed* size that is sufficiently large. As a result, every record in the file has the same size. This has another advantage: It is then easy to skip quickly to, say, the 50th record, without having to read the first 49 records in. Just set the file pointer to 49 × the record size.

When storing numbers in a file with fixed record sizes, it is easier to access them in binary form, rather than text form. For that reason, the RandomAccessFile class stores binary data. The readInt and writeInt methods read and write integers as four-byte quantities. The readDouble and writeDouble methods process double-precision floating-point numbers as eight-byte quantities.

> The RandomAccessFile class reads and writes numbers in binary form.

```
double x = f.readDouble();
f.writeDouble(x);
```

If we save the account number as an integer and the balance as a double value, then each bank account record consists of 12 bytes: 4 bytes for the integer and 8 bytes for the double-precision floating-point value.

Now that we have determined the file layout, we can implement our random access file methods. In the program at the end of this section, we use a BankData class to translate between the random access file format and bank account objects. The size method determines the total number of accounts by dividing the file length by the size of a record.

```
public int size() throws IOException
{
   return (int) (file.length() / RECORD_SIZE);
}
```

To read the nth account in the file, the read method positions the file pointer to the offset n * RECORD_SIZE, then reads the data, and constructs a bank account object:

```
public BankAccount read(int n) throws IOException
{
   file.seek(n * RECORD_SIZE);
   int accountNumber = file.readInt();
   double balance = file.readDouble();
   return new BankAccount(accountNumber, balance);
}
```

Writing an account works the same way:

```
public void write(int n, BankAccount account) throws IOException
{
   file.seek(n * RECORD_SIZE);
   file.writeInt(account.getAccountNumber());
   file.writeDouble(account.getBalance());
}
```

The test program asks the user to enter an account number and an amount to deposit. If the account does not currently exist, it is created. The money is deposited, and then the user can choose to continue or quit. The bank data are saved and reloaded when the program is run again.

**section_3/BankSimulator.java**

```
1   import java.io.IOException;
2   import java.util.Scanner;
3
4   /**
5       This program demonstrates random access. You can access
6       existing accounts and deposit money, or create new accounts.
7       The accounts are saved in a random access file.
8   */
9   public class BankSimulator
10  {
11      public static void main(String[] args) throws IOException
12      {
13          Scanner in = new Scanner(System.in);
14          BankData data = new BankData();
15          try
16          {
17              data.open("bank.dat");
18
19              boolean done = false;
20              while (!done)
21              {
22                  System.out.print("Account number: ");
23                  int accountNumber = in.nextInt();
24                  System.out.print("Amount to deposit: ");
25                  double amount = in.nextDouble();
26
27                  int position = data.find(accountNumber);
28                  BankAccount account;
29                  if (position >= 0)
30                  {
31                      account = data.read(position);
32                      account.deposit(amount);
33                      System.out.println("New balance: " + account.getBalance());
34                  }
35                  else // Add account
36                  {
37                      account = new BankAccount(accountNumber, amount);
38                      position = data.size();
39                      System.out.println("Adding new account.");
40                  }
41                  data.write(position, account);
42
43                  System.out.print("Done? (Y/N) ");
44                  String input = in.next();
45                  if (input.equalsIgnoreCase("Y")) { done = true; }
46              }
47          }
48          finally
49          {
50              data.close();
51          }
52      }
53  }
```

**section_3/BankData.java**

```
 1  import java.io.IOException;
 2  import java.io.RandomAccessFile;
 3
 4  /**
 5     This class is a conduit to a random access file
 6     containing bank account records.
 7  */
 8  public class BankData
 9  {
10     private RandomAccessFile file;
11
12     public static final int INT_SIZE = 4;
13     public static final int DOUBLE_SIZE = 8;
14     public static final int RECORD_SIZE = INT_SIZE + DOUBLE_SIZE;
15
16     /**
17        Constructs a BankData object that is not associated with a file.
18     */
19     public BankData()
20     {
21        file = null;
22     }
23
24     /**
25        Opens the data file.
26        @param filename the name of the file containing bank
27        account information
28     */
29     public void open(String filename)
30           throws IOException
31     {
32        if (file != null) { file.close(); }
33        file = new RandomAccessFile(filename, "rw");
34     }
35
36     /**
37        Gets the number of accounts in the file.
38        @return the number of accounts
39     */
40     public int size()
41           throws IOException
42     {
43        return (int) (file.length() / RECORD_SIZE);
44     }
45
46     /**
47        Closes the data file.
48     */
49     public void close()
50           throws IOException
51     {
52        if (file != null) { file.close(); }
53        file = null;
54     }
55
56     /**
57        Reads a bank account record.
58        @param n the index of the account in the data file
```

```
59          @return a bank account object initialized with the file data
60       */
61       public BankAccount read(int n)
62             throws IOException
63       {
64          file.seek(n * RECORD_SIZE);
65          int accountNumber = file.readInt();
66          double balance = file.readDouble();
67          return new BankAccount(accountNumber, balance);
68       }
69
70       /**
71          Finds the position of a bank account with a given number.
72          @param accountNumber the number to find
73          @return the position of the account with the given number,
74          or -1 if there is no such account
75       */
76       public int find(int accountNumber)
77             throws IOException
78       {
79          for (int i = 0; i < size(); i++)
80          {
81             file.seek(i * RECORD_SIZE);
82             int a = file.readInt();
83             if (a == accountNumber) { return i; }
84                // Found a match
85          }
86          return -1; // No match in the entire file
87       }
88
89       /**
90          Writes a bank account record to the data file.
91          @param n the index of the account in the data file
92          @param account the account to write
93       */
94       public void write(int n, BankAccount account)
95             throws IOException
96       {
97          file.seek(n * RECORD_SIZE);
98          file.writeInt(account.getAccountNumber());
99          file.writeDouble(account.getBalance());
100      }
101   }
```

**Program Run**

```
Account number: 1001
Amount to deposit: 100
Adding new account.
Done? (Y/N) N
Account number: 1018
Amount to deposit: 200
Adding new account.
Done? (Y/N) N
Account number: 1001
Amount to deposit: 1000
New balance: 1100.0
Done? (Y/N) Y
```

SELF CHECK

6. Why doesn't System.out support random access?
7. What is the advantage of the binary format for storing numbers? What is the disadvantage?

**Practice It**   Now you can try these exercises at the end of the chapter: R19.12, R19.13, P19.6, P19.7.

# 19.4 Object Streams

In the program of Section 19.3 you read BankAccount objects by reading each input value separately. Actually, there is an easier way. The ObjectOutputStream class can save entire objects out to disk, and the ObjectInputStream class can read them back in. Objects are saved in binary format; hence, you use streams and not writers.

For example, you can write a BankAccount object to a file as follows:

```
BankAccount b = . . .;
ObjectOutputStream out = new ObjectOutputStream(
      new FileOutputStream("bank.dat"));
out.writeObject(b);
```

> Use object streams to save and restore all instance variables of an object automatically.

The object output stream automatically saves all instance variables of the object to the stream. When reading the object back in, you use the readObject method of the ObjectInputStream class. That method returns an Object reference, so you need to remember the types of the objects that you saved and use a cast:

```
ObjectInputStream in = new ObjectInputStream(
      new FileInputStream("bank.dat"));
BankAccount b = (BankAccount) in.readObject();
```

The readObject method can throw a ClassNotFoundException—it is a checked exception, so you need to catch or declare it.

You can do even better than that, though. You can store a whole bunch of objects in an array list or array, or inside another object, and then save that object:

```
ArrayList<BankAccount> a = new ArrayList<BankAccount>();
// Now add many BankAccount objects into a
out.writeObject(a);
```

With one instruction, you can save the array list and *all the objects that it references*. You can read all of them back with one instruction:

```
ArrayList<BankAccount> a = (ArrayList<BankAccount>) in.readObject();
```

Of course, if the Bank class contains an ArrayList of bank accounts, then you can simply save and restore a Bank object. Then its array list, and all the BankAccount objects that it contains, are automatically saved and restored as well. The sample program at the end of this section uses this approach.

This is a truly amazing capability that is highly recommended.

> Objects saved to an object stream must belong to classes that implement the Serializable interface.

To place objects of a particular class into an object stream, the class must implement the Serializable interface. That interface has no methods, so there is no effort involved in implementing it:

```
class BankAccount implements Serializable
{
   . . .
}
```

The process of saving objects to a stream is called **serialization** because each object is assigned a serial number on the stream. If the same object is saved twice, only the serial number is written out the second time. When the objects are read back in, duplicate serial numbers are restored as references to the same object.

Following is a sample program that puts serialization to work. The Bank class manages a collection of bank accounts. Both the Bank and BankAccount classes implement the Serializable interface. Run the program several times. Whenever the program exits, it saves the Bank object (and all bank account objects that the bank contains) into a file bank.dat. When the program starts again, the file is loaded, and the changes from the preceding program run are automatically reflected. However, if the file is missing (either because the program is running for the first time, or because the file was erased), then the program starts with a new bank.

**section_4/Bank.java**

```java
1   import java.io.Serializable;
2   import java.util.ArrayList;
3
4   /**
5      This bank contains a collection of bank accounts.
6   */
7   public class Bank implements Serializable
8   {
9      private ArrayList<BankAccount> accounts;
10
11     /**
12        Constructs a bank with no bank accounts.
13     */
14     public Bank()
15     {
16        accounts = new ArrayList<BankAccount>();
17     }
18
19     /**
20        Adds an account to this bank.
21        @param a the account to add
22     */
23     public void addAccount(BankAccount a)
24     {
25        accounts.add(a);
26     }
27
28     /**
29        Finds a bank account with a given number.
30        @param accountNumber the number to find
31        @return the account with the given number, or null if there
32        is no such account
33     */
34     public BankAccount find(int accountNumber)
35     {
36        for (BankAccount a : accounts)
37        {
38           if (a.getAccountNumber() == accountNumber) // Found a match
39           {
40              return a;
41           }
42        }
43        return null;  // No match in the entire array list
```

```
44      }
45  }
```

## section_4/SerialDemo.java

```
 1  import java.io.File;
 2  import java.io.IOException;
 3  import java.io.FileInputStream;
 4  import java.io.FileOutputStream;
 5  import java.io.ObjectInputStream;
 6  import java.io.ObjectOutputStream;
 7
 8  /**
 9     This program demonstrates serialization of a Bank object.
10     If a file with serialized data exists, then it is loaded.
11     Otherwise the program starts with a new bank.
12     Bank accounts are added to the bank. Then the bank
13     object is saved.
14  */
15  public class SerialDemo
16  {
17     public static void main(String[] args)
18           throws IOException, ClassNotFoundException
19     {
20        Bank firstBankOfJava;
21
22        File f = new File("bank.dat");
23        if (f.exists())
24        {
25           ObjectInputStream in = new ObjectInputStream(
26                 new FileInputStream(f));
27           firstBankOfJava = (Bank) in.readObject();
28           in.close();
29        }
30        else
31        {
32           firstBankOfJava = new Bank();
33           firstBankOfJava.addAccount(new BankAccount(1001, 20000));
34           firstBankOfJava.addAccount(new BankAccount(1015, 10000));
35        }
36
37        // Deposit some money
38        BankAccount a = firstBankOfJava.find(1001);
39        a.deposit(100);
40        System.out.println(a.getAccountNumber() + ":" + a.getBalance());
41        a = firstBankOfJava.find(1015);
42        System.out.println(a.getAccountNumber() + ":" + a.getBalance());
43
44        ObjectOutputStream out = new ObjectOutputStream(
45              new FileOutputStream(f));
46        out.writeObject(firstBankOfJava);
47        out.close();
48     }
49  }
```

## Program Run

```
1001:20100.0
1015:10000.0
```

**Second Program Run**

```
1001:20200.0
1015:10000.0
```

8. Why is it easier to save an object with an `ObjectOutputStream` than a `RandomAccess-File`?

9. What do you have to do to the `Country` class from Section 9.6.2 so that its objects can be saved in an `ObjectOutputStream`?

**Practice It**    Now you can try these exercises at the end of the chapter: R19.8, R19.9, P19.9.

---

**HOW TO 19.1**    **Choosing a File Format**

Many programs allow users to save their work in files. Program users can later load those files and continue working on the data, or send the files to other users. When you develop such a program, you need to decide how to store the data. This How To lets you choose the appropriate mechanisms for saving and loading your program's data.

**Step 1**    Select a data format.

The most important questions you need to ask yourself concern the format to use for saving your data:

- Does your program manipulate text, such as plain text files? If so, use readers and writers.
- Does your program update portions of a file? Then use random access.
- Does your program read or write individual bytes of binary data, such as image files or encrypted data? Then use streams.
- Does your program save and restore objects? Then use object streams.

**Step 2**    Use scanners and writers if you are processing text.

Use a scanner to read the input.

```
Scanner in = new Scanner(new File("input.txt"));
```

Then use the familiar methods `next`, `nextInt`, and so on. See Chapter 7 for details.
    To write output, turn the file output stream into a `PrintWriter`:

```
PrintWriter out = new PrintWriter("output.txt");
```

Then use the familiar `print` and `println` methods:

```
out.println(text);
```

**Step 3**    Use the `RandomAccessFile` class if you need random access.

The `RandomAccessFile` class has methods for moving a file pointer to an arbitrary position:

```
file.seek(position);
```

You can then read or write individual bytes, characters, binary integers, and binary floating-point numbers.

**Step 4** Use streams if you are processing bytes.

Use this loop to process input one byte at a time:

```
InputStream in = new FileInputStream("input.bin");
boolean done = false;
while (!done)
{
   int next = in.read();
   if (next == -1)
   {
      done = true;
   }
   else
   {
      Process next. // next is between 0 and 255
   }
}
```

Similarly, write the output one byte at a time:

```
OutputStream out = new FileOutputStream("output.bin");
. . .
while (. . .)
{
   int b = . . .; // b is between 0 and 255
   out.write(b);
}
out.close();
```

Use binary streams only if you are ready to process the input one byte at a time. This makes sense for encryption/decryption or processing the pixels in an image. In other situations, binary streams are not appropriate.

**Step 5** Use object streams if you are processing objects.

First go through your classes and tag them with `implements Serializable`. You don't need to add any additional methods.

Also go to the online API documentation to check that the library classes that you are using implement the `Serializable` interface. Fortunately, many of them do. In particular, `String` and `ArrayList` are serializable.

Next, put all the objects you want to save into a class (or an array or array list—but why not make another class containing that?).

Saving all program data is a trivial operation:

```
ProgramData data = . . .;
ObjectOutputStream out = new ObjectOutputStream(new FileOutputStream("program.dat"));
out.writeObject(data);
out.close();
```

Similarly, to restore the program data, you use an `ObjectInputStream` and call

```
ProgramData data = (ProgramData) in.readObject();
```

The `readObject` method can throw a `ClassNotFoundException`. You must catch or declare that exception.

## CHAPTER SUMMARY

### Describe the Java class hierarchy for handling input and output.

- Streams access sequences of bytes. Readers and writers access sequences of characters.

### Write programs that carry out input and output of binary data.

- Use `FileInputStream` and `FileOutputStream` classes to read and write binary data from and to disk files.
- The `InputStream.read` method returns an integer, either –1 to indicate end of input, or a byte between 0 and 255.
- The `OutputStream.write` method writes a single byte.

### Describe random access and use the `RandomAccessFile` class.

- In sequential file access, a file is processed one byte at a time.
- Random access allows access at arbitrary locations in the file, without first reading the bytes preceding the access location.
- A file pointer is a position in a random access file. Because files can be very large, the file pointer is of type `long`.
- The `RandomAccessFile` class reads and writes numbers in binary form.

### Use object streams to automatically read and write entire objects.

- Use object streams to save and restore all instance variables of an object automatically.
- Objects saved to an object stream must belong to classes that implement the `Serializable` interface.

## STANDARD LIBRARY ITEMS INTRODUCED IN THIS CHAPTER

```
java.io.FileInputStream              java.io.RandomAccessFile
java.io.FileOutputStream                getFilePointer
java.io.InputStream                      length
   close                                 readChar
   read                                  readDouble
java.io.ObjectInputStream                readInt
   readObject                            seek
java.io.ObjectOutputStream               writeChar
   writeObject                           writeChars
java.io.OutputStream                     writeDouble
   close                                 writeInt
   write                              java.io.Serializable
```

## REVIEW EXERCISES

**■ R19.1** What is the difference between a stream and a reader?

**■ R19.2** Write a few lines of text to a new `FileWriter("output1.txt", "UTF-8")` and the same text to a new `FileWriter("output2.txt", "UTF-16")`. How do the output files differ?

**■ R19.3** How can you open a file for both reading and writing in Java?

**■■ R19.4** What happens if you try to write to a file reader?

**■■ R19.5** What happens if you try to write to a random access file that you opened only for reading? Try it out if you don't know.

**■ R19.6** How can you break the Caesar cipher? That is, how can you read a document that was encrypted with the Caesar cipher, even though you don't know the key?

**■■ R19.7** What happens if you try to save an object that is not serializable in an object stream? Try it out and report your results.

**■■ R19.8** Of the classes in the `java.lang` and `java.io` packages that you have encountered in this book, which implement the `Serializable` interface?

**■■ R19.9** Why is it better to save an entire `ArrayList` to an object stream instead of programming a loop that writes each element?

**■ R19.10** What is the difference between sequential access and random access?

**■ R19.11** What is the file pointer in a file? How do you move it? How do you tell the current position? Why is it a long integer?

**■ R19.12** How do you move the file pointer to the first byte of a file? To the last byte? To the exact middle of the file?

**■■ R19.13** What happens if you try to move the file pointer past the end of a file? Try it out and report your result.

**■■ R19.14** Can you move the file pointer of `System.in`?

## PROGRAMMING EXERCISES

**■■ P19.1** *Random monoalphabet cipher.* The Caesar cipher, which shifts all letters by a fixed amount, is far too easy to crack. Here is a better idea. For the key, don't use numbers but words. Suppose the key word is FEATHER. Then first remove duplicate letters, yielding FEATHR, and append the other letters of the alphabet in reverse order. Now encrypt the letters as follows:

```
A B C D E F G H I J K L M N O P Q R S T U V W X Y Z
↓ ↓ ↓ ↓ ↓ ↓ ↓ ↓ ↓ ↓ ↓ ↓ ↓ ↓ ↓ ↓ ↓ ↓ ↓ ↓ ↓ ↓ ↓ ↓ ↓ ↓
F E A T H R Z Y X W V U S Q P O N M L K J I G D C B
```

Write a program that encrypts or decrypts a file using this cipher. The key word is specified with the -k command line option. The -d command line option specifies decryption. For example,

```
java Encryptor -d -k FEATHER encrypt.txt output.txt
```

decrypts a file using the keyword FEATHER. It is an error not to supply a keyword.

- **P19.2** *Letter frequencies.* If you encrypt a file using the cipher of Exercise P19.1, it will have all of its letters jumbled up, and will look as if there is no hope of decrypting it without knowing the keyword. Guessing the keyword seems hopeless, too. There are just too many possible keywords. However, someone who is trained in decryption will be able to break this cipher in no time at all. The average letter frequencies of English letters are well known. The most common letter is E, which occurs about 13 percent of the time. Here are the average frequencies of English letters:

| A | 8% | H | 4% | O | 7% | V | 1% |
|---|-----|---|-----|---|-----|---|-----|
| B | <1% | I | 7% | P | 3% | W | 2% |
| C | 3% | J | <1% | Q | <1% | X | <1% |
| D | 4% | K | <1% | R | 8% | Y | 2% |
| E | 13% | L | 4% | S | 6% | Z | <1% |
| F | 3% | M | 3% | T | 9% | | |
| G | 2% | N | 8% | U | 3% | | |

Write a program that reads an input file and prints the letter frequencies in that file. Such a tool will help a code breaker. If the most frequent letters in an encrypted file are H and K, then there is an excellent chance that they are the encryptions of E and T.

- **P19.3** *Vigenère cipher.* The trouble with a monoalphabetic cipher is that it can be easily broken by frequency analysis. The so-called Vigenère cipher overcomes this problem by encoding a letter into one of several cipher letters, depending on its position in the input document. Choose a keyword, for example TIGER. Then encode the first letter of the input text like this:

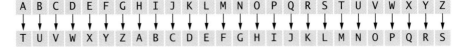

That is, the encoded alphabet is just the regular alphabet shifted to start at T, the first letter of the keyword TIGER. The second letter is encrypted according to this map:

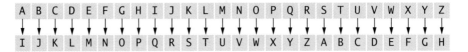

The third, fourth, and fifth letters in the input text are encrypted using the alphabet sequences beginning with characters G, E, and R. Because the key is only five letters long, the sixth letter of the input text is encrypted in the same way as the first.

Write a program that encrypts or decrypts an input text using this cipher. Use command line arguments as in Exercise P19.1.

■■ **P19.4** *Playfair cipher*. Another way of thwarting a simple letter frequency analysis of an encrypted text is to encrypt pairs of letters together. A simple scheme to do this is the Playfair cipher. You pick a keyword and remove duplicate letters from it. Then you fill the keyword, and the remaining letters of the alphabet, into a 5 × 5 square. (Because there are only 25 squares, I and J are considered the same letter.) Here is such an arrangement with the keyword PLAYFAIR:

```
P L A Y F
I R B C D
E G H K M
N O Q S T
U V W X Z
```

To encrypt a letter pair, say AT, look at the rectangle with corners A and T:

```
P L A Y F
I R B C D
E G H K M
N O Q S T
U V W X Z
```

The encoding of this pair is formed by looking at the other two corners of the rectangle—in this case, FQ. If both letters happen to be in the same row or column, such as GO, simply swap the two letters. Decryption is done in the same way.

Write a program that encrypts or decrypts an input text using this cipher. Use command line arguments as in Exercise P19.1.

■ **P19.5** Write a program that opens a binary file and prints all ASCII characters from that file, that is, all bytes with values between 32 and 126. Print a new line after every 64 characters. What happens when you use your program with word processor documents? With Java class files?

■■ **P19.6** Modify the BankSimulator program so that it is possible to delete an account. To delete a record from the data file, fill the record with zeroes.

■■ **P19.7** The data file in Exercise P19.6 may end up with many deleted records that take up space. Write a program that compacts such a file, moving all active records to the beginning and shortening the file length. *Hint:* Use the setLength method of the RandomAccessFile class to truncate the file length. Look up the method's behavior in the API documentation.

■■■ **P19.8** Write a program that manipulates a database of product records. Records are stored in a binary file. Each record consists of these items:
- Product name: 30 characters at two bytes each = 60 bytes
- Price: one double = 8 bytes
- Quantity: one int = 8 bytes

The program should allow the user to add a record, find a record that matches a product name, and change the price and quantity of a product by a given amount.

■■ **P19.9** Enhance the SerialDemo program to demonstrate that it can save and restore a bank that contains a mixture of savings and checking accounts.

■■ **Graphics P19.10** Implement a graphical user interface for the BankSimulator program in Section 19.3.

■■■ **Graphics P19.11** Write a graphical application in which the user clicks on a panel to add shapes (rectangles, ellipses, cars, etc.) at the mouse click location. The shapes are stored in an array list. When the user selects File->Save from the menu, save the selection of shapes in a file. When the user selects File->Open, load in a file. Use serialization.

■■■ **P19.12** Write a toolkit that helps a cryptographer decrypt a file that was encrypted using a monoalphabet cipher. A monoalphabet cipher encrypts each character separately. Examples are the Caesar cipher and the cipher in Exercise P19.1. Analyze the letter frequencies as in Exercise P19.2. Use brute force to try all Caesar cipher keys, and check the output against a dictionary file. Allow the cryptographer to enter some substitutions and show the resulting text, with the unknown characters represented as ?. Try out your toolkit by decrypting files that you get from your classmates.

## ANSWERS TO SELF-CHECK QUESTIONS

1. Image data is stored in a binary format—try loading an image file into a text editor, and you won't see much text. Therefore, you should use an InputStream.

2. For HTML files, a reader would be useful. But URLs can also point to binary files, such as http://horstmann.com/bigjava/duke.gif.

3. It returns a special value of -1 to indicate that no more input is available. If the return type had been byte, no special value would have been available that is distinguished from a legal data value.

4. It is "Hello, World!", encrypted with a key of 3.

5. Yes—the program uses streams and encrypts each byte.

6. Suppose you print something, and then you call seek(0), and print again to the same location. It would be difficult to reflect that behavior in the console window.

7. Advantage: The numbers use a fixed amount of storage space, making it possible to change their values without affecting surrounding data. Disadvantage: You cannot read a binary file with a text editor.

8. You can save the entire object with a single writeObject call. With a RandomAccessFile, you have to save each instance variable separately.

9. Add implements Serializable to the class definition.

# THE BASIC LATIN AND LATIN-1 SUBSETS OF UNICODE

This appendix lists the Unicode characters that are most commonly used for processing Western European languages. A complete listing of Unicode characters can be found at http://unicode.org.

### Table 1  Selected Control Characters

| Character | Code | Decimal | Escape Sequence |
|-----------|------|---------|-----------------|
| Tab | '\u0009' | 9 | '\t' |
| Newline | '\u000A' | 10 | '\n' |
| Return | '\u000D' | 13 | '\r' |
| Space | '\u0020' | 32 | |

## Table 2  The Basic Latin (ASCII) Subset of Unicode

| Char. | Code | Dec. | Char. | Code | Dec. | Char. | Code | Dec. |
|-------|------|------|-------|------|------|-------|------|------|
|  |  |  | @ | '\u0040' | 64 | ` | '\u0060' | 96 |
| ! | '\u0021' | 33 | A | '\u0041' | 65 | a | '\u0061' | 97 |
| " | '\u0022' | 34 | B | '\u0042' | 66 | b | '\u0062' | 98 |
| # | '\u0023' | 35 | C | '\u0043' | 67 | c | '\u0063' | 99 |
| $ | '\u0024' | 36 | D | '\u0044' | 68 | d | '\u0064' | 100 |
| % | '\u0025' | 37 | E | '\u0045' | 69 | e | '\u0065' | 101 |
| & | '\u0026' | 38 | F | '\u0046' | 70 | f | '\u0066' | 102 |
| ' | '\u0027' | 39 | G | '\u0047' | 71 | g | '\u0067' | 103 |
| ( | '\u0028' | 40 | H | '\u0048' | 72 | h | '\u0068' | 104 |
| ) | '\u0029' | 41 | I | '\u0049' | 73 | i | '\u0069' | 105 |
| * | '\u002A' | 42 | J | '\u004A' | 74 | j | '\u006A' | 106 |
| + | '\u002B' | 43 | K | '\u004B' | 75 | k | '\u006B' | 107 |
| , | '\u002C' | 44 | L | '\u004C' | 76 | l | '\u006C' | 108 |
| - | '\u002D' | 45 | M | '\u004D' | 77 | m | '\u006D' | 109 |
| . | '\u002E' | 46 | N | '\u004E' | 78 | n | '\u006E' | 110 |
| / | '\u002F' | 47 | O | '\u004F' | 79 | o | '\u006F' | 111 |
| 0 | '\u0030' | 48 | P | '\u0050' | 80 | p | '\u0070' | 112 |
| 1 | '\u0031' | 49 | Q | '\u0051' | 81 | q | '\u0071' | 113 |
| 2 | '\u0032' | 50 | R | '\u0052' | 82 | r | '\u0072' | 114 |
| 3 | '\u0033' | 51 | S | '\u0053' | 83 | s | '\u0073' | 115 |
| 4 | '\u0034' | 52 | T | '\u0054' | 84 | t | '\u0074' | 116 |
| 5 | '\u0035' | 53 | U | '\u0055' | 85 | u | '\u0075' | 117 |
| 6 | '\u0036' | 54 | V | '\u0056' | 86 | v | '\u0076' | 118 |
| 7 | '\u0037' | 55 | W | '\u0057' | 87 | w | '\u0077' | 119 |
| 8 | '\u0038' | 56 | X | '\u0058' | 88 | x | '\u0078' | 120 |
| 9 | '\u0039' | 57 | Y | '\u0059' | 89 | y | '\u0079' | 121 |
| : | '\u003A' | 58 | Z | '\u005A' | 90 | z | '\u007A' | 122 |
| ; | '\u003B' | 59 | [ | '\u005B' | 91 | { | '\u007B' | 123 |
| < | '\u003C' | 60 | \' | '\u005C' | 92 | \| | '\u007C' | 124 |
| = | '\u003D' | 61 | ] | '\u005D' | 93 | } | '\u007D' | 125 |
| > | '\u003E' | 62 | ^ | '\u005E' | 94 | ~ | '\u007E' | 126 |
| ? | '\u003F' | 63 | _ | '\u005F' | 95 |  |  |  |

## Table 3  The Latin-1 Subset of Unicode

| Char. | Code | Dec. | Char. | Code | Dec. | Char. | Code | Dec. |
|---|---|---|---|---|---|---|---|---|
| | | | À | '\u00C0' | 192 | à | '\u00E0' | 224 |
| ¡ | '\u00A1' | 161 | Á | '\u00C1' | 193 | á | '\u00E1' | 225 |
| ¢ | '\u00A2' | 162 | Â | '\u00C2' | 194 | â | '\u00E2' | 226 |
| £ | '\u00A3' | 163 | Ã | '\u00C3' | 195 | ã | '\u00E3' | 227 |
| ¤ | '\u00A4' | 164 | Ä | '\u00C4' | 196 | ä | '\u00E4' | 228 |
| ¥ | '\u00A5' | 165 | Å | '\u00C5' | 197 | å | '\u00E5' | 229 |
| ¦ | '\u00A6' | 166 | Æ | '\u00C6' | 198 | æ | '\u00E6' | 230 |
| § | '\u00A7' | 167 | Ç | '\u00C7' | 199 | ç | '\u00E7' | 231 |
| ¨ | '\u00A8' | 168 | È | '\u00C8' | 200 | è | '\u00E8' | 232 |
| © | '\u00A9' | 169 | É | '\u00C9' | 201 | é | '\u00E9' | 233 |
| ª | '\u00AA' | 170 | Ê | '\u00CA' | 202 | ê | '\u00EA' | 234 |
| « | '\u00AB' | 171 | Ë | '\u00CB' | 203 | ë | '\u00EB' | 235 |
| ¬ | '\u00AC' | 172 | Ì | '\u00CC' | 204 | ì | '\u00EC' | 236 |
| | '\u00AD' | 173 | Í | '\u00CD' | 205 | í | '\u00ED' | 237 |
| ® | '\u00AE' | 174 | Î | '\u00CE' | 206 | î | '\u00EE' | 238 |
| ¯ | '\u00AF' | 175 | Ï | '\u00CF' | 207 | ï | '\u00EF' | 239 |
| ° | '\u00B0' | 176 | Ð | '\u00D0' | 208 | ð | '\u00F0' | 240 |
| ± | '\u00B1' | 177 | Ñ | '\u00D1' | 209 | ñ | '\u00F1' | 241 |
| ² | '\u00B2' | 178 | Ò | '\u00D2' | 210 | ò | '\u00F2' | 242 |
| ³ | '\u00B3' | 179 | Ó | '\u00D3' | 211 | ó | '\u00F3' | 243 |
| ´ | '\u00B4' | 180 | Ô | '\u00D4' | 212 | ô | '\u00F4' | 244 |
| µ | '\u00B5' | 181 | Õ | '\u00D5' | 213 | õ | '\u00F5' | 245 |
| ¶ | '\u00B6' | 182 | Ö | '\u00D6' | 214 | ö | '\u00F6' | 246 |
| · | '\u00B7' | 183 | × | '\u00D7' | 215 | ÷ | '\u00F7' | 247 |
| ¸ | '\u00B8' | 184 | Ø | '\u00D8' | 216 | ø | '\u00F8' | 248 |
| ¹ | '\u00B9' | 185 | Ù | '\u00D9' | 217 | ù | '\u00F9' | 249 |
| º | '\u00BA' | 186 | Ú | '\u00DA' | 218 | ú | '\u00FA' | 250 |
| » | '\u00BB' | 187 | Û | '\u00DB' | 219 | û | '\u00FB' | 251 |
| ¼ | '\u00BC' | 188 | Ü | '\u00DC' | 220 | ü | '\u00FC' | 252 |
| ½ | '\u00BD' | 189 | Ý | '\u00DD' | 221 | ý | '\u00FD' | 253 |
| ¾ | '\u00BE' | 190 | Þ | '\u00DE' | 222 | þ | '\u00FE' | 254 |
| ¿ | '\u00BF' | 191 | ß | '\u00DF' | 223 | ÿ | '\u00FF' | 255 |

# JAVA OPERATOR SUMMARY

The Java operators are listed in groups of decreasing *precedence* in the table below. The horizontal lines in the table indicate a change in operator precedence. Operators with higher precedence bind more strongly than those with lower precedence. For example, x + y * z means x + (y * z) because the * operator has higher precedence than the + operator. Looking at the table below, you can tell that x && y || z means (x && y) || z because the || operator has lower precedence.

The *associativity* of an operator indicates whether it groups left to right, or right to left. For example, the - operator binds left to right. Therefore, x - y - z means (x - y) - z. But the = operator binds right to left, and x = y = z means x = (y = z).

| Operator | Description | Associativity |
|---|---|---|
| . | Access class feature | |
| [] | Array subscript | Left to right |
| () | Function call | |
| ++ | Increment | |
| -- | Decrement | |
| ! | Boolean *not* | |
| ~ | Bitwise *not* | |
| + *(unary)* | (Has no effect) | Right to left |
| - *(unary)* | Negative | |
| (*TypeName*) | Cast | |
| new | Object allocation | |
| * | Multiplication | |
| / | Division or integer division | Left to right |
| % | Integer remainder | |
| + | Addition, string concatenation | |
| - | Subtraction | Left to right |
| << | Shift left | |
| >> | Right shift with sign extension | Left to right |
| >>> | Right shift with zero extension | |

| Operator | Description | Associativity |
|:---:|:---|:---:|
| < | Less than | |
| <= | Less than or equal | |
| > | Greater than | Left to right |
| >= | Greater than or equal | |
| instanceof | Tests whether an object's type is a given type or a subtype thereof | |
| == | Equal | Left to right |
| != | Not equal | |
| & | Bitwise *and* | Left to right |
| ^ | Bitwise exclusive *or* | Left to right |
| \| | Bitwise *or* | Left to right |
| && | Boolean "short circuit" *and* | Left to right |
| \|\| | Boolean "short circuit" *or* | Left to right |
| ? : | Conditional | Right to left |
| = | Assignment | |
| *op=* | Assignment with binary operator (*op* is one of +, -, *, /, &, \|, ^, <<, >>, >>>) | Right to left |

# JAVA RESERVED WORD SUMMARY

| Reserved Word | Description |
| --- | --- |
| abstract | An abstract class or method |
| assert | An assertion that a condition is fulfilled |
| boolean | The Boolean type |
| break | Breaks out of the current loop or labeled statement |
| byte | The 8-bit signed integer type |
| case | A label in a switch statement |
| catch | The handler for an exception in a try block |
| char | The 16-bit Unicode character type |
| class | Defines a class |
| const | Not used |
| continue | Skip the remainder of a loop body |
| default | The default label in a switch statement |
| do | A loop whose body is executed at least once |
| double | The 64-bit double-precision floating-point type |
| else | The alternative clause in an if statement |
| enum | An enumeration type |
| extends | Indicates that a class is a subclass of another class |
| final | A value that cannot be changed after it has been initialized, a method that cannot be overridden, or a class that cannot be extended |
| finally | A clause of a try block that is always executed |
| float | The 32-bit single-precision floating-point type |
| for | A loop with initialization, condition, and update expressions |
| goto | Not used |
| if | A conditional branch statement |
| implements | Indicates that a class realizes an interface |

| Reserved Word | Description |
|---|---|
| import | Allows the use of class names without the package name |
| instanceof | Tests whether an object's type is a given type or a subtype thereof |
| int | The 32-bit integer type |
| interface | An abstract type with only abstract methods and constants |
| long | The 64-bit integer type |
| native | A method implemented in non-Java code |
| new | Allocates an object |
| package | A collection of related classes |
| private | A feature that is accessible only by methods of the same class |
| protected | A feature that is accessible only by methods of the same class, a subclass, or another class in the same package |
| public | A feature that is accessible by all methods |
| return | Returns from a method |
| short | The 16-bit integer type |
| static | A feature that is defined for a class, not for individual instances |
| strictfp | Use strict rules for floating-point computations |
| super | Invoke the superclass constructor or a superclass method |
| switch | A selection statement |
| synchronized | A block of code that is accessible to only one thread at a time |
| this | The implicit parameter of a method; or invocation of another constructor of the same class |
| throw | Throws an exception |
| throws | The exceptions that a method may throw |
| transient | Instance variables that should not be serialized |
| try | A block of code with exception handlers or a finally handler |
| void | Tags a method that doesn't return a value |
| volatile | A variable that may be accessed by multiple threads without synchronization |
| while | A loop statement |

# THE JAVA LIBRARY

This appendix lists all classes and methods from the standard Java library that are used in this book.

In the following inheritance hierarchy, superclasses that are not used in this book are shown in gray type. Some classes implement interfaces not covered in this book; they are omitted. Classes are sorted first by package, then alphabetically within a package.

```
java.io.Serializable
java.lang.Object
    java.awt.BorderLayout implements Serializable
    java.awt.Color implements Serializable
    java.awt.Component implements Serializable
        java.awt.Container
            javax.swing.JComponent
                javax.swing.AbstractButton
                    javax.swing.JButton
                    javax.swing.JMenuItem
                        javax.swing.JMenu
                    javax.swing.JToggleButton
                        javax.swing.JCheckBox
                        javax.swing.JRadioButton
                javax.swing.JComboBox
                javax.swing.JFileChooser
                javax.swing.JLabel
                javax.swing.JMenuBar
                javax.swing.JPanel
                javax.swing.JOptionPane
                javax.swing.JScrollPane
                javax.swing.JSlider
                javax.swing.text.JTextComponent
                    javax.swing.JTextArea
                    javax.swing.JTextField
        java.awt.Window
            java.awt.Frame
                javax.swing.JFrame
    java.awt.Dimension2D
        java.awt.Dimension implements Serializable
    java.awt.FlowLayout implements Serializable
    java.awt.Font implements Serializable
    java.awt.Graphics
    java.awt.GridLayout implements Serializable
    java.awt.event.MouseAdapter implements MouseListener
    java.io.File implements Comparable<File>, Serializable
    java.io.InputStream
        java.io.FileInputStream
        java.io.ObjectInputStream
    java.io.OutputStream
        java.io.FileOutputStream
        java.io.FilterOutputStream
            java.io.PrintStream
        java.io.ObjectOutputStream
```

```
            java.io.RandomAccessFile
        java.io.Writer
            java.io.PrintWriter
        java.lang.Boolean implements Comparable<Boolean>, Serializable
        java.lang.Character implements Comparable<Character>, Serializable
        java.lang.Class implements Serializable
        java.lang.Math
        java.lang.Number implements Serializable
            java.math.BigDecimal implements Comparable<BigDecimal>
            java.math.BigInteger implements Comparable<BigInteger>
            java.lang.Double implements Comparable<Double>
            java.lang.Integer implements Comparable<Integer>
        java.lang.String implements Comparable<String>, Serializable
        java.lang.System
        java.lang.Thread implements Runnable
        java.lang.Throwable
            java.lang.Error
            java.lang.Exception
                java.lang.InterruptedException
                java.io.IOException
                    java.io.EOFException
                    java.io.FileNotFoundException
                java.lang.RuntimeException
                    java.lang.IllegalArgumentException
                        java.lang.NumberFormatException
                    java.lang.IllegalStateException
                    java.util.NoSuchElementException
                        java.util.InputMismatchException
                    java.lang.NullPointerException
                java.sql.SQLException
                javax.xml.xpath.XPathException
                    javax.xml.xpath.XPathExpressionException
    java.net.ServerSocket
    java.net.Socket
    java.net.URL implements Serializable
    java.net.URLConnection
        java.net.HttpURLConnection
    java.sql.DriverManager
    java.text.Format implements Serializable
        java.text.DateFormat
    java.util.AbstractCollection<E>
        java.util.AbstractList<E>
            java.util.AbstractSequentialList<E>
                java.util.LinkedList<E> implements List<E>, Queue<E>, Serializable
            java.util.ArrayList<E> implements List<E>, Serializable
        java.util.AbstractQueue<E>
            java.util.PriorityQueue<E> implements Serializable
        java.util.AbstractSet<E>
            java.util.HashSet<E> implements Serializable, Set<E>
            java.util.TreeSet<E> implements Serializable, SortedSet<E>
    java.util.AbstractMap<K, V>
        java.util.HashMap<K, V> implements Map<K, V>, Serializable
            java.util.LinkedHashMap<K, V>
        java.util.TreeMap<K, V> implements Serializable, Map<K, V>
    java.util.Arrays
    java.util.Collections
    java.util.Calendar
        java.util.GregorianCalendar
    java.util.Date implements Serializable
    java.util.Dictionary<K, V>
```

```
        java.util.Hashtable<K, V>
            java.util.Properties implements Serializable
    java.util.EventObject implements Serializable
        java.awt.AWTEvent
            java.awt.event.ActionEvent
            java.awt.event.ComponentEvent
                java.awt.event.InputEvent
                    java.awt.event.KeyEvent
                    java.awt.event.MouseEvent
        javax.swing.event.ChangeEvent
    java.util.Random implements Serializable
    java.util.Scanner
    java.util.TimeZone implements Serializable
    java.util.concurrent.locks.ReentrantLock implements Lock, Serializable
    java.util.logging.Level implements Serializable
    java.util.logging.Logger
    javax.swing.ButtonGroup implements Serializable
    javax.swing.ImageIcon implements Serializable
    javax.swing.Keystroke implements Serializable
    javax.swing.Timer implements Serializable
    javax.swing.border.AbstractBorder implements Serializable
        javax.swing.border.EtchedBorder
        javax.swing.border.TitledBorder
    javax.xml.parsers.DocumentBuilder
    javax.xml.parsers.DocumentBuilderFactory
    javax.xml.xpath.XPathFactory
java.lang.Comparable<T>
java.lang.Runnable
java.sql.Connection
java.sql.ResultSet
java.sql.ResultSetMetaData
java.sql.Statement
    java.sql.PreparedStatement
java.util.Collection<E>
    java.util.List<E>
    java.util.Set<E>
        java.util.SortedSet<E>
java.util.Comparator<T>
java.util.EventListener
    java.awt.event.ActionListener
    java.awt.event.KeyListener
    java.awt.event.MouseListener
    javax.swing.event.ChangeListener
java.util.Iterator<E>
    java.util.ListIterator<E>
java.util.Map<K, V>
java.util.Queue<E> extends Collection<E>
java.util.concurrent.locks.Condition
java.util.concurrent.locks.Lock
javax.xml.xpath.XPath
org.w3c.dom.DOMConfiguration
org.w3c.dom.DOMImplementaton
org.w3c.dom.Node
    org.w3c.dom.CharacterData
        org.w3c.dom.Text
    org.w3c.dom.Document
    org.w3c.dom.Element
org.w3c.dom.ls.DOMImplementationLS
org.w3c.dom.ls.LSSerializer
```

In the following descriptions, the phrase "this object" ("this component", "this container", and so forth) means the object (component, container, and so forth) on which the method is invoked (the implicit parameter, `this`).

# Package java.awt

## Class java.awt.BorderLayout

- **BorderLayout**()
  This constructs a border layout. A border layout has five regions for adding components, called "NORTH", "EAST", "SOUTH", "WEST", and "CENTER".

- static final int CENTER
  This value identifies the center position of a border layout.

- static final int EAST
  This value identifies the east position of a border layout.

- static final int NORTH
  This value identifies the north position of a border layout.

- static final int SOUTH
  This value identifies the south position of a border layout.

- static final int WEST
  This value identifies the west position of a border layout.

## Class java.awt.Color

- **Color**(int red, int green, int blue)
  This creates a color with the specified red, green, and blue values between 0 and 255.
  **Parameters:**    red  The red component
  green  The green component
  blue  The blue component

## Class java.awt.Component

- void **addKeyListener**(KeyListener listener)
  This method adds a key listener to the component.
  **Parameters:**    listener  The key listener to be added

- void **addMouseListener**(MouseListener listener)
  This method adds a mouse listener to the component.
  **Parameters:**    listener  The mouse listener to be added

- int **getHeight**()
  This method gets the height of this component.
  **Returns:**    The height in pixels

- int **getWidth**()
  This method gets the width of this component.
  **Returns:**        The width in pixels

- void **repaint**()
  This method repaints this component by scheduling a call to the paint method.

- void **setFocusable**(boolean focusable)
  This method controls whether or not the component can receive input focus.
  **Parameters:**      focusable  true to have focus, or false to lose focus

- void **setPreferredSize**(Dimension preferredSize)
  This method sets the preferred size of this component.

- void **setSize**(int width, int height)
  This method sets the size of this component.
  **Parameters:**      width  the component width
                       height   the component height

- void **setVisible**(boolean visible)
  This method shows or hides the component.
  **Parameters:**      visible  true to show the component, or false to hide it

## Class java.awt.Container

- void **add**(Component c)
- void **add**(Component c, Object position)
  These methods add a component to the end of this container. If a position is given, the layout manager is called to position the component.
  **Parameters:**      c  The component to be added
                       position  An object expressing position information for the layout manager

- void **setLayout**(LayoutManager manager)
  This method sets the layout manager for this container.
  **Parameters:**      manager  A layout manager

## Class java.awt.Dimension

- **Dimension**(int width, int height)
  This constructs a Dimension object with the given width and height.
  **Parameters:**      width  The width
                       height  The height

## Class java.awt.FlowLayout

- **FlowLayout**()
  This constructs a new flow layout. A flow layout places as many components as possible in a row, without changing their size, and starts new rows when necessary.

## Class java.awt.Font

- **Font**(String name, int style, int size)
  This constructs a font object from the specified name, style, and point size.
  **Parameters:**   name   The font name, either a font face name or a logical font name, which must be one of "Dialog", "DialogInput", "Monospaced", "Serif", or "SansSerif"
  style   One of Font.PLAIN, Font.ITALIC, Font.BOLD, or Font.ITALIC+Font.BOLD
  size   The point size of the font

## Class java.awt.Frame

- void **setTitle**(String title)
  This method sets the frame title.
  **Parameters:**   title   The title to be displayed in the border of the frame

## Class java.awt.Graphics

- void **drawLine**(int x1, int y1, int x2, int y2)
  Draws a line between two points
  **Parameters:**   x1, y1   The starting point
  x2, y2 The endpoint
- void **drawOval**(int x, int y, int width, int height)
- void **fillOval**(int x, int y, int width, int height)
  **Parameters:**   x1, y1   The top-left corner of the bounding rectangle
  width, height   The width and height of the bounding rectangle
- void **drawRect**(int x, int y, int width, int height)
- void **fillRect**(int x, int y, int width, int height)
  **Parameters:**   x1, y1   The top-left corner of the rectangle
  width, height   The width and height of the rectangle
- void **drawString**(String s, int x, int y)
  This method draws a string in the current font and color.
  **Parameters:**   s   The string to draw
  x, y   The basepoint of the first character in the string
- void **setColor**(Color c)
  This method sets the current color. After the method call, all graphics operations use this color.
  **Parameters:**   c   The new drawing color

## Class java.awt.GridLayout

- **GridLayout**(int rows, int cols)
  This constructor creates a grid layout with the specified number of rows and columns. The components in a grid layout are arranged in a grid with equal widths and heights. One, but not both, of rows and cols can be zero, in which case any number of objects can be placed in a row or in a column, respectively.
  **Parameters:**   rows   The number of rows in the grid
  cols   The number of columns in the grid

# Class `java.awt.Rectangle`

- `Rectangle()`
  This constructs a rectangle with a top-left corner at (0, 0) and width and height set to 0.

- `Rectangle(int x, int y, int width, int height)`
  This constructs a rectangle with given top-left corner and size.
  **Parameters:**    x, y  The top-left corner
                     width  The width
                     height  The height

- `double getHeight()`
- `double getWidth()`
  These methods get the height and width of the rectangle.

- `double getX()`
- `double getY()`
  These methods get the $x$- and $y$-coordinates of the top-left corner of the rectangle.

- `void grow(int dw, int dh)`
  This method adjusts the width and height of this rectangle.
  **Parameters:**    dw  The amount to add to the width (can be negative)
                    dh  The amount to add to the height (can be negative)

- `Rectangle intersection(Rectangle other)`
  This method computes the intersection of this rectangle with the specified rectangle.
  **Parameters:**    other  A rectangle
  **Returns:**       The largest rectangle contained in both `this` and `other`

- `void setLocation(int x, int y)`
  This method moves this rectangle to a new location.
  **Parameters:**    x, y  The new top-left corner

- `void setSize(int width, int height)`
  This method sets the width and height of this rectangle to new values.
  **Parameters:**    width  The new width
                   height  The new height

- `void translate(int dx, int dy)`
  This method moves this rectangle.
  **Parameters:**    dx  The distance to move along the $x$-axis
                   dy  The distance to move along the $y$-axis

- `Rectangle union(Rectangle other)`
  This method computes the union of this rectangle with the specified rectangle. This is not the set-theoretic union but the smallest rectangle that contains both `this` and `other`.
  **Parameters:**    other  A rectangle
  **Returns:**       The smallest rectangle containing both `this` and `other`

# Package `java.awt.event`

## Interface `java.awt.event.ActionListener`

- void **actionPerformed**(ActionEvent e)
  The event source calls this method when an action occurs.

## Class `java.awt.event.KeyEvent`

This event is passed to the KeyListener methods. Use the KeyStroke class to obtain the key information from the key event.

## Interface `java.awt.event.KeyListener`

- void **keyPressed**(KeyEvent e)
- void **keyReleased**(KeyEvent e)
  These methods are called when a key has been pressed or released.

- void **keyTyped**(KeyEvent e)
  This method is called when a keystroke has been composed by pressing and releasing one or more keys.

## Class `java.awt.event.MouseEvent`

- int **getX**()
  This method returns the horizontal position of the mouse as of the time the event occurred.
  **Returns:** The *x*-position of the mouse

- int **getY**()
  This method returns the vertical position of the mouse as of the time the event occurred.
  **Returns:** The *y*-position of the mouse

## Interface `java.awt.event.MouseListener`

- void **mouseClicked**(MouseEvent e)
  This method is called when the mouse has been clicked (that is, pressed and released in quick succession).

- void **mouseEntered**(MouseEvent e)
  This method is called when the mouse has entered the component to which this listener was added.

- void **mouseExited**(MouseEvent e)
  This method is called when the mouse has exited the component to which this listener was added.

- void **mousePressed**(MouseEvent e)
  This method is called when a mouse button has been pressed.

- void **mouseReleased**(MouseEvent e)
  This method is called when a mouse button has been released.

# Package `java.io`

## Class `java.io.EOFException`

- `EOFException`(String message)
  This constructs an "end of file" exception object.
  **Parameters:**     message   The detail message

## Class `java.io.File`

- `File`(String name)
  This constructs a `File` object that describes a file (which may or may not exist) with the given name.
  **Parameters:**     name   The name of the file
- `static final String pathSeparator`
  The sytem-dependent separator between path names. A colon (:) in Linux or Mac OS X; a semicolon (;) in Windows.

## Class `java.io.FileInputStream`

- `FileInputStream`(File f)
  This constructs a file input stream and opens the chosen file. If the file cannot be opened for reading, a `FileNotFoundException` is thrown.
  **Parameters:**      f   The file to be opened for reading
- `FileInputStream`(String name)
  This constructs a file input stream and opens the named file. If the file cannot be opened for reading, a `FileNotFoundException` is thrown.
  **Parameters:**     name   The name of the file to be opened for reading

## Class `java.io.FileNotFoundException`

This exception is thrown when a file could not be opened.

## Class `java.io.FileOutputStream`

- `FileOutputStream`(File f)
  This constructs a file output stream and opens the chosen file. If the file cannot be opened for writing, a `FileNotFoundException` is thrown.
  **Parameters:**      f   The file to be opened for writing
- `FileOutputStream`(String name)
  This constructs a file output stream and opens the named file. If the file cannot be opened for writing, a `FileNotFoundException` is thrown.
  **Parameters:**     name   The name of the file to be opened for writing

## Class `java.io.InputStream`

- void `close`()
  This method closes this input stream (such as a `FileInputStream`) and releases any system resources associated with the stream.

- int **read**()
  This method reads the next byte of data from this input stream.
  **Returns:** The next byte of data, or −1 if the end of the stream is reached

## Class java.io.InputStreamReader

- **InputStreamReader**(InputStream in)
  This constructs a reader from a specified input stream.
  **Parameters:** in The stream to read from

## Class java.io.IOException

This type of exception is thrown when an input/output error is encountered.

## Class java.io.ObjectInputStream

- **ObjectInputStream**(InputStream in)
  This constructs an object input stream.
  **Parameters:** in The stream to read from
- Object **readObject**()
  This method reads the next object from this object input stream.
  **Returns:** The next object

## Class java.io.ObjectOutputStream

- **ObjectOutputStream**(OutputStream out)
  This constructs an object output stream.
  **Parameters:** out The stream to write to
- Object **writeObject**(Object obj)
  This method writes the next object to this object output stream.
  **Parameters:** obj The object to write

## Class java.io.OutputStream

- void **close**()
  This method closes this output stream (such as a FileOutputStream) and releases any system resources associated with this stream. A closed stream cannot perform output operations and cannot be reopened.
- void **write**(int b)
  This method writes the lowest byte of b to this output stream.
  **Parameters:** b The integer whose lowest byte is written

## Class java.io.PrintStream / Class java.io.PrintWriter

- **PrintStream**(String name)
- **PrintWriter**(String name)
  This constructs a PrintStream or PrintWriter and opens the named file. If the file cannot be opened for writing, a FileNotFoundException is thrown.
  **Parameters:** name The name of the file to be opened for writing

- void **close**()
  This method closes this stream or writer and releases any associated system resources.
- void **print**(int x)
- void **print**(double x)
- void **print**(Object x)
- void **print**(String x)
- void **println**()
- void **println**(int x)
- void **println**(double x)
- void **println**(Object x)
- void **println**(String x)

  These methods print a value to this PrintStream or PrintWriter. The println methods print a newline after the value. Objects are printed by converting them to strings with their toString methods.

  **Parameters:**     x   The value to be printed

- PrintStream **printf**(String format, Object... values)
- Printwriter **printf**(String format, Object... values)

  These methods print the format string to this PrintStream or PrintWriter, substituting the given values for placeholders that start with %.

  **Parameters:**     format   The format string

  values   The values to be printed. You can supply any number of values

  **Returns:**     The implicit parameter

## Class java.io.RandomAccessFile

- **RandomAccessFile**(String name, String mode)
  This method opens a named random access file for reading or read/write access.

  **Parameters:**     name   The file name

  mode   "r" for reading or "rw" for read/write access

- long **getFilePointer**()
  This method gets the current position in this file.

  **Returns:**     The current position for reading and writing

- long **length**()
  This method gets the length of this file.

  **Returns:**     The file length

- char **readChar**()
- double **readDouble**()
- int **readInt**()

  These methods read a value from the current position in this file.

  **Returns:**     The value that was read from the file

- void **seek**(long position)
  This method sets the position for reading and writing in this file.

  **Parameters:**     position   The new position

- void **writeChar**(int x)
- void **writeChars**(String x)
- void **writeDouble**(double x)
- void **writeInt**(int x)

  These methods write a value to the current position in this file.

  **Parameters:**   x   The value to be written

## Interface java.io.Serializable

A class should implement this interface in order to enable serialization of objects.

# Package java.lang

## Class java.lang.Boolean

- **Boolean**(boolean value)

  This constructs a wrapper object for a boolean value.

  **Parameters:**     value   The value to store in this object

- boolean **booleanValue**()

  This method returns the value stored in this boolean object.

  **Returns:**         The Boolean value of this object

## Class java.lang.Character

- static boolean **isDigit**(ch)

  This method tests whether a given character is a Unicode digit.

  **Parameters:**       ch   The character to test
  **Returns:**          true if the character is a digit

- static boolean **isLetter**(ch)

  This method tests whether a given character is a Unicode letter.

  **Parameters:**       ch   The character to test
  **Returns:**          true if the character is a letter

- static boolean **isLowerCase**(ch)

  This method tests whether a given character is a lowercase Unicode letter.

  **Parameters:**       ch   The character to test
  **Returns:**          true if the character is a lowercase letter

- static boolean **isUpperCase**(ch)

  This method tests whether a given character is an uppercase Unicode letter.

  **Parameters:**       ch   The character to test
  **Returns:**          true if the character is an uppercase letter

## Class java.lang.Class

- static Class **forName**(String className)

  This method loads a class with a given name. Loading a class initializes its static variables.

  **Parameters:**       className   The name of the class to load
  **Returns:**          The type descriptor of the class

## Interface java.lang.Comparable<T>

- int **compareTo**(T other)
  This method compares this object with the other object.
  **Parameters:**    other  The object to be compared
  **Returns:**       A negative integer if this object is less than the other, zero if they are equal, or a positive integer otherwise

## Class java.lang.Double

- **Double**(double value)
  This constructs a wrapper object for a double-precision floating-point number.
  **Parameters:**    value  The value to store in this object

- double **doubleValue**()
  This method returns the floating-point value stored in this Double wrapper object.
  **Returns:**       The value stored in the object

- static double **parseDouble**(String s)
  This method returns the floating-point number that the string represents. If the string cannot be interpreted as a number, a NumberFormatException is thrown.
  **Parameters:**    s  The string to be parsed
  **Returns:**       The value represented by the string argument

## Class java.lang.Error

This is the superclass for all unchecked system errors.

## Class java.lang.IllegalArgumentException

- **IllegalArgumentException**()
  This constructs an IllegalArgumentException with no detail message.

## Class java.lang.IllegalStateException

This exception is thrown if the state of an object indicates that a method cannot currently be applied.

## Class java.lang.Integer

- **Integer**(int value)
  This constructs a wrapper object for an integer.
  **Parameters:**    value  The value to store in this object

- int **intValue**()
  This method returns the integer value stored in this wrapper object.
  **Returns:**       The value stored in the object

- static int **parseInt**(String s)
  This method returns the integer that the string represents. If the string cannot be interpreted as an integer, a NumberFormatException is thrown.
  **Parameters:**    s  The string to be parsed
  **Returns:**       The value represented by the string argument

- static Integer **parseInt**(String s, int base)
  This method returns the integer value that the string represents in a given number system. If the string cannot be interpreted as an integer, a NumberFormatException is thrown.
  **Parameters:**    s   The string to be parsed
                    base   The base of the number system (such as 2 or 16)
  **Returns:**        The value represented by the string argument

- static String **toString**(int i)
- static String **toString**(int i, int base)
  This method creates a string representation of an integer in a given number system. If no base is given, a decimal representation is created.
  **Parameters:**    i   An integer number
                    base   The base of the number system (such as 2 or 16)
  **Returns:**        A string representation of the argument in the specified number system

- static final int MAX_VALUE
  This constant is the largest value of type int.

- static final int MIN_VALUE
  This constant is the smallest (negative) value of type int.

## Class java.lang.InterruptedException

This exception is thrown to interrupt a thread, usually with the intention of terminating it.

## Class java.lang.Math

- static double **abs**(double x)
  This method returns the absolute value $|x|$.
  **Parameters:**    x   A floating-point value
  **Returns:**        The absolute value of the argument

- static double **acos**(double x)
  This method returns the angle with the given cosine, $\cos^{-1} x \in [0, \pi]$.
  **Parameters:**    x   A floating-point value between –1 and 1
  **Returns:**        The arc cosine of the argument, in radians

- static double **asin**(double x)
  This method returns the angle with the given sine, $\sin^{-1} x \in [-\pi/2, \pi/2]$.
  **Parameters:**    x   A floating-point value between –1 and 1
  **Returns:**        The arc sine of the argument, in radians

- static double **atan**(double x)
  This method returns the angle with the given tangent, $\tan^{-1} x \ (-\pi/2, \pi/2)$.
  **Parameters:**    x   A floating-point value
  **Returns:**        The arc tangent of the argument, in radians

- `static double` `atan2`(double y, double x)

  This method returns the arc tangent, $\tan^{-1}(y/x) \in (-\pi, \pi)$. If $x$ can equal zero, or if it is necessary to distinguish "northwest" from "southeast" and "northeast" from "southwest", use this method instead of atan(y/x).

  **Parameters:**  y, x  Two floating-point values

  **Returns:**  The angle, in radians, between the points (0,0) and $(x,y)$

- `static double` `ceil`(double x)

  This method returns the smallest integer $\geq x$ (as a `double`).

  **Parameters:**  x  A floating-point value

  **Returns:**  The smallest integer greater than or equal to the argument

- `static double` `cos`(double radians)

  This method returns the cosine of an angle given in radians.

  **Parameters:**  radians  An angle, in radians

  **Returns:**  The cosine of the argument

- `static double` `exp`(double x)

  This method returns the value $e^x$, where $e$ is the base of the natural logarithms.

  **Parameters:**  x  A floating-point value

  **Returns:**  $e^x$

- `static double` `floor`(double x)

  This method returns the largest integer $\leq x$ (as a `double`).

  **Parameters:**  x  A floating-point value

  **Returns:**  The largest integer less than or equal to the argument

- `static double` `log`(double x)
- `static double` `log10`(double x)

  This method returns the natural (base $e$) or decimal (base 10) logarithm of $x$, ln $x$.

  **Parameters:**  x  A number greater than 0.0

  **Returns:**  The natural logarithm of the argument

- `static int` `max`(int x, int y)
- `static double` `max`(double x, double y)

  These methods return the larger of the given arguments.

  **Parameters:**  x, y  Two integers or floating-point values

  **Returns:**  The maximum of the arguments

- `static int` `min`(int x, int y)
- `static double` `min`(double x, double y)

  These methods return the smaller of the given arguments.

  **Parameters:**  x, y  Two integers or floating-point values

  **Returns:**  The minimum of the arguments

- `static double` `pow`(double x, double y)

  This method returns the value $x^y$ ($x > 0$, or $x = 0$ and $y > 0$, or $x < 0$ and $y$ is an integer).

  **Parameters:**  x, y  Two floating-point values

  **Returns:**  The value of the first argument raised to the power of the second argument

- `static long` **`round`**`(double x)`
  This method returns the closest `long` integer to the argument.
  **Parameters:**    x   A floating-point value
  **Returns:**       The argument rounded to the nearest `long` value

- `static double` **`sin`**`(double radians)`
  This method returns the sine of an angle given in radians.
  **Parameters:**    radians   An angle, in radians
  **Returns:**       The sine of the argument

- `static double` **`sqrt`**`(double x)`
  This method returns the square root of $x$, $\sqrt{x}$ .
  **Parameters:**    x   A nonnegative floating-point value
  **Returns:**       The square root of the argument

- `static double` **`tan`**`(double radians)`
  This method returns the tangent of an angle given in radians.
  **Parameters:**    radians   An angle, in radians
  **Returns:**       The tangent of the argument

- `static double` **`toDegrees`**`(double radians)`
  This method converts radians to degrees.
  **Parameters:**    radians   An angle, in radians
  **Returns:**       The angle in degrees

- `static double` **`toRadians`**`(double degrees)`
  This methods converts degrees to radians.
  **Parameters:**    degrees   An angle, in degrees
  **Returns:**       The angle in radians

- `static final double E`
  This constant is the value of $e$, the base of the natural logarithms.

- `static final double PI`
  This constant is the value of $\pi$.

## Class java.lang.NullPointerException

This exception is thrown when a program tries to use an object through a `null` reference.

## Class java.lang.NumberFormatException

This exception is thrown when a program tries to parse the numerical value of a string that is not a number.

## Class java.lang.Object

- `boolean` **`equals`**`(Object other)`
  This method tests whether `this` and the other object are equal. This method tests only whether the object references are to the same object. Subclasses should redefine this method to compare the instance variables.
  **Parameters:**    other   The object with which to compare
  **Returns:**       `true` if the objects are equal, `false` otherwise

- void **notify**()
  This method notifies one of the threads that is currently on the wait list for the lock of this object.
- void **notifyAll**()
  This method notifies all of the threads that are currently on the wait list for the lock of this object.
- String **toString**()
  This method returns a string representation of this object. This method produces only the class name and locations of the objects. Subclasses should redefine this method to print the instance variables.
  **Returns:**        A string describing this object
- void **wait**()
  This method blocks the currently executing thread and puts it on the wait list for the lock of this object.

## Interface java.lang.Runnable

- void **run**()
  This method should be overridden to define the tasks to be carried out when this runnable is executed.

## Class java.lang.RuntimeException

This is the superclass for all unchecked exceptions.

## Class java.lang.String

- int **compareTo**(String other)
  This method compares this string and the other string lexicographically.
  **Parameters:**    other   The other string to be compared
  **Returns:**        A value less than 0 if this string is lexicographically less than the other, 0 if the strings are equal, and a value greater than 0 otherwise
- boolean **equals**(String other)
- boolean **equalsIgnoreCase**(String other)
  These methods test whether two strings are equal, or whether they are equal when letter case is ignored.
  **Parameters:**    other   The other string to be compared
  **Returns:**        true if the strings are equal
- static String **format**(String format, Object... values)
  This method formats the given string by substituting placeholders beginning with % with the given values.
  **Parameters:**    format   The string with the placeholders
  values   The values to be substituted for the placeholders
  **Returns:**        The formatted string, with the placeholders replaced by the given values
- int **length**()
  This method returns the length of this string.
  **Returns:**        The count of characters in this string

- String **replace**(String match, String replacement)
  This method replaces matching substrings with a given replacement.
  **Parameters:**   match   The string whose matches are to be replaced
  replacement   The string with which matching substrings are
  replaced
  **Returns:**   A string that is identical to this string, with all matching sub-
  strings replaced by the given replacement
- String **substring**(int begin)
- String **substring**(int begin, int pastEnd)
  These methods return a new string that is a substring of this string, made up of
  all characters starting at position begin and up to either position pastEnd - 1, if it is
  given, or the end of the string.
  **Parameters:**   begin   The beginning index, inclusive
  pastEnd   The ending index, exclusive
  **Returns:**   The specified substring
- String **toLowerCase**()
  This method returns a new string that consists of all characters in this string con-
  verted to lowercase.
  **Returns:**   A string with all characters in this string converted to lowercase
- String **toUpperCase**()
  This method returns a new string that consists of all characters in this string con-
  verted to uppercase.
  **Returns:**   A string with all characters in this string converted to uppercase

## Class java.lang.System

- static long **currentTimeMillis**()
  This method returns the difference, measured in milliseconds, between the current time and midnight, Universal Time, January 1, 1970.
  **Returns:**   The current time in milliseconds since January 1, 1970.
- static void **exit**(int status)
  This method terminates the program.
  **Parameters:**   status   Exit status. A nonzero status code indicates abnormal
  termination
- static final InputStream in
  This object is the "standard input" stream. Reading from this stream typically
  reads keyboard input.
- static final PrintStream out
  This object is the "standard output" stream. Printing to this stream typically
  sends output to the console window.

## Class java.lang.Thread

- boolean **interrupted**()
  This method tests whether another thread has called the interrupt method on the current thread.
  **Returns:**          true if the thread has been interrupted

- static void **sleep**(int millis)
  This method puts the calling thread to sleep.
  **Parameters:**     millis  The number of millseconds to sleep

- void **start**()
  This method starts the thread and executes its run method.

## Class java.lang.Throwable

This is the superclass of exceptions and errors.

- **Throwable**()
  This constructs a Throwable with no detail message.

- String **getMessage**()
  This method gets the message that describes the exception or error.
  **Returns:**          The message

- void **printStackTrace**()
  This method prints a stack trace to the "standard error" stream. The stack trace contains a printout of this object and of all calls that were pending at the time it was created.

# Package java.math

## Class java.math.BigDecimal

- **BigDecimal**(String value)
  This constructs an arbitrary-precision floating-point number from the digits in the given string.
  **Parameters:**     value  A string representing the floating-point number

- BigDecimal **add**(BigDecimal other)
- BigDecimal **multiply**(BigDecimal other)
- BigDecimal **subtract**(BigDecimal other)
  These methods return a BigDecimal whose value is the sum, difference, product, or quotient of this number and the other.
  **Parameters:**     other  The other number
  **Returns:**          The result of the arithmetic operation

## Class java.math.BigInteger

- **BigInteger**(String value)
  This constructs an arbitrary-precision integer from the digits in the given string.
  **Parameters:**     value  A string representing an arbitrary-precision integer

- BigInteger **add**(BigInteger other)
- BigInteger **divide**(BigInteger other)
- BigInteger **mod**(BigInteger other)
- BigInteger **multiply**(BigInteger other)
- BigInteger **subtract**(BigInteger other)

These methods return a BigInteger whose value is the sum, quotient, remainder, product, or difference of this number and the other.

**Parameters:** other The other number

**Returns:** The result of the arithmetic operation

# Package java.net

## Class java.net.HttpURLConnection

- int **getResponseCode**()
  This method gets the response status code from this connection. A value of HTTP_OK indicates success.
  **Returns:** The HTTP response code

- String **getResponseMessage**()
  This method gets the response message of this connection's HTTP request.
  **Returns:** The message, such as "OK" or "File not found"

- static int HTTP_OK
  This response code indicates a successful fulfillment of the request.

## Class java.net.ServerSocket

- **ServerSocket**(int port)
  This constructs a server socket that listens to the given port.
  **Parameters:** port The port number to listen to

- Socket **accept**()
  This method waits for a client to connect to the port to which this server socket listens. When a connection occurs, the method returns a socket through which the server can communicate with the client.
  **Returns:** The socket through which the server can communicate with the client

- void **close**()
  This method closes the server socket. Clients can no longer connect.

## Class java.net.Socket

- **Socket**(String host, int port)
  This constructs a socket that connects to a server.
  **Parameters:** host The host name
  port The port number to connect to

- void **close**()
  This method closes the connection with the server.

- InputStream **getInputStream**()
  This method gets the input stream through which the client can read the information that the server sends.
  **Returns:**       The input stream associated with this socket

- OutputStream **getOutputStream**()
  This method gets the output stream through which the client can send information to the server.
  **Returns:**       The output stream associated with this socket

## Class java.net.URL

- **URL**(String s)
  This constructs a URL object from a string containing the URL.
  **Parameters:**       s  The URL string, such as "http://horstmann.com/index.html"

- InputStream openStream()
  This method gets the input stream through which the client can read the information that the server sends.
  **Returns:**       The input stream associated with this URL

## Class java.net.URLConnection

- **URLConnection**(URL u)
  This constructs a URLConnection object from a URL object.
  **Parameters:**       u  The resource to which you intend to connect

- int **getContentLength**()
  This method gets the value of the content-length header of this URL connection.
  **Returns:**       The number of bytes in the content that the server is sending

- String **getContentType**()
  This method gets the value of the content-type header of this URL connection.
  **Returns:**       The MIME type of the content that the server is sending, such as
                      "text/plain" or "image/gif"

- InputStream **getInputStream**()
  This method gets the input stream through which the client can read the information that the server sends.
  **Returns:**       The input stream associated with this URL

- void **setIfModifiedSince**(Date d)
  This method instructs the connection to request that the server send data only if the content has been modified since a given date.
  **Parameters:**       d  The modification date

# Package `java.sql`

## Interface `java.sql.Connection`

- void **close**()
  This method closes the connection with the database.

- void **commit**()
  This method commits all database changes since the last call to `commit` or `rollback`.

- Statement **createStatement**()
  This method creates a statement object, which can be used to issue database commands.
  **Returns:**      A statement object

- PreparedStatement **prepareStatement**(String command)
  This method creates a prepared statement for a SQL command that is issued repeatedly.
  **Parameters:**     command   The SQL command
  **Returns:**      The statement object for setting parameters and executing the call

- void **rollback**()
  This method abandons all database changes since the last call to `commit` or `rollback`.

- void **setAutoCommit**(boolean b)
  This method sets the auto commit mode. By default, it is `true`. If it is set to `false`, then transactions are indicated with calls to `commit` or `rollback`.
  **Parameters:**     b   The desired auto commit mode

## Class `java.sql.DriverManager`

- static Connection **getConnection**(String url, String username, String password)
  This method obtains a connection to the database specified in the database URL.
  **Parameters:**     url   The database URL
                       username   The database user name
                       password   The password for the database user
  **Returns:**      A connection to the database

## Interface `java.sql.PreparedStatement`

- boolean **execute**()
  This method executes this prepared statement.
  **Returns:**      `true` if the execution yielded a result set

- ResultSet **executeQuery**()
  This method executes this prepared query.
  **Returns:**      The query result

- int **executeUpdate**()
  This method executes this prepared update command.
  **Returns:**      The number of records affected by the update

- void **setDouble**(int index, double value)
  This method sets a floating-point parameter for a call of this prepared statement.
  **Parameters:**    index  The parameter index (starting with 1)
                      value  The parameter value

- void **setInt**(int index, int value)
  This method sets an integer parameter for a call of this prepared statement.
  **Parameters:**    index  The parameter index (starting with 1)
                      value  The parameter value

- void **setString**(int index, String value)
  This method sets a string parameter for a call of this prepared statement.
  **Parameters:**    index  The parameter index (starting with 1)
                      value  The parameter value

## Interface java.sql.ResultSet

- void **close**()
  This method closes the result set.

- double **getDouble**(int column)
  This method returns the floating-point value at the cursor row and the given column.
  **Parameters:**    column  The column index (starting with 1)
  **Returns:**       The data value

- double **getDouble**(String columnName)
  This method returns the floating-point value at the cursor row and the given column name.
  **Parameters:**    columnName  The column name
  **Returns:**       The data value

- int **getInt**(int column)
  This method returns the integer value at the cursor row and the given column.
  **Parameters:**    column  The column index (starting with 1)
  **Returns:**       The data value

- int **getInt**(String columnName)
  This method returns the integer value at the cursor row and the given column name.
  **Parameters:**    columnName  The column name
  **Returns:**       The data value

- ResultSetMetaData **getMetaData**()
  This method returns the metadata associated with this result set.
  **Returns:**       The metadata

- String **getString**(int column)
  This method returns the value at the cursor row and the given column.
  **Parameters:**    column  The column index (starting with 1)
  **Returns:**       The data value, as a string

- `String` **`getString`**`(String columnName)`
  This method returns the value at the cursor row and the given column name.
  **Parameters:** `columnName`   The column name
  **Returns:**       The data value, as a string

- `boolean` **`next`**`()`
  This method positions the cursor to the next row. You must call `next` once before calling any of the `get` methods to move the cursor to the first row.
  **Returns:**       `true` if the cursor has been positioned on a row, `false` at the end of the result set

## Interface `java.sql.ResultSetMetaData`

- `int` **`getColumnCount`**`()`
  This method returns the number of columns of this result set.
  **Returns:**       The number of columns

- `int` **`getColumnDisplaySize`**`(int column)`
  This method returns the number of characters that should be used to display the specified column in this result set.
  **Parameters:** `column`   The column index (starting with 1)
  **Returns:**       The number of characters that should be used to display this column

- `String` **`getColumnLabel`**`(int column)`
  This method returns the label for a column in this result set.
  **Parameters:** `column`   The column index (starting with 1)
  **Returns:**       The column label

## Class `java.sql.SQLException`

This exception is thrown when a database error occurs.

## Interface `java.sql.Statement`

- `void` **`close`**`()`
  This method closes this statement.

- `boolean` **`execute`**`(String command)`
  This method executes a SQL command.
  **Parameters:** `command`   The command to execute
  **Returns:**       `true` if the execution yielded a result set

- `ResultSet` **`executeQuery`**`(String command)`
  This method executes a SQL query.
  **Parameters:** `command`   The query command to execute
  **Returns:**       The query result

- `int` **`executeUpdate`**`(String command)`
  This method executes a SQL update command.
  **Parameters:** `command`   The update command to execute
  **Returns:**       The number of records affected by the update

- `ResultSet getResultSet()`
  This method gets the result of the last command.
  **Returns:**      The query result from the last command
- `int getUpdateCount()`
  This method gets the update count of the last command.
  **Returns:**      The number of records affected by the last command

# Package java.text

## Class java.text.DateFormat

- `String format(Date aDate)`
  This method formats a date.
  **Parameters:**    aDate  The date to format
  **Returns:**      A string containing the formatted date
- `static DateFormat getTimeInstance()`
  This method returns a formatter that formats only the time portion of a date.
  **Returns:**      The formatter object
- `void setTimeZone(TimeZone zone)`
  This method sets the time zone to be used when formatting dates.
  **Parameters:**    zone  The time zone to use

# Package java.util

## Class java.util.ArrayList<E>

- `ArrayList()`
  This constructs an empty array list.
- `boolean add(E element)`
  This method appends an element to the end of this array list.
  **Parameters:**    element  The element to add
  **Returns:**      true (This method returns a value because it overrides a method in the List interface.)
- `void add(int index, E element)`
  This method inserts an element into this array list at the given position.
  **Parameters:**    index  Insert position
                      element  The element to insert
- `E get(int index)`
  This method gets the element at the specified position in this array list.
  **Parameters:**    index  Position of the element to return
  **Returns:**      The requested element

- E **remove**(int index)
  This method removes the element at the specified position in this array list and returns it.
  **Parameters:**     index   Position of the element to remove
  **Returns:**         The removed element

- E **set**(int index, E element)
  This method replaces the element at a specified position in this array list.
  **Parameters:**     index   Position of element to replace
                       element   Element to be stored at the specified position
  **Returns:**         The element previously at the specified position

- int **size**()
  This method returns the number of elements in this array list.
  **Returns:**         The number of elements in this array list

## Class java.util.Arrays

- static int **binarySearch**(Object[] a, Object key)
  This method searches the specified array for the specified object using the binary search algorithm. The array elements must implement the Comparable interface. The array must be sorted in ascending order.
  **Parameters:**     a   The array to be searched
                       key   The value to be searched for
  **Returns:**         The position of the search key, if it is contained in the array; otherwise, *-index* – 1, where *index* is the position where the element may be inserted

- static *T*[] **copyOf**(*T*[] a, int newLength)
  This method copies the elements of the array a, or the first newLength elements if a.length > newLength, into an array of length newLength and returns that array. *T* can be a primitive type, class, or interface type.
  **Parameters:**     a   The array to be copied
                       key   The value to be searched for
  **Returns:**         The position of the search key, if it is contained in the array; otherwise, *-index* – 1, where *index* is the position where the element may be inserted

- static void **sort**(Object[] a)
  This method sorts the specified array of objects into ascending order. Its elements must implement the Comparable interface.
  **Parameters:**     a   The array to be sorted

- static String **toString**(*T*[] a)
  This method creates and returns a string containing the array elements. *T* can be a primitive type, class, or interface type.
  **Parameters:**     a   An array
  **Returns:**         A string containing a comma-separated list of string representations of the array elements, surrounded by brackets.

## Class `java.util.Calendar`

- `int get(int field)`
  This method returns the value of the given field.
  **Parameters:**  `field`  One of `Calendar.YEAR`, `Calendar.MONTH`,
  `Calendar.DAY_OF_MONTH`, `Calendar.HOUR`, `Calendar.MINUTE`,
  `Calendar.SECOND`, or `Calendar.MILLISECOND`

## Interface `java.util.Collection<E>`

- `boolean add(E element)`
  This method adds an element to this collection.
  **Parameters:**  `element`  The element to add
  **Returns:**  `true` if adding the element changes the collection
- `boolean contains(E element)`
  This method tests whether an element is present in this collection.
  **Parameters:**  `element`  The element to find
  **Returns:**  `true` if the element is contained in the collection
- `Iterator iterator()`
  This method returns an iterator that can be used to traverse the elements of this collection.
  **Returns:**  An object of a class implementing the `Iterator` interface
- `boolean remove(E element)`
  This method removes an element from this collection.
  **Parameters:**  `element`  The element to remove
  **Returns:**  `true` if removing the element changes the collection
- `int size()`
  This method returns the number of elements in this collection.
  **Returns:**  The number of elements in this collection

## Class `java.util.Collections`

- `static <T> int binarySearch(List<T> a, T key)`
  This method searches the specified list for the specified object using the binary search algorithm. The list elements must implement the `Comparable` interface. The list must be sorted in ascending order.
  **Parameters:**  a  The list to be searched
  key  The value to be searched for
  **Returns:**  The position of the search key, if it is contained in the list; otherwise, −*index* − 1, where *index* is the position where the element may be inserted
- `static <T> void sort(List<T> a)`
  This method sorts the specified list of objects into ascending order. Its elements must implement the `Comparable` interface.
  **Parameters:**  a  The list to be sorted

## Interface java.util.Comparator<T>

- int **compare**(T first, T second)
  This method compares the given objects.
  **Parameters:**      first, second   The objects to be compared
  **Returns:**          A negative integer if the first object is less than the second, zero if
  they are equal, or a positive integer otherwise

## Class java.util.Date

- **Date**()
  This constructs an object that represents the current date and time.

## Class java.util.EventObject

- Object **getSource**()
  This method returns a reference to the object on which this event initially
  occurred.
  **Returns:**          The source of this event

## Class java.util.GregorianCalendar

- **GregorianCalendar**()
  This constructs a calendar object that represents the current date and time.

- **GregorianCalendar**(int year, int month, int day)
  This constructs a calendar object that represents the start of the given date.
  **Parameters:**      year, month, day   The given date

## Class java.util.HashMap<K, V>

- **HashMap**<K, V>()
  This constructs an empty hash map.

## Class java.util.HashSet<E>

- **HashSet**<E>()
  This constructs an empty hash set.

## Class java.util.InputMismatchException

This exception is thrown if the next available input item does not match the type
of the requested item.

## Interface java.util.Iterator<E>

- boolean **hasNext**()
  This method checks whether the iterator is past the end of the list.
  **Returns:**          true if the iterator is not yet past the end of the list

- E **next**()
  This method moves the iterator over the next element in the linked list. This method throws an exception if the iterator is past the end of the list.
  **Returns:**        The object that was just skipped over

- void **remove**()
  This method removes the element that was returned by the last call to next or previous. This method throws an exception if there was an add or remove operation after the last call to next or previous.

## Class java.util.LinkedHashMap<K, V>

- **LinkedHashMap**<K, V>()
  This constructs an empty linked hash map. The iterator of a linked hash map visits the entries in the order in which they were added to the map.

## Class java.util.LinkedList<E>

- void **addFirst**(E element)
- void **addLast**(E element)
  These methods add an element before the first or after the last element in this list.
  **Parameters:**        element  The element to be added

- E **getFirst**()
- E **getLast**()
  These methods return a reference to the specified element from this list.
  **Returns:**        The first or last element

- E **removeFirst**()
- E **removeLast**()
  These methods remove the specified element from this list.
  **Returns:**        A reference to the removed element

## Interface java.util.List<E>

- ListIterator<E> **listIterator**()
  This method gets an iterator to visit the elements in this list.
  **Returns:**        An iterator that points before the first element in this list

## Interface java.util.ListIterator<E>

  Objects implementing this interface are created by the listIterator methods of list classes.

- void **add**(E element)
  This method adds an element after the iterator position and moves the iterator after the new element.
  **Parameters:**        element  The element to be added

- boolean **hasPrevious**()
  This method checks whether the iterator is before the first element of the list.
  **Returns:**        true if the iterator is not before the first element of the list

- E **previous**()
  This method moves the iterator over the previous element in the linked list. This method throws an exception if the iterator is before the first element of the list.
  **Returns:**     The object that was just skipped over

- void **set**(E element)
  This method replaces the element that was returned by the last call to next or previous. This method throws an exception if there was an add or remove operation after the last call to next or previous.
  **Parameters:**     element   The element that replaces the old list element

## Interface java.util.Map<K, V>

- V **get**(K key)
  Gets the value associated with a key in this map.
  **Parameters:**     key   The key for which to find the associated value
  **Returns:**     The value associated with the key, or null if the key is not present in the map

- Set<K> **keySet**()
  This method returns all keys this map.
  **Returns:**     A set of all keys in this map

- V **put**(K key, V value)
  This method associates a value with a key in this map.
  **Parameters:**     key   The lookup key
                      value   The value to associate with the key
  **Returns:**     The value previously associated with the key, or null if the key was not present in the map

- V **remove**(K key)
  This method removes a key and its associated value from this map.
  **Parameters:**     key   The lookup key
  **Returns:**     The value previously associated with the key, or null if the key was not present in the map

## Class java.util.NoSuchElementException

This exception is thrown if an attempt is made to retrieve a value that does not exist.

## Class java.util.PriorityQueue<E>

- PriorityQueue<E>()
  This constructs an empty priority queue. The element type E must implement the Comparable interface.

- E **remove**()
  This method removes the smallest element in the priority queue.
  **Returns:**     The removed value

# Class `java.util.Properties`

- String **getProperty**(String key)

  This method gets the value associated with a key in this properties map.

  **Parameters:**   key   The key for which to find the associated value

  **Returns:**            The value, or `null` if the key is not present in the map

- void **load**(InputStream in)

  This method loads a set of key/value pairs into this properties map from a stream.

  **Parameters:**   in   The stream from which to read the key/value pairs (it must be a sequence of lines of the form `key=value`)

# Interface `java.util.Queue<E>`

- E **peek**()

  Gets the element at the head of the queue without removing it.

  **Returns:**            The head element or `null` if the queue is empty

# Class `java.util.Random`

- **Random**()

  This constructs a new random number generator.

- double **nextDouble**()

  This method returns the next pseudorandom, uniformly distributed floating-point number between 0.0 (inclusive) and 1.0 (exclusive) from this random number generator's sequence.

  **Returns:**            The next pseudorandom floating-point number

- int **nextInt**(int n)

  This method returns the next pseudorandom, uniformly distributed integer between 0 (inclusive) and the specified value (exclusive) drawn from this random number generator's sequence.

  **Parameters:**   n   Number of values to draw from

  **Returns:**            The next pseudorandom integer

# Class `java.util.Scanner`

- **Scanner**(File in)
- **Scanner**(InputStream in)
- **Scanner**(Reader in)

  These construct a scanner that reads from the given file, input stream, or reader.

  **Parameters:**   in   The file, input stream, or reader from which to read

- void **close**()

  This method closes this scanner and releases any associated system resources.

- boolean **hasNext**()
- boolean **hasNextDouble**()
- boolean **hasNextInt**()
- boolean **hasNextLine**()

These methods test whether it is possible to read any non-empty string, a floating-point value, an integer, or a line, as the next item.

**Returns:** true if it is possible to read an item of the requested type, false otherwise (either because the end of the file has been reached, or because a number type was tested and the next item is not a number)

- String **next**()
- double **nextDouble**()
- int **nextInt**()
- String **nextLine**()

These methods read the next whitespace-delimited string, floating-point value, integer, or line.

**Returns:** The value that was read

- Scanner **useDelimiter**(String pattern)

Sets the pattern for the delimiters between input tokens.

**Parameters:** pattern A regular expression for the delimiter pattern
**Returns:** This scanner

## Interface java.util.Set<E>

This interface describes a collection that contains no duplicate elements.

## Class java.util.TimeZone

- static String[] **getAvailableIDs**()

This method gets the supported time zone IDs.

**Returns:** An array of ID strings

- static TimeZone **getTimeZone**(String id)

This method gets the time zone for a time zone ID.

**Parameters:** id The time zone ID, such as "America/Los_Angeles"
**Returns:** The time zone object associated with the ID, or null if the ID is not supported

## Class java.util.TreeMap<K, V>

- TreeMap<K, V>()

This constructs an empty tree map. The iterator of a TreeMap visits the entries in sorted order.

## Class java.util.TreeSet<E>

- TreeSet<E>()

This constructs an empty tree set.

# Package java.util.concurrent.locks

## Interface java.util.concurrent.locks.Condition

- void await()
  This method blocks the current thread until it is signalled or interrupted.
- void signal()
  This method unblocks one thread that is waiting on this condition.
- void signalAll()
  This method unblocks all threads that are waiting on this condition.

## Interface java.util.concurrent.locks.Lock

- void lock()
  This method causes the current thread to acquire this lock. The thread blocks if the lock is not available.
- Condition newCondition()
  This method creates a new condition object for this lock.
  **Returns:**          The condition object
- void unlock()
  This method causes the current thread to relinquish this lock.

## Class java.util.concurrent.locks.ReentrantLock

- ReentrantLock()
  This constructs a new reentrant lock.

# Package java.util.logging

## Class java.util.logging.Level

- static final int INFO
  This value indicates informational logging.
- static final int OFF
  This value indicates logging of no messages.

## Class java.util.logging.Logger

- static Logger getGlobal()
  This method gets the global logger. For Java 5 and 6, use getLogger("global") instead.
  **Returns:**          The global logger that, by default, displays messages with level INFO or a higher severity on the console.

- void **info**(String message)
  This method logs an informational message.
  **Parameters:**     message   The message to log

- void **setLevel**(Level aLevel)
  This method sets the logging level. Logging messages with a lesser severity than the current level are ignored.
  **Parameters:**     aLevel   The minimum level for logging messages

# Package javax.swing

## Class javax.swing.AbstractButton

- void **addActionListener**(ActionListener listener)
  This method adds an action listener to the button.
  **Parameters:**     listener   The action listener to be added

- boolean **isSelected**()
  This method returns the selection state of the button.
  **Returns:**          true if the button is selected

- void **setSelected**(boolean state)
  This method sets the selection state of the button. This method updates the button but does not trigger an action event.
  **Parameters:**     state   true to select, false to deselect

## Class javax.swing.ButtonGroup

- void **add**(AbstractButton button)
  This method adds the button to the group.
  **Parameters:**     button   The button to add

## Class javax.swing.ImageIcon

- **ImageIcon**(String filename)
  This constructs an image icon from the specified graphics file.
  **Parameters:**     filename   A string specifying a file name

## Class javax.swing.JButton

- **JButton**(String label)
  This constructs a button with the given label.
  **Parameters:**     label   The button label

## Class javax.swing.JCheckBox

- **JCheckBox**(String text)
  This constructs a check box with the given text, which is initially deselected.
  (Use the setSelected method to make the box selected; see the javax.swing.
  AbstractButton class.)
  **Parameters:**     text  The text displayed next to the check box

## Class javax.swing.JComboBox

- **JComboBox**()
  This constructs a combo box with no items.
- void **addItem**(Object item)
  This method adds an item to the item list of this combo box.
  **Parameters:**     item  The item to add
- Object **getSelectedItem**()
  This method gets the currently selected item of this combo box.
  **Returns:**          The currently selected item
- boolean **isEditable**()
  This method checks whether the combo box is editable. An editable combo box
  allows the user to type into the text field of the combo box.
  **Returns:**          true if the combo box is editable
- void **setEditable**(boolean state)
  This method is used to make the combo box editable or not.
  **Parameters:**     state  true to make editable, false to disable editing
- void **setSelectedItem**(Object item)
  This method sets the item that is shown in the display area of the combo box as
  selected.
  **Parameters:**     item  The item to be displayed as selected

## Class javax.swing.JComponent

- protected void **paintComponent**(Graphics g)
  Override this method to paint the surface of a component. Your method needs to
  call super.paintComponent(g).
  **Parameters:**     g  The graphics context used for drawing
- void **setBorder**(Border b)
  This method sets the border of this component.
  **Parameters:**     b  The border to surround this component
- void **setFont**(Font f)
  Sets the font used for the text in this component.
  **Parameters:**     f  A font

## Class `javax.swing.JFileChooser`

- `JFileChooser()`
  This constructs a file chooser.

- `File getSelectedFile()`
  This method gets the selected file from this file chooser.
  **Returns:**      The selected file

- `int showOpenDialog(Component parent)`
  This method displays an "Open File" file chooser dialog box.
  **Parameters:**      parent  The parent component or `null`
  **Returns:**      The return state of this file chooser after it has been closed by
  the user: either `APPROVE_OPTION` or `CANCEL_OPTION`. If `APPROVE_OPTION` is
  returned, call `getSelectedFile()` on this file chooser to get the file

- `int showSaveDialog(Component parent)`
  This method displays a "Save File" file chooser dialog box.
  **Parameters:**      parent  The parent component or `null`
  **Returns:**      The return state of the file chooser after it has been closed by the
  user: either `APPROVE_OPTION` or `CANCEL_OPTION`

## Class `javax.swing.JFrame`

- `void setDefaultCloseOperation(int operation)`
  This method sets the default action for closing the frame.
  **Parameters:**      operation  The desired close operation. Choose among
  `DO_NOTHING_ON_CLOSE`, `HIDE_ON_CLOSE` (the default), `DISPOSE_ON_CLOSE`,
  or `EXIT_ON_CLOSE`

- `void setJMenuBar(JMenuBar mb)`
  This method sets the menu bar for this frame.
  **Parameters:**      mb  The menu bar. If `mb` is `null`, then the current menu bar is
  removed

- `static final int EXIT_ON_CLOSE`
  This value indicates that when the user closes this frame, the application is to exit.

## Class `javax.swing.JLabel`

- `JLabel(String text)`
- `JLabel(String text, int alignment)`
  These containers create a `JLabel` instance with the specified text and horizontal
  alignment.
  **Parameters:**      text  The label text to be displayed by the label
                      alignment  One of `SwingConstants.LEFT`, `SwingConstants.CENTER`, or
                      `SwingConstants.RIGHT`

## Class `javax.swing.JMenu`

- `JMenu()`
  This constructs a menu with no items.

- JMenuItem **add**(JMenuItem menuItem)
  This method appends a menu item to the end of this menu.
  **Parameters:**    menuItem  The menu item to be added
  **Returns:**        The menu item that was added

## Class javax.swing.JMenuBar

- JMenuBar()
  This constructs a menu bar with no menus.
- JMenu **add**(JMenu menu)
  This method appends a menu to the end of this menu bar.
  **Parameters:**    menu  The menu to be added
  **Returns:**        The menu that was added

## Class javax.swing.JMenuItem

- JMenuItem(String text)
  This constructs a menu item.
  **Parameters:**    text  The text to appear in the menu item

## Class javax.swing.JOptionPane

- static String **showInputDialog**(Object prompt)
  This method brings up a modal input dialog box, which displays a prompt and waits for the user to enter an input in a text field, preventing the user from doing anything else in this program.
  **Parameters:**    prompt  The prompt to display
  **Returns:**        The string that the user typed
- static void **showMessageDialog**(Component parent, Object message)
  This method brings up a confirmation dialog box that displays a message and waits for the user to confirm it.
  **Parameters:**    parent  The parent component or null
                   message  The message to display

## Class javax.swing.JPanel

This class is a component without decorations. It can be used as an invisible container for other components.

## Class javax.swing.JRadioButton

- JRadioButton(String text)
  This constructs a radio button having the given text that is initially deselected. (Use the setSelected method to select it; see the javax.swing.AbstractButton class.)
  **Parameters:**    text  The string displayed next to the radio button

## Class javax.swing.JScrollPane

- JScrollPane(Component c)
  This constructs a scroll pane around the given component.
  **Parameters:**    c  The component that is decorated with scroll bars

## Class javax.swing.JSlider

- JSlider(int min, int max, int value)
  This constructor creates a horizontal slider using the specified minimum, maximum, and value.
  **Parameters:**     min   The smallest possible slider value
  max   The largest possible slider value
  value   The initial value of the slider
- void **addChangeListener**(ChangeListener listener)
  This method adds a change listener to the slider.
  **Parameters:**     listener   The change listener to add
- int **getValue**()
  This method returns the slider's value.
  **Returns:**        The current value of the slider

## Class javax.swing.JTextArea

- JTextArea()
  This constructs an empty text area.
- JTextArea(int rows, int columns)
  This constructs an empty text area with the specified number of rows and columns.
  **Parameters:**     rows   The number of rows
  columns   The number of columns
- void **append**(String text)
  This method appends text to this text area.
  **Parameters:**     text   The text to append

## Class javax.swing.JTextField

- JTextField()
  This constructs an empty text field.
- JTextField(int columns)
  This constructs an empty text field with the specified number of columns.
  **Parameters:**     columns   The number of columns

## Class javax.swing.KeyStroke

- static KeyStroke **getKeyStrokeForEvent**(KeyEvent event)
  Gets a KeyStroke object describing the key stroke that caused the event.
  **Parameters:**     event   The key event to be analyzed
  **Returns:**        A KeyStroke object. Call toString on this object to get a string representation such as "pressed LEFT"

## Class javax.swing.Timer

- **Timer**(int millis, ActionListener listener)
  This constructs a timer that notifies an action listener whenever a time interval has elapsed.
  **Parameters:**   millis   The number of milliseconds between timer notifications
  listener   The object to be notified when the time interval has elapsed

- void **start**()
  This method starts the timer. Once the timer has started, it begins notifying its listener.

- void **stop**()
  This method stops the timer. Once the timer has stopped, it no longer notifies its listener.

# Package javax.swing.border

## Class javax.swing.border.EtchedBorder

- **EtchedBorder**()
  This constructor creates a lowered etched border.

## Class javax.swing.border.TitledBorder

- **TitledBorder**(Border b, String title)
  This constructor creates a titled border that adds a title to a given border.
  **Parameters:**   b   The border to which the title is added
  title   The title the border should display

# Package javax.swing.event

## Class javax.swing.event.ChangeEvent

Components such as sliders emit change events when they are manipulated by the user.

## Interface javax.swing.event.ChangeListener

- void **stateChanged**(ChangeEvent e)
  This event is called when the event source has changed its state.
  **Parameters:**   e   A change event

# Package javax.swing.text

## Class javax.swing.text.JTextComponent

- String **getText**()
  This method returns the text contained in this text component.
  **Returns:** The text

- boolean **isEditable**()
  This method checks whether this text component is editable.
  **Returns:** true if the component is editable

- void **setEditable**(boolean state)
  This method is used to make this text component editable or not.
  **Parameters:** state  true to make editable, false to disable editing

- void **setText**(String text)
  This method sets the text of this text component to the specified text. If the argument is the empty string, the old text is deleted.
  **Parameters:** text  The new text to be set

# Package javax.xml.parsers

## Class javax.xml.parsers.DocumentBuilder

- Document **newDocument**()
  This constructs a new document object.
  **Returns:** An empty document

- Document **parse**(File in)
  This method parses an XML document in a file.
  **Parameters:** in  The file containing the document
  **Returns:** The parsed document

- Document **parse**(InputStream in)
  This method parses an XML document in a stream.
  **Parameters:** in  The stream containing the document
  **Returns:** The parsed document

## Class javax.xml.parsers.DocumentBuilderFactory

- DocumentBuilder **newDocumentBuilder**()
  This method creates a new document builder object.
  **Returns:** The document builder

- static DocumentBuilderFactory **newInstance**()
  This method creates a new document builder factory object.
  **Returns:**           The document builder factory object
- void **setIgnoringElementContentWhitespace**(boolean b)
  This method sets the parsing mode for ignoring white space in element content for all document builders that are generated from this factory.
  **Parameters:**      b   true if white space should be ignored
- void **setValidating**(boolean b)
  This method sets the validation mode for all document builders that are generated from this factory.
  **Parameters:**      b   true if documents should be validated during parsing

# Package javax.xml.xpath

## Interface javax.xml.xpath.XPath

- String **evaluate**(String path, Object context)
  This method evaluates the given path expression in the given context.
  **Parameters:**      path   An XPath expression
                       context   The starting context for the evaluation, such as a document, node, or node list
  **Returns:**           The result of the evaluation

## Class javax.xml.xpath.XPathExpressionException

This exception is thrown when an XPath expression cannot be evaluated.

## Class javax.xml.xpath.XPathFactory

- static XPathFactory **newInstance**()
  This method returns a factory instance that can be used to construct XPath objects.
  **Returns:**           An XPathFactory instance
- XPath **newXPath**()
  This method returns an XPath object that can be used to evaluate XPath expressions.
  **Returns:**           An XPath object

# Package `org.w3c.dom`

## Interface `org.w3c.dom.Document`

- `Element` **`createElement`**`(String tagName)`
  This method creates a new document element with a given tag.
  **Parameters:**     `tagName`   The name of the XML tag
  **Returns:**        The created element

- `Text` **`createTextNode`**`(String text)`
  This method creates a text node with the given text.
  **Parameters:**     `text`   The text for the text node
  **Returns:**        The created text node

- `DOMImplementation` **`getImplementation`**`()`
  This method returns the `DOMImplementation` object associated with this document.

## Interface `org.w3c.dom.DOMConfiguration`

- `void` **`setParameter`**`(String name, Object value)`
  This method sets the value of a configuration parameter.
  **Parameters:**     `name`   The name of the parameter to set
                  `value`   The new value or `null` to unset the parameter

## Interface `org.w3c.dom.DOMImplementation`

- `Object` **`getFeature`**`(String feature, String version)`
  This method gets an object that implements a specialized API (such as loading and saving of DOM trees).
  **Parameters:**     `feature`   The feature version (such as "LS")
                  `version`   The version number (such as "3.0")
  **Returns:**        The feature object

## Interface `org.w3c.dom.Element`

- `String` **`getAttribute`**`(String attributeName)`
  This method returns the value of a given attribute.
  **Parameters:**     `attributeName`   The name of the XML attribute
  **Returns:**        The attribute value, or the empty string "" if that attribute does not exist for this element

- `void` **`setAttribute`**`(String name, String value)`
  This method sets the value of a given attribute.
  **Parameters:**     `name`   The name of the XML attribute
                  `value`   The desired value of the XML attribute

## Interface `org.w3c.dom.Text`

This interface describes a node that contains the textual content of an XML element.

# Package org.w3c.dom.ls

## Interface org.w3c.dom.ls.DOMImplementationLS

- LSSerializer **createLSSerializer**()
  This method creates a serializer object that can be used to convert a DOM tree to a string or stream.
  **Returns:**        The serializer object

## Interface org.w3c.dom.ls.LSSerializer

- DOMConfiguration **getDomConfig**()
  This method gets the configuration object that allows customization of the serializer behavior.

- String **writeToString**(Node root)
  This method converts the DOM tree starting at the given node to a string.
  **Parameters:**    node  The root node of the tree
  **Returns:**        The string representation of the tree

# JAVA SYNTAX SUMMARY

In this syntax summary, we use a monospaced font for actual Java reserved words and tokens such as `while`. An italic font denotes language constructs such as *condition* or *variable*. Items enclosed in brackets [ ] are optional. Items separated by vertical bars | are alternatives. Do not include the brackets or vertical bars in your code!

The summary reflects the parts of the Java language that were covered in this book. For a full overview of the Java syntax, see `http://download.oracle.com/javase/7/docs/api/`.

Please be careful to distinguish an ellipsis . . . from the ... token. The latter appears twice in this appendix in the "variable parameters" discussion in the "Methods" section.

## Types

A type is a primitive type or a reference type. The primitive types are

- The numeric types `int`, `long`, `short`, `char`, `byte`, `float`, `double`
- The `boolean` type

The reference types are

- Classes such as `String` or `Employee`
- Enumeration types such as `enum Sex { FEMALE, MALE }`
- Interfaces such as `Comparable`
- Array types such as `Employee[]` or `int[][]`

## Variables

Local variable declarations have the form

    [final] *Type variableName* [= *initializer*];

Examples:

```
int n;
double x = 0;
String harry = "Harry Handsome";
Rectangle box = new Rectangle(5, 10, 20, 30);
int[] a = { 1, 4, 9, 16, 25 };
```

The variable name consists only of letters, numbers, and underscores. It must begin with a letter or underscore. Names are case-sensitive: `totalscore`, `TOTALSCORE`, and `totalScore` are three different variables.

The scope of a local variable extends from the point of its definition to the end of the enclosing block.

A variable that is declared as final can have its value set only once.

Instance variables will be discussed under "Classes".

# Expressions

An *expression* is a variable, a method call, or a combination of subexpressions joined by operators. Examples are:

```
x
Math.sin(x)
x + Math.sin(x)
x * (1 + Math.sin(x))
x++
x == y
x == y && (z > 0 || w > 0)
p.x
e.getSalary()
v[i]
```

Operators can be *unary*, *binary*, or *ternary*. A unary operator acts on a single expression, such as x++. A binary operator combines two expressions, such as x + y. A ternary operator combines three expressions. Java has one ternary operator, ? : (see Special Topic 3.1).

Unary operators can be *prefix* or *postfix*. A prefix operator is written before the expression on which it operates, as in -x. A postfix operator is written after the expression on which it operates, such as x++.

Operators are ranked by *precedence* levels. Operators with a higher precedence bind more strongly than operators with a lower precedence. For example, * has a higher precedence than +, so x + y * z is the same as x + (y * z), even though the + comes first.

Most operators are *left-associative*. That is, operators of the same precedence are evaluated from the left to the right. For example, x - y + z is interpreted as (x - y) + z, not x - (y + z). The exceptions are the unary prefix operators and the assignment operator which are right-associative. For example, z = y = Math.sin(x) means the same as z = (y = Math.sin(x)).

Appendix B has a list of all Java operators.

# Classes

The syntax for a *class* is

```
[public] [abstract|final] class ClassName
      [extends SuperClassName]
      [implements InterfaceName₁, InterfaceName₂, . . .]
{
   feature₁
   feature₂
   . . .
}
```

Each *feature* is either a declaration of the form

> *modifiers  constructor|method|instance variable|class*

or an initialization block

> [static] { *body* }

See the section "Constructors" for more information about initialization blocks.
Potential *modifiers* include `public`, `private`, `protected`, `static`, and `final`.
An *instance variable* declaration has the form

> *Type variableName* [= *initializer*];

A *constructor* has the form

> *ClassName*(*parameter*$_1$, *parameter*$_2$, . . .)
>      [throws *ExceptionType*$_1$, *ExceptionType*$_2$, . . .]
> {
>      *body*
> }

A *method* has the form

> *Type methodName*(*parameter*$_1$, *parameter*$_2$, . . .)
>      [throws *ExceptionType*$_1$, *ExceptionType*$_2$, . . .]
> {
>      *body*
> }

An *abstract method* has the form

> abstract *Type methodName*(*parameter*$_1$, *parameter*$_2$, . . .);

Here is an example:

```java
public class Point
{
    private double x;   // Instance variable
    private double y;

    public Point()   // Constructor with no arguments
    {
        x = 0; y = 0;
    }

    public Point(double xx, double yy)   // Constructor
    {
        x = xx; y = yy;
    }

    public double getX()   // Method
    {
        return x;
    }

    public double getY()   // Method
    {
        return y;
    }
}
```

A class can have both instance variables and static variables. Each object of the class has a separate copy of the instance variables. There is only a one per-class copy of the static variables.

A class that is declared as abstract cannot be instantiated. That is, you cannot construct objects of that class.

A class that is declared as final cannot be extended.

# Interfaces

The syntax for an interface is

```
[public] interface InterfaceName
        [extends InterfaceName₁, InterfaceName₂, . . .]
{
    feature₁
    feature₂
    . . .
}
```

Each feature has the form

*modifiers  method | instance variable*

Potential modifiers are public, static, final. However, modifiers are never necessary because methods are automatically public and instance variables are automatically public static final.

An instance variable declaration has the form

*Type variableName = initializer;*

A method declaration has the form

*Type methodName(parameter₁, parameter₂, . . .);*

Here is an example:

```
public interface Measurable
{
    int CM_PER_INCH = 2.54;

    int getMeasure();
}
```

# Enumeration Types

The syntax for an enumeration type is

```
[public] enum EnumerationTypeName
{
    constant₁, constant₂, . . .;
    feature₁
    feature₂
    . . .
}
```

Each constant is a constant name, followed by optional construction parameters.

*constantName[(parameter₁, parameter₂, . . .)]*

The semicolon after the constants is only required if the enumeration declares additional features. An enumeration can have the same features as a class. Each feature has the form

*modifiers  method | instance variable*

Potential modifiers are `public`, `static`, `final`.

Here are two examples:

```
public enum Suit { HEARTS, DIAMONDS, SPADES, CLUBS };
public enum Card
{
   TWO(2), THREE(3), FOUR(4), FIVE(5), SIX(6),
       SEVEN(7), EIGHT(8), NINE(9), TEN(10),
       JACK(10), QUEEN(10), KING(10), ACE(11);
   private int value;

   public void Card(int aValue) { value = aValue; }
   public int getValue() { return value; }
}
```

# Methods

A method definition has the form

*modifiers Type methodName*(*parameter*$_1$, *parameter*$_2$, . . ., *parameter*$_n$)
    [throws *ExceptionType*$_1$, *ExceptionType*$_2$, . . .]
{
    *body*
}

The return type *Type* is any Java type, or the special type `void` to indicate that the method returns no value.

Each *parameter variable* has the form

[`final`] *Type parameterName*

A method has variable parameters if the last parameter variable has the special form

*Type . . . parameterName*

Such a method can be called with a sequence of values of the given type of any length. The parameter variable with the given name is an array of the given type that holds the arguments. For example, the method

```
public static double sum(double... values)
{
   double s = 0;
   for (double v : values) { s = s + v; }
   return s;
}
```

can be called as

```
double result = sum(1, -2.5, 3.14);
```

In Java, all parameters are passed by *value*. Each parameter variable is a local variable whose scope extends to the end of the method body. It is initialized with a copy of the value supplied in the call. That value may be a primitive type or a reference type. If it is a reference type, invoking a mutator on the reference will modify the object whose reference has been passed to the method.

Changing the value of the parameter variable has no effect outside the method. Tagging the parameter variable as final disallows such a change altogether. This is commonly done to allow access to the parameter variable from an inner class declared in the method.

Java distinguishes between *instance* methods and *static* methods. Instance methods have a special parameter, the *implicit* parameter, supplied in the method call with the syntax

*implicitParameterValue*.*methodName*(*parameterValue*$_1$, *parameterValue*$_2$, . . .)

Example:

```
harry.setSalary(30000)
```

The type of the implicit parameter must be the same as the type of the class containing the method definition. A static method does not have an implicit parameter.

In the method body, the this variable is initialized with a copy of the implicit parameter value. Using an instance variable name without qualification means to access the instance variable of the implicit parameter. For example,

```
public void setSalary(double s)
{
    salary = s; // i.e., this.salary = s
}
```

By default, Java uses *dynamic method lookup*. The virtual machine determines the class to which the implicit parameter object belongs and invokes the method declared in that class. However, if a method is invoked on the special variable super, then the method declared in the superclass is invoked on this. For example,

```
public class MyPanel extends JPanel
{
    . . .
    public void paintComponent(Graphics g)
    {
        super.paintComponent(g);
        // Calls JPanel.paintComponent
        . . .
    }
    . . .
}
```

The return statement causes a method to exit immediately. If the method type is not void, you must return a value. The syntax is

```
return [value];
```

For example,

```
public double getSalary()
{
    return salary;
}
```

A method can call itself. Such a method is called *recursive:*

```
public static int factorial(int n)
{
    if (n <= 1) { return 1; }
    return n * factorial(n - 1);
}
```

# Constructors

A constructor definition has the form

> *modifiers ClassName*(*parameter*$_1$, *parameter*$_2$, . . .)
>     [throws *ExceptionType*$_1$, *ExceptionType*$_2$, . . .]
> {
>    *body*
> }

You invoke a constructor to allocate and construct a new object with a new expression

> new *ClassName*(*parameterValue*$_1$, *parameterValue*$_2$, . . .)

A constructor can call the body of another constructor of the same class with the syntax

> this(*parameterValue*$_1$, *parameterValue*$_2$, . . .)

For example,

```
public Employee()
{
    this("", 0);
}
```

It can call a constructor of its superclass with the syntax

> super(*parameterValue*$_1$, *parameterValue*$_2$, . . .)

The call to this or super must be the first statement in the constructor.
Arrays are constructed with the syntax

> new *ArrayType* [ = { *initializer*$_1$, *initializer*$_2$, . . . }]

For example,

```
new int[] = { 1, 4, 9, 16, 25 }
```

When an object is constructed, the following actions take place:

- All instance variables are initialized with 0, false, or null.
- The initializers and initialization blocks are executed in the order in which they are declared.
- The body of the constructor is invoked.

When a class is loaded, the following actions take place:

- All static variables are initialized with 0, false, or null.
- The initializers of static variables and static initialization blocks are executed in the order in which they are declared.

# Statements

A *statement* is one of the following:

- An expression followed by a semicolon
- A branch or loop statement
- A return statement

- A throw statement
- A block, that is, a group of variable declarations and statements enclosed in braces {. . .}
- A try block

Java has two branch statements (if and switch), three loop statements (while, for, and do), and two mechanisms for nonlinear control flow (break and continue).

The if statement has the form

if (*condition*) *statement*$_1$ [else *statement*$_2$]

If the *condition* is true, then the first *statement* is executed. Otherwise, the second *statement* is executed.

The switch statement has the form

```
switch (expression)
{
    group₁
    group₂
    . . .
      [default:
      statement₁
      statement₂
      . . .]
}
```

Where each group has the form

```
case constant₁:
case constant₂:

. . .
    statement₁
    statement₂

    . . .
```

The *expression* must be an integer or an enumeration type. Depending on its value, control is transferred to the first statement following the matching case label, or to the first statement following the default label if none of the case labels match. Execution continues with the next statement until a break or return statement is encountered, an exception is thrown, or the end of the switch is reached. Execution skips over any case labels.

The while loop has the form

while (*condition*) *statement*

The *statement* is executed while the *condition* is true.

The for loop has the form

```
for (initExpression|variableDeclaration;
     condition;
     updateExpression₁, updateExpression₂, . . .)
    statement
```

The initialization expression or the variable declaration are executed once. While the *condition* remains true, the loop *statement* and the *updateExpressions* are executed.

Examples:

```
for (i = 0; i < 10; i++)
{
    sum = sum + i;
}

for (int i = 0, j = 9; i < 10; i++, j--)
{
    a[j] = b[i];
}
```

The enhanced for loop has the form

```
for (Type variable : array|iterableObject)
    statement
```

When this loop traverses an array, it is equivalent to

```
for (int i = 0; i < array.length; i++)
{
    Type variable = array[i];
    statement
}
```

Otherwise, the *iterableObject* must belong to a class that implements the Iterable interface. Then the loop is equivalent to

```
Iterator i = iterableObject.iterator();
while (i.hasNext())
{
    Type variable = i.next();
    statement
}
```

The do loop has the form

```
do statement while (condition);
```

The *statement* is repeatedly executed until the *condition* is no longer true. In contrast to a while loop, the statement of a do loop is executed at least once.

The break statement exits the innermost enclosing while, do, for, or switch statement (not counting if or block statements).

Any statement (including if and block statements) can be tagged with a label:

*label*: *statement*

The labeled break statement

```
break label;
```

exits the labeled statement.

The continue statement skips past the end of the *statement* part of a while, do, or for loop. In the case of the while or do loop, the loop *condition* is executed next. In the case of the for loop, the *updateExpressions* are executed next.

The labeled continue statement

```
continue label;
```

skips past the end of the *statement* part of a while, do, or for loop with the matching label.

# Exceptions

The throw statement

```
throw expression;
```

abruptly terminates the current method and resumes control inside the innermost matching catch clause of a surrounding try block. The *expression* must evaluate to a reference to an object of a subclass of Throwable.

The try statement has the form

```
try tryBlock
[catch (ExceptionType₁ exceptionVariable₁) catchBlock₁
catch (ExceptionType₂ exceptionVariable₂) catchBlock₂
. . .]
[finally finallyBlock]
```

- The try statement must have at least one catch or finally clause.
- All blocks are block statements in the usual sense, that is, { . . . }-delimited statement sequences.

The statements in the *tryBlock* are executed. If one of them throws an exception object whose type is a subtype of one of the types in the catch clauses, then its *catchBlock* is executed. As soon as the catch block is entered, that exception is handled.

If the *tryBlock* exits for any reason at all (because all of its statements executed completely; because one of its statements was a break, continue, or return statement; or because an exception was thrown), then the *finallyBlock* is executed.

If the *finallyBlock* was entered because an exception was thrown and it itself throws another exception, then that exception masks the prior exception.

# Packages

A class can be placed in a package by putting the package declaration

```
package packageName;
```

as the first non-import declaration of the source file.

A package name has the form

$identifier_1 . identifier_2 . \ . \ . $

For example,

```
java.util
com.horstmann.bigjava
```

A fully qualified name of a class is

*packageName . ClassName*

Classes can always be referenced by their fully qualified class names. However, this can be inconvenient. For that reason, you can reference imported classes by just their *ClassName*. All classes in the package java.lang and in the package of the current source file are always imported.

To import additional classes, use an import directive

    import *packageName*.*ClassName*;

or

    import *packageName*.*;

The second version imports all classes in the package.

# Generic Types and Methods

A generic type is declared with one or more type parameters, placed after the type name:

*modifiers* class|interface *TypeName*<*typeParameter*₁, *typeParameter*₂, . . .>

Similarly, a generic method is declared with one or more type parameters, placed before the method's return type:

*modifiers* <*typeParameter*₁, *typeParameter*₂, . . .> *returnType* *methodName*

Each type parameter has the form

*typeParameterName* [extends *bound*₁ & *bound*₂ & . . .]

For example,

```
public class BinarySearchTree<T extends Comparable>
public interface Comparator<T>
public <T extends Comparable & Cloneable> T cloneMin(T[] values)
```

Type parameters can be used in the definition of the generic type or method as if they were regular types. They can be replaced with any types that match the bounds. For example, the BinarySearchTree<String> type substitutes the String type for the type parameter T.

Type parameters can also be replaced with *wildcard types*. A wildcard type has the form

    ? [super|extends *Type*]

It denotes a specific type that is unknown at the time that it is declared. For example, Comparable<? super Rectangle> is a type Comparable<S> for a specific type S, which can be Rectangle or a supertype such as RectangularShape or Shape.

# Comments

There are three kinds of comments:

    /* *comment* */
    // *one-line-comment*
    /** *documentationComment* */

The one-line comment extends to the end of the line. The other comments can span multiple lines and extend to the */ delimiter.

Documentation comments are further explained in Appendix H.

# HTML SUMMARY

## A Brief Introduction to HTML

A web page is written in a language called HTML (Hypertext Markup Language). Like Java code, HTML code is made up of text that follows certain strict rules. When a browser reads a web page, the browser *interprets* the code and *renders* the page, displaying characters, fonts, paragraphs, tables, and images.

HTML files are made up of text and *tags* that tell the browser how to render the text. Nowadays, there are dozens of HTML tags—see Table 1 for a summary of the most important tags. Fortunately, you need only a few to get started. Most HTML tags come in pairs consisting of an opening tag and a closing tag, and each pair applies to the text between the two tags. Here is a typical example of a tag pair:

```
Java is an <i>object-oriented</i> programming language.
```

The tag pair `<i> </i>` directs the browser to display the text inside the tags in *italics*:

Java is an *object-oriented* programming language.

The closing tag is just like the opening tag, but it is prefixed by a slash (/). For example, bold-faced text is delimited by `<b> </b>`, and a paragraph is delimited by `<p> </p>`.

```
<p><b>Java</b> is an <i>object-oriented</i> programming language.</p>
```

The result is the paragraph

**Java** is an *object-oriented* programming language.

Another common construct is a bulleted list. For example:

Java is

- object-oriented
- safe
- platform-independent

Here is the HTML code to display it:

```
<p>Java is</p>
<ul><li>object-oriented</li>
<li>safe</li>
<li>platform-independent</li></ul>
```

Each item in the list is delimited by `<li> </li>` (for "list item"), and the whole list is surrounded by `<ul> </ul>` (for "unnumbered list").

| Table 1 | Selected HTML Tags | | |
|---|---|---|---|
| Tag | Meaning | Children | Commonly Used Attributes |
| html | HTML document | head, body | |
| head | Head of an HTML document | title | |
| title | Title of an HTML document | | |
| body | Body of an HTML document | | |
| h1 . . . h6 | Heading level 1 . . . 6 | | |
| p | Paragraph | | |
| ul | Unnumbered list | li | |
| ol | Ordered list | li | |
| dl | Definition list | dt, dd | |
| li | List item | | |
| dt | Term to be defined | | |
| dd | Definition data | | |
| table | Table | tr | |
| tr | Table row | th, td | |
| th | Table header cell | | |
| td | Table cell data | | |
| a | Anchor | | href, name |
| img | Image | | src, width, height |
| pre | Preformatted text | | |
| hr | Horizontal rule | | |
| br | Line break | | |
| i or em | Italic | | |
| b or strong | Bold | | |
| tt or code | Typewriter or code font | | |
| s or strike | Strike through | | |
| u | Underline | | |
| super | Superscript | | |
| sub | Subscript | | |
| form | Form | | action, method |

### Table 1 Selected HTML Tags

| Tag | Meaning | Children | Commonly Used Attributes |
|---|---|---|---|
| `input` | Input field | | `type, name, value, size, checked` |
| `select` | Combo box style selector | `option` | `name` |
| `option` | Option for selection | | |
| `textarea` | Multiline text area | | `name, rows, cols` |

As in Java, you can freely use white space (spaces and line breaks) in HTML code to make it easier to read. For example, you can lay out the code for a list as follows:

```
<p>Java is</p>
<ul>
<li>object-oriented</li>
<li>safe</li>
<li>platform-independent</li>
</ul>
```

The browser ignores the white space.

If you omit a tag (such as a `</li>`), most browsers will try to guess the missing tags—sometimes with differing results. It is always best to include all tags.

You can include images in your web pages with the `img` tag. In its simplest form, an image tag has the form

```
<img src="hamster.jpeg"/>
```

This code tells the browser to load and display the image that is stored in the file `hamster.jpeg`. This is a slightly different type of tag. Rather than text inside a tag pair `<img> </img>`, the `img` tag uses an attribute to specify a file name. Attributes have names and values. For example, the `src` attribute has the value `"hamster.jpeg"`. Table 2 contains commonly used attributes.

### Table 2 Selected HTML Attributes

| Attribute | Description | Commonly Contained in |
|---|---|---|
| `name` | Name of form element or anchor | `input, select, textarea, a` |
| `href` | Hyperlink reference | `a` |
| `src` | Source (as of an image) | `img` |
| `code` | Applet code | `applet` |
| `width, height` | Width, height of image or applet | `img, applet` |
| `rows, cols` | Rows, columns of text area | `textarea` |
| `type` | Type of input field, such as `text`, `password`, `checkbox`, `radio`, `submit`, `hidden` | `input` |
| `value` | Value of input field, or label of submit button | `input` |

| Table 2 Selected HTML Attributes | | |
|:---:|:---:|:---:|
| Attribute | Description | Commonly Contained in |
| size | Size of text field | input |
| checked | Check radio button or checkbox | input |
| action | URL of form action | form |
| method | GET or POST | form |

It is considered polite to use several additional attributes with the img tag, namely the *image size* and an *alternate description*:

```
<img src="hamster.jpeg" width="640" height="480"
alt="A photo of Harry, the Horrible Hamster"/>
```

These additional attributes help the browser lay out the page and display a temporary description while gathering the data for the image (or if the browser cannot display images, such as a voice browser for blind users). Users with slow network connections really appreciate this extra effort.

Because there is no closing </img> tag, we put a slash / before the closing >. This is not a requirement of HTML, but it is a requirement of the emerging XHTML standard, the XML-based successor to HTML. See www.w3c.org/TR/xhtml1 for more information on XHTML.

The most important tag on a web page is the <a> </a> tag pair, which makes the enclosed text into a *link* to another file. The links between web pages are what makes the Web into, well, a web. The browser displays a link in a special way (for example, underlined text in blue color). Here is the code for a typical link:

```
<a href="http://horstmann.com">Cay Horstmann</a> is the author of this book.
```

When the viewer of the web page clicks on the words Cay Horstmann, the browser loads the web page located at horstmann.com. (The value of the href attribute is a *Universal Resource Locator* (URL), which tells the browser where to go. The prefix http:, for *Hypertext Transfer Protocol*, tells the browser to fetch the file as a web page. Other protocols allow different actions, such as ftp: to download a file, mailto: to send e-mail to a user, and file: to view a local HTML file.)

| Table 3 Selected HTML Entities | | |
|:---:|:---:|:---:|
| Entity | Description | Appearance |
| &lt; | Less than | < |
| &gt; | Greater than | > |
| &amp; | Ampersand | & |
| &quot; | Quotation mark | " |
|   | Nonbreaking space | |
| &copy; | Copyright symbol | © |

You have noticed that tags are enclosed in angle brackets (less-than and greater-than signs). What if you want to show an angle bracket on a web page? HTML provides the notations &lt; and &gt; to produce the < and > symbols, respectively. Other codes of this kind produce symbols such as accented letters. The & (ampersand) symbol introduces these codes; to get that symbol itself, use &amp;. See Table 3 for a summary.

You may already have created web pages with a web editor that works like a word processor, giving you a WYSIWYG (what you see is what you get) view of your web page. But the tags are still there, and you can see them when you load the HTML file into a text editor. If you are comfortable using a WYSIWYG web editor, you don't need to memorize HTML tags at all. But many programmers and professional web designers prefer to work directly with the tags at least some of the time, because it gives them more control over their pages.

# TOOL SUMMARY

In this summary, we use a monospaced font for actual commands such as javac. An italic font denotes descriptions of tool command components such as *options*. Items enclosed in brackets [...] are optional. Items separated by vertical bars | are alternatives. Do not include the brackets or vertical bars when typing the commands.

## The Java Compiler

javac [*options*] *sourceFile*$_1$|@*fileList*$_1$ *sourceFile*$_2$|@*fileList*$_2$ . . .

A file list is a text file that contains one file name per line. For example,

**Greeting.list**

```
1    Greeting.java
2    GreetingTester.java
```

Then you can compile all files with the command

javac @Greeting.list

The Java compiler options are summarized in Table 1.

**Table 1  Common Compiler Options**

| Option | Description |
|---|---|
| -classpath *locations* or -cp *locations* | The compiler is to look for classes on this path, overriding the CLASSPATH environment variable. If neither is specified, the current directory is used. Each *location* is a directory, JAR file, or ZIP file. Locations are separated by a platform-dependent separator (: on Unix, ; on Windows). |
| -sourcepath *locations* | The compiler is to look for source files on this path. If not specified, source files are searched in the class path. |
| -d *directory* | The compiler places files into the specified directory. |
| -g | Generate debugging information. |
| -verbose | Include information about all classes that are being compiled (useful for troubleshooting). |
| -deprecation | Give detailed information about the usage of deprecated messages. |
| -Xlint:*errorType* | Carry out additional error checking. If you get warnings about unchecked conversions, compile with the -Xlint:unchecked option. |

# The Java Virtual Machine Launcher

The following command loads the given class and starts its main method, passing it an array containing the provided command line arguments:

java [*options*] *ClassName* [*argument*$_1$ *argument*$_2$ . . . ]

The following command loads the main class of the given JAR file and starts its main method, passing it an array containing the provided command line arguments:

java [*options*] -jar *jarFileName* [*argument*$_1$ *argument*$_2$ . . . ]

The Java virtual machine options are summarized in Table 2.

| Option | Description |
| --- | --- |
| -classpath *locations*<br>or<br>-cp *locations* | Look for classes on this path, overriding the CLASSPATH environment variable. If neither is specified, the current directory is used.<br>Each *location* is a directory, JAR file, or ZIP file. Locations are separated by a platform-dependent separator (: on Unix, ; on Windows). |
| -verbose | Trace class loading |
| -D*property*=*value* | Set a system property that you can retrieve with the System.getProperties method. |

**Table 2 Common Virtual Machine Launcher Options**

# The JAR Tool

To combine one or more files into a JAR (Java Archive) file, use the command

jar cvf *jarFile* *file*$_1$ *file*$_2$ . . .

The resulting JAR file can be included in a class path.

To build a program that can be launched with java -jar, you must create a *manifest file*, such as

**myprog.mf**

```
1   Main-Class: com/horstmann/MyProg
```

The manifest must specify the path name of the class file that launches the application, but with the .class extension removed. Then build the JAR file as

jar cvfm *jarFile* *manifestFile* *file*$_1$ *file*$_2$ . . .

You can also use JAR as a replacement for a ZIP utility, simply to compress and bundle a set of files for any purpose. Then you may want to suppress the generation of the JAR manifest, with the command

jar cvfM *jarFile* *file*$_1$ *file*$_2$ . . .

To extract the contents of a JAR file into the current directory, use

jar xvf *jarFile*

To see the files contained in a JAR file without extracting the files, use

jar tvf *jarFile*

# JAVADOC SUMMARY

## Documentation Comments

A documentation comment is delimited by /** and */. You can comment

- Classes
- Methods
- Instance variables

Each comment is placed *immediately above* the feature it documents.

Each /** . . . */ documentation comment contains introductory text followed by tagged documentation. A tag starts with an @ character, such as @author or @param. Tags are summarized in Table 1. The *first sentence* of the introductory text should be a summary statement. The javadoc utility automatically generates summary pages that extract these sentences.

You can use HTML tags such as em for emphasis, code for a monospaced font, img for images, ul for bulleted lists, and so on.

### Table 1  Common javadoc Tags

| Tag | Description |
| --- | --- |
| @param *parameter explanation* | A parameter of a method. Use a separate tag for each parameter. |
| @return *explanation* | The return value of a method. |
| @throws *exceptionType explanation* | An exception that a method may throw. Use a separate tag for each exception. |
| @deprecated | A feature that remains for compatibility but that should not be used for new code. |
| @see *packageName.ClassName*<br>@see *packageName.ClassName*<br>   *#methodName(Type$_1$, Type$_2$, . . .)*<br>@see *packageName.ClassName#variableName* | A reference to a related documentation entry. |
| @author | The author of a class or interface. Use a separate tag for each author. |
| @version | The version of a class or interface. |

Here is a typical example. The summary sentence (in color) will be included with the method summary.

```java
/**
   Withdraws money from the bank account. Increments the
   transaction count.
   @param amount the amount to withdraw
   @return the balance after the withdrawal
   @throws IllegalArgumentException if the balance is not sufficient
*/
public double withdraw(double amount)
{
   if (balance - amount < minimumBalance)
   {
      throw new IllegalArgumentException();
   }
   balance = balance - amount;
   transactions++;
   return balance;
}
```

# Generating Documentation from Commented Source

To extract the comments, run the javadoc program:

javadoc [*options*] *sourceFile$_1$*|*packageName$_1$*|*@fileList$_1$*
        *sourceFile$_2$*|*packageName$_2$*|*@fileList$_2$* . . .

See the documentation of the javac command in Appendix G for an explanation of file lists. Commonly used options are summarized in Table 2.

To document all files in the current directory, use (all on one line)

```
javadoc -link http://download.oracle.com/javase/7/docs/api -d docdir *.java
```

| Table 2 **Common javadoc Command Line Options** | |
|---|---|
| Option | Description |
| -link *URL* | Link to another set of javadoc files. You should include a link to the standard library documentation, either locally or at http://download.oracle.com/javase/7/docs/api. |
| -d *directory* | Store the output in *directory*. This is a useful option, because it keeps your current directory from being cluttered up with javadoc files. |
| -classpath *locations* | Look for classes on the specified paths, overriding the CLASSPATH environment variable. If neither is specified, the current directory is used. Each *location* is a directory, JAR file, or ZIP file. Locations are separated by a platform-dependent separator (: Unix, ; Windows). |
| -sourcepath *locations* | Look for source files on the specified paths. If not specified, source files are searched in the class path. |
| -author, -version | Include author, version information in the documentation. This information is omitted by default. |

# NUMBER SYSTEMS

## Binary Numbers

Decimal notation represents numbers as powers of 10, for example

$$1729_{decimal} = 1 \times 10^3 + 7 \times 10^2 + 2 \times 10^1 + 9 \times 10^0$$

There is no particular reason for the choice of 10, except that several historical number systems were derived from people's counting with their fingers. Other number systems, using a base of 12, 20, or 60, have been used by various cultures throughout human history. However, computers use a number system with base 2 because it is far easier to build electronic components that work with two values, which can be represented by a current being either off or on, than it would be to represent 10 different values of electrical signals. A number written in base 2 is also called a *binary* number.

For example,

$$1101_{binary} = 1 \times 2^3 + 1 \times 2^2 + 0 \times 2^1 + 1 \times 2^0 = 8 + 4 + 1 = 13$$

For digits after the "decimal" point, use negative powers of 2.

$$1.101_{binary} = 1 \times 2^0 + 1 \times 2^{-1} + 0 \times 2^{-2} + 1 \times 2^{-3}$$

$$= 1 + \frac{1}{2} + \frac{1}{8}$$

$$= 1 + 0.5 + 0.125 = 1.625$$

In general, to convert a binary number into its decimal equivalent, simply evaluate the powers of 2 corresponding to digits with value 1, and add them up. Table 1 shows the first powers of 2.

To convert a decimal integer into its binary equivalent, keep dividing the integer by 2, keeping track of the remainders. Stop when the number is 0. Then write the remainders as a binary number, starting with the *last* one. For example,

$$100 \div 2 = 50 \text{ remainder } 0$$
$$50 \div 2 = 25 \text{ remainder } 0$$
$$25 \div 2 = 12 \text{ remainder } 1$$
$$12 \div 2 = 6 \text{ remainder } 0$$
$$6 \div 2 = 3 \text{ remainder } 0$$
$$3 \div 2 = 1 \text{ remainder } 1$$
$$1 \div 2 = 0 \text{ remainder } 1$$

Therefore, $100_{decimal} = 1100100_{binary}$.

Conversely, to convert a fractional number less than 1 to its binary format, keep multiplying by 2. If the result is greater than 1, subtract 1. Stop when the number is 0. Then use the digits before the decimal points as the binary digits of the fractional part, starting with the *first* one. For example,

$$0.35 \cdot 2 = 0.7$$
$$0.7 \cdot 2 = 1.4$$
$$0.4 \cdot 2 = 0.8$$
$$0.8 \cdot 2 = 1.6$$
$$0.6 \cdot 2 = 1.2$$
$$0.2 \cdot 2 = 0.4$$

Here the pattern repeats. That is, the binary representation of 0.35 is 0.01 0110 0110 0110...

To convert any floating-point number into binary, convert the whole part and the fractional part separately.

### Table 1 Powers of Two

| Power | Decimal Value |
|-------|---------------|
| $2^0$ | 1 |
| $2^1$ | 2 |
| $2^2$ | 4 |
| $2^3$ | 8 |
| $2^4$ | 16 |
| $2^5$ | 32 |
| $2^6$ | 64 |
| $2^7$ | 128 |
| $2^8$ | 256 |
| $2^9$ | 512 |
| $2^{10}$ | 1,024 |
| $2^{11}$ | 2,048 |
| $2^{12}$ | 4,096 |
| $2^{13}$ | 8,192 |
| $2^{14}$ | 16,384 |
| $2^{15}$ | 32,768 |
| $2^{16}$ | 65,536 |

# Overflow and Roundoff Errors

In Java, an int value is an integer that is 32 bits long. When combining two such values, it is possible that the result does not fit into 32 bits. In that case, only the last 32 bits of the results are used, yielding an incorrect answer. For example,

```
int fiftyMillion = 50000000;
System.out.println(100 * fiftyMillion); // Expected: 5000000000
```

displays 705032704.

To see why this curious value is the result, one can carry out the long multiplication by hand:

```
1 1 0 0 1 0 0 * 1 0 1 1 1 1 1 0 1 0 1 1 1 1 0 0 0 0 1 0 0 0 0 0 0 0

1 0 1 1 1 1 1 0 1 0 1 1 1 1 0 0 0 0 1 0 0 0 0 0 0 0
  1 0 1 1 1 1 1 0 1 0 1 1 1 1 0 0 0 0 1 0 0 0 0 0 0 0
    0
      0
          1 0 1 1 1 1 1 0 1 0 1 1 1 1 0 0 0 0 1 0 0 0 0 0 0 0
            0
              0
_____
1 0 0 1 0 1 0 1 0 0 0 0 0 0 0 1 0 1 1 1 1 1 0 0 1 0 0 0 0 0 0 0 0 0
```

The result has 33 bits. However, you can't fit a 33-bit result into a 32-bit int, and the top bit is discarded. The last 32 bits are the binary representation of 705032704. (Note that the top bit is $2^{32}$ = 4294967296, and the two values add up to 5000000000, the correct result.)

With floating-point numbers, you can encounter another type of error: roundoff error. Consider this example:

```
double price = 4.35;
double quantity = 100;
double total = price * quantity; // Should be 100 * 4.35 = 435
System.out.println(total); // Prints 434.99999999999999
```

To see why the error occurs, carry out the long multiplication:

```
1 1 0 0 1 0 0 * 1 0 0.0 1|0 1 1 0|0 1 1 0|0 1 1 0 ...

1 0 0.0 1|0 1 1 0|0 1 1 0|0 1 1 0 ...
  1 0 0.0 1|0 1 1 0|0 1 1 0|0 1 1 ...
    0
      0
          1 0 0.0 1|0 1 1 0|0 1 1 0 ...
            0
              0
_____
1 1 0 1 1 0 0 1 0.1 1 1 1 1 1 1 1 ...
```

That is, the result is 434, followed by an infinite number of 1s. The fractional part of the product is the binary equivalent of an infinite decimal fraction 0.999999 . . . , which is equal to 1. But the CPU can store only a finite number of 1s, and it discards some of them when converting the result to a decimal number.

# Two's Complement Integers

To represent negative integers, there are two common representations, called "signed magnitude" and "two's complement". Signed magnitude notation is simple: use the leftmost bit for the sign (0 = positive, 1 = negative). For example, when using 8-bit numbers,

$$-13 = 10001101_{\text{signed magnitude}}$$

However, building circuitry for adding numbers gets a bit more complicated when one has to take a sign bit into account. The two's complement representation solves this problem. To form the two's complement of a number,

- Flip all bits.
- Then add 1.

For example, to compute −13 as an 8-bit value, first flip all bits of 00001101 to get 11110010. Then add 1:

$$-13 = 11110011_{\text{two's complement}}$$

Now no special circuitry is required for adding two numbers. Simply follow the normal rule for addition, with a carry to the next position if the sum of the digits and the prior carry is 2 or 3. For example,

```
       1 1111 111
+13      0000 1101
-13      1111 0011
       ─────────────
       1 0000 0000
```

But only the last 8 bits count, so +13 and −13 add up to 0, as they should.

In particular, −1 has two's complement representation 1111 . . . 1111, with all bits set.

The leftmost bit of a two's complement number is 0 if the number is positive or zero, 1 if it is negative.

Two's complement notation with a given number of bits can represent one more negative number than positive numbers. For example, the 8-bit two's complement numbers range from −128 to +127.

This phenomenon is an occasional cause for a programming error. For example, consider the following code:

```
short b = ...;
if (b < 0) { b = (byte) -b; }
```

This code does not guarantee that b is nonnegative afterwards. If b happens to be −128, then computing its negative again yields −128. (Try it out—take 10000000, flip all bits, and add 1.)

# IEEE Floating-Point Numbers

The Institute for Electrical and Electronics Engineering (IEEE) defines standards for floating-point representations in the IEEE-754 standard. Figure 1 shows how single-precision (`float`) and double-precision (`double`) values are decomposed into

- A sign bit
- An exponent
- A mantissa

Floating-point numbers use scientific notation, in which a number is represented as

$$b_0.b_1 b_2 b_3 \ldots \times 2^e$$

In this representation, $e$ is the exponent, and the digits $b_0.b_1 b_2 b_3 \ldots$ form the mantissa. The *normalized* representation is the one where $b_0 \neq 0$. For example,

$$100_{\text{decimal}} = 1100100_{\text{binary}} = 1.100100_{\text{binary}} \times 2^6$$

In the binary number system, because the first bit of a normalized representation must be 1, it is not actually stored in the mantissa. Therefore, you always need to add it on to represent the actual value. For example, the mantissa 1.100100 is stored as 100100.

The exponent part of the IEEE representation uses neither signed magnitude nor two's complement representation. Instead, a *bias* is added to the actual exponent. The bias is 127 for single-precision numbers and 1023 for double-precision numbers. For example, the exponent $e = 6$ would be stored as 133 in a single-precision number. Thus,

$$100_{\text{decimal}} = 0\ 10000101\ 10010000000000000000000\ \text{single-precision IEEE}$$

In addition, there are several special values. Among them are:

- *Zero:* biased exponent = 0, mantissa = 0.
- *Infinity:* biased exponent = 11...1, mantissa = ±0.
- *NaN* (not a number): biased exponent = 11...1, mantissa ≠ ±0.

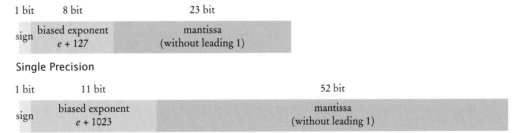

Figure 1  IEEE Floating-Point Representation

# Hexadecimal Numbers

Because binary numbers can be hard to read for humans, programmers often use the hexadecimal number system, with base 16. The digits are denoted as 0, 1, …, 9, A, B, C, D, E, F. (See Table 2.)

Four binary digits correspond to one hexadecimal digit. That makes it easy to convert between binary and hexadecimal values. For example,

$$11 | 1011 | 0001_{\text{binary}} = 3B1_{\text{hexadecimal}}$$

In Java, hexadecimal numbers are used for Unicode character values, such as \u03B1 (the Greek lowercase letter alpha). Hexadecimal integers are denoted with a 0x prefix, such as 0x3B1.

| Table 2 Hexadecimal Digits | | |
|:---:|:---:|:---:|
| Hexadecimal | Decimal | Binary |
| 0 | 0 | 0000 |
| 1 | 1 | 0001 |
| 2 | 2 | 0010 |
| 3 | 3 | 0011 |
| 4 | 4 | 0100 |
| 5 | 5 | 0101 |
| 6 | 6 | 0110 |
| 7 | 7 | 0111 |
| 8 | 8 | 1000 |
| 9 | 9 | 1001 |
| A | 10 | 1010 |
| B | 11 | 1011 |
| C | 12 | 1100 |
| D | 13 | 1101 |
| E | 14 | 1110 |
| F | 15 | 1111 |

# BIT AND SHIFT OPERATIONS

There are four bit operations in Java: the unary negation (~) and the binary *and* (&), *or* (|), and *exclusive or* (^), often called *xor*.

Tables 1 and 2 show the truth tables for the bit operations in Java. When a bit operation is applied to integer values, the operation is carried out on corresponding bits.

For example, suppose you want to compute 46 & 13. First convert both values to binary. $46_{\text{decimal}} = 101110_{\text{binary}}$ (actually 00000000000000000000000000101110 as a 32-bit integer), and $13_{\text{decimal}} = 1101_{\text{binary}}$. Now combine corresponding bits:

$$
\begin{array}{r}
0\ldots\ldots0101110 \\
\&\ \ 0\ldots\ldots0001101 \\
\hline
0\ldots\ldots0001100
\end{array}
$$

The answer is $1100_{\text{binary}} = 12_{\text{decimal}}$.

You sometimes see the | operator being used to combine two bit patterns. For example, the symbolic constant BOLD is the value 1, and the symbolic constant ITALIC is 2. The binary *or* combination BOLD | ITALIC has both the bold and the italic bit set:

$$
\begin{array}{r}
0\ldots\ldots0000001 \\
|\ \ 0\ldots\ldots0000010 \\
\hline
0\ldots\ldots0000011
\end{array}
$$

Don't confuse the & and | bit operators with the && and || operators. The latter work only on boolean values, not on bits of numbers.

### Table 1  The Unary Negation Operation

| a | ~a |
| --- | --- |
| 0 | 1 |
| 1 | 0 |

### Table 2  The Binary And, Or, and Xor Operations

| a | b | a & b | a \| b | a ^ b |
| --- | --- | --- | --- | --- |
| 0 | 0 | 0 | 0 | 0 |
| 0 | 1 | 0 | 1 | 1 |
| 1 | 0 | 0 | 1 | 1 |
| 1 | 1 | 1 | 1 | 0 |

Besides the operations that work on individual bits, there are three *shift* operations that take the bit pattern of a number and shift it to the left or right by a given number of positions. There are three shift operations: left shift (<<), right shift with sign extension (>>), and right shift with zero extension (>>>).

The left shift moves all bits to the left, filling in zeroes in the least significant bits. Shifting to the left by $n$ bits yields the same result as multiplication by $2^n$. The right shift with sign extension moves all bits to the right, propagating the sign bit. Therefore, the result is the same as integer division by $2^n$, both for positive and negative values. Finally, the right shift with zero extension moves all bits to the right, filling in zeroes in the most significant bits. (See Figure 1.)

Note that the right-hand-side value of the shift operators is reduced modulo 32 (for int values) or 64 (for long values) to determine the actual number of bits to shift.

For example, `1 << 35` is the same as `1 << 3`. Actually shifting 1 by 35 bits to the left would make no sense—the result would be 0.

The expression

```
1 << n
```

yields a bit pattern in which the nth bit is set (where the 0 bit is the least significant bit).

To set the nth bit of a number, carry out the operation

```
x = x | 1 << n
```

To check whether the nth bit is set, execute the test

```
if ((x & 1 << n) != 0) . . .
```

Note that the parentheses around the & are required—the & operator has a lower precedence than the relational operators.

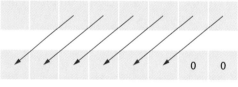

Left shift (<<)

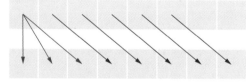

Right shift with sign extension (>>)

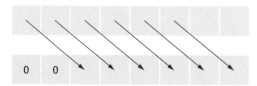

**Figure 1**
The Shift Operations    Right shift with zero extension (>>>)

# UML
# SUMMARY

In this book, we use a very restricted subset of the UML notation. This appendix lists the components of the subset.

## CRC Cards

CRC cards are used to describe in an informal fashion the responsibilities and collaborators for a class. Figure 1 shows a typical CRC card.

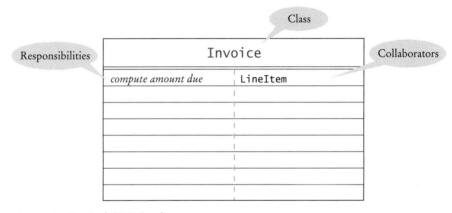

**Figure 1** Typical CRC Card

## UML Diagrams

Figure 2 shows the UML notation for classes and interfaces. You can optionally supply attributes and methods in a class diagram, as in Figure 3.

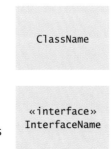

**Figure 2**
UML Symbols for Classes
and Interfaces

**Figure 3**
Attributes and Methods
in a Class Diagram

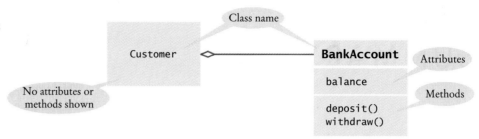

Table 1 shows the arrows used to indicate relationships between classes. Multiplicity can be indicated in a diagram, as in Figure 4.

| Table 1 UML Relationship Symbols | | | |
|---|---|---|---|
| Relationship | Symbol | Line Style | Arrow Tip |
| Inheritance | ⟶ | Solid | Triangle |
| Interface Implementation | ⤍ | Dotted | Triangle |
| Aggregation | ◇⟶ | Solid | Diamond |
| Dependency | ⤏ | Dotted | Open |

**Figure 4**
An Aggregation Relationship
with Multiplicities

Dependencies between objects are described by a dependency diagram. Figure 5 is a typical example.

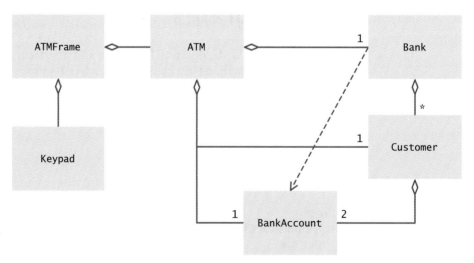

**Figure 5**
UML Class Diagram for
the ATM Simulation

State diagrams are used when an object goes through a discrete set of states that affects its behavior (see Figure 6).

For a complete discussion of the UML notation, see *The Unified Modeling Language User Guide,* Grady Booch, James Rumbaugh, and Ivar Jacobson (Addison-Wesley, 2005, 1999).

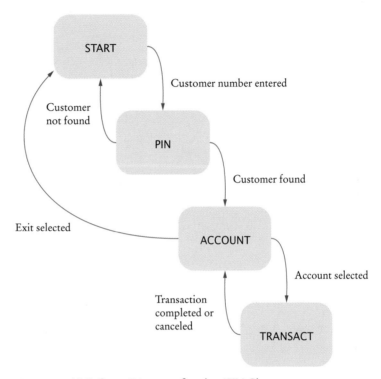

**Figure 6**   UML State Diagram for the ATM Class

# JAVA LANGUAGE CODING GUIDELINES

## Introduction

This coding style guide is a simplified version of one that has been used with good success both in industrial practice and for college courses.

A style guide is a set of mandatory requirements for layout and formatting. Uniform style makes it easier for you to read code from your instructor and classmates. You will really appreciate that if you do a team project. It is also easier for your instructor and your grader to grasp the essence of your programs quickly.

A style guide makes you a more productive programmer because it reduces gratuitous choice. If you don't have to make choices about trivial matters, you can spend your energy on the solution of real problems.

In these guidelines, several constructs are plainly outlawed. That doesn't mean that programmers using them are evil or incompetent. It does mean that the constructs are not essential and can be expressed just as well or even better with other language constructs.

If you already have programming experience, in Java or another language, you may be initially uncomfortable at giving up some fond habits. However, it is a sign of professionalism to set aside personal preferences in minor matters and to compromise for the benefit of your group.

These guidelines are necessarily somewhat dull. They also mention features that you may not yet have seen in class. Here are the most important highlights:

- Tabs are set every three spaces.
- Variable and method names are lowercase, with occasional upperCase characters in the middle.
- Class names start with an Uppercase letter.
- Constant names are UPPERCASE, with an occasional UNDER_SCORE.
- There are spaces after reserved words and surrounding binary operators.
- Braces must line up horizontally or vertically.
- No magic numbers may be used.
- Every method, except for main and overridden methods, must have a comment.
- At most 30 lines of code may be used per method.
- No continue or break is allowed.
- All non-final variables must be private.

Note to the instructor: Of course, many programmers and organizations have strong feelings about coding style. If this style guide is incompatible with your own preferences or with local custom, please feel free to modify it. For that purpose, this coding style guide is available in electronic form at www.wiley.com/college/horstmann and in the WileyPLUS course for this book.

# Source Files

Each Java program is a collection of one or more source files. The executable program is obtained by compiling these files. Organize the material in each file as follows:

- package statement, if appropriate
- import statements
- A comment explaining the purpose of this file
- A public class
- Other classes, if appropriate

The comment explaining the purpose of this file should be in the format recognized by the javadoc utility. Start with a /**, and use the @author and @version tags:

```
/**
    Classes to manipulate widgets.
    Solves CS101 homework assignment #3
    COPYRIGHT (C) 2013 Harry Morgan. All Rights Reserved.
    @author  Harry Morgan
    @version 1.01 2013-02-15
*/
```

# Classes

Each class should be preceded by a class comment explaining the purpose of the class.
First list all public features, then all private features.
Within the public and private sections, use the following order:

1. Instance variables
2. Static variables
3. Constructors
4. Instance methods
5. Static methods
6. Inner classes

Leave a blank line after every method.

All non-final variables must be private. (However, instance variables of a private inner class may be public.) Methods and final variables can be either public or private, as appropriate.

All features must be tagged public or private. Do not use the default visibility (that is, package visibility) or the protected attribute.

Avoid static variables (except final ones) whenever possible. In the rare instance that you need static variables, you are permitted one static variable per class.

# Methods

Every method (except for `main`) starts with a comment in `javadoc` format.

```
/**
    Convert calendar date into Julian day.
    Note: This algorithm is from Press et al., Numerical Recipes
    in C, 2nd ed., Cambridge University Press, 1992.
    @param day  day of the date to be converted
    @param month  month of the date to be converted
    @param year  year of the date to be converted
    @return  the Julian day number that begins at noon of the
    given calendar date.
*/
public static int getJulianDayNumber(int day, int month, int year)
{
    . . .
}
```

Parameter variable names must be explicit, especially if they are integers or Boolean:

```
public Employee remove(int d, double s)
    // Huh?
public Employee remove(int department, double severancePay)
    // OK
```

Methods must have at most 30 lines of code. The method signature, comments, blank lines, and lines containing only braces are not included in this count. This rule forces you to break up complex computations into separate methods.

# Variables and Constants

Do not define all variables at the beginning of a block:

```
{
    double xold; // Don't
    double xnew;
    boolean done;
    . . .
}
```

Define each variable just before it is used for the first time:

```
{
    . . .
    double xold = Integer.parseInt(input);
    boolean done = false;
    while (!done)
    {
        double xnew = (xold + a / xold) / 2;
        . . .
    }
    . . .
}
```

Do not define two variables on the same line:

```
int dimes = 0, nickels = 0; // Don't
```

Instead, use two separate definitions:

```
int dimes = 0; // OK
int nickels = 0;
```

In Java, constants must be defined with the reserved word `final`. If the constant is used by multiple methods, declare it as `static final`. It is a good idea to define static final variables as `private` if no other class has an interest in them.

Do not use magic numbers! A magic number is a numeric constant embedded in code, without a constant definition. Any number except –1, 0, 1, and 2 is considered magic:

```
if (p.getX() < 300) // Don't
```

Use `final` variables instead:

```
final double WINDOW_WIDTH = 300;
. . .
if (p.getX() < WINDOW_WIDTH) // OK
```

Even the most reasonable cosmic constant is going to change one day. You think there are 365 days per year? Your customers on Mars are going to be pretty unhappy about your silly prejudice. Make a constant

```
public static final int DAYS_PER_YEAR = 365;
```

so that you can easily produce a Martian version without trying to find all the 365s, 364s, 366s, 367s, and so on, in your code.

When declaring array variables, group the [] with the type, not the variable.

```
int[] values; // OK
int values[]; // Ugh—this is an ugly holdover from C
```

When using collections, use type parameters and not "raw" types.

```
ArrayList<String> names = new ArrayList<String>(); // OK
ArrayList names = new ArrayList(); // Not OK
```

# Control Flow

## Statement Bodies

Use braces to enclose the bodies of branch and loop statements, even if they contain only a single statement. For example,

```
if (x < 0)
{
   x++;
}
```

and not

```
if (x < 0)
   x++;  // Not OK--no braces
```

## The for Statement

Use for loops only when a variable runs from somewhere to somewhere with some constant increment/decrement:

```
for (int i = 0; i < a.length; i++)
{
    System.out.println(a[i]);
}
```

Or, even better, use the enhanced for loop:

```
for (int e : a)
{
    System.out.println(e);
}
```

Do not use the for loop for weird constructs such as

```
for (a = a / 2; count < ITERATIONS; System.out.println(xnew))    // Don't
```

Make such a loop into a while loop. That way, the sequence of instructions is much clearer:

```
a = a / 2;
while (count < ITERATIONS) // OK
{
    . . .
    System.out.println(xnew);
}
```

## Nonlinear Control Flow

Avoid the switch statement, because it is easy to fall through accidentally to an unwanted case. Use if/else instead.

Avoid the break or continue statements. Use another boolean variable to control the execution flow.

## Exceptions

Do not tag a method with an overly general exception specification:

```
Widget readWidget(Reader in) throws Exception // Bad
```

Instead, specifically declare any checked exceptions that your method may throw:

```
Widget readWidget(Reader in)
        throws IOException, MalformedWidgetException // Good
```

Do not "squelch" exceptions:

```
try
{
    double price = in.readDouble();
}
catch (Exception e)
{ } // Bad
```

Beginners often make this mistake "to keep the compiler happy". If the current method is not appropriate for handling the exception, simply use a throws specification and let one of its callers handle it.

# Lexical Issues

## Naming Conventions

The following rules specify when to use upper- and lowercase letters in identifier names:

- All variable and method names are in lowercase (maybe with an occasional upperCase in the middle); for example, `firstPlayer`.
- All constants are in uppercase (maybe with an occasional UNDER_SCORE); for example, `CLOCK_RADIUS`.
- All class and interface names start with uppercase and are followed by lowercase letters (maybe with an occasional UpperCase letter); for example, `BankTeller`.
- Generic type variables are in uppercase, usually a single letter.

Names must be reasonably long and descriptive. Use `firstPlayer` instead of `fp`. No drppng f vwls. Local variables that are fairly routine can be short (`ch`, `i`) as long as they are really just boring holders for an input character, a loop counter, and so on. Also, do not use `ctr`, `c`, `cntr`, `cnt`, `c2` for variables in your method. Surely these variables all have specific purposes and can be named to remind the reader of them (for example, `current`, `next`, `previous`, `result`, . . .). However, it is customary to use single-letter names, such as `T` or `E` for generic types.

## Indentation and White Space

Use tab stops every three columns. That means you will need to change the tab stop setting in your editor!

Use blank lines freely to separate parts of a method that are logically distinct.

Use a blank space around every binary operator:

```
x1 = (-b - Math.sqrt(b * b - 4 * a * c)) / (2 * a);
// Good

x1=(-b-Math.sqrt(b*b-4*a*c))/(2*a);
// Bad
```

Leave a blank space after (and not before) each comma or semicolon. Do not leave a space before or after a parenthesis or bracket in an expression. Leave spaces around the ( . . . ) part of an `if`, `while`, `for`, or `catch` statement.

```
if (x == 0) { y = 0; }

f(a, b[i]);
```

Every line must fit in 80 columns. If you must break a statement, add an indentation level for the continuation:

```
a[n] = .................................................
         + .................;
```

Start the indented line with an operator (if possible).

## Braces

Opening and closing braces must line up, either horizontally or vertically:

```java
while (i < n) { System.out.println(a[i]); i++; }

while (i < n)
{
   System.out.println(a[i]);
   i++;
}
```

Some programmers don't line up vertical braces but place the { behind the reserved word:

```java
while (i < n) { // DON'T
   System.out.println(a[i]);
   i++;
}
```

Doing so makes it hard to check that the braces match.

## Unstable Layout

Some programmers take great pride in lining up certain columns in their code:

```java
firstRecord = other.firstRecord;
lastRecord  = other.lastRecord;
cutoff      = other.cutoff;
```

This is undeniably neat, but the layout is not stable under change. A new variable name that is longer than the preallotted number of columns requires that you move all entries around:

```java
firstRecord = other.firstRecord;
lastRecord  = other.lastRecord;
cutoff      = other.cutoff;
marginalFudgeFactor = other.marginalFudgeFactor;
```

This is just the kind of trap that makes you decide to use a short variable name like mff instead. Use a simple layout that is easy to maintain as your programs change.

# GLOSSARY

**Abstract class**   A class that cannot be instantiated.

**Abstract method**   A method with a name, parameter variable types, and return type but without an implementation.

**Accessor method**   A method that accesses an object but does not change it.

**Aggregation**   The *has-a* relationship between classes.

**Algorithm**   An unambiguous, executable, and terminating specification of a way to solve a problem.

**Anonymous class**   A class that does not have a name.

**Anonymous object**   An object that is not stored in a named variable.

**API (Application Programming Interface)**   A code library for building programs.

**API Documentation**   Information about each class in the Java library.

**Applet**   A graphical Java program that executes inside a web browser or applet viewer.

**Argument**   A value supplied in a method call, or one of the values combined by an operator.

**Array**   A collection of values of the same type stored in contiguous memory locations, each of which can be accessed by an integer index.

**Array list**   A Java class that implements a dynamically-growable array of objects.

**Assignment**   Placing a new value into a variable.

**Association**   A relationship between classes in which one can navigate from objects of one class to objects of the other class, usually by following object references.

**Asymmetric bounds**   Bounds that include the starting index but not the ending index.

**Attribute**   A named property that an object is responsible for maintaining.

**Auto-boxing**   Automatically converting a primitive type value into a wrapper type object.

**Balanced tree**   A tree in which each subtree has the property that the number of descendants to the left is approximately the same as the number of descendants to the right.

**Big-Oh notation**   The notation $g(n) = O(f(n))$, which denotes that the function $g$ grows at a rate that is bounded by the growth rate of the function $f$ with respect to $n$. For example, $10n^2 + 100n - 1000 = O(n^2)$.

**Binary file**   A file in which values are stored in their binary representation and cannot be read as text.

**Binary operator**   An operator that takes two arguments, for example + in $x + y$.

**Binary search**   A fast algorithm for finding a value in a sorted array. It narrows the search down to half of the array in every step.

**Binary search tree**   A binary tree in which *each* subtree has the property that all left descendants are smaller than the value stored in the root, and all right descendants are larger.

**Binary tree**   A tree in which each node has at most two child nodes.

**Bit**   Binary digit; the smallest unit of information, having two possible values: 0 and 1. A data element consisting of $n$ bits has $2^n$ possible values.

**Black-box testing**    Testing a method without knowing its implementation.

**Block**    A group of statements bracketed by {}.

**Boolean operator**    An operator that can be applied to Boolean values. Java has three Boolean operators: &&, ||, and !.

**Boolean type**    A type with two possible values: true and false.

**Border layout**    A layout management scheme in which components are placed into the center or one of the four borders of their container.

**Boundary test case**    A test case involving values that are at the outer boundary of the set of legal values. For example, if a method is expected to work for all nonnegative integers, then 0 is a boundary test case.

**Bounds error**    Trying to access an array element that is outside the legal range.

**break statement**    A statement that terminates a loop or switch statement.

**Buffer**    A temporary storage location for holding values that have been produced (for example, characters typed by the user) and are waiting to be consumed (for example, read a line at a time).

**Bug**    A programming error.

**Byte**    A number made up of eight bits. Essentially all currently manufactured computers use a byte as the smallest unit of storage in memory.

**Bytecode**    Instructions for the Java virtual machine.

**Call stack**    The ordered set of all methods that currently have been called but not yet terminated, starting with the current method and ending with main.

**Case sensitive**    Distinguishing upper- and lowercase characters.

**Cast**    Explicitly converting a value from one type to a different type. For example, the cast from a floating-point number x to an integer is expressed in Java by the cast notation (int) x.

**catch clause**    A part of a try block that is executed when a matching exception is thrown by any statement in the try block.

**Central processing unit (CPU)**    The part of a computer that executes the machine instructions.

**Character**    A single letter, digit, or symbol.

**Check box**    A user-interface component that can be used for a binary selection.

**Checked exception**    An exception that the compiler checks. All checked exceptions must be declared or caught.

**Class**    A programmer-defined data type.

**Client**    A computer program or system that issues requests to a server and processes the server responses.

**Cohesion**    A class is cohesive if its features support a single abstraction.

**Collection**    A data structure that provides a mechanism for adding, removing, and locating elements.

**Collaborator**    A class on which another class depends.

**Combo box**    A user-interface component that combines a text field with a drop-down list of selections.

**Command line**   The line the user types to start a program in DOS or UNIX or a command window in Windows. It consists of the program name followed by any necessary arguments.

**Comment**   An explanation to help the human reader understand a section of a program; ignored by the compiler.

**Compiler**   A program that translates code in a high-level language (such as Java) to machine instructions (such as bytecode for the Java virtual machine).

**Compile-time error**   An error that is detected when a program is compiled.

**Component**   See **User-interface component**

**Composition**   An aggregation relationship where the aggregated objects do not have an existence independent of the containing object.

**Computer program**   A sequence of instructions that is executed by a computer.

**Concatenation**   Placing one string after another to form a new string.

**Concrete class**   A class that can be instantiated.

**Condition object**   An object that manages threads that currently cannot proceed.

**Console program**   A Java program that does not have a graphical window. A console program reads input from the keyboard and writes output to the terminal screen.

**Constant**   A value that cannot be changed by a program. In Java, constants are defined with the reserved word `final`.

**Constructor**   A sequence of statements for initializing a newly instantiated object.

**Container**   A user-interface component that can hold other components and present them together to the user. Also, a data structure, such as a list, that can hold a collection of objects and present them individually to a program.

**Content pane**   The part of a Swing frame that holds the user-interface components of the frame.

**Coupling**   The degree to which classes are related to each other by dependency.

**CRC card**   An index card representing a class that lists its responsibilities and collaborating classes.

**De Morgan's Law**   A law about logical operations that describes how to negate expressions formed with *and* and *or* operations.

**Deadlock**   A state in which no thread can proceed because each thread is waiting for another to do some work first.

**Deadly embrace**   A set of blocked threads, each of which could only be unblocked by the action of other threads in the set.

**Debugger**   A program that lets a user run another program one or a few steps at a time, stop execution, and inspect the variables in order to analyze it for bugs.

**Dependency**   The *uses* relationship between classes, in which one class needs services provided by another class.

**Directory**   A structure on a disk that can hold files or other directories; also called a folder.

**Dot notation**   The notation *object.method(arguments)* or *object.variable* used to invoke a method or access a variable.

**Doubly-linked list**   A linked list in which each link has a reference to both its predecessor and successor links.

**DTD (Document Type Definition)**   A sequence of rules that describes the legal child elements and attributes for each element type in an SGML or XML document.

**Dynamic method lookup**   Selecting a method to be invoked at run time. In Java, dynamic method lookup considers the class of the implicit parameter object to select the appropriate method.

**Editor**   A program for writing and modifying text files.

**Embedded system**   The processor, software, and supporting circuitry that is included in a device other than a computer.

**Encapsulation**   The hiding of implementation details.

**Enumeration type**   A type with a finite number of values, each of which has its own symbolic name.

**Escape character**   A character in text that is not taken literally but has a special meaning when combined with the character or characters that follow it. The \ character is an escape character in Java strings.

**Escape sequence**   A sequence of characters that starts with an escape character, such as \n or \".

**Event**   See **User-interface event**

**Event class**   A class that contains information about an event, such as its source.

**Event adapter**   A class that implements an event listener interface by defining all methods to do nothing.

**Event handler**   A method that is executed when an event occurs.

**Event listener**   An object that is notified by an event source when an event occurs.

**Event source**   An object that can notify other classes of events.

**Exception**   A class that signals a condition that prevents the program from continuing normally. When such a condition occurs, an object of the exception class is thrown.

**Exception handler**   A sequence of statements that is given control when an exception of a particular type has been thrown and caught.

**Explicit parameter**   A parameter of a method other than the object on which the method is invoked.

**Expression**   A syntactical construct that is made up of constants, variables, method calls, and the operators combining them.

**Extension**   The last part of a file name, which specifies the file type. For example, the extension .java denotes a Java file.

**Fibonacci numbers**   The sequence of numbers 1, 1, 2, 3, 5, 8, 13, . . . , in which every term is the sum of its two predecessors.

**File**   A sequence of bytes that is stored on disk.

**File pointer**   The position within a random-access file of the next byte to be read or written. It can be moved so as to access any byte in the file.

**finally clause**   A part of a try block that is executed no matter how the try block is exited.

**Flag**   See **Boolean type**

**Floating-point number**   A number that can have a fractional part.

**Flow layout**   A layout management scheme in which components are laid out left to right.

**Flushing a stream**   Sending all characters that are still held in a buffer to their destination.

**Folder**   See **Directory**

**Font**   A set of character shapes in a particular style and size.

**Foreign key**   A reference to a primary key in a linked table.

**Frame**   A window with a border and a title bar.

**Garbage collection**   Automatic reclamation of memory occupied by objects that are no longer referenced.

**Generic class**   A class with one or more type parameters.

**Generic method**   A method with one or more type parameters.

**Generic programming**   Providing program components that can be reused in a wide variety of situations.

**Grammar**   A set of rules that specifies which sequences of tokens are legal for a particular document set.

**Graphics context**   A class through which a programmer can cause shapes to appear on a window or off-screen bitmap.

**grep**   The "global regular expression print" search program, useful for finding all strings matching a pattern in a set of files.

**Grid layout**   A layout management scheme in which components are placed into a two-dimensional grid.

**GUI (Graphical User Interface)**   A user interface in which the user supplies inputs through graphical components such as buttons, menus, and text fields.

**Hard disk**   A device that stores information on rotating platters with magnetic coating.

**Hardware**   The physical equipment for a computer or another device.

**Hash code**   A value that is computed by a hash function.

**Hash collision**   Two different objects for which a hash function computes identical values.

**Hash function**   A function that computes an integer value from an object in such a way that different objects are likely to yield different values.

**Hash table**   A data structure in which elements are mapped to array positions according to their hash function values.

**Hashing**   Applying a hash function to a set of objects.

**Heap**   A balanced binary tree that is used for implementing sorting algorithms and priority queues.

**Heapsort algorithm**   A sorting algorithm that inserts the values to be sorted into a heap.

**High-level programming language**   A programming language that provides an abstract view of a computer and allows programmers to focus on their problem domain.

**HTML (Hypertext Markup Language)**   The language in which web pages are described.

**HTTP (Hypertext Transfer Protocol)**   The protocol that defines communication between web browsers and web servers.

**IDE (Integrated Development Environment)**   A programming environment that includes an editor, compiler, and debugger.

**Implementing an interface**   Implementing a class that defines all methods specified in the interface.

**Implicit parameter**   The object on which a method is invoked. For example, in the call x.f(y), the object x is the implicit parameter of the method f.

**Importing a class or package**   Indicating the intention of referring to a class, or all classes in a package, by the simple name rather than the qualified name.

**Inheritance**   The *is-a* relationship between a more general superclass and a more specialized subclass.

**Initialization**   Setting a variable to a well-defined value when it is created.

**Inner class**   A class that is defined inside another class.

**Instance method**   A method with an implicit parameter; that is, a method that is invoked on an instance of a class.

**Instance of a class**   An object whose type is that class.

**Instance variable**   A variable defined in a class for which every object of the class has its own value.

**Instantiation of a class**   Construction of an object of that class.

**Integer**   A number that cannot have a fractional part.

**Integer division**   Taking the quotient of two integers and discarding the remainder. In Java the / symbol denotes integer division if both arguments are integers. For example, 11/4 is 2, not 2.75.

**Interface**   A type with no instance variables, only abstract methods and constants.

**Internet**   A worldwide collection of networks, routing equipment, and computers using a common set of protocols that define how participants interact with each other.

**Iterator**   An object that can inspect all elements in a container such as a linked list.

**JavaBean**   A class with a no-argument constructor that exposes properties through its get and set methods.

**javadoc**   The documentation generator in the Java SDK. It extracts documentation comments from Java source files and produces a set of linked HTML files.

**JavaServer Faces (JSF)**   A framework for developing web applications that aids in the separation of user interface and program logic.

**JDBC (Java Database Connectivity)**   The technology that enables a Java program to interact with relational databases.

**JDK**   The Java software development kit that contains the Java compiler and related development tools.

**Join**   A database query that involves multiple tables.

**JSF container**   A program that executes JSF applications.

**JVM**   The Java Virtual Machine.

**Layout manager**   A class that arranges user-interface components inside a container.

**Lazy evaluation**   Deferring the computation of a value until it is needed, thereby avoiding the computation if the value is never needed.

**Lexicographic ordering**   Ordering strings in the same order as in a dictionary, by skipping all matching characters and comparing the first non-matching characters of both strings. For example, "orbit" comes before "orchid" in lexicographic ordering. Note that in Java, unlike a dictionary, the ordering is case sensitive: Z comes before a.

**Library**    A set of precompiled classes that can be included in programs.

**Linear search**    Searching a container (such as an array or list) for an object by inspecting each element in turn.

**Linked list**    A data structure that can hold an arbitrary number of objects, each of which is stored in a link object, which contains a pointer to the next link.

**Literal**    A constant value in a program that is explicitly written as a number, such as –2 or 6.02214115E23, or as a character sequence, such as "Harry".

**Local variable**    A variable whose scope is a block.

**Lock**    A data structure to regulate the scheduling of multiple threads. Once a thread has acquired a lock, other threads that also wish to acquire it must wait until the first thread relinquishes it.

**Lock object**    An object that allows a single thread to execute a section of a program.

**Logging**    Sending messages that trace the progress of a program to a file or window.

**Logical operator**    See **Boolean operator**.

**Logic error**    An error in a syntactically correct program that causes it to act differently from its specification. (A form of run-time error.)

**Loop**    A sequence of instructions that is executed repeatedly.

**Loop and a half**    A loop whose termination decision is neither at the beginning nor at the end.

**Machine code**    Instructions that can be executed directly by the CPU.

**Magic number**    A number that appears in a program without explanation.

**main method**    The method that is first called when a Java application executes.

**Managed bean**    A JavaBean that is managed by a JSF container.

**Map**    A data structure that keeps associations between key and value objects.

**Markup**    Information about data that is added as humanly readable instructions. An example is the tagging of HTML documents with elements such as <h1> or <b>.

**Memory location**    A value that specifies the location of data in computer memory.

**Merge sort**    A sorting algorithm that first sorts two halves of a data structure and then merges the sorted subarrays together.

**Metadata**    Data that describe properties of a data set.

**Method**    A sequence of statements that has a name, may have parameter variables, and may return a value. A method can be invoked any number of times, with different values for its parameter variables.

**Method expression**    In JSF, an expression describing a bean and a method that is to be applied to the bean at a later time.

**Mixed content**    In XML, a markup element that contains both text and other elements.

**Modifier**    A reserved word that indicates the accessibility of a feature, such as private or public.

**Modulus**    The % operator that computes the remainder of an integer division.

**Mutator method**    A method that changes the state of an object.

**Mutual recursion**    Cooperating methods that call each other.

**Name clash**    Accidentally using the same name to denote two program features in a way that cannot be resolved by the compiler.

**Navigation rule**    In JSF, a rule that describes when to move from one web page to another.

**Nested loop**    A loop that is contained in another loop.

**Networks**    An interconnected system of computers and other devices.

**new operator**    An operator that allocates new objects.

**Newline**    The '\n' character, which indicates the end of a line.

**Null reference**    A reference that does not refer to any object.

**Number literal**    A constant value in a program this is explicitly written as a number, such as −2 or 6.02214115E23.

**Object**    A value of a class type.

**Object-oriented programming**    Designing a program by discovering objects, their properties, and their relationships.

**Object reference**    A value that denotes the location of an object in memory. In Java, a variable whose type is a class contains a reference to an object of that class.

**Off-by-one error**    A common programming error in which a value is one larger or smaller than it should be.

**Opening a file**    Preparing a file for reading or writing.

**Operating system**    The software that launches application programs and provides services (such as a file system) for those programs.

**Operator**    A symbol denoting a mathematical or logical operation, such as + or &&.

**Operator associativity**    The rule that governs in which order operators of the same precedence are executed. For example, in Java the - operator is left-associative because a - b - c is interpreted as (a - b) - c, and = is right-associative because a = b = c is interpreted as a = (b = c).

**Operator precedence**    The rule that governs which operator is evaluated first. For example, in Java the && operator has a higher precedence than the || operator. Hence a || b && c is interpreted as a || (b && c). (See Appendix B.)

**Overloading**    Giving more than one meaning to a method name.

**Overriding**    Redefining a method in a subclass.

**Package**    A collection of related classes. The import statement is used to access one or more classes in a package.

**Panel**    A user-interface component with no visual appearance. It can be used to group other components.

**Parallel arrays**    Arrays of the same length, in which corresponding elements are logically related.

**Parameter**    An item of information that is specified to a method when the method is called. For example, in the call System.out.println("Hello, World!"), the parameters are the implicit parameter System.out and the explicit parameter "Hello, World!".

**Parameter passing**    Specifying expressions to be arguments for a method when it is called.

**Parameter variable**   A variable of a method that is initialized with a value when the method is called.

**Parse tree**   A tree structure that shows how a string conforms to the rules of a grammar.

**Parser**   A program that reads a document, checks whether it is syntactically correct, and takes some action as it processes the document.

**Partially filled array**   An array that is not filled to capacity, together with a companion variable that indicates the number of elements actually stored.

**Permutation**   A rearrangement of a set of values.

**Polymorphism**   Selecting a method among several methods that have the same name on the basis of the actual types of the implicit parameters.

**Postfix operator**   A unary operator that is written after its argument.

**Prefix operator**   A unary operator that is written before its argument.

**Prepared statement**   A SQL statement with a precomputed query strategy.

**Primary key**   A column (or combination of columns) whose value uniquely specifies a table record.

**Primitive type**   In Java, a number type or `boolean`.

**Priority queue**   An abstract data type that enables efficient insertion of elements and efficient removal of the smallest element.

**Programming**   The act of designing and implementing computer programs.

**Project**   A collection of source files and their dependencies.

**Prompt**   A string that tells the user to provide input.

**Property**   A named value that is managed by a component.

**Pseudocode**   A high-level description of the actions of a program or algorithm, using a mixture of English and informal programming language syntax.

**Pseudorandom number**   A number that appears to be random but is generated by a mathematical formula.

**Public interface**   The features (methods, variables, and nested types) of a class that are accessible to all clients.

**Queue**   A collection of items with "first in, first out" retrieval.

**Quicksort**   A generally fast sorting algorithm that picks an element, called the pivot, partitions the sequence into the elements smaller than the pivot and those larger than the pivot, and then recursively sorts the subsequences.

**Race condition**   A condition in which the effect of multiple threads on shared data depends on the order in which the threads are scheduled.

**Radio button**   A user-interface component that can be used for selecting one of several options.

**RAM (random-access memory)**   Electronic circuits in a computer that can store code and data of running programs.

**Random access**   The ability to access any value directly without having to read the values preceding it.

**Reader**   In the Java input/output library, a class from which to read characters.

**Recursion**  A method for computing a result by decomposing the inputs into simpler values and applying the same method to them.

**Recursive method**  A method that can call itself with simpler values. It must handle the simplest values without calling itself.

**Red-black tree**  A kind of binary search tree that rebalances itself after each insertion and removal.

**Redirection**  Linking the input or output of a program to a file instead of the keyboard or display.

**Reference**  See **Object reference**

**Regular expression**  A string that defines a set of matching strings according to their content. Each part of a regular expression can be a specific required character; one of a set of permitted characters such as [abc], which can be a range such as [a-z]; any character not in a set of forbidden characters, such as [^0-9]; a repetition of one or more matches, such as [0-9]+, or zero or more, such as [ACGT]; one of a set of alternatives, such as and|et|und; or various other possibilities. For example, "[A-Za-z][0-9]+" matches "Cloud9" or "007" but not "Jack".

**Relational database**  A data repository that stores information in tables and retrieves data as the result of queries that are formulated in terms of table relationships.

**Relational operator**  An operator that compares two values, yielding a Boolean result.

**Reserved word**  A word that has a special meaning in a programming language and therefore cannot be used as a name by the programmer.

**Return value**  The value returned by a method through a return statement.

**Reverse Polish notation**  A style of writing expressions in which the operators are written following the operands, such as 2 3 4 * + for 2 + 3 * 4.

**Roundoff error**  An error introduced by the fact that the computer can store only a finite number of digits of a floating-point number.

**Runnable thread**  A thread that can proceed provided it is given a time slice to do work.

**Run-time error**  An error in a syntactically correct program that causes it to act differently from its specification.

**Run-time stack**  The data structure that stores the local variables of all called methods as a program runs.

**Scope**  The part of a program in which a variable is defined.

**Secondary storage**  Storage that persists without electricity, e.g., a hard disk.

**Selection sort**  A sorting algorithm in which the smallest element is repeatedly found and removed until no elements remain.

**Sentinel**  A value in input that is not to be used as an actual input value but to signal the end of input.

**Sequential access**  Accessing values one after another without skipping over any of them.

**Sequential search**  See **Linear search**

**Serialization**  The process of saving an object, and all the objects that it references, to a stream.

**Set**  An unordered collection that allows efficient addition, location, and removal of elements.

**Shadowing**  Hiding a variable by defining another one with the same name.

**Shell script**   A file that contains commands for running programs and manipulating files. Typing the name of the shell script file on the command line causes those commands to be executed.

**Shell window**   A window for interacting with an operating system through textual commands.

**Short-circuit evaluation**   Evaluating only a part of an expression if the remainder cannot change the result.

**Sign bit**   The bit of a binary number that indicates whether the number is positive or negative.

**Socket**   An object that encapsulates a TCP/IP connection. To communicate with the other endpoint of the connection, you use the input and output streams attached to the socket.

**Software**   The intangible instructions and data that are necessary for operating a computer or another device.

**Source code**   Instructions in a programming language that need to be translated before execution on a computer.

**Source file**   A file containing instructions in a programming language such as Java.

**SQL (Structured Query Language)**   A command language for interacting with a database.

**Stack**   A data structure with "last-in, first-out" retrieval. Elements can be added and removed only at one position, called the top of the stack.

**Stack trace**   A printout of the call stack, listing all currently pending method calls.

**State**   The current value of an object, which is determined by the cumulative action of all methods that were invoked on it.

**State diagram**   A diagram that depicts state transitions and their causes.

**Statement**   A syntactical unit in a program. In Java a statement is either a simple statement, a compound statement, or a block.

**Static method**   A method with no implicit parameter.

**Static variable**   A variable defined in a class that has only one value for the whole class, and which can be accessed and changed by any method of that class.

**Stepwise refinement**   The process of solving a problem that starts out with a subdivision into steps, then continues by further subdividing those steps.

**Stored procedure**   A database procedure that is executed in the database kernel.

**Stream**   An abstraction for a sequence of bytes from which data can be read or to which data can be written.

**String**   A sequence of characters.

**Stub**   A method with no or minimal functionality.

**Subclass**   A class that inherits variables and methods from a superclass but adds instance variables, adds methods, or redefines methods.

**Substitution principle**   The principle that a subclass object can be used in place of any superclass object.

**Superclass**   A general class from which a more specialized class (a subclass) inherits.

**Swing**   A Java toolkit for implementing graphical user interfaces.

**Symmetric bounds**   Bounds that include the starting index and the ending index.

**Synchronized block**   A block of code that is controlled by a lock. To start execution, a thread must acquire the lock. Upon completion, it relinquishes the lock.

**Synchronized method**   A method that is controlled by a lock. In order to execute the method, the calling thread must acquire the lock.

**Syntax**   Rules that define how to form instructions in a particular programming language.

**Syntax diagram**   A graphical representation of grammar rules.

**Syntax error**   An instruction that does not follow the programming language rules and is rejected by the compiler. (A form of compile-time error.)

**Tab character**   The '\t' character, which advances the next character on the line to the next one of a set of fixed positions known as tab stops.

**TCP/IP (Transmission Control Protocol/Internet Protocol)**   The pair of communication protocols that is used to establish reliable transmission of data between two computers on the Internet.

**Ternary operator**   An operator with three arguments. Java has one ternary operator, a ? b : c.

**Text field**   A user-interface component that allows a user to provide text input.

**Text file**   A file in which values are stored in their text representation.

**Thread**   A program unit that is executed independently of other parts of the program.

**Three-tier application**   An application that is composed of separate tiers for presentation logic, business logic, and data storage.

**Throwing an exception**   Indicating an abnormal condition by terminating the normal control flow of a program and transferring control to a matching catch clause.

**throws specifier**   Indicates the types of the checked exceptions that a method may throw.

**Time slice**   A small amount of time used when scheduling threads. Each thread is given a small amount of time (a slice) in which to do its work, then control is given to another thread.

**Token**   A sequence of consecutive characters from an input source that belongs together for the purpose of analyzing the input. For example, a token can be a sequence of characters other than white space.

**Trace message**   A message that is printed during a program run for debugging purposes.

**Transaction**   A set of database operations that should either succeed in their entirety, or not happen at all.

**Tree**   A data structure consisting of nodes, each of which has a list of child nodes, and one of which is distinguished as the root node.

**try block**   A block of statements that contains exception processing clauses. A try block contains at least one catch or finally clause.

**Turing machine**   A very simple model of computation that is used in theoretical computer science to explore computability of problems.

**Two-dimensional array**   A tabular arrangement of elements in which an element is specified by a row and a column index.

**Type**   A named set of values and the operations that can be carried out with them.

**Type parameter**   A parameter in a generic class or method that can be replaced with an actual type.

**Type variable**    A variable in the declaration of a generic type that can be instantiated with a type.

**Unary operator**    An operator with one argument.

**Unchecked exception**    An exception that the compiler doesn't check.

**Unicode**    A standard code that assigns code values consisting of two bytes to characters used in scripts around the world. Java stores all characters as their Unicode values.

**Unified Modeling Language (UML)**    A notation for specifying, visualizing, constructing, and documenting the artifacts of software systems.

**Uninitialized variable**    A variable that has not been set to a particular value. In Java, using an uninitialized local variable is a syntax error.

**Unit test**    A test of a method by itself, isolated from the remainder of the program.

**URL (Uniform Resource Locator)**    A pointer to an information resource (such as a web page or an image) on the World Wide Web.

**User-interface component**    A building block for a graphical user interface, such as a button or a text field. User-interface components are used to present information to the user and allow the user to enter information to the program.

**User-interface event**    A notification to a program that a user action such as a key press, mouse move, or menu selection has occurred.

**Value expression**    In JSF, an expression describing a bean and a property that is to be accessed at a later time.

**Variable**    A symbol in a program that identifies a storage location that can hold different values.

**Virtual machine**    A program that simulates a CPU that can be implemented efficiently on a variety of actual machines. A given program in Java bytecode can be executed by any Java virtual machine, regardless of which CPU is used to run the virtual machine itself.

**void**    A reserved word indicating no type or an unknown type.

**Walkthrough**    A step-by-step manual simulation of a computer program.

**Web application**    An application that executes on a web server and whose user interface is displayed in a web browser.

**White space**    Any sequence of only space, tab, and newline characters.

**Wrapper class**    A class that contains a primitive type value, such as Integer.

**Writer**    In the Java input/output library, a class to which characters are to be sent.

**XML (Extensible Markup Language)**    A simple format for structured data in which the structure is indicated by markup instructions.

# INDEX

# ILLUSTRATION CREDITS

Page 74: © José Luis Gutiérrez/iStockphoto.
Page 75: © Captainflash/iStockphoto.
Page 77: © TebNad/iStockphoto.

## Chapter 3

Page 81, 82: © zennie/iStockphoto.
Page 82: © DrGrounds/iStockphoto.
Page 83, 120: © Media Bakery.
Page 86: © TACrafts/iStockphoto.
Page 87: Photo by Vincent LaRussa/John Wiley & Sons, Inc.
Page 88, 120: © arturbo/iStockphoto.
Page 91: © caracterdesign/iStockphoto.
Page 92, 120: Corbis Digital Stock.
Page 93: © MikePanic/iStockphoto.
Page 95: Bob Daemmrich/Getty Images.
Page 96, 120: © kevinruss/iStockphoto.
Page 99: © travelpixpro/iStockphoto.
Page 100, 120: © ericsphotography/iStockphoto.
Page 103: © thomasd007/iStockphoto.
Page 105: © mikie11/iStockphoto.
Page 108: © Ekspansio/iStockphoto.
Page 110: Bananastock/Media Bakery.
Page 111, 121: Cusp/SuperStock.
Page 112: © toos/iStockphoto.
Page 115: © YouraPechkin/iStockphoto.
Page 116, 121: Tetra Images/Media Bakery.
Page 118 (top): © jeanma85/iStockphoto.
Page 118 (bottom): © benjaminalbiach/iStockphoto.
Page 119: Vaughn Youtz/Zuma Press.
Page 128 (top): © rotofrank/iStockphoto.
Page 1298 (bottom): © lillisphotography/iStockphoto.
Page 130: © Straitshooter/iStockphoto.
Page 131: © Mark Evans/iStockphoto.
Page 132: © drxy/iStockphoto.
Page 133 (top): © nano/iStockphoto
Page 133 (bottom): © Photobuff/iStockphoto.
Page 134: © rotofrank/iStockphoto.
Page 135: Courtesy NASA/JPL-Caltech.

## Chapter 4

Page 139, 140 (top): © photo75/iStockphoto.
Page 140 (middle): © AlterYourReality/iStockphoto.
Page 140 (bottom), 182: © mmac72/iStockphoto.
Page 144: © MsSponge/iStockphoto.
Page 145: © ohiophoto/iStockphoto.
Page 146: Courtesy of the Naval Surface Warfare Center, Dahlgren, VA., 1988. NHHC Collection.
Pages 147–149 (paperclip): © Yvan Dubé/iStockphoto.
Page 151, 183: © Enrico Fianchini/iStockphoto.
Page 156: © akaplummer/iStockphoto.

Page 158, 183: © Rhoberazzi/iStockphoto.

Page 161: © Michal_edo/iStockphoto.

Page 162: Courtesy of Martin Hardee.

Page 166 (top): © Hiob/iStockphoto.

Page 166 (bottom): © drflet/iStockphoto.

Page 167: © CEFutcher/iStockphoto.

Page 168: © tingberg/iStockphoto.

Page 169: © Stevegeer/iStockphoto.

Page 172 (top): © MorePixels/iStockphoto.

Page 172 (bottom), 183: © davejkahn/iStockphoto.

Page 175: Cay Horstmann.

Page 177, 183: © ktsimage/iStockphoto.

Page 178: © timstarkey/iStockphoto.

Page 181: © Rpsycho/iStockphoto.

Page 182 (top): © RapidEye/iStockphoto.

Page 182 (bottom): © thomasd007/iStockphoto.

Page 189: © Anthony Rosenberg/iStockphoto.

Page 191: © GlobalP/iStockphoto.

Page 194: © hatman12/iStockphoto.

Page 195 (top): © Charles Gibson/iStockphoto.

Page 195 (bottom): © MOF/iStockphoto.

Page 196 (top): *Introduction to Engineering Programming: Solving Problems with Algorithms*, James P. Holloway (John Wiley & Sons, Inc., 2004) Reprinted with permission of John Wiley & Sons, Inc.

Page 196 (middle): © Snowleopard1/iStockphoto.

Page 196 (bottom): © zig4photo/iStockphoto.


## Chapter 5

Page 201, 202: © attator/iStockphoto.

Page 203, 234: © yenwen/iStockphoto.

Page 204: © studioaraminta/iStockphoto.

Page 205, 234: © princessdlaf/iStockphoto.

Page 207 (collage), 234: © christine balderas/iStockphoto (cherry pie); © inhauscreative/iStockphoto (apple pie); © RedHelga/iStockphoto (cherries); © ZoneCreative/iStockphoto (apples).

Page 210, 234: © Tashka/iStockphoto.

Page 212: © holgs/iStockphoto.

Page 214, 234: © jgroup/iStockphoto.

Page 217: © Lawrence Sawyer/iStockphoto.

Page 218, 234: © AdShooter/iStockphoto.

Page 219: © YinYang/iStockphoto.

Page 224: © lillisphotography/iStockphoto.

Page 225: © pkline/iStockphoto.

Page 226 (collage): © jchamp/iStockphoto (Railway and Main) (also 235); © StevenCarrieJohnson/iStockphoto (Main and N. Putnam); © jsmith/iStockphoto (Main and South St.).

Page 228: © Janice Richard/iStockphoto.

Page 230, 235: © nicodemos/iStockphoto.

Page 233 (top): © Kenneth C. Zirkel/iStockphoto.

Page 358: © Chris Dascher/iStockphoto.

## Chapter 8

Page 361, 362 (top): © Stephanie Strathdee/iStockphoto.
Page 362 (bottom), 403: Media Bakery.
Page 363, 403: © Damir Cudic/iStockphoto.
Page 364 (top): © Christian Waadt/iStockphoto.
Page 364 (bottom): © Jasmin Awad/iStockphoto.
Page 367, 403: © Mark Evans/iStockphoto.
Page 368, 403: Glow Images.
Page 371, 403: © migin/iStockphoto.
Page 374, 403: © James Richey/iStockphoto.
Page 376, 403: © Ann Marie Kurtz/iStockphoto.
Page 380, 404: © Chris Fertnig/iStockphoto.
Page 382: © Mark Evans/iStockphoto.
Page 386: © Pavel Mitrofanov/iStockphoto.
Page 388: © Hunteerwagstaff/Dreamstime.com.
Page 390, 404: © paul prescott/iStockphoto.
Page 391, 404: © John Alexander/iStockphoto.
Page 393: © Llya Terentyev/iStockphoto.
Page 394 (left): © Peter Nguyen/iStockphoto.
Page 394 (center): © Lisa F. Young/iStockphoto.
Page 395, 404: © Jacob Wackerhausen/iStockphoto.
Page 400, 404: © Diane Diederich/iStockphoto.
Page 402: Courtesy of Richard Stallman.
Page 406: © Miklos Voros/iStockphoto.
Page 407: © pixhook/iStockphoto.
Page 410: © ThreeJays/iStockphoto.
Page 411: © Maria Toutoudaki/iStockphoto.

## Chapter 9

Page 415, 416: © Lisa Thornberg/iStockphoto.
Page 416, 455: © Richard Stouffer/iStockphoto (vehicles);
    © Ed Hidden/iStockphoto (motorcycle); © YinYang/iStockphoto (car);
    © Robert Pernell/iStockphoto (truck); © nicholas belton/iStockphoto (sedan);
    Cezary Wojtkowski/Age Fotostock America (SUV).
Page 417: © paul kline/iStockphoto.
Page 421, 455: Media Bakery.
Page 432, 455: © Alpophoto/iStockphoto.
Page 441 (top): © Sean Locke/iStockphoto.
Page 441 (bottom): © vm/iStockphoto.
Page 444: © granata1111/Shutterstock.
Page 448, 455: © gregory horler/iStockphoto.
Page 452: © Janis Dreosti/iStockphoto.
Page 455: Courtesy of John Reid.
Page 460: © Pali Rao/iStockphoto.

## Chapter 10

Page 465, 466: © Trout55/iStockphoto.
Page 466: © Mark Goddard/iStockphoto.

Page 467, 500: © Eduardo Jose Bernardino/iStockphoto.
Page 469: © TommL/iStockphoto.
Page 471, 500: © Seriy Tryapitsyn/iStockphoto.
Page 473, 500: © maureenpr/iStockphoto.
Page 483, 500: © Kyoungil Jeon/iStockphoto.
Page 487, 501: © Alexey Avdeev/iStockphoto.
Page 497: Punchstock.
Page 500 (Video Example): © paul jantz/iStockphoto.
Page 506: © Juanmonino/iStockphoto.

**Chapter 11**

Page 507, 508: © Carlos Santa Maria/iStockphoto.
Page 508, 541: © Felix Mockel/iStockphoto.
Page 510, 541: © Michele Cornelius/iStockphoto.
Page 522, 541: © lillisphotography/iStockphoto.
Page 528: © René Mansi/iStockphoto.
Page 533, 542: © jeff giniewicz/iStockphoto.
Page 536, 542: © james Brey/iStockphoto.
Page 540: © Dmitry Shironosov/iStockphoto.
Page 541: © Nancy Ross/iStockphoto.
Page 545: © Kathy Muller/iStockphoto.

**Chapter 12**

Page 549, 550: © Petrea Alexandru/iStockphoto.
Page 551, 577: © Oleg Prikhodko/iStockphoto.
Page 556, 577: © bojan fatur/iStockphoto.
Page 563: © Scott Cramer/iStockphoto.
Page 573: © Mark Evans/iStockphoto.
Page 575, 577: © Don Wilkie/iStockphoto.

**Chapter 13**

Page 585, 586: © Nicolae Popovici/iStockphoto.
Page 586, 618: © Davis Mantel/iStockphoto.
Page 590, 618: © Nikada/iStockphoto.
Page 594, 618: © gerenme/iStockphoto.
Page 596, 619: © Christina Richards/iStockphoto.
Page 601, 619: © Jeanine Groenwald/iStockphoto.
Page 604: Science Photo Library/Photo Researchers, Inc.
Page 612, 619: © Lanica Klein/iStockphoto.

**Chapter 14**

Page 627, 628: © Volkan Ersoy/iStockphoto.
Page 628, 660: © Zone Creative/iStockphoto.
Page 638, 660: © Kirby Hamilton/iStockphoto.
Page 639, 660: © Rich Legg/iStockphoto.
Page 645: © Christopher Futcher/iStockphoto.
Page 650: Topham/The Image Works.
Page 651–655, 660, 667 (on/off lightbulb):
    © Kraska/Shutterstock.

## Chapter 15

Page 669, 670: © nicholas belton/iStockphoto.
Page 671 (top left): © Filip Fuxa/iStockphoto.
Page 671 (top center), 702: © parema/iStockphoto.
Page 671 (top right): © Vladimir Trenin/iStockphoto.
Page 671 (bottom), 702: © david franklin/iStockphoto.
Page 673, 701: © andrea laurita/iStockphoto.
Page 678: © Denis Vorob'yev/iStockphoto.
Page 679, 702: © Alfredo Ragazzoni/iStockphoto.
Page 680, 702: © Volkan Ersoy/iStockphoto.
Page 686, 701: © Tom Hahn/iStockphoto.
Page 688, 702: © one clear vision/iStockphoto.
Page 690 (top), 702: © John Madden/iStockphoto.
Page 690 (left): © budgetstockphoto/iStockphoto.
Page 691, 700, 702: Photodisc/Punchstock.
Page 692: © paul kline/iStockphoto.
Page 695, 702: © Jorge Delgado/iStockphoto.
Page 698: © Skip ODonnell/iStockphoto.
Page 701 (top): Courtesy of Nigel Tout.
Page 701 (middle): © Ermin Gutenberger/iStockphoto.
Page 706: © martin mcelligott/iStockphoto.
Page 708: © Luis Carlos Torres/iStockphoto.

## Chapter 16

Page 713, 714: © andrea laurita/iStockphoto.
Page 722, 748: © Kris Hanke/iStockphoto.
Page 731, 749: © Craig Dingle/iStockphoto.
Page 736, 749: © ihsanyildizli/iStockphoto.
Page 740, 749: © Neil Kurtzman/iStockphoto.
Page 751: © Philip Dyer/iStockphoto.

## Chapter 17

Page 759, 760: © DNY59/iStockphoto.
Page 760, 806: Courtesy of takato marui.
Page 763: © Yvette Harris/iStockphoto.
Page 764 (right), 806: © kali9/iStockphoto.
Page 764 (left): © AlbanyPictures/iStockphoto.
Page 766: © Emrah Turudu/iStockphoto.
Page 768: Charlotte and Emily Horstmann.
Page 779, 807: © Pawel Gaul/iStockphoto.
Page 781: © David Jones/iStockphoto.
Page 785, 807: © Virginia N/iStockphoto.
Page 791, 807: © Lisa Marzano/iStockphoto.

## Chapter 18

Page 817, 818: © Don Bayley/iStockphoto.
Page 825, 834: © Mike Clark/iStockphoto.
Page 829, 834: © VikramRaghuvanshi/iStockphoto.

## Chapter 19
Page 839, 840: © Claude Dagenais/iStockphoto.

## Icons
Common Error icon: © Scott Harms/iStockphoto.
How To icon: © Steve Simzer/iStockphoto.
Paperclip: © Yvan Dubé/iStockphoto.
Programming Tip icon: Macdaddy/Dreamstime.com.
Random Fact icon: Mishella/Dreamstime.com.
Self Check icon: © Nicholas Homrich/iStockphoto.
Special Topic icon: © nathan winter/iStockphoto.
Worked Example icon: © Tom Horyn/iStockphoto.

## Chapters Available on the Web

## Chapter 20 ✛
Page W861, W862: © Rubén Hidalgo/iStockphoto.
Page W877, W894: Creatas/Punchstock.
Page W893: Courtesy of Professor Naehyuck Chang, Computer Systems Lab, Department of Computer Engineering, Seoul National University.

## Chapter 21 ✛
Page W901, W902: © Felix Alim/iStockphoto.

## Chapter 22 ✛
Page W927, W928: © Jason Allen/iStockphoto.
Page W942: © Greg Nicholas/iStockphoto.

## Chapter 23 ✛
Page W971, W972: © Krzysztof Zmij/iStockphoto.

## Chapter 24 ✛
Page W1011, W1012: © Philip Toy/iStockphoto.
Page W1038: Google Earth™ mapping services screenshot © Google, Inc. Reprinted with permission.